The **Hallmark Features**

A COMPLETE LEARNING PACKAGE

- **LIVES IN CONTEXT BOXES** offer compelling examples that illustrate how we all are embedded in multiple layers of context, including family, culture, neighborhood, community, norms, values, and historical events. Learners will engage with and consider topics such as cultural influence on childbirth, the practice of co-sleeping (infants sleeping with their parents), the impact of community violence, and the influence of media on infant learning. Lives in Context topics:
    - Biological Influences
    - Community Context
    - Cultural Context
    - Family and Peer Context
    - Media and Technology

- **APPLYING DEVELOPMENTAL SCIENCE BOXES** illustrate current research in developmental science and how it may be applied. Examples include the effects of postpartum depression, infant sign language, autism and theory of mind, children's suggestibility, and the effects of adolescent employment.

SAGE Publishing: **Our Story**

At SAGE, we mean business. We believe in creating evidence-based, cutting-edge content that helps you prepare your students to succeed in today's ever-changing business world. We strive to provide you with the tools you need to develop the next generation of leaders, managers, and entrepreneurs.

- We invest in the right **AUTHORS** who distill research findings and industry ideas into practical applications.
- We keep our prices **AFFORDABLE** and provide multiple **FORMAT OPTIONS** for students.
- We remain permanently independent and fiercely committed to **QUALITY CONTENT** and **INNOVATIVE RESOURCES**.

CHILD & ADOLESCENT DEVELOPMENT IN CONTEXT

To FHM

With love always, TKM

TARA L. KUTHER
Western Connecticut State University

Los Angeles | London | New Delhi
Singapore | Washington DC | Melbourne

FOR INFORMATION:

SAGE Publications, Inc.
2455 Teller Road
Thousand Oaks, California 91320
E-mail: order@sagepub.com

SAGE Publications Ltd.
1 Oliver's Yard
55 City Road
London, EC1Y 1SP
United Kingdom

SAGE Publications India Pvt. Ltd.
B 1/I 1 Mohan Cooperative Industrial Area
Mathura Road, New Delhi 110 044
India

SAGE Publications Asia-Pacific Pte. Ltd.
18 Cross Street #10-10/11/12
China Square Central
Singapore 048423

Acquisitions Editor: Lara Parra
Content Development Editor: Jennifer Thomas
Production Editor: Olivia Weber-Stenis
Copy Editor: Christina West
Typesetter: Hurix Digital
Proofreader: Scott Oney
Indexer: Jeanne R. Busemeyer
Cover Designer: Gail Buschman
Marketing Manager: Katherine Hepburn

Printed in Canada

Library of Congress Cataloging-in-Publication Data

Names: Kuther, Tara L., author.

Title: Child and adolescent development : lives in context / Tara L. Kuther, Western Connecticut State University.

Description: Los Angeles, : SAGE, [2020] | Includes bibliographical references.

Identifiers: LCCN 2019030603 | ISBN 9781544324814 (hardcover) | ISBN 9781544324791 (epub) | ISBN 9781544324807 (epub) | ISBN 9781544324821 (ebook)

Subjects: LCSH: Child psychology. | Child development. | Adolescent psychology. | Adolescence.

Classification: LCC BF721 .K88 2020 | DDC 155.4—dc23 LC record available at https://lccn.loc.gov/2019030603

This book is printed on acid-free paper.

20 21 22 23 24 10 9 8 7 6 5 4 3 2 1

BRIEF CONTENTS

DETAILED CONTENTS

©iStockphoto.com/AJ_Watt

©iStockphoto.com/video1

©iStockphoto.com/Eva-Katalin

©iStockphoto.com/FatCamera

©iStockphoto.com/romrodinka

Chapter 5: Cognitive Development in Infancy and Toddlerhood 128

©iStockphoto.com/FatCamera

©iStockphoto.com/ArtMarie

©iStockphoto.com/Linda Raymond

©iStockphoto.com/DGLimages

©iStockphoto.com/FatCamera

©iStockphoto.com/gradyreese

©iStockphoto.com/FatCamera

©iStockphoto.com/monkeybusinessimages

©iStockphoto.com/Tomwang112

©iStockphoto.com/martin-dm

LIST OF BOXED FEATURES

PREFACE

Child and Adolescent Development in Context has its origins in 24 years of interactions with students, in and out of class. The most central tenet of development is that it occurs in context. At all points in life, human development is the result of dynamic interactions among individuals and the many interacting contexts in which they are embedded. The most rapid developmental changes occur from infancy through adolescence. One of the greatest challenges child and adolescent development instructors face is helping students understand the complex influences on development, that outcomes do not vary randomly or simply "depend on the person." With enough information, we can predict and understand development. My goal in writing this text is to explain the sophisticated interactions that constitute development in a way that is comprehensive yet concise.

Child and Adolescent Development in Context focuses on two key themes that promote understanding of how infants, children, and adolescents develop: the centrality of context and the applied value of developmental science. These two themes are highlighted throughout the text as well as in boxed features. This text also conveys findings from current and classic research in a student-friendly writing style.

CONTEXTUAL PERSPECTIVE

Development does not occur in a vacuum but is a function of dynamic transactions among individuals, their physical, cognitive, and socioemotional capacities, and a multitude of contextual influences. We are all embedded in many interacting layers of context, including tangible and intangible circumstances that influence and are influenced by our development, such as family, ethnicity, culture, neighborhood, community, norms, values, and historical events. *Child and Adolescent Development in Context* explains this process, emphasizing how individual factors combine with the places, sociocultural environments, and ways in which we are raised to influence children's development.

The contextual theme is infused throughout the text and highlighted specifically in Lives in Context boxed features that appear in each chapter. The Lives in Context features are labeled to illustrate the various contexts in which children and adolescents are immersed: Family and Peer Context, Community Context, Cultural Context, and Media and Technology. Examples of these features include the effects of parental military deployment (Family and Peer Context), the effects of exposure to community violence (Community Context), and culture and theory of mind (Cultural Context). Advances in technology and the advent of social media have led to a new but highly relevant online context that is depicted in Lives in Context features labeled Media and Technology, such as the effects of screen time on children's health or screen use and infant motor development. Finally, when considering context, it is tempting to overlook biology, but our biology influences and is influenced by our contexts. The Lives in Context feature labeled Biological Influences calls attention to the role of biology in development. Sample topics include pregnancy and the maternal brain, genetic engineering, and the effects of poverty on brain development.

APPLIED EMPHASIS

The field of developmental science is unique because so much of its content has immediate relevance to our daily lives. Students may wonder: Do the first 3 years shape the brain for a lifetime of experiences? Can we teach babies to communicate through sign language? Is learning more than one language beneficial to children? What does it mean to be a transgender child? Developmental science is increasingly applied to influence social policy. For example, why vaccinate infants? Can we outlaw bullying? Research in child and adolescent development can inform our understanding of each of these topics. Moreover, these topics fascinate students because they illustrate clear-cut examples of why developmental science matters. The Applying Developmental Science feature highlights the above topics and more.

CURRENT RESEARCH

Developmental science instructors face the challenge of covering the growing mass of research findings within the confines of a single semester. *Child and Adolescent Development in Context* integrates recently published and classic findings. Rather than present an exhaustive review of current work simply for the sake of including recent references, I carefully select the most relevant findings. I integrate cutting-edge and classic research to present a unified story of what is currently known in developmental psychology.

ACCESSIBLE WRITING STYLE

Having taught at a regional public university for 24 years, I write in a style intended to engage undergraduate readers like my own students. This text is intended to help them understand challenging concepts in language that will not overwhelm: I have avoided jargon but maintained the use of professional and research terms that students need to know in order to digest classic and current literature in the lifespan development field. I attempt to write in the same voice as I teach, carefully structuring sections to build explanations and integrating content with examples that are relevant to students. I regularly use my own texts in class, students work with me in preparing elements of each text, and my students' responses and learning guide my writing.

ORGANIZATION

Child and Adolescent Development in Context is organized into 15 chronological chapters, within five units, that depict the wide range of developments that occur over the lifespan. Unit 1 (Foundations of Child and Adolescent Development) includes Chapters 1, 2, and 3. Chapter 1 combines developmental theory and research design within a single chapter. I chose this approach because, given limited class time, many instructors do not cover stand-alone research chapters. The streamlined approach combines comprehensive coverage of methods of data collection, research design, developmental designs (such as sequential designs), and ethical issues in research with full coverage of the major theories in developmental psychology. Chapter 2 presents the biological foundations of development, including patterns of genetic inheritance, gene–environment interactions, and epigenetics. Chapter 3 describes prenatal development and birth, from conception to the newborn, including the emerging family system. I chose to present prenatal development, birth, and the newborn as a single chapter (rather than birth and the newborn as a stand-alone chapter) to reflect continuity in the perinatal period.

The remaining units contain three chapters each on physical development, cognitive development, and socioemotional development to reflect the major areas of development during infancy (Unit 2, Chapters 4 to 6), early childhood (Unit 3, Chapters 7 to 9), middle childhood (Unit 4, Chapters 10 to 12), and adolescence (Unit 5, Chapters 13 to 15). Therefore, *Child and Adolescent Development in Context* contains 15 chapters that correspond to the 15 weeks of the typical college semester.

PEDAGOGY

My day-to-day experiences in the classroom have helped me to keep college students' interests and abilities at the forefront. Unlike many textbook authors, I teach four classes each semester at a comprehensive regional public university (and have done so since 1996). I taught my first online course in 2002 and have taught online and hybrid courses regularly since. My daily exposure to multiple classes and many students helps keep me grounded in the ever-changing concerns and interests of college students. I teach a diverse group of students. Some live on campus but most commute. Most of my students are ages 18 to 24, but my classes also include many so-called adult learners over the age of 24. Many are veterans, a rapidly increasing population at my institution with unique perspectives and needs. I have many opportunities to try new examples and activities. I believe that what works in my classroom will be helpful to readers and instructors. I use the pedagogical elements of *Child and Adolescent Development in Context* in my own classes and modify them based on my experiences.

LEARNING OBJECTIVES AND SUMMARIES

Core learning objectives are listed at the beginning of each chapter. The end-of-chapter summary returns to each learning objective, recapping the key concepts presented in the chapter related to that objective.

CRITICAL THINKING

Critical Thinking Questions: At the end of each main section within the chapter, these Thinking in Context critical thinking questions encourage readers to compare concepts, apply theoretical perspectives, and consider applications of research findings presented.

A Lives in Context box program illustrate contexts drawn from the real world and their connections to one another, including international adoption and child outcomes, exposure to war and terrorism and children's development, the effects of neighborhood on development, HIV infection in newborns, and the impact of family stress on health.

Lives in Context: Biological Influences boxes tied to each chapter's learning objectives cover cutting-edge biological topics and prompt students to think critically about each concept.

Lives in Context: Community Context boxes raise issues related to the context of community and push students to consider real world implications of concepts connected to chapter learning objectives.

Lives in Context: Cultural Context boxes ask students to consider traditions from the cultural context and then to think critically about how culture affects development.

Lives in Context: Family and Peer Context boxes discuss the family context related to each chapter and challenge learners to apply chapter content to the real world.

Lives in Context: Media and Technology boxes address media and technology and their effects on development at each stage. Learners are prompted to synthesize chapter learning and apply knowledge to real world examples.

Case-Based Application: Each chapter closes with a case scenario, Apply Your Knowledge, followed by questions that require students to apply their understanding to address a particular situation or problem.

SUPPLEMENTS

Engage, Learn, Soar with **SAGE vantage**, an intuitive digital platform that delivers ***Child and Adolescent Development in Context*** textbook content in a learning experience carefully designed to ignite student engagement and drive critical thinking. With evidence-based instructional design at the core, SAGE vantage creates more time for engaged learning and empowered teaching, keeping the classroom where it belongs—in your hands.

Easy to access across mobile, desktop, and tablet devices, SAGE vantage enables students to engage with the material you choose, learn by applying knowledge, and soar with confidence by performing better in your course.

HIGHLIGHTS INCLUDE:

eReading Experience. Makes it easy for students to study wherever they are—students can take notes, highlight content, look up definitions, and more!

Pedagogical Scaffolding. Builds on core concepts, moving students from basic understanding to mastery.

Confidence Builder. Offers frequent knowledge checks, applied-learning multimedia tools, and chapter tests with focused feedback to assure students know key concepts.

Time-saving Flexibility. Feeds auto-graded assignments to your gradebook, with real-time insight into student and class performance.

Quality Content. Written by expert authors and teachers, content is not sacrificed for technical features.

Honest Value. Affordable access to easy-to-use, quality learning tools students will appreciate.

FAVORITE SAGE VANTAGE FEATURES

3-step course setup is so fast you can complete it in minutes!

Control over assignments, content selection, due dates, and grading empowers you to teach your way.

Quality content authored by the experts you trust.

eReading experience makes it easy to learn and study by presenting content in easy-to-digest segments featuring note-taking, highlighting, definition look-up, and more.

LMS integration provides single sign-on with streamlined grading capabilities and course management tools.

Auto-graded assignments include:

- formative knowledge checks for each major section of the text that quickly reinforce what students have read and ensure they stay on track;
- dynamic, hands-on **multimedia activities** that tie real world examples and motivate students to read, prepare for class;
- summative **chapter tests** that reinforce important themes; and
- **helpful hints and feedback** (provided with all assignments) that offer context and explain why an answer is correct or incorrect, allowing students to study more effectively.

Compelling polling questions bring concepts to life and drive meaningful comprehension and classroom discussion.

Short-answer questions provide application and reflection opportunities connected to key concepts.

Instructor reports track student activity and provide analytics so you can adapt instruction as needed.

A student dashboard offers easy access to grades, so students know exactly where they stand in your course and where they might improve.

Honest value gives students access to quality content and learning tools at a price they will appreciate.

SAGE coursepacks

SAGE COURSEPACKS FOR INSTRUCTORS

The **SAGE coursepack** for *Child and Adolescent Development in Context* makes it easy to import our quality instructor materials and student resources into your school's learning management system (LMS), such as Blackboard, Canvas, Brightspace by D2L, or Moodle. Intuitive and simple to use, **SAGE coursepack** allows you to integrate only the content you need, with minimal effort, and requires no access code. Don't use an LMS platform? You can still access many of the online resources for *Child and Adolescent Development in Context* via the **SAGE edge** site.

Within the SAGE coursepack content are pedagogically robust **assessment tools** that foster review, practice, and critical thinking, offering a more complete way to measure student engagement, including:

Diagnostic **coursepack chapter quizzes** that identify opportunities for improvement, track student progress, and ensure mastery of key learning objectives.

Test banks built on Bloom's taxonomy that provide a diverse range of test items.

Activity and quiz options that allow you to choose only the assignments and tests you want.

Editable, chapter-specific **PowerPoint®** slides that offer flexibility when creating multimedia lectures so you don't have to start from scratch but can customize to your exact needs.

Instructions on how to use and integrate the comprehensive assessments and resources provided.

SAGE edge™

SAGE edge is a robust online environment featuring an impressive array of tools and resources for review, study, and further exploration, keeping both instructors and students on the cutting edge of teaching and learning. SAGE edge content is open access and available on demand. Learning and teaching has never been easier!

SAGE edge for Students at **http://edge.sagepub.com/kutherchild1e** provides a personalized approach to help students accomplish their course learning objectives.

ACKNOWLEDGMENTS

Books such as this are not solitary endeavors. I am fortunate to work with a talented team at SAGE and I am grateful for their support. I thank Lara Parra, Reid Hester, Jennifer Thomas, Olivia Weber-Stenis, and Katherine Hepburn. Christina West's copyediting is very much appreciated.

I thank my students for asking the questions and engaging in the discussions that inform these pages. I am especially appreciative of those who have shared their feedback and helped me to improve this book. Lauren Schwarz provided invaluable brainstorming assistance and I appreciate Ed Lindblom's input on the boxed features. Thank you to the many instructors who have reviewed and provided feedback on these chapters.

Finally, I thank my family, especially my parents, Phil and Irene Kuther. Most of all, I am thankful for the support of my husband, Fred, for his encouragement, optimism, and support, both tangible and intangible, and for our exciting, impromptu road trips.

SAGE wishes to thank the following reviewers for their valuable contributions to the development of this manuscript:

Brenda Beagle, *John Tyler Community College*
Cassendra Bergstrom, *University of Northern Colorado*
Brian Bramstedt, Professor, *Georgia Gwinnett College*
Connie Casha, *Middle Tennessee State University*
Elaine Cassel, *Lord Fairfax Community College*
Chun Chu, *Fayetteville State University*
Ryan Clayton, *Bunker Hill Community College*
Carmen Culotta, *Wright State University*
Elizabeth Degiorgio, *Mercer County Community College*
Joan Dolamore, *Lasell College*
Linda Dove, *Western Michigan University*
Angel Dunlap, *Alabama A&M University*
Jia Fanli, *Seton Hall University*
Kathryn Frazier, *Worcester State University*
Ahni Fritton, *Lesley University*
Veronica Fruiht, *Dominican University of California*
Diana Gal-Szabo, *Arizona State University*
Shinder Gill, *California State University Sacramento*
Sara Goldstein, *Montclair State University*
Elizabeth Goncy, *Cleveland State University*
Heidi Heft Laporte, *Barry University School of Social Work*
Erron Huey, *Texas Woman's University*
Matthew Jamnik, *Southern Illinois University Carbondale*
Fu Jun, *Oklahoma State University*
Dawn Kriebel, *Immaculata University*
Deborah Laible, *Lehigh University*
Emily Lewis, *Tulane University*
Miriam Linver, *Montclair State University*
Robert Martinez, *University of the Incarnate*
John Masters, *Middlesex Community College*
Martha Mendez-Baldwin, *Manhattan College*
Krisztina Micsinai, *Palomar College*
Pamela Parent, *J. Sargeant Reynolds Community College*
Gerra Perkins, *Northwestern State University*
Catherine Phillips, *Northwest Vista College*
George Randall, *Sam Houston State University*
Kara Recker, *Coe College*
Amy Reesing, *Arizona State University*
Lisa Reynolds, *Western Connecticut State University*
Erin Sappio, *Stockton University*
Bob Sasse, *Palomar College*
Debra Schwiesow, *Creighton University*
Carla Sewer, *Texas Woman's University*
Christina Sinisi, *Charleston Southern University*
Patrick Smith, *Florida Southern College*
Jerrie Smith Jackson, *Our Lady of the Lake University*
Tara Stoppa, *Eastern University*
Colleen Sullivan, *Worcester State University*
Jill Trumbell, *University of New Hampshire*
Jolie Van Schoik, *California State University San Marcos*
Gina Wilson, *RTI International*

ABOUT THE AUTHOR

Tara L. Kuther is professor of psychology at Western Connecticut State University, where she has taught courses in child, adolescent, and adult development since 1996. She earned her BA in psychology from Western Connecticut State University and her MA and PhD in developmental psychology from Fordham University. Dr. Kuther is the author of the award-winning title *Lifespan Development: Lives in Context*, as well as *The Psychology Major's Handbook* and *Careers in Psychology: Opportunities in a Changing World*. She is fellow of the Society for the Teaching of Psychology (American Psychological Association, Division 2), has served in various capacities in the Society for the Teaching of Psychology and the Society for Research on Adolescence, and is the former chair of the Teaching Committee for the Society for Research in Child Development. Her research interests include social cognition and risky activity in adolescence and adulthood. She is also interested in promoting undergraduate and graduate students' professional development and helping them navigate the challenges of pursuing undergraduate and graduate degrees in psychology.

UNIT I

Foundations of Child and Adolescent Development

CHAPTER 1:
Understanding Human Development: Approaches and Theories

CHAPTER 2:
Biological and Environmental Foundations of Development

CHAPTER 3:
The Prenatal Period, Birth, and the Newborn

©iStockphoto.com/AJ_W

1 Understanding Human Development

Approaches and Theories

It was a sunny day. I looked up at the bright sky as I leaned back in my stroller and pulled my hat down onto my head. The simplest of events, but it is one of my first memories. How old was I? Probably on the brink of early childhood. What is your first memory? Is it similarly vague? Were you engaging in an activity? Do you recall your surroundings and the people around you? How have you changed in the time since that early memory? Are there ways in which you remain the same? We will examine these questions and more throughout this book.

Learning Objectives

1.1 Describe the periods, domains, and contexts of development.

Video Activity 1.1: Sociocultural Influences on Development: Desegregation

1.2 Explain three basic issues in developmental science.

Video Activity 1.2: How Poverty Affects Development Across Lifespan

1.3 Summarize six theoretical perspectives on human development.

1.4 Describe the methods and research designs used to study human development and the ethical principles that guide researchers' work.

Chapter Contents

UNDERSTANDING DEVELOPMENT

Individuals undergo innumerable changes as they progress through infancy, childhood, and adolescence, a process known as **development**. Development refers to the processes by which we grow and change, as well as the ways in which we stay the same over time. The field of **developmental science** studies human development at all points in life, from conception to death. In this book we will examine child development; however, individuals undergo complex changes at every period in life, beginning before birth and continuing throughout adulthood.

Periods of Development

One of the challenges of studying infants and children is that a great many changes occur over just a few years. Researchers divide the time between conception and adolescence into a series of periods, summarized below. Each developmental period is characterized by a predictable pattern of physical, cognitive, and social abilities, or **domains of development**.

Prenatal Period (Conception to Birth)

Upon conception a single cell is formed. This cell multiples repeatedly to form the body structures and organs that will compose the newborn.

Infancy and Toddlerhood (Birth to 2 Years)

Newborns' senses and early learning abilities enable them to adapt to the world. Dramatic changes occur in physical growth as well as motor, perceptual, and intellectual abilities. Infants begin to use language and form emotional bonds with caregivers. Infancy comprises the first year of life; toddlerhood spans the second.

Early Childhood (2 to 6 Years)

Children's muscles strengthen and they become more coordinated. As thinking, language, and self-regulation improve, children establish ties with peers and engage in make-believe play.

Middle Childhood (6 to 11 Years)

As children enter school, their memory and reasoning improve and they learn academic skills such as reading, writing, and arithmetic. As children advance cognitively and gain social experience, their self-understanding and self-control improves. Friendships develop and become more complex and peer group memberships become more important.

Adolescence (11 to 18 Years)

With puberty, adolescents become physically and sexually mature. Adolescents' thinking becomes more complex and abstract. Adolescents spend more time with peers and friendships become more important. They are driven to learn about themselves, become independent from their parents, and define their values and goals. Whether adolescence ends at age 18 is debated by developmental scientists. Some argue that adolescence persists through the college years, ending at about age 21. Others propose an additional period of development called **emerging adulthood**, extending from the completion of secondary education at about age 18 to the adoption of adult roles at about age 25 (Arnett, 2000).

Domains of Development

Consider the many changes that mark each period of development and it is apparent that development is multidimensional. That is, development includes changes in multiple domains of development. Perhaps the most obvious set of changes includes **physical development**, body maturation, and growth, such as body size, proportion, appearance, health, and perceptual abilities. **Cognitive development** refers to the maturation of thought processes and the tools that we use to obtain knowledge, become aware of the world around us, and solve problems. **Socioemotional development** includes changes in emotions, social abilities, self-understanding, and interpersonal relationships with family and friends. These domains of development overlap and interact. For example, the onset of walking precedes advances in language development in infants in the United States and China (He, Walle, & Campos, 2015; Walle & Campos, 2013). Babies who walk tend to spend more time interacting with caregivers; they can initiate interactions with caregivers, such as by bringing objects to them (Clearfield, 2011). They also evoke more verbal responses and warnings from caregivers as they interact with items and explore their environment. Therefore, walking (motor development) is associated with language and social development. Figure 1.1 illustrates how the three domains of development interact, a central principle of development.

Contexts of Development

Where did you grow up? Describe your childhood neighborhood. Did you play in a park or on a playground? Did you ride your bike outside? What was your elementary school like? Did you have

FIGURE 1.1

Domains of Development

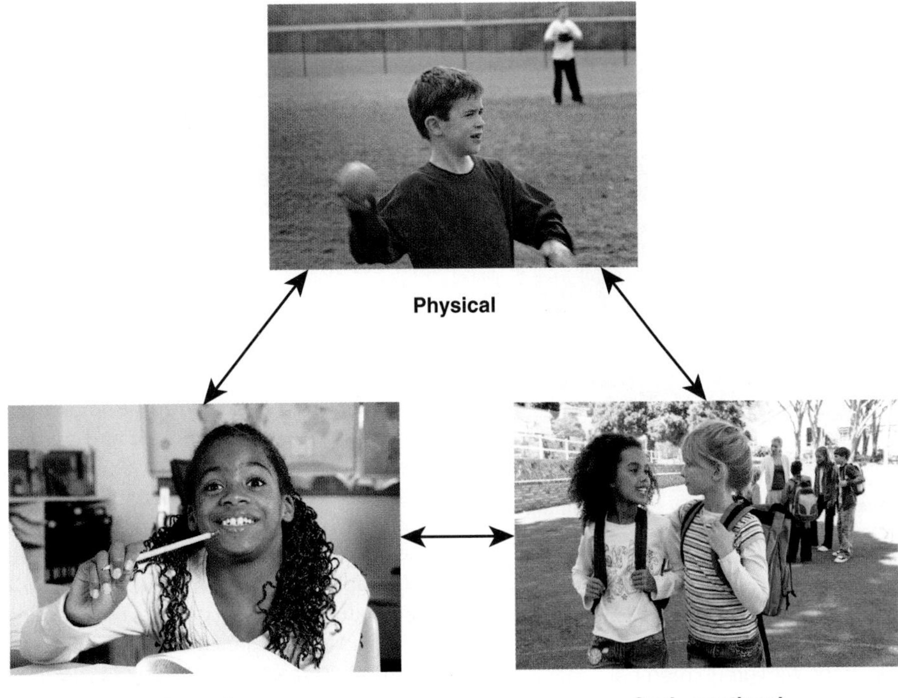

Advances in physical, cognitive, and socioemotional development interact, permitting children to play sports, learn more efficiently, and develop close friendships.

iStock/Essentials; iStock/Signature; Jupiter/Pixland/Thinkstock

access to technology such as tablets and computers? Did you learn to type in school? How large is your family? What were some of your family traditions? What holidays did you celebrate? Did you share family meals often? Your responses to these questions reveal aspects of your context.

Context refers to where and when a person develops. Context encompasses many aspects of the physical and social environment, such as family, neighborhood, country, and historical time period. It includes intangible factors, characteristics that are not visible to the naked eye, such as values, customs, ideals, and culture. In order to understand a given individual's development, we must look to his or her context, including the subtle, less easily viewed, factors. For example, were you encouraged to be assertive and actively question the adults around you, or were you expected to be quiet and avoid confrontation? How large a part was spirituality or religion in your family's life? How did religious values shape your parent's childrearing practices and your own values? How did your family's economic status affect your development? These questions examine a critical context for our development, home and family. However, we are embedded in many more contexts that influence us, and that we influence, such as our peer group, school, neighborhood or community, and culture (see the Lives in Context feature). Our development plays out within the contexts in which we live, a theme that we will return to throughout this book.

1. Consider the multidimensional nature of your development. Provide personal examples of physical, cognitive, and socioemotional development. What changes have you experienced in each of these areas over your childhood? How have these abilities influenced one another?
2. Describe the multiple contexts in which you were raised. How might these have influenced your physical, cognitive, and socioemotional development? Provide examples.
3. In what ways might your physical, cognitive, or socioemotional development have influenced aspects of your context?

LIVES IN CONTEXT: CULTURAL CONTEXT

Defining Culture

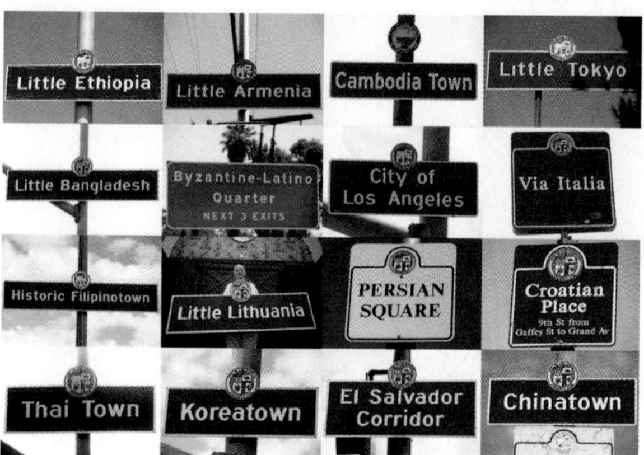

Cultural influences on development include the many ethnic communities that comprise most U.S. cities, and the unique foods, customs, and values that accompany each community.
Reuters/Lucy Nicholson

One broad aspect of context is **culture**. Culture refers to a set of customs, knowledge, attitudes, and values that are shared by members of a group and are learned early in life through interactions with group members (Markus & Kitayama, 1991). Early studies of culture and human development took the form of *cross-cultural research*, comparing individuals and groups from different cultures to examine how these universal processes worked in different contexts (Mistry & Dutta, 2015).

Most classic theories and research on human development are based on Western samples, and developmental researchers once believed that the processes of human development were universal. More recent observations suggest that development varies dramatically with context (Keller, 2017). For example, consider milestones, such as the average age that infants begin to walk. In Uganda, infants begin to walk at about 10 months of age, in France at about 15 months, and in the United States at about 12 months. These differences are influenced by parenting practices that vary by culture. African parents tend to handle infants in ways that stimulate walking, by playing games that allow infants to practice jumping and walking skills (Hopkins & Westra, 1989; Super, 1981). The cultural context in which individuals live influences the timing and expression of many aspects of development, even physical developments long thought to be influenced only by biological maturation (Mistry, 2013). Some scientists argue that applying principles of development derived from Western samples to children of other cultures is unscientific and even unethical because it may yield misleading conclusions about children's capacities (Keller, 2017).

There is a growing trend favoring *cultural research*, which examines how culture itself influences development, over cross-cultural research, which simply examines differences across cultures (Cole & Packer, 2015). Cultural research examines development and culture as fused entities that mutually interact, with culture inherent in all domains of development and a contributor to the context in which we are embedded, transmitting values, attitudes, and beliefs that shape our thoughts, beliefs, and behaviors (Mistry & Dutta, 2015). The shift toward cultural research permits the examination of the multiple subcultures that exist within a society (Oyserman, 2016, 2017). For example, North American culture is not homogeneous; many subcultures exist, defined by factors such as ethnicity (e.g., African American, Asian American), religion (e.g., Christian, Muslim), geography (e.g., southern, midwestern), and others, as well as combinations of these factors. Current trends in cultural research document diversity and emphasize understanding how the historical, cultural, and subcultural contexts in which we live influence development throughout our lives.

What Do You Think?

1. What subcultures can you identify in your own neighborhood, state, or region of the country? What characterizes each of these subcultures?
2. Consider your own experience. With which culture or subculture do you identify?
3. How much of a role do you think your cultural membership has had in your own development?

BASIC ISSUES IN DEVELOPMENTAL SCIENCE

Developmental scientists agree that the biological, cognitive, and socioemotional changes that occur from infancy through adolescence are indisputable. Yet they sometimes disagree on several fundamental questions about how development proceeds and its influences. Developmental scientists' explanations of how infants, children, and adolescents grow and change are influenced by their perspectives on several basic issues, or fundamental questions, about human development:

1. To what extent is development influenced by inborn genetic characteristics, and to what extent is it affected by the environment in which children live?
2. What role do children play in their own development—how much are they influenced by their surroundings, and how much do they influence their surroundings?
3. In what ways do children change gradually, often imperceptibly, over time, and to what extent is developmental change sudden and dramatic?

The following sections examine each of these questions.

Nature and Nurture: How Do Nature and Nurture Influence Development?

Perhaps the oldest question about development concerns its origin. Referred to as the **nature–nurture debate**, researchers once asked whether development is caused by nature (genetics) or nurture (environment). Explanations that rely on nature point to inborn genetic traits and maturational processes as causes of developmental change. For example, most infants take their first steps at roughly the same age, suggesting a maturational trend that supports the role of nature in development (Payne & Isaacs, 2016). An alternative explanation for developmental change emphasizes nurture, the environment. From this perspective, children are molded by the physical and social environment in which they are raised. Therefore, children tend to walk at about the same time because they experience similar environmental circumstances and parenting practices.

Today, developmental scientists generally agree that the nature–nurture debate is, in fact, not a debate. Instead, most now agree that *both* nature and nurture are important contributors to development, and the question has changed to "How do genetics and environment work together to influence child development?" (Rutter, 2014; Sasaki & Kim, 2017). For example, walking is heavily influenced by maturation (nature), but experiences and environmental conditions can speed up or slow down the process (nurture). Although most infants begin to walk at about the same time, infants who experience malnutrition may walk later than well-nourished infants, and those who are given practice making stepping or jumping movements may walk earlier (Siekerman et al., 2015; Worobey, 2014). Developmental scientists attempt to determine *how* nature and nurture interact and work together to influence children's development (Bjorklund, 2018b; Lickliter & Witherington, 2017). Developmental scientists' research on the dynamic interaction of nature and nurture has important applied implications, as discussed in the Applying Developmental Science feature.

APPLYING DEVELOPMENTAL SCIENCE

The Real-World Significance of Developmental Research

In its early years, the study of child development was based on laboratory research devoted to uncovering universal aspects of development by stripping away contextual influences. This basic research was designed to examine how development unfolds, with the assumption that development is a universal process with all children changing in similar ways and in similar time frames. In the early 1980s, influenced by contextual theories (such as Bronfenbrenner's bioecological approach, discussed later in this chapter) and the growing assumption that children are active in their development, scientists began to examine developmental processes outside of the laboratory (Lerner, Johnson, & Buckingham, 2015b). It quickly became apparent that there are a great many individual differences in development that vary with a myriad of contextual influences. The field of **applied developmental science** emerged, studying individuals within the contexts in which they live and applying research findings to improve people's lives.

Applied developmental science is a multidisciplinary field that unites scientists from around the world to examine and contribute to policies on issues that affect children, adolescents, adults, and their families, such as health and health care delivery, violence, and school failure. For example, some study contextual influences on development, such as the impact of environmental contaminants or poor

(Continued)

(Continued)

access to clean water or the ways in which poverty influences children's development and economic status later in life (Aizer, 2017; Gauvain, 2018; Golinkoff, Hirsh-Pasek, Grob, & Schlesinger, 2017; Huston, 2018). Developmental science research can help address global problems. For example, in September 2016, the United Nations defined and adopted the Sustainable Development Goals, a global consensus on 17 goals for supporting individuals and ensuring equity and health in all countries (United Nations General Assembly, 2015). Sample goals include ending poverty in all its forms everywhere; improving nutrition, health, and well-being for all people; promoting education and lifelong learning opportunities; and achieving gender equality and empowering all women and girls. The goals are broad in scope, and reaching them will require the knowledge and skills of applied developmental scientist researchers and practitioners from many disciplines working in interdisciplinary teams (Gauvain, 2018).

What Do You Think?

What are some of the practical challenges a researcher might face in studying applied problems, such as risks to children's health, how to advance education in underserved communities, or how to promote health and well-being in children of developing nations? ●

The Active Child: How Do Children Influence Their Own Development?

Children's development is influenced by their genes and environment, but children also play an active role in guiding their own development. For example, Baby Joey smiles at each adult he passes by as his mother pushes his stroller in the park. Adults often respond with smiles, use "baby talk," and make faces. Baby Joey's actions, even simple smiles, influence adults, bringing them into close contact, making one-on-one interactions, and creating opportunities for learning. By engaging the world around them, thinking, being curious, and interacting with people and objects, infants and children are "manufacturers of their own development" (Flavell, 1992, p. 998).

The prevailing view among developmental scientists is that individuals are active contributors to their own development (Lerner, Agans, DeSouza, & Hershberg, 2014). Children are influenced by the physical and social contexts in which they live, but they also play a role in influencing their development by interacting with and changing those contexts (Elder, Shanahan, & Jennings, 2016). Children interact with and influence the people and things around them, creating experiences that influence their physical, cognitive, and emotional development. That is, they play an active role in influencing their own development.

Infants influence their own development by smiling at adults, making adults more likely to smile, use "baby talk," and play with them in response.
©iStockphoto.com/monkeybusinessimages

Continuities and Discontinuities: In What Ways Is Development Continuous and Discontinuous?

Some aspects of development unfold slowly and gradually over time, demonstrating **continuous change**. For example, children slowly gain experience and learn strategies to become quicker at problem solving (Siegler, 2016). Others are best described as **discontinuous change**, characterized by abrupt change. For example, puberty transforms children's bodies into more adult-like adolescent bodies (Wolf & Long, 2016), infants' understanding and capacity for language is qualitatively different from that of school-aged children (Hoff, 2015), and children make leaps in their reasoning abilities over the course of childhood, such as from believing that robotic dogs and other inanimate objects are alive to understanding that life is a biological process (Beran, Ramirez-Serrano, Kuzyk, Fior, & Nugent, 2011; Zaitchik, Iqbal, & Carey, 2014). As shown in Figure 1.2, a discontinuous view of development emphasizes sudden transformation, whereas a continuous view emphasizes gradual and steady changes.

It was once believed that development was either continuous or discontinuous—but not both. Today, developmental scientists agree that development includes both continuity and discontinuity (Lerner et al., 2014). Whether a particular developmental change appears continuous or discontinuous depends in part on our point of view. For example, consider physical growth. We often think of increases in height as involving a slow and steady process; each month, an infant is taller than the prior month, illustrating continuous change. However, as shown in Figure 1.3, when researchers measured infants' height every day, they discovered that infants have growth days and nongrowth days,

FIGURE 1.2

Continuous and Discontinuous Development

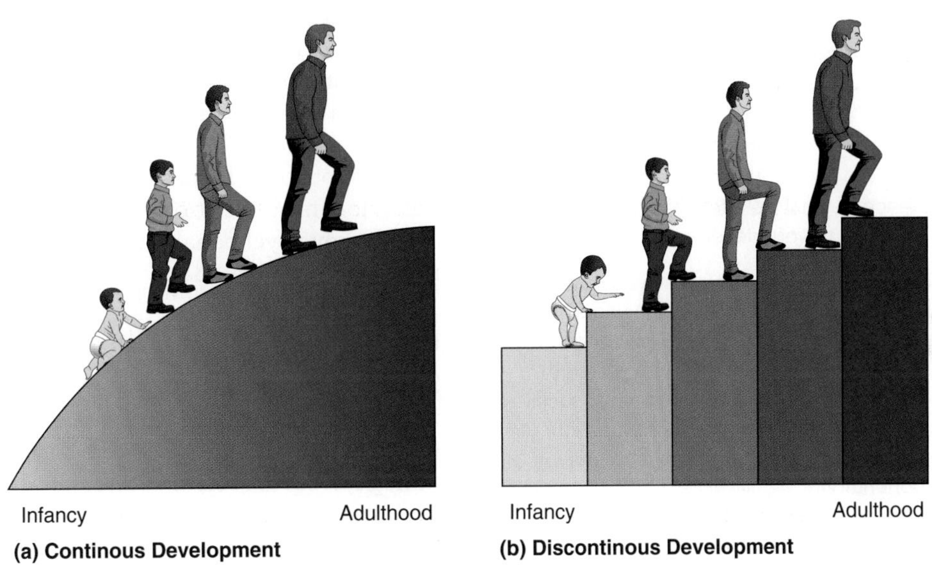

Source: Adapted from End of the Game (2014) Child Development 101, History and Theory, https://endofthegame.net/2014/04/15/child-development-101-history-and-theory/3/

FIGURE 1.3

Infant Growth: A Continuous or Discontinuous Process?

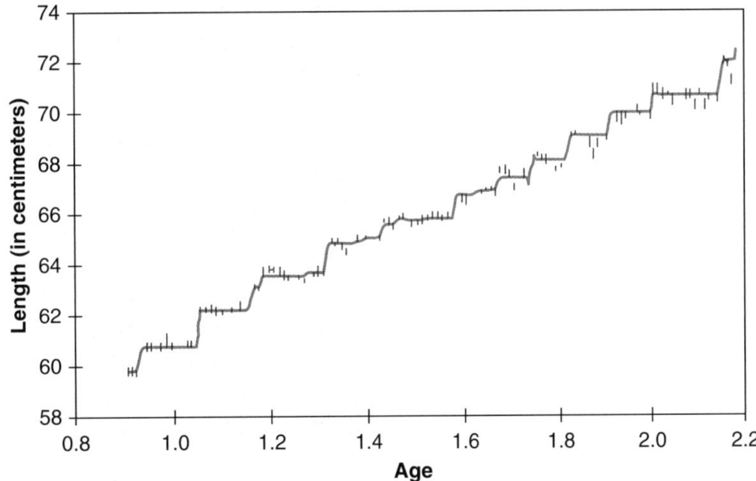

Infants' growth occurs in a random series of roughly 1-centimeter spurts in height that occur over 24 hours or less. The overall pattern of growth entails increases in height, but whether the growth appears to be continuous or discontinuous depends on our point of view.

Source: Figure 1 from Lampl, M., Veldhuis, J. D., & Johnson, M. L. (1992). Saltation and stasis: A model of human growth. *Science, 258*, 801–803. With permission from AAAS.

days in which they show rapid change in height interspersed with days in which there is no change in height, illustrating discontinuous change (Lampl, Johnson, & Frongillo, 2001). In this example, monthly measurements of infant height suggest gradual increases, but daily measurements show spurts of growth, each lasting 24 hours or less. Thus, whether a given phenomenon, such as height, is described as continuous or discontinuous can vary depending on perspective. Most developmental scientists agree that some aspects of development are best described as continuous and others as discontinuous (Miller, 2016).

THINKING IN CONTEXT 1.2

1. In what ways are your traits and abilities influenced by nature? How has nurture contributed to your development?
2. Can you identify ways in which you have changed very gradually over the years? Were there other times in which you showed abrupt change, such as physical growth, strength and coordination, thinking abilities, or social skills? In other words, in what ways is your development characterized by continuity? Discontinuity?
3. Identify examples of how a child might play an active role in his or her development. How do children influence the world around them?

THEORIES OF CHILD DEVELOPMENT

Over the past century, developmental scientists have learned much about how children progress from infancy through adolescence and into adulthood. Developmental scientists organize their observations to construct theories that explain how development unfolds. A **theory** is a way of organizing a set of observations or facts into a comprehensive explanation of how something works. Theories are important tools for compiling and interpreting the growing body of research in child development as well as determining gaps in our knowledge and making predictions about what is not yet known.

Effective theories pose specific explanations, or **hypotheses**, for a given phenomenon that can be tested by research. Scientists conduct research to find flaws in the hypothesis—not to "prove" that it is "correct." A good theory is one that is *falsifiable*, or capable of generating hypotheses that can be tested and, potentially, refuted. As scientists conduct research and learn more about a topic, they modify their theories. Updated theories often give rise to new questions and new research studies, whose findings may further modify theories. The great body of research findings about child development has been organized into several theories to account for the developmental changes that occur in infancy, childhood, and adolescence.

Psychoanalytic Theories

Is children's development guided or pushed by powerful inner forces that they cannot control? **Psychoanalytic theories** describe development and behavior as a result of the interplay of inner drives, memories, and conflicts we are unaware of and cannot control. These inner forces influence our behavior throughout our lives. Freud and Erikson are two key psychoanalytic theorists whose theories remain influential today.

Freud's Psychosexual Theory

Sigmund Freud (1856–1939), a Viennese physician, is credited as the father of the psychoanalytic perspective. Freud believed that much of our behavior is driven by unconscious impulses that are outside of our awareness. He described development as the progression through a series of *psychosexual stages*, periods in which unconscious drives are focused on different parts of the body, making stimulation to those parts a source of pleasure. Freud explained that the task for parents is to strike a balance between overgratifying and undergratifying a child's desires at each stage to

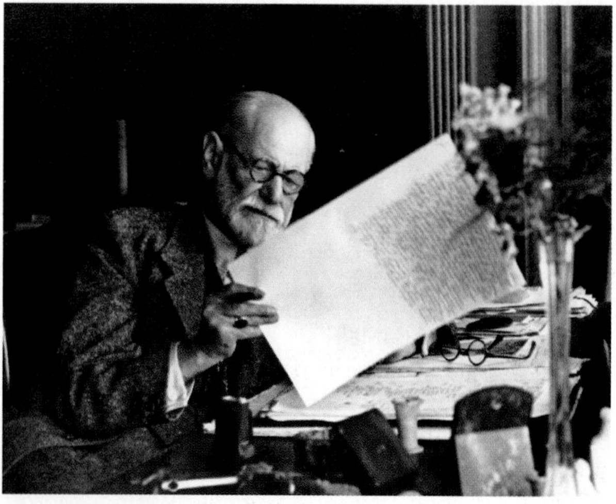

Sigmund Freud (1856–1939), the father of the psychoanalytic perspective, believed that much of our behavior is driven by impulses that we are unaware of and cannot control.
Bettmann/Getty Images

help the child develop a healthy personality with the capacity for mature relationships throughout life. Notably, Freud did not study children; his theory grew from his work with female psychotherapy patients (Crain, 2016).

Many of Freud's ideas, such as the notion of unconscious processes of which we are unaware, have stood up well to the test of time and have permeated popular culture. Notably, Freud's theory was the first to emphasize the importance of early family experience and especially the parent–child relationship for development (Bargh, 2013). However, the psychosexual stage framework's emphasis on childhood sexuality, especially the phallic stage, is unpopular and not widely accepted (Westen, 1998). In addition, unconscious drives and other psychosexual constructs are not falsifiable. They are not supported by research because they cannot be directly observed and tested (Miller, 2016).

Erikson's Psychosocial Theory

Erik Erikson (1902–1994) was influenced by Freud, but he placed less emphasis on unconscious motivators of development and instead focused on the role of the social world, society, and culture. According to Erikson, throughout their lives, individuals progress through eight *psychosocial stages* that include changes in how they understand and interact with others, as well as changes in how they understand themselves and their roles as members of society (Erikson, 1950) (see Table 1.1 for a comparison of Freud's and Erikson's theories). Each stage presents a unique developmental task, which Erikson referred to as a crisis or conflict that must be resolved. How well individuals address the crisis determines their ability to deal with the demands made by the next stage of development. For example, children's success in achieving a sense of trust in others influences their progress in developing a sense of autonomy, the ability to be independent and guide their own behavior. Regardless of their success in resolving a crisis of a given stage, individuals are driven by biological maturation and social expectations to the next psychosocial stage. No crisis is ever fully resolved, and unresolved crises are revisited throughout life.

As one of the first lifespan views of development, Erikson's psychosocial theory views development as spanning well beyond childhood. Erikson's theory offers a positive view of development and includes the role of society and culture, largely ignored by Freud. In addition, Erikson based his theory on a broad range of cases, including larger and more diverse samples of people than did Freud. Largely viewed as unfalsifiable, Erikson's theory is criticized as difficult to test. Yet it has nonetheless sparked research on specific stages, most notably on the development of identity during adolescence and the drive to guide youth and contribute to the next generation during middle adulthood (Crain, 2016). Erikson's ideas can help us understand children's socioemotional development. We will revisit his theory throughout this book.

Erik Erikson (1902–1994) posited that throughout their lifetime, people progress through eight stages of psychosocial development.
Ted Streshinsky Photographic Archive/Corbis Historical/Getty Images

Behaviorist and Social Learning Theories

In response to psychoanalytic theorists' emphasis on the unconscious as an invisible influence on development and behavior, some scientists pointed to the importance of studying observable behavior rather than thoughts and emotion, which cannot be seen or objectively verified. Theorists who study **behaviorism** examine only behavior that can be observed and believe that all behavior is influenced by the physical and social environment. For example, consider this famous quote from John Watson (1925), a founder of behaviorism:

TABLE 1.1

Psychodynamic Theories of Development

APPROXIMATE AGE	FREUD'S PSYCHOSEXUAL THEORY		ERIKSON'S PSYCHOSOCIAL THEORY	
0 to 18 months	Oral	Basic drives focus on the mouth, tongue, and gums. Feeding and weaning influence personality development. Freud believed that failure to meet oral needs influences adult habits centering on the mouth, such as fingernail biting, overeating, smoking, or excessive drinking.	Trust vs. Mistrust	Infants learn to trust that others will fulfill their basic needs (nourishment, warmth, comfort) or to lack confidence that their needs will be met.
18 months to 3 years	Anal	Basic drives are oriented toward the anus, and toilet training is an important influence on personality development. If caregivers are too demanding, pushing the child before he or she is ready, or if caregivers are too lax, individuals may develop issues of control such as a need to impose extreme order and cleanliness on their environment or extreme messiness and disorder.	Autonomy vs. Shame and Doubt	Toddlers learn to be self-sufficient and independent through toilet training, feeding, walking, talking, and exploring or to lack confidence in their own abilities and doubt themselves.
3 to 6 years	Phallic	In Freud's most controversial stage, basic drives shift to the genitals. The child develops a romantic desire for the opposite-sex parent and a sense of hostility and/or fear of the same-sex parent. The conflict between the child's desires and fears arouses anxiety and discomfort. It is resolved by pushing the desires into the unconscious and spending time with the same-sex parent and adopting his or her behaviors and roles, adopting societal expectations and values. Failure to resolve this conflict may result in guilt and a lack of conscience.	Initiative vs. Guilt	Young children become inquisitive, ambitious, and eager for responsibility or experience overwhelming guilt for their curiosity and overstepping boundaries.
6 years to puberty	Latency	This is not a stage but a time of calm between stages when the child develops talents and skills and focuses on school, sports, and friendships.	Industry vs. Inferiority	Children learn to be hard-working, competent, and productive by mastering new skills in school, friendships, and home life or experience difficulty, leading to feelings of inadequacy and incompetence.
Adolescence	Genital	With the physical changes of early adolescence, the basic drives again become oriented toward the genitals. The person becomes concerned with developing mature adult sexual interests and sexual satisfaction in adult relationships throughout life.	Identity vs. Role Confusion	Adolescents search for a sense of self by experimenting with roles. They also look for answers to the question, "Who am I?" in terms of career, sexual, and political roles or remain confused about who they are and their place in the world.

APPROXIMATE AGE	FREUD'S PSYCHOSEXUAL THEORY		ERIKSON'S PSYCHOSOCIAL THEORY	
Early adulthood			Intimacy vs. Isolation	Young adults seek companionship and a close relationship with another person or experience isolation and self-absorption through difficulty developing intimate relationships and sharing with others.
Middle adulthood			Generativity vs. Stagnation	Adults contribute to, establish, and guide the next generation through work, creative activities, and parenting or stagnate, remaining emotionally impoverished and concerned about themselves.
Late adulthood			Integrity vs. Despair	Older adults look back at life to make sense of it, accept mistakes, and view life as meaningful and productive or feel despair over goals never reached and fear of death.

> Give me a dozen healthy infants, well formed, and my own specified world to bring them up in and I'll guarantee to take any one at random and train him to become any type of specialist I might select—doctor, lawyer, artist, merchant, chief, and yes, even beggar-man and thief, regardless of his talents, penchants, tendencies, abilities, vocations, and race of his ancestors. (p. 82)

By controlling an infant's physical and social environment, Watson believed he could control the child's destiny. Behaviorist theory is also known as *learning theory* because it emphasizes how people and animals learn new behaviors as a function of their environment. As discussed in the following sections, classical and operant conditioning are two forms of behaviorist learning; social learning integrates elements of behaviorist theory and information processing theories.

Classical Conditioning

Classical conditioning is a form of learning in which a person or animal comes to associate environmental stimuli with physiological responses. Ivan Pavlov (1849–1936), a Russian physiologist, discovered the principles of classical conditioning when he noticed that dogs naturally salivate when they taste food, but they also salivate in response to various sights and sounds that occur before they taste food, such as their bowl clattering or their owner opening the food cupboard. Pavlov tested his observation by pairing the sound of a tone with the dogs' food; the dogs heard the tone, then received their food. Soon the tone itself began to elicit the dogs' salivation. Through classical conditioning, a neutral stimulus (in this example,

Ivan Pavlov (1849–1936) discovered classical conditioning when he noticed that dogs naturally salivate when they taste food, but they also salivate in response to various sights and sounds that they associate with food.
Sovfoto/Universal Images Group/Getty Images

the sound of the tone) comes to elicit a response originally produced by another stimulus (food). Many fears, as well as other emotional associations, are the result of classical conditioning. For example, some children may fear a trip to the doctor's office because they associate the doctor's office with the discomfort they felt upon receiving a vaccination shot. Classical conditioning applies to physiological and emotional responses only, yet it is a cornerstone of psychological theory. A second behaviorist theory accounts for voluntary, nonphysiological responses, as described in the following section.

Operant Conditioning

Perhaps it is human nature to notice that the consequences of our behavior influence our future behavior. A teenager who arrives home after curfew and is greeted with a severe scolding may be less likely to return home late in the future. A child who is praised for setting the dinner table may be more likely to spontaneously set the table in the future. These two examples illustrate the basic tenet of B. F. Skinner's (1904–1990) theory of **operant conditioning**, which holds that behavior becomes more or less probable depending on its consequences. According to Skinner, a behavior followed by a rewarding or pleasant outcome, called **reinforcement**, will be more likely to recur, but one followed by an aversive or unpleasant outcome, called **punishment**, will be less likely to recur.

Operant conditioning explains much about human behavior, including how we learn skills and habits. Behaviorist ideas about operant conditioning are woven into the fabric of North American culture and are often applied to understand parenting and parent–child interactions (Troutman, 2015). Developmental scientists, however, tend to disagree with operant conditioning's emphasis on external events (reinforcing and punishing consequences) over internal events (thoughts and emotions) as influences on behavior (Crain, 2016). That is, controlling a child's environment can influence his or her development, but recall that children are active in their own development. Change can occur through a child's own thoughts and actions. A child can devise new ideas and learn independently, without experiencing reinforcement or punishment.

Social Learning Theory

Like behaviorists, Albert Bandura (1925–) believed that the physical and social environments are important, but he also advocated for the role of thought and emotion as contributors to development. According to Bandura's **social learning theory**, children actively process information—they think and they feel emotion—and their thoughts and feelings influence their behavior. The physical and social environment influences children's behavior through their effect on their thoughts and emotions. For example, the teenager who breaks his curfew and is met by upset parents may experience remorse, which may then make him less likely to come home late in the future. In this example, the social environment (a discussion with upset parents) influenced the teen's thoughts and emotions (feeling bad for upsetting his parents), which then influenced the teen's behavior (not breaking curfew in the future). In other words, our thoughts and emotions about the consequences of our behavior influence our future behavior. We do not need to experience punishment or reinforcement to change our behavior (Bandura, 2012). We can learn by thinking about the potential consequences of our actions.

One of Bandura's most enduring ideas about development is that people learn through observing and imitating others, which he referred to as **observational learning** (Bandura, 2010). This finding suggests that children who observe violence rewarded, such as a child grabbing (and successfully obtaining) another child's toy, may imitate what they see and use aggressive means to take other children's toys. People also learn by observing the consequences of others' actions. A child observer might be less likely to imitate a child who takes another child's toy if the aggressor is scolded by a teacher and placed in timeout. Observational learning is one of the most powerful ways in which we learn.

Bandura believed that children are active contributors to their development as described by his concept of **reciprocal determinism**, according to which individuals' personal characteristics, behaviors, and environments interact and influence each other (Bandura, 2011). Children's characteristics determine their behavior and the environments they seek. Children who are athletically inclined (personal characteristic) tend to engage in sports activities (behavior) and seek out environments that support their athletic interests, such as groups of children who play sports, like softball or dodgeball. Environments (children's softball team), in turn, influence children's personal characteristics (interest in athletic ability) and behaviors (playing softball). This is an example of the complex interplay among person, behavior, and physical and social environment that underlies much of what we will discuss throughout this book.

Behaviorist theories have made important contributions to understanding child development.

TABLE 1.2

Piaget's Stages of Cognitive Development

STAGE	APPROXIMATE AGE	DESCRIPTION
Sensorimotor	Birth to 2 years	Infants understand the world and think using only their senses and motor skills, by watching, listening, touching, and tasting.
Preoperations	2 to 7 years	Preschoolers explore the world using their own thoughts as guides and develop the language skills to communicate their thoughts to others. Despite these advances, their thinking is characterized by several errors in logic.
Concrete Operations	7 to 11 years	School-aged children become able to solve everyday logical problems. Their thinking is not yet fully mature because they are able to apply their thinking only to problems that are tangible and tied to specific substances.
Formal Operations	12 years to adulthood	Adolescents and adults can reason logically and abstractly about possibilities, imagined instances and events, and hypothetical concepts.

Concepts such as observational learning, reinforcement, and punishment hold implications for parents, teachers, and anyone who works with children. Social learning theory and reciprocal determinism offer a more complex explanation for development and behavior than do behaviorist theories. We will revisit these concepts in later chapters.

Cognitive Theories

Cognitive theorists view cognition—thought—as essential to understanding children's functioning. In this section, we look at some of the ideas offered by cognitive-developmental theory and information processing theory.

Piaget's Cognitive-Developmental Theory

Swiss scholar Jean Piaget (1896–1980) was the first scientist to systematically examine infants' and children's thinking and reasoning. Piaget believed that to understand children, we must understand how they think, because thinking influences all behavior. Piaget's **cognitive-developmental theory** views children and adults as active explorers of their world, driven to learn by interacting with the world around them and organizing what they learn into **cognitive schemas**, or concepts, ideas, and ways of interacting with the world. Through these interactions, they construct and refine their own cognitive schemas, thereby contributing to their own cognitive development.

Piaget proposed that children's drive to explore and understand the world—to construct more sophisticated cognitive schemas—propels them through four stages of cognitive development, as shown in Table 1.2.

Piaget's cognitive-developmental theory transformed the field of developmental psychology and remains one of the most widely cited developmental theories. It was the first to consider *how* infants and children think and to view people as active contributors to their development. In addition, Piaget's concept of cognitive stages and the suggestion that children's reasoning is limited by their stage has implications for education—specifically, the idea that effective instruction must match the child's developmental level.

Some critics of cognitive-developmental theory argue that Piaget focused too heavily on cognition and ignored emotional and social factors in development (Crain, 2016). Others believe that Piaget neglected the influence of contextual factors by assuming that cognitive-developmental stages are universal—that all individuals everywhere progress through the stages in a sequence that does not vary. Some cognitive theorists argue that cognitive development is not a discontinuous, stage-like process but instead is a continuous process (Birney & Sternberg, 2011), as described in the following section.

Information Processing Theory

A developmental scientist presents a 5-year-old child with a puzzle in which a dog, cat, and mouse must find their way to a bone, piece of fish, and hunk of cheese. To solve the puzzle, the child must move all three animals to the appropriate locations. How will the child approach this task? Which item will she move first? What steps will she take? What factors influence whether and how quickly a child completes this task? Finally, how does the 5-year-old child's process and performance differ from that of children older and younger than her?

The problem described above illustrates the questions studied by developmental scientists who favor **information processing theory**, which posits that the mind works in ways similar to a computer in that information enters and then is manipulated, stored, recalled, and used to solve problems (Halford & Andrews, 2011). Unlike the theories we have discussed thus far, information processing theory is not one theory that is attributed to an individual theorist. Instead, there are many information processing theories, and each emphasizes a different aspect of thinking (Callaghan & Corbit, 2015; Müller & Kerns, 2015; Ristic & Enns, 2015). Some theories focus on how children perceive, focus on, and take in information. Others examine how people store information, create memories, and remember information. Still others examine problem solving—how children approach and solve problems at home, at school, and in the peer group.

According to information processing theorists, children are born with the ability to think, or process information. Mental processes, such as noticing, taking in, manipulating, storing, and retrieving information, do not show the radical changes associated with stage theories. Instead, development is continuous and entails changes in the efficiency and speed of thought. Maturation of the brain and nervous system contributes to changes in information processing abilities. Children become more efficient at attending to, storing, and processing information (Luna, Marek, Larsen, Tervo-Clemmens, & Chahal, 2015). Experience and interaction with others also contribute by helping children learn new ways of managing and manipulating information.

Information processing theory offers a complex and detailed view of how children think, which permits scientists to make specific predictions about behavior and performance that can be tested in research studies. Indeed, information processing theory has generated a great many research studies and has garnered much empirical support (Halford & Andrews, 2011). Critics of the information processing perspective argue that a computer model cannot capture the complexity of the human mind and children's unique cognitive abilities. In addition, findings from laboratory research may not extend to everyday contexts in which children must adapt to changing circumstances and challenges to attention (Miller, 2016).

Contextual Theories

Contextual theories emphasize the role of the sociocultural context in development. Children are immersed in their social contexts; they are inseparable from the cultural beliefs and societal, neighborhood, and familial contexts in which they live. The origins of sociocultural systems theory lie with two theorists, Lev Vygotsky and Urie Bronfenbrenner.

Vygotsky's Sociocultural Theory

Writing at the same time as Piaget, Russian scholar Lev Vygotsky (1896–1934) offered a different perspective on development, especially cognitive development, that emphasized the importance of culture. Recall that culture refers to the beliefs, values, customs, and skills of a group; it is a product of people's interactions in everyday settings (Markus & Kitayama, 2010). Vygotsky's (1978) **sociocultural theory** examines how cultural tools, such as language and patterns of thought and behavior, are transmitted from one generation to the next through social interaction. Children interact with adults and more experienced peers as they talk, play, and work alongside them. It is through these formal and informal social contacts that children learn about their culture and adopt the ways of thinking and behaving that characterize their culture. By participating in cooperative dialogues and receiving guidance from adults and more expert peers, children adopt their culture's perspectives and practices, learning to think and behave as members of their society (Rogoff, 2016). Over time, they become able to apply these ways of thinking to guide their own

Lev Vygotsky's (1896–1934) sociocultural theory examines how cultural tools, such as language, are transmitted from one generation to the next through social interaction.
Heritage Images/Hulton Archive/Getty Images

actions, thus requiring less assistance from adults and peers (Rogoff, Moore, Correa-Chavez, & Dexter, 2014).

Vygotsky's sociocultural theory holds important implications for understanding cognitive development. Like Piaget, Vygotsky emphasized that children actively participate in their development by engaging with the world around them. However, Vygotsky also viewed cognitive development as a social process that relies on interactions with adults, more mature peers, and other members of their culture. Vygotsky also argued that acquiring language is a particularly important milestone for children because it enables them to think in new ways and have more sophisticated dialogues with others, advancing their learning about culturally valued perspectives and activities. We will revisit Vygotsky's ideas about the roles of culture, language, and thought in Chapter 8.

Vygotsky's sociocultural theory is an important addition to the field of human development because it is the first theory to emphasize the role of the cultural context in influencing children's development. Critics argue that sociocultural theory overemphasizes the role of context, minimizes the role of children in their own development, and neglects the influence of genetic and biological factors (Crain, 2016).

Bronfenbrenner's Bioecological Systems Theory

Similar to other developmental theorists, Urie Bronfenbrenner (1917–2005) believed that children are active in their own development. Specifically, Bronfenbrenner's **bioecological systems theory** poses that development is a result of the ongoing interactions among biological, cognitive, and psychological changes within the person and his or her changing context (Bronfenbrenner & Morris, 2006). Bronfenbrenner proposed that all individuals are embedded in, or surrounded by, a series of contexts: home, school, neighborhood, culture, and society, as shown in Figure 1.4. The bioecological systems theory thus offers a comprehensive perspective on the role of context as an influence on development. As shown in Figure 1.4, contexts are organized into a series of systems in which individuals are embedded and that interact with one another and the person to influence development.

At the center of the bioecological model is the individual. The developing person's genetic, psychological, socioemotional, and personality traits interact, influencing each other. For example, physical development, such as brain maturation, may influence cognitive development, which in turn may influence social development, such as a child's understanding of friendship. Social development then may influence cognitive development, as children may learn activities or ideas from each other. In this way, the various forms of development interact. The individual interacts with the contexts in which he or she is embedded, influencing and being influenced by them (Bronfenbrenner & Morris, 2006).

The individual is embedded in the innermost level of context, the *microsystem*, which includes interactions with the immediate physical and social environment surrounding the person, such as family, peers, and school. Because the microsystem contains the developing person, it has an immediate and direct influence on his or her development. For example, peer relationships can influence a person's sense of self-esteem, social skills, and emotional development.

The next level, the *mesosystem*, refers to the relations and interactions among microsystems, or connections among contexts. For example, experiences in the home (one microsystem) influence those at school (another microsystem); therefore, parents who encourage and provide support for reading will influence the child's experiences in the classroom. Like the microsystem, the mesosystem has a direct influence on the individual because he or she is a participant in it.

The *exosystem* consists of settings in which the individual is not a participant but that nevertheless influence him or her. For example, a child typically does not participate in a parent's work setting, yet the work setting has an indirect influence on the child because it affects the parent's mood. The availability of funding for schools, another exosystem factor, indirectly affects children by influencing the availability of classroom resources. The exosystem is an important contribution to our understanding of development because it shows us how the effects of outside factors trickle down and indirectly affect children and adults.

The *macrosystem* is the greater sociocultural context in which the microsystem, mesosystem, and exosystem are embedded. It includes cultural values, legal and political practices, and other elements of the society at large. The macrosystem indirectly influences the child because it affects each of the other contextual levels. For example, cultural beliefs about the value of education (macrosystem) influence funding decisions made at national and local levels (exosystem), as well as what happens in the classroom and in the home (mesosystem and microsystem).

A final element of the bioecological system is the *chronosystem*, which refers to how the bioecological system changes over time. As people grow and

FIGURE 1.4

Bronfenbrenner's Bioecological Systems Theory

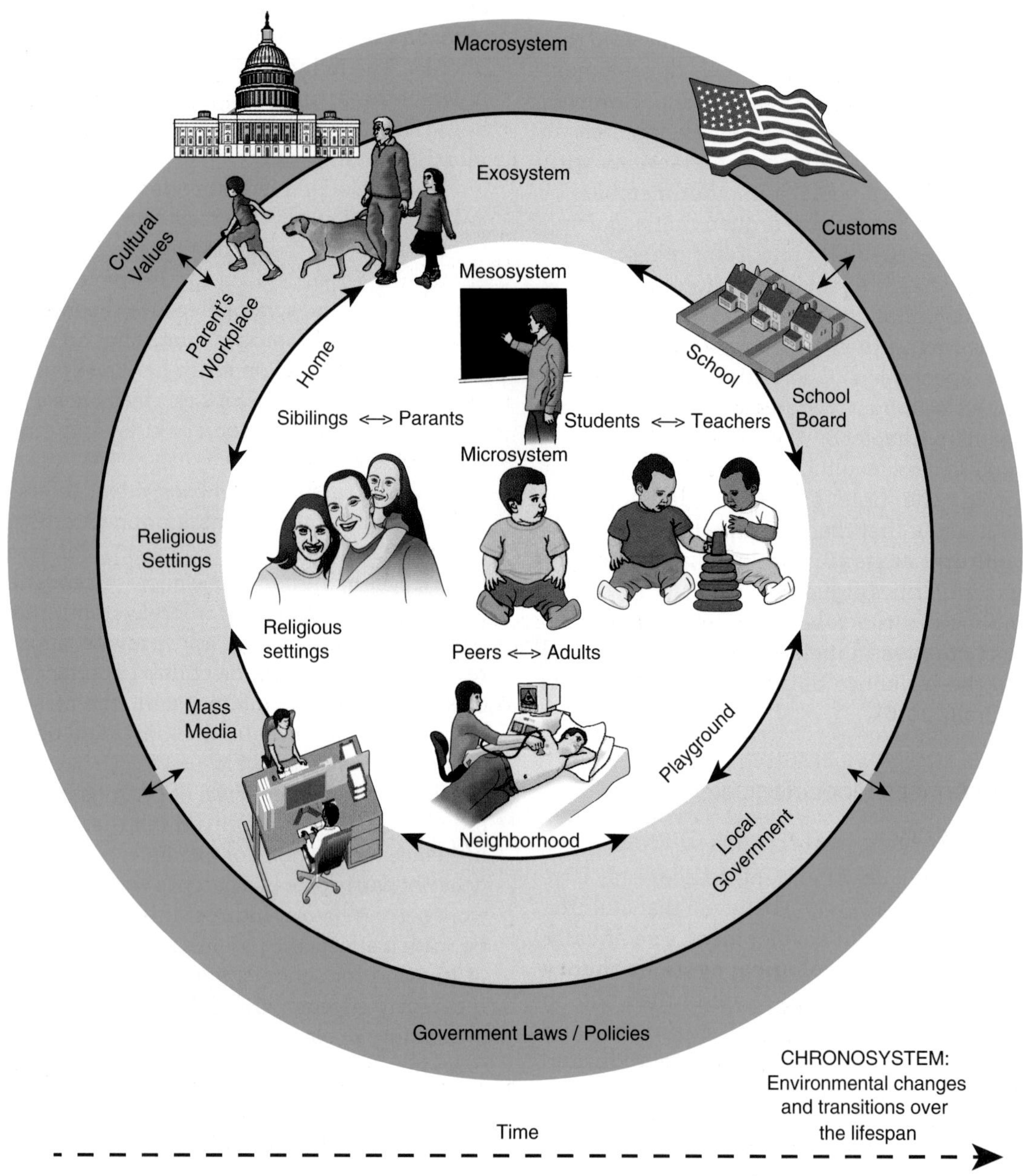

Source: Adapted from Bronfenbrenner and Morris (2006).

change, they take on and let go of various roles. For example, graduating from college, getting married, and becoming a parent involve changes in roles and shifts in microsystems. These shifts in contexts, called *ecological transitions*, occur throughout life.

The bioecological model was criticized recently for its vague explanation of development, especially the role of culture (Vélez-Agosto, Soto-Crespo, Vizcarrondo-Oppenheimer, Vega-Molina, & García Coll, 2017). Situated in the macrosystem, culture is said to influence development through the interdependence of the systems. Yet current conceptualizations of culture describe it as all the processes used by people as they make meaning or think through interactions with group members (Mistry et al., 2016; Yoshikawa, Mistry, & Wang, 2016). Critics therefore argue that since culture is manifested in our daily activities, it is inherent in each bioecological level (Vélez-Agosto et al., 2017). Moreover, cultural changes derive from interactions and pressures at each ecological level, not simply

LIVES IN CONTEXT: CULTURAL CONTEXT

Effects of Exposure to Community Violence

The neighborhoods and communities where children reside are important contextual factors that influence their development. It is estimated that over one-third of all children and adolescents witness violence within their communities (Kennedy & Ceballo, 2014), and the number is much higher in some inner-city neighborhoods. Community violence is particularly damaging to development because it is experienced across multiple contexts—school, playground, and home. The chronic and random nature of community violence presents a constant threat to children and parents' sense of safety. In such environments, children learn that the world is a dangerous and unpredictable place and that parents are unable to offer protection.

Children exposed to chronic community violence display anxiety and symptoms of post-traumatic stress disorder, commonly seen in individuals exposed to the extreme trauma of war and natural disasters, including exaggerated startle responses, difficulty eating and sleeping, and academic and cognitive problems (Fowler, Tompsett, Braciszewski, Jacques-Tiura, & Baltes, 2009; Kennedy & Ceballo, 2014). The periodic and unpredictable experience of intense emotions may interfere with children's ability to identify and regulate their emotions and can disrupt the development of empathy and prosocial responses. Children who are exposed to community violence tend to be less socially aware, to be less skilled, and to display more aggressive and disruptive behavior than other children (McMahon et al., 2013).

Community violence also affects parents. Parents who are exposed to community violence may feel alienated from the community and unsafe (Guo, O'Connor Duffany, Shebl, Santilli, & Keene, 2018). The parental distress, frustration, and sense of helplessness that accompany community violence can compromise parenting (Vincent, 2009). When dealing with their own grief, fear, and anxiety, parents may be less available for physical and emotional caregiving, which in turn predicts poor child adjustment (Farver, Xu, Eppe, Fernandez, & Schwartz, 2005). They also experience a heightened risk for depression (Jacoby, Tach, Guerra, Wiebe, & Richmond, 2017), posing risks to parenting (Dempsey, McQuillin, Butler, & Axelrad, 2016).

Community violence is unquestionably detrimental to developmental outcomes. However, some children display more resilience to its negative effects than others. Three factors appear to protect children from the most negative effects of exposure to community violence: (1) having a supportive person in the environment; (2) having a protected place in the neighborhood that provides a safe haven from violence exposure; and (3) having personal resources such as adaptable temperament, intelligence, or coping capacities (Jain & Cohen, 2013). Unfortunately, the fear that accompanies community violence influences all members of the community, reducing supports and safe havens. Effective interventions to combat the effects of community violence include after-school community centers that allow children to interact with each other and caring adults in a safe context that permits them to develop skills in coping, conflict resolution, and emotional regulation.

What Do You Think?

Consider the problem of community violence from a bioecological perspective.

1. How might community violence influence individuals through the mesosystem and microsystem?
2. Identify exosystem and macrosystem factors that might influence the prevalence of community violence.
3. How can we help children and families? Identify microsystem, mesosystem, and exosystem factors that might help children and families cope with community violence. ●

the macrosystem as Bronfenbrenner believed (Varnum & Grossmann, 2017).

A second criticism arises from the sheer complexity of the bioecological model and its attention to patterns and dynamic interactions. We can never measure and account for all of the potential individual and contextual influences on development at once, making it difficult to devise research studies to test the validity of the model. Proponents, however, argue that it is not necessary to test all of the model's components at once. Instead, smaller studies can examine each component over time (Jaeger, 2016; Tudge et al., 2016). In any case, bioecological systems theory remains an important contribution toward explaining children's development and is a theory that we will consider throughout this book. The Lives in Context feature further examines the effects of contextual factors on development.

Ethology and Evolutionary Developmental Theory

What motivates parents of most species to care for their young? Some researchers argue that caregiving behaviors have an evolutionary basis. **Ethology** is the scientific study of the evolutionary basis of behavior (Bateson, 2015). In 1859, Charles Darwin proposed his theory of evolution, explaining that all species adapt and evolve over time. Specifically, traits that enable a species to adapt, thrive, and mate tend to be passed to succeeding generations because they improve the likelihood of the individual and species' survival. Several early theorists applied the concepts of evolution to behavior. Konrad Lorenz and Niko Tinbergen, two European zoologists, observed animal species in their natural environments and noticed patterns of behavior that appeared to be inborn, emerged early in life, and ensured the animals' survival. For example, shortly after birth, goslings imprint to their mother, meaning that they bond to her and follow her. Imprinting aids the goslings' survival because it ensures that they stay close to their mother, get fed, and remain protected. In order for imprinting to occur, the mother goose must be present immediately after the goslings hatch; mothers instinctively stay close to the nest so that their young can imprint (Lorenz, 1952).

According to John Bowlby (1969), humans also display biologically preprogrammed behaviors that have survival value and promote development. For example, caregivers naturally respond to infants' cues. Crying, smiling, and grasping are inborn ways that infants get attention from caregivers, bring caregivers into physical contact, and ensure that they will be safe and cared for. Such behaviors have adaptive significance because they meet infants' needs and promote the formation of bonds with caregivers, ensuring that the caregivers will feel a strong desire and obligation to care for them (Bowlby, 1973). In this way, innate biological drives and behaviors work together with experience to influence adaptation and ultimately an individual's survival.

Another theory, **evolutionary developmental theory**, applies principles of evolution and scientific knowledge about the interactive influence of genetic and environmental mechanisms to understand the changes people undergo throughout their lives (Bjorklund, 2018a; Witherington & Lickliter, 2016). You may have wondered, for example, whether you—your abilities, personality, and competencies—result from your genes or from the physical and social environment in which you were raised. Evolutionary developmental scientists explain that this is the wrong question to ask. From an evolutionary development perspective, genes and context interact in an ever-changing way such that it is impossible to isolate the contributions of each to development (Witherington & Lickliter, 2016). While all of our traits and characteristics are influenced by

FIGURE 1.5

Interaction of Genetic and Environmental Factors

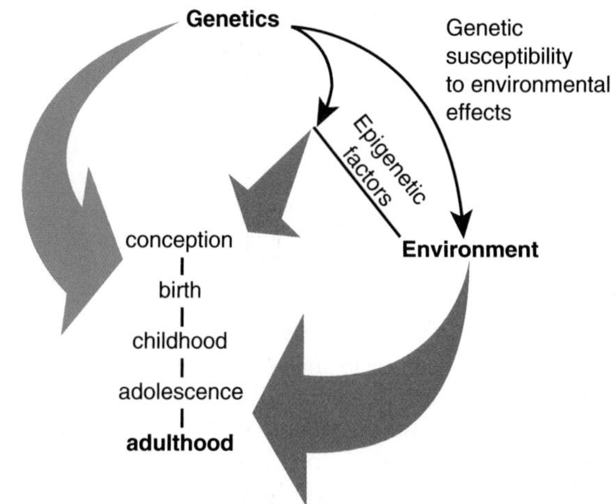

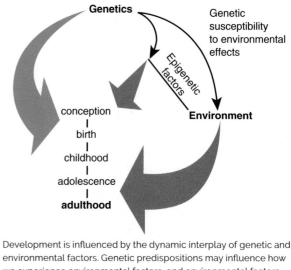

Development is influenced by the dynamic interplay of genetic and environmental factors. Genetic predispositions may influence how we experience environmental factors, and environmental factors may influence how genes are expressed.

Source: Picker (2005).

genes, contextual factors influence the expression of genetic instructions. This process is known as **epigenetics** (Moore, 2017). The term *epigenetics* literally means "above the gene." Individuals are influenced by both genetic and contextual factors; however, as shown in Figure 1.5, some contextual factors can determine whether and how genetic capacities are expressed or shown.

As an example, contextual factors such as gravity, light, temperature, and moisture influence how genes are expressed and therefore how individuals develop (Meaney, 2017). For instance, in some reptiles such as crocodiles, sex is determined by the temperature in which the organism develops. Eggs incubated at one range of temperatures produce male crocodiles and at another temperature produce female crocodiles (Pezaro, Doody, & Thompson, 2017).

According to evolutionary developmental theory, genetic factors and biological predispositions interact with the physical and social environment to influence development, and Darwinian natural selection determines what genes and traits are passed on to the next generation (Bjorklund, 2018a; Witherington & Lickliter, 2016). Children are viewed as active in their development, influencing their contexts, responding to the demands for adaptation posed by their contexts, and constantly interacting with and adapting to the world around them. The relevance of both biological and contextual factors to human development is indisputable, and most developmental scientists appreciate the contributions of evolutionary developmental theory (DelGiudice, 2018; Frankenhuis & Tiokhin, 2018; Legare, Clegg, & Wen, 2018). The ways in which biology and context interact and their influence on development change over the course of the lifetime, as we will discuss throughout this book.

Dynamic Systems Theory

Some of the major concepts that we have discussed throughout this chapter include the interaction of genetics and environment and the active role of children in their own development. Children are motivated to understand their experience and control their environment. Each child's characteristics and environmental circumstances and interactions are unique and influence how the child approaches developmental tasks and problems, resulting in unique patterns of functioning. Esther Thelen's **dynamic systems theory** posits that children's developmental domains, maturation, and environment form an integrated system that is constantly changing, resulting in developmental change and the emergence of new abilities (Thelen, 1995, 2000).

Many childhood milestones, such as an infant's first steps or first word, might look like isolated achievements, but they actually develop systematically and are the result of skill-building, with each new skill (such as pulling up to stand or babbling sounds) preparing an infant to tackle the next (Thelen, 1995, 2000). Simple actions and abilities are combined to provide more complex and effective ways for babies to explore and engage the world. An infant might combine the distinct abilities to sit upright, hold the head upright, match motor movements to vision, reach out an arm, and grasp to coordinate reaching movements to obtain a desired object (Corbetta & Snapp-Childs, 2009; Spencer, Vereijken, Diedrich, & Thelen, 2000). Development reflects goal-oriented behavior because it is initiated by the infant or child's desire to accomplish something, such as picking up a toy or expressing him- or herself. Infants' abilities and their immediate environments, including environmental supports and constraints, determine whether and how the goal can be achieved (Spencer et al., 2000). Although Esther Thelen described developmental systems theory with motor development in mind, theorists are applying it to understand children's cognitive and emotional development as well as mental health (Guo, Garfin, Ly, & Goldberg, 2017; Mascolo, van Geert, Steenbeek, & Fischer, 2016).

The many theories of human development offer complementary and contrasting views of how we change throughout our lifetimes. Table 1.3 provides a comparison of theories of human development.

TABLE 1.3

Comparing Theories of Human Development

	HOW DO NATURE AND NURTURE INFLUENCE DEVELOPMENT?	HOW DO CHILDREN INFLUENCE THEIR DEVELOPMENT?	IS DEVELOPMENT CONTINUOUS OR DISCONTINUOUS?
Freud's psychosexual theory	Greater emphasis on nature: Children are driven by inborn drives, but the extent to which the drives are satisfied influences developmental outcomes.	Children are driven by inborn instincts and are not active participants in their development.	Discontinuous stages
Erikson's psychosocial theory	Both nature and nurture: Biological and social forces propel people through the stages, and social and psychosocial influences determine the outcome of each stage.	Children are active in their development because they interact with their social world to resolve psychosocial tasks.	Discontinuous stages
Behaviorist theory	Nurture: Environmental influences shape behavior.	Individuals are shaped and molded by their environment.	Continuous process of learning new behaviors
Bandura's social learning theory	Both nature and nurture: Inborn characteristics and the physical and social environment influence behavior.	Individuals play an active role in their development; their characteristics and behavior interact with the environment.	Continuous process of learning new behaviors

(Continued)

TABLE 1.3 (Continued)

	HOW DO NATURE AND NURTURE INFLUENCE DEVELOPMENT?	HOW DO CHILDREN INFLUENCE THEIR DEVELOPMENT?	IS DEVELOPMENT CONTINUOUS OR DISCONTINUOUS?
Piaget's cognitive-developmental theory	Both nature and nurture: An innate drive to learn, coupled with brain development, leads people to interact with the world. Opportunities provided by the physical and social environment influence development.	Children actively interact with the world to create their own schemas.	Discontinuous stages
Information processing theory	Both nature and nurture: People are born with processing capacities that develop through maturation and environmental influences.	Children attend to, process, and store information.	Continuous increase of skills and capacities
Vygotsky's sociocultural theory	Both nature and nurture: People learn through interactions with more skilled members of their culture; however, capacities are influenced by genes, brain development, and maturation.	Children actively interact with members of their culture.	Continuous interactions with others lead to developing new reasoning capacities and skills.
Bronfenbrenner's bioecological systems theory	Both nature and nurture: People's inborn and biological characteristics interact with an ever-changing context to influence behavior.	Children interact with their contexts, being influenced by their contexts but also determining what kinds of physical and social environments are created and how they change.	Continuous: People constantly change through their interactions with the contexts in which they are embedded.
Ethology and evolutionary developmental theory	Both nature and nurture: Genetic programs and biological predispositions interact with the physical and social environment to influence development, and Darwinian natural selection determines what genes and traits are passed on to the next generation.	Active individuals interact with their physical and social environment.	Both continuous and discontinuous: People gradually grow and change throughout life, but there are sensitive periods in which specific experiences and developments must occur.
Dynamic systems theory	Both nature and nurture: Biological factors, maturation, and the environment form an integrated system, resulting in developmental change.	Children are active in their development because they are motivated to achieve goals and master skills.	Both: Continuous process of systemic change. Behaviors may show stage-like transformations.

THINKING IN CONTEXT 1.3

Just after their healthy baby girl is born, Latisha and Devonne are overwhelmed by the intense love they feel for her. Like most new parents, they also worry about their new responsibility. They hope that their baby will develop a strong, secure, and close bond to them. They want their baby to feel loved and to love them.

1. What advice would a psychoanalytic theorist give Latisha and Devonne? Contrast psychoanalytic with behaviorist or social learning perspectives. How might a behaviorist theorist approach this question?
2. How might an evolutionary developmental theorist explain bonding between parents and infants? What advice might an evolutionary developmental theorist give to Latisha and Devonne?
3. Considering bioecological systems theory, what microsystem and mesosystem factors influence the parent–child bond? What role might exosystem and macrosystem factors take?

RESEARCH IN HUMAN DEVELOPMENT

Developmental scientists conduct research to gather information and answer questions about how children grow and change. They devise theories to organize what they learn from research and to suggest new hypotheses to test in research studies. In turn, research findings are used to modify theories. By conducting multiple studies over time, developmental scientists refine their theories about child development and determine new questions to ask.

The Scientific Method

Researchers employ the **scientific method**, a process of posing and answering questions by making careful and systematic observations and gathering information. The scientific method provides an organized way of formulating questions, gathering and evaluating information, and determining and communicating answers. Its basic steps are as follows:

1. Identify the research question or problem to be studied and formulate the hypothesis, or proposed explanation, to be tested.
2. Gather information to address the research question.
3. Summarize the information gathered and determine whether the hypothesis is refuted, or shown to be false.
4. Interpret the summarized information, consider the findings in light of prior research studies, and share them with the scientific community and world at large.

In practice, the scientific method usually does not proceed in such a straightforward, linear fashion. Frequently, research studies raise as many questions as they answer—and sometimes more. Unexpected findings can prompt new studies. For example, researchers may repeat an experiment (called a *replication*) to see whether the results are the same as previous ones. Sometimes analyses reveal flaws in data collection methods or research design, prompting a revised study. Experts may also disagree on the interpretation of a study. Researchers may then conduct new studies to test new hypotheses and shed more light on a given topic. For all of these reasons, scientists often say the scientific method is "messy."

Methods of Data Collection

The basic challenge that developmental scientists face in conducting research is determining how to measure their topic of interest. Scientists use the term *data* to refer to the information they collect. How can we gather data about children? Should we simply talk with them? Watch them as they play? Hook them up to machines that measure physiological activity such as heart rate or brain waves? Developmental scientists use a variety of different methods to collect information.

Observational Measures

Some developmental scientists collect data by watching and recording children's behavior. Developmental scientists employ two types of observational measures: naturalistic observation and structured observation.

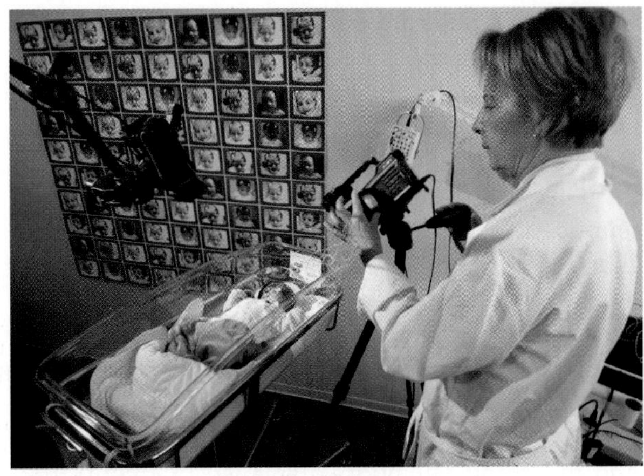

This researcher is using a video camera to observe and record the facial expressions a newborn baby makes while it sleeps.
Thierry Berrod, Mona Lisa Production/Science Source

Scientists who use **naturalistic observation** observe and record behavior in natural, real-world settings. For example, Salo, Rowe, and Reeb-Sutherland (2018) observed 12-month-old infants playing with their parents. They recorded infants' gestures and how often they participated with parents in paying attention to or interacting with an object (such as a toy). One year later, infants who used more gestures and engaged in more joint attention, especially responses to parents' efforts to direct their attention, showed more advanced language development; they understood and produced more words.

Sometimes the presence of an observer causes those being observed to behave in unnatural ways or ways that are not typical for them. This is known as *participant reactivity*, and it poses a challenge to gathering data by naturalistic observation. One way of reducing the effect of observation is to conduct multiple observations so that the children get used to the observer and return to their normal behavior. Another promising method of minimizing participant reactivity is to use an electronically activated voice recorder (EAR) (Mehl, 2017). Participants carry the EAR as they go about their daily lives. The EAR captures segments of information over time: hours, days, or even weeks. It yields a log of people's activities as they naturally unfold. The EAR minimizes participant reactivity because the participant is unaware of exactly when the EAR is recording. For example, researchers who study child trauma use the EAR to sample conversations between parents and children to understand how parent–child interactions influence children's adjustment and how the family environment can aid children's recovery from trauma (Alisic, Krishna, Robbins, & Mehl, 2016).

Naturalistic observation permits researchers to observe patterns of behavior in everyday settings, such as whether an event or behavior typically precedes another. Such observations can help researchers determine which behaviors are important to study in the first place. For example, a scientist who studies bullying by observing children's play may notice that some victims act aggressively *before* a bullying encounter (Kamper-DeMarco & Ostrov, 2017). The scientist may then decide to examine aggression in victims not only after a bullying incident but also beforehand. Naturalistic observation is a useful way of studying events and behaviors that are common. However, some behaviors and events occur infrequently, requiring a researcher to observe for very long periods of time to obtain data on the behavior of interest. For this reason, many researchers make structured observations.

Structured observation entails observing and recording behaviors displayed in a controlled environment, a situation constructed by the experimenter. For example, children might be observed in a laboratory setting as they play with another child or complete a puzzle-solving task. The challenges of identifying and categorizing which behaviors to record are similar to those involved in naturalistic observation. However, the laboratory environment permits researchers to exert more control over the situation than is possible in natural settings. In addition to cataloging observable behaviors, some researchers use technology to measure biological functions such as heart rate, brain waves, and blood pressure. One challenge to conducting structured observations is that children do not always behave in laboratory settings as they do in real life.

Self-Report Measures

Interviews and questionnaires are known as self-report measures because the child under study answers questions about his or her experiences, attitudes, opinions, beliefs, and behavior. Interviews can take place in person, over the phone, or over the Internet.

One type of interview is the **open-ended interview**, in which a trained interviewer uses a conversational style that encourages the child under study to expand his or her responses. Interviewers may vary the order of questions, probe, and ask additional questions based on responses. The scientist begins with a question and then follows up with prompts to obtain a better view of the person's reasoning (Ginsburg, 1997). An example of this is the Piagetian Clinical Interview, which requires specialized training to administer. Consider this dialogue between Piaget and a 6-year-old child:

> You know what a dream is?
>
> *When you are asleep and you see something.*
>
> Where does it come from?
>
> *The sky.*
>
> Can you see it?
>
> *No! Yes, when you're asleep.*
>
> Could I see it if I was there?
>
> *No.*
>
> Why not?
>
> *Because it is in front of us.... When you are asleep you dream and you see them, but when you aren't asleep you don't see them.*
>
> (Piaget, 1929, p. 93)

Open-ended interviews allow children to explain their thoughts thoroughly and in their own words. They also enable scientists to gather a large amount of information quickly. Open-ended interviews are very flexible as well. However, their flexibility poses a challenge: When questions are phrased differently for each child, responses may not capture real differences in how children think about a given topic and instead may reflect differences in how the questions were posed and followed up by the interviewer.

A **structured interview** poses the same set of questions to each child in the same way. On one hand, structured interviews are less flexible than open-ended interviews. On the other hand, because all children receive the same set of questions, differences in responses are more likely to reflect true differences among children and not merely differences in the manner of interviewing. For example, Evans, Milanak, Medeiros, and Ross (2002) used a structured interview to examine American children's beliefs about magic. Children between the ages of 3 and 8 were asked the following set of questions:

> What is magic? Who can do magic?
>
> Is it possible to have special powers? Who has special powers?
>
> Does someone have to learn to do magic? Where have you seen magic? (p. 49)

After compiling and analyzing the children's responses as well as administering several cognitive tasks, the researchers concluded that even older children, who have the ability to think logically and perform concrete operations, may display magical beliefs.

To collect data from large samples of people, scientists may compile and use **questionnaires**, also called surveys, made up of sets of questions, typically multiple choice. Questionnaires can be administered in person, online, or by telephone, email, or postal mail. Questionnaires are popular data collection methods with adolescents because they are easy to use and enable scientists to collect information from many people quickly and inexpensively. Scientists who conduct research on sensitive topics, such as sexual interest and experience, often use questionnaires because they can easily be administered anonymously, protecting participants' privacy. For example, the

Monitoring the Future Study is an annual survey of 50,000 eighth-, tenth-, and twelfth-grade students that collects information about their behaviors, attitudes, and values concerning drug and alcohol use (Miech et al., 2017). The survey permits scientists to gather an enormous amount of data, yet its anonymity protects the adolescents from the consequences of sharing personal information that they might not otherwise reveal. Questionnaires, however, rely on a child's ability to read and understand questions and provide responses. It is not until late childhood and, more often, adolescence that questionnaires become feasible sources of data.

Despite their ease of use, self-report measures are not without challenges. Sometimes children give socially desirable answers: They respond in ways they would like themselves to be perceived or believe researchers desire. A fifth-grade student completing a survey about cheating, for example, might sometimes peek at other students' tests, but she might choose survey answers that do not reflect this behavior. Her answers might instead match the person she aspires to be or the behavior she believes her teacher expects—that is, someone who does not cheat on exams. Self-report data, then, may not always reflect children's understanding, attitudes, or behavior.

Physiological Measures

Physiological measures are increasingly used in developmental research because cognition, emotion, and behavior have physiological indicators. For example, when you are speaking in public, such as when you give a class presentation, do you feel your heart beat more rapidly or your palms grow sweaty? Increases in heart rate and perspiration are physiological measures of anxiety that might be measured by researchers. Other researchers might measure cortisol, a hormone triggered by the experience of stress (Simons, Cillessen, & de Weerth, 2017).

Some researchers measure eye movements or pupil dilation as indicators of attention and interest. For example, researchers in one study examined infants' pupil dilation to determine whether they detect and attend to an unusual sound (Wetzel, Buttelmann, Schieler, & Widmann, 2016). Another study examined older children's eye movements to determine their attention to healthy and unhealthy foods depicted in a cartoon (Spielvogel, Matthes, Naderer, & Karsay, 2018). The children paid more attention to unhealthy foods than healthy foods, especially when the characters were shown interacting with and eating the unhealthy food.

In recent decades, researchers have increasingly used physiological measures of brain activity to study human behavior. There are many ways of measuring brain activity, and each measure provides a different perspective, as noted in the Lives in Context feature. An advantage of physiological measures is that they do not rely on verbal reports and generally cannot be faked. A challenge to physiological measures is that, although physiological responses can be recorded, they may be difficult to interpret. For example, excitement and anger may both cause an increase in heart rate. Data collection methods are summarized in Table 1.4.

TABLE 1.4

Data Collection Methods

MEASURE	ADVANTAGE	DISADVANTAGE
OBSERVATIONAL MEASURES		
Naturalistic observation	Gathers data on everyday behavior in a natural environment as behaviors occur.	The observer's presence may influence the children's behavior. No control over the observational environment.
Structured observation	Observation in a controlled setting.	May not reflect real-life reactions and behavior.
SELF-REPORT MEASURES		
Open-ended or clinical interview	Gather a large amount of information quickly and inexpensively.	Nonstandardized questions. Characteristics of the interviewer may influence children's responses.
Structured interview	Permits gathering a large amount of information quickly and inexpensively.	Characteristics of the interviewer may influence children's responses.
Questionnaire	Permits collecting data from a large sample more quickly and inexpensively than by interview methods.	Some participants may respond in socially desirable or inaccurate ways. Children may be too young to understand and participate.
Physiological measures	Assesses biological indicators and does not rely on participant report.	May be difficult to interpret.

LIVES IN CONTEXT: CULTURAL CONTEXT

Methods of Studying the Brain

What parts of the brain are active when children solve problems or feel emotions? How does the brain change with development? Until recently, the brain was a mystery. Over the past hundred years, researchers have devised several ways of studying brain activity that have increased our understanding of how the brain functions and how it develops.

The earliest instrument created to measure brain activity was the electroencephalogram, first used with humans in the 1920s (Collura, 1993). Electroencephalography (EEG) measures electrical activity patterns produced by the brain via electrodes placed on the scalp. Researchers study fluctuations in activity that occur when participants are presented with stimuli or when they sleep. EEG recordings measure electrical activity in the brain, but they do not provide information about the location of activity.

Not until the invention of positron emission tomography (PET) in the early 1950s did researchers obtain the first glimpse of the inner workings of the brain (Portnow, Vaillancourt, & Okun, 2013). Researchers inject a small dose of radioactive material into the participant's bloodstream and the PET scan measures its flow throughout the brain. The resulting images can illustrate what parts of the brain are active as participants view stimuli and solve problems. Developed in 1971, computerized tomography, known as the CT scan, produces X-ray images of brain structures that are combined to make a three-dimensional picture of the person's brain, providing images of bone, brain vasculature, and tissue (Cierniak, 2011). Because both PET and CT scans rely on the use of radioactive material, these methods are generally only used for diagnosis rather than research.

Commonly used for research, functional magnetic resonance imaging (fMRI) measures brain activity by monitoring changes in blood flow in the brain (Bandettini, 2012). Developed in the 1990s, MRI machines house a powerful magnet that uses radio waves to measure the blood oxygen level. Active areas of the brain require more oxygen-rich blood. Like PET scans, fMRI enables researchers to determine what parts of the brain are active as individuals complete cognitive tasks.

Near-infrared spectroscopy (NIRS) involves directing infrared light into brain tissue and detecting its differential absorption in response to neural activity. Unlike fMRI, NIRS does not require the child to remain motionless (Yücel, Selb, Huppert, Franceschini, & Boas, 2017). The infant wears a cap with sensors and can move and interact with others during testing (McDonald & Perdue, 2018). NIRS, however, measures activity only on the outer part of the brain, the cortex, limiting its use somewhat.

What Do You Think?

1. If you were going to study the brain, which measure would you choose and why?
2. Would you use the same measure for an infant and older child? Why or why not?
3. Identify a research question that your measure might help you answer. What type of information would you obtain from your chosen measure?

Research Designs

Conducting research entails determining a question, deciding what information to collect, and choosing a research design—a technique for conducting the research study. Developmental scientists employ several types of designs.

Case Study

A **case study** is an in-depth examination of a single individual (or small group of individuals). It is conducted by gathering information from many sources, such as through observations, interviews, and conversations with family, friends, and others who know the individual. A case study may include samples or interpretations of a person's writing, such as poetry or journal entries, artwork, and other creations. A case study provides a rich description of a person's life and influences on his or her development. It is often employed to study individuals who have unique and unusual experiences, abilities, or disorders. Conclusions drawn from a case study may shed light on an individual's development but may not be generalized or applied to others. Case studies can be a source of hypotheses to examine in large-scale research.

Correlational Research

Are children with high self-esteem more likely to excel at school? Are toddlers with working parents more aggressive? Do children who participate in athletic activities have a positive body image? All of these questions can be studied with **correlational research**, which permits researchers to examine relations among measured characteristics, behaviors, and events. For example, in one study, scientists examined the relationship between physical fitness and academic performance in middle school students and found that children with higher aerobic capacity scored higher on achievement tests than did children with poorer aerobic capacity (Bass, Brown, Laurson, & Coleman, 2013). Note that this correlation does not tell us *why* aerobic capacity was associated with academic achievement. Correlational research cannot answer this question because it simply describes relationships that exist among variables; it does not enable us to reach conclusions about the causes of those relationships. It is likely that other variables influence both a child's aerobic ability and achievement (e.g., health), but correlation does not enable us to determine the causes for behavior—for that we need an experiment.

Experimental Research

Developmental scientists who seek to test hypotheses about *causal* relationships, such as whether media exposure influences behavior or whether hearing particular types of music influences mood, employ **experimental research**. An experiment is a procedure that uses control to determine causal relationships among variables. Specifically, one or more variables thought to influence a behavior of interest are changed, or manipulated, while other variables are held constant. Researchers can then examine how the changing variable influences the behavior under study. If the behavior changes as the variable changes, this suggests that the variable caused the change in the behavior.

For example, Gentile, Bender, and Anderson (2017) examined the effect of playing violent video games on children's physiological stress and aggressive thoughts. Children were randomly assigned to play a violent video game (*Superman*) or a nonviolent video game (*Finding Nemo*) for 25 minutes in the researchers' lab. The researchers measured physiological stress as indicated by heart rate and cortisol levels before and after the children played the video game. Children also completed a word completion task that the researchers used to measure the frequency of aggressive thoughts. Gentile et al. (2017) found that children who played violent video games showed higher levels of physiological stress and aggressive thoughts than did the children who played nonviolent video games. The researchers concluded that the type of video game changed children's stress reactions and aggressive thoughts.

Let's take a closer look at the components of an experiment. Conducting an experiment requires choosing at least one **dependent variable**, the behavior under study (e.g., physiological stress—heart rate and cortisol—and aggressive thoughts), and one **independent variable**, the factor proposed to change the behavior under study (e.g., type of video game). The independent variable is manipulated or varied systematically by the researcher during the experiment (e.g., a child plays with a violent or a nonviolent video game). The dependent variable is expected to change as a result of varying the independent variable, and how it changes is thought to depend on how the independent variable is manipulated (e.g., physiological stress and aggressive thoughts vary in response to the type of video game).

In an experiment, the independent variable is administered to one or more *experimental groups*, or test groups. The *control group* is treated just like the experimental group except that it is not exposed to the independent variable. For example, in an experiment investigating whether particular types of music influence mood, the experimental group would experience a change in music (e.g., from "easy listening" to rock), whereas the control group would hear only one type of music (e.g., "easy listening"). **Random assignment**, whereby each participant has an equal chance of being assigned to the experimental or control group, is essential for ensuring that the groups are as equal as possible in all preexisting characteristics (e.g., age, ethnicity, and biological sex). Random assignment makes it less likely that any observed differences in the outcomes of the experimental and control groups are due to preexisting differences between the groups. After the independent variable is manipulated, if the experimental and control groups differ on the dependent variable, it is concluded that the independent variable *caused* the change in the dependent variable. That is, a cause-and-effect relationship has been demonstrated.

As another example, consider a study designed to examine whether massage therapy improves outcomes in preterm infants (infants who were born well before their due date) (Abdallah, Badr, & Hawwari, 2013). Infants housed in a neonatal unit were assigned to a massage group (independent variable), who were touched and their arms and legs moved for 10-minute periods once each day,

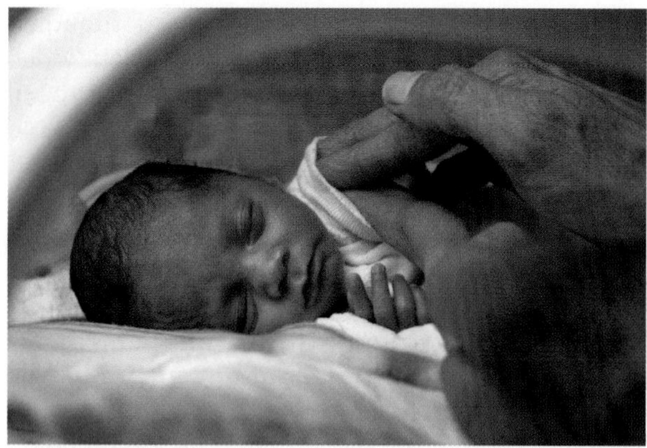

By experimentally manipulating which infants receive massage therapy, researchers determined that massage can help preterm infants gain weight.
AP Photo / AL GOLDIS

or to a control group, which received no massage. Other than the massage/no-massage periods, the two groups of infants were cared for in the same way. Infants who were massaged scored lower on the measure of infant pain and discomfort (including indicators such as heart rate, oxygen saturation, and facial responses) at discharge (dependent variable). The researchers concluded that massage therapy reduces pain responses in preterm infants.

Developmental scientists conduct studies that use both correlational and experimental research. Studying development, however, requires that scientists pay close attention to age and how people change over time, which requires the use of specialized research designs, as described in the following sections.

Developmental Research Designs

Do children outgrow shyness? Are infants' bonds with their parents associated with their peer relationships in adolescence? These challenging questions require that developmental scientists examine relationships among variables over time. There are several approaches to examining developmental change.

Cross-Sectional Research Design

A **cross-sectional research study** compares groups of children of different ages at a single point in time. For example, to examine how vocabulary improves in elementary school, a researcher might measure the vocabulary size of children in first, third, fifth, and seventh grades. The resulting comparison describes how the vocabulary of first-grade children differs from older children in Grades 3, 5, and 7. However, the results do not tell us whether the observed age differences in vocabulary reflect age-related or developmental change. In other words, we don't know whether the first graders will show the same pattern of vocabulary ability and use as the seventh graders, 6 years from now, when they are in seventh grade.

Cross-sectional research permits age comparisons, but participants differ not only in age but also in cohort, limiting the conclusions researchers can draw about development. A cohort is a group of people of the same age who are exposed to similar historical events and cultural and societal influences. Although the first-grade and seventh-grade children may attend the same school, they are different ages and different cohorts and thus may have different experiences. For example, suppose the elementary school changed the language curriculum, leading the first-grade children to be taught a new, improved curriculum, whereas the seventh graders received the old curriculum. The first graders and seventh graders therefore have different experiences because they were taught different curricula. Any differences in vocabulary may be due to age but also to different experiences. Therefore, cross-sectional research is an important source of information about age differences (how the first graders differ from seventh graders), but it cannot provide information about age change (whether the first graders will show similar development as the seventh graders).

Longitudinal Research Design

A **longitudinal research study** follows the same group of participants over many points in time. Returning to the previous example, to examine how vocabulary changes between Grades 1 and 7, a developmental scientist using longitudinal research would measure children's vocabulary size in first grade, then follow up 2 years later in third grade, then 2 years later in fifth grade, and finally 2 years later in seventh grade. This longitudinal study would take 6 years to complete.

Longitudinal research provides information about age change because it follows people over time, enabling scientists to describe how the first graders' vocabulary progressed through childhood. However, longitudinal research studies only one cohort or age-group over time. Are the findings due to developmental change or are they specific to the children studied? Is the pattern of change experienced by these children over a 6-year span similar to other cohorts or groups of children?

Because only one cohort is assessed, it is not possible to determine whether the observed changes are age related or unique to the cohort examined.

Cross-Sequential Research Design

A **cross-sequential research study** combines the best features of cross-sectional and longitudinal research by assessing multiple cohorts over time, enabling scientists to make comparisons that disentangle the effects of cohort and age (see Table 1.5). Consider the vocabulary study of children in Grades 1 through 7 once more. A cross-sequential design would begin by measuring vocabulary in first-, third-, fifth-, and seventh-grade children. The children are followed up 2 years later: the first graders are in third grade, the third graders are now in fifth grade, and the fifth graders are in seventh grade (assume the seventh graders graduated elementary school and have left the study). A new group of first-grade children are introduced to the study. Two years later, the first graders are in third grade, the third graders are in fifth grade, the fifth graders are in seventh grade, the seventh graders have aged out of the study, a new group of first-grade children are introduced to the study, and so on (Figure 1.6).

The cross-sequential design provides information about age, cohort, and age-related change. The cross-sectional data (comparisons of first through seventh graders during a given year) permit comparisons across age-groups. But, as we have seen, these cross-sectional comparisons may reflect cohort effects rather than developmental differences. The longitudinal data (annual follow-up of participants in Grades 1 through 7) allow researchers to examine age-changes; that is, how the group of first graders develop throughout elementary school. However, studying only one cohort can also be misleading. A cross-sequential design helps developmental scientists separate cohort effects from age-related change. Because several cohorts are examined at once and over time, researchers can determine the effect of cohort. The sequential design is complex, but it permits developmental scientists to effectively answer questions about development.

In summary, scientists use the scientific method to systematically ask and seek answers to questions

TABLE 1.5

Comparing Research Designs

DESIGN	STRENGTHS	LIMITATIONS
RESEARCH DESIGNS		
Case study	Provides a rich description of an individual.	Conclusions may not be generalized to other individuals.
Correlational	Permits the analysis of relationships among variables as they exist in the real world.	Cannot determine cause-and-effect relations.
Experimental	Permits a determination of cause-and-effect relations.	Data collected from artificial environments may not represent behavior in real-world environments.
DEVELOPMENTAL RESEARCH DESIGNS		
Cross-sectional	More efficient and less costly than the longitudinal design. Permits the determination of age differences.	Does not permit inferences regarding age change. Confounds age and cohort.
Longitudinal	Permits the determination of age-related changes in a sample of participants assessed for a period of time.	Time-consuming and expensive. Participant attrition may limit conclusions. Cohort-related changes may limit the generalizability of conclusions.
Cross-sequential	More efficient and less costly than the longitudinal model. Allows for both longitudinal and cross-sectional comparisons, which reveal age differences and age change, as well as cohort effects.	Time-consuming, expensive, and complicated in data collection and analysis.

about human development. Researchers' decisions about measures and research designs influence the information that they collect and the conclusions that they make about development. Researchers have responsibilities to conduct sound research and also to adhere to standards of ethical conduct in research, as the next section describes. See Table 1.5 for a comparison of research designs.

Research Ethics

Researchers have responsibilities to conduct research that is scientifically sound. They are also obligated to adhere to standards of ethical conduct in research. Suppose a researcher wanted to determine the effects of malnutrition on development or the effects of bullying on emotional development. Would it be possible to design a study in which some children are exposed to bullying or some kindergarteners are deprived of food? Of course not. These studies violate the basic ethical principles that guide developmental scientists' work: (1) beneficence and nonmaleficence, (2) responsibility, (3) integrity, (4) justice, and (5) respect for autonomy (American Psychological Association, 2010).

Beneficence and nonmaleficence are the dual responsibilities to do good and to avoid doing harm. Researchers must protect and help the individuals, families, and communities with which they work by maximizing the benefits and minimizing the potential harms of their work. Above all, participating in research must never pose threats to children beyond those they might encounter in everyday life. Researchers also have the responsibility to help participants. For example, when interviewing children about their experiences with violence in their community, a developmental scientist pays attention to their participants' demeanor. If adolescents show distress in response to a particular set of questions, the scientist might direct, or even accompany, the participant to a therapist or mental health professional who can help him or her manage the distress.

The ethical principle of **responsibility** requires that researchers act responsibly by adhering to professional standards of conduct and clarifying their obligations and roles to others. For example, a researcher conducting interviews with children and parents must clarify her role as scientist and not counselor and help her participants understand that she is simply gathering information from them rather than conducting therapy. Researchers' responsibility extends beyond their participants to society at large to ensure that their research findings are accurately portrayed in the media. The principle of responsibility means that researchers must attempt to foresee ways in which their results may be misinterpreted and correct any misinterpretations that occur (Lilienfeld, 2002; Society for Research in Child Development, 2007).

The principle of **integrity** requires that scientists be accurate, honest, and truthful in their work. Researchers should be mindful of the promises they make to participants and make every effort to keep their promises to the people and communities with which they work. In addition, the risks and benefits of research participation must be spread equitably across individuals and groups. This is the principle of **justice**. Scientists must take care to ensure that all people have access to the contributions and benefits of research. For example, when a study testing an intervention finds that it is

FIGURE 1.6

Cross-Sequential Research Design

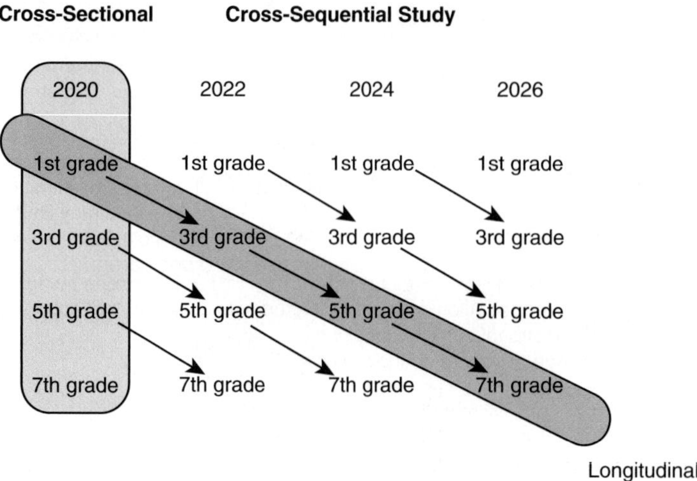

successful, the participants who did not receive it (those who were in the control group) must be given the opportunity to benefit from the intervention.

Perhaps the most important principle of research ethics is **respect for autonomy**. Scientists have a special obligation to respect participants' autonomy, their ability to make and implement decisions. Ethical codes of conduct require that researchers protect participants' autonomy by obtaining **informed consent**—participants' informed, rational, and voluntary agreement to participate. Soliciting informed consent requires providing the individuals under study information about the research study, answering questions, and ensuring that they understand that they are free to decide not to participate in the research study and that they will not be penalized if they refuse.

Respecting people's autonomy also means protecting those who are not capable of making judgments and asserting themselves. Parents provide parental permission for their minor children to participate because researchers (and lawmakers) assume that minors are not able to meet the rational criteria of informed consent. Although children cannot provide informed consent, researchers respect their growing capacities for decision making in ways that are appropriate to their age by seeking **child assent**, children's agreement to participate (Tait & Geisser, 2017). For a toddler or young child, obtaining assent may involve simply asking if he or she wants to play with the researcher (Brown, Harvey, Griffith, Arnold, & Halgin, 2017b). With increasing cognitive and social development, children are better able to understand the nature of science and engage meaningfully in decisions about research participation. In short, discussions about research participation should be tailored to children's development, including offering more detailed information and seeking more comprehensive assent as children grow older (Roth-Cline & Nelson, 2013). Moreover, seeking assent helps children learn how to make decisions and participate in decision making within safe contexts (Oulton et al., 2016).

Developmental science is a broad field of study that integrates theory and research from many disciplines to describe, predict, and explain how children grow and change. Developmental scientists apply their knowledge to identify, prevent, and solve problems and to improve opportunities for individuals, families, and communities. Throughout this book, you will learn the fundamentals of child development, including physical, cognitive, and socioemotional change, as well as the implications of developmental science for social issues. We begin our journey in Chapter 2 by considering the role of genetics and environment in shaping child development.

THINKING IN CONTEXT 1.4

Lua is interested in understanding academic achievement in elementary school students. Specifically, she believes that too much screen time harms students' achievement.

1. How might Lua gather information to address her hypothesis?
2. What kind of research design should Lua use? What are the advantages and disadvantages of this design?
3. What are some of the challenges of measuring behaviors such as screen time?
4. Suppose Lua wanted to interview children at school. What ethical principles are most relevant to her work? Why? What challenges might she anticipate?

APPLY YOUR KNOWLEDGE

Nine-year-old Christopher taunts his classmate, Josh, at recess: "Chicken! What are you afraid of? Everything!" He shoves Josh. Josh quietly walks away, head down and sniffling. This happens several times each week. Christopher and Josh's classmates usually notice and most watch. Some laugh at the funny things Christopher says or when Josh trips as he slinks away and hopes that Christopher will leave him alone.

Christopher walks home alone after school. He usually takes the long way, walking around the block to avoid the older kids who hang out outside the convenience store on the corner. The older kids are friends with Christopher's brother and they often tease Christopher, especially when his brother is there. Sometimes the kids take Christopher's hat and laugh when he tries to retrieve it. No one in the neighborhood seems to notice. Christopher thinks it's because no one cares.

Christopher returns to an empty home. After entering, he quickly and quietly walks through his home to be sure that it's empty. His mother always reminds him to be sure that it's safe before settling in. He feels silly but also a little bit nervous as he looks around. "You can't be too careful," he thinks to himself. Afterward Christopher locks the door and makes a snack.

Christopher's mother usually doesn't get home from work until 7 p.m. Christopher knows he should do his homework like his mother says, but what's the point when he keeps getting Ds and Fs? Instead, Christopher plays video games. He likes to pretend that he's in the game, running, leaping, and shooting at the bad guys. Christopher wants to be strong and tough so that nobody messes with him. "Not like that weakling Josh," he thinks.

1. Describe Christopher's behavior and interactions at school, in his neighborhood, and at home.
2. How might behaviorist and social learning theorists explain Christopher's behavior at school? In his neighborhood? At home?
3. How might Erikson explain Christopher's development and behavior?
4. Consider Christopher's development and behavior from the perspective of Bronfenbrenner's bioecological systems theory. Specifically:
   a. Identify macrosystem influences on Christopher's behavior.
   b. Discuss the interactions among mesosystem factors that might influence Christopher.
   c. Give examples of exosystem factors and discuss how they might influence Christopher's behavior and development.
   d. How might the macrosystem affect Christopher?

WANT A BETTER GRADE?

KEY TERMS

SUMMARY

1.1 Describe the periods, domains, and contexts of development.

Development begins at conception and continues prenatally and through several periods from infancy to adolescence. Each period is characterized by a predictable pattern of physical, cognitive, and socioemotional developments that unfold across a variety of contexts in which the developing person interacts, such as home, school, and peer group.

1.2 Explain three basic issues in developmental science.

Developmental scientists sometimes disagree on several fundamental questions about how development proceeds and its influences. First, in what ways is developmental change continuous, characterized by slow and gradual change, or discontinuous, characterized by sudden and abrupt change? Second, to what extent do people play an active role in their own development, interacting with and influencing the world around them? Finally, is development caused by nature or nurture—heredity or the environment? Most developmental scientists agree that some aspects of development appear continuous and others discontinuous, that individuals are active in influencing their development, and that development reflects the interactions of nature and nurture.

1.3 Summarize six theoretical perspectives on human development.

Freud's psychosexual theory explains personality development as progressing through a series of psychosexual stages during childhood. Erikson's psychosocial theory suggests that individuals move through eight stages of psychosocial development across the lifespan, with each stage presenting a unique psychosocial task, or crisis. Behaviorist and social learning theory emphasizes environmental influences on behavior, specifically, classical conditioning and operant conditioning, as well as observational learning. Piaget's cognitive-developmental theory describes cognitive development as an active process and proceeding through four stages. Information processing theorists study the steps involved in cognition: perceiving and attending, representing, encoding, retrieving, and problem solving. Sociocultural systems theorists, such as Vygotsky, look to the importance of context in shaping development. Bronfenbrenner's bioecological model explains development as a function of the ongoing reciprocal interaction among biological and psychological changes in the person and his or her changing context. Evolutionary developmental psychology integrates Darwinian principles of evolution and scientific knowledge about the interactive influence of genetic and environmental mechanisms. Dynamic systems theory views children's developmental capacities, goals, and context as an integrated system that influences the development of new abilities.

1.4 Describe the methods and research designs used to study human development and the ethical principles that guide researchers' work.

A case study is an in-depth examination of an individual. Interviews and questionnaires are called self-report measures because they ask the persons under study questions about their own experiences, attitudes, opinions, beliefs, and behavior. Observational measures are methods that scientists use to collect and organize information based on watching and monitoring people's behavior. Physiological measures gather the body's physiological responses as data. Scientists use correlational research to describe relations among measured characteristics, behaviors, and events. To test hypotheses about causal relationships among variables, scientists employ experimental research. Developmental designs include cross-sectional research, which compares groups of people at different ages simultaneously, and longitudinal research, which studies one group of participants at many points in time. Cross-sequential research combines the best features of cross-sectional and longitudinal designs by assessing multiple cohorts over time. Researchers must maximize the benefits to research participants and minimize the harms, safeguarding participants' welfare. They also must respect participants' autonomy by seeking informed consent and child assent.

REVIEW QUESTIONS

1.1 What are the periods, domains, and contexts of development?

1.2 What position do most developmental scientists take on three basic issues in developmental science?

1.3 How do six theoretical perspectives explain development?

1.4 What methods are used for collecting data and answering research questions?

1.5 What designs do researchers use to study development?

1.6 To what ethical principles must researchers adhere?

©iStockphoto.com/vic

2 Biological and Environmental Foundations of Development

The average person cannot tell twin siblings apart because twins are virtually identical. Or are they? Consider these twin girls: Maria has strikingly dark hair and deep brown eyes, similar to her father. Maria's twin sister, Anna, seems to take after their mother, with blond hair and blue eyes. Maria and Anna not only differ in appearance, but they like different foods, have different interests, and have somewhat different personalities. Although Maria is more outgoing and sociable than Anna, they both enjoy spending quiet solitary time in their room reading, drawing, and daydreaming. As twins, Maria and Anna shared a womb and many early experiences. Shouldn't they be more similar? We tend to expect twins to share similarities, as they are often depicted in the media as identical in appearance, personality, and interests, yet they tend to differ in many unpredictable ways despite sharing parents and a home environment. Twins illustrate the complexity of how characteristics and tendencies are inherited. In this chapter, we discuss

Learning Objectives

2.1 Discuss the genetic foundations of development.

Video Activity 2.1: Twins

2.2 Identify examples of genetic disorders and chromosomal abnormalities.

2.3 Examine the choices available to prospective parents in having healthy children.

Video Activity 2.1: Genetics and Pregnancy

2.4 Summarize the interaction of heredity and environment, including behavioral genetics and the epigenetic framework.

Chapter Contents

the process of genetic inheritance and principles that can help us to understand how members of a family—even twins—can share a great many similarities and also many differences.

GENETIC FOUNDATIONS OF DEVELOPMENT

What determines our traits, such as appearance, physical characteristics, health, and personality? We are born with a hereditary "blueprint" that influences our development. The following sections examine the role of heredity in our development.

Genetics

The human body is composed of trillions of units called cells, each with a nucleus containing 23 matching pairs of rod-shaped structures called **chromosomes** (Plomin, DeFries, Knopik, & Neiderhiser, 2013). Each chromosome holds the basic units of heredity, known as **genes**, composed of stretches of **deoxyribonucleic acid (DNA)**, a complex molecule shaped like a twisted ladder or staircase. Genes carry the plan for creating all of the traits that organisms carry. It is estimated that 20,000 to 25,000 genes reside within the chromosomes, comprising the human genome and influencing all genetic characteristics (Finegold, 2017).

Much of our genetic material is not unique to humans. Every species has a different genome, yet we share genes with all organisms, from bacteria to primates. We share 99% of our DNA with our closest genetic relative, the chimpanzee. There is even less genetic variation among humans. People around the world share 99.7% of their genes (Lewis, 2017). Although all humans share the same basic genome, every person has a slightly different code, making him or her genetically distinct from other humans.

Cell Reproduction

Most cells in the human body reproduce through a process known as **mitosis** in which DNA replicates itself, duplicating chromosomes, which ultimately form new cells with identical genetic material (Sadler, 2018). The process of mitosis accounts for the replication of all body cells. However, sex cells reproduce in a different way, through **meiosis**. First, the 46 chromosomes begin to replicate as in mitosis, duplicating themselves. But before the cell completes dividing, a critical process called crossing over takes place. The chromosome pairs align and DNA segments cross over, moving from one member of the pair to the other, essentially "mixing up" the DNA. Crossing over thereby creates unique combinations of genes (Sadler, 2018). The resulting cell consists of only 23 single, unpaired chromosomes. Known as **gametes**, these cells are specialized for sexual reproduction: sperm in males and ova in females. Ova and sperm join at fertilization to produce a fertilized egg, or **zygote**, with 46 chromosomes, forming 23 pairs with half from the biological mother and half from the biological father. Each gamete has a unique genetic profile, and it is estimated that individuals can produce millions of genetically different gametes (National Library of Medicine, 2019).

Sex Determination

Whether a zygote will develop into a male or female is controlled by the sex chromosomes. As shown in Figure 2.1, 22 of the 23 pairs of chromosomes are matched; they contain similar genes in almost identical positions and sequence, reflecting the distinct genetic blueprint of the biological mother and father. The 23rd pair of chromosomes are sex chromosomes that specify the biological sex of the individual. In females, sex chromosomes consist of two large X-shaped chromosomes (XX). Males'

FIGURE 2.1

Chromosomes

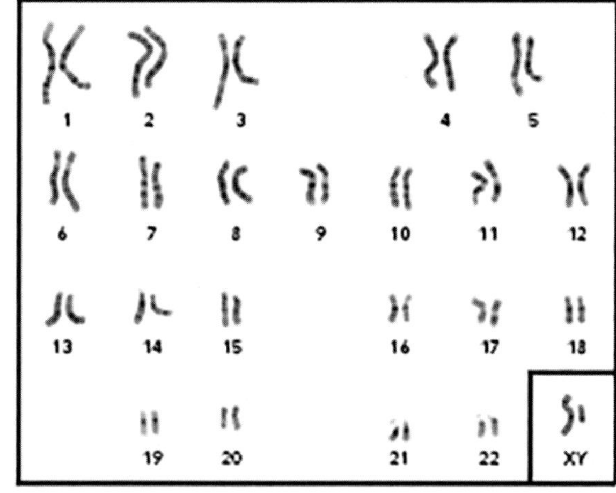

sex chromosomes consist of one large X-shaped chromosome and one much smaller Y-shaped chromosome (XY).

Because females have two X sex chromosomes, all ova contain one X sex chromosome. A male's sex chromosome pair includes both X and Y chromosomes; therefore, one-half of the sperm males produce contains an X chromosome and one-half contains a Y. The Y chromosome contains genetic instructions that will cause the fetus to develop male reproductive organs. Thus, whether the fetus develops into a boy or girl is determined by which sperm fertilizes the ovum. If the ovum is fertilized by a Y sperm, a male fetus will develop, and if the ovum is fertilized by an X sperm, a female fetus will form, as shown in Figure 2.2. (The introduction of sex selection methods has become more widely available, and some parents may seek to choose the sex of their child. For more on this topic, see the Applying Developmental Science feature.)

Genes Shared by Twins

All biological siblings share the same parents, inheriting chromosomes from each. Despite this genetic similarity, siblings are often quite different from one another. Twins are siblings who share the same womb. Twins occur in about 1 out of every 33 births in the United States (Martin, Hamilton, Osterman, Driscoll, & Drake, 2018).

The majority of naturally conceived twins are **dizygotic (DZ) twins**, or fraternal twins, conceived when a woman releases more than one ovum and each is fertilized by a different sperm. DZ twins share about one-half of their genes, and like other siblings, most fraternal twins differ in appearance,

FIGURE 2.2

Sex Determination

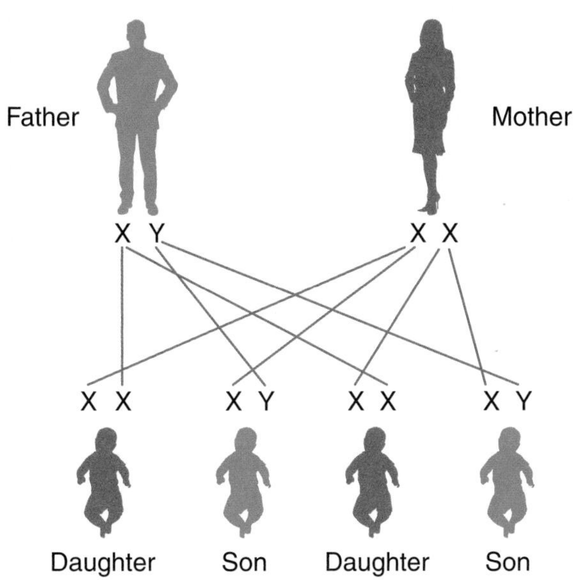

such as hair color, eye color, and height. In about half of fraternal twin pairs, one twin is a boy and the other a girl. DZ twins tend to run in families, suggesting a genetic component that controls the tendency for a woman to release more than one ovum each month. However, rates of DZ twins also increase with in vitro fertilization, maternal age, and each subsequent birth (Pison, Monden, & Smits, 2015; Umstad, Calais-Ferreira, Scurrah, Hall, & Craig, 2019).

Monozygotic (MZ) twins, or identical twins, originate from the same zygote, sharing the same **genotype**, or set of genetic instructions for all physical and psychological characteristics. MZ twins occur when the zygote splits into two distinct separate but identical zygotes that develop into two infants. It is estimated that MZ twins occur in 1 in every 250 births (Parazzini et al., 2016; Umstad et al., 2019). The causes of MZ twinning are not well understood. Rates of MZ twins are not related to maternal age or the number of births, but in vitro fertilization appears to increase the risk of MZ twins (Knopman et al., 2014; Umstad et al., 2019).

APPLYING DEVELOPMENTAL SCIENCE

Prenatal Sex Selection

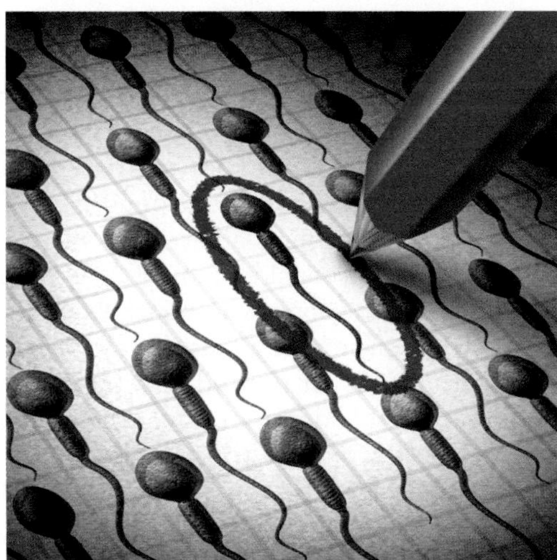

Sperm cells can be sorted by whether they carry the X or Y chromosome. Through in vitro fertilization, a zygote with the desired sex is created.
Brain light/Alamy Stock Photo

Parents have long shown a preference for giving birth to a girl or boy, depending on circumstances such as cultural or religious traditions, the availability of males or females to perform certain kinds of work important to the family or society, or the sex of the couple's other children. Until recently, the sex of an unborn child was a matter of hope, prayer, and folk rituals. It is only in the past generation that science has made it possible for parents to reliably choose the sex of their unborn child. The introduction of sex selection has been a boon to couples carrying a genetically transmitted disease (i.e., a disease carried on the sex chromosomes), enabling them to have a healthy baby of the sex unaffected by the disease they carried.

Sex selection is generally conducted using two methods: preimplantation genetic diagnosis (PGD) or preconception sperm sorting (Bhatia, 2018). PGD creates zygotes within the laboratory by removing eggs from the woman and fertilizing them with sperm. This is known as in vitro (literally, "in glass") fertilization because fertilization takes place in a test tube, outside of the woman's body. After 3 days, a cell from the organism is used to examine the chromosomes and determine its sex. The desired male or female embryos are then implanted into the woman's uterus. PGD is generally conducted only when the risk of family genetic disorders is high and is about 99% effective.

(Continued)

(Continued)

Preconception sperm sorting entails spinning sperm in a centrifuge to separate those that carry an X or a Y chromosome. Because X sperm are denser than Y sperm, they are easily separated. Sperm with the desired chromosomes are then used to fertilize the ovum. Sperm sorting has been available and commonly used since the 1970s. The success rate is about 75% (Bhatia, 2018).

The availability of sex selection procedures enables parents to choose the sex of their child because of personal desires, such as to create family balance or to conform to cultural valuing of one sex over the other, rather than simply to avoid transmitting genetic disorders (Robertson & Hickman, 2013). Critics argue that sex selection can lead down a "slippery slope" of genetic engineering and selecting for other characteristics, such as appearance, intelligence, and more (Dondorp et al., 2013). Others express concerns about societal sex ratio imbalances if sex selection becomes widely practiced (Colls et al., 2009; Robertson & Hickman, 2013). Such sex ratio imbalances favoring males have occurred in India and China because of female infanticide, gender-driven abortion, and China's one-child family policy (see the Lives in Context: Cultural Context feature in Chapter 12 for more information; Bhatia, 2010, 2018).

Most Canadian, U.K., and European countries restrict the use of PGD and prohibit it for nonmedical reasons (Bayefsky, 2016). The United States does not have a formal policy regarding sex selection (Deeney, 2013). Sex selection remains hotly debated in medical journals, by hospital and university ethics boards, and by the public.

What Do You Think?

1. Should parents be able to choose the sex of their baby? Under what conditions is sex selection acceptable?
2. If you were able to selectively reproduce other characteristics, apart from sex, what might you choose? Why or why not? ●

Patterns of Genetic Inheritance

Although the differences among various members of a given family may appear haphazard, they are the result of a genetic blueprint unfolding. Researchers are just beginning to uncover the instructions contained in the human genome, but we have learned that traits and characteristics are inherited in predictable ways.

Dominant–Recessive Inheritance

Lynn has red hair but her brother, Jim, does not—and neither do their parents. How did Lynn end up with red hair? These outcomes can be explained by patterns of genetic inheritance, how the sets of genes from each parent interact. As we have discussed, each person has 23 pairs of chromosomes, one pair inherited from the mother and one from the father. The genes within each chromosome can be expressed in different forms, or **alleles**, that influence a variety of physical characteristics. When alleles of the pair of chromosomes are alike with regard to a specific characteristic, such as hair color, the person is said to be *homozygous* for the characteristic and will display the inherited trait. If they are different, the person is *heterozygous*, and the trait expressed will depend on the relations among the genes (Lewis, 2017). Some genes are passed through **dominant–recessive inheritance** in which some genes are *dominant* and are always expressed regardless of the gene they are paired with. Other genes are *recessive* and will be expressed only if paired with another recessive gene. Lynn and Jim's parents are heterozygous for red hair; both have dark hair, but they each carry a recessive gene for red hair.

When an individual is heterozygous for a particular trait, the dominant gene is expressed, and the person becomes a carrier of the recessive gene. For example, consider Figure 2.3. Both parents have nonred hair. People with nonred hair may have homozygous or heterozygous genes for hair color because the gene for nonred hair (symbolized by N in Figure 2.3) is dominant over the gene for red hair (r). In other words, both a child who inherits a homozygous pair of dominant genes (NN) and one who inherits a heterozygous pair consisting of both a dominant and recessive gene (Nr) will have nonred hair, even though the two genotypes are different. Both parents are heterozygous for red hair (Nr). They each carry the gene for red hair and can pass it on to their offspring. Red hair can result only from having two recessive genes (rr); both parents must carry the recessive gene for red hair. Therefore, a child with red hair can be born to parents who have nonred hair if they both carry heterozygous genes for hair color. As shown in Table 2.1, several characteristics are passed through dominant–recessive inheritance.

TABLE 2.1

Dominant and Recessive Characteristics

DOMINANT TRAIT	RECESSIVE TRAIT
Dark hair	Blond hair
Curly hair	Straight hair
Hair	Baldness
Nonred hair	Red hair
Facial dimples	No dimples
Brown eyes	Blue, green, hazel eyes
Second toe longer than big toe	Big toe longer than second toe
Type A blood	Type O blood
Type B blood	Type O blood
Rh-positive blood	Rh-negative blood
Normal color vision	Colorblindness

Source: McKusick (1998) and McKusick-Nathans Institute of Genetic Medicine (2019).

Incomplete Dominance

In most cases, dominant–recessive inheritance is an oversimplified explanation for patterns of genetic inheritance. **Incomplete dominance** is a genetic inheritance pattern in which both genes influence the characteristic (Finegold, 2017). For example, consider blood type. The alleles for blood types A and B do not dominate each other. A heterozygous person with the alleles for blood type A and B will express both A and B alleles and have blood type AB.

A different type of inheritance pattern is seen when a person inherits heterozygous alleles in which one allele is stronger than the other yet does not completely dominate. In this situation, the stronger allele does not mask all of the effects of the weaker allele. Therefore, some, but not all, characteristics of the recessive allele appear. For example, the trait for developing normal blood cells does not completely mask the allele for developing sickle-shaped blood cells. About 5% of African American newborns (and relatively few Caucasians or Asian Americans) carry the recessive **sickle cell trait** (Ojodu, Hulihan, Pope, & Grant, 2014). Sickle cell alleles cause red blood cells to become crescent, or sickle, shaped. Cells that are sickle shaped cannot distribute oxygen effectively throughout the circulatory system (Ware, de Montalembert, Tshilolo, & Abboud, 2017). The average life expectancy for individuals with sickle cell anemia is 55 years in North America (Pecker & Little, 2018). Alleles for normal blood cells do not mask

FIGURE 2.3

Dominant–Recessive Inheritance

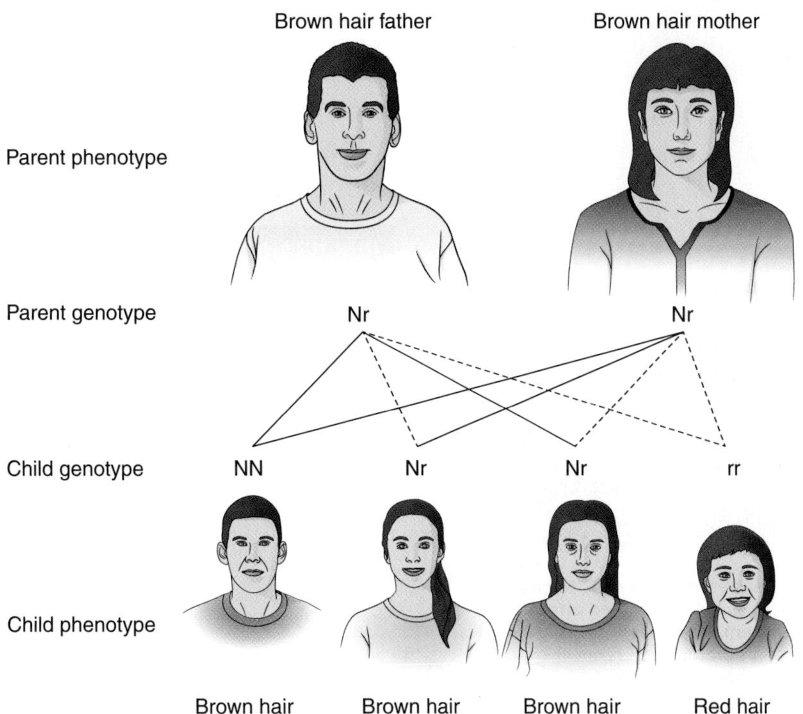

all of the characteristics of recessive sickle cell alleles, illustrating incomplete dominance. Sickle cell carriers do not develop full-blown sickle cell anemia (Chakravorty & Williams, 2015). Carriers of the trait for sickle cell anemia may function normally but may show some symptoms such as reduced oxygen distribution throughout the body and exhaustion after exercise. Only individuals who are homozygous for the recessive sickle cell trait develop sickle cell anemia.

Polygenic Inheritance

Whereas dominant-recessive and codominant-recessive patterns account for some genotypes, most traits are a function of the interaction of many genes, known as **polygenic inheritance**. Hereditary influences act in complex ways, and researchers cannot trace most characteristics to only one or two genes. Instead, polygenic traits are the result of interactions among many genes. Examples of polygenic traits include height, intelligence, personality, and susceptibility to certain forms of cancer (Bouchard, 2014; Kremen, Panizzon, & Cannon, 2016; Penke & Jokela, 2016). As the number of genes that contribute to a trait increases, so does the range of possible traits. Genetic propensities interact with environmental influences to produce a wide range of individual differences in human traits.

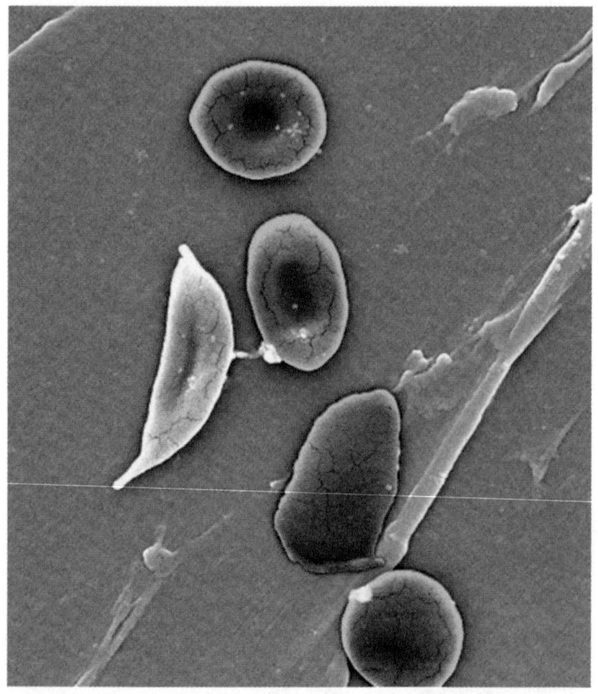

Recessive sickle cell alleles cause red blood cells to become crescent shaped and unable to distribute oxygen effectively throughout the circulatory system. Alleles for normal blood cells do not mask all of the characteristics of recessive sickle cell alleles, illustrating incomplete dominance.

Genomic Imprinting

The principles of dominant-recessive and incomplete dominance inheritance can account for over 1,000 human traits (Amberger & Hamosh, 2017; McKusick, 2007). However, a few traits are determined by a process known as **genomic imprinting**. Genomic imprinting refers to the instance in which the expression of a gene is determined by whether it is inherited from the mother or the father (Kelly & Spencer, 2017; National Library of Medicine, 2019). For example, consider two conditions that illustrate genomic imprinting: Prader-Willi syndrome and Angelman syndrome. Both syndromes are caused by an abnormality in the 15th chromosome (Kalsner & Chamberlain, 2015). As shown in Figure 2.4, if the abnormality occurs on chromosome 15 acquired by the father, the individual—whether a daughter or son—will develop Prader-Willi syndrome, a set of specific physical and behavioral characteristics including obesity, insatiable hunger, short stature, motor slowness, and mild to moderate intellectual impairment (Butler, Manzardo, Heinemann, Loker, & Loker, 2016). If the abnormal chromosome 15 arises from the mother, the individual—again, whether a daughter or a son—will develop Angelman syndrome, characterized by hyperactivity, thin body frame, seizures, disturbances in gait, and severe learning disabilities, including severe problems with speech (Buiting, Williams, & Horsthemke, 2016). Prader-Willi and Angelman syndromes are rare, occurring on average in 1 in 12,000 to 20,000 persons (Kalsner & Chamberlain, 2015; Spruyt, Braam, & Curfs, 2018). Patterns of genetic inheritance can be complex, yet they follow predictable principles. For a summary of patterns of genetic inheritance, refer to Table 2.2.

TABLE 2.2

Summary of Patterns of Genetic Inheritance

INHERITANCE PATTERN	DESCRIPTION
Dominant–recessive inheritance	Genes that are dominant are always expressed, regardless of the gene they are paired with, and recessive genes are expressed only if paired with another recessive gene.
Incomplete dominance	Both genes influence the characteristic, and aspects of both genes appear.
Polygenic inheritance	Polygenic traits are the result of interactions among many genes.
Genomic imprinting	The expression of a gene is determined by whether it is inherited from the mother or the father.

FIGURE 2.4

Genomic Imprinting

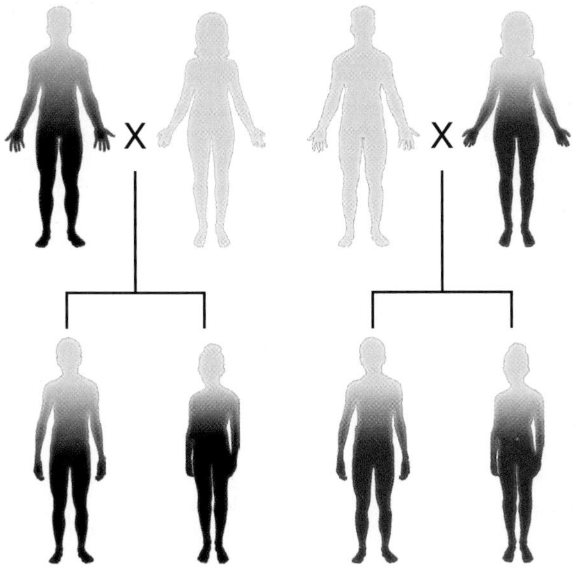

Source: C. Cristofre Martin (1998).

THINKING IN CONTEXT 2.1

1. Consider the evolutionary developmental perspective discussed in Chapter 1. From an evolutionary developmental perspective, why are some characteristics dominant and others recessive? Is it adaptive for some traits to dominate over others? Why or why not?
2. Consider your own physical characteristics, such as hair and eye color. Are they indicative of recessive traits or dominant ones? Which of your traits are likely polygenic?
3. From an evolutionary developmental perspective, why do twins occur? Do you think twinning serves an adaptive purpose? Explain.

CHROMOSOMAL AND GENETIC PROBLEMS

Many disorders are passed through genetic inheritance or are the result of chromosomal abnormalities. Hereditary and chromosomal abnormalities can often be diagnosed prenatally. Others are evident at birth or can be detected soon after an infant begins to develop. Some are discovered only over a period of many years.

Genetic Disorders

Disorders and abnormalities that are inherited through the parents' genes are passed through the inheritance processes that we have discussed. These include well-known conditions such as sickle cell anemia, as well as others that are rare. Some are highly visible and others go unnoticed during an individual's life.

Dominant–Recessive Disorders

Recall that in dominant-recessive inheritance, dominant genes are always expressed regardless of the gene they are paired with and recessive genes are expressed only if paired with another recessive gene. Table 2.3 illustrates diseases that are inherited through dominant–recessive patterns. Few severe disorders are inherited through dominant inheritance because individuals who inherit the allele often do not survive long enough to reproduce and pass it to the next generation. One exception is Huntington disease, a fatal disease in which the central nervous system deteriorates (National Library of Medicine, 2019). Individuals with the Huntington allele develop normally in childhood, adolescence, and young adulthood. Symptoms of Huntington disease do not appear until age 35 or later. By then, many individuals have already had children, and one-half of them, on average, will inherit the dominant Huntington gene.

Phenylketonuria (PKU) is a common recessive disorder that prevents the body from producing an enzyme that breaks down phenylalanine, an amino acid, from proteins (Kahn et al., 2016; Romani et al., 2017). Without treatment, the phenylalanine builds up quickly to toxic levels that damage the central nervous system, contributing to intellectual developmental disability, once known as mental retardation, by 1 year of age. The United States and Canada require all newborns to be screened for PKU (Blau, Shen, & Carducci, 2014).

PKU illustrates how genes interact with the environment to produce developmental outcomes. Intellectual disability results from the interaction of the genetic predisposition and exposure to phenylalanine from the environment (Blau, 2016). Children with PKU can process only very small amounts of phenylalanine. If the disease is discovered, the infant is placed on a diet low in phenylalanine. Yet it is very difficult to remove nearly all phenylalanine from the diet. Individuals who maintain a strict diet usually attain average levels of intelligence, although they tend to score lower than those without PKU (Jahja et al., 2017).

TABLE 2.3

Diseases Inherited Through Dominant–Recessive Inheritance

DISEASE	OCCURRENCE	MODE OF INHERITANCE	DESCRIPTION	TREATMENT
Huntington disease	1 in 20,000	Dominant	Degenerative brain disorder that affects muscular coordination and cognition	No cure; death usually occurs 10 to 20 years after onset
Cystic fibrosis	1 in 2,000 to 2,500	Recessive	An abnormally thick, sticky mucus clogs the lungs and digestive system, leading to respiratory infections and digestive difficulty	Bronchial drainage, diet, gene replacement therapy
Phenylketonuria (PKU)	1 in 10,000 to 15,000	Recessive	Inability to digest phenylalanine that, if untreated, results in neurological damage and death	Diet
Sickle cell anemia	1 in 500 African Americans	Recessive	Sickling of red blood cells leads to inefficient distribution of oxygen throughout the body that leads to organ damage and respiratory infections	No cure; blood transfusions, treat infections, bone marrow transplant; death by middle age
Tay-Sachs disease	1 in 3,600 to 4,000 descendants of Central and Eastern European Jews	Recessive	Degenerative brain disease	None; most die by 4 years of age

Source: McKusick-Nathans Institute of Genetic Medicine (2019).

Some cognitive and psychological problems may appear in childhood and persist into adulthood, particularly difficulty in attention and planning skills, emotional regulation, depression, and anxiety (Hawks, Strube, Johnson, Grange, & White, 2018; Jahja et al., 2017). The emotional and social challenges associated with PKU, such as the pressure of a strict diet and surveillance from parents, may worsen these symptoms, and dietary compliance tends to decline in adolescence as young people push boundaries and seek independence (Medford, Hare, & Wittkowski, 2017).

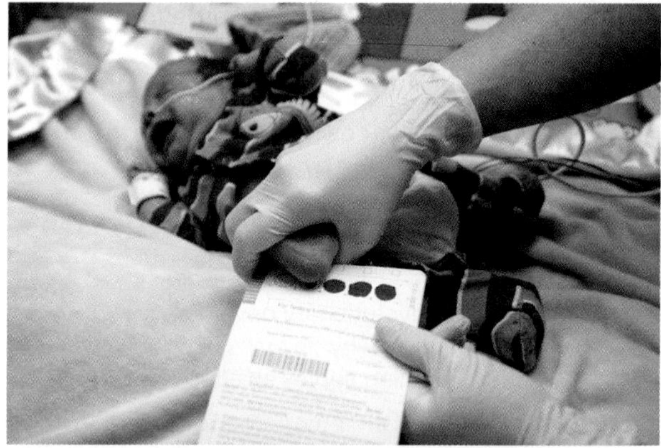

A newborn's blood is tested for phenylketonuria (PKU), a genetic disorder in which the body lacks the enzyme that breaks down phenylalanine. Without treatment, the phenylketonuria builds up to toxic levels and can damage the central nervous system.
Marmaduke St. John/Alamy Stock Photo

X-Linked Disorders

A special instance of the dominant–recessive pattern occurs with genes that are located on the X chromosome (Shah, DeRemigis, Hageman, Sriram, & Waggoner, 2017). Recall that males (XY) have both an X and a Y chromosome. Some recessive genetic disorders, like the gene for red-green colorblindness, are carried on the X chromosome. Males are more likely to be affected by X-linked genetic disorders because they have only one X chromosome and therefore any genetic marks on their X chromosome are displayed. Females (XX) have two X chromosomes; a recessive gene located on one X chromosome will be masked by a dominant gene on the other X chromosome. Females are thereby less likely to display X-linked genetic disorders because both of their X chromosomes must carry the recessive genetic disorder for it to be displayed.

Hemophilia, a condition in which the blood does not clot normally, is another example of a recessive disease inherited through genes on the X chromosome (Shah et al., 2017). Daughters who inherit the gene for hemophilia typically do not show the disorder because the gene on their second X chromosome promotes normal blood clotting and is a dominant gene. Females, therefore, can carry the gene for hemophilia without exhibiting the disorder. A female carrier has a 50/50 chance of transmitting the gene to each child. Sons who inherit the gene will display the disorder because the Y chromosome does not have the corresponding genetic information to counter the gene. Daughters who inherit the gene, again, will be carriers (unless their second X chromosome also carries the gene). Table 2.4 illustrates diseases acquired through X-linked inheritance.

In contrast, **fragile X syndrome** is an example of a dominant disorder carried on the X chromosome (Hagerman et al., 2017). Because the gene is dominant, it need appear on only one X chromosome to be displayed. That means that fragile X syndrome occurs in both males and females, although females tend to experience more mild symptoms. Males with fragile X syndrome typically have large ears, large testes, and a long, narrow face. Fragile X syndrome is the most common known inherited form of intellectual disability (Doherty & Scerif, 2017), and children with fragile X syndrome tend to show moderate to severe intellectual disability (Raspa, Wheeler, & Riley, 2017). Cardiac defects are common as well as several behavioral mannerisms, including poor eye contact and repetitive behaviors such as hand flapping, hand biting, and mimicking others, behaviors common in individuals with autistic spectrum disorders (Hagerman et al., 2017). Fragile X syndrome is often codiagnosed with autism, with estimates of 30% to 54% of boys and 16% to 20% of girls with fragile X syndrome meeting the diagnostic criteria for autism (Kaufmann et al., 2017).

Chromosomal Abnormalities

Chromosomal abnormalities are the result of errors during cell reproduction, meiosis or mitosis, or damage caused afterward. Occurring in about 1 of every 1,500 births, the most widely known chromosome disorder is trisomy 21, more commonly called **Down syndrome** (de Graaf, Buckley, Dever, & Skotko, 2017; Morrison & McMahon, 2018). Down syndrome occurs when a third chromosome appears alongside the 21st pair of chromosomes. Down syndrome is associated with marked physical, health, and cognitive attributes, including a short, stocky build, and striking facial features mark the disorder, such as a round face, almond-shaped eyes, and a flattened nose, as shown in Figure 2.5 (Davis & Escobar, 2013; Kruszka et al., 2017). Children with Down syndrome tend to show delays in physical and

TABLE 2.4

Diseases Acquired Through X-Linked Inheritance

SYNDROME/ DISEASE	OCCURRENCE	DESCRIPTION	TREATMENT
Colorblindness	1 in 12 males	Difficulty distinguishing red from green; less common is difficulty distinguishing blue from green	No cure
Duchenne muscular dystrophy	1 in 3,500 males	Weakness and wasting of limb and trunk muscles; progresses slowly but will affect all voluntary muscles	Physical therapy, exercise, body braces; survival rare beyond late 20s
Fragile X syndrome	1 in 4,000 males and 1 in 8,000 females	Symptoms include cognitive impairment, attention problems, anxiety, unstable mood, long face, large ears, flat feet, and hyper-extensible joints, especially fingers	No cure
Hemophilia	1 in 3,000 to 7,000 males	Blood disorder in which the blood does not clot	Blood transfusions

Source: McKusick-Nathans Institute of Genetic Medicine (2019).

FIGURE 2.5

Down Syndrome

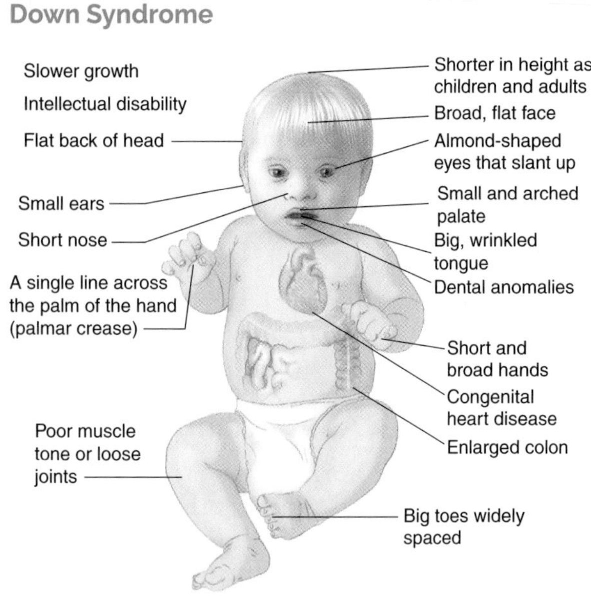

motor development relative to other children and health problems, such as congenital heart defects, vision impairments, poor hearing, and immune system deficiencies (Ram & Chinen, 2011; Zampieri et al., 2014). Down syndrome is the most common genetic cause of intellectual developmental disability (Vissers, Gilissen, & Veltman, 2016), but children's abilities vary. Generally, children with Down syndrome show greater strengths in nonverbal learning and memory relative to their verbal skills (Grieco, Pulsifer, Seligsohn, Skotko, & Schwartz, 2015). Expressive language is delayed relative to comprehension. Infants and children who participate in early intervention and receive sensitive caregiving and encouragement to explore their environment show positive outcomes, especially in the motor, social, and emotion areas of functioning (Næss, Nygaard, Ostad, Dolva, & Lyster, 2017; Wentz, 2017).

Advances in medicine have addressed many of the physical health problems associated with Down syndrome so that today, the average life expectancy is 60 years of age, compared with about 25 in the 1980s (Glasson, Dye, & Bittles, 2014; National Association for Down Syndrome, 2017). However, Down syndrome is associated with premature aging and an accelerated decline of cognitive functioning (Covelli, Raggi, Meucci, Paganelli, & Leonardi, 2016; Ghezzo et al., 2014). Individuals with Down syndrome are at risk to show signs of Alzheimer's disease very early relative to other adults (Hithersay, Hamburg, Knight, & Strydom, 2017; Wiseman et al., 2015). This is an example of how disorders and illnesses can be influenced by multiple genes and complex contextual interactions; in this case, Down syndrome and Alzheimer's disease share genetic markers (Lee, Chien, & Hwu, 2017).

Some chromosomal abnormalities concern the 23rd pair of chromosomes: the sex chromosomes. These abnormalities result from either an additional or missing sex chromosome. Given their different genetic makeup, sex chromosome abnormalities yield different effects in males and females. They are summarized in Table 2.5.

Mutation

Not all inborn characteristics are inherited. Some result from **mutations**, sudden changes and abnormalities in the structure of genes that occur spontaneously or may be induced by exposure to environmental toxins such as radiation and agricultural chemicals in food (Lewis, 2017). A mutation may involve only one gene or many. It is estimated that as many as one-half of all conceptions include mutated chromosomes (Plomin et al., 2013). Most mutations are fatal—the developing organism often dies very soon after conception, often before the woman knows she is pregnant (Sadler, 2018).

Sometimes mutations are beneficial. This is especially true if the mutation is induced by stressors in the environment and provides an adaptive advantage to the individual. For example, the sickle cell gene (discussed earlier in this chapter) is a mutation that originated in areas where malaria is widespread, such as Africa (Ware et al., 2017). Children who inherited a single sickle cell allele were more resistant to malarial infection and more likely to survive and pass it along to their offspring (Croke et al., 2017; Gong, Parikh, Rosenthal, & Greenhouse, 2013). The sickle cell gene is not helpful in places of the world where malaria is not a risk. The frequency of the gene is decreasing in areas of the world where malaria is uncommon. For example, only 8% of African Americans are carriers, compared with as much as 30% of Black Africans in some African countries (Maakaron & Taher, 2012). Therefore, the developmental implications of genotypes—and mutations—are context specific, posing benefits in some contexts and risks in others. Recent advances in genetic engineering hold important implications for understanding and treating genetic disorders, as discussed in the Lives in Context feature.

TABLE 2.5

Sex Chromosome Abnormalities

FEMALE GENOTYPE	SYNDROME	DESCRIPTION	PREVALENCE
XO	Turner	As adults, girls are short in stature, often have small jaws with extra folds of skin around their necks (webbing), lack prominent female secondary sex characteristics such as breasts, and show abnormal development of the ovaries. Elevated risk for early puberty, thyroid disease, vision and hearing problems, heart defects, diabetes, and autoimmune disorders.	1 in 2,500 females
XXX	Triple X	Females grow about an inch or so taller than average with unusually long legs and slender torsos, as well as normal development of sexual characteristics and fertility. Some may show intelligence in the low range of normal with small learning difficulties. Because cases of triple X syndrome often go unnoticed, little is known about the syndrome.	1 in 1,000
MALE GENOTYPE	**SYNDROME**	**DESCRIPTION**	**PREVALENCE**
XXY	Klinefelter	Symptoms range in severity from going unnoticed to severe symptoms such as a high-pitched voice, feminine body shape, breast enlargement, and infertility. Many boys and men with Klinefelter syndrome have long legs, a tendency to be overweight, and language and short-term memory impairments that can cause difficulties in learning.	1 in 500 to 1 in 1,000
XYY	XYY, Jacob's syndrome	The syndrome is accompanied by high levels of testosterone. Males may be slender with severe acne and poor coordination in adolescence, but most go unnoticed.	Prevalence of XYY syndrome is uncertain, as most men with XYY syndrome are unaware that they have a chromosomal abnormality.

Source: Ammerman et al. (2015); McKusick-Nathans Institute of Genetic Medicine (2019); Pappas and Migeon (2017); Wigby et al. (2016); and Wistuba, Brand, Zitzmann, and Damm (2017).

LIVES IN CONTEXT: BIOLOGICAL INFLUENCES

Genetic Engineering

We have seen that DNA influences many of our expressed traits. DNA, however, can be changed. Genetic engineering is a technology that permits scientists to change an organism's DNA. Genetic engineering is commonly used in agriculture and can be applied to modify plants to promote growth, strengthen crop resilience, and improve their nutritional value. In a process known as gene editing, genetic material can be added, removed, or changed at specific places on the genome (National Library of Medicine, 2019). One popular method of gene editing, CRISPR-Cas9 (commonly referred to as CRISPR), has generated a lot of excitement in the scientific community because it is faster, more cost-effective, more accurate, and more efficient than existing genome editing methods (National Library of Medicine, 2019).

Although gene editing is in its infancy, it is an experimental treatment for some genetic illnesses, including cancer and sickle cell anemia. Often referred to as gene therapy, the CRISPR method is used to manipulate the ill person's genome. At present, gene therapy is generally available only in research settings such as in experimental cancer treatment, for example

(Continued)

(Continued)

(Stein, 2019). However, it holds promise. In recent clinical trials, some patients with sickle cell anemia have shown no signs of the disease after gene editing (Kolata, 2019).

Ethical concerns arise when gene editing is used to alter the human genome. Research on gene editing is limited to somatic cells, or body cells, because these changes affect only certain tissues and are not passed from generation to generation. Changes to sperm and egg cells, however, can be passed to future generations, posing ethical dilemmas such as the use of gene editing to enhance normal human traits. Because of these ethical issues as well as safety concerns, gene editing is not permitted on sperm and egg cells or embryos.

In late 2018, Chinese scientist He Jiankui garnered global media attention after using CRISPR to edit the DNA of two embryos. The embryos were implanted and carried to term by their mother. Jiankui's work was judged as unethical, and he was criticized for using untested, unregulated, and unsafe methods. In addition, the developmental consequences for the infants are unknown and any genetic abnormalities may be passed on to their kin. Jiankui argued that the infants' genomes were sequenced or mapped after birth, suggesting that only the intended genes were deleted. Nevertheless, the scientific community has condemned Jiankui's work and Jiankui is facing allegations of scientific misconduct and will also face criminal charges in his home country, China.

What Do You Think?

1. What are some of the pros and cons of genetic engineering?
2. What kinds of conditions should be treated by gene therapy? Are there any conditions that should be off limits to gene therapy? ●

THINKING IN CONTEXT 2.2

1. Give advice to prospective parents. Explain how genetic and chromosomal disorders are transmitted. What can parents do to reduce the risks?
2. Recall from Chapter 1 that most developmental scientists agree that nature and nurture interact to influence development. Choose a genetic or chromosomal disorder discussed in this section and explain how it illustrates the interaction of genes and context.

REPRODUCTIVE CHOICES

The likelihood of genetic disorders often can be predicted before conception. Our growing understanding of genetic inheritance has led many couples to wonder about their own genetic inheritance and what genes they will pass on to their children.

Genetic Counseling

Many prospective parents seek **genetic counseling** to determine the risk that their children will inherit genetic defects and chromosomal abnormalities (Ioannides, 2017; Uhlmann, Schuette, & Yashar, 2009). Candidates for genetic counseling include those whose relatives have a genetic condition, couples who have had difficulties bearing children, women over the age of 35, and couples from the same ethnic group. Genetic testing can also determine whether a couple's difficulty conceiving or recurrent miscarriage is influenced by sperm chromosomal abnormalities in the male (Kohn, Kohn, Darilek, Ramasamy, & Lipshultz, 2016).

The genetic counselor interviews the couple to construct a family history of heritable disorders for both prospective parents. This service is particularly valuable when one or both prospective parents have relatives with inborn disorders. If a disorder is common in either parent's family or it appears that they are likely to carry a genetic disorder, genetic screening blood tests may be carried out on both parents to detect the presence of dominant and recessive genes and chromosomal abnormalities associated with various disorders. The tests determine whether each parent is a carrier for recessive disorders and estimate the likelihood that a child may be affected by a genetic disorder. The genetic counselor interprets the results and helps the parents understand genetic concepts by tailoring the explanation to match the parents' knowledge (Nance, 2017).

Once prospective parents learn about the risk of conceiving a child with a disorder, they can determine how to proceed—whether it is to conceive a child naturally or through the use of in vitro fertilization—after screening gametes for the disorders of concern. Given advances in our knowledge of genetic disorders and the ability to screen for them, some argue that genetic counseling should be available to all prospective parents (Minkoff & Berkowitz, 2014). Others argue that abnormalities are rare and so few would be discovered that universal screening is of little utility (Larion, Warsof, Maher, Peleg, & Abuhamad, 2016). Whether to seek genetic counseling is a personal decision for prospective parents based on their history, view of their risks, and their values. Adults who carry significant risks of conceiving a child with a genetic disorder sometimes consider alternative methods of reproduction.

Assisted Reproductive Technology

Couples turn to assisted reproductive technology for a variety of reasons. As noted, some couples at risk for bearing children with genetic or chromosomal abnormalities seek alternative methods of conception. About 15% of couples in the United States experience infertility, the inability to conceive (Thoma et al., 2013). About 35% of the time, factors within the male are identified as contributors to infertility (Centers for Disease Control and Prevention, 2017c). In addition, single men and women, as well as gay and lesbian couples, often opt to conceive with the use of reproductive technology. However, there are racial, ethnic, and socioeconomic disparities in the use of assisted reproductive technologies. Women and couples who are White, college educated, and of high socioeconomic status (SES) are more likely to use infertility services than African American and Hispanic couples (Janitz, Peck, & Craig, 2016). Race and ethnicity are often linked with socioeconomic status and disparities in health care in the United States. Socioeconomic factors play a large role in access to infertility treatment and assisted reproductive technology (Dieke, Zhang, Kissin, Barfield, & Boulet, 2017).

One assisted reproduction technique is **artificial insemination**, the injection of sperm into a woman. The male partner's sperm may be used or, if the male experiences reproductive difficulties, a donor's sperm may be used. Artificial insemination through a donor also enables women without male partners, whether single or lesbian, to conceive. The most expensive assisted reproductive technology, in vitro fertilization, tends to average over $12,000 per trial, not including medication, and often requires multiple cycles, posing a financial burden too great for low SES women and couples (Teoh & Maheshwari, 2014).

In vitro fertilization, introduced in the United States in 1981, permits conception to occur outside of the womb. A woman is prescribed hormones that stimulate the maturation of several ova, which are surgically removed. The ova are placed in a dish and sperm are added. One or more ova are fertilized, and the resulting cell begins to divide. After several cell divisions, the cluster of cells is placed in the woman's uterus. If they implant into the uterus and begin to divide, a pregnancy has occurred. The success rate of in vitro fertilization is about 50% and varies with the mother's age. For example, the success rate is 47% in 35-year-old women, 27% in 41- to 42-year-old women, and 16% in 43- to 44-year-old women (Sunderam et al., 2017).

Assisted reproductive technology contributed to 1.6% of all infants born in the United States in 2014 (Sunderam et al., 2017). As shown in Figure 2.6, about 50% of assisted reproduction technology procedures that progress to the embryo-transfer stage result in pregnancy and about 40% result in a live birth. Infants conceived by in vitro fertilization are at higher risk of low birth weight (Fauser et al., 2014), although it has been suggested that it is because of maternal factors, such as advanced age, and not in vitro fertilization per se (Seggers et al., 2016). Infants conceived by in vitro fertilization show no differences in growth, health, development, and cognitive function relative to infants conceived naturally (Fauser et al., 2014). Because in vitro fertilization permits cells to be screened for genetic problems prior to implantation, in vitro infants are not at higher risk of birth defects (Fauser et al., 2014). However, about 40% of births from in vitro fertilization include more than one infant (38% twins and 2% triplets and higher). Multiple gestations increase risk for low birth weight, prematurity, and other poor outcomes (Sullivan-Pyke, Senapati, Mainigi, & Barnhart, 2017).

Surrogacy is an alternative form of reproduction in which a woman (the surrogate) is impregnated and carries a fetus to term and agrees to turn the baby over to a woman, man, or couple who will raise the child. Single parents, same-sex couples, and couples in which one or both members are infertile choose surrogacy. Sometimes the surrogate carries a zygote composed of one or both of the couple's gametes. Other times, the ova, sperm, or zygote are donated. Despite several highly publicized cases of surrogate mothers deciding not to relinquish the infant, most surrogacies are successful. In 2015, 2,807 babies were born through surrogacy in the United States, up from 738 in 2004, according to the American Society for Reproductive Medicine (Beitsch, 2017). Longitudinal research suggests no psychological differences through age 14 between children born

FIGURE 2.6

Number of Outcomes of Assisted Reproductive Technology Procedures, by Type of Outcome—United States and Puerto Rico, 2014

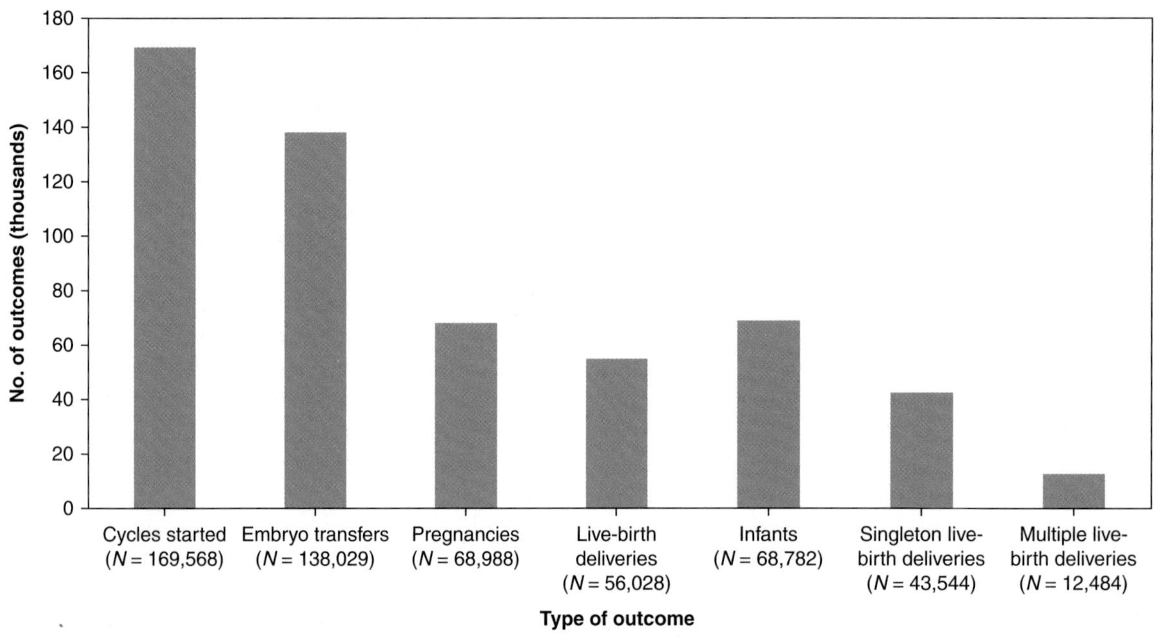

Source: Sunderam et al. (2017).

through surrogacy compared with other methods, including children born to gay father and lesbian mother families (Carone, Lingiardi, Chirumbolo, & Baiocco, 2018; Golombok, 2013; Golombok, Ilioi, Blake, Roman, & Jadva, 2017). In addition, mothers of children who were the product of surrogates do not differ from those whose children were conceived using other methods, and surrogate mothers show no negative effects (Jadva, Imrie, & Golombok, 2015; Söderström-Anttila et al., 2015). Like other forms of reproductive technology, surrogacy is expensive, limiting its access to parents with high SES. Finally, some argue that surrogacy may pose ethical issues. For example, women are often paid at least $30,000 to surrogate a fetus (Beitsch, 2017), creating financial incentives that may be difficult for women with low SES to resist.

Adoption

Another reproductive option for prospective parents is **adoption**. Adults who choose to adopt have similar motives for parenthood as those who raise biological children, such as valuing family ties, continuing a family line, feeling that parenting is a life task, and desiring to have a nurturing relationship with a child (Jennings, Mellish, Tasker, Lamb, & Golombok, 2014; Malm & Welti, 2010). Heterosexual and same-sex adults report similar reasons for choosing adoption (Goldberg, Downing, & Moyer, 2012).

Adoptive children tend to be raised by parents with higher levels of education and income than other parents. This is partly due to self-selection and partly because of the screening that adoptive parents must undergo before they are allowed to adopt. It is estimated that transracial adoptions, in which a child (typically of color) is adopted by parents of a different race (most often White), account for about one-quarter of adoptions (Marr, 2017). Although there is little research, transracial adoptive children, and especially adolescents, may face challenges in ethnic and racial socialization and identity development (Wiley, 2017). Research reviews are mixed, with some suggesting no clear relation among racial or ethnic identity, parental socialization efforts, and adjustment (Boivin & Hassan, 2015) and more recent analyses suggesting that racial and ethnic socialization is associated with healthy adoptee outcomes (Montgomery & Jordan, 2018). Parents can foster their adoptive children's ethnic and racial socialization by exposing children to their racial and ethnic heritage and providing opportunities for children to learn about and interact with people who identify with their birth race and ethnicity (Hrapczynski & Leslie, 2018).

Overall, adoptive children tend to spend more time with their parents and have more educational resources than other children (Zill, 2015). Yet some adopted children show less engagement in class and tend to have more academic difficulties than other children. Longitudinal research suggests that adoption is associated with lower academic achievement across childhood, adolescence, and emerging adulthood compared with nonadopted comparison groups (Brown, Waters, & Shelton, 2017). Adopted children tend to experience greater stress prenatally, early in life, prior to adoption, and during the adoption process that likely influences their long-term adjustment after adoption (Grotevant & McDermott, 2014). Adopted children therefore may show more psychological problems and adjustment difficulties than their nonadoptive peers, in some cases persisting into adulthood (A. Brown et al., 2017; Palacios & Brodzinsky, 2010).

Children's experiences prior to adoption and their developmental status at the time of adoption influence their outcomes (Balenzano, Coppola, Cassibba, & Moro, 2018). Children who experience neglect or fear and lack an early bond to a caregiver may experience difficulty regulating emotion and conflict. Biological mothers who choose to adopt may have experienced physical or mental health problems that interfered with their ability to care and form a bond and might be passed on. In other cases, the child may have experienced neglect, deprivation, and trauma, which influence adjustment (Grotevant & McDermott, 2014). Many children adopted from international orphanages arrive with experiences that are harmful, as discussed in the accompanying Lives in Context feature.

For many children, emotional differences are transitional. Research has suggested that most children show resilience in the years after adoption, but some issues continue (Palacios & Brodzinsky, 2010). Those who develop a close bond with adoptive parents tend to show better emotional understanding and regulation, social competence, and also self-esteem (Juffer & van IJzendoorn, 2007). This is true also of children who have experienced emotional neglect, and those effects hold regardless of age at adoption (Barone, Lionetti, & Green, 2017).

Prenatal Diagnosis

Prenatal testing is recommended when genetic counseling has determined a risk for genetic abnormalities, when the woman is older than age

LIVES IN CONTEXT: CULTURAL CONTEXT

Development of Internationally Adopted Children

Over the past 5 decades, international adoption has become commonplace. In many countries throughout the world, children are reared in orphanages with substandard conditions—without adequate food, clothing, or shelter and with poorly trained caregivers. Such orphanages have been found in a number of countries, including China, Ethiopia, Ukraine, Congo, and Haiti, accounting for over two-thirds of internationally adopted children (U.S. Department of State, 2014). Underfunded and understaffed orphanages often provide poor, nonnurturing care for children, increasing the risks for malnutrition, infections, physical disabilities, and growth retardation (Leiden Conference on the Development and Care of Children Without Permanent Parents, 2012). With high infant-to-caregiver ratios, children available for adoption often spend a significant amount of time deprived of consistent human contact.

Few internationally adopted children enter the United States healthy and at age-appropriate developmental norms. Not surprisingly, the longer the children are institutionalized, the more developmental challenges they face (Jacobs, Miller, & Tirella, 2010). Physical growth stunting is directly associated with the length of institutionalization, but catch-up growth is commonly seen after adoption (Wilson & Weaver, 2009). As with growth, the time spent in an orphanage predicts the degree of developmental delay. Longer institutionalization is associated with delays in the development of language, fine motor skills, social skills, attention, and other cognitive skills (Mason & Narad, 2005; Wiik et al., 2011).

Speech and language delays are among the most consistent deficiencies experienced by internationally

(Continued)

(Continued)

adopted children, especially those adopted after the age of 1 (Eigsti, Weitzman, Schuh, de Marchena, & Casey, 2011). However, more children reach normative age expectations 1 to 2 years postadoption (Glennen, 2014; Rakhlin et al., 2015). Generally, the younger the child is at adoption, the more quickly he or she will adapt to the new language and close any gaps in language delays (Glennan & Masters, 2002; Mason & Narad, 2005). Some research suggests that internationally adopted children are prone to long-term deficits in executive function likely due to neurological factors (Merz, Harlé, Noble, & McCall, 2016). The presence of a high-quality parent–child relationship promotes development of language, speech, or academic outcomes, and most children reach age-expected language levels (Glennen, 2014; Harwood, Feng, & Yu, 2013).

As adolescents, all children struggle to come to a sense of identity, to figure out who they are. This struggle may be especially challenging for internationally adopted children who may wonder about their native culture and homeland (Rosnati et al., 2015). Frequently, adolescents may want to discuss and learn more yet inhibit the desire to talk about this with parents (Garber & Grotevant, 2015). Parents who assume a multicultural perspective and provide opportunities for their children to learn about their birth culture support adopted children's development and promote healthy outcomes (Pinderhughes, Zhang, & Agerbak, 2015). Internationally adopted children seek to understand their birth culture and integrate their birth and adopted cultures into their sense of self (Grotevant, Lo, Fiorenzo, & Dunbar, 2017). A positive sense of ethnic identity is associated with positive outcomes such as self-esteem in international adoptees (Mohanty, 2015). Although there are individual differences in the degree of resilience and in functioning across developmental domains, adopted children overall show great developmental gains and resilience in physical, cognitive, and emotional development (Misca, 2014; Palacios, Román, Moreno, León, & Peñarrubia, 2014; Wilson & Weaver, 2009).

What Do You Think?

In your view, what are the most important challenges internationally adopted children and their families face? Identify sources and forms of support that might help adopted children and their parents. ●

35, when both parents are members of an ethnicity at risk for particular genetic disorders, or when fetal development appears abnormal (Barlow-Stewart & Saleh, 2012). Technology has advanced rapidly, equipping professionals with an array of tools to assess the health of the fetus. Table 2.6 summarizes methods of prenatal diagnosis.

The most widespread and routine diagnostic procedure is **ultrasound**, in which high-frequency sound waves directed at the mother's abdomen provide clear images of the womb represented on a video monitor. Ultrasound enables physicians to observe the fetus, measure fetal growth, judge gestational age, reveal the sex of the fetus, detect multiple pregnancies (twins, triplets, etc.), and determine physical abnormalities in the fetus. Many deformities can be observed, such as cardiac abnormalities, cleft palate, and microencephaly (small head size). At least 80% of women in the United States receive at least one prenatal ultrasound scan (Sadler, 2018). Three to four screenings over the duration of pregnancy are common to evaluate fetal development (Papp & Fekete, 2003). Repeated ultrasound of the fetus does not appear to affect growth and development (Stephenson, 2005).

Fetal MRI applies MRI technology to image the fetus's body and diagnose malformations (Griffiths et al., 2017). Most women will not have a fetal MRI. It is often used as a follow-up to ultrasound imaging to provide more detailed views of any suspected abnormalities (Milani et al., 2015). Fetal MRI can detect abnormalities throughout the body, including the central nervous system (Saleem, 2014). MRI in the obstetrical patient is safe for mother and fetus in the second and third trimesters but is expensive and has limited availability in some areas (Patenaude et al., 2014).

Amniocentesis is a prenatal diagnostic procedure in which a small sample of the amniotic fluid that surrounds the fetus is extracted from the mother's uterus through a long, hollow needle that is guided by ultrasound as it is inserted into the mother's abdomen (Odibo, 2015). The amniotic fluid contains fetal cells, which are grown in a laboratory dish to create enough cells for genetic analysis. Genetic analysis is then performed to detect genetic and chromosomal anomalies and defects. Amniocentesis is less common than ultrasound, as it poses greater risk to the fetus. It is recommended for women aged 35 and older, especially if the woman and partner are both known carriers of genetic diseases (Vink & Quinn, 2018a). Usually amniocentesis is conducted between the 15th and 18th weeks of pregnancy. Conducted any earlier, an amniocentesis may increase the risk of miscarriage (Akolekar et al., 2015). Test results generally are available about

TABLE 2.6

Methods of Prenatal Diagnosis

	EXPLANATION	ADVANTAGES	DISADVANTAGES
Ultrasound	High-frequency sound waves directed at the mother's abdomen provide clear images of the womb projected onto a video monitor.	Ultrasound enables physicians to observe the fetus, measure fetal growth, reveal the sex of the fetus, and determine physical abnormalities in the fetus.	Many abnormalities and deformities cannot be easily observed.
Fetal MRI	Fetal MRI uses a magnetic scanner to record detailed images of fetal organs and structures.	Fetal MRI provides the most detailed and accurate images available.	It is expensive. At present, there is no evidence to suggest that it is harmful to the fetus.
Amniocentesis	A small sample of the amniotic fluid that surrounds the fetus is extracted from the mother's uterus through a long, hollow needle inserted into the mother's abdomen. The amniotic fluid contains fetal cells. The fetal cells are grown in a laboratory dish to create enough cells for genetic analysis.	Amniocentesis permits a thorough analysis of the fetus's genotype. There is a nearly 100% diagnostic success rate.	It is safe, but poses a greater risk to the fetus than ultrasound. If conducted before the 15th week of pregnancy, it may increase the risk of miscarriage.
Chorionic villus sampling (CVS)	CVS requires studying a small amount of tissue from the chorion, part of the membrane surrounding the fetus, for the presence of chromosomal abnormalities. The tissue sample is obtained through a long needle inserted either abdominally or vaginally, depending on the location of the fetus.	It permits a thorough analysis of the fetus's genotype. CVS is relatively painless, and there is a 100% diagnostic success rate. It can be conducted earlier than amniocentesis, between 10 and 12 weeks.	It may pose a higher rate of spontaneous abortion and limb defects when conducted prior to 10 weeks' gestation.
Noninvasive prenatal testing (NIPT)	Cell-free fetal DNA is examined by drawing blood from the mother.	There is no risk to the fetus. NIPT can diagnose several chromosomal abnormalities.	It cannot yet detect the full range of abnormalities. It may be less accurate than other methods. Researchers have identified the entire genome sequence using NIPT, suggesting that someday, NIPT may be as effective as other, more invasive techniques.

Source: Akolekar, Beta, Picciarelli, Ogilvie, and D'Antonio (2015); Chan, Kwok, Choy, Leung, and Wang (2013); Gregg et al. (2013); Odibo (2015); Shahbazian, Barati, Arian, and Saadati (2012); Shim et al. (2014); and Theodora et al. (2016).

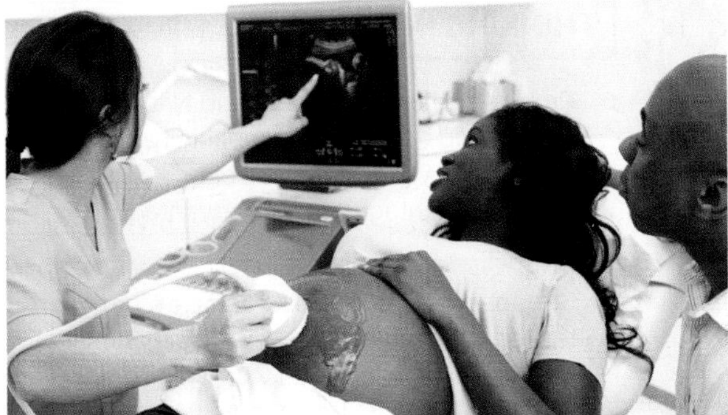

Ultrasound technology enables health care professionals to observe the fetus, measure fetal growth, detect physical abnormalities, and more.
©iStockphoto.com/monkeybusinessimages

2 weeks after the procedure because it takes that long for the genetic material to grow and reproduce to the point where it can be analyzed.

Chorionic villus sampling (CVS) also samples genetic material and can be conducted earlier than amniocentesis, between 10 and 12 weeks of pregnancy (Vink & Quinn, 2018b). CVS requires studying a small amount of tissue from the chorion, part of the membrane surrounding the fetus. The tissue sample is obtained through a long needle inserted either abdominally or vaginally, depending on the location of the fetus. Results are typically available about 1 week following the procedure. CVS is relatively painless and, like amniocentesis, has a 100% diagnostic success rate. Generally, CVS poses few risks to the fetus (Beta, Lesmes-

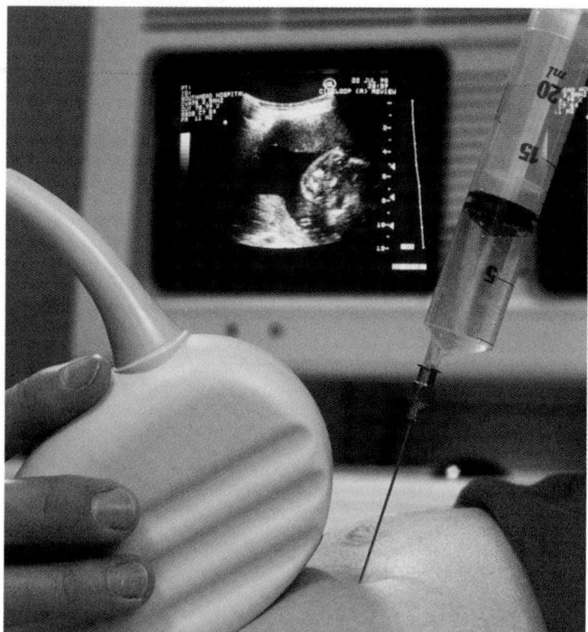

During amniocentesis, ultrasound is used to guide the insertion of a long, hollow needle into the mother's abdomen in order to extract a sample of the amniotic fluid that surrounds the fetus. The amniotic fluid contains fetal cells, which are grown in a laboratory dish and tested for genetic and chromosomal anomalies and defects.
Saturn Stills/Science Source

Heredia, Bedetti, & Akolekar, 2018; Shim et al., 2014). However, CVS should not be conducted prior to 10 weeks' gestation, as some studies suggest an increased risk of limb defects and miscarriages (Shahbazian et al., 2012).

Noninvasive prenatal testing (NIPT) screens the mother's blood to detect chromosomal abnormalities. Cell-free fetal DNA (chromosome fragments that result in the breakdown of fetal cells) circulates in maternal blood in small concentrations that can be detected and studied by sampling the mother's blood (Warsof, Larion, & Abuhamad, 2015). Testing can be done after 10 weeks, typically between 10 and 22 weeks. Given that the test involves drawing blood from the mother, there is no risk to the fetus. The use of NIPT has increased dramatically in the United States and other countries (Hui, Angelotta, & Fisher, 2017). However, NIPT cannot detect as many chromosomal abnormalities as amniocentesis or CVS and does so with less accuracy (Chan et al., 2013; National Coalition for Health Professional Education in Genetics, 2012). Researchers have identified the entire genome sequence using NIPT, suggesting that someday, NIPT may be as effective as other, more invasive techniques (Tabor et al., 2012). Pregnant women and their partners, in consultation with their obstetrician, should carefully weigh the risks and benefits of any procedure designed to monitor prenatal development.

Prenatal Treatment of Genetic Disorders

What happens when a genetic or chromosomal abnormality is found? Advances in genetics and in medicine have led to therapies that can be administered prenatally to reduce the effects of many genetic abnormalities. Fetoscopy is a technique that uses a small camera, inserted through a small incision on the mother's abdomen or cervix and placed into the amniotic sac that encases the fetus, to examine and perform procedures on the fetus during pregnancy. Risks of fetoscopy include infection, rupture of the amniotic sac, premature labor, and fetal death. However, when serious abnormalities are suspected, fetoscopy permits a visual assessment of the fetus, which aids in diagnosis and treatment. Hormones and other drugs, as well as blood transfusions, can be given to the fetus by inserting a needle into the uterus (Fox & Saade, 2012; Lindenburg, van Kamp, & Oepkes, 2014). Surgeons rely on the images provided by fetoscopy to surgically repair defects of the heart, lung, urinary tract, and other areas (Deprest et al., 2010; P. Sala et al., 2014).

In addition, researchers believe that one day, we may be able to treat many heritable disorders thorough genetic engineering by synthesizing normal genes to replace defective ones. It may someday be possible to sample cells from an embryo, detect harmful genes and replace them with healthy ones, and then return the healthy cells to the embryo where they reproduce and correct the genetic defect (Coutelle & Waddington, 2012). This approach has been used to correct certain heritable disorders in animals and holds promise for treating humans.

THINKING IN CONTEXT 2.3

1. Provide advice to Eduardo and Natia, a couple in their mid-30s who are seeking reproductive assistance. What are their options and what are the advantages and disadvantages of each?
2. Suppose that you are a health care provider tasked with explaining prenatal diagnostic choices to a 38-year-old woman pregnant with her first child. How would you explain the tests? What would you advise? Why?

HEREDITY AND ENVIRONMENT

Our brief introduction to the processes of heredity illustrates the complexity of genetic inheritance. In fact, most human traits are influenced by a combination of genes (polygenic) working in concert with environmental influences. Our genotype, or genetic makeup, inherited from our biological parents is a biological contributor to all of our traits, from hair and eye color to personality, health, and behavior. However, our **phenotype**, the traits we ultimately show, such as our specific eye or hair color, is not determined by genotype, our genetic blueprint, alone. Phenotypes result from the interaction of genotypes and our experiences.

Behavioral Genetics

Behavioral genetics is the field of study that examines how genes and experience combine to influence the diversity of human traits, abilities, and behaviors (Krüger, Korsten, & Hoffman, 2017; Plomin et al., 2013). Behavioral geneticists have discovered that even traits with a strong genetic component, such as height, are modified by environmental influences (Dubois et al., 2012; Plomin, DeFries, Knopik, & Neiderhiser, 2016). Moreover, most human traits, such as intelligence, are influenced by multiple genes, and there are often multiple variants of each gene and each might interact with the environment in a different way (Bouchard, 2014; Chabris, Lee, Cesarini, Benjamin, & Laibson, 2015; Knopik, Neiderhiser, DeFries, & Plomin, 2017).

Methods of Behavioral Genetics

Behavioral geneticists seek to estimate the heritability of specific traits and behaviors. **Heritability** refers to the extent to which variation among people on a given characteristic is due to genetic differences. The remaining variation not due to genetic differences is instead a result of the environment and experiences. Heritability research therefore examines the contributions of the genotype but also provides information on the role of experience in determining phenotypes (Plomin et al., 2016). Behavioral geneticists assess the hereditary contributions to behavior by conducting selective breeding and family studies.

Selective breeding studies entail deliberately modifying the genetic makeup of animals to examine the influence of heredity on attributes and behavior. For example, mice can be bred to be very physically active or sedentary by mating highly active mice only with other highly active mice and, similarly, by breeding mice with very low levels of activity with each other. Over subsequent generations, mice bred for high levels of activity become many times more active than those bred for low levels of activity (Knopik et al., 2017). Selective breeding in rats, mice, and other animals such as chickens has revealed genetic contributions to many traits and characteristics, such as aggressiveness, emotionality, sex drive, and even maze learning (Plomin et al., 2016).

For many reasons, especially ethical reasons, people cannot be selectively bred. However, we can observe people who naturally vary in shared genes and environment. Behavioral geneticists conduct *family studies* to compare people who live together and share varying degrees of relatedness. Two kinds of family studies are common: twin studies and adoption studies (Koenen, Amstadter, & Nugent, 2012). *Twin studies* compare identical and fraternal twins to estimate how much of a trait or behavior is attributable to genes. Recall that identical (monozygotic) twins share 100% of their genes because they originated from the same zygote. Like all nontwin siblings, fraternal (dizygotic) twins share 50% of their genes, as they resulted from two different fertilized ova and from two genetically different zygotes. If genes affect a given attribute, identical twins should be more similar than fraternal twins because identical twins share 100% of their genes, whereas fraternal twins share about half.

Adoption studies, on the other hand, compare the degree of similarity between adopted children and their biological parents whose genes they share (50%) and their adoptive parents with whom they share an environment but not genes. If the adopted children share similarities with their biological parents, even though they were not raised by them, it suggests that the similarities are genetic. The similarities are influenced by the environment if the children are more similar to their adoptive parents. Observations of adoptive siblings also shed light on the extent to which attributes and behaviors are influenced by the environment. For example, the degree to which two genetically unrelated adopted children reared together are similar speaks to the role of environment. Comparisons of identical twins reared in the same home with those reared in different environments can also illustrate environmental contributions to phenotypes. If identical twins reared together are more similar than those reared apart, an environmental influence can be inferred.

Genetic Influences on Personal Characteristics

Research examining the contribution of genotype and environment to intellectual abilities has found a moderate role for heredity. Twin studies have shown that identical twins consistently have more highly correlated scores than do fraternal twins. For example, a classic study of intelligence in over 10,000 twin pairs showed a correlation of .86 for identical and .60 for fraternal twins (Plomin & Spinath, 2004). Table 2.7 summarizes the results of comparisons of intelligence scores from individuals who share different genetic relationships with each other. Note that correlations for all levels of kin are higher when they are reared together, supporting the role of environment. Average correlations also rise with increases in shared genes.

Genes contribute to many other traits, such as sociability, temperament, emotionality, and susceptibility to various illnesses such as obesity, heart disease and cancer, anxiety, poor mental health, and a propensity to be physically aggressive (Esposito et al., 2017; McRae et al., 2017; Ritz et al., 2017). Yet even traits that are thought to be heavily influenced by genetics can be modified by physical and social interventions. For example, growth, body weight, and body height are largely predicted by genetics, yet environmental circumstances and opportunities influence whether genetic potentials are realized (Dubois et al., 2012; Jelenkovic et al., 2016). Even identical twins who share 100% of their genes are not 100% alike. Those differences are due to the influence of environmental factors, which interact with genes in a variety of ways.

TABLE 2.7

Average Correlation of Intelligence Scores From Family Studies for Related and Unrelated Kin Reared Together or Apart

	REARED TOGETHER	REARED APART
Monozygotic twins (100% shared genes)	.86	.72
Dizygotic twins (50% shared genes)	.60	.52
Siblings (50% shared genes)	.47	.24
Biological parent/child (50% shared genes)	.42	.22
Half-siblings (25% shared genes)	.31	–
Unrelated (adopted) siblings (0% shared genes)[a]	.34	–
Nonbiological parent/child (0% shared genes)[a]	.19	–

Source: Adapted from Bouchard and McGue (1981).

[a] Estimated correlation for individuals sharing neither genes nor environment = .0.

Gene–Environment Interactions

We have seen that genes and the environment work together in complex ways to determine our characteristics, behavior, development, and health (Chabris et al., 2015; Ritz et al., 2017; Rutter, 2012). **Gene–environment interactions** refer to the dynamic interplay between our genes and our environment. Several principles illustrate these interactions.

Range of Reaction

Everyone has a different genetic makeup and therefore responds to the environment in a unique way. In addition, any one genotype can be expressed in a variety of phenotypes. There is a **range of reaction** (see Figure 2.7), a wide range of potential expressions of a genetic trait, depending on environmental opportunities and constraints (Gottlieb, 2000, 2007). For example, consider height. Height is largely a function of genetics, yet an individual may show a range of sizes depending on environment and behavior. Suppose that a child is born to two very tall parents. She may have the genes to be tall, but unless she has adequate nutrition, she will not fulfill her genetic potential for height. In societies in which nutrition has improved dramatically over a generation, it is common for children to tower over their parents. The enhanced environmental opportunities (in this case, nutrition) enabled the children to fulfill their genetic potential for height. Therefore, a genotype sets boundaries on the range of possible phenotypes, but the phenotypes ultimately displayed vary in response to different environments (Manuck & McCaffery, 2014). In this way, genetics sets the range of development outcomes and the environment influences where, within the range, that person will fall.

Canalization

Some traits illustrate a wide reaction range. Others are examples of **canalization**, in which heredity narrows the range of development to only one or a few outcomes. Canalized traits are biologically programmed, and only powerful environmental forces can change their developmental path (Flatt, 2005; Posadas & Carthew, 2014; Waddington, 1971).

FIGURE 2.7

Range of Reaction

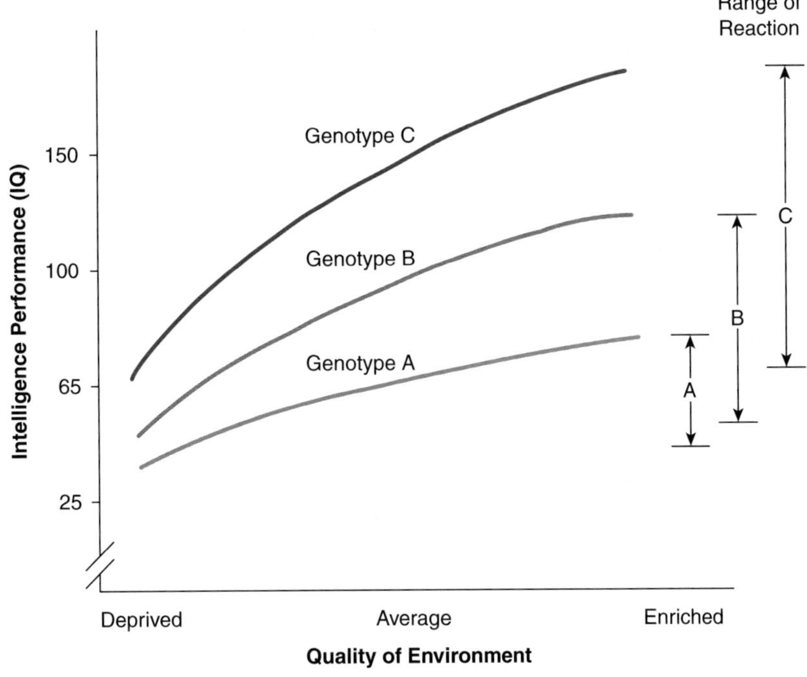

Source: Adapted from Gottlieb (2007).

For example, infants follow an age-related sequence of motor development, from crawling, to walking, to running. Around the world, most infants walk at about 12 months of age. Generally, only extreme experiences or changes in the environment can prevent this developmental sequence from occurring. For example, children reared in impoverished international orphanages and exposed to extreme environmental deprivation demonstrated delayed motor development, with infants walking 5 months to a year later than expected (Chaibal, Bennett, Rattanathanthong, & Siritaratiwat, 2016; Miller, Tseng, Tirella, Chan, & Feig, 2008).

Motor development is not entirely canalized, however, because some minor changes in the environment can subtly alter its pace and timing. For example, practice facilitates stepping movements in young infants, prevents the disappearance of stepping movements in the early months of life, and leads to an earlier onset of walking (Adolph & Franchak, 2017; Ulrich, Lloyd, Tiernan, Looper, & Angulo-Barroso, 2008). These observations demonstrate that even highly canalized traits, such as motor development, which largely unfolds via maturation, can be subtly influenced by contextual factors.

Gene–Environment Correlations

Heredity and environment are powerful influences on development. Not only do they interact, but environmental factors often support hereditary traits (Plomin et al., 2016; Scarr & McCartney, 1983). **Gene–environment correlation** refers to the finding that many genetically influenced traits tend to be associated with environmental factors that promote their development (Lynch, 2016). That is, genetic traits influence children's behavior, which is often supported or encouraged by the environment (Knafo & Jaffee, 2013). There are three types of gene–environment correlations—passive, evocative, and active.

Parents create homes that reflect their own genotypes. Because parents are genetically similar to their children, the homes that parents create support their own preferences but also correspond to their child's genotype—an example of a *passive gene–environment correlation* (Wilkinson, Trzaskowski, Haworth, & Eley, 2013). It is a passive gene–environment correlation because it occurs regardless of the child's behavior. For example, a parent might provide genes that predispose a child to develop music ability and create a home environment that reflects the parent's interest and ability in music, which then also happens to support the child's musical ability, as shown in the top photo in Figure 2.8. This type of gene-environment correlation tends to occur early in life because parents create rearing environments for their infants and young children.

Children naturally evoke responses from others and the environment, just as the environment and the actions of others evoke responses from the individual. In an *evocative gene-environment correlation*, a child's genetic traits (e.g., personality characteristics, including openness to experience) influence the social and physical environment, which in turn shape development in ways that support the genetic trait (Burt, 2009; Klahr, Thomas, Hopwood, Klump, & Burt, 2013). For example, active, happy infants tend to receive more adult attention than do passive or moody infants (Deater-Deckard & O'Connor, 2000), and even among infant twins reared in the same family, the more outgoing and happy twin receives more positive attention than does the more subdued twin (Deater-Deckard, 2001). Why? Babies who are cheerful and smile often influence their social world by evoking smiles from others, which in turn supports the tendency to be cheerful. In this way, genotypes influence the physical and social environment to respond in ways that support the genotype. Children who engage in disruptive play tend to later experience problems with peers (Boivin et al., 2013). To return to the music example, a child with a genetic trait for music talent will evoke pleasurable responses (e.g., parental approval) when she plays music; this environmental support, in turn, encourages further development of the child's musical trait. In addition, individuals vary in their sensitivity to environmental stimuli; some children may be more affected by environmental stimuli due to their genetic makeup (Belsky & Hartman, 2014; Pluess, 2015).

Children also take a hands-on role in shaping their development. Recall from Chapter 1 that a major theme in understanding human development is the finding that individuals are active in their development. Here we have an example of this theme. As children grow older, they have increasing freedom in choosing their own activities and environments. An *active gene-environment correlation* occurs when the child actively creates experiences and environments that correspond to and influence his genetic predisposition. For

FIGURE 2.8

Gene–Environment Correlation

The availability of instruments in the home corresponds to the child's musical abilities, and she begins to play guitar (passive gene–environment correlation). As she plays guitar, she evokes positive responses in others, increasing her interest in music (evocative gene–environment correlation). Over time, she seeks opportunities to play, such as performing in front of an audience (niche-picking).

iStock/Essentials; iStock/Signature

example, the child with a genetic trait for interest and ability in music actively seeks experiences and environments that support that trait, such as friends with similar interests and after-school music classes. This tendency to actively seek out experiences and environments compatible with and supportive of our genetic tendencies is called **niche-picking** (Corrigall & Schellenberg, 2015; Scarr & McCartney, 1983).

The strength of passive, evocative, and active gene–environment correlations changes with development, as shown in Figure 2.9 (Scarr, 1992). Passive gene–environment correlations are common at birth, as caregivers determine infants' experiences. Correlations between their genotype and environment tend to occur because their environments are made by genetically similar parents. Evocative gene–environment correlations also occur from birth, as infants' inborn traits and tendencies influence others, evoking responses that support their own genetic predispositions. In contrast, active gene–environment correlations take place as children grow older and more independent. As they become increasingly capable of controlling parts of their environment, they engage in niche-picking by choosing their own interests and activities, actively shaping their own development. Niche-picking contributes to the differences we see in siblings, including fraternal twins, as they grow older. But identical twins tend to become more similar over time perhaps because they are increasingly able to select the environments that best fit their genetic propensities. As they age, identical twins—even those reared apart—become alike in attitudes, personality, cognitive ability, strength, mental health, and preferences, as well as select similar spouses and best friends (McGue & Christensen, 2013; Plomin & Deary, 2015; Plomin et al., 2016; Rushton & Bons, 2005).

Epigenetic Influences on Development

We have seen that development is influenced by the dynamic interaction of biological and contextual forces. Genes provide a blueprint for development, but phenotypic outcomes, individuals' characteristics, are not predetermined. Our genes are expressed as different phenotypes in different contexts or situations, known as epigenetics (Moore, 2017). The term *epigenetics* literally means "above the gene." The epigenome is a molecule that stretches along the length of DNA and provides instructions to genes, determining how they are expressed, whether they are turned on or off. The epigenome carries the instructions that determine what each cell in your body will become, whether heart cell, muscle cell, or brain cell, for example. Those instructions are carried out by turning genes on and off.

At birth, each cell in our body turns on only a fraction of its genes. The epigenome instructs genes to be turned on and off over the course of development and also in response to the environment (Meaney, 2017). Epigenetic mechanisms determine how genetic instructions are carried out to determine the phenotype (Lester, Conradt, & Marsit, 2016). Environmental factors such as toxins, injuries, crowding, diet, and responsive parenting can influence the expression of genetic traits. In this way, even traits that are highly canalized can be influenced by the environment.

FIGURE 2.9

Development Stage and Gene–Environment Correlations

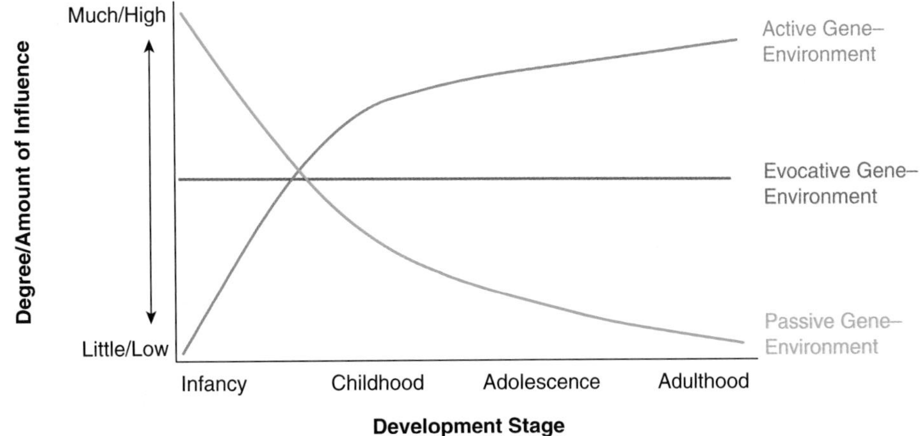

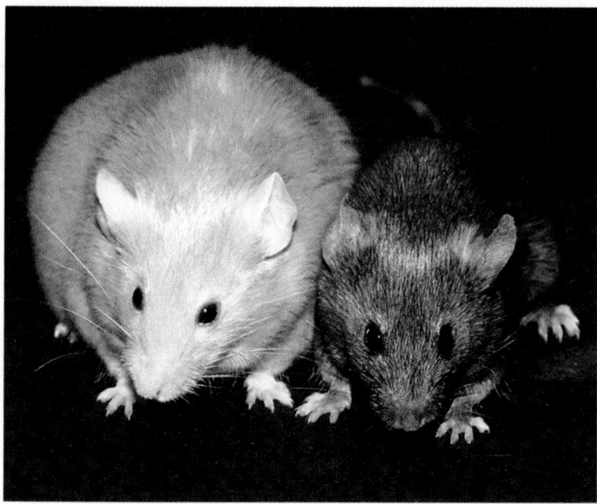

These two mice are genetically identical. Both carry the agouti gene, but it is turned on all the time in the yellow mouse and turned off in the brown mouse.

One of the earliest examples of epigenetics is the case of agouti mice, which carry the agouti gene. Mice that carry the agouti gene have yellow fur, are extremely obese, are shaped much like a pincushion, and are prone to diabetes and cancer. When agouti mice breed, most of the offspring are identical to the parents—yellow, obese, and susceptible to life-shortening disease. However, a groundbreaking study showed that yellow agouti mice can produce offspring that look very different (Waterland & Jirtle, 2003). The mice in the photo both carry the agouti gene, yet they look very different; the brown mouse is slender and lean and has a low risk of developing diabetes and cancer, living well into old age. Why are these mice so different? Epigenetics. In the case of the yellow and brown mice, the phenotype of the brown mice has been altered, but the DNA remains the same. Both carry the agouti gene, but it is turned on all the time in the yellow mouse and turned off in the brown mouse.

In 2003, Waterland and Jertle discovered that the pregnant agouti female's diet can determine her offspring's phenotype. In this study, female mice were fed foods containing chemicals that attach to a gene and turn it off. Yellow agouti mothers fed extra nutrients passed along the agouti gene to their offspring, but it was turned off. The mice looked radically different from their mother (brown) and were healthier (lean, not susceptible to disease) even though they carried the same genes.

Epigenetic processes also influence human development. For example, consider brain development. Providing an infant with a healthy diet and opportunities to explore the world will support the development of brain cells, governed by epigenetic mechanisms that switch genes on and off. Brain development influences motor development, further supporting the infant's exploration of the physical and social world and thereby promoting cognitive and social development. Active engagement with the world encourages connections among brain cells. Conversely, epigenetic changes that accompany exposure to toxins or extreme trauma might suppress the activity of some genes, potentially negatively influencing brain development and its cascading effects on motor, cognitive, and social development. In this way, an individual's neurological capacities are the result of epigenetic interactions among genes and contextual factors that determine his or her phenotype (Lerner & Overton, 2017). These complex interactions are illustrated in Figure 2.10 (Dodge & Rutter, 2011). Interactions between heredity and environment change throughout development, as does the role we play in constructing environments that support our genotypes, influence our epigenome, and determine who we become (Lickliter & Witherington, 2017).

Perhaps the most surprising finding emerging from animal studies of epigenetics, however, is that not only can the epigenome be influenced by the environment before birth but it can be passed by males and females from one generation to the next without changing the DNA itself (Soubry, Hoyo, Jirtle, & Murphy, 2014; Szyf, 2015). This means that what you eat and do today could affect the epigenome—the development, characteristics, and health—of your children, grandchildren, and great-grandchildren (Bale, 2015; Vanhees, Vonhögen, van Schooten, & Godschalk, 2014).

FIGURE 2.10

Epigenetic Framework

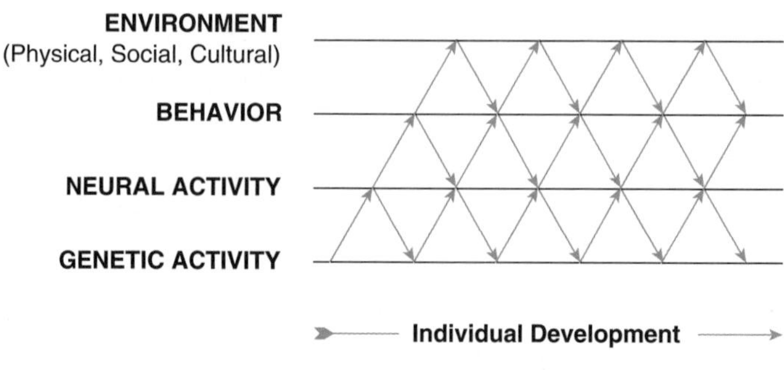

Source: Gottlieb (2007). With permission from John Wiley & Sons.

THINKING IN CONTEXT 2.4

1. Describe a skill or ability in which you excel. How might your ability be influenced by your genes and your context?
   a. Identify passive gene–environment correlation that may contribute to your ability. How has your environment influenced your ability?
   b. Provide an example of an evocative gene–environment correlation. How have you evoked responses from your context that influenced your ability?
   c. Explain how your ability might reflect an active gene–environment correlation.
   d. Which of these types of gene–environment correlations do you think best accounts for your ability? Why?
2. Considering the research on epigenetics, what can you do to protect your epigenome? What kinds of behavioral and contextual factors might influence your epigenome?

APPLY YOUR KNOWLEDGE

Zennia is sitting in her doctor's office. She tells Dr. Rasheed, "I want to have a baby. I have no partner, but I'm ready. I'm in my late 30s and financially stable. It's time. What are my options?" Dr. Rasheed replies, "There are a number of choices. It's a matter of figuring out what's right for you. In addition to a full examination to assess your health, we will seek assistance from a genetic counselor to determine the risk for genetic disorders. This information can help you decide among reproductive options."

1. Identify three ways that genetic disorders are passed. Why does Dr. Rasheed advise genetic testing?
2. What are some of the reproductive options available to Zennia? What are some of the advantages and disadvantages of each option?
3. Which option do you suggest? Why?
4. Suppose that Zennia became pregnant. What types of prenatal screening tests might Dr. Rasheed prescribe? Discuss some of the advantages and disadvantages of each.
5. What advice would you give Zennia? Why?

WANT A BETTER GRADE?

Get the tools you need to sharpen your study skills. **SAGE edge** offers a robust online environment featuring an impressive array of free tools and resources. Access practice quizzes, eFlashcards, video, and multimedia at **edge.sagepub.com/kutherchild1e** SAGE edge™

KEY TERMS

SUMMARY

2.1 Discuss the genetic foundations of development.

The human body is composed of trillions of units called cells, each with a nucleus containing 23 matching pairs of chromosomes, which contain genes, composed of stretches of deoxyribonucleic acid (DNA) that carry the plan for creating all of the traits that organisms carry. Some genes are passed through dominant–recessive inheritance, in which some genes are dominant and will always be expressed regardless of the gene they are paired with. Other genes are recessive and will only be expressed if paired with another recessive gene. When a person is heterozygous for a particular trait, the dominant gene is expressed and the person remains a carrier of the recessive gene. Some traits are carried on the X chromosome. Some traits are passed through incomplete dominance in which both genes influence the characteristic. Polygenic traits are the result of interactions among many genes. Some traits are determined by genomic imprinting, determined by whether it is inherited from the mother or the father.

2.2 Identify examples of genetic disorders and chromosomal abnormalities.

Genetic disorders carried through dominant–recessive inheritance include phenylketonuria (PKU), a recessive disorder, and Huntington disease, carried by a dominant allele. Some recessive genetic disorders, like the gene for hemophilia, are carried on the X chromosome. Males are more likely to be affected by X-linked genetic disorders, such as hemophilia. Fragile X syndrome is an example of a dominant–recessive disorder carried on the X chromosome. Because the gene is dominant, it must appear on only one X chromosome to be displayed. Other X-linked genetic disorders include Klinefelter syndrome, Jacob's syndrome, triple X syndrome, and Turner syndrome. Some disorders, such as trisomy 21, known as Down syndrome, are the result of chromosomal abnormalities. Others result from mutations, genetic abnormalities that may occur randomly or as a result of exposure to toxins.

2.3 Examine the choices available to prospective parents in having healthy children.

Genetic counseling is a medical specialty that helps prospective parents determine the likelihood that their children will inherit genetic defects and chromosomal abnormalities. Single women, gay and lesbian couples, and individuals at risk for bearing children with genetic or chromosomal abnormalities may seek alternative methods of conception such as artificial insemination, in vitro fertilization, and surrogacy. Others consider adopting a child. Prenatal diagnosis is recommended when genetic testing has determined a risk for genetic abnormalities. Some prenatal tests, such as ultrasound, are conducted routinely. Advances in genetics and in medicine have led to therapies that can be administered prenatally to reduce the effects of many genetic abnormalities.

2.4 Summarize the interaction of heredity and environment, including behavioral genetics and the epigenetic framework.

Behavioral genetics is the field of study that examines how genes and experience combine to influence the diversity of human traits, abilities, and behaviors. Heritability research examines the contributions of the genotype in determining phenotypes but also provides information on the role of experience through three types of studies: selective breeding studies, family studies, and adoption studies. Genetics contributes to many traits, such as intellectual ability, sociability, anxiety, agreeableness, activity level, obesity, and susceptibility to various illnesses. Passive, evocative, and active gene–environment correlations illustrate how traits often are supported by both our genes and environment. Reaction range refers to the idea that there is a wide range of potential expressions of a genetic trait, depending on environmental opportunities and constraints. Some traits illustrate canalization and require extreme changes in the environment to alter their course. The epigenetic framework is a model for understanding the dynamic ongoing interactions between heredity and environment whereby the epigenome's instructions to turn genes on and off throughout development are influenced by the environment.

REVIEW QUESTIONS

2.1 What genes are shared by twins?

What are four types of genetic inheritance?

2.2 Give an example of the following:

- a dominant–recessive disorder
- an X-linked disorder
- a chromosomal abnormality

What is imprinting?

What is a mutation?

2.3 What is genetic counseling?

What are the differences between artificial insemination, in vitro fertilization, surrogacy, and adoption?

What are the five common methods of prenatal diagnosis?

2.4 What is behavioral genetics?

What are three types of gene—environment correlations?

What is the range of reaction?

What is the epigenetic framework?

©iStockphoto.com/Eva-Kat

3 The Prenatal Period, Birth, and the Newborn

"There's a baby in here," explained Mia as she patted her nearly flat stomach and looked down as her 3-year-old son, Miguel, stared incredulously. "Yes," she smiled, "Your little brother or sister is very tiny now but will grow and make Mommy's tummy really big and round, like a ball." "When?" asked Miguel. "When will your tummy grow? I like it now," he pouted. Miguel will be in for a surprise as his mother's body will undergo dramatic changes over the next few months. In this chapter, we examine **prenatal development**, how individuals develop before birth.

Learning Objectives

3.1 Describe the three periods of prenatal development.

Video Activity 3.1: Pregnancy and Ultrasound

3.2 Explain how exposure to teratogens and other environmental factors can influence the prenatal environment.

3.3 Summarize the process of childbirth.

Video Activity 3.2: The Process of Childbirth

3.4 Discuss the neonate's physical capacities, including development in low-birthweight infants.

Chapter Contents

PRENATAL DEVELOPMENT

Conception, the union of ovum and sperm, marks the beginning of prenatal development. Over 266 days (or 38 weeks), the human progresses from fertilization to birth. During this transformation, the zygote progresses through several periods of development, finally emerging from the womb as a neonate.

Conception

A woman can conceive only during a short window of time each month. About every 28 days, an ovum bursts from one of the ovaries into the long, thin fallopian tube that leads to the uterus; this event is known as **ovulation** (see Figure 3.1). The ovum is the largest cell in the human body, yet it is only 1/175th of an inch in diameter (about

FIGURE 3.1

Female Reproductive System

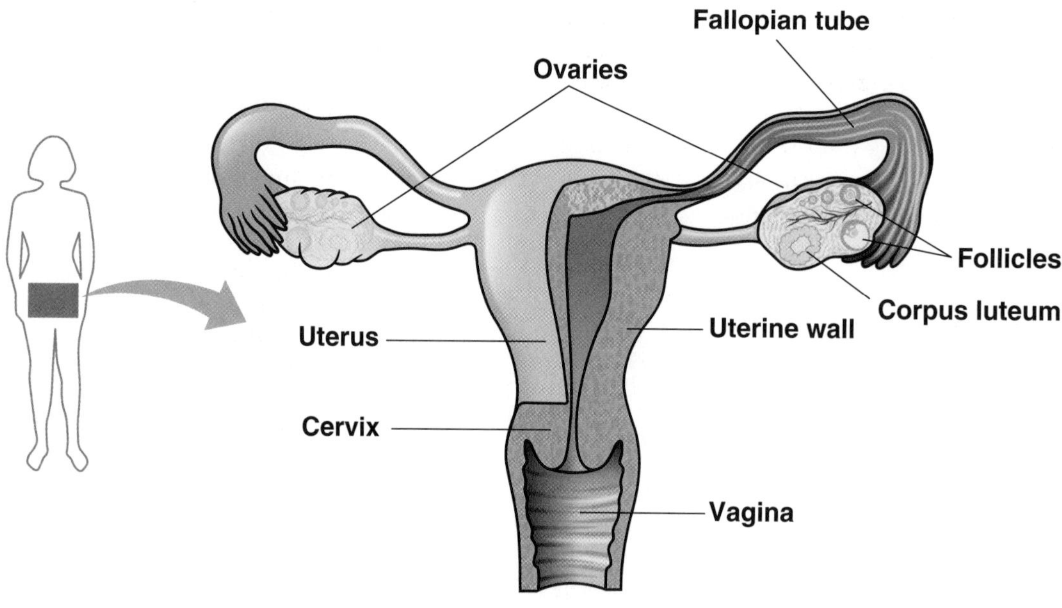

Source: Levine and Munsch (2010, p. 102).

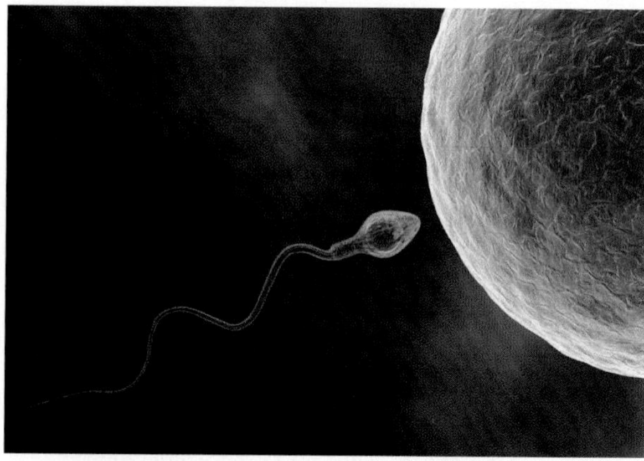

A tiny sperm is fertilizing the much larger ovum.
©iStockphoto.com/Dr_Microbe

the size of the period at the end of this sentence). Over several days, the ovum travels down the **fallopian tube**, which connects the ovaries to the uterus, while the corpus luteum, the spot on the ovary from which the ovum was released, secretes hormones that cause the lining of the uterus to thicken in preparation for the fertilized ovum (Sadler, 2018). If fertilization does not occur, the lining of the uterus is shed through menstruation about 2 weeks after ovulation.

Conception, of course, also involves the male. Each day, a man's testes produce millions of sperm, which are composed of a pointed head packed with 23 chromosomes' worth of genetic material and a long tail. During ejaculation, about 360 million, and as many as 500 million, sperm are released, bathed in a protective fluid called semen (Moore & Persaud, 2016). After entering the female's vagina, sperm travel through the cervix into the uterus and onward toward the ovum. After about 6 hours the sperm reach the fallopian tube, where an ovum may—or may not—be present. The journey is difficult: Some sperm get tangled up with other sperm, some travel up the wrong fallopian tube, and others do not swim vigorously enough to reach the ovum. On average, about 300 sperm reach the ovum, if one is present (Webster, Morris, & Kevelighan, 2018). Those that travel up the fallopian tube can live up to 6 days, able to fertilize a yet unreleased ovum. The ovum, however, remains viable for only about a day after being released into the fallopian tube.

Both sperm and the woman's reproductive tract play a role in fertilization (Suarez, 2016). Sperm are guided by temperature, tracking the heat of an expectant ovum, as well as by chemical signal (Lottero-Leconte, Isidro Alonso, Castellano, & Perez Martinez, 2017). In the presence of an ovum, sperm become hyperactivated, they swim even more vigorously, and the sperm's head releases enzymes to help it penetrate the protective layers of the ovum (Bianchi & Wright, 2016). As soon as one sperm penetrates the ovum, a chemical reaction makes the ovum's membrane impermeable to other sperm. The sperm's tail falls off, and the sperm's genetic contents merge with that of the ovum.

At the moment of conception, the zygote contains 46 chromosomes, half from the ovum and half from the sperm. After fertilization, the zygote rapidly transforms into a multicelled organism. Prenatal development takes place over three developmental periods: (1) the germinal period, (2) the embryonic period, and (3) the fetal period.

Germinal Period (0 to 2 Weeks)

During the **germinal period**, also known as the period of the zygote, the newly created zygote begins cell division as it travels down the fallopian tube, where fertilization took place, toward the uterus. About 30 hours after conception, the zygote then splits down the middle, forming two identical cells (Webster et al., 2018). This process is called **cleavage**, and it continues at a rapid pace. As shown in Figure 3.2, the two cells each split to form four cells, then eight, and so on. Each of the resulting cells is identical until about the third set of cell divisions. This process of cell division continues rapidly. Any of these cells may become a person (and sometimes two, in the case of monozygotic or identical twins).

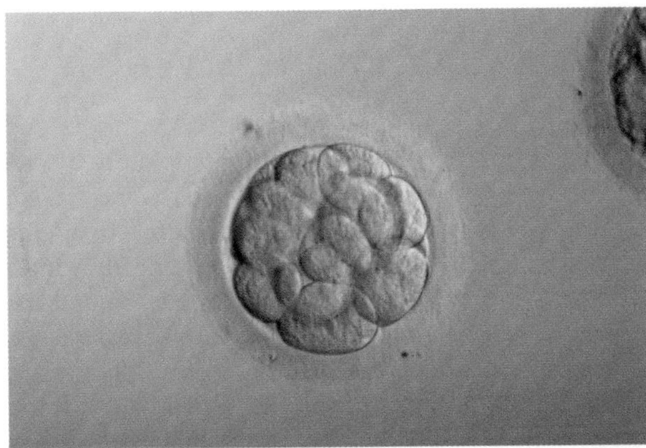

This ball of cells, known as a morula, is formed at about 3 days after conception. Each of these cells is identical. Differentiation has not yet begun.
Pascal Goetgheluck/Science Source

Cell differentiation begins roughly 72 hours after fertilization when the organism consists of about 16 to 32 cells. Differentiation means that the cells begin to specialize and are no longer identical. By 4 days, the organism consists of about 60 to 70 cells formed into a hollow ball called a **blastocyst**, a fluid-filled sphere with cells forming a protective circle around an inner cluster of cells from which the embryo will develop. **Implantation**, in which the blastocyst burrows into the wall of the uterus, begins at about day 6 and is complete by about day 11 (Moore & Persaud, 2016).

Embryonic Period (3 to 8 Weeks)

After implantation, by the third week after conception, the developing organism, now called an **embryo**, begins the most rapid period of structural development in the lifespan. All of the organs and major body systems form during the **embryonic period**. The mass of cells composing the *embryonic disk* forms layers, which will develop into all of the major organs of the body. The *ectoderm*, the upper layer, will become skin, nails, hair, teeth, sensory organs, and the nervous system. The *endoderm*, the lower layer, will become the digestive system, liver, lungs, pancreas, salivary glands, and respiratory system. The middle layer, the *mesoderm*, forms later and will become muscles, skeleton, circulatory system, and internal organs.

As the embryo develops, support structures form to protect it, provide nourishment, and remove

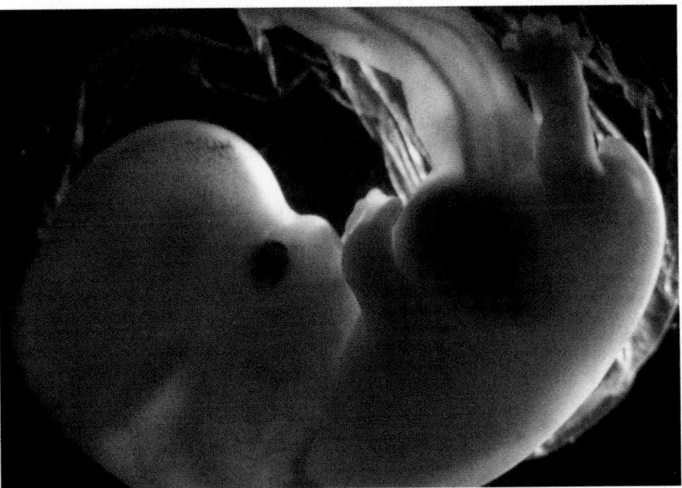

Development proceeds very quickly during the embryonic period. Note the dramatic changes from the fifth week (left) to the seventh week (right) of prenatal development.
Petit Format/Science Source

FIGURE 3.2

Germinal Period

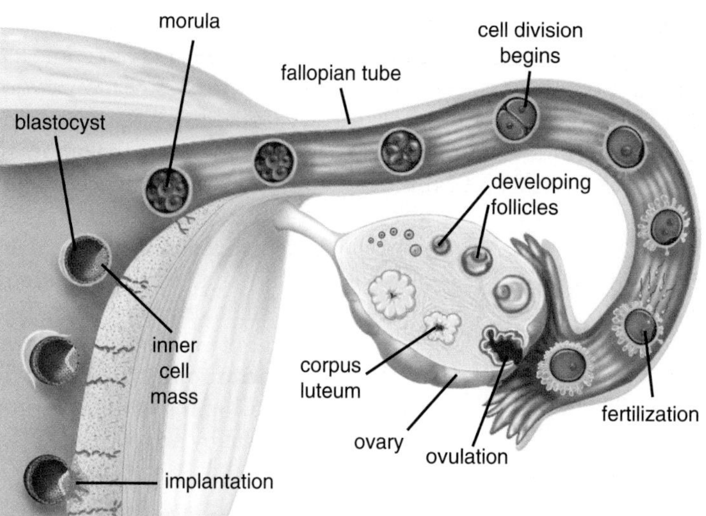

Source: Levine and Munsch (2010, p. 102).

wastes. The **amnion**, a membrane that holds amniotic fluid, surrounds the embryo, providing temperature regulation, cushioning, and protection from shocks. The **placenta**, a principal organ of exchange between the mother and developing organism, begins to form. It contains tissue from both the mother and embryo and, once formed, will act as a filter, enabling the exchange of nutrients, oxygen, and wastes to occur through the umbilical cord. The placenta is also a protective barrier, preventing some toxins from entering the embryo's bloodstream as well as keeping the mother and embryo's bloodstreams separate. Many toxins, however, are able to pass through the placenta, including drugs and chemicals such as alcohol, cannabis, and opioids (Gupta, 2017; Neradugomma et al., 2018; Serra et al., 2017).

About 22 days after conception marks a particularly important change. The endoderm folds to form the **neural tube**, which will develop into the central nervous system (brain and spinal cord) (Webster et al., 2018). Now the head can be distinguished. A blood vessel that will become the heart begins to pulse and blood begins to circulate throughout the body. During days 26 and 27, arm buds appear, followed by leg buds on days 28 through 30. At about this time, a tail-like appendage extends from the spine, disappearing at about 55 days after conception (Sadler, 2018). The brain develops rapidly and the head grows faster than the other parts of the body during the fifth week of development. The eyes, ears, nose, and mouth begin to form during the sixth week. Upper arms, forearms, palms, legs, and feet appear. The embryo shows reflex responses to touch.

During the seventh week, webbed fingers and toes are apparent; they separate completely by the end of the eighth week. A ridge called the indifferent gonad appears; it will develop into the male or female genitals, depending on the fetus's sex chromosomes (Moore & Persaud, 2016). The Y chromosome of the male embryo instructs it to secrete testosterone, causing the **indifferent gonad** to create testes. In female embryos, no testosterone is released, and the indifferent gonad produces ovaries. The sex organs take several weeks to develop. The external genital organs are not apparent until about 12 weeks.

At the end of the embryonic period, 8 weeks after conception, the embryo weighs about one-seventh of an ounce and is 1 inch long. All of the basic organs and body parts have formed in a very rudimentary way. The embryo displays spontaneous reflexive movements, but it is still too small for the movements to be felt by the mother (Hepper, 2015). Serious defects that emerge during the embryonic period often cause a miscarriage, or spontaneous abortion (loss of the fetus); indeed, most miscarriages are the result of chromosomal abnormalities. The most severely defective organisms do not survive beyond the first trimester, or third month of pregnancy. It is estimated that up to 45% of all conceptions abort spontaneously, and most occur before the pregnancy is detected (Bienstock, Fox, & Wallach, 2015).

Fetal Period (9 Weeks to Birth)

During the **fetal period**, from the ninth week to birth, the organism, called a **fetus**, grows rapidly, and its organs become more complex and begin to function. Now all parts of the fetus's body can move spontaneously, the legs kick, and the fetus can suck its thumb (an involuntary reflex). By the end of the 12th week, the upper limbs have almost reached their final relative lengths, but the lower limbs are slightly shorter than their final relative lengths (Sadler, 2018).

By the 14th week, limb movements are coordinated, but they will be too slight to be felt by the mother until about 17 to 20 weeks. The heartbeat gets stronger. Eyelids, eyebrows, fingernails, toenails, and tooth buds form. The first hair to appear is **lanugo**, a fine down-like hair that covers the fetus's body; it is gradually replaced by human hair. The skin is covered with a greasy material called the **vernix caseosa**, which protects the fetal skin from abrasions, chapping, and hardening that can occur with exposure to amniotic fluid (Moore & Persaud, 2016). At 21 weeks, rapid eye movements begin, signifying an important time of growth and development for the fetal brain. The brain begins to become more responsive. For example, startle responses have been reported at 22 to 23 weeks in response to sudden vibrations and noises (Hepper, 2015). During weeks 21 to 25, the fetus gains substantial weight, and its body proportions become more like those of a newborn infant. Growth of the fetal body begins to catch up to the head, yet the head remains disproportionately larger than the body at birth.

During the last 3 months of pregnancy, the fetal body grows substantially in weight and length; specifically, it typically gains over 5 pounds and grows 7 inches. At about 28 weeks after conception, brain development grows in leaps and bounds. The cerebral cortex develops convolutions and furrows, taking on the brain's characteristic wrinkly appearance (Andescavage et al., 2016). The fetal brain wave pattern shifts to include occasional bursts of activity, similar to the sleep-wake cycles of newborns. By 30 weeks, the pupils of the eyes dilate in response to light. At 35 weeks, the fetus has a firm hand grasp and spontaneously orients itself toward light.

Although the expected date of delivery is 266 days or 38 weeks from conception (40 weeks from the mother's last menstrual period), about 1 in every 10 American births is premature (Centers for Disease Control and Prevention, 2017e). The **age of viability**—the age at which advanced medical care permits a preterm newborn to survive outside the womb—begins at about 22 weeks after conception (Sadler, 2018). Infants born before 22 weeks rarely survive more than a few days, because their brain and lungs have not begun to function. Although a 23-week fetus born prematurely may survive in intensive care, its immature respiratory system places it at risk; only about one-third of infants born at 23 weeks' gestation survive (Stoll et al., 2015). At about 26 weeks, the lungs become capable of breathing air and the premature infant stands a better chance of surviving if given intensive care. About 80% of infants born at 25 weeks survive, and 94% of those born at 27 weeks also survive. Premature birth has a variety of causes, including many environmental factors.

Our discussion thus far has emphasized fetal development; however, expectant mothers also experience radical physical changes during pregnancy. In addition to changes in body weight and shape, pregnancy is accompanied by changes in brain structure and function, as discussed in the Lives in Context feature.

LIVES IN CONTEXT: BIOLOGICAL INFLUENCES

Pregnancy and the Maternal Brain

The developing embryo and fetus receive a great deal of research attention, but what does pregnancy mean for mothers' development? Women's bodies undergo a radical transformation during pregnancy. For example, the hormone progesterone increases up to 15-fold and is accompanied by a flood of estrogen that is greater than the lifelong exposure prior to pregnancy. Hormonal shifts are associated with brain changes during puberty as well as later in life. Do the hormonal changes with pregnancy influence women's brain structure? Animal research suggests that pregnancy is accompanied by neurological changes, including changes in neural receptors, neuron generation, and gene expression, that are long-lasting (Kinsley & Amory-Meyer, 2011). It is likely that pregnancy is also associated with neural changes in humans, but there is little research to date (Hillerer, Jacobs, Fischer, & Aigner, 2014).

In a recent groundbreaking study, Elseine Hoekzema and colleagues (2017) conducted brain scans of women who were attempting to become pregnant for the first time as well as their partners. Women who became pregnant were scanned again after giving birth and at

(Continued)

(Continued)

least 2 years later. The fathers and women who had not become pregnant were also assessed. The new mothers experienced reductions in the brain's gray matter, signifying increased neural efficiency in regions of the brain involved in social cognition, specifically, the ability to sense another person's emotions and perspective. This corresponds with prior findings suggesting that pregnancy is associated with the enhanced ability to recognize faces, especially those displaying emotions (Pearson, Lightman, & Evans, 2009). Gestational alterations in the brain structures that are implicated in social processes may offer an adaptive advantage to mothers by facilitating their ability to recognize the needs of their children and to promote mother–infant bonding (Hoekzema et al., 2017). The changes in gray matter volume predicted mothers' attachment to their infants in the postpartum period, as indicated by mothers' increased neural activity in response to viewing photos of their infant compared with other infants. The pregnancy-related neurological changes were so marked and predictable that all of the women could be classified as having undergone pregnancy or not on the basis of the volume changes in gray matter. Notably, fathers did not show a change in gray matter volume, suggesting that the neural effects of pregnancy are biological in nature rather than associated with the contextual changes that occur with the transition to parenthood.

Pregnancy is not only a period of development for the embryo, but for the mother as well. Brain plasticity during pregnancy and the postpartum period is adaptive, as it helps women adapt to motherhood and the challenges of caring for a newborn. Moreover, research suggests that increased plasticity continues well after birth. One study of brain images of women 1 to 2 days after childbirth and 4–6 weeks later found a rejuvenation effect whereby women's brains showed enhanced plasticity, appearing on average about 5 years younger in the weeks after birth (Luders et al., 2018). However, some scientists argue that enhanced plasticity can promote development but it may also increase women's sensitivity to stress and vulnerability to mental disorders, such as depression (Barba-Müller, Craddock, Carmona, & Hoekzema, 2019), underlining the importance of support for new mothers.

What Do You Think?

1. From an evolutionary developmental perspective (see Chapter 1), why might these pregnancy-related brain changes occur?
2. How can mothers take advantage of the plasticity that accompanies pregnancy and the postpartum period?
3. What are some ways to support women during the transition to motherhood? ●

THINKING IN CONTEXT 3.1

1. "The most critical time in prenatal development is the end because the fetus is most like a baby," explains Rita. To what extent do you agree with Rita? What do we know about the process of prenatal development?
2. What might be some of the implications of the timing of prenatal development for the behavior of pregnant women and those who are considering becoming pregnant?

ENVIRONMENTAL INFLUENCES ON PRENATAL DEVELOPMENT

Prenatal development unfolds along a programmed path, a predictable pattern of change. However, environmental factors can interfere with the processes of prenatal development. A **teratogen** is an agent, such as a disease, drug, or other environmental factor, that disrupts prenatal development, increasing the risk of abnormalities, defects, and even death. The field of *teratology* attempts to find the causes of birth defects so that they may be avoided. Health care providers help pregnant women and those who intend to become pregnant to be aware of teratogens and avoid them, as much as possible, to maximize the likelihood of having a healthy baby.

Principles of Teratology

Different teratogens affect development in different ways. Moreover, it is not always easy to predict the harm caused by teratogens. Generally, several principles can account for the varied effects of exposure to teratogens on prenatal development (Moore & Persaud, 2016; Sadler, 2015).

- **Critical Periods.** The extent to which exposure to a teratogen disrupts prenatal development depends on the stage of prenatal development when exposure occurs. That is, there are critical periods during prenatal development in which the developing organism is more susceptible to damage from exposure to teratogens. Exposure to teratogens during the germinal stage can interfere with cell division and prevent implantation; however, during this stage most women are unaware that they are pregnant and the effects of teratogens often go unnoticed. It is during the embryonic period that the embryo is most sensitive to the harmful effects of teratogens (Webster et al., 2018). Structural defects occur when the embryo is exposed to a teratogen while that part of the body is developing. As shown in Figure 3.3, each organ of the body has a sensitive period in development during which it is most susceptible to damage from teratogens such as drugs, alcohol, and environmental contaminants. Once a body part is fully formed, it is less likely to be harmed by exposure to teratogens; however, some body parts, like the brain, remain vulnerable throughout pregnancy.

- **Dose.** The amount of exposure (i.e., dose level) to a teratogen influences its effects. Generally, the greater the dose and the longer the period of exposure, the more damage to development. However, teratogens also differ in their strength. Some teratogens, like alcohol, display a powerful dose–response relationship so that larger doses, or heavier and more frequent drinking, result in greater damage (Muggli et al., 2017).
- **Individual Differences.** Individuals vary in their susceptibility to particular teratogens based on the genetic makeup of both the organism and mother, as well as the quality of the prenatal environment. How an organism responds to a teratogen may vary with its genetic vulnerability. That is, teratogens increase the risk of defects for all organisms, but responses may vary such that some organisms show severe defects, others show more mild defects, and some may display normal development. The mother's genetic makeup and the prenatal environment (e.g., nutrition) may also increase or decrease the likelihood of teratogenic defects.
- **Complicated Effects.** Different teratogens can cause the same birth defect, and a variety of birth defects can result from the same teratogen. Also, some teratogenic effects may not be noticeable at birth but instead emerge later in life. **Sleeper effects** refer to detrimental outcomes of exposure to teratogens and early risks that appear only later in development.

FIGURE 3.3

Sensitive Periods in Prenatal Development

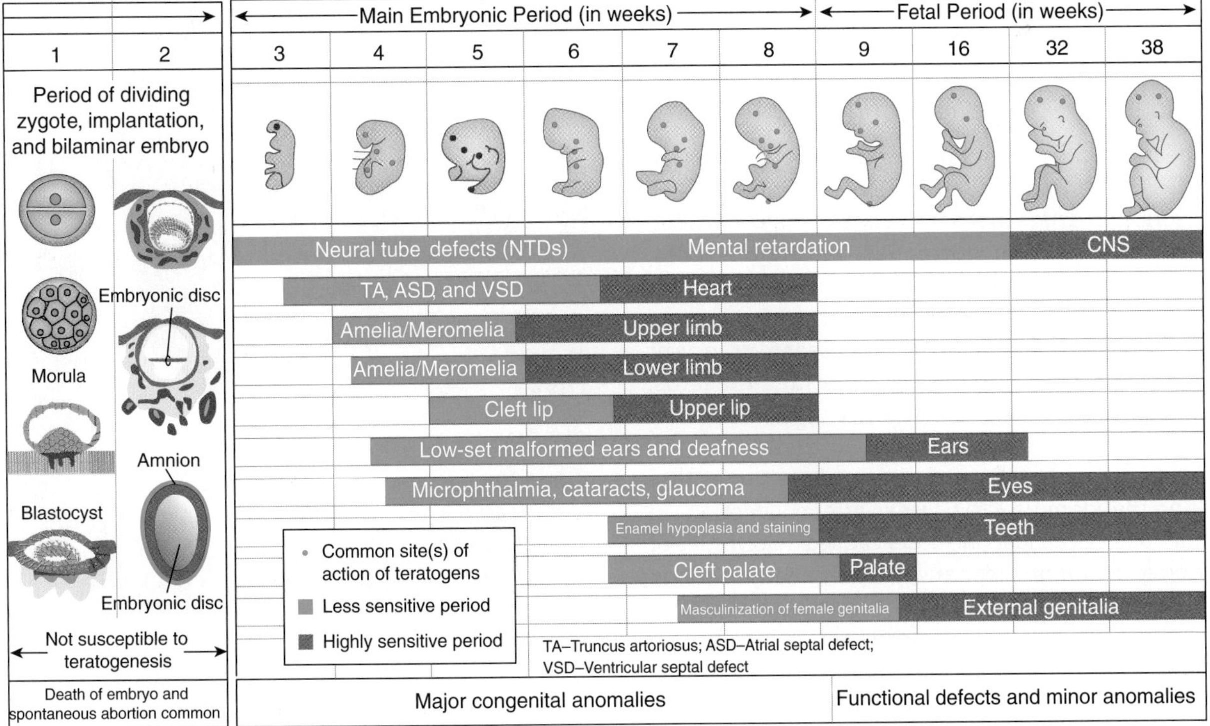

Source: Levine and Munsch (2010, p. 113).

For example, infants born to women who consumed diethylstilbestrol (DES), a hormone that was widely prescribed between 1945 and 1970 to prevent miscarriages, were born healthy but as adults were more likely to experience problems with their reproductive systems. Daughters born to mothers who took DES were more likely to develop a rare form of cervical cancer, have miscarriages, and give birth to infants who were premature or low birthweight (Conlon, 2017).

Types of Teratogens

Prenatal development can be influenced by many contextual factors, including environmental factors, maternal illness, and maternal consumption of over-the-counter (OTC), prescription, and recreational drugs, among others. Sometimes a pregnant woman and her doctor must make a difficult choice between forgoing a needed prescription drug and putting the fetus at risk. In those cases, the woman and her doctor must weigh not just the risks to the fetus but the benefits of the medication to the mother and the potential harm from forgoing it. Frequently, the risks are deemed as justified to protect the woman's mental and physical health. In most cases, women are unaware of their pregnancies until after the first few weeks of the embryonic stage. Thus, in the real world, almost no pregnancy can be entirely free of exposure to teratogens. However, each year, about 97% of infants are born without defects (Centers for Disease Control and Prevention, 2017a). Next, we examine common teratogens.

Prescription and Nonprescription Drugs

More than 90% of pregnant women take prescription or OTC medications (Servey & Chang, 2014). Prescription drugs that can act as teratogens include antibiotics, certain hormones, antidepressants, anticonvulsants, and some acne drugs (Webster et al., 2018). In several cases, physicians have unwittingly prescribed drugs to ease pregnant women's discomfort that caused harm to the fetus. For example, in the late 1950s and early 1960s, many pregnant women were prescribed thalidomide to prevent morning sickness. However, it was found that taking thalidomide 4 to 6 weeks after conception (in some cases, even just one dose) caused deformities of the child's arms and legs and, less frequently, damage to the ears, heart, kidneys, and genitals (Fraga et al., 2016). Isotretinoin, a form of vitamin A used to treat acne, is a potent teratogen associated with miscarriage as well as severe face, heart, and central nervous system abnormalities, as well as intellectual disability (Henry et al., 2016; Wilson, 2016). The teratogenic effect of isotretinoin is so severe that the U.S. Food and Drug Administration (2010) requires that women prescribed isotretinoin take physician-administered pregnancy tests for 2 months prior to beginning treatment and agree to use two methods of birth control and complete a monthly pregnancy test each month while taking it.

Nonprescription drugs, such as diet pills and cold medicine, can also cause harm, but research on OTC drugs lags far behind research on prescription drugs, and we know little about the teratogenic effect of many OTC drugs (Hussain & Ashmead, 2017). Frequently, findings regarding the teratogenic effects of drugs are mixed, with some studies suggesting potential harm and others suggesting no ill effects of a given drug. For example, although high doses of the common painkiller aspirin may be associated with an increased risk of miscarriage and poor fetal growth (Li, Liu, & Odouli, 2003), low doses are often prescribed to pregnant women to prevent and treat high blood pressure and preeclampsia (dangerously high blood pressure late in pregnancy that can cause organ damage) (Roberge, Bujold, & Nicolaides, 2017). Likewise, the most common OTC drug consumed during pregnancy, caffeine, found in coffee, tea, cola drinks, and chocolate, appears to be safe in low doses (200 milligrams or about one cup per day; March of Dimes, 2015). Heavy caffeine consumption, however, is associated with an increased risk for miscarriage and low birthweight (Chen et al., 2014, 2016).

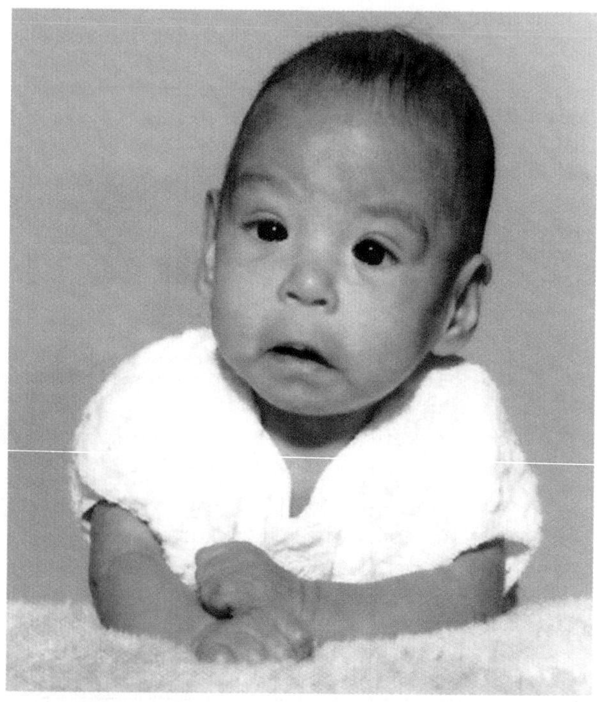

Fetal alcohol syndrome is associated with distinct facial characteristics, growth deficiencies, and deficits in physical and cognitive abilities that persist throughout childhood into adulthood.

Alcohol

An estimated 10% to 20% of Canadian and U.S. women report consuming alcohol during pregnancy (Alshaarawy, Breslau, & Anthony, 2016; Popova, Lange, Probst, Parunashvili, & Rehm, 2017). Alcohol abuse during pregnancy has been identified as the leading cause of developmental disabilities (Webster et al., 2018). **Fetal alcohol spectrum disorders** refer to the continuum of effects of exposure to alcohol, which vary with the timing and amount of exposure (Hoyme et al., 2016). Fetal alcohol spectrum disorders are estimated to affect as many as 2% to 5% of younger schoolchildren in the United States and Western Europe (P. A. May et al., 2014, 2018). At the extreme end of the spectrum is **fetal alcohol syndrome (FAS)**, a cluster of defects appearing after heavy prenatal exposure to alcohol. FAS is associated with a distinct pattern of facial characteristics (such as small head circumference, short nose, small eye opening, and small midface), pre- and postnatal growth deficiencies, and deficits in intellectual development, school achievement, memory, visuospatial skills, attention, language, problem solving, motor coordination, and the combined abilities to plan, focus attention, problem solve, and use goal-directed behavior (Gupta, Gupta, & Shirasaka, 2016; Wilhoit, Scott, & Simecka, 2017). The effects of exposure to alcohol within the womb persist throughout childhood and adolescence and are associated with cognitive, learning, and behavioral problems from childhood and adolescence through adulthood (Mamluk et al., 2016; Panczakiewicz et al., 2016; Rangmar et al., 2015).

Even moderate drinking is harmful, as children may be born displaying some but not all of the problems of FAS, termed *fetal alcohol effects* (Hoyme et al., 2016). Consuming 7 to 14 drinks per week during pregnancy is associated with lower birth size, growth deficits through adolescence, and deficits in attention, memory, and cognitive development (Alati et al., 2013; Flak et al., 2014; Lundsberg, Illuzzi, Belanger, Triche, & Bracken, 2015). Even less than one drink per day has been associated with poor fetal growth and preterm delivery (Mamluk et al., 2017). Sleeper effects may also occur with exposure to alcohol, as infants exposed prenatally to as little as an ounce of alcohol a day may display no obvious physical deformities at birth but later, as children, may demonstrate cognitive delays (Charness, Riley, & Sowell, 2016). Scientists have yet to determine if there is a safe level of drinking, but the only way to be certain of avoiding alcohol-related risks is to avoid alcohol during pregnancy altogether.

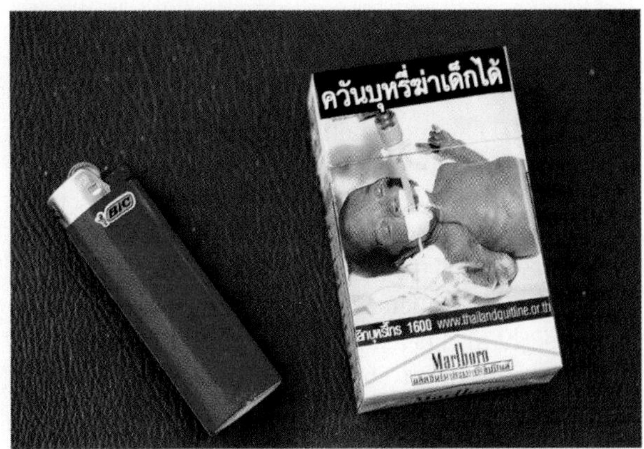

Cigarette packages in many countries include warnings of the dangers smoking poses to prenatal development.
©iStockphoto.com/Jan-Otto

Cigarette Smoking

Every package of cigarettes sold in the United States includes a warning about the dangers of smoking while pregnant. Fetal deaths, premature births, and low birthweight are up to twice as frequent in mothers who are smokers than in those who do not smoke (Juárez & Merlo, 2013). Infants exposed to smoke while in the womb are prone to congenital heart defects, respiratory problems, and sudden infant death syndrome and, as children, show more behavior problems, have attention difficulties, and score lower on intelligence and achievement tests (He, Chen, Zhu, Hua, & Ke, 2017; Lee & Lupo, 2013; Sutin, Flynn, & Terracciano, 2017). Moreover, maternal smoking during pregnancy shows epigenetic effects on offspring, influencing predispositions to illness and disease in childhood, adolescence, and even middle adulthood (Joubert et al., 2016; Tehranifar et al., 2018). There is no safe level of smoking during pregnancy. Even babies born to light smokers (one to five cigarettes per day) show higher rates of low birthweight than do babies born to nonsmokers (Berlin, Golmard, Jacob, Tanguy, & Heishman, 2017; Tong, England, Rockhill, & D'Angelo, 2017). Although e-cigarettes are commonly believed to be "safer" than cigarettes, animal research suggests that exposure to e-cigarette vapor prenatally is associated with an increased risk for asthma and cognitive and neurological changes (T. Nguyen et al., 2018; Sharma et al., 2017). Research is sparse and just emerging, but it is likely that e-cigarettes have similar effects as smoking traditional cigarettes. Quitting smoking before or during pregnancy reduces the risk of adverse pregnancy outcomes.

Cannabis

The effects of cannabis, also referred to as marijuana, on prenatal development are not well understood because there are few long-term studies of its effects and existing studies vary both in quality and in conclusions (El Marroun et al., 2018). The main active ingredient of cannabis, tetrahydrocannabinol, or THC, readily crosses the placenta to affect the fetus in lower doses than experienced by the mother (Alvarez, Rubin, Pina, & Velasquez, 2018). Cannabis use during early pregnancy negatively affects fetal length and birthweight and is associated with a thinner cortex, the outer layer of the brain, in late childhood, suggesting that there are long-term neurological effects (El Marroun et al., 2016; Gunn et al., 2016). In fact, a growing body of research suggests that exposure to THC prenatally may lead to subtle long-term effects in cognition, including impairments in attention, memory, and executive function as well as impulsivity in children, adolescents, and young adults (Grant, Petroff, Isoherranen, Stella, & Burbacher, 2018; Sharapova et al., 2018; Smith et al., 2016). Researchers and health practitioners have thus concluded that it is important to educate the public about the impact of cannabis, even medical cannabis, on pregnancy (Chasnoff, 2017).

Cocaine

Prenatal exposure to cocaine is associated with low birthweight, impaired motor skills, and reduced brain volume at birth and in infancy (Grewen et al., 2014; Gupta, 2017). For example, 1 month after birth, babies who were exposed to cocaine have difficulty regulating their arousal states and show poor movement skills, poor reflexes, and greater excitability (Fallone et al., 2014). Prenatal cocaine exposure has long-term effects on children through its effect on brain development, particularly the regions associated with attention, arousal, regulation, and executive function (Bazinet, Squeglia, Riley, & Tapert, 2016).

Although it was once believed that cocaine-exposed infants would suffer lifelong cognitive deficits, research suggests more subtle effects (Behnke & Smith, 2013; Lambert & Bauer, 2012). Prenatal cocaine exposure has a small but lasting effect on attention and behavioral control, as well as language skills through early adolescence (Buckingham-Howes, Berger, Scaletti, & Black, 2013; Lewis et al., 2013; Singer, Minnes, Min, Lewis, & Short, 2015). However, once home factors (such as parenting and socioeconomic status) are controlled, cocaine-exposed children do not show more behavioral problems in preschool and elementary school (Viteri et al., 2015). However, in adolescence, prenatal exposure to cocaine is associated with behavior problems and substance use (Min, Minnes, Yoon, Short, & Singer, 2014; Richardson, Goldschmidt, Larkby, & Day, 2015). The relationship between cocaine exposure and behavior problems in adolescence is reduced when contextual factors such as home caregiving environment and exposure to violence are controlled, suggesting that the postnatal environment contributes to children's adjustment (Buckingham-Howes et al., 2013).

Opioids

Prenatal exposure to opioids—a class of drugs that includes the illegal drugs heroin and synthetic opioids such as fentanyl, as well as pain relievers available legally by prescription, such as oxycodone, morphine, and others—poses serious risks to development. Newborns exposed to opioids prenatally may show signs of addiction and withdrawal symptoms, including tremors, irritability, abnormal crying, disturbed sleep, and impaired motor control (Gupta, 2017; Raffaeli et al., 2017). Prenatal exposure to opioids is associated with low birthweight, smaller head circumference, and altered brain development in newborns (Monnelly et al., 2018; Nørgaard, Nielsson, & Heide-Jørgensen, 2015; Towers et al., 2019). Children exposed to opioids prenatally tend to show difficulty with attention, managing arousal, learning, and inhibitory control (Bazinet et al., 2016; Levine & Woodward, 2018). They perform more poorly than their peers on tasks measuring executive functioning (such as planning) in preschool (Konijnenberg & Melinder, 2015), score lower in measures of intelligence in late childhood (Nygaard, Moe, Slinning, & Walhovd, 2015), and show reduced volume and a smaller cortical surface area in adolescence (Nygaard et al., 2018; Sirnes et al., 2017).

The challenge of determining the effects of prenatal exposure to illegal drugs is that most infants exposed to opioids or cocaine are also exposed to other substances, including tobacco, alcohol, and marijuana, making it difficult to isolate the effect of each drug on prenatal development. We must be cautious in interpreting findings about illicit drug use and the effects on prenatal development because many other contextual factors often co-occur with parental substance use and also pose risks for development. These risks include poverty, malnutrition, inconsistent parenting, stress, and diminished parental responsiveness (Smith et al., 2016). For example, parents who abuse drugs tend to provide poorer quality care, a home environment less conducive to cognitive development, and parent-child interaction that is less sensitive and positive than the environments provided by other parents (Hatzis, Dawe, Harnett, & Barlow, 2017). Children raised by substance-abusing parents are at risk for

APPLYING DEVELOPMENTAL SCIENCE

Maternal Drug Use While Pregnant

Maternal alcohol and substance use harms prenatal development. Is it abuse?
©iStockphoto.com/vchal

We have seen that exposure to teratogens such as drugs and alcohol adversely affects the developing fetus. Is maternal substance use fetal abuse? For many states, the answer is yes. Although laws are generally intended to promote health and protect fetuses, some developmental scientists and policy analysts argue that state laws are punitive because they potentially threaten women with involuntary treatment or protective custody during pregnancy (Seiler, 2016). As of 2017, 34 states had laws related to reporting of alcohol consumption during pregnancy (Alcohol Policy Information System, 2018). One-half of states classify controlled substance use during pregnancy as child abuse, which may lead to removing the infant from parental custody or even terminating parental rights (Guttmacher Institute, 2018). In some cases, these consequences have been extended to include alcohol abuse and dependence (Paltrow & Flavin, 2013; Seiler, 2016).

Both the American College of Obstetricians and Gynecologists (2011) and the American Medical Association (2014) argue that criminal sanctions for maternal drug use are ineffective because they increase the risk of harm by discouraging prenatal and postnatal care and undermining the physician–patient relationship. Such policies can cause women to develop a mistrust in medical professionals that ultimately harms their care if they become reluctant to seek medical care for themselves and their children. Others argue that these policies are discriminatory toward women of color and those in low socioeconomic status brackets because low-income African American and Hispanic women are disproportionately tested and tried for substance use (Paltrow & Flavin, 2013). For example, a study of one California county with universal screening policies requiring drug and alcohol testing for all pregnant women found that although Black and White women showed similar rates of drug and alcohol use, Black women were four times more likely than White women to be reported to child protective services after delivery (Roberts & Nuru-Jeter, 2012).

Moreover, some experts argue that mandatory drug testing violates women's rights because they are treated differently under the law compared with men because of their sex and pregnancy status (Hui, Angelotta, & Fisher, 2017). Punitive approaches to maternal substance use that favor criminal charges over substance abuse treatment may pit the interdependent interests of the mother and fetus against each other. Some argue that there is no evidence that punitive measures improve maternal or fetal outcomes. Instead, fetal outcomes as supported by substance abuse treatment that rewards abstention, invests in family and community supports, and promotes contact with health care and social support services hold the most promise (Bada et al., 2012; Hui et al., 2017).

What Do You Think?

1. In your view, is substance use during pregnancy a form of abuse? Why or why not?
2. What do you think could be done to reduce the prevalence of substance use by pregnant women? ●

being subjected to overly harsh discipline and lack of supervision as well as disruptions in care due to factors such as parental incarceration, inability to care for a child, and even death (e.g., from a drug overdose or violence).

At the same time, quality care can lessen the long-term impact of prenatal exposure to substances (Calhoun, Conner, Miller, & Messina, 2015). Some evidence suggests, for example, that developmental differences in exposed infants are reduced and often disappear when medical and environmental factors are considered (Behnke & Smith, 2013). Disentangling the long-term effects of prenatal exposure to substances, subsequent parenting, and contextual factors is challenging. Researchers and health care providers who construct interventions must address the contextual and parenting-related risk factors to improve the developmental outlook for children exposed to drugs prenatally. The accompanying Applying Developmental Science feature examines the difficulties of addressing maternal drug use in the legal system.

Maternal Illness

Depending on the type and when it occurs, an illness experienced by the mother during pregnancy can have devastating consequences for the developing fetus. For example, rubella (German measles) prior to the 11th week of pregnancy can cause a variety of defects, including blindness, deafness, heart defects, and brain damage, but after the first trimester, adverse consequences become less likely (Bouthry et al., 2014). Other illnesses have varying effects on the fetus. For example, chicken pox can produce birth defects affecting the arms, legs, eyes, and brain; mumps can increase the risk of miscarriage (Mehta, 2016; Webster et al., 2018). In addition to posing risks to development, some sexually transmitted infections, such as syphilis, can be transmitted to the fetus during pregnancy (Tsimis & Sheffield, 2017). Others, such as gonorrhea, genital herpes, and HIV, can be transmitted as the child passes through the birth canal during birth or through bodily fluids after birth. Since some diseases, such as mumps and rubella, can be prevented with vaccinations, it is important for women who are considering becoming pregnant to discuss their immunization status with their health care provider.

Some illnesses with teratogenic effects, such as the mosquito-borne Zika virus, are not well understood. Children born to women infected with the Zika virus are at greater risk of microencephaly, reduced head size (Prakalapakorn, Meaney-Delman, Honein, & Rasmussen, 2017). They may also show a pattern of defects now known as *congenital Zika syndrome*, which includes severe microcephaly characterized by partial skull collapse, damage to the back of the eye, and body deformities, including joints and muscles with restricted range of motion (Centers for Disease Control and Prevention, 2017d; Moore, 2017).

Environmental Hazards

Prenatal exposure to chemicals, radiation, air pollution, and extremes of heat and humidity can impair development. Infants prenatally exposed to heavy metals, such as lead and mercury, whether through ingestion or inhalation, score lower on tests of cognitive ability and intelligence and have higher rates of childhood illness (Sadler, 2018; Vigeh, Yokoyama, Matsukawa, Shinohara, & Ohtani, 2014; Xie et al., 2013). Exposure to radiation can cause genetic mutations. Infants born to mothers pregnant during the atomic bomb explosions in Hiroshima and Nagasaki and after the nuclear power accident at Chernobyl displayed many physical deformities, mutations, and intellectual deficits. Prenatal exposure to radiation is associated with Down syndrome, reduced head circumference, intellectual disability, reduced intelligence scores and school performance, and heighted risk for cancer (Chang, Lasley, Das, Mendonca, & Dynlacht, 2014). About 85% of the world's birth defects occur in developing countries, supporting the role of context in influencing prenatal development directly via environmental hazards but also indirectly through the opportunities and resources for education, health, and financial support (Weinhold, 2009).

Maternal Characteristics

Teratogens—and the avoidance of them—are, of course, not the only determinants of how healthy a baby will be. A pregnant woman's characteristics, such as her age and her behavior during pregnancy, including nutrition and emotional well-being, also influence prenatal outcomes.

Nutrition

Nutrition plays a role in prenatal development both before and after conception. The quality of men's and women's diets influences the health of the sperm and egg (Sinclair & Watkins, 2013). Most women need to consume 2,200 to 2,900 calories per day to sustain a pregnancy (Kaiser, Allen, & American Dietetic Association, 2008). Yet about 41 million people in the United States (about 12% of households) reported food insecurity in 2016 (U.S. Department of Agriculture, 2017). That is, at least sometimes they lacked access to enough food for an active healthy lifestyle for all members of the household. About 795 million people

Good nutrition promotes healthy prenatal development.
©iStockphoto.com/becon

of the 7.3 billion people in the world, or one in nine, suffer from chronic undernourishment, almost all of whom live in developing countries (World Hunger Education Service, 2017). Fetal malnutrition is associated with increased susceptibility to complex diseases in postnatal life (Chmurzynska, 2010). Dietary supplements can reduce many of the problems caused by maternal malnourishment, and infants who are malnourished can overcome some of the negative effects if they are raised in enriched environments. However, most children who are malnourished before birth remain malnourished; few have the opportunity to be raised in enriched environments after birth.

Some deficits resulting from an inadequate diet cannot be remedied. For example, inadequate consumption of folic acid (a B vitamin) very early in pregnancy can result in the formation of neural tube defects stemming from the failure of the neural tube to close. **Spina bifida** occurs when the lower part of the neural tube fails to close and spinal nerves begin to grow outside of the vertebrae, often resulting in paralysis. Surgery must be performed before or shortly after birth, but lost capacities cannot be restored (Adzick, 2013). Spina bifida is often accompanied by malformations in brain development and impaired cognitive development (Donnan et al., 2017). Another neural tube defect, **anencephaly**, occurs when the top part of the neural tube fails to close and all or part of the brain fails to develop, resulting in death shortly after birth. As researchers have learned and disseminated the knowledge that folic acid helps prevent these defects, the frequency of neural tube defects has declined to about 1 in 1,000 births (Viswanathan et al., 2017; Williams et al., 2015). However, in a national study of U.S. mothers, only 24% consumed the recommended dose of folic acid during pregnancy (Tinker, Cogswell, Devine, & Berry, 2010).

Emotional Well-Being

Although stress is inherently part of almost everyone's life, exposure to chronic and severe stress during pregnancy poses risks, including low birthweight, premature birth, and a longer postpartum hospital stay (Field, 2011; Schetter & Tanner, 2012). Maternal stress influences prenatal development because stress hormones cross the placenta, raising the fetus's heart rate and activity level. Long-term exposure to stress hormones in utero is associated with higher levels of stress hormones in newborns (Kapoor, Lubach, Ziegler, & Coe, 2016). As a result, the newborn may be more irritable and active than a low-stress infant and may have difficulties in sleep, digestion, and self-regulation (Davis, Glynn, Waffarn, & Sandman, 2011; Kingston, Tough, & Whitfield, 2012). Later in childhood, he or she may have symptoms of anxiety, attention-deficit/hyperactivity disorder, and aggression (Glover, 2011). Prenatal stress may also have epigenetic effects on development, influencing stress responses throughout the lifespan (Van den Bergh et al., 2017). Stress in the home may make it difficult for parents to respond with warmth and sensitivity to an irritable infant (Crnic & Ross, 2017). Social support can mitigate the effects of stress on pregnancy and infant care (Feldman, Dunkel-Schetter, Sandman, & Wadhwa, 2000; Ghosh, Wilhelm, Dunkel-Schetter, Lombardi, & Ritz, 2010).

Maternal Age

U.S. women are becoming pregnant at later ages than ever before. As shown in Figure 3.4, since 1990, the pregnancy rate has increased for women ages 35 to 39 and 40 to 44 and decreased slightly for women in their 20s (Hamilton et al., 2017). Does maternal age matter? Women who give birth over the age of 35, and especially over 40, are at greater risk for pregnancy and birth complications, including miscarriage and stillbirth, than are younger women. They are more vulnerable to pregnancy-related illnesses such as hypertension and diabetes, and their pregnancies involve increased risks to the newborn, including low birthweight, preterm birth, respiratory problems, and related conditions requiring intensive neonatal care (Frederiksen et al., 2018; Grotegut et al., 2014; Kenny et al., 2013; Khalil, Syngelaki, Maiz, Zinevich, & Nicolaides, 2013). The risk of having a child with Down syndrome also increases sharply with maternal age, especially after age 40 (Diamandopoulos & Green, 2018; Hazlett, Hammer, Hooper, & Kamphaus, 2011) (see Figure 3.5).

Although risks for complications rise linearly with each year (Yaniv et al., 2011), it is important to realize that the majority of women over age 35 give birth to healthy infants. Differences in context and behavior may compensate for some of the risks of advanced maternal age. For example, longer use of oral contraceptives is associated with a lower risk of giving birth to a child with Down syndrome (Nagy, Győrffy, Nagy, & Rigó, 2013).

Paternal Characteristics

It is easy to see how mothers' health, behavior, and contexts influence prenatal development, but what about fathers? It was once thought that fathers had no influence on prenatal development and researchers thus neglected to study the father's role. Most obviously, fathers influence the home context. Second-hand smoke from fathers is harmful to the developing organism (Wang et al., 2018). Fathers' interactions with pregnant mothers can increase maternal stress, with potential negative implications

FIGURE 3.4

Birthrates by Age of Mother, United States, 2017

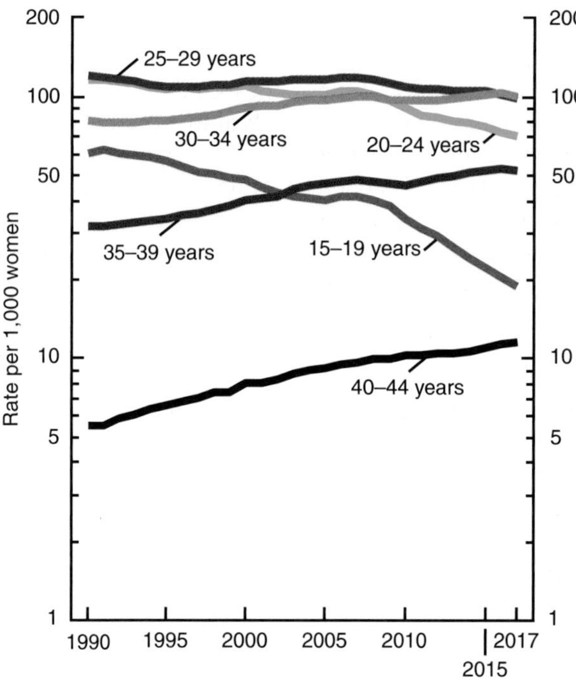

Source: J. A. Martin et al. (2018).

FIGURE 3.5

Maternal Age and Down Syndrome

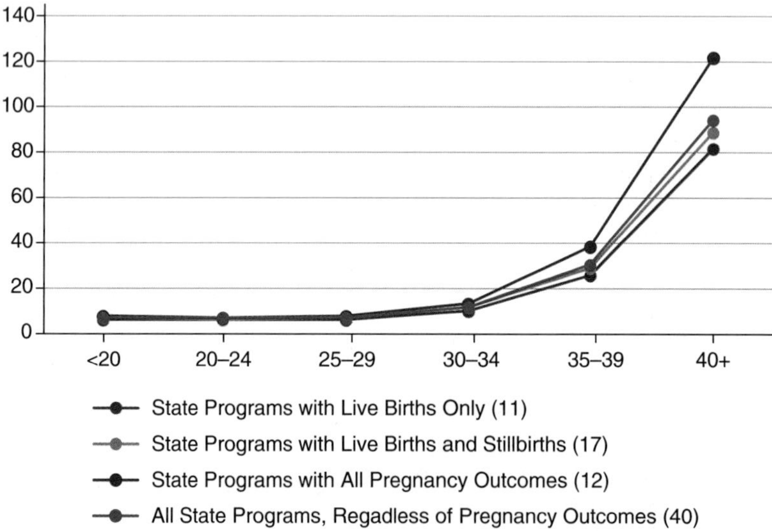

Source: Data are from Mai et al. (2015).

for prenatal development. We know less about how fathers' health, behaviors, and contextual factors act as biological influences on prenatal development.

Advanced paternal age is associated with an increased risk of birth defects, chromosomal abnormalities, Down syndrome, and autism spectrum disorder (Day, Savani, Krempley, Nguyen, & Kitlinska, 2016; Herati, Zhelyazkova, Butler, & Lamb, 2017). Paternal alcohol and substance use and exposure to toxins such as lead can impair sperm production and quality (Borges et al., 2018; Estill & Krawetz, 2016). For example, smoking is associated with DNA damage and mutations in sperm (Beal, Yauk, & Marchetti, 2017; Esakky & Moley, 2016).

In addition to DNA, fathers (and mothers) also pass on epigenetic marks that can influence their offspring's health throughout life and may even be passed to their offspring's children. Recall from Chapters 1 and 2 that the epigenome determines how DNA is expressed, what genes are turned on and off. The epigenome contains a molecular record or "memory" of a person's life experiences, including health behaviors, exposure to toxins, nutritional status, and more (Abbasi, 2017). Moreover, epigenetic marks are heritable, passed through ova and sperm, meaning that they can be inherited from parents or even grandparents (Immler, 2018). Exposure to substances and contaminants can alter the epigenome that is passed to offspring and potentially from generation to generation (Bošković & Rando, 2018). For example, in one study, men whose fathers smoked when they were conceived had a 50% lower sperm count than the men with nonsmoking fathers (Axelsson et al., 2018). It is important to remember, however, that the epigenetic marks we are born with are not set in stone. Some epigenetic marks can be changed after birth through experiences, health care, and behaviors such as diet and exercise (Champagne, 2018).

Contextual and Cultural Influences on Prenatal Care

Prenatal care, a set of services provided to improve pregnancy outcomes and engage the expectant mother, family members, and friends in health care decisions, is critical for the health of both mother and infant. About 26% of pregnant women in the United States do not seek prenatal care until after the first trimester; 6% seek prenatal care at the end of pregnancy or not at all (U.S. Department of Health and Human Services, 2014). Inadequate prenatal care is a risk factor for low-birthweight and preterm births as well as infant mortality during the first year (Partridge, Balayla, Holcroft, & Abenhaim, 2012). In addition, use of prenatal care predicts pediatric care, and thereby health and development, throughout childhood (Deaton, Sheiner, Wainstock, Landau, & Walfisch, 2017).

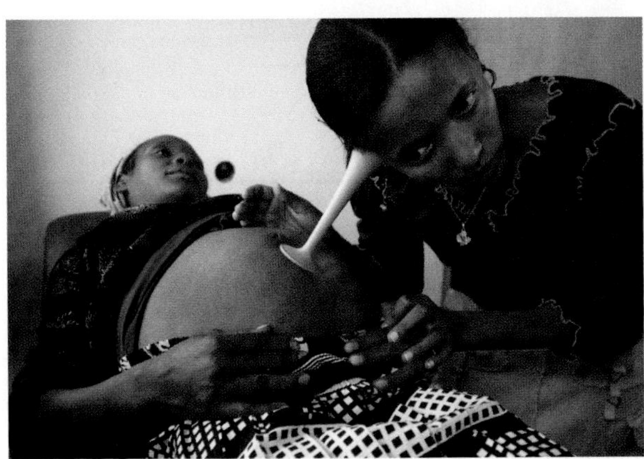

Prenatal care and birth practices vary by culture. Here, a pregnant woman receives prenatal care from an extension worker in Ethiopia.
Jenny Matthews / Alamy Stock Photo

Why do women delay or avoid seeking prenatal care? A common reason is the lack of health insurance (Baer et al., 2019). Although government-sponsored health care is available for the poorest mothers, many low-income mothers do not qualify for care or lack information on how to take advantage of care that may be available. Figure 3.6 lists other barriers to seeking prenatal care, including difficulty in finding a doctor, lack of transportation, demands of caring for young children, ambivalence about the pregnancy, depression, lack of education about the importance of prenatal care, lack of social support, poor prior experiences in the health care system, and family crises (Daniels, Noe, & Mayberry, 2006; Heaman et al., 2015; Mazul, Salm Ward, & Ngui, 2016).

Moreover, there are significant ethnic and socioeconomic disparities in prenatal care. As shown in Figure 3.7, prenatal care is linked with maternal education. About 86% of women with a college degree obtain first-trimester care, compared with less than two-thirds of women with less than a high school diploma (U.S. Department of Health and Human Services, 2014). In addition, women of color are disproportionately less likely to receive prenatal care during the first trimester and are more likely to receive care beginning in the third trimester or no care (see Figure 3.8). Native Hawaiian and Native American women are least likely to obtain prenatal care during the first trimester, followed by Hispanic, African American, Asian American, and White American women (Hamilton, Martin, Osterman, Driscoll, & Rossen, 2017). In the most extreme case, only about half of Native Hawaiian or other Pacific Islander women obtain first-trimester care, and one in five obtains late or no prenatal care. Ethnic differences are thought to be largely influenced by socioeconomic factors, as the ethnic groups least likely to seek early prenatal care are also the most economically disadvantaged members of society and are most likely to live in communities with fewer health resources, including access to physicians and hospitals, sources of health information, and nutrition and other resources.

Although prenatal care predicts better birth outcomes, cultural factors also appear to protect some women and infants from the negative consequences of inadequate prenatal care. In a phenomenon termed the *Latina paradox*, Latina

FIGURE 3.6

Reasons for Delayed Prenatal Care Among Women, 2009–2010

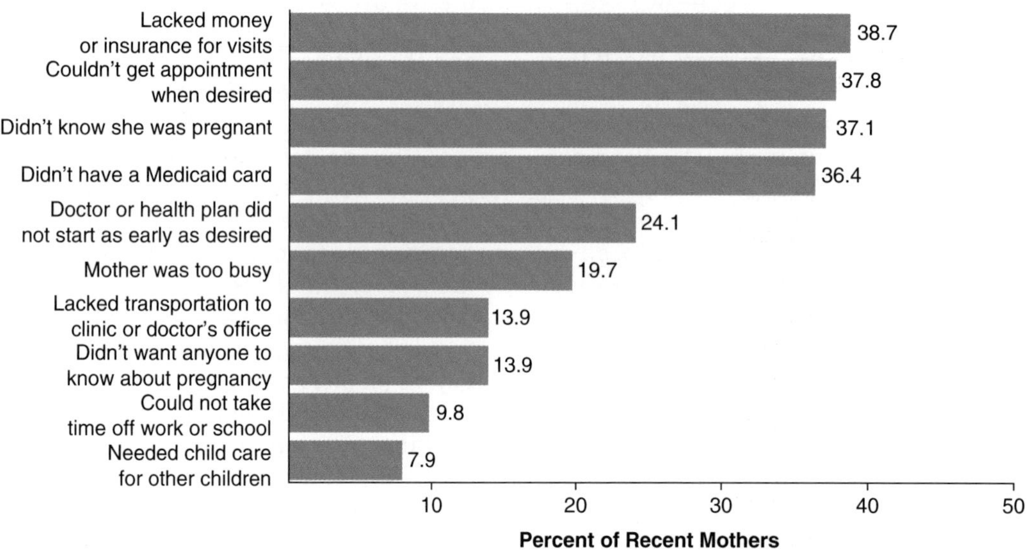

Source: U.S. Department of Health and Human Services et al. (2013).

FIGURE 3.7

Timing of Prenatal Care Initiation, by Maternal Education, 2012

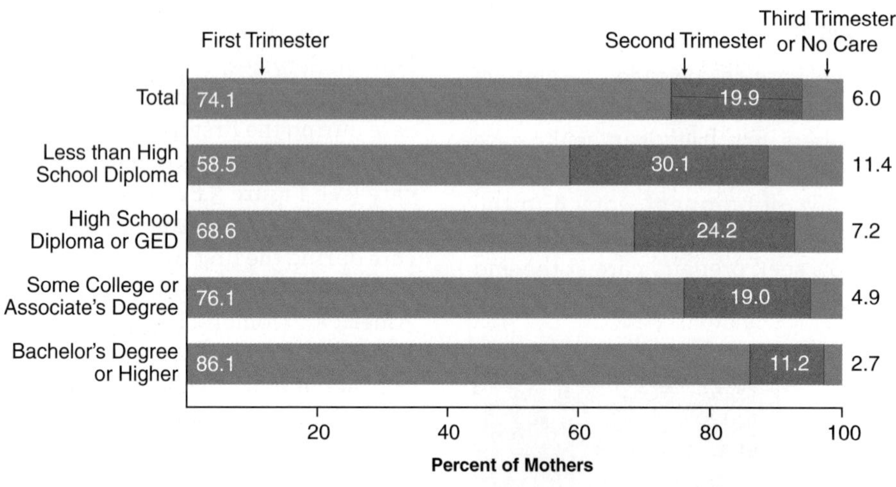

Source: U.S. Department of Health and Human Services et al. (2013).

mothers, despite low rates of prenatal care, tend to experience low-birthweight and mortality rates below national averages. These favorable birth outcomes are striking because of the strong and consistent association between socioeconomic status and birth outcomes and because Latinos as a group are among the most socioeconomically disadvantaged ethnic populations in the United States (McGlade, Saha, & Dahlstrom, 2004; Ruiz, Hamann, Mehl, & O'Connor, 2016).

Several factors are thought to account for the Latina paradox, including strong cultural support for maternity, healthy traditional dietary practices, and the norm of selfless devotion to the maternal

FIGURE 3.8

Prenatal Care Beginning in the First Trimester and Late or No Care, by Race and Ethnicity, in the United States, 2016

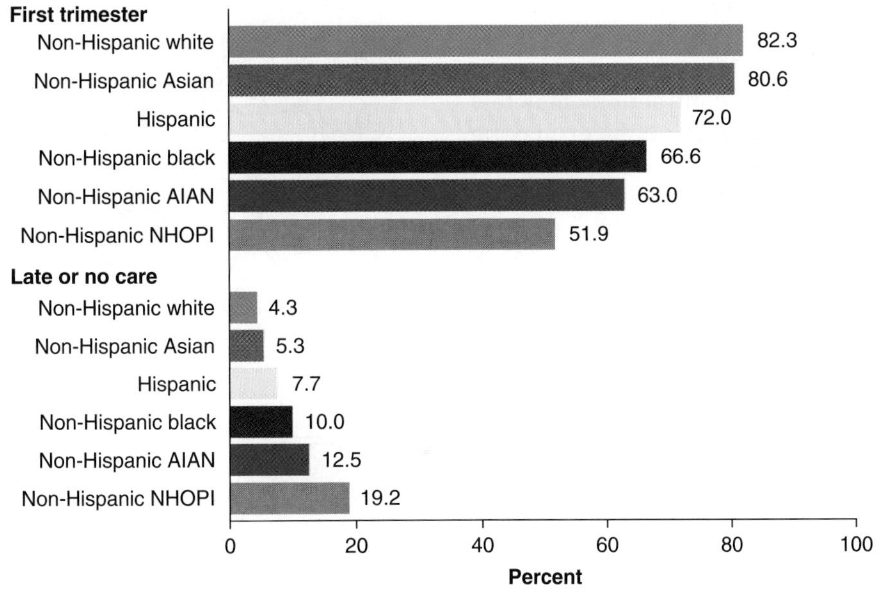

Source: Hamilton et al. (2017).

role (known as *marianismo*) (Fracasso & Busch-Rossnagel, 1992; McGlade et al., 2004). These protective cultural factors interact with strong social support networks and informal systems of health care among Latino women, in which women tend to take responsibility for the health needs of those beyond their nuclear households. Mothers benefit from the support of other family members such as sisters, aunts, and other extended family. In this way, knowledge about health is passed down from generation to generation. There is a strong tradition of women helping other women in the community, and warm interpersonal relationships, known as *personalismo*, are highly valued (Fracasso & Busch-Rossnagel, 1992; McGlade et al., 2004).

Although these cultural factors are thought to underlie the positive birth outcomes seen in Latino women, they appear to erode as Latino women acculturate to American society. The birth advantage has been found to decline in subsequent American-born generations. Recent findings have called the existence of the Latina paradox into question, as some samples have illustrated that the negative effects of socioeconomic disadvantage cannot be easily ameliorated by cultural supports (Hoggatt, Flores, Solorio, Wilhelm, & Ritz, 2012; Sanchez-Vaznaugh et al., 2016).

THINKING IN CONTEXT 3.2

1. From the perspective of Bronfenbrenner's bioecological model (see Chapter 1), identify environmental influences on prenatal development that are examples of microsystem, mesosystem, exosystem, and macrosystem, factors.
2. Suppose you were creating a program to support pregnant women and their families in delivering healthy babies. Identify factors that you might address at each level of Bronfenbrenner's model. Discuss your program and how it may help promote healthy infants.
3. What specific advice would you provide to a pregnant woman to help her promote a healthy pregnancy?

CHILDBIRTH

Thirty-eight weeks after conception (or 40 weeks after the last menstruation), childbirth (also known as **labor**) begins.

Labor

Labor progresses in three stages. The first stage of labor, dilation, is the longest. It typically lasts 8 to 14 hours for a woman having her first child; for later-born children, the average is 3 to 8 hours. Labor begins when the mother experiences regular uterine contractions spaced at 10- to 15-minute intervals. Initial contractions may feel like a backache or menstrual cramps or may be extremely sharp. The amniotic sac, a membrane containing the fetus surrounded by fluid, may rupture at any time during this stage, often referred to as the "water breaking." The contractions, which gradually become stronger and closer together, cause the cervix to dilate so that the fetus's head can pass through, as shown in Figure 3.9.

The second stage of labor, delivery, begins when the cervix is fully dilated to 10 centimeters and the fetus's head is positioned at the opening of the cervix—known as "crowning." It ends when the baby emerges completely from the mother's body. It is during this stage that the mother typically feels an urge to push or bear down with each contraction to assist the birth process. Delivery can take from 30 minutes to an hour and a half.

In the third stage of labor, the placenta separates from the uterine wall and is expelled by uterine contractions. This typically happens about 5 to 15 minutes after the baby has emerged, and the process can take up to a half hour.

FIGURE 3.9

Stages of Labor

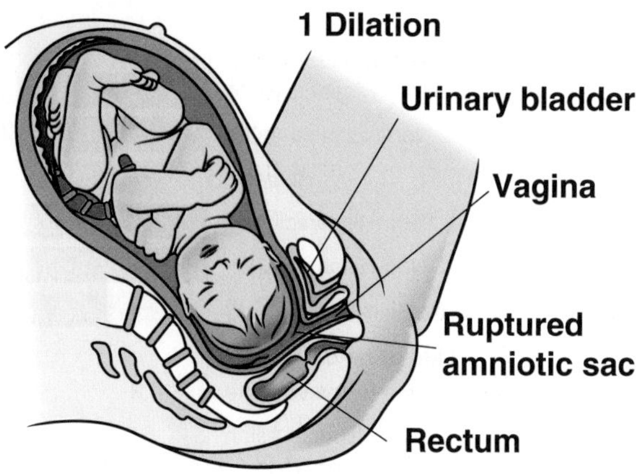

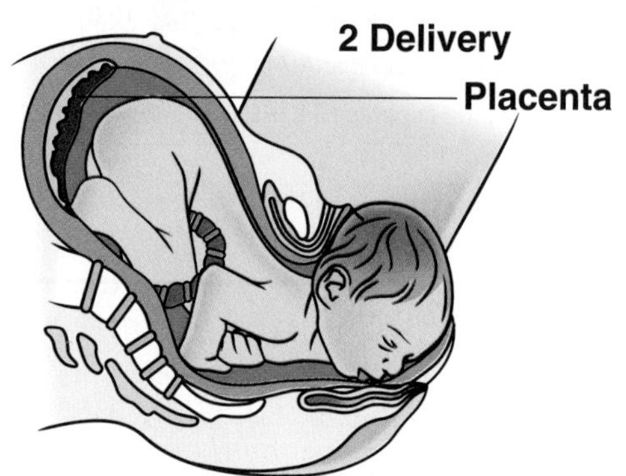

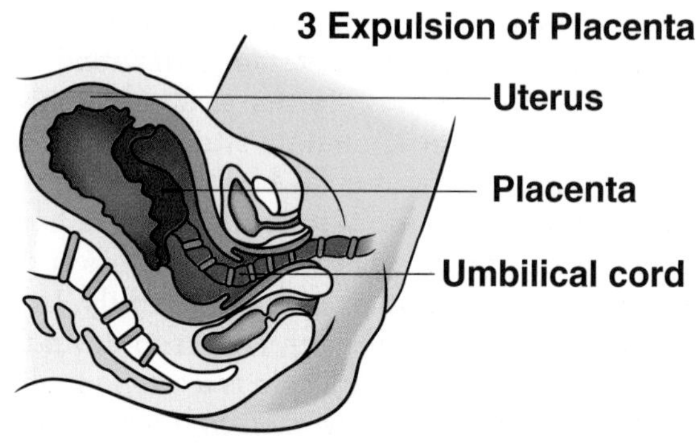

Source: Adapted from Tortora and Derrickson (2009).

Medication During Delivery

Medication is administered in over 80% of births in the United States (Declercq, Sakala, Corry, Applebaum, & Herrlich, 2014). Several drugs are used during labor, with varying effects. *Analgesics*, such as tranquilizers, reduce the perception of pain. They may be used in small doses to relieve pain and to help the mother relax. However, these drugs pass through the placenta to the fetus and are associated with decreases in heart rate and respiration (Hacker, Gambone, & Hobel, 2016). Newborns exposed to some medications show signs of sedation and difficulty regulating their temperature (Gabbe et al., 2016). *Anesthetics* are painkillers that block overall sensations or feelings. General anesthesia (getting "knocked out") blocks consciousness entirely; it is no longer used because it is transmitted to the fetus and can slow labor and harm the fetus.

Today, the most common anesthetic is an *epidural*, in which a pain-relieving drug

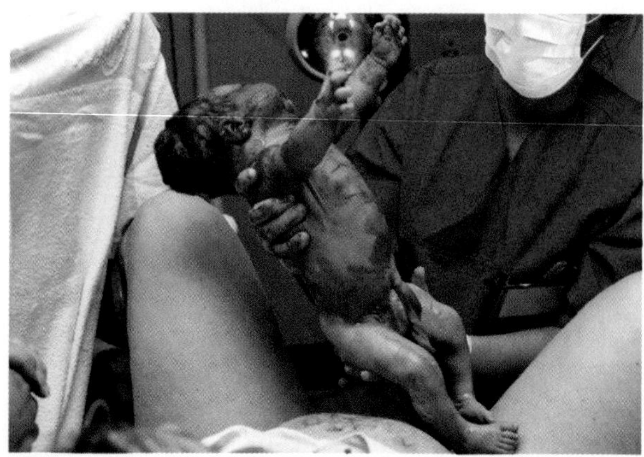

The newborn emerges during the second stage of labor.
©iStockphoto.com/delectus

is administered to a small space between the vertebrae of the lower spine, numbing the woman's lower body. There are several types of epidurals, with varying numbing effects ranging from immobilizing the lower body to numbing only the pelvic region, enabling the mother to move about (a so-called walking epidural). Epidurals, however, are associated with a longer delivery, as they weaken uterine contractions and may increase the risk of a cesarean section, as discussed next (Gabbe et al., 2016; Herrera-Gómez et al., 2017). An analysis of nearly 15,500 deliveries suggested that newborns exposed to epidural anesthesia did not differ from those exposed to no anesthesia (Q. Wang et al., 2018). The American College of Obstetricians and Gynecologists (2017) has concluded that the proper administration of medication poses few risks to the newborn and pain medication should be available to all women.

Cesarean Delivery

Sometimes a vaginal birth is not possible because of concerns for the health or safety of the mother or fetus. For example, normally the baby's head is the first part of the body to exit the vagina. A baby facing feet-first is said to be in a **breech position**, which poses risks to the health of the baby. Sometimes the obstetrician can turn the baby so that it is head-first. In other cases, a **cesarean section**, or C-section, is common. A cesarean section is a surgical procedure that removes the fetus from the uterus through the abdomen. About 32% of U.S. births were by cesarean section in 2016 (J. A. Martin et al., 2018). Cesarean sections are performed when labor progresses too slowly, the fetus is in breech position or transverse position (crosswise in the uterus), the head is too large to pass through the pelvis, or the fetus or mother is in danger (Jha, Baliga, Kumar, Rangnekar, & Baliga, 2015; Visscher & Narendran, 2014). Babies delivered by cesarean section are exposed to more maternal medication and secrete lower levels of the stress hormones that occur with vaginal birth that are needed to facilitate respiration, enhance circulation of blood to the brain, and help the infant adapt to the world outside of the womb. Interactions between mothers and infants, however, are similar for infants delivered vaginally and by cesarean section (Durik, Hyde, & Clark, 2000).

Natural Childbirth

Natural childbirth is an approach to birth that reduces pain through the use of breathing and relaxation exercises. Natural childbirth methods emphasize preparation by educating mothers and their partners about childbirth, helping them to reduce their fear, and teaching them pain management techniques. Although most women use at least some medication in childbirth, many women adopt some natural childbirth methods.

The most widely known natural childbirth method—the Lamaze method—was created by a French obstetrician, Ferdinand Lamaze (1956). The Lamaze method entails teaching pregnant women about their bodies, including detailed anatomical information, with the intent of reducing anxiety and fear. When women know what to expect and learn a breathing technique to help them relax, they are better able to manage the pain of childbirth. The Lamaze method relies on the spouse or partner as coach, providing physical and emotional support and reminding the mother to use the breathing techniques.

In addition to the expectant mother's partner, a doula can be an important source of support. A **doula** is a caregiver who provides support to an expectant mother and her partner throughout the birth process (Kang, 2014). Doulas provide education about anatomy, delivery, and pain management practices, such as breathing. The doula is present during birth, whether at a hospital or other setting, and helps the woman carry out her birth plans. The presence of a doula is associated with less pain medication, fewer cesarean deliveries, and higher rates of satisfaction in new mothers (Gabbe et al., 2016; Kozhimannil et al., 2016).

Home Birth

Although common in nonindustrialized nations, home birth is rare, comprising 1.5% of all births in 2016 in the United States (MacDorman & Declercq, 2016). The remaining 98% of births occur in hospitals. Most home births are managed by a midwife, a health care professional, usually a nurse, who specializes in childbirth. Midwives provide health care throughout pregnancy and supervise home births. One review of 50 studies found that the use of midwives, whether as part of a home birthing plan or as part of a plan to birth in a hospital setting, is associated with reduced neonatal mortality, reduced preterm birth, fewer interventions, and more efficient use of medical resources (Renfrew et al., 2014).

Is a home birth safe? A healthy woman, who has received prenatal care and is not carrying twins, is unlikely to encounter problems requiring intervention—and may be a good candidate for a home birth (Wilbur, Little, & Szymanski, 2015). Although unpredictable events can occur and immediate access to medical facilities can improve outcomes, studies from Europe indicate that home birth is not associated with greater risk of perinatal mortality. However, home birth is far more common in many European countries than the United States (20% in the Netherlands, 8% in the United Kingdom, and about 1% in the United

LIVES IN CONTEXT: CULTURAL CONTEXT

Cultural Differences in Childbirth

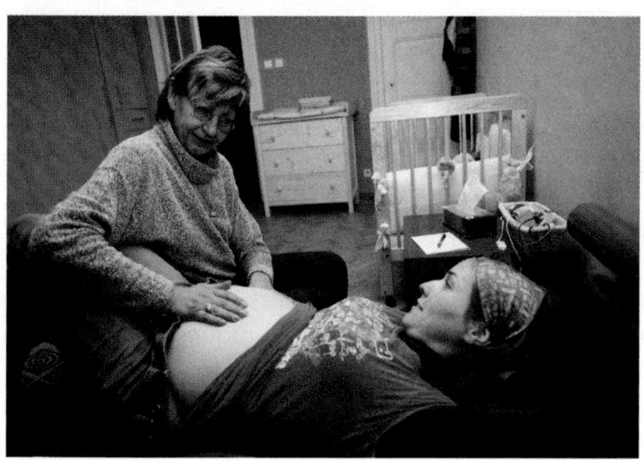

A midwife prepares a mother to give birth in her home. Birth practices vary by culture.
Liba Taylor / Alamy Stock

Societies vary in their customs and perceptions of childbirth, including the privacy afforded to giving birth and how newborns are integrated into the community. In the United States, birth is a private event that usually occurs in a hospital, attended by medical personnel and one or two family members. In most cases, the first-time mother has never witnessed a birth but is well educated and may have well-informed expectations. After birth, the mother and infant are often visited by family within designated hospital visiting hours; the newborn usually rooms with the mother all or part of the day.

In a small village in southern Italy, birth is a community event. It usually takes place in a hospital, attended by a midwife (Fogel, 2007; Schreiber, 1977). Just after birth, the midwife brings the mother's entire family (immediate and extended) to the mother's room and they take turns congratulating the mother and baby, kissing them. The family provides a party, including pastries and liqueurs. During labor and afterward, the mother is supported and visited by many of her friends and relatives to recognize the contribution that the mother has made to the community. The mother-in-law is an example of the social support system in place because a few days before and until about 1 month after the birth, she brings and feeds the mother ritual foods of broth, marsala, and fresh cheeses.

In some other cultures, birth is an even more public process. The Jahara of South America give birth under a shelter in full view of everyone in the village (Fogel, 2007). On the Indonesian island of Bali, it is assumed that the husband, children, and other family will want to be present. The birth occurs in the home with the aid of a midwife and female relatives. As a result, Balinese women know what to expect in giving birth to their first child because they have been present at many births (Diener, 2000). The baby is immediately integrated into the family and community as he or she is considered a reincarnated soul of an ancestor. Many kin are present to support the mother and baby since the child is considered to be related to many more people than its parents.

Childbirth is tied to social status in the Brong-Ahafo Region in Ghana. After a delivery, women achieve a higher social position and can then give advice to other women (Jansen, 2006). Home deliveries are highly valued. The more difficult the delivery and the less skilled assistance she receives, the more respect a woman attains, the higher her position will be, and the more influence she has on the childbirth decisions of other women, such as whether to give birth at home or in a medical setting and how to combine traditional and modern practices (Bazzano, Kirkwood, Tawiah-Agyemang, Owusu-Agyei, & Adongo, 2008).

Many cultures conduct rites that they believe protect newborns from evil and spirits. Among the Maya of the Yucatan region of Mexico, there are few changes in the expectant mother's surroundings; the Mayan woman lies in the same hammock in which she sleeps each night. The father-to-be is expected to be present during labor and birth to take an active role but also to witness the suffering that accompanies labor. If the father is not present and the child is stillborn, it is blamed on the father's absence. The pregnant woman's mother is present, often in the company of other females, including sisters, sisters-in-law, mothers-in-law, godmothers, and sometimes neighbors and close friends. The mother and child must remain inside the house for 1 week before returning to normal activity after birth because it is believed that the mother and newborn are susceptible to the influence of evil spirits from the bush (Gardiner & Kosmitzki, 2018).

A neighboring ethnic group, the Zinacanteco, place their newborns naked before a fire. The midwife who assisted the mother says prayers asking the gods to look kindly upon the infant. The infant is dressed in a long skirt made of heavy fabric extending beyond the feet; this garment is to be worn throughout the first year. The newborn is then wrapped in several layers of blankets, even covering the face, to protect against losing parts of the soul. These traditional practices are believed to protect the infant from illnesses as well as evil spirits (Brazelton, 1977; Fogel, 2007).

What Do You Think?

1. Which of these birthing customs most appeals to you? Why?
2. If you, a family member, or friend have given birth, describe the process. Where did the birth occur? Who witnessed it? What happened afterward? When did family and friends meet the baby? ●

States) (Brocklehurst et al., 2011; de Jonge et al., 2015). The few U.S. studies that have examined planned home birth compared with hospital birth have found no difference in neonatal deaths or Apgar scores, and women who have a planned home birth report high rates of satisfaction (Jouhki, Suominen, & Åstedt-Kurki, 2017; Zielinski, Ackerson, & Kane Low, 2015). Cultures vary in their approach to birth, as discussed in the Lives in Context feature.

THINKING IN CONTEXT 3.3

1. How might contextual issues influence parents' decisions about birthing? How might contextual factors account for differences in the rates of home birth, natural birth, and cesarean birth?
2. Create a birth plan for a healthy woman in her 20s. What type of birth will you choose? Why? How might you address pain relief? Consider a healthy 39-year-old woman. In what ways might your birth plan change (or not)? Why?

THE NEWBORN

The average newborn is about 20 inches long and weighs about 7½ pounds. Boys tend to be slightly longer and heavier than girls. Newborns have distinctive features, including a large head (about one-quarter of body length) that is often long and misshapen from passing through the birth canal. The newborn's skull bones are not yet fused—and will not be until about 18 months of age—permitting the bones to move and the head to mold to the birth canal, easing its passage. A healthy newborn is red-skinned and wrinkly at birth; skin that is bluish in color indicates that the newborn has experienced oxygen deprivation. Some babies emerge covered with *lanugo*, the fuzzy hair that protects the skin in the womb; for other babies, the lanugo falls off prior to birth. The newborn's body is covered with *vernix caseosa*, a white waxy substance that protects against infection; this dries up within the first few days. Although many hospital staff wash the vernix caseosa away after birth, research suggests that it is a naturally occurring barrier to infection and should be retained at birth (Jha et al., 2015).

Medical and Behavioral Assessment of Newborns

After birth, newborns are routinely screened with the **Apgar scale**, which provides a quick and easy overall assessment of the baby's immediate health. As shown in Table 3.1, the Apgar scale is composed of five subtests: appearance (color), pulse (heart rate), grimace (reflex irritability), activity (muscle tone), and respiration (breathing). The newborn is rated 0, 1, or 2 on each subscale for a maximum total score of 10. A score of 4 or lower means that the newborn is in serious condition and requires immediate medical attention. The rating is conducted twice, 1 minute after delivery and again 5 minutes after birth; this timing ensures that hospital staff will monitor the newborn over several minutes. Over 98% of all newborns in the United States achieve a 5-minute score of 7 to 10, indicating good health (Martin, Hamilton, Osterman, Curtin, & Mathews, 2013).

The **Brazelton Neonatal Behavioral Assessment Scale (NBAS)** is a neurobehavioral assessment commonly administered to newborns, especially those who are judged to be at risk (Bartram, Barlow, & Wolke,

TABLE 3.1

Apgar Scale

	RATING (ABSENCE–PRESENCE)		
INDICATOR	**0**	**1**	**2**
Appearance (color)	Blue	Pink body, blue extremities	Pink
Pulse (heart rate)	Absent	Slow (below 100)	Rapid (over 100)
Grimace (reflex irritability)	No response	Grimace	Coughing, crying
Activity (muscle tone)	Limp	Weak and inactive	Active and strong
Respiration (breathing)	Absent	Irregular and slow	Crying, good

Source: Apgar (1953).

2015). It is administered in the first few days after birth to assess the newborn's neurological competence as indicated by the responsiveness to the physical and social environment, perception, and motor skills such as activity level and the ability to bring a hand to the mouth (Nugent, 2013). The NBAS also assesses infants' attention and state changes, including excitability and ability to settle down after being upset. When parents observe and participate in their baby's NBAS screening, they learn about their newborn's perceptual and behavioral capacities and are better able to elicit gazes, quiet fussiness, and tend to be more responsive to their infants (Benzies et al., 2013).

The Newborn's Perceptual Capacities

Until recent decades, it was widely believed that the newborn was perceptually immature—blind and deaf at birth. Developmental researchers now know that the newborn is more perceptually competent than ever imagined. For example, both taste and smell are well developed at birth. Taste appears to function well before birth because research has shown that fetuses swallow sweetened amniotic fluid more quickly than bitter fluid (Ventura & Worobey, 2013). Newborns can discriminate smells and calm in response to the scent of amniotic fluid and other familiar smells (Neshat et al., 2016; Rotstein et al., 2015). The visual capacities of the newborn are more limited and focused primarily on the near environment. Newborn vision is blurry and best at about 18 inches away—the typical distance to a parent's face when holding the infant.

The most remarkable newborn capacities for perception and learning are auditory in nature. Pregnant women often report that they notice fetal movements in response to a loud sound like a car horn or a door slamming. The fetus responds to auditory stimulation as early as 23 to 25 weeks after conception (Hepper, 2015). By 32 to 34 weeks, the fetus responds to the mother's voice as indicated by a change in heart rate (Kisilevsky & Hains, 2011). Prior to birth, the fetus can discriminate voices and speech sounds (Granier-Deferre, Ribeiro, Jacquet, & Bassereau, 2011). At birth, newborns show preferences for speech sounds, their mother's voice, their native language, and even stories and music heard prenatally (Moon, Cooper, & Fifer, 1993). Moreover, from birth, the newborn is an active listener, paying attention to sounds and naturally taking advantage of opportunities to learn (Vouloumanos, Hauser, Werker, & Martin, 2010).

Newborn States of Arousal

Newborns display regular cycles of eating, elimination, and **states of arousal** or degrees of wakefulness. In a typical day, newborns move in and out of five infant states or levels of arousal, as shown in Table 3.2. Most newborns spend about 70% of their time sleeping and wake every 2 to 3 hours. These short stretches of sleep alternate with shorter periods of wakefulness that are primarily devoted to feeding. During the first month, infants often move rapidly from one state to another, dozing off during feeding, for example. Naps are punctuated by periods of drowsiness, alert and unalert activity, and crying.

Newborn sleep cycles are brief, lasting from 45 minutes to 2 to 3 hours, but similar to those of adults in that they consist of both **REM sleep**, or rapid eye

TABLE 3.2

Newborn States of Arousal

STATE	DESCRIPTION	DAILY DURATION IN NEWBORNS
Regular sleep	This is being fully asleep with little or no body movement. The eyes are closed with no eye movements. The face is relaxed, and breathing is slow and regular.	8–9 hours
Irregular sleep	Facial grimaces, limb movements, occasional stirring, and eye movement behind closed lids indicate rapid eye movement (REM) sleep. Breathing is irregular.	8–9 hours
Drowsiness	Falling asleep or waking up, eyes open and closed and have a glazed look. Breathing is even but faster than in regular sleep.	Varies
Quiet alertness	The eyes are open and attentive, exploring the world; the body is relatively inactive. Breathing is even.	2–3 hours
Waking activity	There are frequent bursts of uncoordinated activity. Breathing is irregular; the face may be relaxed or tense. Fussiness and crying may occur.	1–4 hours

Sources: Prechtl (1974) and Wolff (1966).

movement sleep, and non-REM sleep (Korotchikova, Stevenson, Livingstone, Ryan, & Boylan, 2016). When a person is in REM sleep, the brain wave activity is remarkably similar to that of the waking state. The eyes move back and forth beneath closed lids; heart rate, blood pressure, and breathing are uneven; and there are slight body movements. It is sleep. Newborns spend about half of their sleep time in REM, but by ages 3 to 5, children spend about 15% to 20% of their sleep in REM, similar to adults (Grigg-Damberger & Wolfe, 2017; Kobayashi, Good, Mamiya, Skinner, & Garcia-Rill, 2004).

Why do newborns spend so much time in REM sleep? REM sleep is associated with dreaming in both children and adults. Neonates spend about 18 hours sleeping each day and therefore spend little time in the active alert state in which they get stimulation from the environment. REM is a way that the brain stimulates itself, which is important for the growth of the central nervous system (Grigg-Damberger & Wolfe, 2017). This view of REM sleep as serving a self-stimulation function is supported by findings that fetuses and preterm babies, who are even less able to take advantage of external stimulation than are newborns, spend even more time in REM sleep. In addition, neonates with low REM sleep activity tend to score lower on mental tests at 6 months of age (Arditi-Babchuk, Feldman, & Eidelman, 2009).

Low-Birthweight Infants: Preterm and Small-for-Date Babies

About 8% of infants born in the United States each year are low birthweight (J. A. Martin et al., 2018). Low-birthweight infants may be **preterm**, or premature (born before their due date), or **small for date**, who are full term but have experienced slow growth and are smaller than expected for their gestational age. Infants are classified as **low birthweight** when they weigh less than 2,500 grams (5.5 pounds) at birth; **very low birthweight** refers to a weight less than 1,500 grams (3.5 pounds), and **extremely low birthweight** refers to a weight less than 750 grams (1 pound, 10 ounces). Infants who are born with low birthweight are at risk for a variety of developmental difficulties. Indeed, their very survival is far from certain; the Centers for Disease Control and Prevention lists prematurity and low birthweight among the leading causes of infant mortality, accounting for 35% of mortality cases in infancy (Mathews & MacDorman, 2013). Infants most at risk for developmental challenges, disabilities, and difficulty surviving are those with extremely low birthweight

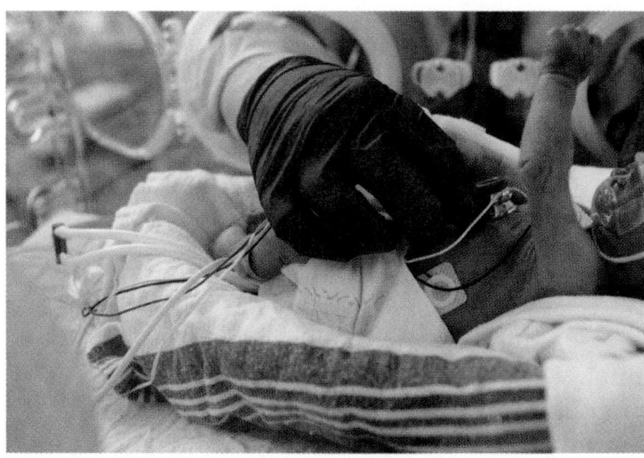

Low-birthweight infants require extensive care. They are at risk for poor developmental outcomes and even death.
Andrew Lichtenstein/Corbis News/Getty Images

Contextual Risks for Low Birthweight

The prevalence of low birthweight varies with ethnicity and socioeconomic status, as shown in Figure 3.10. In 2016, non-Hispanic Black infants were more than twice as likely to be born low birthweight (11%) as non-Hispanic White and Hispanic infants (5% and 6%, respectively) (Womack, Rossen, & Martin, 2018). Contextual influences, such as neighborhood and socioeconomic factors, interact in complex ways to influence low birthweight. For example, neighborhood disadvantage and the stressors that accompany it are associated with an increased risk for low birthweight (Ncube, Enquobahrie, Albert, Herrick, & Burke, 2016). In one study, low birthweight rates were higher in non-Hispanic Black mothers than non-Hispanic White mothers, but the racial difference declined (but did not disappear) when the researchers took into account financial and relationship stresses (Almeida, Bécares, Erbetta, Bettegowda, & Ahluwalia, 2018). These findings suggest that contextual factors, such as differences in experienced stress, may influence some of the racial differences in low birthweight.

Socioeconomic disadvantage interacts with race and ethnicity in complex ways to influence low birthweight. For example, in one study of over 10,000 Californian women, the most economically disadvantaged Black and White women showed similar low-birthweight rates, regardless of race (Braveman et al., 2015). Rates of low birthweight declined with a rise in income for all women, but the racial disparity in low birthweight grew such that greater socioeconomic advantage was more strongly associated with lower low-birthweight rates among White but not Black women.

In the United States, socioeconomic status is associated not simply with income but also with access to social services such as health care. The socioeconomic inequalities that influence women's ability to seek early prenatal care also influence birth outcomes. A comparison of U.S., U.K., Canadian, and Australian births illustrates the role of SES

FIGURE 3.10

Very Low and Low Birthweight Rates, by Maternal Race/Ethnicity, 2015

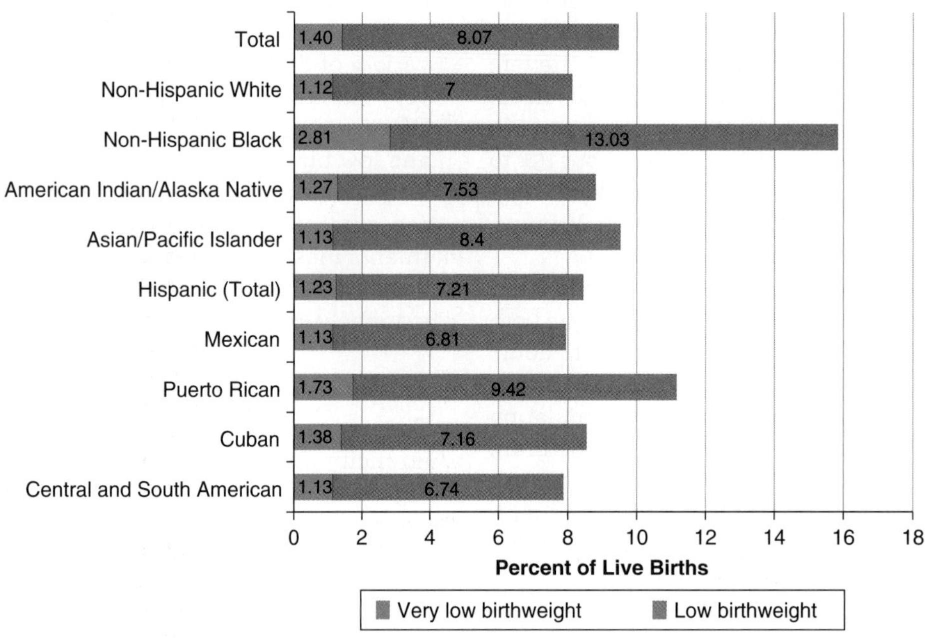

Source: Centers for Disease Control and Prevention (2018c).

in predicting low birthweight. Although the most disadvantaged women were more likely to give birth to low-birthweight infants in all four countries, SES was most strongly linked with low birthweight in the United States (Martinson & Reichman, 2016). In contrast with the privatization of health care in the United States, health care and other social services are readily available to all individuals in the United Kingdom, Canada, and Australia. Access to health care is an important influence on low birthweight. A recent comparison among five North American cities (Baltimore, Boston, Chicago, Philadelphia, and Toronto, Canada) illustrates the role of contextual factors in low birthweight (De Maio, Ansell, & Shah, 2018). In this study, unemployment and living in a racial or ethnically segregated community were not associated with low birthweight in Toronto, but they were strongly associated with low birthweight across communities in the four U.S. cities in the analysis. Unfortunately, poor access to health care can prevent low-birthweight infants from getting the help that they need to overcome the formidable challenges ahead of them.

Characteristics of Low-Birthweight Infants

Low-birthweight infants are at a disadvantage when it comes to adapting to the world outside the womb. At birth, they often experience difficulty breathing and are likely to suffer from respiratory distress syndrome, in which the newborn breathes irregularly and at times may stop breathing. Low-birthweight infants have difficulty maintaining homeostasis, a balance in their biological functioning. Their survival depends on care in neonatal hospital units, where they are confined in isolettes that separate them from the world, regulating their body temperature, aiding their breathing with the use of respirators, and protecting them from infection. Many low-birthweight infants cannot yet suck from a bottle, so they are fed intravenously.

The deficits that low-birthweight infants endure range from mild to severe and correspond closely to the infant's birthweight, with extremely low-birthweight infants suffering the greatest deficits (Hutchinson et al., 2013). Low-birthweight infants are at higher risk for poor growth, cerebral palsy, seizure disorders, neurological difficulties, respiratory problems, and illness (Adams-Chapman et al., 2013; Durkin et al., 2016; Miller et al., 2016). Higher rates of sensory, motor, and cognitive problems mean that low-birthweight children are more likely to require special education and display poor academic achievement in childhood, adolescence, and even adulthood (Eryigit Madzwamuse, Baumann,

LIVES IN CONTEXT: COMMUNITY CONTEXT

HIV Infection in Newborns

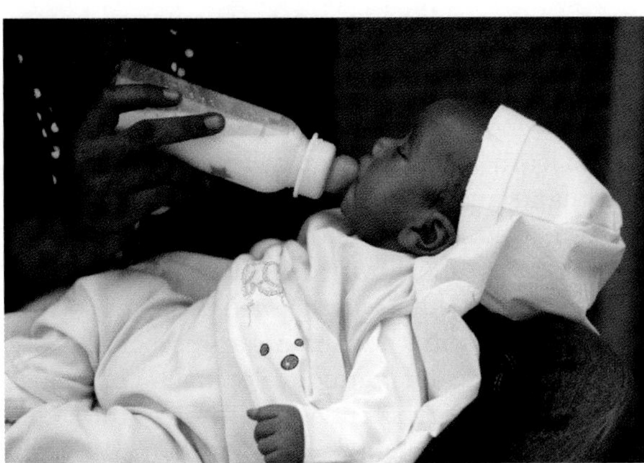

Mother-to-child transmission of HIV has declined as scientists have learned more about HIV. However, HIV remains a worldwide problem especially in developing nations where cultural, economic, and hygienic reasons prevent mothers from seeking alternatives to breastfeeding, a primary cause of mother-to-child transmission of HIV.

Godong/Universal Images Group/Getty Images

The global rate of mother-to-child transmission of HIV has dropped in recent years as scientists have learned more about HIV. The use of cesarean delivery as well as prescribing anti-HIV drugs to the mother during the second and third trimesters of pregnancy, as well as to the infant for the first 6 weeks of life, has reduced mother-to-child HIV transmission to less than 2% in the United States and Europe (from over 20%) (Torpey et al., 2010). However, the incidence of perinatal HIV remains at about 1.75 per 100,000 live births in the United States. Over two-thirds of the HIV infected children born in 2002–2013 were to Black or African American mothers (63%) and about 18% to Hispanic or Latina mothers (A. W. Taylor et al., 2017). A combination of socioeconomic factors influence these health disparities, such as lack of insurance, limited health literacy, and poverty and its associated sense of powerlessness which may prevent women from seeking assistance. HIV medications and treatment are expensive and an HIV diagnosis is often stigmatizing and may alienate individuals from their communities. Aggressive treatment may further reduce the transmission of HIV to newborns, and research suggests that it may even induce remission (National Institute of Allergy and Infectious Diseases, 2014; Pollack & McNeil, 2013; Rainwater-Lovett, Luzuriaga, & Persaud, 2015). However, women of color and those in poverty are less likely to experience HIV treatment.

HIV rates are highest for infants in developing countries where interventions are widely unavailable. Worldwide, mother-to-child HIV transmission remains a serious issue. About 80% of children living with HIV reside in Sub-Saharan African countries (Kassa, 2018). Globally, 20% to 30% of neonates with HIV develop AIDS during the first year of life and most die in infancy (United Nations Children's Fund, 2013). Breastfeeding accounts for 30% to 50% of HIV transmission in newborns (Sullivan, 2003; World Health Organization, 2011). The World Health Organization (2010) recommends providing women who test positive for HIV with information about how HIV may be transmitted to their infants and counseling them not to breastfeed. Yet cultural, economic, and hygienic reasons often prevent mothers in developing nations from seeking alternatives to breastfeeding. For example, the widespread lack of clean water in some countries makes the use of powdered formulas dangerous. Also, in some cultures, women who do not breastfeed may be ostracized from the community (Sullivan, 2003). Balancing cultural values with medical needs is a challenge.

Children with HIV are at high risk for a range of illnesses and health conditions, including chronic bacterial infections; disorders of the central nervous system, heart, gastrointestinal tract, lungs, kidneys, and skin; growth stunting; neurodevelopmental delays, including brain atrophy, which contribute to cognitive and motor impairment; and delays in reaching developmental milestones (Blanchette, Smith, Fernandes-Penney, King, & Read, 2001; Laughton, Cornell, Boivin, & Van Rie, 2013; Sherr, Mueller, & Varrall, 2009).

What Do You Think?

How might you help women to reduce the potential for HIV transmission to their infants? What challenges might you face in working with U.S. mothers? How might these differ from those experienced by women in an underdeveloped country? ●

Jaekel, Bartmann, & Wolke, 2015; Hutchinson et al., 2013; MacKay, Smith, Dobbie, & Pell, 2010). Low-birthweight children often experience difficulty in self-regulation, poor social competence, and poor peer relationships, including peer rejection and victimization in adolescence (Georgsdottir, Haraldsson, & Dagbjartsson, 2013; Ritchie, Bora, & Woodward, 2015; Yau et al., 2013). As adults, low-birthweight individuals tend to be less socially engaged, show poor communication skills, and may score high on measures of anxiety (Eryigit Madzwamuse et al., 2015). Frequently, the risk factors for low birthweight, such as prenatal exposure to substances or maternal illness, also pose challenges for postnatal survival. The Lives in Context feature discusses HIV, a risk factor for neonate development.

Not only are low-birthweight infants at a physical disadvantage, but they often begin life at an emotional disadvantage because they are at risk for experiencing difficulties in their relationships with parents. Parenting a low-birthweight infant is stressful even in the best of circumstances (Howe, Sheu, Wang, & Hsu, 2014). Such infants tend to be easily overwhelmed by stimulation and difficult to soothe; they smile less and fuss more than their normal-weight counterparts, making caregivers feel unrewarded for their efforts. Often these infants are slow to initiate social interactions and do not attend to caregivers, looking away or otherwise resisting attempts to attract their attention (Eckerman, Hsu, Molitor, Leung, & Goldstein, 1999). Because low-birthweight infants often do not respond to attempts to solicit interaction, they can be frustrating to interact with, can be difficult to soothe, and are at risk for less secure attachment to their parents (Jean & Stack, 2012; Wolke, Eryigit-Madzwamuse, & Gutbrod, 2014). Research also indicates that they may experience higher rates of child abuse (Cicchetti & Toth, 2015).

Outcomes of Low-Birthweight Infants

Parental responses to having a low-birthweight infant influence the child's long-term health outcomes, independently of perinatal risk, suggesting that the parenting context is an important influence on infant health (Pierrehumbert, Nicole, Muller-Nix, Forcada-Guex, & Ansermet, 2003). When mothers have knowledge about child development and how to foster healthy development, are involved with their children, and create a stimulating home environment, low-birthweight infants tend to have good long-term outcomes (Benasich & Brooks-Gunn, 1996; Jones, Rowe, & Becker, 2009). For example, one study of low-birthweight children demonstrated that those who experienced sensitive parenting showed faster improvements in executive function and were indistinguishable from their normal-weight peers by age 5; however, those who experienced below-average levels of sensitive parenting showed lasting deficits (Camerota, Willoughby, Cox, Greenberg, & the Family Life Project Investigators, 2015). Likewise, exposure to sensitive, positive parenting predicted low-birthweight children's catching up to their normal-birthweight peers at age 8 in academic achievement, but exposure to insensitive parenting predicted much poorer functioning (Jaekel, Pluess, Belsky, & Wolke, 2015). Longitudinal research has found that low-birthweight children raised in unstable, economically disadvantaged families tend to remain smaller in stature, experience more emotional problems, and show more long-term deficits in intelligence and academic performance than do those raised in more advantaged homes (Taylor, Klein, Minich, & Hack, 2001).

Interventions to promote the development of low-birthweight children often emphasize helping parents learn coping strategies for interacting with their infants and managing parenting stress (Chang et al., 2015; Lau & Morse, 2003). Interventions focused on teaching parents how to massage and touch their infants in therapeutic ways as well as increase skin-to-skin contact with their infants are associated with better cognitive and neurodevelopmental outcomes at age 2 (Procianoy, Mendes, & Silveira, 2010). One intervention common in developing countries where mothers may not have access to hospitals is **kangaroo care**, in which the infant is placed vertically against the parent's chest, under the shirt, providing skin-to-skin contact (Charpak et al., 2005). As the parent goes about daily activities, the infant remains warm and close, hears the voice and heartbeat, smells the body, and feels constant skin-to-skin contact. Kangaroo care is so effective that the majority of hospitals in the United States offer kangaroo care to preterm infants. Babies who receive early and consistent kangaroo care grow more quickly, sleep better, score higher on measures of health, and show more cognitive gains throughout the first year of life (Boundy et al., 2015; Jefferies, 2012).

In summary, a remarkable amount of growth and development takes place between conception and birth. In 9 short months, the zygote transforms into a newborn. Although there are a variety of risks to healthy development within the womb, most newborns are healthy. Infants are born with a surprising array of competencies, such as well-developed hearing, taste, and smell. Additional physical, cognitive, and psychosocial capacities develop shortly after birth, as we will see in upcoming chapters.

THINKING IN CONTEXT 3.4

1. In what ways might newborns' shifting states of arousal be adaptive?
2. Parental responses to having a low-birthweight infant influence the child's long-term health outcome. How might contextual factors influence parents' responses? What supports from the family, community, and broader society can aid parents in helping their low-birthweight infants adapt and develop healthily?

APPLY YOUR KNOWLEDGE

Best friends since first grade, Charmayne and Latisha were inseparable throughout childhood, adolescence, and now adulthood. Shortly after Charmayne discovered she was pregnant, Latisha revealed that she too was expecting. Together they learned about their developing babies, brainstormed baby names, and planned how to fit an infant into their cramped homes.

Charmayne and Latisha also commiserated about the challenges of pregnancy. Charmayne worked as a nail technician at a busy nail and hair salon. It's not uncommon for her customers to complain about the chemical odors, but she usually doesn't notice the smell. Charmayne's boss suggests that she wear a surgical mask and sometimes Charmayne complies but it's hard to converse with her customers from behind a mask. Charmayne has always found it uncomfortable to sit at the manicurist table all day, but now her rapidly expanding pregnancy "bump" makes sitting and leaning over the table very difficult. Most days she takes an over-the-counter painkiller to ease the discomfort. In the past, her doctor has prescribed medical cannabis for her symptoms. Charmayne still has some and consumes it occasionally when the pain is overpowering. She figures that once in a while can't hurt, especially if it helps her do her job.

Latisha works as a server and bartender at a popular local restaurant. She loves her job, but most shifts leave her exhausted because she's on her feet all day. Large tables of customers mean that she often carries heavy platters of food. Her pregnant body is changing so quickly that Latisha often finds herself off-balance, straining her back to compensate for her growing belly. After Latisha nearly dropped a heavy tray, her boss suggested that she work at the bar instead of serving food. Latisha happily complied, as she enjoys interacting with customers at the bar. Most of her customers are friendly. Sometimes regular customers will order alcoholic drinks for a big group of friends and ask her to share one with them. Sometimes the idea of an alcoholic drink makes her nauseous, but she usually agrees because happy customers mean big tips and she has a new baby to support. Usually the drink makes her feel better. Most nights Latisha stands outside during her breaks. She used to smoke during breaks, but she gave up cigarettes when she learned she was pregnant. Giving up nicotine was difficult, and Latisha missed the habit of smoking, so she tried vaping instead. Electronic cigarettes don't give off smoke, so they can't be that bad, she reasoned.

One spring morning several weeks before her due date, Latisha gave birth to a baby girl. She seemed healthy, but tiny. Charmayne carried her daughter to term, giving birth a few days before her due date. Several months later, the best friends visited, placing their babies on the floor together for tummy time.

1. Most women are exposed to some teratogens during pregnancy. Generally speaking, what are some examples of teratogens and other environmental influences on prenatal development?
2. What teratogens and environmental influences on prenatal development did Charmayne and Latisha encounter?
3. Suppose that Charmayne and Latisha give birth to full-term newborns, but one had a defect that was visible at birth. How might the principles of teratology account for variability in outcomes such as these?
4. Latisha's daughter is a low-birthweight infant. What are characteristics of low-birthweight infants and what can Latisha expect? How can she best care for her daughter?

WANT A BETTER GRADE?

Get the tools you need to sharpen your study skills. **SAGE edge** offers a robust online environment featuring an impressive array of free tools and resources. Access practice quizzes, eFlashcards, video, and multimedia at **edge.sagepub.com/kutherchild1e.** SAGE edge™

KEY TERMS

Lanugo 67

Vernix caseosa 67

Age of viability 67

Teratogen 68

Sleeper effects 69

Fetal alcohol spectrum disorders 71

Fetal alcohol syndrome (FAS) 71

Spina bifida 75

Anencephaly 75

Prenatal care 77

Labor 79

Breech position 81

Cesarean section 81

Natural childbirth 81

Doula 81

Apgar scale 83

Brazelton Neonatal Behavioral Assessment Scale (NBAS) 83

States of arousal 84

REM sleep 84

Preterm 85

Small for date 85

Low birthweight 85

Very low birthweight 85

Extremely low birthweight 85

Kangaroo care 88

SUMMARY

3.1 Describe the three periods of prenatal development.

Conception occurs in the fallopian tube. During the germinal period, the zygote begins cell division and travels down the fallopian tube toward the uterus. During the embryonic period from weeks 2 to 8, the most rapid developments of the prenatal period take place. From 9 weeks until birth, the fetus grows rapidly, and the organs become more complex and begin to function.

3.2 Explain how exposure to teratogens and other environmental factors can influence the prenatal environment.

Teratogens include diseases, drugs, and other agents that influence the prenatal environment to disrupt development. Generally, the effects of exposure to teratogens on prenatal development vary depending on the stage of prenatal development and dose. There are individual differences in effects, different teratogens can cause the same birth defect, a variety of birth defects can result from the same teratogen, and some teratogens have subtle effects that result in developmental delays that are not obvious at birth or not visible until many years later. Prescription and nonprescription drugs, maternal illnesses, and smoking and alcohol use can harm the developing fetus. Prenatal development can also be harmed by factors in the environment.

3.3 Summarize the process of childbirth.

Childbirth progresses through three stages. The first stage of labor begins when the mother experiences regular uterine contractions that cause the cervix to dilate. During the second stage, the fetus passes through the birth canal. The placenta is passed during the third stage. Medication is used in most births, often in combination with breathing and relaxation techniques characteristic of natural births. About one-third of U.S. births are by cesarean section.

3.4 Discuss the neonate's physical capacities, including development in low-birthweight infants.

Developmental researchers now know that the newborn is more perceptually competent than ever imagined. The most well-developed sense is audition. Newborns display regular cycles of eating, elimination, and states of arousal or degrees of wakefulness, spending about 50% of their sleep time in REM, thought to permit the brain to stimulate itself. There are two types of low-birthweight infants, those who are preterm and those who are small for date. Low-birthweight infants struggle to survive. Low-birthweight infants experience higher rates of sensory, motor, and language problems as well as learning disabilities, behavior problems, and deficits in social skills into adolescence. The long-term outcomes of low birthweight vary considerably and depend on the environment in which the children are raised.

REVIEW QUESTIONS

3.1 What are the three periods of prenatal development?

What major milestones occur in each period?

What are influences on prenatal care?

3.2 Define and provide three examples of teratogens.

What are four principles that determine the effects of exposure to teratogens during prenatal development?

3.3 What are the three stages of childbirth?

Describe characteristics of each stage.

What are the differences among cesarean delivery, natural childbirth, and home birth?

3.4 How are neonates assessed at birth?

Describe the neonate's perceptual capabilities.

What are two types of low-birthweight infants?

What factors determine long-term outcomes for low-birthweight babies?

UNIT II

INFANCY AND TODDLERHOOD

4 Physical Development in Infancy and Toddlerhood

Oscar has his first well-baby visit at 2 weeks of age. His arms and legs flail as he is placed on the scale to be weighed and he cries in response to feeling the chilly metal scale against his body. Although seemingly helpless, Oscar is born with powerful capacities for adapting to the world around him. In this chapter, we examine the physical capacities of infants, including their growth, brain development, and sensory and motor capacities.

Learning Objectives

4.1 Discuss growth and influences and threats to growth during infancy and toddlerhood.

▶ **Video Activity 4.1:** Body Proportions in Infancy and Early Childhood

4.2 Summarize brain development during infancy and toddlerhood.

4.3 Compare infants' early learning capacities for habituation, classical conditioning, operant conditioning, and imitation.

4.4 Describe infants' developing sensory abilities.

4.5 Analyze the roles of maturation and contextual factors in infant and toddler motor development.

▶ **Video Activity 4.2:** Motor Development in Infancy

Chapter Contents

BODY GROWTH

Perhaps the most obvious change that infants undergo during the first year of life is very rapid growth.

Growth Trends

It is easy to observe that infants grow substantially larger and heavier over time—but there are many individual differences in growth. How can parents and caregivers tell if a child's growth is normal? By compiling information about the height and weight of large samples of children from diverse populations, researchers have determined that growth follows distinct patterns. **Growth norms** are expectations for typical gains and variations in height and weight for children based on their chronological age and ethnic background.

In the first few days after birth, newborns shed excess fluid and typically lose 5% to 10% of their body weight. After this initial loss, however, infants gain weight quickly. Infants typically double their birthweight at about 4 months of age, triple it by 12 months, and quadruple it by 2.5 years (Kliegman et al., 2016). The average 3-year-old weighs about 31 pounds. Gains in height of 10 to 12 inches can be expected over the first year of life, making the average 1-year-old child about 30 inches tall. Most children grow about 5 inches during their second year of life and 3 to 4 inches during their third. To parents, growth may appear slow and steady, but research has shown that it tends to occur in spurts in which an infant or toddler can grow up to one-quarter of an inch overnight (Lampl et al., 2001). Infant growth appears to be tied to sleep, as increased bouts of sleep predict small bursts of growth (Lampl & Johnson, 2011). At about 2 years of age, both girls and boys have reached one-half of their adult height (Kliegman et al., 2016).

Patterns of Growth

Over the course of infancy, children get larger and heavier, but growth is uneven. Different parts of the body grow at different rates. Growth during the prenatal period and infancy proceeds in two systematic patterns. **Cephalocaudal development** refers to the principle that growth proceeds from the head downward. The head and upper regions of the body develop before the lower regions. For example, recall the fetus's disproportionately large head. During prenatal development, the head grows before the other body parts. Even at birth, the newborn's head is about one-fourth the total body length, as shown in Figure 4.1. As the lower parts of the body develop, the head becomes more proportionate to the body. By 3 years of age, the child is less top-heavy. **Proximodistal development** refers to the principle that growth and development proceed from the center of the body outward (Figure 4.2). During prenatal development, the internal organs develop before the arms and legs. After birth, the trunk grows ahead of the arms and legs, and the arms and legs tend to grow ahead of the hands and feet.

Growth is largely maturational, but it can be influenced by health and environmental factors. Today's children grow taller and faster than ever before, and the average adult is taller today than a century ago. Increases in children's growth over the past century are influenced by contextual changes such as improved sanitation, nutrition, and access to medical care (Mummert, Schoen, & Lampl, 2018). Large gains have occurred in North America and Europe, followed by South Asia (NCD Risk Factor Collaboration, 2016). Although children of sub-Saharan Africa showed growth gains into the mid-1990s, mass poverty and starvation, poor infrastructure to provide clean water and sanitation, and exposure to the emotional and physical stresses of war and terror have affected growth (Simmons, 2015). Contextual factors can both help and harm children's development.

Nutrition and Growth

Good nutrition is essential to healthy growth during infancy and toddlerhood. Many infants' first nutritional experiences are through breast milk.

Breastfeeding

The U.S. Department of Health and Human Services (2011) has recommended that mothers breastfeed their babies, and breastfeeding has increased in popularity in the United States in recent years. In 1990, about one-half of mothers breastfed their babies, whereas about 83% breastfed in 2014 (Centers for Disease Control and Prevention, 2017b). Over one-half of women continue to breastfeed after 6 months and over one-third at 12 months.

Breastfeeding practices vary by maternal age, education, and socioeconomic status (Hauck, Fenwick, Dhaliwal, & Butt, 2011). In the United States and the United Kingdom, for example, the lowest rates of breastfeeding are among low-income mothers, mothers who are young, and mothers with low levels of education. Researchers

FIGURE 4.1

Body Proportions Throughout Life

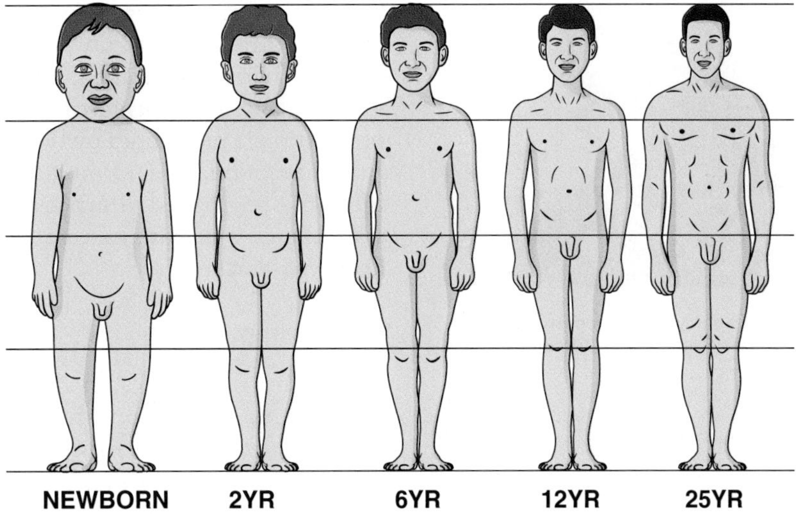

Source: Huelke (1998).

FIGURE 4.2

Cephalocaudal and Proximodistal Development

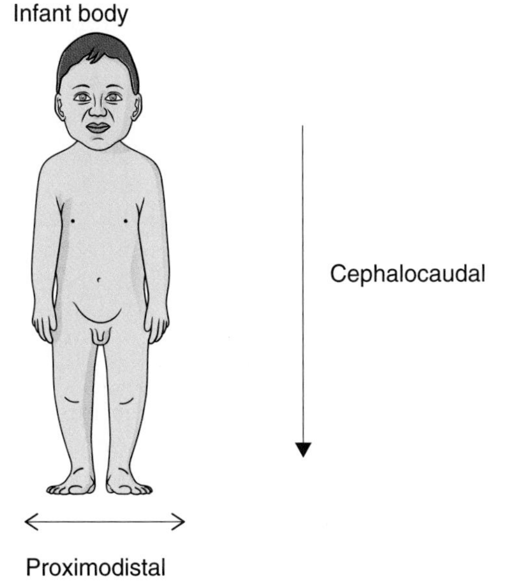

have observed that the employment settings of low-income mothers may offer few resources to support breastfeeding, such as private places for women to use breast pumps (Griffiths, Tate, & Lucy, 2007; Racine, Frick, Guthrie, & Strobino, 2009). In contrast, women in developing countries who have low educational levels and are in the poorest social classes are *more* likely to breastfeed their children. Educated women of higher income brackets in these countries tend to shun breastfeeding, viewing it as an option primarily for poor women (Victora et al., 2016). Other factors affecting breastfeeding practices include ethnicity and social policies. In the United States, for instance, Hispanic mothers breastfeed at higher rates than non-Hispanic White mothers, who are more likely to breastfeed than non-Hispanic Black mothers (Centers for Disease Control and Prevention, 2013; Smith-Gagen, Hollen, Walker, Cook, & Yang, 2014). And unsurprisingly, countries where working women are allowed paid maternity leave for part or all of their infant's first year of life, such as Denmark, Norway, Sweden, and Australia, show very high breastfeeding rates of 94% and more (Hauck et al., 2011; Imdad, Yakoob, & Bhutta, 2011; Roelants, Hauspie, & Hoppenbrouwers, 2010).

Breastfeeding offers benefits for mothers and infants. Mothers who breastfeed have lower rates of diabetes, cardiovascular disease, and depression, and after they reach menopause, they are at lower risk for ovarian and breast cancer and bone fractures (Godfrey & Lawrence, 2010; Islami et al., 2015). A mother's milk is tailored to her infant and has the right amount of fat, sugar, water, and protein needed for the baby's growth and development. Most babies find it easier to digest breast milk than formula. In addition, breast milk contains immunizing agents that

Breastfeeding is associated with many health benefits for infants and mothers and provides opportunities for infant–mother bonding.
©iStockphoto.com/kate_sept2004

protect the infant against infections, and breastfed infants tend to experience lower rates of allergies and gastrointestinal symptoms as well as have fewer visits to physicians (Cabinian et al., 2016; Turfkruyer & Verhasselt, 2015). Breastfeeding for more than 6 months is associated with reduced risk of obesity and childhood cancer, especially lymphomas (Amitay, Dubnov Raz, & Keinan-Boker, 2016; Victora et al., 2016). Recent research suggests that exclusively breastfeeding during the first 4 to 6 weeks of life may be associated with longer telomeres, protective caps on chromosomes that predict longevity, at age 4 and 5 (Wojcicki et al., 2016).

Research on the effects of breastfeeding on cognitive development yields mixed findings. In some studies, infants breastfed for more than 6 months perform better on tests of cognitive ability compared with their formula-fed counterparts (Kramer et al., 2008; Sloan, Stewart, & Dunne, 2010). Others suggest that the differences in test scores are influenced by the characteristics of mothers who breastfeed, such as higher levels of education and socioeconomic status (Der, Batty, & Deary, 2006; Schulze & Carlisle, 2010; Tanaka, Kon, Ohkawa, Yoshikawa, & Shimizu, 2009). Yet studies that control for maternal factors still support a cognitive advantage to breastfed infants (Sloan et al., 2010). The cognitive advantages may persist throughout childhood into adolescence. The duration of breastfeeding, specifically longer than 6 months, is associated with higher scores in language ability at ages 5 and 10 (Whitehouse, Robinson, Li, & Oddy, 2011) and intelligence in adolescence (Isaacs et al., 2010). Although breastfeeding appears to be associated with positive cognitive outcomes, it is important to recognize that differences in cognitive development between breastfed and formula-fed infants are small (Jenkins & Foster, 2014; Schulze & Carlisle, 2010).

Although breastfeeding is recommended by pediatricians, it is not essential for a healthy infant. Many mothers do not breastfeed whether by choice or circumstance. Infant formula is a safe and healthy alternative to breast milk. Formula production is monitored by the U.S. Food and Drug Administration. Most formulas are made from cow's milk, but soy-based alternatives exist for infants with allergies or parents who choose to raise their child vegetarian.

Malnutrition

Many infants experience malnutrition, with devastating effects on physical growth. One in four children in the world suffer from **growth stunting**, a reduced growth rate. Children in developing countries are at especially high risk of chronic malnutrition and growth stunting. For example, growth stunting affects 43% of children in East African countries, 34% in West Africa, and 35% in South-Central Asia (de Onis & Branca, 2016). Infants who consume a diet that is chronically insufficient in calories, nutrients, and protein can develop **marasmus**, a wasting disease in which the body's fat and muscle are depleted (Kliegman et al., 2016). Growth stops, the body wastes away, the skin becomes wrinkly and aged looking, the abdomen shrinks, and the body takes on a hollow appearance. Another disease related to malnutrition is **kwashiorkor**, found in children who experience an insufficient intake of protein, which may occur when a child prematurely abandons breastfeeding, such as after the birth of a younger sibling. Kwashiorkor is characterized by lethargy, wrinkled skin, and fluid retention appearing as bloating and swelling of the stomach, face, legs, and arms. Because the vital organs of the body take all of the available nutrients, the other parts of the body deteriorate. Marasmus occurs most often in infants, whereas kwashiorkor tends to occur in older infants and young children (Morley, 2016).

Malnutrition influences development in multiple ways. Malnourished children show cognitive deficits as well as impairments in motivation, curiosity, language, and the ability to effectively interact with the environment throughout childhood and adolescence and even into adulthood (Galler et al., 2012; C. J. Peter et al., 2016). Malnourishment damages neurons, as shown in Figure 4.3, and the resulting neurological and cognitive deficits from early malnutrition last. For example, among Ghannan

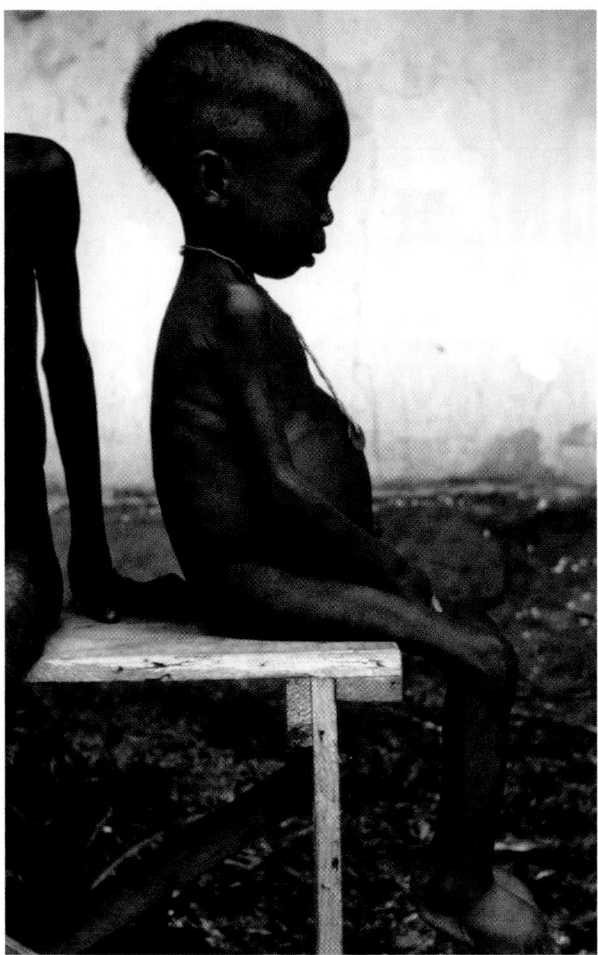

A swollen belly is characteristic of kwashiorkor, an extreme nutritional deficiency.
Lyle Conrad/CDC

children who survived a severe famine in 1983, those who were youngest at the time of the famine (under age 2) scored lower on cognitive measures throughout childhood and into adulthood than did those who were older (ages 6 to 8) (Ampaabeng & Tan, 2013). Malnutrition during the first year of life is associated with depression years later, when those children are 11 to 17 years old (Galler et al., 2010). Some of the damage caused by malnutrition can be reversed. For example, motor and mental development can be enhanced if nutrition is reinstated early. However, long-term difficulties in attention, learning, and intelligence often remain, even into middle adulthood (Kim, Fleisher, & Sun, 2017; Schoenmaker et al., 2015; Waber et al., 2014).

Although malnutrition is common in developing countries, it is also found in some of the world's wealthiest countries. Because of socioeconomic factors, many children in the United States and other developed countries are deprived of diets that support healthy growth. In 2017, about 16% of U.S. households with children were categorized as *food insecure*. That is, they lacked consistent access to food to support a healthy lifestyle for all members of the family at some point during the year (Coleman-Jensen, Rabbitt, Gregory, & Singh, 2018). As shown in Figure 4.4, rates of food insecurity are higher in Black and Hispanic households (22% and 18%, respectively) and those headed by single parents (20% for homes headed by single men and 30% for those headed by single women). In the United States and other developed nations, food insecurity is linked with stunted growth, poor school performance, and health and behavior problems (Shankar, Chung, & Frank, 2017; Zhu, Mangini, Dong, & Forman, 2017).

FIGURE 4.3

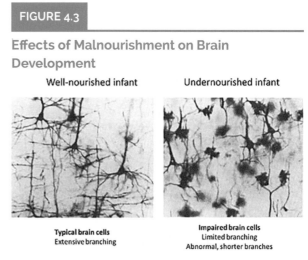

Effects of Malnourishment on Brain Development

Well-nourished infant

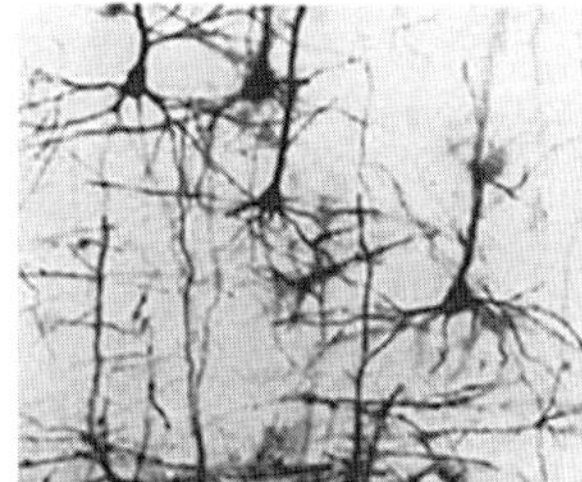

Undernourished infant

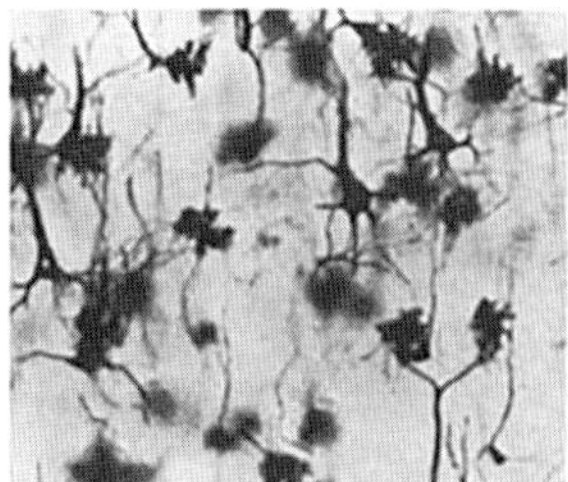

Source: de Onis and Branca (2016), https://onlinelibrary.wiley.com/doi/epdf/10.1111/mcn.12231 licensed under CC BY 3.0 IGO, https://creativecommons.org/licenses/by/3.0/igo/legalcode

Health Threats

We have seen that poor nutrition and poverty can contribute to poor physical growth. Sometimes developmental difficulties occur despite access to nutrition.

Growth Faltering

Although growth follows particular norms, children's rate of growth varies with hereditary and contextual factors. Some children, however, show significantly slower growth than other children their age. Some infants demonstrate **growth faltering**, also known as *failure to thrive*, a condition in which their growth and weight are substantially lower than other children their age. Specifically, growth faltering refers to weight below the fifth percentile for the child's age, meaning that the child weighs less than 95% of same-age children

FIGURE 4.4

Food Insecurity

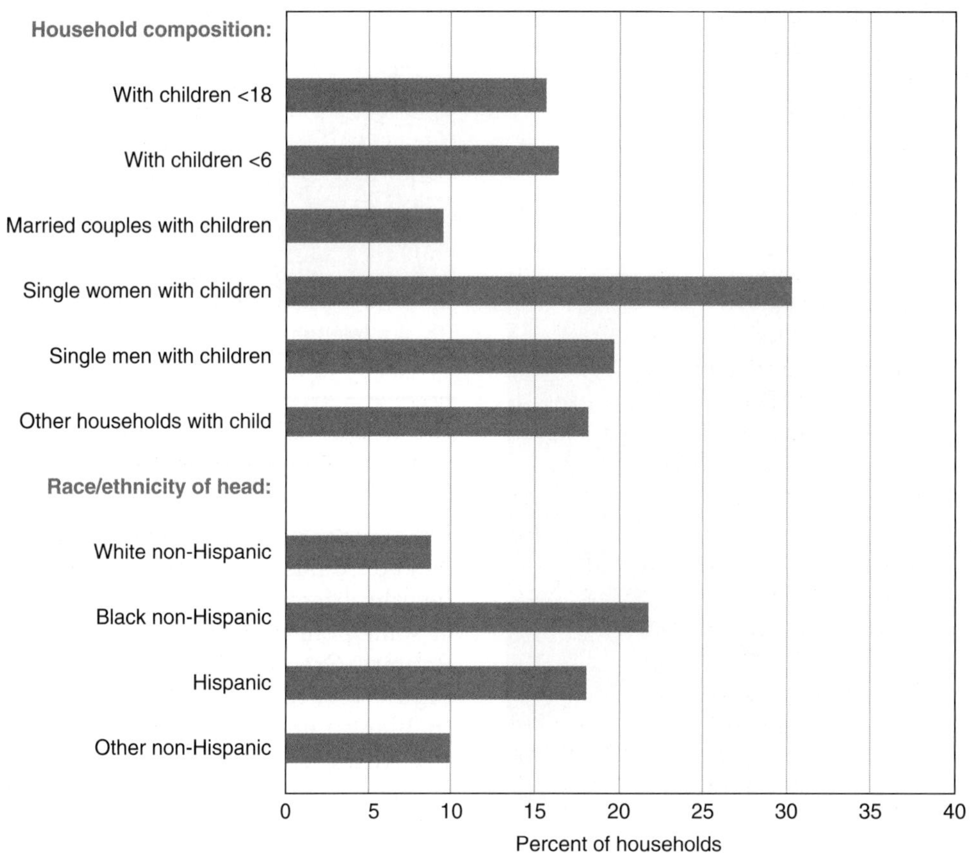

Source: Coleman-Jensen et al. (2018).

(Raab, 2017). Their caloric intake is insufficient to maintain growth (Larson-Nath & Biank, 2016). Children with growth faltering may be irritable and emotional, lack age-appropriate social responses such as smiling and eye contact, and show delayed motor development. Untreated, growth faltering is accompanied by delays in cognitive, verbal, and behavioral skills that make it difficult for the child to achieve success in school, home, and peer environments (Homan, 2016).

Growth faltering may be influenced by medical conditions. Sometimes socioemotional and contextual factors contribute to growth faltering, such as an insecure attachment to caregivers, parents with physical or mental health problems, emotional neglect and abuse, and, especially, living in poverty and experiencing contextual stressors such as violence within the community (Feigelman & Keane, 2017). Pediatricians typically treat growth faltering by providing the child with the nutrients necessary to grow normally. They may also work with other health professionals such as psychologists and social workers to address underlying medical and psychosocial contributors. Although nutritional interventions can alleviate many of the effects of malnutrition on physical development, some children might show long-term cognitive and psychosocial deficits (Homan, 2016; Larson-Nath & Biank, 2016).

Sudden Infant Death Syndrome

The leading cause of death of infants under the age of 1 is **sudden infant death syndrome (SIDS)** (Bajanowski & Vennemann, 2017). SIDS is the diagnostic term used to describe the sudden unexpected death of an infant less than 1 year of age that occurs seemingly during sleep and remains unexplained after a thorough investigation, including an autopsy and review of the circumstances of death and the infant's clinical history (Task Force on Sudden Infant Death Syndrome, 2016).

What causes SIDS? It is believed to be the result of an interaction of factors, including an infant's biological vulnerability to SIDS coupled with exposure to a trigger or stressor that occurs during a critical period of development (Moon & Task Force on Sudden Infant Death Syndrome, 2016; Spinelli, Collins-Praino, Van Den Heuvel, & Byard, 2017). The first factor is unknown biological vulnerabilities, such as genetic abnormalities and mutations and prematurity, that may place infants at risk for SIDS. For example, a recent 10-year review of hundreds of SIDS cases in Australia confirmed that, although the underlying cause of SIDS remains unknown, mutations and genetic variants likely play a role (Evans, Bagnall, Duflou, & Semsarian, 2013). Second, environmental stressors or events that might trigger SIDS include risks such as having the infant sleep on his or her stomach or side, use of soft bedding or other inappropriate sleep surfaces (including sofas), bed sharing, and exposure to tobacco smoke (Carlin & Moon, 2017). One review of several hundred cases in the United Kingdom found that in over a third of SIDS deaths, infants were co-sleeping with adults at the time of death (Blair, Sidebotham, Berry, Evans, & Fleming, 2006). Finally, there are developmental periods in which infants are most vulnerable to SIDS. Most cases of SIDS occur between the second and fifth months of life (Bajanowski & Vennemann, 2017). Therefore, it is thought that SIDS is most likely to occur when the triple risks—biological vulnerability, triggering events, and critical period of development—converge (Filiano & Kinney, 1994; Spinelli et al., 2017).

Ethnic differences appear in the prevalence of SIDS, with Native Americans and Blacks showing the highest rates of SIDS in the United States, followed by non-Hispanic Whites. Asian American and Hispanic infants show lower rates of SIDS than White infants (Parks, Erck Lambert, & Shapiro-Mendoza, 2017). Ethnic differences in SIDS are likely due to differences in socioeconomic and lifestyle factors associated with SIDS, such as lack of prenatal care, low rates of breastfeeding, maternal smoking, and low maternal age. Cultural practices such as adult–infant bed sharing, providing infants with soft bedding, and placing the sleeping baby in a separate room from caregivers increase SIDS risk (Colson et al., 2013; Parks et al., 2017; Shapiro-Mendoza et al., 2014). However, ethnic differences in SIDS are complex and influenced by context. For example, in one study of infants, those of Mexican American U.S.-born mothers had a 50% greater rate of SIDS than infants of Mexican foreign-born mothers after controlling for factors associated with SIDS, including birthweight, maternal age, education, marital status, prenatal care, and socioeconomic status (Collins, Papacek, Schulte, & Drolet, 2001). Differences in acculturation and associated child care practices likely play a role in influencing SIDS risk, but they are not well understood (Parks et al., 2017).

In the 1990s, SIDS declined dramatically after the American Academy of Pediatrics, based on data from Europe, Australia, and the United States, recommended that infants be placed for sleep in a nonprone position (i.e., a supine position: on their backs) as a strategy to reduce the risk of SIDS (see Figure 4.5) (American Academy of Pediatrics, 1992). Initiated in 1992, the "Back to Sleep" campaign publicized the importance of nonprone sleeping. Between 1992 and 2001, the SIDS rate declined dramatically in the United States and other countries that implemented nonprone/supine sleeping campaigns (Bajanowski & Vennemann, 2017; Bergman, 2015; Moon & Task Force on Sudden Infant Death Syndrome, 2016), consistent with the steady increase in the prevalence of supine sleeping. In addition to placing infants on their backs to sleep, other recommendations for a safe sleep environment include the use of a firm sleep surface, avoidance of soft bedding and infant overheating, and sharing a room with the infant without sharing a bed. Avoid placing infants in sitting devices, such as car seats, strollers, and infant carriers, for routine sleep. Couches and armchairs are extremely dangerous places for infants. SIDS poses grave risks to infants, but the risks can be reduced.

Failure to Vaccinate

Failure to vaccinate is a preventable risk to infants' health. Over the past 60 years, childhood diseases such as measles, mumps, and whooping cough have declined dramatically because of widespread immunization of infants. A **vaccine** is a small dose of inactive virus that is injected into the body to stimulate the production of antibodies to guard against the disease. Vaccines control infectious diseases that once spread quickly and killed thousands of people. The Centers for Disease Control and Prevention recommends that infants be vaccinated against most vaccine-preventable diseases by the time they are 2 years of age. Currently, 10 vaccines are included

FIGURE 4.5

Trends in Sudden Unexpected Infant Death (SUID) by Cause, 1990–2015

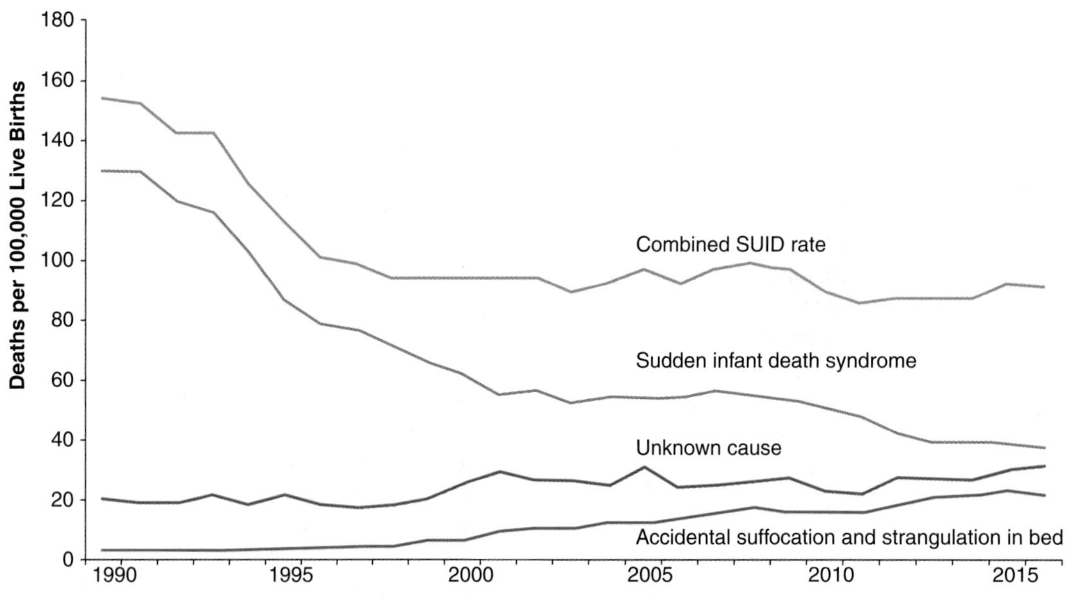

Source: Centers for Disease Control and Prevention National Center for Health Statistics, National Vital Statistics System, Compressed Mortality File.

in the standard recommendations for children at specific ages between birth and 10 years. Immunization rates vary by vaccine, but overall vaccination coverage in the United States tends to be high. For example, in 2016, 91% of children 19 to 35 months of age were vaccinated for measles, mumps, and rubella (MMR) (National Center for Health Statistics, 2018). However, the percentage of children who have received no vaccines has increased over the past 2 decades, from .3% of 19- to 35-month-old children in 2001 to 1.3% for children born in 2015 (Hill, Elam-Evans, Yankey, Singleton, & Kang, 2018).

Although only a small minority of children are unvaccinated, highly contagious diseases, such as measles, can spread quickly among them. For example, in 2019, nearly 900 cases of measles were reported, largely confined to geographic areas where vaccination is less common (Centers for Disease Control and Prevention, 2019b). The Applying Developmental Science feature examines some of the reasons parents cite for not vaccinating their children.

Interventions to increase vaccination rates tend to focus on education and counseling and improving access to vaccines (Ventola, 2016). Health care workers can inform parents about vaccination by describing the infections that they prevent, discussing the research supporting their use, and dispelling myths. Offering combination vaccines that include several at once minimizes the number of injections and visits. Providing opportunities to administer vaccinations during all pediatric visits—well, sick, and follow-up—as well as by nurses can increase compliance. At the community level, advertising, public messaging campaigns, and social media and text messaging educational materials and reminders can inform parents of the benefits of vaccinations. Access to free vaccines and opportunities for vaccination within the community, such as at day care facilities, walk-in clinics, pharmacies, and financial aid offices, can help remove financial barriers to vaccination.

THINKING IN CONTEXT 4.1

1. Identify ways in which contextual factors influence growth. What do parents need to know about these factors? How might you increase parents' knowledge?
2. Prepare a brief presentation for parents of newborns explaining SIDS, risk factors for it, and what parents can do to help protect their infants.

APPLYING DEVELOPMENTAL SCIENCE

Why Don't Parents Vaccinate?

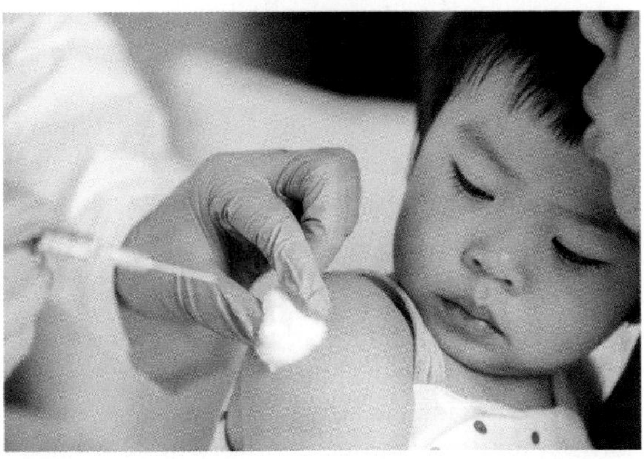

Vaccines protect children and communities from diseases that once spread quickly and killed thousands of people.
©iStockphoto.com/spukkato

In 2000, the highly contagious infection measles was declared eliminated from the United States. Yet as of May 2019, 880 cases have been reported, linked to individuals who have not been vaccinated for the disease. Some parents decline or delay vaccinating their children or follow alternative immunization schedules because of medical, religious, philosophical, or socioeconomic reasons (Ventola, 2016). This has caused a resurgence of many infectious diseases.

Vaccination is compulsory for school-age children in the United States, but all states permit exemptions. Currently, exemptions due to medical reasons are allowed in all states, religious grounds in nearly all states, and philosophical objections in 20 states (Bednarczyk, King, Lahijani, & Omer, 2019; Wang, Clymer, Davis-Hayes, & Buttenheim, 2014). It has been estimated that 1% to 3% of children are excused from immunization because of these exemptions, but in some communities the exemption rate is as high as 20% (Ventola, 2016). Even when a low percentage of children are excused from immunization, the risk of disease outbreaks in schools increases.

Some researchers argue that, paradoxically, one reason that parents may hesitate to vaccinate their children is the widespread success of immunization (Temoka, 2013). Because of high vaccination rates, most vaccine-preventable diseases have declined to historically low levels in the United States, which can mask the health dangers of once-common infections. With little to no experience with vaccine-preventable diseases, young parents may be unaware of the threat these diseases pose or the need to seek protection.

Another reason is that many families in the United States do not have access to the health care they need. Children in families with incomes below the poverty level are less likely to receive the combined series vaccination (Child Trends, 2015). Many parents are unaware that children from low-income families who do not have medical insurance can receive vaccinations through the federal Vaccines for Children program, begun in 1994.

Some parents choose not to vaccinate their children because of the common misconception that vaccines are linked with autism (Salmon, Dudley, Glanz, & Omer, 2015). Extensive research indicates that there is no association between vaccination and autism (Modabbernia, Velthorst, & Reichenberg, 2017; Taylor, Swerdfeger, & Eslick, 2014). Instead, children tend to receive vaccines at the age when some chronic illnesses and developmental disorders—such as autism—tend to emerge, but this correlation is not indicative of a cause-and-effect relationship. (Recall from Chapter 1 that correlational research documents phenomena that occur together but cannot demonstrate causation.) As we discuss later in this chapter, although specific causes of autism spectrum disorders have yet to be fully identified, these disorders appear to have a strong genetic component (Lee & McGrath, 2015; Waltes et al., 2014). Other parents report concerns about chemicals in vaccines and possible unforeseen future effects of vaccination (Martin & Petrie, 2017). Yet longitudinal research has suggested no negative long-term effects of vaccines administered in infancy (Henry et al., 2018; Su et al., 2017; Wessel, 2017).

A challenge to immunizing children is that the vaccination schedule is complicated, with specific vaccines administered at specific times in development (Kurosky, Davis, & Krishnarajah, 2017). Even when children receive the full schedule of vaccinations, many do not receive them on the timetable recommended by the National Vaccine Advisory Committee. Vaccine timeliness is important because the efficacy of early and late vaccination is not always known and may vary by disease. When a child receives a vaccination may be just as important as whether the child receives it in promoting disease resistance.

What Do You Think?

What do you think are the most compelling reasons parents might choose not to vaccinate their children? How might you counter these reasons? ●

BRAIN DEVELOPMENT DURING INFANCY AND TODDLERHOOD

Infants' bodies grow rapidly, but the most dramatic changes during infancy are much less visible. All of the developments in infants' physical and mental capacities are influenced by the changes that occur in the brain. At birth, the brain is about 25% of its adult weight, and it grows rapidly throughout infancy, reaching about 70% of its adult weight by 2 years of age (Lyall et al., 2015). As the brain develops, it becomes larger and more complex.

The Neuron

The brain is made up of billions of cells called **neurons**. Neurons are specialized to communicate with one another to make it possible for people to sense the world, think, move their bodies, and carry out their lives. As shown in Figure 4.6, neurons have distinct structures that set them apart from other cells and enable the communicative functions characteristic of neurons. Dendrites are branching receptors that receive chemical messages (called neurotransmitters) from other neurons that are translated into an electrical signal (Stiles, 2017). The axon is a long tube-like structure that extends from the neuron and carries electrical signals to other neurons. Neurons do not touch. Instead, there are gaps between neurons called **synapses**. Once the electrical signal reaches the end of the axon, it triggers the release of the neurotransmitter, which crosses the synapse to communicate with the dendrites of another neuron (Carson, 2014). This process of neural transmission is how neurons communicate with other neurons. Neurons also communicate with sensory and motor cells. Some axons synapse with muscle cells and are responsible for movement. The dendrites of some neurons synapse with sensory cells, such as those in the eyes or ears, to transfer sensory information such as vision and hearing (Gibb & Kovalchuk, 2018). Finally, axons are often coated with a fatty substance called **myelin**, which speeds the transmission of electrical impulses and neurological function.

Processes of Neural Development

The first neurons form early in prenatal development, in the embryo's neural tube, through a process called **neurogenesis**. We are born with more than 100 billion neurons, more than we will ever need—and more than we will ever have at any other time in our lives. Some of our neurons die, but neurogenesis continues throughout life and new neurons are formed, although at a much slower pace than during prenatal development (Stiles et al., 2015). As the brain develops, new neurons migrate along a network of **glial cells**, a second type of brain cell that outnumbers neurons (Gibb & Kovalchuk, 2018). Glial cells nourish neurons and move throughout the brain to provide a physical structure to the brain. As shown in Figure 4.7, neurons travel along glial cells to the location of the brain where they will function, often the outer layer of the brain, known as the cortex, and glial cells instruct neurons to form connections with other neurons (Kolb, Whishaw, & Teskey, 2016).

At birth, the networks of neurons are simple, with few connections, or synapses, between neurons (Kolb et al., 2016). Early in infancy, major growth takes place. Neurons and glial cells enlarge. The

FIGURE 4.6

The Neuron

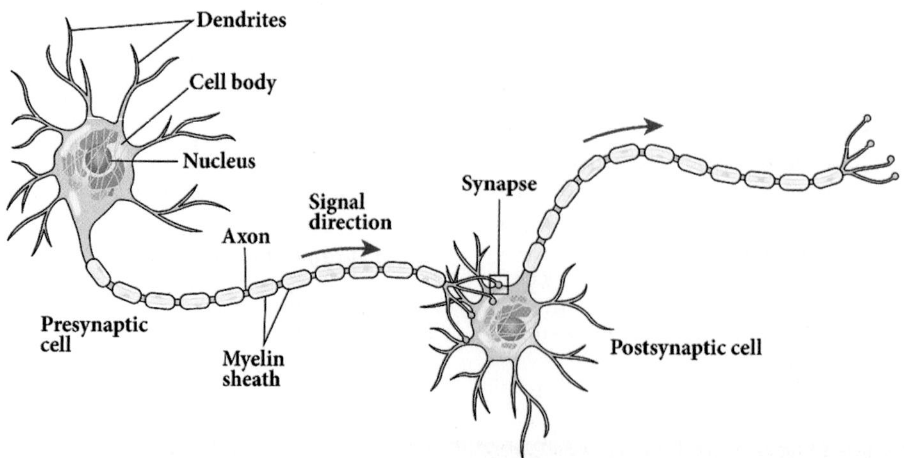

FIGURE 4.7

Glial Cell–Neuron Relationship

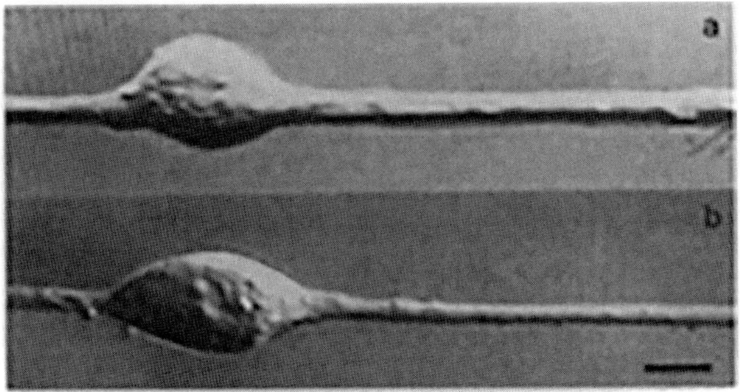

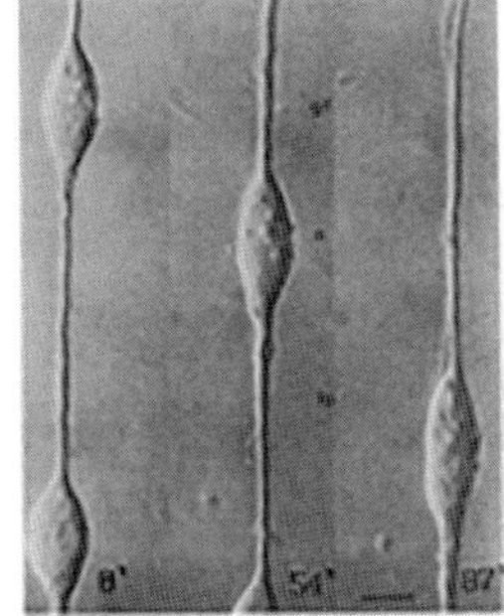

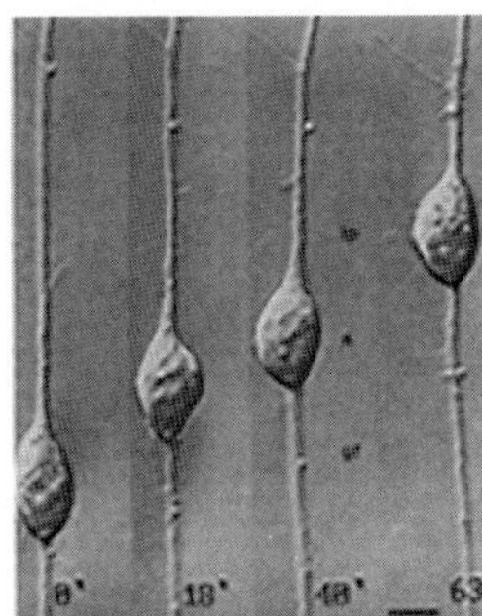

Neurons migrate along thin strands of glial cells.

Source: Gasser and Hatten (1990).

dendrites grow and branch out, increasing synapses with other neurons, a process called **synaptogenesis**. Synaptogenesis peaks in different brain regions at different ages (Remer et al., 2017). The most active areas of synaptogenesis during the first 5 weeks of life are in the sensorimotor cortex and subcortical parts of the brain, which are responsible for respiration and other essential survival processes. The visual cortex develops very rapidly between 3 and 4 months and reaches peak density by 12 months of age. The prefrontal cortex—responsible for planning and higher thinking—develops more slowly and is not complete until early adulthood (Tamnes et al., 2017).

In response to exposure to stimulation from the outside world, the number of synapses initially rises meteorically in the first year of life, and the dendrites increase 500% by age 2 (Schuldiner & Yaron, 2015). Cortical thickness peaks by 2 years of age, but surface area continues to develop throughout childhood (Gilmore, Knickmeyer Santelli, & Gao, 2018). Toddlers have more synapses than at any other point in life (see Figure 4.8). This explosion in connections in the early years of life means that the brain makes more connections than it needs, in preparation to receive any and all conceivable kinds of stimulation (Schuldiner & Yaron, 2015). Those connections that are used become stronger and more efficient, while those unused eventually shrink, atrophy, and disappear. This loss of unused neural connections is a process called **synaptic pruning**, which can improve the efficiency of neural communication by removing "clutter"—excess unused connections. Little-used synapses are pruned in response to experience, an important part of neurological development that leads to more efficient thought (Lyall et al., 2015).

Another important process of brain development is **myelination**, in which glial cells produce and coat the axons of neurons with a fatty substance called myelin. Myelination begins prenatally but accelerates after birth (Gilmore et al., 2018). Myelination contributes to advances in neural communication because axons coated with myelin transmit neural impulses more quickly than unmyelinated axons (Lebel & Deoni, 2018). With increases in myelination, infants and children process information more quickly. Their thought and behaviors become faster more coordinated, and complex (Chevalier et al., 2015). Myelination proceeds most rapidly from birth to age 4, first in the sensory and motor cortex in infancy, and continues through childhood into adolescence and early adulthood (Qiu, Mori, & Miller, 2015).

The Cerebral Cortex

The wrinkled and folded outermost layer of the brain is known as the **cortex**. The cortex comprises about 85% of the brain's mass and develops throughout childhood and some parts mature into early adulthood.

The cortex is composed of different structures with differing functions, located across four lobes. The various parts of the brain work together; however, as shown in Figure 4.9, each lobe is specialized to a certain extent. The four lobes progress on different developmental timetables. The sensory and motor areas tend to develop first (for example, the visual cortex regions of the occipital lobe). The frontal lobe, specifically a part called the **prefrontal cortex**, develops throughout infancy, childhood, and adolescence, maturing into early adulthood (Hodel, 2018; Tamnes et al., 2017). The prefrontal cortex is the part of the brain responsible for higher thought, such as planning, goal setting, controlling impulses, and using cognitive skills and memory to solve problems.

FIGURE 4.8

Synaptogenesis From Birth to Age 2

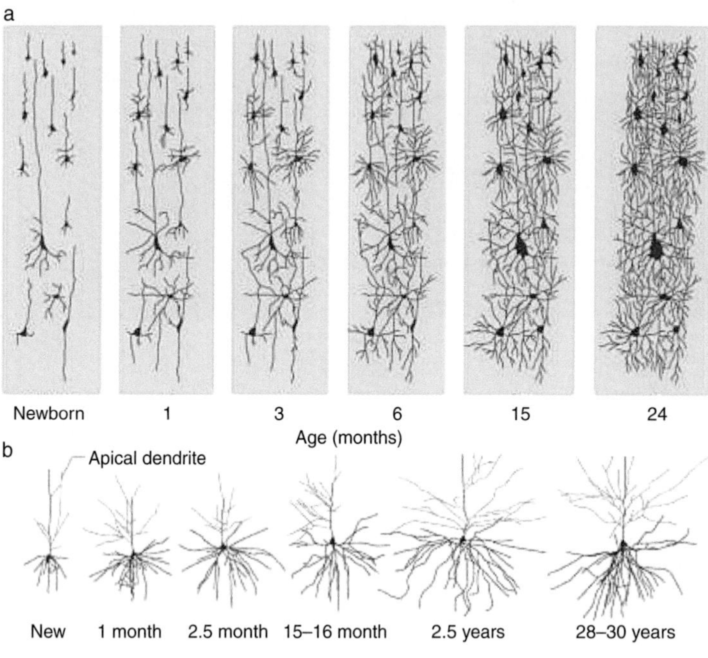

Source: Gilmore et al. (2018).

In addition, the cortex is composed of two hemispheres that are joined by a thick band of neural fibers known as the corpus collosum. Although all four lobes appear on both hemispheres, the hemispheres are not identical. Over childhood, the right and left hemispheres become specialized to carry out different functions, a process known as **lateralization** (Duboc, Dufourcq, Blader, & Roussigné, 2015). For most people, language is governed by the left hemisphere. Each hemisphere of the brain (and the parts of the brain that comprise each hemisphere) is specialized for particular functions and becomes more specialized with experience.

Lateralization ("of the side" in Latin) begins before birth and is influenced both by genes and by early experiences (Young, 2016). For example, in the womb, most fetuses face toward the left, freeing the right side of the body, which permits more movement on that side and the development of greater control over the right side of the body (Previc, 1991). In newborns, the left hemisphere tends to have greater structural connectivity and efficiency than the right—more connections and pathways, suggesting that they are better able to control the right side of their bodies (Ratnarajah et al., 2013). Newborns tend to have slightly better hearing from their right ear (Ari-Even Roth, Hildesheimer, Roziner, & Henkin, 2016). Infants generally display a hand preference, usually right, and their subsequent activity makes the hand more dominant because experience strengthens the hand and neural connections and improves agility. In this way, one hemisphere becomes stronger and more adept over the course of childhood, a process known as hemispheric dominance. Most adults experience hemispheric dominance, usually with the left hemisphere dominating over the right, making about 90% of adults in Western countries right-handed (Duboc et al., 2015).

Experience and Brain Development

Stimulation and experience are key components needed to maximize neural connections and brain development throughout life, but especially in infancy. Much of what we know about brain development comes from studying animals. Animals raised in stimulating environments with many toys and companions to play with develop brains that are heavier and have more synapses than do those who grow up in standard laboratory conditions (Berardi, Sale, & Maffei, 2015). Likewise, when animals raised in stimulating environments are moved to unstimulating standard laboratory conditions, their brains lose neural connections. This is true for humans, too. Infants who are understimulated, such as those who experience child maltreatment, or who are reared in deprivation, such as in poor

FIGURE 4.9

The Human Brain

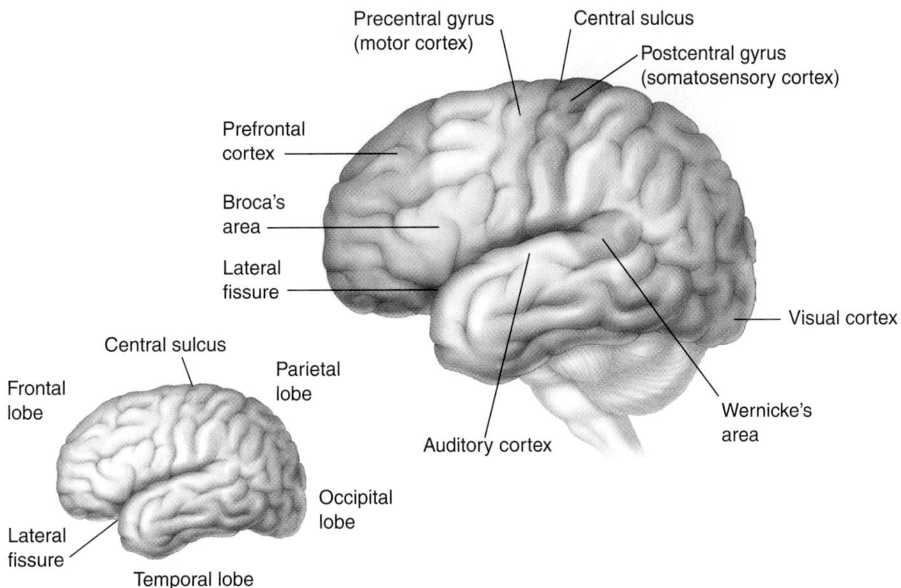

The brain develops in response to experiences that are unique to each individual, such as playing with specific toys or participating in social interactions.
©iStockphoto.com/kate_sept2004

understaffed orphanages in developing countries, show deficits in brain volume as well as cognitive and perceptual deficiencies that may persist into adolescence (Hodel et al., 2015; Nelson et al., 2016; Sheridan & McLaughlin, 2014). In this way, infancy is said to be a sensitive period for brain development, a period in which experience has a particularly powerful role (Hensch, 2018).

The powerful role that experience plays in brain development can be categorized into two types. First, the brain depends on experiencing certain basic events and stimuli at key points in time to develop normally (Bick & Nelson, 2017; Hensch, 2018); this is referred to as **experience-expectant brain development**. Experience-expectant brain development is demonstrated in sensory deprivation research with animals. If animals are blindfolded and prevented from using their visual system for the first several weeks after birth, they never acquire normal vision because the connections among the neurons that transmit sensory information from the eyes to the visual cortex fail to develop; instead, they decay (DiPietro, 2000). If only one eye is prevented from seeing, the animal will be able to see well with one eye but will not develop binocular vision, the ability to focus two eyes together on a single object. Similarly, human infants born with a congenital cataract in one eye (an opaque clouding that blocks light from reaching the retina) will lose the capacity to process visual stimuli in the affected eye if they do not receive treatment. Even with treatment, subtle differences in facial processing may remain (Maurer, 2017). Deprivation of sound has similar effects on the auditory cortex (Mowery, Kotak, & Sanes, 2016). Brain organization depends on experiencing certain ordinary events early in life, such as opportunities to hear language, see the world, touch objects, and explore the environment (Kolb, Mychasiuk, & Gibb, 2014; Maurer, 2017). All infants around the world need these basic experiences during specific times in development, known as sensitive periods, to develop normally, and it is difficult to repair errors that are the result of severe deprivation and neglect (Berardi et al., 2015; McLaughlin, Sheridan, & Nelson, 2017).

A second type of development, experience-dependent brain development, refers to the growth that occurs in response to learning experiences (Bick & Nelson, 2017). For example, experiences such as learning to stack blocks

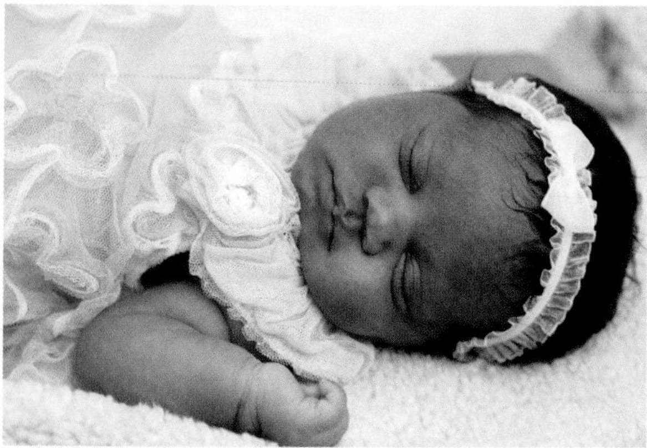

One hypothesis for infants' increased time in sleep is that it provides stimulation and promotes brain development.
©iStockphoto.com/Imagesbybarbara

or crawl on a slippery wood floor are unique to individual infants, and they influence what particular brain areas and functions are developed and reinforced. Experience-dependent development is the result of lifelong experiences that vary by individual based on contextual and cultural circumstances (Kolb, 2018; Kolb et al., 2014). Exposure to enriching experiences, such as interactive play with toy cars and other objects that move; hands-on play with blocks, balls, and cups; and stimulating face-to-face play can all enhance children's development (Kolb, 2018). For example, a longitudinal study that followed more than 350 infants from 5 to 24 months of age found that the quality of mother–infant interactions at 5 months predicted greater brain activity in the prefrontal cortex at 10 and 24 months of age, suggesting that parenting quality may contribute to brain development in infancy (Bernier, Calkins, & Bell, 2016). On the other hand, exposure to deprivation and trauma can have lasting negative effects on brain development (Harker, 2018).

Sleep and Brain Development

Whereas adults sleep approximately 8 hours each day, the typical neonate sleeps about 16 to 18 hours each day. Sleep declines steadily. Six-month-old infants sleep about 12 hours (Figueiredo, Dias, Pinto, & Field, 2016). Infant rats, rabbits, cats, and rhesus monkeys also sleep much longer than adults, suggesting that sleep serves a developmental function (Blumberg, Gall, & Todd, 2014). Sleep promotes physical growth and development (Tham, Schneider, & Broekman, 2017). In adults, sleep is thought to permit the body to repair itself, as indicated by increased cell production and the removal of metabolic wastes during sleep (Tononi & Cirelli, 2014). Sleep is also associated with increases in connections among neurons (Krueger, Frank, Wisor, & Roy, 2016).

In adults, sleep is associated with memory consolidation, "cementing" memories, and sleep deficits are associated deficits in attention, memory, and learning (Chambers, 2017; Doyon, Gabitov, Vahdat, Lungu, & Boutin, 2018; Spencer, Walker, & Stickgold, 2017). Rapid eye movement (REM) sleep, during which adults' eyes flutter and dreaming occurs, is particularly important for cognitive functioning (Lewis, 2017). Infants spend about half of their sleep time in REM sleep, decreasing to about 20% in adulthood. REM sleep is thought to provide infants with stimulation and promote brain development and cognitive growth (Friedrich, Wilhelm, Mölle, Born, & Friederici, 2017; Tham et al., 2017). Neonates with poor sleep patterns showed poor attention at 4 months and increased distractibility at 18 months of age (Geva, Yaron, & Kuint, 2016). Similar to findings with adults, one study found that sleep was associated with memory formation in 3- to 8-month-old infants (Friedrich et al., 2017). Sleep may have long-term effects on cognitive development. An examination of infants at 12 months of age and again at 3 to 4 years old showed that lower-quality sleep in infancy was associated with problems with attention and behavioral control in early childhood (Sadeh et al., 2015).

Sleeping serves a developmental function, yet young infants wake often (Mäkelä et al., 2018). The typical newborn wakes every 2 hours to eat, and babies continue to require nighttime feedings until they are 4 or 5 months old. Many continue to wake at night. Cultures differ in infant sleep practices. For example, parents in the United States typically look forward to the time when their infant will sleep through the night, viewing the newborn's unpredictable sleep pattern as something to fix. In contrast, many European parents view newborn sleep as part of normal development and do not intervene to shape newborn sleep cycles. Children in Pacific-Asian countries tend to sleep an hour less than those in North America, Europe, and Australia (Galland, Taylor, Elder, & Herbison, 2012; Mindell, Sadeh, Wiegand, How, & Goh, 2010). Parental behavior influences infants' sleep patterns. Infants are more likely to continue waking overnight when their parents play with them during nighttime feedings, as stimulation and attention may reinforce nighttime waking (Sadeh et al., 2015). Cultures also have different practices around sleeping arrangements for infants, toddlers, and older children—including co-sleeping and bedsharing (see the Lives in Context feature).

LIVES IN CONTEXT: CULTURAL CONTEXT

Co-sleeping

While sharing a bedroom can enhance the infant–parent bond and make nighttime feedings easier, infants are safest in their own bassinets, such this one, which is adapted to promote safe parent–infant contact.
Jennie Hart / Alamy Stock Photo

The practice of *co-sleeping*, which refers to the infant sharing a bed with the mother or with both parents, is common in many countries yet controversial in others. In Japan, China, Kenya, Bangladesh, and the Mayan peninsula of Mexico, co-sleeping in infancy and early childhood is the norm and is believed to enhance the child's sense of security and attachment to the mother (Huang, Wang, Zhang, & Liu, 2010; Morelli, Rogoff, Oppenheim, & Goldsmith, 1992; Super & Harkness, 1982). In Latin America and Asia, infants are not usually expected to go to bed and sleep alone at a regular time each night. Instead, they are held until they fall asleep and then are placed in the parental bed (Lozoff, Wolf, & Davis, 1984). In contrast, in many industrialized countries, such as the United States and the United Kingdom, newborns are placed to sleep in their own bassinets, whether in their parents' room or in a separate nursery. In these countries, learning to sleep by oneself is viewed as fostering independence and the ability to self-regulate (Ball, Hooker, & Kelly, 1999; McKenna & Volpe, 2007). Parents' decisions of whether to co-sleep are influenced by their own values and beliefs, which are often shaped by the context in which they live.

Proponents of co-sleeping argue that it best meets the developmental needs of human newborns and aids in forming the attachment bond (McKenna, 2001). Infants who sleep with their mothers synchronize their sleep patterns with hers, permitting more awakenings for breastfeeding, yet lengthening the total time that infants sleep (Gettler & McKenna, 2011). Both mothers and babies benefit from skin-to-skin contact, as it enhances breast milk production, stabilizes infants' heart rate, increases the prevalence and duration of breastfeeding, and is associated with more positive mother–infant interactions (McKenna & Volpe, 2007; Taylor, Donovan, & Leavitt, 2008). Fathers report that they find co-sleeping rewarding rather than an intrusion on the marital bed (Ball, Hooker, & Kelly, 2000).

Pediatricians in Western nations tend to advise separate sleeping arrangements for parents and infants. Opponents of co-sleeping point to an increased risk of accidental suffocation and an increased risk of SIDS (sudden infant death syndrome), especially among mothers who smoke (Mitchell, 2009). The American Academy of Pediatrics and the U.K. Department of Health have declared sharing a bed with an infant to be an unsafe practice; instead, they advise having infants sleep in a crib in the parents' room (Task Force on Sudden Infant Death Syndrome, 2016; U.K. Department of Health, 2005). Despite these warnings, co-sleeping has become more common among Western families. Some believe that co-sleeping can be safe if appropriate precautions are taken, such as using light bed coverings and a firm mattress and avoiding comforters and pillows (McKenna, 2001). The American Academy of Pediatrics advises that bedsharing should be abandoned in favor of room sharing, to provide the developmental advantages of co-sleeping and minimize the dangers (Task Force on Sudden Infant Death Syndrome, 2016).

What Do You Think?

1. In your view, what are the advantages and disadvantages of co-sleeping?
2. In what ways might parent–child sleeping arrangements influence emotional development?
3. How might safety concerns be addressed?

Brain development is a multifaceted process that is not a result of maturational or environmental input alone. Brains do not develop normally in the absence of a basic genetic code or in the absence of essential environmental input. At all points in development, intrinsic and environmental factors interact to support the increasingly complex and elaborate structures and functions of the brain.

THINKING IN CONTEXT 4.2

1. Consider the role of contextual factors in brain development. What role does experience play in brain development and how might the different contexts in which children live influence their development?
2. Marta hopes to promote her baby's brain development. Explain the processes that influence infants' brain development and provide advice to help Marta promote her infant's development.

FIGURE 4.10

Habituation

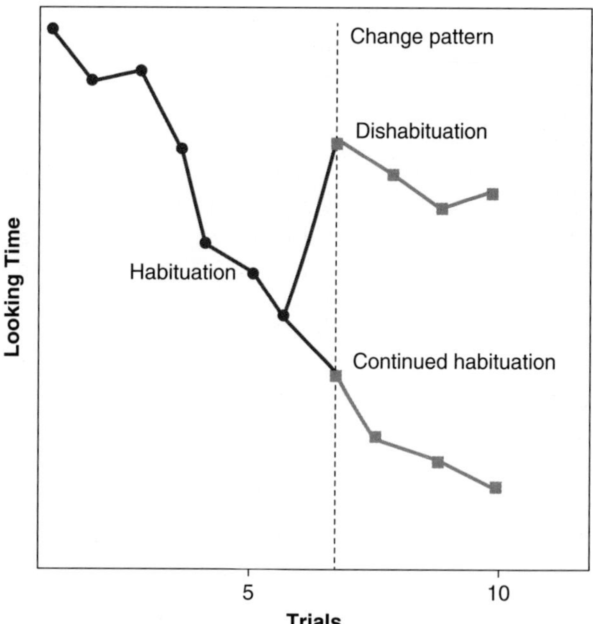

Looking time declines with each trial as the infant habituates to the pattern. Dishabituation, renewed interest, signifies that the infant detects a change in stimulus pattern.

Source: Visual development by Marcela Salamanca and Donald Kline, University of Calgary (http://psych.ucalgary.ca/PACE/VA-Lab/). Reprinted by permission of the authors.

EARLY LEARNING CAPACITIES

Can newborns learn? If we define learning as changing behavior in response to experience, certainly: Animals and even insects learn. Yet infants were once believed to be born incapable of sensing and understanding the physical world around them. Most new parents will quickly tell you that this is far from the truth. At birth, and even before, neonates can perceive their physical world and have powerful capacities for learning about it.

Habituation

Less than 1 day old, cradled next to his mother in the hospital maternity center, Tommy is already displaying the earliest form of learning. He no longer cries each time he hears the loud beep made by the machine that reads his mother's blood pressure. This type of learning is called **habituation**; it occurs when repeated exposure to a stimulus results in the gradual decline in the intensity, frequency, or duration of a response (see Figure 4.10). All animals and humans are programmed to learn. Even before birth, humans demonstrate habituation, as early as 22 to 24 weeks' gestation (Hepper, 2015). For example, 27- to 36-week-old fetuses demonstrate habituation to vibration as well as auditory stimuli, such as the sound of a tone. Initially, the fetus moves in response to the vibration, suggesting interest in a novel stimulus. After repeated stimulation, the fetus no longer responds to the stimulus, indicating that it has habituated to it (McCorry & Hepper, 2007; Muenssinger et al., 2013). Not only can the fetus habituate to stimuli but it can recall a stimulus for at least 24 hours (van Heteren, Boekkooi, Jongsma, & Nijhuis, 2000).

Habituation improves with development. For example, the performance of fetuses on habituation tasks improves with gestational age (James, 2010). After birth, habituation is often measured by changes in an infant's heart rate and in attention or looking at a stimulus (Domsch, Thomas, & Lohaus, 2010). Younger infants require more time to habituate than older infants (Kavšek & Bornstein, 2010). Five- to 12-month-old babies habituate quickly—even after just a few seconds of sustained attention—and in some cases, they can recall the stimulus for weeks, such as recalling faces that they have encountered for brief periods of time (Richards, 1997).

Neural development, specifically development of the prefrontal cortex, is thought to underlie age-related gains in habituation skill (Nakano, Watanabe, Homae, & Taga, 2009). As the brain matures, infants process information more quickly and learn more about stimuli in fewer exposures. Younger infants and those with low birthweight require more time to habituate than do older and more fully developed infants (Kavšek & Bornstein, 2010; Krafchuk, Tronick, & Clifton, 1983; Rovee-Collier, 1987). Fetuses with more mature nervous systems require fewer trials to habituate than do those with less well-developed nervous systems, even at the same gestational age (Morokuma et al., 2004). Fetal habituation predicts measures of information processing ability at 6 months of age (Gaultney & Gingras, 2005).

There are also individual differences in habituation among healthy, developmentally normal infants. Some habituate quickly and recall what they have learned for a long time. Other infants require many more exposures to habituate and quickly forget what they have learned. The speed at which infants habituate is associated with cognitive development when they grow older. Infants who habituate quickly during the first 6 to 8 months of life tend to show more advanced capacities to learn and use language during the second year of life (Tamis-LeMonda & Bornstein, 1989). Rapid habituation is also associated with higher scores on intelligence tests in childhood (Kavšek, 2004). The problem-solving skills measured by intelligence tests tap information processing skills such as attention, processing speed, and memory—all of which influence the rate of habituation (McCall, 1994).

Innate learning capacities permit young infants to adapt quickly to the world, a skill essential for survival. Researchers use these capacities to study infant perception and cognition (Aslin, 2014). For example, to examine whether an infant can discriminate between two stimuli, a researcher presents one until the infant habituates to it. Then a second stimulus is presented. If dishabituation, or the recovery of attention, occurs, it indicates that the infant detects that the second stimulus is different from the first. If the infant does not react to the new stimulus by showing dishabituation, it is assumed that the infant does not perceive the difference between the two stimuli. The habituation method is very useful in studying infant perception and cognition and underlies many of the findings discussed later in this chapter.

Classical Conditioning

In addition to their capacity to learn by habituation, infants are born with a second powerful tool for learning. They can learn through association. Classical conditioning entails making an association between a neutral stimulus and an unconditioned stimulus that triggers an innate reaction. Eventually, the neutral stimulus (now conditioned stimulus) produces the same response as the unconditioned stimulus.

Newborns demonstrate classical conditioning. For example, when stroking the forehead was paired with tasting sugar water, 2-hour-old infants were conditioned to suck in response to having their heads stroked (Blass, Ganchrow, & Steiner, 1984). Let's look at this example more closely. Sugar water is an unconditioned stimulus, as it naturally evokes the unconditioned response of sucking in infants. Touching or stroking the forehead yielded no response from the 2-hour-old infants; it was a neutral stimulus. When the researcher paired the neutral stimulus (stroke) with the unconditioned stimulus (sugar water), infants soon showed the conditioned response. That is, they associated the stroking with sugar water and thereby responded to the stroke with sucking movements.

Similarly, Lipsitt and Kaye (1964) paired a tone with the presentation of a nipple to 2- and 3-day-old infants. Soon, the infants began to make sucking movements at the sound of the tone. Sleeping neonates can be conditioned to respond to a puff of air to the eye (Tarullo et al., 2016). Even premature infants can demonstrate associative learning, although at slower rates than full-term infants (Herbert, Eckerman, Goldstein, & Stanton, 2004). Research with chimpanzee fetuses has shown that they display classical conditioning before birth (Kawai, 2010). It is likely that the human fetus can as well. Although classical conditioning is innate, neurological damage can hinder infants' abilities to learn by association. Infants with fetal alcohol syndrome (FAS) require much more time than other infants to associate eye blinking with external stimuli, such as sounds (Cheng et al., 2016).

Newborns tend to require repeated exposures to conditioning stimuli because they process information slowly (Little, Lipsitt, & Rovee-Collier, 1984). As infants grow older, classical conditioning occurs more quickly and to a broader range of stimuli. For example, in a classic study, Watson and Raynor (1920) paired a white rat with a loud banging noise to evoke fear in an 11-month-old boy known as Little Albert. Repeated pairings of the white rat with the loud noise made Albert cry even when the rat was presented without the noise. In other words, Little Albert was conditioned to associate the neutral stimulus with the conditioned stimulus. Albert demonstrated fear in response to seeing the rat, indicating that emotional responses can be classically conditioned. Our capacities to learn through classical conditioning are evident at birth—and persist throughout life.

Operant Conditioning

At birth, babies can learn to engage in behaviors based on their consequences, known as operant conditioning. Behaviors increase when they are followed by reinforcement and decrease when they are followed by punishment. For example, newborns will change their rate of sucking on a pacifier, increasing or decreasing the rate of sucking, to hear a tape recording of their mother's voice, a reinforcer (Moon, Cooper, & Fifer, 1993). Reinforcers are experienced as pleasurable. Infants (and people of all ages) change their behavior to experience reinforcement, in this example, changing the rate of sucking on a pacifier to hear the mother's voice. Other research shows that newborns will change their rate of sucking to see visual designs or hear human voices that they find pleasing (Floccia, Christophe, & Bertoncini, 1997). Premature infants and even third-trimester fetuses can be operantly conditioned (Thoman & Ingersoll, 1993). For example, a 35-week-old fetus will change its rate of kicking in response to hearing the father talk against the mother's abdomen (Dziewolska & Cautilli, 2006).

As infants develop, they process information more quickly and require fewer trials pairing behavior and consequence to demonstrate operant conditioning. It requires about 200 trials for 2-day-old infants to learn to turn their heads in response to a nippleful of milk, but 3-month-old infants require about 40 trials, and 5-month-olds require less than 30 trials (Papousek, 1967). Infants' early capacities for operant conditioning imply that they are active and responsive to their environments and adapt their behavior from birth.

FIGURE 4.11

Neonate Imitation

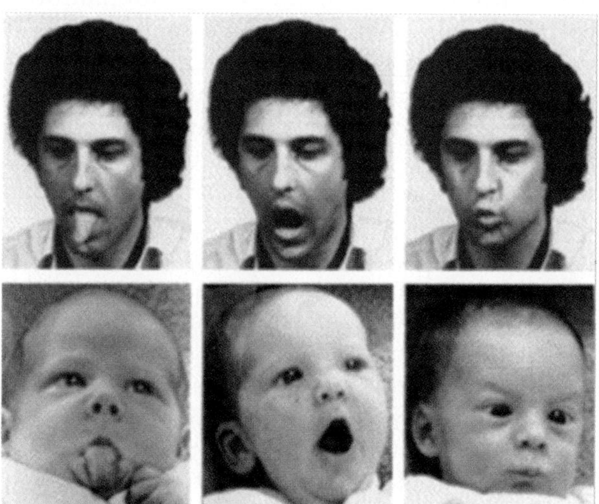

In this classic experiment, Meltzoff and Moore demonstrated that neonates imitated the adults' facial expression more often than chance, suggesting that they are capable of facial imitation—a groundbreaking finding.

Source: Meltzoff and Moore (1977). Reprinted with permission of AAAS.

Imitation

Toddler Tula puts a bowl on her head and pats it just as she watched her older sister do yesterday. Imitation is an important way in which children and adults learn. Can newborns imitate others? Believe it or not, some research suggests that newborns have a primitive ability to learn through imitation. In a classic study (see Figure 4.11), 2-day-old infants mimicked adult facial expressions, including sticking out the tongue, opening and closing the mouth, and sticking out the lower lip (Meltzoff & Moore, 1977). The prevalence and function of neonate imitation is debated (Suddendorf, Oostenbroek, Nielsen, & Slaughter, 2013). Some studies have failed to replicate this ability (Oostenbroek et al., 2016) and have suggested that tongue protruding simply reflects a general spontaneous newborn behavior (Keven & Akins, 2017), that it reflects arousal (Vincini, Jhang, Buder, & Gallagher, 2017), and that neonate imitation is not developmentally similar to later social imitation (Suddendorf et al., 2013). Others have confirmed that newborns from several ethnic groups and cultures display early capacities for imitation (Meltzoff & Kuhl, 1994; Nadel & Butterworth, 1999). In one study, newborns made corresponding mouth movements to both vowel and consonant vocal models; when the adult model made an *a* sound, newborns opened their mouths, and when the model made an *m* sound, newborns clutched their mouths (Chen, Striano, & Rakoczy, 2004). Studies that require infants to imitate several behaviors in response to different stimuli suggest that neonate imitation is not simply an arousal response (Nagy, Pilling, Orvos, & Molnar, 2013).

Newborns mimic facial expressions, but they are simply carrying out an innate program thought to be controlled by the mirror neuron system, located in the premotor cortex (Binder et al., 2017). The mirror neuron system, an inborn capacity to make associations and respond to the actions of others by mirroring their actions in our own neural circuits, is apparent in both newborn humans and monkeys (Cook, Bird, Catmur, Press, & Heyes, 2014; Olsen, 2006; Shaw & Czekóová, 2013). The ability to copy others' actions likely serves an evolutionarily adaptive purpose in humans, perhaps to aid the development of social communication (Tramacere, Pievani, & Ferrari, 2017). Newborns do not understand imitation; rather, the action of mirror neurons naturally syncs their body movements with the model. The regulatory mechanisms to inhibit imitative responding develop during infancy (Rizzolatti, Sinigaglia, & Anderson, 2008).

In summary, infants enter the world equipped with several basic learning capacities that permit them to learn even before birth. Newborns display classical and operant conditioning, imitation, and habituation, illustrating that they are wired to attend to their environment. Not only do infants display early competencies that permit them to learn quickly but they are also surprisingly adept at sensing and perceiving stimuli around them.

THINKING IN CONTEXT 4.3

Consider the developmental issue, nature and nurture, discussed in Chapter 1. From your perspective, do infants' learning abilities reflect nature, inborn capacities, or nurture, capacities influenced by experience?

SENSATION AND PERCEPTION DURING INFANCY AND TODDLERHOOD

Meeting the pediatrician for the first time in her young life, newborn Kerry stared intently at the object the doctor held about 6 inches from her face. "I think she sees it!" said her surprised mother. "She most certainly does," said the doctor. "Even as a newborn, your Kerry can sense the world better than you realize." Newborns can see, hear, smell, taste, and respond to touch, but it is unclear how they perceive sensory stimuli.

Developmental researchers draw a distinction between sensation and perception. **Sensation** occurs when our senses detect a stimulus. Our sense organs—the eyes, ears, tongue, nostrils, and skin—convert visual, auditory, taste, olfactory (smell), and tactile (touch) stimuli into electrical impulses that travel on sensory nerves to the brain where they are processed. **Perception** refers to the sense our brain makes of the stimulus and our awareness of it. The newborn is equipped with a full range of senses, ready to experience the world. They can both detect and perceive stimuli, but many of their abilities are immature relative to those of adults. Yet infants' sensory abilities develop rapidly, achieving adult levels within the first year of life (Johnson & Hannon, 2015).

Methods for Studying Infant Perception

How do researchers study infant perception? The simplest method is through *preferential looking tasks*, experiments designed to determine whether infants prefer to look at one stimulus or another. For example, consider an array of black and white stripes. As shown in Figure 4.12, an array with more stripes (and therefore, many more narrow stripes) tends to appear gray rather than black and white because the pattern becomes more difficult to see as the stripes become more narrow. Researchers determine infants' **visual acuity**, sharpness of vision or the ability to see, by comparing infants' responses to stimuli with different frequencies of stripes because infants who are unable to detect the stripes lose interest in the stimulus and look away from it.

FIGURE 4.12

Visual Acuity

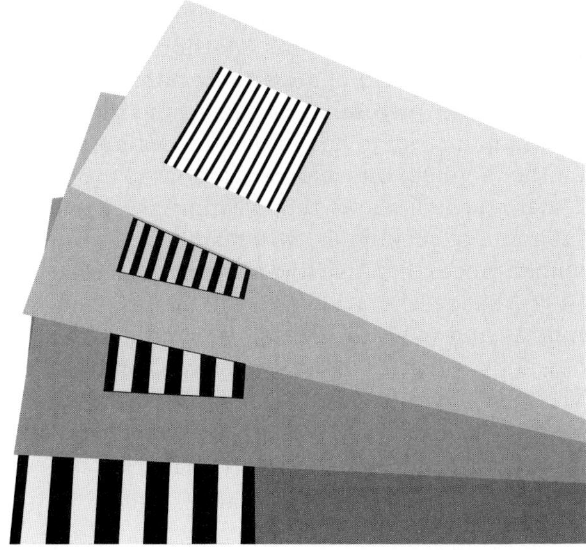

Researchers and pediatricians use stimuli such as the Teller Acuity Cards illustrated here to determine what infants can see. Young infants attend to stimuli with wider lines and stop attending as the lines become smaller.

Source: Leat, Yadev, and Irving (2009).

Another method of studying infant perception relies on infants' capacity for habituation, a gradual decline in the intensity, frequency, or duration of a response to an unchanging stimulus. For example, to examine whether an infant can discriminate between two stimuli, a researcher presents one until the infant habituates to it. Then a second stimulus is presented. If dishabituation, or the recovery of attention, occurs, it indicates that the infant detects that the second stimulus is different from the first. If the infant does not react to the new stimulus by showing dishabituation, it is assumed that the infant does not perceive the difference between the two stimuli. The habituation method is very useful in studying infant perception and cognition and underlies many of the findings discussed in this chapter.

Operant conditioning is the basis for a third method researchers use to study perception in infants. Recall from Chapter 1 that operant conditioning entails learning behaviors based on their consequences, whether they are followed by reinforcement or punishment. Behaviors increase when they are followed by reinforcement and decrease when they are followed by punishment. Research employing this method has shown that newborns will change their rate of sucking on a pacifier, increasing or decreasing the rate of sucking, in order to hear a tape recording of their mother's voice, a reinforcer (Moon et al., 1993). Other research shows that newborns will change their rate of sucking to see visual designs or hear human voices that they find pleasing (Floccia et al., 1997). Researchers have found that premature infants and even third-trimester fetuses can be operantly conditioned (Dziewolska & Cautilli, 2006; Thoman & Ingersoll, 1993). For example, a 35-week-old fetus will change its rate of kicking in response to hearing the father talk against the mother's abdomen, suggesting that hearing begins in the womb (Dziewolska & Cautilli, 2006).

Vision

It is impossible to know whether the fetus has a sense of vision, but the fetus responds to bright light directed at the mother's abdomen as early as 28 weeks' gestation (Johnson & Hannon, 2015). At birth, vision is the least developed sense, but it improves rapidly. Newborn visual acuity is approximately 20/400 (Farroni & Menon, 2008). Preferential looking studies show that infants reach adult levels of visual acuity between 6 months and 1 year of age (Mercuri, Baranello, Romeo, Cesarini, & Ricci, 2007). Improvement in vision is due to the increasing maturation of the structures of the eye and the visual cortex, the part of the brain that processes visual stimuli.

Face Perception

Newborns are born with preferences for particular visual stimuli. Newborns prefer to look at patterns, such as a few large squares, rather than a plain stimulus such as a black or white oval shape (Fantz, 1961). Newborns also prefer to look at faces, and the preference for faces increases with age (Frank, Vul, & Johnson, 2009). Face processing is influenced by experience with faces (Quinn, Lee, & Pascalis, 2018). Infants generally tend to see more female than male faces and more own- than other-race faces (Sugden, Mohamed-Ali, & Moulson, 2014). For example, between birth and 3 months, infants begin to prefer to look at and can more easily see female faces as compared with male faces, when their caregivers are female, but do not show similar preferences when their caregivers are male (Bayet et al., 2015; Rennels & Kayl, 2017).

Infants show similar preferences and abilities to discriminate same-race faces over other-race faces. That is, between approximately 3 and 9 months of age, infants tend to prefer and are better able to distinguish faces of frequently experienced groups, typically faces of members of their own race. However, differentiation of faces from within unfamiliar groups, such as other races, becomes more difficult with age (Markant & Scott, 2018). After about 9 months, infants show difficulty discriminating among unfamiliar faces, such as other-race faces. This decline in sensitivity to discriminate faces within unfamiliar groups is called **perceptual narrowing** (Scott, Pascalis, & Nelson, 2007). Experience influences perceptual narrowing. Specifically, babies who are extensively exposed to other-race faces (e.g., through adoption, training, or living in racially diverse communities) show less perceptual narrowing (Ellis, Xiao, Lee, & Oakes, 2017). Some researchers speculate that early perceptual differences in infancy may be associated with the emergence of implicit racial bias in childhood, but more research is needed to understand the social implications of same- and other-race face recognition (K. Lee, Quinn, & Pascalis, 2017; Quinn, Lee, & Pascalis, 2019).

Object Exploration

How infants explore visual stimuli changes with age (Colombo, Brez, & Curtindale, 2015). Until about 1 month of age, infants tend to scan along the outer perimeter of stimuli. For example, when presented with a face, the infant's gaze will scan along the hairline and not move to the eyes and mouth. This is known as the **externality effect** because infants scan along the outer contours of complex visual stimuli. By 6 to 7 weeks of age, infants study the eyes and mouth, which hold more information than the hairline, as shown in Figure 4.13 (Hunnius & Geuze, 2004). Similarly, the ability to follow an object's movement with the eyes, known as visual tracking, is very limited at birth but improves quickly. By 2 months of age, infants can follow a slow-moving object smoothly, and by 3 to 5 months, their eyes can dart ahead to keep pace with a fast-moving object (Agyei, van der Weel, & van der Meer, 2016; Richards & Holley, 1999). The parts of the brain that process motion in adults are operative in infants by 7 months of age (Weaver, Crespi, Tosetti, & Morrone, 2015).

Color Vision

Like other aspects of vision, color vision improves with age. Newborns see color, but they have trouble distinguishing among colors. That is, although they can see both red and green, they do not perceive

FIGURE 4.13

Externality Effect and Face Perception

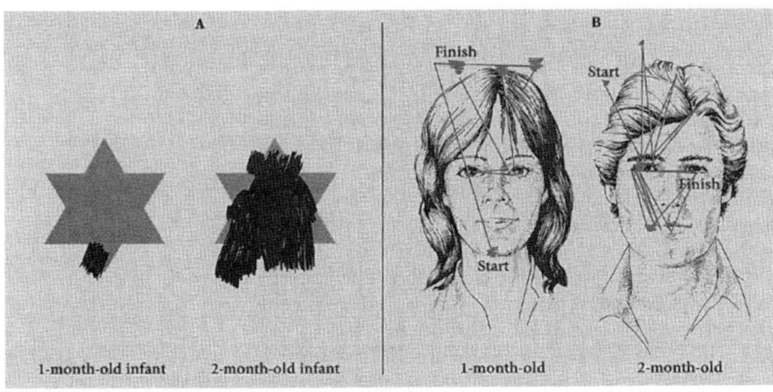

The externality effect refers to a particular pattern of infant visual processing. When presented with a complex stimulus, such as a face, infants under 2 months of age tend to scan along the outer contours, such as along the hairline. Older infants scan the internal features of complex images and faces, thereby processing the entire stimulus.

Source: Shaffer (2002, p. 190); adapted from Salapatek (1975).

red as different from green. Early visual experience with color is necessary for normal color perception to develop (Colombo et al., 2015; Sugita, 2004). Habituation studies show that by 1 month of age, infants can distinguish among red, green, and white (Teller, 1997). By 2 to 3 months of age, infants are as accurate as adults in discriminating the basic colors of red, yellow, and blue (Matlin & Foley, 1997; Teller, 1998). By 3 to 4 months of age, infants can distinguish many more colors as well as distinctions among closely related colors (Bornstein & Lamb, 1992; Haith, 1993). Seven-month-old infants detect color categories similar to those of adults; they can group slightly different shades (e.g., various shades of blue) into the same basic color categories as adults do (Clifford, Franklin, Davies, & Holmes, 2009).

Depth Perception

Depth perception is the ability to perceive the distance of objects from each other and from ourselves. Depth perception is what permits infants to successfully reach for objects and, later, to crawl without bumping into furniture. By observing that newborns prefer to look at three-dimensional objects rather than two-dimensional figures, researchers have found that infants can perceive depth at birth (Slater, Rose, & Morison, 1984). Three- to 4-week-old infants blink their eyes when an object is moved toward their face as if to hit them, suggesting that they are sensitive to depth cues (Kayed, Farstad, & van der Meer, 2008; Náñez & Yonas, 1994). Infants learn about depth by observing and experiencing motion.

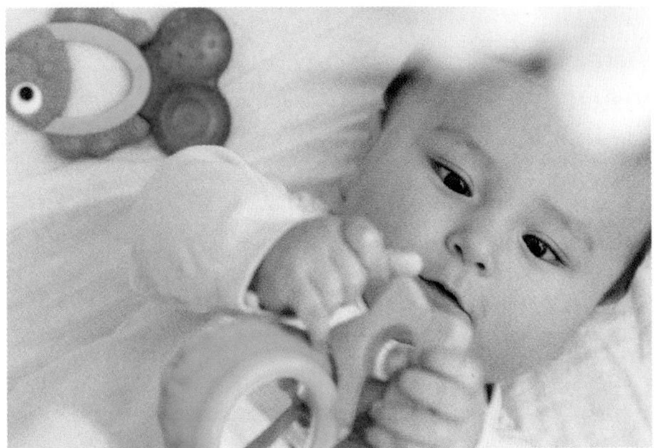

Infants see color at birth, and color discrimination improves over the first few months of life.
©iStockphoto.com/alexey_ds

A classic series of studies using an apparatus called the *visual cliff* demonstrated that crawling influences how infants perceive depth. The visual cliff, as shown in Figure 4.14, is a Plexiglas-covered table bisected by a plank so that one side is shallow, with a checkerboard pattern right under the glass, and the other side is deep, with the checkerboard pattern a few feet below the glass (Gibson & Walk, 1960). In this classic study, crawling babies readily moved from the plank to the shallow side but not to the deep side, even if coaxed by their mothers, suggesting that they perceive the difference in depth (Walk, 1968). The more crawling experience infants have, the more likely they are to refuse to cross the deep side of the visual cliff (Bertenthal, Campos, & Barrett, 1984).

Does this mean that babies cannot distinguish the shallow and deep sides of the visual cliff until they crawl? No, because even 3-month-old infants who are too young to crawl distinguish shallow from deep drops. When placed face down on the glass surface of the deep side of the visual cliff, 3-month-old infants became quieter and showed a decrease in heart rate compared with when they were placed on the shallow side of the cliff (Dahl et al., 2013). The young infants can distinguish the difference between shallow and deep drops but do not yet associate fear with deep drops.

As infants gain experience crawling, their perception of depth changes. Newly walking infants avoid the cliff's deep side even more consistently than do crawling infants (Dahl et al., 2013; Witherington, Campos, Anderson, Lejeune, & Seah, 2005). A new perspective on the visual cliff studies argues that infants avoid the deep side of the cliff not out of fear but simply because they perceive that they are unable to successfully navigate the drop; fear might be conditioned through later experiences, but infants are not naturally fearful of heights (Adolph, Kretch, & LoBue, 2014).

FIGURE 4.14

Visual Cliff

Three-month-old infants show a change in heart rate when placed face down on the glass surface of the deep side of the visual cliff, suggesting that they perceive depth, but do not fear it. Crawling babies, however, move to the shallow side of the visual cliff and refuse to cross the deep side of the visual cliff.

Source: Levine and Munsch (2010).

Hearing

The capacity to hear develops in the womb; in fact, hearing is the most well-developed sense at birth. Newborns are able to hear about as well as adults (Northern & Downs, 2014). Shortly after birth, neonates can discriminate among sounds, such as tones (Hernandez-Pavon, Sosa, Lutter, Maier, & Wakai, 2008). By 3 days of age, infants will turn their head and eyes in the general direction of a sound, and this ability to localize sound improves over the first 6 months (Clifton, Rochat, Robin, & Berthier, 1994; Litovsky & Ashmead, 1997).

As we will discuss in Chapter 5, the process of learning language begins at birth, through listening. Newborns are attentive to voices and can detect their mothers' voices. Newborns only 1 day old prefer to hear speech sounds over similar-sounding nonspeech sounds (May, Gervain, Carreiras, & Werker, 2018). Newborns can perceive and discriminate nearly all sounds in human languages, but from birth, they prefer to hear their native language (Kisilevsky, 2016). Brain activity in the temporal and left frontal cortex in response to auditory stimuli indicates that newborns can discriminate speech patterns, such as differences in cadence among languages, suggesting an early developing neurological specialization for language (Gervain, Macagno, Cogoi, Peña, & Mehler, 2008; Gervain & Mehler, 2010).

Touch

Compared with vision and hearing, we know much less about the sense of touch in infants. In early infancy, touch, especially with the mouth, is a critical means of learning about the world (Piaget, 1936/1952). The mouth is the first part of the body to show sensitivity to touch prenatally and remains one of the most sensitive areas to touch after birth.

Touch, specifically a caregiver's massage, can reduce stress responses in preterm and full-term neonates and is associated with weight gain in newborns (Álvarez et al., 2017). Skin-to-skin contact with a caregiver, as in kangaroo care (see Chapter 3), has an analgesic effect, reducing infants' pain response to being stuck with a needle for vaccination (Pandita et al., 2018). Although it was once believed that newborns were too immature to feel pain, we now know that the capacity to feel pain develops even before birth. In one study, fetuses as early as 24 weeks of age observed with sophisticated ultrasound technology showed facial expressions suggesting distress or pain in response to a needle prick (Reissland, Francis, & Mason, 2013). The neonate's capacity to feel pain has influenced debates about infant circumcision, as discussed in the Lives in Context feature.

Smell and Taste

Smell and taste receptors are functional in the fetus and preferences are well developed at birth (Bloomfield, Alexander, Muelbert, & Beker, 2017). Just hours after birth, newborns display facial expressions signifying disgust in response to odors of ammonia, fish, and other scents that adults find offensive (Steiner, 1979). Within the first days of life, newborns detect and recognize their mother's odor (Macfarlane, 1975; Marin, Rapisardi, & Tani, 2015). Infants are calmed by their mother's scent. Newborns who smelled their mother's odor displayed less agitation during a heel-stick test and cried less afterward than infants presented with unfamiliar odors (Rattaz, Goubet, & Bullinger, 2005). Familiar scents are reinforcing and can reduce stress responses in infants (Goubet, Strasbaugh, & Chesney, 2007; Nishitani et al., 2009; Schaal, 2017). For example, the scent of breast milk can slow heart rate in premature neonates who are under stress (Neshat et al., 2016).

Infants show innate preferences for some tastes (E. S. Ross, 2017). For example, both bottle-fed and breastfed newborns prefer human milk—even milk from strangers—to formula (Marlier & Schaal, 2005). Newborns prefer sugar to other substances, and a small dose of sugar can serve as an anesthetic, distracting newborns from pain (Gradin, Eriksson, Schollin, Holmqvist, & Holstein, 2002). Experience

LIVES IN CONTEXT: FAMILY AND PEER CONTEXT

Neonatal Circumcision

Neonatal circumcision, removal of the foreskin of the penis, is the oldest known planned surgery (Alanis & Lucidi, 2004). Although it is uncommon throughout much of the world, about three-quarters of males in the United States are circumcised (Morris et al., 2016). As shown in Figure 4.15, there are regional differences, with nearly twice as many infant circumcisions in the Midwest as in the West (Owings, Uddin, & Williams, 2013). In recent years, circumcision has come under increasing scrutiny within the United States as some charge that it places the newborn under great distress and confers few medical benefits.

For decades, many scientists and physicians believed that newborns did not feel pain, leading many to perform circumcision without pain management. We now know that even the fetus feels pain (Benatar & Benatar, 2003). Newborns show many indicators of distress during circumcision, such as a high-pitched wail, flailing, grimacing, and dramatic rises in heart rate, blood pressure, palm sweating, pupil dilation, muscle tension, and cortisol levels (Paix & Peterson, 2012). Analgesia (pain relief in which the newborn remains conscious) is safe and effective in reducing the pain associated with circumcision (AAP Task Force on Circumcision, 2012). Treatment as simple as administering a sugar solution to infants aids in pain management (Matsuda, 2017).

The medical benefits of circumcision are debated (Beal, 2017; Freedman, 2016). Benefits include reduced risk of having urinary tract infections, developing penile cancer, and acquiring HIV (AAP Task Force on Circumcision, 2012; American Medical Association, 1999; Morris et al., 2017). Some argue that these are relatively rare conditions and that the evidence regarding HIV transmission comes from research with adult males in Africa. Whether the same effects apply to infants in Western industrialized countries is uncertain (Alanis & Lucidi, 2004). Moreover, behavior is a more important factor in preventing HIV infection than is circumcision.

In 1999, both the American Medical Association and the American Academy of Pediatrics (AAP) joined medical associations in Canada, Europe, and Australia in concluding that the benefits of circumcision are not large enough to recommend routine circumcision; instead, it is a parental decision. However, in 2012, the AAP modified its view to note that although it is a parental decision, the benefits of circumcision justify providing access to the procedure (by insurance companies) to families who choose it. Critical physicians and representatives of medical associations in Canada, Australia, and several European countries counter that the revised recommendation was not based on medical evidence but instead reflected cultural bias on the part of the AAP to support social practices common in the United States (Frisch et al., 2013).

FIGURE 4.15

Rates of Circumcision Performed, 1979–2010

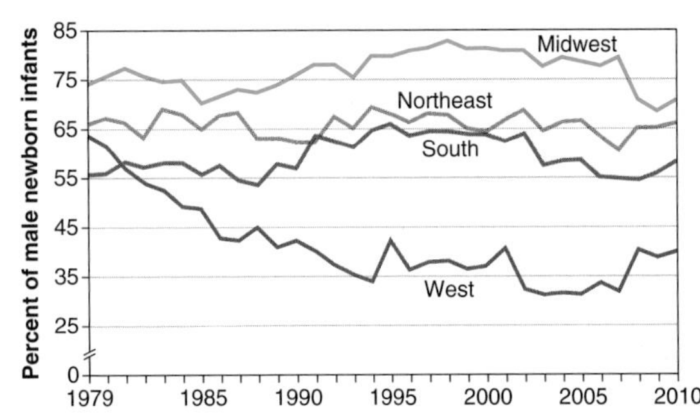

Source: Owings et al. (2013).
Notes: Rates represent circumcisions performed during the birth hospitalization. Circumcision is identified by International Classification of Diseases, Ninth Revision, Clinical Modification (ICD-9-CM) procedure code 64.0.

Regardless, formal recommendations by medical associations may ultimately have little sway on parents (Freedman, 2016). Cultural traditions and religious factors influence parental decisions about circumcision. For example, in Jewish cultures, a boy is circumcised on the eighth day after birth in a ritual celebration known as a bris, in which the boy is welcomed as a member of the community. Parents' decisions are also influenced by social factors such as whether the father is circumcised and the desire that the child resemble his peers (Bo & Goldman, 2008). The decision is complicated, as parents weigh health risks and benefits with contextual factors such as religious and cultural beliefs, as well as personal desires, to determine what is best for their child.

What Do You Think?

1. In your view, what are the most important considerations in making a decision about whether to circumcise a newborn boy?
2. Imagine that you had a newborn boy. Would you choose to circumcise your son? Why or why not? ●

can modify taste preferences, beginning before birth: Fetuses are exposed to flavors in amniotic fluid that influence their preferences after birth (Beauchamp & Mennella, 2011; Forestell, 2016). In one study, the type of formula fed to infants influenced their taste preferences at 4 to 5 years of age (Mennella & Beauchamp, 2002). Infants who were fed milk-based formulas and protein-based formulas were more likely to prefer sour flavors at 4 to 5 years of age compared with infants who were fed soy-based formulas, who, in turn, were more likely to prefer bitter flavors.

Intermodal Perception

All stimuli we encounter involve more than one type of sensory information. For example, we see a dog but we also hear its bark. Not only are infants able to sense in multiple modalities, but they are able to coordinate their senses. **Intermodal perception** is the process of combining information from more than one sensory system (Johnson & Hannon, 2015). Sensitivity to intermodal relations among stimuli is critical to perceptual development and learning—and this sensitivity emerges early in life (Lewkowicz, Leo, & Simion, 2010). That is, infants expect vision, auditory, and tactile information to occur together (Sai, 2005). For example, newborns turn their heads and eyes in the direction of a sound source, suggesting that they intuitively recognize that auditory and visual information co-occur and provide information about spatial location (Newell, 2004).

Newborns show a preference for viewing their mother's face at 72, 12, and even just 4 hours after birth (Pascalis, Dechonen, Morton, Duruelle, & Grenet, 1995). It was once believed that infants' preference for their mother's face was innate. Are infants born knowing their mother's face? In one study, neonates were able to visually recognize their mother's face only if the face was paired with their mother's voice at least once after birth (Sai, 2005). Thus, intermodal perception is evident at birth because neonates can coordinate auditory (voice) and visual stimuli (face) to recognize their mother. They quickly remember the association and demonstrate a preference for her face even when it is not paired with her voice.

Infants integrate touch and vision very early in life. In one classic study, 1-month-old infants were presented with a smooth-surfaced pacifier or one with nubs on it. After exploring it with their mouths, the infants were shown two pacifiers—one smooth and one nubbed. The infants preferred to look at the shape they had sucked, suggesting that they could match tactile and visual stimuli (Meltzoff & Borton, 1979). In another example, 8- to 31-day-old infants fitted with special goggles were presented with a virtual object created by a shadow caster (Bower, Broughton, & Moore, 1970). The virtual object was an illusory object that could be seen by the infant but not touched. When the infant reached for the object, his or her hand felt nothing and flailed through the air. Infants exposed to the virtual object attempted to reach for it and became distressed when they did not feel it, suggesting that vision and touch are integrated and infants expect to feel objects that they can see and reach. Infants' ability to integrate sensory information has implications for learning as discussed in the Lives in Context feature.

Although young infants show impressive capacities to integrate visual and tactile information, these senses are not completely integrated at birth. Newborns can visually recognize an object previously held but not seen, but they cannot tactually recognize an object previously seen and not held, suggesting that intermodal relations among senses are not bidirectional at birth (Sann & Streri, 2007). Instead, development may be triggered by experience.

Infant–Context Interactions and Perceptual Development

We have seen that individuals are embedded in and interact dynamically with their context. James and Eleanor Gibson studied perceptual development from an ecological perspective, emphasizing that perception arises through interactions with the environment (Adolph & Kretch, 2015). Rather than collecting small pieces of sensory information and building a representation of the world, the Gibsons argued that the environment itself provides all the information needed and we perceive the environment directly, without constructing or manipulating sensory information.

Perception arises from action. Infants actively explore their environment with their eyes, moving their heads and, later, reaching their hands and, eventually, crawling. Perception provides the information infants need to traverse their environment. Through their exploration, infants perceive **affordances**—the nature, opportunities, and limits of objects (Gibson & Pick, 2000). The features of objects tell infants about their affordances and their possibilities for action, such as whether an object is squeezable, mouthable, catchable, or reachable. Infants explore their environment, not randomly but rather systematically searching to discover the properties of the things around

LIVES IN CONTEXT: BIOLOGICAL INFLUENCES

Intermodal Perception and Learning

Infants can integrate information from multiple senses from birth. Do they process sensory information in similar ways as older children and adults? We cannot be certain of how they make sense of intermodal sensations; however, fMRI research suggests that when very young infants (11–36 days old) are perceiving intermodal stimuli, they show activity in similar sensory regions of the brain as adults (Sours et al., 2017).

Infants are particularly responsive to touch (recall kangaroo care in Chapter 3). When given soft brush strokes to the skin of their leg, 11- to 36-day-old infants show similar neural responses as children and adults in areas linked with sensory, social, and affective processing (Tuulari et al., 2019). Infants' early sensitivity to touch and its links with socio-affective brain regions may play an important role in development.

Infants' sensitivity to touch and their ability to integrate auditory with tactile information may aid learning. In one set of studies, researchers examined the integration of tactile and auditory senses in 5- to 7-month-old infants (Lew-Williams, Ferguson, Abu-Zhaya, & Seidl, 2019). Specifically, infants listened to abstract patterns of tones while being touched on the knee or elbow. The infants were more likely to learn auditory sequences when the accompanying touches matched the auditory pattern. The findings suggest that social touch not only arouses infants but also influences how they process stimuli and learn.

Touch, particularly caregivers' touch, promotes learning. For example, in one study, 4-month-old infants habituated to a face while their forehead was either stroked with a soft paintbrush, stroked by a caregiver, or was not stroked. The infants who were stroked by caregivers looked significantly longer than their peers when shown a new face, suggesting that caregiver touch promoted learning (Della Longa, 2019). Social touch is rewarding and may play a special role in learning, as suggested by a recent study of 7- to 8-month-old infants (Tanaka, Kanakogi, Kawasaki, & Myowa, 2018). In this study, infants heard a short string of syllables while being tickled (multisensory) or while not being tickled. When infants were tickled while listing to the string of syllables, they displayed more brain activity in regions of the brain related to sensory processing and attention than when they listened without being tickled. In addition, the difference in brain activity was related to engagement. When infants showed more engagement, such as laughing, they showed more activity in the sensory and attention regions. Social touch may play a special role in facilitating sensory integration and learning.

What Do You Think?

How can parents apply these findings about intermodal integration to help infants learn? ●

them (Savelsbergh, van der Kamp, & van Wermeskerken, 2013). From this perspective, perception arises from action, just as it influences action (Gibson, 1979). Exploration and discovery of affordances depends on infants' capacities for action, which is influenced by their development, genetics, and motivation. For example, a large pot might offer a 10-year-old the possibility of cooking because the child has developed this capacity and can perceive this affordance of the pot. An 18-month-old infant may perceive very different affordances from the pot based on her capacities, such as a drum to bang or a bucket to fill. We naturally perceive affordances, such as knowing when a surface is safe for walking, by sensing information from the environment and coordinating it with our body sensations, such as our sense of balance (Kretch, Franchak, & Adolph, 2014). In this way, our perception of affordances, the opportunities for exploration, influences how we move and interact within our environments (Adolph & Kretch, 2015).

THINKING IN CONTEXT 4.4

1. Infants show both remarkable early competencies as well as deficiencies. Explain this statement.
2. From an evolutionary developmental perspective, how might infants' varied competencies be adaptive?
3. In which ways do infants' perceptual abilities influence their interactions with others in their context?

MOTOR DEVELOPMENT DURING INFANCY AND TODDLERHOOD

Newborns are equipped to respond to the stimulation they encounter in the world. The earliest ways in which infants adapt are through the use of their **reflexes**, involuntary and automatic responses to stimuli such as touch, light, and sound. Each reflex has its own developmental course (Payne & Isaacs, 2016). Some disappear early in life and others persist throughout life, as shown in Table 4.1. Infants show individual differences in how reflexes are displayed, specifically the intensity of the response. Preterm newborns, for example, show reflexes suggesting a more immature neurological system than full-term newborns (Barros, Mitsuhiro, Chalem, Laranjeira, & Guinsburg, 2011). The absence of reflexes, however, may signal neurological deficits.

Gross Motor Development

Gross motor development refers to the ability to control the large movements of the body, actions that help us move around in our environment. Like physical development, motor skills evolve in a predictable sequence. By the end of the first month of life, most infants can reach the first milestone, or achievement, in motor development: lifting their heads while lying on their stomachs. After lifting the head, infants progress through an orderly series of motor milestones: lifting the chest, reaching for objects, rolling over, and sitting up with support (see Table 4.2). Notice that these motor achievements reflect a cephalocaudal progression of motor control, proceeding from the head downward (see Chapter 3) (Payne & Isaacs, 2016). Researchers have long believed that all motor control proceeds from the head downward, but we now know that motor development is more variable. Instead, some infants may sit up before they roll over or not crawl at all before they walk (Adolph & Robinson, 2015). Similarly, infants reach for toys with their feet weeks before they use their hands, suggesting that early leg movements can be precisely controlled, the development of skilled reaching need not involve lengthy practice, and early motor behavior does not necessarily follow a strict cephalocaudal pattern (Galloway & Thelen, 2004).

Success at initiating forward motion, or crawling (6–10 months), is particularly significant for both infants and parents. Infants vary in how they crawl (Adolph & Robinson, 2015). Some use their arms to pull and legs to push, some use only their arms or only their legs, and others scoot on their bottoms. Once infants can pull themselves upright while holding on to a chair or table, they begin "cruising," moving by holding on to furniture to maintain their balance while stepping sideways. In many Western industrialized countries, most infants walk alone by about 1 year of age.

Once babies can walk, their entire visual field changes. Whereas crawling babies are more likely to look at the floor as they move, walking babies

TABLE 4.1

Newborn Reflexes

NAME OF REFLEX	RESPONSE	DEVELOPMENTAL COURSE
Palmar grasp	Curling fingers around objects that touch the palm	Birth to about 4 months, when it is replaced by voluntary grasp
Rooting	Turning head and tongue toward stimulus when cheek is touched	Disappears over first few weeks of life and is replaced by voluntary head movement
Sucking	Sucking on objects placed into the mouth	Birth to about 6 months
Moro	Giving a startle response in reaction to a loud noise or sudden change in the position of the head, resulting in throwing out the arms, arching the back, and bringing the arms together as if to grasp something	Birth to about 5 to 7 months
Babinski	Fanning and curling the toes in response to stroking the bottom of the foot	Birth to about 8 to 12 months
Stepping	Making stepping movements as if to walk when held upright with feet touching a flat surface	Birth to about 2 to 3 months
Swimming	Holding breath and moving arms and legs, as if to swim, when placed in water	Birth to about 4 to 6 months

TABLE 4.2

Motor Skills Timetable

AVERAGE AGE ACHIEVED	MOTOR SKILL
2 months	Lifts head Holds head steady when held upright
3 months	Pushes head and chest up with arms Rolls from stomach to back
4 months	Grasps cube
6 months	Sits without support
7 months	Rolls from back to stomach Attempts crawling Uses opposable thumb to grasp objects
8 months	Achieves sitting position alone Pulls to a stand
9 months	"Cruises" by holding on to furniture
10 months	Plays patty-cake
11 months	Stands alone
12 months	Walks alone
14 months	Builds tower of two cubes Scribbles
17 months	Walks up steps
18 months	Runs

gaze straight ahead at caregivers, walls, and toys (Kretch et al., 2014). Most beginning walkers, even through 19 months of age, tend to walk in short spurts, a few steps at a time, often ending in the middle of the floor (Cole, Robinson, & Adolph, 2016). Independent walking holds implications for cognitive, social, and emotional development, as it is associated not only with more attention and manipulation of objects but also with more sophisticated social interactions with caregivers, such as directing mothers' attention to particular objects and sharing. These behaviors, in turn, are associated with advanced language development relative to nonwalkers in both U.S. and Chinese infants (Ghassabian et al., 2016; He et al., 2015).

Fine Motor Development

Fine motor development refers to the ability to control small movements of the fingers such as reaching and grasping. Voluntary reaching plays an important role in cognitive development because it provides new opportunities for interacting with the world. Like other motor skills, reaching and grasping begin as gross activity and are refined with time. Newborns begin by engaging in *prereaching,* swinging their arms and extending them toward nearby objects (Ennouri & Bloch, 1996; von Hofsten & Rönnqvist, 1993). Newborns use both arms equally and cannot control their arms and hands, so they rarely succeed in making contact with objects of interest (Lynch, Lee, Bhat, & Galloway, 2008). Prereaching stops at about 7 weeks of age.

Voluntary reaching appears at about 3 months of age and slowly improves in accuracy. At 5 months, infants can successfully reach for moving objects. By 7 months, the arms can reach independently, and infants are able to reach for an object with one arm rather than both (Spencer et al., 2000). By 10 months, infants can reach for moving objects that change direction (Fagard, Spelke, & von Hofsten, 2009). As they gain experience with reaching and acquiring objects, infants develop cognitively because they learn by exploring and playing with objects—and object preferences change with experience. In one study, 4- to 6-month-old infants with less reaching experience spent more time looking at and exploring larger objects, whereas 5- to 6-month-old infants with more reaching experience spent more time looking at and touching smaller objects. The older infants

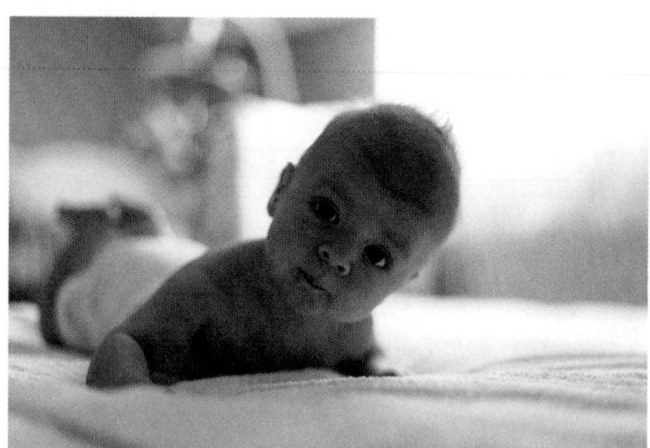

By the end of the first month of life, most infants can lift their head while lying on their stomach.
©iStockphoto.com/aywan88

did this despite first looking at and touching the largest object (Libertus et al., 2013). With experience, infants' attention moves away from the motor skill (like the ability to coordinate their movement to hit a mobile), to the object (the mobile), as well as to the events that occur before and after acquiring the object (how the mobile swings and how grabbing it stops the swinging or how batting at it makes it swing faster). In this way, infants learn about cause and how to solve simple problems.

Biological and Contextual Determinants of Motor Development

Motor development illustrates the complex interactions that take place between maturation and contextual factors.

Biological Influences on Motor Development

Maturation plays a very strong role in motor development. Preterm infants reach motor milestones later than do full-term infants (Gabriel et al., 2009). Cross-cultural research also supports the role of maturation because around the world, infants display roughly the same sequence of motor milestones. Among some Native Americans and other ethnic groups around the world, it is common to follow the tradition of tightly swaddling infants to cradleboards and strapping the board to the mother's back during nearly all waking hours for the first 6 to 12 months of the child's life. Although this might lead one to expect that swaddled babies will not learn to walk as early as babies whose movements are unrestricted, studies of Hopi Native American infants have shown that swaddling has little impact on when Hopi infants initiate walking (Dennis & Dennis, 1991; Harriman & Lukosius, 1982). Such research suggests that walking is very much maturationally programmed. Other evidence for the maturational basis of motor development comes from twin studies. Identical twins, who share the same genes, have more similarities in the timing and pace of motor development than do fraternal twins, who share half of their genes (Fogel, 2007; Wilson & Harpring, 1972). Samples of young children in the United States show no ethnic or socioeconomic status differences in gross motor skills such as running, hopping, kicking, and catching (Kit, Akinbami, Isfahani, & Ulrich, 2017).

Advancements in motor skill are influenced by body maturation and especially brain development. The pruning of unused synapses contributes to increases in motor speed and reaction time so that 11-year-old children tend to respond twice as quickly as 5-year-olds (Kail, 2003). Growth of the cerebellum (responsible for balance, coordination, and some aspects of emotion and reasoning) and myelination of its connections to the cortex contribute to advances in gross and fine motor skills and speed (Tiemeier et al., 2010). Brain development improves children's ability to inhibit actions, which enables children to carry out more sophisticated motor activities that require the use of one hand while controlling the other, such as throwing a ball, or that require both hands to do different things, such as playing a musical instrument (Diamond, 2013). As infants and children gain experience coordinating their motor skills, activity in the areas of the brain responsible for motor skills becomes less diffuse and more focused, consistent with the lifespan principle that domains of development interact (Nishiyori, Bisconti, Meehan, & Ulrich, 2016).

Contextual Influences on Motor Development

Much of motor development is driven by maturation, yet opportunities to practice motor skills are also important. In a classic naturalistic study of institutionalized orphans in Iran who had spent their first 2 years of life lying on their backs in their cribs and were never placed in sitting positions or played with, none of the 1- to 2-year-old infants could walk, and fewer than half of them could sit up; the researchers also found that most of the 3- to 4-year-olds could not walk well alone (Dennis, 1960). Recent research suggests that infants raised in orphanages score lower on measures of gross motor milestones at 4, 6, and 8 months of age and walk later compared with home-reared infants (Chaibal et al., 2016). While maturation is necessary for motor development, it is not sufficient; we must also have opportunities to practice our motor skills.

In fact, practice can enhance motor development (Lobo & Galloway, 2012). For example, when infants from 1 to 7 weeks of age practice stepping reflexes each day, they retain the movements and walk earlier than infants who receive no practice (Vereijken & Thelen, 1997; Zelazo, 1983). Newborns show improvement in stepping after practicing on a treadmill (Siekerman et al., 2015). Practice in sitting has a similar effect (Zelazo, Zelazo, Cohen, & Zelazo, 1993). Even 1-month-old infants given postural training showed more advanced control of their heads and necks than other infants (Lee & Galloway, 2012). Similarly, infants who spend supervised playtime prone on their stomachs each day reach many motor milestones, including rolling over and crawling, earlier than do infants who spend little time on their stomachs (Fetters & Huang, 2007; Kuo, Liao, Chen, Hsieh, & Hwang, 2008). In one study, over a 2-week period, young infants received daily play experience with "sticky mittens"—Velcro-covered mitts that enabled them to independently pick up objects. These infants showed advances in their reaching behavior and greater visual exploration of objects, while a comparison group of young infants who passively watched an adult's actions on the objects showed no change (Libertus & Needham, 2010). Sticky mittens training in reaching at 3 months of age predicts object exploration at 15 months of age (Libertus, Joh, & Needham, 2016).

Practice contributes to cross-cultural differences in infant motor development. Different cultures provide infants with different experiences and opportunities for development. For example, in many cultures, including several in sub-Saharan Africa and in the West Indies, infants attain motor goals like sitting up and walking much earlier than do North American infants. Among the Kipsigi of Kenya, parents seat babies in holes dug in the ground and use rolled blankets to keep babies upright in the sitting position (Keller, 2003). The Kipsigis help their babies practice walking at 2 to 3 months of age by holding their hands, putting them on the floor, and moving them slowly forward. Notably, Kipsigi mothers do not encourage their infants to crawl; crawling is seen as dangerous as it exposes the child to dirt, insects, and the dangers of fire pits and roaming animals. Crawling is therefore virtually nonexistent in Kipsigi infants (Super & Harkness, 2015). Infants of many sub-Saharan villages, such as the !Kung San, Gusii, and Wolof, are also trained to sit using holes or containers for support and are often held upright and bounced up and down, a social interaction practice that contributes to earlier walking (Lohaus et al., 2011). Caregivers in some of these cultures further encourage walking by setting up two parallel bamboo poles that infants can hold on to with both hands, learning balance and stepping skills (Keller, 2003). Similarly, mothers in Jamaica and other parts of the West Indies use a formal handling routine to exercise their babies' muscles and help them to grow up strong and healthy (Dziewolska & Cautilli, 2006; Hopkins, 1991; Hopkins & Westra, 1989, 1990).

Infants' motor development varies with cultural styles of interaction, such as a Western cultural emphasis on individualism and Eastern cultural emphasis on collectivism. In one cross-cultural study comparing infants in Germany and in the Cambodian Nso culture, the Nso infants showed overall more rapid motor development. The Nso practices of close proximity, lots of close body contact, and less object play are related to the socialization goals of fostering relationships; they also provide infants with body stimulation that fosters gross motor skills. German mothers displayed a parenting style with less body contact but more face-to-face contact and object play, socialization practices that emphasize psychological autonomy but less gross motor exploration. However, the German infants learned how to roll from back to stomach earlier than the Nso infants, likely because Nso infants are rarely placed on their backs and instead are carried throughout the day (Lohaus et al., 2011).

Although practice can speed development and caregivers in many cultures provide their infants with opportunities for early practice of motor skills, sometimes survival and success require continued dependence on caregivers and delaying motor milestones. For example, crawling may not be encouraged in potentially dangerous environments, such as those with many insects, rodents, and/or reptiles on the ground. The nomadic Ache of eastern Paraguay discourage their infants from crawling or moving independently. Ache infants walk at 18 to 20 months, compared with the 12-month average of North American infants (Kaplan & Dove, 1987).

Even simple aspects of the child-rearing context, such as choice of clothing, can influence motor development. In the 19th century, 40% of American infants skipped crawling, possibly because the long, flowing gowns they wore impeded movement on hands and knees (Trettien, 1990). One study of 13- and 19-month-old infants compared their gait while wearing a disposable diaper, a thicker cloth diaper, and no diaper (Cole, Lingeman, & Adolph, 2012). When naked, infants demonstrated the most sophisticated walking with fewer missteps and falls. While wearing a diaper, infants walked as poorly as they would have done several weeks earlier had they been walking naked. In sum, motor development is largely maturational, but subtle differences in context and cultural emphasis play a role in its timing.

Motor Development as a Dynamic System

Motor milestones, such as the ability to crawl, might look like isolated achievements, but they actually develop systematically and build on each other with each new skill preparing an infant to tackle the next (Thelen, 1995, 2000). According to dynamic systems theory (see Chapter 1), motor development reflects an interaction among developmental domains, maturation, and environment (Thelen, 1995, 2000). Simple motor skills are combined in increasingly complex ways, permitting advances in movement, including a wider range and more precise movements that enable babies to more effectively explore and control their environments. Separate abilities are blended together to provide more complex and effective ways of exploring and controlling the environment. For example, the abilities to sit upright, hold the head upright, match motor movements to vision, reach out an arm, and grasp are all combined into coordinated reaching movements to obtain a desired object (Corbetta & Snapp-Childs, 2009; Spencer et al., 2000). Motor skills become more specialized, coordinated, and precise with practice, permitting infants to reach for an object with one hand without needlessly flailing the other, for example (D'Souza, Cowie, Karmiloff-Smith, & Bremner, 2017).

Motor skills also reflect the interaction of multiple domains of development. All movement relies on the coordination of our senses and cognitive abilities to plan and predict actions. Sensory abilities such as binocular vision and the ability to direct gaze combine with exploratory hand and foot movements, designed to determine the opportunities a given surface provides for movement. For example, when 14-month-old infants were tested on a "bridge" of varying widths, they explored the bridge first with quick glances (Kretch & Adolph, 2017). When faced with an impossibly narrow width, infants with walking experience tended to engage in more extensive and time-consuming perceptual and motor exploration, such as touching with hands and feet, to determine whether to cross the bridge.

Motor development reflects goal-oriented behavior because it is initiated by the infant or child's desire to accomplish something, such as picking up a toy or moving to the other side of the room. Infants' abilities and their immediate environments (e.g., whether they are being held, lying in a crib, or lying freely on the floor) determine whether and how the goal can be achieved (Spencer et al., 2000). The infant tries out behaviors and persists at those that enable him or her to move closer to the goal, practicing and refining the behavior. For example, infants learn to walk by taking many steps and making many falls, but they persist even though, at the time, crawling is a much faster and more efficient means of transportation (Adolph et al., 2012). Why? Perhaps because upright posture leads to many more interesting sights, objects, and interactions. The upright infant can see more and do more, with two hands free to grasp objects, making walking a very desirable goal (Adolph & Tamis-LeMonda, 2014). New motor skills provide new possibilities for exploration of the environment and new interactions with caregivers that influence opportunities. Differences in caregiver interactions and caregiving environments affect children's motor skills, the form they take, the ages of onset, and the overall developmental trend (Adolph & Franchak, 2017).

Social and cultural influences provide context to our movements. Motor skills do not develop in isolation; rather, they are influenced by the physical and social context in which they occur. For example, a naturalistic study of video records of at-home interactions of mother–infant pairs from six countries revealed large differences in opportunities for infant sitting and infant performance (Karasik, Tamis-LeMonda, Adolph, & Bornstein, 2015). Infants from the United States, Argentina, South Korea, and Italy spent most of their sitting time in places that offered postural support, such as child furniture. In contrast, infants from Kenya and Cameroon, who spent most of their sitting time in places that offered little postural support, such as the ground or adult furniture, tended to show the longest bouts of independent sitting and at the earliest age. Cultural differences in daily activities influence motor skills across the lifespan. Long-distance running is part of daily life for Tarahumaran children, who routinely run 10 to 40 kilometers in a few hours and adults run 150 to 300 kilometers in 24 to 48 hours (Adolph & Franchak, 2017). From childhood, East African females carry heavy loads balanced on their heads, altering their posture and gait to complete a contextually important activity.

Therefore, from a dynamic systems perspective, motor development is the result of several processes: central nervous system maturation, the infant's physical capacities, environmental supports, and the infant's desire to explore the world. It is learned by revising and combining abilities and skills to fit the infant's goals. In this way, motor development is highly individualized because each infant has goals and opportunities that are particular to his or her specific environment (Adolph & Franchak, 2017). For example, an infant might respond to slippery hardwood floors by crawling on her stomach rather than all fours or by shuffling her feet and hands rather than raising each. Infants attain the same motor tasks, such as climbing down stairs, at about the same age, yet differ in how they approach the task. Some, for example, might turn around and back down, others descend on their bottoms, and others slide down face first (Berger, Theuring, & Adolph, 2007). By viewing motor development as dynamic systems of action produced by an infant's abilities, goal-directed behavior, and environmental supports and opportunities, we can account for the individual differences that we see in motor development.

THINKING IN CONTEXT 4.5

1. From a bioecological perspective, describe contextual influences on motor development. How do factors in an infant's microsystem and exosystem influence their motor development? How might exosystem factors play a distal, or distant, influence on motor skills? Identify macrosystem cultural factors that might influence an infant's development.
2. Misha is concerned that her 14-month-old baby is not walking. All of her friends' babies walked by 12 months of age. What would you tell Misha?
3. How might you explain Misha's baby's development from a dynamic systems approach?

APPLY YOUR KNOWLEDGE

Theo pushes into a crawling position onto all fours and rocks back and forth. Theo will soon crawl, about 2 months later than the other babies in the child care center. Much smaller than his peers, Theo is new to the child care center, recently adopted from an overcrowded orphanage in a developing country. At first tiny Theo didn't eat much. The adults around him worried about his poor eating habits and lack of growth. Soon, however, Theo became comfortable in his new, affectionate and nurturing home and he began to grow quickly.

1. What are patterns of normative growth in infancy? What are influences on growth and how might they explain Theo's development?
2. How do motor skills unfold during infancy? Should Theo's parents worry about his progress? Why or why not?
3. Theo's mother worries about how his early experiences of deprivation might influence Theo's brain development. Discuss processes of brain development and the role of experience in development. Should Theo's mother worry? What can she do to help Theo?

WANT A BETTER GRADE?

Get the tools you need to sharpen your study skills. **SAGE edge** offers a robust online environment featuring an impressive array of free tools and resources. Access practice quizzes, eFlashcards, video, and multimedia at **edge.sagepub.com/kutherchild1e.** SAGE edge™

KEY TERMS

Growth norm 96

Cephalocaudal development 96

Proximodistal development 96

Growth stunting 98

Marasmus 98

Kwashiorkor 98

Growth faltering 99

Sudden infant death syndrome (SIDS) 100

Vaccine 101

Neuron 104

Synapse 104

Myelin 104

Neurogenesis 104

Glial cell 104

Synaptogenesis 105

Synaptic pruning 105

Myelination 105

Cortex 105

Prefrontal cortex 105

Lateralization 106

Experience-expectant brain development 107

Habituation 110

Sensation 113

Perception 113

Visual acuity 113

Perceptual narrowing 114

Externality effect 114

Depth perception 115

Intermodal perception 118

Affordance 118

Reflex 120

Gross motor development 120

Fine motor development 121

SUMMARY

4.1 Discuss growth and influences and threats to growth during infancy and toddlerhood.

Growth proceeds from the head downward (cephalocaudal) and from the center of the body outward (proximodistal). Breastfeeding is associated with many benefits for mothers and infants. Malnourishment is associated with growth stunting and impaired learning, concentration, and language skills throughout childhood and adolescence. Severely malnourished children may suffer from diseases such as marasmus and kwashiorkor or, more common in the United States, growth faltering. Other threats to infants' health include SIDS and underimmunization.

4.2 Summarize brain development during infancy and toddlerhood.

The brain develops through several processes: neurogenesis (the creation of neurons), synaptogenesis (the creation of synapses), pruning (reducing unused neural connections), and myelination (coating the axons with myelin to increase the speed of transmission). Experience shapes the brain structure through pruning. Sleep also plays a role in brain development. Although infancy is a particularly important time for the formation and strengthening of synapses, experience shapes the brain structure at all ages of life.

4.3 Compare infants' early learning capacities for habituation, classical conditioning, operant conditioning, and imitation.

Innate learning capacities permit young infants to quickly adapt to the world. Habituation is a type of innate learning in which repeated exposure to a stimulus results in the gradual decline in the intensity, frequency, or duration of a response. In classical conditioning, an association is formed between a neutral stimulus and one that triggers an innate reaction. Infants also learn based on the consequences of their behaviors, whether they are followed by reinforcement or punishment, known as operant conditioning. Neonates mimic simple facial and finger expressions but do so without control. The regulatory mechanisms to inhibit imitative responding develop during infancy.

4.4 Describe infants' developing sensory abilities.

Visual acuity, pattern perception, visual tracking, and color vision improve over the first few months of life. Neonates are sensitive to depth cues and young infants can distinguish depth, but crawling stimulates the perception of depth and the association of fear with sharp drops. Newborns can perceive and discriminate nearly all sounds in human languages, but from birth, they prefer to hear their native language. Intermodal perception is evident at birth as infants can combine information from more than one sensory system.

4.5 Analyze the roles of maturation and contextual factors in infant and toddler motor development.

Infants are born with reflexes, each with its own developmental course. Gross and fine motor skills develop systematically and build on each other, with each new skill preparing the infant to tackle the next. Much of motor development is influenced by maturation, but infants benefit from opportunities to practice motor skills. Different cultures provide infants with different experiences and opportunities for practice, contributing to cross-cultural differences in motor development. Viewing motor development as dynamic systems of action produced by an infant's abilities, goal-directed behavior, and environmental supports and opportunities accounts for the individual differences that we see in motor development.

REVIEW QUESTIONS

4.1 What are two patterns that describe growth in infancy and childhood?

What are two types of malnutrition found primarily in developing nations?

What is failure to thrive?

4.2 Describe processes of neural development in infancy and toddlerhood.

What is the cerebral cortex?

What are examples of experience-expectant brain development and experience-dependent brain development?

4.3 Provide examples of how babies learn through

- habituation
- classical conditioning
- operant conditioning
- imitation

4.4 How does vision develop during infancy?

Describe infants' abilities to smell and hear.

What is intermodal perception?

How does intermodal perception contribute to early learning?

4.5 How do gross and fine motor development proceed in infancy and toddlerhood?

What are examples of biological and contextual influences on motor development?

What is dynamic systems theory?

©iStockphoto.com/romrod

5 Cognitive Development in Infancy and Toddlerhood

Dominic eagerly crawled toward the open cupboard. Just as he began to peer inside, his father bent down and swooped Dominic into his arms. His father said, "That's not for you, Dominic. Let's find something for you to play with." Soon Dominic sat amidst several toys: a set of stacking rings, cups and bowls, and a giant telephone with wheels and a string. "Overdoing it?" asked Dominic's mother. "Just giving Dominic options," his father explained. "Everyone wants a choice, right?" Soon Dominic placed several stacking rings in a bowl and then tried to balance the bowl on the giant telephone. His father said, "See? Dominic's figuring it all out in his own, unorthodox, way." Dominic's father grasps an important principle: individuals actively contribute to their own development, as noted in Chapter 1. We learn by acting on the world and making sense of our observations. In this chapter, we examine how infants interact with the world around them to influence their cognitive development.

Learning Objectives

5.1 Discuss the cognitive-developmental perspective on infant reasoning.

▶ **Video Activity 5.1:** Object Permanence

5.2 Describe the information processing system in infants.

▶ **Video Activity 5.2:** Infants, Young Children, and Technology

5.3 Discuss individual differences in infant intelligence.

5.4 Summarize the patterns of language development during infancy and toddlerhood.

Chapter Contents

PIAGET'S COGNITIVE-DEVELOPMENTAL THEORY

Swiss scholar Jean Piaget (1896–1980) was the first scientist to systematically examine children's thinking. Piaget viewed infants and children as active explorers who learn by interacting with the world, building their own understanding of everyday phenomena, and applying it to adapt to the world around them.

Processes of Development

According to Piaget (1952), infants and children are active in their own development not simply because they engage other people and the world, adapting their ways of thinking in response to their experiences. Through these interactions, individuals organize what they learn to construct and refine their own cognitive schemas, or concepts, ideas, and ways of interacting with the world. The earliest schemas are inborn motor responses, such as the reflex response that causes infants to close their fingers around an object when it touches their palm. As infants grow and develop, these early motor schemas are transformed into cognitive schemas, or thoughts and ideas. At every age, we rely on our schemas to make sense of the world, and our schemas are constantly adapting and developing in response to our experiences. Piaget also emphasized the importance of two developmental processes that enable us to cognitively adapt to our world: assimilation and accommodation.

Assimilation involves integrating a new experience into a preexisting schema. For example, suppose that 1-year-old Makayla uses the schema of "grab and shove into the mouth" to learn. She grabs and shoves a rattle into her mouth, learning about the rattle by using her preexisting schema. When Makayla comes across another object, such as Mommy's keys, she transfers the schema to it—and assimilates the keys by grabbing and shoving them into her mouth. Makayla develops an understanding of the new objects through assimilation, by fitting them into her preexisting schema.

Sometimes we encounter experiences or information that do not fit within an existing schema, so we must change the schema, adapting and modifying it in light of the new information. This process is called **accommodation**. For example, suppose Makayla encounters another object, a beach ball. She tries her schema of grab and shove, but the beach ball won't fit into her mouth; perhaps she cannot even grab it. She must adapt her schema or create a new one in order to incorporate the new information—to learn about the beach ball. Makayla may squeeze and mouth the ball instead, accommodating or changing her schema to interact with the new object.

The processes of assimilation and accommodation enable people to adapt to their environment, absorbing the constant flux of information they encounter daily (see Figure 5.1). People—infants, children, and adults—constantly integrate new information into their schemas and continually encounter new information that requires them to modify their schemas. Piaget proposed that people naturally strive for **cognitive equilibrium**, a balance between the processes of assimilation and accommodation. When assimilation and accommodation are balanced, individuals are neither incorporating new information into their schemas nor changing their schemas in light of new information; instead, our schemas match the outside world and represent it clearly. But a state of cognitive equilibrium is rare and fleeting. More frequently, people experience a mismatch, or **cognitive disequilibrium**, between their schemas and the world.

Disequilibrium leads to cognitive growth because of the mismatch between schemas and reality. This mismatch leads to confusion and discomfort, which in turn motivate children to modify their cognitive schemas so that their view of the world matches reality. It is through assimilation and accommodation that this modification takes place so that cognitive equilibrium is restored. Children's drive for cognitive equilibrium is the basis for cognitive change, propelling them through the four stages of cognitive development proposed by Piaget (refer to Chapter 1). With each advancing stage, children create and use more sophisticated

FIGURE 5.1

Assimilation and Accommodation

Bobby sees a cat that fits his schema for kitty (left). He has never seen a cat like this before (middle). He must accommodate his schema for kitty to include a hairless cat (right).
iStock/GlobalP; iStock/YouraPechkin

cognitive schemas, enabling them to think, reason, and understand their world in more complex ways.

Sensorimotor Substages

"There you go, little guy," Mateo's uncle says, placing a rattle within the infant's grasp. Six-month-old Mateo shakes the toy and puts it in his mouth, sucking on it. He then removes the rattle from his mouth and gives it a vigorous shake, dropping it to the ground. "Mateo! Where's your rattle?" asks his mother. "Whenever he drops his toy, he never looks for it," she explains to Nico's uncle, "Not even when it's his favorite toy." Mateo displays sensorimotor thinking. During the sensorimotor stage, from birth to about 2 years old, infants learn about the world through their senses and motor skills. To think about an object, they must act on it by viewing it, listening to it, touching it, smelling it, and tasting it. Piaget (1952) believed that infants are not capable of **mental representation**—thinking about an object using mental pictures. They also lack the ability to remember and think about objects and events when they are not present. Instead, in order to think about an object, an infant must experience it through both the visual and tactile senses. The sensorimotor period of reasoning, as Piaget conceived of it, progresses through six substages in which cognition develops from reflexes to intentional action to symbolic representation. At each stage infants are driven to learn and explore the world.

Substage 1: Reflexes (Birth to 1 Month)

In the first substage, newborns use their reflexes, such as the sucking and palmar grasp reflexes, to react to stimuli. During the first month of life, infants use these reflexes to learn about their world, through the process of assimilation; they apply their sucking schema to assimilate information and learn about their environment. At about 1 month of age, newborns begin to accommodate, or modify, their sucking behaviors to specific objects, sucking differently in response to a bottle versus a pacifier. For example, they may modify their sucking schema when they encounter a pacifier, perhaps sucking less vigorously and without swallowing. During the first month of life, newborns strengthen and modify their original reflexive schemas to explore the world around them.

In the first substage (birth to 1 month), newborns use their reflexes, such as the grasping reflex, to respond to stimuli, such as to grasp an adult's finger.
©iStockphoto.com/damircudic

Substage 2: Primary Circular Reactions (1 to 4 Months)

During the second substage, infants begin to make accidental discoveries. Early cognitive growth in the sensorimotor period comes through engaging in circular reactions, the repetition of an action and its response. Infants learn to repeat pleasurable or interesting events that originally occurred by chance. Between 1 and 4 months, infants engage in behaviors called **primary circular reactions**, which consist of repeating actions involving parts of the body that produce pleasurable or interesting results. A primary circular reaction begins by chance, as the infant produces a pleasurable sensation and learns to repeat the behavior to make the event happen again and experience the pleasurable effect again. For

In the second substage (1 to 4 months), infants discover that they can control their bodies and repeat the behavior to experience and explore their bodies. This infant enjoys repeatedly grasping her feet.
©iStockphoto.com/NickyLloyd

example, an infant flails her arms and accidentally puts her hand in her mouth. She is surprised at the outcome (her hand in her mouth) and tries to make it happen again. Therefore, the infant repeats the behavior to experience and explore her body.

Substage 3: Secondary Circular Reactions (4 to 8 Months)

During the third sensorimotor substage, as infants' awareness extends further, they engage in **secondary circular reactions**, repetitions of actions that trigger responses in the external environment. Now the patterns of repetition are oriented toward making interesting events occur in the infant's environment. For example, the infant shakes a rattle to hear its noise or kicks his legs to move a mobile hanging over the crib. Secondary circular reactions indicate that infants' attention has expanded to include the environment outside their bodies and that they are beginning to understand that their actions cause results in the external world. In this way, infants discover new ways of interacting with their environments to continue experiencing sensations and events that they find pleasing.

Substage 4: Coordination of Secondary Circular Reactions (8 to 12 Months)

Unlike primary and secondary circular reactions, behaviors that are discovered by accident, the coordination of secondary circular reactions substage represents true means–end behavior and signifies the beginning of intentional behavior. During this substage, infants purposefully coordinate two secondary circular reactions and apply them in new situations to achieve a goal. For example, Piaget described how his son, Laurent, combined the two activities of knocking a barrier out of his way and grasping an object. When Piaget put a pillow in front of a matchbox that Laurent desired, the boy pushed the pillow aside and grabbed the box. In this way, Laurent integrated two secondary circular reactions to achieve a goal. Now planning and goal-directed behavior have emerged.

During the third sensorimotor substage (4 to 8 months), infants' awareness extends to include objects. They repeat actions that have effects on objects.
©iStockphoto.com/kieferpix

During the fourth substage (8 to 12 months), infants demonstrate object permanence, the understanding that objects exist outside of sensory awareness.
Doug Goodman/Science Source

One of the most important advances during the coordination of secondary circular reactions stage is **object permanence**, the understanding that objects continue to exist outside of sensory awareness (e.g., when they are no longer visible). According to Piaget, infants younger than 8 months of age do not yet have object permanence—out of sight is literally out of mind. An infant loses interest and stops reaching for or looking at a small toy after it is covered by a cloth. Not until 8 to 12 months, during the coordination of secondary circular reactions stage, will an infant search for hidden objects, thus displaying object permanence. This development is an important cognitive advance because it signifies a capacity for mental representation, or internal thought. The ability to think about an object internally is an important step toward learning language because language uses symbols: Sounds symbolize and stand for objects (e.g., infants must understand that the sound "ball" represents an object, a ball).

Substage 5: Tertiary Circular Reactions (12 to 18 Months)

During the fifth substage, infants begin to experiment with new behaviors to see the results. Piaget described infants as "little scientists" during this period because they move from intentional behavior to systematic exploration. In what Piaget referred to as **tertiary circular reactions**, infants now engage in mini-experiments: active, purposeful, trial-and-error exploration to search for new discoveries. They vary their actions to see how the changes affect the outcomes. For example, many infants begin to experiment with gravity by dropping objects to the floor while sitting in a high chair. First an infant throws a ball and watches it bounce. Next

During the fifth substage (12 to 18 months), infants begin to experiment with new behaviors to see the results.
©iStockphoto.com/MartinPrescott

Through play, infants quickly learn about the physical properties of objects.
©iStockphoto.com/Image Source

FIGURE 5.2

Primary, Secondary, and Tertiary Circular Reactions

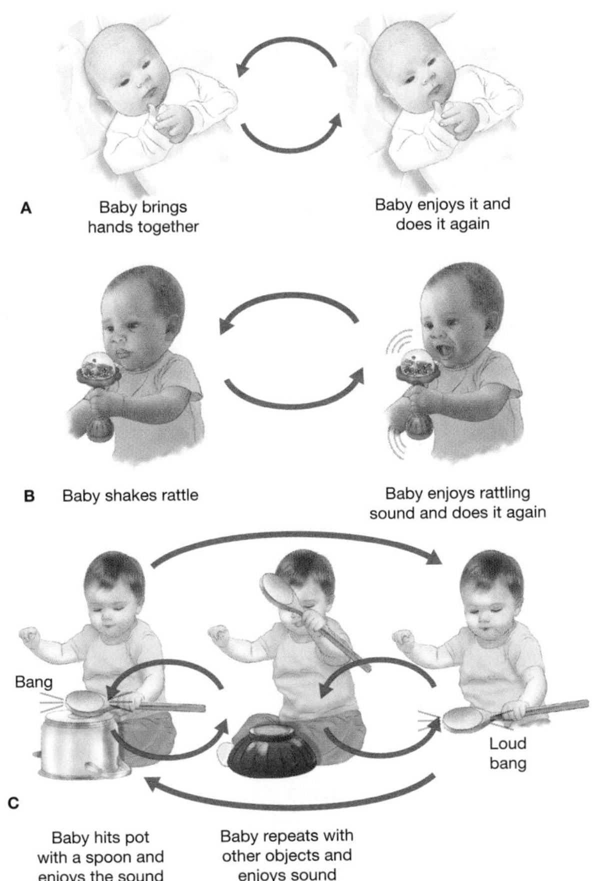
A
Baby brings hands together
Baby enjoys it and does it again
B
Baby shakes rattle
Baby enjoys rattling sound and does it again
Bang
Loud bang
C
Baby hits pot with a spoon and enjoys the sound
Baby repeats with other objects and enjoys sound

Source: Adapted from Papalia et al. (2001).

a piece of paper floats slowly down. Then Mommy's keys clatter to the floor. And so on. This purposeful exploration is how infants search for new discoveries and learn about the world. When presented with a problem, babies in the tertiary circular reactions substage engage in trial-and-error analyses, trying out behaviors until they find the best one to attain their goal. Figure 5.2 illustrates primary, secondary, and tertiary reactions.

Substage 6: Mental Representation (18 to 24 Months)

The sixth sensorimotor substage marks a transition between the sensorimotor and preoperational reasoning stages. Between 18 and 24 months of age, infants develop representational thought, the ability to use symbols such as words and mental pictures to represent objects and actions in memory. In developing this ability, infants are freed from immediate experience: They can think about objects that they no longer see directly in front of them and can engage in deferred imitation, imitating actions of an absent model. Now, external physical exploration of the world gives way to internal mental exploration. Children can think through potential solutions and create new solutions without engaging in physical trial and error simply by considering the potential solutions and their consequences. Table 5.1 summarizes the substages of sensorimotor reasoning.

Evaluating Sensorimotor Reasoning

Piaget's contributions to understanding cognitive development are invaluable. Piaget was the first scientist to examine infants' and children's thinking and ask what develops during childhood and how it occurs. Piaget recognized that motor action and cognition are inextricably linked, a view still accepted by today's developmental scientists (Libertus et al., 2016).

Piaget's work has stimulated a great deal of research as developmental scientists have tested his theory. However, measuring the cognitive capabilities of infants and toddlers is very challenging because, unlike older children and adults, babies cannot fill out questionnaires or answer questions

TABLE 5.1

Substages of Sensorimotor Reasoning

SUBSTAGE	MAJOR FEATURES	EXAMPLE
Reflexes (0–1 month)	Strengthens and adapts reflexes	Newborn shows a different sucking response to a nipple versus a pacifier.
Primary circular reactions (1–4 months)	Repeats motor actions that produce interesting outcomes that are centered toward the body	Infant bats a mobile with her arm and watches her arm move.
Secondary circular reactions (4–8 months)	Repeats motor actions that produce interesting outcomes that are directed toward the environment	Infant bats a mobile with his arm and watches the mobile move.
Coordination of secondary circular reactions (8–12 months)	Combines secondary circular reactions to achieve goals and solve problems; the beginnings of intentional behavior	Infant uses one hand to lift a bucket covering a ball and the other to grasp the ball. Infant uses both hands to pull a string attached to a ball and eventually reach the ball.
Tertiary circular reactions (12–18 months)	Experiments with different actions to achieve the same goal or observe the outcome and make new discoveries	Toddler hits a pot with a wooden spoon and listens to the sound, then hits other objects in the kitchen, such as the refrigerator, stove, or plates, to hear the sound that the spoon makes against the objects.
Mental representation (18–24 months)	Internal mental representation of objects and events; thinking to solve problems rather than relying on trial and error	When confronted with a problem, like a toy that is out of reach on the counter, the toddler considers possible solutions to a problem in his mind, decides on a solution, and implements it.

orally. Researchers have had to devise methods of measuring observable behavior that can provide clues to what an infant is thinking. For example, researchers measure infants' looking behavior by determining what infants look at and for how long. Using such methods, they have found support for some of Piaget's claims and evidence that challenges others. One of the most contested aspects of Piaget's theory concerns his assumption that infants are not capable of mental representation until late in the sensorimotor period (Carey, Zaitchik, & Bascandziev, 2015). A growing body of research conducted with object permanence and imitation tasks suggests otherwise, as described in the following sections.

Violation-of-Expectation Tasks

Piaget's method of determining an infant's understanding of object permanence relied on the infant's ability to demonstrate it by uncovering a hidden object. Researchers have posited that many infants may understand that the object is hidden but lack the motor ability to coordinate their hands to physically demonstrate their understanding. Studying infants' looking behavior enables researchers to study object permanence in younger infants with undeveloped motor skills because it eliminates the need for infants to use motor activity to demonstrate their cognitive competence.

One such research design uses a **violation-of-expectation task**, a task in which a stimulus appears to violate physical laws (Hespos & Baillargeon, 2008). Specifically, in a violation-of-expectation task, an infant is shown two events: one that is labeled *expected* because it follows physical laws and a second that is called *unexpected* (or "impossible") because it violates physical laws. If the infant looks longer at the unexpected event, it suggests that he or she is surprised by it, is aware of physical properties of objects, and can mentally represent them.

In a classic study, developmental researcher Renée Baillargeon (1987) used the violation-of-expectation method to study the mental representation capacities of very young infants. Infants were shown a drawbridge that rotated 180 degrees. Then the infants watched as a box was placed behind the drawbridge to impede its movement. Infants watched as either the drawbridge rotated and stopped upon hitting the box (expected event) or did not stop and appeared to move through the box (an "impossible" event). As shown in Figure 5.3, 4½-month-old infants looked longer when the drawbridge appeared to move through the box (the unexpected "impossible" event) than

FIGURE 5.3

Object Permanence in Young Infants: Baillargeon's Drawbridge Study

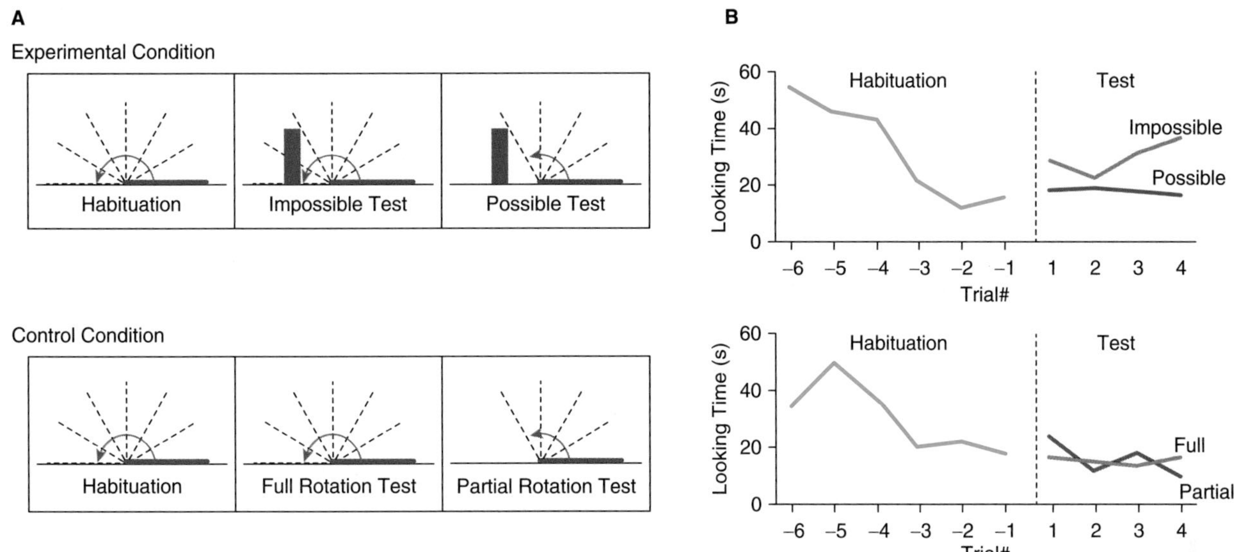

(A) Side view of habituation and test displays. Infants were habituated to a 180-degree drawbridge-like motion. (B) In the Experimental Condition, infants completed two types of test trials with a new object, a box. The Impossible Test involved the same full 180-degree rotation from habituation, but now the screen surprisingly passed through the box as it completed its rotation (with the box disappearing as it became obscured). The Possible Test involved a novel shorter rotation of the screen up to the point where it would contact the box, where it stopped; this motion was "possible" in terms of solidity and object permanence. In the Control Condition, the screen rotations were identical, but no box was presented (such that both motions were equally possible). The results from the test phase are depicted in the right panels of (B). In the Experimental Condition, infants looked longer at the Impossible Test but not the Possible Test. However, in the Control Condition, no preference was observed. They looked equally at the full and partial rotation. These results suggest a violation of infants' expectations regarding object permanence.

Source: Baillargeon (1987).

when it stopped upon hitting the box, as expected. Baillargeon and colleagues interpreted infants' behavior as suggesting that the infants maintained a mental representation of the box, even though they could not see it, and therefore understood that the drawbridge could not move through the entire box.

Other researchers counter that these results do not demonstrate object permanence but rather illustrate infants' preference for novelty or for greater movement (Bogartz, Shinskey, & Schilling, 2000; Heyes, 2014). For example, when the study was replicated without the box, 5-month-old infants looked longer at the full rotation, suggesting that infants looked at the unexpected event not because it violated physical laws but because it represented greater movement (Rivera, Wakely, & Langer, 1999). Nevertheless, studies that use simpler tasks have shown support for young infants' competence. Four- and 5-month-old infants will watch a ball roll behind a barrier, gazing to where they expect it to reappear (von Hofsten, Kochukhova, & Rosander, 2007). When 6-month-old infants are shown an object and the lights are then turned off, they will reach in the dark for the object (Shinskey, 2012), suggesting that they maintain a mental representation of the object and therefore have object permanence earlier than Piaget believed.

A-Not-B Tasks

Other critics of Piaget's views of infants' capacity for object permanence focus on an error that 8- to 12-month-old infants make, known as the **A-not-B error**. The A-not-B error involves the following scenario: An infant repeatedly uncovers a toy hidden behind a barrier. He then sees the toy moved from behind one barrier (Place A) to another (Place B), but he continues to look for the toy in Place A, even after watching it be moved to Place B (see Figure 5.4). Piaget believed that the infant incorrectly, but persistently, searches for the object in Place A because he lacks object permanence.

Some researchers, however, point out that infants look at Place B, the correct location, at the same time as they mistakenly reach for Place A, suggesting that they understand the correct location of the object (Place B) but cannot keep themselves from reaching for Place A because of neural and motor immaturity (Diamond, 1991). Other researchers

FIGURE 5.4

A-Not-B Error

The infant continues to look for the ball under Place A despite having seen the ball moved to Place B.

propose that infants cannot restrain the impulse to repeat a behavior that was previously rewarded (Zelazo, Reznick, & Spinazzola, 1998). When looking-time procedures are used to study the A-not-B error (Ahmed & Ruffman, 1998), infants look longer when the impossible event occurs (when the toy is moved from Place A to Place B but is then found at Place A) than when the expected event occurs (when the toy is moved from Place A to Place B and is found at Place B). This suggests that infants have object permanence, but their motor skills prohibit them from demonstrating it in A-not-B tasks. One longitudinal study followed infants from 5 to 10 months of age and found that between 5 and 8 months, infants showed better performance on an A-not-B looking task than on a reaching task. Nine- and 10-month-old infants performed equally well on A-not-B looking and reaching tasks (Cuevas & Bell, 2010). Age-related changes in performance on A-not-B and other object permanence tasks may be due to maturation of the brain circuitry controlling motor skills and inhibition as well as advances in the ability to control attention (Cuevas & Bell, 2010; Marcovitch, Clearfield, Swingler, Calkins, & Bell, 2016).

Deferred Imitation Tasks

Another method of studying infants' capacities for mental representation relies on **deferred imitation**, the ability to repeat an act performed some time ago. Piaget (1962) believed that infants younger than 18 months cannot engage in deferred imitation because they lack mental representation abilities. Yet laboratory research on infant facial imitation has found that 6-week-old infants who watch an unfamiliar adult's facial expression will imitate it when they see the same adult the next day (Meltzoff & Moore, 1994). Six- and 9-month-old infants also display deferred imitation of unique actions performed with toys, such as taking a puppet's glove off, shaking it to ring a bell inside, and replacing it over a 24-hour delay (Barr, Marrott, & Rovee-Collier, 2003).

When infants engage in deferred imitation, they act on the basis of stored representations of actions—memories—a contradiction of Piaget's beliefs about infants' capabilities (Jones & Herbert, 2006). Many researchers now suggest that deferred imitation, along with object permanence itself, is better viewed as a continuously developing ability rather than the stage-like shift in representational capacities that Piaget proposed (Miller, 2016). For example, a 3-year longitudinal study of infants 12, 18, and 24 months old showed that performance on deferred imitation tasks improved throughout the second year of life (Kolling, Goertz, Stefanie, & Knopf, 2010). Between 12 and 18 months, infants remember modeled behaviors for several months and imitate peers as well as adults (Hayne, Boniface, & Barr, 2000). They also imitate across contexts, imitating behaviors that they learn in child care at home (Patel, Gaylord, & Fagen, 2013).

Increases in imitative capacity are observed with development up to 30 months of age. In addition, imitative capacity increases when shorter sequences of action are used, for example, a sequence of fewer than eight unique actions (Kolling et al., 2010; Kressley-Mba, Lurg, & Knopf, 2005). Furthermore, research following infants from 9 to 14 months of age suggests that individual differences in imitation are stable; children who show lower levels of imitation at 9 months of age continue to score lower on imitation at 14 months (Heimann & Meltzoff, 1996). These gradual changes suggest that infants and toddlers increase their representational capacities in a continuous developmental progression.

Core Knowledge Theory

Developmental psychologists generally agree with Piaget's description of infants as eagerly interacting with the world, actively taking in information, and constructing their own thinking. However, most researchers no longer agree with Piaget's belief that all mental abilities arise from sensorimotor activity. Instead, infants are thought to have some innate, or inborn, cognitive capacities. Conservative theorists believe that infants are born with limited learning capacities such as a set of perceptual biases that cause them to attend to features of the environment that will help them to learn quickly (Bremner, Slater, & Johnson, 2015). Alternatively, **core knowledge theory** proposes that infants are born with several innate knowledge systems, or core domains of thought, that promote early rapid learning and adaptation (Spelke, 2016a, 2016b).

According to core knowledge theorists, infants learn so quickly and encounter such a great amount of sensory information that some prewired evolutionary understanding, including the early ability to learn rules, must be at work (Spelke, 2016a, 2016b). Using the violation-of-expectation method, core knowledge researchers have found that young infants have a grasp of the physical properties of objects, including the knowledge that objects do not disappear out of existence (permanence), cannot pass through another object (solidity), and will fall without support (gravity) (Baillargeon, Scott, & Bian, 2016). Developmental researchers have made significant advances in understanding the origins of this ability in infancy. This evidence indicates that when infants observe an agent act in a simple scene, they infer the agent's mental states and then use these mental states, together with a principle of rationality (and its corollaries of efficiency and consistency). Infants also display early knowledge that liquids are nonsolid substances able to pass through grids (Hespos, Ferry, Anderson, Hollenbeck, & Rips, 2016).

Infants are also thought to have early knowledge of numbers (Spelke, 2017). Five-month-old infants can discriminate between small and large numbers of items (Christodoulou, Lac, & Moore, 2017). Even newborns are sensitive to large differences in number, distinguishing nine items from three, for example, but newborns show difficulty distinguishing small numbers from each other (two versus three items) (Coubart, Izard, Spelke, Marie, & Streri, 2014). Comparative research has shown that animals display these systems of knowledge early in life and without much experience (Piantadosi & Cantlon, 2017), suggesting that it is possible—and perhaps evolutionarily adaptive—for infants to quickly yet naturally construct an understanding of the world (Bjorklund, 2018a). Increasingly, infants are viewed as statistical learners, able to quickly identify patterns in the world around them (Saffran & Kirkham, 2018).

Much core knowledge research employs the same looking paradigms described earlier, in which infants' visual preferences are measured as indictors of what they know, and this approach has come under criticism. Critics argue that it is unclear whether we can interpret looking in the same way in infants as in adults. Such measures demonstrate

LIVES IN CONTEXT: MEDIA AND TECHNOLOGY

Baby Videos and Infant Learning

Infants and toddlers learn more from interaction with their parents and other caregivers than they do watching infant-directed educational content.
©iStockphoto.com/LucaLorenzelli

Infants and toddlers spend 1 to 2 hours a day engaged with screen media, including television and tablets, and are exposed to over 5 hours daily of background television intended for adults (Courage, 2017). Infant-directed videos and programming, which offer educational content embedded in an engaging video format, are often advertised as aids to babies' brain development, intelligence, and learning (Fenstermacher et al., 2010; Vaala & LaPierre, 2014). Most parents believe that age-appropriate videos can have a positive impact on early child development while providing good entertainment for babies and convenience for parents (Robb, Richert, & Wartella, 2009). Certainly, even very young infants attend to video material, as its movement, color, and rapid scene changes are attractive (Courage, 2017).

But do baby videos really aid development? Brain-building claims made by baby media manufacturers are not supported by longitudinal studies, which offer no evidence of long-term benefits of media use in early childhood (American Academy of Pediatrics Council on Communications and Media, 2016; Courage & Howe, 2010; Ferguson & Donnellan, 2014). For example, one study tested a popular DVD program that claims to help young infants learn to read. Ten- to 18-month-old infants who regularly watched the program for 7 months did not differ from other infants in intelligence, cognitive skills, reading skill, or word knowledge (Neuman, Kaefer, Pinkham, & Strouse, 2014). Baby videos are often advertised as aiding language development, yet several studies found that children under 2 years of age showed no learning of target words after viewing a language-learning DVD up to 20 times (DeLoache et al., 2010; Ferguson & Donnellan, 2014).

(Continued)

(Continued)

Infants learn more readily from people than from television, a finding known as the video deficit effect (Anderson & Pempek, 2005). For example, when 12- to 18-month-old infants watched a best-selling DVD that labels household objects, the infants learned very little from it compared with what they learned though interaction with parents (DeLoache et al., 2010). Recently, the video deficit effect has been relabeled as a transfer deficit because infants are less able to transfer what they see on the screen to their own behavior than to transfer what they learn in active interactions with adults (Barr, 2010). The transfer deficit is reduced somewhat for older infants when their memory capacities are taken into account, that is, when content is repeated and verbal cues are added (Barr, 2013). When parents watch videos along with their infants and talk to them about the content, the infants spend more time looking at the screen, learn more from the media, and show greater knowledge of language as toddlers (Linebarger & Vaala, 2010). However, it is not clear that parent coviewing of media provides a better alternative to learning than parent–infant interaction by itself (Courage, 2017).

Infants learn from contingent interactions with others—and baby videos do not provide contingent stimulation. Infants can, however, learn from screens when contingent interactions with people are involved (McClure, Chentsova-Dutton, Holochwost, Parrott, & Barr, 2018). For example, 12- to 25-month-olds were presented with on-screen partners who taught novel words, actions, and patterns via real-time FaceTime conversations or prerecorded videos (Myers, LeWitt, Gallo, & Maselli, 2017). All of the infants were attentive and responsive, but only children in the FaceTime group responded to the partner in a time-synchronized manner. One week later, the children in the FaceTime group preferred and recognized their partner, learned more novel patterns, and (among the older infants) learned more novel words. Although baby media will not transform babies into geniuses or even guarantee learning, babies can learn from real-time interactions with others—in person or on screen.

What Do You Think?

1. Imagine that you are a parent. What are some of the reasons why you might allow your young child to play with your mobile phone or tablet? In your view, what are some disadvantages to screen use by infants and toddlers?
2. How might you teach infants and toddlers how to learn from screens, such as from televisions, cell phones, and tablets? ●

discrimination—that young infants can tell the difference between stimuli—yet perceiving the difference between two stimuli does not necessarily mean that infants understand how the two stimuli differ (Bremner et al., 2015). Others have suggested that infants are not detecting differences in number but rather differences in area (Mix, Huttenlocher, & Levine, 2002). For example, it may be that the infant differentiates nine items from three not because of the change in number but simply because nine items take up more space than three. More recent research has shown that 7-month-old infants can differentiate changes in number and area, are more sensitive to changes in number than area, and prefer to look at number changes than area changes (Libertus, Starr, & Brannon, 2014). Infants apply basic inferential mechanisms to quickly yet naturally construct an understanding of the world (Xu & Kushnir, 2013).

Overall, Piaget's theory has had a profound influence on how we view cognitive development. However, infants and toddlers are more cognitively competent than Piaget imagined, showing signs of representational ability and conceptual thought that he believed were not possible. Developmental scientists agree with Piaget that immature forms of cognition give way to more mature forms, that the individual is active in development, and that interaction with the environment is critical for cognitive growth. Today, electronic media are an important part of almost everyone's environment. Do infants interact with electronic media? The Lives in Context feature examines infants' learning from electronic media.

THINKING IN CONTEXT 5.1

1. Design a child care environment for infants at each sensorimotor stage.
   a. What toys and surroundings might suit an infant in the primary circular reaction substage?
   b. Secondary circular reaction substage?
   c. Coordination of secondary schemas substage?
   d. Tertiary circular reactions substage?
2. Identify contextual influences on cognitive development. Given your current understanding, what do you think Piaget would say about contextual influences on sensorimotor reasoning? What do you think?

INFORMATION PROCESSING THEORY

Information processing theorists describe cognition as a set of interrelated components that permit people to process information—to notice, take in, manipulate, store, and retrieve. Newborns are ready to learn and adapt to their world because they are born information processors. In the following sections we examine the information processing system and how cognition changes in infancy.

Information Processing System

According to information processing theory, the mind is composed of three mental stores: sensory memory, working memory, and long-term memory (Atkinson & Shiffrin, 1968). All throughout our lives, information moves through these three stores, and we use them to manipulate and store information (see Figure 5.5).

Sensory memory is the first step in getting information into the mind; it holds incoming sensory information in its original form (Vandenbroucke et al., 2014). For example, look at this page, then close your eyes. Did you "see" the page for a fraction of a second after you closed your eyes? That image, or icon, represents your sensory memory. Information fades from sensory memory quickly if it is not processed. Visual information decays in about a quarter of a second and auditory information lasts about 4 seconds (Radvansky, 2017).

A great deal of information is taken in and rapidly moves through sensory memory. Not surprisingly, much of it is discarded. When we direct our **attention**, or awareness, on information, it passes to the next part of the information processing system, **working memory**. Working memory holds and processes information that is being "worked on" in some way. Working memory consists of at least three components: a short-term store, a processing component, and a control mechanism (Baddeley, 2016). Just as your thoughts are constantly changing, so are the contents of working memory. We can hold only so much information in working memory (perhaps as many as nine and as few as four or five), and we can hold it for a short period, from seconds to minutes (Radvansky, 2017). Indeed, a core assumption of the information processing approach is the idea of limited capacity (Bjorklund & Myers, 2015; Oberauer, Farrell, Jarrold, & Lewandowsky, 2016).

Working memory is responsible for manipulating (considering, comprehending), encoding (transforming into a memory), and retrieving (recalling) information. All of your thoughts—that is, all conscious mental activities—occur within working memory. For example, reading this paragraph, remembering assignments, and considering how this material applies to your own experience taps your working memory.

An important part of working memory is the **central executive**, a control mechanism or processor that directs the flow of information and regulates cognitive activities such as attention, action, and problem solving (Just & Carpenter, 1992). The central executive determines what is important to attend to, combines new information with information already in working memory, and selects and applies strategies for manipulating the information in order to understand it, make decisions, and solve problems (Baddeley, 2012). Collectively, these cognitive activities are known as **executive function**.

As information is manipulated in working memory, it becomes more likely that it will enter long-term memory, the third mental store. **Long-term memory** is an unlimited store that holds information indefinitely. Information is not manipulated or processed in long-term memory; it is simply stored until it is retrieved to manipulate in working memory (e.g., in remembering events and thinking about them).

FIGURE 5.5

Information Processing System

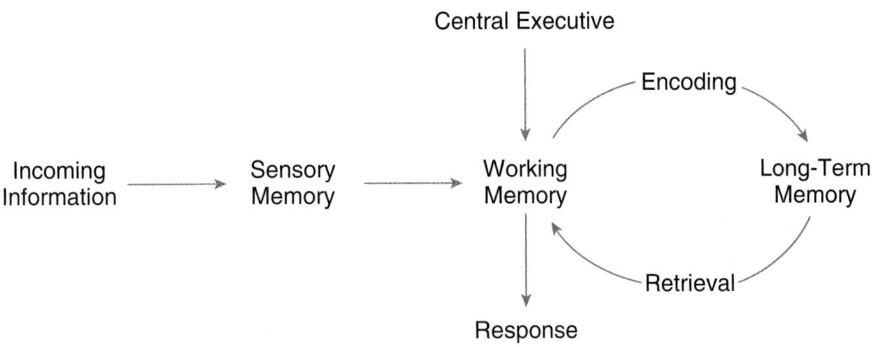

Although the information processing model was created to explain cognition in adults, research has shown that infants, children, and adolescents have the same memory stores and the structure of the information processing system remains the same throughout the lifespan. We are born with the ability to take in, store, and manipulate information through our sensory, working, and long-term memory. With development, we get better at moving information through our cognitive system in ways that allow us to adapt to our world. We can process more information, retain more information, and do so more quickly and efficiently.

Attention

Attention refers to our ability to direct our awareness. The ability to focus and switch attention is critical for selecting information to process in working memory and is influenced by neurological development, including advances in myelination (Reynolds & Romano, 2016). Important developments in attention occur over the course of infancy and continue throughout childhood.

Infant attention is often studied using the same methods used to learn about their visual perception (Chapter 4). Preferential-looking procedures (measuring and comparing the length of time infants look at two stimuli) and habituation procedures (measuring the length of time it takes infants to show a reduction in how long they look at a nonchanging stimulus) are used to study infants' attention to visual stimuli, such as geometric patterns (Ristic & Enns, 2015a). Infants show more attentiveness to dynamic stimuli—stimuli that change over time—than to static, unchanging stimuli (Reynolds, Zhang, & Guy, 2013).

By around 10 weeks of age, infants show gains in attention. As infants' capacities for attention increase, so do their preferences for complex stimuli. For example, in one experiment, 3- to 13-month-old infants were shown displays that included a range of static and moving stimuli (Courage, Reynolds, & Richards, 2006). From about 6½ months of age, infants' looking time varied with stimulus complexity, decreasing for simple stimuli such as dot patterns, increasing slightly for complex stimuli such as faces, and increasing more for very complex stimuli such as video clips (Courage et al., 2006). Overall, looking time peaked at 14 weeks of age and dropped steadily, demonstrating infants' growing cognitive efficiency. As infants become more efficient at directing their attention to scan and process visual information, they require less exposure to stimuli to habituate.

Infants are more attentive to dynamic stimuli, stimuli that move and change over time, than to static, unchanging stimuli.
©iStockphoto.com/kamsta

The development of infant attention is thought to be closely related to neurological development in the areas underlying attentional control (Reynolds & Romano, 2016). In response to tasks that challenge attention, infants show activity in the frontal cortex (used for thinking and planning) that is diffuse (widely spread) at 5½ months of age but more specific or localized by 7½ months of age (Richards, 2010).

Memory

We have memory capacities at birth. For example, newborn infants display sensory memory, but it is much shorter in duration than adults' memory (Cheour et al., 2002). Given that infants are unable to speak and tell us what they are thinking, it is difficult to assess memory.

Working Memory

Working memory is thought to improve alongside development of the prefrontal cortex. Infants' working memory is assessed by observing reaching and looking behaviors. For example, the duration of working memory can be assessed by the use of delayed response tasks in which an object is hidden among several boxes; the infant is allowed to search for the object after a short delay (such as 10 seconds) (Simmering, 2016). Delayed response tasks can be used as soon as infants are able to reliably reach for items, at about 5 to 6 months of age. Results across a host of studies suggest a rapid increase in memory durability from 6 to 12 months and continued increases through age 2 (Reznick, 2009). Similar techniques are used to study the capacity of working memory, the number of items an infant can recall. Infants' memory capacity has been estimated to reach three objects at 12 to 14 months of age (Feigenson & Carey, 2003).

Long-Term Memory

Recognition memory, the ability to recognize a previously encountered stimulus, appears early in life. Habituation studies measuring looking time and brain activity demonstrate that neonates can recall visual and auditory stimuli (Muenssinger et al., 2013; Streri, Hevia, Izard, & Coubart, 2013). With age, infants require fewer trials or presentations to recall a stimulus and are able to retain material for progressively longer periods of time (Howe, 2015). Infants can also remember motor activities. In one study, 2- to 3-month-old infants were taught to kick their foot, which was tied to a mobile with a ribbon, to make the mobile move. One week later, when the infants were reattached to the mobile, they kicked vigorously, indicating their memory of the first occasion. The infants would kick even 4 weeks later if the experimenter gave the mobile a shake to remind them of its movement (Rovee-Collier & Bhatt, 1993).

Infants' long-term memory, the ability to recall information encountered some time in the past, has been assessed with tasks that measure deferred imitation, imitating a model after a delay. For example, the infant watches an experimenter engage in a novel behavior with an unfamiliar object. After a period of time, the infants are given the object. If they display the novel behavior more often than infants who have not viewed the object, it suggests that they have formed a long-term memory for the object and action. Results from deferred imitation studies suggest that infants can form memories that last a year and sometimes longer (Bauer, Burch, & Kleinknecht, 2002; Bauer, Wenner, Dropik, & Wewerka, 2000).

With age infants can remember more complicated sets of actions, with fewer exposures, and for a longer period of time. Nine-month-old infants shown a two-step sequence of actions (for example, hanging a plate from a bar and striking it with a mallet) could imitate the action after a 1-month delay if they viewed the event at least three times, but not if it was viewed less than three times. Long-term memory appears to increase rapidly, because 13-, 16-, and 20-month-old infants can imitate a more complicated three-step sequence of actions over a longer delay, with older infants showing higher levels of deferred imitation than younger infants (see Figure 5.6) (Bauer et al., 2000).

Infants' memory is influenced by situational factors. They are most likely to remember events that take place in familiar contexts and in which they are actively and emotionally engaged (Courage & Cowan, 2009; Rose, Feldman, Jankowski, & Van Rossem, 2011). One method for testing the effect of emotional engagement on memory is the still-face interaction paradigm. In this experimental task, an infant interacts with an adult who first engages in normal social interaction and then suddenly lets his or her face become still and expressionless, not responsive to the infant's actions (Tronick, Als, Adamson, Wise, & Brazelton, 1978). Infants usually respond to the adult's still face with brief smiles followed by displaying negative facial expressions, crying, looking away, sucking their

FIGURE 5.6

Recall in Infancy and Toddlerhood

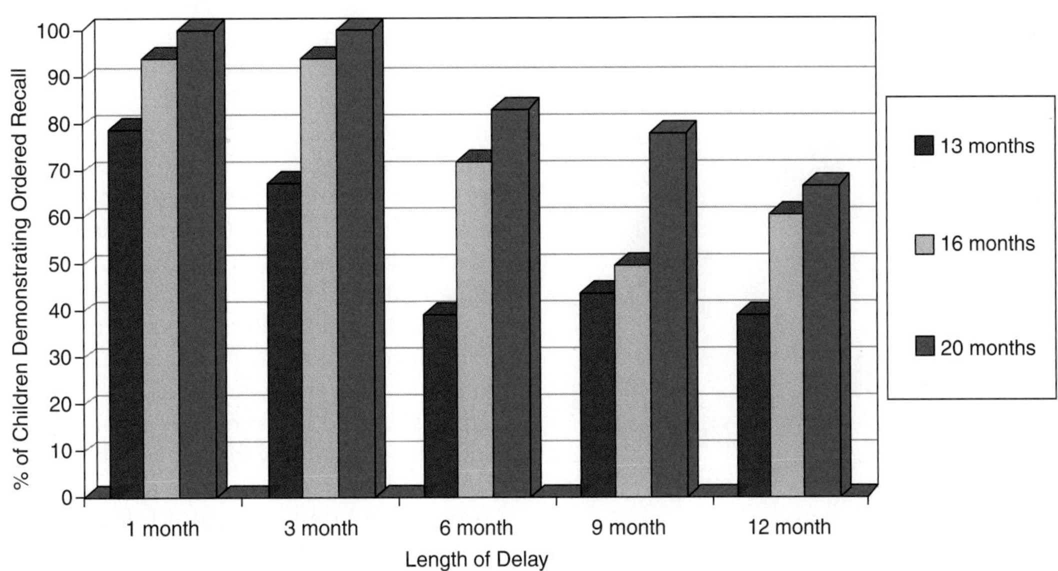

Source: Bauer et al. (2000).

thumb, and showing other indications of emotional distress (Shapiro, Fagen, Prigot, Carroll, & Shalan, 1998; Weinberg & Tronick, 1994). In one study, 5-month-old infants who were exposed to the still face demonstrated recall over a year later, at 20 months of age, by looking less at the woman who had appeared in the earlier still-face paradigm than at two other women whom the infants had never previously seen (Bornstein, Arterberry, & Mash, 2004). Generally, with age, infants create memories more quickly and retain them for longer periods, but at all ages infants are more likely to recall events that take place in familiar surroundings in which they are actively engaged and that are emotionally salient (Courage & Cowan, 2009; Learmonth, Lamberth, & Rovee-Collier, 2004). As we develop, we amass a great deal of information in long-term memory, organize it in increasingly sophisticated ways, and encode and retrieve it more efficiently and with less effort.

Infants' Thinking

In infants' eyes, all of the world is new—"one great blooming, buzzing confusion," in the famous words of 19th-century psychologist William James (1890). How do infants think about and make sense of the world? As infants are bombarded with a multitude of stimuli, encountering countless new objects, people, and events, they form concepts by naturally grouping stimuli into classes or categories. **Categorization**, grouping different stimuli into a common class, is an adaptive mental process that allows for organized storage of information in memory, efficient retrieval of that information, and the capacity to respond with familiarity to new stimuli from a common class (Quinn, 2016). Infants naturally categorize information, just as older children and adults do (Rosenberg & Feigenson, 2013). Without the ability to categorize, we would have to respond anew to each novel stimulus we experience.

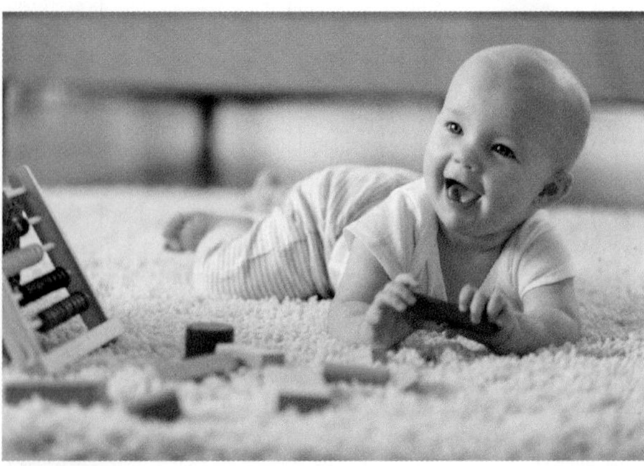

Infants naturally categorize stimuli, such as toys and other objects, enabling them to respond adaptively.
©iStockphoto.com/Steve Debenport

Just as in studying perception and attention, developmental researchers must rely on basic learning capacities, such as habituation, to study how infants categorize objects (Rigney & Wang, 2015). For example, infants are shown a series of stimuli belonging to one category (e.g., fruit: apples and oranges) and then are presented with a new stimulus of the same category (e.g., a pear or a lemon) and a stimulus of a different category (e.g., a cat or a horse). If an infant dishabituates or shows renewed interest by looking longer at the new stimulus (e.g., cat), it suggests that he or she perceives it as belonging to a different category from that of the previously encountered stimuli (Cohen & Cashon, 2006). Using this method, researchers have learned that 3-month-old infants categorize pictures of dogs and cats differently based on perceived differences in facial features (Quinn, Eimas, & Rosenkrantz, 1993).

Infants' earliest categories are based on the perceived similarity of objects (Rakison & Butterworth, 1998). By 4 months, infants can form categories based on perceptual properties, grouping objects that are similar in appearance, including shape, size, and color (Quinn, 2016). As early as 7 months of age, infants use conceptual categories based on perceived function and behavior (Mandler, 2004). Moreover, patterns in 6- to 7-month-old infants' brain waves correspond to their identification of novel and familiar categories (Quinn, Doran, Reiss, & Hoffman, 2010). Seven- to 12-month-old infants use many categories to organize objects, such as food, furniture, birds, animals, vehicles, kitchen utensils, and more, based on both perceptual similarity and perceived function and behavior (Bornstein & Arterberry, 2010; Mandler & McDonough, 1998; Oakes, 2010).

Researchers also use sequential touching tasks to study the conceptual categories that older infants create (Perry, 2015). Infants are presented with a collection of objects from two categories (e.g., four animals and four vehicles) and their patterns of touching are recorded. If the infants recognize a categorical distinction among the objects, they touch those from within a category in succession more than would be expected by chance. Research using sequential touching procedures has shown that 12- to 30-month-old toddlers organize objects first at a global level and then at more specific levels. They categorize at more inclusive levels (e.g., animals or vehicles) before less inclusive levels (e.g., types of animals or types of vehicles) and before even less inclusive levels (e.g., specific animals or vehicles) (Bornstein & Arterberry, 2010). Infants' and toddlers' everyday experiences and exploration contribute to their growing capacity to recognize commonalities among objects, group them in meaningful ways,

APPLYING DEVELOPMENTAL SCIENCE

Baby Signing

Few things are as frustrating for parents as trying to decipher their baby's cry. What does she need? Is she hungry? Cold? Does she have a wet diaper? Is she hurt? Imagine how nice it would be if infants could communicate their needs! Is baby signing the answer?

The baby signing movement promotes early communication between infants and parents by teaching infants to communicate with symbolic gestures. The assumption behind baby signing is that the cognitive and gross motor skills needed for signing develop before the relatively fine motor control of the mouth, tongue, and breath needed to articulate speech (Goodwyn & Acredolo, 1998). Researchers Linda Acredolo and Susan Goodwyn demonstrated that babies readily acquire symbolic gestures when exposed to the enhanced gestural training that they refer to as baby signs (Acredolo, Goodwyn, & Abrams, 2009). They propose that the rewards of baby signing include larger and more expressive vocabulary, advanced mental development, improved parent–child relationships, and fewer tantrums and behavior problems (Acredolo & Goodwyn, 1988; Goodwyn & Acredolo, 1998). Based on their findings, Acredolo and Goodwyn created a signing program for infants with videos, classes, books, and cue cards (Acredolo et al., 2009). Numerous companies have been created to promote and sell baby signing materials, often advertising benefits such as facilitating spoken language, reducing tantrums, and increasing IQ.

It is generally recognized that gesture and language are linked and that babies naturally make early gestures that precede their use of language (Iverson & Goldin-Meadow, 2005). Sensitive responses from caregivers tend to result in more pointing and gesturing from infants, suggesting that gestures are a form of communication (Vallotton, Decker, Kwon, Wang, & Chang, 2017). But will baby signing programs and videos accelerate language and cognitive development? One review of 33 websites associated with various baby signing products revealed that all promoters claimed benefits such as faster language development, and many claimed to foster cognitive and emotional development, including higher IQs, improvements in parent–child interactions, and fewer child tantrums (Nelson, White, & Grewe, 2012). Yet almost none provided evidence to support these claims. A review of research studies examining the outcomes of baby signing programs found that although some of the studies suggested some benefits, nearly all contained methodological weaknesses such as a lack of control groups or no random assignment (see Chapter 1), suggesting insufficient evidence to support these claims (Johnston, 2005).

More recently, a longitudinal study tested the effects of baby signing products. Infants were followed from 8 months of age until 20 months of age (Kirk, Howlett, Pine, & Fletcher, 2013). Babies were randomly assigned to one of three conditions: baby sign training, verbal training (i.e., mothers modeled words without signs), and nonintervention. At 20 months of age, the language development was similar for all babies, regardless of intervention. Encouraging gestures did not result in higher scores on language measures, providing no support for the claims of baby signing proponents.

Nevertheless, many parents report that baby signing has improved their child's ability to communicate, cognitive ability, and overall parent–infant interactions (Doherty-Sneddon, 2008; Mueller & Sepulveda, 2014). For example, although U.K. infants enrolled in a baby signing class showed no differences in language development compared with their nonsigning peers, mothers who enrolled their infants in the baby signing class tended to use more mental terms and refer to thinking ("You want the toy, huh?") in their infant-directed interactions (Zammit & Atkinson, 2017). Baby signing may not have research support for accelerating language development, but if it promotes frequent parent–infant interaction, does not rush or pressure infants, and is helpful in parents' estimation, there is no reason to discourage its use.

What Do You Think?

Should we encourage parents to teach their babies how to sign? Why or why not? Identify advantages and disadvantages of teaching babies how to sign. ●

and use these concepts to think and solve problems. Recognizing categories is a way of organizing information that allows for more efficient thinking, including storage and retrieval of information in memory. Therefore, advances in categorization are critical to cognitive development. The cognitive abilities that underlie categorization also influence language development as words represent categories, ways of organizing ideas and things. In the Applying Developmental Science feature, we look at the baby signing movement, which proposes that infants can apply gestures as symbols in order to communicate.

As shown in Table 5.2, information processing capacities, such as attention, memory, and categorization skill, show continuous change over the first 3 years of life (Rose, Feldman, & Jankowski, 2009). Infants get better at attending to the world around them, remembering what they encounter, and organizing and making sense of what they learn. Infants' emerging cognitive capacities influence all aspects of their development and functioning, including intelligence. Cognitive development is also influenced by the contexts in which infants and children live.

Culture and Cognitive Development

Theories of infant cognition tend to emphasize infants' construction of new ways of thinking through interactions with the world (such as Piaget) and development of information processing capacities, through advances in attention and memory. A criticism of cognitive-developmental and information processing approaches is that they give little attention to the role of context in cognitive development. The social and cultural contexts in which infants are embedded provide opportunities for social interactions that affect how infants think and view their world. For example, caregivers convey relevant information about the nature of objects and people through social play with infants (Deák, Krasno, Triesch, Lewis, & Sepeta, 2014; Wu, Gopnik, Richardson, & Kirkham, 2011).

Children's social learning opportunities are facilitated and constrained by culture (Legare, Wen, Herrmann, & Whitehouse, 2015). Research with Western samples suggests that caregivers promote children's learning through shared attention, by directing their attention to objects by using clear visual cues such as pointing and alternating their gaze between the infant and object. However, emphasis on instruction, stimulation, and engagement with infants during object play is more common in Western cultures, such as Germany and Greece, than nonwestern cultures, such as

TABLE 5.2

Changes in Information Processing Skills During Infancy

ABILITY	DESCRIPTION
Attention	Attention increases steadily over infancy. From birth, infants attend more to dynamic than static stimuli. During the second half of their first year, infants attend more to complex stimuli such as faces and video clips. Attention is linked with diffuse frontal lobe activity in young infants and localized frontal lobe activity by 7½ months of age. Individual differences appear at all ages and are stable over time. Attention is associated with performance on visual recognition memory tasks.
Memory	Memory improves with age. Three-month-old infants can remember a visual stimulus for 24 hours. By the end of the first year, infants can remember a visual stimulus for several days or even weeks. Infants are most likely to remember events in familiar, engaging, and emotionally salient contexts.
Categorization	Infants first categorize objects based on perceived similarity. By 4 months, infants can form categories based on perceptual properties such as shape, size, and color. By 6 to 7 months of age, infants' brain waves correspond to their identification of novel and familiar categories. Seven- to 12-month-old infants can organize objects such as food, furniture, animals, and kitchen utensils, based on perceived function and behavior. Twelve- to 30-month-old infants categorize objects first at a global level and then at more specific levels. Infants categorize objects at more global and inclusive levels (such as motor vehicles) before more specific and less inclusive levels (such as cars, trucks, and construction equipment). The use of categories improves memory efficiency.

rural Cameroon and rural India (Keller et al., 2009). For example, visual face-to-face contact is common in Western communities, yet many nonwestern communities, such as the !Kung, Gusii, and Samoan communities, emphasize physical contact with infants instead of visual, face-to-face contact (Konner, 2017).

In many communities learning may occur without direct adult instruction and often through observation, without any direct instructional cues (Gaskins & Paradise, 2010). For example, when children grow up in cultural communities where observational learning is valued, such as in agricultural communities where children learn to participate in household tasks at an early age, they tend to become skilled observational learners, even as infants, which influences how they process stimuli in their world. In one study, 14- to 20-month-old Guatemalan Mayan and middle-class U.S. children were exposed to co-occurring events, such as being given a new toy to explore while other events were happening in the room. U.S. children tended to focus on only one event at a time, whereas the Mayan children tended to simultaneously monitor multiple events by rapidly shifting their attention from one to another or by manipulating the toy while observing the other events (Chavajay & Rogoff, 1999). Attending to events in this way fosters learning from observation by permitting children the opportunity to learn from interactions that do not involve them.

Caregivers of different cultures interact with infants and objects in different ways. One recent study compared caregiver–child interactions among Western parents from the United States and those on the island of Tanna in Vanuatu, an isolated agricultural country in which children learn from a very young age to be responsible for assisting adults in cooking, planting and harvesting crops, prepping for ceremonial gatherings, and helping with the child care of younger siblings (Little, Carver, & Legare, 2016). Vanuatu children learn through observing and participating in daily activities (Rogoff, Mistry, Göncü, & Mosier, 1993a; Rogoff et al., 2003). When female caregivers were observed interacting with their infant with a novel object, both the U.S. and Vanuatu caregivers engaged in similar amounts of interactions with the infant and object, but Vanuatu caregivers spent more time physically engaging infants with the object compared with U.S. caregivers who used visual cues, such as eye gaze, to direct the infants. In addition, after they observed an experimenter interact with a novel object, U.S. caregivers were more likely to spontaneously teach the action during play than the Vanuatu and the U.S. caregivers tended to use visual transmission. Although infants learn from their social world, the means by which they learn appears to vary by cultural context.

THINKING IN CONTEXT 5.2

1. What are some of the challenges of studying information processing capacities, such as attention and memory, in infants?
2. Recall from Chapter 1 that developmental scientists vary in whether they view development as continuous, gradual, or discontinuous and stage-like. Consider cognition in infancy. To what degree do you view it as continuous or discontinuous? Why?
3. How might contextual influences, such as child care environment, home, interaction with others, neighborhood, and media, influence infants' information processing abilities?

INDIVIDUAL DIFFERENCES IN COGNITIVE ABILITIES

As we have discussed, infants are born with cognitive abilities that develop rapidly. Infants vary, however, in their set of mental skills. Most simply put, **intelligence** refers to an individual's ability to adapt to the world. Different people have different levels of intelligence—an example of the concept of individual differences or variation from one individual to another (see Chapter 1). Intelligence tests are used to measure these differences; they include questions that measure memory, pattern recognition, verbal knowledge, quantitative abilities, and logical reasoning. Measuring intelligence in infancy is challenging because, as noted earlier, infants cannot answer questions. Instead, researchers who study infant intelligence rely on an assortment of nonverbal tasks—the same kinds of methods that are used to study cognitive development. There are two general approaches to studying intelligence in infancy. As discussed next, the testing approach emphasizes standardized tests that compare infants with age-based norms. A second approach, the information processing approach, examines specific processing skills.

Testing Infant Intelligence

At 3 months of age, baby Lourdes can lift and support her upper body with her arms when she is on her stomach. She grabs and shakes toys with her hands and enjoys playing with other people. Lourdes's pediatrician tells her parents that her development is right on track for babies her age and that she shows typical levels of infant intelligence. Standardized tests permit the pediatrician to determine Lourdes's development relative to other infants her age.

The most often used standardized measure of infant intelligence is the Bayley Scales of Infant Development III (BSID-III), commonly called "Bayley-III." This test is appropriate for infants from 1 month through 42 months of age (Bayley, 1969, 2005). The Bayley-III consists of five scales: three consisting of infant responses and two of parent responses. The *Motor Scale* measures gross and fine motor skills, such as grasping objects, drinking from a cup, sitting, and climbing stairs. The *Cognitive Scale* includes items such as attending to a stimulus or searching for a hidden toy. The *Language Scale* examines comprehension and production of language, such as following directions and naming objects. The *Social-Emotional Scale* is derived from parental reports regarding behavior such as the infant's responsiveness and play activity. Finally, the *Adaptive Behavior Scale* is based on parental reports of the infant's ability to adapt in everyday situations, including the infant's ability to communicate, regulate his or her emotions, and display certain behavior.

The Bayley-III provides a comprehensive profile of an infant's current functioning, but the performance of infants often varies considerably from one testing session to another (Bornstein, Slater, Brown, Roberts, & Barrett, 1997). Scores vary with infants' states of arousal and motivation. This suggests that pediatricians and parents must exert great care in interpreting scores—particularly poor scores—because an infant's performance may be influenced by factors other than developmental functioning. Infants who perform poorly on the Bayley-III should be reexamined.

Although Bayley-III scores offer a comprehensive profile of an infant's abilities, scores do not predict performance on intelligence tests in childhood (Luttikhuizen dos Santos, de Kieviet, Königs, van Elburg, & Oosterlaan, 2013; Rose & Feldman, 1995).

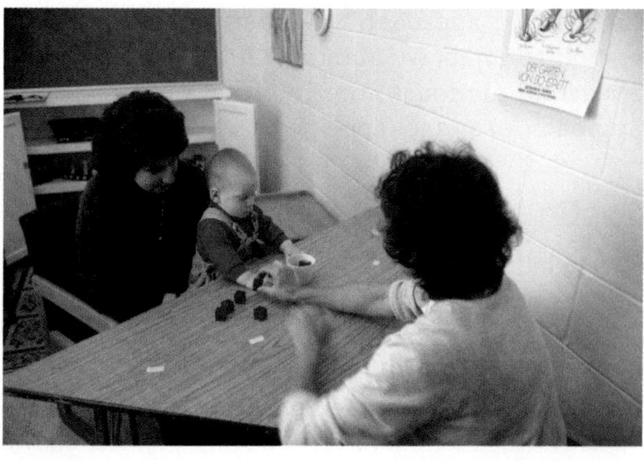

Infant assessment tests, such as the BSID-III, examine cognitive, language, socioemotional, and motor abilities, such as infants' skill in manipulating objects.
Cliff Moore/Science Source

Even Nancy Bayley, who invented the Bayley Scales, noted in a longitudinal study (1949) that infant performance was not related to intelligence scores at age 18. Why is infant intelligence relatively unrelated to later intelligence? Consider what is measured by infant tests: perception and motor skills, responsiveness, and language skills. The ability to grasp an object, crawl up stairs, or search for a hidden toy—items that appear on the Bayley-III—are not measured by childhood intelligence tests. Instead, intelligence tests administered in childhood examine more complex and abstract abilities such as verbal reasoning, verbal comprehension, and problem solving.

If the Bayley-III does not predict later intelligence, why administer it? Infants whose performance is poor relative to age norms may suffer from serious developmental problems that can be addressed. The abilities measured by the Bayley-III are critical indicators of neurological health and are useful for charting developmental paths, diagnosing neurological disorders, and detecting intellectual disabilities in infants and toddlers. Thus, the Bayley-III is primarily used as a screening tool to identify infants who can benefit from medical and developmental intervention. As discussed in the accompanying Lives in Context feature, contextual conditions, especially exposure to poverty, can place some infants and children at risk for poor developmental outcomes.

Information Processing as Intelligence

The challenge in determining whether intelligence in infancy predicts performance in childhood and beyond rests in identifying measures that evaluate cognitive functioning from infancy through childhood. Information processing abilities, such as those related to attention, working memory, and processing speed, underlie performance in all cognitive tasks, including intelligence tests, and are therefore important indicators of intellectual ability that are evident at birth and persist for a lifetime (Baddeley, 2016; Müller & Kerns, 2015; Ristic & Enns, 2015a).

Individuals who process information more efficiently are thought to acquire knowledge more quickly. This is true for infants as well as for older children and adults. Indeed, information processing capacities in infancy, such as attention, memory, and processing speed, have been shown to predict cognitive ability and intelligence through late adolescence.

Information processing abilities can be assessed in simple ways that allow us to study intelligence

LIVES IN CONTEXT: BIOLOGICAL INFLUENCES

Poverty and Brain Development

Forty-five percent of U.S. children under 3 years of age (including two-thirds of black, Hispanic, and Native American children) live in low-income families (income less than $48,000 per year for a family of four), and 23% live in poor families (income less than $24,000) (Koball & Jiang, 2018) (see Figure 5.7). In 2013, the American Academy of Pediatrics added child poverty to its Agenda for Children in recognition of poverty's broad and enduring effects on child health and development (American Academy of Pediatrics, 2017). Infants and children from poor families experience higher rates of malnutrition, growth stunting, and susceptibility to illness than do their peers (Yoshikawa, Aber, & Beardslee, 2012).

Exposure to chronic long-term poverty has negative effects on brain growth and is associated with lower volumes in parts of the brain associated with memory and learning, cognitive control, and emotional processing (Johnson, Riis, & Noble, 2016; Ursache & Noble, 2016; Wijeakumar, Kumar, Delgado Reyes, Tiwari, & Spencer, 2019). For example, a longitudinal study of 77 children from birth to age 4 revealed a link between poverty and lower gray matter volume especially in the frontal and parietal regions associated with executive function (Hanson et al., 2013). In another study, 5-week-old infants in low socioeconomic status (SES) homes tended to have smaller brain volumes than other infants, suggesting that poverty may influence biological and cognitive development during the first few weeks of life or earlier (Betancourt et al., 2016).

The effects of SES on development vary. SES is more closely related with brain structure and cognition in children from poor homes than high SES homes (Hair, Hanson, Wolfe, Pollak, & Knight, 2015; Noble et al., 2015). That is, the detrimental effect of low SES contexts is a greater influence on children's development than the positive effect of high SES contexts. Chronic poverty is especially damaging because the neurological and cognitive deficits accumulate over childhood (Dickerson & Popli, 2016). One way in which poverty affects development is through the quality of parent–infant interactions and infants' exposure to language (Hackman, Gallop, Evans, & Farah, 2015). Infants in higher SES homes are talked to more and the speech they hear is often more stimulating and supportive of language development than is the case in lower SES homes (Fernald, Marchman, & Weisleder, 2013; Sheridan, Sarsour, Jutte, D'Esposito, & Boyce, 2012).

Poverty is also thought to affect children's outcomes indirectly by contributing to household chaos, a combination of household instability and disorder (Berry et al., 2016). Children reared in economic uncertainty are more likely to experience disruptions in home settings and relationships through household moves and adults moving in and out of the home (Pascoe, Wood, Duffee, & Kuo, 2016). Impoverished environments often include household crowding, lack of structure, and excessive ambient noise in the home or neighborhood (Evans & Kim, 2013). Infants and children reared in environments

FIGURE 5.7

Percentage of Children in Low-Income and Poor Families by Race/Ethnicity, 2016

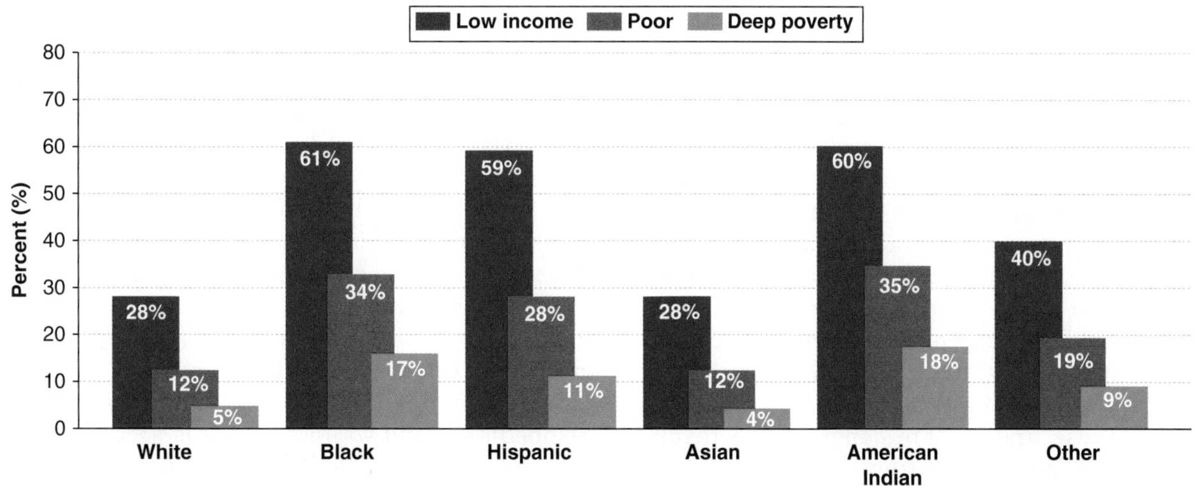

(Continued)

(Continued)

of household chaos may be overwhelmed by stimulation combined with little developmentally appropriate support, with negative effects for cognitive development. The effects of a chaotic home environment begin early. For example, a chaotic environment has been shown to negatively affect visual processing speed for complex stimuli in 5½-month-old infants (Tomalski et al., 2017). Poverty has early effects on children's brain development that increase over time with lifelong implications for cognitive and language development.

What Do You Think?

Infants and children reared in poverty face many contextual risks to development. Their contexts may also offer opportunities for resilience. Identify factors within the family and home that can promote the development of infants and children who are exposed to poverty. How might the extended family, neighborhood, and community help to buffer the effects of challenging environments on development? ●

in infants who are too young to tell us what they think and understand. For example, infants' visual reaction time (how quickly they look when shown a stimulus) and preference for novelty (the degree to which they prefer new stimuli over familiar ones) are indicators of attention, memory, and processing speed and have been shown to predict intelligence in childhood and adolescence (Fagan, 2011). Habituation tasks also provide information about the efficiency of information processing because they indicate how quickly an infant learns: Infants who learn quickly look away from an unchanging stimulus (or habituate) rapidly. Longitudinal studies suggest that infants who are fast habituators score higher on measures of intelligence in childhood and adolescence than do those who are slower habituators (Kavšek, 2013; Rose, Feldman, & Jankowski, 2012). One study demonstrated that, compared with average and slow habituators, infants who were fast habituators had higher IQs and higher educational achievement when they were followed up 20 years later in emerging adulthood (Fagan et al., 2007).

Many other studies confirm that infant information processing abilities are associated with measures of intelligence throughout life. For example, working memory and visuospatial short-term memory in infancy are associated with IQ in fourth- and fifth-grade children (Giofrè, Mammarella, & Cornoldi, 2013). Working memory and processing speed are also associated with intelligence in children and adults (Redick, Unsworth, Kelly, & Engle, 2012; Rose, Feldman, Jankowski, & Van Rossem, 2012; Sheppard, 2008). Information processing skills in infancy are effective predictors of intelligence in childhood; however, these findings are generally the result of laboratory research. Although pediatricians might test an infant's attention and habituation as part of an examination, there is no standardized information processing test of intelligence to apply to infants comparable to the Bayley-III.

Child Care and Mental Development

Infants are immersed in a system of contexts that influence their development. Parents shape infants' physical world, providing food, health care, a home, and stimulation that influences their cognitive development. Infants also are influenced by the child care context.

In the United States, more than half of all mothers of infants younger than 1 year old, and over two-thirds of mothers of children under 6, are employed (U.S. Bureau of Labor Statistics, 2016). The infants and young children of working mothers are cared for in a variety of settings: in center-based care, in the home of someone other than a relative, or with a relative such as a father, grandparent, or older sibling (Federal Interagency Forum on Child and Family Statistics, 2014). A common misconception is that nonfamilial center-based care is damaging to children's development and places children at risk for insecure attachment. However, this belief is not supported by research. What are the effects of nonparental care?

One of the best sources of information about the effects of nonparental care is a longitudinal study of over 1,300 children conducted by the National Institute of Child Health and Human Development (NICHD). This study found that infants' developmental outcomes are influenced more by characteristics of the family, such as parenting, maternal education, and maternal sensitivity, than by the type of child care (Axe, 2007; Dehaan, 2006). Center-based care did not predispose infants to forming insecure attachments (Belsky, 2005; Harrison & Ungerer, 2002). Some research suggests that center-based care is associated with more disobedience and aggression but is accompanied by greater sociability (Jacob, 2009). Other work suggests that behavior problems may be more common in low-quality care but do not appear in high-quality care (Gialamas, Mittinty, Sawyer, Zubrick, & Lynch, 2014; Huston, Bobbitt, & Bentley,

2015). Indicators of high-quality child care include a low child-to-teacher ratio and positive teacher–child interactions.

Quality of child care matters. Infants and young children exposed to poor-quality child care score lower on measures of cognitive and social competence, regardless of demographic variables such as parental education and SES (NICHD Early Child Care Research Network, 2005). In contrast, high-quality child care that includes specific efforts to stimulate children is associated with gains in cognitive and language development over the first 3 years of life and can even compensate for lower-quality and chaotic home environments (Berry et al., 2016; Gialamas et al., 2014; Mortensen & Barnett, 2015; Watamura, Phillips, Morrissey, McCartney, & Bub, 2011).

Child care quality has long-term effects as well. A recent study of Dutch infants showed that high-quality care, defined as providing high levels of emotional and behavioral support, predicted children's social competence a year later; specifically, children who spent at least 3½ days a week in care showed lower levels of behavioral problems (Broekhuizen, van Aken, Dubas, & Leseman, 2018). Longitudinal research in Sweden showed that older children and adolescents who had received high-quality care as infants and toddlers scored higher on measures of cognitive, emotional, and social competence later in childhood (Andersson, 1989; Broberg, Wessels, Lamb, & Hwang, 1997). In addition, a longitudinal analysis of over 1,200 children from the NICHD study revealed that the quality of care predicted academic grades and behavioral adjustment at the end of high school, at age 15 and 18, as well as admission to more selective colleges (Vandell, Belsky, Burchinal, Steinberg, & Vandergrift, 2010; Vandell, Burchinal, & Pierce, 2016).

The challenge is that high-quality child care is expensive. For example, the annual cost of center-based care in the United States ranged from about $6,000 in Arkansas to $22,000 in Washington, D.C., from 2012 to 2016 (Child Care Aware of America, 2014; Schulte & Durana, 2016). In some countries, such as Sweden, Norway, and Finland, child care is heavily subsidized by the government (Gothe-Snape, 2017). In the United States, however, it remains a private responsibility. The few public subsidies for child care available in the United States are tied to economic need and are mainly targeted at low-income families who receive other forms of public assistance. Because of this, child care settings vary dramatically from large commercial centers to nonprofit facilities supported by churches and community groups, to in-home and informal centers.

THINKING IN CONTEXT 5.3

1. To what extent do you think cognitive development, such as sensorimotor stage or information processing abilities, influences scores on infant intelligence measures? Why?
2. Can contextual factors influence infant scores on intelligence measures? Consider specific aspects of context, such as home, adult interactions, child care center, neighborhood, and others. How might these factors influence intelligence?

LANGUAGE DEVELOPMENT IN INFANCY AND TODDLERHOOD

"You just love to hear Mommy talk, don't you?" Velma asked as newborn Jayson stared up at her. Is Jayson attending to his mother? Is he interested in his mother's speech? As described in Chapter 4, hearing emerges well before birth, and evidence suggests that newborns can recall sounds heard in the womb (Dirix, Nijhuis, Jongsma, & Hornstra, 2009). Jayson recognizes his mother's voice and naturally tunes in, which will help him learn language, a critical task for infancy and toddlerhood. Language development has important implications for the child's cognitive, social, and emotional development. Gaining the ability to use words to represent objects, experiences, thoughts, and feelings permits children to think and to communicate with others in increasingly flexible and adaptive ways.

Early Preferences for Speech Sounds

Newborn infants are primed to learn language. Recall from Chapter 4 that neonates naturally attend to speech and prefer to hear human speech sounds, especially their native language, as well as stories and sounds that they heard prenatally (L. May et al., 2018). Infants naturally notice the complex patterns of sounds around them and organize sounds into meaningful units. They recognize frequently heard words, such as their names. By 4½ months of age, infants will turn their heads to hear their own names but not to hear other names, even when the other names have a similar sound pattern (e.g., Annie and

Johnny) (Mandel, Jusczyk, & Pisoni, 1995). Infants pay particular attention to vowel sounds at 6 months of age and to consonants at 9 months of age (Kuhl, 2015).

Although infants can perceive and discriminate sounds that comprise all human languages at birth, their developing capacities and preferences are influenced by context (Hoff, 2015). For example, the Japanese language does not discriminate between the consonant sounds of "r" in rip and "l" in lip. Japanese adults who are learning English find it very difficult to discriminate between the English pronunciations of these "r" and "l" sounds, yet up until about 6 to 8 months of age, Japanese and U.S. infants are equally able to distinguish these sounds. By 10 to 12 months, however, discrimination of "r" and "l" improves for U.S. infants and declines for Japanese infants. This likely occurs because U.S. infants hear these sounds often, whereas Japanese infants do not (Kuhl et al., 2006). As they are exposed to their native language, they become more attuned to the sounds (and distinctions between sounds) that are meaningful in their own language and less able to distinguish speech sounds that are not used in that language (Werker, Yeung, & Yoshida, 2012). Native-language discrimination ability between 6 and 7 months predicts the rate of language growth between 11 and 30 months (Kuhl, 2015).

Infants' speech discrimination abilities remain malleable in response to the social context (Kuhl, 2016). In one study, Kuhl and her colleagues exposed 9-month-old English-learning American infants to 12 live interaction sessions with an adult speaker of Mandarin Chinese over the course of 4 to 5 weeks (Kuhl, Tsao, & Liu, 2003). After the sessions, the infants were tested on a Mandarin phonetic contrast that does not occur in English. The infants discriminated the contrast as well as same-aged Mandarin-learning infants and retained the contrast for several days. The relevance of context is also illustrated by the infants' loss of the ability to discriminate the Mandarin contrast several days after training, presumably in the absence of ongoing exposure to the Mandarin language (Fitneva & Matsui, 2015).

Social interaction is vital to language learning. In the study just described, the English-learning infants did not learn the Mandarin phonetic contrast when they were exposed to it only by audio or video. Live interaction may have increased infants' motivation to learn by increasing their attention and arousal. Or perhaps live interaction provides specific information that fosters learning, like the speaker's eye gaze and pointing coupled with interactive contingency (Kuhl et al., 2003).

In addition, social input, such as the quality of mother–infant interactions, plays a critical role in determining the timing of infants' narrowing of speech sound discrimination. Specifically, infants who experience high-quality interactions with their mothers, characterized by frequent speech, show a narrowing of speech sound discrimination earlier, as early as 6 months of age (Elsabbagh et al., 2013).

Prelinguistic Communication

At birth, crying is the infant's only means of communication. Infants soon learn to make many more sounds, like gurgles, grunts, and squeals. Between 2 and 3 months of age, infants begin **cooing**, making deliberate vowel sounds like "ahhhh," "ohhhh," and "eeeee." Infants' first coos sound like one long vowel. These vocal sounds are a form of vocal play; they are likely to be heard when babies are awake, alert, and contented. At the cooing stage, infants already use pauses that are consistent with the turn-taking pattern of spoken conversations. With age, the quality of coos changes to include different vowel-like sounds and combinations of vowel-like sounds (Owens, 2016). **Babbling**, repeating strings of consonants and vowels such as "ba-ba-ba" and "ma-ma-ma," begins to appear at about 6 months of age.

At first, babbling is universal. All babies do it, and the sounds they make are similar no matter what language their parents speak or in what part of the world they are raised. However, infants soon become sensitive to the ambient language around them, and it influences their vocalizations (Chen & Kent, 2010). In one study, French adults listened to the babbling of a French 8-month-old and a second 8-month-old from either an Arabic-speaking or a Cantonese-speaking family. Nearly three-quarters of the time, the adults correctly indicated which baby in the pair was French (Boysson-Bardies et al., 1984). By the end of the first year, infants' babbling sounds more like real speech as they begin to vary the pitch of their speech in ways that reflect the inflections

By the end of the first year, infants' babbling sounds like real speech.
Eric Scouten/Alamy Stock Photo

of their native languages (Andruski, Casielles, & Nathan, 2013). For example, in spoken English, declarative sentences are characterized by pitch that falls toward the end of the sentence, whereas in questions, the pitch rises at the end of the sentence. Older babies' babbling mirrors these patterns when they are raised by English-speaking parents, while babies reared with Japanese or French as their native languages show intonation patterns similar to those of the respective languages (Levitt et al., 1992). Longitudinal observations of infants raised in Catalan-speaking environments likewise show that their babbling shifts to mirror intonations in native speech (Esteve-Gilbert et al., 2013).

Language acquisition, as mentioned, is a socially interactive process: Babies learn by hearing others speak and by noticing the reactions that their vocalizations evoke in caregivers (Hoff, 2015; Kuhl, 2016). Social interaction elicits cooing, and infants modify their babbling in response to caregiver interactions (Tamis-LeMonda, Kuchirko, & Song, 2014). For example, when mothers of 9½-month-old infants speak in response to their infants' babbling, infants restructure their babbling, changing the phonological pattern of sounds in response to their mother's speech (Goldstein & Schwade, 2008). Babbling repertoires reflect infants' developing morphology and are a foundation for word learning (Ramsdell, Oller, Buder, Ethington, & Chorna, 2012). Language development follows a predictable pattern.

First Words

Eleven-month-old William was wide-eyed as his father handed him a ball and said, "Ball!" "Ba!" said William. William now understands many words and is beginning to try to utter them. Throughout language development, babies' **receptive language** (what they can understand) exceeds their **productive language** (what they can produce themselves) (Tamis-Lemonda & Bornstein, 2015). That is, infants understand more words than they can use. Research suggests that infants may understand some commonly spoken words as early as 6 to 9 months of age, long before they are able to speak (Bergelson & Swingley, 2012; Dehaene-Lambertz & Spelke, 2015).

At about 1 year of age, the average infant speaks his or her first word. At first, infants use one-word expressions, called **holophrases**, to express complete thoughts. A first word might be a complete word or a syllable. Usually, the word has more than one meaning, depending on the context in which it is used. For example, "Da" might mean, "I want that," "There's Daddy!" or "What's that?" Caregivers usually hear and understand first words before other adults do. The first words that infants use are those that they hear often or are meaningful for them, such as their own name, the word *no*, or the word for their caregiver. Infants reared in English-speaking homes tend to use nouns first, as they are most concrete and easily understood (Waxman et al., 2013). For example, the word *dog* refers to a concrete thing—an animal—and is easier to understand than a verb, such as *goes*. In contrast, infants reared in homes in which Mandarin Chinese, Korean, or Japanese is spoken tend to learn verbs very early in their development in response to the greater emphasis on verbs in their native languages (Waxman et al., 2013).

Regardless of what language a child speaks, early words tend to be used in the following ways (MacWhinney, 2015; Owens, 2016):

- Request or state the existence or location of an object or person by naming it (car, dog, outside).
- Request or describe the recurrence of an event or receipt of an object (again, more).
- Describe actions (eat, fall, ride).
- Ask questions (What? That?).
- Attribute a property to an object (hot, big).
- Mark social situations, events, and actions (no, bye).

Learning Words: Semantic Growth

"I can't believe how quickly Matthew picks up new words. It's time for us to be more careful about what we say around him," warned Elana. Her husband agreed. "He's only 2 years old and he has quite a vocabulary. Who would think that he'd learn so many words so quickly?" By 13 months of age, children begin to quickly learn the meaning of new words and understand that words correspond to particular things or events (Woodward, Markman, & Fitzsimmons, 1994). Most infants of Matthew's age expand their vocabularies rapidly, often to the surprise of their parents. Infants learn new words through **fast mapping**, a process of quickly acquiring and retaining a word after hearing it applied a few times (Kan & Kohnert, 2008; Marinellie & Kneile, 2012). At 18 months, infants are more likely to learn a new word if both they and the speaker are attending to the new object when the speaker introduces the new word (Baldwin et al., 1996). Two-year-olds have been shown to be able to learn a word even after a single brief exposure under ambiguous conditions (Spiegel & Halberda, 2011) or after overhearing a speaker use the word when talking to someone else (Akhtar, Jipson, & Callanan, 2001).

Between 24 and 30 months, infants can learn new words even when their attention is distracted by other objects or events (Moore, Angelopoulos, & Bennett, 1999). Children's knowledge and interests influence their vocabulary development. They are more likely to learn words that are related to those they know and label objects, actions, and events that they find interesting (Mani & Ackermann, 2018).

Fast mapping improves with age and accounts for the naming explosion, or vocabulary spurt—a period of rapid vocabulary learning that occurs between 16 and 24 months of age (Owens, 2016). During this period, infants apply their word-learning strategies to learn multiple words of varying difficulty seemingly at once. Within weeks, a toddler may increase her vocabulary from 50 words to over 400 (Bates, Bretherton, & Snyder, 1988). As shown in Figure 5.8, however, infants vary in the speed of word acquisition, with some showing a rapid increase in vocabulary before others (Samuelson & McMurray, 2017). In addition, although fast mapping helps young children learn many new words, their own speech lags behind what they can understand because young children have difficulty retrieving words from memory (McMurray, 2007). The speed at which young children acquire words during the vocabulary spurt predicts the size of their vocabulary as preschoolers at 54 months of age (Rowe, 2012). That is, children who rapidly expand their knowledge of words during the vocabulary spurt tend to have larger vocabularies in preschool than their peers who acquire new words at a slower pace.

As children learn words, we see two interesting kinds of mistakes that tell us about how words are acquired (Gershkoff-Stowe, 2002). **Underextension** refers to applying a word more narrowly than it is usually applied so that the word's use is restricted to a single object. For example, *cup* might refer to Daddy's cup but not to the general class of cups. Later, the opposite tendency appears. **Overextension** refers to applying a word too broadly. *Cow* might refer to cows, sheep, horses, and all farm animals. Overextension suggests that the child has learned that a word can signify a whole class of objects. As children develop a larger vocabulary and get feedback on their speech, they demonstrate fewer errors of overextension and underextension (Brooks & Kempe, 2014).

Two-Word Utterances

At about 21 months of age, or usually about 8 to 12 months after they say their first word, most children compose their first simple two-word sentences, such as "Kitty come" or "Mommy milk." **Telegraphic speech**, like a telegram, includes only a few essential words. Like other milestones in language development, telegraphic speech is universal among toddlers. Children around the world use two-word phrases to express themselves.

Language development follows a predictable path, as shown in Table 5.3. Between 20 and 30 months of age, children begin to follow the rules for forming sentences in a given language. Soon they become more comfortable with using plurals, past tense, articles (such as *a* and *the*), prepositions (such as *in* and *on*), and conjunctions (such as *and* and *but*). By 2½ years of age, children demonstrate an

FIGURE 5.8

Number of Words Known as a Function of Time for Individual Children

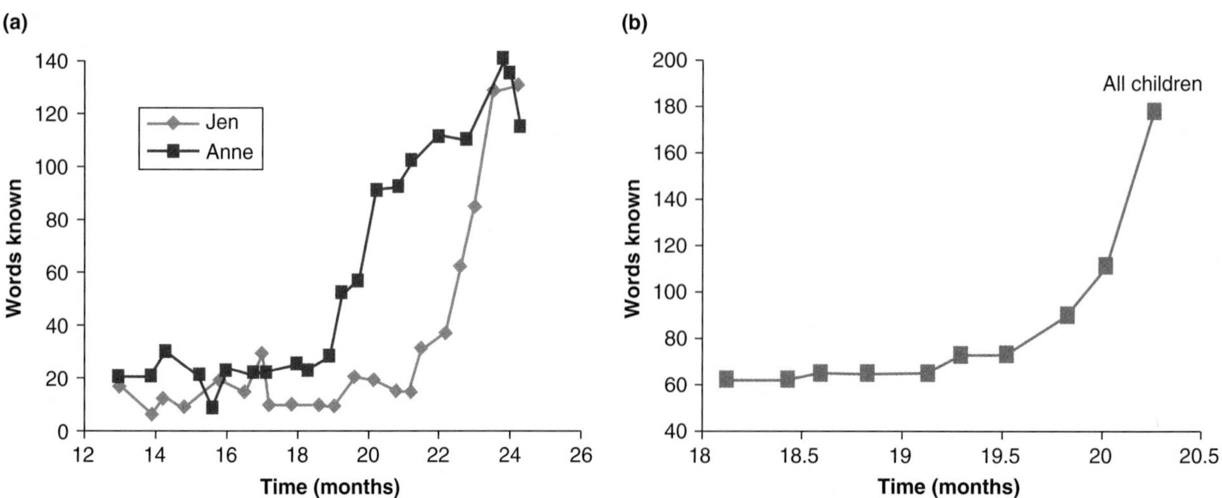

Source: Samuelson and McMurray (2017).

learning influenced by exposure to two languages? Brain scans suggest that 12-month-old bilingual infants' responses to language are similar to those of monolingual infants, suggesting that they are on the same timetable for language learning (Ferjan Ramírez, Ramírez, Clarke, Taulu, & Kuhl, 2017). Notably, however, bilingual infants retain the ability to discriminate phonetic speech sounds of other languages long after their monolingual peers have narrowed their perception to native language sounds (Garcia-Sierra et al., 2011; Petitto et al., 2012).

Language development is promoted through exposure to speech during frequent, high-quality social interactions. In bilingual babies, the amount of infant-directed speech heard in one-to-one interactions influences the growth of that language but is unrelated to growth of the second language (Kuhl & Ramirez, 2016). For example, hearing lots of high-quality Spanish in interactions with a caregiver predicts the growth of Spanish but not English. Bilingual infants' brain responses to hearing each language vary with the amount and quality of speech they hear in each (Garcia-Sierra et al., 2011). Language growth, therefore, is related to the quality and quantity of speech heard, whether in one language or two.

Typically, infants exposed to two languages from birth babble and produce their first words at the same rate as those exposed to one language. Bilingual infants' vocabulary develops in similar ways as monolingual infants (Kuhl & Ramirez, 2016). Although bilingual infants show a smaller vocabulary than monolingual infants on a single language when both languages are considered, bilingual children do not lag behind their monolingual peers (Hoff, Core, Place, & Rumiche, 2012). For example, combined across both languages, bilingual children's vocabulary tends to be equal to or greater than that of monolingual children (Hoff & Core, 2015). Infants' language skills reflect the quantity of language that they hear. The rate of vocabulary and grammatical growth in bilingual children correlates with the quality and quantity of speech that they hear in each language (Ramírez-Esparza, García-Sierra, & Kuhl, 2017). Moreover, some research suggests that bilingual infants are better at learning new words than their monolingual peers (Singh, Fu, Tay, & Golinkoff, 2018). Their exposure to the sounds of multiple languages contributes to their ability to flexibly learn new sounds.

Therefore, the interactionist perspective on language development points to the dynamic and reciprocal influence of biology and context. Infants are equipped with biological propensities and information processing capacities that permit them to perceive and analyze speech and learn to speak. Infants are motivated to communicate with others, and language is a tool for communication. Interactions with others provide important learning experiences, which help infants expand their language capacities and learn to think in ways similar to members of their culture (Fitneva & Matsui, 2015). Theories of language development are summarized in Table 5.4.

Language Development in Deaf Infants. About 2 in 1,000 U.S. infants are born with profound hearing loss (Centers for Disease Control and Prevention, 2019a). We have seen that infants are sensitive to language from birth and language develops rapidly over the first year of life, placing deaf infants at risk for impaired language development. Advances in technology have led nearly all industrialized countries

TABLE 5.4

Theories of Language Development

THEORY	DESCRIPTION
Learning theory	Language is learned through reinforcement, punishment, and imitation. The quantity and quality of the parents' verbal interactions with the child and responses to the child's communication attempts influence the child's rate of language development. Learning theory cannot account for the unique utterances and errors that young children make.
Nativist theory	Despite wide variations in circumstances, living situations, and contexts, infants around the world achieve language milestones at about the same time. An inborn language acquisition device (LAD) equipped with universal grammar permits infants to quickly and efficiently analyze everyday speech and determine its rules. Researchers have not identified the LAD or universal grammar Chomsky thought underlies all languages. Language does not emerge in a finished form. Instead, children learn to string words together over time based on their experiences and trial and error.
Interactionist theory	Infants have an inborn sensitivity to language and discriminate a wide variety of speech sounds, including those that adults can no longer distinguish. Exposure to language influences infants' sensitivity to speech sounds, and the ability to detect sounds not used in their native language declines throughout the first year of life. Language acquisition occurs in a social context. Babies learn language by interacting with more mature, expert speakers who can speak at their developmental level.

to adopt policies for universal neonatal hearing screening (National Center for Hearing Assessment and Management, 2019) and provide early intervention promoting access to visual and/or spoken language (Lederberg, Schick, & Spencer, 2013). Researchers have documented dramatic improvements in language outcomes when hearing disabilities are identified at birth and intervention is implemented by 6 months of age (Cole & Flexer, 2016). Typically, infants with hearing loss wear hearing aids and those with profound hearing loss eventually obtain cochlear implants, electrical devices that convert auditory information into electric signals that are transmitted to the brain. The U.S. Food and Drug Administration advises cochlear implantation after 12 months of age, but research suggests that earlier age of cochlear implantation, as early as 6 months of age, improves language outcomes (McKinney, 2017). However, early administration of cochlear implants is often not covered by health insurance, limiting access to early intervention to families with greater economic means.

Deaf and hard of hearing infants do not experience the range of sensory input that hearing infants receive. Early hearing disability affects the development of cognitive skills, such as memory, attention, learning, and information processing, skills that are also essential for speech and spoken language development (Kronenberger & Pisoni, 2018). Moreover, auditory deprivation early in life may affect brain development, reducing the neurological ability to detect and respond to speech signals and making it difficult to learn language (Wang, Shafto, & Houston, 2018). We have seen that sensory deprivation at birth has dramatic effects on the organization of the brain that interfere with its normal development.

In addition to the availably of early intervention, deaf and hard of hearing infants' outcomes are influenced by contextual factors such as the availability and use of family support from professionals, access to and the ability of family members to learn sign language, and access to professional services and technology (Lederberg et al., 2013). Language environments vary and children with hearing disabilities may be especially sensitive to variations in environmental quality, such as the quality and quantity of parent speech (Levine, Strother-Garcia, Golinkoff, & Hirsh-Pasek, 2016). A dynamic web of factors influence the development of deaf and hard of hearing infants, such as parental knowledge and involvement, socioeconomic status, access to quality early childhood education, and community support.

Infancy represents an important time for development that illustrates the interaction of biology, maturation, and the sociocultural context. Infants are equipped with early and rapidly emerging capacities to move and control their bodies, sense the world around them, and learn and think. However, interactions with their sociocultural context strengthen and modify infants' capacities in every domain of development. In turn, babies' actions influence elements of their sociocultural context. Infants' active role in their own cognitive development cannot be denied. Infants also play an active role in their socioemotional development, as discussed in Chapter 6.

THINKING IN CONTEXT 5.4

1. Consider language development from Bronfenbrenner's bioecological systems theory. Identify four microsystem and mesosystem factors that might influence children's language learning. Provide at least two examples of exosystem factors that might influence children's language development. How might the macrosystem influence language?
2. Consider the various perspectives on language development. From the nativist perspective, what can parents do to promote language development in their infants? What advice would learning theorists provide? Provide advice to parents about language development from the interactionist perspective.

APPLY YOUR KNOWLEDGE

Joshua is 1½ years old and attends an exclusive local nursery school called Three Trees, all day Monday through Friday. Three Trees Nursery School emphasizes interactive play with peers. The staff is culturally diverse and the child-to-staff ratio is 1:3, which allows each child to have individualized care, attention, and specialized learning opportunities.

The staff at Three Trees are informed about new and important findings from research in child development. They are trained in effective ways to promote and develop skills in attention, memory, and categorization. Joshua's mother, a lawyer, chose Three Trees because of its emphasis on the early introduction of learning concepts. The school has an indoor classroom accompanied with stimulating toys and an ample acre-large play area outside.

At school, Joshua's personal teacher Malika speaks to him frequently—she asks questions, names objects, and encourages verbal communication.

Joshua frequently engages other children in play. Joshua's mother is impressed with how quickly he learns new words. His vocabulary is exploding. One of Joshua's favorite games to play with Malika is hide-and-seek. When Joshua first joined Three Trees at age 6 months, Malika would hide objects right in front of him and he wouldn't even attempt to find them. But at 1½ years of age, Joshua is eager to search every corner of the room to find them.

Joshua has recently become a bit mischievous. One day, he was hiding and bumped up against a bookshelf that was adorned with a potted plant. The potted plant fell and shattered on the ground. Now, Joshua picks up different objects on countertops and purposefully drops them on the ground, interested in how they fall and what happens when they hit the ground.

1. Evaluate Joshua's child care setting. Specifically, what factors indicate its quality? What effects can Joshua expect, given his interactions at Three Trees Nursery School?
2. Provide examples of Joshua's behavior that illustrate sensorimotor reasoning.
3. In what ways do Joshua's experiences at Three Trees influence his language development? Why?

WANT A BETTER GRADE?

Get the tools you need to sharpen your study skills. **SAGE edge** offers a robust online environment featuring an impressive array of free tools and resources. Access practice quizzes, eFlashcards, video, and multimedia at **edge.sagepub.com/kutherchild1e.** SAGE edge™

KEY TERMS

Assimilation 130
Accommodation 130
Cognitive equilibrium 130
Cognitive disequilibrium 130
Mental representation 131
Primary circular reaction 131
Secondary circular reaction 132
Object permanence 132
Tertiary circular reaction 132
Violation-of-expectation task 134
A-not-B error 135
Deferred imitation 136
Core knowledge theory 136
Sensory memory 139
Attention 139
Working memory 139
Central executive 139
Executive function 139
Long-term memory 139
Recognition memory 140
Categorization 142
Intelligence 145
Cooing 150
Babbling 150
Receptive language 151
Productive language 151
Holophrase 151
Fast mapping 151
Underextension 152
Overextension 152
Telegraphic speech 152
Language acquisition device (LAD) 153
Broca's area 154
Wernicke's area 154
Infant-directed speech 156

SUMMARY

5.1 Discuss the cognitive-developmental perspective on infant reasoning.

During the sensorimotor period, infants move through six substages that transition the infant from strengthening basic reflexes to engaging in primary, secondary, and tertiary circular reactions and demonstrating representational thought. Core knowledge researchers using violation of expectation and other tasks have shown that young infants may have a grasp of the physical properties of objects, such as object permanence, earlier than Piaget indicated.

5.2 Describe the information processing system in infants.

According to information processing theory, we are born with a functioning information processing system comprising sensory memory, working memory (which includes a short-term store, a processing component, and the central executive), and long-term memory. We are born with the ability to attend and remember, and these abilities improve rapidly. Infants are able to categorize objects, at first based on the perceived similarity. Later in the first year, infants use conceptual categories based on perceived function and behavior and apply them to organize objects, such as food, furniture, birds, animals, vehicles, kitchen utensils, and more.

5.3 Discuss individual differences in infant intelligence.

Intelligence refers to an individual's ability to adapt to the world. The most commonly used measure of infant intelligence is the Bayley Scales of Infant Development III (BSID-III), or Bayley-III, which assesses indicators of neurological health useful for charting developmental paths, diagnosing neurological disorders, and detecting developmental disabilities very early in life. New approaches to understanding intelligence examine information processing as an indicator of intellectual skill.

5.4 Summarize the patterns of language development during infancy and toddlerhood.

Newborns are able to hear all of the sounds of which the human voice is capable, but their ability to perceive nonnative speech sounds declines over the first year of life. Infants progress from cooing to babbling and then first words. Infants learn words through fast mapping, but their own speech lags behind what they can understand, and they display underextension and overextension errors. At about 21 months of age, most children compose their first simple two-word sentences, telegraphic speech. Learning theory poses that language is learned through operant conditioning. Nativist theorists pose that the human brain has an innate capacity to learn language. An interactionist perspective integrates nature and nurture, noting that we have innate perceptual biases for discriminating and listening to language and are reared in a social context in which adults use infant-directed speech to facilitate language development.

REVIEW QUESTIONS

5.1 What are two processes that influence cognitive development?

How do infants progress through six substages of sensorimotor reasoning?

What are criticisms of Piaget's sensorimotor period?

What is the core knowledge perspective?

5.2 How is the information processing system organized?

Describe developmental changes in attention, memory, and thinking during infancy.

5.3 Describe the most often used standardized measure of infant intelligence.

How useful are infant intelligence tests for predicting developmental outcomes?

What is the information processing approach to intelligence?

5.4 Describe the process of language development through infancy and toddlerhood.

How do learning theory and nativist theory explain language development?

Provide examples to illustrate the interactionist approach to language development.

6 Socioemotional Development in Infancy and Toddlerhood

Newborn Micah wailed, arms and legs flailing. "Why hello, you're awake. Did you sleep well? Hungry?" his mother cooed as she picked Micah up and cradled him. Micah quickly learned the routine: he cried and his mother or father would hold him and comfort him. At 2 months of age, Baby Micah smiled at the sight of his parents and gurgled happily when held. In turn, Micah's parents played with him and were delighted to see his animated, excited responses. As a toddler, his emerging language skills enabled Micah to express his needs in words. He quickly learned that words are powerful tools that can convey emotions ("I love you, Mommy"). Micah learned to use words to help him manage his emotions and reactions to challenging situations, such as when his parents drop him off at the child care center. When Daddy leaves, Micah says, "Bye Daddy! I'm going to play," and distracts himself by singing. As Micah is increasingly able to express his ideas and feelings, he develops new and more complex relationships with the people around him.

Learning Objectives

6.1 Summarize the psychosocial tasks of infancy and toddlerhood.

6.2 Describe emotional development and the role of contextual influences on emotional development in infants and toddlers.

6.3 Discuss temperament and the role of goodness of fit in development during infancy and toddlerhood.

6.4 Examine the development of attachment and influences on attachment stability and outcomes in infancy and toddlerhood.

Video Activity 6.1: Childhood Attachment: The Strange Situation Study

6.5 Explain infants and toddlers' emerging sense of self and self-control.

Chapter Contents

As Micah illustrates, babies learn new ways of expressing their emotions in the first 2 years of life. They become capable of new and more complex emotions and develop a greater sense of self-understanding, social awareness, and self-management. These abilities influence their interactions with others and their emerging social relationships. These processes collectively are referred to as socioemotional development. In this chapter, we examine the processes of socioemotional development in infancy and toddlerhood.

PSYCHOSOCIAL DEVELOPMENT IN INFANCY AND TODDLERHOOD

According to Erik Erikson (1950), as we travel through the lifespan, we proceed through a series of psychosocial crises, or developmental tasks. As discussed in Chapter 1, how well each crisis is resolved influences psychological development and how the individual approaches subsequent developmental tasks. Erikson believed that infants and toddlers progress through two psychosocial stages that influence their personality development: trust versus mistrust and autonomy versus shame and doubt.

Toddlers take pride in completing tasks, such as tooth brushing, all by themselves, developing a sense of autonomy.
©iStockphoto.com/dszc

Trust Versus Mistrust

From the day she was born, each time Carla cried, her mother or father would come to her bassinet and hold her, check her diaper, and feed her if necessary. Soon, Carla developed the basic expectation that her parents would meet her needs. According to Erikson (1950), developing a sense of **trust versus mistrust** is the first developmental task of life. Infants must develop a view of the world as a safe place where their basic needs will be met. Throughout the first year of life, infants depend on their caregivers for food, warmth, and affection. If parents and caregivers attend to infants' physical and emotional needs and consistently fulfill them, infants will develop a basic sense of trust in their caregivers and, by extension, in the world in general.

However, if caregivers are neglectful or inconsistent in meeting infants' needs, infants will develop a sense of mistrust, feeling that they cannot count on others for love, affection, or the fulfillment of other basic human needs. The sense of trust or mistrust developed in infancy influences how people approach the subsequent stages of development. Specifically, when interaction with adults inspires trust and security, babies are more likely to feel comfortable exploring the world, which enhances their learning, social development, and emotional development.

Autonomy Versus Shame and Doubt

Two-and-a-half-year-old Sarah is an active child who vigorously explores her environment, tests new toys, and attempts to learn about the world on her own. At dinnertime, she wants to feed herself and gets angry when her parents try to feed her. Each morning, she takes pleasure in attempting to dress herself and expresses frustration when her mother helps. Sarah is progressing through the second stage in Erikson's scheme of psychosocial development—**autonomy versus shame and doubt**—which is concerned with establishing a sense of autonomy, or the feeling that one can make choices and direct oneself.

Toddlers walk on their own, express their own ideas and needs, and become more independent. Their developmental task is to learn to do things for themselves and feel confident in their ability to maneuver in their environment. According to Erikson (1950), if parents encourage toddlers' initiative and allow them to explore, experiment, make mistakes, and test limits, toddlers will develop autonomy, self-reliance, self-control, and confidence. If parents are overprotective or disapprove of their toddlers' struggle for independence, the children may begin to doubt their abilities to do things by themselves, may feel ashamed of their desire for autonomy, may passively observe, and may not develop a sense of independence and self-reliance.

Both trust and autonomy develop out of warm and sensitive parenting and developmentally appropriate expectations for exploration and behavioral control. Without a secure sense of trust in caregivers, toddlers will struggle to establish and maintain close relationships with others and will find it challenging to develop autonomy. Adjustment difficulties are more likely when children do not develop a sense of individuality and confidence in their own abilities to meet new challenges. Much of the research on parenting examines mothers, but infants' interaction relationships with fathers also predict autonomy and social competence. This is true across cultures, and the accompanying Lives in Context feature looks at father–infant interactions.

LIVES IN CONTEXT: CULTURAL CONTEXT

Father–Infant Interactions

Across cultures, father–infant interaction tends to be play oriented, promotes close father–infant bonds, and promotes socioemotional development.
©iStockphoto.com/worklater1

We know a great deal about the influence of mother–infant relationships on infant attachment and adjustment, but fathers are also part of the family system and infants also develop attachments to their fathers (Cabrera, Fitzgerald, Bradley, & Roggman, 2014; Lickenbrock & Braungart-Rieker, 2015). At birth, fathers interact with their newborns much like mothers do. They provide similar levels of care by cradling the newborn and performing tasks like diaper changing, bathing, and feeding the newborn (Combs-Orme & Renkert, 2009). This is true of fathers in Western contexts as well as those in non-Western contexts, such as the Kadazan of Malaysia and Aka and Bofi of Central Africa (Hewlett & MacFarlan, 2010; Hossain, Roopnarine, Ismail, Hashmi, & Sombuling, 2007; Tamis-LeMonda, Kahana-Kalman, & Yoshikawa, 2009b).

Early in an infant's life, however, fathers and mothers develop different play and communicative styles. Fathers tend to be more stimulating, while mothers are more soothing (Feldman, 2003; Grossmann et al., 2002). Father–infant play is more physical and play oriented compared with the social exchanges centered on mutual gaze and vocalization that are characteristic of mother–infant play (Feldman, 2003). Fathers tend to engage in more unpredictable rough-and-tumble play that is often met with more positive reactions and arousal from infants; when young children have a choice of an adult play partner, they tend to choose their fathers (Feldman, 2003; Lamb & Lewis, 2016).

Differences in mothers' and fathers' interaction styles appear in many cultures, including France, Switzerland, Italy, and India, as well as among White non-Hispanic, African American, and Hispanic American families in the United States (Best, House, Barnard, & Spicker, 1994; Hossain, Field, Pickens, Malphurs, & Del Valle, 1997; Roopnarine, Talukder, Jain, Joshi, & Srivastav, 1992). However, interaction styles differ more in some cultures than in others. For example, German, Swedish, and Israeli kibbutzim fathers, as well as fathers in the Aka ethnic group of Africa's western Congo basin, are not more playful than mothers (Frodi, Lamb, Hwang, & Frodi, 1983; Hewlett, 2008; Hewlett, Lamb, Shannon, Leyendecker, & Scholmerich, 1998; Sagi et al., 1985). Furthermore, overall and across cultures, most of the differences between mothers and fathers are not large (Lamb & Lewis, 2016).

Father–child interaction is associated with social competence, independence, and cognitive development in children (Cabrera, Volling, & Barr, 2018; Sethna et al., 2016). Rough-and-tumble play contributes to advances in emotional and behavioral regulation in children (Flanders, Leo, Paquette, Pihl, & Séguin, 2009). Fathers provide opportunities for babies to practice arousal management by providing high-intensity stimulation and excitement, like tickling, chasing, and laughing. Fathers who are sensitive, supportive, and appropriately challenging during play promote father–infant attachment relationships (Grossmann et al., 2002; Lickenbrock & Braungart-Rieker, 2015). When fathers are involved in the caregiving of their infants, their children are more likely to enjoy a warm relationship with their father as they grow older, carry out responsibilities, follow parents' directions, and become well adjusted. Similar to findings with mothers, sensitive parenting on the part of fathers predicts secure attachments with their children through age 3 (Brown, Mangelsdorf, & Neff, 2012; Lucassen et al., 2011). The positive social, emotional, and cognitive effects of father–child interaction continue from infancy into childhood and adolescence (Cabrera et al., 2018; Sarkadi, Kristiansson, Oberklaid, & Bremberg, 2008).

What Do You Think?

1. What are some of the challenges of studying father–child relationships? How might researchers address these challenges?
2. Why do you think fathers are more likely to be "play mates" than mothers?

THINKING IN CONTEXT 6.1

1. What kinds of parental behaviors foster a sense of trust in infants? What behaviors promote the development of autonomy? To what extent are these two sets of behaviors similar? Do behaviors that foster trust also foster autonomy? Why or why not?
2. How might contextual factors, such as neighborhood, parents' jobs, or urban or rural community, for example, influence infants' progress on developing trust and autonomy?

EMOTIONAL DEVELOPMENT IN INFANCY AND TODDLERHOOD

What emotions do infants feel? Infants cannot describe their experiences and feelings, which makes studying their emotional development quite challenging. Most people, including infants, show their emotions on their faces, such as by smiling or frowning. If we use facial expressions as a guide to what emotions infants might feel, the first and most reliable emotion that newborns show is distress. They cry, wail, and flail their arms and bodies, alerting caregivers to their need for attention. Newborns also show interest with wide-eyed gazes when something catches their attention, and they smile when they are happy.

Infants' Emotional Experience

Observation of newborns' facial expressions suggests that they experience interest, distress, disgust, and happiness or contentment from birth or shortly after birth (Izard, Woodburn, & Finlon, 2010). Of course, we do not know whether internal emotional states accompany these facial expressions, but infants' facial expressions are remarkably similar to those of adults (Sullivan & Lewis, 2003).

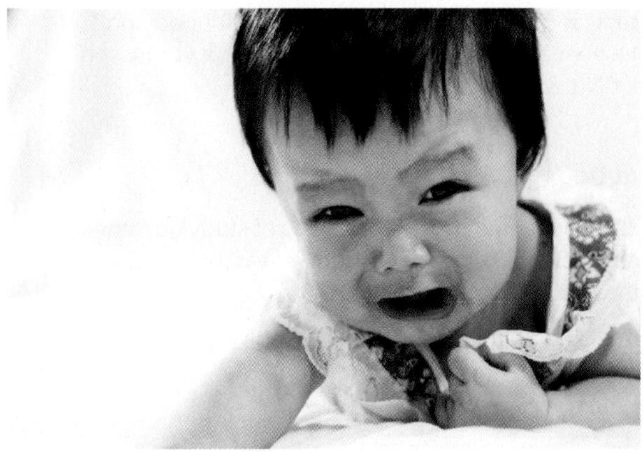

Young infants display a wide range of emotions. Intense emotions are often accompanied by crying.
©iStockphoto.com/Sasiistock

Basic Emotions

Basic emotions, also known as primary emotions (happiness, sadness, interest, surprise, fear, anger, and disgust), are universal, experienced by people around the world (Cordaro et al., 2018; Lench, Baldwin, An, & Garrison, 2018). Basic emotions emerge in all infants at about the same ages and are seen and interpreted similarly in all cultures that have been studied, suggesting that they are inborn (Izard et al., 2010). Between 2 and 7 months of age, infants begin to display anger, sadness, joy, surprise, and fear (Bennett, Bendersky, & Lewis, 2005).

Research with adults suggests that emotions are the result of interactions among richly connected, subcortical brain structures, including the brainstem and the limbic system, as well as parts of the cerebral cortex (Celeghin, Diano, Bagnis, Viola, & Tamietto, 2017; Kragel & LaBar, 2016). These structures develop prenatally and are present in animals, suggesting that emotions serve a biological purpose, are crucial to survival, and are likely experienced by infants (Rolls, 2017; Turner, 2014).

Emotions develop in predictable ways, as shown in Table 6.1. Although basic emotions are thought to be inborn, the ways that they are expressed and the conditions that elicit them change during the first few months of life. For example, in adults, smiling indicates happiness. Newborns smile, and smiling is one of the most important emotional expressions in infancy. Newborn smiles are reflexive, involuntary, and linked with shifts in arousal state (e.g., going from being asleep to drowsy wakefulness), and they occur frequently during periods of rapid eye movement (REM) sleep (Kawakami et al., 2008). At about 3 weeks, infants smile while awake and alert

TABLE 6.1

Milestones in Emotional Development

APPROXIMATE AGE	MILESTONE
Birth	Basic emotions Discriminates mother
2–3 months	Social smile Distinguishes happiness, anger, surprise, and sadness
6–8 months	Fear, stranger anxiety, and separation protest occur
7–12 months	Social referencing
18–24 months	Self-conscious emotions appear. Develops vocabulary for talking about emotions

Smiling plays a role in initiating and maintaining social interactions between infants and adults.
©iStockphoto.com/monkeybusinessimages

and in response to familiarity—familiar sounds, voices, and tastes (Sroufe & Waters, 1976).

During the second month of life, as infants' vision improves, they smile more in response to visual stimuli—sights that catch their attention, such as bright objects coming into view (Sroufe, 1997). The **social smile**, which occurs in response to familiar people, emerges between 6 and 10 weeks of age and is an important milestone in infant development because it shows social engagement (Lewis, Hitchcock, & Sullivan, 2004; Messinger & Fogel, 2007). The social smile plays a large role in initiating and maintaining social interactions between infants and adults, especially by enhancing caregiver–child bonding. Parents are enthralled when their baby shows delight in seeing them, and the parents' happy response encourages their baby to smile even more (Beebe et al., 2016).

As infants grow, laughs begin to accompany their smiles, and they laugh more often and at more things. Infants may show clear expressions of joy and intense happiness as early as 2½ months of age while playing with a parent and at 3 to 4 months of age in response to stimuli that they find highly arousing (Bornstein & Lamb, 2011). At 6 months of age, an infant might laugh at unusual sounds or sights, such as when Mommy puts a bowl on her head or makes a funny face. Laughing at unusual events illustrates the baby's increasing cognitive competence as he or she knows what to expect and is surprised when something unexpected occurs. By a year of age, infants can smile deliberately to engage an adult.

Negative emotions change over time as well. Distress is evident at birth when newborns experience the discomfort of hunger, a heel prick, or a chilly temperature. Anger appears at about 6 months of age and develops rapidly, becoming more complex in terms of elicitors and responses (Lemerise & Dodge, 2008). Initially, physical restrictions such as being restrained in a high chair or when being dressed can elicit anger. The inability to carry out a desired act, such as unsuccessfully reaching to obtain a desired toy, can also provoke frustration and anger (Sullivan & Lewis, 2003). Between 8 and 20 months of age, infants gradually become more reactive, and anger is more easily aroused (Braungart-Rieker, Hill-Soderlund, & Karrass, 2010). They become aware of the actions of others, so that anger can be elicited by others' behavior. For example, an infant may become upset when Mommy goes to the door to leave or when Grandma takes out the towels in preparation for bath time. During the second year of life, temper tantrums become common when the toddler's attempts at autonomy are thwarted and he or she experiences frustration or stress. The anger escalates with the child's stress level (Potegal, Robison, Anderson, Jordan, & Shapiro, 2007). Some toddlers show extreme tantrums, lie on the floor, scream, and jerk their arms and legs. Other children's tantrums are more subtle. They may whine, mope, and stick out their lower lip.

Self-Conscious Emotions

Emotional development is an orderly process in which complex emotions build on the foundation of simple emotions. The development of **self-conscious emotions**, or secondary emotions—such as empathy, pride, embarrassment, shame, and guilt—depends on cognitive development, as well as an awareness of self. Self-conscious emotions do not begin to emerge until about 15 to 18 months, and they largely develop during the second and third years of life (Goodvin, Thompson, & Winer, 2015). To experience self-conscious emotions, toddlers must be able to have a sense of self, observe themselves and others, be aware of standards and rules, and compare their behavior with those standards (Lewis, 2016). Feelings of pride, for example, arise from accomplishing a personally meaningful goal, whereas guilt derives from realizing that one has violated a standard of conduct. Parental evaluations are the initial basis for many secondary emotions (Stipek, 1995).

Emotion Regulation

As children become aware of social standards and rules, **emotion regulation**—the ability to control their emotions—becomes important. How do infants regulate emotions? Very young infants have been observed to manage negative emotions by sucking vigorously on objects or turning their bodies away from distressing stimuli (Mangelsdorf, Shapiro, & Marzolf, 1995).

Smiling is also thought to serve a purpose in regulating emotions, as it allows the infant to control aspects of a situation without losing touch with it. When an infant gets excited and smiles, she looks away briefly. This may be a way of breaking herself away from the stimulus and allowing her to regroup, preventing overstimulation. Smiling is associated with a decline in heart rate, suggesting that it is a relaxation response to decrease an infant's level of arousal.

Whereas 6-month-old infants are more likely to use gaze aversion and fussing as primary emotion regulatory strategies, 12-month-old infants are more likely to use self-soothing (e.g., thumb sucking, rocking themselves) and distraction (chewing on objects, playing with toys). By 18 months of age, toddlers actively attempt to change the distressing situation, such as by moving away from upsetting stimuli, and begin to use distraction, such as by playing with toys or talking (Crockenberg & Leerkes, 2004; Feldman, Dollberg, & Nadam, 2011).

After 18 months of age, toddlers' vocabulary for talking about feelings develops rapidly, and their ability to tell caregivers how they feel presents new opportunities for emotion regulation (Bretherton, Fritz, Zahn-Waxler, & Ridgeway, 1986). Vocabulary predicts self-regulation abilities in 24-month-old infants (Vallotton & Ayoub, 2011). In one longitudinal study of children from 18 to 48 months, toddlers with better language skill tended to engage in more support seeking and distracted themselves more, which was linked with showing less anger at 48 months (Roben, Cole, & Armstrong, 2013). Researchers have also found that infants' abilities to self-regulate at 15 months predict executive functioning at 4 years (Ursache, Blair, Stifter, Voegtline, & The Family Life Project Investigators, 2013).

Social Interaction and Emotional Development

Infants and young children often need outside assistance in regulating their emotions. Warm and supportive interactions with parents and other caregivers can help infants understand their emotions and learn how to manage them.

Parental Interaction

Responsive parenting that is attuned to infants' needs helps infants develop skills in emotion regulation, especially in managing negative emotions like anxiety, as well as their physiological correlates, such as accelerated heart rate (Feldman et al., 2011). For example, sensitive responses coupled with soft vocalizations aid 3-month-old infants in regulating distress (Spinelli & Mesman, 2018). Likewise, when mothers responded promptly to their 2-month-old infants' cries, these same infants, at 4 months of age, cried for shorter durations, were better able to manage their emotions, and stopped crying more quickly than other infants (Jahromi & Stifter, 2007).

Responsive parenting helps infants learn to regulate their emotions.
©iStockphoto.com/AleksandarNakic

Parents help their infants learn to manage emotions through a variety of strategies, including direct intervention, modeling, selective reinforcement, control of the environment, verbal instruction, and touch (Waters, West, Karnilowicz, & Mendes, 2017). These strategies change as the infants grow older. For example, touching becomes a less common regulatory strategy with age, whereas vocalizing and distracting techniques increase (Meléndez, 2005). When mothers provide guidance in helping infants regulate their emotions, the infants tend to engage in distraction and mother-oriented strategies, such as seeking help, during frustrating events (Thomas, Letourneau, Campbell, Tomfohr-Madsen, & Giesbrecht, 2017).

Parent–infant interactions undergo continuous transformations as infants develop. For example, infants' growing motor skills influence their interactions with parents, as well as their socioemotional development. Crawling, creeping, and walking introduce new challenges to parent–infant interaction and socioemotional growth (Adolph & Franchak, 2017). As crawling begins, parents and caregivers respond with happiness and pride, positive emotions that encourage infants' exploration. As infants gain motor competence, they wander further from parents (Thurman & Corbetta, 2017). Crawling increases a toddler's capability to attain goals—a capability that, while often satisfying to the toddler, may involve hazards.

As infants become more mobile, emotional outbursts become more common. Parents report that advances in locomotion are accompanied by increased frustration as toddlers attempt to move in ways that often exceed their abilities or are not permitted by parents (Clearfield, 2011; Pemberton Roben et al., 2012). When mothers recognize the dangers posed to toddlers by objects such as houseplants, vases, and electrical appliances, they sharply increase their expressions of anger and fear, often leading to fear and frustration in their toddlers. At this stage, parents actively monitor toddlers' whereabouts, protect them from dangerous situations, and expect them to comply—a dynamic that is often a struggle, amounting to a test of wills. At the same time, these struggles help the child to begin to develop a grasp of mental states in others that are different from his or her own.

Changes in emotional expression and regulation are dynamic because the changing child influences the changing parent. In particular, mothers and infants systematically influence and regulate each other's emotions and behaviors. Mothers regulate infant emotional states by interpreting their emotional signals, providing appropriate arousal, and reciprocating and reinforcing infant reactions. Infants regulate their mother's emotions through their receptivity to her initiations and stimulation and by responding to her emotions (Bornstein, Hahn, Suwalsky, & Haynes, 2011; Bornstein, Suwalsky, & Breakstone, 2012). By experiencing a range of emotional interactions—times when their emotions mirror those of their caregivers and times when their emotions are different from those of their caregivers—infants learn how to transform negative emotions into neutral or positive emotions and regulate their own emotional states (Guo, Leu, Barnard, Thompson, & Spieker, 2015).

Social Referencing

Early in life, the ability emerges to discriminate facial expressions that indicate emotion. In one study, 2-day-old infants initially did not show a preference for a happy or disgust face, but after being habituated to either a happy or disgust face, they successfully discriminated between the two, suggesting an early sensitivity to dynamic-faced expressions of emotions (Addabbo, Longhi, Marchis, Tagliabue, & Turati, 2018). Likewise, newborns are able to discriminate happy faces from fearful ones (Farroni, Menon, Rigato, & Johnson, 2007). It is thought that infants are innately prepared to attend to facial displays of emotion, because such displays are biologically significant and the ability to recognize them is important for human survival (Leppanen, 2011). Between 2 and 4 months of age, infants can distinguish emotional expressions, including happiness as opposed to anger, surprise, and sadness (Bornstein, Arterberry, & Lamb, 2013). Infants 6½ months old can identify and match happy, angry, and sad emotions portrayed on faces but also body movements indicating emotion (Hock et al., 2017).

Beyond recognizing the emotional expressions of others, infants also respond to them. Between 6 and 10 months of age, infants begin to use **social referencing**, looking to caregivers' or other adults' emotional expressions to find clues for how to interpret ambiguous events, which influences their emotional responses and subsequent actions (Walle, Reschke, & Knothe, 2017). For example, when a toddler grabs the sofa to pull herself up, turns, and tumbles over as she takes a step, she will look to her caregiver to determine how to interpret her fall. If the caregiver has a fearful facial expression, the infant is likely to be fearful also, but if the caregiver smiles, the infant will probably remain calm and return to attempts at walking. The use of social referencing is one way that infants demonstrate their understanding that others experience their own emotions and thoughts.

Older infants tend to show a negativity bias when it comes to social referencing. That is, they attend to and follow social referencing cues more closely when the cues indicate negative attitudes toward an object, compared with neutral or happy attitudes (Vaish, Grossmann, & Woodward, 2008). In addition, infants may be more influenced by the vocal information conveyed in emotional messages than the facial expressions themselves, especially within the context of fearful messages (Biro, Alink, van IJzendoorn, & Bakermans-Kranenburg, 2014).

How infants employ social referencing changes with development. Ten-month-old infants show selective social referencing. They monitor the caregiver's attention and do not engage in social referencing when the adult is not attending or engaged (Stenberg, 2017). At 12 months, infants use referential cues such as the caregiver's body posture, gaze, and voice direction to determine to what objects caregivers' emotional responses refer (Brooks & Meltzoff, 2008). Twelve-month-old infants are more likely to use a caregiver's cues as guides in ambivalent situations when the caregiver responds promptly to the infants' behavior (Stenberg, 2017). In sum, social referencing reflects infants' growing understanding of the emotional states of others; it signifies that infants can observe, interpret, and use emotional information from others to form their own interpretation and response to events.

Cultural Influences on Emotional Development

As we've already seen, emotional development does not occur in a vacuum. Contextual factors, such as culture, influence how infants interpret and express emotions, as well as what emotions they feel. In this section, we explore the role of context in shaping children's knowledge about the appropriate display of emotions, as well as the degree to which children experience a fear common in infancy: stranger wariness.

Emotional Display Rules

Every society has a set of **emotional display rules** that specify the circumstances under which various

In some cultures, infants cry very little, perhaps because they are in constant contact with their mother.
John S Lander/LightRocket/Getty Images

emotions should or should not be expressed (Safdar et al., 2009). We learn these rules very early in life through interactions with others. Every interaction between parent and infant is shaped by the culture in which they live, which influences their emotional expressions (Bornstein et al., 2013). When North American mothers play with their 7-month-old babies, for instance, they tend to model positive emotions, restricting their own emotional displays to show joy, interest, and surprise (Malatesta & Haviland, 1982). They also are more attentive to infants' expression of positive emotions, such as interest or surprise, and respond less to negative emotions (Broesch, Rochat, Olah, Broesch, & Henrich, 2016). Thus, babies are socialized to respond and display their emotions in socially acceptable ways.

Which emotions are considered acceptable, as well as how they should be expressed, differ by culture and context. North American parents tickle and stimulate their babies, encouraging squeals of pleasure. The Gusii and Aka people of Central Africa prefer to keep babies calm and quiet; they engage in little face-to-face play (Hewlett et al., 1998; LeVine et al., 1994). These differences communicate cultural expectations about emotions (Halberstadt & Lozada, 2011). North American infants learn to express positive emotions, and Central African babies learn to restrain strong emotions.

Similarly, cultures often have particular beliefs about how much responsiveness is appropriate when babies cry and fuss, as well as expectations about infants' abilities to regulate their own emotions (Halberstadt & Lozada, 2011). The !Kung hunter-gatherers of Botswana, Africa, respond to babies' cries nearly immediately (within 10 seconds), whereas Western mothers tend to wait a considerably longer period of time before responding to infants' cries (e.g., 10 minutes) (Barr, Konner, Bakeman, & Adamson, 1991). Fijian mothers tend to be more responsive than U.S. mothers to negative facial expressions in their infants (Broesch et al., 2016). Gusii mothers believe that constant holding, feeding, and physical care are essential for keeping an infant calm, which in turn protects the infant from harm and disease; therefore, like !Kung mothers, Gusii mothers respond immediately to their babies' cries (LeVine et al., 1994). Non-Western infants are thought to cry very little because they are carried often (Bleah & Ellett, 2010). In one study, infants born to parents who were recent immigrants from Africa cried less than U.S. infants, illustrating the role of culture in influencing infant cries (Bleah & Ellett, 2010). Caregivers' responses to infant cries influence infants' capacity for self-regulation and responses to stress. Babies who receive more responsive and immediate caregiving when distressed show lower rates of persistent crying, spend more time in happy and calm states, and cry less overall as they approach their first birthday (Axia & Weisner, 2002; Papoušek & Papoušek, 1990).

Stranger Wariness

Many infants around the world display **stranger wariness** (also known as *stranger anxiety*), a fear of unfamiliar people. Whether infants show stranger wariness depends on the infants' overall temperament, their past experience, and the situation in which they meet a stranger (Thompson & Limber, 1991). In many, but not all, cultures, stranger wariness emerges at about 6 months and increases throughout the first year of life, beginning to decrease after about 15 months of age (Bornstein et al., 2013; Sroufe, 1977).

Recent research has suggested that the pattern of stranger wariness varies among infants. Some show rapid increases and others show slow increases in stranger wariness; once wariness has been established, some infants show a steady

As attachments form, infants in many cultures become more wary and display "stranger anxiety" when in the presence of unfamiliar people.
©iStockphoto.com/manonallard

decline and others show more rapid changes. Twin studies suggest that these patterns are influenced by genetics, because the patterns of change are more similar among monozygotic twins (identical twins who share 100% of their genes) than dizygotic twins (fraternal twins who share 50% of their genes) (Brooker et al., 2013).

Among North American infants, stranger wariness is so common that parents and caregivers generally expect it. However, infants of the Efe people of Zaire, Africa, show little stranger wariness. This is likely related to the Efe collective caregiving system, in which Efe babies are passed from one adult to another, relatives and nonrelatives alike (Tronick, Morelli, & Ivey, 1992), and the infants form relationships with the many people who care for them (Meehan & Hawks, 2013). In contrast, babies reared in Israeli kibbutzim (cooperative agricultural settlements that tend to be isolated and subjected to terrorist attacks) tend to demonstrate widespread wariness of strangers. By the end of the first year, when infants look to others for cues about how to respond emotionally, kibbutz babies display far greater anxiety than babies reared in Israeli cities (Saarni, Mumme, & Campos, 1998). In this way, stranger wariness may be adaptive, modifying infants' drive to explore in light of contextual circumstances (Easterbrooks, Bartlett, Beeghly, & Thompson, 2012).

Stranger wariness illustrates the dynamic interactions among the individual and context. The infant's tendencies toward social interaction and past experience with strangers are important, of course, but so is the mother's anxiety. Infants whose mothers report greater stress reactivity, who experience more anxiety and negative affect in response to stress, show higher rates of stranger wariness (Brooker et al., 2013; Waters, West, & Mendes, 2014). Characteristics of the stranger (e.g., his or her height), the familiarity of the setting, and how quickly the stranger approaches influence how the infant appraises the situation. Infants are more open when the stranger is sensitive to the infant's signals and approaches at the infant's pace (Mangelsdorf, 1992).

In sum, over the first few months of life, infants display the full range of basic emotions. More complex self-conscious emotions emerge with cognitive development and social interaction. Adults interact with infants, provide opportunities to observe and practice emotional expressions, and assist in regulating emotions. Much of emotional development is the result of the interplay of infants' emerging capacities and the contexts in which they are raised, especially the emotional contexts within the home. The accompanying Applying Developmental Science feature discusses the challenges maternal depression poses for emotional development.

APPLYING DEVELOPMENTAL SCIENCE

Maternal Depression and Emotional Development in Infancy

We have seen that parent–infant interactions are critical to infants' emotional development. Maternal depression poses significant risks to infants' well-being. Depression is not simply sadness; rather, it is characterized by a lack of emotion and a preoccupation with the self that makes it difficult for depressed mothers to recognize their infants' needs and provide care. Both mothers and fathers can become depressed, but most of the research examines mothers. The hormonal and social changes that accompany pregnancy and new motherhood place women at risk for postpartum depression, depression that occurs in the months after childbirth. However, depression can occur at any time in life.

Depression poses risks to parenting. Mothers who are depressed tend to view their infants differently than nondepressed mothers and independent observers (Newland, Parade, Dickstein, & Seifer, 2016). They are more likely to identify negative emotions (i.e., sadness) than positive emotions (i.e., happiness) in infant faces (Webb & Ayers, 2015). Challenging behaviors, such as fussiness and crying, and difficult temperaments tend to elicit more negative responses from depressed mothers (Newland et al., 2016). When depressed and nondepressed mothers were shown images of their own and unfamiliar infants' joy and distress faces, mothers with depression showed blunted brain activity in response to their own infants' joy and distress faces, suggesting muted responses to infants' emotional cues (Laurent & Ablow, 2013). Depressed women tend to disengage faster from positive and negative infant emotional expressions (Webb & Ayers, 2015).

In practice, mothers who are depressed tend to be less responsive to their babies, show less affection,

(Continued)

(Continued)

use more negative forms of touch, and show more negative emotions and behaviors such as withdrawal, intrusiveness, hostility, coerciveness, and insensitivity (Jennings et al., 2008). Given the poor parent–child interaction styles that accompany maternal depression, it may not be surprising that infants of depressed mothers show a variety of negative outcomes, including overall distress, withdrawn behavior, poor social engagement, and difficulty regulating emotions (Granat, Gadassi, Gilboa-Schechtman, & Feldman, 2017; Leventon & Bauer, 2013). They tend to show greater physiological arousal in response to stressors, have difficulty reading and understanding others' emotions, and are at risk for later problems in emotional development but also cognitive and language development (Liu et al., 2017; Prenoveau et al., 2017; Suurland et al., 2017).

The ongoing reciprocal interactions between mothers and infants account for the long-term negative effects of maternal depression (Granat et al., 2017). In one study, maternal depressive symptoms 9 months after giving birth predicted infants' negative reactions to maternal behavior at 18 months of age and, in turn, higher levels of depressive symptoms on the part of mothers when the children reached 27 months of age (Roben et al., 2015). Similarly, in a sample of infants studied from 4 to 18 months of age, family factors such as maternal depression and the mother's experience of relationship stress were associated with the infants' developing strong negative emotions early in infancy, which compromised their emotion regulation capacities (Bridgett et al., 2009). Declines in infants' regulatory control were in turn associated with negative parenting in toddlerhood, because parents and children interact with and influence each other reciprocally.

Depression can be treated with therapy with or without the accompaniment of antidepressant medication (Hollon et al., 2016; Swartz et al., 2016). Experts argue that in addition to treating maternal depression, parenting interventions are particularly important in helping children of depressed mothers (Goodman & Garber, 2017). Interventions that teach parents how to interact with their children will foster the parent–child relationships that promote healthy development (Dempsey et al., 2016; Messer et al., 2018).

What Do You Think?

In your view, how can we best support mothers? If you were to create a program to help prevent depression or to help depressed mothers, what might you include? ●

THINKING IN CONTEXT 6.2

1. Identify examples of how infants' experience and expression of basic and self-conscious emotions are influenced by their interactions with others and their physical and cultural context. How might these interactions and contexts influence the development of emotion regulation?
2. How might social referencing and stranger wariness reflect adaptative responses to a context? Why does stranger wariness vary among children and cultures?

TEMPERAMENT IN INFANCY AND TODDLERHOOD

"Jayla is such an easygoing baby!" gushed her babysitter. "She eats everything, barely cries, and falls asleep without a fuss. I wish all my babies were like her." The babysitter is referring to Jayla's temperament. **Temperament**, the characteristic way in which an individual approaches and reacts to people and situations, is thought to be one of the basic building blocks of emotion and personality. Temperament has strong biological determinants; behavior genetics research has shown genetic bases for temperament (Saudino & Micalizzi, 2015). Yet the expression of temperament reflects reciprocal interactions among genetic predispositions, maturation, and experience (Goodvin et al., 2015; Rothbart, 2011). Every infant behaves in a characteristic, predictable style that is influenced by his or her inborn tendencies toward arousal and stimulation as well as by experiences with adults and contexts. In other words, every infant displays a particular temperament style.

Styles of Temperament

The New York Longitudinal Study (NYLS), begun in 1956, is a pioneering study of temperament that has followed 133 infants into adulthood. Early in life, the infants in the study demonstrated differences in nine characteristics that are thought to capture the essence of temperament (Buss & Plomin, 1984; Chess & Thomas, 1991; Goldsmith et al., 1987).

- *Activity level.* Some babies wriggle, kick their legs, wave their arms, and move around a great deal, whereas other babies tend to be more still and stay in one place.
- *Rhythmicity.* Some infants are predictable in their patterns of eating, sleeping, and defecating; other babies are not predictable.
- *Approach-withdrawal.* Some babies tend to approach new situations, people, and objects, whereas others withdraw from novelty.
- *Adaptability.* Some babies get used to new experiences and situations quickly; others do not.
- *Intensity of reaction.* Some babies have very extreme reactions, giggling exuberantly and crying with piercing wails. Other babies show more subdued reactions, such as simple smiles and soft, whimpering cries.
- *Threshold of responsiveness.* Some babies notice many types of stimuli—sights, sounds, and touch sensations—and react to them. Other infants notice few types of stimuli and seem oblivious to changes.
- *Quality of mood.* Some babies tend toward near-constant happiness, while others tend toward irritability.
- *Distractibility.* Some babies can be easily distracted from objects or situations, while others cannot.
- *Attention span.* Some babies play with one toy for a long time without becoming bored, whereas others get bored easily and change toys often.

Some aspects of infant temperament, particularly activity level, irritability, attention, and sociability or approach-withdrawal, show stability for months and years at a time and in some cases even into adulthood (Lemery-Chalfant, Kao, Swann, & Goldsmith, 2013; Papageorgiou et al., 2014). Infants' growing ability to regulate their attention and emotions holds implications for some components of temperament, such as rhythmicity, distractibility, and intensity of reaction. The components of infant temperament cluster into three profiles (Thomas & Chess, 1977; Thomas, Chess, & Birch, 1970):

- **Easy temperament:** Easy babies are often in a positive mood, even-tempered, open, adaptable, regular, and predictable in biological functioning. They establish regular feeding and sleeping schedules easily.
- **Difficult temperament:** Difficult babies are active, irritable, and irregular in biological rhythms. They are slow to adapt to changes in routine or new situations, show intense and frequent unpleasant moods, react vigorously to change, and have trouble adjusting to new routines.
- **Slow-to-warm-up temperament:** Just as it sounds, slow-to-warm-up babies tend to be inactive, moody, and slow to adapt to new situations and people. They react to new situations with mild irritability but adjust more quickly than do infants with difficult temperaments.

Although it may seem as if all babies could be easily classified, about one-third of the infants in the New York Longitudinal Study did not fit squarely into any of the three categories but displayed a mix of characteristics, such as eating and sleeping regularly but being slow to warm up to new situations (Thomas & Chess, 1977; Thomas et al., 1970).

Another influential model of temperament, by Mary Rothbart, includes three dimensions (Rothbart, 2011; Rothbart & Bates, 2007):

- *Extraversion/surgency*—the tendency toward positive emotions. Infants who are high in extraversion/surgency approach experiences with confidence, energy, and positivity, as indicated by smiles, laughter, and approach-oriented behaviors.
- *Negative affectivity*—the tendency toward negative emotions, such as sadness, fear, distress, and irritability.
- *Effortful control*—the degree to which one can focus attention, shift attention, and inhibit responses in order to manage arousal. Infants who are high in effortful control are able to regulate their arousal and soothe themselves.

From this perspective, temperament reflects how easily we become emotionally aroused or our reactivity to stimuli, as well as how well we are able to control our emotional arousal (Rothbart, 2011). Some infants and children are better able to distract themselves, focus their attention, and inhibit impulses than others. The ability to self-regulate and manage emotions and impulses is associated with positive long-term adjustment, including academic achievement, social competence, and resistance to stress, in both Chinese and North American samples (Chen & Schmidt, 2015).

Infant temperament tends to be stable over the first year of life but less so than childhood temperament, which can show stability over years, even into adulthood (Bornstein et al., 2015). In infancy, temperament is especially open to environmental influences, such as interactions with others (Gartstein, Putnam, Aron, & Rothbart, 2016). Young infants' temperament can change with experience, neural development, and sensitive caregiving (e.g., helping babies regulate their negative emotions) (Jonas et al., 2015; Thompson et al., 2013). As infants gain experience and learn how to regulate their states and emotions, those who are cranky and difficult may become less so. By the second year of life, styles of responding to situations and people are better established, and temperament becomes more stable. Temperament at age 3 remains stable, predicting temperament at age 6 and personality traits at age 26 (Dyson et al., 2015).

Context and Goodness of Fit

Like all aspects of development, temperament is influenced by reciprocal reactions among individuals and their contexts. An important influence on socioemotional development is the **goodness of fit** between the child's temperament and the environment around him or her, especially the parents' temperaments and childrearing methods (Chess & Thomas, 1991). Infants are at particular risk for poor outcomes when their temperaments show poor goodness of fit to the settings in which they live (Rothbart & Bates, 1998). For example, if an infant who is fussy, difficult, and slow to adapt to new situations is raised by a patient and sensitive caregiver who provides time for him or her to adapt to new routines, the infant may become less cranky and more flexible over time. The infant may adapt her temperament style to match her context so that later in childhood, she may no longer be classified as difficult and no longer display behavioral problems (Bates, Pettit, Dodge, & Ridge, 1998). If, on the other hand, a child with a difficult temperament is reared by a parent who is insensitive, coercive, and difficult in temperament, the child may not learn how to regulate her emotions and may have behavioral problems and adjustment difficulties that worsen with age, even into early adolescence and beyond (Pluess, Birkbeck, & Belsky, 2010). Accordingly, when children are placed in low-quality caregiving environments, those with difficult temperaments respond more negatively and show more behavior problems than do those with easy temperaments (Poehlmann et al., 2011). The Lives in Context feature examines the impact of extremely negative experiences, trauma, on development.

LIVES IN CONTEXT: BIOLOGICAL INFLUENCES

Trauma and Emotional Development

Can infants remember early life experiences? Does exposure to adversity, such as maltreatment, poverty, and violence, influence infants' development? Very young infants likely do not recall specific experiences and events, but early exposure to trauma may affect infants' development in ways that can last a lifetime. For example, maladaptive contexts may pose risks of physical harm to children, directly influencing neurological development. However, trauma also poses invisible long-term risks to children's emotional development and mental health (Blair, 2010).

How does early trauma affect emotional development? The experience of early social adversity may have epigenetic effects on the genes that regulate the endocrine system, which controls hormone production and release at all ages in life (Conradt, 2017). Infancy may be a particularly plastic time in development, with heightened potential for lifelong epigenetic changes that may sensitize responses to stress throughout the lifespan (Laurent, Harold, Leve, Shelton, & Van Goozen, 2016). For example, research with adults reveals that childhood maltreatment is associated with increased stress reactivity in adulthood (Turecki & Meaney, 2016).

However, not all infants respond to early life stress with heightened reactivity. Some infants exposed to trauma show lower levels of stress hormones and reduced reactivity to stress (Turecki & Meaney, 2016). The timing and intensity of adversity influences developmental outcomes. Exposure to particularly intense chronic stress early in development can lead to hyperactive stress responses that may be followed by blunted responses (Laurent et al., 2016). Blunted responses may reflect adaptations to chronically stressful situations. Unpredictable stressors, on the other hand, may lead to heightened stress reactivity as the individual adapts to volatile and unexpected situations (Blair, 2010). Both heightened and blunted stress responses may be adaptive attempts to optimize survival in nonoptimal caregiving environments, yet these adaptations may carry behavioral costs, such as heightened distress when confronted with stress and longer-term anxiety and depressive symptoms, which negatively affect developmental trajectories (Laurent et al., 2016).

Early life stress poses risks to emotional development, but the caregiving environment also influences the developing stress response system. For example, maternal presence buffers and regulates infants' hormonal and behavioral responses to threats (Howell et al., 2017). Sensitive mothers tend to have infants who display better self-regulation during stressful events; intrusive mothers tend to have the opposite effect (Enlow et al., 2014). Warm parenting within a predictable stimulating environment with supportive adults and family can help infants develop the self-regulation skills to adapt to adverse contexts (Blair, 2010). Unfortunately, trauma often disrupts the caregiving system, making adaptation quite difficult.

What Do You Think?

Consider protective factors for infants' adjustment to experiencing trauma. What individual characteristics and developmental competencies can help infants adapt? How might the home and caregiving context influence infants' adjustment? How might neighborhood and community factors influence infants' adaptation? ●

An infant's temperament may be stable over time because certain temperamental qualities evoke certain reactions from others, promoting goodness of fit. Easy babies usually get the most positive reactions from others, whereas babies with a difficult temperament receive mixed reactions (Chess & Thomas, 1991). For example, an "easy" baby tends to smile often, eliciting smiles and positive interactions from others, which in turn reinforce the baby's "easy" temperamental qualities (Planalp, Van Hulle, Lemery-Chalfant, & Goldsmith, 2017). Conversely, a "difficult" baby may evoke more frustration and negativity from caregivers as they try unsuccessfully to soothe the baby's fussing. Researchers found that mothers who view their 6-month-old infants as difficult may be less emotionally available to them (Kim & Teti, 2014). Babies' emotionality and negative emotions predict maternal perceptions of parenting stress and poor parenting (Oddi, Murdock, Vadnais, Bridgett, & Gartstein, 2013; Paulussen-Hoogeboom, Stams, Hermanns, & Peetsma, 2007). Goodness of fit at 4 and 8 months of age predicts a close bond with caregivers at 15 months (Seifer et al., 2014).

Temperament can also be related to mothers' own temperament, as well as their expectations about their infants and their ability to parent (Grady & Karraker, 2017). In one study, mothers who, *prior to giving birth,* considered themselves less well equipped to care for their infants were found to be more likely to have infants who showed negative aspects of temperament, such as fussiness, irritability, and difficulty being soothed (Verhage, Oosterman, & Schuengel, 2013). This suggests that perceptions of parenting may shape views of infant temperament—and thereby shape temperament itself. In other research, new mothers' feelings of competence 3 months after giving birth were positively associated with infant temperament. Mothers' beliefs about their ability to nurture are shaped by the interaction between their infants' traits and their own parenting self-efficacy, as well as their opportunities for developing successful caregiving routines (Verhage et al., 2013). This contextual dynamic has been found to hold true across cultures. Both British and Pakistani mothers in the United Kingdom reported fewer problems with their infants' temperaments at 6 months of age when the mothers had a greater sense of parenting efficacy and displayed more warm and less hostile parenting styles (Prady, Kiernan, Fairley, Wilson, & Wright, 2014).

As mentioned earlier, socioemotional development is a dynamic process in which infants' behavior and temperament styles influence the family processes that shape their development. Sensitive and patient caregiving is not always easy with a challenging child, and adults' own temperamental styles influence their caregiving. A poor fit between the caregiver's and infant's temperament can make an infant more fussy and cranky. When a difficult infant is paired with a parent with a similar temperament—one who is impatient, irritable, and forceful—behavioral problems in childhood and adolescence are likely (Chess & Thomas, 1984; Rubin, Hastings, Chen, Stewart, & McNichol, 1998).

The most adaptive matches between infant temperament and context can sometimes be surprising. Consider the Maasai, an African semi-nomadic ethnic group. In times of drought, when the environment becomes extremely hostile, herds of cattle and goats die, and infant mortality rises substantially. Under these challenging conditions, infants with difficult temperaments tend to survive at higher rates than do those with easy temperaments. Infants who cry and are demanding are attended to, are fed more, and are in better physical condition than easy babies, who tend to cry less and therefore are assumed to be content (Gardiner & Kosmitzki, 2018).

Thus, the Maasai infants with difficult temperaments demonstrate higher rates of survival because their temperaments better fit the demands of the hostile context in which they are raised. Our temperament interacts with our family and community context to influence our development.

Cultural Differences in Temperament

Researchers have observed consistent cultural differences in temperament that are rooted in cultural norms for how individuals are perceived. Japanese mothers, for example, view their infants as interdependent beings who must learn the importance of relationships and connections with others (Rothbaum, Weisz, Pott, Miyake, & Morelli, 2000b). North American mothers, on the other hand, view their task as shaping babies into autonomous beings (Kojima, 1986). Whereas Japanese mothers tend to interact with their babies in soothing ways, discouraging strong emotions, North American mothers are active and stimulating (Rothbaum et al., 2000a). Differences in temperament result, such that Japanese infants tend to be more passive, less irritable and vocal, and more easily soothed when upset than North American infants (Kojima, 1986; Lewis, Ramsay, & Kawakami, 1993; Rothbaum et al., 2000b). Culture influences the behaviors that parents view as desirable and the means that parents use to socialize their infants (Chen & Schmidt, 2015; Kagan, 2013). Culture, therefore, plays a role in how emotional development—in this case, temperament—unfolds.

Asian cultures often prioritize low arousal and emotionality and socialize infants in line with these values. Chinese American, Japanese American, and Hmong children tend to display lower levels of irritability, exhibit less physical activity, and engage in more self-quieting and self-control than do European American children (Friedlmeier, Çorapçi, & Benga, 2015; Super & Harkness, 2010). Similarly, a recent comparison of toddlers from Chile, South Korea, Poland, and the United States showed that the South Korean toddlers scored highest on measures of control (Krassner et al., 2016).

If infants from Asian cultures engage in more self-soothing, are they more temperamentally resistant to stress? One study examined levels of the hormone cortisol in infants receiving an inoculation (Lewis et al., 1993). Cortisol, which is released as part of the fight-or-flight response, is often used as a marker of stress. Four-month-old Japanese infants showed a pronounced cortisol response, suggesting that they were experiencing great stress, coupled with little crying. The U.S. infants, on the other hand, displayed intense behavioral reactions to the pain and took longer to calm down, yet they displayed a lower cortisol response. In other words, although the Japanese babies appeared quiet and calm, they were more physiologically stressed than the U.S. infants. It seems that cultural views of the nature of arousal and emotional regulation influence parenting behaviors and ultimately infants' responses to stressors (Friedlmeier et al., 2015).

In summary, we have seen that the cultures in which we are immersed influence how we interpret stimuli and respond to the world, including how we manifest stress. Culture also influences attachment.

THINKING IN CONTEXT 6.3

1. In your view, are extreme changes in temperament possible, such as moving from an easy temperament to difficult, or the reverse? Why? If so, how might these changes occur?
2. Give examples of contextual factors that might influence goodness of fit, and thereby infants' temperament and adjustment.

ATTACHMENT IN INFANCY AND TODDLERHOOD

Raj gurgles and cries out while lying in his crib. As his mother enters the room, he squeals excitedly. Raj's mother smiles as she reaches into the crib, and Raj giggles with delight as she picks him up. Raj and his mother have formed an important emotional bond, called attachment. **Attachment** refers to a lasting emotional tie between two people who each strive to maintain closeness to the other and act to ensure that the relationship continues.

Attachment relationships serve as an important backdrop for emotional and social development. Our earliest attachments are with our primary caregivers, most often our mothers. It was once thought that feeding determined patterns of attachment. Freud, for example, emphasized the role of feeding and successful weaning on infants' personality and well-being. Behaviorist theorists explain attachment as the result of the infants associating their mothers with food, a powerful reinforcer that satisfies a biological need. Certainly, feeding is important for infants' health and well-being and offers opportunities for the close contact needed to develop attachment bonds, but feeding itself does not determine attachment. In one famous study, baby rhesus monkeys were reared with two inanimate surrogate "mothers": one made of wire mesh and a second covered with terrycloth (see

FIGURE 6.1

Harlow's Study: Contact Comfort and the Attachment Bond

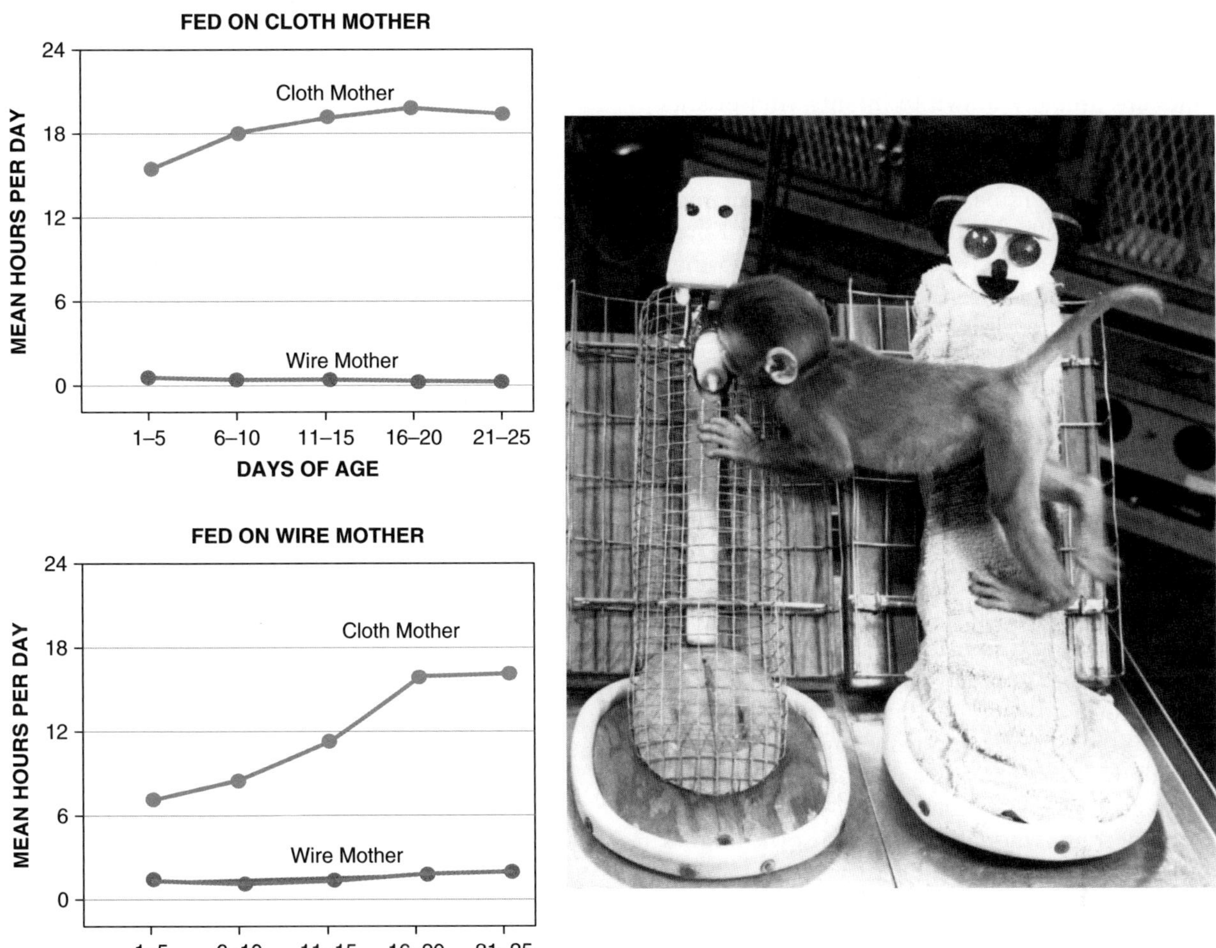

This infant monkey preferred to cling to the cloth-covered mother even if fed by the wire mother. Harlow concluded that attachment is based on contact comfort rather than feeding.

Source: Harlow, H. F. (1958); Photo Researchers Inc.

Figure 6.1). The baby monkeys clung to the terrycloth mother despite being fed only by the wire mother, suggesting that attachment bonds are not based on feeding but rather on contact comfort (Harlow & Zimmerman, 1959). So how does an attachment form, and what is its purpose?

Bowlby's Ethological Perspective on Attachment

John Bowlby, a British psychiatrist, posed that early family experiences influence emotional disturbances not through feeding practices, conditioning, or psychoanalytic drives but via inborn tendencies to form close relationships. Specifically, Bowlby (1969, 1988) developed an ethological theory of attachment that characterizes it as an adaptive behavior that evolved because it contributed to the survival of the human species. Inspired by ethology, particularly by Lorenz's work on the imprinting of geese (see Chapter 1) and by observations of interactions of monkeys, Bowlby posited that humans are biologically driven to form attachment bonds with other humans. An attachment bond between caregivers and infants ensures that the two will remain in close proximity, thereby aiding the survival of the infant and, ultimately, the species. From this perspective, caregiving responses are inherited and are triggered by the presence of infants and young children.

Infants' Signals and Adults' Responses

From birth, babies develop a repertoire of behavior signals to which adults naturally attend and respond, such as smiling, cooing, and clinging. Crying is a particularly effective signal because it conveys negative emotion that adults can judge reliably, and it motivates adults to relieve the infants' distress. Adults are innately drawn to infants, find infants' signals irresistible, and respond in kind. For example, one recent study found that nearly 700 mothers in 11 countries (Argentina, Belgium, Brazil, Cameroon, France, Kenya, Israel, Italy, Japan, South Korea, and the United States) tended to respond to their infants' cries and distress by picking up, holding, and talking to their infants (Bornstein et al., 2017). Infants' behaviors, immature appearance, and even smell draw adults' responses (Kringelbach, Stark, Alexander, Bornstein, & Stein, 2016). Infants, in turn, are attracted to caregivers who respond consistently and appropriately to their signals. During the first months of life, infants rely on caregivers to regulate their states and emotions—to soothe them when they are distressed and help them establish and maintain an alert state (Thompson, 2013). Attachment behaviors provide comfort and security to infants because they bring babies close to adults who can protect them.

Magnetic resonance imaging (MRI) scans support a biological component to attachment, as first-time mothers show specific patterns of brain activity in response to infants. Mothers' brains light up with activity when they see their own infants' faces, and areas of the brain that are associated with rewards are activated specifically in response to happy, but not sad, infant faces (Strathearn, Jian, Fonagy, & Montague, 2008). In response to their infants' cries, U.S., Chinese, and Italian mothers show brain activity in regions associated with auditory processing, emotion, and the intention to move and speak, suggesting automatic responses to infant expressions of distress (Bornstein et al., 2017).

Phases of Attachment

Bowlby proposed that attachment formation progresses through several developmental phases during infancy, from innate behaviors that bring the caregiver into contact to a mutual attachment relationship. With each phase, infants' behavior becomes increasingly organized, adaptable, and intentional.

Phase 1: Preattachment–Indiscriminate Social Responsiveness (Birth to 2 Months): Infants instinctively elicit responses from caregivers by crying, smiling, and making eye contact with adults. Infants respond to any caregiver who reacts to their signals, whether parent, grandparent, child care provider, or sibling.

Phase 2: Early Attachments–Discriminating Sociability (2 Through 6-7 Months): When caregivers are sensitive and consistent in responding to babies' signals, babies learn to associate their caregivers with the relief of distress, forming the basis for an initial bond. Babies begin to discriminate among adults and prefer familiar people. They direct their responses toward a particular adult or adults who are best able to soothe them.

Phase 3: Attachments (7-24 Months): Infants develop attachments to specific caregivers who attend, accurately interpret, and consistently respond to their signals. Infants can gain proximity to caregivers through their own motor efforts, such as crawling.

Phase 4: Reciprocal Relationships (24-30 Months and Onward): With advances in cognitive and language development, children can engage in interactions with their primary caregiver as partners, taking turns and initiating interactions within the attachment relationship. They begin to understand others' emotions and goals and apply this understanding through strategies such as social referencing.

Secure Base, Separation Anxiety, and Internal Working Models

The formation of an attachment bond is crucial for infants' development because it enables infants to begin to explore the world, using their attachment figure as a secure base, or foundation, to return to when frightened. When infants are securely attached to their caregivers, they feel confident to explore the world and to learn by doing so. As clear attachments form, starting at about 7 months, infants are likely to experience **separation anxiety** (sometimes called separation protest), a reaction to separations from an attachment figure that is characterized by distress and crying (Lamb & Lewis, 2015). Infants may follow, cling to, and climb on their caregivers in an attempt to keep them near.

Separation anxiety tends to increase between 8 and 15 months of age, and then it declines. This pattern appears across many cultures and environments as varied as those of the United States, Israeli kibbutzim, and !Kung hunter-gatherer groups in Africa (Kagan et al., 1994). It is the formation of the attachment bond that makes separation anxiety possible, because infants must feel connected to their caregivers in order to feel distress in the caregivers' absence. Separation anxiety declines as infants develop reciprocal relationships with caregivers, increasingly use them as secure bases, and can understand and predict parents' patterns of separation and return, reducing their confusion and distress.

The attachment bond developed during infancy and toddlerhood influences personality development because it comes to be represented as an **internal working model**, which includes the children's expectations about whether they are worthy of love, whether their attachment figures will be available during times of distress, and how they will be treated. The internal working model influences the development of self-concept, or sense of self, in infancy and becomes a guide to later relationships throughout life (Bretherton & Munholland, 2016).

Ainsworth's Strange Situation and Attachment Classifications

Virtually all infants form an attachment to their parents, but Canadian psychologist Mary Salter Ainsworth proposed that infants differ in security of attachment—the extent to which they feel that parents can reliably meet their needs. Like Bowlby, Ainsworth believed that infants must develop a dependence on parents, viewing them as a metaphorical secure base, in order to feel comfortable exploring the world (Salter, 1940). To examine attachment, Mary Ainsworth developed the **Strange Situation**, a structured observational procedure that reveals the security of attachment when the infant is placed under stress. As shown in Table 6.2, the Strange Situation is a heavily structured observation task consisting of eight 3-minute-long episodes. In each segment, the infant is with the parent (typically the mother), with a stranger, with both, or alone. Observations center on the infant's exploration of the room, his or her reaction when the mother leaves the room, and, especially, his or her responses during reunions, when the mother returns.

Mary Salter Ainsworth proposed that infants differ in security of attachment—the extent to which they feel that parents can reliably meet their needs. To examine attachment, Mary Ainsworth developed the Strange Situation.
JHU Sheridan Libraries/Gado/Archive Photos/Getty Images

TABLE 6.2

The Strange Situation

EVENT	ATTACHMENT BEHAVIOR OBSERVED
Experimenter introduces mother and infant to playroom and leaves	
Infant plays with toys and parent is seated	Mother as secure base
Stranger enters, talks with caregiver, and approaches infant	Reaction to unfamiliar adult
Mother leaves room; stranger responds to baby if upset	Reaction to separation from mother
Mother returns and greets infant	Reaction to reunion
Mother leaves room	Reaction to separation from mother
Stranger enters room and offers comfort to infant	Reaction to stranger and ability to be soothed by stranger
Mother returns and greets infant; tries to interest the infant in toys	Reaction to reunion

On the basis of responses to the Strange Situation, infants are classified into one of several attachment types (Ainsworth, Blehar, Waters, & Wall, 1978).

Secure Attachment: The securely attached infant uses the parent as a secure base, exploring the environment and playing with toys in the presence of the parent, but regularly checking in (e.g., by looking at the parent or bringing toys). The infant shows mild distress when the parent leaves. On the parent's return, the infant greets the parent enthusiastically, seeks comfort, and then returns to individual play. About two-thirds of North American infants who complete the Strange Situation are classified as securely attached (Lamb & Lewis, 2015).

Insecure-Avoidant Attachment: Infants who display an insecure-avoidant attachment show little interest in the mother and busily explore the room during the Strange Situation. The infant is not distressed when the mother leaves and may react to the stranger in similar ways as to the mother. The infant ignores or avoids the mother on return or shows subtle signs of avoidance, such as failing to greet her or turning away from her. About 15% of samples of North American infants' responses to the Strange Situation reflect this style of attachment (Lamb & Lewis, 2015).

The most important determinant of infant attachment is the caregiver's ability to consistently and sensitively respond to the child's signal.
©iStockphoto.com/aywan88

Insecure-Resistant Attachment: Infants with an insecure-resistant attachment show a mixed pattern of responses to the mother. The infant remains preoccupied with the mother throughout the procedure, seeking proximity and contact, clinging even before the separation. When the mother leaves, the infant is distressed and cannot be comforted. During reunions, the infant's behavior suggests resistance, anger, and distress. The infant might seek proximity to the mother and cling to her while simultaneously pushing her away, hitting, or kicking. About 10% of North American infants tested in the Strange Situation fall into this category (Lamb & Lewis, 2015).

Insecure-Disorganized Attachment: A fourth category was added later to account for the small set of infants (10% or below) who show inconsistent, contradictory behavior in the Strange Situation. The infant with insecure-disorganized attachment shows a conflict between approaching and fleeing the caregiver, suggesting fear (Main & Solomon, 1986). Infants showing insecure-disorganized attachment experience the greatest insecurity, appearing disoriented and confused. They may cry unexpectedly and may show a flat, depressed emotion and extreme avoidance or fearfulness of the caregiver.

Attachment-Related Outcomes

Secure parent–child attachments are associated with positive socioemotional development in infancy, childhood, and adolescence. Preschool and school-age children who were securely attached as infants tend to be more curious, empathetic, self-confident, and socially competent, and they will have more positive interactions and close friendships with peers (Groh, Fearon, van IJzendoorn, Bakermans-Kranenburg, & Roisman, 2017; Veríssimo, Santos, Fernandes, Shin, & Vaughn, 2014). The advantages of secure attachment continue into adolescence. Adolescents who were securely attached in infancy and early childhood are more socially competent, tend to be better at making and keeping friends and functioning in a social group, and demonstrate greater emotional health, self-esteem, ego resiliency, and peer competence (Boldt, Kochanska, Yoon, & Koenig Nordling, 2014; Sroufe, 2016; Stern & Cassidy, 2018).

In contrast, insecure attachment in infancy, particularly disorganized attachment, is associated with long-term negative outcomes, including poor peer relationships, poor social competence, and higher rates of antisocial behavior, depression, and anxiety from childhood into adulthood (Groh et al., 2017; Kochanska & Kim, 2013; Wolke et al., 2014). Insecure attachments tend to correlate with difficult life circumstances and contexts, such as parental problems, low socioeconomic status (SES), and environmental stress, that persist throughout childhood and beyond, influencing the continuity of poor outcomes (Granqvist et al., 2017). One longitudinal study suggested that infants with an insecure-disorganized attachment at 12 and 18 months of age were, as adults, more likely to have children with insecure-disorganized attachment, suggesting the possibility of intergenerational transmission of insecure attachment (and associated negative outcomes) (Raby, Steele, Carlson, & Sroufe, 2015). Conversely, attachment is not set in stone. Quality parent–child interactions can at least partially make up for poor interactions early in life. Children with insecure attachments in infancy who experience subsequent sensitive parenting show more positive social and behavioral outcomes in childhood and adolescence than do those who receive continuous care of poor quality (Sroufe, 2016). In addition, infants can form attachments to multiple caregivers with secure attachments, perhaps buffering the negative effects of insecure attachments (Boldt et al., 2014).

Influences on Attachment

The most important determinant of infant attachment is the caregiver's ability to consistently and sensitively respond to the child's signals (Ainsworth et al., 1978; Behrens, Parker, & Haltigan, 2011). Infants become securely attached to mothers who are sensitive and offer high-quality responses to their signals, who accept their role as caregiver, who are accessible and cooperative with infants, who are not distracted by their own thoughts and needs, and who feel a sense of efficacy (Gartstein & Iverson, 2014). Mothers of securely attached infants provide stimulation and warmth and consistently synchronize or match their interactions with their infants' needs (Beebe et al., 2010). Secure mother–infant dyads show more positive interactions and fewer negative interactions compared with insecure dyads (Guo et al., 2015). The goodness of fit between the infant and parent's temperament influences attachment, supporting the role of reciprocal interactions in attachment (Seifer et al., 2014).

Infants who are insecurely attached have mothers who tend to be more rigid, unresponsive, inconsistent, and demanding (Gartstein & Iverson, 2014). The insecure-avoidant attachment pattern is associated with parental unavailability or rejection. Insecure-resistant attachment is associated with inconsistent and unresponsive parenting. Parents may respond inconsistently, offering overstimulating and intrusive caregiving at times and unresponsive care that is not attentive to the infant's signals at other times. Frightening parental behavior (at the extreme, child abuse) is thought to play a role in insecure-disorganized attachment (Duschinsky, 2015). Disorganized attachment is more common among infants who have been abused or raised in particularly poor caregiving environments; however, disorganized attachment itself is not an indicator of abuse (Granqvist et al., 2017; Lamb & Lewis, 2015).

Parent–infant interactions and relationships are influenced by many contextual factors. For example, conflict among parents is associated with lower levels of attachment security (Tan, McIntosh, Kothe, Opie, & Olsson, 2018). Insecure attachment responses may therefore represent adaptive responses to poor caregiving environments (Weinfield, Sroufe, Egeland, & Carlson, 2008). For example, not relying on an unsupportive parent (such as by developing an insecure-avoidant attachment) may represent a good strategy for infants. Toddlers who show an avoidant attachment tend to rely on self-regulated coping rather than turning to others, perhaps an adaptive response to an emotionally absent parent (Zimmer-Gembeck et al., 2017).

Stability of Attachment

Attachment patterns tend to be stable over infancy and early childhood, especially when securely attached infants receive continuous responsive care (Ding, Xu, Wang, Li, & Wang, 2014; Marvin, Britner, & Russell, 2016). The continuity of care influences the stability of attachment. For example, negative experiences can disrupt secure attachment. The loss of a parent, parental divorce, a parent's psychiatric disorder, and physical abuse, as well as changes in family stressors, adaptive processes, and living conditions, can transform a secure attachment into an insecure attachment pattern later in childhood or adolescence (Feeney & Monin, 2016; Lyons-Ruth & Jacobvitz, 2016). Contextual factors such as low SES, family and community stressors, and the availability of supports influence the stability of attachment through their effect on parents' emotional and physical resources and the quality of parent–infant interactions (Booth-LaForce et al., 2014; Thompson, 2016; Van Ryzin, Carlson, & Sroufe, 2011). Securely attached infants reared in contexts that pose risks to development are at risk to develop insecure attachments, whereas risky contexts tend to stabilize insecure attachment over time (Pinquart, Feußner, & Ahnert, 2013). An insecure attachment between child and parent can be overcome by changing maladaptive interaction patterns, increasing sensitivity on the part of the parent, and fostering consistent and developmentally appropriate responses to children's behaviors. Pediatricians, counselors, and social workers can help parents identify and change ineffective parenting behaviors to improve parent–child interaction patterns.

Although most research on attachment has focused on the mother–infant bond, we know that infants form multiple attachments (Dagan & Sagi-Schwartz, 2018). Consider the Efe foragers of the Democratic Republic of Congo, among whom infants are cared for by many people, as adults' availability varies with their hunting and gathering duties (Morelli, 2015). Efe infants experience frequent changes in residence and camp, exposure to many adults, and frequent interactions with multiple caregivers. It is estimated that the Efe infant will typically come into contact with 9 to 14 and as many as 20 people within a 2-hour period. Efe infants are reared in an intensely social community and develop many trusting relationships—many attachments to many people (Morelli, 2015). On a smaller scale, Western infants also develop multiple attachments to mothers, fathers, family members, and caregivers. Multiple attachment relationships offer important developmental opportunities. For example, an infant's secure attachment relationship with a father can compensate for the negative effects of an insecure attachment to a mother (Dagan & Sagi-Schwartz, 2018; Kochanska & Kim, 2013). It is important that infants develop attachments with some caregivers—but which caregivers, whether mothers, fathers, or other responsive adults, matters less than the bond itself. The Lives in Context feature discusses a challenge to attachment that many military families face: parental absence due to military deployment.

LIVES IN CONTEXT: FAMILY AND PEER CONTEXT

Infant Adjustment to Parental Deployment

The parent–infant relationship is vital to cognitive and especially socioemotional development. How does parental absence influence children's development? Infants who are raised in military families may experience the prolonged absence of a parent who is deployed abroad. Parental absence is a significant stressor for infants and young children.

Infants thrive on predictable routine environments and may experience more stress than older children when deployment and unexpected changes disrupt the family (Paris, DeVoe, Ross, & Acker, 2010). Wartime deployments increase stress for families. Rates of marital conflict and domestic violence rise along with increases in parental anxiety and depression, a sense of ambiguous loss, and perceived parenting stress (Trautmann, Alhusen, & Gross, 2015). These factors may limit a parent's emotional availability and sensitivity, vital to supporting their children's adjustment. Children's stress, in turn, influences parents' responses (Paley, Lester, & Mogil, 2013).

Sometimes adults dismiss infants' awareness and grasp of deployment separations. While they likely do not understand deployment itself, infants and toddlers are aware of deployment separations and likely are able to mourn parental separations (Osofsky & Chartrand, 2013). They can sense the varied emotions that caregivers and other nearby adults experience, such as sadness, anger, and anxiety. However, most infants and young children are resilient and, although they miss the absent parent, fare well.

The ability of infants and young children to manage a parent's deployment successfully is influenced by the available parent's ability to manage stress, cope with the changes in roles and responsibilities, and respond sensitively and consistently to the infant (Osofsky & Chartrand, 2013; Paris et al., 2010). To help infants and toddlers, parents should maintain consistent and predictable routines. Stay connected to the deployed parent through online video communication and by creating videos prior to deployment to permit the child to regularly see and hear the parent. Help toddlers label their emotions and link them to specific behaviors or events. Warm sensitive parenting that fosters emotional connections and security can help infants weather parental separations. Interventions to help military families before, during, and after deployment tend to focus on helping parents be mindful and aware of their own and their child's emotions and experience, learn effective skills for interacting with children, and learn how to manage emotions and promote adjustment (Julian et al., 2018a, 2018b).

What Do You Think?

1. Consider the effects of parental deployment from a bioecological perspective. Identify factors within the infant and parents that might influence successful adaptation. What are some microsystem and mesosystem factors that might contribute to infants' adaptation?
2. Identify two exosystem factors that might influence infant's experience of and adjustment to parental deployment.
3. Consider the macrosystem and identify two potential influences on adaptation to parental deployment. ●

Cultural Variations in Attachment Classifications

Attachment occurs in all cultures, but whether the Strange Situation is applicable across cultural contexts is a matter of debate. Research has shown that infants in many countries, including Germany, Holland, Japan, and the United States, approach the Strange Situation in similar ways (Sagi, Van IJzendoorn, & Koren-Karie, 1991). In addition, the patterns of attachment identified by Ainsworth occur in a wide variety of cultures in North America, Europe, Asia, Africa, and the Middle East (Bornstein et al., 2013; Cassibba, Sette, Bakermans-Kranenburg, & van IJzendoorn, 2013; Huang, Lewin, Mitchell, & Zhang, 2012; Jin, Jacobvitz, Hazen, & Jung, 2012; Thompson, 2013).

Nevertheless, there are differences. For example, insecure-avoidant attachments are more common in Western European countries, and insecure-resistant attachments are more prevalent in Japan and Israel (Van IJzendoorn & Kroonenberg, 1988). This pattern may result from the fact that Western cultures tend to emphasize individuality and independence, whereas Eastern cultures are more likely to emphasize the importance of relationships and connections with others, collectivism. Individualist and collectivist cultural perspectives interpret children's development in different ways; Western parents might interpret insecure-resistant behavior as clingy, whereas Asian parents might interpret it as successful bonding (Gardiner & Kosmitzki, 2018).

Many Japanese and Israeli infants become highly distressed during the Strange Situation and

Dogon infants from Mali, West Africa, show rates of secure attachment that are similar to those of Western infants, but the avoidant attachment style is not observed in samples of Dogon infants because infants are in constant proximity to mothers who respond to infant distress and feed infants on demand.
Danita Delimont / Alamy Stock Photo

show high rates of insecure resistance. Resistance in Japanese samples of infants can be attributed to cultural childrearing practices that foster mother-infant closeness and physical intimacy that leave infants unprepared for the separation episodes; the Strange Situation may be so stressful for them that they resist comforting (Takahashi, 1990). In other words, the Strange Situation may not accurately measure the attachment of these infants. Similarly, infants who are raised in small, close-knit Israeli kibbutz communities do not encounter strangers in their day-to-day lives, so the introduction of a stranger in the Strange Situation procedure can be overly challenging for them. At the same time, kibbutz-reared infants spend much of their time with their peers and caregivers and see their parents infrequently and therefore may prefer to be comforted by people other than their parents (Sagi et al., 1985).

Dogon infants from Mali, West Africa, show rates of secure attachment that are similar to those of Western infants, but the avoidant attachment style is not observed in samples of Dogon infants (McMahan True, Pisani, & Oumar, 2001). Dogon infant care practices diminish the likelihood of avoidant attachment because the infant is in constant proximity to the mother. Infant distress is promptly answered with feeding and infants feed on demand, so mothers cannot behave in ways that would foster avoidant attachment.

As shown in Figure 6.2, although secure attachment is most common, the prevalence of other attachment styles varies internationally. The behaviors that characterize sensitive caregiving

FIGURE 6.2

Cross-Cultural Variations in Attachment

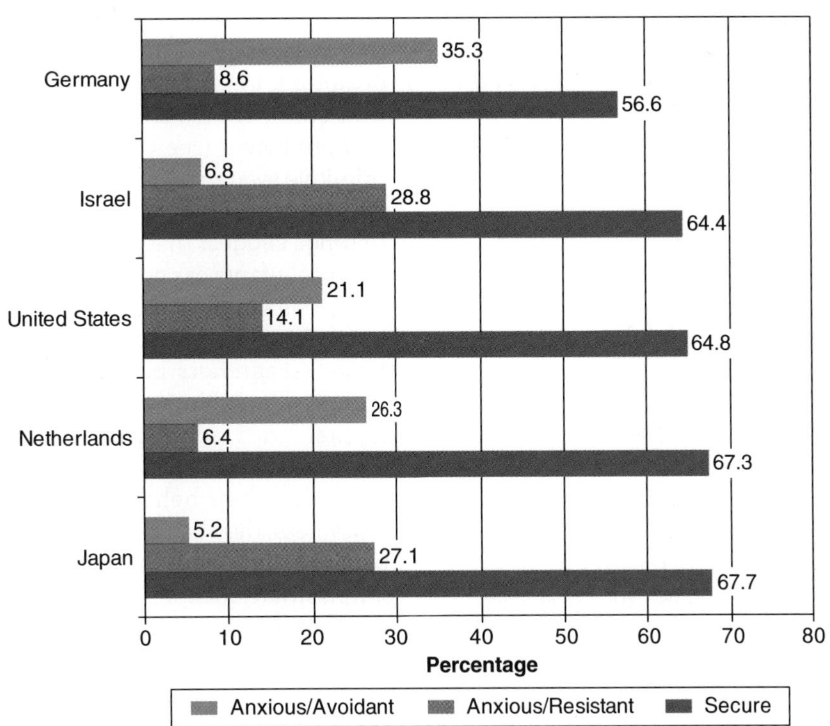

Source: Adapted from Van IJzendoorn and Kroonenberg (1988).

vary with culturally specific socialization goals, values, and beliefs of the parents, family, and community (Mesman, van IJzendoorn, & Sagi-Schwartz, 2016). For example, Puerto Rican mothers often use more physical control in interactions with infants, such as picking up crawling infants and placing them in desired locations, over the first year of life than do European American mothers. They actively structure interactions in ways consistent with long-term socialization goals oriented toward calm, attentive, and obedient children. Typically, attachment theory conceptualizes this type of control as insensitive, yet physical control is associated with secure attachment status at 12 months in Puerto Rican infants (but not White non-Hispanic infants) (Carlson & Harwood, 2003; Harwood, Scholmerich, Schulze, & Gonzalez, 1999). Similarly, German mothers operate according to the shared cultural belief that infants should become independent at an early age and should learn that they cannot rely on the mother's comfort at all times. German mothers may seem unresponsive to their children's crying, yet they are demonstrating sensitive childrearing within their context (Grossmann, Spangler, Suess, & Unzner, 1985). In other words, the behaviors that reflect sensitive caregiving vary with culture because they are adaptations to different circumstances (Rothbaum et al., 2000a).

In summary, attachment is an adaptive process in which infants and caregivers become attuned to each other and develop an enduring bond. Infants become attached to caregivers—mothers, fathers, and other adults—who are sensitive to their needs. Secure attachment in infancy is associated with emotional and social competence in infancy, early childhood, and even later childhood and adolescence. The attachment bond formed in infancy, whether secure or insecure, influences the child's developing internal working model of self and thereby his or her self-concept, as described in the next section.

THINKING IN CONTEXT 6.4

1. Recall from Chapter 1 that individuals are thought to play an active role in their development. How might this be true with regard to attachment? How might infants contribute to the development of attachments?
2. Infants reared in impoverished orphanages may receive little attention and experience few meaningful interactions with caregivers. What might these experiences mean for the development of attachment? What outcomes and behaviors might you expect from children reared under such conditions? In your view, what can be done to help such children?

THE SELF IN INFANCY AND TODDLERHOOD

What do babies know about themselves? When do they begin to know that they have a "self"—that they are separate from the people and things that surround them? We have discussed the challenges that researchers who study infants face. Infants cannot tell us what they perceive, think, or feel. Instead, researchers must devise ways of inferring infants' states, feelings, and thoughts. As you might imagine, this makes it very challenging to study infants' conceptions of self, as well as their awareness and understanding of themselves.

Self-Awareness

Maya, 4 months of age, delights in seeing that she can make the mobile above her crib move by kicking her feet. Her understanding that she can influence her world suggests that she has a sense of herself as different from her environment (Rochat, 1998). Before infants can take responsibility for their own actions, they must begin to see themselves as physically separate from the world around them.

Some developmental researchers believe that infants are born with a capacity to distinguish the self from the surrounding environment (Meltzoff, 1990). Newborns show distress at hearing a recording of another infant's cries but do not show distress at hearing their own cries, suggesting that they can distinguish other infants' cries from their own and thereby have a primitive notion of self (Dondi, Simion, & Caltran, 1999). Newborns' facial imitation, that is, their ability to view another person's facial expression and produce it (see Chapter 4), may also suggest a primitive awareness of self and others (Meltzoff, 2007; Rochat, 2013). It is unclear, however, whether these findings suggest that newborns have self-awareness because infants cannot tell us what they know.

Others argue that an awareness of oneself is not innate but emerges by 3 months of age (Neisser, 1993). Some researchers believe that this emergence is indicated by infants' awareness of the consequences of their own actions on others (Langfur, 2013). As infants interact with people and objects, they learn that their behaviors have effects. With this awareness, they begin to experiment to see how their behaviors influence the world around them, begin to differentiate themselves from their environments, and develop a sense of self (Bigelow, 2017).

Self-Recognition

How do we know whether self-awareness is innate or develops in the early months of life? One way of

This toddler recognizes herself in the mirror, as shown by her touching the rouge mark on her face.
Thierry Berrod, Mona Lisa Production/Science Source

studying self-awareness in infants is to examine infants' reactions to viewing themselves in a mirror. **Self-recognition**, the ability to recognize or identify the self, is assessed by the "rouge test." In this experiment, a dab of rouge or lipstick is applied to an infant's nose without the infant's awareness—for example, under the pretext of wiping his or her face. The infant is then placed in front of a mirror (Bard, Todd, Bernier, Love, & Leavens, 2006). Whether the infant recognizes himself or herself in the mirror depends on cognitive development, especially the ability to engage in mental representation and hold images in one's mind. Infants must be able to retain a memory of their own image in order to display self-recognition in the mirror task. If the infant has an internal representation of her face and recognizes the infant in the mirror as herself, she will notice the dab of rouge and reach for her own nose.

Mirror recognition develops gradually and systematically (Brandl, 2018). From 3 months of age, infants pay attention and react positively to their mirror image, and by 8 to 9 months of age, they show awareness of the tandem movement of the mirror image with themselves and play with the image, treating it as if it is another baby (Bullock & Lutkenhaus, 1990). Some 15- to 17-month-old infants show signs of self-recognition, but it is not until 18 to 24 months that most infants demonstrate self-recognition by touching their nose when they notice the rouge mark in the mirror (Cicchetti, Rogosch, Toth, & Spagnola, 1997). Does experience with mirrors influence how infants respond to the rouge test? Interestingly, infants from nomadic tribes with no experience with mirrors demonstrate self-recognition at the same ages as infants reared in surroundings with mirrors (Priel & deSchonen, 1986). This suggests that extensive experience with a mirror is not needed to demonstrate self-recognition in the mirror task. In addition, research with Canadian toddlers shows that their performance on the mirror task is unrelated to their experience with mirrors in the home (Courage, Edison, & Howe, 2004).

Mirror recognition is not the only indicator of a sense of self—and may not be the earliest indicator. A recent study suggests that self-recognition may develop before infants can succeed on the mirror task (Stapel, van Wijk, Bekkering, & Hunnius, 2017). Eighteen-month-old infants viewed photographs of their own face, the face of an unfamiliar infant, the face of their caregiver, and the face of an unfamiliar caregiver while their brain activity was registered via electroencephalography (EEG). The infants showed more brain activity in response to their own face, suggesting self-recognition, yet only half of these infants succeeded on the mirror task.

By 18 to 24 months of age, children begin to recognize themselves in pictures and refer to themselves in the pictures as "me" or by their first names (Lewis & Brooks-Gunn, 1979). One study of 20- to 25-month-old toddlers showed that 63% could pick themselves out when they were presented with pictures of themselves and two similar children (Bullock & Lutkenhaus, 1990). By 30 months of age, nearly all of the children could pick out their own picture.

With advances in self-awareness, toddlers begin to experience more complex emotions, including self-conscious emotions, such as embarrassment, shame, guilt, jealousy, and pride (Lewis & Carmody, 2008). An understanding of self is needed before children can be aware of being the focus of attention and feel embarrassment, identify with others' concerns and feel shame, or desire what someone else has and feel jealousy toward that person. In a study of 15- to 24-month-old infants, only those who recognized themselves in the mirror looked embarrassed when an adult gave them overwhelming praise. They smiled, looked away, and covered their faces with their hands. The infants who did not recognize themselves in the mirror did not show embarrassment (Lewis, 2011). A developing sense of self and the self-conscious emotions that accompany it lead toddlers to have more complex social interactions with caregivers and others, all of which contribute to the development of self-concept.

Emerging Self-Concept

In toddlerhood, between 18 and 30 months of age, children's sense of self-awareness expands beyond self-recognition to include a **categorical self**, a self-description based on broad categories such as sex, age, and physical characteristics (Stipek, Gralinski, & Kopp, 1990). Toddlers describe themselves as "big," "strong," "girl/boy," and "baby/big kid." Children use their categorical self as a guide to behavior. For example, once toddlers label themselves by gender, they spend more time playing with toys stereotyped for their own gender. Applying the categorical self as a guide to behavior illustrates toddlers' advancing capacities for self-control.

At about the same time as toddlers display the categorical self, they begin to show another indicator of their growing self-understanding. As toddlers become proficient with language and their vocabulary expands, they begin to use many personal pronouns and adjectives, such as "I," "me," and "mine," suggesting a sense of self in relation to others (Bates, 1990). Claims of possession emerge by about 21 months and illustrate children's clear representation of "I" versus other (Levine, 1983), a milestone in self-definition and the beginnings of self-concept (Rochat, 2010).

Self-Control

Self-awareness and the emerging self-concept permit self-control, as one must be aware of oneself as separate from others to comply with requests and modify behavior in accordance with caregivers' demands. In order to engage in self-control, the infant must be able to attend to a caregiver's instructions, shift his or her attention from an attractive stimulus or task, and inhibit a behavior. Cortical development, specifically development of the frontal lobes, is responsible for this ability (Posner & Rothbart, 2018). Between 12 and 18 months, infants begin to demonstrate self-control by their awareness of, and compliance to, caregivers' simple requests (Kaler & Kopp, 1990).

Although toddlers are known for asserting their autonomy, such as by saying no and not complying with a caregiver's directive, compliance is much more common (Kochanska, 2000). Paradoxically, when parents encourage autonomous, exploratory behavior, their children are more likely to show compliance to parental instructions in toddlerhood through early childhood (Laurin & Joussemet, 2017). Secure attachment relationships and warm parenting are associated with effortful control, likely as securely attached infants feel comfortable exploring their environment, which promotes autonomy (Pallini et al., 2018). Toddlers' capacities for self-control improve rapidly. For example, delay of gratification tasks suggest that between 18 and 36 months, toddlers become better able to control their impulses and wait before eating a treat or playing with a toy (Białecka-Pikul, Byczewska-Konieczny, Kosno, Białek, & Stępień-Nycz, 2018; Cheng, Lu, Archer, & Wang, 2018).

Infants make great strides in socioemotional development over the first 2 years of life, as summarized in Table 6.3. Infants' advances in emotional expression and regulation represent the interaction of biological predispositions, such as inborn capacities for basic emotions and temperament, and experience—particularly parent–child interactions—the contexts in which they are raised, and the goodness of fit between infants' needs and what their contexts provide. Infants' gains in emotional and social development and a growing sense of self form a socioemotional foundation for the physical and cognitive changes that they will experience in the early childhood years.

TABLE 6.3

The Developing Self

CONCEPT	DESCRIPTION	EMERGENCE
Self-concept	Self-description and thoughts about the self	Begins as a sense of awareness in the early months of life
Self-awareness	Awareness of the self as separate from the environment	Innate or develops in the early months of life
Self-recognition	The ability to recognize or identify the self; typically tested in mirror recognition tasks	18–24 months
Categorical self	Self-description based on broad categories such as sex, age, and physical characteristics; indicates the emergence of self-concept	18–30 months

Source: Adapted from Butterworth (1992).

THINKING IN CONTEXT 6.5

1. How might culture influence infants' developing sense of self? Consider Western cultures that emphasize individuality and Eastern cultures that value collectivism. How might parents and other adults interact with babies and promote their developing sense of self? How might babies in each of these cultures come to understand themselves?
2. Provide examples of how infants' temperament, emotional development, and sense of self interact. How do changes in one influence the others? How do interactions with others influence these developments?

APPLY YOUR KNOWLEDGE

Eighteen-month-old Stefana toddles across the floor to her mother, gripping her leg as she cries. "Ah, come here, hija," her mother, Perda, says as she scoops Stefana into her arms and soothes her. "Are you tired? Let's take a nap," Perda says. As she puts Stefana in her crib, Perda reminds herself that Stefana has come a long way.

Stefana was a challenge from day 1, as Perda's mother puts it. She cried through the day and night on most days. It was hard to determine what caused her to cry. Was the room too loud or too cold? Did she just wake up on the "wrong side of the crib"? Stefana was unpredictable, to say the least, sometimes liking specific foods—and other times spitting them out. Sometimes she napped and often she didn't. "Challenging or not, I'm here for my little girl," Perda thought.

At 18 months, Stefana is still unpredictable, but she is more easily soothed. Now when she hears a loud noise, like a truck backfiring outside, she no longer wails. Instead she looks to her mother and soon goes back to playing.

The child care center teacher has noted that Stefana adjusts much more easily to her mother leaving. When Perda goes to work, Stefana cries at first but sucks her thumb and begins to play shortly thereafter. She beams and runs to Perda when she returns every afternoon.

1. How would you describe Stefana's temperament? How do Stefana and Perda's temperament styles interact?
2. How would you describe Stefana's attachment style?
3. What long-term outcomes do you expect for Stefana?
4. Suppose Stefana lived in a different context, with a caregiver who shares her temperament or perhaps as an orphan in an orphanage that is understaffed and underfunded. Or perhaps she lives with a loving mother but in an unsafe, unpredictable war zone. How might these contexts contribute to Stefana's emotional development?

WANT A BETTER GRADE?

Get the tools you need to sharpen your study skills. **SAGE edge** offers a robust online environment featuring an impressive array of free tools and resources. Access practice quizzes, eFlashcards, video, and multimedia at **edge.sagepub.com/kutherchild1e.** SAGE edge™

KEY TERMS

Trust versus mistrust 164
Autonomy versus shame and doubt 164
Basic emotions 166
Social smile 167
Self-conscious emotions 167
Emotion regulation 167
Social referencing 169
Emotional display rule 169
Stranger wariness 170
Temperament 172
Easy temperament 173
Difficult temperament 173
Slow-to-warm-up temperament 173
Goodness of fit 174
Attachment 176
Separation anxiety 178
Internal working model 179
Strange Situation 179
Secure attachment 179
Insecure-avoidant attachment 179
Insecure-resistant attachment 180
Insecure-disorganized attachment 180
Self-recognition 185
Categorical self 186

SUMMARY

6.1 Summarize the psychosocial tasks of infancy and toddlerhood.

The psychosocial task of infancy is to develop a sense of trust. If parents and caregivers are sensitive to the infant's physical and emotional needs and consistently fulfill them, the infant will develop a basic sense of trust in his or her caregivers and the world. The task for toddlers is to learn to do things for themselves and feel confident in their ability to maneuver themselves in their environment. Psychosocial development is supported by warm and sensitive parenting and developmentally appropriate expectations for exploration and behavioral control.

6.2 Describe emotional development and the role of contextual influences on emotional development in infants and toddlers.

Newborns display some basic emotions, such as interest, distress, and disgust. Self-conscious emotions, such as empathy, embarrassment, shame, and guilt, depend on cognitive development, as well as an awareness of self, and do not emerge until about late infancy. With development, infants use different and more effective strategies for regulating their emotions. At about 6 months old, infants begin to use social referencing. Social referencing occurs in ambiguous situations, provides children with guidance in how to interpret the event, and influences their emotional responses and subsequent actions. Parents socialize infants to respond to and display their emotions in socially acceptable ways. The emotions that are considered acceptable, as well as ways of expressing them, differ by culture and context.

6.3 Discuss temperament and the role of goodness of fit in development during infancy and toddlerhood.

Temperament is the characteristic way in which an individual approaches and reacts to people and situations. Children are classified into three temperament styles: easy, slow to warm up, and difficult. Temperament is influenced by the interaction of genetic predispositions, maturation, and experience. Temperament tends to be stable, but there are developmental and individual differences. An important influence on socioemotional development is the goodness of fit between the child's temperament and the environment around him or her, especially the parent's temperament and childrearing methods.

6.4 Examine the development of attachment and influences on attachment stability and outcomes in infancy and toddlerhood.

From an ethological perspective, attachment is an adaptive behavior that evolved because it ensures that the infant and caregiver will remain in close proximity, aiding the survival of the infant. The Strange Situation is used to classify infants as securely attached or insecurely attached (insecure–avoidant, insecure–resistant, or disorganized–disoriented). Secure attachments in infancy are associated with social competence and socioemotional health. Attachment patterns are seen in a wide variety of cultures around the world, but the behaviors that make up sensitive caregiving vary depending on the socialization goals, values, and beliefs of the family and community, which may vary by culture. Generally, infants become securely or insecurely attached to caregivers based on the caregiver's ability to respond sensitively to the child's signals.

6.5 Explain infants and toddlers' emerging sense of self and self-control.

The earliest notion of self-concept, self-awareness, is evident in a primitive fashion at 3 months of age. Self-recognition, as indicated by mirror self-recognition, develops gradually and systematically in infants, but it is not until 18 to 24 months that a majority of infants demonstrate self-recognition in the mirror test. Once children have a sense of self, they can experience more complex emotions, such as self-conscious emotions. Self-awareness permits self-control, as one must be aware of oneself as an agent apart from others to comply with requests and modify behavior in accord with caregivers' demands.

REVIEW QUESTIONS

6.1 What are the two psychosocial tasks of infancy and toddlerhood, according to Erikson's theory?

How can parents promote positive psychosocial development during infancy and toddlerhood?

6.2 What are examples of basic and self-conscious emotions?

How do infants regulate their emotions?

How do social interactions influence emotional development?

Describe cultural influences on emotional development

6.3 What is temperament?

What are three temperament styles?

What are three dimensions of temperament?

How stable is temperament?

How does goodness of fit influence emotional development?

What are cultural differences in temperament?

6.4 What is attachment? How do researchers measure infant attachment?

What are four patterns of infant attachment?

Describe cultural influences on attachment.

What are ways of promoting a secure parent–child attachment bond?

6.5 What is self-awareness, and how is it measured in infancy?

What is self-concept and when does it first emerge?

How does self-control develop?

UNIT III

EARLY CHILDHOOD

©iStockphoto.com/ArtM

7 Physical Development in Early Childhood

Sophia's parents watched with pride as their 4-year-old daughter kicked the soccer ball to the other children. Sophia has grown from a bowlegged, round-tummied, and top-heavy toddler into a strong, well-coordinated young child. Her body slimmed, grew taller, and reshaped into proportions similar to that of an adult. As a toddler, she often stumbled and fell, but Sophia can now run, skip, and throw a ball. She has also gained better control over her fingers; she can draw recognizable pictures of objects, animals, and people. All of these physical developments help Sophia interact with the world in new ways, helping her to form new relationships, learn, and influence her own health and development. In this chapter, we examine the many physical changes that children undergo in early childhood and their far-reaching effects.

Learning Objectives

7.1 Describe patterns of growth and motor development in early childhood.

▶ **Video Activity 7.1:** Fostering Gross Motor Skills in Early Childhood

7.2 Summarize patterns of typical and atypical brain development.

▶ **Video Activity 7.2:** MRI of Brain Changes Through Childhood

7.3 Examine the influence of nutrition, physical activity, sleep, and screen use on young children's health.

7.4 Discuss threats to young children's physical health and well-being.

Chapter Contents

GROWTH AND MOTOR DEVELOPMENT

In early childhood, young children get taller, stronger, and better able to control their bodies. Their developing motor skills permit them to engage in new activities and interact with others in new ways.

Patterns of Growth

Compared with the first 2 years of life, growth slows during early childhood. From ages 2 through 6, the average child grows about 2.5 inches taller and gains nearly 5 pounds in weight each year. The typical 6-year-old child weighs about 45 pounds and is about 46 inches tall.

Body proportions change during early childhood as the body "catches up" with the head. The proportion of body fat to muscle changes. Young children become leaner. Boys and girls both gain muscle and lose fat; at 5 years of age, girls tend to have slightly more fat than boys and boys tend to have more muscle (Lloyd, Coller, & Miller, 2019). The cephalocaudal trend of infancy continues as the trunk, arms, and legs grow rapidly and body proportions become similar to those of adults. Specifically, the long bones of the arms and legs form new tissue through a process known as **ossification**. Ossification results in gains in height and arm span as the legs and arms grow; bones also become stronger and harder (Lloyd et al., 2019). As a result, during early childhood young children's bodies become less top-heavy, their bodies slim and their legs become longer, and they start to take on proportions that are similar to adults.

Biological factors play a large role in physical development. Children's height and rate of growth are closely related to that of their parents (Kliegman et al., 2016). Genes influence the rate of growth by stipulating the amount of hormones to be released. **Hormones** are chemicals that are produced and secreted into the bloodstream by glands. One hormone, growth hormone, is secreted from birth and influences the growth of nearly all parts of the body. Children with growth hormone deficiencies show slowed growth, but growth hormone supplements can stimulate growth when needed (Stagi, Scalini, Farello, & Verrotti, 2017).

Ethnic differences in patterns of growth appear in developed nations such as England, France, Canada, Australia, and the United States (Natale & Rajagopalan, 2014). Generally, children of African descent tend to be tallest, followed by children of European descent, then Asian, then Latino. However, there are many individual differences. Even within a given culture, some families are much taller than others (Stulp & Barrett, 2016). It is difficult to assess ethnic differences in growth patterns of children in developing nations because malnutrition and growth stunting are common (de Onis & Branca, 2016). In addition, there is little research examining normative patterns of development in developing countries. Contextual factors also play a role in growth because differences in nutrition, health care access, stress, and well-being influence physical development, as we will discuss later in this chapter.

Gross Motor Skills

Between the ages of 3 and 6, children become physically stronger, with increases in bone and muscle strength as well as lung capacity. Children make gains in coordination as the parts of the brain responsible for sensory and motor skills develop, permitting them to play harder and engage in more complicated play activities such as throwing and catching a ball. They can balance and coordinate their bodies to run, stop suddenly and turn, jump, hop, and climb. Watch a child fighting, bouncing, and jumping about wherever possible—outside, inside, and everywhere in between—and it's quickly apparent that young children are very active. In fact, 3-year-old children show the highest level of activity in the lifespan (Gabbard, 2018). Young children are driven to move and to practice motor skills. As children practice their motor skills, they become more agile.

Coordinating complex movements, like those entailed in riding a bicycle, is challenging for young children because it requires controlling multiple limbs, balancing, and more. As they grow and gain competence in their motor skills, young children become more coordinated and begin to show interest in balancing games and those that involve feats of coordination, such as running while kicking a ball. By age 5, most North American children can throw and catch a ball, climb a ladder, and ride a tricycle. Some 5-year-olds can even skate or ride a bicycle (Gabbard, 2018). Table 7.1 summarizes gross motor milestones in young children.

TABLE 7.1

Gross and Fine Motor Skill Development in Early Childhood

AGE	GROSS MOTOR SKILL
2–3 years	Walks more smoothly, runs but cannot turn or stop suddenly, jumps, throws a ball with a rigid body and catches by trapping the ball against the chest, rides push toys using feet
3–4 years	Runs, ascends stairs alternating feet, jumps 15 to 24 inches, hops, pedals and steers a tricycle
4–5 years	Runs more smoothly with control over stopping and turning, descends stairs alternating feet, jumps 24 to 33 inches, skips, throws a ball by rotating the body and transferring weight to one foot, catches a ball with hands, rides tricycle and steers effectively
5–6 years	Runs more quickly, skips more effectively, throws and catches a ball like older children, makes a running jump of 28 to 36 inches, rides bicycle with training wheels

Young children's motor abilities unfold with maturation and are also influenced by their context. For example, children in low socioeconomic status (SES) homes in the United States and United Kingdom tend to perform more poorly on measures of gross and fine motor development, perhaps because of nutritional deficits, reduced opportunities for outside play, and other reductions in supports (Bellows et al., 2017; Morley, Till, Ogilvie, & Turner, 2015). A caregiver's encouragement or discouragement of vigorous active play influences children's opportunities to practice and refine motor skills. There is continuity in motor development throughout childhood. For example, motor experience and achievements in infancy are associated with motor skills in early childhood. Children who learn to crawl early tend to show more advanced motor skills in early childhood than their late-crawling peers (Payne & Isaacs, 2016). These differences may be influenced by genetics; however, contextual experiences, such as opportunities to practice motor skills, may influence development in infancy and early childhood.

Children learn new motor skills by experimenting with movement and discovering new abilities. They also learn by observing other children and through play. Boys and girls show similar motor abilities, with subtle differences (Barnett et al., 2016; Morley, Till, Ogilvie, & Turner, 2015; Thomas & French, 1985). Boys tend to be more active than girls and can typically throw a ball and kick better as well as jump farther than girls. Girls tend to be better at coordinated activities such as balancing on

Climbing requires strength, coordination, and balance.
©iStockphoto.com/FatCamera

one foot. The games that boys and girls are typically encouraged to play contribute to sex differences in motor skills. For example, boys often have more practice in games involving balls and girls often play balancing games such as hopscotch.

The activities favored for children, and those that children therefore practice and master, vary with cultural context. For example, young children of some nations can swim in rough ocean waves that many adults of other nations would not attempt. In one comparison, Brazilian children, raised in a culture that stresses spontaneous, informal, playful, and physically active behavior, tended to outperform British children in comparisons of vigorous activities such as running and jumping (Victora, Victora, & Barros, 1990). The British children, immersed in a culture that tended to encourage quiet, independent, and self-contained activities that foster academic achievement, excelled on fine motor movements compared with the Brazilian children. Advances in gross motor skills help children move about and develop a sense of mastery of their environment, but it is fine motor skills that permit young children to take responsibility for their own care.

Fine Motor Skills

Motor development follows the proximodistal principle (see Chapter 4) and children therefore gain motor control from the body outward toward the fingers and toes. Fine motor skills rely on controlling and coordinating the small muscles of the body. The ability to button a shirt, pour milk into a glass, assemble puzzles, and draw pictures all involve eye-hand and small muscle coordination. As children get better at these skills, they are able to become more independent and do more for themselves. Young children become better at grasping eating utensils and become more self-sufficient at feeding. Many fine motor skills are very difficult for young children because they involve both hands and both sides of the brain. Tying a shoelace is a complex act requiring attention, memory for an intricate series of hand movements, and the dexterity to perform them. Although preschoolers struggle with this task, most children can tie their shoes by 5 to 6 years of age (Payne & Isaacs, 2016). Recent research suggests that children's fine motor ability influences cognition—specifically, their ability to use their fingers to aid in counting predicts their mathematical skills (Fischer, Suggate, Schmirl, & Stoeger, 2018).

"Very pretty! What is it?" asks Jessica as she examines the marked-up page. "A flower," answers 3-year-old Demitri. "It's a beautiful flower," Jessica responds as she tries to see a flower in the messy scribbles on the page. Young children's skills in drawing and writing illustrate the interaction of cognitive and motor domains of development. Drawing reflects fine motor control, planning skills, spatial understanding, and the recognition that pictures can symbolize objects, people, and events (Yamagata, 2007). Young children's emerging fine motor skills enable them to draw using large crayons and, eventually, pencils.

Young children's drawing skills progress through a predictable sequence alongside cognitive, motor, and brain maturation (Kellogg, 1970). Toddlers scribble when given a crayon (Dunst & Gorman, 2009; Toomela, 2003). At first, the physical gestures children use *are* the content, not the drawing itself. For example, an 18-month-old bounces a crayon around the page, making dots, to indicate that a rabbit jumps (Winner, 1986). One- and 2-year-olds engage in random scribbling, taking great pleasure in moving the crayon over the paper and becoming interested in the paper only when they notice that their movements result in drawings. Over time, the scribbles of 2-year-olds begin to become patterns, such as vertical and zigzag lines (Dunst & Gorman, 2009). If asked to draw a human figure, 2- to 3-year-olds usually draw a tadpole-like figure with a circle for the head with eyes and sometimes a smiley mouth, and they then draw a line or two beneath to represent the rest of the body (Figure 7.1). Tadpole-like forms are characteristic of young children's art in all cultures (Cox, 1993).

By 3 years of age, children's scribbles become more controlled, often recognizable, pictures (Dunst & Gorman, 2009; Toomela, 2003). This sometimes happens by accident, in that they begin drawing, notice that the shape is recognizable, and label it (Winner, 1986). Most 3-year-olds can draw circles, squares, rectangles, triangles, crosses, and Xs and they begin to combine shapes into more complex designs. Some 3-year-olds create drawings that are recognizable enough for others to identify what their picture represents. Other young children begin to understand the representational function

FIGURE 7.1

A Typical 2- to 3-Year-Old's Drawing of a Person

Source: Claire Marley, 2009.

of drawings after adults show them how pictures can be used to stand for people, objects, and places (Callaghan, 1999).

Between 3 and 4, young children begin to understand the representational function of drawings. Even when drawings appear to be nothing more than scribbles, young children often label them as representing a particular object and remember the label. In one study, children were asked to draw a balloon and a lollipop. The drawings looked the same to adults, but the children were adamant about which was which (Bloom, 2000), suggesting that it is important to ask a child what his or her drawing is rather than guess, because children's creations reflect their perspectives. Between ages 4 and 5, children's drawings loosely begin to depict actual objects, demonstrating the convergence of fine motor skills and the cognitive development of representational ability.

By age 4, children's drawings of people consist of simple figures, mostly heads with legs and arms, and a circle is often used to represent a stomach (Cox, 1997). As cognitive and fine motor skills improve, children create more sophisticated drawings of the human form in which the head and body are differentiated. Five-year-olds include a torso; after 5, children include arms and hands in their drawings (Cox, 1997). However, even older preschoolers' drawings contain perceptual distortions. During middle childhood, the use of depth improves and children's drawings become more perceptually realistic (Cox & Littlejohn, 1995). Overall, fine motor skills, such as the ability to copy a design and write letters, predict cognitive and academic achievement at kindergarten entry and in second grade (Cameron et al., 2012; Dinehart & Manfra, 2013) (Table 7.2).

THINKING IN CONTEXT 7.1

Recall from Chapter 1 that domains of development interact. Consider this principle with regard to physical development in early childhood.

1. How might changes in growth or motor skills influence other aspects of a child's development? Give examples.
2. Might other aspects of development, such as cognitive, emotional, or social, have implications for physical development? Why or why not?

BRAIN DEVELOPMENT

Early childhood is a period of rapid brain growth. The increase in synapses and connections among brain regions helps the brain to reach 90% of its adult weight by age 5 (Dubois et al., 2013.) The greatest increases in cortical surface area during early childhood are in the frontal and temporal cortex, which play a role in thinking, memory, language, and planning (Gilmore et al., 2018). Children's brains tend to grow in spurts, with very rapid periods of growth followed by little growth or even reductions in volume with synaptic pruning (Jernigan & Stiles, 2017).

Normative Processes of Brain Development

Synaptogenesis occurs in early childhood but slows relative to infancy. Pruning and remolding of synapses continues in response to experience. Recall from Chapter 4 that experience plays a critical role in

TABLE 7.2

Fine Motor Skill Development in Early Childhood

AGE	FINE MOTOR SKILL
2–3 years	Unzips large zippers, puts on and removes some clothing, uses a spoon
3–4 years	Serves food, can work large buttons, copies vertical lines and circles, uses scissors
4–5 years	Uses scissors to cut along a line, uses a fork effectively, copies simple shapes and some letters
5–6 years	Ties shoes, uses a knife to cut soft food, copies numbers and simple words

brain development. Little-used synapses are pruned in response to experience, an important part of neurological development that leads to more efficient thought. The natural forming and pruning of synapses enables the human brain to demonstrate **plasticity**, the brain's ability to change its organization and function in response to experience (Stiles, 2017). For example, young children given training in music demonstrated structural brain changes over a period of 15 months that corresponded with increases in music and auditory skills (Hyde et al., 2009). Plasticity enables the young child's brain to reorganize itself in response to injury in ways that the adult's brain cannot. Adults who suffered brain injuries during infancy or early childhood often have fewer cognitive difficulties than do adults who were injured later in life.

Yet the immature young brain, while offering opportunities for plasticity, is also uniquely sensitive to injury. If a part of the brain is damaged at a critical point in development, functions linked to that region will be irreversibly impaired. Generally speaking, plasticity is greatest when neurons are forming many synapses, and it declines with pruning (Stiles, 2017). However, brain injuries sustained before age 2 and, in some cases, age 3 can result in more global, severe, and long-lasting deficits than do those sustained later in childhood (Anderson et al., 2014), suggesting that a reserve of neurons is needed for the brain to show plasticity. Overall, the degree to which individuals recover from an injury depends on the injury, its nature and severity, age, experiences after the injury, and contextual factors supporting recovery such as interventions (Bryck & Fisher, 2012).

Myelination contributes to many of the changes that we see in children's capacities. As the neuron's axons become coated with fatty myelin, children's thinking becomes faster, more coordinated, and complex. Myelination aids quick, complex communication between neurons and makes coordinated behaviors possible (Chevalier et al., 2015). Patterns of myelination correspond with the onset and refinement of cognitive functions and behaviors (Dean et al., 2014). Myelination proceeds most rapidly from birth to age 4, first in the sensory and motor cortex, and then spreads to other cortical areas through childhood into adolescence and early adulthood (Qiu et al., 2015).

Lateralization, the process of the hemispheres becoming specialized to carry out different functions, becomes more pronounced in early childhood and is associated with children's development (Duboc et al., 2015). Recall from Chapter 4 that infants generally display a hand preference, left or right, which tends to strengthen with use. Hemispheric domination increases over childhood and the left hemisphere tends to dominate over the right in most adults (Duboc et al., 2015). Language tends to be lateralized to the left hemisphere in adults, and lateralization predicts children's language skills. Young children who show better performance on language tasks use more pathways in the left hemisphere and fewer in the right than those who are less skilled in language tasks (Walton, Dewey, & Lebel, 2018). The Lives in Context feature discusses handedness and lateralization.

Atypical Brain Development

So far, we have discussed typical brain development. Some children, however, experience brain development that is atypical, not normative. Two examples of atypical brain development in early childhood are autism spectrum disorder and sensory processing disorder.

Autism Spectrum Disorder

Autism spectrum disorder (ASD) is a family of neurodevelopmental disorders that range in severity and are characterized by deficits in social communication and a tendency to engage in repetitive behaviors (Hall, 2018). About 1 in 68 U.S. children is diagnosed with ASD, with males about four times more likely to be diagnosed than females (Masi, DeMayo, Glozier, & Guastella, 2017). The social and communication impairments related to ASD vary widely from minor difficulties in social comprehension and perspective taking to the inability to use nonverbal or spoken language. A common characteristic of ASD is repetitive behavior, such as rocking, hand flapping, twirling, and repeating sounds, words, or phrases. Some children with ASD experience sensory dysfunction, feeling visual, auditory, and tactile stimulation as intense and even painful.

There is evidence for a hereditary influence on ASD but ASD is likely epigenetic, the result of multiple interacting genes and environmental factors rather than a single gene (Eshraghi et al., 2018; Sandin et al., 2017). Some of the genes associated with ASD influence the availability of proteins that affect synaptic strength or number and neural connectivity in the brain (Bourgeron, 2015). ASD is associated with atypical brain connectivity (Hahamy, Behrmann, & Malach, 2015). The sensorimotor areas of the brain tend to show heightened connectivity, perhaps accounting for the sensory difficulties and motor features associated with ASD (Hull et al., 2017; Khan et al., 2015). Areas responsible for inhibitory control, or self-regulation, tend to show less connectivity, suggesting that children with ASD may experience difficulty controlling impulses (Voorhies et al., 2018). The areas of the brain implicated for facial

LIVES IN CONTEXT: BIOLOGICAL INFLUENCES

Handedness

What hand do you use to write, use a mouse, or eat? Do you consistently use one hand, either your right or left, for these activities? Most people do—an indicator of brain lateralization, the specialization of brain functions to a particular hemisphere. About 90% of U.S. adults report a right hand preference (Gilbert & Wysocki, 1992), signifying that the left hemisphere dominates in fine motor control. Hand preferences emerge early in life. For example, 18-month-old infants tend to prefer their right hand (Suzuki, Ando, & Satou, 2009) and this preference has even been observed prenatally (Hepper, 2013).

Do lefties differ from righties? Is there an advantage (or disadvantage) to being a lefty? Although left handedness was once considered a deficit to correct, such as by requiring left-handed children to learn to write with their right hand, research suggests that there are few differences between left- and right-handed children. Left-handed children are not more prone to injury than their peers (Johnston, Nicholls, Shah, & Shields, 2009). Some research has suggested that left-handed children score slightly lower on measures of cognitive development than their right-handed peers (Johnston, Nicholls, Shah, & Shields, 2013; Somers, Shields, Boks, Kahn, & Sommer, 2015). Why? Left-handed young children must adjust to a right-handed world. Children learn to write and draw using notebooks, desks, and other materials designed for right-handed children and tend to show poorer handwriting than their right-handed peers (Hawkyard, Dempsey, & Arthur-Kelly, 2014). Perhaps it is not surprising that left-handed young children tend to perform more poorly on fine motor tasks (Giagazoglou, Fotiadou, Angelopoulou, Tsikoulas, & Tsimaras, 2001). We have seen that penmanship is a fine motor skill that is associated with academic performance (Dinehart, 2015). However, the effect of handedness on cognitive ability is small (Resch et al., 1997). In fact, some studies of adults suggest that lefties show better performance on tasks that require executive function, including working memory, inhibitory control, and mental flexibility (Beratis, Rabavilas, Kyprianou, Papadimitriou, & Papageorgiou, 2013). Left-handed children and adults tend to have a larger corpus callosum, a thick band of neural fibers that connect and enable the two hemispheres to communicate (Cowell & Gurd, 2018; Luders, Thompson, & Toga, 2010). Lefties must adapt their motor skills to use right-handed tools, often using their left hand for some tasks and their right for others. This requires greater communication between their right and left hemispheres, stimulating growth of the corpus callosum.

What causes handedness? Given observations of fetal behavior, it appears that handedness preferences are largely inborn. Research suggests a role for genetics; however, specific genes have not been reported (de Kovel, Carrión-Castillo, & Francks, 2019; Paracchini & Scerri, 2017). The APOE gene may play a role in handedness, but handedness is likely a polygenic trait influenced by multiple genes (Bloss, Delis, Salmon, & Bondi, 2010; Brandler et al., 2013). However, monozygotic (identical) twins often differ in handedness, and the left-handed twin tends to develop a larger corpus callosum (Cowell & Gurd, 2018; Gurd, Schulz, Cherkas, & Ebers, 2006). Experience also matters. In the United States and United Kingdom, elementary school teachers used to require left-handed children to write with their right hand. As this practice declined, the percentage of left-handed children has increased (Levy, 1976). For example, more adults in Great Britain and the United States claim to be left-handed today (about 10%) than in 1900 (about 3%) (McManus, Moore, Freegard, & Rawles, 2010).

What Do You Think?

1. How might contextual factors and cultural preferences influence the prevalence of left or right handedness?
2. Imagine that you are left-handed (or if you're a lefty, imagine being right-handed). What would it be like to write, use a spiral notebook, use a mouse, or even turn a doorknob? Practice using your nondominant hand. Suppose you were permitted to only use this hand. How might it affect your day-to-day experience and learning? Why? ●

expression involved in social behavior, emotion, social communication, and theory of mind show reduced and less efficient connectivity within and between each area (Cheng, Rolls, Gu, Zhang, & Feng, 2015; Dajani & Uddin, 2016; Doyle-Thomas et al., 2015). Collectively these neurological differences mean that children with ASD may experience a poor theory of mind (Kana et al., 2015; Senju, 2012). That is, they may find it difficult to consider mental states, which is essential to communication.

Although children are typically not diagnosed until age 3, some ASD symptoms are apparent in infancy. Some infants may demonstrate delays in milestones such as following another person's gaze, smiling at others, and vocalizing back at others (Tchaconas & Adesman, 2013). In one study, researchers found that infants who were later diagnosed with ASD began showing less attention to other people's eyes by 2 months of age (Jones & Klin, 2013). Likewise, brain scans show that infants' brains differentiate people's faces from objects, but infants with ASD show similar brain activity in response to faces and objects, suggesting that they view faces and objects similarly (McCleery, Akshoomoff, Dobkins, & Carver, 2009). Early recognition that faces are special stimuli that are linked with social stimulation is important for developing communication skills, emotional attachments, and theory of mind.

Some children with ASD are intellectually disabled; others show average or above-average intelligence (Hall, 2018). Children with ASD often show difficulties with working memory, requiring additional time to process information (Y. Wang et al., 2017). They may benefit from instruction that emphasizes modeling, hands-on activities, and concrete examples and teaches skills for generalizing learning from one setting or problem to another (Lewis, Wheeler, & Carter, 2017).

Sensory Processing Disorder

"No!! It's too loud!" Ryan cries and retreats to the corner, rocking. The other children, unperturbed by the sound, watch Ryan and then go back to playing. It is estimated that, perhaps like Ryan, between 5 and 16% of children experience **sensory processing disorder (SPD)**, an extreme difficulty processing and responding to sensory stimuli that interferes with daily functioning (Ahn, Miller, Milberger, & McIntosh, 2004; Ben-Sasson, Carter, & Briggs-Gowan, 2009). Children with SPD may overreact or underreact to sensory stimuli, making it difficult to respond appropriately to everyday sights, sounds, smells, and tactile stimuli. SPD is caused by atypical processing of sensory stimuli in the brain. Children with SPD show abnormalities in the parts of the brain involved in multimodal sensory integration, especially the parietal and occipital regions (Chang et al., 2016). Brain scans also tend to show structural abnormalities in the connections among sensory pathways and the parts of the brain responsible for higher-order thinking, the frontal cortex, suggesting that children with SPD may experience difficulty making sense of sensory stimuli, integrating sensory and social stimuli, and inhibiting inappropriate responses to stimuli (Owen et al., 2013).

Children with ASD can benefit from hands-on activities that enable them to explore objects of different sizes, shapes, and textures.
©iStockphoto.com/FatCamera

SPD may take several forms. Some children with SPD experience sensory over-responsivity. These children have a very low sensory threshold and their sensory system overreacts to stimuli, causing them to be easily overwhelmed (Miller, Nielsen, Schoen, & Brett-Green, 2009). Other children with SPD experience sensory under-responsivity, a high sensory threshold in which they often do not notice or process sensory input (Goodman-Scott & Lambert, 2015). For example, a child with sensory under-responsivity may not hear the teacher and may miss social signals because the child does not notice visual cues like facial expression. A third group of children with SPD crave and seek intense stimulation (Miller et al., 2009). These children may appear impulsive and unpredictable because they are often constantly in motion, running, jumping, tapping, humming, and fidgeting to receive sensations from their environment.

SPD often co-occurs with other disorders, such as ASD and attention-deficit/hyperactivity disorder (ADHD) (Owen et al., 2013). Because of this and a general lack of research, SPD is included as a diagnosis in only some diagnostic manuals, such as the *Diagnostic Manual for Infancy and Early Childhood* and the *Diagnostic Classification of Mental Health and Developmental Disorders of Infancy and Early Childhood–Revised*, but not in the American Psychiatric Association's *Diagnostic and Statistical Manual of Mental Disorders (DSM)* or the World Health Organization's *International Statistical Classification of Diseases* (Goodman-Scott & Lambert, 2015). However, brain research suggests that SPD is neurologically distinct from other disorders; children with ASD and ADHD tend to show abnormal connectivity in the temporal and frontal lobes (compared with the parietal and occipital lobes in SPD), suggesting that the disorders are neurologically distinct (Owen et al., 2013)

SPD poses social and cognitive risks for children. Children with SPD often have difficulty playing with other children and experience more internalizing problems (Boterberg & Warreyn, 2016). They tend to experience frequent conflict with peers because of their difficulty in processing and generating adaptive responses to sensory input (Cosbey, Johnston, Dunn, & Bauman, 2012). Children with SPD find it harder to make and sustain friendships. They tend to be less aware of other children's social cues and spend more time in solitary play and play that is less mature than their peers. Moreover, parents of children with SPD report higher levels of parental stress than parents of children without sensory deficits (Gourley, Wind, Henninger, & Chinitz, 2013).

Treatment for SPD involves exposing children to sensory stimuli in a controlled environment. Sensory integration therapy is a form of treatment that is specialized to meet a child's specific sensory challenges. Through therapy and play, children are exposed to sensory stimuli and aided in developing coping and problem-solving skills to help them organize sensory input and promote self-regulation and appropriate responses (Critz, Blake, & Nogueira, 2015).

THINKING IN CONTEXT 7.2

1. How might the contexts in which children are immersed influence brain development?
   a. Consider the home and child care or school environment. Provide examples of how factors within these contexts can influence brain development.
   b. How might the larger cultural context matter in influencing children's brain development? Consider the experiences of children from a Western country compared with children from a non-Western, underdeveloped country. Do you expect cultural differences? Why or why not?
2. Many disorders, such as ASD and SPD, are much more common in Western countries than in underdeveloped countries. Why? How might contextual factors influence the prevalence of these disorders?

PROMOTING HEALTH IN EARLY CHILDHOOD

Early childhood is a healthy time in life. It is also a time in which children begin to develop health interests and patterns of behaviors. Habits developed in early childhood can influence children's interests and health throughout childhood and beyond. Parents and caregivers can help young children develop heathy eating, exercise, sleep, and screen use habits, as discussed next.

Nutrition

From ages 2 to 6, young children's appetites vary with their growth. Children's appetite is usually very good during active growth periods, but their appetite declines as their growth slows (Marotz, 2015). This decline is normal but is often an undue concern for parents. Children eat when they are hungry and should be provided with frequent opportunities to eat. For example, when a child doesn't finish breakfast, a small nutritious midmorning snack can make up for lost nutrients. Generally, preschool children tend to balance their eating, making up for short periods of little food intake with greater consumption later (Ball, Bindler, Cowen, & Shaw, 2017). The Applying Developmental Science feature examines picky eating.

Food attitudes are often formed in early childhood, influencing eating patterns into childhood and even to adulthood. Children's food preferences are influenced by their experiences. Repeated exposure to sweet and salty snacks increases children's preference for sugary and salty foods (Remington, Añez, Croker, Wardle, & Cooke, 2012). Young children are often sensitive to the sensory quality of foods, including appearance, texture, and shape (Marotz, 2015). Parents model food preferences and children can acquire food preferences and dislikes through observation (Hannon, Bowen, Moinpour, & McLerran, 2003). Children often dislike trying new foods. Encouraging the child to try the food several times over a few weeks can help him or her become familiar with the taste and texture, which can increase the likelihood of the child eating. Involving children in meal preparation can improve children's interest in and acceptance of new foods.

Young children require a healthy diet, with the same foods that adults need. Most children in developed nations eat enough calories, but their diets are often insufficient in vitamins and minerals, such as vitamin D, calcium, and potassium, and often excessive in calories and sugar (Hess & Slavin, 2014). In one study of 96 child care centers, 90% served high-sugar or high-salt food or did not serve whole grains in a day's meals (Benjamin Neelon, Vaughn, Ball, McWilliams, & Ward, 2012). Nutrient-dense snacks, such as cheese, yogurt, or hummus, can increase children's intake of nutrients without contributing to dietary excess (Figure 7.2).

Children with developmental disabilities and health conditions may have different food needs and experience feeding challenges (Samour & King, 2013). For example, impaired motor skills may make it difficult or impossible for a child to feed himself. Medications may influence children's appetite or their needs for particular nutrients. Children may have difficulty recognizing the body signals for hunger or fullness. Children with ASD and sensory disorders such as SPD may restrict their eating to particular textures or colors and require coaxing to eat, especially new foods (Shmaya, Eilat-Adar, Leitner, Reif, & Gabis, 2017). Food allergies, such as to dairy, wheat, or gluten, may make it difficult for children to gain the calories that they need.

Physical Activity

"Try to catch me!" 4-year old Eduardo called out to his playmates in the yard and broke into a sprint. Young children's play often involves physical activity, with

APPLYING DEVELOPMENTAL SCIENCE

Picky Eating

Many parents pressure children to eat, but picky eating is a common phase with no effect on growth in most children.
©iStockphoto.com/skynesher

At around age 3, it is not uncommon for children to go through a fussy eating phase where previously tolerated food is no longer accepted and it is hard to introduce new foods (Fildes et al., 2014). Estimates of picky eating vary widely, but it is highest (14%–50%) in preschool children and tends to decline with time (Taylor, Wernimont, Northstone, & Emmett, 2015). Parents of picky eaters report that their children consume a limited variety of foods, require foods to be prepared in specific ways, express strong likes and dislikes, and throw tantrums over feeding. Children who are picky eaters are likely to consume fewer calories, fruits and vegetables, and vitamins and minerals than other children. This behavior often raises parental concerns about nutrition (Berger, Hohman, Marini, Savage, & Birch, 2016). Pediatricians tend to view picky eating as a passing phase, often to the frustration of parents.

The overall incidence of picky eating declines with time, but picky eating is chronic for some children and lasts for several years. Persistent picky eating poses risks for poor growth (Taylor et al., 2015). One longitudinal study of Dutch children assessed at 1½, 3, and 6 years of age suggested that persistent picky eating was associated with symptoms common to developmental problems such as attention-deficit disorder, autism, and oppositional defiant disorder at age 7 (Cardona Cano et al., 2016). Another study found that sensory sensitivity predicted picky eating at age 4 and at age 6 (Steinsbekk, Bonneville-Roussy, Fildes, Llewellyn, & Wichstrøm, 2017). Children who are more sensitive to touch in general are also more sensitive to the tactile sensation of food in their mouths, whether the food is crispy or slimy, thick or with bits, for example (Nederkoorn, Jansen, & Havermans, 2015). They then reject foods of a particular texture. Likewise, children with a difficult temperament at 1½ years of age are more likely to be picky eaters 2 years later (Hafstad, Abebe, Torgersen, & von Soest, 2013).

Persistent picky eating illustrates the dynamic interaction of developmental domains. Physical and emotional factors, such as sensory sensitivity and temperament, can place children at risk for picky eating, which in turn influences physical development. Moreover, picky eating tends to elicit parental pressure to eat, which is associated with continued pickiness, suggesting that picky eating is sustained through bidirectional parent–child interactions (Jansen et al., 2017). Interventions for picky eating can help children learn to tolerate tactile sensations and help parents to understand that parental responses to pickiness can influence children's behavior and sustain picky eating (Walton, Kuczynski, Haycraft, Breen, & Haines, 2017).

In most cases, picky eating is a normative phase in preschool, with no significant effect on growth (Jansen et al., 2017). Regardless, picky eating is an important concern for parents and may remain so through much of childhood.

What Do You Think?

Were you a picky eater? Do you know a child with picky eating habits? What factors do you think influence picky eating in general? What would you tell a parent of a preschooler with picky eating habits? ●

important benefits for development. An analysis of nearly 100 studies conducted in 36 countries suggests that physical activity enhances growth and is consistently associated with advances in motor development, fitness, and bone and skeletal health (Carson et al., 2017). The recently updated Physical Activity Guidelines for Americans (U.S. Department of Health and Human Services, 2018b) advise that preschool children require daily physical activity, and they suggest a target of about 3 hours of activity (at any level ranging from light, such as walking at a comfortable pace, to vigorous, such as running)

FIGURE 7.2

MyPlate Food Groups for Children

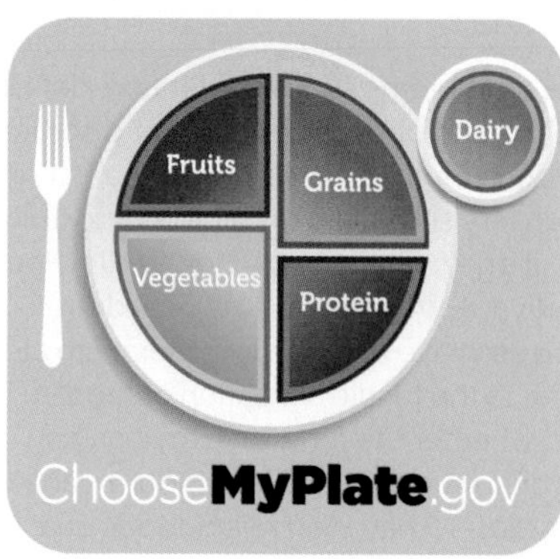

Source: U.S. Department of Agriculture (2018), https://www.choosemyplate.gov/kids.

per day. For example, over the course of a day, a child might go for a walk with a caregiver, engage in active play with peers, and practice dancing and balancing games in preschool. Canada, the United Kingdom, and the Commonwealth of Australia have published similar recommendations (Piercy et al., 2018).

Unfortunately, only about half of children meet the physical activity guidelines (Hesketh, Lakshman, & van Sluijs, 2017; Pate et al., 2015). One important predictor of physical activity is time spent outdoors. Children are more active when they are enrolled in care centers that schedule more than 1 hour of outside time each day (Copeland, Khoury, & Kalkwarf, 2016). Access to safe play environments is also associated with greater physical activity. Children from low-income homes tend to spend less time outdoors, engage in less physically active play, and spend more time in sedentary behaviors, such as watching television, as reported by parents (Lindsay, Greaney, Wallington, Mesa, & Salas, 2017). Although children of color are more likely to reside in communities that may pose challenges to outside play, ethnic and racial differences are not apparent in preschoolers' physical activity (Pate et al., 2015).

Sleep

Sleep plays an important role in development in infancy, childhood, and adolescence (Gómez & Edgin, 2015). We sleep most as infants, and sleep duration naturally declines about 20% from infancy into early childhood (Honaker & Meltzer, 2014). The American Academy of Sleep Medicine advises that young children 3 to 5 years of age should sleep 10 to 13 hours (including naps) each day (Paruthi et al., 2016). Most young children meet these goals, sleeping 10 to 11 hours each night (Magee, Gordon, & Caputi, 2014).

Some children, however, experience sleep problems, such as awakening often, difficulty falling asleep, and poor sleep duration. Sleep problems pose risks to young children's development, such as cognitive difficulties, including problems with attention, working memory, and slower processing speed (Schumacher et al., 2017). For example, when preschoolers who nap during the day are deprived of their usual naptime, they show poorer cognitive and emotion processing and poor self-control (Berger, Miller, Seifer, Cares, & Lebourgeois, 2012; Miller, Seifer, Crossin, & Lebourgeois, 2015). Persistent sleep deficits are linked with cognitive and neurological difficulties, including problems with attention, working memory, and slower processing speed (Schumacher et al., 2017).

Nightmares and **sleep terrors**, sometimes called night terrors, commonly occur in early childhood. Nightmares are anxiety-provoking dreams, whereas sleep terrors are more severe. Over the course of the evening, sleep patterns typically shift so that rapid eye movement (REM) sleep, in which the eyes move under closed lids and the individual dreams, increases. Deep non-REM sleep declines over the sleep period. Sleep terrors occur during deep sleep and tend to occur earlier in the evening when periods of deep sleep are longest.

Sleep terrors are most common in early childhood but may continue into adolescence. They are often triggered by stress and anxiety. During a sleep terror, the child may scream, violently thrash around in bed, and gasp for air. The child may wake or may remain asleep and unaware of the event. Children who experience nightmares and night terrors may dislike going to sleep. They may develop insomnia, insist on leaving the lights on, or cry at bedtime. Providing a consistent sleep routine, limiting evening access to electronic screens, allowing perhaps a security object such as a stuffed animal, and providing understanding and affection can help children develop healthy sleep habits.

Sleep is influential to young children's socioemotional functioning. Poor sleep is associated with anxiety, depression, hyperactivity, and impulsivity (Keefe-Cooperman & Brady-Amoon, 2014). Persistent sleep problems and insufficient sleep in early childhood may have consequences that persist into the school-age years and beyond, posing long-term risks to development (Schumacher et al., 2017).

Poor sleep may have a cascading effect on development through its influence on brain function. For example, sleep deprivation affects the neural connectivity between the prefrontal cortex and parts of the brain responsible for emotion, resulting in overreactive and exaggerated emotional responses to positive and negative stimuli (Magee et al., 2014). Poor sleep is associated with impaired behavioral and emotional self-regulation in young children, which can manifest as anxiety, depression, and impulsivity (Vaughn, Elmore-Staton, Shin, & El-Sheikh, 2015). These emotional problems can, in turn, interfere with sleep in a perpetual cycle, with increasing negative effects for young children.

One longitudinal study of over 5,000 Australian children followed from infancy through age 9 suggested that sleep problems predicted deficits in emotional regulation across childhood, which in turn affected children's ability to regulate their attention and contributed to ongoing sleep problems (Magee et al., 2014). Children experiencing difficulty with emotional regulation may be preoccupied with attempts to regulate their emotional system, resulting in limited capacity to focus their attention, with implications for learning and social interactions. When children are unable to control their emotions and attention, they are unprepared to cope with social interactions and everyday frustrations—and they tend to have difficulty learning in and out of school.

Parents can promote good sleep habits through the use of a bedtime routine, including a consistent bedtime (before 9:00 p.m.) and nightly bedtime reading (Mindell, Meltzer, Carskadon, & Chervin, 2009). In addition, young children should refrain from caffeinated products, sleep in a room without a television, and avoid the use of computer screens before bed. The Lives in Context feature describes cultural influences on sleep in early childhood.

Screen Use

In 2017, an estimated 95% of families with children younger than age 8 had a smartphone (up from 63% in 2013). Approximately 42% of children have their own tablet device (up from 7% in 2013) (Rideout, 2018). Research has suggested that children from

LIVES IN CONTEXT: CULTURAL CONTEXT

Cultural Influences on Sleep in Early Childhood

Sleep is a biological necessity, but it is also influenced by contextual factors. There are substantial cultural differences in sleep patterns and norms (Jenni & O'Connor, 2005). In one study, over 2,500 parents in Eastern (China, Hong Kong, India, Japan, Korea, Malaysia, Philippines, Singapore, and Thailand) and Western (Australia/New Zealand, Canada, United Kingdom, United States) countries reported on their preschool-aged child's sleep (Mindell, Sadeh, Kwon, & Goh, 2013). Children from Eastern countries had later sleep times (as late as nearly 10:30 p.m. in India) compared to nearly 8:00 p.m. in Australia and New Zealand (nearly 3 hours earlier). Although all children slept about the same amount of time over a 24-hour period, they showed different sleep patterns. Most children from Eastern countries continued to nap during the day and engage in bed sharing and room sharing at night (see Chapter 4 for more on bed sharing and room sharing). Young children's sleep patterns are influenced by cultural attitudes about the goals of childrearing.

Parents in Western countries tend to emphasize individualism, fostering children's independence. Bedtime provides opportunities for children to learn self-regulation. Young children in Western countries tend to have a distinct presleep bedtime ritual, consisting of an organized set of activities and procedures (Jenni & O'Connor, 2005). Bedtime rituals include activities such as bathing, dressing in pajamas, telling stories and singing lullabies, putting the child to bed with goodnight kisses, and then leaving the child alone in his or her room (Beltramini & Hertzig, 1983). Frequently, children insist on sleeping with a light on or taking a doll, stuffed animal, or blanket to bed with them or they repeatedly call their parents after being put to bed for various reasons such as getting a drink of water.

Collectivist values that characterize many Eastern countries favor relatedness and emphasize the roles of children as group members rather than as individuals. In many collectivist societies, the wake-to-sleep transition, bedtime, is not recognized as a distinct event with specific activities. That is, there is no "bedtime" or bedtime ritual. For example, Mayan young children fall asleep when they are tired, often in someone's arms or when taken to bed with a family member, as parents and children sleep in the same room and usually share a bed (Jenni & O'Connor, 2005). Mayan parents do not report bedtime rituals—there are no specific sleep clothes, stories, or songs to put young children to sleep. Mayan children typically do not use sleep aids (such as dolls) nor do they resist sleep. Similarly, children in Bali show similar sleep habits. Balinese culture centers around ritual and spiritual observances that often take place at night, can last throughout the night, and are attended by children and adults (Mead, 1970). People of all ages slip in and out of sleep during the celebrations. Balinese young children therefore learn to transition from sleep to wakefulness smoothly and under conditions of high stimulation. They do not require bedtime rituals and can fall asleep easily under conditions that children from other cultures might find difficult. How children (and adults) sleep—where, with whom, and for how long—is influenced by cultural customs (Owens, 2004).

What Do You Think?

Did you have bedtime routines as a child? What purpose did they serve? How might your context and culture support your childhood sleep habits?

lower-income homes and with parents with less education spend about 90 minutes more on screen media than children from higher-income homes (3:39 vs. 1:50) (Przybylski & Weinstein, 2019; Rideout, 2018). Children of color are disproportionately more likely to live in lower-income homes and are more likely to experience household chaos, which are associated with increased screen use (Emond et al., 2018). Some research suggests that White children engage in less screen time than children of color, but the difference is small (Przybylski & Weinstein, 2019).

Parents report that children tend to spend their screen time watching videos. A smaller proportion watch educational programs or play early-learning apps and some play games (Reid Chassiakos et al., 2016). About one-half of children from higher-income homes watch educational content on mobile devices compared with about one-quarter of those from the lowest income families (Rideout, 2018).

Although many parents and pediatricians are concerned with the effect of screen time on well-being, a recent study suggested that there is little or no support for harmful links between digital screen use and young children's psychological well-being (specifically, attachment, curiosity, resilience, and positive mood) (Przybylski & Weinstein, 2019). Screen time, however, may negatively affect physical development. Children who engage in more screen time use may be less engaged in the physical play that contributes to the growth of motor skills and overall physical health (Fakhouri, Hughes, Brody, Kit, & Ogden, 2013). Screen use also negatively affects sleep. Greater exposure to screens, such as a television, computer, or mobile phone, in the bedroom is associated with fewer minutes of sleep per night in young children (Reid Chassiakos et al., 2016). Small doses of supervised screen time may permit children to enjoy fun games and learn from educational apps while reserving time for the physical play and activity that children require to build healthy bodies.

THINKING IN CONTEXT 7.3

1. Provide advice to a parent of a 4-year-old. Explain the relevance of nutrition, physical activity, sleep, and screen use to young children's development and make recommendations for each.
2. Suppose you wanted to help young children be "healthy." What does "health" mean to you, and how should we help children be more "healthy"?

THREATS TO HEALTH AND WELL-BEING

We have seen that there are many opportunities to promote young children's health. However, there are several common threats that pose risks to children's health and well-being. Next we examine these threats as well as how to protect children.

Illness

Young children tend to experience more colds and illnesses than older children. Their immune systems are still developing and they are more susceptible to germs than older children and adults. Immunization (discussed in Chapter 4) prevents serious, sometimes fatal, diseases that were once common. Young children receive booster shots to bolster the effectiveness of vaccines received in infancy. A measles outbreak in 20 U.S. states in 2019 illustrates the value of immunization in preventing illness (Centers for Disease Control and Prevention, 2019b). Measles, a disease thought to be eliminated in the United States in 2000, spread quickly among unvaccinated children and adults in 2019. In New York City, one child was thought to be the source of the infection that affected more than 500 other children (New York City Department of Health, 2019). Symptoms of measles include high fever, cough, inflamed eyes, spots inside the mouth, and a rash on the body. Complications are common and include pneumonia, bronchitis, diarrhea, and ear infections.

Most children experience minor illnesses such as colds and flu. Most colds must run their course. Preventing dehydration and alleviating a child's discomfort is appropriate treatment for a cold and flu. Fevers can be treated with a lukewarm bath. Aspirin must never be administered to young children because it places children at risk to develop Reye's syndrome, a rare condition in which the brain and liver swell. Seek medical treatment if a fever lasts longer than a day or is accompanied by pain, or if the child's temperature reaches 104 degrees.

Diarrhea is common, but children who are well hydrated and perhaps administered electrolytes to replace the salts and minerals lost typically feel better within a few days. Although diarrhea is not generally serious in the United States and other developed countries, it is a leading cause of death in underdeveloped countries with poor sanitation and health resources. Like diarrhea, nausea is common and can result from a variety of conditions ranging from eating too quickly, to flu, to poisoning. Multiple instances of vomiting can lead to dehydration. Seek medical assistance if vomiting persists longer than a day or is accompanied by pain.

Perhaps the more effective way to prevent illness is to encourage young children to wash their hands. Provide assistance and teach children how to use soap, rub all parts of their hands, and rinse off. Completing vaccinations and booster shots prevents many illnesses. Finally, keeping sick children home, away from child care settings and preschool, can prevent illness from spreading. Unfortunately, many parents have few other child care options without staying home from work. Parents who work shift-work, are paid by the hour, or do not have personal days often have little choice than to send their sick child to school.

Allergies

Food allergies are common in young children. Allergic reactions can range from mild to severe and include symptoms such as itchy eyes or skin, hives and red spots, swelling, stomach pain, vomiting and diarrhea, and trouble breathing. About 90% of children's allergic reactions are to the following eight foods: milk, eggs, peanuts, tree nuts (such as almonds, cashews, or walnuts), fish (such as bass, cod, or flounder), shellfish (such as crab, lobster, or shrimp), soy, and wheat (Mayo Clinic, 2016). Peanut allergies are most common, affecting up to 2% of children.

Pediatricians who counsel families with young children generally emphasize preventing contact with allergens. Children are advised to avoid the food; however, avoiding some allergens, such as peanuts, is very difficult. Some schools are peanut free and no children are allowed to bring any peanut-containing foods for lunch. Children with serious allergies may be triggered by cross-contamination. For example, a knife that is used to spread peanut butter and simply wiped with a napkin rather than washed may contain small amounts of peanut, enough to trigger a very sensitive child's allergy. It is very difficult and, in some cases, nearly impossible to avoid allergens.

The National Institute of Allergy and Infectious Diseases recently revised its guidelines for the diagnosis and management of food allergy, surprising many parents and pediatricians by offering counterintuitive advice to introduce infants to small amounts of peanut powder (Togias et al., 2017). A large longitudinal study, Learning Early About Peanut Allergy (LEAP), examined 640 infants between 4 and 11 months of age who were at high risk of developing a peanut allergy (Du Toit et al., 2015). At 5 years of age, children who had consumed the peanut powder as infants were much less likely to show peanut allergies than the children who avoided peanuts, and this effect persisted at 6 years of age (Du Toit et al., 2016). The introduction of small amounts of peanut at 4 to 6 months in infancy appears to help children develop a tolerance to peanuts. Parents should consult their pediatrician before introducing peanuts into an infant's diet. These findings are promising and the new guidelines may reduce childhood allergies.

Toxins

Some hazards to young children's development are invisible. Young children are more sensitive to the negative effects of toxins than adolescents and adults because their brains and bodies are undergoing rapid development. Exposure to air pollution, such as carbon monoxide, nitrogen dioxide, particulate matter, black carbon, wood smoke, and car exhausts, negatively affects children's respiratory health, leading to breathing problems and asthma (a chronic disease involving the inflammation of the lungs, discussed in Chapter 10) (Goldizen, Sly, & Knibbs, 2016; Landrigan et al., 2019).

There are many substances in the air, water, and food that can affect children's development. Many substances are untested; however, lead, mercury, pesticides, and bisphenol A (BPA) in plastic are known to harm development (Vrijheid, Casas, Gascon, Valvi, & Nieuwenhuijsen, 2016). Children encounter pesticides in their food, but also in the environment. It is estimated that children are exposed to more pesticides around their homes than in food (Bradman et al., 2015). Exposure to pesticides is associated with increased risk for ADHD. Pesticides likely interact with other factors in an epigenetic fashion to influence the development of ADHD (Roberts, Dawley, & Reigart, 2019). Using

Peanut allergies are the most common food allergy. Children with severe allergies cannot be exposed to any amount of peanut.
©iStockphoto.com/Image Source

safer alternatives in gardening and around the home and keeping pesticides in clearly labeled containers away from children can limit children's pesticide exposure.

Exposure to lead poses serious risks to brain development. Peeling paint can expose children to lead chips or dust that contaminates their surroundings. Lead is associated with increased risk for poor growth and damage to the brain that can result in learning and behavior problems, including disorders such as ADHD and delinquency in childhood and adolescence (Thapar, Cooper, Eyre, & Langley, 2013; Zhang et al., 2013). For example, one study of New Zealand children assessed the level of lead in their blood at age 11 and found that childhood lead exposure was associated with lower cognitive function and socioeconomic status at age 38 (Reuben et al., 2017). Although lead is no longer included as an ingredient in household paint, older houses still contain lead paint. Children from low-SES homes are more likely to live in older housing and be exposed to lead paint as well as other toxins. Exposure to toxic substances can have long-term negative effects on children's health and well-being (Landrigan et al., 2019; Suk et al., 2016).

Unintentional Injury

Unintentional injuries, accidents, are the leading cause of death in young children. Drowning is the most common cause of injury-related death, followed by car accidents, unintentional suffocation, and fire (Centers for Disease Control and Prevention, 2017f). Falls are the most common type of nonfatal injury or accident that requires a visit to the emergency room (Centers for Disease Control and Prevention, 2018a). Other common reasons include being hit by an object, stung, or cut or burned.

Although they are "accidental," many unintentional injuries can be prevented. A variety of individual and contextual influences place children at risk for injury. Children who are impulsive, overactive, and difficult, as well as those diagnosed with ADHD, experience higher rates of unintentional injuries (Acar et al., 2015; Lange et al., 2016; Morrongiello, Corbett, McCourt, & Johnston, 2006). These children are more likely to test limits and protest safety restraints, such as wearing a seat belt or helmet or holding an adult's hand when crossing the street.

Parents of these children are sometimes less likely to intervene and prevent dangerous behavior. Children's risk of injury rises when their parents report feeling little control over their child's behavior (Acar et al., 2015). Poor parental and adult supervision is closely associated with childhood injury (Ablewhite et al., 2015; Morrongiello et al., 2006). Moreover, some parents hold the belief that injuries are an inevitable part of child development (Ablewhite et al., 2015) and they may therefore provide less supervision and intervention. Childhood injury is also associated with parental distraction, such as talking to another parent or using a phone (Huynh, Demeter, Burke, & Upperman, 2017). Parents who work long hours or multiple jobs and who live in challenging environments may find it difficult to keep tabs on their children or may feel overwhelmed.

Neighborhood disadvantage, specifically low SES and lack of resources, is associated with higher rates of injuries and bone fractures in children in the United States, Canada, and the United Kingdom (Lyons et al., 2000; McClure, Kegler, Davey, & Clay, 2015; Stark, Bennet, Stone, & Chishti, 2002). Disadvantaged neighborhoods may also contribute to children's injuries due to factors that increase overall injury risk, such as poor surface maintenance of streets or sidewalks and poor design or maintenance of housing and playgrounds. In addition to having few opportunities to be active, children in unsafe disadvantaged neighborhoods often have inadequate access to sources of healthy nutrition; this combination of circumstances can interfere with children developing healthy strong bodies.

Just as there are multiple contextual factors that place children at risk of injury, there are many opportunities for preventing and reducing childhood injuries. Parenting interventions that improve supervision and monitoring, teach parents about safety risks, and model safe practices can help parents reduce injuries in their children (Kendrick, Barlow, Hampshire, Stewart-Brown, & Polnay, 2008). School programs can help students learn and practice safety skills. At the community level, installing and maintaining safe playground equipment and protected floor surfaces can reduce the injuries that accompany falls. Disadvantaged communities, however, may lack the funding to provide safe play spaces, placing residing children at risk.

Child Maltreatment

According to the Child Abuse Prevention and Treatment Act, child abuse, also known as **child maltreatment**, is any intentional harm to a minor (an individual under 18 years of age), including actions that harm the child physically, emotionally, sexually, and through neglect (U.S. Department of Health and Human Services, 2016). Many children experience more than one form of abuse.

Physical abuse refers to any intentional physical injury to the child and can include striking, kicking, burning, or biting the child, or any other action that results in a physical impairment of the child.

Emotional abuse is sometimes called psychological abuse. It refers to speech and behavior that impairs a child's emotional development and feelings of worth.

Sexual abuse refers to engaging in any sexual activity, coerced or persuaded, with a child. It also includes inappropriate touching or comments. Neglect occurs when a child is deprived of adequate food, clothing, shelter, or medical care.

Each year, there are over 700,000 confirmed cases of child abuse or neglect in the United States (U.S. Department of Health and Human Services, 2016). Child maltreatment results in over 1,500 fatalities per year, about three-quarters in children younger than 3 years. Parents are the most common perpetrators (in more than 80% of cases, on average), with relatives other than parents and unmarried partners of parents constituting an additional 10% of perpetrators (U.S. Department of Health and Human Services, 2016). It is estimated that about 27% of children younger than age 17 have experienced sexual abuse (Kim, Wildeman, Jonson-Reid, & Drake, 2017). Sexual abuse may occur at any time during infancy, childhood, or adolescence, but it is most often reported in early and middle childhood, with about half of cases occurring between ages 4 and 12 (U.S. Department of Health and Human Services, 2013). Although these statistics are alarming, they underestimate the incidence of abuse because many children experience maltreatment that is not reported. Moreover, abuse often is not a one-time event; some children experience maltreatment that persists for years.

Effects of Child Maltreatment

The physical effects of child maltreatment are immediate, ranging from bruises to broken bones to internal bleeding and more. Some physical effects are long lasting. Child abuse can impair brain development and functioning through physical injuries, such as blows to the head and shaking. Physical harm and prolonged stress can alter the course of brain development, increasing the child's risk for ADHD, emotion-regulation problems, conduct disorder, and learning and memory difficulties (Cicchetti & Toth, 2015; Hein & Monk, 2017).

It follows that child maltreatment and its neurological and emotional consequences may negatively affect cognitive development (Font & Berger, 2014). Preschool children who are abused score lower on measures of school readiness and problem solving. Children who are abused experience difficulty understanding and completing day-to-day schoolwork and demonstrate serious learning difficulties, often resulting in academic failure (Widom, 2014). Teachers report maltreated children as inattentive, uninvolved, passive, and angry, as well as lacking in creativity, initiative, persistence, and confidence.

Maltreated children may display symptoms of posttraumatic stress disorder (PTSD), an anxiety disorder that occurs after experiencing a traumatic event and includes flashbacks, nightmares, and feelings of helplessness (Maniglio, 2013). The socioemotional effects of child maltreatment are especially daunting and long lasting. Young children who are abused tend to have poor coping skills, low self-esteem, and difficulty regulating their emotions and impulses, and they tend to show more negative affect, such as anger and frustration, and less positive affect than other children (Barth et al., 2007). They tend to have difficulty understanding their own and other people's emotions and often have difficulty making and maintaining friendships (Cicchetti & Banny, 2014).

Children and adolescents who are abused also are at risk for a range of psychological disorders. These include anxiety, eating, and depressive disorders as well as behavioral problems in adolescence, such as delinquency, teen pregnancy, illicit drug use, and risky behavior (Carlson, Oshri, & Kwon, 2015; Cecil, Viding, Fearon, Glaser, & McCrory, 2017; Jones et al., 2013).

Risk Factors for Child Maltreatment

Risk factors for child abuse exist at all ecological levels: the child, parent, community, and society, as shown in Figure 7.3 (Cicchetti, 2016). Certain child characteristics have been found to increase the risk or potential for maltreatment. Children with special needs, such as those with physical and mental disabilities, preterm birth status, or serious illness, require a great deal of care that can overwhelm or frustrate caregivers, placing such children at risk of maltreatment. Similarly, children who are temperamentally difficult, inattentive, overactive, or have other developmental problems are also at risk because they may be especially taxing for caregivers (Font & Berger, 2014). Other characteristics might buffer or reduce the negative effects of maltreatment, as discussed in the Lives in Context feature.

Parents who engage in child maltreatment tend to perceive their child as stubborn and noncompliant and tend to evaluate the child's misdeeds as worse than they are, leading them to use strict and physical methods of discipline (Casanueva et al., 2010). They often lack knowledge about child development and have unrealistic expectations for their children. They may be less skilled in recognizing emotions displayed on their children's faces; find it difficult to recognize, manage, and express their own feelings appropriately; and have poor impulse control, coping, and problem-solving skills (Wagner et al., 2015). Abuse is more common in homes characterized by poverty, marital instability, and drug and alcohol abuse (Cicchetti & Toth, 2015). Children who are raised in homes in which adults come and go, as a result of repeated marriages, separations, revolving romantic partners, and so forth, are at higher risk of sexual abuse. However, sexual abuse also occurs in intact middle-class families. In these families, children's victimization often remains undetected and unreported (Hinkelman & Bruno, 2008).

Community factors, such as inadequate housing, community violence, and poverty, place children at risk for abuse (Cuartas, 2018; Widom, 2014). Neighborhoods with few community-level support resources, such as parks, child care centers, preschool programs, recreation centers, and churches, increase the likelihood of child maltreatment (Molnar et al., 2016). In contrast, neighborhoods with a low turnover of residents, a sense of community, and connections among neighbors support parents and protect against child maltreatment (van Dijken, Stams, & de Winter, 2016).

At the societal level, several factors contribute to the problem of child abuse. Legal definitions of violence and abuse and political or religious views that value independence, privacy, and noninterference in families may influence the prevalence of child abuse within a given society (Tzeng, Jackson, & Karlson, 1991). Social acceptance of violence—for example, as expressed in video games, music lyrics, and television shows and films—can send the message that violence is an acceptable method of managing conflict. Overall, there are many complex influences on child maltreatment.

Along with recognizing risk factors, it is important to be aware of signs that abuse may be taking place. Table 7.3 provides a nonexhaustive list of signs of abuse. Not all children who display one

FIGURE 7.3

Bioecological Perspective of Risk Factors for Child Maltreatment

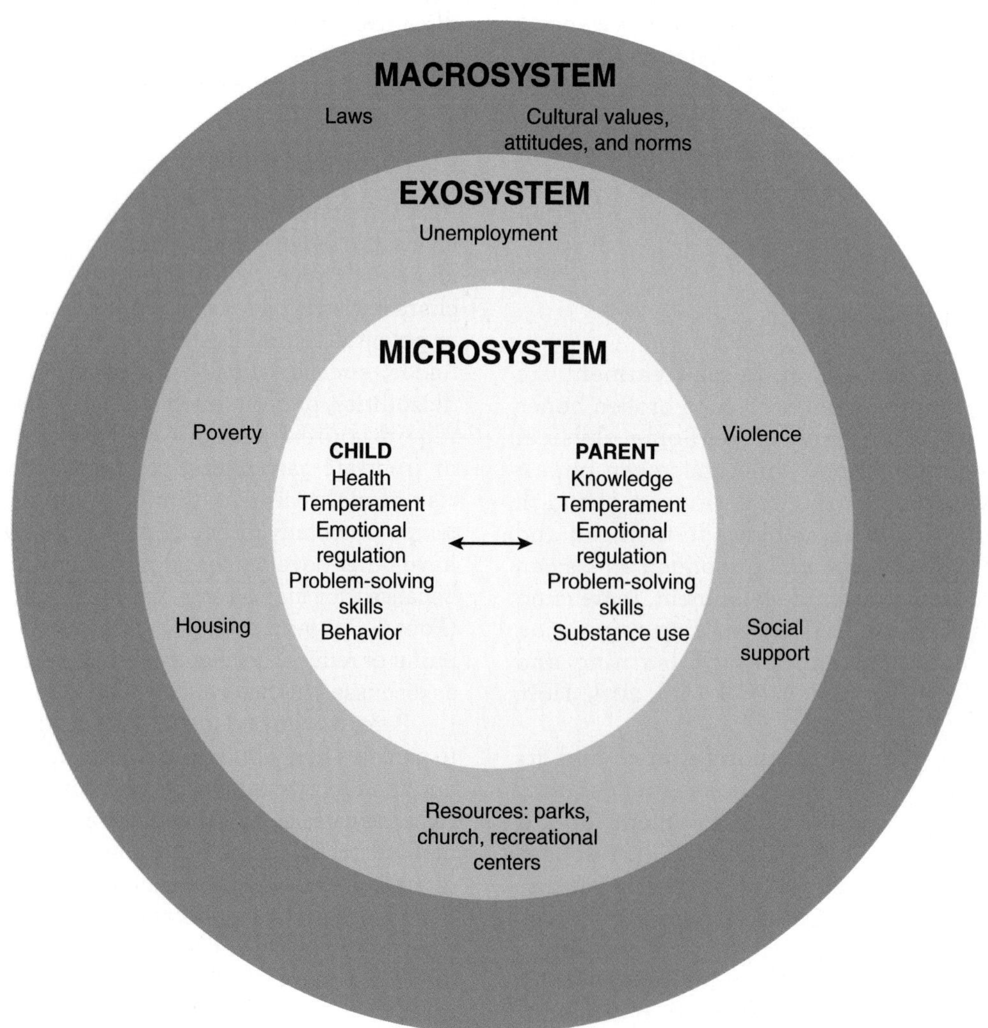

LIVES IN CONTEXT: FAMILY AND PEER CONTEXT

Gene × Environment Interaction and Responses to Adversity

Children who are maltreated or abused by their parents are at risk for developing many problems, including aggression and violent tendencies. Yet not all children who are maltreated become violent adolescents and adults. Why? A classic study examined this question.

Caspi and colleagues (2002) followed a sample of males from birth until adulthood and observed that only some boys who were maltreated developed problems with violence. Upon further study, the researchers were surprised to find that the link between maltreatment and violence varied with the gene that controls monoamine oxidase A (MAOA), an enzyme that regulates specific chemicals in the brain. Only boys who carried a certain form of this gene were at risk for becoming violent after experiencing maltreatment. Specifically, there are two versions of the gene that controls MAOA; one produces high levels of the enzyme, and the other produces low levels.

Boys who experienced abuse and other traumatic experiences were about twice as likely to develop problems with aggression, to display violent behaviors, and to even be convicted of a violent crime—but only if they carried the low-MAOA gene. Maltreated boys who carried the high-MAOA gene were no more likely to become violent than nonmaltreated boys. In addition, the presence of the low-MAOA gene itself was not associated with violence. The low-MAOA gene predicted violence only for boys who experience abuse early in life. These findings have been replicated in another 30-year longitudinal study of boys (Fergusson, Boden, Horwood, Miller, & Kennedy, 2011) and in a meta-analysis of 27 studies (Byrd & Manuck, 2014).

Similar findings of an MAOA gene × environment interaction in which low MAOA, but not high MAOA, predicts negative outcomes in response to childhood adversity has been extended to include other mental health outcomes such as antisocial personality disorder and depression (Beach et al., 2010; Cicchetti, Rogosch, & Sturge-Apple, 2007; Manuck & McCaffery, 2014; Nikulina, Widom, & Brzustowicz, 2012). Many of these studies have examined only males. Females show a more mixed pattern, with some studies demonstrating that girls display the MAOA gene × environment interaction on emotional reactivity and aggression but to a much lesser extent than boys, whereas other studies suggest no relationship (Byrd & Manuck, 2014; Byrd et al., 2018).

In addition, some genes might increase our sensitivity to, and the effectiveness of, environmental interventions (Bakermans-Kranenburg & van IJzendoorn, 2015; Chhangur et al., 2017). Just as we may adjust contextual factors to contribute to successful developmental outcomes and resilience, in the future we might learn how to "turn on" protective genes and "turn off" those that contribute to risk.

What Do You Think?

If some genes may be protective in particular contexts, should scientists learn how to turn them on? Should scientists learn to turn off genes that might increase risks in particular contexts? Why or why not? Identify advantages and disadvantages. ●

or more of the signs on this list have experienced maltreatment, but each sign is significant enough to merit attention. All U.S. states and the District of Columbia identify mandated reporters, individuals who are legally obligated to report suspected child maltreatment to the appropriate agency, such as child protective services, a law enforcement agency, or a state's child abuse reporting hotline (Child Welfare Information Gateway, 2013). Individuals designated as mandatory reporters typically have frequent contact with children: teachers, principals, and other school personnel; child care providers; physicians, nurses, and other health care workers; counselors, therapists, and other mental health professionals; and law enforcement officers. Of course, anyone can, and is encouraged to, report suspected maltreatment of a child.

THINKING IN CONTEXT 7.4

1. Provide advice to a child care center director who wishes to keep the children in her center safe and well. What does the director need to know about children's allergies, illnesses, and threats to their well-being?
2. Child maltreatment is a problem with a complex set of influences at multiple bioecological levels. The most effective prevention and intervention programs target risk and protective factors in the child, parent, and community. Referring to the bioecological model, discuss factors at each bioecological level that might be incorporated into prevention and intervention programs to prevent child abuse and promote positive outcomes.

TABLE 7.3

Signs of Child Abuse and Neglect

The Child
• Exhibits extremes in behavior, such as overly compliant or demanding behavior, extreme passivity, withdrawal, or aggression. • Has not received help for physical or medical problems (e.g., dental care, eyeglasses, immunizations) brought to the parents' attention. • Has difficulty concentrating or learning problems that appear to be without cause. • Is very watchful, as if waiting for something bad to happen. • Frequently lacks adult supervision. • Has unexplained burns, bruises, broken bones, or black eyes. • Is absent from school often, especially with fading bruises upon return. • Is reluctant to be around a particular person, or shrinks at the approach of a parent or adult. • Reports injury by a parent or another adult caregiver. • Lacks sufficient clothing for the weather. • Is delayed in physical or emotional development. • States that there is no one at home to provide care.
The Parent
• Shows indifference and little concern for the child. • Denies problems at home. • Blames problems on the child. • Refers to the child as bad or worthless, or berates the child. • Has demands that are too high for the child to achieve. • Offers conflicting, unconvincing, or no explanation for the child's injury. • Uses harsh physical discipline with the child, or suggests that caregivers use harsh physical discipline if the child misbehaves. • Is abusing alcohol or other drugs.

Source: Adapted from Child Welfare Information Gateway (2013).

APPLY YOUR KNOWLEDGE

"I don't want to be 'it'! I just can't catch them!" Jorge cried as the other 4-year-old children ran from him during a game of tag. Frustrated, Jorge sat on the curb. "Aren't you going to chase us?" asked Lilli. "Nope," Jorge replied. "Ha! That's because you're too short. Your legs can't beat mine!" she called out as she ran off.

At the end of the school day, Jorge's grandmother walked with him the short distance home. "Are you ready for ice cream?" she asked. "With fudge and whipped cream?" Jorge asked. "Of course!" she replied. Every afternoon Jorge's grandmother offered treats like ice cream, candy, and chips. Then Jorge settled in to watch his favorite cartoons and play video games. Jorge's grandmother preferred that he play inside because Jorge was too young to play outside without supervision. Jorge didn't mind. He was slower and heavier than the other children, and he didn't like balancing games or playing catch. "Your uncles—and even your mother—played outside all day when they were kids. They were fast and played hard, often with scrapes and bruises," Jorge's grandmother recalled. "I bet you can be as fast as them, but it's better for you to stay home. I can't sit outside all day and today kids can't be outside alone," she said. Jorge didn't mind because he didn't like going to the playground and would rather play at home on his tablet, which he did until dinnertime.

Jorge's mother often didn't get home from work until nearly bedtime, so his grandmother cooked dinner every night. Jorge preferred his grandmother's meals because she didn't make him eat yucky vegetables and didn't mind if he didn't eat his meat. After dinner Jorge and his grandmother watched their favorite television programs until Jorge's mother returned home.

1. Describe Jorge's physical and motor abilities.
2. Identify contextual influences on Jorge's development and health.
3. What changes can Jorge's family make to improve his health?
4. How might Jorge's health and physical development influence his relationships with peers? How might his relationships with peers influence his health?

WANT A BETTER GRADE?

Get the tools you need to sharpen your study skills. **SAGE edge** offers a robust online environment featuring an impressive array of free tools and resources. Access practice quizzes, eFlashcards, video, and multimedia at **edge.sagepub.com/kutherchild1e.** SAGE edge™

KEY TERMS

Ossification 193

Hormone 193

Plasticity 197

Autism spectrum disorder (ASD) 197

Sensory processing disorder (SPD) 199

Nightmare 202

Sleep terror 202

Child maltreatment 206

SUMMARY

7.1 Describe patterns of growth and motor development in early childhood.

During early childhood, growth slows relative to infancy, bones begin to ossify, and body proportions change as young children gain muscle and become leaner. Advances in gross motor skills permit young children to balance and coordinate their bodies and engage in more complicated physical activities, such as throwing and catching a ball. As children's fine motor skills improve, they learn to write and engage in self-care activities such as buttoning a shirt.

7.2 Summarize patterns of typical and atypical brain development.

Synaptogenesis, pruning, myelination, and lateralization continue in early childhood. Synaptogenesis and pruning contribute to enhanced plasticity. Two examples of atypical brain development include autism spectrum disorder (ASD) and sensory processing disorder (SPD). ASD is a family of neurodevelopmental disorders that range in severity and are characterized by deficits in social communication and a tendency to engage in repetitive behaviors. ASD has epigenetic causes and is associated with atypical brain connectivity in areas responsible for sensorimotor functioning, inhibitory control, theory of mind, communication, and self-regulation. SPD is an extreme difficulty processing and responding to sensory stimuli that interferes with daily functioning. Children with SPD show abnormalities in the parts of the brain involved in multimodal sensory integration, especially the parietal and occipital regions, and in the part of the brain responsible for higher-order thinking, the frontal cortex. ASD and SPD cannot be cured, but specialized instruction and therapy can help children and families cope.

7.3 Examine the influence of nutrition, physical activity, sleep, and screen use on young children's health.

Most children in developed nations eat enough calories, but their diets are often insufficient in vitamins and minerals. Physical activity enhances growth and is consistently associated with advances in motor development, fitness, and bone and skeletal health. Only about half of children meet recommended physical activity guidelines. Time spent outdoors and access to safe play environments are associated with greater physical activity. Sleep plays an important role in development. Sleep problems pose risks to young children's development such as cognitive difficulties, including problems with attention, working memory, and slower processing speed. Screen time may adversely affect young children's health through its inverse relationship with physical activity and sleep quality.

7.4 Discuss threats to young children's physical health and well-being.

Young children tend to experience more colds and illnesses than older children. Immunization prevents serious, sometimes fatal, diseases. Some children experience allergic reactions. Exposure to toxins, such as lead, pollution, pesticides, and bisphenol A (BPA), can harm children's physical and cognitive development. Unintentional injuries, accidents, are the leading cause of death in young children but many can be prevented by addressing the contextual factors that may place children at risk for injury. Child maltreatment refers to intentional harm to a minor through physical, emotional, or sexual means or through neglect. Child maltreatment is associated with a variety of short- and long-term negative effects. Risk factors occur at multiple contextual levels, and prevention and intervention programs can target these levels.

REVIEW QUESTIONS

7.1 How do gross and fine motor skills change in early childhood?

How do advances in motor skills influence children's development?

7.2 What is plasticity?

What are characteristics of autism spectrum disorder?

What is sensory processing disorder?

7.3 Why is nutrition important in early childhood?

What are the benefits of physical activity in early childhood?

How do children's sleep and screen time influence their development?

7.4 What are common threats to children's health?

What are ways of preventing unintentional injuries?

What are risk factors for child maltreatment?

©iStockphoto.com/Linda Raymond

8 Cognitive Development in Early Childhood

Four-year-old Damius stands up on his toes and releases his parachute toy, letting the action figure dangling from a parachute drift a few feet from him and collapse on the floor. "I'm going to go up high and make it faster," he says, imagining standing on the sofa and making the toy sail far into the clouds. He stands on the sofa and releases the toy, which sails a bit further this time. "Next time he'll jump out of the plane even higher!" Damius thinks, excitedly. His friend Isaiah calls out, "Let's make him land on the moon! He can meet space people!"

Damius and Isaiah can plan, think of solutions to problems, and use language to communicate their ideas. They learn through play by interacting with people and objects around them. In this chapter, we examine the processes of cognitive development and their implications for children's behavior.

Learning Objectives

8.1 Compare Piaget's cognitive-developmental and Vygotsky's sociocultural theories of cognitive development in early childhood.

8.2 Describe information processing abilities during early childhood.

▶ **Video Activity 8.1:** False Belief

8.3 Summarize young children's advances in language development.

▶ **Video Activity 8.2:** Children's Understanding of Language

8.4 Contrast social learning and cognitive-developmental perspectives on moral development in early childhood.

8.5 Identify and explain various approaches to early childhood education.

Chapter Contents

COGNITIVE-DEVELOPMENTAL AND SOCIOCULTURAL REASONING IN EARLY CHILDHOOD

Young children take an active role in their development by engaging with objects and people around them. According to Piaget, young children construct their understanding of the world through assimilation and accommodation (see Chapter 5). From the cognitive-developmental perspective, young children's thought progresses from the sensory and motor schemes of infancy to more sophisticated representational thought.

Piaget's Cognitive-Developmental Theory: Preoperational Reasoning

According to Piaget, preoperational reasoning appears in young children from about ages 2 to 6. **Preoperational reasoning** is characterized by a dramatic leap in the use of symbolic thinking that permits young children to use language, interact with others, and play using their own thoughts and imaginations to guide their behavior. It is symbolic thought that enables Damius and Isaiah to use language to communicate their thoughts and desires—and it is also what allows them to send their toy on a mission to the moon to visit with pretend space people.

Characteristics of Preoperational Reasoning

Young children in the preoperational stage show impressive advances in representational thinking, but they are unable to grasp logic and cannot understand complex relationships. Children who show preoperational reasoning tend to make several common errors, including egocentrism, animism, centration, and irreversibility.

Egocentrism. "See my picture?" Jessica asks as she holds up a blank sheet of paper. Mr. Seris answers, "You can see your picture, but I can't. Turn your page around so that I can see your picture. There it is! It's beautiful," he proclaims after Jessica flips the piece of paper, permitting him to see her drawing. Jessica did not realize that even though she could see her drawing, Mr. Seris could not. Jessica displays egocentrism, the inability to take another person's point of view or perspective. The egocentric child views the world from his or her own perspective, assuming that other people share the child's feelings, knowledge, and even physical view of the world.

A classic task used to illustrate preoperational children's egocentrism is the **three-mountains task**. As shown in Figure 8.1, the child sits at a table facing three large mountains. A doll is placed in a chair across the table from the child. The child is asked how the mountains look to the doll. Piaget found that young children in the preoperational stage demonstrated egocentrism because they described the scene from their own perspective rather than the doll's. They did not understand that the doll would have a different view of the mountains (Piaget & Inhelder, 1967).

FIGURE 8.1

The Three-Mountains Task

Children who display preoperational reasoning cannot describe the scene depicted in the three-mountains task from the point of view of the teddy bear.

FIGURE 8.2

Appearance vs. Reality: Is It a Cat or Dog?

Young children did not understand that Maynard the cat remained a cat despite wearing a dog mask and looking like a dog.

Source: DeVries, R. (1969). Constancy of generic identity in the years three to six. *Monographs of the Society for Research in Child Development, 34*(3, serial no 127), May. With permission from Blackwell Publishing.

Animism. Egocentric thinking can also take the form of **animism**, the belief that inanimate objects are alive and have feelings and intentions. "It's raining because the sun is sad and it is crying," 3-year-old Melinda explains. Children accept their own explanations for phenomena because they are unable to consider another viewpoint or alternative reason.

Centration. Preoperational children exhibit **centration**, the tendency to focus on one part of a stimulus or situation and exclude all others. For example, a boy may believe that if he wears a dress, he will become a girl. He focuses entirely on the appearance (the dress) rather than the other characteristics that make him a boy.

Centration is illustrated by a classic task that requires the preoperational child to distinguish what something appears to be from what it really is, the **appearance–reality distinction**. In a classic study illustrating this effect, DeVries (1969) presented 3- to 6-year-old children with a cat named Maynard (see Figure 8.2). The children were permitted to pet Maynard. Then, while his head and shoulders were hidden behind a screen (and his back and tail were still visible), a dog mask was placed onto Maynard's head. The children were then asked, "What kind of animal is it now?" "Does it bark or meow?" Three-year-old children, despite Maynard's body and tail being visible during the transformation, replied that he was now a dog. Six-year-old children were able to distinguish Maynard's appearance from reality and explained that he only *looked* like a dog.

One reason that 3-year-old children fail appearance–reality tasks is because they are not yet capable of effective dual encoding, the ability to mentally represent an object in more than one way at a time (Flavell, Green, & Flavell, 1986). For example, young children are not able to understand that a scale model (like a dollhouse) can be both an object (something to play with) and a symbol (of an actual house) (MacConnell & Daehler, 2004).

Irreversibility. "You ruined it!" cried Johnson after his older sister, Monique, placed a triangular block atop the tower of blocks he had just built. "No, I just put a triangle there to show it was the top and finish it," she explains. "No!" insists Johnson. "Okay, I'll take it off," says Monique. "See? Now it's just how you left it." "No. It's ruined," Johnson sighs. Johnson continued to be upset after his sister removed the triangular block, not realizing that by removing the block, she has restored the block structure to its original state. Young children's thinking is characterized by irreversibility, meaning that they do not understand that reversing a process can often undo it and restore the original state.

Preoperational children's irreversible thinking is illustrated by their performance on tasks that measure **conservation**, the understanding that the physical quantity of a substance, such as number, mass, or volume, remains the same even when its appearance changes. For example, a child is shown two identical glasses. The same amount of liquid is poured into each glass. After the child agrees that the two glasses contain the same amount of water, the liquid from one glass is poured into a taller, narrower glass and the child is asked whether one glass contains more liquid than the other. Young children in the preoperational stage reply that the taller narrower glass contains more liquid. Why? It has a higher liquid level than the shorter, wider glass has. They center on the appearance of the liquid without realizing that the process can be reversed by pouring the liquid back into the shorter, wider glass. They focus on the height of the water, ignoring

FIGURE 8.3

Additional Conservation Problems

Conservation Task	Original Presentation	Transformation
Number	Are there the same number of pennies in each row?	Now are there the same number of pennies in each row, or does one row have more?
Mass	Is there the same amount of clay in each ball?	Now does each piece have the same amount of clay, or does one have more?
Liquid	Is there the same amount of water in each glass?	Now does each glass have the same amount of water, or does one have more?

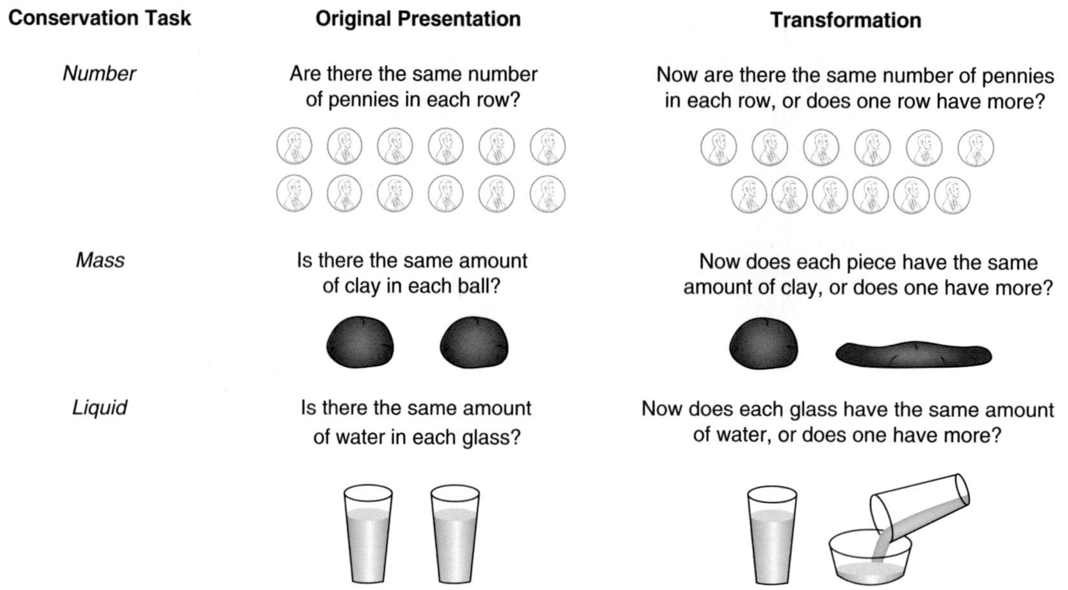

other aspects such as the change in width, not understanding that it is still the same water. Figure 8.3 illustrates other types of conservation problems. Characteristics of preoperational children's reasoning are summarized in Table 8.1.

Evaluating Preoperational Reasoning

Research with young children has suggested that Piaget's tests of preoperational thinking underestimated young children. Success on Piaget's tasks appears to depend more on the child's language abilities than his or her actions. As we discussed earlier, to be successful at the three-mountains task, the child must not only understand how the mounds look from the other side of the table but also must be able to communicate that understanding. Appearance–reality tasks require not simply an understanding of dual representation but the ability to express it. However, if the task is nonverbal, such as requiring reaching for an object rather than talking about it, even 3-year-old children can distinguish appearance from reality (Sapp, Lee, & Muir, 2000).

TABLE 8.1

Characteristics of Preoperational Children's Reasoning

CHARACTERISTIC	DESCRIPTION
Egocentrism	The inability to take another person's point of view or perspective
Animism	The belief that inanimate objects are alive and have feelings and intentions
Centration	Tendency to focus attention on one part of a stimulus or situation and exclude all others
Irreversibility	Failure to understand that reversing a process can often undo the process and restore the original state

Research Findings on Egocentrism and Animism. Simple tasks demonstrate that young children are less egocentric than Piaget posited. When a 3-year-old child is shown a card that depicts a dog on one side and a cat on the other, and the card is held up between the researcher who can see the cat and the child who can see the dog, the child correctly responds that the researcher can see the cat (Flavell, Everett, Croft, & Flavell, 1981). When the task is relevant to children's everyday lives (i.e., hiding), their performance suggests that they are not as egocentric as Piaget posited (Newcombe & Huttenlocher, 1992). Other research suggests that 3- to 5-year-old children can learn perspective-taking skills through training and retain their perspective-taking abilities 6 months later (Mori & Cigala, 2016).

Likewise, 3-year-old children do not tend to describe inanimate objects with lifelike qualities, even when the object is a robot that can move (Jipson, Gülgöz, & Gelman, 2016). Most 4-year-old children understand that animals grow, and even plants grow, but objects do not (Backschneider, Shatz, & Gelman, 1993). Sometimes, however, young children provide animistic responses. Gjersoe, Hall, and Hood (2015) suggest an emotional component to animistic beliefs. They found that 3-year-olds attribute mental states to toys to which they are emotionally attached but not to other favorite toys, even those with which they frequently engage in imaginary play. Finally, children show individual differences in their expressions of animism and reasoning about living things, and these differences are linked with aspects of cognitive development such as memory, working memory, and inhibition (Zaitchik et al., 2014).

Research Findings on Reversibility and the Appearance–Reality Distinction. Although young children typically perform poorly on conservation tasks, 4-year-old children can be taught to conserve, suggesting that children's difficulties with reversibility and conservation tasks can be overcome (Gallagher, 2008). In addition, making the task relevant improves children's performance. For example, when children are asked to play a trick on someone (i.e., "let's pretend that this sponge is a rock and tell Anne that it is a rock when it really is a sponge") or choose an object that can be used to clean up spilled water, many choose the sponge, illustrating that they can form a dual representation of the sponge as an object that looks like a rock (Sapp et al., 2000). Three-year-old children can shift between describing the real and fake or imagined aspects of an object or situation. In addition, they can describe misleading appearances and functions of objects in response to natural conversational prompts, as compared with the more formal language in the typical prompts used in traditional appearance–reality tasks (e.g., "What is it really and truly?") (Deák, 2006). In sum, preschoolers show an understanding of the appearance–reality distinction, and it develops throughout childhood (Woolley & Ghossainy, 2013).

Educational Implications of Preoperational Reasoning

In early childhood, advances in symbolic thinking enable young children to use language, engage in imaginative play (as we will discuss in Chapter 9), and learn in new ways. Piaget's rich descriptions of children's abilities have implications for teaching young children and creating supportive child care and preschool settings (Gray & MacBlain, 2015). Like infants, young children learn by exploring the world. Specifically, they construct their cognitive schemes or concepts about the world through interacting with other people, objects, and environments. Children learn by integrating new information into their existing schemes (assimilation), and when they encounter material that differs from what they know, children modify their schemes or concepts (accommodation). Discovery learning, in which children are encouraged to explore and "discover" knowledge for themselves rather than be taught rote facts, embodies Piaget's theory about the active role children play in constructing their understanding of the world.

Education must be age appropriate as, in Piaget's view, cognitive development cannot be rushed. However, teachers can help young children understand their own ideas in more sophisticated ways by asking open-ended questions that encourage children to express themselves. Children learn by doing; therefore, helpful interactions focus on the process, such as building a tower, rather than the product, the final height of the tower. Child care and preschool settings that are designed with children's hands, bodies, and minds in mind, such as with child-sized desks and chairs, seating in small groups rather than rows, and toys that are easily manipulated by tiny hands, reflect the needs of children in the preoperational stage of reasoning.

Vygotsky's Sociocultural Theory

According to Russian psychologist Lev Vygotsky, we are embedded in a cultural context that shapes how we think and who we become. Mental activity—cognition—is influenced by culture, specifically, the cultural tools that members of a culture share (Robbins, 2005; Vygotsky, 1978). Cultural tools include physical items such as computers, pencils, and paper but also ways of thinking about phenomena, including how to approach math and

Children learn culturally valued skills by interacting with and helping skilled partners.
John Scofield/National Geographic Image Collection/Getty Images

scientific problems. Spoken language is a vital cultural tool of thought.

Children learn how to use the tools of their culture by interacting with skilled partners who provide guidance. For example, suppose a child wanted to bake cookies for the first time. Rather than send the child into the kitchen alone, we would probably accompany the child and provide the tools needed to accomplish the task, such as the ingredients, a rolling pin to roll the dough, cookie cutters, and a baking sheet. We would probably show the child how to use each tool, such as how to roll out the dough. With interaction and experience, the child adopts and internalizes the tools and knowledge, becoming able to apply them independently. That is, the child learns to bake. Vygotsky argued that in this way, culturally valued ways of thinking and problem solving get passed on to children.

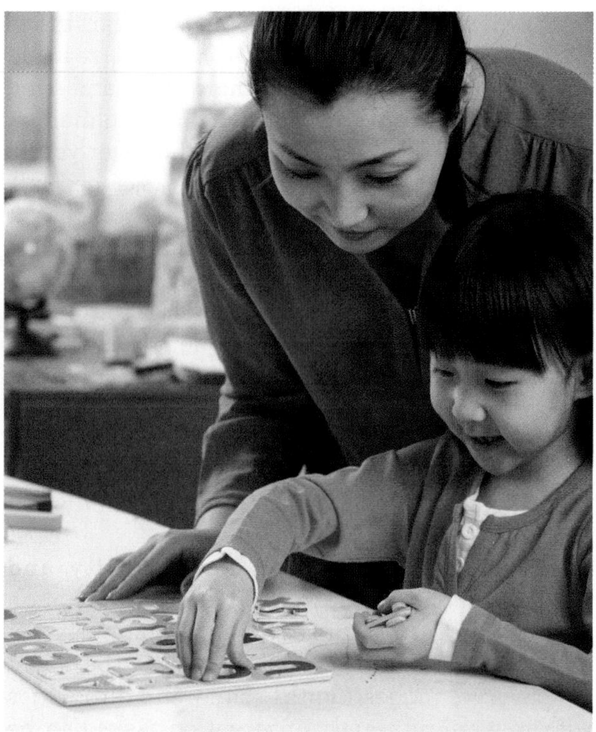

Parents' guidance acts as a scaffold within the zone of proximal development to help children accomplish challenging tasks. Soon children become able to complete the task independently.
©iStockphoto.com/XiXinXing

Guided Participation and Scaffolding

As mentioned, children learn through social experience, by interacting with more experienced partners who offer assistance in completing tasks. Children learn through **guided participation** (also known as an *apprenticeship in thinking*), a form of sensitive teaching in which the partner is attuned to the needs of the child and helps him or her to accomplish more than the child could do alone (Rogoff, 2014). As novices, children learn from more skilled, or expert, partners by observing them and asking questions. In this way, children are apprentices, learning how others approach problems. The expert partner provides **scaffolding** that permits the child to bridge the gap between his or her current competence level and the task at hand (Mermelshtine, 2017). For example, consider a child working on a jigsaw puzzle. She is stumped, unable to complete it on her own. Suppose a more skilled partner, such as an adult, sibling, or another child who has more experience with puzzles, provides a little bit of assistance, a scaffold. The expert partner might point to an empty space on the puzzle and encourage the child to find a piece that fits that spot. If the child remains stumped, the partner might point out a piece or rotate it to help the child see the relationship. The partner acts to motivate the child and provide support to help the child finish the puzzle, emphasizing that they are working together. The child novice and expert partner interact to accomplish the goal and the expert adjusts his or her responses to meet the needs of the child.

Scaffolding occurs in formal educational settings, but also informally, anytime a partner adjusts his or her interactional style to fit the needs of a child and guide the child to complete a task that he or she could not complete alone (Rogoff, Callanan, Gutiérrez, & Erickson, 2016). Mothers vary their scaffolding behaviors in response to children's attempts at tasks. For example, they spontaneously use different behaviors depending on the child's attention skills, using more verbal engagement, strategic questions, verbal hints, and verbal prompts when children show difficulty paying attention during a task (Robinson, Burns, & Davis, 2009). Moreover, maternal reading, scaffolding, and verbal guidance are associated with 2- to 4-year-olds' capacities for cognitive control and planning (Moriguchi, 2014). Parents and child care providers often provide this informal instruction, but anyone who is more skilled at a given task, including older siblings and peers, can promote children's cognitive development (Rogoff et al., 2016). Collaboration with more skilled peers improves performance on cognitive tasks such as card-sorting tasks, Piagetian tasks, planning, and academic tasks (Sills, Rowse, & Emerson, 2016).

Zone of Proximal Development

As Vygotsky explained, "What the child can do in cooperation today, he can do alone tomorrow" (1962, p. 104). Effective scaffolding works within the **zone of proximal development**, the gap between the child's competence level—what he can accomplish independently—and what he can do with the assistance of a skilled partner. With time, the child internalizes the scaffolding lesson and learns to accomplish the task on her own—and her zone of

FIGURE 8.4

Zone of Proximal Development

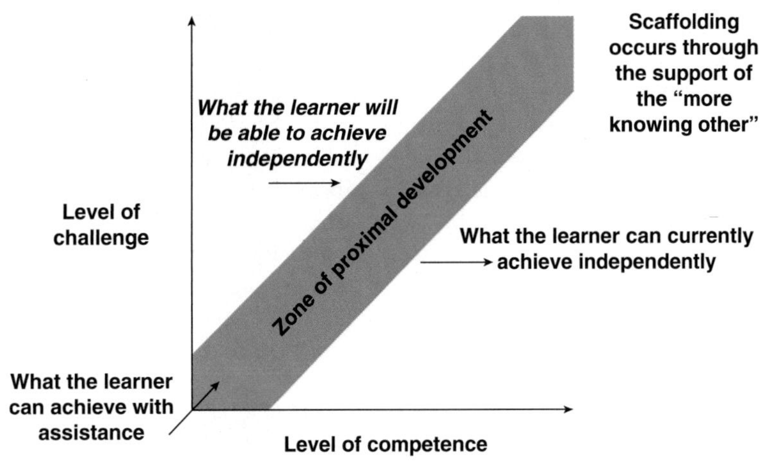

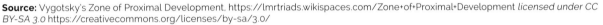

Source: Vygotsky's Zone of Proximal Development, https://lmrtriads.wikispaces.com/Zone+of+Proximal+Development *licensed under CC BY-SA 3.0* https://creativecommons.org/licenses/by-sa/3.0/

proximal development shifts, as shown in Figure 8.4. Adults tend to naturally provide children with instruction within the zone of proximal development (Rogoff, 2014). For example, adults reading a book to a child tend to point to items, label and describe characters' emotional states, explain, ask questions, listen, and respond sensitively, helping the child understand challenging material that is just beyond what the child can understand on his or her own (Silva, Strasser, & Cain, 2014).

The quality of scaffolding influences children's development. In one study of preschool teachers and children, the degree to which the adult matched the child's needs for help in playing predicted more autonomous play on the part of children over a 6-month period (Trawick-Smith & Dziurgot, 2011). Adults may act intentionally to encourage and support children's learning (Zuckerman, 2007). For example, one study of parents and young children visiting a science museum found that when parents provided specific guidance in considering a conservation of volume problem, such as discussing the size of the containers, asking "how" and "why" questions, and talking about simple math, children were more likely to give correct responses to scientific reasoning problems, including those involving conservation (Vandermaas-Peeler, Massey, & Kendall, 2016).

Parents and preschool teachers can take advantage of the social nature of learning by assigning children tasks that they can accomplish with some assistance, providing just enough help so that children learn to complete the tasks independently. This helps to create learning environments that stimulate children to complete more challenging tasks on their own (Wass & Golding, 2014). Through guided play, teachers can develop play environments and settings with materials that encourage exploration and guide children with comments, encouraging them to explore, question, or extend their interests (Bodrova & Leong, 2018).

Private Speech

As Leroy played alone in the corner of the living room, he pretended to drive his toy car up a mountain and said to himself, "It's a high mountain. Got to push it all the way up. Oh no! Out of gas. Now they will have to stay here." Young children like Leroy often talk aloud to themselves, with no apparent intent to communicate with others. This self-talk, called **private speech**, accounts for 20% to 50% of the utterances of children ages 4 to 10 (Berk, 1986). Private speech serves developmental functions. It is thinking. Young children use self-talk to guide their own learning (Vygotsky & Minick, 1987).

Private speech plays a role in self-regulation, the ability to control one's impulses and appropriately direct behavior; this increases during the preschool years (Berk & Garvin, 1984). Children use private speech to plan strategies, solve problems, and regulate themselves so that they can achieve goals. Children are more likely to use private speech while working on challenging tasks and attempting to solve problems, especially when they encounter obstacles or do not have adult supervision (Winsler, Fernyhough, & Montero, 2009). As children grow older, they use private speech more effectively to accomplish tasks. Children who use private speech during a challenging activity are more attentive and involved and show better performance than children who do not (Alarcón-Rubio, Sánchez-Medina, &

Prieto-García, 2014). For example, in one study, 4- and 5-year-old children completed a complex multistep planning task over six sessions. Children who used on-task private speech showed dramatic improvements between consecutive sessions (Benigno, Byrd, McNamara, Berg, & Farrar, 2011).

During elementary school, children's private speech becomes a whisper or a silent moving of the lips (Manfra & Winsler, 2006). Private speech is the child's thinking and eventually becomes internalized as *inner speech*, or word-based internal thought, a silent internal dialogue that individuals use every day to regulate and organize behavior (Al-Namlah, Meins, & Fernyhough, 2012). However, there is some evidence that private speech may not be as private as suggested. That is, private speech often occurs in the presence of others. When children ages 2½ to 5 years completed a challenging task in the presence of an experimenter who sat a few feet behind the child, not interacting, or alone, the children engaged in more private speech in the presence of a listener than they did when alone (McGonigle-Chalmers, Slater, & Smith, 2014). This suggests that private speech may have social value and may not be simply a tool for self-regulation.

Although Vygotsky considered the use of private speech a universal developmental milestone, further research suggests that there are individual differences, with some children using private speech little or not at all (Berk, 1992). Preschool girls tend to use more mature forms of private speech than boys. The same is true of middle-income children as compared with low-income children (Berk, 1986). This pattern corresponds to the children's relative abilities in language use. Talkative children use more private speech than do quiet children (McGonigle-Chalmers et al., 2014). Bright children tend to use private speech earlier, and children with learning disabilities tend to continue its use later in development (Berk, 1992). One of the educational implications of private speech is that parents and teachers must understand that talking to oneself or inaudible muttering is not misbehavior but rather indicates an effort to complete a difficult task or self-regulate behavior.

Evaluating Vygotsky's Sociocultural Theory

Although relatively unknown until recent decades, Vygotsky's ideas about the sociocultural nature of cognitive development have influenced prominent theories of development, such as Bronfenbrenner's bioecological theory (Bronfenbrenner, 1979). They have been applied in educational settings, supporting the use of assisted discovery, guiding children's learning, and cooperative learning with peers.

Similar to Piaget, Vygotsky has been criticized for developing a theory that lacks precision. The mechanisms or processes underlying the social transmission of thought are not described (Göncü & Gauvain, 2012). Moreover, constructs such as the zone of proximal development are not easily testable (Wertsch, 1998). In addition, underlying cognitive capacities, such as attention and memory, are not addressed. It is understandable, however, that Vygotsky's theory is incomplete, as he died of tuberculosis at the age of 37. We can only speculate about how his ideas might have evolved over a longer lifetime. Nevertheless, Vygotsky provided a new framework for understanding development as a process of transmitting culturally valued tools that influence how we look at the world, think, and approach problems.

THINKING IN CONTEXT 8.1

1. Compare and contrast Vygotsky and Piaget's theories of cognitive development.
2. If children can be taught to respond correctly to problems assessing animism, egocentrism, or conservation, should they? Why or why not?
3. What role does context take in Piaget and Vygotsky's theories? To what extent is cognitive development influenced by the sociocultural contexts in which children live, according to Piaget and Vygotsky?
4. What similarities might classrooms designed by Piaget and Vygotsky share? How might they differ?

INFORMATION PROCESSING IN EARLY CHILDHOOD

From an information processing perspective, cognitive development entails developing mental strategies to guide one's thinking and use one's cognitive resources more effectively. In early childhood, children become more efficient at attending, encoding and retrieving memories, and problem solving.

Attention

Early childhood is accompanied by dramatic improvements in attention, particularly **sustained attention**, the ability to remain focused on a stimulus for an extended period of time (Rueda, 2013). Young children often struggle with selective attention. **Selective attention** refers to the ability to systematically deploy one's attention, focusing on relevant information and ignoring distractors.

Young children do not search thoroughly when asked to compare detailed pictures and explain what's missing from one. They have trouble focusing on one stimulus and switching their attention to compare it with other stimuli (Hanania & Smith, 2010). For example, young children who sort cards according to one dimension such as color may later be unable to successfully switch to different sorting criteria (Honomichl & Zhe, 2011). Young children's selective attention at age 2½ predicts working memory and response inhibition at age 3 (Veer, Luyten, Mulder, van Tuijl, & Sleegers, 2017).

Working Memory and Executive Function

Young children simply get better at thinking. Recall from Chapter 5 that working memory is where all thinking or information processing takes place. Working memory consists of a short-term store (*short-term memory*), a processor, and a control mechanism known as the central executive, responsible for executive function (Baddeley, 2016; Miyake & Friedman, 2012). Children get better at holding information in working memory, manipulating it, inhibiting irrelevant stimuli, and planning, which allows them to set and achieve goals (Carlson, Zelazo, & Faja, 2013).

Short-term memory is commonly assessed by a memory span task in which individuals are asked to recall a series of unrelated items (such as numbers) presented at a rate of about 1 per second. The greatest lifetime improvements on memory span tasks occur in early childhood. In a classic study, 2- to 3-year-old children could recall about two digits, increasing to about five items at age 7, but only increasing another two digits, to seven, by early adulthood (Bjorklund & Myers, 2015).

As their short-term memory increases, young children are able to manipulate more information in working memory and become better at planning, considering the steps needed to complete a particular act and carrying them out to achieve a goal (Rueda, 2013). Preschoolers can create and abide by a plan to complete tasks that are familiar and not too complex, such as systematically searching for a lost object in a yard (Wellman, Somerville, & Haake, 1979). But they have difficulty with more complex tasks. Young children have difficulty deciding where to begin and how to proceed to complete a task in an orderly way (Ristic & Enns, 2015a). When they plan, young children often skip important steps. One reason why young children get better at attention, memory, and cognitive tasks is because they get better at inhibiting impulses to engage in task-irrelevant actions and can keep focused on a task.

Memory

Young children's memory for events and information acquired during events, **episodic memory**, expands rapidly (Roediger & Marsh, 2003; Tulving, 2002). For example, a researcher might study episodic memory by asking a child, "Where did you go on vacation?" or "Remember the pictures I showed you yesterday?" Most laboratory studies of memory examine episodic memory, including memory for specific information, for scripts, and for personal experiences.

Memory for Information

Shana turns over one card and exclaims, "I've seen this one before. I know where it is!" She quickly selects its duplicate by turning over a second card from an array of cards. Shana recognizes a card she has seen before and recalls its location. Children's memory for specific information, such as the location of items, lists of words or numbers, and directions, can be studied using tasks that examine recognition memory and recall memory. Recognition memory, the ability to recognize a stimulus one has encountered before, is nearly perfect in 4- and 5-year-old children, but they are much less proficient in **recall memory**, the ability to generate a memory of a stimulus encountered before without seeing it again (Myers & Perlmutter, 2014).

Why do young children perform so poorly in recall tasks? Young children are not very effective at using **memory strategies**, cognitive activities that make us more likely to remember. For example, rehearsal, repeating items over and over, is a strategy that older children and adults use to recall lists of stimuli. Children do not spontaneously and reliably apply rehearsal until after the first grade (Bjorklund & Myers, 2015). Preschool-age children can be taught strategies, but they generally do not transfer their learning and apply it to new tasks (Titz & Karbach, 2014). This utilization deficiency seems to occur because of their limited working memories and difficulty inhibiting irrelevant stimuli. They cannot apply the strategy at the same time as they have to retain both the material to be learned and the strategy to be used. Instead, new information competes with the information the child is attempting to recall (Aslan & Bäuml, 2010). Overall, advances in executive function, working memory, and attention predict strategy use (Stone, Blumberg, Blair, & Cancelli, 2016).

However, young children do not always show more poor performance relative to adults. In one study, parents read a novel rhyming verse and a word list as their 4-year-old children's bedtime story on 10 consecutive days. When asked to recall the verse, the 4-year-old children outperformed their parents and a set of young adults who also listened to the verse

(Király, Takács, Kaldy, & Blaser, 2017). The children and adults did not differ in the ability to recall the gist of the verse. Unlike adults, young children are immersed in a culture of verse and rely on oral transmission of information, likely underlying their skill relative to adults.

Memory for Scripts

Young children remember familiar repeated everyday experiences, like the process of eating dinner, taking a bath, or going to nursery school or preschool, as **scripts**, or descriptions of what occurs in a particular situation. When young children begin to use scripts, they remember only the main details. A 3-year-old might describe a trip to a restaurant as follows: "You go in, eat, then pay." These early scripts include only a few acts but usually are recalled in the correct order (Bauer, 1996). As children grow older and gain cognitive competence, scripts become more elaborate. Consider a 5-year-old child's explanation of a trip to a restaurant: "You go in, you can sit at a booth or a table, then you tell the waitress what you want, you eat, if you want dessert, you can have some, then you go pay, and go home" (Hudson, Fivush, & Kuebli, 1992). Scripts are an organizational tool that help children understand and remember repeated events and help them to predict future events. However, scripts may inhibit memory for new details. For example, in one laboratory study, children were presented with a script of the same series of events repeated in order multiple times as well as a single alternative event. Preschoolers were less likely than older children to spontaneously recall and provide a detailed account of the event (Brubacher, Glisic, Roberts, & Powell, 2011).

Autobiographical Memory

Autobiographical memory refers to memory of personally meaningful events that took place at a specific time and place in one's past (Bauer, 2015). Autobiographical memory emerges as children become proficient in language and executive function and develops steadily from 3 to 6 years of age (Nieto, Ros, Ricarte, & Latorre, 2018). Young children report fewer memories for specific events than do older children and adults (Baker-Ward, Gordon, Ornstein, Larus, & Clubb, 1993). But by age 3, they are able to retrieve and report specific memories, especially those that have personal significance, are repeated, or are highly stressful (Nuttall, Valentino, Comas, McNeill, & Stey, 2014). For example, in one study, children who were at least 26 months old at the time of an accidental injury and visit to the emergency room accurately recalled the details of these experiences even after a 2-year delay (Goodman, Rudy, Bottoms, & Aman, 1990). Eight-year-old children have been found to accurately remember events that occurred when they were as young as 3½ years of age (Goodman & Aman, 1990).

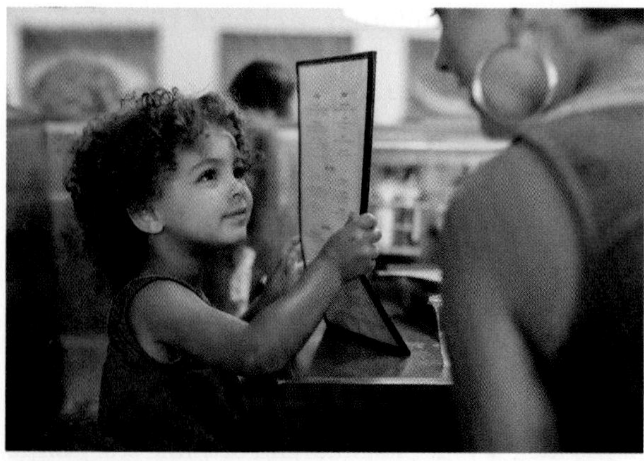

This child demonstrates a script as she explains the process of going to a restaurant and ordering from a menu.
Inti St Clair Blend Images/Newsco

Events that are unique or new, such as a trip to the circus, are better recalled; 3-year-old children will recall them for a year or longer (Fivush, Hudson, & Nelson, 1983). Frequent events, however, tend to blur together. Young children are better at remembering things they did than things they simply watched. For example, one study examined 5-year-old children's recall of an event they observed, were told about, or experienced. A few days later, the children who actually experienced the event were more likely to recall details in a more accurate and organized way and to require fewer prompts (Murachver, Pipe, Gordon, Owens, & Fivush, 1996).

The way adults talk with the child about a shared experience can influence how well the child will remember it (Haden & Fivush, 1996). Parents with an elaborative conversational style discuss new aspects of an experience, provide more information to guide a child through a mutually rewarding conversation, and affirm the child's responses. They may ask questions, expand children's responses, and help the children tell their story. Three-year-olds of parents who use an elaborative style engage in longer conversations about events, remember more details, and tend to remember the events better at ages 5 and 6 (Fivush, 2011).

Young children can have largely accurate memories, but they can also tell tall tales, make errors, and succumb to misleading questions. Children's ability to remember events can be influenced by information and experiences that may interfere with their memories. These can include conversations with parents and adults, exposure to media, and sometimes intentional suggestions directed at changing the child's view of what transpired. Children's vulnerability to suggestion is discussed in the Applying Developmental Science feature.

APPLYING DEVELOPMENTAL SCIENCE

Children's Suggestibility

The accuracy of children's memory, especially their vulnerability to suggestion, is an important topic because children as young as 3 years have been called upon to relate their memories of events that they have experienced or witnessed, including abuse, maltreatment, and domestic violence (Pantell & Committee on Psychosocial Aspects of Child and Family Health, 2017). Young children can recall much about their experiences, often material that is relevant and accurate (Cauffman, Shulman, Bechtold, & Steinberg, 2015). How suggestible are young children? Can we trust their memories?

Research suggests that repeated questioning may increase suggestibility in children (La Rooy, Lamb, & Pipe, 2011). For example, in one study, preschoolers were questioned every week about events that had either happened or not happened to them; by the 11th week, nearly two-thirds of the children falsely reported having experienced an event (Ceci, Huffman, Smith, & Loftus, 1994). Preschool-age children may be more vulnerable to suggestion than school-age children or adults (Brown & Lamb, 2015). When children were asked if they could remember several events, including a fictitious instance of getting their finger caught in a mousetrap, almost none of them initially recalled these events. However, after repeated suggestive questioning, more than half of 3- and 4-year-olds and two-fifths of 5- and 6-year-olds said they recalled these events—often vividly (Poole & White, 1991, 1993).

Young children's natural trust in others may enhance their suggestibility. In one study, 3-year-olds who received misleading verbal and visual information from an experimenter about a sticker's location continued to search in the wrong, suggested location despite no success (Jaswal, 2010). In another study, 3- to 5-year-old children watched as an adult hid a toy in one location, then told the children that the toy was in a different location. When retrieving the toy, 4- and 5-year-olds relied on what they had seen and disregarded the adult's false statements, but 3-year-olds deferred to what the adult had said, despite what they had directly observed (Ma & Ganea, 2010).

In some cases, children can resist suggestion. For example, in one study, 4- and 7-year-old children either played games with an adult confederate (e.g., dressing up in costumes, playing tickle, being photographed) or merely watched the games (Ceci & Bruck, 1998). Eleven days later, each child was interviewed by an adult who included misleading questions that were often followed up with suggestions relevant to child abuse. Even the 4-year-olds resisted the false suggestions about child abuse. Children also vary. Some children are better able to resist social pressure and suggestive questioning than others (Uhl, Camilletti, Scullin, & Wood, 2016).

Children are more vulnerable than adults, but adults are not entirely resistant to suggestion. For example, recent research suggests that in some situations, adults are *more* likely than children to make quick associations between suggestive details about unexperienced events and prior experiences, making them more vulnerable to suggestion (Otgaar, Howe, Merckelbach, & Muris, 2018). Like children, adults who are exposed to information that is misleading or inconsistent with their experiences are more likely to perform poorly during memory interviews—and repeated questioning has a similar effect on performance (Wysman, Scoboria, Gawrylowicz, & Memon, 2014).

What Do You Think?

Suppose you need to question a preschool child about an event. What kinds of questions would you ask? How would you maximize your likelihood of the child's giving an accurate account of what occurred? ●

Theory of Mind

Over the childhood years, thinking becomes more complex. In particular, children become increasingly aware of the process of thinking and of their own thoughts. **Theory of mind** refers to children's awareness of their own and other people's mental processes. This awareness of the mind can be considered under the broader concept of **metacognition**, knowledge of how the mind works and the ability to control the mind (Lockl & Schneider, 2007). Let's explore these concepts.

Young children's theory of mind grows and changes between the ages of 2 and 5 (Bower, 1993; Flavell, Green, & Flavell, 1995; Wellman, 2017). For example, 3-year-old children understand the difference between thinking about a cookie and having a cookie. They know that having a cookie means that one can touch, eat, or share it, while thinking about a cookie does not permit such

Culture shapes children's thinking. Samoan and Vanuatu cultures de-emphasize internal mental states as explanations for behavior. Children are not exposed to discussions about the mind and they get little experience considering other people's thoughts.
age fotostock / Alamy Stock Photo

actions (Astington, 1993). Young children also understand that a child who wants a cookie will be happy upon receiving one and sad upon not having one (Moses, Coon, & Wusinich, 2000). Similarly, they understand that a child who believes he is having hot oatmeal for breakfast will be surprised upon receiving cold spaghetti (Wellman & Banerjee, 1991). Theory of mind is commonly assessed by examining children's abilities to understand that people can hold different beliefs about an object or event.

False Belief

Young children do not yet understand that people can hold different beliefs and that some may be incorrect. Three-year-old children tend to perform poorly on **false-belief tasks,** tasks that require them to understand that someone can have an incorrect belief. In a classic false-belief task, children who are presented with a Band-Aid box that contains pencils rather than Band-Aids will show surprise but tend to believe that other children will share their knowledge and expect the Band-Aid box to hold pencils (Flavell, 1993), similar to Figure 8.5. The children do not yet understand that the other children hold different, false beliefs. In addition, the children will claim that they knew all along that the Band-Aid box contained pencils (Birch, 2005). They confuse their present knowledge with their memories for prior knowledge and have difficulty remembering ever having believed something that contradicts their current view (Bernstein, Atance, Meltzoff, & Loftus, 2007).

FIGURE 8.5

False-Belief Task

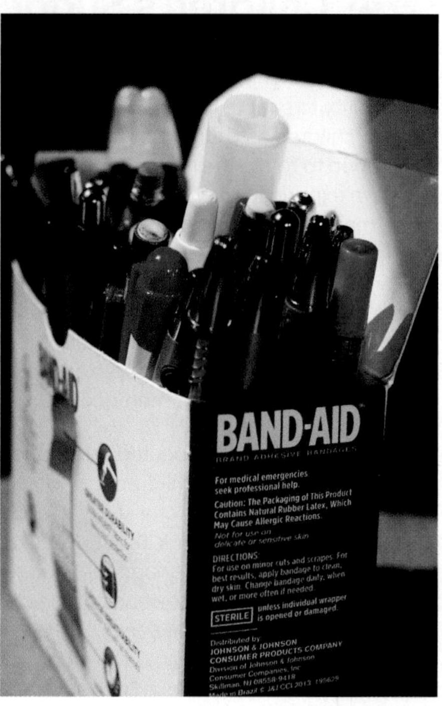

Source: Nathan Davidson.

Some researchers, however, assert that young children are much more competent than they appear. Research with infants using preferential looking and habituation tasks has suggested an understanding of false belief as early as 15 months of age (Scott & Baillargeon, 2017). Similar to arguments regarding object permanence in infancy and egocentrism in early childhood (see Chapter 5), it may be that children understand the concept (that another person will understand that the Band-Aid box contains bandages, not pencils) but may have difficulty communicating their understanding to the researcher (Helming, Strickland, & Jacob, 2014). Yet many researchers counter that false-belief findings with infants reflect perceptual preferences, that is, a desire to look at one object over another, not theory of mind (Heyes, 2014). Indeed, the research to date suggests that theory of mind as evidenced by false-belief tasks emerges at about 3 years of age and shifts reliably between 3 and 4 years of age (Grosse Wiesmann, Friederici, Singer, & Steinbeis, 2017). By age 3, children can understand that two people can believe different things (Rakoczy, Warneken, & Tomasello, 2007). Four-year-old children can understand that people who are presented with different versions of the same event develop different beliefs (Eisbach, 2004). By age 4 or 5, children become aware that they and other people can hold false beliefs (Moses et al., 2000).

Advanced cognition is needed for children to learn abstract concepts such as belief. Performance on false-belief tasks, such as the Band-Aid task, is associated with measures of executive function, the abilities that enable complex cognitive functions such as planning, decision making, and goal setting (Doenyas, Yavuz, & Selcuk, 2018; Sabbagh, Xu, Carlson, Moses, & Lee, 2006). Advances in executive functioning facilitate children's abilities to reflect on and learn from experience and promote development of theory of mind (Benson, Sabbagh, Carlson, & Zelazo, 2013). For example, one longitudinal study following children from ages 2 to 4 found that advances in executive functioning predicted children's performance on false-belief tasks (Hughes & Ensor, 2007). Children's performance on false-belief tasks is closely related with language development and competence in sustaining conversations (Hughes & Devine, 2015).

Context

The contexts in which children are embedded contribute to their developing understanding of the mind. Children in many countries, including Canada, India, Thailand, Norway, China, and the United States, show the onset and development of theory of mind between the ages of 3 and 5 (Callaghan et al., 2005; Wellman, Fang, & Peterson, 2011). However, social and contextual factors may influence the specific pattern of theory of mind development. North American and Chinese children develop theory of mind in early childhood, but along different paths (Wellman, 2017). Chinese culture emphasizes collectivism, commonality, and interdependence among community members. Chinese parents' comments to children tend to refer to knowing and shared knowledge that community members must learn. U.S. parents emphasize Western values such as individuality and independence. They comment more on thinking, including differences in thoughts among individuals. U.S. children, and other children from individualist cultures, develop an understanding of beliefs before knowledge. Chinese children tend to show the reverse pattern: they have an early understanding of the knowledge aspect of theory of mind and later come to understand beliefs (Wellman, 2017). Children from Iran and Turkey follow a similar pattern in theory of mind development (Shahaeian, Peterson, Slaughter, & Wellman, 2011).

Everyday conversations aid children in developing theory of mind because such conversations tend to center on and provide examples of mental states and their relation with behavior. When parents and other adults speak with children about mental states, emotions, and behaviors, as well as discuss causes and consequences, children develop a more sophisticated understanding of other people's perspectives (Devine & Hughes, 2018; Pavarini, Hollanda Souza, & Hawk, 2012). In addition, siblings provide young children with opportunities for social interaction, pretend play, and practice with deception. Children with siblings perform better on false-belief tests than do only children (McAlister & Peterson, 2013). Success in false-belief attribution tasks is most frequent in children who are the most active in shared pretend play (Schwebel, Rosen, & Singer, 1999).

Children's interactions with people in their immediate contexts can also influence the development of theory of mind. Children can be trained in perspective taking. For example, when children are presented with a series of objects that look like a certain thing but are actually something else (candle and apple) and are shown the appearance and real states of the objects, along with explanation, 3-year-olds showed improvements on false-belief tasks (Lohmann & Tomasello, 2003). Discussion emphasizing the existence of a variety of possible perspectives in relation to an object can improve performance in false-belief tasks—dialogue can facilitate the development of theory of mind (Bernard & Deleau, 2007). Other studies have engaged North American and European children in discussion about the thoughts, beliefs, and desires of characters in stories, especially stories in which characters play tricks to surprise or deceive one another. Children who received the training improved their performance in subsequent false-belief tasks (Liu, Wellman, Tardif, & Sabbagh, 2008; Milligan, Astington, & Dack, 2007; Slaughter & Perez-Zapata, 2014). Similarly, conversation about deceptive objects (e.g., a pen that looked like a flower) also improves performance on false-belief tasks (Lohmann & Tomasello, 2003).

Metacognition

Theory of mind is a precursor to the development of metacognition (Lecce, Demicheli, Zocchi, & Palladino, 2015). Young children know that the mind is where thinking takes place. Between 3 and 5, children come to understand that they can know something that others do not (essential for success on false-belief tasks), that their thoughts cannot be observed, and that there are individual differences in mental states (Pillow, 2008). They begin to understand that someone can think of one thing while doing something else, that a person whose eyes and ears are covered can think, and that thinking is different from talking, touching, and knowing (Flavell et al., 1995). However, young children's

TABLE 8.2

Development of Information Processing Skills During Early Childhood

SKILL	DESCRIPTION
Attention	Young children are better able to focus and sustain their attention to complete tasks but have difficulty with complex tasks that require them to switch their attention among stimuli.
Memory	Young children's limited capacity to store and manipulate information in working memory influences their performance on memory and problem-solving tasks. Young children show advances in recognition memory and the ability to use scripts, but recall memory lags behind because they are not able to effectively use memory strategies. They often can be taught memory strategies but do not spontaneously apply them in new situations. Episodic memory emerges in early childhood, but the extent and quality of memories increase with age.
Theory of mind	Theory of mind refers to children's awareness of their own and other people's mental processes. When researchers use vocabulary that children are familiar with, observe them in everyday activities, and use concrete examples and simple problems such as those involving belief and surprise, it is clear that young children's understanding of the mind grows and changes between the ages of 2 and 5.
Metacognition	In early childhood theory of mind, an awareness of one's own and others' minds emerges. Young children demonstrate a growing ability for metacognition, understanding the mind. However, young children's abilities are limited, and they tend to fail false-belief and appearance–reality tasks, suggesting that their abilities to understand the mind and predict what other people are thinking are limited.

understanding of the mind is far from complete. Three- and four-year-old children do not understand that we think even when we are inactive. They look for visible indicators of thinking—perhaps one reason why teachers of young children refer to "putting on your thinking cap"—and assume their absence indicates the absence of thought. It is not until middle childhood that children understand that the mind is always active (Flavell, 1999). Likewise, preschoolers tend to think of the mind as simply a container for items, but older children tend to see the mind as an active constructor of knowledge that receives, processes, and transforms information (Chandler & Carpendale, 1998).

Young children show limited knowledge of memory functions, contributing to their poor performance on memory tasks. Four-year-olds recognize that increasing the number of items on a list makes recall more difficult and that longer retention intervals increase the likelihood of forgetting (Pillow, 2008). But they know little about the effectiveness of deliberate memory strategies. For example, whereas 6- and 7-year-olds demonstrated an understanding of the role of deliberate practice in memory and practiced without being prompted, 5-year-olds showed an understanding of deliberate practice and some capacity to practice but 4-year-olds showed neither of these capabilities (Brinums, Imuta, & Suddendorf, 2018). The advances that take place in information processing during early childhood are summarized in Table 8.2.

THINKING IN CONTEXT 8.2

1. How might brain development account for the changes in information processing capacity that we experience in childhood, such as increases in working memory, processing speed, and changes in reasoning?
2. How can information processing theory be applied in the classroom? From an information processing perspective, how should preschool classrooms be organized and what can teachers do to help children learn?
3. How might contextual influences—family, neighborhood, sociocultural context, and even cohort or generation—influence cognitive development? Consider attention, working memory, autobiographical memory, and theory of mind.

LANGUAGE DEVELOPMENT IN EARLY CHILDHOOD

Toddlers transitioning from infancy to early childhood tend to use telegraphic speech. They learn to use multiple elements of speech, such as plurals, adjectives, and the past tense. Children's vocabulary and grammar become dramatically more complex during early childhood, enabling them to communicate, but also think, in new ways.

Vocabulary

At 2 years of age, the average child knows about 500 words; vocabulary acquisition continues at a rapid pace. The average 3-year-old child has a vocabulary of 900 to 1,000 words. By 6 years of age, most children have a vocabulary of about 14,000 words, which means that the average child learns a new word every 1 to 2 hours, every day (Owens, 2016). How is language learned so quickly? Children continue to use fast mapping (see Chapter 5) as a strategy to enable them to learn the meaning of a new word after hearing it once or twice based on contextual association and understanding (Kucker, McMurray, & Samuelson, 2015). Fast mapping improves with age.

Children learn words that they hear often, that label things and events that interest them, and that they encounter in contexts that are meaningful to them (Harris, Golinkoff, & Hirsh-Pasek, 2011). Preschoolers can learn words from watching videos with both human and robot speakers, but they learn more quickly in response to human speakers (Moriguchi, Kanda, Ishiguro, Shimada, & Itakura, 2011), especially when the speaker responds to them, such as through videoconferencing (e.g., Skype) (Roseberry, Hirsh-Pasek, & Golinkoff, 2014). Children learn best in interactive contexts with parents, teachers, siblings, and peers that entail turn-taking, joint attention, and scaffolding experiences that provide hints to the meaning of new words (MacWhinney, 2015).

Another strategy that children use to increase their vocabulary is **logical extension**. When learning a word, children extend it to other objects in the same category. For example, when learning that a dog with spots is called a Dalmatian, a child may refer to a Dalmatian bunny (a white bunny with black spots) or a Dalmatian horse. Children tend to make words their own and apply them to all situations they want to talk about (Behrend, Scofield, & Kleinknecht, 2001). At about age 3, children demonstrate the **mutual exclusivity assumption** in learning new words: They assume that objects have only one label or name. According to mutual exclusivity, a new word is assumed to be a label for an unfamiliar object, not a synonym or second label for a familiar object (Markman, Wasow, & Hansen, 2003). In one study, young children were shown one familiar object and one unfamiliar object. They were told, "Show me the X," where X is a nonsense syllable. The children reached for the unfamiliar object, suggesting that they expect new words to label new objects rather than acting as synonyms (Markman & Wachtel, 1988). Similarly, young children use the mutual exclusivity assumption to learn the names of parts of objects, such as the brim of a hat, the cab of a truck, or a bird's beak (Hansen & Markman, 2009). Four- and 5-year-old children continue to apply the mutual exclusivity principle, but they can also understand that a given object can have multiple labels (Kalashnikova, Mattock, & Monaghan, 2016).

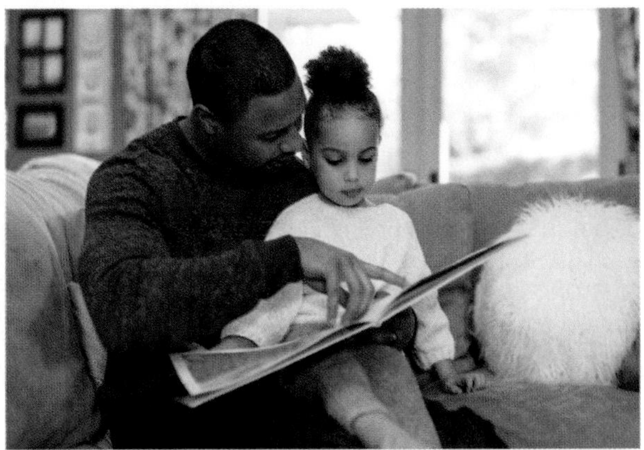

Children learn new words through reading.
©iStockphoto.com/monkeybusinessimages

By 5 years of age, many children can quickly understand and apply most words that they hear. If a word is used in context or explained with examples, most 5-year-olds can learn it. Preschoolers learn words by making inferences given the context—and inferential learning is associated with better retention than learning by direct instruction (Zosh, Brinster, & Halberda, 2013). Certain classes of words are challenging for young children. For example, they have difficulty understanding that words that express comparisons—tall and short or high and low—are relative in nature and are used in comparing one object to another. Thus, the context defines their meaning, such that calling an object tall is often meant in relation to another object that is short. Children may erroneously interpret *tall* as referring to all tall things and therefore miss the relative nature of the term (Ryalls, 2000). Children also have difficulty with words that express relative place and time, such as *here, there, now, yesterday,* and *tomorrow.* Despite these errors, children make great advances in vocabulary, learning thousands of words each year. One way in which children learn new words is through exposure to media, such as television programs, as discussed in the Lives in Context feature.

Grammar

Young children quickly learn to combine words into sentences in increasingly sophisticated ways that follow the complex rules of grammar (de Villiers & de Villiers, 2014). Three-year-old children tend to use plurals (cats), possessives (cat's), and past tense

LIVES IN CONTEXT: MEDIA AND TECHNOLOGY

Television and Children's Development

Over two-thirds of preschoolers watch television each day. In 2017, preschoolers spent on average about 2 hours each day watching television, DVDs, or videos (Rideout, 2018). Does television watching influence children's development? It depends on the program.

Educational television can teach children skills such as problem solving, reading, and language (Moses, 2008). *Sesame Street*, created to simultaneously entertain and teach children, especially those who may be unprepared for school, is a particularly successful educational program. Preschoolers who watch the show frequently display increases in many school readiness skills, such as knowing letters and numbers as well as writing their name. They tend to remember what they learn from the program. Viewers also earn higher scores on standardized measures of vocabulary, view school and people of other ethnicities more positively, and adapt better to school (Kirkorian, Wartella, & Anderson, 2008). These changes are long lasting. Young children from low-income families who watch *Sesame Street* and other educational programs demonstrate better performance in reading, math, language ability, and overall school readiness 3 years later (Wright et al., 2001). Young children's learning from educational television programs is influenced by their developing social relationships with on-screen characters, such as Ernie and Elmo from *Sesame Street* (Richert, Robb, & Smith, 2011). Preschool children who watch more educational television tend to read more books, be more achievement oriented, and earn higher grades in English, math, and science as adolescents (Anderson, Huston, Schmitt, Lineberger, & Wright, 2001).

On the other hand, noneducational programs and those created for general audiences, particularly those that contain violence, have been associated with attention problems, motivation problems, and aggressive behavior in early childhood and later (Barr, Lauricella, Zack, & Calvert, 2010). Televised violence provides models that imply that aggression is an appropriate response to provocation and a way to obtain desired outcomes, providing models and offering messages that aggressive behaviors and attitudes are appropriate (Comstock & Scharrer, 1999; Slaby, Roedell, Arezzo, & Hendrix, 1995). Experimental studies have shown that young children exposed to media displaying aggressive models, such as adults hitting an inflated doll, are more likely to hit the doll themselves (Bandura, Ross, & Ross, 1963). In sum, viewing aggression on television is associated with aggressive behavior. The relation is small but long lasting and consistent over many research studies (Kirkorian et al., 2008; Moses, 2008).

For these reasons, many professional organizations dedicated to promoting the well-being of children (including the American Psychological Association [APA], American Academy of Pediatrics [AAP], American Medical Association, and American Psychiatric Association) advise parents to protect their children from violent media, including violent cartoons, the evening news, and programs designed for general audiences (Anderson & Bushman, 2002). Fortunately, one recent analysis of 88 current children's shows suggested that the most popular children's programs were animated and tended to contain little violent content; however, they also contained little educational and prosocial content (Taggart, Eisen, & Lillard, 2019). Although not harmful, most popular children's shows likely do not promote cognitive and socioemotional development in young children.

What Do You Think?

1. What guidelines might you use to determine whether a television program is appropriate for a young child?
2. Is noneducational television ever appropriate for young children? If so, under what conditions? Explain. ●

(walked) (Park, Yelland, Taffe, & Gray, 2012). They also tend to understand the use of pronouns such as *I*, *you*, and *we*.

Similar to telegraphic speech, young children's sentences are short, leaving out words like *a* and *the*. However, their speech is more sophisticated than telegraphic speech because they include some pronouns, adjectives, and prepositions. Four- and 5-year-olds use four- to five-word sentences and can express declarative, interrogative, and imperative sentences (Turnbull & Justice, 2016). Context influences the acquisition of syntax. Four-year-old children will use more complex sentences with multiple clauses, such as "I'm resting because I'm tired," if their parents use such sentences (Huttenlocher, Vasilyeva, Cymerman, & Levine, 2002). Parental conversations and support for language learning are associated with faster and more correct language use (MacWhinney, 2015). Children often use run-on sentences, in which ideas and sentences are strung together.

"See? I goed on the slide!" called out Leona. **Overregularization errors** such as Leona's are very common in young children. They occur because young children are still learning exceptions to grammatical rules. Overregularization errors are grammatical mistakes that young children make because they are applying grammatical rules too stringently (Marcus, 2000). For example, to create a plural noun, the rule is to add *s* to the word. However, there are many exceptions to this rule. Overregularization is expressed when children refer to *foots, gooses, tooths,* and *mouses*, which illustrates that the child understands and is applying the rules. Adult speakers find this usage awkward, but it is actually a sign of the child's increasing grammatical sophistication. And despite all of the common errors young children make, one study of 3-year-olds showed that nearly three-quarters of their utterances were grammatically correct. The most common error was in making tenses (e.g., *eat/eated, fall/falled*) (Eisenberg, Guo, & Germezia, 2012). By the end of the preschool years, most children use grammar rules appropriately and confidently.

In addition to advances in vocabulary and grammar, children demonstrate increasingly sophisticated understanding of the pragmatics of language, how to use language to communicate effectively (Owens, 2016). Young children engage the people around them in conversation. They get better at turn-taking, alternating between listening and speaking. Parents often marvel at the sophistication of their "baby's" thoughts. Young children carry on conversations about objects, their surroundings, and their feelings. The content of their conversations is limited by young children's cognitive skills, especially egocentrism. For example, young children may find it difficult to take another's perspective. As children's ability to think ahead and consider the future improves, they can increasingly talk about things that have not yet happened, such as a trip or party. Preschoolers recognize the need to adjust their speech to their conversational partner; for example, they speak more simply to a toddler sibling than a peer or an adult.

Bilingual Language Learning

As we discussed in Chapter 5, current research suggests that children who are exposed to two languages build distinct language systems from birth (MacWhinney, 2015). The pace of learning two languages is influenced by the degree to which the two languages differ, how often the child hears each language, and how clearly the speakers enunciate speech sounds (Petitto et al., 2012; Werker, 2012).

Typically, bilingual children have words in both languages for the same thing, which conflicts with the mutual exclusivity assumption that characterizes most children's vocabulary learning. For example, a bilingual child might say "all done" in English and "*pau*" in Hawaiian. In contrast, monolingual children learn synonyms for words much later (Littschwager & Markman, 1994). This difference suggests that bilingual children are aware that the words are part of two separate language systems and that a label is appropriate to a specific language (Hoff, 2015). Bilingual children also learn two sets of rules for combining words, grammar, and do not appear to mix the grammatical rules for the two languages. For example, bilingual children learning French and German do not incorrectly use German words with French syntax or vice versa (Meisel, 1989). Moreover, bilingual children tend to select the appropriate language to use with other speakers, suggesting that they are aware that they know two languages (and that others may not) (Genesee & Nicoladis, 2007).

The course of language development is similar for each language the bilingual child learns. The pattern of vocabulary and grammatical development in each language tends to follow the developmental course for each language (Conboy & Thal, 2006; Parra, Hoff, & Core, 2011). The pace of simultaneous language learning, however, is not the same as learning one language. Similar to acquiring one language, the rate of acquisition for two languages depends on the quantity and quality of the input in each language (Hoff & Core, 2015).

Frequently, bilingual children hear one language spoken more than another; in their dominant language they may seem similar to monolingual children in terms of development. But because children who hear two languages will tend to hear less of either language than their monolingual peers, their rate of growth in each language tends to be slower than those who hear and acquire a single language. That is, a bilingual child may hear Spanish two-thirds of the time and English one-third of the time, whereas a child learning English hears English 100% of the time. Bilingual children therefore hear less of each language than monolingual children and tend to lag behind monolingual children in vocabulary and grammar in each language, when measured separately (Hindman & Wasik, 2015; Hoff et al., 2012).

The gap in vocabulary between monolingual and bilingual children persists but narrows with age (Hoff, Rumiche, Burridge, Ribot, & Welsh, 2014). Likewise, a lag in grammatical development can be observed throughout the school years, but with continued and consistent exposure to two languages, bilingual children may catch up to monolingual peers by the age of 10 years (Gathercole & Thomas, 2009). It is important to note, however, that bilingual children acquire language at a similar rate as monolingual peers. The combined vocabularies for both languages are similar in size to the vocabulary of monolingual children; some research suggests that the total vocabulary growth in bilingual children may be greater than that of monolingual children (Bosch & Ramon-Casas, 2014; Hoff et al., 2014).

THINKING IN CONTEXT 8.3

1. Should children's language development unfold naturally, or should parents and teachers guide children in expanding their vocabulary and learning grammar? If adults should help children, how can they advance children's language development?
2. How might advances in language development influence other domains of development, such as cognitive or socioemotional development?
3. How does children's context influence their language development? How might the home, school, and community context influence language development?

MORAL DEVELOPMENT IN EARLY CHILDHOOD

Young children's cognitive capacities and skills in theory of mind influence moral reasoning, how they view and make judgments in their social world (Skitka, Bauman, & Mullen, 2016). Two-year-old children classify behavior as good or bad. They respond with distress when viewing or experiencing aggressive or potentially harmful actions (Kochanska, Casey, & Fukumoto, 1995). By age 3, children judge a child who knocks another child off a swing intentionally as worse than one who does so accidentally (Yuill & Perner, 1988). Four-year-old children can understand the difference between truth and lies (Bussey, 1992). By age 5, children are aware of many moral rules, such as those regarding lying and stealing. They also demonstrate conceptions of justice or fairness (e.g., "It's my turn," "Hers is bigger," "It's not fair!"). How do these capacities develop?

There are many perspectives on moral development, as discussed in later chapters. Here we consider two classic views of moral development: social learning theory and cognitive-developmental theory. Both consider a young child's moral values and behavior as first influenced by outside factors. With development, moral values become internalized and moral behavior becomes guided by inner standards.

Social Learning Theory

Social learning theory views all behavior, including moral behavior, as acquired through reinforcement and modeling (Bandura, 1977; Grusec, 1992). Bandura and McDonald (1963) demonstrated that the moral judgments of young children could be modified through a training procedure involving social reinforcement and modeling. Parents and others naturally dole out reinforcement and punishment that shapes the child's behavior. Modeling also plays a role in children's moral development. Adults and other children serve as models for the child, demonstrating appropriate (and sometimes not!) actions and verbalizations. When children observe a model touching a forbidden toy, they are more likely to touch the toy. Some research suggests that children who observe a model resisting temptation are less likely to do so themselves (Rosenkoetter, 1973). However, models are more effective at encouraging rather than inhibiting behavior that violates a rule or expectation. Children are more likely to follow a model's transgressions rather than his or her appropriate behavior.

Children are more likely to imitate behavior when the model is competent and powerful (Bandura, 1977). They are also more likely to imitate a model that is perceived as warm and responsive rather than cold and distant (Yarrow, Scott, & Waxler, 1973). Over the course of early childhood, children develop internalized standards of conduct based on reinforcements, punishments, and observations of models (Bandura, 1986; Mussen & Eisenberg-Berg, 1977). Those adopted standards and moral values are then internalized and used by children as guides for behavior (Grusec & Goodnow, 1994). In this way, children's behavior is shaped to conform with the rules of society.

Cognitive-Developmental Theory

The cognitive-developmental perspective views moral development through a cognitive lens and examines reasoning about moral issues: Is it ever right to steal even if it would help another person? Is lying ever acceptable? Similar to cognitive development, children are active in constructing their own moral understanding through social experiences with adults and peers (Smetana, 1995; Smetana & Braeges, 1990). Young children's reasoning about moral problems changes with development as they construct concepts about justice and fairness from their interactions in the world (Gibbs, 1991, 2003).

Heteronomous Morality

Cognitive-developmental theorist Jean Piaget (1932) studied children's moral development—specifically, how children understand rules. He observed children playing marbles, a common game played in every schoolyard during Piaget's time, and asked them questions about the rules. What are the rules to the game? Where do the rules come from? Have they always been the same? Can they be changed? Piaget found that preschool-age children's play was not guided by rules. The youngest children engaged in solitary play without regard for rules, tossing the marbles about in random ways. Piaget posited that moral thinking develops in stages similar to those in his theory of cognition.

By 6 years of age, children enter the first stage of Piaget's theory of morality, **heteronomous morality** (also known as the morality of constraint). In this stage, as children first become aware of rules, they view them as sacred and unalterable. For example, the children interviewed by Piaget believed that people have always played marbles in the same way and that the rules cannot be changed. At this stage, moral behavior is behavior that is consistent with the rules set by authority figures. Young children see rules, even those created in play, as sacred, absolute, and unchangeable; they see behavior as either right or wrong; and they view the violation of rules as meriting punishment regardless of intent (DeVries & Zan, 2003; Nobes & Pawson, 2003). Young children may proclaim, without question, that there is only one way to play softball: As their coach advocates, the youngest children must be first to bat. Preschoolers will hold to this rule, explaining that it is simply the "right way" to play.

At first young children engage in solitary play with marbles, without concern for rules. By about age 6, they become interested in the rules and engage in group play.

Preconventional Reasoning

Lawrence Kohlberg (1969, 1976) investigated moral development by posing hypothetical dilemmas about justice, fairness, and rights that place obedience to authority and law in conflict with helping someone. For example, is stealing ever permissible—even in order to help someone? Individuals' responses change with development; moral reasoning progresses through a universal order of stages representing qualitative changes in conceptions of justice. Young children who display cognitive reasoning at the preoperational stage are at the lowest level of Kohlberg's scheme: **preconventional reasoning**. Similar to Piaget, Kohlberg argued that young children's behavior is governed by self-interest, avoiding punishment and gaining rewards. "Good" or moral behavior is a response to external pressure. Young children have not internalized societal norms, and their behavior is motivated by desires rather than internalized principles. Similar to cognitive development, children are active in constructing their own moral understanding through social experiences with adults and peers (Smetana, 1995; Smetana & Braeges, 1990). The ability to take other people's perspectives contributes to advances in moral development. The Lives in Context feature discusses cultural influences on theory of mind, how individuals understand other people's thinking. We will examine Kohlberg's perspective in greater detail when we discuss middle and late childhood.

LIVES IN CONTEXT: CULTURAL CONTEXT

Culture and Theory of Mind

As children develop, they show improvements in theory of mind and get better at communicating and taking other people's perspectives. Cultural differences in social norms might influence children's emerging understanding of the mind. Collectivist cultures emphasize the community, whereas individualist cultures focus on the needs of the individual. These differing perspectives may influence how children come to understand mental states as well as their ability to take their perspectives (Taumoepeau, 2015). For example, children from Japan tend to show delayed development on false-belief tasks compared with Western children (Wellman, Cross, & Watson, 2001). When researchers probed children's understanding of the false-belief task by asking them to explain why the actor searched in the wrong location for his chocolate, Japanese children failed to use thoughts as explanations (Naito & Koyama, 2006). Instead of giving explanations associated with mental states, such as "He didn't know it was moved," Japanese children provided justifications that referenced the physical situation (e.g., "The chocolate is now in a different place") or interpersonal factors (e.g., "He promised to do so"). The findings suggest a cultural difference in mind reading, whereby Japanese children who are raised

(Continued)

(Continued)

with collectivist values focus less on an actor's mental states and more on his physical and social situation when answering questions about his behavior.

Culture shapes children's thinking. A study of 8-year-old children from Peru used a culturally appropriate version of the Band-Aid box task in which a sugar bowl contained tiny potatoes (Vinden, 1996). At first the children believed the bowl contained sugar. After learning that it contained potatoes, they answered typical false-belief questions incorrectly, predicting that others would respond that the bowl contained potatoes. Even at age 8, well after Western children succeed on similar tasks, the Peruvian children responded incorrectly, unable to explain why others might initially believe that the bowl contained sugar and be surprised to learn otherwise. One explanation is that the children in this study were raised in an isolated farming village where farmers worked from dawn to dusk and there was no reason or time for deception (Vinden, 1996). The Peruvian children's culture did not include ideas such as false belief, or deceiving others, as their day-to-day world was concerned more with tangible activities and things rather than considerations of people's thoughts.

Other research with Samoan and Vanuatu children of the South Pacific has confirmed the relevance of culture on theory of mind. Samoan children ages 3 to 14 years showed delayed development in theory of mind and a prolonged transition to succeeding on theory of mind tasks relative to Western samples (Dixson, Komugabe-Dixson, Dixson, & Low, 2018; Mayer & Träuble, 2015). Samoan and Vanuatu children's slow progression on theory of mind tasks is consistent with the Pacific Island doctrine of opacity of mind (Slaughter & Perez-Zapata, 2014). Samoan and Vanuatu cultures de-emphasize internal mental states as explanations for behavior. Samoan and Vanuatu children, therefore, are not exposed to discussions about the mind. They get little experience considering other people's thoughts. Research with English-speaking Western samples has shown that having conversations about people's thoughts predicts children's understanding of false beliefs (Slaughter, Peterson, & Mackintosh, 2007). Therefore, Samoan and Vanuatu children's delayed success on false-belief tasks is likely a result of their culture's views. In support of this idea is a study of Pacific families living in New Zealand, in which mothers with a stronger Pacific cultural identity referred to beliefs less often when talking to their children than mothers whose Pacific identities were weaker (Slaughter & Perez-Zapata, 2014; Taumoepeau, 2015). Samoan and Vanuatu children may be relatively slow to attribute false beliefs because they take longer to recognize that such beliefs exist relative to cultures where minds are less opaque. Interestingly, however, Vanuatu children's performance varied by context. Vanuatu children who lived in towns showed more advanced performance than those who lived in rural settings, suggesting that the social contexts within a given cultural setting also influence how children come to understand the nature of people's thoughts (Dixson et al., 2018).

What Do You Think?

1. Is the development of theory of mind universally important? That is, is theory of mind important in all cultures? How might context determine the relevance of theory of mind?
2. How does theory of mind contribute to moral reasoning and behavior? ●

Conceptions of Moral, Social, and Personal Issues

Social experiences—disputes with siblings over toys, for example—help young children develop conceptions about justice and fairness (Killen & Nucci, 1995). As early as 3 years of age, children can differentiate between moral issues, imperatives which concern people's rights and welfare, and social conventions, or social customs (Smetana & Braeges, 1990). For example, they judge stealing an apple, a moral violation, more harshly than violating a social convention, such as eating with one's fingers (Smetana, 1995; Turiel, 1998). In one study, 3- and 4½-year-old children viewed an interchange in which one puppet struggled to achieve a goal, was helped by a second puppet, and was violently hindered by a third puppet. When asked to distribute biscuits, the 4½-year-olds but not 3-year-olds were more likely to give more biscuits to the helper than the hinderer puppet. Most explained the unequal distribution by referring to the helper's prosocial behavior or the hinderer's antisocial behavior (Kenward & Dahl, 2011). In addition to moral and conventional issues, between ages 3 and 5, children come to differentiate personal issues, matters of personal choice that do not violate rights, across home and school settings (Turiel & Nucci, 2017). Individuals, including preschoolers, believe that they have control over matters of personal choice, unlike moral issues whose violations are inherently wrong.

Cross-cultural research suggests that children in diverse cultures in Europe, Africa, Asia, Southeast Asia, and North and South America differentiate moral, social conventional, and personal issues (Killen, McGlothlin, & Lee-Kim, 2002; Turiel, 1998; Yau & Smetana, 2003). However, cultural differences in socialization contribute to children's conceptions. For example, a study of Chinese children ages 3 to 4 and 5 to 6 showed that, similar to Western children, the Chinese children overwhelmingly considered personal issues as permissible and up to the child, rather than the adults.

The children's consideration of moral transgressions varied. The Chinese children tended to focus on the intrinsic consequences of the acts for others' welfare and fairness, as compared with the emphasis on avoiding punishment common in Western samples of preschoolers (Yau & Smetana, 2003). These differences are consistent with cultural preferences for collectivism and individualism. Whereas Western parents tend to emphasize individuality and independence, Chinese parents tend to emphasize children's obligations to the family and community (Chao, 1995; Yau & Smetana, 2003). One study of 4-year-old Chinese children and their mothers showed that mothers consistently drew children's attention to transgressions, emphasizing the consequences for others. The children learned quickly and were able to spontaneously discuss their mothers' examples and strategies, as well as reenact them in their own interactions, and their explanations reflected their own understanding of rules and expectations in their own terms, rather than reflecting simple memorization (Wang, Bernas, & Eberhard, 2008).

How adults discuss moral issues, such as truth telling, harm, and property rights, influences how children come to understand these issues. When adults discuss moral issues in ways that are sensitive to the child's developmental needs, children develop more sophisticated conceptions of morality and advance in their moral reasoning (Janssens & Dekovic, 1997; Walker & Taylor, 1991). As we have seen, there are cultural differences in how people think about moral and conventional issues—and these conceptualizations are communicated, internalized, and transformed by children as they construct their own concepts about morality.

THINKING IN CONTEXT 8.4

1. Compare the social learning and cognitive-developmental perspectives on moral development. What are the strengths and weaknesses of each? In your view, is one better able to account for moral development than another? Why or why not?
2. How might cultural context and values influence young children's views of issues as moral, conventional, or personal choices? In what ways might home and neighborhood contexts influence young children's views?

EARLY CHILDHOOD EDUCATION

Many children attend kindergarten prior to entering elementary school, but only 15 states require children to complete kindergarten (Education Commission of the States, 2014). Early education

Effective education emphasizes active learning through creative play, artwork, physical activity, and social play.
AP Photo/ Lori Wolfe

is important for children's cognitive, social, and emotional development. Preschool programs provide educational experiences for children ages 2 to 5.

Child-Centered and Academically Centered Preschool Programs

There are two general approaches to early childhood education. **Academically centered preschool programs** emphasize providing children with structured learning environments in which teachers deliver direct instruction on letters, numbers, shapes, and academic skills. **Child-centered preschool programs** take a constructivist approach that encourages children to actively build their own understanding of the world through observing, interacting with objects and people, and engaging in a variety of activities that allow them to manipulate materials and interact with teachers and peers (Kostelnik, Soderman, Whiren, & Rupiper, 2015). Children learn by doing, through play, and learn to problem solve, get along with others, communicate, and self-regulate.

Montessori schools, first created in the early 1900s by the Italian physician and educator Maria Montessori (1870–1952), exemplify the child-centered approach, in which children are viewed as active constructors of their own development and are given freedom in choosing their activities. Teachers act as facilitators, providing a range of activities and materials, demonstrating ways of exploring them, and providing help when the child asks. The Montessori approach is credited with fostering independence, self-regulation, and cognitive and problem-solving skills.

In contrast, problems have been documented with teacher-directed rigid academic programs. Children immersed in such programs sometimes show signs of stress such as rocking, may have less confidence in their skills, and may avoid challenging tasks compared with children who are immersed in more active forms of play-based learning (Stipek,

Feiler, Daniels, & Milburn, 1995). Such programs are also negatively associated with reading skills in first grade (Lerkkanen et al., 2016).

Instead of a purely academic approach, many practitioners advocate for a **developmentally appropriate practice**, which tailors instruction to the age of the child, recognizing individual differences and the need for hands-on active teaching methods (Kostelnik et al., 2015). Teachers provide educational support in the form of learning goals, instructional support, and feedback, but they also emphasize emotional support and help children learn to manage their own behavior (Anderson & Phillips, 2017). Moreover, teachers are provided with explicit instruction in how to teach and the teaching strategies needed to support young children's literacy, language, math, social, and self-regulatory development (Markowitz, Bassok, & Hamre, 2018). Responsive child-centered teaching is associated with higher reading and math scores during first grade (Lerkkanen et al., 2016).

Effective early childhood educational practice is influenced by cultural values (Gordon & Browne, 2016). In the United States, a society that emphasizes individuality, a child-centered approach in which children are given freedom of choice is associated with the most positive outcomes (Marcon, 1999). Yet in Japan, the most effective preschools tend to foster collectivist values and are society centered with an emphasis on social and classroom routines, skills, and promoting group harmony (Holloway, 1999; Nagayama & Gilliard, 2005). Japanese preschools prepare children for their roles in society and provide formal instruction in academic areas as well as art, swordsmanship, gymnastics, tea ceremonies, and Japanese dance. Much instruction is teacher directed, and children are instructed to sit, observe, and listen. Teachers are warm but address the group as a whole rather than individuals. This structured approach is associated with positive outcomes in Japanese children (Holloway, 1999; Nagayama & Gilliard, 2005), illustrating the role of culture in influencing outcomes of early childhood education. Even within a given country such as the United States, there exist many ethnicities and corresponding cultures, such as those of Native Americans and Mexican Americans. In each case, instruction that is informed by an understanding of children's home and community culture fosters a sense of academic belongingness that ultimately influences academic achievement (Gilliard & Moore, 2007; Gordon & Browne, 2016).

In Western countries, children spend most of their day at school and, aside from household chores such as picking up their toys or cleaning their dinner plates, work is not a part of the typical Western child's day. Most children are segregated from adult work and know little about their parents' workplace. Some educators advocate for applying neuroscience findings to improve early childhood education, as discussed in the Lives in Context feature.

LIVES IN CONTEXT: BIOLOGICAL INFLUENCES

Brain-Based Learning

Children play an active role in their own cognitive development by interacting with the world. Some educators advocate for brain-based learning that capitalizes on children's natural inclinations toward active learning. Brain-based learning encourages children to explore a variety of activities to develop all aspects of their brains, tapping physical, musical, creative, cognitive, and other abilities. Given that the brain changes with experience, enriched everyday experiences such as learning a musical instrument, role-playing, and expanding vocabulary may alter children's brains (Jensen, 2008).

Neurological researchers, however, are critical of some brain-based learning approaches, such as those that emphasize teaching different parts of the brain separately (Howard-Jones, 2014). For example, a common brain-based education instructional strategy is to teach for the left or right lateralized brain. The "left brain" is said to be the "logical" hemisphere, concerned with language and analysis, while the "right brain" is said to be the "intuitive" hemisphere concerned with spatial patterns and creativity (Sousa, 2001). Brain-based learning theorists may then encourage teachers to teach to specific hemispheres during adapted lessons, such as teaching reading and writing to support the left hemisphere and creating visual representations of concepts to support the right. Brain researchers, however, are sharply critical of left/right brain teaching because, although the brain is lateralized, it functions as a whole (Howard-Jones, 2014). Language and spatial information—and, for that matter, most other abilities—are processed differently but simultaneously by the two hemispheres (Corballis, Lalueza-Fox, Orlando, Enard, & Green, 2014). It is highly improbable, then, that any given lesson, regardless of analytic or spatial type, can stimulate activation of only one hemisphere.

Some experts argue that the leap from neurological research to the classroom is large and unsupported

(Alferink & Farmer-Dougan, 2010). For many researchers, the problem of brain-based learning is the oversimplification of complex research findings (Alferink & Farmer-Dougan, 2010; Busso & Pollack, 2014). Neuroscience researchers make many new discoveries about brain activity, but it requires a different set of research strategies to determine how to apply neuroscience findings in the classroom; currently we know little about how to apply brain research to draw direct inferences about teaching (Bowers, 2016; Bruer, 2008). Many researchers, therefore, find it problematic to state that specific teaching strategies should be derived from brain research.

In a move away from brain-based learning, the growing field of educational neuroscience emphasizes the educational value of understanding neurological development, such as how and when the parts of the brain develop (Byrnes & Vu, 2015; Thomas, Ansari, & Knowland, 2019). Unlike brain-based learning theorists, educational neuroscientists do not advocate activities to develop specific parts of the brain. Instead, from an educational neuroscience perspective, understanding when the parts of the brain responsible for attention, working memory, or executive function develop can help educators understand their students and may influence the material and types of assignments presented to students. Applications of neuroscience research to enhance brain development, however, are largely unknown. Teachers who wish to support their students' cognitive development should engage in activities that foster active learning and encourage students to become engaged and participate in their own learning, such as being creative in artwork, physical activity, and story making.

What Do You Think?

Identify an advantage and a disadvantage to brain-based learning. In your view, should preschools emphasize teaching specifically to a specific part of the brain, such as the left or right hemisphere? ●

Early Childhood Education Interventions

Recognizing that young children's developmental needs extend beyond education, one of the most successful early childhood education and intervention programs in the United States, **Project Head Start**, was created by the federal government to provide economically disadvantaged children with nutritional, health, and educational services during their early childhood years, prior to kindergarten (Ramey & Ramey, 1998). Parents of Head Start children also receive assistance, such as education about child development, vocational services, and programs addressing their emotional and social needs (Zigler & Styfco, 2004).

Over the past 4 decades, a great deal of research has been conducted on the effectiveness of Head Start. The most common finding is that Head Start improves cognitive performance, with gains in IQ and achievement scores in elementary school (Zhai, Brooks-Gunn, & Waldfogel, 2011). Compared with children who do not participate in Head Start, those who do so have greater parental involvement in school, show higher math achievement scores in middle school, are less likely to be held back a grade or have problems with chronic absenteeism in middle school, and are more likely to graduate from high school (Duncan, Ludwig, & Magnuson, 2007; Joo, 2010; Phillips, Gormley, & Anderson, 2016). Head Start is associated with other long-lasting social and physical effects, such as gains in social competence and health-related outcomes, including immunizations (Huston, 2008). Yet some research has suggested that the cognitive effects of Head Start may fade over time such that, by late childhood, Head Start participants perform similarly to control group low socioeconomic status children who have not participated in Head Start (U.S. Department of Health and Human Services & Administration for Children and Families, 2010). Early intervention may not compensate for the pervasive and long-lasting effects of poverty-stricken neighborhoods and inadequate public schools (Schnur & Belanger, 2000; Welshman, 2010). At the same time, long-term advantageous effects of attending Head Start include higher graduation rates and lower rates of adolescent pregnancy and criminality for low-income children who attend Head Start compared with their control group peers (Duncan & Magnuson, 2013). Despite these findings, only about one-third of poor children are enrolled in Head Start, and this proportion has shrunk over the past decade, as shown in Figure 8.6.

Additional evidence for the effectiveness of early childhood education interventions comes from the Carolina Abecedarian Project and the Perry Preschool Project, carried out in the 1960s and 1970s. Both of these programs enrolled children from families with incomes below the poverty line and emphasized the provision of stimulating preschool experiences to promote motor, language, and social skills as well as cognitive skills, including literacy and math. Special emphasis was placed on rich, responsive adult–child verbal communication as well as nutrition and health services. Children in these programs achieved higher reading and math scores in elementary school than their nonenrolled peers (Campbell & Ramey, 1994). As adolescents, they showed higher rates of high school graduation and college enrollment, as well as lower rates of substance abuse and pregnancy

FIGURE 8.6

Number of Children (in Thousands) Enrolled in Head Start and Early Head Start, and Children Enrolled as a Percentage of Children in Poverty, 2006–2014

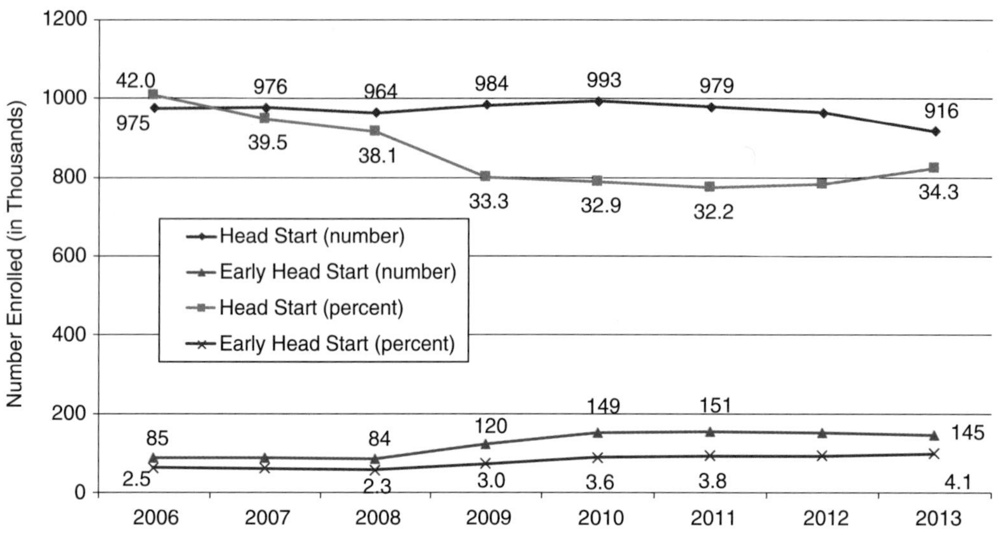

Source: Child Trends (2015).

(Campbell, Ramey, Pungello, Sparling, & Miller-Johnson, 2002; Muennig et al., 2011). At ages 30 and 40, early intervention participants showed higher levels of education and income (Campbell et al., 2012; Schweinhart et al., 2005).

The success of early education intervention programs has influenced a movement in the United States toward comprehensive prekindergarten (pre-K). Young children who participate in high-quality pre-K programs enter school with greater readiness to learn and score higher on reading and math tests than their peers (Gormley, Phillips, Adelstein, & Shaw, 2010). About one-half of states offer some form of state-funded pre-K without income restrictions (Barnett, Carolan, Squires, Clarke Brown, & Horowitz, 2015). A few states, including Oklahoma, Georgia, and Florida, provide universal pre-K to all children, and many more states are moving in this direction (Williams, 2015). Beginning in the fall of 2017, New York City initiated a city-funded "3-K for all" program of free full-day preschool to all 3-year-olds (Taylor, 2017). Although some research suggests that half-day and more intense full-day programs do not differ in academic and social outcomes, full-day preschool incorporates the benefit of free child care to working parents that is likely of higher quality than they might have otherwise been able to afford (Leow & Wen, 2017). Funding public preschool programs is daunting, but the potential rewards are tremendous.

THINKING IN CONTEXT 8.5

1. What are the pros and cons of academically centered and child-centered preschool programs? Design a preschool setting and program that combines aspects of both types of programs, as you see fit. Discuss your choices.
2. Consider early childhood interventions such as Head Start from the perspective of bioecological theory. Identify factors at the microsystem, mesosystem, and exosystem levels that programs may address to promote children's development.

APPLY YOUR KNOWLEDGE

On the first day of softball practice, Coach Kim explained how to throw the ball. She modeled the steps: "Grip the ball with all five fingers. Point your shoulder at the target. Keep your elbow up. Throw. Then point your chest at the target after your throw." The children nodded. "Remember: Grip, shoulder, elbow, chest," Coach Kim instructed, "Now you all say it." The children repeated, "Grip, shoulder, elbow, chest."

"Now let's try throwing," Coach Kim suggested. Five-year-old Jenna grasped the ball, stood tall, and repeated the instructions "Grip, shoulder, elbow, chest" to herself as she threw the ball and it swooped far to the left. "Almost, Jenna. Try it this way," Coach Kim instructed as she moved Jenna's arm into the proper position. Jenna threw a perfect pitch, amazed. "I did it!" she exclaimed. "Yes, just remember to keep your elbow up," Coach Kim said.

Next week, Jenna stood at the pitcher's mound during their first game. Breathing deeply, she reminded herself of the four points. "Grip, shoulder, elbow, chest. Grip it with all five fingers," she said as she talked herself through the process. "I did it!" she cried as the ball sailed to the batter. Later she explained to her mother, "At first I was scared, but I told myself to think and remember what we did in practice."

1. What cognitive abilities are needed to play a game like softball?
2. Explain Jenna's learning from the perspective of Vygotsky's sociocultural theory.
3. How might theory of mind and metacognition contribute to children's participation in everyday activities like softball?

WANT A BETTER GRADE?

Get the tools you need to sharpen your study skills. **SAGE edge** offers a robust online environment featuring an impressive array of free tools and resources. Access practice quizzes, eFlashcards, video, and multimedia at **edge.sagepub.com/kutherchild1e.** SAGE edge™

KEY TERMS

Preoperational reasoning 216
Egocentrism 216
Three-mountains task 216
Animism 217
Centration 217
Appearance–reality distinction 217
Irreversibility 217
Conservation 217
Guided participation 220
Scaffolding 220
Zone of proximal development 220
Private speech 221
Sustained attention 222
Selective attention 222
Episodic memory 223
Recall memory 223
Memory strategy 223
Script 224
Autobiographical memory 224
Theory of mind 225
Metacognition 225
False-belief task 226
Logical extension 229
Mutual exclusivity assumption 229
Overregularization errors 230
Heteronomous morality 233
Preconventional reasoning 233
Academically centered preschool program 235
Child-centered preschool program 235
Montessori school 235
Developmentally appropriate practice 236
Project Head Start 237

SUMMARY

8.1 Compare Piaget's cognitive-developmental and Vygotsky's sociocultural theories of cognitive development in early childhood.

Piaget explained that children in the preoperational stage of reasoning are able to think using mental symbols, but their thinking is limited because they cannot grasp logic. Simplified and nonverbal tasks demonstrate that young children are more cognitively advanced and less egocentric than Piaget posed. From Vygotsky's sociocultural perspective, children's learning occurs through guided participation, scaffolding within the zone of proximal development. With time, the child internalizes the lesson and learns to accomplish the task on his or her own. In this way, cognitive development entails actively internalizing the tools of our culture.

8.2 Describe information processing abilities during early childhood.

The ability to sustain attention improves in early childhood through the preschool years. Episodic memory also improves steadily but young children's limited working memory makes it difficult for them to use memory strategies. Autobiographical memory develops steadily and is accompanied by increases in the length, richness, and complexity of recall memory. Advances in theory of mind enable children to understand that people can believe different things, that beliefs can be inaccurate, and that sometimes people act on the basis of false beliefs. Children thereby become able to lie or use deception in play.

8.3 Summarize young children's advances in language development.

Young children apply strategies such as logical extension and the mutual exclusivity assumption to increase their vocabulary rapidly. Young children quickly move from telegraphic speech to combining words into sentences in increasingly sophisticated ways, using multiple elements of speech, such as plurals, adjectives, and the past tense, yet they often make overregularization errors. Parental conversations and support for language learning are associated with faster and more correct language use. At the end of the preschool years, most children use main grammar rules appropriately and confidently. Children who are exposed to two languages build two distinct systems with similar patterns of development. The rate of acquisition for two languages depends on the quantity and quality of the input in each language. When considering one language, bilingual children tend to show a gap in vocabulary compared to their monolingual peers; however, when both languages are considered, the gap closes.

8.4 Contrast social learning and cognitive-developmental perspectives on moral development in early childhood.

Social learning theory explains that children develop internalized standards of conduct based on observation, reinforcements, and punishments. The cognitive-developmental perspective examines reasoning about moral issues, specifically concerns of justice. Kohlberg explained that young children display preconventional moral reasoning, motivated by self-interest. Young children in diverse cultures can differentiate between moral concerns from social conventions, or social customs. Social experiences with parents, caregivers, siblings, and peers help young children develop conceptions about justice and fairness.

8.5 Identify and explain various approaches to early childhood education.

Child-centered preschool programs encourage children to manipulate materials, interact with teachers and peers, and learn by doing, through play. Academically oriented preschool programs provide children with structured learning environments through which they learn letters, numbers, shapes, and academic skills via drills and formal lessons. Head Start and other early childhood education interventions can promote children's learning and development.

REVIEW QUESTIONS

8.1 What are characteristics of preoperational reasoning?

What are criticisms of Piaget's explanation of thinking in early childhood?

Provide an example of scaffolding and the zone of proximal development.

What is a criticism of Vygotsky's theory?

8.2 How does social learning theory explain the development of moral behavior in children?

How does the cognitive-developmental perspective account for moral development?

Differentiate moral, conventional, and personal issues.

8.3 What strategies do children use to increase their vocabulary?

Provide an example of overregularization.

How does language development occur in bilingual children?

8.4 How does social learning theory explain moral development?

What is heteronomous morality?

What is preconventional reasoning?

Give examples of moral, social, and personal issues.

8.5 Compare two common approaches to preschool education.

What is Project Head Start?

What are characteristics of successful early intervention programs?

©iStockphoto.com/DGLimages

9 Socioemotional Development in Early Childhood

"Oww!" Ren cried out as he tripped. "Are you okay?" asked his mother. Ren nodded. "I'm okay but I don't like that step." "I agree," smiled Ren's mother, marveling at how Ren has matured. Just a short while ago he would react to frustration by crying. Now he used words to express his wants and needs, at least most of the time. Early childhood is a time of transition from the dependence of infancy and toddlerhood to the increasing capacities for autonomy and emotional regulation characteristic of childhood. How do young children learn to understand and control their emotions? Do they experience the same complex emotions that older children and adolescents experience? What is the role of parents in children's emotional and social development? What is the function of play in development? In this chapter, we explore children's experience and understanding of their social and emotional world and how socioemotional development changes over the early childhood years.

Learning Objectives

9.1 Discuss young children's sense of initiative, self-concept, and self-esteem.

9.2 Discuss the development of emotional regulation and prosocial and aggressive behavior in early childhood.

9.3 Summarize styles of parenting and discipline and their associations with child outcomes.

▶ **Video Activity 9.1:** Parenting and Discipline

9.4 Compare biological, cognitive, and contextual theoretical explanations of gender role development.

▶ **Video Activity 9.2:** Gender Schemas and Play Preferences

9.5 Discuss the range of forms play takes in early childhood and its influence on social development and relationships.

Chapter Contents

EMERGING SENSE OF SELF

When assigned a task, such as dusting off a bookcase shelf, 3-year-old Shawna calls out, "I'll do it!" After completing the task, she proudly proclaims, "I did it!" The autonomy that Shawna developed during the toddler years has prepared her to master the psychosocial task of the preschool years: developing a sense of initiative (Erikson, 1950).

Participating in household work is one way in which children develop initiative, a sense of purpose, and pride in their accomplishments.
©iStockphoto.com/Halfpoint

Psychosocial Development in Early Childhood

During Erikson's third psychosocial stage, **initiative versus guilt**, young children develop a sense of purpose and take pride in their accomplishments. As they develop a sense of initiative, young children make plans, tackle new tasks, set goals (e.g., climbing a tree, writing their name, counting to 10), and work to achieve them, persisting enthusiastically in tasks, whether physical or social, even when frustrated (Lambert & Kelley, 2011).

Much of the work of this stage occurs through play. During play, young children experiment and practice new skills in a safe context and learn to work cooperatively with other children to achieve common goals. Children in all societies practice adult roles in play, such as mother, father, doctor, teacher, and police officer (Gaskins, 2014). For example, Hopi Indian children pretend to be hunters and potters, and the Baka of West Africa pretend to be hut builders and spear makers (Roopnarine, Lasker, Sacks, & Stores, 1998). The sense of pride that children feel from accomplishment fuels their play and fosters curiosity. Children become motivated to concentrate, persist, and try new experiences, such as climbing to the top of the monkey bars. Through play, children also learn how to manage their emotions and develop self-regulation skills (Goldstein & Lerner, 2018).

During early childhood, children come to identify with their parents and internalize parental rules. Young children feel guilt when they fail to uphold rules and when they fail to achieve a goal. If parents are controlling—not permitting children to carry out their sense of purpose—or are highly punitive, critical, or threatening, children may not develop high standards and the initiative to meet them. Instead, children may be paralyzed by guilt and worry about their inability to measure up to parental expectations. They may develop an overly critical conscience and be less motivated to exert the effort to master new tasks.

Children who develop a sense of initiative demonstrate independence and act purposefully. Their success in taking initiative and the feeling of competence and pride that accompanies it contributes to young children's developing sense of self.

Self-Concept

Three- and 4-year-old children tend to understand and describe themselves concretely, using observable descriptors including appearance, general abilities, favorite activities, possessions, and simple psychological traits (Harter, 2012). For example, Wanda explains, "I'm 4 years old. I have black hair. I'm happy, my doggie is white, and I have a television in my room. I can run really fast. Watch me!" Wanda's self-description, her **self-concept**, is typical of children her age. Soon children begin to include emotions and attitudes in their self-descriptions, such as "I'm sad when my friends can't play," suggesting an emerging awareness of their internal characteristics (Thompson & Virmani, 2010).

Children's conceptions of themselves are influenced by their interactions with parents and the cultural context in which they are raised. In one study, preschool through second-grade U.S. and Chinese children were asked to recount autobiographical events and describe themselves in response to open-ended questions (Wang, 2004). The U.S. children often provided detailed accounts of their experiences. They focused on their own roles, preferences, and feelings and described their personal attributes and inner traits positively. In contrast, Chinese children provided relatively skeletal accounts of past experiences that focused on social interactions and daily routines. They often described themselves in neutral or modest tones, referring to social roles and context-specific personal characteristics. These differences are consistent with cultural values of independence in the United States and collectivism in China. In another study, U.S. preschool children reported feeling more sadness and shame in response to failure and more pride in response to success than did Japanese preschool children (Lewis, Takai-Kawakami, Kawakami, & Sullivan, 2010). The Japanese preschool children displayed few negative emotions in response to failure but showed self-conscious embarrassment in response to success. Culture, then, influences how children come to define and understand themselves and even the emotions with which they self-identify (Thompson & Virmani, 2010).

Self-Esteem

Young children tend to evaluate themselves positively. That is, they generally have a high sense of **self-esteem**. For example, 3-year-old Dorian exclaims, "I'm the smartest! I know all my ABCs! Listen! A, B, C, F, G, L, M!" Like Dorian, many young children are excited but also unrealistically positive about their abilities, underestimating the difficulty of tasks and believing that they will always be successful (Harter, 2012). Preschoolers often fail to recognize deficits in their abilities and tend to view their performance favorably, even when it is not up to par (Boseovski, 2010). Even after failing at a task several times, they often continue to believe that the next try will bring success.

Young children's overly optimistic perspective on their skills can be attributed to their cognitive development, attachment with caregivers, and the overwhelmingly positive feedback they usually receive when they attempt a task (Goodvin, Meyer, Thompson, & Hayes, 2008). These unrealistically positive expectations serve a developmental purpose: They contribute to young children's growing sense of initiative and aid them in learning new skills. Young children maintain their positive views about themselves because they do not yet engage in **social comparison**. In other words, they do not compare their performance with that of other children. With advances in cognition and social experience, children begin to learn their relative strengths and weaknesses, and their self-evaluations become more realistic (Rochat, 2013). Between ages 4 and 7, children's self-evaluations become linked with their performance. For example, in one study, children's self-evaluations declined when they failed tasks assigned by an adult as well as those they perceived as important (Cimpian, Hammond, Mazza, & Corry, 2017). Sensitive parenting that supports children's attempts at difficult tasks emphasizes the value of effort and helps children identify and take pride in success that promotes self-esteem.

In what ways might young children's inaccurate views of themselves and their abilities be adaptive? How might their developing sense of self influence their ability to tackle the psychosocial task of this stage, developing a sense of initiative?

EMOTIONAL DEVELOPMENT IN EARLY CHILDHOOD

Young children's advances in cognitive development and growing sense of self influence the emotions they show and the contexts in which they display these emotions. Moreover, young children come to understand people and social relationships in more complex ways, leading to new opportunities for emotional development. Emotional development includes an increasing awareness and management of emotion, as well as an ability to recognize others' emotions and infer causes and consequences of others' emotions (Camras & Halberstadt, 2017).

Emotional Understanding

Donald begins to cry as his mother leaves, dropping him off at preschool. Watching Donald, Amber explains to her mother, "Donald is sad because he misses his mommy," and she brings Donald a toy. "Don't be sad," she says. By 3 to 4 years of age, children recognize and name emotions based on their expressive cues. By age 4, children begin to understand that external factors (such as losing a toy) can affect emotion and can predict a peer's emotion and behavior (such as feeling sad and crying or feeling angry and hitting things) (Goodvin et al., 2015).

The emergence of theory of mind has profound implications for emotional development. As children begin to take other people's perspectives, they can apply their understanding of emotions to understand and help others, such as recognizing that a sibling is sad and offering a hug. Children's growing understanding of the mind leads them to appreciate the role of internal factors, such as desires, on emotion and behavior (Wellman, 2017). By age 5, most children understand that desire can motivate emotion, and many understand that people's emotional reactions to an event can vary based on their desires.

Theory of mind influences the development and expression of self-conscious emotions, such as pride and guilt. Self-conscious emotions emerge as children become aware of rules and standards that define socially appropriate behavior and that others have expectations for their behavior (Muris & Meesters, 2014). For example, in response to success, children's joy may be accompanied by the self-conscious emotion of pride. Likewise, shame results from recognizing that poor outcomes are the result of their behavior.

Interactions with others play an important role in advancing children's understanding of emotions. When parents talk to their preschoolers about emotions and explain their own and their children's emotions, the children are better able to evaluate and label others' emotions (Camras & Halberstadt, 2017). Preschool teachers also engage in emotion coaching, helping young children to understand the emotions they feel and see in others (Silkenbeumer, Schiller, & Kärtner, 2018). Young children often discuss emotional experiences with parents and peers. They also often enact emotions in pretend sociodramatic play, providing experience and practice in understanding emotions and their influence on social interactions (Goodvin et al., 2015). Pretend play with siblings and peers gives children practice in acting out feelings, considering others' perspectives, and implementing self-control, improving the children's understanding of emotion (Hoffmann & Russ, 2012). In one study, preschoolers' engagement in sociodramatic play predicted their expressiveness, knowledge, and regulation of emotion 1 year later (Lindsey & Colwell, 2013). Children's interactions with siblings offer important opportunities to practice identifying emotions, decoding the causes of emotions, anticipating the emotional responses of others, and using their emotional understanding to influence their relationships and affect the behavior of others (Kramer, 2014).

Emotion Regulation

Over the course of childhood, children make great strides in regulating their emotions and become better able to manage how they experience and display emotions. Advances in emotion regulation are influenced by cognition, executive function, theory of mind, and language development. By age 4, children can explain simple strategies for reducing emotional arousal, such as limiting sensory input (covering their eyes), talking to themselves ("It's not scary"), or changing their goals ("I want to play blocks," after having been excluded by children who were playing another game) (Thompson & Goodvin, 2007). Emotion regulation strategies are a response to emotions, change with age, and also influence children's emotional experience (Eisenberg, Spinrad, & Knafo-Noam, 2015).

Parents remain important resources for emotional management in childhood. Mothers' emotional awareness and management skills influence children's emotional regulation skills (Crespo, Trentacosta, Aikins, & Wargo-Aikins, 2017). Parents who are responsive when children are distressed, who frame experiences for children (e.g., by acting cheery during a trip to the doctor), and who explain expectations and strategies for emotional management both model and foster emotion regulation (Sala, Pons, & Molina, 2014). In contrast, dismissive or hostile reactions to children's emotions prevent them from learning how to manage and not be overwhelmed by their emotions (Zeman, Cassano, & Adrian, 2013). Emotion regulation skill is associated with both social competence and overall adjustment (Deneault & Ricard, 2013). Children who are able to direct their attention and distract themselves when distressed or frustrated become well-behaved students and are well liked by peers (McClelland & Cameron, 2011).

Empathy and Prosocial Behavior

In early childhood, young children develop the cognitive and language skills that permit them to reflect on emotions, talk about emotions, and convey feelings of **empathy**, the ability to understand someone's feelings (Stern & Cassidy, 2018). Empathy stems from the perspective-taking ability that emerges with theory of mind. The child must imagine another's perspective in order to understand how that person feels (Eisenberg et al., 2015). A secure attachment to a caregiver helps children develop the emotional understanding and regulation skills on which empathy depends (Ştefan & Avram, 2018).

Empathy influences how young children make judgments in their social world. Children who score higher on measures of empathy tend to rate moral transgressions involving physical and psychological harm as more serious and are more likely to rate unfairness as more deserving of punishment than other children (Ball, Smetana, & Sturge-Apple, 2017). Children who feel empathy for another person often are primed to engage in **prosocial behavior**, voluntary behavior intended to benefit another (Eisenberg et al., 2015). However, sometimes feelings of empathy for distressed others can result in personal distress, leading the child to focus on relieving his or her own distress rather than helping the person in need.

Prosocial Behavior

When does prosocial behavior emerge? A series of research studies using the violation-of-expectation method (see Chapter 5) have suggested that infants as young as 3 months may possess simple conceptions

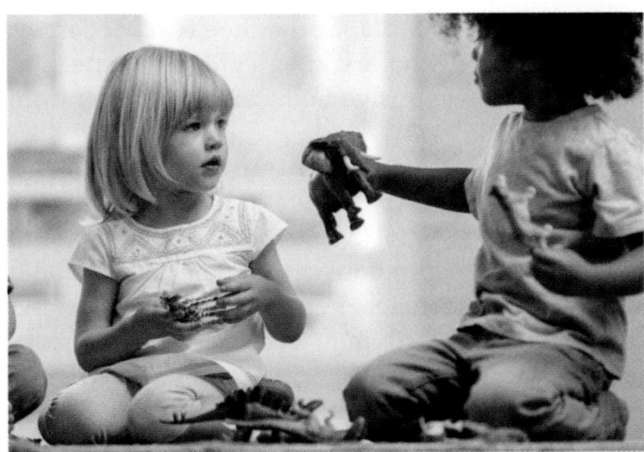

One example of prosocial behavior is sharing. Sharing becomes more equitable and complex with development.
©iStockphoto.com/FatCamera

of prosocial behavior, such as preferring to look at characters that help rather than hinder others (Van de Vondervoort & Hamlin, 2016). For toddlers as young as 18 months, prosocial behavior is simple, such as the tendency to help adults, even unfamiliar experimenters, by picking up markers that have fallen (Thompson & Newton, 2013). Between 18 and 24 months of age, toddlers show increasingly prosocial responses to others' emotional and physical distress, but their responses are limited to their own perspective. That is, they tend to offer the aid that they themselves would prefer, such as bringing their own mother to help a distressed peer (Hepach, Vaish, & Tomasello, 2012). Although toddlers are capable of prosocial responding to distressed others, spontaneous prosocial behavior not prompted by adults is rare in toddlerhood (Eisenberg et al., 2015).

At 3½ years of age, children show more complex forms of **instrumental assistance**, or tangible help. Compared to 18-month-old children, 3½-year-olds are more likely to help an adult by bringing a needed object, to do so autonomously without the adult's specific request, and to select an object appropriate to the adult's need (Svetlova, Nichols, & Brownell, 2010). Young children may engage in prosocial behavior for egocentric motives, such as the desire for praise and to avoid punishment and disapproval. With development, children become less egocentric and more aware of others' perspectives. Their prosocial behavior becomes motivated by empathy as well as internalized societal values for good behavior (Eisenberg, Spinrad, & Morris, 2013).

In addition to helping, children display prosocial behavior by sharing. Children's views of sharing change over time. Three-year-old children conceptualize fair sharing as strict equality—for example, each child should get the same amount of candy, no matter what (Damon, 1977; Enright et al., 1984). Using nonverbal measures, researchers have shown that 3-year-old children identify and react negatively to unfair distributions of stickers, especially if they receive fewer than another child (LoBue, Nishida, Chiong, DeLoache, & Haidt, 2011). Despite endorsing norms of sharing, behavioral studies show that 3-year-old children tend to favor themselves but become more likely to share with age (Smith, Blake, & Harris, 2013). However, sharing is influenced by context. For example, after working together actively to obtain rewards in a collaboration task, most 3-year-old children share equally with a peer (Warneken, Lohse, Melis, & Tomasello, 2011).

Between 3 and 5 years of age, young children show selectivity in sharing. Four- and 5-year-olds believe in an obligation to share, but they often allocate rewards based on observable characteristics, such as age, size, or other obvious physical characteristics (e.g., "The oldest should get more candy"). Often these decisions are based on personal desires and characteristics that adults would deem irrelevant, such as, "Girls should get more because they're girls!" When told that they must make an unequal distribution, 5-year-olds tend to share more with others whom they expect will reciprocate and more with friends than with peers they dislike (Paulus & Moore, 2014). Young children share more with children and adults who show prosocial behaviors such as sharing and helping others (Kuhlmeier, Dunfield, & O'Neill, 2014).

Early childhood prosocial behavior is associated with positive peer relationships, mental health, and social competence in preschool and beyond (Malti & Dys, 2018). Prosocial children tend to show low levels of aggressive and problem behaviors. They tend to be successful in school and score high on measures of vocabulary, reading, and language—perhaps because prosocial children are friendly and engage in interaction with teacher and peers (Eisenberg et al., 2015).

Influences on Prosocial Behavior

Prosocial behavior is influenced by many interacting factors, including biology and genes, family contexts, the larger social context, and the development of reasoning skills. Let's explore each of these influences.

Biological Influences. Genetic factors are thought to contribute to individual differences in prosocial behavior (Waldman et al., 2011). Twin studies, for example, have revealed that adult identical twins show more similar reports of prosocial behavior than do their fraternal twin peers (Knafo-Noam, Uzefovsky, Israel, Davidov, & Zahn-Waxler, 2015). Several genes have been implicated in prosocial tendencies, including one that influences the hormone oxytocin, which is associated with attachment and other socioemotional behaviors (Carter, 2014). A child's inborn temperament influences how the child regulates emotion, which is related to feelings of empathy for a distressed child or adult and, in turn, whether empathetic feelings result in personal distress or prosocial behavior (Eisenberg et al., 2015). Children who are unable to successfully regulate their emotions tend to react to distressed others with heightened physiological arousal, including increases in heart rate and brain activity in regions known to process negative emotions, suggesting a feeling of being overwhelmed that can interfere with prosocial responding (Miller, 2018).

Emotional Influences. Self-conscious emotions, such as guilt and pride, influence prosocial behavior. For example, in response to guilt, 2- and 3-year-olds are motivated to repair damage that they have caused (Vaish, 2018). When 3- and 4-year-old children feel pride in response to an achievement, they are more likely to offer spontaneous help to a person in need (Ross, 2017). Self-conscious emotions and the self-evaluations inherent in them might motivate prosocial behavior in an attempt to maintain an ideal self.

Family Influences. Rich interactions with parents engage the emotions, cognitions, and behaviors critical to prosocial responding (Brownell, 2016). The secure attachment that accompanies warm, sensitive parenting aids in the development of emotional regulation, a predictor of empathy and prosocial responding (Spinrad & Gal, 2018). Parents of prosocial children draw attention to models of prosocial behavior in peers and in media, such as in storybooks, movies, and television programs. As suggested earlier, parents may also describe feelings and model sympathetic concern and the use of language to discuss feelings. Young children whose parents do these things are more likely to use words to describe their thoughts and emotions and attempt to understand others' emotional states (Taylor, Eisenberg, Spinrad, Eggum, & Sulik, 2013).

Parents also actively encourage prosocial behavior by including young children in their household and caregiving activities (Dahl, 2015). Parents' encouragement of children's participation in household cleanup routines predicts children's willingness to help another adult in a new context (Hammond & Carpendale, 2015). Children's prosocial behavior emerges out of prosocial activity shared with adults, and parental encouragement promotes its development (Brownell, 2016).

At the same time as parents influence children, children play a role in their own development by influencing their parents. One study that followed children from 4½ years of age through sixth grade found that maternal sensitivity influenced children's prosocial behavior and that prosocial behavior, in turn, predicted mothers' subsequent sensitivity, suggesting that mothers and children influence each other (Newton, Laible, Carlo, Steele, & McGinley, 2014). Children who are kind, compassionate, and helpful elicit responsive and warm parenting from their mothers.

Siblings offer opportunities to learn and practice helping and other prosocial behavior. Older siblings who display positive emotional responsiveness promote preschoolers' emotional and social competence. Researchers have observed that children with siblings tend to develop a theory of mind earlier than those without siblings (Kramer, 2014). As we have seen, the perspective-taking and cognitive skills that compose theory of mind promote emotional understanding and prosocial behavior.

Contextual Influences. The broader social world also influences the development of prosocial behavior. Collectivist cultures, in which people live with extended families, work is shared, and the maintenance of positive relationships with others is emphasized, tend to promote prosocial values and behavior more so than do cultures that emphasize the individual, as is common in most Western cultures (Eisenberg et al., 2015). One study of mother–child dyads in Japan and the United States found that the Japanese mothers of 4-year-old children tended to emphasize mutuality in their interactions, stressing the relationship (e.g., "This puzzle is difficult for us. Let's see if we can solve it."). In contrast, the U.S. mothers tended to emphasize individuality (e.g., "This puzzle is hard for you, isn't it? Let's see you try again.") (Dennis, Cole, Zahn-Waxler, & Mizuta, 2002). These different styles influence how children display empathy, whether as sharing another's emotion or simply understanding another's emotion.

These cultural differences extend to children's reasons for sharing. When Filipino and American fifth graders were presented with hypothetical scenarios that required them to determine how resources should be shared, both the Filipino and American children preferred equal division of the resources regardless of merit or need (Carson & Banuazizi, 2008). However, the children offered different explanations of their choices. U.S. children emphasized that the characters in the scenario preformed equally and therefore deserved equal amounts of the resources, reflecting U.S. culture's emphasis on individuality and merit. Filipino children, on the other hand, tended to be more concerned with the interpersonal and emotional consequences of an unequal distribution, in line with their culture's emphasis on the collective and the importance of interpersonal relationships (Carson & Banuazizi, 2008). Norms and expectations for children vary dramatically with culture, as illustrated in the Lives in Context feature.

LIVES IN CONTEXT: CULTURAL CONTEXT

Children's Participation in Household Work

Societies differ along many dimensions that have implications for children's socioemotional development. Children in collectivist societies that foster group orientation tend to show more other-oriented behavior than do children in more individualist societies. For example, Israeli children from kibbutz communities, which typically emphasize communal living and high cooperation to meet shared goals, have been shown to display more prosocial, cooperative, and otherwise other-oriented behaviors compared with their urban-dwelling peers.

In a groundbreaking study of children in six cultures, Whiting and Whiting (1975) observed that children's prosocial behavior varied with culture. Children in Mexico and the Philippines were more often observed offering help and support (e.g., by offering food, toys, and information) than were children in Okinawa, India, and the United States. Children in rural Kenya, the most traditional society of those studied, demonstrated the most pronounced levels of helpful behavior. The differences in prosocial behavior are influenced by cultural and contextual differences, such as the tendency for people to live together in extended families. The most prosocial children lived in cultures where the female role was important to the family's economic well-being, and children were assigned chores and responsibilities at an early age and were expected to contribute to the family's well-being.

Cultures vary widely in the degree to which children are expected to aid the family by participating in household and economic work—activities that offer opportunities for prosocial development (Lancy, 2008; Ochs & Izquierdo, 2009). Although Western industrialized societies tend to conceptualize childhood as an innocent, playful period free from labor, children in many societies participate extensively in household and economic labor. In these societies, adults naturally scale down responsibilities to match children's developmental stage and capabilities (Lancy, 2008). Participation in work often begins by children simply being present and watching adults' activities (Paradise & Rogoff, 2009). Young children and toddlers might perform simple tasks in close proximity to adults and later on their own (Ochs & Izquierdo, 2009). For example, Tarong parents express strong expectations for prosocial behavior and expect children as young as 3 or 4 years of age to contribute to household and wage labor by performing simple tasks such as pushing a baby's hammock or helping string tobacco leaves (Guzman, Do, & Kok, 2014). Alternatively, children might engage in work alongside adults but be expected to produce less, as in the case of Mikea children in Madagascar who forage for edibles as part of adult groups but are not expected to accomplish the same level of success (Tucker & Young, 2005). Compared with able-bodied adults, children might gather younger tubers that are easier to dig for or gather and carry fewer nuts and fruits. Older Tarong children, at 6 or 7 years of age, are expected to participate in more sophisticated ways, such as tending to animals or helping to gather weeds, prepare food, or clean the home (Guzman et al., 2014). From these examples, we can see that cultures and economic environments vary dramatically in their expectations for children's behavior, with implications for their development.

What Do You Think?

1. In your view, what role does participation in household work or responsibility play in prosocial development?
2. To what extent and in what ways should parents and other adults require children to participate in household work? What expectations are appropriate, in your view? ●

Aggression

Although their capacities for empathy and prosocial responses increase, young children commonly show **aggressive behavior**, behavior that harms or violates the rights of others. Most infants and children engage in some physically aggressive behaviors—hitting, biting, or kicking—some of the time (Tremblay et al., 2004). Some aggression is normal and not an indicator of poor adjustment.

The most common form of aggression seen in infancy and early childhood is **instrumental aggression**, aggression used to achieve a goal, such as obtaining a toy. Instrumental aggression is often displayed as physical aggression (Hay, Hurst, Waters, & Chadwick, 2011). For example, a child who grabs a crayon out of another child's hand is often motivated to obtain the crayon, not to hurt the other child. In addition to toys, preschool children often battle over space ("I was sitting there!"). Instrumental aggression increases from toddlerhood into early childhood, around age 4, as children begin to play with other children and act in their own interests. Indeed, instrumental aggression usually occurs during play. It is often displayed by sociable and confident preschoolers, suggesting that it is a normal aspect of development.

By ages 4 to 5, most children develop the self-control to resist aggressive impulses and the language skills to express their needs. Now physical aggression declines and verbal aggression becomes more frequent (Eisner & Malti, 2015). **Verbal aggression** is a form of relational aggression, intended to harm others' social relationships (Ostrov & Godleski, 2010). In preschool and elementary school, relational aggression often takes the form of name calling and excluding peers from play (Pellegrini & Roseth, 2006).

Most children learn to inhibit aggressive impulses; however, a small minority of children show high levels of aggression (e.g., repeated hitting, kicking, biting) that increase during childhood (Tremblay, 2014). Young children who show high levels of aggression are more likely to have experienced coercive parenting, family dysfunction, and low income; they are also more likely to have mothers with a history of antisocial behavior and early childbearing (Wang, Christ, Mills-Koonce, Garrett-Peters, & Cox, 2013). Children who do not develop the impulse control and self-management skills to inhibit their aggressive responses may continue and escalate aggressive behavior over the childhood years and show poor social and academic outcomes during the school age years and beyond (Gower, Lingras, Mathieson, Kawabata, & Crick, 2014).

THINKING IN CONTEXT 9.2

1. How might the contexts in which young children are embedded, such as family, school, and neighborhood, influence the development of empathy and prosocial behavior? What factors might contribute to aggressive behavior?
2. How might peer interactions contribute to young children's understanding and regulation of emotions?
3. Recall from Chapter 1 that children are active contributors to their own development. In what ways might young children's interactions with their contexts contribute to the development of prosocial and antisocial behavior?

FAMILIES

The relationship that develops between parents and children has a tremendous influence on children's social and emotional development. Parenting style is the emotional climate of the parent–child relationship—the degree of warmth, support, and boundaries that parents provide. Parenting style influences parents' efficacy, their relationship with their children, and their children's development.

Parenting Styles

Parenting styles are displayed as enduring sets of parenting behaviors that occur across situations to form childrearing climates. These behaviors combine warmth and acceptance with limits and rule setting in various degrees. In a classic series of studies, Diana Baumrind (1971, 2013) examined 103 preschoolers and their families through interviews, home observations, and other measures. She identified several parenting styles and their effects on children (see Table 9.1).

Authoritarian Parenting

In Baumrind's classification, parents who use an **authoritarian parenting style** emphasize behavioral control and obedience over warmth. Children are to conform to parental rules without question, simply "because I say so." Violations are often accompanied by forceful punishment, such as yelling, threatening, or spanking. Parents with an authoritarian style are less supportive and warm and more detached, perhaps even appearing cold.

Children raised by authoritarian parents tend to be withdrawn, mistrustful, anxious, and angry (Rose, Roman, Mwaba, & Ismail, 2018). They show more behavioral problems than other children, both as preschoolers and as adolescents (Baumrind, Larzelere, & Owens, 2010). Children reared in authoritarian homes tend to be disruptive in their interactions with peers and react with hostility in response to frustrating peer interactions (Gagnon et al., 2013). A recent meta-analysis of over 1,400 studies concluded that harsh parenting and psychological control show the strongest associations with behavior problems in childhood and adolescence (Pinquart, 2017). Moreover, parents and children influence each other. As parenting becomes more harsh, children tend to display more behavior problems, which may increase negative interactions with parents. The Lives in Context feature examines the effects of one type of negative parent–child interaction, physical punishment, on children.

Permissive Parenting

Parents who adopt a **permissive parenting style** are warm and accepting, even indulgent. They emphasize self-expression and have few rules and behavioral expectations for their children. When rules are set, they often are not enforced or are enforced inconsistently. Parents with a permissive parenting style often allow children to monitor their own behavior. Autonomy is not granted

TABLE 9.1

Parenting Styles

PARENTING STYLE	WARMTH	CONTROL
Authoritative	High	Firm, consistent, coupled with discussion
Authoritarian	Low	High, emphasizing control and punishment without discussion or explanation
Permissive	High	Low
Indifferent	Low	Low

LIVES IN CONTEXT: FAMILY AND PEER CONTEXT

Physical Punishment

Time-out removes the child from overstimulating situations and stops inappropriate behaviors. It is effective when accompanied by explanation and a warm parent–child relationship.
Cynthia Dopkin/Science Source

Physical punishment—spanking—is against the law in over 50 countries (Grogan-Kaylor, Ma, & Graham-Bermann, 2018), yet hotly contested in many countries. For example, parents in many countries within Asia, Africa, the Middle East, and North and South America report that spanking is acceptable, appropriate, and sometimes necessary (Hicks-Pass, 2009; Oveisi et al., 2010). In the United States, the majority of adults report that they were spanked as children without harm, and 80% of a sample of U.S. parents report spanking their young children (Gershoff, 2013). Why the controversy on spanking if it occurs in most cultures?

Research suggests that physical punishment tends to increase compliance only temporarily. Furthermore, physical punishment is associated with behavior problems at ages 1 and 3 and continued behavior problems at age 5 (Choe, Olson, & Sameroff, 2013; Lee, Altschul, & Gershoff, 2013; Mendez, Durtschi, Neppl, & Stith, 2016). Physical punishment is also damaging to the parent–child relationship. When a parent loses self-control and yells, screams, or hits a child, the child may feel helpless, become fearful of the parent, avoid him or her, and become passive. Parental use of spanking is associated with internalizing problems (such as anxiety and depression), externalizing problems (such as aggression), impaired cognitive ability, and low self-esteem in childhood and adolescence and mental health problems and antisocial behavior in adulthood (Balan, Dobrean, Roman, & Balazsi, 2017; Coley, Kull, & Carrano, 2014; Gershoff & Grogan-Kaylor, 2016).

Moreover, physical punishment can foster the very behavior that parents seek to stop. Parents often punish children for aggressive behavior, yet physical punishment models the use of aggression as an effective way of resolving conflict and other problems, teaching children that might makes right (D'Souza, Russell, Wood, Signal, & Elder, 2016). In one recent study, parents who reported using physical discipline were nearly three times as likely to report aggressive behaviors like hitting and kicking in their young children than parents who did not use physical discipline (Thompson et al., 2017). In addition,

(Continued)

(Continued)

physical punishment tends to become less effective with repeated use and as children grow older (AAP Committee on Psychosocial Aspects of Child and Family Health, 1998). For example, the use of spanking is impractical with teenagers.

What can parents do about their children's undesirable behavior? While physical punishment is not generally effective, noncorporal punishment can be effective, in small doses and within specific contexts. Running into the street or touching a hot stove, for example, are behaviors that are dangerous to children or to others. These behaviors must be stopped immediately to prevent injury. To be effective, punishment should occur immediately after the dangerous behavior, be applied consistently, and be clearly connected to the behavior. The purpose of such punishment is to keep the child from engaging in the dangerous behavior, to make him or her comply but not to feel guilt. Time-out, which entails removing a child from the situation and from social contact for a short period of time, is often effective in reducing inappropriate behavior (Morawska & Sanders, 2011). Effective punishment is administered calmly, privately, and within the context of a warm parent–child relationship, and it is accompanied by an explanation so that the child understands the reason for the punishment (Baumrind, 2013).

What Do You Think?

1. Under what circumstances do you think it is appropriate to punish a child? Identify two examples of nonphysical punishment.
2. Considering operant conditioning (review learning theory in Chapter 1), how might you use reinforcement to shape a child's behavior?
3. Suppose that a child receives a punishment, such as time-out, yet continues to repeat the behavior that was punished. Considering operant conditioning, why might the child continue to engage in the forbidden behavior? ●

gradually and in developmentally appropriate ways in permissive households. Instead, children are permitted to make their own decisions at an early age, often before they are able. For example, children may decide their own bedtime or monitor their own screen time. Many children lack the self-regulation capacities to appropriately limit their activity. Preschoolers raised by permissive parents tend to be more socioemotionally immature and show little self-control and self-regulatory capacity compared with their peers (Piotrowski, Lapierre, & Linebarger, 2013). They often tend to be impulsive, rebellious, and bossy, and they show less task persistence, low levels of school achievement, and more behavior problems (Jewell, Krohn, Scott, Carlton, & Meinz, 2008). In short, a permissive parenting style interferes with the development of self-regulatory skills that are needed to develop academic and behavioral competence in childhood and adolescence (Hoeve, Dubas, Gerris, van der Laan, & Smeenk, 2011).

Uninvolved Parenting

Parents with an **uninvolved parenting style** focus on their own needs rather than those of their children. Parents who are under stress, emotionally detached, or depressed often lack time or energy to devote to their children, putting them at risk for an uninvolved parenting style (Baumrind, 2012). Uninvolved parents provide little support or warmth, exert little control, and fail to recognize their children's need for affection and direction. At the extreme, uninvolved parenting is neglectful and a form of child maltreatment. Uninvolved parenting can have negative consequences for all forms of children's development—cognitive, emotional, social, and even physical. For example, young children reared in neglectful homes show less knowledge about emotions than do children raised with other parenting styles (Sullivan, Carmody, & Lewis, 2010).

Authoritative Parenting

The most positive developmental outcomes are associated with what Baumrind termed the **authoritative parenting style.** Authoritative parents are warm and sensitive to children's needs but also are firm in their expectations that children conform to appropriate standards of behavior. While exerting firm, reasonable control, they engage their children in discussions about standards and grant them developmentally appropriate levels of autonomy, permitting decision making that is appropriate to the children's abilities (Baumrind, 2013). When a rule is violated, authoritative parents explain what the children did wrong and impose limited, developmentally appropriate punishments that are closely connected to the misdeed. Authoritative parents value and foster children's individuality. They encourage their children to have their own interests, opinions, and decisions, but ultimately, they control the children's behavior.

Children of authoritative parents display confidence, higher self-esteem, social skills, curiosity, and high academic achievement, and they score higher on measures of executive functioning; these positive effects persist throughout childhood into adolescence (Fay-Stammbach, Hawes, & Meredith,

2014; Sosic-Vasic et al., 2017). Parents in a given household often share a common parenting style, but when they do not, the presence of authoritative parenting in at least one parent buffers the negative outcomes associated with the other style and predicts positive adjustment (Hoeve et al., 2011; McKinney & Renk, 2011).

Discipline

Discipline refers to the methods a parent uses to teach and socialize children toward acceptable behavior. Learning theory can account for the effect of parents' discipline strategies on children's behavior. Specifically, the consequences of a child's behavior, whether it is reinforced or punished, influence the child's future behavior.

Children learn best when they are reinforced for good behavior. Recall from learning theory that the child must view the reinforcement as rewarding in order for it to be effective in encouraging his or her behavior. Reinforcement can be tangible, such as money or candy, or intangible, such as attention or a smile. Effective reinforcement is administered consistently when the desired behavior occurs. Eventually the reinforcement becomes internalized by the child and the behavior itself becomes reinforcing. The child comes to associate the behavior with pleasurable feelings and the behavior itself eventually produces a positive feeling, sense of accomplishment.

Four-year-old Jayden throws blocks at his brother, Harlan. When Harlan cries out to their mother, Sheila, she yells at Jayden and tells him to sit down at the kitchen table while she cooks. Each day Jayden throws blocks or hits Harlan and then is told to sit at the kitchen table. Sometimes he plays nicely with his brother, but soon he returns to his usual behavior of throwing blocks. Sheila becomes frustrated because Jayden continues to torment his brother despite being punished for his misbehavior each day. What is happening here? Frequently parents ignore good behavior but scold bad behavior, drawing attention to it and inadvertently reinforcing it. Jayden's goes unnoticed. Sheila does not reinforce his good behavior by complimenting his attempts to play nicely with Harlan. But Jayden gets attention when he misbehaves, not only by having Sheila notice his behavior, but also by being seated in the kitchen close to her. Sheila believes she is punishing his misbehavior, but requiring him to sit at the table while she cooks may be making Jayden more likely to misbehave.

The strategies parents use to control children's behavior vary with the parent and child's personalities, the age of the child, the parent–child relationship, and cultural customs and expectations (Grusec & Goodnow, 1994). Parents' perceptions of their own efficacy in carrying out strategies influence which strategies they choose. Parents' strategies also vary with the situation. For example, swift enforcement of parental control may be appropriate in situations when children are in danger, whereas discipline that relies on communication may be used to teach sharing (Grusec & Goodnow, 1994).

Inductive discipline, methods that use reasoning, are effective alternatives to spanking in changing a child's behavior (AAP Committee on Psychosocial Aspects of Child and Family Health, 1998). Examples of inductive methods include helping children find and use words to express their feelings. Another inductive method is to provide children with choices (e.g., peas or carrots), permitting them to feel some control over the situation and be empowered. Parents who use inductive techniques model effective conflict resolution and help children to become aware of the consequences of their actions. Inductive methods are very effective in helping children to internalize rules and standards (Choe et al., 2013). Children are more likely to comply with rules that they understand. One study of 54 African American kindergarten-aged children from an inner city found that those whose mothers used inductive reasoning were more likely to see that hurting other people is not just a question of breaking rules but is wrong, as compared with children whose mothers reported taking away privileges (Jagers, Bingham, & Hans, 1996). Authoritative parents apply inductive discipline.

The American Academy of Pediatrics recommends that parents positively reinforce good behavior and, when necessary, discourage inappropriate behavior with the use of time-out, removal of privileges, and verbal reprimands aimed at the behavior rather than the child (AAP Committee on Psychosocial Aspects of Child and Family Health, 1998). Researchers advise that punishment be used sparingly, as it often directs children's attention to themselves and their own feelings rather than to how their behavior affects others, increasing children's emphasis on themselves rather than empathetic and prosocial motives (McCord, 1996). Overall, developmental professionals agree that discipline that relies on a warm parent–child relationship, clear expectations, communication, and limit-setting is most effective in modifying children's behavior.

Culture, Context, and Parenting

The strategies parents use to control children's behavior vary with the parent's and child's personalities, the age of the child, the parent–child relationship, and cultural customs and expectations. One concern that researchers have regarding

Parents rearing children in challenging contexts sometimes pair vigilant, strict control with warmth for positive childrearing outcomes.
©iStockphoto.com/kalig

discussions of discipline is that there is not just one effective way to parent. Instead, there are many cultural variations in parenting, and the effectiveness of disciplinary techniques may differ by cultural context (Cauce, 2008).

Expectations for behavior as well as methods of discipline vary with culture. North American parents permit and encourage children to express emotions, including anger, while Japanese parents encourage children to refrain from displaying strong emotions. In one cross-cultural experiment, U.S. preschoolers exposed to situations designed to elicit stress and anger demonstrated more aggressive behaviors than did Japanese children (Zahn-Waxler, Friedman, Cole, Mizuta, & Hiruma, 1996). In comparison with North American mothers, Japanese mothers are more likely to use reasoning, empathy, and disapproval to discipline their children. Such techniques are effective for Japanese mothers because of the strong mother–child relationship and collectivist values that are prevalent in Japan, illustrating the importance of relationships in that culture (Rothbaum, Pott, Azuma, Miyake, & Weisz, 2000).

Chinese parents tend to describe their parenting as relatively controlling and as not emphasizing individuality and choice (Chao, 2001). They are directive and view exerting control as a way of teaching children self-control and encouraging high achievement (Huntsinger, Jose, & Larson, 1998). Yet most Chinese parents couple the emphasis on control with warmth (Xu et al., 2005). The combination of warmth and control is linked with cognitive and social competence. As in North American samples, however, excessive control without warmth is associated with depression, social difficulties, and poor academic achievement in Chinese children (Cheah, Leung, Tahseen, & Schultz, 2009).

Is strict control always harmful to North American children? Researchers have identified a disciplinary style common in African American families that combines strict parental control with affection (Tamis-LeMonda, Briggs, McClowry, & Snow, 2009a). This style stresses obedience and views strict control as important in helping children develop self-control and attentiveness. African American parents who use controlling strategies tend to raise children who are more cognitively mature and socially competent than their peers who are being raised in other ways. This difference is particularly apparent in children reared in low-income homes and communities, where vigilant, strict parenting enhances children's safety (Weis & Toolis, 2010). Whereas physical discipline is associated with behavioral problems in European American children, it appears to protect some African American children from conduct problems in adolescence (Lansford, Deater-Deckard, Dodge, Bates, & Pettit, 2004). The warmth and affection buffer some of the negative consequences of strictness (McLoyd & Smith, 2002; Stacks, Oshio, Gerard, & Roe, 2009). Children's perception of parental discipline and intention is important in determining its effect. Children evaluate parental behavior in light of their culture and the emotional tone of the relationship. African American and low-income children reared in homes with strict but warm parents often see this style of discipline as indicative of concern about their well-being (Y.-E. Lee et al., 2016).

In the United States, it is often difficult to disentangle the effects of culture and neighborhood context on parenting behaviors because African American families are disproportionately represented in disadvantaged neighborhoods. Does strict discipline embody cultural beliefs about parenting? Or is it a response to raising children in a disadvantaged environment (Murry, Brody, Simons, Cutrona, & Gibbons, 2008)? Parents' perceptions of danger and their own distress influence how they parent (Cuellar, Jones, & Sterrett, 2013). Parenting behaviors, including discipline, must be considered within a cultural and environmental context, as parenting is "not one size fits all" (Sorkhabi, 2005).

Siblings

Over 80% of children have at least one brother or sister (McHale, Updegraff, & Whiteman, 2012). Siblings are an important, yet understudied, context for young children's development. Young children spend a great deal of time with their siblings, often more than with parents. Through interactions with siblings, children practice displaying positive and negative emotions, and sibling relationships are emotionally uninhibited (Aldercotte, White, & Hughes, 2016). Most sibling relationships are characterized by ambivalence, positivity and negativity, because siblings frequently play together but also argue. Siblings provide opportunities to learn about conflict and negotiation.

Sibling relationships vary in quality, and variations are associated with adjustment. Frequent and intense sibling conflict in early childhood is associated with behavior problems later in childhood and adolescence (Pike & Oliver, 2017). In turn, positive relationships with siblings are associated with healthy adjustment, including advanced social skills and good relationships with peers (Hughes, McHarg, & White, 2018).

Positive interactions with siblings and high-quality relationships are associated with advanced social skills. Interactions with siblings offer young children opportunities to understand other people's thoughts and practice taking their perspectives, advancing theory of mind (see Chapter 8) (Devine & Hughes, 2018). The sibling relationship is also a context for informal learning (Howe, Della Porta, Recchia, & Ross, 2016). Children naturally scaffold each other's learning as they play. For example, while playing a game involving cooking, a child might instruct, "Roll the dough like this," and watch as his sibling imitates him. Siblings naturally aid and influence each other's development.

THINKING IN CONTEXT 9.3

1. Consider parenting from a bioecological perspective. Identify microsystem and mesosystem influences on parenting. How do more distant, exosystem, factors influence parents' discipline style and interactions with their children? Identify macrosystem factors that influence parenting.
2. What challenges do parents face in modifying their parenting styles as children grow older?

GENDER STEREOTYPES, GENDER DIFFERENCES, AND GENDER DEVELOPMENT

Many people use the terms sex and gender interchangeably, but to developmental scientists, sex and gender have distinct meanings. Sex is biological and determined by genes—specifically, by the presence of a Y chromosome in the 23rd pair of chromosomes—and is indicated by the genitals. Gender, on the other hand, is determined by socialization and the roles that the individual adopts.

Gender Role Norms and Gender Stereotypes

Most societies have **gender role norms**, normative expectations for males and females that are applied to everyday behavior. Many such norms derive from women's traditional role as child bearer and caregiver (Best & Bush, 2016). Nurturing the young and forming close family bonds requires emotional regulation skills and sensitivity to others. **Expressive traits** such as kindness, creativity, gentleness, and cooperation are key characteristics of the feminine gender role, as are physical traits such as being soft, small, and graceful (Bem, 1974). In contrast, the traditional masculine gender role entails instrumental agency—acting on the world to fulfill the role of provider and protector of the family—as well as physical characteristics such as being strong, powerful, and large. **Instrumental traits** include dominance, independence, and competitiveness. Gender role norms are seen in most cultures. For example, adults in 30 countries generally agree on the instrumental and expressive traits thought to characterize males and females, respectively (Guimond, Chatard, & Lorenzi-Cioldi, 2013; Lockenhoff et al., 2014).

Most people naturally expect that men and women will behave differently according to their society's gender roles. These expectations sometimes reflect **gender stereotypes**, broad generalized judgments of the activities, attitudes, skills, and characteristics deemed appropriate for males or females in a given culture. Gender stereotypes are exaggerated beliefs about what males and females should and should not do. Children show gender stereotypes as early as age 2, and stereotype knowledge increases during the preschool years as children acquire gender role norms, a process called **gender typing** (Liben, Bigler, & Hilliard, 2013). By 5 or 6 years of age, children have extensive knowledge of the activities and interests stereotyped for males and females (Blakemore, Berenbaum, & Liben, 2009). They express this knowledge as rigid rules about the behavior appropriate for boys and girls (Baker, Tisak, & Tisak, 2016). Preschoolers tend to expect males to be independent, forceful, and competitive and females to be warm, nurturing, and expressive (C. L. Martin et al., 2013). They also tend to show positive same-gender and negative other-gender attitudes (Halim et al., 2017).

Stereotypes influence children's preferences and views of their own abilities. For example, by age 6, girls are less likely than boys to believe that members of their gender are "really, really smart." Also at age 6, girls begin to avoid activities said to be for children who are "really, really smart," lump more boys into the "really, really smart" category, and steer themselves away from games intended for the "really, really smart" (Bian, Leslie, & Cimpian, 2017). Gender stereotypes appear in many countries but vary in intensity. For example, in one study of children in 25 countries, high rates of gender stereotyping and stereotyped beliefs were observed in Pakistan, New Zealand, and England, whereas stereotypes were very low in Brazil, Taiwan, Germany, and France (Williams & Best, 1982).

Sex Differences

Despite common views, boys and girls are more alike than different (Leaper, 2013). The largest sex difference is in socioemotional functioning. From an early age, girls are better able to manage and express their emotions than boys. For example, at 6 months of age, males have more difficulty at regulating their emotions in frustrating or ambiguous situations than girls (Weinberg, Tronick, Cohn, & Olson, 1999). In infancy, childhood, and adolescence, girls are more accurate at identifying facial expressions, such as happy or sad, than boys (Thompson & Voyer, 2014). While girls tend to express happiness and sadness more often than boys, boys express more anger (Chaplin & Aldao, 2013). Girls also express shame and guilt, complex emotions that rely on cognitive and social development, more often than boys (Else-Quest, Higgins, Allison, & Morton, 2012).

Gender differences in aggression have been observed as early as 17 months of age, with boys showing more aggression (Hyde, 2014). Beginning at preschool age, boys tend to exhibit more physical and verbal aggression, whereas girls tend to demonstrate more relational aggression—excluding a peer from social activities, withdrawing friendship, spreading rumors, or humiliating the person (Ostrov & Godleski, 2010). Boys and girls also differ in inhibitory control, from as early as 3 months of age (Else-Quest, Hyde, Goldsmith, & Van Hulle, 2006). Differences in activity and the ability to restrain impulses likely play a role in sex differences in aggression. Although intelligence tests show no differences between boys and girls, girls tend to do better at verbal and mathematical computation tasks as well as those requiring fine motor skills (Miller & Halpern, 2014). Boys tend to perform better on a specific type of spatial reasoning task—mental rotation, or the ability to recognize a stimulus that is rotated in space (Hines, 2015). Even as infants, boys are more likely than girls to recognize stimuli that have been rotated (Quinn & Liben, 2014). Yet sex differences are not apparent on other spatial tasks (Hyde, 2016).

In all, as suggested earlier, there are few differences between boys and girls. In addition, there is a great deal of variability within each sex—more so than between the sexes. In other words, there is a greater number and variety of differences among boys and among girls than between boys and girls.

Biological Influences on Gender Role Development

Because most cultures have similar gender roles, sex differences may be a function of biology. Biological explanations point to the role of evolution and look to differences in biological structures, especially the brain, as well as hormones as contributors to sex differences in psychological and behavioral functioning (Hines, 2015).

From an evolutionary perspective, males adapted to become aggressive and competitive because these traits were advantageous in securing a mate and thereby passing along their genetic inheritance (Côté, 2009). Females became more nurturing, as it was adaptive to care for the young to ensure that their genes survived to be passed along to the next generation. Studies show that most mammalian species demonstrate a preference for same-sex playmates, males are more active and aggressive, and females are more nurturing (de Waal, 1993). These findings suggest that such gender differences in behavior are adaptive across species, including our own.

Gender differences begin at conception with the union of sex chromosomes, either XX (female) or XY (male; recall from Chapter 2). Genetic information on the Y chromosome leads to the formation of testes. The subsequent production of testosterone results in the formation of the male genitals and reproductive system. Estrogens in the absence of testosterone lead to the formation of the female reproductive system (Sadler, 2018). In animals, testosterone produced prenatally influences neural survival and neural connectivity, leading to subtle sex differences in brain structure and function (Nugent & McCarthy, 2011).

Hormonal differences have effects on behavior as well. Animal and human studies have demonstrated that exposure to relatively high levels of testosterone promotes male-typical behavior development. When females are exposed to male sex hormones prenatally (e.g., in the case of congenital adrenal hyperplasia, a genetic disorder that causes excess androgen production beginning prenatally), they show more active play and fewer caregiving activities in early childhood compared with their female peers (Hines et al., 2016). Testosterone is linked with aggression. Higher levels of testosterone, prenatally and after birth, can account for boys' tendency to be more aggressive than girls. Hormonally influenced differences in behavioral styles then influence play styles; children choose to play with children who have similar styles, resulting in a preference for same-sex playmates (Berenbaum, 2018). In this way, biological factors influence the behaviors that are associated with gender roles. Other explanations for gender role development rely on understanding children's thinking, as described in the next section.

Cognitive Influences on Gender Role Development

From the cognitive-developmental perspective, children's understanding of gender is constructed in the same manner as their understanding of the world: by interacting with people and things and thinking about their experiences. Infants as young as 3 to 4 months of age distinguish between female and male faces, as shown by habituation and preferential looking studies (Quinn, Yahr, Kuhn, Slater, & Pascalis, 2002). By 10 months of age, infants are able to form stereotypic associations between faces of women and men and gender-typed objects (scarf, hammer), suggesting that they have the capacity to form primitive stereotypes (Levy & Haaf, 1994). Most children develop the ability to label gender groups and to use gender labels in their speech between 18 and 24 months (Martin & Ruble, 2010).

Gender identity, awareness of whether one is a boy or a girl, occurs at about age 2 (Bussey, 2013). Once children label themselves as male or female, they classify the world around them, as well as their own behaviors, according to those labels (e.g., like me, not like me) (Kohlberg, 1966). In this way, children construct their own understandings of what it means to be a boy or a girl and thereby begin to acquire gender roles. By 2 to 2½ years of age, once children have established gender identity, they show more interest in gender-appropriate toys (e.g., dolls for girls, cars for boys) and a preference for playing with children of their own sex (Zosuls et al., 2009).

Recently, increased attention has been drawn to **transgender** children—those who do not identify with their sex assigned at birth but instead adopt an opposite-sex identity. Although there is much to learn, a recent study compared transgender and **cisgender** (children who identify with their sex assigned at birth), gender-conforming children on cognitive measures of gender preferences (Olson, Key, & Eaton, 2015). Transgender children showed a clear preference for peers and objects endorsed by peers who shared their expressed gender, as well as an explicit and implicit identity that aligned with their expressed gender. Their implicit preferences were indistinguishable from those of other children, when matched by gender identity. The prevalence of transgender identity is not well documented, but it appears to be rare. About .5% to 1% of the population of adults identify themselves as transgender (Conron, Scott, Stowell, & Landers, 2012; Gates, 2011), although the true figure may be higher. The vast majority of children adopt a gender identity that is congruent with their biological sex. The Applying Developmental Science feature provides additional information about transgender children and adolescents.

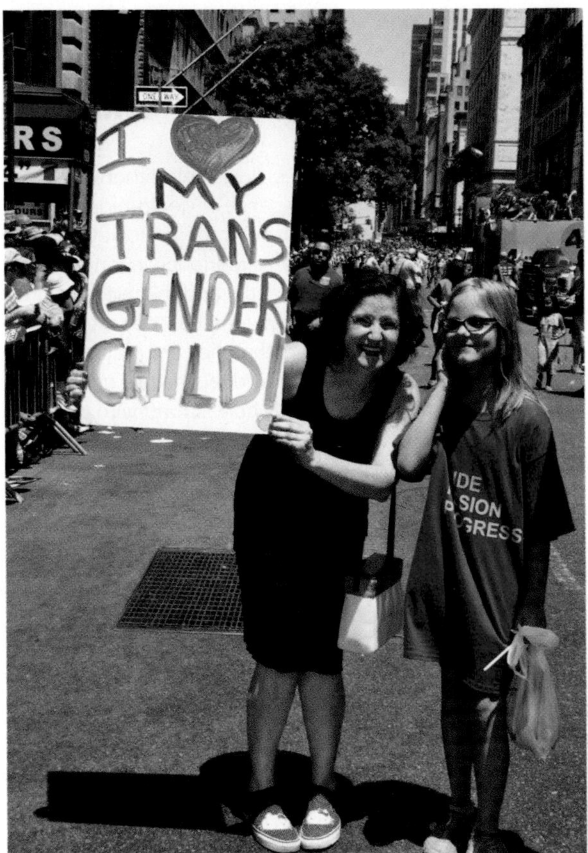

Support from parents and family can help transgender children.
LEE SNIDER/Alamy Stock Photo

Between ages 3 and 5, children show an increase in stereotype knowledge, evaluate their own gender more positively, and tend to show more rigid sex-typed behaviors (Halim et al., 2013). For example, in one study of diverse children from Mexican, Chinese, Dominican, and African American ethnic backgrounds, gender stereotypes held at age 4 predicted positive attitudes about their gender and more gender-stereotyped behavior at age 5 (Halim, Ruble, Tamis-LeMonda, Shrout, & Amodio, 2017).

Three-year-old children associate gender with external behaviors and traits, but they do not yet understand gender as a biological construct. Young children tend to focus on appearance and therefore tend to believe that wearing a dress, for example, can change a child from boy to girl. Only later in childhood, when children come to understand Piagetian conservation tasks, do they come to believe that a boy will always be a boy, even if he grows long hair and wears a skirt, and that a girl will remain a girl no matter what she wears or which activities she chooses.

APPLYING DEVELOPMENTAL SCIENCE

Transgender Children

By 2 years of age, most children label themselves as boy or girl. This early sense of gender identity tends to intensify with development. However, a small minority of children experience incongruence between their gender identity and their sex assigned at birth. That is, some boys feel that they are really girls, and some girls feel that they are really boys. Although transgender individuals have a gender identity that does not fully correspond with their sex assigned at birth, their gender development is quite similar to that of other children. For example, like gender-typical children, transgender children show preferences for peers, toys, and clothing typically associated with their expressed gender, choose stereotypically gendered outfits, and say that they are more similar to children of their expressed gender than to children of the other gender (Fast & Olson, 2018).

Parents, peers, and teachers tend to discourage gender nonconformity in children, especially boys who show interest in girls' activities and toys (Halpern & Perry-Jenkins, 2016; C. L. Martin et al., 2013). Transgender children resist such pressure, insisting on their true gender identity. While in the past parents may have ignored children's wishes or outright prohibited them from adopting a transgender identity, some parents today adopt a different approach, permitting their children to "socially transition" to the gender identity that feels right to them. This type of social transitioning is reversible and nonmedical. It may entail changing the pronoun used to describe a child, the child's name, and the child's appearance, including hair and clothing. In this way, children are raised according to their gender identity rather than their biological sex.

Whether or not parents should support children's desire to live presenting as their gender identity is hotly debated (Steensma & Cohen-Kettenis, 2011; Zucker, Wood, Singh, & Bradley, 2012). The few studies that have examined transgender children have found that children who have not socially transitioned reported increased rates of anxiety and depression, with more than 50% of older children in some samples falling in the clinical range of internalizing symptoms (Ryan, Russell, Huebner, Diaz, & Sanchez, 2010; Simons, Schrager, Clark, Belzer, & Olson, 2013). In contrast, studies of transitioned transgender children suggest levels of depression and anxiety similar to gender-consistent children and overall norms (Olson, Durwood, DeMeules, & McLaughlin, 2016). There is growing evidence that social support is linked to better mental health outcomes among transgender adolescents and adults (Durwood, McLaughlin, & Olson, 2017). These findings suggest that social transitions in children, indicating parents' affirmation and support, may be associated with positive mental health in transgender children (Fuss, Auer, & Briken, 2015; Ryan et al., 2010). A sense of acceptance and the ability to live as one's perceived gender may buffer stresses that tend to accompany gender nonconformity.

In contrast to social transition, biological transition is a medical process. It typically involves both developmental changes, induced by means of hormone therapy, and permanent changes to the external genitals, accomplished by means of gender reassignment surgery. Older children who identify as transgender, in consultation with their parents and pediatrician, may take medication to delay the onset of puberty and the reproductive maturation that goes with it. Postponing puberty provides children with additional time to socially transition, decide whether biological transition is the right decision for them, and make a mature, informed choice.

What Do You Think?

1. What challenges might children with an incongruent gender identity face, and how might these challenges change with age?
2. What advice do you give to a parent who is concerned about gender-atypical behavior, such as a boy who is interested in playing with dolls or a girl who wishes to play with trucks and dress like a superhero? ●

Gender constancy refers to the child's understanding that gender does not change—that he or she will always be the same regardless of appearance, activities, or attitudes (Kohlberg, 1966). Initially, gender constancy may further gender typing, as children become more aware of and pay more attention to gender norms (Arthur, Bigler, & Ruble, 2009). For example, the more positively children view their own gender and the more they understand that gender categories remain stable over time, the more likely girls are to insist on wearing dresses, and the more likely boys are to refuse to wear anything with a hint of femininity (Halim et al., 2014). When children develop positive other-gender attitudes, they tend to show less gender rigidity and less gender-stereotyped behavior (Halim et al., 2017). A full understanding of gender constancy includes the awareness that a person's sex is a biological characteristic, which typically occurs by about 7 years of age (Halim, 2016). Children with a more mature grasp of gender constancy may be less afraid to engage in cross-gender-typed activities than they had been previously because they understand that despite their engagement in cross-gender-typed activities, their gender will still remain the same (Halim et al., 2017).

Once children develop the ability to label their sex, they begin to form a **gender schema**, a concept or a mental structure that organizes gender-related information and embodies their understanding of what it means to be a male or female. Researchers have proposed a gender schema theory, a cognitive explanation of gender role development that emphasizes cognitive processing and environmental influences (Canevello, 2016; Weisgram, 2016). A child's gender schema becomes an organizing principle, and children notice more differences between males and females, such as preferred clothes, toys, and activities. Children also notice that their culture classifies males and females as different and encompassing different roles. Children then use their gender schemas as guides for their behavior and attitudes, and gender typing occurs. For example, when given gender-neutral toys, children first try to figure out whether they are boys' or girls' toys before deciding whether to play with them (Miller, Trautner, & Ruble, 2006). When told that an attractive toy is for the opposite sex, children will avoid playing with it and expect same-sex peers to avoid it as well. Young children play with peers who engage in similar levels of gender-typed activities (e.g., playing dress-up, playing with tools) and, over time, engage in increasingly similar levels of gender-typed activities, contributing to sex segregation in children's play groups (C. L. Martin et al., 2013).

Gender schemas are such an important organizing principle that they can influence children's memory. For example, preschool children tend to notice and recall information that is consistent with their gender schemas (Liben et al., 2013). Children who see others behaving in gender-inconsistent ways, such as a boy baking cookies or a girl playing with toy trucks, often will misrecall the event, distorting it in ways that are gender consistent. They may not even recall gender-inconsistent information (Signorella & Liben, 1984). Not until around age 8 do children notice and recall information that contradicts their gender schemas. Yet even elementary school children have been shown to misrecall gender-inconsistent story information (Frawley, 2008). Clearly, children's knowledge and beliefs about gender and gender roles influence their own gender role and behavior. However, the world around the child also holds implications for gender role development. Terms that pertain to gender role development are summarized in Table 9.2.

Contextual Influences on Gender Role Development

A contextual approach to understanding gender development emphasizes social learning and the influence of the sociocultural context in which children are raised. According to this approach, gender typing occurs through socialization, through children's interpretation of the world around them, influenced by parents, peers, teachers, and culture. Social learning theory emphasizes the importance of models in acquiring gender-typical behavior (Bandura & Bussey, 2004). Children observe models—typically the same-sex parent, but also peers, other adults, and even characters in stories and television programs. They use models as guides to their own behavior, resulting in gender-typed behavior. Feedback from others serves as reinforcement. Sometimes parents or other adults will directly teach a child about

TABLE 9.2

Gender Role Development: Terms

TERM	DEFINITION
Gender differences	Psychological or behavioral differences between males and females
Gender constancy	The understanding that gender remains the same throughout life, despite superficial changes in appearance or attitude
Gender identity	A person's awareness of being a male or female
Gender role	The behaviors and attitudes deemed appropriate for a given gender
Gender schema	A mental structure that organizes gender-related information
Gender stability	The understanding that gender generally does not change over time; however, superficial changes in appearance might bring a change in gender
Gender typing	The process of acquiring gender roles

gender-appropriate behavior or provide positive reinforcement for behaving in sex-consistent ways: Boys get approval for building bridges and running fast, whereas girls get approval for preparing a make-believe meal or keeping a pretty dress neat. Each of these contextual factors also influences the cognitive components of gender, such as gender schema.

Parents

Boys and girls have different social experiences from birth (Martin & Ruble, 2010). Parents perceive sons and daughters differently and have different expectations for them. For example, parents often describe competition, achievement, and activity as important for sons and warmth, politeness, and closely supervised activities as important for daughters. Many parents encourage their children to play with gender-appropriate toys. Boys tend to receive toys that emphasize action and competition, such as cars, trains, and sports equipment, and girls tend to receive toys that focus on cooperation, nurturance, and physical attractiveness, such as baby dolls, Easy-Bake Ovens, and play makeup (Hanish et al., 2013). In one study, 3- and 5-year-old children were asked to identify "girl toys" and "boy toys" and then asked to predict parents' reactions to their preferences about gender-specific toys and behaviors (Freeman, 2007). Children predicted that parents would approve of their playing with gender-stereotyped toys and disapprove of choices to play with cross-gender toys.

Gender-consistent behavior is socially regulated through approval. Parents tend to encourage boys' independent play, demands for attention, and even attempts to take toys from other children, whereas parents tend to direct girls' play, provide assistance, refer to emotions, and encourage girls to participate in household tasks (Hines, 2015). Girls are often reinforced for behavior emphasizing closeness and dependency. Children internalize expectations about gender-related behavior and tend to feel good about themselves when their behavior is in accord with their internal standards and experience negative feelings when their behavior is not (Leaper, 2013).

Boys tend to be more strongly gender socialized than girls. Parents, especially fathers, tend to show more discomfort with sex-atypical behavior in boys (e.g., playing with dolls) than girls (e.g., playing with trucks) (Basow, 2008). Fathers play an important role in influencing gender typing. A study of preschool children in England and Hungary revealed that children whose fathers did more housework and child care tended to demonstrate less awareness of gender stereotypes and less gender-typed play (Turner & Gervai, 1995). Dutch fathers with strong stereotypical gender role attitudes tended to use more physical control strategies with their 3-year-old boys than with girls, whereas fathers with counter-stereotypical

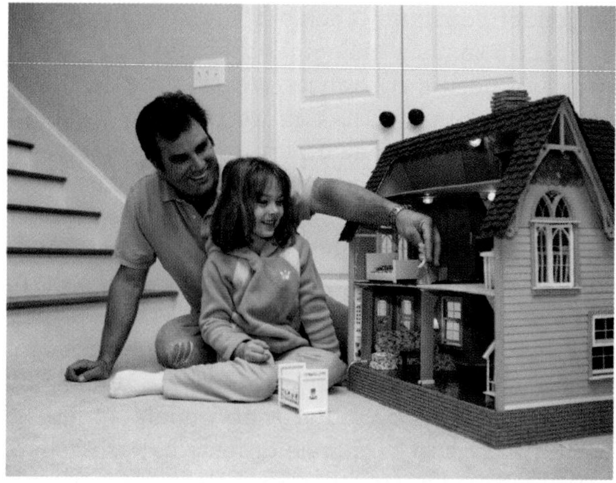

Parents often have different expectations for boys and girls and encourage their children to play with gender-appropriate toys.
©iStockphoto.com/gregoryelang

attitudes used more physical control with girls; this differential treatment predicted gender differences in aggression 1 year later (Endendijk et al., 2017).

Peers

The peer group also serves as a powerful influence on gender typing in young children. As early as age 3, peers reinforce gender-typed behavior with praise, imitation, or participation. They criticize cross-gender activities and show more disapproval of boys who engage in gender-inappropriate behavior than of girls who are tomboys (Hanish et al., 2013). Among older children, gender-atypical behavior is associated with exclusion and peer victimization (Zosuls, Andrews, Martin, England, & Field, 2016).

Girls and boys show different play styles. Boys use more commands, threats, and force; girls use more gentle tactics, such as persuasion, acceptance, and verbal requests, which are effective with other girls but ignored by boys (Leaper, 2013). Girls, therefore, may find interacting with boys unpleasant, as boys pay little attention to their attempts at interaction and are generally nonresponsive. Differences in play styles influence boys' and girls' choices of play partners and contribute to sex segregation (Martin, Fabes, Hanish, Leonard, & Dinella, 2011). Peer and parental attitudes tend to be similar and reinforce each other, as both are part of a larger sociocultural system of socialization agents (Bandura & Bussey, 2004).

Media

Children's television and G-rated movies tend to depict the world as gender stereotyped, and these media depictions can promote gender-typed behavior in children. Typical children's media display more male than female characters, with male characters in action roles such as officers or soldiers in the military and female characters as more likely to have domestic roles and be in romantic relationships (England, Descartes, & Collier-Meek, 2011). Television commercials advertising toys tend to illustrate only one gender or the other, depending on the toy (Kahlenberg & Hein, 2010). In support of television's influence on gender typing, several Canadian towns that gained access to television for the first time showed a marked increase in children's gender-stereotyped attitudes 2 years after gaining access to television (Kimball, 1986).

One study of 4- and 5-year-old children found that nearly all had viewed media featuring Disney princess heroines, and two-thirds of girls played with Disney princess toys at least once a week as compared with only 4% of the boys. Engagement with Disney princess toys and media was associated with more female gender-stereotypical behavior in girls 1 year later, even after controlling for initial levels of gender-stereotypical behavior (Coyne, Linder, Rasmussen, Nelson, & Birkbeck, 2016). Overall, there have been traditionally more male than female characters in children's literature, and female characters often need help while male characters tend to provide help (Evans, 1998). Coloring books display similar patterns, with more male than female characters, and male characters are depicted as older, stronger, more powerful, and more active than female characters (e.g., as superheroes vs. princesses) (Fitzpatrick & McPherson, 2010). Even cereal boxes depict twice as many male as female characters (Black, Marola, Littman, Chrisler, & Neace, 2009).

Culture

The larger culture and its many aspects also influence gender typing, as most cultures emphasize gender differences. Some societies closely link activities and dress with gender; girls and boys may attend sex-segregated schools, wear contrasting types of school uniforms, and never interact (Beal, 1994). Societies vary in the types of behavior that are considered appropriate for men and women. For example, farming is a task for women in many parts of the world, but in North America, it is men who are traditionally in charge of farming tasks. The exact behaviors may vary across societies, but all societies have values regarding gender-appropriate behavior for males and females, and all societies transmit these values to young children.

Children's television and movies tend to depict the world as gender stereotyped.
Album/Alamy Stock Photo

Reducing Gender Stereotyping

We have seen that young children are immersed in a gendered world. They quickly learn and internalize messages about gender as they interact with people and things around them. Parents who wish to reduce gender stereotyping in their children must begin by examining their own views and gender-related behavior. Parents can model gender-neutral attitudes and beliefs by engaging in nontraditional activities, such as men baking cookies and women taking out the garbage. Parents can encourage mixed gender play dates that include a broad range of activities.

Teachers can organize classrooms to be less gender salient, such as by encouraging all children to take turns playing in the kitchen, block area, and sandbox. Some preschools are committed to creating "gender-neutral" classroom environments in which teachers typically refrain from using gendered language and actively work to counteract gender stereotypes. Children in these settings typically show more gender-neutral behaviors and attitudes. For example, one study examined preschool children in Sweden, a country with relatively egalitarian gender attitudes (Shutts, Kenward, Falk, Ivegran, & Fawcett, 2017). Some of the children attended a traditional preschool and others attended a gender-neutral preschool with policies and practices aimed at actively creating a gender-neutral environment. Although all Swedish schools are required by law to aim for gender equality in classrooms, the gender-neutral preschool included additional practices to reduce the salience of gender. For example, teachers avoided using gendered language (including the use of a gender-neutral pronoun and not "boy" or "girl"), modifying stories and songs to counteract rather than reinforce traditional gender roles and family structures, and avoiding some behaviors traditionally directed at one gender (e.g., commenting on the attractiveness of girls' clothes). Children exposed to the gender-neutral preschool setting showed less in-gender favoritism ("Girls are better than boys!") and less stereotyping. They were less likely to limit their play to same-sex peers.

In addition to encouraging children to befriend boys and girls and play with a wide range of toys, including nontraditional toys, parents and teachers can help children recognize gender stereotyping and sexism in the world around them. Parents and teachers

TABLE 9.3

Theories of Gender Role Development

THEORY	EXPLANATION
Biological	Describes gender role development in evolutionary and biological terms. Males adapted to become more aggressive and competitive and females more nurturing as it ensured that their genes were passed to the next generation. Gender differences may also be explained by subtle differences in brain structure as well as differences in hormones.
Cognitive	The emergence of gender identity leads children to classify the world around them according to gender labels, and they begin to show more interest in gender-appropriate toys. Children show an increase in stereotype knowledge, evaluate their own gender more positively, and demonstrate rigidity of gender-related beliefs. Gender constancy furthers gender typing as children attend more to norms of their sex. According to gender schema theory, once children can label their sex, their gender schema forms and becomes an organizing principle. Children notice differences between males and females in preferred clothes, toys, and activities, as well as how their culture classifies males and females as different and encompassing different roles. Children then use their gender schemas as guides for their behavior and attitudes, and gender typing occurs.
Contextual	Contextual explanations rely on social learning and the influence of the sociocultural context in which children are raised. Males and females have different social experiences from birth. Gender typing occurs through socialization, through a child's interpretation of the world around him or her, and modeling and reinforcement from parents, peers, and teachers.

can point out and correct stereotypes. Opportunities arise daily. For example, when 4-year-old Aaron insisted, "Only boys can be doctors!" his father replied, "Is that true? Remember Dr. Lopes? She's a woman—and a doctor. And remember the nurse who gave you a shot, Aaron?" "He's a man." "Yes—and he's a nurse. Men can be nurses and women can be doctors." Young children encounter messages about gender daily. Each of these instances is an opportunity to reduce stereotyping and encourage children to be more flexible and tolerant. Table 9.3 summarizes theoretical explanations of gender role development.

THINKING IN CONTEXT 9.4

1. Recall from Chapter 1 that development is influenced by nature and nurture. In what ways is gender role development influenced by nature? Nurture? In your view, does either have greater influence?
2. How might contextual factors contribute to the sex differences that we see in socioemotional development? How might parents, teachers, peers, and environments influence sex differences?
3. Provide advice to parents and teachers on how to reduce gender stereotyping in young children. Consider the home, school, and peer environment.

PLAY AND PEER RELATIONSHIPS IN EARLY CHILDHOOD

In early childhood, the social world expands to include peers. "Let's be pirates!" declared Ramon. "Okay. Here's my sword," Billy said as he held up the plastic Wiffle ball bat. Ramon and Billy ran to the playhouse at the end of the yard. "There's the boat. Let's get them!" Billy cried as he chased after his sister. Billy explained, "You're on the boat, and we're pirates coming to get you." "I'll run!" she said. Their grandmother watched from the porch as the children created stories, acted them out together, and climbed on every available surface. Play offers important learning opportunities for young children. Play contributes to physical, cognitive, emotional, and social development. Children learn how to use their muscles, control their bodies, coordinate their senses, and learn new motor skills. Play helps children to perspective take and understand other children's viewpoints, manage challenging situations, regulate emotions, practice creativity, learn to express their thoughts and desires, and problem solve (Coplan & Arbeau, 2009).

Play and Development

Running, jumping, and balancing games help young children develop their motor skills and strengthen their muscles and bones. Organized sports are increasingly accessible to young children. For example, gymnastics lessons are often available to children as young as 3. Five-year-old children may play soccer or softball. These adult-directed activities offer children opportunities to develop physical skills and learn how to be part of a team. However, child-directed play in which children play freely without direction from adults is especially important for cognitive and social development.

Cognitive and Emotional Development

Children learn though play. Piaget (1962) explained play as an important way in which children of all ages contribute to their own knowledge by actively exploring the world around them. Early play is simple, such as a toddler's bouncing a ball and then chasing it across the room. Simple forms of dramatic play begin in toddlerhood, when a

LIVES IN CONTEXT: FAMILY AND PEER CONTEXT

Young Children's Understanding of Peers With Disabilities

Children learn through physical and social play with other children. Sometimes disabilities may interfere with children's ability to play with their peers. How do young children understand physical and cognitive disabilities in peers?

Young children can identify physical and sensory disabilities in peers; however, they are less likely to identify intellectual and behavioral disabilities (Diamond & Kensinger, 2002; Yu, Ostrosky, & Fowler, 2012). In one study, preschool children were able to identify children who did not "walk as well" or "talk as well" as the other children but they were much less likely to identify children who had "difficulty behaving well" (Yu, Ostrosky, & Fowler, 2015). In this study, typically developing children generally were less likely to play with children they identified as having a disability; however, their play preferences depended on whether they liked the child. That is, typically developing children were more likely to play with a classmate with a disability if they rated him or her positively, regardless of their identification of the classmate as having a disability, suggesting that likability is more influential in determining play preferences (Yu et al., 2015). However, young children with disabilities often experience difficulties developing friendships and they have limited social interactions with peers (Guralnick, Hammond, Connor, & Neville, 2006). As a result, young children with disabilities may be less accepted, and often rejected, by their typically developing peers (Odom et al., 2006; Yu et al., 2015).

Preschool children's decisions to include a peer with a disability in a play activity are influenced by the play context. For example, young children's preference ratings for a hypothetical child with a physical disability were more positive when the activity required modest physical skills (e.g., eating lunch) than when more complicated motor skills were required (e.g., throwing a ball) (Diamond & Tu, 2009; Nabors & Keyes, 1995).

Theory of mind plays a role in determining how children understand their peers. For example, children with well-developed theory-of-mind skills were more likely to say that they would include a child with a physical disability. Their inclusion decisions were also influenced by information about the other child's previous play experiences. They were more likely to choose or play with a peer with a disability when the peer had more experience with the activity than they did (Diamond & Hong, 2010).

Generally, young children who have more interactions with disabled peers, such as through inclusive child care and classroom settings, have more positive attitudes toward peers with disabilities (Dyson, 2005; Yu et al., 2012). However, including children with disabilities in inclusive classrooms is unlikely to spontaneously enhance interactions between children with and without disabilities (Diamond & Hong, 2010; Diamond & Tu, 2009). Activities or programs such as reading and discussing children's books about disabilities, arranging inclusive cooperative learning group activities, or assisting parents in the promotion of children's positive attitude development can help children understand and accept their classmates with disabilities (Dorsey, Mouzourou, Park, Ostrosky, & Favazza, 2016; Ostrosky, Mouzourou, Dorsey, Favazza, & Leboeuf, 2015).

What Do You Think?

What actions and activities might a teacher use to help preschool children understand and accept their peers with disabilities? ●

2-year-old feeds or punishes a stuffed animal (Frahsek, Mack, Mack, Pfalz-Blezinger, & Knopf, 2010). In early childhood, children develop more sophisticated ways of interacting with play partners. Their cognitive capacities (such as their growing theory of mind) and emotional capacities (their ability to regulate their emotions) enable them to join peer groups more easily, manage conflict more effectively, and select and keep playmates. Playing with other children may push them to learn to take the perspective of others and develop less egocentric ways of thinking (Piaget, 1962). Moreover, successfully playing with peers requires that young children learn to manage their emotions and carefully control their behavior to match their peers and the setting (Coplan & Arbeau, 2009). The Lives in Context feature examines young children's understanding of peers with disabilities.

Young children's emerging cognitive abilities make certain types of play possible. For example, in make-believe or **representational play**, children often pretend that one object is something else. Understanding that an object, such as a block, can also symbolize something else, such as a make-believe telephone, is a cognitive feat that prepares children for learning symbols such as letters and numbers (Berk & Winsler, 1995; Vygotsky, 1976). Following the "rules" of pretend play, that a block is a telephone, gives children practice in controlling their impulses and regulating their own behavior. Preschool children can observe the rules in simple games, such as Simon Says, matching games, and games with spinners and dice (Rubin, Bukowski, & Bowker, 2015a), opening new opportunities for playing with other children and for social development.

Social Development and Early Friendships

Advances in social development in early childhood enable children to include others in their play. Social play develops over a series of steps that take place over the ages of 2 through 5 (Parten, 1932). Toddlers' play is characterized by *nonsocial activity*, including inactivity, onlooker behavior, and solitary play. *Parallel play* then emerges, in which children play alongside each other but do not interact. Play shifts to include social interaction in *associative play*, in which children play alongside each other but exchange toys and talk about each other's activities. Finally, *cooperative play* represents the most advanced form of play because children play together and work toward a common goal, such as building a bridge or engaging in make-believe play. These forms of play emerge in order but are not a strict developmental sequence because later behaviors do not replace earlier ones (Yaoying & Xu, 2010). For example, solitary play declines with age but may take up to a third of kindergarteners' playtime (Dyer & Moneta, 2006).

Children engage in solitary play for a variety of reasons. Some activities, such as coloring, are best completed alone. Sometimes young children play alone to have time for self-reflection (Katz & Buchholz, 1999). Solitary play may afford opportunities to regulate themselves or control their environment (Luckey & Fabes, 2005). Over the preschool years, social play becomes more common, and children have more playmates, longer play episodes, and more varied contacts (Pellegrini, 2013).

The earliest friendships emerge through children's play. Most young children can name a friend (Quinn & Hennessy, 2010). Young children generally understand friends as companions who live nearby and share toys and expectations for play. Friends are a source of amusement and excitement. Friends share with each other, imitate each other, and initiate social interactions with each other (van Hoogdalem, Singer, Eek, & Heesbeen, 2013). As children enter preschool, they spend more time interacting with peers, especially same-sex peers. Although researchers emphasize the proximity and play dimensions of young children's friendships, some research suggests that preschool friendships can be characterized by emotional qualities such as support and closeness, and high-quality friendships are more likely to endure over the school year (Sebanc, Kearns, Hernandez, & Galvin, 2007). Through peer interactions, young children gain social competence, communication, and emotional regulation skills that permit them to have more complicated—and rewarding—relationships in later childhood and adolescence.

Sociodramatic Play

Children act out themes and stories in their play. Simple forms of dramatic play begin in toddlerhood, when a 2-year-old feeds or punishes a stuffed animal (Frahsek et al., 2010). With advances in reasoning and opportunities to interact with other children, the most advanced type of play, **sociodramatic play**, emerges. In sociodramatic play, children interact with other children, taking on roles and acting out stories (Lillard, 2015). They imitate people and experiences they have had or observed. Representational play is part of sociodramatic play as children make believe that they are adults, animals, or superheroes, for example, and incorporate pretend objects into their play. Sociodramatic play is social, involving two or more children, and it is interactive, requiring children to talk with each other as they act out their stories. It emerges in early childhood and becomes more frequent and more complex from ages 3 to 6, often with intricate storylines (Rubin et al., 2015a).

By pretending to be mothers, astronauts, cartoon characters, and other persons, children learn how to explain their ideas and emotions and develop a sense of self-concept as they differentiate themselves from the roles they play (Coplan & Arbeau, 2009). Practicing being sad, angry, or afraid in pretend scenarios helps children develop emotional control (Goldstein & Lerner, 2018). Both boys and girls engage in sociodramatic play, with girls engaging in more such play than boys. Sociodramatic play offers important opportunities for development as children learn through social interactions. Children model higher-level thinking and interaction skills, scaffold less skilled peers, and help them to reach their potential (Vygotsky, 1978). Sociodramatic play helps children explore social rules and conventions, promotes language skills, and is associated with social competence (Gioia & Tobin, 2010; Newton & Jenvey, 2011).

Rough-and-tumble play, which includes running, climbing, chasing, jumping, and play fighting, is seen around the world.
©iStockphoto.com/yellowsarah

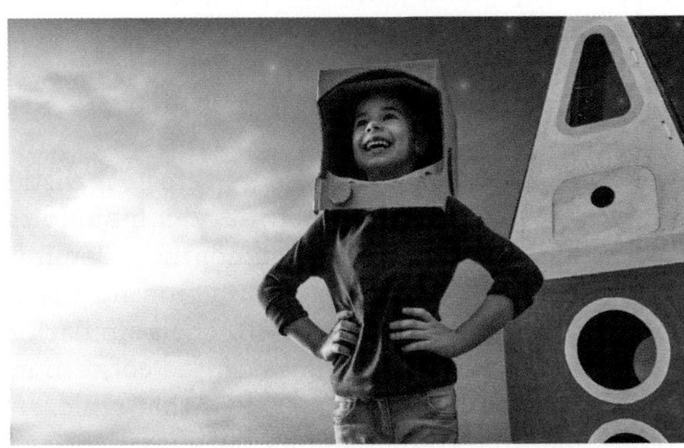

This child is pretending to be an astronaut. She is engaged in sociodramatic play and is learning to act out a role.
©iStockphoto.com/Choreograph

Rough-and-Tumble Play

Some sociodramatic play is accompanied by **rough-and-tumble play**, characterized by vigorous physical activity such as running, climbing, chasing, jumping, and play fighting. Children's rough-and-tumble play is seen around the world and can be distinguished from aggression by the presence of a play face, smiling, and laughing (Pellegrini, 2013). Rough-and-tumble play serves developmental purposes. It is carefully orchestrated and requires self-control, emotional regulation, and social skills. Children learn how to assert themselves, interact with other children, and engage in physical play without hurting other children (Ginsburg, 2007). Rough-and-tumble play exercises children's gross motor skills and helps them to develop muscle strength and control. Research with animals has shown that rough-and-tumble play elicits positive affect that buffers the effects of stress, suggesting that it promotes resilience (Burgdorf, Kroes, & Moskal, 2017).

Both boys and girls engage in rough-and-tumble play, but boys do so at much higher rates. For example, in one observation of preschool children, about 80% of the instances of rough-and-tumble play occurred in boys (Tannock, 2011). It is estimated that preschool children engage in rough-and-tumble play in 5% of play in the preschool period, rising to about 10% in late childhood and falling to about 4% in adolescence (Pellegrini, 2013).

Rough-and-tumble play often accompanies sociodramatic play. Many children engage in superhero play, pretending to be media characters with extraordinary abilities, including strength, the ability to fly, or power to transform themselves into other beings. Children act out scenarios, running, jumping, and chasing. They take turns pretending to be "bad guys" and "good guys" (Frost, Wortham, & Reifel, 2012). Similar to other forms of sociodramatic play, superhero play promotes children's emotional and social development. Children pretend to be powerful characters and pretend to experience different emotions, advancing their understanding of and ability to regulate their emotions. Superhero play promotes friendships between children as they share their common interests and cooperate with each other.

Pretend Playmates

"You stay here, and I'll get the cookies," Katie told her friend Madison. "Does Madison want cookies too?" asked Mommy. "Of course!" replied Katie as she placed two cookies at a place setting in front of an empty chair. **Imaginary companions** or friends are common in early childhood, as early as ages 2 to 3, and occur in about 40% of young children (Taylor, Shawber, & Mannering, 2009). According to parents' reports, there is no clear triggering event that marks the emergence of most imaginary companions (Taylor et al., 2009). Children who experience adversity, such as those in foster care, are no more or less likely to report imaginary friends (Aguiar, Mottweilier, Taylor, & Fisher, 2017). Children appear to come up with them on their own. Imaginary companions often represent extensions of real people known to the child, especially those whom the child admires or characters from stories, television, or movies. Imaginary companions are usually human, although they may take the form of animals, aliens, and monsters (Gleason, Sebanc, & Hartup, 2000). The sense of what an invisible friend looks like is stable and can be retained for years. Imaginary companions may be a marker for creativity. Children who create imaginary companions are more likely to report vivid imagery and elaborate storylines in daydreams, dreams, and pretend games (Bouldin, 2006; Trionfi & Reese, 2009).

Relationships with imaginary friends appear to resemble those with real friends and provide similar benefits, especially companionship (Gleason & Kalpidou, 2014). Children create realistic relationships with their imaginary companions that include imagining pretend conflicts, feeling angry with their companion, and finding them unavailable to play (Taylor, 1999). Their similarity with real friends has sometimes caused concern in parents and professionals who fear that children create imaginary companions because they are lonely and have no playmates. However, research suggests that children with pretend friends are particularly sociable by nature and do not differ from other children in terms of the number of playmates or peer acceptance (Gleason & Kalpidou, 2014). By interacting with imaginary companions, children may practice social interactions, social roles, and emotions (Gleason, 2017). In fact, children with imaginary companions are better at communicating with peers and show more advanced theory of mind and understanding of emotion than their peers (Giménez-Dasí, Pons, & Bender, 2016; Roby & Kidd, 2008). One study of 5-year-olds found that those with imaginary friends were better able to understand and talk about mental characteristics in actual friends (Davis, Meins, & Fernyhough, 2014). Perhaps imaginary companions and the mental gymnastics that create and sustain them indicate psychosocial health rather than deficits.

Imaginary friends are common in early childhood and are indicative of a child's creativity and imagination.
Kansas City Star/Tribune News Service/Getty Images

Culture and Play

Although children around the world play, peer activities take different forms in different cultures. Children in collectivist societies tend to play games that emphasize cooperation. For example, children in India often engage in sociodramatic play that involves acting in unison coupled with close physical contact. In a game called *bhajtto*, for instance, the children imaginatively enact a script about going to the market, pretending to cut and share a vegetable, and touching each other's elbows and hands (Roopnarine, Hossain, Gill, & Brophy, 1994). In contrast, children from Western cultures that tend to emphasize the rights of the individual are inclined to play competitive games such as Follow the Leader, Hide and Seek, and Duck, Duck, Goose! Play, like other aspects of development, is shaped by the context in which it occurs.

Children's play varies with contextual circumstances, such as the amount of household work that is common for children in a given culture, the availability of toys, and parental encouragement of play. The amount of household work expected of children and adults' encouragement for play is linked with children's styles of play (Gaskins, 2014). For example, children of the Nyansongo community of Kenya help with household and agricultural work as well as child and animal care (Edwards, 2000). Parents tend to discourage outside play to minimize aggression with neighbors and they do not stimulate children's play by joining or making suggestions. Children, however, tended to combine play with work and play with kin. For example, when boys were herding cattle and goats in the lineage pastures, they played tag and created hurdles out of sticks. The children engaged in little role play, likely because they had real babies to play with and adult work to do.

In contrast, young children in Juxtlahuaca, Mexico, have much more unstructured time

(Edwards, 2000). Although adults generally do not stimulate play, they do not discourage it. Children's work entails running for adults, but they spend much of their time in the courtyard playing simple games such as tag and ball. Children, especially girls, tend to engage in role play, pretending to tend house, sew, and make tortillas. Boys tend to spin tops, or play with toy cars on roads they create with mud.

As expectations for work decline and support for play increases, more sophisticated forms of play become common. For example, parents in Taira, Okinawa, tend to be heavily involved in physical work but their young children are seldom given chores and are permitted to wander and play in the courtyards (Edwards, 2000). The children attend a community nursery in the morning where they are taught turn-taking and other cooperative skills that are useful in play. Older children supervise younger ones as they play in large groups. Children play rule-based games, such as marbles. They draw in the sand, construct houses of bamboo sticks, and dig. Taira children also engage in a great deal of sociodramatic play including house, animal care, and robber and ghost themes. Children's play varies with contextual opportunities to play and adult supports for play.

THINKING IN CONTEXT 9.5

1. "Five-year-old children can't have friends," argued Janelle. "They're too young." Respond to Janelle. What do we know about young children's relationships and capacities for friendship?
2. How do social settings contribute to children's social development and relationships? What kinds of settings might promote social development and the formation of relationships and friendships?

APPLY YOUR KNOWLEDGE

"I want that!" Julissa exclaimed as she kicked a ball out of Daryl's hands. "Hey!" he yelled as the ball hurtled toward his friend, knocking him down. "Are you okay? Don't cry," Daryl told his friend as Julissa chased the ball. Daryl handed his friend a toy truck. "You can play with this," he instructed.

Later that day during snack time the teacher told Daryl to distribute the crackers. He gave each child exactly three crackers. Julissa protested, claiming that girls should get more than boys. "Why?" Daryl asked. "Because girls are better," Julissa answered. When Daryl counted three crackers for Julissa, she announced, "You're not invited to my birthday party!"

After school Daryl told his mother about Julissa's proclamation. "She wasn't very nice, was she?" Daryl's mother asked. "How did that make you feel?" "Bad," he answered. After she gave him a hug, Daryl's mother encouraged him to go play outside with his best friend who lived next door.

1. Compare Julissa's and Daryl's prosocial and aggressive behavior. What is typical for young children?
2. How does children's understanding of sharing change over time?
3. What role do parents play in influencing children's prosocial and aggressive behavior?
4. What advice would you provide Daryl's parents? Julissa's parents?

WANT A BETTER GRADE?

Get the tools you need to sharpen your study skills. **SAGE edge** offers a robust online environment featuring an impressive array of free tools and resources. Access practice quizzes, eFlashcards, video, and multimedia at **edge.sagepub.com/kutherchild1e.** SAGE edge™

KEY TERMS

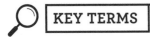

Initiative versus guilt 244
Self-concept 244
Self-esteem 245
Social comparison 245
Empathy 246
Prosocial behavior 246
Instrumental assistance 247
Aggressive behavior 249
Instrumental aggression 249
Verbal aggression 250
Parenting styles 250
Authoritarian parenting style 250

SUMMARY

9.1 Discuss young children's sense of initiative, self-concept, and self-esteem.

Young children's psychosocial task is to develop a sense of initiative over guilt, a sense of purpose and pride in their accomplishments. Young children tend to understand and describe themselves concretely and have unrealistically positive views about their abilities. As children gain life experience and develop cognitively, their self-evaluations become more realistic and correlated with skills, accomplishments, evaluations by others, and other external indicators of competence.

9.2 Discuss the development of emotional regulation and prosocial and aggressive behavior in early childhood.

In early childhood, young children become better able to understand their own and others' emotions. Young preschoolers tend to engage in prosocial behavior for egocentric motives, to gain praise and avoid punishment. With development, their prosocial behavior becomes motivated by empathy and internalized societal perspectives of good behavior. Parents of prosocial children model prosocial behavior and empathetic concern. Aggression, especially instrumental aggression, is common in early childhood. By age 4, most children have developed the self-control to express their desires and to wait for what they want, moving from using physical aggression to expressing desires with words.

9.3 Summarize styles of parenting and discipline and their associations with child outcomes.

Parenting styles are enduring sets of parenting behaviors. Authoritarian parents emphasize control and obedience over warmth and raise children who tend to be withdrawn and anxious, and often react to frustration with hostility. Parents who are permissive are warm and accepting but have few rules and expectations for children, resulting in children who have little self-control and are immature, impulsive, and rebellious. Uninvolved parents provide little support or warmth and little control, with negative consequences for all forms of development. Authoritative parents are warm and sensitive to children's needs but also are firm in their expectations that children conform to appropriate standards of behavior. Children of authoritative parents show the most positive outcomes. Parenting behaviors must be considered within their cultural context, as parenting is not one size fits all.

9.4 Compare biological, cognitive, and contextual theoretical explanations of gender role development.

Gender roles appear in all societies, and young children acquire gender roles early. Biological explanations of gender development cite evolutionary perspectives and look to differences in biological structures and hormones as contributors to sex differences in psychological and behavioral functioning. Cognitive-developmental perspectives on gender development posit that children's understanding of gender is constructed in the same manner as their understanding of the world, by interacting with the world and thinking about their experiences. Cognitive explanations of gender development focus on the gender schema as a guide for their behavior and attitudes. Contextual explanations of gender development emphasize the influence of various contextual settings and socialization.

9.5 Discuss the range of forms play takes in early childhood and its influence on social development and relationships.

Play contributes to all aspects of development. All children play, but the form that play takes varies with development. Types of play include parallel, associative, cooperative, and sociodramatic play. Children's first friends are playmates. Although all children around the world play, peer activities take different forms by culture.

REVIEW QUESTIONS

9.1 What are the benefits of developing a sense of initiative in early childhood?

Contrast self-esteem with self-concept in early childhood.

9.2 What influences children's ability to understand and control their emotions?

What individual and contextual factors influence the development of empathy and prosocial behavior?

What is the most common form of aggression in early childhood, and how does this typically change?

9.3 Discuss characteristics and outcomes associated with four parenting styles.

How do parenting styles differ by culture?

9.4 What are gender role norms, gender stereotyping, and gender typing?

What sex differences exist between boys and girls?

Differentiate gender identity, gender constancy, and gender schema.

What are biological and contextual influences on gender role development?

9.5 Identify types of play in early childhood.

What are the benefits of rough-and-tumble play and sociodramatic play?

How do peer interactions change in early childhood?

Middle Childhood

10 Physical Development in Middle Childhood

"Can you believe I scored another goal?" asked Jacinto. "It's my third so far this season! Coach says I'm on a roll." "I think he's right and I can tell you're excited. I saw your backflip off the field," Jacinto's mother said with a smile. At 8 years old Jacinto can run faster and kick a ball farther than ever before. He has the strength and coordination to perform physical stunts, such as backflips, and he enjoys practicing and testing his skills. In this chapter, we examine the physical changes that children undergo in middle childhood, from about ages 6 to 11.

Learning Objectives

10.1 Discuss patterns of growth and motor development and influences on each in middle childhood.

10.2 Describe processes of brain development in middle childhood and two examples of atypical brain development.

10.3 Identify the benefits of physical activity and common opportunities for physical activity in middle childhood.

Video Activity 10.1: Movement to Increase Engagement

10.4 Summarize common threats to school-age children's health.

Video Activity 10.2: U.S. Peanut Allergy

Chapter Contents

GROWTH AND MOTOR DEVELOPMENT

In middle childhood, physical development is more subtle and continuous than earlier in life. School-age children's bodies gradually get bigger, and they show advances in gross and fine motor development and coordination.

Patterns of Growth

Growth slows considerably in middle childhood. Despite a slower growth rate, though, gradual day-to-day increases in height and weight add up quickly and can seem to sneak up on a child. In middle childhood, children grow 2 to 3 inches and gain 5 to 8 pounds per year, so that the average 10-year-old child weighs about 70 pounds and is about 4½ feet tall. In late childhood, at about age 9, girls begin a period of rapid growth that will continue into adolescence. During this time, girls gain about 10 pounds a year, becoming taller and heavier than same-age boys. As we will discuss in Chapter 13, not until early adolescence, at about age 12, do boys enter a similar period of rapid growth.

As in infancy and early childhood, growth follows a cephalocaudal pattern, proceeding from the head downward (Kliegman et al., 2016). As children grow taller, their body proportions become more like those of adults, slimmer and with longer limbs. Physical growth is often accompanied by **growing pains**, intermittent aches and stiffness in the legs often experienced at night that are caused by the stretching and molding of the muscles to fit the child's growing skeleton (Pavone et al., 2011).

"Marcus is so much smaller than the other children. I thought I'd bring him in for a checkup to be sure that he's okay," started Mr. Petrulli. "Is there anything we can do to boost his growth?" he asks Marcus's pediatrician. Marcus is healthy, eats well, and gets plenty of exercise because he plays several sports. Should Mr. Petrulli be concerned about his son? Just as in other aspects of development, there are many individual differences and variations in growth. Sometimes children's growth lags behind their peers. Growth is regulated by human growth hormone. Growth deficiencies can be caused by too little growth hormone circulating in the blood, known as a **growth hormone deficiency**. When such a deficiency is diagnosed, pediatricians can prescribe synthetic growth hormone injections to encourage growth. Typically children on growth hormone therapy grow about 4 inches or more in the first year and 3 or more inches in the following 2 years, before the rate of growth declines (Toft, 2018). However, growth is contingent on adhering to the treatment schedule (van Dommelen, Koledova, & Wit, 2018). Treatment efficacy and thereby children's growth are compromised when injections are late or skipped altogether. Growth hormones are only prescribed for children with a growth hormone deficiency, not those who are simply shorter than their peers (Grimberg & Allen, 2017). Moreover, growth hormone deficiency is rare, diagnosed in about 1 in 4,000 children (Murray, Dattani, & Clayton, 2016). Marcus, discussed above, will most likely catch up to his peers without medical intervention.

What determines growth? Genes and nutrition interact to influence the rate of children's growth. African American children grow faster and are taller and heavier than White children of the same age. For example, 6-year-old African American girls tend to have greater muscle and bone mass than White or Mexican American girls their age (Ellis, Abrams, & Wong, 1997). Children who enter middle childhood with stunted growth and nutritional deficits often do not catch up (Stein et al., 2010). Instead, stunting often continues and worsens in middle childhood, especially if children remain in the same environments that caused malnourishment (Kitsao-Wekulo et al., 2013). For example, growth stunting in children in sub-Saharan Africa tends to persist and worsen throughout the school years (Senbanjo, Oshikoya, Odusanya, & Njokanma, 2011). Children who enter middle childhood with stunted growth are likely to experience a variety of problems, including cognitive deficits, aggression, behavior problems, and a greater risk of chronic illnesses and other health problems (Hoddinott, Alderman, Behrman, Haddad, & Horton, 2013). Growth stunting, however, is not common in children from developed nations, such as the United States.

Gross Motor Development

Like growth, motor development advances gradually throughout childhood. Motor skills from birth to age 4 predict school-age children's motor abilities (Piek, Dawson, Smith, & Gasson, 2008). During middle childhood, children's body movements become more fluid and coordinated. The gross motor skills developed in early childhood refine and combine into more complex abilities, such as running and turning to dodge a ball, walking heel to toe down the length of a balance beam and turning around, or creating elaborate jump rope routines that include twisting, turning, and hopping (Gabbard, 2018). Increases in body size and strength contribute to advances in motor skills, which are accompanied by advances in flexibility, balance, agility, and strength. Now children can bend their bodies to do a somersault or carry out a dance routine, balance to jump rope, demonstrate agility to run and change speed and direction rapidly, and have the strength to jump higher and throw a ball farther than ever before, as shown in Figure 10.1.

Fine Motor Development

Not only are older children better at running, jumping, and other physical activities than young children, but they also show advances in fine motor control that allow them to develop new interests. School-age children build model cars, braid friendship bracelets, and learn to play musical instruments—all tasks that depend on fine motor control. Fine motor development is particularly important for penmanship. Most 6-year-old children can write the alphabet, their names, and numbers in large print, making strokes with their entire arm. With development, children become able to use their wrists and fingers to write. Uppercase letters are usually mastered first; the lowercase alphabet requires smaller movements of the hand that require much practice. By third grade, most children can write in cursive (writing using flowing strokes and connected letters, sometimes referred to as script). Girls tend to outperform boys in fine motor skills (Junaid & Fellowes, 2006). Success in fine motor skills, particularly writing skills, may influence academic skills. Children who write with ease may be better able to express themselves in writing, for example.

As computers are increasingly used in classrooms, handwriting has become less commonly used in class. Several states have eliminated instruction in cursive writing in favor of keyboard instruction. The U.S. Common Core State Standards (http://www.corestandards.org) for education include handwriting only in kindergarten and first grade. However, many educational experts believe that writing by hand stimulates neural connections that promote reading and cognitive skills (Chemin, 2014). In fact, early instruction in handwriting is associated with academic achievement (Dinehart, 2015).

FIGURE 10.1

Gross Motor Skills

In middle childhood, gross motor skills combine and become more complex, permitting faster running, higher jumping, and greater coordination, such as the ability to balance on a balance beam.
canstock/sergeevspb; canstock/kzenon; Comstock/Stockbyte/Thinkstock

Influences on Growth and Motor Development

Children's motor skills are influenced by body growth and increases in strength. Brain development also plays a role in advancing motor skills. The pruning of unused synapses contributes to increases in motor speed and reaction time so that 11-year-old children tend to respond twice as quickly as 5-year-old children (Gabbard, 2018). Growth of the **cerebellum** (responsible for balance, coordination, and some aspects of emotion and reasoning) and myelination of its connections to the cortex contribute to advances in gross and fine motor skills and speed (Tiemeier et al., 2010). Brain development improves children's ability to inhibit actions, which enables children to carry out more sophisticated motor activities that require the use of one hand while controlling the other, such as throwing a ball, or that require the hands to do different things, such as playing an instrument (Diamond, 2013).

In addition to maturational advances in physical growth and brain development, motor development is also influenced by contextual factors, such as nutrition, opportunities to practice motor skills, and health. For example, children in different contexts have different opportunities to practice motor skills through vigorous physical play and other activities (Laukkanen, Pesola, Havu, Sääkslahti, & Finni, 2014). In addition, there are long-term implications of motor development for other domains of development. In one study, children's motor development and activity at age 8 predicted measures of cognitive development and academic achievement 8 years later, at age 16 (Kantomaa et al., 2013). The ability to physically explore and engage the world influences opportunities to interact and play with other children, and thereby social skills and, potentially, cognitive development.

THINKING IN CONTEXT 10.1

1. Consider your own physical and motor development. What physical activities did you engage in during childhood? How did your abilities change? What factors in the home, school, peer, or neighborhood context have influenced you and your physical skills?
2. Why might a body movement skill, specifically fine motor development, be associated with academic achievement? To what degree should parents encourage the development of fine motor skills? How might they do so?

BRAIN DEVELOPMENT

Brain development proceeds throughout childhood. By about age 6 the brain has reached about 95% of its adult size. Size, however, is deceiving because the brain will undergo substantial development and changes over the coming years.

Normative Brain Development

Brain volume continues to increase throughout middle childhood into early adolescence, especially in the prefrontal cortex (Stiles et al., 2015). Located in the frontal lobe, behind the forehead, the prefrontal cortex is responsible for executive function, the highest level of thinking. Executive function plays a role in attention, working memory, reasoning, planning, and inhibition. Brain development in middle childhood is influenced by a subtle shift in hormones that generally go unnoticed. The Lives in Context feature discusses **adrenarche**, the maturation of the adrenal glands.

With experience and learning, neurons make new connections with other neurons. This increase in synaptic density results in an overall increase in **gray matter**, unmyelinated neurons. Synaptogenesis is responsible for increases in cortical thickness in middle childhood. As in earlier periods of life, unused synapses are pruned, or eliminated. Pruning leads children to show more focused brain activity on cognitive tasks. Rather than show diffuse patterns of activity throughout multiple parts of the brain when considering a problem, the greater connectivity that occurs as a result of pruning contributes to more focused brain activation (Gibb & Kovalchuk, 2018). As children use fewer regions of the brain they free up processing capacity, leading to improvements in working memory (Ullman, Almeida, & Klingberg, 2014). Gray matter tends to increase into early adolescence when a new burst of synaptic pruning occurs. The processes of synaptogenesis and pruning contribute to advances in information processing as new connections form among neurons and unused "clutter" is eliminated (Mills et al., 2016).

Myelination continues throughout middle childhood. Myelinated brain tissue is known as **white matter** because myelin, the fatty substance that coats neurons, is white. Insulating neurons with myelin increases the speed of neural transmission and contributes to more efficient processing of information. As a result, children's performance on cognitive tasks improves (Gibb & Kovalchuk, 2018).

LIVES IN CONTEXT: BIOLOGICAL INFLUENCES

Adrenarche

Somewhere between ages 6 and 8, children experience a shift in hormones that trigger the activation of the adrenal glands, located above the kidneys (Witchel & Topaloglu, 2019). This process is known as adrenarche. As the adrenal glands mature, they begin to secrete androgens, sex hormones that influence psychological and physical development in older children.

Physical changes that accompany adrenarche include the eruption of the first permanent molars, the development of body hair and odor, and more efficient and mature body movements (Auchus & Rainey, 2004; Utriainen, Laakso, Liimatta, Jaaskelainen, & Voutilainen, 2015). Adrenal hormones influence the body's metabolism, leading to an increase in fat needed to cause the onset of puberty, sexual maturation, discussed in Chapter 13. Although some of the body changes that accompany adrenarche are often associated with puberty, the two processes are independent (DelGiudice, 2018).

Adrenal androids influence brain development, prolonging neurogenesis and synaptogenesis, especially in the prefrontal cortex, responsible for executive function, promoting brain plasticity, advancing myelination, and increasing brain volume to near adult levels (Barendse et al., 2018; Utriainen et al., 2015). The presence of adrenal androids in the brain is associated with cognitive changes in attention, working memory, inhibitory control, and decision making (Byrne et al., 2017; Tobiansky, Wallin-Miller, Floresco, Wood, & Soma, 2018).

Adrenarche is also thought to influence interests and behavior. For example, the brain converts adrenal androgens into estrogen and testosterone, feminizing and masculinizing hormones, which may influence the timing of initial sexual attraction (Campbell, 2011; Witchel & Topaloglu, 2019). Many adults recall their first memorable sexual attractions to peers occurring at about age 9 or 10 (Diamond, Bonner, & Dickinson, 2015). At present, we know little about adrenarche; however, researchers are showing increasing interest in understanding how adrenal hormones influence children.

What Do You Think?

1. Why do you think adrenarche is less studied than other biological transitions, like puberty? What are some of the challenges in studying adrenarche?
2. When did you experience the physical and psychological changes of adrenarche? How old were you? Do you think these changes influenced your relationships with family and peers? Why or why not? ●

Myelination increases throughout the brain but, like synaptogenesis, it is especially prominent in the prefrontal cortex. Myelination continues throughout adolescence and into early adulthood.

In addition to the cerebral cortex, the **hippocampus**, a structure located in the inner region of the temporal lobe, undergoes important changes in middle childhood. The hippocampus plays a role in memory, specifically encoding or forming memories (Kolb et al., 2016). The hippocampus develops rapidly in infancy, doubling its size, then slows (Gilmore et al., 2012). This early development is linked with the emergence of episodic memory in late infancy (Bauer, 2007). The hippocampus develops throughout childhood, especially the lower regions, which show reductions in volume with pruning.

Neural connections within the hippocampus and between the hippocampus and other brain structures increase in middle to late childhood (Blankenship, Redcay, Dougherty, & Riggins, 2017). Cross-sectional and longitudinal studies show that white matter tracts, myelinated neural fibers, connecting the hippocampus and parts of the prefrontal and parietal cortex strengthen in middle childhood through adulthood (Lebel & Beaulieu, 2011; Lebel, Walker, Leemans, Phillips, & Beaulieu, 2008). Hippocampal development is linked with advances in episodic memory in childhood (Blankenship et al., 2017; Riggins et al., 2018). With hippocampal development the specificity of memory improves and children become increasingly able to recall highly specific details of events and stimuli (Keresztes, Ngo, Lindenberger, Werkle-Bergner, & Newcombe, 2018). Brain development, therefore, has clear implications for how children think and learn.

Atypical Brain Development

All children experience developmental shifts in gray and white matter. Brain development contributes to advances in cognitive capacities in all children. Some children, however, experience patterns of brain activity and development that can pose challenges to school success, as discussed next.

Attention-Deficit/Hyperactivity Disorder

Attention-deficit/hyperactivity disorder (ADHD) is the most commonly diagnosed disorder in children, diagnosed in about 10% of schoolchildren in the United States (Visser et al., 2014). ADHD is a neurodevelopmental disorder characterized by persistent difficulties with attention and/or hyperactivity/impulsivity that interferes with performance and behavior in school and daily life (Hinshaw, 2018). Difficulty with attention and distractibility may manifest as failing to attend to details, making careless mistakes, not appearing to listen when spoken to directly, not following through on instructions, or difficulty organizing tasks or activities. Impulsivity may include frequent fidgeting, squirming in one's seat, and leaving one's seat in class; often running or climbing in situations where it is not appropriate; talking excessively, often blurting out an answer before a question is completed; and having trouble waiting a turn. While most children show one or two symptoms of inattention or hyperactivity at some point in their development, a diagnosis of ADHD requires consistent display of a minimum number of specific symptoms over a 6-month period, and the symptoms must interfere with behavior in daily life (Hinshaw, 2018).

Children with ADHD have difficulty attending, which may appear as boredom.

ADHD is associated with differences in brain development—specifically, structural abnormalities in parts of the brain responsible for attentional and motor control (Jacobson et al., 2018). ADHD has biological causes and is nearly 80% heritable, or genetic (Aguiar, Eubig, & Schantz, 2010; Schachar, 2014). Research studying identical twins in which only one twin has been diagnosed with ADHD has suggested a role for epigenetics in determining the degree to which genetic propensities are expressed (Chen et al., 2018). Environmental influences on ADHD include premature birth, maternal smoking, drug and alcohol use, lead exposure, and brain injuries (Tarver, Daley, & Sayal, 2014; Thapar et al., 2013).

Stimulant medication is the most common treatment for ADHD. Stimulant medication increases activity in the parts of the brain that are responsible for attention, self-control, and behavior inhibition (Hawk et al., 2018). Behavioral interventions can help children learn strategies to manage impulses and hyperactivity, direct their attention, and monitor their behavior (Evans, Owens, Wymbs, & Ray, 2018).

Specific Learning Disorder

Once referred to as learning disability, the DSM-5 replaced this term with **specific learning disorder (SLD)**. SLDs are diagnosed in children who demonstrate a measurable discrepancy between aptitude and achievement in a particular academic area given their age, intelligence, and amount of schooling (American Psychiatric Association, 2013). Children with SLDs have difficulty with academic achievement despite having normal intelligence and sensory function. An estimated one in five children in the United States has a SLD (Horowitz, Rawe, & Whittaker, 2017). There are several SLDs that influence reading, writing skills, mathematics, and other cognitive skills.

Developmental dyslexia is the most commonly diagnosed SLD. Children with dyslexia tend to be bright children yet they have difficulty reading, with reading achievement below that predicted by age or IQ. Children with dyslexia demonstrate age-inappropriate difficulty in matching letters to sounds and difficulty with word recognition and spelling despite adequate instruction and intelligence and intact sensory abilities (Peterson & Pennington, 2012; Ramus, 2014). Dyslexia is estimated to affect 5% to nearly 18% of the school population, boys and girls equally.

Dyslexia is influenced by genetics (Carrion-Castillo, Franke, & Fisher, 2013). Children with dyslexia have a neurologically based difficulty in processing speech sounds. During speech tasks, they use different regions of the brain than other children, and they often have difficulty recognizing that words consist of small units of sound, strung together and represented visually by letters (Lonigan, 2015; Schurz et al., 2015). Abnormalities in the brain areas responsible for reading can be seen in 11-year-olds with dyslexia but not in young children who have not been exposed to reading, suggesting that the brain abnormalities associated with dyslexia occur after reading commences (Clark et al., 2014). Successful interventions include not only training in phonics but also supporting emerging skills by linking letters, sounds, and words through writing and reading from developmentally appropriate texts (Snowling, 2013).

Another common SLD is **developmental dyscalculia**, a disorder that affects mathematics ability. Children with developmental dyscalculia find it challenging to learn mathematical concepts such as counting, addition, and subtraction and often have a poor understanding of these concepts (Gilmore, McCarthy, & Spelke, 2010; Kucian & von Aster, 2015). In early elementary school, they may use relatively ineffective strategies for solving math problems, such as using their fingers to add large sums. Dyscalculia

Children with developmental dyscalculia show extreme difficulties in mathematics.

is thought to affect about 5% of students and is not well understood (Kaufmann et al., 2013; Rapin, 2016). Research suggests that it is influenced by brain functioning and difficulty with working memory and executive function, specifically visuospatial short-term memory and inhibitory function (Menon, 2016; Watson & Gable, 2013). Children with dyscalculia are usually given intensive practice to help them understand numbers, but there is much to learn about this disorder (Bryant et al., 2016; Fuchs, Malone, Schumacher, Namkung, & Wang, 2017).

Developmental dysgraphia is a disorder that affects writing abilities. It may appear as difficulties with spelling, poor handwriting, and trouble conveying thoughts on paper leading a child to show writing performance below that expected based on the child's class level (Döhla & Heim, 2016). The prevalence for developmental writing disorders is about 7–15% among school-aged children, with boys being more affected than girls (Horowitz et al., 2017). Similar to dyscalculia, children with dysgraphia experience difficulties with working memory and executive function, especially response inhibition; however, fMRI scans suggest different patterns of brain connectivity (Richards et al., 2015).

Writing relies on motor and sensory skills, in addition to cognition. Children with dysgraphia may hold their pencil in a tight awkward grip, show poor body posture while writing, and produce illegible handwriting. Children with dysgraphia may avoid writing tasks, say words out loud or get easily tired while writing, omit words in sentences, and have difficulty organizing and conveying ideas on paper. Teachers may identify children with dysgraphia when they notice a large discrepancy between the child's understanding demonstrated by speech compared with written work.

Teachers and parents can help children with dysgraphia by focusing on the sensory and motor aspects (Berninger & Wolf, 2009). Paper with raised lines can provide a sensory guide to help children learn to write within the lines. Provide children with dysgraphia a range of pens and pencils to sample for comfort. Train children in handwriting, but permit them to use print or cursive letters, whichever is most comfortable. Children with dysgraphia often benefit from the use of a keyboard, which is often easier than manipulating a pen; however, a keyboard should not completely replace handwriting. Like other SLDs, managing dysgraphia often requires learning and practicing skills.

THINKING IN CONTEXT 10.2

1. How would you explain the process of brain development in middle childhood to a third-grade teacher? In your view, what is the most important development of which teachers should be aware?
2. Consider the relevance of contextual factors in understanding disorders such as ADHD and SLDs. Choose a disorder. Identify factors in the home, school, peer, and community context that might influence how children experience the disorder, posing challenges for children as well as supporting them.

PHYSICAL ACTIVITY IN MIDDLE CHILDHOOD

Children's advances in motor skills, strength, and coordination influence their capacity for physical activity and exercise. During the school years, physical activity is often interwoven into outdoor play carried out with peers on playgrounds, school yards, and recreation centers. The Physical Activity Guidelines for Americans recommends that children get 60 minutes or more of moderate to vigorous physical activity daily (U.S. Department of Health and Human Services, 2018b). Much of children's play, such as running and chasing, entails physical activity. Dancing, biking, and brisk walking also count, as does any activity that increases children's heart rate. Gross motor activities that use the large muscles of the body, such as jumping rope, skipping, and playing basketball, also strengthen muscles and bones.

Benefits of Physical Activity for Children

Regular physical activity—moving around and increasing the heart rate—has important health benefits for children. One review of 162 research studies conducted in 31 countries linked moderate physical activity with positive physical, psychological, and cognitive health in children (Poitras et al., 2016). Physical activity improves cardiovascular health, bone and muscle strength, blood pressure, and immune system health and is associated with a lower incidence of obesity (Bangsbo et al., 2016; Caldas & Reilly, 2018).

Physical activity benefits children's bodies, but it also benefits their minds. Aerobic exercise, in particular, has cognitive benefits. A single session of moderate physical activity improves brain function and cognitive performance (Bangsbo et al., 2016). Children who engage in regular physical activity score higher on measures of attention, memory, and executive function, especially planning and cognitive control (Carson et al., 2013; Janssen et al., 2010; van der Niet et al., 2015), and tend to have greater math and reading achievement (Best, 2012; Caldas & Reilly, 2018). In addition, physical activity has been linked to higher levels of self-esteem and lower levels of anxiety, which are associated with higher academic performance in the classroom (Caldas & Reilly, 2018; Liu, Wu, & Ming, 2015). As children feel more competent in their motor skills, they tend to engage in more physical activity (De Meester et al., 2016) and the benefits compound.

Unfortunately, the majority of children and adolescents in the United States do not meet the recommended guidelines of at least 60 minutes of moderate to vigorous physical activity every day. It is estimated that only about one-quarter of children and adolescents age 6 to 15 are at least moderately active for 60 minutes per day on at least 5 days per week, with activity dropping with age such that only 8% of 12- to 15-year-old adolescents meet the guideline (Kann et al., 2014). Physical activity tends to decline beginning in middle childhood, about age 7, and is frequently displaced by screen time (Farooq et al., 2018). The Lives in Context feature examines the effects of screen time on another behavior critical to health: sleep. In addition to reducing screen time, a way of increasing children's physical activity is to provide opportunities to exercise at school.

Physical Education

School-based physical activity most often occurs during physical education (PE) classes. PE is structured and designed to educate students about movement, fitness, and health. On days when elementary school children have PE, they are more active and take more steps, over one-third as many steps and two-thirds as many moderately vigorous steps as on non-PE days (Calvert, Mahar, Flay, & Turner, 2018; Castillo, Clark, Butler, & Racette, 2015). Although boys tend to be more active than girls,

LIVES IN CONTEXT: MEDIA AND TECHNOLOGY

Screen Time and Sleep

We have seen that the more time children spend with screens, the less time they have to engage in physical activity, suggesting that screen time poses risks to children's health. Screen time may also affect children's health through changes in sleep patterns. Insufficient sleep among school-aged children is associated with an increased risk of poor academic performance, obesity, poor health, and depression (Poitras et al., 2016; Wu, Gong, Zou, Li, & Zhang, 2017).

Is screen use related to sleep? A review of 67 studies suggests so. Screen time was inversely associated with sleep quality, specifically, going to bed later and sleeping fewer hours (Hale & Guan, 2015). Screen time interferes with quality sleep for several reasons. First is time displacement; with more time spent in front of screens, children have less time available to sleep. For example, one study of fourth- and seventh-grade students found that greater use of screens was associated with later bedtimes despite having to get up early for school (Falbe et al., 2015). Typically, screen content is engaging and arousing and may include social interaction (via chatting or gaming, for example), which make it difficult for children to relax and fall asleep. Finally, the light emitted by screens may interfere with the production of melatonin, a hormone associated with sleep (Hale & Guan, 2015). Children are more sensitive to light than adults and show greater reductions in melatonin after exposure to light than adults (Turner & Mainster, 2008).

Although the use of all types of screens is negatively associated with sleep quality, use of computers, video games, and mobile phones is more consistently associated with poor sleep than television, perhaps because television watching is more passive and less interactive and stimulating than the use of other screens (Falbe et al., 2015; Hale & Guan, 2015).

How much is too much screen time? Sleep duration declines progressively after 4 to 6 hours of daily screen time for preadolescents (Parent, Sanders, & Forehand, 2016). A recent survey of parents of children ages 6–17 found that each hour devoted to digital screens was associated with 3–8 fewer minutes of nightly sleep and more variations in bedtimes (Przybylski, 2019). However, the researcher concluded that, although screen use is associated with sleep, the observed relation was small, suggesting that other factors, such as family functioning (El-Sheikh & Kelly, 2017), also play a role in influencing the quality of children's sleep.

The American Academy of Pediatrics suggests that parents create a media plan that addresses what type of and how much media is appropriate for a child and to place consistent limits on hours per day of media use as well as types of media used. Children should not sleep with devices, such as a television, computer, or smartphone, in their bedrooms. Reduce stimulation and exposure to light before bedtime by encouraging children to avoid exposure to devices or screens for 1 hour before bedtime. Moreover, parents should designate media-free times and locations together (e.g., family dinner and bedrooms) and spend time interacting media free such as reading, teaching, talking, and playing together.

What Do You Think?

1. In your view, how can parents monitor screen use in children?
2. As a parent, what rules might you set regarding children's use of electronic media? ●

both are more active on PE days. PE interventions designed to increase children's physical activity tend to be successful in increasing physical activity over the school day but are less consistent in influencing out-of-school physical activity (Errisuriz, Golaszewski, Born, & Bartholomew, 2018).

Support for physical education varies. Although over three-quarters of states require elementary school students to enroll in physical education class, only 15% of elementary schools require students to take PE classes on at least 3 days per week for the entire school year (Centers for Disease Control and Prevention, 2014). Over 85% of school districts permit students to substitute other activities, such as dance team, marching band, cheerleading, and after-school sports, for physical education (Centers for Disease Control and Prevention, 2018b). Most experts agree that students need more opportunities to engage in physical activity; however, many schools increasingly devote less time to PE in favor of academic activities. Moreover, when PE is offered, it tends to fall short of the recommended 50% of time spent on moderately vigorous activity. Instead, schoolchildren tend to spend about one-third of PE class engaged in moderately vigorous physical activity (Hollis et al., 2016). Children, however, often have unstructured opportunities for physical activity and play.

Recess

Recess, unstructured play, allocates time for free play and social growth. Children can accrue substantial amounts of physical activity during recess. About two-thirds of school districts require elementary schools to offer students regularly scheduled recess; however, only about 16% require schools to provide daily recess (Centers for Disease Control and Prevention, 2018b).

Children may have few opportunities for free outdoor play outside of school hours for a variety of reasons (Frost et al., 2012). After-school activities reduce the time for free play. Students in urban areas or whose parents work may not be allowed to play outside after school. Recess can provide children with much-needed social interaction as well as physical play.

Recess has benefits for physical, cognitive, and social development (Murray, Ramstetter, Council on School Health, & American Academy of Pediatrics, 2013). Periods of vigorous free play give children opportunities to exercise their bodies. They also offer a needed break from academic activity, helping children regain their focus, fidget less in class, and show better behavior. Unstructured play helps children develop social skills such as learning how to resolve conflicts, cooperate, compete constructively, and make decisions. How children spend recess tends to change over time. Seven-year-olds tend to spend their time running around and playing games, such as ball and chase (Frost et al., 2012). By 11 years, girls tend to talk and pretend as well as engage in jump rope and skipping games; boys tend to play organized games, such as football.

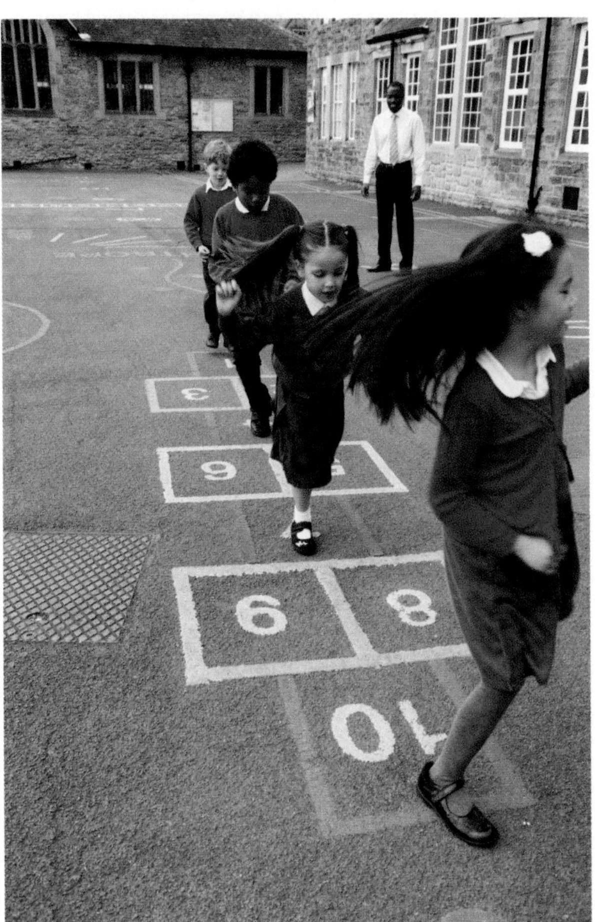

Recess benefits children's physical and social development, but most school districts do not require schools to provide recess daily.
©iStockphoto.com/omgimages

Organized Sports

About one-half of 6- to 12-year-old children reported playing on a team sport at least once a year, while 37% reported playing on a team sport on a regular basis (National Physical Activity Plan Alliance, 2018). Children join team sports like football, basketball, or soccer, or pursue individual sports like track, swimming, or gymnastics. Organized sports offer children opportunities to exercise and develop their motor skills, form peer relationships, and develop self-esteem, motivation, and the ability to work with others to achieve goals. Typically organized by an adult coach, sports usually include regular practice sessions in which children develop strength, endurance, and sport-specific motor skills.

Unfortunately, not all children have access to organized sports. The availability of sports depends on resources, such as fields for football or baseball, and access to playing and safety equipment. Communities and schools with less space and fewer economic resources may not offer children opportunities to participate in organized sports. Children from low-income homes are less likely to participate in organized sports than their peers from high-income homes (National Physical Activity Plan Alliance, 2018). When organized sports teams require that children purchase their own play and safety equipment, children from low socioeconomic status (SES) homes may be unable to participate. Parents who work may be unable to pick children up from after-school practices or may be unable to take children to games. It is perhaps for these reasons that only about a third of children report playing on sports teams regularly.

Sports achievements can be a source of pride and self-esteem (Slutzky & Simpkins, 2009). However, children may feel pressured to win, and criticism from teammates, coaches, parents, and the sidelines at games may sting. The time spent practicing and playing a sport can erode a student's personal time and distract from schoolwork. Children may be unprepared for the competition involved in organized sports. If coaches or parents emphasize winning, children, especially those who are less physically developed or less skilled, may experience stress and poor well-being. Sports participation is also a source of injuries, often from overuse. We discuss injuries later.

THINKING IN CONTEXT 10.3

1. What kinds of physical activities did you engage in as a child? Did you participate in organized sports? How did these activities change over childhood? What are some of the advantages and disadvantages of physical activity and organized sports?
2. Veronica would like to help her 8-year-old daughter become more physically active. What do you suggest? Consider Veronica and her daughter's personalities, interests, and interactions. Next, consider the home context and how it might promote (or hinder) physical activity. What about the world outside? What about her peers, school, and neighborhood? Help Veronica become aware of opportunities and risks for physical activity in each of these settings.

THREATS TO HEALTH IN MIDDLE CHILDHOOD

Middle childhood generally is a healthy time. Colds are less common in middle childhood compared with infancy and early childhood. The typical school-age child experiences five to seven episodes of colds, flu, or viruses per year (Thompson, 2014). About two-thirds of children age 5–11 miss 2 days or less per year because of illness or injury (National Center for Health Statistics, 2017). Less than 4% miss 11 or more days. Childhood mortality declines after infancy and has declined over the last 4 decades (Child Trends, 2018a). As shown in Figure 10.2, the mortality, or death, rate for children age 5 to 14 is about one-half of the rate for infants and young children age 1 to 4 and about twice that of adolescents age 15 to 19.

Unintentional Injury

Unintentional injuries from accidents are the most common cause of death in children and adolescents in the United States, causing about one in five deaths (Dellinger & Gilchrist, 2018; Xu, Murphy, Kochanek, & Bastian, 2016).

Rates for nonfatal injuries vary dramatically with age and are highest in infancy and adolescence (specifically, ages 15–19 and increases into emerging adulthood at ages 20–24) (Centers for Disease Control and Prevention, 2019d). At all ages, males experience more injuries than females, likely due to their higher levels of activity and risk taking. Motor vehicle accidents are the most common source of injury at all ages. Other common types of injuries also vary with age, as shown in Table 10.1. Falls are the most common source of injuries in children age 5 to 9; from age 10 to 14, children are equally likely to be injured by a fall or being struck by an object or person. Overall, children from low SES homes have higher rates of injury and mortality than do

FIGURE 10.2

Death Rates for Children Ages 1 to 19 (per 100,000), 1980–2017

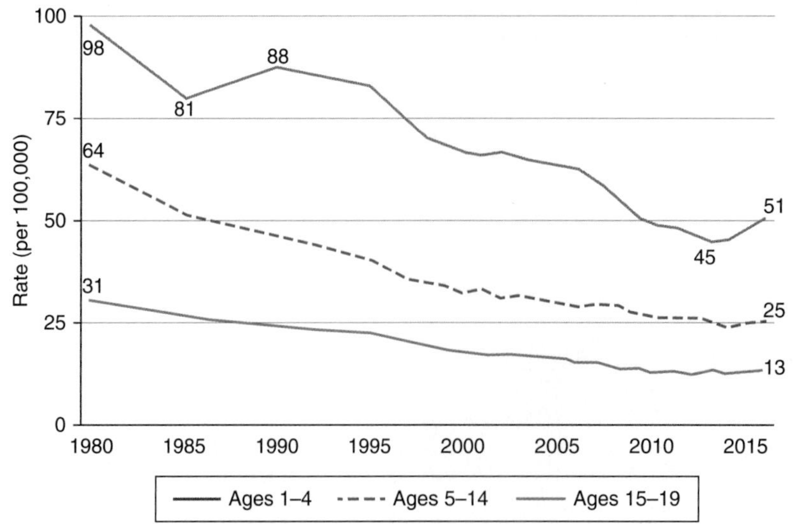

Source: Child Trends (2018a).

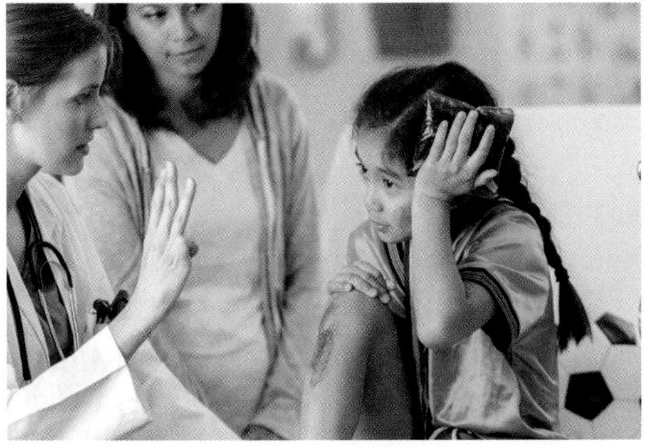

Unintentional injuries, especially falls, are common in middle childhood.
©iStockphoto.com/Steve Debenport

TABLE 10.1

Leading Causes of Nonfatal Injury, United States, 2017

RANK	AGE-GROUPS 1–4	5–9	10–14
1	Unintentional fall	Unintentional fall	Unintentional struck by/ against
2	Unintentional struck by/ against	Unintentional struck by/ against	Unintentional fall
3	Unintentional other bite/sting	Unintentional other bite/sting	Unintentional overexertion
4	Unintentional foreign body	Unintentional cut/pierce	Unintentional cut/pierce
5	Unintentional cut/pierce	Unintentional overexertion	Unintentional unknown/ unspecified

Source: Centers for Disease Control and Prevention (2019d).

other children, because of poor access to health care, poor nutrition, and stressful home and neighborhood environments (Singh & Kogan, 2007; Yuma-Guerrero, Orsi, Lee, & Cubbin, 2018).

About 25% of children in the United States under age 18 are diagnosed with chronic medical conditions that require special health services (National Survey of Children's Health, 2014). The most commonly experienced chronic illness in childhood is asthma.

Asthma

Diego steps off the basketball court, leaning over to catch his breath. Coach Santos asks, "Are you OK? Have you been taking your inhaler?" "Not always, Coach. I've been feeling good," Diego says. Coach Santos replies, "Diego, that's why you should take your medication. You can't stop taking it when you feel good because asthma doesn't go away. You will always have to be aware and take care of yourself."

The most common chronic medical condition among children is **asthma**, a chronic inflammatory disorder of the airways that causes wheezing and coughing (Akinbami, Moorman, Garbe, & Sondik, 2009). Exposure to triggers such as cold weather, exercise, allergens, emotional stress, and infection cause the bronchial tubes to contract and fill with mucus, making it difficult for children to breathe. Asthma affects about 10% of children age 5 to 11 (Centers for Disease Control, 2019c). Figure 10.3 demonstrates ethnic differences in asthma prevalence rates.

Asthma appears to be heritable, but its genetic underpinnings are not well understood (Willis-Owen, Cookson, & Moffatt, 2018). In recent decades, asthma diagnoses have become more common in industrialized nations, suggesting that environmental factors also play a role (Thomsen, van der Sluis, Kyvik, Skytthe, & Backer, 2010). For example, better insulation of homes makes them

FIGURE 10.3

Ethnic Differences in Asthma Prevalence Rates

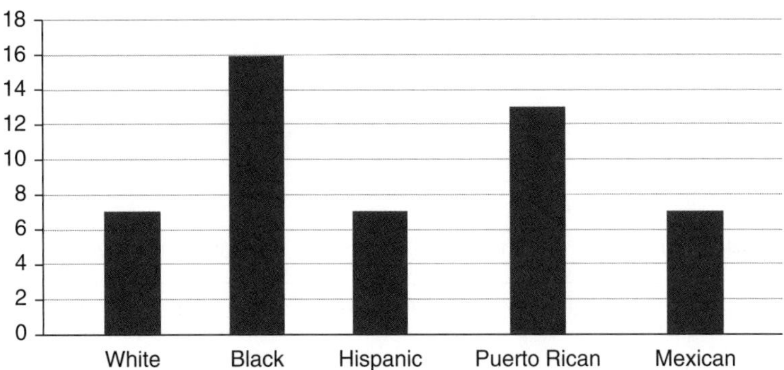

Source: Centers for Disease Control and Prevention (2019c).

more efficient at retaining heat but permits less air circulation, exposing family members to more allergens and toxins from sources such as mold, furry pets living in the home, and carpeting in the home (Ding, Ji, & Bao, 2014; Heinrich, 2011). Urbanization, less outdoor play, and poor access to health care (all of which tend to accompany low socioeconomic status, another correlate of asthma) increase children's risk of developing asthma (Kiechl-Kohlendorfer et al., 2007). One study of South African 6- to 7-year-old children found that those who lived in urban areas were more likely to be diagnosed with asthma than those from rural areas, supporting the role of exposure to pollution and toxins in developing asthma (Wichmann, Wolvaardt, Maritz, & Voyi, 2009). Other risk factors for developing asthma include low birthweight, stress, low socioeconomic status, and exposure to secondhand smoke in the home (Ding et al., 2014; Kiechl-Kohlendorfer et al., 2007).

Asthma poses risks to children's development and functioning because children with asthma are more likely to report only fair or poor overall health and well-being, and to be treated for a mental health problem, than are children without asthma (Collins et al., 2008; Miller, Wood, & Smith, 2010). Asthma is the most common cause of school absence (Akinbami et al., 2009). In addition to more school absences, children with asthma tend to report more unhappiness at school and are less likely to report having a group of friends to play with (Chen, 2014; Petteway, Valerio, & Patel, 2011). Moreover, many asthmatic children report being teased or bullied (van den Bemt et al., 2010). Physical health influences, and is influenced by, psychosocial development, as demonstrated by findings on childhood obesity.

Childhood Obesity

Byron looked up at the menu and the pictures of each item and tried to decide what to order for dinner. "What will it be?" Dad asks. "Bacon cheeseburger and large french fries. Can I have a chocolate milkshake too?" "Sure! It's our night out," Dad answers. A calorie-packed junk food dinner like Byron's is a fun splurge once in a while, but for some children this is a regular everyday dinner. Children today weigh more than ever before. Obesity is a serious health problem for children today. Health care professionals determine whether someone's weight is in the healthy range by examining **body mass index (BMI)**, calculated as weight in kilograms divided by height in meters squared (kg/m^2; World Health Organization, 2009). **Obesity** is defined as having a BMI at or above the 95th percentile for height and age, as indicated by the 2000 Centers for Disease Control and Prevention (CDC) growth charts (Reilly, 2007). About 18% of school-age children are classified as obese (Hales, Fryar, Carroll, Freedman, & Ogden, 2018). Obesity is a growing problem as in 2015–2016 children were over four times as likely to be obese as they were in 1971–1974 as shown in Figure 10.4 (Child Trends, 2018b).

FIGURE 10.4

Percentage of Children Ages 2 to 19 Who Are Obese, 1971–2016

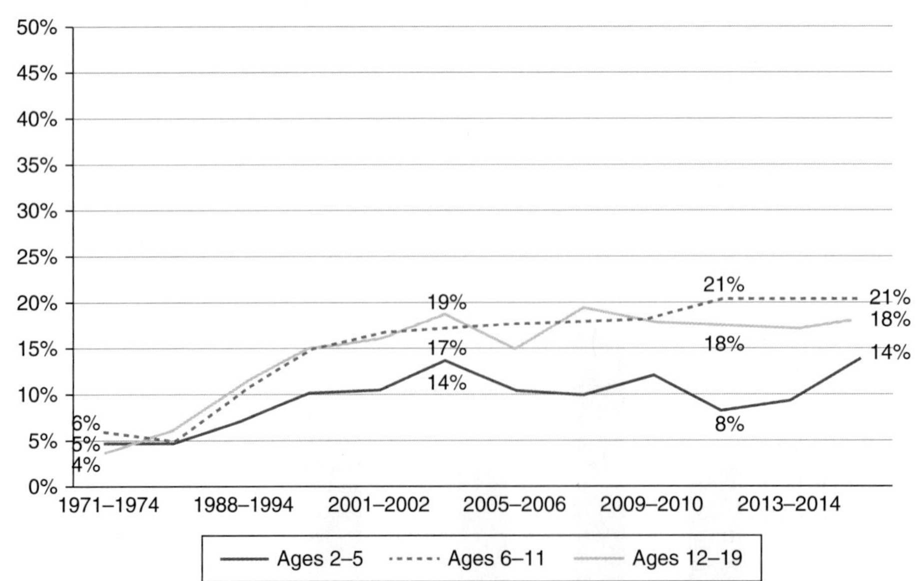

Source: Child Trends (2018b).

Rising rates of overweight and obesity among children and adolescents are a problem not only in the United States but also in all other developed nations, including Australia, Canada, Denmark, Finland, Germany, Great Britain, Ireland, Japan, Hong Kong, and New Zealand (Figure 10.5) (de Onis, Blössner, & Borghi, 2010; Janssen et al., 2005; Lobstein et al., 2015; Wang & Lim, 2012). Obesity is also becoming more common in developing nations, such as India, Pakistan, and China, as they

FIGURE 10.5

Worldwide Prevalence of Overweight Children (Ages 5–17) in 2010

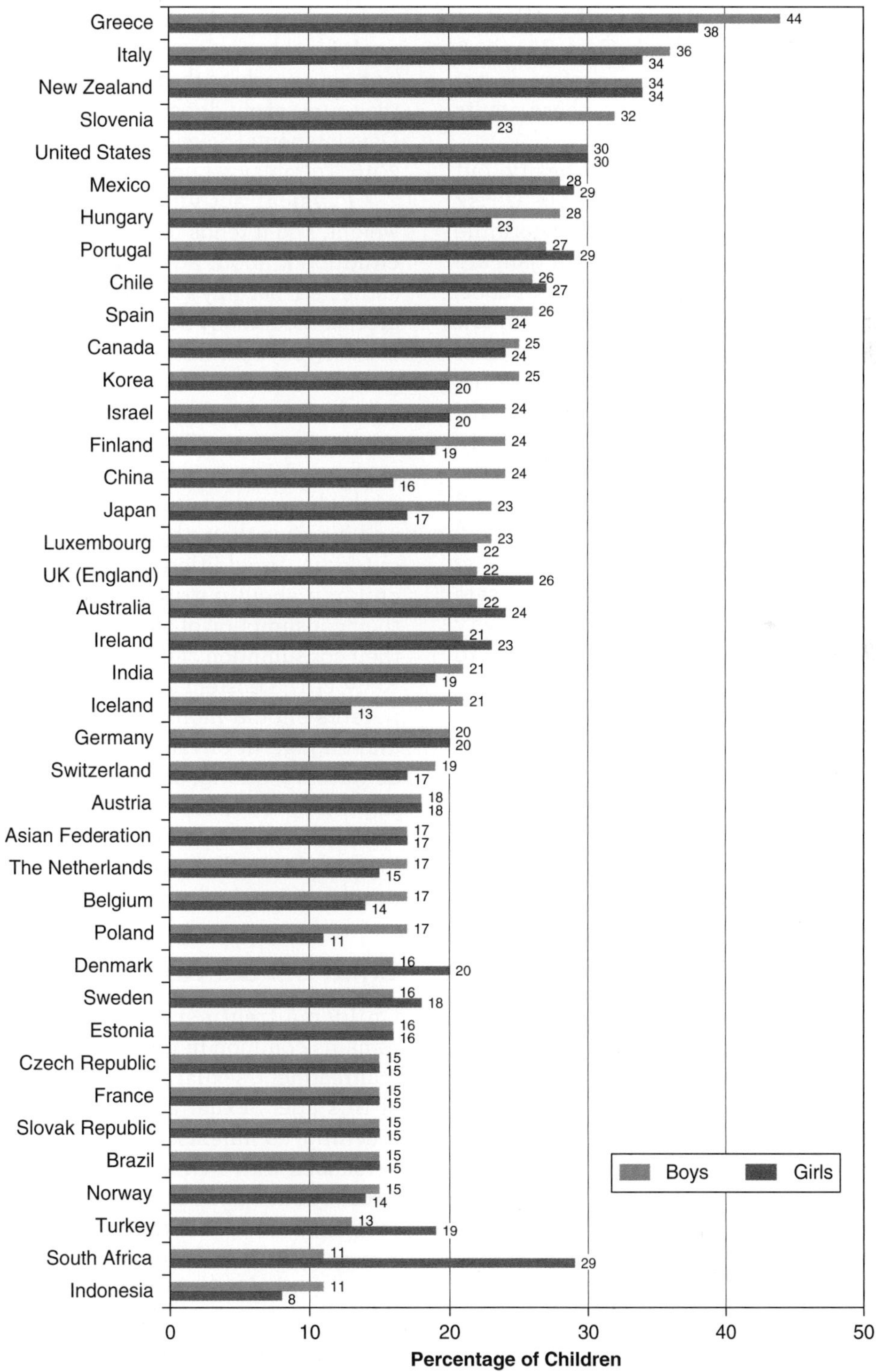

Source: Organization for Economic Co-operation and Development (2014).

adopt Western-style diets higher in meats, fats, and refined foods and as they show the increased snacking and decreased physical activity linked with watching television and screen use (Afshin, Reitsma, & Murray, 2017).

Child and adolescent obesity is associated with short- and long-term health problems, including heart disease, high blood pressure, orthopedic problems, and diabetes (Pulgarón, 2013). Obese children and adolescents are at risk for peer rejection, depression, low self-esteem, and body dissatisfaction (Harrist et al., 2016; Pulgarón, 2013; Quek, Tam, Zhang, & Ho, 2017). The majority of obese youngsters do not outgrow obesity but instead become obese adults (Simmonds, 2016).

Heredity plays a strong role in obesity, but contextual factors also place individuals at risk for obesity and interact with biology to determine whether genetic predispositions to weight gain are fulfilled (Albuquerque, Nóbrega, Manco, & Padez, 2017; Goodarzi, 2018). For example, children in low SES homes are at higher risk for obesity than their peers who live in high SES homes (Chung et al., 2016). The effects of SES may interact with individuals' genetic predispositions. For example, in one study, children who were carriers of a particular allele of the *OXTR* gene had greater BMI when reared in low SES environments but had the lowest BMI when reared in high SES homes (Bush et al., 2017). Community-level influences on obesity include the lack of safe playgrounds with equipment that encourages activity and even the proximity of fast-food restaurants to schools (Alviola, Nayga, Thomsen, Danforth, & Smartt, 2014; Black, Menzel, & Bungum, 2015; Fan & Jin, 2014).

U.S. children who eat an evening meal with parents are less likely to be overweight than other children (Horning et al., 2017) and are less likely to be overweight as young adults (Berge et al., 2015). These children tend to have healthier diets that include more fruits and vegetables and less fried foods and soft drinks. The frequency of family dinnertimes drops sharply between ages 9 and 14, however, and family dinners have become less common in recent decades (Fink, Racine, Mueffelmann, Dean, & Herman-Smith, 2014). Screen time—time spent in front of a television, computer, or electronic device screen—is a sedentary activity that places children at risk for obesity (Mitchell, Rodriguez, Schmitz, & Audrain-McGovern, 2013a). Eight- to 12-year-old children average more than 4.5 hours of screen time each day (Rideout, 2015). Children also show individual differences in screen use. On any given day, 6% report no use of screen media and 28% use it for 2 hours or less; on the other hand, 27% spend between 4 and 8 hours with screen media and 11% spend more than 8 hours. Screen time increases with age and the sedentary nature of screen time and snacking that tends to accompany it both place children at risk for overweight and obesity (Rideout, 2015; Robinson et al., 2017).

At the same time that screen time is associated with overweight and obesity, media consumption, especially exposure to media depictions of unrealistically thin celebrities, influences how children view their bodies. **Body image dissatisfaction**, dissatisfaction with one's physical appearance as shown by a discrepancy between one's ideal body figure and actual body figure, can be seen as early as the preschool years and rises over the course of childhood, as discussed in the Applying Developmental Science feature (Slater & Tiggemann, 2016; Tremblay & Limbos, 2009).

Physical activity also contributes to body weight, and it tends to decline beginning in middle childhood, about age 7 (Farooq et al., 2018). It is estimated that only about 10% of 12- to 15-year-olds are at least moderately active for 60 minutes per day on at least 5 days per week, in accord with recommended guidelines (Kann, Kinchen, Shanklin, Flint, Kawkins, Harris, Lowry, Olsen, McManus, Chyen, Whittle, Taylor, Demissie, Brener, Thornton, Moore, Zaza, et al., 2014). Programs that effectively reduce obesity in children and adolescents target their screen time and increase their physical activity and time spent outdoors. In addition, successful programs teach children about nutrition and help them to reduce their consumption of high-calorie foods and increase their consumption of fruits and vegetables (Kumar & Kelly, 2017; Lobstein et al., 2015). To prevent obesity, parents should monitor their children's activities and engage in physical activities with them such as walking, biking, and swimming. Intervention is important to reduce childhood obesity, but it must be done sensitively, as children who are pressured to lose weight may become obsessed with body size and develop a poor body image.

Child Sexual Abuse

Child maltreatment, discussed in Chapter 7, remains common in middle childhood. One form of maltreatment, sexual abuse, is particularly prevalent at this age. Sexual abuse refers to inappropriate touching, comments, or sexual activity, coerced or persuaded with a child. Once considered rare, child sexual abuse is now understood as a widespread problem around the world (Hillis, Mercy, Amobi, & Kress, 2016). It is estimated that about one-quarter to one-third of U.S. children under the age of 17 have experienced sexual abuse (Finkelhor, Shattuck, Turner, & Hamby, 2014). Many cases are unreported, as many children do not disclose abuse (Leclerc & Wortley, 2015). Although both boys and girls

APPLYING DEVELOPMENTAL SCIENCE

Body Image Dissatisfaction

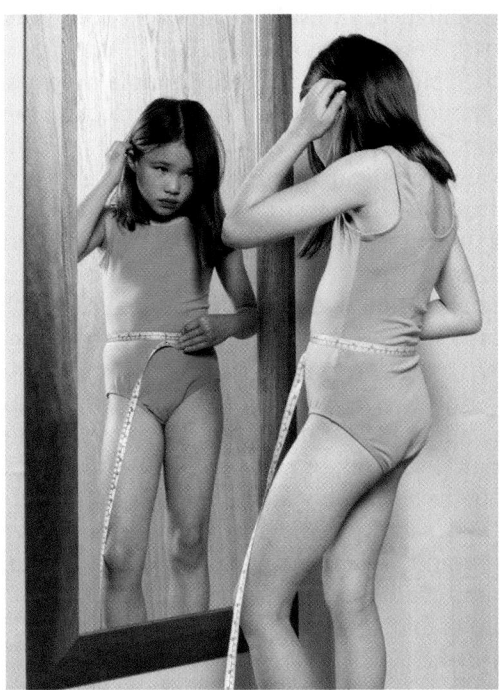

Body image dissatisfaction often emerges in middle childhood.
Peter Dazeley/Photographer's Choice/Getty Images

"See how my stomach sticks out?" asked Amanda. "I have to wear baggy tops to hide it. I want to wear cropped tops like that one," Amanda said, pointing to a page in a magazine. "But I'm too fat." "Me too," said her best friend, Betsy. At 9 years of age, Amanda and Betsy display signs of body image dissatisfaction.

Up to half of elementary school children (6–12 years) are dissatisfied with some aspect of their body and shape (Dion et al., 2016; Smolak, 2011). Perhaps it is not surprising, then, that dieting behaviors often begin in childhood, and about half of 8- to 10-year-old children report dieting at least some of the time (Dohnt & Tiggemann, 2005). Body image dissatisfaction is associated with poor self-esteem, depression, unhealthy eating and exercise behaviors, and inadequate weight gain in childhood (Dion et al., 2016; Duchin et al., 2015). Although less well researched, boys also are vulnerable to body dissatisfaction, often desiring a taller and more muscular physique (Costa, Silva, Alvarenga, & de Assis Guedes de Vasconcelos, 2016).

Peer interactions play a role in body image dissatisfaction. Girls often bond over "fat talk," criticizing their bodies (McVey, Levine, Piran, & Ferguson, 2013). Many school-age girls believe that being thin would make them more likable by their peers and less likely to be teased (Michael et al., 2014). Girls with a higher BMI report experiencing more teasing and bullying, which in turn is associated with body dissatisfaction (McVey et al., 2013; Williams et al., 2013). Even without being teased, simply having a higher BMI relative to peers predicts present body image concerns and those 1 year later in 9- to 12-year-old girls (Clark & Tiggemann, 2008).

Individuals' perceptions of body ideals and their own bodies are influenced by multiple contextual factors. Exposure to media images of thin models has often been associated with dieting awareness, weight concerns, and body dissatisfaction in girls and women (Evans, Tovée, Boothroyd, & Drewett, 2013; Gattario, Frisén, & Anderson-Fye, 2014). The influence of the media is perhaps best illustrated by longitudinal studies of teenagers in the Pacific island nation of Fiji before and after television became widely available in the islands. Disordered eating attitudes and behaviors arose after the introduction of television (Dasen, 1994). With the emergence of U.S. television programming, girls from rural Fiji reported comparing their bodies unfavorably to those of the program characters (Becker, Keel, Anderson-Fye, & Thomas, 2004).

School-based programs aim to educate students about body image using strategies such as lessons, group discussions, and role play as well as encouraging supportive peer groups (McCabe, Connaughton, Tatangelo, Mellor, & Busija, 2017; O'Dea & Yager, 2011). Improving media literacy is an important focus of many programs. The programs may include lessons about advertising, the homogeneity of body shapes shown on television and in magazines, and the airbrushing of photos (Richardson, Paxton, & Thomson, 2009). For example, as part of a 2011 governmental initiative in British schools, Britney Spears allowed pre-airbrushed images of herself in a bikini to be shown alongside the airbrushed ones for children aged 10 to 11 to show how media might try to alter and improve images (Gattario et al., 2014). Effective programs emphasize providing children with alternative ways of thinking about beauty and body ideals (Gattario et al., 2014).

What Do You Think?

In what ways might body image dissatisfaction be experienced similarly by girls and boys? How might girls' and boys' experience of body image dissatisfaction differ? Would you expect boys and girls to react to body image dissatisfaction in similar ways? Why or why not? ●

are victims of sexual abuse, girls are more often victimized. Sexual abuse may occur at any time during infancy, childhood, or adolescence, but it is most often reported in middle childhood, with about half of cases occurring between ages 4 and 12 (U.S. Department of Health and Human Services, 2018a). Older children are more likely to disclose sexual abuse, whereas sexual abuse of young children is most likely discovered accidentally, through eyewitness detection, or in response to questions (Alaggia, Collin-Vézina, & Lateef, 2018). Although, as mentioned, girls are more often victims of sexual abuse, boys are much less likely to report abuse, perhaps because of internalized gender stereotypes about masculinity and perceived weakness associated with victimization (Gagnier & Collin-Vézina, 2016). It is often difficult for children who are sexually abused to cope and heal because sexual abuse often is not a one-time event; some children experience sexual abuse that persists for years.

Reported cases of child sexual abuse are more common in homes characterized by poverty, food and housing insecurity, marital instability, and drug and alcohol abuse (Berger, Font, Slack, & Waldfogel, 2017; Kim, Drake, & Jonson-Reid, 2018; U.S. Department of Health and Human Services, 2018a). Children who are raised in homes in which adults come and go—repeated marriages, separations, and revolving romantic partners—are at higher risk of sexual abuse. However, sexual abuse also occurs in intact families and at all socioeconomic levels. Some researchers argue that maltreatment is more likely to be discovered in children of disadvantaged families than in children at higher socioeconomic levels, because disadvantaged children are likelier to come into contact with social services, such as when parents seek welfare and other forms of financial assistance or when parental substance use is discovered.

Perpetrators of sexual abuse are most often males whom the child knows, trusts, and has frequent contact with, such as parents, stepparents, and live-in boyfriends; stepfathers are likelier than fathers to be perpetrators (U.S. Department of Health and Human Services, 2018a). Most sexual assaults occur in the home of the victim or the perpetrator, not in dark alleys or during abduction by a stranger (Kenny, 2018). Children comply with the abuser for a variety of reasons. Some are bribed by gifts or privileges and are told that they are special and that the activity is a secret that they share. Others are intimidated and threatened by physical harm and reprisal for noncompliance or for telling another adult.

Both boys and girls show similar emotional responses to sexual abuse, including symptoms of anxiety and depression and behavioral responses such as social withdrawal, aggression, sleep disturbances, poor academic achievement, and risky behaviors (Maikovich-Fong & Jaffee, 2010; Pérez-Fuentes et al., 2013). Childhood sexual abuse is associated with mental and behavioral health problems in adolescence and adulthood, including depression, anxiety, antisocial behavior, substance dependence, and suicide attempts (Maniglio, 2011, 2013; Pérez-González, Guilera, Pereda, & Jarne, 2017). Moreover, the chronic trauma of sexual abuse is thought to alter neuron functioning in brain areas responsible for emotion regulation in adulthood, a physiological risk for mental health problems, difficulties managing stress, and an increased prevalence of disease (Nemeroff, 2016). Lifelong physical health issues associated with sexual victimization in childhood include gastrointestinal distress, reproductive problems, generalized pain, and overall poor health (Fergusson, McLeod, & Horwood, 2013; Herrenkohl, Hong, Klika, Herrenkohl, & Russo, 2013). As adolescents and adults, victims of sexual abuse are also likely to show sexual problems such as risky and unprotected sexual activity, avoidance of sex, and sexual anxiety and guilt (Homma, Wang, Saewyc, & Kishor, 2012; Jones et al., 2013). Sexual abuse victims of all ages are at risk to display symptoms of posttraumatic stress disorder (PTSD), an anxiety disorder that includes flashbacks, nightmares, and feelings of helplessness (Kenny, 2018). Note, though, that not all children who experience traumatic events such as sexual abuse experience dire outcomes. Some children function well and even thrive despite adversity, as we will see later in this chapter.

Prevention and early identification of sexual abuse is essential. When abuse is identified and stopped early, children display more positive adjustment (Fryda & Hulme, 2015). Effective prevention and early identification of sexual abuse relies on training parents and teachers to recognize the signs of abuse and report suspicions to law enforcement and child protection agencies. As noted in Chapter 7, teachers and other professionals who come into contact with children are mandated reporters, legally obligated to report suspicions to authorities. Children tend to experience fewer long-term consequences of abuse if the child's account is believed, the abuse is stopped, and the home environment is structured, stable, and nurturing (Kenny, 2018). In addition to targeting parents, caregivers, and other adults, effective prevention programs educate children about their bodies and their right to not be touched. When children are exposed to school-based education programs that help them learn how to recognize inappropriate touches, they are more apt to report them to teachers and other adults (Brassard & Fiorvanti, 2015). Table 10.2 summarizes characteristics of effective sexual abuse prevention programs.

TABLE 10.2

Characteristics of Effective Child Sexual Abuse Prevention Programs

CHARACTERISTIC	DESCRIPTION
Early identification	Train parents and teachers to recognize the risk factors and early signs of sexual abuse and report suspicions to law enforcement and child protection agencies.
Educate children	Educate children in a developmentally appropriate way about their bodies and their rights to not be touched. Provide children with the vocabulary to describe their bodies. Help children learn how to recognize inappropriate touches and learn what to do if touched.
Engage parents	Educate parents and assist them in discussing sexual abuse prevention with their children. Encourage them to support school efforts by discussing school activities.
Repeat exposure	Repeatedly expose children to the material in school and at home via homework and discussions with parents.
Strengthen parenting and families	Provide parents with support, parenting education, and other resources to help them improve the bond with their child, reducing children's attention-seeking behaviors.

Resilience in Middle Childhood

Best friends Jane and Margarita walk to school together every day, partly because they live next door to each other, but also in response to several neighborhood shootings and the growing problem of violence in their community. The contexts in which children are embedded pose both opportunities and risks for development. Recall that risk factors are associated with a higher likelihood of negative outcomes. In contrast, contexts also include protective factors, which may reduce or protect the child from the poor outcomes associated with adverse circumstances.

In Jane and Margarita's case, one contextual risk factor is neighborhood violence. Other contextual risk factors include child maltreatment, parental mental health problems, poverty, homelessness, and war (Luthar, Crossman, & Small, 2015; Masten & Cicchetti, 2016). Risk factors are cumulative; the more risks children face, the more difficult it is for them to adjust (Ungar, 2015). For example, children exposed to war in Bosnia showed higher rates of PTSD and mental health and learning problems the more they witnessed the atrocities of war, such as death, violence, and forced displacement (Layne et al., 2008). In all contexts, poor responses to adversity include psychological, behavioral, and health problems, including anxiety, depression, frequent illnesses and hospitalizations, poor academic achievement, and delinquent activity (Cutuli et al., 2017). The Lives in Context feature examines the developmental challenges posed by war.

Acts of war and terror affect children, families, and communities with dire consequences for development.
SOPA Images/LightRocket/Getty Images

Culture can influence how risk and protective factors manifest. In one striking example, over 5,000 Aboriginal children who participated in the Western Australian Aboriginal Child Health Survey showed that risk factors such as harsh parenting, family violence, and caregiver unemployment cumulatively predicted children's problems (Hopkins, Taylor, D'Antoine, & Zubrick, 2012). And for these children, living in a high SES neighborhood and demonstrating more knowledge of their culture were associated with lower levels of resilience to adversity. These unusual results were explained by the context. About 90% of Aboriginal people lived in lower SES neighborhoods. Growing up in a more economically advantaged community may separate a child from social supports and expose the child to prejudice. Likewise, children's knowledge of their culture when they are members of a minority group and are ostracized from their community may create heightened sensitivity to oppression and lead to higher levels of depression and delinquency.

Even children from Western cultures show a range of outcomes in response to adversity. For example, like many of her classmates, Jane worries about her and her family's safety. Jane

LIVES IN CONTEXT: COMMUNITY CONTEXT

Exposure to War and Terrorism and Children's Development

Acts of war and terror affect children, families, and communities, with dire consequences for children's development. Living through chronic, unexpected bouts of terror and trauma, such as listening to bomb blasts, fleeing a home and community in search of safety, and losing loved ones to military service, confinement, or death, disrupts the contextual and social fabric of children's and families' lives (Masten, Narayan, Silverman, & Osofsky, 2015; Werner, 2012). Traumatic experiences may be particularly challenging for school-age children, as they are able to understand the gravity of the situation but have not yet developed the emotion regulation, abstract reasoning, and psychosocial maturity to process such events (Saraiya, Garakani, & Billick, 2013). Children exposed to acts of terror may show anxiety and symptoms of PTSD, fear of being alone, safety concerns, and behavior problems, such as aggression (Huesmann et al., 2016; Slone & Mann, 2016).

Parents influence how children process and adapt to trauma. Parents' ability to regulate their own experience of trauma and manage their stress and emotions influences children's adjustment (Halevi, Djalovski, Vengrober, & Feldman, 2016). The economic and physical hardships that accompany war can interfere with parents' ability to meet children's basic needs for food, shelter, and safety. Distress can contribute to harsh parenting, and community insecurity can result in increased parental control (Sim, Fazel, Bowes, & Gardner, 2018). Parents face many challenges, but those who are able to instill a sense of warmth and security are best able to support their children's needs and promote resilience (Saraiya et al., 2013).

It is important to note, however, that many children show resilience. For example, one study of Palestinian children exposed to the 2008–2009 War on Gaza found that about three-quarters of the children showed some recovery from PTSD symptoms (Punamäki, Palosaari, Diab, Peltonen, & Qouta, 2014). Likewise, one comprehensive review showed that most child survivors of war who participated in long-term follow-up studies showed no enduring patterns of emotional distress or poor psychosocial outcomes (Werner, 2012).

Nevertheless, exposure to war and ongoing, unpredictable terrorism is challenging for all children. The loss of a sense of safety and the familiar environment and routines of school, social networks, and patterns of family life poses risks for adjustment (Cummings, Goeke-Morey, Merrilees, Taylor, & Shirlow, 2014; Masten et al., 2015). Interventions to assist children promote children's attachment with parents and caregivers by ensuring that children stay physically and emotionally close to their parents. In addition to having their physical needs met, children must have opportunities to express ideas and feelings directly and through play, such as drawing, storytelling, drama, and games. Establishing routines is an important way of instilling a sense of security. No intervention can erase the effects of exposure to the trauma of war and terror, but interventions can help to bolster the factors that promote resilience to adversity.

What Do You Think?

Consider the problem of war or terrorism from the standpoint of Bronfenbrenner's bioecological theory. Identify factors within the microsystem that may help children adjust to experiencing terror. What factors might make it more challenging for children to adjust? What about mesosystem factors? Exosystem? Macrosystem? ●

sometimes feels paralyzed by her fear and finds it hard to concentrate in class. She performs poorly in reading and math. Margarita also worries about her family and her own safety, but she can put her worries aside to focus on the teacher's lesson and earns As on many of her assignments. Margarita displays **resilience**, the ability to respond or perform positively in the face of adversity, to achieve despite the presence of disadvantages, or to significantly exceed expectations given poor home, school, and community circumstances (Masten, 2016).

Despite experiencing a variety of intense stressors, some children display little trauma and are able to manage their anxiety to succeed at home and school, showing high self-esteem, low levels of depression, and few behavioral problems (Cicchetti, 2016; Pérez-González et al., 2017). Adaptation to adversity is a dynamic process involving interactions among a child's developmental capacities and his or her changing context, which includes both risk factors and protective factors. Protective factors may help shield children from risk factors, buffering the poor outcomes that accompany adverse circumstances and contexts. For example, Margarita often attends an after-school program, where she learned to play basketball and use a computer. She has a close relationship with her mother and uncle, who visits each week to accompany them to church. Each of these factors—school and community connections, warm relationships with adults, routines, and church

TABLE 10.3

Characteristics of Resilient Children

INDIVIDUAL COMPETENCIES	FAMILY COMPETENCIES AND CHARACTERISTICS	SCHOOL AND COMMUNITY CHARACTERISTICS
Coping skills Easy temperament Emotional regulation abilities Good cognitive abilities Intelligence Positive outlook Positive self-concept Religiosity Self-efficacy (feeling of control over one's destiny) Talents valued by others	Close relationships with parents and caregivers Organized home Parental involvement in children's education Positive family climate Postsecondary education of parents Provision of support Religiosity and engagement with the church Socioeconomic advantage Warm but assertive parenting	Access to local churches After-school programs Availability of emergency services Mentoring programs and opportunities to form relationships with adults Health care availability Instruction in conflict management Opportunity to develop and practice leadership skills Peer programs, such as big brother/big sister programs Programs to assist developing self-management skills Public safety Support networks outside of the family, such as supportive adults and peers Ties to prosocial organizations Well-funded schools with highly qualified teachers Youth programs

Source: Child Trends (2013).

attendance—is a protective factor that promotes adjustment and can reduce the negative outcomes associated with adversity (Masten & Monn, 2015; Ungar, 2015).

Protective factors may arise from within the child, from the family or extended family, and from the community (Pérez-González et al., 2017; Traub & Boynton-Jarrett, 2017). Resilient children tend to have personal characteristics that protect them from adversity and help them learn from experience, such as an easy temperament, a sense of competence, self-control, good information processing and problem-solving skills, friendliness, and empathy (Afifi & MacMillan, 2011; Domhardt, Münzer, Fegert, & Goldbeck, 2015; Marriott, Hamilton-Giachritsis, & Harrop, 2014). A fundamental characteristic is that they are successful in regulating their emotions and behavior (Eisenberg et al., 2010). Resilient individuals also have a proactive orientation, take initiative, believe in their own effectiveness, and have a positive sense of self (Luthar et al., 2015; Pérez-González et al., 2017). Avenues for fostering resilience include promoting children's strengths and bolstering children's executive function skills, self-appraisals, and sense of efficacy (B. J. Ellis, Bianchi, Griskevicius, & Frankenhuis, 2017; Traub & Boynton-Jarrett, 2017). Children who are resilient tend to have strong and supportive relationships with at least one parent, caregiver, or adult who provides warm guidance and firm support (Domhardt et al., 2015; Labella, Narayan, McCormick, Desjardins, & Masten, 2018). Effective supports for children at risk target parents' mental health and self-care skills, aid parents in establishing routines, promote parenting skills, and help parents understand the impact of trauma on children (Masten & Monn, 2015; Ungar, 2015). Table 10.3 illustrates characteristics that promote resilience in children. Resilient children illustrate an important finding: Exposure to adversity in childhood does not necessarily lead to maladjustment; many children thrive despite challenging experiences.

THINKING IN CONTEXT 10.4

1. We have seen that development takes place through dynamic interactions between the individual and the world around him or her. Consider childhood obesity within the context of these interactions. What are some physical and socioemotional correlates of childhood obesity? How might these outcomes influence children's subsequent interactions with the people, objects, and places around them?
2. What are some barriers to the early reporting of child sexual maltreatment? What factors might influence children and adults' awareness of sexual abuse? What factors might determine whether abuse is reported? Consider all levels of context: variables within the child and adult, home, school, and neighborhood and community. How might larger macrosystem factors, such as societal and cultural attitudes, influence awareness and reporting of sexual abuse?
3. Suppose that you are an intervention researcher who wants to create a program to promote resilience in children. What might the program include? What traits or abilities would you seek to improve in children? Why? What activities might you include? Explain your choices.

APPLY YOUR KNOWLEDGE

Nine-year-old Lavette walks home from school alone, quietly singing to herself as she passes the empty playground around the corner from her home. "Mom says don't go in there alone," she reminds herself. "Sure, I might fall off the slide or something, but Mom's not worried about that. It's those high school kids," she thinks. Lavette continues, stepping around the glass from a shattered car window. "Another one," she mutters. "Mom says to be careful and look around before going into our building," Lavette reminds herself as she pulls her keys out of her pocket. Finally, she enters the quiet apartment and settles down with her tablet to watch some videos. Lavette's phone rings and she answers. "Hi, Mom. Yes, I'm home. No problems."

Lavette's schoolmate, Tasha, dribbles a basketball as she walks home in another neighborhood. Tasha stops at the playground near her home, walks onto the basketball court, and calls out, "Ready to play?" to the handful of other elementary school kids playing ball and jumping rope. After playing two games, Tasha sprints home just in time for dinner with her family.

1. Compare Lavette and Tasha's experiences. How might their differing contexts influence their growth and motor development?
2. What factors might promote physical activity? What are some barriers to physical activity? How might parents, schools, and communities address these barriers?
3. Identify potential threats to Lavette and Tasha's health.
4. Suppose a counselor at the community center wanted to foster resilience in the local children. What characteristics within children would the counselor seek to foster? Within the environment? Make suggestions for both Lavette and Tasha.

WANT A BETTER GRADE?

Get the tools you need to sharpen your study skills. **SAGE edge** offers a robust online environment featuring an impressive array of free tools and resources. Access practice quizzes, eFlashcards, video, and multimedia at **edge.sagepub.com/kutherchild1e.** SAGE edge™

KEY TERMS

Growing pains 273

Growth hormone deficiency 274

Cerebellum 275

Adrenarche 276

Gray matter 276

White matter 276

Hippocampus 277

Attention-deficit/hyperactivity disorder (ADHD) 277

Specific learning disorder (SLD) 278

Developmental dyslexia 278

Developmental dyscalculia 278

Developmental dysgraphia 278

Recess 281

Asthma 283

Body mass index (BMI) 284

Obesity 284

Body image dissatisfaction 286

Resilience 290

SUMMARY

10.1 Discuss patterns of growth and motor development and influences on each in middle childhood.

Growth and motor development advance gradually throughout middle childhood. During middle childhood, children's body movements become more fluid and coordinated. Increases in fine motor skills influence children's interests and enable them to write fluidly, with implications for academic achievement. In addition to maturational advances in physical growth and brain development, motor development is also influenced by contextual factors, such as nutrition, opportunities to practice motor skills, and health.

10.2 Describe processes of brain development in middle childhood and two examples of atypical brain development.

Although nearly adult size, brain volume continues to increase in middle childhood, especially in the prefrontal cortex. Increases in synaptic density result in an overall increase in gray matter and cortical thickness. Pruning leads children to show more focused brain activity on cognitive tasks. Myelination continues throughout middle childhood, creating white matter and contributing to more efficient processing of information. One example of atypical brain development is attention-deficit/hyperactivity disorder (ADHD), a neurodevelopmental disorder characterized by persistent difficulties with attention and/or hyperactivity/impulsivity that interferes with performance and behavior in school and daily life. Specific learning disorders are diagnosed in children who demonstrate a measurable discrepancy between aptitude and achievement in a particular academic area. There are several SLDs that influence reading (developmental dyslexia), writing skills (developmental dysgraphia), mathematics (developmental dyscalculia), and other cognitive skills.

10.3 Identify the benefits of physical activity and common opportunities for physical activity in middle childhood.

The Physical Activity Guidelines for Americans recommends that children get 60 minutes or more of moderate to vigorous physical activity daily. Moderate physical activity is associated with positive physical, psychological, and cognitive health in children, yet most children do not meet this guideline. School-based physical activity most often occurs during physical education classes but support for physical education as well as recess, unstructured active time, varies. About a third of children play organized sports, but the availability of sports and children's ability to take advantage of opportunities depends on contextual factors, such as resources, community socioeconomic status, and family socioeconomic status.

10.4 Summarize common threats to school-age children's health.

Middle childhood generally is a healthy time. Unintentional injuries from accidents are the most common cause of death in school-age children. Asthma is the most common chronic illness. Rising rates of obesity pose risks to children's physical and psychological health. In middle childhood, child maltreatment often takes the form of child sexual abuse, with devastating consequences for children's physical and socioemotional development. Contextual factors play an important role in each of these threats to development. Some children show resilience and are able to show positive adjustment in spite of exposure to threats to development.

REVIEW QUESTIONS

10.1 What are examples of gross and fine motor development?

What are influences on growth and motor development?

10.2 What are ways in which children's brains grow in middle childhood?

What are characteristics of ADHD?

What are specific learning disabilities?

10.3 What are benefits of physical activity?

What opportunities do children have for physical activity?

How do contextual factors influence children's physical activity?

10.4 What is asthma?

What are influences on obesity?

What are effects of child sexual abuse?

How can abuse be prevented?

What are characteristics that signify resilience?

©iStockphoto.com/grady

11 Cognitive Development in Middle Childhood

We have seen that children make impressive gains in physical development, becoming bigger, stronger, and capable of a broader range of motor activities. Their leaps in cognitive development are even more impressive. Children's capacities to take in, process, and retain information all increase dramatically. In this chapter, we examine how cognitive development unfolds and its implications for how children understand and operate in their world.

Learning Objectives

11.1 Examine school-age children's capacities for reasoning and processing information.

Video Activity 11.1: Piaget's Conservation Tasks

Video Activity 11.2: Executive Function

11.2 Summarize views of intelligence, including the uses, correlates, and criticisms of intelligence tests.

11.3 Discuss patterns of moral development during middle childhood.

11.4 Explain processes of language development during middle childhood.

11.5 Discuss children's learning at school.

Chapter Contents

COGNITIVE DEVELOPMENT IN MIDDLE CHILDHOOD

School-age children grasp the world around them in new, more adultlike ways and become capable of thinking logically, although their reasoning remains different from that of adults. Children become faster, more efficient thinkers, and they develop more sophisticated perspectives on the nature of knowledge and how the mind works.

Piaget's Cognitive-Developmental Theory: Concrete Operational Reasoning

When children enter Piaget's **concrete operational stage of reasoning**, at about age 6 or 7, they become able to use logic to solve problems but are still unable to apply logic to abstract and hypothetical situations. Older children's newly developed ability for logical thinking enables them to reason about physical quantities and is evident in their skills for conservation and classification.

Classification

What hobbies did you enjoy as a child? Did you collect and trade coins, stamps, rocks, or baseball cards? School-age children develop interests and hobbies that require advanced thinking skills, such as the ability to compare multiple items across several dimensions. **Classification** is the ability to understand hierarchies, to simultaneously consider relations between a general category and more specific subcategories. Several types of classification skills emerge during the concrete operational stage: transitive inference, seriation, and class inclusion.

The ability to infer the relationship between two objects by understanding each object's relationship to a third is called **transitive inference**. For example, present a child with three sticks: A, B, and C. She is shown that Stick A is longer than Stick B and Stick B is longer than Stick C. The concrete operational child does not need to physically compare Sticks A and C to know that Stick A is longer than Stick C. She uses the information given about the two sticks to infer their relative lengths (Wright & Smailes, 2015). Transitive inference emerges earlier than other concrete operational skills. By about 5 years of age, children are able to infer that A is longer than C (Goodwin & Johnson-Laird, 2008).

Seriation is the ability to order objects in a series according to a physical dimension such as height, weight, or color. For example, ask a child to arrange a handful of sticks in order by length, from shortest to longest. Four- to 5-year-old children can pick out the smallest and largest stick but will arrange the others haphazardly. Six- to 7-year-old children, on the other hand, arrange the sticks by picking out the smallest, and next smallest, and so on (Inhelder & Piaget, 1964).

Class inclusion involves understanding hierarchical relationships among items. For example, suppose that a child is shown a bunch of flowers, seven daisies and two roses. She is told that there are nine flowers; seven are called daisies and two are called roses. The child is then asked, "Are there more daisies or flowers?" Preoperational children will answer that there are more daisies, as they do not understand that daisies are a subclass of flowers. By age 5, children have some knowledge of classification hierarchies and may grasp that daisies are flowers but still not fully understand and apply classification hierarchies to correctly solve the problem (Deneault & Ricard, 2006). By about age 8, children not only can classify objects, in this case flowers, but they also can make quantitative judgments and respond that there are more flowers than daisies (Borst, Poirel, Pineau, Cassotti, & Houdé, 2013).

Children's ability and interest in hierarchical classification becomes apparent in middle childhood when they begin to collect items and spend hours sorting their collections along various dimensions. For example, one day Susan sorts her rock collection by geographic location (e.g., the part of the world in which it is most commonly found), with subcategories based on hardness and color. She might then reorganize her rocks based on other characteristics, such as age or composition.

Conservation

In a classic conservation problem, a child is shown two identical balls of clay and watches while the experimenter rolls one ball into a long hotdog shape. When asked which piece contains more clay, a child who reasons at the preoperational stage will say that the hotdog shape contains more clay because it is longer. Eight-year-old Julio, in contrast, notices that the ball shape is shorter than the hotdog shape, but it is also thicker. He knows that the two shapes contain the same amount of clay. At the concrete operational stage of reasoning, Julio understands that certain characteristics of an object do not change despite superficial changes to the object's appearance. An understanding of reversibility—that an object can be returned to its original state—means Julio realizes that the hotdog-shaped clay can be reformed into its original ball shape.

Most children solve this conservation problem of substance by age 7 or 8. At about age 9 or 10,

Older children understand conservation, that clay can be molded into many shapes but retains the same mass.
Ryhor Bruyeu/EyeEm/Getty Images

children also correctly solve conservation of weight tasks (after presenting two equal-sized balls of clay and rolling one into a hotdog shape, "Which is heavier, the hotdog or the ball?"). Conservation of volume tasks (after placing the hotdog- and ball-shaped clay in glasses of liquid: "Which displaces more liquid?") are solved last, at about age 12. The ability to conserve develops slowly, and children show inconsistencies in their ability to solve different types of conservation problems.

Recent theorists link children's success on conservation tasks with the development of information processing capacities, such as working memory and the ability to control impulses (Borst et al., 2013). In response to conservation of number tasks, for example, older children show more activity in parts of the temporal and prefrontal cortex as well as other parts of the brain associated with working memory, inhibitory control, and executive control (Houdé et al., 2011; Poirel et al., 2012). With practice, the cognitive abilities tested in Piagetian tasks become automatic and require less attention and fewer processing resources, enabling children to think in more complex ways (Case, 1999). For example, once a child solves a conservation task, the problem becomes routine and requires less attention and mental resources than before, enabling the child to tackle more complex problems.

Culture and Concrete Operational Reasoning

Piaget emphasized the universal nature of cognitive development, assuming that all children around the world progressed through the same stages. Today's researchers, however, find that the cultural context in which children are immersed plays a critical role in development (Goodnow, Lawrence, Goodnow, & Lawrence, 2015). Studies of children in non-Western cultures suggest that they achieve conservation and other concrete operational tasks later than children from Western cultures. However, cultural differences in children's performance on tasks that measure concrete operational reasoning may be influenced by methodology (e.g., how questions are asked and the cultural identity of the experimenter) rather than children's abilities (Gauvain & Perez, 2015). For instance, when 10- and 11-year-old Canadian Micmac Indian children were tested in English on conservation problems (substance, weight, and volume), they performed worse than 10- to 11-year-old White English-speaking children. But when tested in their native language, by researchers from their own culture, the children performed as well as the English-speaking children (Collette & Van der Linden, 2002).

Children around the world demonstrate concrete operational reasoning, but experience, specific cultural practices, and education play a role in how it is displayed (Manoach et al., 1997). Children are more likely to display logical reasoning when considering substances with which they are familiar. Mexican children who make pottery understand at an early age that clay remains the same when its shape is changed. They demonstrate conservation of substance earlier than other forms of conservation (Fry & Hale, 1996) and earlier than children who do not make pottery (Hitch, Towse, & Hutton, 2001; Leather & Henry, 1994).

Despite having never attended school and scoring low on measures of mathematics achievement, many 6- to 15-year-old children living in the streets of Brazil demonstrate sophisticated logical and computational reasoning. Why? These children sell items such as fruit and candy to earn their living. In addition to pricing their products, collecting money, making change, and giving discounts, the children must adjust prices daily to account for changes in demand, overhead, and the rate of inflation (Gathercole, Pickering, Ambridge, & Wearing, 2004). Researchers found that these children's competence in mathematics was influenced by experience, situational demands, and learning from others. Nevertheless, schooling also matters; children with some schooling were more adept at these tasks than were unschooled children (Siegel, 1994).

Schooling influences the rate at which principles are understood. For example, children who have been in school longer tend to do better on transitive inference tasks than same-age children with less schooling (Artman & Cahan, 1993). Likewise, Zimbabwean children's understanding of conservation is influenced by academic experience, age, and family socioeconomic status (Mpofu & Vijver, 2000). Japanese children's understanding of mathematical concepts tends to follow a path consistent with Piaget's maturational view, but other mathematical concepts are understood because of formal instruction, supportive of Vygotsky's principle of scaffolding (see Chapter 8).

Implications of Cognitive-Developmental Theory for Education

The constructive nature of thinking, that children actively engage with their surroundings to make sense of the world, is highly relevant to education. The simplest implication for parents and teachers is to encourage curiosity (McDevitt & Ormrod, 2016). School-age children often believe that they should be mastering facts. Parents and teachers should encourage and validate children's questions, even if ill-timed. "What a great question, Narvesha! I'll write it on the board so that we can discuss it after this activity," Mr. Lopes said. Older children benefit from opportunities to learn from each other, such as through group work and in free-play recess.

Like infants and young children, older children learn by exploring the physical world. Provide children with opportunities to explore and experiment with physical objects. Hands-on activities might include grouping objects with similar characteristics, working with clay, and building structures with sticks. Unlike their younger peers, school-age children engage in intellectual exploration and generate simple logical explanations for phenomena. Pose problems and probe children's reasoning and conclusions. Sometimes children misinterpret their observations, confirming misconceptions or drawing the wrong conclusions (Fitzsimmons, Leddy, Johnson, Biggam, & Locke, 2013). By creating lessons that combine exploration and guided instruction, teachers can help children interpret their observations and draw accurate conclusions.

School-age children's emerging capacities for reasoning influence their understanding of a variety of phenomena, including their conceptions of illness (Brodie, 1974). We explore this concept more in the accompanying Lives in Context feature.

Information Processing Theory

"If you're finished, put your head down on your desk and rest for a moment," Mrs. McCalvert advised. She was surprised to see that three-quarters of her students immediately put their heads down. "They are getting quicker and quicker," she thought to herself. Information processing theorists would agree with Mrs. McCalvert's observation, because the information processing perspective describes development as entailing changes in the efficiency of cognition rather than qualitative changes in reasoning. School-age children can take in more information, process it more accurately and quickly, and retain it more effectively than younger children. They are better able to determine what information is important, attend to it, and use their understanding of how memory works to choose among strategies to retain information more effectively.

Working Memory and Executive Function

Children's working memory expands rapidly but is more limited than that of adults. By 8 years of age, children on average recall about half as many items as adults (Kharitonova, Winter, & Sheridan, 2015). Steady increases in working memory and executive function continue throughout childhood and are responsible for the cognitive changes seen during childhood. Advanced executive function capacities enable older children to control their attention and deploy it selectively, focusing on the relevant information and ignoring other information, compared with younger children, who are easily distracted and fidget (Ristic & Enns, 2015a). Children not only get better at attending to and manipulating information, but they get better at storing it in long-term memory, organizing it in more sophisticated ways, and encoding and retrieving it more efficiently and with less effort.

Improvements in memory, attention, and processing speed are possible because of brain development, particularly myelination and pruning in the prefrontal cortex and corpus callosum (Crone & Steinbeis, 2017; Perone, Almy, & Zelazo, 2018). Between ages 3 and 7, children show increasing prefrontal cortex engagement while completing tasks that measure working memory (Perlman, Huppert, & Luna, 2016). Neural systems for visuospatial working memory, auditory working memory, and response inhibition differentiate into separate parts to enable faster and more efficient processing of these critical cognitive functions (Crone & Steinbeis, 2017; Tsujimoto, Kuwajima, & Sawaguchi, 2007). Older children are quicker at matching pictures and recalling spatial information than younger children, and they show more activity in the frontal regions of the brain compared with younger children (Farber & Beteleva, 2011). Development of the prefrontal cortex leads to advances in response inhibition, the ability to withhold a behavioral response inappropriate in the current context. These advances improve children's capacity for self-regulation, controlling their thoughts and behavior. Advances in working memory and executive function are associated with language, reading, writing, and mathematics skills (Berninger, Abbott, Cook, & Nagy, 2017; Peng et al., 2018).

Age changes in performance on working memory tasks are also influenced by context. For example, the amount of schooling is a better predictor of working memory in Australian schoolchildren than chronological age (Roberts et al., 2015). High-quality relations with teachers are associated

LIVES IN CONTEXT: CULTURAL CONTEXT

Children's Understanding of Illness

Older children can hold both biological and cultural explanations about the causes of illness.
REUTERS/Ilya Naymushin

Cognitive development influences how children understand biology, their bodies, and the causes of illness. For example, young children tend to attribute contagious illnesses such as colds, coughs, and stomachaches to immanent justice—the belief that illness is caused by misdeeds and naughtiness (Myant & Williams, 2005). Other nonbiological explanations (e.g., magic or fate) are also common. As children advance in cognitive maturity, they develop more mature conceptions of illness, distinguish specific symptoms and diseases, and appreciate the biological causes of illness and contagiousness (Mouratidi, Bonoti, & Leondari, 2016).

Beliefs about biology and the causes of illness may vary by cultural setting. Research has suggested that nonbiological explanations of illness are common in adults from non-Western societies. For example, Murdock (1980) examined evidence from 139 nonindustrial societies around the world and found that most emphasized nonbiological causes of illness. Among the Zande of southern Sudan, for example, illness is thought to be caused by jealous or angry neighbors practicing witchcraft (Allen, 2007).

Cultural differences in beliefs about the causes of illness may arise from exposure to different explanations for illness. For example, most children in the United States are exposed to a germ and infection model of illness. Young children show a simple understanding of germs, and older children develop a more elaborate understanding. Children growing up in China have traditionally been exposed to Chinese medicine, which concerns the balance of yin and yang; breaking the balance is thought to lead to illness. In recent decades, however, Chinese children have been increasingly exposed to Western medicine. With age and the cognitive development that accompanies it, Chinese children tend to integrate these two perspectives, emphasizing biological causes but also referring to concepts from traditional Chinese medicine (Zhu, Liu, & Tardif, 2009).

When exposed to biological concepts of illness, children of all cultures tend to incorporate them into their understanding. For example, one study of 5- to 15-year-old children and adults from Sesotho-speaking South African communities showed that the participants, who were exposed to Western medicine, most commonly endorsed biological explanations for illness but also often endorsed witchcraft (Legare & Gelman, 2008). Both natural and supernatural explanations were viewed as complementary. Likewise, comparisons of older children, adolescents, and adults from Tanna and Vanuatu, remote islands off the coast of Malaysia, find that as individuals are confronted with scientific understandings of the world, they integrate scientific explanations with preexisting supernatural and other kinds of natural (e.g., folk-biological) explanations (Watson-Jones, Busch, & Legare, 2015). Tanna and Vanuatu children endorsed biological just as frequently as supernatural explanations, but adolescents and adults most commonly endorsed biological explanations.

With age and across cultural groups, when individuals are exposed to biological explanations of illness, such explanations tend to be most frequently endorsed (Legare, Evans, Rosengren, & Harris, 2012). Moreover, the coexistence of biological and nonbiological reasoning about causes of illness is not confined to specific cultures. For example, in the United States and other industrialized societies, many alternative medicine practitioners attribute illness to negative thinking and other psychological problems. U.S. children and adults tend to retain some supernatural explanations alongside biological explanations (Legare et al., 2012). Among people in all cultures, diverse, culturally constructed belief systems about illness coexist with factual understanding, and explanations of illness change with development.

What Do You Think?

1. How does our knowledge of individuals' understanding of illness compare with Piaget's cognitive-developmental theory?
2. Consider your own views and experience. Do you remember "catching a cold" when you were a child? What did that mean to you? ●

with higher scores on working memory tasks during elementary school (de Wilde, Koot, & van Lier, 2016).

Metacognition and Metamemory

Whereas young children tend to see the mind as a static container for information, older children view the mind in more sophisticated terms, as an active manipulator of information. Development of the prefrontal cortex influences children's growing capacities for metacognition. Children become mindful of their thinking and better able to consider the requirements of a task, determine how to tackle it, and monitor, evaluate, and adjust their activity to complete the task (Ardila, 2013).

Metamemory, an aspect of metacognition, includes the understanding of one's memory and the ability to use strategies to enhance it. Metamemory improves steadily throughout the elementary school years and contributes to advances in memory (Cottini, Basso, & Palladino, 2018; Schneider & Ornstein, 2015). Kindergarten and first-grade children understand that forgetting occurs with time and studying improves memory, but not until they are age 8 or 9 can children accurately evaluate their knowledge and apply it to learn more effectively. Older children perform better on cognitive tasks because they can evaluate the task; determine how to approach it given their cognitive resources, attention span, motivation, and knowledge; and choose and monitor the use of memory strategies that will permit them to successfully store and retrieve needed information (Schneider & Pressley, 2013). These abilities improve with neural maturation and experience.

Memory Strategies

Advances in executive function, working memory, and attention enable children to use memory strategies—cognitive activities ("tricks") that make them more likely to remember (Coughlin, Leckey, & Ghetti, 2018). Common memory strategies include rehearsal, organization, and elaboration. **Rehearsal** refers to systematically repeating information in order to retain it in working memory. A child may say a phone number over and over so that he does not forget it before writing it down. Children do not spontaneously and reliably apply rehearsal until after the first grade (Miller, McCulloch, & Jarrold, 2015; Morey, Mareva, Lelonkiewicz, & Chevalier, 2018). Shortly after rehearsal appears, children start to use **organization**, categorizing or chunking items to remember by grouping them by theme or type, such as animals, flowers, and furniture. When memorizing a list of words, a child might organize them into meaningful groups, or chunks—foods, animals, objects, and so forth. Growth in working memory is partially attributed to an increase in the number of chunks children can retain with age (Cowan et al., 2010). A third strategy, **elaboration**, entails creating an imagined scene or story to link the material to be remembered. To remember to buy bread, milk, and butter, for example, a child might imagine a slice of buttered bread balancing on a glass of milk. It is not until the later school years that children use elaboration without prompting and apply it to a variety of tasks (Schneider & Ornstein, 2015). As metacognition and metamemory skills, and the executive function that underlies these abilities, improve, children get better at choosing, using, and combining memory strategies, and their recall improves dramatically (Stone et al., 2016). For example, fifth-grade students who use more complex memory strategies are more successful in delayed recall tasks in which they are asked to read a passage and then recall it after a delay (Jonsson, Wiklund-Hörnqvist, Nyroos, & Börjesson, 2014).

Context and Cognition

As children go about their daily lives, they acquire increasing amounts of information, which they naturally organize in meaningful ways. As children learn more about a topic, their knowledge structures become more elaborate and organized, while the information becomes more familiar and meaningful. It is easier to recall new information about topics with which we are already familiar, and existing knowledge about a topic makes it easier to learn more about that topic (Ericsson & Moxley, 2013). During middle childhood, children develop vast knowledge bases and organize information into elaborate hierarchical networks that enable them to apply strategies in more complex ways and remember more material than ever before—and more easily than ever before. For example, fourth-grade students who are experts at soccer show better recall of a list of soccer-related items than do students who are soccer novices, although the groups of children do not differ on the non-soccer-related items (Schneider & Bjorklund, 1992). The soccer experts tend to organize the lists of soccer items into categories; their knowledge helps them to organize the soccer-related information with little effort, using fewer resources on organization and permitting the use of more working memory for problem solving and reasoning. Novices, in contrast, lack a knowledge base to aid their attempts at organization. Children's experiences, then, influence their memory, thinking, and reasoning.

The strategies that children use to tackle cognitive tasks vary with culture. In fact, daily tasks themselves vary with our cultural context. Children in Western cultures receive lots of experience with tasks that require them to recall bits of information, leading them to develop considerable expertise in the use of memory strategies such as rehearsal, organization, and elaboration. In contrast, research shows that people in non-Western cultures with no formal schooling do not use or benefit from instruction in memory strategies such as rehearsal (Rogoff & Chavajay, 1995). Instead, they refine memory skills that are adaptive to their way of life. For example, they may rely on spatial cues for memory, such as when recalling items within a three-dimensional miniature scene. Australian aboriginal and Guatemalan Mayan children perform better at these tasks than do children from Western cultures (Rogoff & Waddell, 1982). Culture and contextual demands influence the cognitive strategies that we learn and prefer, as well as how we use our information processing system to gather, manipulate, and store knowledge. Children of all cultures amass a great deal of information, and as they get older, they organize it in more sophisticated ways and encode and retrieve it more efficiently and with less effort.

Implications for Education

Children's capacities for executive function hold important implications for education. Parents and teachers can help children learn about the mind and how memory works. They can teach memory strategies, and especially the role of elaboration in learning. We learn more efficiently when we relate new material to what we already know. Parents and teachers can help children relate what they are learning to existing knowledge. They can point out connections, such as that subtraction is the reverse of addition.

Although school-age children's attention and working memory improve, their thinking remains limited as compared with adults. Children can only process a small amount of information at once, so parents and teachers should pace their presentation of new information. Give children time to process information and reduce the working memory demands of tasks by using scaffolds such as presenting complex instructions on the board or asking children to write them down (McDevitt & Ormrod, 2016). Practice in basic skills, such as multiplication table drills, can help children memorize them and free cognitive resources so that they can solve more complex problems.

THINKING IN CONTEXT 11.1

1. In what ways might children's increasing ability to apply logic influence their social relationships and their interactions with others?
2. How do children's surroundings influence their thinking? How might your surroundings—culture, neighborhood, media, home, school, and peers—have influenced specific aspects of your thinking, such as what strategies you use and your capacities for metacognition? Provide examples of how your context has influenced your cognitive development.
3. Imagine that you are an elementary school teacher. How would cognitive-developmental and information processing theories influence your teaching? What parts of each theory do you think are most useful for helping children learn in a classroom setting?

INTELLIGENCE

At its simplest, intelligence refers to an individual's ability to adapt to the world in which he or she lives (Sternberg, 2014a). Individuals differ in intelligence, an example of the lifespan concept of individual differences. There are many ways of defining and measuring intelligence. Intelligence is most commonly assessed through the use of **intelligence tests (IQ tests)**, which measure intellectual aptitude, an individual's capacity to learn.

Intelligence Tests

Individually administered intelligence tests are conducted in a one-on-one setting by professionally trained examiners. The most widely used, individually administered measures of intelligence today are a set of tests constructed by David Wechsler, who viewed intelligence as "the global capacity of a person to act purposefully, to think rationally, and to deal effectively with his environment" (Wechsler, 1944, p. 3). The Wechsler Intelligence Scale for Children (WISC-V), appropriate for children aged 6 through 16, is the most widely used individually administered intelligence test for children. In addition to the WISC, there are Wechsler tests for preschoolers

Intelligence tests are often administered individually, one-on-one.
BSIP/Universal Images Group/Getty Images

(the Wechsler Preschool and Primary Scale of Intelligence, or WPPSI) and adults (the Wechsler Adult Intelligence Scale, or WAIS).

The WISC-V is composed of 10 subtests that comprise an overall measure of IQ as well as five indexes: verbal comprehension, visual spatial, fluid reasoning, working memory, and processing speed (Wechsler, 2014a). The WISC tests verbal abilities that tap vocabulary and knowledge and factual information that is influenced by culture. It also tests nonverbal abilities, such as tasks that require the child to arrange materials such as blocks and pictures, that are thought to be less influenced by culture. The nonverbal subtests require little language proficiency, which enables children with speech disorders and those who do not speak English to be fairly assessed. Supplemental subtests are included to aid examiners in further assessing a child's capacities in a given area. Table 11.1 presents the subtests and sample items that compose the WISC-V. By carefully examining a child's pattern of subtest scores, a professional can determine whether a child has specific learning needs, whether gifted or challenged (Flanagan & Alfonso, 2017).

The WISC is standardized on samples of children who are geographically and ethnically representative of the total population of the United States, creating norms that permit comparisons among children who are similar in age and ethnic background (Sattler, 2014). In Canada, an adapted WISC, standardized with children representative of the Canadian population, is available in English and French (Wechsler, 2014b). The WISC has been adapted and used in many other countries, including the United Kingdom, Greece, Japan, Taiwan, Sweden, Lithuania, Slovenia, Germany, Austria, Switzerland, France, and the Netherlands (Georgas, Weiss, van de Vijver, & Saklofske, 2003).

IQ scores are a strong predictor of academic achievement. Children with high IQs tend to earn higher-than-average grades at school and are more likely to stay in school (Mackintosh, 2011). School, in turn, provides children with exposure to information and ways of thinking that are valued by the majority culture and reflected in IQ tests. Same-age children with more years of schooling tend to have higher IQs than their less educated peers (Cliffordson & Gustafsson, 2008), and correlations between IQ and school achievement tests tend to increase with age (Sternberg, Grigorenko, & Bundy, 2001), suggesting that schooling is also an influence on IQ.

Individual and Group Differences in IQ

A consistent and controversial finding in the intelligence literature is that African American children as a group tend to score 10 to 15 points below non-Hispanic White Americans on standardized IQ tests (Rindermann & Thompson, 2013). The IQ scores of Hispanic children as a group tend to fall between those of children of African American and non-Hispanic White descent, and the scores of Asian American children tend to fall at the same level or slightly higher than those of non-Hispanic White children (Neisser et al., 1996; Nisbett et al., 2013). It is important to remember, however, that emphasizing differences between groups overlooks important facts. For one thing, individuals of all races and ethnicities show a wide range of functioning, from severely disabled to exceptionally gifted. In addition, the IQ scores of children of all races and ethnicities overlap. For example, at least 20% of African American children score higher on IQ than all other children, whether African American or non-Hispanic White (Rindermann & Thompson, 2013). Because there are more differences among African American

TABLE 11.1

Sample Items Measuring the Five Wechsler Intelligence Scale for Children Indices

WISC-V INDEX	SAMPLE ITEM
Verbal Comprehension Index (VCI)	Vocabulary: What does *amphibian* mean?
Visual Spatial Index (VSI)	Block design: In this timed task, children are shown a design composed of red and white blocks, are given a set of blocks, and are asked to put together the blocks in order to copy the design.
Fluid Reasoning Index (FRI)	Matrix reasoning: Children are shown an array of pictures with one missing. They must select the picture that completes the array.
Working Memory Index (WMI)	Digit span: Children are read lists of numbers and asked to repeat them as heard or in reverse order.
Processing Speed Index (PSI)	Coding: In this timed task, children are shown a code that converts numbers into symbols and are asked to transcribe lists of numbers into code.

children and among non-Hispanic White children than between the two groups, many researchers conclude that group comparisons are meaningless (Daley & Onwuegbuzie, 2011).

Contextual Influences on IQ

Like all facets of development, intelligence is influenced by dynamic interactions among genetic or biological factors and context. Heredity is thought to play a role in intelligence, but to date, researchers have not identified any specific genes that are responsible for IQ (Franić et al., 2015). Genes likely do not act independently but instead in conjunction with the environment (Dubois et al., 2012; Plomin et al., 2016). Perhaps most telling is that the heritability of IQ tends to vary with context.

Genes appear to play a large role in determining IQ scores of children from high SES homes but play less of a role in determining IQ scores for children in low SES homes (Nisbett et al., 2013). Because high SES homes tend to provide consistent support, such as cognitive stimulation, to help children achieve their genetic potential, differences in IQ among children reared in high SES homes are more likely due to genetics. Children from impoverished homes, however, often lack consistent access to the basic support needed for intellectual development, such as nutrition, health care, and stimulating environments and activities. In these cases, IQ scores are often heavily influenced by the context and opportunities that children have experienced (Nisbett et al., 2013). African American children are disproportionately likely to live in poverty, and impoverished children's IQ scores tend to be more influenced by the disadvantaged contexts in which they are immersed than by the genes with which they are born. Likewise, children who are adopted from low SES homes into higher SES homes typically score 12 points higher on IQ tests than siblings who are raised by birth parents or adopted into lower SES homes (Duyme, Dumaret, & Tomkiewicz, 1999).

Socioeconomic status contributes to IQ through differences in culture, nutrition, living conditions, school resources, intellectual stimulation, and life circumstances such as the experience of discrimination. Any or all of these factors can influence cognitive and psychosocial factors related to IQ, such as motivation, self-concept, and academic achievement (Plomin & Deary, 2015). Education plays a particularly important role in IQ. As noted earlier, school provides children with exposure to information and ways of thinking that are valued by the majority culture and reflected in IQ tests. IQ rises with each year spent in school, improves during the school year—which generally runs from September to May in the United States—and drops over the summer vacation (Huttenlocher, Levine, & Vevea, 1998). The seasonal drop in IQ scores each summer is larger for children from low SES homes (Nisbett et al., 2013).

Some experts argue that IQ tests tap the thinking style and language of the majority culture (Heath, 1989; Helms, 1992). Language difficulties also may explain some group differences. For example, Latino and Native American children tend to do better on nonverbal tasks than ones that require the use of language (Neisser et al., 1996). However, even nonverbal sorting tasks can be influenced by culture. When presented with a series of cards depicting objects and activities and told to sort the cards into meaningful categories, children from Western cultures tend to sort the cards by category, putting bird and dog in the same category of animal. Children of the Kpelle tribe in Nigeria instead sort the cards by function, placing bird with fly, for example, because birds fly (Sternberg, 1985). Learning experiences and opportunities influence children's scores on nonverbal tasks. For example, performance on spatial reasoning tasks is associated with experience with spatially oriented video games (Subrahmanyam & Greenfield, 1996).

Finally, sociohistorical context influences intelligence. Since the 1930s, some researchers have noted that intelligence scores increase with each generation (Lynn, 2013). Over the past 60 years, intelligence scores have increased by about 9 points for measures of general knowledge and 15 points for nonverbal measures of fluid reasoning with each generation (Flynn, 1987, 1998). Referred to as the **Flynn effect**, this generational increase in IQ is thought to be a function of contextual factors—specifically, changes in education and environmental stimulation that improve children's reasoning and problem-solving skills (Flynn & Weiss, 2007). Each generation of children is exposed to more information and ideas than the generation before, and this exposure likely influences thinking itself (te Nijenhuis, 2013).

Alternative Views of Intelligence

Arguments about the cultural bias of IQ tests have led some researchers to reconsider what it means to be intelligent. Howard Gardner and Robert Sternberg propose that intelligence entails more than academics. Their theories link intelligence to everyday problems and situations.

Multiple Intelligences

A skilled dancer, a champion athlete, an award-winning musician, and an excellent communicator all have talents that are not measured by traditional IQ tests. According to Howard Gardner (2017), intelligence is the ability to solve problems or create

TABLE 11.2

Multiple Intelligences

INTELLIGENCE	DESCRIPTION
Verbal-linguistic intelligence	Ability to understand and use the meanings and subtleties of words ("word smarts").
Logical-mathematical intelligence	Ability to manipulate logic and numbers to solve problems ("number smarts").
Spatial intelligence	Ability to perceive the visual-spatial world accurately, navigate an environment, and judge spatial relationships ("spatial smarts").
Bodily-kinesthetic intelligence	Ability to move the body skillfully ("body smarts").
Musical intelligence	Ability to perceive and create patterns of pitch and melody ("music smarts").
Interpersonal intelligence	Ability to understand and communicate with others ("people smarts").
Intrapersonal intelligence	Ability to understand the self and regulate emotions ("self-smarts").
Naturalist intelligence	Ability to distinguish and classify elements of nature: animals, minerals, and plants ("nature smarts").

Source: Gardner (2017).

culturally valued products. Specifically, Gardner's **multiple intelligence theory** proposes at least eight independent kinds of intelligence, shown in Table 11.2. Multiple intelligence theory expands the use of the term *intelligence* to refer to skills not usually considered intelligence by experts and has led to a great deal of debate among intelligence theorists and researchers (Kaufman, Kaufman, & Plucker, 2013).

According to multiple intelligence theory, each person has a unique pattern of intellectual strengths and weaknesses. A person may be gifted in dance (bodily-kinesthetic intelligence), communication (verbal-linguistic intelligence), or music (musical intelligence), yet score low on traditional measures of IQ. Each form of intelligence is thought to be biologically based, and each develops on a different timetable (Gardner, 2017). Assessing multiple intelligences requires observing the products of each form of intelligence (e.g., how well a child can learn a tune, navigate an unfamiliar area, or learn dance steps), which at best is a lengthy proposition and at worst is nearly impossible (Barnett, Ceci, & Williams, 2006). However, through extended observations, an examiner can identify patterns of strengths and weaknesses in individuals and help them understand and achieve their potential (Gardner, 2016).

The theory of multiple intelligences is an optimistic perspective that allows everyone to be intelligent in his or her own way, viewing intelligence as broader than book-learning and academic skills. If intelligence is multidimensional, as Gardner suggests, perhaps school curricula should target the many forms that intelligence may take and help students to develop a range of talents (Gardner, 2013). Although the theory of multiple intelligences has been criticized as not being grounded in research (Waterhouse, 2006), neuroscientists have noted that each type of intelligence corresponds to specific neurological processes (Shearer & Karanian, 2017). The theory of multiple intelligences draws attention to the fact that IQ tests measure a specific set of mental abilities and ignore others.

Triarchic Theory of Intelligence

Jason Bourne, hero of the popular spy-action novel and movie series *The Bourne Trilogy*, is highly adaptive. He can quickly gather information, such as a villain's plot, process it, and devise a plan. He adapts his plan on the fly as the situation changes and thinks creatively in order to escape seemingly impossible situations—traps, car chases, and other dangerous scenarios. Certainly Jason Bourne is a fictional character, but he illustrates another view of intelligence, articulated by Robert Sternberg. According to Sternberg (1985), intelligence is a set of mental abilities that permit individuals to adapt to any context and to select and modify the sociocultural contexts in which they live and behave. Sternberg's **triarchic theory of intelligence** poses three interacting forms of

FIGURE 11.1

Triarchic Theory of Intelligence

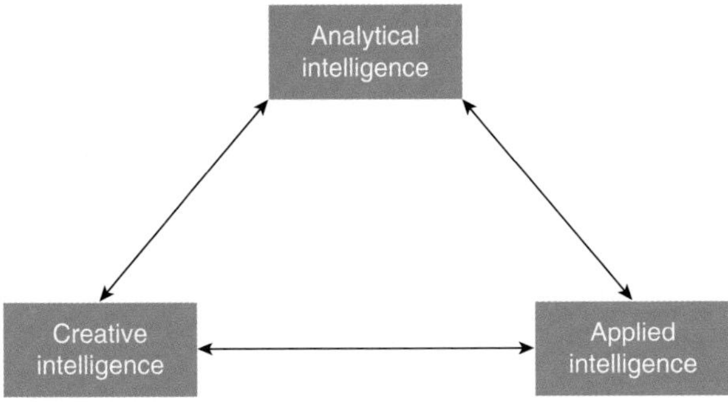

intelligence: analytical, creative, and applied (Sternberg, 2011) (see Figure 11.1). Individuals may have strengths in any or all of them.

Analytical intelligence refers to information processing capacities, such as how efficiently people acquire knowledge, process information, engage in metacognition, and generate and apply strategies to solve problems—much like Bourne's ability to process information quickly and consider different solutions. *Creative intelligence* taps insight and the ability to deal with novelty. People who are high in creative intelligence, like Bourne, respond to new tasks quickly and efficiently. They learn easily, compare information with what is already known, come up with new ways of organizing information, and display original thinking. *Applied intelligence* influences how people deal with their surroundings: how well they evaluate their environment, selecting and modifying it, and adapting it to fit their own needs and external demands—similar to Bourne's ability to modify his plans on the fly, using whatever resources are available. Intelligent people apply their analytical, creative, and applied abilities to suit the setting and problems at hand (Sternberg, 2011). Some situations require careful analysis, others the ability to think creatively, and yet others the ability to solve problems quickly in everyday settings. Many situations tap more than one form of intelligence.

Traditional IQ tests measure analytical ability, which is thought to be associated with school success. However, IQ tests do not measure creative and practical intelligence, which predict success outside of school. Some people are successful in everyday settings but less so in school settings and therefore may obtain low scores on traditional IQ tests despite being successful in their careers and personal lives. In this way, traditional IQ tests can underestimate the intellectual strengths of some children.

Cultures vary in the specific skills thought to constitute intelligence, but the three mental abilities that underlie intelligent behavior—analytic, creative, and applied intelligence—are recognized across cultures. Still, the relative importance ascribed to each may differ (Sternberg & Grigorenko, 2008). In Western cultures, the intelligent person is one who invests a great deal of effort into learning, enjoys it, and enthusiastically seeks opportunities for lifelong learning. In contrast, other cultures emphasize applied intelligence. For example, the Chinese Taoist tradition emphasizes the importance of humility, freedom from conventional standards of judgment, and awareness of the self and the outside world (Yang & Sternberg, 1997). In many African cultures, conceptions of intelligence revolve around the skills that maintain harmonious interpersonal relations (Ruzgis & Grigorenko, 1994). Chewa adults in Zambia emphasize social responsibilities, cooperativeness, obedience, and respectfulness as being important to intelligence. Likewise, Kenyan parents emphasize responsible participation in family and social life (Serpell, 1974; Serpell & Jere-Folotiya, 2008; Super & Harkness, 1982).

Views of intelligence even vary within a given context (Sternberg, 2014b). For example, when parents were asked of the characteristics of an intelligent child in the first grade of elementary school, White American parents emphasized cognitive capacities. Parents who were immigrants from Cambodia, the Philippines, Vietnam, and Mexico, on the other hand, pointed to motivation, self-management, and social skills (Okagaki & Sternberg, 1993), suggesting that characteristics valued as intelligent vary across cultures and that children within the same context may be immersed in different cultures (Sternberg, 2014). Once again, we see the complexity of context and culture as influences on development.

THINKING IN CONTEXT 11.2

1. To what extent do you think the WISC-V subscales match the content taught in elementary school classes? What kinds of experiences might help children improve their verbal comprehension skills? How about spatial reasoning, fluid reasoning, working memory, and processing speed? Are some abilities more easily modified than others? In your view, do schools offer opportunities for children to modify the abilities assessed by the WISC-V?

2. Compare and contrast the multiple intelligence and triarchic perspectives on intelligence. What is the role of context in each theory? In your view, which theory most effectively integrates biological and contextual influences on intelligence?

MORAL REASONING IN MIDDLE CHILDHOOD

The development of moral reasoning is influenced by childhood advances in cognitive development, social experience, and opportunities to consider issues of fairness. Specifically, children's reasoning about justice changes in middle childhood.

Moral Reasoning: Piaget's Theory

As elementary school children spend more time with peers and become better at taking their friends' perspectives, their understanding of rules becomes more flexible. Recall from Chapter 8 that according to Piaget (1932), young children view rules rigidly. Piaget referred to this stage as heteronomous morality. In middle childhood, at about age 7, children enter the second stage of Piaget's scheme, **autonomous morality** (also known as the morality of cooperation). Now children begin to see rules as products of group agreement and tools to improve cooperation. For example, older children are likely to recognize that the teacher's rule that the youngest children must be the first to bat at the piñata at a children's party is a way to help the youngest children, who are less likely to be successful. Some children might agree that the rule promotes fairness, while others might argue to abandon the rule as it gives younger children an unfair advantage. At this stage, children view a need for agreement on rules and consequences for violations. Piaget's theory of moral reasoning inspired Lawrence Kohlberg, who created perhaps the most well-known theory of moral reasoning.

Children's Conceptions of Justice: Kohlberg's Cognitive-Developmental Theory

Kohlberg (1976) proposed that moral reasoning reflects cognitive development and is organized into stages and levels. Each level of moral reasoning is composed of two stages. Beginning in early childhood and persisting until about age 9, children demonstrate what Kohlberg called preconventional reasoning. Similar to Piaget, Kohlberg argued that young children's behavior is governed by self-interest, the desire to gain rewards and avoid punishments ("Don't steal because you don't want to go to jail"). Moral behavior is a response to external pressure, and children's reasoning illustrates their difficulty in taking another person's perspective. Instead, young children's moral reasoning is motivated by their desires. The preconventional level comprises two stages, in which children move from avoiding punishment as a motivator of moral judgments (Stage 1) to self-interest, rewards, and concern about what others can do for them (Stage 2).

At about age 9 or 10, children transition to the second level of Kohlberg's scheme, **conventional moral reasoning**. Children are now able to take others' perspectives and are motivated by reciprocity, seeking to be accepted and avoid disapproval. Rules maintain relationships. At Stage 3, children uphold rules in order to please others, gain affection, and be a good person—honest, caring, and nice. The Golden Rule motivates their behavior: "Do unto others as you would have them do unto you." At Stage 4, which emerges in adolescence, perspective taking expands beyond individuals to include society's rules. Adolescents accept rules as a tool to maintain social order and believe that everyone has a duty to uphold the rules. Reasoning is no longer influenced by relationships and a desire to be a good person. Instead, rules are universal and must be enforced for everyone. Many people demonstrate conventional reasoning throughout their lives. Not everyone develops the third and final level of reasoning, postconventional reasoning, discussed in Chapter 14. Preconventional and conventional moral reasoning are compared in Table 11.3.

Moral development is influenced by how parents and caregivers discuss moral issues, such as those involving telling the truth, harming others, and respecting property rights (Malti & Latzko, 2010). Reasoning advances when children have opportunities to engage in discussions that are characterized by mutual perspective taking and opportunities to discuss different points of view. When children encounter reasoning that is slightly more advanced than their own, they may be prompted to reconsider their own thinking and advance their reasoning. Parents who are warm and engage their children in discussion, listen with sensitivity, and use humor promote the development of moral reasoning (Carlo, Mestre, Samper, Tur, & Armenta, 2011; Killen & Smetana, 2015).

Distributive Justice Reasoning

Every day, children are confronted with moral issues of **distributive justice**—how to divide goods fairly (Damon, 1977, 1988). For example, how should a candy bar be divided among three siblings? Does age matter? Height? Hunger? How much the child likes chocolate?

As with moral reasoning, children progress from self-serving reasons for sharing, expressed

TABLE 11.3

Moral Development in Middle Childhood: Comparison of Piaget's and Kohlberg's Theories

	PIAGET'S STAGES		KOHLBERG'S LEVELS	
	STAGE 1: MORALITY OF CONSTRAINT	STAGE 2: MORALITY OF COOPERATION	LEVEL 1: PRECONVENTIONAL MORAL REASONING	LEVEL 2: CONVENTIONAL MORAL REASONING
Cognitive-developmental stage	Preoperational	Concrete operational	Preoperational	Concrete operational
Perspective	Individualistic. Children cannot take the perspective of others; they assume that everyone sees the world as they do.	Multiple. Children can take the perspective of others; they see that more than one point of view is possible and that others do not necessarily view issues as they do.	Individualistic. Children cannot take the perspective of others; they focus on their own needs.	Community. Children take the perspective of the community at large; there is an emphasis on societal rules and welfare.
View of justice	Absolute. Children see acts as either right or wrong, with no shades of gray. The wrongness of an act is defined by punishment.	Relative. Children see that there is often more than one point of view. Acts are seen as right or wrong regardless of punishment.	Absolute. Acts are either right or wrong, defined by punishment and rewards.	Absolute. Right or wrong acts are defined by social approval.
Understanding of rules	Rules are unalterable and sacred.	Rules are created by people and can be changed if it suits people's needs.	Rules are unalterable and imposed by authority figures.	Rules are unalterable and act to uphold the community.
Reason for compliance with rules	Rules are obeyed out of a sense of obligation to conform to authority and to avoid punishment.	Rules perceived as just are obeyed for their own sake rather than under threat of punishment.	Rules are followed in order to gain rewards and avoid punishment.	Rules are followed out of a sense of duty, in order to please others and gain social approval, which is more important than other rewards.

Source: Adapted from Hoffman (1970), Kohlberg (1981), and Piaget (1932).

in early childhood (e.g., "I get more candy because I want it" or "I share candy so that Mikey will play with me"), to more sophisticated and mature conceptions of distributive justice in middle childhood (Damon, 1977). At about 7 years of age, children take merit into account and believe that extra candy should go to the child who has excelled or worked especially hard. At around 8 years of age, children can act on the basis of benevolence, believing that others at a disadvantage should get special consideration. For example, extra candy should go to the child who does not get picked to play on a sports team or a child who is excluded from an activity. Between ages 8 and 10, children come to understand that people can have different yet equally valid reasons for claiming a reward. They begin to reflect on the need to balance competing claims, such as those of merit and need (Smith & Warneken, 2016). Older children also tend to differentiate among their relationships, which may influence their judgments. For example, older children often see relationships with acquaintances as relationships of mutual exchange (e.g., you scratch my back and I'll scratch yours), whereas relationships with their best friends might be seen as communal and reciprocal; decisions may be guided by concern for the other and a desire to maintain the relationship (Frederickson & Simmonds, 2008). Preadolescents and young adolescents try to coordinate claims of merit, need, and equality and provide increasingly sophisticated answers that often cannot be expressed in a single sentence (Damon, 1980).

Culture subtly influences children's ideas about distributive justice. Research with young children from rural and urban areas of China, Peru, Fiji, the United States, Brazil, and Tibet showed a similar pattern of development from self-interest to increasing fairness (Robbins, Starr, & Rochat, 2016; Rochat et al., 2009). Cultures varied in the magnitude of young children's self-interest. Children reared in small-scale urban and traditional societies thought to promote more collective values showed less self-interest and more fairness. When Filipino and American fifth graders were presented with hypothetical scenarios that required that they distribute resources, both the Filipino and American children preferred equal division of the resources regardless of merit or need, but the children offered different explanations of their choices that are based in differences in Filipino and U.S. culture (Carson & Banuazizi, 2008). U.S. children emphasized that the characters in the scenario performed equally and therefore deserved equal amounts of the resources, reflecting U.S. culture's emphasis on individuality and merit. Filipino children, on the other hand, tended to be more concerned with the interpersonal and emotional consequences of an unequal distribution, in line with their culture's emphasis on the collective and the importance of interpersonal relationships (Carson & Banuazizi, 2008).

Distinguishing Moral and Conventional Rules

Like younger children, school-age children distinguish between moral and conventional rules, judging moral imperatives as more absolute than conventional rules (see Chapter 8) (Turiel & Nucci, 2017). Moral rules are seen as less violable, less contingent on authority, and less alterable than social conventions (Smetana, Jambon, & Ball, 2013). Children anticipate feeling positive emotions after following moral imperatives and are likely to label violations of moral imperatives as disgusting (Danovitch & Bloom, 2009). With advances in cognitive development, children can consider multiple perspectives and become better able to consider the situation and weigh a variety of variables in making decisions. They discriminate social conventions that have a purpose from those with no obvious purpose. Social conventions that serve a purpose, such as preventing injuries (e.g., not running indoors), are evaluated as more important and more similar to moral issues than social conventions with no obvious purpose (e.g., avoiding a section of the school yard despite no apparent danger) (Smetana et al., 2013). School-age children also consider intent and context. For example, Canadian 8- to 10-year-old children understood that a flag serves as a powerful symbol of a country and its values—and that burning it purposefully is worse than accidentally burning it. The 10-year-old children also understood that flag burning is an example of freedom of expression and can be used to express disapproval of a country or its activities. They agreed that if a person were in a country that is unjust, burning its flag would be acceptable (Helwig & Prencipe, 1999).

School-age children also distinguish among moral issues. For example, elementary school children judged bullying as wrong independent of rules and more wrong than other moral issues, such as lapses in truth-telling—and both were judged more wrong than etiquette transgressions (Thornberg, Thornberg, Alamaa, & Daud, 2016). School-age children become increasingly able to demonstrate nuanced judgments in response to complex moral dilemmas. For example, 5- to 11-year-old children become increasingly tolerant of necessary harm—that is, violating moral rules in order to prevent injury to others (Jambon & Smetana, 2014).

Children develop and hone their understanding of morality through social interaction, at home, at school, and with peers. Children regularly encounter moral and conventional issues, such as lying to a friend, not completing homework, or violating a household rule. Everyday social interactions can advance moral reasoning. When children engage in issue-focused discussions involving reasoning that is slightly more advanced than their own, it may prompt them to reconsider their own thinking. As a result, they often internalize the new reasoning, advancing their moral thinking to a new level.

As children grow older, they are more likely to view relational aggression as morally wrong and comparable to physical aggression.
©iStockphoto.com/LSOphoto

THINKING IN CONTEXT 11.3

1. In what ways might children's moral reasoning, such as conventional moral reasoning, influence their decisions about distributive justice? Do children who show more mature moral reasoning view moral and conventional issues differently? Why or why not?
2. How might moral development influence socioemotional development, such as children's experience of emotion, self-understanding, and relationships?
3. Theories of moral reasoning emphasize cognition. In what ways might children's decisions about right and wrong reflect other factors, such as physical maturation or socioemotional development?

LANGUAGE DEVELOPMENT IN MIDDLE CHILDHOOD

School-age children expand their vocabulary and develop a more complex understanding of grammar, rules that permit combining words to express ideas and feelings. Children's understanding of pragmatics, how language is used in everyday contexts, grows and becomes more sophisticated during middle childhood.

Vocabulary

School-age children's increases in vocabulary are not as noticeable to parents as the changes that occurred in infancy and early childhood. Nevertheless, 6-year-old children's vocabularies expand by four times by the end of the elementary school years and six times by the end of formal schooling (Clark, 2017).

Children learn that many words can describe a given action, but the words often differ slightly in meaning (e.g., walk, stride, hike, march, tread, strut, and meander) (Hoff, 2014). They become more selective in their use of words, choosing the right word to meet their needs. As their vocabularies grow, children learn that some words can have more than one meaning, such as run ("The jogger runs down the street," "The clock runs fast," etc.). They begin to appreciate that some words have psychological meanings as well as physical ones (e.g., a person can be smooth and a surface can be smooth). This understanding that words can be used in more than one way leads 8- to 10-year-old children to understand similes and metaphors (e.g., a person can be described as "cold as ice" or "sharp as a tack") (Katz, 2017).

One influence on children's growing vocabulary in middle childhood is reading.
©iStockphoto.com/FangXiaNuo

Everyday experiences shape our vocabulary, how we think, and how we speak. Words are often acquired incidentally from writing and verbal contexts rather than through explicit vocabulary instruction (Owens, 2016). Some complex words, such as scientific terms, require the acquisition of conceptual knowledge over repeated exposure in different contexts. One study examined 4- to 10-year-old children's knowledge of two scientific terms, eclipse and comet, before and after the natural occurrence of a solar eclipse. Two weeks after the solar eclipse and without additional instruction, the children showed improvement in their knowledge of eclipses but not comets; older and younger children did not differ in their knowledge (Best, Dockrell, & Braisby, 2006).

Grammar

Older children become increasingly aware of and knowledgeable about the nature and qualities of language, known as metalinguistic awareness (Simard & Gutiérrez, 2018). Language arts classes in elementary school teach children about the parts of language and the syntax of sentences, aiding children as they further develop their ability to think about their use of language. By 8 years of age, children can analyze the grammatical acceptability of their utterances and spontaneously self-correct many of their errors (Hanley, Cortis, Budd, & Nozari, 2016).

In middle childhood, schoolchildren become better able to understand complex grammatical structures. They begin to use the passive voice ("The dog is being fed"), complex constructions such as the use of the auxiliary "have" ("I have already fed the dog"), and conditional sentences ("If I had been home earlier, I would have fed the dog") (Clark, 2017). Despite these advances, school-age children often have difficulty understanding spoken sentences when the meaning depends on subtle shifts in intonation (Turnbull & Justice, 2016). An example can be found in the sentence, "John gave a lollipop to David, and he gave one to Bob." With the emphasis placed on "and," the sentence can be taken to mean that John gave a lollipop to both David and Bob, whereas if the emphasis is on "he," the sentence can be assumed to mean that John gave a lollipop to David, and David gave a lollipop to Bob.

Experience with language and exposure to complex constructions influence grammatical development. For example, most English-speaking children find passive-voice sentences (such as "The boy was struck by the car") difficult to understand and therefore master passive-voice sentences later than other structures (Armon-Lotem et al., 2016). In contrast, the Inuit children of Arctic Canada hear and speak the Inuktitut language, which emphasizes full passives; they produce passive-voice sentences in their language sooner than do children from other cultures (Allen & Crago, 1996). The culture and language systems in which children are immersed influence their use of language and, ultimately, the ways in which they communicate. Throughout middle childhood, sentence structure and use of grammar become more sophisticated, children become better at communicating their ideas, and their understanding of pragmatics improves.

Pragmatics

Pragmatics refers to the practical application of language to communicate (Owens, 2016). With age and advances in perspective-taking skills that come with cognitive development, children are more likely to change their speech in response to the needs of listeners. For example, when faced with an adult who will not give them a desired object, 9-year-old children are more polite in restating their request than are 5-year-old children (Ninio, 2014). Similarly, 10-year-old Marques asks to share a cookie with his friend ("Yo! Gimme a cookie!") using very different language and intonation than he does when asking his grandmother for a cookie ("May I please have a cookie?"). Children speak to adults differently than to other children, and they speak differently on the playground than in class or at home. In addition, older children begin to understand that there is often a distinction between what people say and what they mean.

One example of pragmatics that develops in middle childhood is the use of irony, choosing a word or expression that conveys the opposite of its literal meaning. Many contextual, linguistic, and developmental factors influence the processing and comprehension of irony, such as the ability to interpret intonation and facial expressions as well as the capacity to evaluate how well a statement matches the situation (Pexman, 2014). Children at the ages of 5 to 6 become capable of recognizing irony when they are able to understand that a speaker might believe something different from what has been said. Yet most children at this age tend to interpret irony as sincere, relying on the person's statement and disregarding other cues in the story, such as intonation and gestures. Cognitive development permits children to detect the discrepancy between what the speaker says and what he or she believes. Children's ability to understand ironic remarks continues to develop through middle childhood, and by age 8, children can recognize and use irony (Glenwright & Pexman, 2010). However, even in adolescence, the understanding of irony is still developing; children as old as 13 do not reliably distinguish irony, intended to joke or mock, from deception, intended to conceal information (Filippova & Astington, 2008).

Bilingual Language Learning

About 22% of school-age children in the United States speak a language other than English at home (Annie E. Casey Foundation, 2017). Of these, about one in five struggle with speaking English at school (Federal Interagency Forum on Child and Family Statistics, 2017). How should children be taught a new language? In the United States, English as a Second Language (ESL) is most often taught to children by English immersion, which places foreign-language-speaking children in English-speaking classes, requiring them to learn English and course content at the same time. Some studies suggest that immersion is associated with a loss in children's native language use (Baus, Costa, & Carreiras, 2013).

Another approach is **dual-language learning** (also called two-way immersion), in which English-speaking and non-English-speaking students learn together in both languages and both languages are valued equally. Advocates of dual-language learning argue that bringing a child's native language into the classroom sends children the message that their cultural heritage is respected and strengthens their cultural identity and self-esteem. Children exposed to dual-language immersion tend to retain their native language while learning the new language (Castro, Páez, Dickinson, & Frede, 2011). Longitudinal research with U.S. samples suggests that dual-language immersion approaches, which encourage students to retain their native language while learning English, are more effective than immersion approaches at promoting successful learning of English as well as overall academic achievement (Relji, Ferring, & Martin, 2015). Approaches to second language learning remain hotly debated, however.

Learning a second language during childhood may affect proficiency in the first or native language. The first language may be lost or the second language may become dominant, used more often

In a dual-language learning classroom, English and non-English language students learn in the same classroom.
Joe Amon/Denver Post/Getty Images

(Hoff, 2015). In one study of Chinese immigrant children in New York City, children who were under the age of 9 when they immigrated reported preferring English to Mandarin 1 year later and were more proficient in English 3 years later than children who were older than 9 at the time of immigration (Jia & Aaronson, 2003). Why the difference? The younger children became friends with children who spoke English and spent more time interacting with peers who spoke English than the older children. Peers and the surrounding community influence bilingual children's language acquisition and use, and the language that is used most becomes dominant.

A similar switch in language preference and dominance has been shown in a study of children in Southern California who first learned Spanish at home and then began to learn English at school at 5 years of age (Kohnert & Bates, 2002). The children improved their proficiency in both Spanish and English but made faster progress in English, so that by middle childhood, they were more proficient in English. Children who are living in the United States or another English-speaking country and are Spanish-English bilingual at 2 years of age often become English dominant by age 4. As a result, many adults who grew up in Spanish-speaking homes retain little ability to speak Spanish (Hoff et al., 2014).

The ability to speak more than one language is associated with many cognitive skills. Individuals who have mastered two or more languages have higher scores on measures of memory, selective attention, analytical reasoning, concept formation, and cognitive flexibility (Bialystok, 2015). Bilingual children tend to score higher on measures of executive function, particularly the ability to control attention and ignore misleading information (Barac & Bialystok, 2012; Barac, Bialystok, Castro, & Sanchez, 2014). These effects emerge slowly over the course of several years. For example, one study of second- and fifth-grade students showed improvements over a 5-year span in tasks such as verbal fluency and executive control (Bialystok, Peets, & Moreno, 2014). Moreover, when children are able to speak, read, and write in two languages, they are more cognitively and socially flexible and can participate in both cultures.

THINKING IN CONTEXT 11.4

1. Children's advances in language enable them to have more complicated relationships with parents and peers. Discuss the social implications of gains in vocabulary, grammar, and pragmatics.
2. Recall from Chapter 1 that development is characterized by continuities and discontinuities. How might you characterize language development in middle childhood? Is it continuous or discontinuous? Why?
3. In your view, why is learning a second language beneficial for children's development? Why is it associated with cognitive gains?

LEARNING AND SCHOOLING IN MIDDLE CHILDHOOD

Schoolchildren's advancing cognitive abilities enable them to learn in more sophisticated ways. As we have discussed, however, their ability to grasp logic is still developing. Effective instruction helps older children grasp complex ideas by identifying connections between new material and prior knowledge, building on what they already know, and keeping pace with their growing abilities. During the school years, older children become proficient at reading, writing, and mathematics.

Approaches to Education

Recall from our discussion of early childhood education (see Chapter 8), that preschool programs vary in orientation from academically centered, emphasizing structured learning, to child centered, an approach that places the child at the center of his or her own learning. A similar distinction characterizes classrooms in elementary school.

Teacher-Centered Classroom

Classrooms that are teacher centered emphasize direct instruction from a teacher who selects the instructional strategies and conveys information to students through direct instruction (Powell, 2019). Learning activities typically include drills, quizzes, presentations, and recitations of definitions, facts, and lists. Children's learning is assessed through quizzes and exams that often involve selecting responses, such as multiple choice or fill-in-the-blank items.

A criticism of teacher-centered instruction is that students tend to have a passive role in instruction because it is often limited to responding to teacher-specified directions (Burden & Byrd, 2019). Critics argue that teacher-centered instruction overemphasizes teacher talk and centers on learning and comprehending facts rather than higher-level thinking. Today facts are easily available via the Internet. Children need to develop skills in evaluating and applying information (Borich, 2017).

Constructivist Classroom

Often referred to as a student-centered approach, constructivist classrooms involve students in their own learning (Powell, 2019). Influenced by Piaget and Vygotsky's perspectives on cognitive development, children are viewed as active constructors of their own understanding through interactions with their worlds.

Constructivist student-centered instruction emphasizes engaging children in problem-solving activities in which students investigate a problem, examine data or information relevant to the problem, and devise conclusions. Teachers ask questions to encourage student exploration and nurture reflection and thought about the process rather than emphasizing a single correct answer. Constructivist approaches also encourage peer interaction. Cooperative learning, role playing, simulations, and debates permit students to interact, share their ideas, and learn from one another (Burden & Byrd, 2019).

Reading and Mathematics Instruction

Cognitive development, especially in executive functioning and working memory, contributes to advances in math achievement and reading comprehension in elementary school (Cormier, McGrew, Bulut, & Funamoto, 2017). Schooling plays a key role in aiding children in mastering reading and math.

In past generations, most children were taught to read via phonics instruction, lessons and drills that emphasized learning the patterns of sound combinations in words. Children learned the sounds of each letter, memorized language rules, and sounded out words (Brady, 2011). In the late 1980s, the whole-language approach to reading instruction was introduced. In this approach, literacy is viewed as an extension of language, and children learn to read and write through trial-and-error discovery that is similar to how they learn to speak—without drills or learning phonics. The emphasis on children as active constructors of knowledge is appealing and in line with cognitive-developmental theory. Today, the whole-language approach is still in widespread use, and many teachers are not trained in phonics instruction. However, the research comparing the two approaches has offered little support for whole-language claims and overwhelming support for the efficacy of phonics training in improving children's reading skills (Cunningham, 2013).

A substantial number of U.S. children are poor readers and thereby at risk for poor academic achievement. In 2017, over one-third of fourth-grade students were unable to meet basic standards for reading at their grade level (National Center for Education Statistics, 2019). Early reading deficits influence all areas of academic competence (math, writing, science, etc.), and children who experience early difficulties in reading often remain behind (Hong & Yu, 2007). Children's attitudes, interests, and motivation in reading and writing tend to decline over the school years, and the drop occurs more rapidly in worse readers (Wigfield, Gladstone, & Turci, 2016). Deficits in reading skill are associated with social adjustment problems, and this association increases over time. For example, poor reading achievement in preschool and third grade predicts behavioral problems in first grade and fifth grade (Guo, Sun, Breit-Smith, Morrison, & Connor, 2015). Children with poor reading skills tend to have poor vocabularies, which may make it more difficult for them to successfully interact with peers (Benner, Nelson, & Epstein, 2002).

Similar to reading, in past generations, math was taught through rote learning activities such as drills, memorization of number facts (e.g., multiplication tables), and completion of workbooks. Many children found these methods boring or restrictive; they learned to dislike math and did not perform well. In 1989, the National Council of Teachers of Mathematics modified the national mathematics curriculum to emphasize mathematical concepts and problem solving, estimating, and probability; teachers were to encourage student interaction and social involvement in solving math problems. The emphasis changed from product—getting correct answers quickly—to process—learning how to understand and execute the steps in getting an answer. Teachers often use strategies that involve manipulatives, opportunities for students to interact physically with objects to learn target information, rather than relying solely on abstraction. Such strategies have been shown to be effective in enhancing problem solving and retention (Carbonneau, Marley, & Selig, 2013).

In contrast with research findings about the whole-language approach to reading, changes in the mathematics curriculum are supported by student achievement, as fourth-grade students' mathematical skills have improved over the past 2 decades. Between 1990 and 2017, the proportion of fourth-grade students performing at or above the proficient level increased from 13% to 40%, and the proportion who could not do math at their grade level fell from 50% in 1990 to 20% in 2017 (National Center for Education Statistics, 2019). Although these represent important gains, the 20% statistic means that one in five U.S. schoolchildren is still deficient in math skills, suggesting that there is more work to be done. The past decades have seen new educational initiatives that emphasize math and reading instruction coupled with frequent assessments of student achievement to ensure that progress is made and children do not fall through the cracks. What should educators do when children fail to meet academic standards for promotion to the next grade level? See the accompanying Applying Developmental Science feature for more discussion on this topic.

Transition to First Grade

Most children go to kindergarten before entering first grade, and many go to preschool before kindergarten. Despite some experience with the educational system, children usually feel a mixture of excitement and anxiety upon entering first grade. For most children and parents, first grade holds symbolic value as the threshold to elementary school and older childhood.

Easing children's transition to first grade is important because adjustment and behavior during the first year of elementary school influence teachers' perceptions as well as children's views of themselves, their academic performance, and class

APPLYING DEVELOPMENTAL SCIENCE

Should Children Get "Left Back"?

What should educators do when children fail to meet academic standards for promotion to the next grade level? In the 1970s, social promotion, the practice of promoting children to the next grade even when they have not met the academic standards, became a common educational practice because grade retention, or "getting left back," became viewed as damaging to children's self-esteem (Bowman, 2005; Kelly, 1999). As social promotion rose in popularity during the 1980s, schoolchildren's standardized test scores declined and school officials were criticized for promoting failing students to the next grade level (Shepard & Smith, 1990). By the 1990s, legislators and the general public called for an end to social promotion and many states banned it in favor of grade retention as a way to remediate poor academic performance (Frey, 2005).

About 10% of U.S. children are retained in a grade at least once between kindergarten and eighth grade (National Center for Education Statistics, 2017a). In addition to state-mandated retention due to low achievement scores, students are retained for other reasons, such as frequent unexcused absences, social and cognitive immaturity, and the belief that an extra year of schooling will produce successful academic and socioemotional outcomes. Black students are more likely to be retained than White and Hispanic students (2.6% of Black students in kindergarten through eighth grade were retained in 2016, compared with 1.5% of White and Hispanic students) (National Center for Education Statistics, 2019). Children of color often face obstacles to education though challenging neighborhood and home environments, lack of access to resources, and discrimination (Warren & Saliba, 2012).

Does grade retention work? In some cases, retention can be a wake-up call to children and parents. Some students show an improvement in grades and are less likely to take remedial courses (Schwerdt, West, & Winters, 2017). However, the cumulative evidence published to date shows that students who are retained in school, even in the first 2 years of elementary school, do not fare as well as promoted students. They later show poor performance in reading, mathematics, and language as well as poor school attendance and more emotional and social difficulties. They also report a dislike for school more than do their peers who were promoted and are more likely to drop out of high school by age 16 (Ehmke, Drechsel, & Carstensen, 2010; Hughes, Cao, West, Allee Smith, & Cerda, 2017; Hughes, Chen, Thoemmes, & Kwok, 2010; Wu, West, & Hughes, 2010). Dropping out of high school has long-term negative effects on postsecondary education, career, and income. As shown in Table 11.4, the National Association of School Psychologists

(Continued)

(Continued)

TABLE 11.4

National Association of School Psychologists' Recommendations to Enhance Academic Achievement and Reduce Retention and Social Promotion

TARGET	ACTION
Parental involvement	Have frequent contact with teachers. Supervise children's homework.
Instruction	Adopt age-appropriate and culturally sensitive instructional strategies. Continuously monitor instructional strategies and effectiveness and modify instructional efforts in response. Implement effective early reading programs. Offer extended year, extended day, and summer school programs to develop and promote academic skills.
Student academic support	Identify students with learning difficulties, design interventions to address academic problems, and evaluate the effectiveness of those interventions. Provide comprehensive education services for children with educational disabilities, including collaboration between regular, remedial, and special education professionals.
Student psychosocial support	Create and implement school-based mental health programs that identify students in need of assistance and devise ways of aiding students. Address student behavior problems with the use of behavior management and cognitive strategies to reduce classroom behavior problems. Establish full-service schools to organize educational, social, and health services to meet the diverse needs of at-risk students.

(2003) recommends providing students and families with a variety of academic and support resources to promote student achievement and address school failure.

What Do You Think?

How can parents and teachers help children avoid getting left back? Should a child ever repeat a grade? Why or why not? ●

involvement (Zafiropoulou, Sotiriou, & Mitsiouli, 2007). Teachers play an important role in aiding children's adjustment to first grade. They provide both instructional and emotional support: For example, they attend to students' interests, promote initiative, provide appropriately challenging learning opportunities, and encourage positive social relationships (Cadima, Doumen, Verschueren, & Buyse, 2015). These forms of support help children develop not only academic skills but also social skills, such as self-control and the ability to follow directions (Lerkkanen et al., 2016).

High-quality, sensitive, responsive, and positive interactions with teachers are associated with greater student motivation and academic achievement and fewer problems with anxiety and poor behavior throughout elementary school (Maldonado-Carreño & Votruba-Drzal, 2011; Van Craeyevelt, Verschueren, Vancraeyveldt, Wouters, & Colpin, 2017). Conversely, teacher–child conflict is associated with aggression, poor social competence, and underachievement throughout elementary school (Runions et al., 2014; Spilt, Hughes, Wu, & Kwok, 2012; White, 2013).

First grade serves as a foundation for a child's educational career because the school curriculum of each grade builds on prior grades. Starting in first grade, reading and math skills build step by step each year, so that doing well in one year helps children perform well the next year (Entwisle, Alexander, & Steffel Olson, 2005). Early academic deficiencies often persist through the school years, and children may fall further behind with each successive year in school. In addition, children's performance in each grade is documented into a cumulative file that follows them from year to year, influencing teachers' perceptions and expectations of them, which, in turn, influences their educational success.

Access to Digital Technology and Learning

All school-age children in the United States have access to computers or tablets at school, and broadband Internet is available to all schools (National Science Foundation, 2018). However, not all schools provide access to current technology, and the quality of Internet access varies across school systems. Schools in rural areas and low SES communities are less likely to have access to current technology or may have fewer opportunities to access computers and tablets, given fewer resources.

Computers and tablets offer children new learning opportunities. Effective educational applications engage children and foster active learning through discovery. For example, children may learn social studies, math, and science by playing and reflecting on computer simulations, games, and interactive cartoons (Chauhan, 2017; Hwang, Chiu, & Chen, 2015; Outhwaite, Gulliford, & Pitchford, 2017). Perhaps not surprising, children report preferring tablet learning to traditional classroom instruction (Dunn, Gray, Moffett, & Mitchell, 2018). Digital learning environments are especially effective in fostering learning outside of the classroom, at home (Chauhan, 2017). Computer and tablet-based games and interventions improve attention, working memory, and other cognitive skills (Ramos & Melo, 2019; Roberts et al., 2016).

Unfortunately, children's home access to technology varies with geography and socioeconomic status (Katz, Moran, & Gonzalez, 2018). About one-quarter of rural families report access to highspeed Internet as a major problem and an additional third report it as a minor problem (Anderson, 2018). While more than 90% of families with school-age children living in low SES homes report having Internet access, more than half of these families report that their connectivity is constrained by interrupted or slow service, outdated devices, or having to share devices (Rideout, 2016). Inequity in home access to technology, often referred to as the homework gap because of the challenges that students face when trying to do their homework, increases as teachers incorporate more technology-based learning into assignments and the effects magnify with each grade (Moore, Vitale, & Stawinoga, 2018). Children with poor access to technology at home typically report using their smartphone and cellular data plan. School and community initiatives that provide children with tablet computers for home use hold promise for improving children's access to technology and closing the homework gap (Wenger, 2018).

Giftedness

Traditionally, **giftedness** has been defined by IQ scores, specifically scores of 130 or greater (Horowitz & O'Brien, 1986), and thereby associated primarily with academic skill. Recent definitions of giftedness are broader, including a wide range of human abilities, talents, and accomplishments in areas such as art, music, creative writing, dance, and sports (Mcclain & Pfeiffer, 2012). Exceptionally talented children share several characteristics. Not only are they smart, but their ability, whether in music, math, or other, is substantially above average (Subotnik, Olszewski-Kubilius, & Worrell, 2011). Moreover, gifted children translate their intellectual abilities and talents into outstanding performance and innovation in areas in which they are passionate. Finally, perhaps most essential to exceptional performance is creativity. Gifted persons are creative, meaning that they are able to come up with new thoughts and actions leading them to produce work that is original—that is, something that others have not thought of, and that is useful (Kaufman, Plucker, & Russell, 2012). Gifted children show creativity in identifying problems, generating ideas, choosing the most promising ideas, and applying their knowledge to understand and solve problems (Guignard & Lubart, 2006).

Many experts view giftedness as a talent that must be developed and nurtured (Pfeiffer, 2012). Without encouragement, support, and stimulation, talent may deteriorate. Talented children require home and school environments that are challenging and supportive, with stimulating peers (Subotnik et al., 2011). There are two general approaches toward educating gifted children: enrichment and acceleration. The enrichment approach covers the same curriculum as a typical class, but in greater depth, breadth, or complexity. Students may share the classroom with their average-ability peers and receive enriched content after school, on Saturday, during the summer, or through more challenging assignments (Kim, 2016). In contrast, an accelerated program covers the curriculum at a more advanced pace, in conjunction with student mastery. A student might skip grade levels in particular subjects, such as mathematics, or may skip a grade entirely.

Some parents and teachers fear that students who accelerate their education may not be emotionally or socially ready to enter college at a young age, but research suggests that gifted children in accelerated programs generally do not report feeling isolated from their peers and do not show negative social or emotional outcomes (Boazman & Sayler, 2011). Instead, some research suggests that they experience fewer emotional problems than their peers and display more emotional maturity (Simonton & Song, 2009; Subotnik et al., 2011). One study of first- through sixth-grade students found that the gifted students scored higher on measures of theory of mind, suggesting that they have greater social understanding than their average-ability peers (Boor-Klip, Cillessen, & van Hell, 2014). As adults, gifted children who accelerated their education report satisfaction with their career, relationships, and life (Lubinski, Benbow, Webb, & Bleske-Rechek, 2006). Longitudinal research following gifted young adolescents through adulthood found that they tend to be, as adults, extraordinarily successful in school and in their careers. For example, more than 15% had been awarded patents and over one-third earned doctorates by age 40 (Kell, Lubinski, Benbow, & Steiger, 2013; Makel, Kell, Lubinski, Putallaz, & Benbow, 2016). Like all children, however, gifted children require supportive environments to help them reach their intellectual potential.

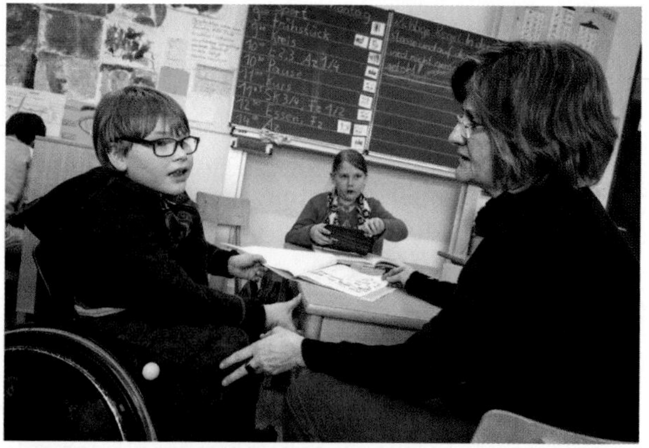

Special education classrooms that practice inclusion integrate all children into a regular classroom with additional teachers and educational support that is tailored to learners' needs.
E.D. Torial / Alamy Stock Photo

Educating Children With Special Needs

School systems must meet the needs of a diverse population of children, many with special educational needs. Children with intellectual and learning disabilities require assistance to help them overcome obstacles to learning. **Special education** is tailored to a child's specific needs. It is individually planned, specialized, goal directed, and guided by student performance (Heward, 2018). In the United States and Canada, legislation mandates that children with disabilities are to be placed in the "least restrictive" environment, or classrooms that are as similar as possible to classrooms for children without learning disabilities. Whenever possible, children are to be educated in the general classroom, with their peers, for all or part of the day. Teachers must be sensitive to the special needs of students with learning disabilities and provide additional instruction and extra time for them to complete assignments. When children are placed in regular classrooms with peers of all abilities, they have multiple opportunities to learn from peers and may be better prepared to learn and work alongside people of all abilities.

A special education approach known as **inclusion** integrates children with learning disabilities in the regular classroom and provides them with a teacher or paraprofessional specially trained to meet their needs (Mastropieri & Scruggs, 2017). Inclusion may take different forms for different children or may vary depending on academic subject. For example, one child with a learning disability may attend class with peers all day, receiving additional handouts, guidance, or extra time to complete assignments. Another student with a learning disability might be placed in the regular classroom, but may receive special instruction for part of the day (or for a specific subject) in a resource room (Salend, 2015).

Children's responses to inclusion vary with the severity of their disabilities as well as the quality and quantity of support provided in the classroom (Lewis et al., 2017). Most experts agree that inclusion works best when children receive instruction in a resource room that meets their

THINKING IN CONTEXT 11.5

1. In your view, what is the purpose of first grade? What kinds of learning experiences are most important for children to have when they start school? Why?
2. Suppose you were tasked with creating a class environment that would address the needs of children with intellectual disabilities and learning disabilities as well as children without disabilities. What would your environment include? What are some of the challenges in creating such an environment?
3. What school and community resources might support children with special education needs and their families? Recalling from Chapter 1 that development is multidimensional, consider resources that support multiple domains of development—physical, cognitive, and socioemotional—relevant to children with special needs.

specialized needs for part of the school day and the regular classroom for the rest of the school day (Heward, 2018). Children with learning disabilities report preferring combining time in the regular classroom with time in a resource room that is equipped with a teacher who is trained to meet their special learning needs (Vaughn & Klingner, 1998). Interaction with peers and cooperative learning assignments that require children to work together to achieve academic goals help students with learning disabilities learn social skills and form friendships with peers.

Although children with disabilities learn strategies to succeed, the disabilities themselves and the academic and social challenges posed by them do not disappear. Like all children, children with disabilities often need to adapt their learning strategies as they gain competence. Parents and teachers who are sensitive to children's changing needs will be better able to help them. Parents and teachers are most helpful when they understand that learning disabilities are not a matter of intelligence or laziness but rather a function of brain differences and when they help children to learn to monitor their behavior.

APPLY YOUR KNOWLEDGE

Five-year-old Kira instructed 3-year-old Romeo how to play hopscotch: "You throw the rock onto the first square, then on one leg, hop over it and onto all of the other squares. Come back and, on one leg, pick up the rock, then jump over the first square back to the beginning." Romeo looked puzzled as he jumped onto the square with two feet. "No! That's against the rules!" Kira argued.

"Romeo's younger and his balance isn't good," advised Kira's 9-year-old sister, Mira. "Let him play this way," she said. "No! It's a rule and you can't play it that way. No breaking the rule," insisted Kira. Mira shook her head at her younger sister and said, "We can make a new rule."

In her room, Mira pulled out her big box of seashells. "What kinds of rules can I use for ordering these?" she wondered. Sometimes she organizes her shells by color, other times by size. Sometimes she sorts them by both color and size. Recently Mira discovered a website that has pictures and names for all kinds of seashells. Mira identified each of her shells and memorized the names. Now she organizes shells by class or type.

1. Contrast Kira and Mira's perspectives on the rules of hopscotch. How does their understanding of rules differ?
2. Compare Kira and Mira's reasoning with the cognitive-developmental approach to morality.
3. Discuss Mira's cognitive development from Piaget's perspective. Give examples.
4. What information processing skills influence how Mira plays with her seashells?

WANT A BETTER GRADE?

KEY TERMS

Concrete operational stage of reasoning 296

Classification 296

Transitive inference 296

Seriation 296

Class inclusion 296

Metamemory 300

Rehearsal 300

Organization 300

Elaboration 300

Intelligence test (IQ test) 301

Flynn effect 303

Multiple intelligence theory 304

Triarchic theory of intelligence 304

Autonomous morality 306

Conventional moral reasoning 306

Distributive justice 306

Pragmatics 310

Dual-language learning 310

Giftedness 315

Special education 316

Inclusion 316

SUMMARY

11.1 Examine school-age children's capacities for reasoning and processing information.

At about age 7, children enter the concrete operational stage of reasoning, permitting them to use mental operations to solve problems and think logically and to demonstrate several different kinds of classification skills and make advances in solving conservation tasks. Concrete operational reasoning is found in children around the world; however, experience, specific cultural practices, and education play a role in development. Brain maturation leads to improvements in executive functioning and attention, memory, response inhibition, and processing speed. As children's understanding of their own thinking and memory increase, they get better at selecting and using mnemonic strategies and become more planful. Experience influences how children organize information and the strategies they use.

11.2 Summarize views of intelligence, including the uses, correlates, and criticisms of intelligence tests.

IQ tests measure intellectual aptitude and are often used to identify children with special educational needs. IQ predicts school achievement, how long a child will stay in school, and career attainment in adulthood. Persistent group differences are found in IQ scores, but contextual factors, such as socioeconomic status, living conditions, school resources, culture, and life circumstances, are thought to account for group differences. Multiple intelligence theory and the triarchic theory of intelligence conceptualize intelligence as entailing a broader range of skills than those measured by IQ tests.

11.3 Discuss patterns of moral development during middle childhood.

Until about age 9, children demonstrate preconventional reasoning in Kohlberg's theory of moral development, moving from concern with punishment as a motivator of moral judgments (Stage 1) to self-interest and concern about what others can do for them (Stage 2). In late childhood, children advance to conventional moral reasoning in which they internalize the norms and standards of authority figures, becoming concerned with pleasing others (Stage 3) and maintaining social order (Stage 4). School-age children's views of fairness become more sophisticated, they differentiate social conventions from moral rules, and they become more likely to consider the situation and weigh a variety of variables in making decisions about distributive justice.

11.4 Explain processes of language development during middle childhood.

Vocabulary expands fourfold during the elementary school years. School-age children learn words through contextual cues and by comparing complex words with simpler words. Understanding of complex grammatical structures, syntax, and pragmatics improves in middle childhood with experience with language and exposure to complex constructions, and children become better communicators. Many children speak more than one language, and bilingualism is associated with cognitive benefits. Dual-language approaches to language learning are more effective than immersion approaches at teaching language and promoting academic achievement in children.

11.5 Discuss children's learning at school.

Teacher-centered classrooms emphasize direct instruction, whereas constructivist classrooms involve students in their own learning. Although phonics methods are highly effective in teaching reading, most schools employ the whole-language approach. However, a substantial number of U.S. children are poor readers and about one in five is deficient in math skills. First grade is often the foundation for children's academic career. Although all schools offer access to technology, quality varies and children's home access to technology varies with geography and socioeconomic status. In the United States and Canada, legislation mandates that, whenever possible, children with developmental learning disabilities are to be educated in the general classroom, with their peers, for all or part of the day. The nature of inclusion varies with the severity of the disability as well as the quality and quantity of support provided in the classroom.

REVIEW QUESTIONS

11.1 What abilities mark concrete operational reasoning?

How do changes in working memory, executive function, and metacognition influence children's thinking and memory?

What is the role of context and experience in cognitive development in middle childhood?

11.2 What is intelligence?

What is the most common IQ test, and how does it define intelligence?

What are contextual influences on IQ scores?

What are two alternative theories of intelligence?

11.3 What is autonomous morality?

What is conventional moral reasoning?

What is distributive justice reasoning?

How do children distinguish moral and conventional rules?

What factors influence moral development?

11.4 What advances in vocabulary and grammar take place during middle childhood?

Provide an example illustrating the development of pragmatics.

What are the developmental correlates of bilingualism?

11.5 What approaches are used to teach reading and mathematics?

What are some common disabilities that are aided by special education?

What are some methods for educating children with special needs?

©iStockphoto.com/FatCamera

12 Socioemotional Development in Middle Childhood

Ten-year-old Dyronne meets the same group of neighborhood boys to play basketball in the park across the street from his home each day after school. Dyronne looks forward to these games because he enjoys kidding around with his buddies, and he's better at basketball than most of his friends. Dyronne is well liked by his friends on the basketball court and is also popular with his classmates. He performs well at school, which is important because his gym teacher has suggested that Dyronne try out for the school's basketball team. Only students with good grades can play, and Dyronne is relieved that he doesn't have to worry about his grades like some of the other players. Overall, Dyronne has successfully navigated many of the socioemotional tasks of middle childhood. He has come to understand himself in more sophisticated ways, and he has established good relationships with his parents and peers. In this chapter, we examine ways in which family and peer contexts shape school-age children's socioemotional development.

Learning Objectives

12.1 Describe school-age children's self-conceptions and motivation.

12.2 Summarize sex differences and gender preferences and stereotypes in middle childhood.

12.3 Examine the roles of friendship, peer acceptance, and peer victimization in school-age children's adjustment.

Video Activity 12.1: Bullying

12.4 Discuss family relationships in middle childhood and the influence of family structure on adjustment.

Video Activity 12.2: Divorce: Parent's Perspective

Chapter Contents

PSYCHOSOCIAL DEVELOPMENT IN MIDDLE CHILDHOOD

Middle childhood, ages 6 to 11, represents an important transition in children's conceptions of themselves and their abilities. According to Erik Erikson (1950), school-age children face the psychosocial crisis of industry verses inferiority. They must develop a sense of competence rather than feel inadequate. Children must learn and master skills that are valued in their society, such as reading, mathematics, writing, and using computers. Success at even simple culturally valued tasks influences children's feelings of competence and curiosity as well as their motivation to persist and succeed in all of the contexts in which they are embedded. Six-year-old Kia tied her shoelace and smiled to herself: "It's easy now. I'm really good at tying my shoelaces—much better than my little brother." When children are unable to succeed or when they receive consistently negative feedback from parents or teachers, they may lose confidence in their ability to succeed and be productive at valued tasks. Children's sense of industry influences their self-concept, self-esteem, and readiness to face the physical, cognitive, and social challenges of middle childhood.

Self-Concept

In middle childhood, children's emerging cognitive capacities enable them to think about themselves in new, more complex ways and develop more sophisticated and comprehensive self-concepts (Goodvin et al., 2015). Self-concept shifts from concrete descriptions of behavior to trait-like psychological constructs (e.g., popular, smart, good-looking). For example, consider this school-age child's self-description: "I'm pretty popular. . . . That's because I'm nice to people and helpful and can keep secrets. Mostly I am nice to my friends, although if I get in a bad mood I sometimes say something that can be a little mean" (Harter, 2012b, p. 59). Like most older children, this child's self-concept focuses on competencies and personality traits rather than specific behaviors.

Older children include both positive and negative traits, unlike younger children, who tend to describe themselves in all-or-none terms. Through interactions with parents, teachers, and peers, children learn more about themselves (Pesu, Viljaranta, & Aunola, 2016). Older children come to understand that their traits can vary with the context—for example, that a person can be nice or mean, depending on the situation. Brain development contributes to self-concept. When processing information about the self, children use many more areas of the brain than do adults, suggesting that, with development, processing becomes more efficient and self-concept becomes more complex and differentiated (Pfeifer & Peake, 2012). As self-concept differentiates, children develop a physical self-concept (referring to physical attributes and attractiveness), academic self-concept (school performance), athletic self-concept (physical skills), social self-concept (social relationships with peers and others), and beliefs about behavioral conduct (whether they can behave appropriately) (Harter, 2012a). The Lives in Context feature discusses the neurological correlates of self-concept.

LIVES IN CONTEXT: BIOLOGICAL INFLUENCES

Self-Concept and the Brain

We have seen that self-concept shifts over childhood from all-or-none trait descriptions in early childhood to complex integrations of psychological traits in middle to late childhood. By about 9 years of age, children describe and evaluate themselves across a range of domains, such as academic, athletic, and social competence (Harter, 2012b). Advances in perspective taking and social comparison abilities contribute to the development of self-concept from childhood through adolescence and adulthood. Brain development also plays a role in children's changing sense of self.

Research with adults has shown that several areas of the brain, especially the medial prefrontal cortex (mPFC), are active during self-reflection tasks (Northoff & Hayes, 2011). The mPFC is one of the last parts of the brain to develop, undergoing significant change into adulthood (Blakemore, 2012). Neuroimaging studies have shown developmental differences in this region that correlate with the emerging sense of self (Mills, Lalonde, Clasen, Giedd, & Blakemore, 2014b; Pfeifer & Peake, 2012). For example, mPFC activity increases from childhood into adolescence in response to self-knowledge and evaluation tasks (Mills, Goddings, Clasen, Giedd, & Blakemore, 2014a). In one longitudinal study, children engaged in a self-evaluation task at age 10 and again at 13 in which they judged their own social skills and those of a familiar fictional character (e.g., Harry Potter) (Pfeifer et al., 2013). With age, the children showed greater activity in the mPFC during self-evaluations than other-evaluations and overall mPFC activity increased from age 10 to 13.

Children and adults also show different patterns of mPFC activity in response to self-knowledge and evaluation tasks (Mills et al., 2014a). For example, 10-year-old children and adults completed a self-knowledge task in which they judged whether phrases such as "I like to read just for fun" better described either themselves or a familiar fictional character (Pfeifer, Lieberman, & Dapretto, 2007). The children showed more activity in the mPFC when retrieving information about themselves. In addition, mPFC activity was more diffuse, spread out across a larger region, in children compared to adults, suggesting that the task required greater neural resources in children. Children's increased mPFC activity indicates that they were actively processing the task, engaging in self-reflection. In addition, the adults showed more activity in the lateral temporal cortex (LTC), which is associated with semantic memory (Cabeza & Nyberg, 2000). The lower levels of mPFC activity and higher LTC activity in adults suggest that the adults engaged in less active processing and instead relied on memory to complete the self-knowledge task, perhaps because they have more extensive knowledge about themselves (Pfeifer et al., 2007). That is, the task was easier for adults. In the children, however, greater involvement of the mPFC and relatively less activation of semantic knowledge stores in the LTC imply that they actively constructed their self-descriptive attributes, evaluating themselves and creating self-descriptions as they completed the task. As children learn more about themselves, they rely on memory, freeing neural resources for more complex reflections about the self and others.

What Do You Think?

1. Why might children and adults show different patterns of brain activity in response to self-reflection tasks?
2. How might cognitive abilities influence children's performance on self-knowledge tasks?
3. What can we do to improve children's knowledge about themselves? ●

Self-Esteem

Whereas preschoolers tend to have unrealistically positive self-evaluations, school-age children's sense of self-esteem becomes more realistic (Boseovski, 2010). Older children's growing ability to take other people's perspectives enables them to consider their abilities more objectively. Children evaluate their characteristics, abilities, and performance in comparison with peers, which influences their overall sense of competence (Harter, 2012b). Children also receive feedback about their abilities from parents, teachers, and peers, and this affects their self-esteem (Hart, Atkins, & Tursi, 2006). Perceived disapproval by peers, for example, is associated with declines in self-esteem (Thomaes et al., 2010). Although children learn about their abilities through their interactions with parents, teachers, and peers, children whose self-evaluations depend on approval from others tend to have low self-esteem (Moore & Smith, 2018). Children with low self-esteem tend to emphasize their weaknesses and downplay their strengths, evaluating their abilities inaccurately.

From late childhood into adolescence, beliefs about the self become more closely related to behavior (Davis-Kean, Jager, & Andrew Collins, 2009). Self-esteem is influenced by children's self-evaluations as well as by the importance they assign to the particular ability being evaluated. This is illustrated by a child's comment: "Even though I'm not doing well in those subjects, I still like myself as a person, because Math and Science just aren't that important to me. How I look and how popular I am are more important" (Harter, 2012b, p. 95). Children tend to report feeling most interested in activities in which they perform well and areas that they view as their strengths (Denissen, Zarrett, & Eccles, 2007).

Positive parent–child interactions and a secure attachment to parents predict a positive sense of self-esteem throughout childhood (Sroufe, 2016). Self-esteem is nurtured by parental warmth. Warm parents express positive emotions and acceptance and foster in their child the feeling that he or she matters. Children internalize the view of themselves as worthy individuals, and this internalized view is at the core of self-esteem (Brummelman, 2018). The home environment influences self-esteem throughout the lifespan. For example, in one longitudinal study, the quality of the early home environment through the first 6 years of life predicted self-esteem at age 8 through early adulthood, age 28 (Orth, 2017a).

Children's ratings of self-esteem vary with ethnic, contextual, and cultural factors. For example, many African American children experience adverse contextual conditions such as poverty, unsafe neighborhoods, ongoing stressors, and the experience of racism and discrimination. As a result, African American children may score lower on measures of self-esteem than White and Hispanic children (Kenny & McEachern, 2009). Despite the fact that their academic achievement is in general higher than that of North American children, Chinese and Japanese children tend to score lower in self-esteem. One reason may be that competition is high and Asian children experience great pressure to achieve (Stevenson, Lee, & Mu, 2000). In addition, Asian cultures emphasize collectivism, social harmony, and modesty, and they do not encourage children to use social comparison to enhance their self-esteem (Toyama, 2001). Instead, children are encouraged to praise others, including their peers, while minimizing attention to themselves in order to foster and maintain relationships (Falbo, Poston, Triscari, & Zhang, 1997).

The cultural emphasis on individuality characteristic of North America contributes to children's high self-esteem. However, when parents overvalue their children's attributes, overpraise their performance, and overencourage them to stand out from others, children may develop a sense of narcissism, viewing themselves as superior to others (Brummelman, 2018). Children's self-esteem is best fostered within the context of warm and accepting parent–child interactions, parental encouragement for realistic and meaningful goals, and praise that is connected to children's performance.

Achievement Motivation

Children's sense of industry and emerging sense of self influences their **achievement motivation**, the willingness to persist at challenging tasks and meet high standards of accomplishment (Wigfield et al., 2015). How children explain their own successes and failures is important for sustaining motivation and ultimately influencing their own achievement. Some children gravitate toward **internal attributions**, emphasizing their own role in the outcome, such as through ability or choice of study techniques. Other children rely on **external attributions**, causes that cannot be controlled, such as luck, to explain their performance.

In addition to attributing success or failure to internal or external causes, children also vary in their mindset, the degree to which they believe that their abilities and characteristics are modifiable (Dweck, 2017). Some show a **growth mindset**, viewing their skills and characteristics as malleable or changeable. In contrast, others show a **fixed mindset**, believing that their characteristics are enduring and unchangeable.

Children who adopt internal explanations and a growth mindset tend to have a strong mastery orientation, a belief that success stems from trying hard and that failures are influenced by factors that can be controlled, like effort (Haimovitz & Dweck, 2017). When faced with challenges, children who are mastery oriented focus on changing or adapting their behavior (Muenks, Wigfield, & Eccles, 2018). They are able to bounce back from failure and take steps, such as learning study strategies to improve their exam scores, to improve their performance.

Other children respond to success and failure in maladaptive ways, by attributing success to external factors such as luck and attributing failure to internal factors such as ability. Some children adopt a **learned helplessness orientation**, characterized by a fixed mindset and the attribution of poor performance to internal factors. Children who show learned helplessness are overwhelmed by challenges, are overly self-critical, feel incompetent, and avoid challenging tasks (Yeager & Dweck, 2012). A learned helplessness orientation can perpetuate poor performance. For example, students in fourth through sixth grades who were self-critical viewed their abilities as fixed, rated their own competence as lower, knew less about study strategies, avoided challenges, and performed more poorly at school than their non-self-critical peers (Pomerantz & Saxon, 2001). Poor performance, in turn, can confirm children's negative views of their ability and their sense of helplessness.

Children who attribute success to factors such as luck and failure to factors such as ability are at risk to develop a learned helplessness orientation.
©iStockphoto.com/FatCamera

Contextual Influences on Achievement Attributions and Motivation

Our views about our abilities and our explanations for our successes and failures are influenced by our interactions with the people around us. The contexts in which we are immersed, including factors such as parents and teachers, socioeconomic status, and culture, also play a role in shaping our views of our abilities.

Parents

Parents influence children's achievement through their own beliefs and attitudes about ability. Children raised by parents with a fixed view of abilities tend to view their own ability as fixed and unchangeable and are more likely to show a learned helplessness orientation (Pomerantz & Dong, 2006). When parents believe that ability cannot be changed, they tend to provide few opportunities for children to improve and may ignore positive changes that children show. In addition, failing to provide opportunities to problem solve or intervening when a child tries a challenging task may inhibit children's desire to succeed and may foster helplessness (Orkin, May, & Wolf, 2017).

Parenting styles also have an effect. Warm and supportive parenting can help children to recognize their worth and appreciate their own competence. Authoritative parents who promote their children's autonomy, encourage their children to explore their environment, and permit them to take an active role in solving their own problems foster a mastery orientation (Raftery, Grolnick, & Flamm, 2012). In contrast, excessive control and harsh criticism can damage children's motivation.

Parents also influence children through the home context they provide. Socioeconomic status (SES) influences children's motivation through the availability of opportunities and resources and through parents' behavior. Research has shown that children who grow up in high SES families are more likely than their middle or low SES peers to show a greater mastery orientation and higher levels of achievement motivation, as well as better academic performance and greater involvement in organized activities after school (Wigfield et al., 2015). Children require not only opportunities to try new things but also parents who are aware of and able to take advantage of opportunities (Archer et al., 2012; Simpkins, Delgado, Price, Quach, & Starbuck, 2013). Parents in low SES families often work jobs that involve long hours, rotating and nonstandard shifts, and high physical demands. As a result, many low SES parents lack the energy and time to devote to children, and they may be unaware of opportunities or unable to take advantage of them (Parra-Cardona, Cordova, Holtrop, Villarruel, & Wieling, 2008).

Teachers

Like parents, teachers support a mastery orientation in students when they are warm and helpful and when they attribute children's failure to lack of effort (Wentzel, 2002). Students who believe that their teachers provide a positive learning environment tend to work harder in class and show higher achievement than students who lack this belief (Wigfield, Muenks, & Rosenzweig, 2015). When students view their teachers as unsupportive, they are more likely to attribute their performance to external factors, such as luck or the teacher, and to withdraw from class participation. As students' achievement declines, they further doubt their abilities, creating a vicious cycle between helpless attributions and poor achievement. Teachers who relate failure back to their students' effort, are supportive of their students, and stress learning goals over performance goals are more likely to have mastery-oriented students (Meece, Anderman, & Anderman, 2006).

Warm and supportive parenting that fosters autonomy can help children to recognize their worth, appreciate their own competence, and develop a mastery orientation.
©iStockphoto.com/JohnnyGreig

Cultural Influences

Children and adolescents of many cultures point to family as an important influence on achievement. Internal attributions for success tend to be more common in Westerners and may be less common among people of other cultural backgrounds (Reyna, 2008). In one study, students from the Pacific islands (e.g., Samoa and Tonga) rated family, teacher, luck, and friends as more important for their best marks than did European, Asian, or Māori (indigenous) students (McClure et al., 2011). Moreover, Māori and other Pacific Islander students were less likely to adopt internal attributions (e.g., ability, effort) for their best and worst marks compared with European and Asian students.

Parents in many Asian countries tend to hold a growth mindset and to view the application of effort as a moral responsibility (Pomerantz, Ng, Cheung, & Qu, 2014). Parents in many Asian cultures tend to focus more on children's failure in order to encourage them to make corrections. North American parents, on the other hand, tend to pay attention to children's success and its relevance for self-esteem. For example, when U.S. and Chinese mothers watched their fourth- and fifth-grade students solve a puzzle, the U.S. mothers offered more praise after the child succeeded, but the Chinese mothers tended to point out poor performance and offer task-oriented statements to make the child try harder (e.g., "You only got 7 of 10"). After the mothers left the room, the children continued to play, and the Chinese children showed greater improvements in performance than the U.S. children (Ng, Pomerantz, & Lam, 2007).

Cultures also vary in the use and perception of criticism and praise. Students from some cultures may feel uncomfortable with praise because it singles them out from the group and, by implication, elevates them above their peers (Markus & Kitayama, 1991). Some students may be more motivated by critical feedback because their goal is to meet the expectations of their teachers and/or family (Pomerantz et al., 2014).

THINKING IN CONTEXT 12.1

1. How does cognitive development influence self-concept, self-esteem, and achievement motivation? Identify aspects of socioemotional development that might influence development in these areas.
2. How might a learned helplessness orientation form? Identify examples of how early and later experiences in and out of the home might place a child at risk for a learned helplessness orientation.
3. As a fourth-grade teacher, what can you do to promote students' academic achievement and academic motivation, as well as help them develop positive views of their own abilities?

GENDER DEVELOPMENT

The processes of gender role development begun in infancy and early childhood continue in middle childhood and are informed by advances in cognition and a developing sense of self. Casual observers often remark that boys and girls are different. Are they? We consider this question next.

Boys and Girls: Similarities and Differences

All children—boys and girls alike—share both similarities and differences. Although many adults may insist that boys and girls are dramatically different, research instead suggests that in childhood, and all periods of life, average sex differences in cognitive abilities and social behaviors are small or negligible (Hyde, 2014; Liben et al., 2013). There is much overlap between the sexes and a great deal of variability within each sex, more so than between the sexes (Blakemore et al., 2009; Hyde, 2016; Miller & Halpern, 2014). In other words, there is a greater number and variety of differences among boys and among girls than there is between boys and girls. Thus, generalizations about males and females should be understood as referring to the average, but not necessarily to any particular individual boy or girl.

Growth

Girls and boys are similar in weight and height and show similar rates of growth in childhood. Yet, at all ages, even before birth, boys tend to be more physically active than girls, and this difference increases during childhood (Alexander & Wilcox, 2012; Leaper, 2013). Boys engage in more physical, active play, including rough-and-tumble interactions that involve playful aggression and overall body contact (Scott & Panksepp, 2003). Boys are also at higher risk of injury. African American boys, followed by Native American boys, experience the highest rates of unintentional injuries (Ballesteros, Williams, Mack, Simon, & Sleet, 2018). Contextual factors, such as exposure to poverty, poor neighborhood resources (such as safe playgrounds), adult supervision, and discrimination contribute to racial and ethnic differences in injury rates.

Verbal Skills

On average, boys and girls do not differ in measures of intelligence (Halpern & LaMay, 2000). Despite similarities in intelligence scores, decades of research have shown that males and females show subtle differences in several aspects of cognition—specifically, certain aspects of verbal ability, spatial ability, and mathematics (Ardila, Rosselli, Matute, & Inozemtseva, 2011; Miller & Halpern, 2014). Sex differences in verbal ability emerge in infancy, as girls begin to talk earlier than boys and have a larger vocabulary than boys through age 5 (Bornstein et al., 2004). However, recall from Chapter 6 that baby girls tend to be held and talked to more often than boys—and infant-directed speech promotes language development. Girls' advanced verbal skills are likely the result of these interactions. Early verbal skills enable girls to interact with caregivers in more advanced ways, further advancing their language development. In all industrialized countries, girls show a small advantage on reading comprehension and verbal fluency tasks through adolescence (Ardila et al., 2011; Miller & Halpern, 2014). Yet these subtle gender differences disappear as children grow up. Most tests of vocabulary and other verbal abilities show a negligible or no sex difference in adults (Hines, 2013; Hyde, 2016).

Spatial Skills

One consistent difference between boys and girls lies in a specific type of spatial reasoning task—*mental rotation*, or the ability to recognize a stimulus that is rotated in space (Hines, 2015). As infants, boys are more likely than girls to recognize stimuli that have been rotated (Alexander & Wilcox, 2012; Quinn & Liben, 2014). Males' advantage in mental rotation ability persists across childhood and into adulthood (Choi & Silverman, 2003; Roberts & Bell, 2002). However, elementary school children tend to agree with gender stereotypes that girls are less proficient in mental rotation tasks than boys—and girls performed worse when spatial tasks were described as art problems verses math problems, suggesting that gender stereotypes may play a role in girls' performance on spatial tasks (Neuburger, Ruthsatz, Jansen, & Quaiser-Pohl, 2015). Sex differences appear only on spatial tasks measuring mental rotation. Boys and girls show similar performance on other spatial tasks (Hyde, 2016; Miller & Halpern, 2014).

Mathematics Skills

Sex differences in math abilities are more complicated. Research conducted over the past few decades has suggested that girls tend to do better at tests of computational mathematics skills in childhood (Hyde, 2014; Wei et al., 2012) and boys tend to perform better at tasks measuring mathematical reasoning in adolescence (Byrnes & Takahira, 1993; Leahey & Guo, 2001). Yet boys and girls have similar understanding of math concepts (Hines, 2015). Sex differences have become smaller in recent decades. For example, adolescent boys used to earn much higher scores on standardized math tests such as the Scholastic Aptitude Test (SAT) but the sex difference has largely disappeared over the past 3 decades (Hyde, 2016; Lindberg, Hyde, Petersen, & Linn, 2010). In a recent comprehensive study of children age 6 to 13, boys and girls demonstrated similar numerical skills, suggesting that any observed difference favoring males is an anomaly, not the norm (Hutchison, Lyons, & Ansari, 2019). This shift in mathematics performance over the past few decades accompanies the increasing emphasis by educational institutions, government, and industry on encouraging females to enter careers in the sciences, suggesting that socialization influences how boys and girls approach math (Ceci, Ginther, Kahn, & Williams, 2014; Dasgupta & Stout, 2014).

Emotional Expression

From an early age, girls are better able to manage and express their emotions than boys. For example, at 6 months of age, males have more difficulty than girls at regulating their emotions in frustrating or ambiguous situations (Weinberg et al., 1999). In infancy, childhood, and adolescence, girls are more accurate at identifying facial expressions, such as happy or sad, than boys (Alexander & Wilcox, 2012; Thompson & Voyer, 2014). While girls tend to express happiness and sadness more often than boys, boys express more anger (Chaplin & Aldao, 2013). Girls also express shame and guilt, complex emotions that rely on cognitive and social development, more often than boys (Else-Quest et al., 2012). Throughout adulthood, females tend to express a greater range of emotions more intensely than do males (Birditt & Fingerman, 2003; Chaplin, 2015; Zimmermann & Iwanski, 2014).

Whereas boys tend to exhibit more physical and verbal aggression, girls tend to demonstrate more relational aggression, such as gossip and social exclusion.

Beginning at preschool age, boys tend to exhibit more physical and verbal aggression, whereas girls tend to demonstrate more relational aggression than boys do, such as excluding a peer from social activities, withdrawing friendship, spreading rumors, or humiliating the person (Björkqvist, 2018). Gender differences in aggression have been observed as early as 17 months of age (Hyde, 2014). Boys and girls also differ in inhibitory control, from as early as 3 months of age (Else-Quest et al., 2006). Differences in activity and the ability to restrain impulses likely play a role in sex differences in terms of aggression. Throughout childhood, adolescence, and adulthood, males tend to demonstrate higher rates of impulsivity (Cross, Copping, & Campbell, 2011).

Gender-Related Preferences and Stereotypes

By about 5 years of age, children have extensive knowledge of the activities and interests stereotyped for males and females. Children express this gender knowledge as rigid rules about the behavior appropriate for boys and girls, and it influences their preferences for toys, activities, and playmates (Baker et al., 2016; Blakemore et al., 2009; Hines, 2015). Young children tend to prefer same-sex peers, and this preference increases as children enter middle childhood. For example, at 4½ years of age, children spend about three times as much time with same-sex peers as with opposite-sex peers, and this difference increases to 10 times by 6½ years of age (Hines, 2013; Maccoby & Jacklin, 1987). The tendency of children to play with others of the same sex is seen in a range of cultures (Whiting & Whiting, 1975). Children's gender stereotypes and expectations extend to their peer interactions. In one study, most of the 3- to 6-year-old children surveyed reported not wanting to be friends with nonconforming children, such as boys who wear nail polish or girls who play with trucks (Ruble et al., 2007).

In middle childhood, knowledge of stereotypes expands to include beliefs about personality and achievement (Bussey, 2013; Serbin, Powlishta, & Gulko, 1993). Gender stereotypes influence children's preferences and views of their own abilities. Elementary school children describe reading, spelling, art, and music as appropriate subjects for girls and mathematics and athletics as for boys (Cvencek, Meltzoff, & Greenwald, 2011; Kurtz-Costes, Copping, Rowley, & Kinlaw, 2014; Passolunghi, Rueda Ferreira, & Tomasetto, 2014).

Stereotypes influence girls' attitudes about math. For example, girls tend to report negative feelings about math and perceive math as a "male subject" (Cvencek et al., 2011). Despite recent initiatives to increase women's representation in quantitative fields such as Science, Technology, Engineering, and Mathematics (STEM), girls show less interest in these areas and are less likely to pursue a career in these areas than boys (Eccles & Wang, 2016). Stereotyped attitudes, beliefs, and interests about math are influenced by early experiences with parents and teachers. Exposure to toys that emphasize acting on the world, such as blocks, vehicles, and building sets, stimulates quantitative interests and abilities. Parents' and teachers' beliefs about gender influence children's attitudes, and research suggests that adults commonly hold stereotypes that girls are less likely to succeed in math than boys (Cimpian, Lubienski, Timmer, Makowski, & Miller, 2016; Ellemers, 2018). As early as first grade, teachers consistently underrate female, relative to male, math performance despite a general lack of evidence for differences in achievement across the genders (Cimpian et al., 2016). Adults' gender-stereotyped expectations influence their interactions with children, encouraging stereotyped behavior (Ellemers, 2018).

Transgender children show similar patterns of gender development and stereotyping as do children with a cisgender identity. For example, one study compared 5- to 12-year-old transgender children, their cisgender siblings, and a group of unrelated cisgender children on self-report and implicit, less controllable, measures of gender identity and preferences (Olson et al., 2015). When transgender children's responses were considered in light of their sex assigned at birth, their responses differed radically from the cisgender children and the stereotyped behavior typical of children their age. However, when transgender children's responses were evaluated in terms of their expressed gender, there was a close match to peers. The transgender children preferred peers and objects endorsed by peers who shared their expressed gender, suggesting a similar developmental trend in gender identity and preferences for transgender and cisgender children. Transgender children, however, demonstrate more flexible views of gender stereotypes than cisgender children. For example, a study suggested that 6- to 8-year-old transgender children and their siblings were less likely to endorse gender stereotypes than unrelated children and viewed gender nonconformity as more acceptable in peers (Olson & Enright, 2018).

Children's beliefs about gender change over the course of middle childhood. By around 7 years of age, children demonstrate gender constancy, the awareness that a person's sex is a biological characteristic (Halim, 2016). Gender rigidity tends to decline as children's understanding of gender constancy develops (Ruble et al., 2007; Trautner et al., 2005). Children with a more mature grasp of gender constancy may be less afraid to engage in cross-gender-typed activities than they had been previously because they understand that they will remain a girl or boy despite engaging in cross-gender-typed activities (Halim et al., 2017). Girls tend to show more flexible gender-stereotyped beliefs than boys. This trend toward flexibility in views of what males and females can do increases with age in both boys and girls (Blakemore et al., 2009).

However, becoming more open-minded about boys' and girls' gendered behavior does not mean that school-age children approve of violating gender stereotypes. School-age children tend to remain intolerant to certain violations, especially boys playing with dolls or wearing dresses and girls playing noisily and roughly, which they rate as severely as moral violations (Blakemore, 2003; Levy, Taylor, & Gelman, 1995). Yet older children tend to understand that gender-stereotyped traits and behaviors are associated with gender but are not defined by gender (Banse, Gawronski, Rebetez, Gutt, & Bruce Morton, 2010; Martin et al., 2002). At about 9 to 10 years of age, children grasp the social basis of gender roles, that they are social conventions rather than biological inevitabilities (Leaper, 2013). Now children increasingly agree that boys and girls follow their own preferences regardless of social conventions.

THINKING IN CONTEXT 12.2

1. Why do many adults perceive sex differences in children if research shows that sex differences are limited to only a few areas? Pretend that you are explaining this to a parent of a 9-year-old child.
2. How are children's sex stereotyped attitudes and behavior influenced by cognitive development? How might contextual factors in the home, peer, school, and neighborhood context influence children's gender-related attitudes and behavior?

PEER RELATIONSHIPS IN MIDDLE CHILDHOOD

As older children's self-concepts expand and they become better able to understand and appreciate others' perspectives, peer relationships become more complex. Older children spend more time with peers and place more importance on those relationships than do younger children (Schneider, 2016). Most school-age children have multiple friendships and are part of a peer group in school and, increasingly, out of school. Friendship and peer acceptance become important influences on adjustment.

Friendship

Friendships serve important developmental purposes throughout the lifespan. They are a source of companionship, stimulation, and affection. Friends provide each other with tangible and emotional support. They are also a source of social comparison, permitting children to judge their competence relative to peers (Erdley & Day, 2017). At all times in life, friendships are rooted in similarity. Children tend to choose friends who share interests, play preferences, and personality characteristics (Laursen, 2017). Friends also show similarities in cognitive ability and intelligence, likely because these characteristics influence the capacity to take other people's perspectives and thus reciprocate (Boutwell, Meldrum, & Petkovsek, 2017; Ilmarinen, Vainikainen, Verkasalo, & Lönnqvist, 2017). In addition, friends tend to share demographics, such as gender, race, and ethnicity (Rubin et al., 2015b). For example, in one study of 6- to 12-year-old U.S. children of Cambodian, Dominican, and Portuguese heritage, children became more proud of their heritage as they grew older and in turn showed a greater preference to form friendships within their ethnic group (Marks, Szalacha, Lamarre, Boyd, & Coll, 2007).

Friends are an important source of companionship, support, and fun in middle childhood.
Jeff Greenberg/Universal Images Group/Getty Images

Contextual characteristics, such as the ethnic diversity of a neighborhood or school, also influence children's choices of friends within and outside of their own ethnic group. In schools that are ethnically, racially, and socioeconomically diverse, children are more likely to report having at least one close friend of another race (Iqbal, Neal, & Vincent, 2017; McGlothlin & Killen, 2006). School-age girls may be more likely to have ethnically diverse social networks and cross-race friendships than boys (Lee, Howes, & Chamberlain, 2007). Once established, cross-race friendships are similar to same-race friendships with regard to intimacy, companionship, and security (McDonald et al., 2013). Compared to children who do not have friends of other races, children in cross-race friendships tend to show a lower tolerance for excluding others (Killen, Kelly, Richardson, Crystal, & Ruck, 2010) and are less prone to peer victimization (Kawabata & Crick, 2011). They also tend to feel socially and emotionally safer and less vulnerable at school (Graham, Munniksma, & Juvonen, 2014; Munniksma & Juvonen, 2012).

In middle childhood, friendship transforms into a reciprocal relationship in which children are responsive to each other's needs and trust each other. Shared values and rules become important components to friendship by 9 to 10 years of age (Rubin et al., 2015a). In middle to late childhood, friends are expected to be loyal and stick up for each other. Violations of trust, such as divulging secrets, breaking promises, and not helping a friend in need, can break up a friendship. Because of their more complex perspectives on friendship, school-age children tend to name only a handful of friends, compared with preschoolers, who say that they have lots of friends. "I know a lot of kids and am inviting them all to my birthday party," explained 9-year-old Shana, "but only a few are really my friends. I don't tell them everything. I only tell everything to my best friend. Only she knows that I like Nicky." As Shana illustrates, with age, children differentiate among best friends, good friends, and casual friends, depending on how much time they spend together and how much they share with one another (Rubin et al., 2015a). Older children, especially girls, tend to have fewer, but closer, friends, and by age 10, most children report having a best friend (Erdley & Day, 2017).

Friendships tend to remain stable from middle childhood into adolescence, especially among children whose friendships are high in relationship quality, characterized by sharing, mutual perspective taking, and compromise (Poulin & Chan, 2010). Nevertheless, because friendship is based largely on similar characteristics, proximity, and opportunities for interaction, friendships may come and go as children develop new interests, competencies, and values (Laursen, 2017). They may also end as children progress into new contexts, such as when they change schools or move to a different neighborhood (Troutman & Fletcher, 2010). Older children become more upset at losing a friend and find making friends more challenging than do young children (Hartup, 2006).

Friendship dissolution may have serious consequences for children who are unable to replace the friendship. Some children who experience disruption and loss of close friendships have problems with depression, loneliness, guilt, anger, anxiety, and acting-out behaviors, yet children with psychosocial problems are also at risk to experience friendship loss and, in turn, show poor adjustment (Rubin et al., 2015a). Many children replace "lost" friendships with "new" friendships. In one study of fifth graders, losing a friend was associated with adjustment difficulties only when the lost friendship was not replaced by a new friendship. For these children, the lost and new friendships were largely interchangeable (Wojslawowicz Bowker, Rubin, Burgess, Booth-Laforce, & Rose-Krasnor, 2006). For many children, the importance of stable best friendships during middle childhood may have less to do with the relationship's length and more to do with simply having a "buddy" by one's side who can provide companionship, recreation, validation, caring, help, and guidance.

Can a child be happy without friends or without a best friend? An estimated 15% to 20% of children are chronically friendless or consistently without a mutual best friend (Rubin et al., 2015a). Children without friends tend to report feeling more lonely than other children, especially when they desire friends. Friendless children may lack social skills or might direct their friendship toward children who are unlikely to reciprocate (Bowker et al., 2010). Some research suggests that young elementary school children without friends score lower on measures of theory of mind, suggesting that they are not cognitively prepared to take another person's perspective, a skill critical to making friends (Fink, Begeer, Peterson, Slaughter, & de Rosnay, 2015). Lacking a best friend itself is not necessarily harmful or indicative of problems or loneliness (Klima & Repetti, 2008). Some children simply prefer solitude; their preference for alone time is not driven by anxiety or fear (Coplan, Ooi, & Nocita, 2015). Although lacking close friends is not associated with maladjustment, social acceptance by the peer group influences children's adjustment, as discussed next.

Peer Acceptance, Popularity, and Rejection

Mykelle announced to her mother, "I heard from the last kid! Everyone in class is coming to my birthday party!" "Fantastic!" her mother replied. "Now I have to figure out how to fit 25 of your friends into our house." Peer acceptance, the degree to which a child is viewed as a worthy social partner by his or her peers, becomes increasingly important in middle childhood. Peer evaluations become vital sources of self-validation, self-esteem, and confidence (LaFontana & Cillessen, 2010). Some children stand out from their peers as exceptionally well liked or exceptionally disliked.

Popularity

Children who are valued by their peers are said to be popular. **Popular children** tend to have a variety of positive characteristics, including helpfulness, trustworthiness, assertiveness, and prosocial habits (Kornbluh & Neal, 2016). They are skilled in emotional regulation and social information processing (van den Berg, Deutz, Smeekens, & Cillessen, 2017). That is, popular children are good at reading social situations, problem solving, self-disclosure, and conflict resolution (Blandon, Calkins, Grimm, Keane, & O'Brien, 2010). For example, theory of mind predicts popularity throughout childhood (Slaughter, Imuta, Peterson, & Henry, 2015). Positive social competencies and prosocial behaviors are cyclical; children who excel at social interaction continue to do so, their peers tend to reciprocate, and positive effects on peer relationships increase (Laible, McGinley, Carlo, Augustine, & Murphy, 2014).

A minority of popular children do not show the prosocial and empathetic characteristics typical of popular children. Often labeled by peers and teachers as tough, these children are socially skilled yet show antisocial and aggressive behavior (Shi & Xie, 2012). Aggressive popular children show social competencies similar to prosocial popular children, yet also share many characteristics of children who are rejected by their peers (Kornbluh & Neal, 2016; Marks, 2017).

Peer Rejection

Children who experience **peer rejection** tend to be disliked and shunned by their peers. Children who have poor communication, language, emotional control, and social information processing skills are at risk for peer rejection (Bierman, Kalvin, & Heinrichs, 2015; Menting, van Lier, & Koot, 2011). For example, kindergarteners who had difficulty controlling their emotions were more likely than their more skilled peers to experience peer rejection through seventh grade (Bierman et al., 2014). Boys and girls with behavior problems are at risk for peer rejection—and peer rejection, in turn, is associated with increases in behavior problems throughout elementary school as well as rule breaking in adolescence (Ettekal &

Ladd, 2015). Rejected children show two patterns of behavior, characterized by either aggression or withdrawal.

Mrs. Connelly turned to a fellow teacher and sighed. "Poor Monica. She tries to force her way into games, like knocking Jamie out of the way to take her spot in line for jump rope. No wonder the other children don't like her." **Aggressive-rejected children** like Monica are confrontational, hostile toward other children, impulsive, and hyperactive. They enter peer groups in destructive ways that disrupt the group's interaction or activity and direct attention to themselves. Aggressive-rejected children tend to have difficulty taking the perspective of others, and they tend to react aggressively to slights by peers, quickly assuming hostile intentions (Fite, Hendrickson, Rubens, Gabrielli, & Evans, 2013; Laible et al., 2014). Children whose parents show little warmth and use coercive discipline and threats are likely to threaten other children, have poor social skills, and show aggressive behavior and are more likely to be rejected by other children (Lansford, 2014).

Other rejected children are socially withdrawn, passive, timid, anxious, and socially awkward. **Withdrawn-rejected children** tend to isolate themselves from peers, rarely initiate contact with peers, and speak less frequently than their peers (Rubin et al., 2009). They tend to spend most of their time playing alone and on the periphery of the social scene, often because of shyness or social anxiety. When socially withdrawn children experience peer rejection, they tend to become more withdrawn and even more disliked by their peers (Coplan et al., 2013). Despite this, socially withdrawn children are just as likely to have a best friend as other children (Rubin, Wojslawowicz, Rose-Krasnor, Booth-LaForce, & Burgess, 2006).

Both aggressive-rejected and withdrawn-rejected children are similar in that they misinterpret other children's behaviors and motives, have trouble understanding and regulating their emotions, are poor listeners, and are less socially competent than other children (Ladd & Kochenderfer-Ladd, 2016). Peer rejection further hinders social development by depriving children of opportunities to learn and practice social skills such as interacting with other children, resolving conflict, and regulating emotions. Peer rejection is associated with short- and long-term problems, such as loneliness, anxiety, depression, low self-esteem, low academic achievement, and, in adolescence, delinquency and school dropout (Cooley & Fite, 2016; Menting, Koot, & van Lier, 2014; Schwartz, Lansford, Dodge, Pettit, & Bates, 2015). Chronic peer rejection is associated with high levels of activity in regions of the brain linked with detecting and experiencing the emotional distress caused by social exclusion. Moreover, the experience of chronic rejection in childhood is associated with heightened neural responses to exclusion in adolescence (Will, van Lier, Crone, & Güroğlu, 2016). Table 12.1 summarizes characteristics associated with popular children and those who are rejected.

Bullying

Bullying, also known as *peer victimization*, refers to an ongoing interaction in which a child repeatedly attempts to inflict physical, verbal, or social harm on another child by, for example, hitting, kicking, name-calling, teasing, shunning, or humiliating the other child (Olweus, 2013). Bullying is a problem for school-age children in many countries. Estimated rates of bullying and victimization range from 15% to 25% of children in Australia, Austria, England, Finland, Germany, Norway, and the United States (Zych, Farrington, Llorent, & Ttofi, 2017). Physical bullying is most common in childhood, and verbal/relational forms of bullying rise in childhood and remain common in adolescence (Finkelhor, Ormrod, & Turner, 2009). Cyberbullying is a type of relational bullying carried out by electronic means by text or electronic communication and social media (Vaillancourt, Faris, & Mishna, 2017). Cyberbullying tends to accompany other types of bullying rather than occur independently and is more common in adolescence than childhood (Waasdorp & Bradshaw, 2015).

Children Who Bully

Boys who bully tend to be above average in size, use physical aggression, and target both boys and girls. Girls who bully tend to be verbally assertive, target other girls, and use verbal or psychological methods of bullying that threaten relationships (Murray-Close, Nelson, Ostrov, Casas, & Crick, 2016). These latter methods, known as relational aggression, include ridiculing, embarrassing, and spreading rumors. Boys and girls who bully tend to be impulsive and domineering, and they show little anxiety or insecurity in peer contexts. Bullying can be motivated by the pursuit of high status and a powerful dominant position in the peer group (Thomas, Connor, & Scott, 2017). Relationally aggressive children, including bullies, are frequently perceived by peers as cool, powerful, and popular; bullying can be helpful in maintaining prestige. Indirect forms of bullying, such as relational bullying, require social skills, which contribute to the relational bully's high social status among peers (Juvonen & Graham, 2014). In support of this, many bullies report making friends easily and receive similar levels of support from their classmates as other children (Menesini & Salmivalli, 2017).

TABLE 12.1

Characteristics of Popular and Rejected Children

<table>
<tr><th></th><th>CHARACTERISTIC</th><th>OUTCOMES</th></tr>
<tr><td>Popular children</td><td>Helpful, trustworthy, assertive
Cognitively skilled and achievement oriented
Socially skilled, able to self-disclose and provide emotional support
Good social problem-solving skills and conflict resolution skills
Prosocial orientation
Assume others have good intentions
A minority are also antisocial and aggressive. They interact with others in a hostile way, using physical or relational aggression, and are likely to bully other children.</td><td>Positive characteristics are strengthened though experience and peer approval.
Positive peer evaluations are sources of self-validation, self-esteem, confidence, and attention from peers, and they influence adjustment.
Without intervention, the minority of popular adolescents who are aggressive are likely to continue patterns of physical or relational aggression in response to peer approval and acceptance.</td></tr>
<tr><td>Aggressive-rejected children</td><td>Confrontational, hostile toward other children
Impulsive and hyperactive
Difficulty with emotional regulation
Difficulty taking others' perspectives
Assume that their peers are out to get them
Poor social skills
Misinterpret other children's behaviors and motives</td><td rowspan="2">Similar outcomes for both types of rejected children
Negative characteristics are strengthened
Few opportunities to learn and practice social skills, conflict resolution, and emotional regulation
Anxiety, depression, and low self-esteem
Behavior problems
Poor academic achievement
Increased physical and relational aggression over time
Withdrawal and loneliness</td></tr>
<tr><td>Withdrawn-rejected children</td><td>Passive, timid, and socially awkward
Socially withdrawn, isolate themselves from others
Anxious
Poor social skills
Fear being disliked by peers
Misinterpret other children's behaviors and motives</td></tr>
</table>

Children who show physically aggressive forms of bullying often demonstrate hyperactive behavior, have poor school achievement, perceive less support from teachers than do other children, and may show higher rates of depression than other children (Turcotte Benedict, Vivier, & Gjelsvik, 2015). Bullies are more likely to experience inconsistent, hostile, and rejecting parenting. Parents of bullies are more likely to provide poor supervision, prefer coercive control and physical discipline, and tend to be permissive toward aggressive behavior, even teaching their children to strike back at perceived provocation (Gómez-Ortiz, Romera, & Ortega-Ruiz, 2016; Rajendran, Kruszewski, & Halperin, 2016).

Rates of bullying may vary with the sociocultural context. One study of Puerto Rican children living in the South Bronx, New York, and San Juan, Puerto Rico, showed that children were more likely to bully others when they were part of a minority group on the mainland than when they were living in their home culture in Puerto Rico (Morcillo et al., 2015). Mainland children who were more acculturated, or acclimated to U.S. culture, engaged in more bullying than did their less acculturated peers. The longer the children lived on the mainland, the greater the demands of navigating cross-cultural worlds. Bullying may be a response to the distress of navigating cross-cultural worlds or a response to perceived discrimination.

Victims of Bullying

Bullies report choosing their victims because they do not like them, often because the victims are perceived as different, as more quiet and cautious than other children (Juvonen & Graham, 2014). Victims of bullying are likely to be inhibited, frail in appearance, and younger than their peers. They often experience intrusive parenting, overprotectiveness, and criticism from parents, which increases their vulnerability to bullying (Menesini & Salmivalli, 2017). Perhaps not surprisingly, children who are bullied often report feeling lonely and less happy at school and having fewer good friends than their classmates (Reavis, Keane, & Calkins, 2010).

Many victim characteristics, including nonassertive styles of interacting with peers, shyness, passivity, and social withdrawal, as well

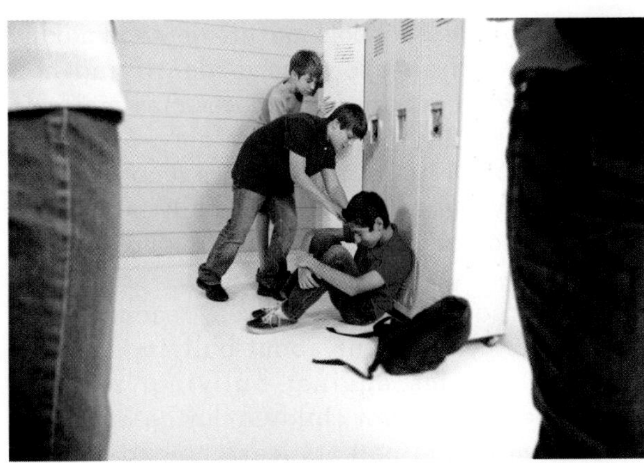

Characteristics such as passivity and nonassertive styles of interacting with peers place children at risk for peer victimization and tend to increase in response to victimization.
©iStockphoto.com/fstop123

as anxiety, depression, and poor emotional control, are present before the child becomes a target of peer victimization and are amplified by victimization (Perren, Ettekal, & Ladd, 2013). Much of the long-term stability of peer victimization and its negative effects can be explained by the dynamic interactions between risk factors for victimization and the effects of victimization (Shetgiri, Lin, & Flores, 2013). Risk factors are circumstances that increase the likelihood of negative outcomes and, in extreme cases, can impede development.

Although children respond in various ways to bullying, avoidance behaviors (such as not going to school and refusing to go certain places) are common (Waasdorp & Bradshaw, 2011). Victims of bullying may respond to victimization in ways that reinforce bullies by becoming defensive, crying, and giving in to bullies' demands. Not all victims of bullying are passive and withdrawn, however. Older children who experience frequent victimization may respond with more intense feelings of anger and greater desires to retaliate, making them more likely to show reactive aggression, an aggressive response to an insult, confrontation, or frustration (Arseneault, 2018).

Some aggressive-rejected children become provocative victims or bully-victims (Hymel & Swearer, 2015). Bully-victims share characteristics of both bullies and victims but function more poorly than either. For example, bully-victims tend to show high levels of anxiety and depression, as well as low rates of social acceptance and self-esteem common to victims, but they also show more aggression, impulsivity, and poor self-control than do other victims (Swearer & Hymel, 2015; van Dijk, Poorthuis, & Malti, 2017). Children who are bully-victims have difficulties managing emotions that may increase their risk for reactive aggression and acting-out behaviors that invite aggressive exchanges with others. These characteristics lead children who are both bullies and victims to have problems in peer relationships. Bully-victims often are among the most disliked members of a classroom (Arseneault, 2018).

Physical and relational bullying have negative emotional and academic consequences that appear as early as in kindergarten and persist over the childhood and adolescent years, often well after the bullying ends (Moore et al., 2017). For example, children who were bully-victims were more likely to experience anxiety and depression in late adolescence and in early adulthood—and even into middle adulthood (Evans-Lacko et al., 2017; McDougall & Vaillancourt, 2015). Like other forms of bullying, cyberbullying is associated with anxiety, depression, academic problems, and behavioral problems (Hamm et al., 2015; Vaillancourt et al., 2017). Cyberbullying may be more damaging, as it not only co-occurs with other types of bullying but also is more difficult for victims to avoid (Kowalski, Giumetti, Schroeder, & Lattanner, 2014). Cyberbullying can occur at any time of the day or any day of the week, and the victim need not be present. Victims of cyberbullying are also less likely to report their abuse or to seek help than victims of traditional bullying (Mishna, Cook, Gadalla, Daciuk, & Solomon, 2010).

Furthermore, the meaning and implications of bullying may vary with context. For example, relational bullying may be more emotionally damaging to children reared in collectivist cultures that highly value relationships. Accordingly, one comparison of Japanese and U.S. fourth graders showed more depression in Japanese victims (Kawabata, Crick, & Hamaguchi, 2010).

Intervening in Bullying

Successful interventions to combat bullying target multiple perspectives, including victims, bullies, and schools (Hutson, Kelly, & Militello, 2018; Nese, Horner, Dickey, Stiller, & Tomlanovich, 2014). Interventions focusing on victims seek to change victims' negative perceptions of themselves by helping them to acquire the skills needed to maintain relationships with peers and teaching them to respond to bullying in ways that do not reinforce their attackers (Olweus & Limber, 2010). Successful interventions stress that victimized children are not to blame for the abuse. Helping victims of bullying is not enough, though—perpetrators of bullying also need help. Parents and teachers should help bullies learn to identify, understand, and manage their and other people's emotions, as well as direct anger in safe and appropriate ways (Hutson et al., 2018).

Teachers need to be aware of bullying and willing to intervene (Espelage, Low, & Jimerson, 2014). In addition, bystanders—children who watch episodes of bullying but do not act—reinforce bullies' behaviors and increase bullying (Kärnä, Voeten, Poskiparta, & Salmivalli, 2010; Salmivalli, 2014). Class norms can influence whether bystanders intervene (Pozzoli, Gini, & Vieno, 2012). So can advice from parents (Grassetti et al., 2018). Classmates can be encouraged to support one another when bullying events occur: Rather than being bystanders or egging the bully on, they can tell a teacher, refuse to watch, and even, if safe, encourage bullies to stop.

Bullying is not simply a child-to-child problem, and it requires more than a child-centered solution. Stopping bullying requires awareness and change within the school. Schools must review and modify practices with an eye toward identifying how class environment and procedures may maintain or increase bullying (Fink, Patalay, Sharpe, & Wolpert, 2018; Nese et al., 2014). In recognition of the pervasiveness and severity of bullying, specific bully-related policies are included in public school laws in most states. Addressing the problem of bullying requires that children, teachers, and parents voice concerns about bullying; schools develop policies against bullying; teachers supervise and monitor children during lunch and recess times; and parents learn how to identify and change victims' and bullies' behaviors (Table 12.2). The Applying Developmental Science feature discusses antibullying legislation.

APPLYING DEVELOPMENTAL SCIENCE

Antibullying Legislation

Schools are responsible for children's physical well-being, but how far does that responsibility extend? What is the role of schools in addressing peer victimization? In a landmark case, the mother of fifth-grader LaShonda Davis filed a suit against the Monroe County (Georgia) Board after the school failed to intervene during the months in which her daughter was the victim of severe harassment, often sexual, by a fellow student. The 1999 decision in *Davis v. Monroe County Board of Education* ruled that sexual harassment by peers violates Title IX of the Education Amendments Act of 1972, which stipulates that "no person in the United States shall, on the basis of sex, be excluded from participation in, be denied the benefits of, or be subjected to discrimination under any education program or activity receiving Federal financial assistance." The court deemed that sexual harassment in the school setting violates students' rights to education. *Davis v. Monroe* applies specifically to peer-to-peer sexual harassment, but researchers and legislators look to this ruling as an important precedent for antibullying legislation because bullying violates students' rights.

In recognition of the pervasiveness and severity of bullying, every state in the United States includes specific bully-related policies in their public school laws (U.S. Department of Health and Human Services, 2017a). Antibullying laws do not criminalize bullying itself but stipulate that school districts must take action to prevent or intervene when bullying occurs (Hinduja & Patchin, 2015). School boards are charged with establishing antibullying policies (Cornell & Limber, 2015). Most developmental researchers agree that a model bullying law should include, at minimum, the following: a clear definition of bullying, explicit articulation of a bullying prohibition, implementation of prevention and treatment programs, and acknowledgment of the association between bullying and public health risks (Limber & Small, 2003; Srabstein et al., 2008). State antibullying laws vary dramatically but, as a whole, are associated with a 7% to 13% reduction in school violence and in reports of bullying (Nikolaou, 2017; Sabia & Bass, 2017).

The Safe Schools Improvement Act, proposed in 2013 and reintroduced to Congress in 2017, is legislation that would require states to collect and report information on the incidence of bullying and harassment. It would also permit schools to use federal grants to prevent and respond to incidents of bullying and harassment, require schools to provide annual reports of bullying prevalence and policies, and establish grievance procedures for students and parents to register complaints regarding such conduct. Although not yet passed by Congress, the Safe Schools Improvement Act sets an important precedent by acknowledging the relevance of peer victimization to children's everyday lives.

What Do You Think?

What role should schools take in addressing bullying? Did your school draw attention to bullying and have rules or policies about bullying? How effective are school bullying policies? ●

TABLE 12.2

Bullying Risks and Interventions

		BULLYING RISK FACTOR	BULLYING INTERVENTION
Child	Victim	Physically weak Younger than peers Anxious, insecure, low self-esteem, dependent Quiet, cautious, withdrawn Little prosocial behavior Poor emotional control Loneliness Unhappiness at school Fewer good friends than peers	Teach assertiveness skills. Teach children alternative responses to bullying. Teach anxiety and emotional management as well as social and coping skills.
	Bully	Above average in size More physically and verbally assertive Impulsive Domineering, hostile toward peers Little anxiety or insecurity in peer contexts Makes friends easily Hyperactive behavior Academic difficulties Poor emotional control	Teach alternatives to violence. Help children develop empathy. Teach emotional management and coping skills to reduce impulsive behavior.
Parent	Victim	Intrusive, overprotective, and/or critical parenting	Teach authoritative parenting skills. Encourage parents to aid children in being independent and developing coping skills.
	Bully	Hostile and rejecting parenting Use of physical punishment Models aggressive behavior Permissive, inconsistent response to aggressive bullying behavior	Teach authoritative parenting skills. Parent with sensitivity and consistency. Model nonaggressive behavior, interpersonal interactions, and conflict management strategies. Provide positive feedback to children for appropriate social behaviors. Use alternatives to physical punishment.
School		Groups students by physical characteristics such as height Policies that discourage reporting bullying incidents Teachers and administrators who ignore bullying Environment of negative feedback and negative attention	Stress that victims are not to blame. Teach social skills and conflict management. Promote a positive school climate that encourages students to feel good about themselves. Encourage fair discipline that is not punitive. Train teachers to identify and respond to potentially damaging victimization. Teachers use positive feedback and modeling to address appropriate social interactions. School personnel never ignore bullying behaviors. Encourage classmates to support one another and, rather than simply watch bullying events occur, tell a teacher, and refuse to watch or encourage the bully. Review and modify school practices with an eye toward identifying how school procedures may contribute to bullying.

THINKING IN CONTEXT 12.3

1. Considering Bronfenbrenner's bioecological theory from Chapter 1, what microsystem factors (such as personal characteristics), mesosystem factors (such as family and school), and exosystem factors (such as neighborhood) might lead a child to be popular or unpopular with peers? Which factors are most important, in your view?
2. As a parent, what might you do to lower the likelihood that your child might become a bully or a victim of bullying? As a teacher, what can you do to foster a bully-free environment in your classroom? What could you do as a school principal?

FAMILIES IN MIDDLE CHILDHOOD

Children are embedded in families that play an important role in their development. Children's relationships with parents and siblings are dynamic and reciprocal. Children influence and are influenced by every member of their family. Families may take many forms, as described in the following sections.

Parent–Child Relationships

As school-age children become more independent, they spend less time with their parents but remain close to their parents. Parents and school-age children tend to spend their time together engaging in task-oriented activities, such as doing homework, preparing meals, cleaning, and shopping. Interactions with parents help children practice, rehearse, and refine skills that are important for peer relationships. The parent–child relationship transforms as parents adapt their parenting styles to match their children's increased ability to reason and desire for independence. Parents tend to use less direct management and instead begin to share power—for example, by guiding and monitoring children's behavior from a distance, communicating expectations, and allowing children to be in charge of moment-to-moment decision making (Lamb & Lewis, 2015). Parents increasingly use reasoning and inductive techniques of discipline, such as pointing out the consequences of a child's behavior, explaining how a child affects others, and appealing to the child's self-esteem and sense of values. Parents of securely attached children tend to be more responsive and supportive of the child's autonomy and use more behavioral and less harsh control strategies (Koehn & Kerns, 2018). Children who are securely attached to parents tend to develop positive emotion regulation skills that aid them in home, peer, and school contexts (Brumariu, 2015).

As in many aspects of development, continuity is typical in parenting and parent–child relationships (Bradley, Iida, Pennar, Owen, & Vandell, 2017). Patterns of harsh verbal discipline (yelling, threatening, punishment, shaming) and insensitive parenting established in early childhood tend to persist in middle childhood (Bradley & Corwyn, 2008; Lansford, Staples, Bates, Pettit, & Dodge, 2013). In turn, harsh parenting styles and poor-quality parent–child relationships in middle childhood tend to worsen and are associated with poor adjustment, antisocial activity, and delinquency into adolescence (Hakvoort, Bos, van Balen, & Hermanns, 2010; Keijsers, Loeber, Branje, & Meeus, 2011; Koehn & Kerns, 2018).

Siblings

Nearly 80% of children in the United States have at least one sibling (Gao, 2015). By middle childhood, children spend more time with siblings than with parents (Dunn, 2002). Siblings are an important influence on each other's development. Through interactions with siblings, children learn relationship skills such as conflict resolution (McHale, Updegraff, & Whiteman, 2012). They learn that relationships continue even through arguments and anger. Siblings offer each other social support and help each other manage academic, family, and peer challenges and the anxiety and depressive symptoms that often accompany them (Gass, Jenkins, & Dunn, 2007; Ji-Yeon, McHale, Crouter, & Osgood, 2007).

Sibling relationships are also often characterized by patterns of ambivalence and conflict, however (Kramer, 2010). Sibling rivalry tends to rise in middle childhood as children increasingly engage in social comparison. Parents, teachers, peers, and other family

Siblings offer each other social support and opportunities to learn relationship skills such as conflict resolution.
©iStockphoto.com/kali9

members—as well as children themselves—naturally compare siblings' characteristics, interests, and accomplishments (McHale et al., 2012). Children who feel that a sibling receives more affection, approval, or resources from parents may feel resentful, which may harm the sibling relationship. Some fighting and violence are common among siblings. In one study, nearly three-quarters of families reported physical violence between siblings, and over 40% of children had been kicked, bitten, or punched by a sibling within the past year (Feinberg, Solmeyer, & McHale, 2012). Sibling conflict is associated with poor adjustment, depression, peer aggression, and antisocial behaviors (Buist & Vermande, 2014; Coyle, Demaray, Malecki, Tennant, & Klossing, 2017). Children who experience chronic victimization by siblings are at higher risk for peer victimization (Tucker, Finkelhor, & Turner, 2019). Sibling victimization tends to increase with family adversities, such as loss, illness, and other transitions, especially in boys, and declines as families adjust and overcome adversity (Tucker et al., 2019). In contrast, research with children in foster care suggests that warm sibling relationships are a source of support and are associated with resilience to adversity (Wojciak, McWey, & Waid, 2018).

Only Children

As shown in Figure 12.1, family size has shrunk over the past 4 decades. In 2016, about 20% of children lived in one-child households, as or only children (Bialik, 2018). Only children are commonly stereotyped as spoiled and overly dependent on parents. Fortunately, research fails to support these biases. Instead, only children tend to show positive adjustment, have high self-esteem, and are high achievers (Falbo & Polit, 1986). Only children tend to receive greater attention from parents and develop closer relationships than children with siblings who must share their parents' attention. We have seen that siblings offer opportunities to learn interpersonal and conflict resolution skills. In both early and middle childhood, only children are more likely than their peers to show poor interpersonal skills and difficulty with self-control (Downey, Condron, & Yucel, 2015). However, only children tend to have

FIGURE 12.1

Percentage of Mothers Who Have Given Birth to One to Two and Three or More Children

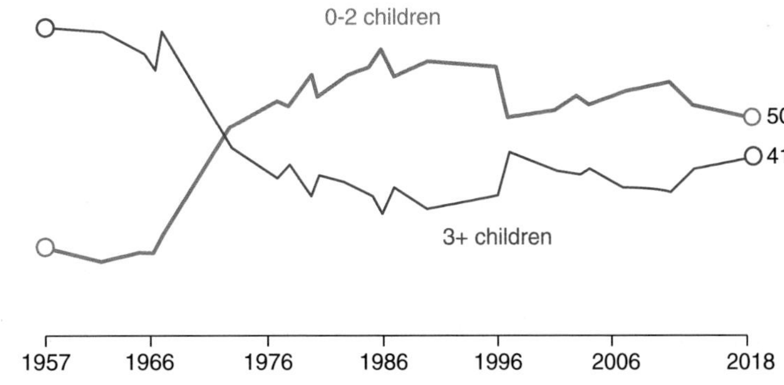

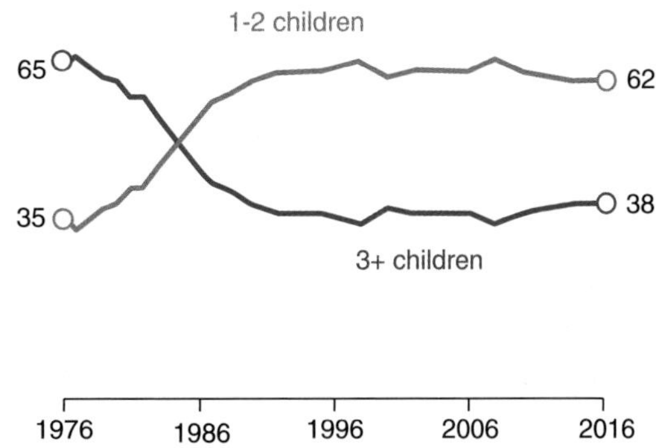

Source: Bialik (2018).

LIVES IN CONTEXT: CULTURAL CONTEXT

China's One-Child Policy

Until recently, married couples in China were permitted to give birth to only one child. The policy was implemented in 1979 in response to a rapidly growing population that posed social, economic, and environmental problems. Known as the one-child policy, it was designed to curb population growth by restricting the number of children married couples could have to one. The one-child policy was most strictly implemented in urban areas (McLoughlin, 2005). Couples in rural areas, especially those who require assistance to manage farms, could request permission for two children if the first child was a girl and the couple waited 4 to 5 years between births (Yang, 2007).

At the core of the one-child policy was a set of incentives as well as penalties for infractions (McLoughlin, 2005). Penalties included stiff fines, reductions in health care and educational opportunities, and even job demotion or job loss. Incentives focused on health and education resources. The official slogan of the one-child policy was "you sheng you yu" ("give birth to fewer children, but give them better care and education"; Yang, 2007). In exchange for limiting parents' childbearing, the Chinese government provided greater opportunities and resources at the national, community, and household levels for only children. The one-child policy was intended to give Chinese school-age only children advantages over those with siblings—specifically, more attention and resources. Early research in the 1980s suggested that Chinese only children scored higher on measures of mathematics and verbal achievement but displayed more egocentrism, uncooperativeness, and difficulty managing emotions and impulses, as well as less sharing, respect of elders, and prosocial behavior than school-age children with siblings (Falbo et al., 1997; McLoughlin, 2005). Later research, however, suggested that Chinese only children scored higher than those with siblings on measures of IQ but did not differ on psychosocial measures such as dependence, helping behaviors, independence, aggression, friendliness, curiosity, self-confidence, peer relationships, social competence, and academic achievement (Chen, Rubin, & Li, 1994; Guo, Yang, Liu, & Song, 2005; Wang et al., 2000).

The one-child policy may have contributed to a gender imbalance in China. Given Chinese culture's tradition of valuing boys, the one-child policy was implicated in high rates of female infanticide and sex-selective abortions, leading to a significant gender imbalance (Mosher, 2006). A population survey of more than 4.5 million Chinese children and teens found that the male to female ratio was 126:100 overall, with several provinces showing ratios of over 130:100 (Zhu, Lu, & Hesketh, 2009). Among second births, the ratio was as high as 149:100, with ratios of over 160:100 in nine provinces (Zhu et al., 2009). A rapidly aging population, coupled with a much smaller workforce, has recently prompted a change in the one-child policy. In 2015, China ended the policy, and now couples may apply to have two children (Buckley, 2015). Initially, fewer couples than expected applied to have a second child, leading to speculation that the one-child policy may have changed perceived norms on family size (Holliday, 2014). However, births in China increased nearly 8% between 2015 and 2016, suggesting that the change is effective (Levenson, 2017).

What Do You Think?

Why do you think fewer Chinese couples than expected initially applied to have a second child? What might have caused the subsequent increase? Do you think the increase in births will continue? Why or why not?

similar numbers of high-quality friendships and generally show similar rates of adjustment as their peers with siblings (Mõttus, Indus, & Allik, 2008). Overall, it appears that only children are similar to those with siblings (Gerhardt, 2016). The Lives in Context feature examines China's One-Child Policy, which resulted in a generation of only children.

Same-Sex Parented Families

Over one-third of adults who identify as lesbian, gay, bisexual, or transgender (LGBT) raise a child (Gates, 2015). Most children raised by LGBT parents are the biological children of these parents, as shown in Figure 12.2. However, LGBT parents are more likely to adopt children than are heterosexual parents. As a result of *Obergefell v. Hodges*, the landmark 2015 U.S. Supreme Court ruling that legalized same-sex marriage nationwide, every state permits joint adoption by married couples, regardless of sexual orientation.

More than 3 decades of research conducted in the United States, the United Kingdom, Belgium, and the Netherlands has failed to reveal important differences in the adjustment or development of children and adolescents reared by same-sex couples compared with those reared by other couples (Fedewa, Black, & Ahn, 2014; Patterson, 2017; Perrin & Siegel, 2013). Specifically, children and adolescents raised by lesbian mothers or gay fathers do not

FIGURE 12.2

Relationship of Children to Parent(s) in Same-Sex Households in the United States, 2011

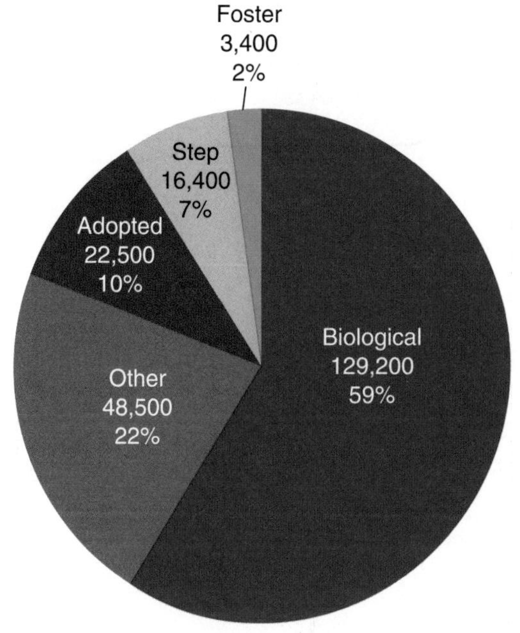

Source: 2011 American Community Survey, as published in Gates, G. J. (2013). *LGBT parenting in the United States*. Los Angeles, CA: The Williams Institute.

Gay and lesbian parents show similar levels of parenting competence as heterosexual parents, but often experience greater well-being.
SHIH WEBER/SIPA/Newscom

differ from other children on measures of emotional development, such as empathy and emotional regulation (Bos, Knox, van Rijn-van Gelderen, & Gartrell, 2016; Farr, 2017). Instead, some studies have suggested that children raised by gay and lesbian parents may score higher in some aspects of social and academic competence, as well as show fewer social and behavioral problems and lower levels of aggression, than other children (Golombok et al., 2014, 2018; Miller, Kors, & Macfie, 2017). Moreover, children raised by lesbian mothers and gay fathers show similar patterns of gender identity and gender role development as children raised by heterosexual parents—they are not more likely to identify as gay or lesbian in adulthood (Fedewa et al., 2014; Tasker & Patterson, 2007). Researchers have concluded that a family's social and economic resources, the strength of the relationships among members of the family, and the presence of stigma are far more important variables than parental gender or sexual orientation in affecting children's development and well-being (Farr, 2017; Perrin & Siegel, 2013).

Single-Parent Families

Over one-quarter of U.S. children under age 18 live with a single parent, most commonly with their mother (U.S. Bureau of the Census, 2018). Figure 12.3 shows the various living arrangements for households with children. African American children are disproportionally likely to live in a single-parent home (Figure 12.4); 49% of African American children live with their mother alone, compared with 26% of Hispanic, 15% of non-Hispanic White, and 11% of Asian American children.

Single-parent families may be created through divorce or death, or the single parent may never have married. In any case, children in such families tend to show more physical and mental health problems, poorer academic achievement, less social competence, and more behavior problems than do children in intact two-parent families (Taylor & Conger, 2017; Waldfogel, Craigie, & Brooks-Gunn, 2010). However, it is important to recognize that these effects tend to be small; the vast majority of children raised in one-parent homes are well adjusted (Lamb, 2012). Moreover, there are more differences among children in single-parent homes than between children in single-parent homes and two-parent homes. Children reared by parents who are single by choice tend to experience few adjustment problems; children of divorced parents tend to experience more difficulties due to the many transitions that accompany divorce, discussed later in this chapter (Golombok & Tasker, 2015).

Children in single-mother homes, regardless of ethnicity, are disproportionately likely to live in poverty (Damaske, Bratter, & Frech, 2017). About one-third of children raised in single-mother homes live in poverty, compared with 16% of children in single-father homes and less than 6% of children in homes of married couples (DeNavas-Walt & Proctor, 2014). Low socioeconomic status poses risks for academic, social, and behavioral problems. Economic disadvantage affects children in a myriad of ways, from having less money for books, clothes, and extracurricular activities to living in poorer school districts and

FIGURE 12.3

Living Arrangements of Children Under 18, 1958–2017

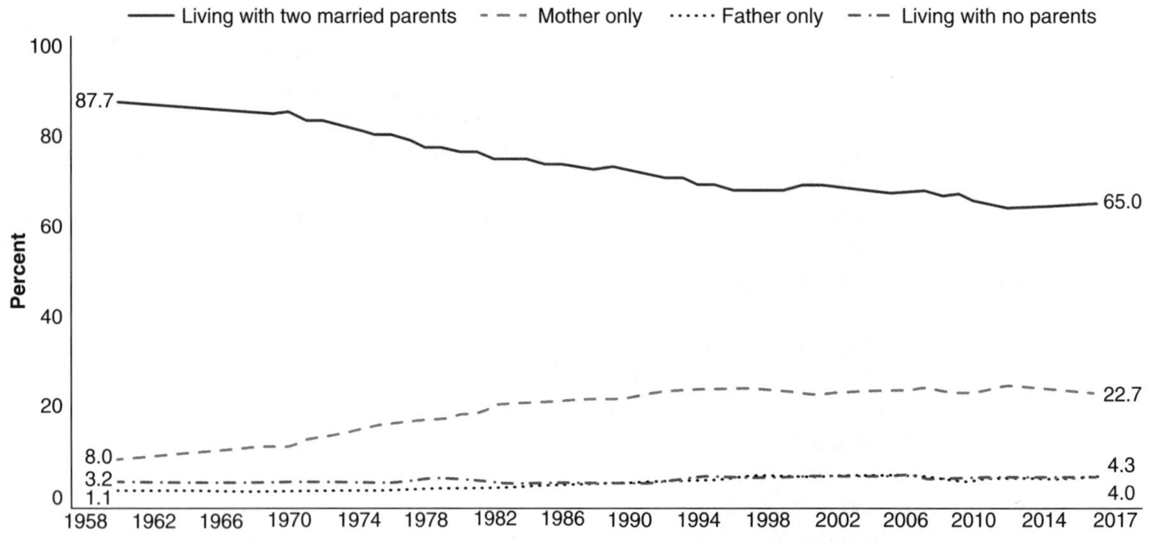

Source: U.S. Bureau of the Census. (2017). Table C3. Retrieved from https://www2.census.gov/programs-surveys/demo/tables/families/2017/cps-2017/tabc3-all.xls

FIGURE 12.4

Living Arrangements of Children, by Race and Hispanic Origin, 2017

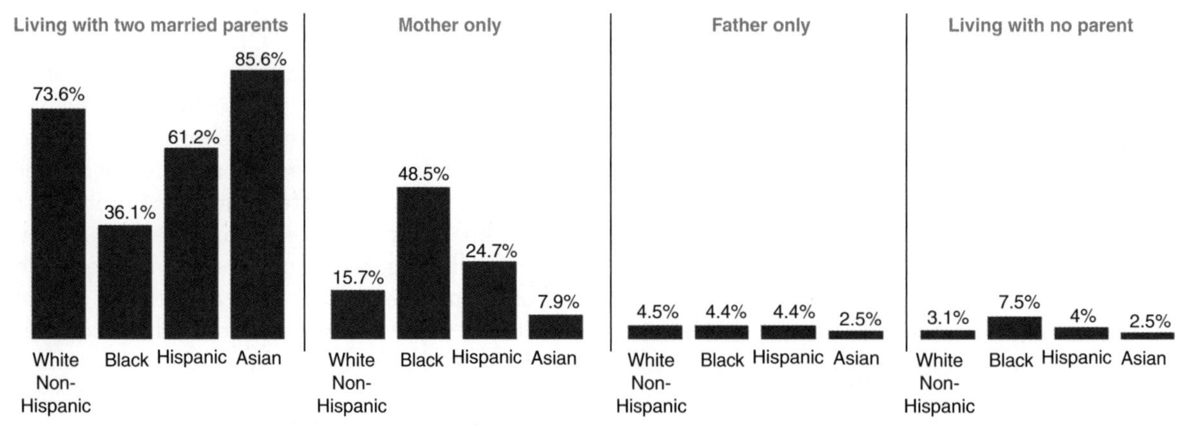

Source: U.S. Bureau of the Census. (2017). Table C3. Retrieved from https://www2.census.gov/programs-surveys/demo/tables/families/2017/cps-2017/tabc3-all.xls

neighborhoods. In addition, families headed by single mothers often experience many transitions, as single mothers tend to change jobs and homes more frequently than other mothers. Each transition poses challenges to children's adjustment (Evans, Li, & Whipple, 2013). In addition, single mothers report more depression and psychological problems than married mothers and, when depressed, undoubtedly function less well as parents (Reising et al., 2013; Waldfogel et al., 2010).

The vast majority of what we know about single-parent families comes from studying mothers. About one-fourth of single-parent households are headed by men, however (Livingston, 2013). Single fathers are more likely than mothers to live with a partner and tend to have higher household incomes, both of which are associated with positive child outcomes. In fact, many of the differences associated with family structure are reduced or disappear when researchers take socioeconomic status into account, suggesting that differences in child well-being across family types are strongly influenced by family income, access to resources, and the stresses that accompany economic difficulties (R. M. Ryan, Claessens, & Markowitz, 2015).

Parenting success, then, is influenced by access to economic and social resources (Taylor & Conger, 2017). The level of social support afforded single mothers influences their abilities to provide emotional support for their children and implement effective parenting strategies. In African American communities, for example, single mothers are often integrated within their community, providing their children with opportunities to interact with many caring adult family members and friends of the family; thus, children are raised as members of a larger African American community (Jayakody & Kalil, 2002). Often, an adult male, such as an uncle or grandfather, takes on a fathering role, helping a child build competence and develop a relationship with a caring adult (Hill, Bush, & Roosa, 2003). In such families, grandmothers often are highly involved, warm, and helpful, taking on important support roles. In one study of U.K. single-parent homes, grandmothers served parental roles and aided their children much as would partners (Harper & Ruicheva, 2010). When children are close to highly involved extended family members, they develop family bonds and a sense of family honor that guides them and encourages them to succeed; this tends to hold true of all children, regardless of family structure (Jaeger, 2012).

Cohabiting Families

There are many kinds of families, and not all are formed through marriage. An estimated 40% of children will spend some time in a cohabiting-parent family before they reach age 12 (Manning, 2015). Children of unmarried cohabiting parents who have close caring relationships with them and whose union is stable develop as well as their counterparts whose parents' marriage is stable (Rose-Greenland & Smock, 2013).

Unmarried cohabiting couples tend to have less stable relationships than married couples, however (Manning, 2015). For example, about one-third of cohabiting couples break up within 3 years (Copen, Daniels, & Mosher, 2013). In contrast, about two-thirds of first marriages are intact after 10 years (Goodwin, Mosher, & Chandra, 2010). Children living in cohabiting households are much more likely to experience their parents' separation, conflict in the home, and transitions in family life than are children of married parents, all of which influence adjustment (Rose-Greenland & Smock, 2013).

Differences in socioeconomic status have an effect on the development of children of cohabiting parents, just as they do on other children's development. On average, children raised in cohabiting-parent families experience economic situations that are better than those of many children in single-parent families (e.g., higher parental education and family earnings) but more economically stressful than those reared by married parents (e.g., greater poverty and food insecurity) (Manning, 2015). About 20% of children living in cohabiting families are poor, compared with about 10% of children from two-parent married households and nearly 40% of children in single-parent households (Kennedy & Fitch, 2012).

The effect of cohabitation on children may vary with contextual norms. Consensual unions and childbearing within cohabiting unions are more common among minority families (Kennedy & Bumpass, 2008). Black and Hispanic children thus spend more time in cohabiting-parent unions than do White children. In addition, the difference in economic advantage between marriage and cohabitation is smaller for cohabiting Black and Hispanic families than for White families, perhaps partially accounting for more positive outcomes for children of color (Manning & Brown, 2006; Osborne, Manning, & Smock, 2007).

Divorced and Divorcing Families

Since 1960, divorce rates have tripled in many industrialized nations. Although the divorce rate in the United States is high relative to that in many countries, it has declined over the past 3 decades from its peak of 5.3 per 1,000 in the total population in 1981 to 3.2 in 2014 (National Center for Health Statistics, 2015). About 40% of marriages in the United States end in divorce within 15 years (Copen, Daniels, Vespa, & Mosher, 2012).

For many decades, it was assumed that divorce caused significant and irreparable harm to children. Most researchers today take a neutral stance, viewing divorce as a common transition that many children experience and that poses some challenges to adjustment. Research has suggested that divorce has some negative effects on children's adjustment, such as internalizing and externalizing problems, but the effects are small, vary by particular outcome, are often transient, and do not apply to all children uniformly (Amato & Anthony, 2014; Weaver & Schofield, 2014). Variations in child, parent, and family characteristics and contexts influence children's adjustment to parental divorce, but most

Divorce tends to be preceded by a period of parental conflict and uncertainty and the tension may continue for several years after the divorce, with implications for children's emotional and psychological health.
©iStockphoto.com/Motortion

children show improved adjustment within 2 years after the divorce, suggesting that the majority of children of divorce are resilient (Lamb, 2012). What initially appear to be effects of divorce are likely to be a complex combination of parent, child, and contextual factors that precede and follow the divorce in conjunction with the divorce itself (Amato & Anthony, 2014; Bennett, 2006).

Divorce triggers a reconfiguration of family roles, and parenting responsibilities shift disproportionately onto the resident parent. After divorce, children are typically raised by their mothers and experience a drop in income that influences their access to resources and opportunities, such as after-school programs and activities (Bratberg & Tjøtta, 2008). Single-parent-headed households often move to more affordable housing, causing additional changes in children's school, community, and circle of friends, reducing children's access to social support and opportunities to play with friends. Custodial parents might also increase the hours they work, leading to less contact with their children. These changes contribute to inconsistencies in family routines, activities, and parental monitoring prior to, during, and after the divorce. High-quality family relationships, including positive interactions with the noncustodial parent and low levels of parent–parent conflict, can buffer children against these stressors (Bastaits & Mortelmans, 2016; Weaver & Schofield, 2015).

Divorce tends to be preceded by a period of uncertainty and tension, often characterized by increases in conflict between parents that may continue for several years after the divorce (Amato, 2010). In fact, harmful family processes, such as parental conflict, poor parent–child interactions, and ineffective parenting strategies, may precede parental divorce by as much as 8 to 12 years (Drapeau, Gagne, Saint-Jacques, Lepine, & Ivers, 2009; Potter, 2010). These processes understandably take a toll on children's emotional and psychological health. Chronic exposure to parental conflict is associated with increased physiological arousal, an elevated stress response, and poorer adjustment (Davidson, O'Hara, & Beck, 2014; Davies & Martin, 2014). In turn, children's difficulties adapting, such as behavior problems, can increase parental conflict (Drapeau et al., 2009). Longitudinal research following children of married parents has found that children whose parents later divorce show many of the problems typical of children of divorce, such as anxiety, depression, delinquency, and poor academics, long before the divorce takes place (Strohschein, 2005). However, not all parents display high levels of conflict. When researchers take into account the quality of parenting and children's exposure to conflict, the link between parental divorce and children's adjustment lessens, suggesting that parenting strategies and relationships are more important influences on children's adjustment than divorce (Bing, Nelson, & Wesolowski, 2009; Whiteside & Becker, 2000).

Blended Families

About 15% of U.S. children live in a blended family: a family composed of a biological parent and a nonrelated adult, most commonly a mother and stepfather (Pew Research Center, 2015). Blended families, also sometimes referred to as stepfamilies or reconstituted families, present children with new challenges and adjustments, as the multiple transitions entailed by divorce and remarriage are stressful. It is often difficult for blended families to integrate and balance the many relationships among custodial, noncustodial, and stepparents, in addition to grandparents and extended family members (Nixon & Hadfield, 2016). As stepfamilies become more complex, that is, as the number of biologically and nonbiologically related individuals in the family increases, so do challenges to children's adjustment (Brown, Manning, & Stykes, 2015).

Age influences adaptation to a blended family. School-age children and adolescents tend to display more difficulties in adjusting to remarriage than do younger children (Ganong, Coleman, & Russell, 2015). Although adjusting to being part of a blended family may pose challenges, most children reared in stepfamilies do not differ from those raised in single-parent families in terms of cognitive, academic, and social outcomes (Ganong & Coleman, 2017). Many are similar to children in first-marriage families. Indeed, entering a stepfamily is associated with improved adjustment, especially when it results in an increase in family income (Ryan et al., 2015). Overall, blended families adapt more easily and children show better adjustment when stepparents build a warm friendship with the child and adopt their new roles slowly rather than rushing or forcing relationships (Doodson & Morley, 2006).

THINKING IN CONTEXT 12.4

1. Parents and children influence each other dynamically. Provide personal examples of this process, and describe how children influence their parents and are also influenced by their parents. How do parent–child interactions change over middle childhood?
2. Considering the many forms that families may take, what contextual factors best support positive development in children?

APPLY YOUR KNOWLEDGE

Every winter Massimo and his father watched ice hockey games on television. Ten-year-old Massimo liked watching the players race across the ice, turn, and shoot, seemingly effortlessly. "I want to play hockey when I'm bigger," Massimo told his father. "Nope, you won't have to wait. A new ice rink opened up nearby. I bet they have a hockey club," Massimo's father said.

Several weeks later, Massimo visited the ice rink and signed up to play hockey. "You should take some ice skating lessons," his father instructed. "I don't need them. It's easy," Massimo responded. Years of watching hockey gave Massimo a good sense of how to skate. Plus, he gracefully glided over every patch of street ice he could find.

Massimo tied the laces on his new ice skates and wobbled to the ice to participate in his first team practice. "These skates feel pretty weird," he thought to himself. Massimo stepped out onto the ice and immediately fell. He scrambled to the wall, pulled himself up, and fell again. "I don't get it! It looks so easy," he said as he tried again.

"Ha! Fall much?" asked Rick, one of the boys on the team. Rick deftly circled Massimo and smoothly stopped, spraying ice onto Massimo. The other boys on the team laughed. Massimo scrambled to stand and fell again. Embarrassed, Massimo clumsily hobbled off of the ice as the boys laughed. Rick called out. Massimo couldn't hear what he said but the boys laughed again.

"I can't do it. I'm just not good at skating," Massimo complained to the coach. "Skating is a talent. Some people naturally do it well. Others have to try hard," the coach explained. "Practice and you will get better," he said.

Massimo sighed and replied, "No, I'm just not good at it and I never will be."

Later Massimo's mother advised, "Go back to the rink, take lessons, and you will learn to skate. Then you'll be ready to play hockey." Massimo cried, "I'm never going back there. There's nothing I can do to get better. Dad said 'Either you have it or you don't,' and I don't."

At school the following week, Rick cornered Massimo in the hall. "You skate like a baby. You're not going to be on our team because you're a loser." The other kids smirked and laughed. Massimo began to cry. A teacher witnessed this exchange and separated the children. "Rick, go to class. Everyone else, go to class. Massimo, come with me," she said.

1. According to Erikson, what is the psychosocial task of middle childhood? How well do Massimo's interests and behaviors match the psychosocial task of middle childhood?
2. How does Massimo view his skating ability? Describe Massimo's mindset and achievement orientation.
3. What role do parents and peers play in influencing older children's sense of self and views of their abilities?
4. To what degree is Massimo at risk for peer victimization? Why?
5. How can parents, teachers, and the school context reduce the incidence of peer victimization and its effects on children?

WANT A BETTER GRADE?

Get the tools you need to sharpen your study skills. **SAGE edge** offers a robust online environment featuring an impressive array of free tools and resources. Access practice quizzes, eFlashcards, video, and multimedia at **edge.sagepub.com/kutherchild1e.** SAGE edge™

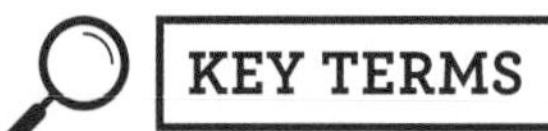

KEY TERMS

Achievement motivation 324
Internal attribution 324
External attribution 324
Growth mindset 324
Fixed mindset 324
Learned helplessness orientation 324
Popular children 330
Peer rejection 330
Aggressive-rejected children 331
Withdrawn-rejected children 331
Bullying 331

SUMMARY

12.1 Describe school-age children's self-conceptions and motivation.

School-age children's conceptions of themselves become more sophisticated, organized, and accurate. They incorporate feedback about their abilities from parents, teachers, and peers as well as engage in social comparison to derive a sense of self-esteem. Children differ in mindset as well as whether they attribute their performance to internal or external causes. A mastery orientation is associated with academic success. A learned helplessness orientation is associated with poor performance. Parents and teachers who are warm and supportive promote a mastery orientation.

12.2 Summarize sex differences and gender preferences and stereotypes in middle childhood.

Research suggests that cognitive abilities and social behaviors in children are small or negligible. School-age children tend to prefer same-sex peers and express gender stereotypes that influence preferences and views of their own abilities. Transgender children show similar patterns of gender development and stereotyping as do children with a cisgender identity, but transgender children demonstrate more flexible views of gender stereotypes. By around 7 years of age, children demonstrate gender constancy, the awareness that a person's sex is a biological characteristic and gender rigidity tends to decline. At about 9 to 10 years of age, children grasp the social basis of gender roles and increasingly agree that boys and girls follow their own preferences regardless of social conventions.

12.3 Examine the roles of friendship, peer acceptance, and peer victimization in school-age children's adjustment.

In middle childhood, friendship becomes a reciprocal relationship characterized by intimacy, loyalty, and commitment. Friendships offer opportunities for children to learn relationship skills and influence children's adjustment. Peer acceptance is a source of self-validation and self-esteem. Popular children tend to be helpful, trustworthy, and bright; they are skilled in self-regulation and conflict resolution. Aggressive-rejected and withdrawn-rejected children show poor emotion regulation skills and are at risk for short- and long-term problems. Children who bully tend to be physically and verbally assertive and impulsive, whereas bullied children are more likely to be inhibited, be anxious, and have low self-esteem and poor social and emotional regulation skills. School procedures can play a role in both increasing and decreasing the prevalence of bullying.

12.4 Discuss family relationships in middle childhood and the influence of family structure on adjustment.

Parents tend to adapt to children's growing independence by guiding and monitoring behavior from a distance, communicating expectations, using reasoning, and permitting children to be in charge of moment-to-moment decision making. Decades of research have failed to reveal important differences in the adjustment or development of children and adolescents reared by same-sex parents. Children's adjustment is influenced by socioeconomic status and family conflict, characteristics that vary with family structure. Divorce has some negative effects on children's adjustment, but the effects are small, vary by particular outcome, and do not apply to all children. Many of children's emotional, psychological, and behavioral problems stem from exposure to parental conflict before and after the divorce. Child sexual abuse poses serious risks to children's physical, psychological, and emotional health and adjustment. Some children show resilience despite experiencing adversity.

REVIEW QUESTIONS

12.1 What is the psychosocial task of middle childhood?

How do self-concept and self-esteem change in middle childhood?

What is achievement motivation and how is it influenced by context?

Differentiate among mindset, mastery orientation, and learned helplessness orientation.

12.2 What sex differences occur in middle childhood?

What gender stereotypes do children show?

How do children's stereotypes change in middle childhood?

12.3 How are children's friendships associated with adjustment?

What are characteristics of popular and rejected children?

Describe common characteristics of bullies and victims of bullying.

What are features of effective bullying interventions?

12.4 What are some of the different forms that families take and how are they associated with children's outcomes?

How do parent–child interactions shift over middle childhood?

What are risk factors and outcomes associated with child sexual abuse?

What are characteristics associated with resilience?

Adolescence

©iStockphoto.com/monkeybusinessimages

13 Physical Development in Adolescence

In second grade, the teacher paired Deja and Carly to work on an in-class assignment. The two girls quickly became best friends. Deja and Carly were inseparable throughout elementary school and middle school. They both participated in dance club, practiced gymnastics, and enjoyed walking around their neighborhood. At age 13, however, Carly was surprised when her friend suddenly quit dance and gymnastics. "Why did you quit? And why didn't you tell me?" she asked. Deja responded, "I feel so big and clumsy. I'm so heavy I can't flip like I used to. Nothing feels right." Self-conscious, Deja sensed that her mature breasts and hips set her apart from her peers. She looked at her short, lean friend, "You don't understand." Carly answered, "Well, I wish I had curves, so maybe you don't understand me either." Although they are the same age, Deja and Carly show different patterns of physical development. In this chapter, we examine the biological changes that accompany adolescence and their influence on adolescents' appearance, behavior, and social world.

Learning Objectives

13.1 Summarize the physical changes that accompany puberty and how context influences how it is experienced.

Video Activity 13.1: The Becoming Years

13.2 Describe brain development during adolescence and its effect on behavior.

Video Activity 13.2: Brain-Body

13.3 Discuss adolescents' health needs and common health problems.

13.4 Distinguish normative sexual development and activity from problematic activities and outcomes.

Chapter Contents

PUBERTY

The dramatic changes that adolescents' bodies undergo are often considered the hallmark of adolescence. **Puberty** is the biological transition to adulthood, in which adolescents mature physically and become capable of reproduction. Although many people view puberty as an event, it is a process that includes many physical changes that occur over about 4 years but can vary dramatically from 1 to 7 years (Mendle, 2014). In late childhood, by about age 8 or 9 in girls and roughly 2 years later in boys, the brain signals the endocrine system to gradually increase the release of hormones that trigger the onset of puberty (Berenbaum, Beltz, & Corley, 2015). Puberty entails the development of reproductive capacity, but that is not the whole story, for puberty influences a great variety of physical changes—not simply those typically associated with sexual maturity, such as changes in body size, shape, and function.

Changes in Body Shape and Size

The first outward sign of puberty is the **adolescent growth spurt**, a rapid gain in height and weight that generally begins in girls at about age 10 (as early as age 7 and as late as 14) and in boys at about age 12 (as early as age 9 and as late as 16) (Tinggaard et al., 2012). The pattern and pace of growth, as shown in Table 13.1, is similar across most children (Sanders et al., 2017). Girls begin their growth spurt about 2 years before boys, so 10- to 13-year-old girls tend to be taller, heavier, and stronger than boys their age. By starting their growth spurts 2 years later than girls, boys begin with an extra 2 years of prepubertal growth on which the adolescent growth spurt builds, leading boys to end up taller than girls (Yousefi et al., 2013). On average, the growth spurt lasts about 2 years, but growth in height continues at a more gradual pace, ending by about 16 in girls and 18 in boys. Adolescents gain a total of about 10 inches in height.

Young adolescents' physical maturation varies dramatically by individual, as illustrated by these girls who are all in the same grade.
Bob Daemmrich/Alamy Stock Photo

Different parts of the body grow at different rates. For example, the extremities grow first, the fingers and toes; then hands and feet; then arms and legs; and finally, the torso (Sheehy, Gasser, & Molinari, 2009). Adolescents' bodies therefore tend to appear lanky and awkward, contributing to a temporary increase in clumsiness as adolescents attempt to control their quickly changing bodies. Adolescents' bodies become taller and heavier before their muscles grow stronger and their internal organs mature (DeRose & Brooks-Gunn, 2006; Seger & Thorstensson, 2000).

Sex differences in body shape emerge during the growth spurt. Boys and girls gain fat and muscle, but in different ratios. Girls gain more fat overall, particularly on their legs and hips, so that fat comes to comprise one-fourth of their body weight—nearly twice as much as boys. Boys gain more muscle than do girls, especially in their upper bodies, doubling

TABLE 13.1

Sequence of Physical Changes with Puberty

GIRLS			BOYS		
CHARACTERISTIC	MEAN AGE	RANGE	CHARACTERISTIC	MEAN AGE	RANGE
Breast growth begins	10	7–13	Growth spurt begins	12.5	10.5–16
Growth spurt begins	10	8–14	Testes and scrotum grow larger	11	9.5–13.5
Pubic hair appears	10.5	7–14	Pubic hair appears	12	10–15
Peak strength spurt	11.5	9.5–14	Penis growth begins	12	11–14.5
Peak height spurt	11.5	10–13.5	Spermarche	13	12–16
Peak weight spurt	12.5	10–14	Peak height spurt	14	12.5–15.5
Menarche	12.5	10–16	Peak weight spurt	14	12.5–15.5
Adult stature	13	10–16	Voice lowers	14	11.5-15.5
Pubic hair growth completed	14.5	14–15	Facial and underarm hair begins	14	12.5–15.5
Breast growth completed	15	10–18	Penis and testes growth completed	14.5	12.5–16
			Peak strength spurt	15	13–17
			Adult stature	15.5	13.5–18
			Pubic hair growth completed	15.5	14–18

their arm strength between ages 13 and 18 (Payne & Isaacs, 2016). Bone density increases in both boys and girls, and the respiratory and cardiovascular systems mature. Boys become much better at taking in and using oxygen as their hearts and lungs grow larger and function more effectively and the number of red blood cells increase (Sadler, 2017). Consequently, once puberty has begun, boys tend to consistently outperform girls in athletics (Tønnessen, Svendsen, Olsen, Guttormsen, & Haugen, 2015).

Secondary Sex Characteristics

Most people associate puberty with the development of **secondary sex characteristics**, body changes that indicate physical maturation but are not directly related to fertility. Examples of changes in secondary sex characteristics include breast development, deepening of the voice, growth of facial and body hair, and, for many, the emergence of acne (Hodges-Simeon, Gurven, Cárdenas, & Gaulin, 2013).

Rapid increases in estrogen cause the budding of breasts, which tends to accompany the growth spurt in girls as the first signs of puberty (Emmanuel & Bokor, 2017). Testosterone causes boys' voices to deepen. As their voices change, boys may occasionally lose control over their voices and emit unpredictable changes in pitch often experienced as high squeaks (Hodges-Simeon et al., 2013). Girls' voices also deepen, but the change is not as noticeable as in boys. Oil and sweat glands become more active, resulting in body odor and acne (Sadler, 2017). Hair on the head, arms, and legs becomes darker, and pubic hair begins to grow, first as straight and downy, and later becomes coarse.

Primary Sex Characteristics

Maturation of the **primary sex characteristics**, the reproductive organs, is less noticeable than secondary sex characteristics but is a function of puberty—reproductive maturation. In females, primary sex characteristics include the ovaries, fallopian tubes, uterus, and vagina. In males, they include the penis, testes, scrotum, seminal vesicles, and prostate gland.

The arrival of menstruation marks the onset of sexual maturity in girls. **Menstruation** refers to the monthly shedding of the uterine lining, which has thickened in preparation for the implantation of a fertilized egg. **Menarche**, the first menstruation, occurs toward the end of puberty, yet most adolescents and adults view it as a critical marker of puberty because it occurs suddenly and is memorable (Brooks-Gunn & Ruble, 2013).

In North America, the average European American girl experiences menarche shortly before turning 13 and the average African American girl shortly after turning 12 (Emmanuel & Bokor, 2017). Generally, African American girls tend to be heavier and enter puberty about a year earlier, reaching pubertal milestones such as the growth spurt and menarche earlier than other girls (Emmanuel & Bokor, 2017). Hispanic American girls enter puberty at about the same time as African American girls, with some studies suggesting earlier menarche and others later (Biro et al., 2018; Deardorff, Abrams, Ekwaru, & Rehkopf, 2014). Frequently, during the first few months after menarche, menstruation takes place without ovulation, the ovaries' release of an ovum (Lacroix & Whitten, 2017). However, this period of temporary sterility is variable and unpredictable.

In boys, the first primary sex characteristic to emerge is the growth of the **testes**, the glands that produce sperm (Tinggaard et al., 2012). About a year later, the penis and scrotum enlarge, and pubic hair, a secondary sex characteristic, appears. As the penis grows, the prostate gland and seminal vesicles begin to produce **semen**, the fluid that contains sperm. At about age 13, boys demonstrate a principal sign of sexual maturation: the first ejaculation, known as **spermarche** (Gaddis & Brooks-Gunn, 1985; Tomova, Lalabonova, Robeva, & Kumanov, 2011). The first ejaculations contain few living sperm. Many boys experience spermarche in the form of **nocturnal emissions**, or wet dreams: involuntary ejaculations that are sometimes accompanied by erotic dreams.

How Do Adolescents Experience Puberty?

Girls' perception of menarche is influenced by their knowledge about menstruation as well as their expectations (Brooke-Gunn & Ruble, 2013). Most girls are surprised by menarche but have some knowledge about it because they have been informed about puberty by health education classes and parents (Stidham-Hall, Moreau, & Trussell, 2012). However, the extent to which adolescents discuss menarche and sexuality varies by context and culture. A study of 12- to 16-year-old Bangladeshi girls revealed that they generally were not informed about menarche, and over two-thirds reacted with fear (Bosch, Hutter, & van Ginneken, 2008). Their mothers also tended to lack an adequate understanding of pubertal processes. Other research has suggested that girls in low- and middle-income countries, such as India, Turkey, Pakistan, Nigeria, and Malaysia, often know little about menarche and, for religious and cultural reasons, may feel shame about menstruation (Behera, Sivakami, & Behera, 2015; Chandra-Mouli & Patel, 2017). In some cultures, girls can be excluded from interaction with others, including attending school, when they are menstruating (see the Lives in Context feature). Girls who view menstruation negatively are

LIVES IN CONTEXT: CULTURAL CONTEXT

Menarche Rituals of the !Xoo

In many cultures, menarche is accompanied by rituals that mark it as a rite of passage to adulthood. For example, the !Xoo of Zutshwa in Botswana expect girls upon experiencing their first menses to immediately run from others and to hide in the bush (Nhlekisana, 2017). Soon the older women of the community search for the girl. The women carry the girl home so that her feet do not touch the ground and she is secluded in a private hut for 1 month. During their seclusion, !Xoo girls learn about the taboos associated with menstruation. For example, it is thought that a menstruating woman should not come into contact with anything that grows. Walking about the community or coming into contact with animals while menstruating, for example, is believed to cause drought or sickness (Nhlekisana, 2017).

While in seclusion, the girl is told not to look outside or make eye contact with others and she must sit with her back against the wall. She is cared for by her mother or grandmother who feeds her, bathes her, and changes the grass that she lies on. The girl is instructed not to touch anything and not to move. She is given a twig to use to scratch her body when it itches but she may not touch herself otherwise. The girl is given meat and roots mixed with medicine believed to strengthen her and reduce the length of her menstruation (Marshall, 1999). She does not touch food with her hands but is fed by her caretaker.

During the month of seclusion, the girl is given instructions and advice in preparation for her new role in the community (Munthali & Zulu, 2007). She is trained in the moral and practical responsibilities of being a wife and child bearer, such as matters concerning womanhood, domestic and agricultural activities, reproduction, and behavior toward men (Denbow & Thebe, 2006). The training is accompanied by singing and dancing.

After the !Xoo girl has been secluded for a month, arrangements for her emergence and reincorporation into the society are made. She is smeared with a reddish powder called *letsoku*. The *letsoku* symbolizes fertility and is intended to make the girl more attractive. Patterns are drawn on her face using white makeup. The girl is adorned with necklaces, armbands, and head bands made from ostrich shells. Her feet are washed with powdered seeds thought to give her freedom to walk safely.

Finally, the girl is accompanied around the community, including the fields and water well. After sunset, she carries a stick to each hut and lights it using the fire burning in each household, offering protection to each household and integrating the girl into the community (Nhlekisana, 2017).

What Do You Think?

1. What purpose does a ritual such as this serve the girl, her family, and the community?
2. What rituals and activities mark menarche in Western girls? ●

at risk to experience menstruation negatively, with more menstrual symptoms and distress (Rembeck, Möller, & Gunnarsson, 2006).

We know less about boys' experience of puberty because they lack easily determined objective markers, such as menarche (Herman-Giddens et al., 2012). Research with small groups of adolescent boys suggests that most boys react positively to first ejaculation, although many experience uneasiness and confusion, especially if they are uninformed about this pubertal change (Frankel, 2002; Stein & Reiser, 1994). Boys who know about ejaculation beforehand are more likely to show positive reactions, such as feeling pleasure, happiness, and pride. Unfortunately, many boys report that health education classes and parents generally do not discuss ejaculation (Omar, McElderry, & Zakharia, 2003; Stein & Reiser, 1994). Parents sometimes report discomfort talking with their sons about reproductive development, particularly ejaculation, because of the close link with sexual desire, sexuality, and masturbation (Frankel, 2002). Perhaps because of its sexual nature, boys are less likely to tell a friend about spermarche than are girls to discuss their own reproductive development (Downs & Fuller, 1991).

Puberty and Sleep Patterns

Adolescents' sleep patterns shift with puberty and they show a **delayed phase preference**, a biologically motivated preference to go to bed later (Carskadon, 2009; Crowley, Acebo, & Carskadon, 2007). Delayed phase preference is triggered by a change in the nightly release of a hormone that influences sleep called **melatonin**. Adolescents who have experienced puberty tend to show a nightly rise in melatonin (and sleep) about 2 hours later than those who have not begun puberty (Carskadon, Acebo, & Jenni, 2004). When adolescents are allowed to regulate their own sleep schedule, they tend to go to bed at about 1:00

a.m. and sleep until about 10:00 a.m. (Colrain & Baker, 2011). As a result, adolescents stay up later, miss out on sleep, and report sleepiness (Carskadon et al., 2004; Loessl et al., 2008).

Adolescents need about 9 hours of sleep each night to support healthy development, but most get far less sleep. From ages 13 to 19, the average hours of sleep reported by adolescents in Western countries, such as the United States and Germany, tends to decrease from about 8 hours to 7 hours, with greater reductions in sleep with each year of age (Carskadon, 2009; Loessl et al., 2008).

Poor sleep in adolescence is associated with anxiety, irritability, and depression and increases the probability of health problems such as illness, obesity, and accidents (Darchia & Cervena, 2014; Fuligni, Arruda, Krull, & Gonzales, 2018; Mitchell et al., 2013b; Wong & Brower, 2012). Poor sleep duration predicts less engagement in extracurricular school activities and declines in academic performance (Fuligni et al., 2018; Minges & Redeker, 2016). Sleep problems are also associated with risky behaviors, including cigarette smoking and alcohol and substance use (Miller, Janssen, & Jackson, 2017; Nguyen-Louie et al., 2018; Pieters et al., 2015; Telzer, Fuligni, Lieberman, & Galván, 2013; Wong, Robertson, & Dyson, 2015).

The tendency for adolescents to go to bed later has increased over the last 3 decades, along with the increased availability of television and electronic media that compete with sleep for adolescents' time (Bartel, Gradisar, & Williamson, 2015; Carskadon & Tarokh, 2014). Greater bedtime screen use is associated with less sleep (Vernon, Modecki, & Barber, 2018) partly because evening exposure to light from screens suppresses adolescents' melatonin production (Crowley, Cain, Burns, Acebo, & Carskadon, 2015).

The home and family context also influences adolescents' sleep. Parental support and cohesive parent–child relationships are linked to longer sleep duration, less sleep variability, and less time spent awake during the night (Tsai et al., 2017). Relatedly, adolescents' perceptions of greater perceived neighborhood cohesion were associated with better sleep and the effect was greater for those of lower socioeconomic status, especially those in homes characterized by lower levels of maternal education (Troxel et al., 2017). Finally, school also affects adolescents' sleep. Most middle and high schools start earlier than elementary school, often to allot time for after-school sports and activities. Earlier school starting times are associated with less total sleep and students generally do not make up for lost sleep on the weekends (Paksarian, Rudolph, He, & Merikangas, 2015). Delaying school start times can increase students' sleep from 25 to as many as 75 minutes each night and improves student school attendance, grades, and disposition (Minges & Redeker, 2016; Owens, Belon, & Moss, 2010; Owens, Dearth-Wesley, Herman, Oakes, & Whitaker, 2017). In 2017, the American Academy of Sleep Medicine (N. F. Watson et al., 2017) issued a policy statement calling on communities, school boards, and educational institutions to implement start times of 8:30 a.m. or later for middle schools and high schools to ensure that every student arrives at school healthy, awake, alert, and ready to learn.

Pubertal Timing

Casual observations of adolescents reveal that although most tend to progress through puberty at about the same time, some begin much earlier or later than others. Children who show signs of physical maturation before age 8 (in girls) or 9 (in boys) are considered early-maturing adolescents, whereas girls who begin puberty after age 13 and boys who begin after age 14 are considered late-maturing adolescents (Dorn, Dahl, Woodward, & Biro, 2006). Early maturation, in particular, poses challenges for both girls' and boys' adaptation (Stroud & Davila, 2016; Ullsperger & Nikolas, 2017).

Early Maturation

Adolescents who mature early tend to look older than their years and are more likely to be treated in ways similar to older adolescents, which adolescents may perceive as stressful (Rudolph, Troop-Gordon, Lambert, & Natsuaki, 2014). Around the world, early-maturing boys and girls show higher rates of risky activity, including smoking, abusing alcohol and substances, and displaying aggressive behavior than do same-age peers (Mrug et al., 2014; Schelleman-Offermans, Knibbe, & Kuntsche, 2013; Skoog & Stattin, 2014).

Early maturation poses specific risks to girls' development. Girls who mature early relative to peers tend to feel less positive about their bodies, physical appearance, and menstruation itself, and they show higher rates of depression, anxiety, and low self-esteem than do girls who mature on time or late (Benoit, Lacourse, & Claes, 2013; Carter, 2015; Carter, Halawah, & Trinh, 2018; Reynolds & Juvonen, 2011; Skoog, Özdemir, & Stattin, 2016; Stojković, 2013). Early-maturing girls tend to date earlier than their peers, are at higher risk of dating violence, and experience more sexual harassment than their peers (Chen, Rothman, & Jaffee, 2017; Skoog & Özdemir, 2016).

Early-maturing boys tend to be athletic, popular with peers, school leaders, and confident (Stojković, 2013). There is less research on boys than on girls, but it appears that early-maturing boys also experience some internalizing and externalizing symptoms (Rudolph et al., 2014; Stroud & Davila, 2016). Early maturers tend to show higher rates of problematic drinking, including consuming alcohol more frequently and in greater quantities, and becoming intoxicated more often than their on-time and late-maturing peers (Biehl, Natsuaki, & Ge, 2007; Schelleman-Offermans et al., 2013). Although all early-maturing adolescents tend to experience more problems, early-maturing girls are at higher risk for early sexual activity and alcohol and substance use and abuse than boys (Ullsperger & Nikolas, 2017). Late maturation shows a different pattern of outcomes.

Late Maturation

In contrast to early maturation, the effects of late maturation tend to differ for boys and girls. Late maturation appears to have a protective effect on girls with regard to depression (Negriff & Susman, 2011). In one study, late-maturing girls experienced less teasing about their appearance and lower rates of appearance-related anxiety compared with other girls (Zimmer-Gembeck, Webb, Farrell, & Waters, 2018). Findings regarding the effects of late maturation on boys are mixed and less consistent (Mendle & Ferrero, 2012). Late-maturing boys may experience more social and emotional difficulties. Similar to girls, perception may matter. For example, in one study African American boys who perceived themselves as late maturers showed more symptoms of anxiety than their peers (Carter, 2015). During early adolescence, they may be less well liked by their peers and may be more likely than their peers to experience a poor body image, overall body dissatisfaction, and depression during early adolescence, but these effects tend to decline with physical maturation (Negriff & Susman, 2011). Other research suggests that late-maturing boys do not differ in anxiety or depression from their on-time peers (Crockett, Carlo, Wolff, & Hope, 2013; Marceau, Ram, Houts, Grimm, & Susman, 2011) or that it is only late-maturing boys with poor peer relationships who experience depression (Benoit et al., 2013).

Context and the Effects of Pubertal Timing

Contextual factors are thought to amplify the effects of pubertal timing on behavior (Natsuaki, Samuels, & Leve, 2015; Seaton & Carter, 2018). For example, some of the problems that early-maturing boys and girls experience arise because they tend to seek relationships with older peers who are more similar to them in physical maturity than their classmates (Kretsch, Mendle, Cance, & Harden, 2016). Spending time with older peers makes early-maturing adolescents, especially girls, more likely to engage in age-inappropriate behaviors, such as early sexual activity and risky sexual activity (Baams, Dubas, Overbeek, & van Aken, 2015; Moore, Harden, & Mendle, 2014). The composition of the peer group may also mater. In one study, early pubertal development was associated with a higher risk for experiencing adolescent dating abuse when the early-maturing girls' friendship groups comprised a higher percentage of boys, but not when the friendship groups contained few boys (Chen et al., 2017).

The school context may also influence the effects of pubertal timing. In one study, elementary school teachers shown drawings of girls at varying stages of pubertal development expected early-developing girls to have more academic and social problems relative to other girls (Carter, Mustafaa, & Leath, 2018). In addition, they expected Black early developers to experience more problems than White early developers, possibly suggesting that race and ethnicity may influence how early puberty is experienced by girls. Other research also suggests that racial identity can influence the effects of pubertal timing. In one study of Black adolescents, early-maturing girls were more likely to experience depressive symptoms when they attended mixed-race schools and believed that others held Blacks in poor regard (Seaton & Carter, 2018). Pubertal development influences girls' sense of self and may interact with their other self-relevant beliefs—as well as the social and racial contexts in which they are immersed—to influence their responses (Seaton & Carter, 2018).

Biological and Contextual Influences on Pubertal Timing

Puberty is a complex trait influenced by many genes that interact with contextual factors (Day et al., 2017; Zhu, Kusa, & Chan, 2018). In support of the role of genetics, pubertal timing for both boys and girls tends to be similar to that of their parents (Wohlfahrt-Veje et al., 2016). Identical twins (who share 100% of their genes) experience menarche more closely in time than fraternal twins (who share only 50% of their genes) (Kretsch, Mendle, & Harden, 2016). Heredity sets the boundaries of pubertal timing, the earliest and latest age when we might begin puberty. But the onset of puberty and whether it is early or late relative to our inherited range is influenced by more than genes. Contextual influences and life experiences play a role in determining when a child begins puberty.

Puberty is triggered by achieving a critical level of body weight, specifically body fat (Das et al., 2017).

From an evolutionary perspective, the link between body weight and the onset of reproductive maturation may be adaptive because it delays fertility when food and resources are scarce and unlikely to support offspring (Roa & Tena-Sempere, 2014). Girls with a greater body mass index (BMI), especially those who are obese (Currie et al., 2012), mature earlier than do their peers, and girls who have a low percentage of body fat, whether from athletic training or severe dieting, often experience menarche late relative to other girls (Tomova, 2016; Villamor & Jansen, 2016).

In contrast, extreme malnutrition can prevent the accumulation of adequate fat stores needed to support pubertal development so that menarche is delayed. In many parts of Africa, for example, menarche does not occur until ages 14 to 17, several years later than in Western nations (Tunau, Adamu, Hassan, Ahmed, & Ekele, 2012). Similarly, some research suggests that weight affects the onset and tempo of puberty in boys, with higher BMI associated with earlier puberty (Lee et al., 2016; Song et al., 2016), but less so as compared with girls (Tinggaard et al., 2012), and the mechanism is not well understood (Cousminer et al., 2014).

Adolescents' social contexts, especially exposure to stress, influence pubertal timing (Joos, Wodzinski, Wadsworth, & Dorn, 2018). Early life stress and the experience of severe stress, such as the experience of sexual abuse and maltreatment, can speed the onset of menarche (Negriff, Blankson, & Trickett, 2015; Noll et al., 2017). Similarly, poor family relationships, harsh parenting, family stress and conflict, parents' marital conflict, and anxiety are associated with early menarche in North American and European girls (Graber, Nichols, & Brooks-Gunn, 2010; Rickard, Frankenhuis, & Nettle, 2014). In industrialized countries such as the United States, Canada, and New Zealand, girls who are raised by single mothers experience puberty earlier than those raised in two-parent homes (Mendle et al., 2006). In addition, the absence of a biological father and the presence in the home of a biological unrelated male, such as a stepfather or a mother's live-in boyfriend, is associated with earlier onset of menarche (Deardorff et al., 2011; Webster, Graber, Gesselman, Crosier, & Schember, 2014). Household stress and economic adversity may hold similar implications for boys' pubertal development, speeding it (Sun, Mensah, Azzopardi, Patton, & Wake, 2017); there is much less research on boys' development (Joos et al., 2018).

Contextual factors outside the home also influence pubertal timing. Adolescents who live in similar contextual conditions, especially those of socioeconomic advantage, reach menarche at about the same age, despite having different genetic backgrounds (Obeidallah, Brennan, Brooks-Gunn, & Earls, 2004). Low socioeconomic status is associated with early pubertal onset in the United States, Canada, and the United Kingdom and may account for some of the ethnic differences in pubertal timing (Kelly, Zilanawala, Sacker, Hiatt, & Viner, 2017; Sun et al., 2017). For example, African American and Latina girls tend to reach menarche before White girls but are also disproportionately likely to live in low SES homes and neighborhoods. Ethnic differences in the timing of menarche are reduced or even disappear when researchers control for the influence of socioeconomic status (Deardorff et al., 2014; Obeidallah, Brennan, Brooks-Gunn, Kindlon, & Earls, 2000). That is, girls growing up in low SES contexts may experience more stress at home and in the community and may have less access to healthy foods and opportunities for safe physical activity. In support of this view, girls' perceptions of their neighborhood safety and their estimates of the likelihood that they will live to age 35 predicted early menarche (Amir, Jordan, & Bribiescas, 2016).

The influence of contextual conditions and physical health in triggering puberty is thought to underlie the **secular trend**, or the lowering of the average age of puberty with each generation from prehistoric to the present times (Papadimitriou, 2016a) (Figure 13.1). Through the 18th century in Europe, puberty occurred as late as age 17; between 1860 and 1970, the age of menarche declined by about 3 to 4 months per decade (Tanner, 1990). In China, the age at menarche declined from 14.25 in girls born before 1976 to 12.60 in girls born after 2000, with an estimated decline of 0.51 years per decade (Meng, Martinez, Holmstrom, Chung, & Cox, 2017). Boys in the United States and Canada begin puberty at least 1 to 1½ years earlier today than in the 1960s (Herman-Giddens, 2006; Herman-Giddens et al., 2012). Likewise, boys reached peak velocity of growth over 1 month earlier each decade between 1946 and 1991 (Bygdell, Vandenput, Ohlsson, & Kindblom, 2014). The secular trend parallels increases in the standard of living and average BMI among children in developed countries and is especially influenced by the growing problem of childhood obesity (Biro, Greenspan, & Galvez, 2012). There are some indications that it has slowed or stopped in most industrialized nations (Kleanthous, Dermitzaki, Papadimitriou, Papaevangelou, & Papadimitriou, 2017; Papadimitriou, 2016b).

The secular trend may be slowing but it is unclear when it will stop (Kleanthous et al., 2017; Papadimitriou, 2016b). Girls have shown precocious puberty as early as age 5 (Scutti, 2015); however, it is unlikely that the average age of puberty will ever drop that low. Nevertheless, the secular trend poses

FIGURE 13.1

Secular Trend in Girls' Pubertal Development, 1830–2010

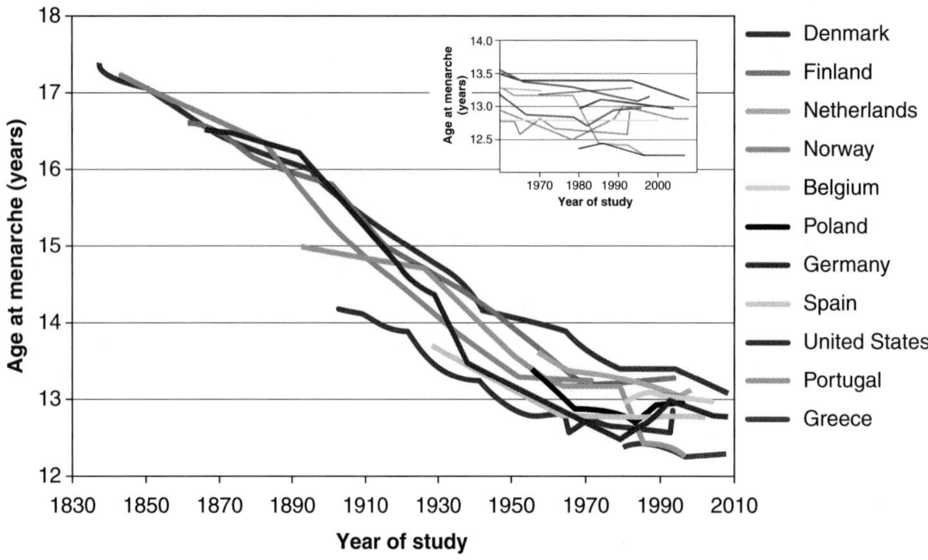

Source: Sørensen et al. (2012). With permission from Karger Publishers.

challenges for young people and parents because the biological entry to adolescence is lowering at the same time as the passage to adulthood is lengthening, making the period of adolescence longer than ever before.

THINKING IN CONTEXT 13.1

1. Suppose that you are a parent to a 9-year-old girl who has suddenly grown much taller than her peers. What does she need to know about puberty? What should you tell her, if anything? What would you tell a boy? Explain your responses.
2. In what ways might pubertal changes influence adolescents' behavior? What are some of the implications of sex differences in body growth? How might girls' earlier maturation contribute to sex differences in behavior?
3. How might contextual factors influence how boys and girls experience pubertal events? Consider interactions with parents and peers, and experiences in school and neighborhood contexts. Might adolescents living in high-, low-, or middle-income neighborhoods experience pubertal changes differently? Why or why not? How might other individual differences, such as race and ethnicity, play a role in adolescents' experiences?

BRAIN DEVELOPMENT IN ADOLESCENCE

Processes of neural development initiated before birth continue throughout childhood and increase in adolescence, leading to changes in brain structure and function that are reflected in adolescents' competencies and behaviors. Although it was once believed that brain development ended in childhood, advances in neuroimaging have revealed that brain structure and function changes dramatically during adolescence (Morris, Squeglia, Jacobus, & Silk, 2018).

Changes in Brain Volume and Structure

The increase in sex hormones with puberty triggers a variety of neurological developments, including a second burst of synaptogenesis, resulting in a rapid increase of connections among neurons (Sisk, 2017). The volume of the cerebral cortex increases, peaking at about 10½ years of age in girls and 14½ in boys (Giedd et al., 2009). There are regional differences in the timing and pace of changes in brain volume. The parietal lobe and parts of the occipital lobe show volume reductions in late childhood and early adolescence as a result of pruning, whereas other parts of the cortex demonstrate an inverted-U

FIGURE 13.2

Developmental Changes in Gray and White Matter Across Adolescence

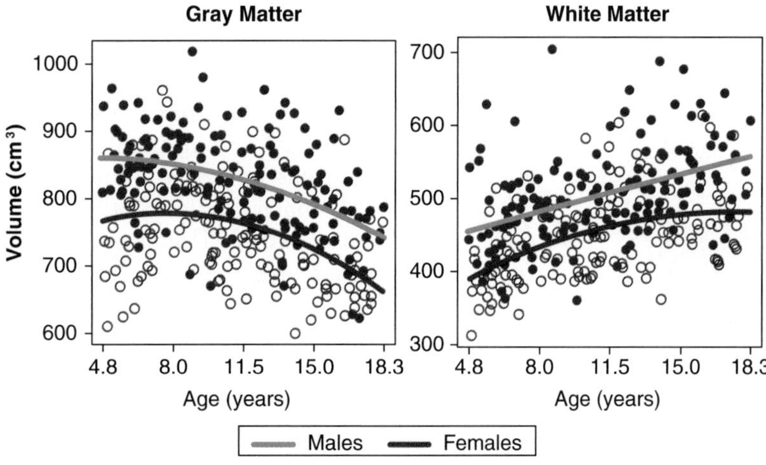

Source: Brain Development Cooperative Group (2012). Reproduced with permission of Oxford University Press.

pattern of growth (Tamnes et al., 2017). For example, one analysis of people age 7 to 29 showed overall declines in brain volume over this period, but increases in the surface area of the prefrontal and temporal cortex, followed by decreases in volume (Mills et al., 2016). Similar patterns of growth were discovered in a longitudinal analysis of participants from ages 3 to 19; the prefrontal cortex and other areas responsible for higher-order social cognitive and brain regulatory functions showed volume increases in early adolescence, followed by decreases in late adolescence (Vijayakumar et al., 2016).

Although the general trend is for an overall decline in cortical volume with pruning, the two main types of tissue in the brain, gray and white matter, show different developmental trajectories, as shown in Figure 13.2. Gray matter includes unmyelinated axons, dendrites, glial cells, and blood vessels and tends to increase and reach its greatest volume in childhood, decrease in adolescence, and stabilize in early adulthood (Mills & Tamnes, 2018). Synaptic pruning in response to experience occurs at an accelerated rate during adolescence and emerging adulthood, decreasing the volume of gray matter and thinning and molding the prefrontal cortex, which is responsible for rational thought and executive function, resulting in markedly more efficient cognition and neural functioning (Giedd, 2018; Zhou, Lebel, Treit, Evans, & Beaulieu, 2015). White matter, myelinated neurons, occupies about half of the brain; it increases linearly through adolescence, until about age 15, then is thought to decrease and stabilize in late adolescence and emerging adulthood (Lebel & Deoni, 2018). Myelination is especially prominent in the prefrontal cortex and the corpus callosum, which increases up to 20% in size, speeding communication between the right and left hemispheres (Lebel & Deoni, 2018).

Over the course of adolescence, adolescents' brains become larger, faster, and more efficient (Richmond, Johnson, Seal, Allen, & Whittle, 2016). However, different parts of the brain develop at different times, leaving adolescents with somewhat lopsided functioning for a time. The prefrontal cortex requires the most time to develop, continuing maturation into emerging adulthood. Research using fMRI scans has shown substantial growth and change in cortical and subcortical structures. For example, the **limbic system**, a set of subcortical structures responsible for emotion, undergoes a burst of development in response to pubertal hormones (Goddings et al., 2014; Sisk, 2017). The **amygdala**, a limbic structure that plays a role in fear learning, reward, aggression, and sexual behavior, increases in volume in childhood and peaks in growth at around 12 to 14 years of age. The hippocampus, also a part of the limbic system, shows linear growth in adolescence, influencing learning, memory, and aspects of emotional function and stress reactivity. In contrast to the limbic system, which shows a burst of growth in early adolescence, the prefrontal cortex continues to develop in emerging adulthood, into the mid-20s (Blakemore & Mills, 2014). The prefrontal cortex is the seat of reasoning and cognitive, emotional, and behavioral control as well as decision making and planning, suggesting that these sophisticated abilities continue to develop into emerging

FIGURE 13.3

Dual-Systems Model: Limbic System and Prefrontal Cortex

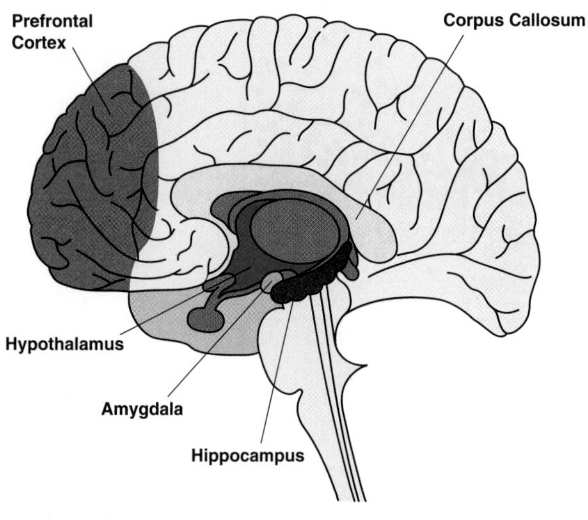

adulthood (Fuhrmann, Knoll, & Blakemore, 2015). The different timing between the limbic system and prefrontal cortex influences adolescents' behavior, as we will discuss.

Experience and the Adolescent Brain

Throughout the lifespan, the brain retains plasticity, the ability to adapt its structure and function in response to environmental demands, experiences, and physiological changes (Nelson, 2011). However, the brain is especially plastic during adolescence. The rapid changes that the adolescent brain undergoes make it is uniquely vulnerable to experience. Exposure to stress and substance use are two examples of experiences toward which adolescents are particularly vulnerable.

Research with rodents suggests that exposure to stress during adolescence may reduce neurogenesis in the hippocampus with potentially long-lasting effects for cognitive function (Hueston, Cryan, & Nolan, 2017). Moreover, adolescents may be uniquely vulnerable to stress because the adolescent brain, especially the hippocampus, amygdala, and prefrontal cortex, is particularly sensitive to stress hormones (Romeo, 2017). Exposure to stress hormones is associated with reduced volume, reduced dendritic growth, and atrophy of dendrites and thereby synapses (Romeo, 2017; Tottenham & Galván, 2016).

In addition to stress, the adolescent brain is sensitive to the effects of substance use. Specifically, cross-sectional and longitudinal studies have shown abnormal gray and white matter trajectories in adolescent alcohol and substance users (Spear, 2018; Squeglia & Gray, 2016). In one prospective 8-year study of youth ages 12 to 24, those who transitioned to heavy drinking showed accelerated decreases in gray matter volume compared with light and nondrinkers (particularly in frontal and temporal regions) and attenuated increases in white matter volume over the follow-up, even after controlling for marijuana and other substance use (Squeglia et al., 2015). This is consistent with other findings that heavy-drinking adolescents and emerging adults have systematically thinner and lower volume in the prefrontal cortex, attenuated white matter development, and altered neural activity, suggesting a toxic effect of consuming alcohol in large quantities on brain development (Cservenka & Brumback, 2017).

Cannabis use during adolescence is also associated with abnormalities in brain structure and patterns of activity and function (Takagi, Youssef, & Lorenzetti, 2016). Longitudinal data indicate that self-reported persistent cannabis use between 13 and 15 years is associated with a significant decline in IQ, and the longer the period of use, the greater the decline in IQ (Meier et al., 2012). A recent longitudinal study tracked heavy cannabis-using youth who also engaged in alcohol use from age 16 to 19 (Jacobus et al., 2015). Heavy cannabis users showed worsening performance on several cognitive domains when compared to non-using youth, including worse performance on tests of complex attention, memory, processing speed, and visuospatial functioning. Earlier onset of cannabis use was associated with poorer processing speed and executive functioning by age 19, suggesting that initiation of cannabis use during early adolescence (before age 16) may be more harmful to the developing brain than later initiation (Jacobus et al., 2015). Research has consistently shown that recreational cannabis use before the age of 18 (but not in adulthood) has been linked to gray matter atrophy (Battistella et al., 2014).

Brain Development and Behavior

We have seen that the limbic system, responsible for emotion, undergoes a burst of development well before the prefrontal cortex, responsible for judgment and executive control (Sisk, 2017). Full development entails the prefrontal cortex catching up to the early-developing limbic system. According to the **dual-systems model**, the different developmental timetables for these structures can account for many "typical" adolescent behaviors (Mills et al., 2014a; Shulman et al., 2016). Let's take a closer look at how these changes influence adolescents' thought and behavior.

Socioemotional Perception

Parents often wonder whether they are speaking in a foreign language when their teens unexpectedly break off a conversation and storm away or when conflict arises over seemingly innocuous events. However, in a way, parents *are* speaking in a foreign language because adolescents' brains do not always lead them to accurately assess situations. Adolescents have difficulty identifying some emotions depicted in facial expressions. Specifically, in studies when both adults and adolescents are shown photographs of people's faces depicting fear, adults tend to correctly identify the emotion shown in the photograph, but many of the adolescents incorrectly identify the emotion as anger (Yurgelun-Todd, 2007). Why? Functional magnetic resonance imaging scans indicate that when adults view facial expressions, both their limbic system and prefrontal cortex are active. Scans of adolescents' brains, however, reveal a highly active limbic system but relatively inactive prefrontal cortex relative to adults, suggesting that adolescents experience emotional activation with relatively little executive processing in response to facial stimuli indicating fear (Yurgelun-Todd, 2007).

When faced with emotionally arousing contexts and stimuli, adolescents tend to show exaggerated activity in the amygdala relative to adults and fewer functional connections between the prefrontal cortex and amygdala, suggesting that adolescents experience more emotional arousal yet less cortical processing and control than adults (Blakemore & Mills, 2014). The ability to control responses to emotionally triggering stimuli develops independently and after the ability to reason about neutral stimuli (Aïte et al., 2018). Generally, amygdala volume increases more in adolescent males than females (Dumontheil, 2016). It seems that adolescents are wired to experience strong emotional reactions and to misidentify emotions in others' facial expressions, which can make communication and social interactions difficult.

Generally speaking, performance on tasks measuring sensitivity to facial expressions improves steadily during the first decade of life but dips in early adolescence, increasing in late adolescence into emerging adulthood (Motta-Mena & Scherf, 2017). For example, research with people ages 7 to 37 reveals developmental changes in brain activation with facial processing with activity in parts of the frontal cortex increasing over childhood, then decreasing in early adolescence, and increasing again in late adolescence continuing into emerging adulthood (Cohen Kadosh, Johnson, Dick, Cohen Kadosh, & Blakemore, 2013). Face recognition, memory for faces, shows a similar pattern (Lawrence, Campbell, & Skuse, 2015). However, recent research suggests that adolescents are better able to process peer faces than adult faces, especially faces with a pubertal status similar to their own (Picci & Scherf, 2016). As the young adolescent's body prepares for sexual maturity, the brain's face processing system may become calibrated toward peers, potential reproductive partners, rather than caregivers.

Reward Perception

Most adults look back on their own adolescence and recall engaging in activities that included an element of risk or were even outright dangerous, such as racing bikes off ramps to soar through the air or driving at fast speeds. Risk taking and adolescence go hand in hand, and the brain plays a large part in such behavior. In early adolescence, the balance of neurotransmitters shifts. At 9 to 10 years of age, the prefrontal cortex and limbic system experience a marked shift in levels of serotonin and dopamine, neurotransmitters that are associated with impulsivity, novelty seeking, and reward salience (Luna et al., 2015; Mills et al., 2014a). Sensitivity to rewards peaks at the same time as adolescents experience difficulty with response inhibition, the ability to control a response. A heightened response to motivational cues coupled with immature behavioral control results in a bias toward immediate goals rather than long-term consequences (van Duijvenvoorde, Peters, Braams, & Crone, 2016). The shift is larger for boys than girls and is thought to make potentially rewarding stimuli even more rewarding for teens (Steinberg, 2008). As a result, risky situations, those that entail an element of danger, become enticing and experienced as thrills (Spielberg, Olino, Forbes, & Dahl, 2014). Adolescents may find themselves drawn to extreme sports, for example, enjoying the high and element of the unknown when they direct their skateboard into the air for a daring turn. These same mechanisms, adolescents' attraction to novelty and enhanced sensitivity to immediate rewards, serve to increase

Adolescents are driven to take risks, including positive risks, such as extreme sports.
©iStockphoto.com/yanik88

their vulnerability to the lure of drugs and alcohol (Bava & Tapert, 2010; Geier, 2013).

Developmental shifts in risky behavior are common among adolescents around the world (Duell et al., 2018). For example, one study examined adolescents in 11 countries in Africa, Asia, Europe, and the Americas and found that sensation seeking increased in preadolescence, peaked at around age 19, and declined thereafter (Steinberg et al., 2018). Risky activity is thought to decline in late adolescence in part because of increases in adolescents' self-regulatory capacities and the capacities for long-term planning that accompany maturation of the frontal cortex (Dumontheil, 2016). However, the imbalance between frontal and limbic activity and fine-tuning of behavioral control continues into emerging adulthood (Giedd, 2018).

Contextual factors, such as adult supervision, exposure to stressors, and impoverished communities, influence adolescents' brain development and hence their propensities for risk taking (Scott, Duell, & Steinberg, 2018; Smith, Chein, & Steinberg, 2013; Tottenham & Galván, 2016). For example, one study of Australian adolescents revealed that neighborhood socioeconomic disadvantage was associated with altered brain development from early to late adolescence (Whittle et al., 2017). Positive parenting reduced the effects of family and neighborhood disadvantage, supporting the role of contextual factors as influences—risk and protective factors—for neural development. This conclusion is supported by other research suggesting that parenting influences the neural circuitry governing emotion (Morris, Criss, Silk, & Houltberg, 2017). The adolescent brain retains plasticity and may change in response to experiences.

THINKING IN CONTEXT 13.2

1. Stereotypes about adolescents abound; for example, some suggest that they are prone to risk taking and poor decision making. In your view, are these stereotypes accurate? Do they have weight? How might brain development inform discussions about adolescent behavior?
2. How might contextual factors such as parenting, relationships with peers, interactions at school, and neighborhood resources influence brain development? Through what means might socioeconomic status influence brain development?
3. Adolescence is a vulnerable period for brain development. Identify factors that pose risks to brain development. What are some protective factors, ways of promoting healthy brain development?

ADOLESCENT HEALTH

Adolescents share many of the same health concerns as children, such as access to good nutrition and opportunities for physical activity, safe schools and neighborhoods, and health care. With puberty adolescents experience new health issues.

Nutrition

As boys and girls enter the adolescent growth spurt, their bodies require more energy and their caloric demands increase rapidly to about 2,200 (for girls) and 2,700 (for boys) calories a day (Jahns, Siega-Riz, & Popkin, 2001). Good nutrition is essential to support adolescents' growth, yet young people's diets tend to worsen as they enter adolescence (Frazier-Wood, Banfield, Liu, Davis, & Chang, 2015). Adolescents tend to consume only about one-half of the U.S. dietary recommendations for vegetables, whole grains, and fruits (Banfield, Liu, Davis, Chang, & Frazier-Wood, 2016). In addition, adolescents tend to skip meals, especially breakfast, and drink less milk (Stang & Stotmeister, 2017; Vikraman, Fryar, & Ogden, 2015). One nationally representative sample of over 11,000 high school students showed that girls and Black and Hispanic adolescents are more likely to skip breakfast than boys and White non-Hispanic adolescents (Demissie, Eaton, Lowry, Nihiser, & Foltz, 2018). Skipping breakfast increased over high school with eleventh- and twelfth-grade students more likely to skip breakfast than ninth and tenth graders.

Fast food consumption tends to increase over adolescence and is associated with less consumption of fruits and vegetables (Gopinath et al., 2016; Stang & Stotmeister, 2017). Fast food is high in calories; when adolescents eat a fast-food meal, they do not appear to adjust their other meals to make up for the

Good nutrition is essential to support adolescents' growth, yet young people's diets tend to worsen as they enter adolescence.
©iStockphoto.com/p_ponomareva

excess calories and instead consume more calories overall (Bowman, Gortmaker, Ebbeling, Pereira, & Ludwig, 2004). When a fast-food restaurant is near school, students in the United States, United Kingdom, Australia, and Finland show more irregular eating habits, greater consumption of fast food, and higher rates of overweight and obesity (Janssen, Davies, Richardson, & Stevenson, 2018; Virtanen et al., 2015).

Family meals are an important way of establishing healthy eating habits. U.S. children and adolescents who eat an evening meal at home with parents tend to have healthier diets that include more fruits and vegetables and they tend to have a lower BMI than their peers who do not share family meals (Watts, Loth, Berge, Larson, & Neumark-Sztainer, 2017). Young people who participate in preparing and eating family meals at least once or twice a week tend to have healthier eating habits 5 years later, from early to middle adolescence through young adulthood (Berge, MacLehose, Larson, Laska, & Neumark-Sztainer, 2016; Berge et al., 2015). Research with families in the Netherlands, Poland, Portugal, and the United Kingdom suggests that family meals are associated with healthier eating habits and enhanced self-control over eating (de Wit et al., 2015). However, the frequency of family dinnertimes drops sharply between ages 9 and 14, and family dinners have become less common in recent decades (Walton & Spencer, 2009). When family meals are irregular, parents can encourage healthy eating by educating adolescents about nutrition, providing access to fruits and vegetables in the home, and supporting healthy eating habits by modeling fruit and vegetable consumption and healthy eating habits (Watts et al., 2017).

Mortality

Although adolescence is a generally healthy time in which young people tend to report good or excellent health and low rates of illness, mortality (the death rate) rises in adolescence (Kochanek, Murphy, Xu, & Arias, 2017; U.S. Department of Health and Human Services, 2017). Adolescent mortality is largely influenced by the risky behavior that is common in adolescence and accompanies neurological development.

As shown in Figure 13.4, adolescent mortality showed an overall decline between 1999 and 2016 but has increased 12% since 2013. The increase in mortality is attributable to a rise in injury-related deaths. Specifically, about 70% of deaths by adolescents age 10 to 19 in 2016 were due to fatal injuries caused by unintentional injury (accident), suicide, and homicide. These types of fatal injuries have declined in prevalence from 1999 through

FIGURE 13.4

Total Injury and Noninjury Death Rates for Children and Adolescents Aged 10–19 Years, United States, 1999–2016

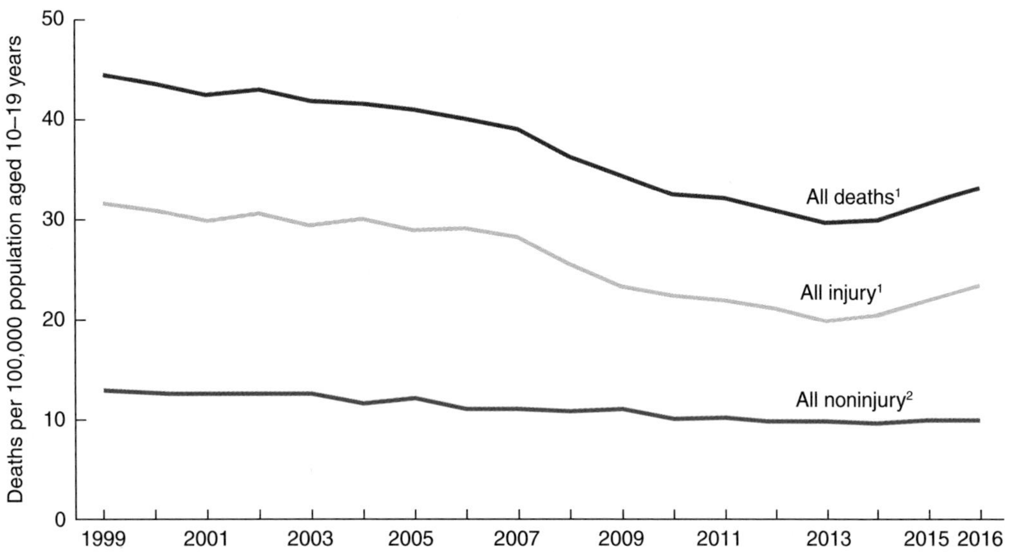

Source: Figure 1 from Curtin et al. (2018). Retrieved from https://www.cdc.gov/nchs/data/nvsr/nvsr67/nvsr67_04.pdf.

FIGURE 13.5

Unintentional Injuries in Adolescence, 2001–2017

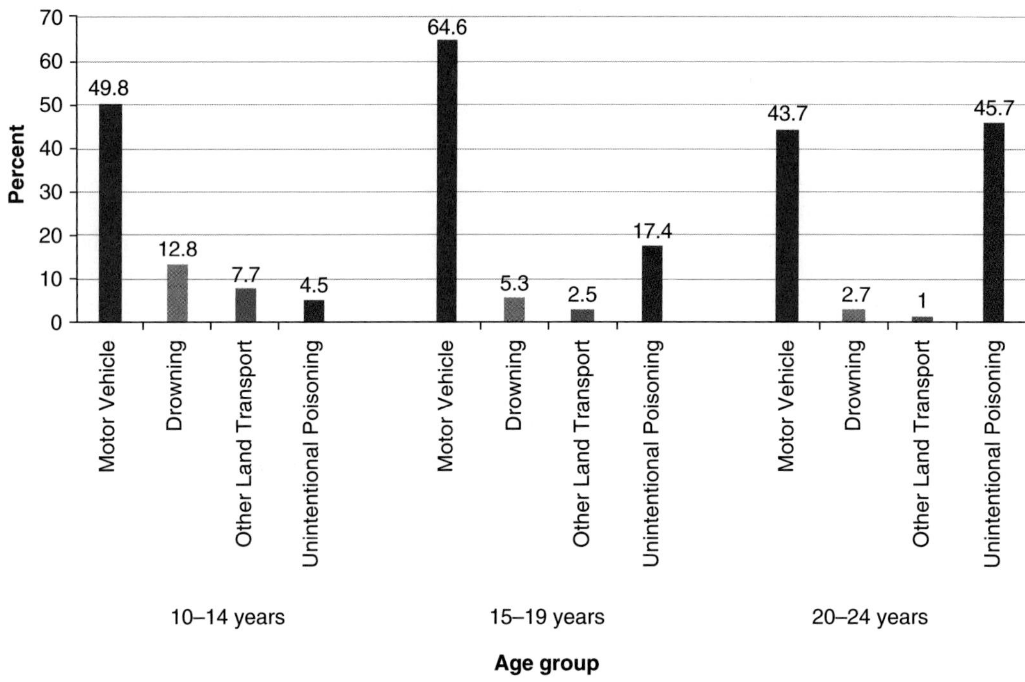

Unintentional All Injury Causes Nonfatal Injuries and Rates per 100,000
2001–2017, United States
All Races, Both Sexes, Ages 10 to 29
Disposition: All Cases

Source: Centers for Disease Control and Prevention (2019e).

2013 and since increased (Curtin, Heron, Miniño, & Warner, 2018). Boys and girls show similar patterns in death rates, with boys consistently showing about twice the mortality rate as girls.

Generally, older adolescents age 15–19 show higher rates of injury-related deaths than those age 10–14, but emerging adults age 20–24 show the highest rates of injury-related deaths. Fatal injuries—specifically, traffic accidents, suicide, unintentional poisoning, and homicide—remain the leading causes of death, respectively, into emerging adulthood. Notably, unintentional poisoning, most often drug overdoses, becomes increasingly common from adolescence into adulthood, as indicated in Figure 13.5.

Ethnic differences in mortality emerge in late adolescence, in both death rates and causes of fatal injuries. As shown in Figure 13.6, Black adolescents show dramatically higher rates of death by homicide than their peers. American Indian and Alaskan Native adolescents show the highest rates of unintentional injury and suicide, as compared with other adolescents (Ballesteros, Williams, Mack, Simon, & Sleet, 2018). White non-Hispanic adolescents show higher rates of suicide than Black, Hispanic, and Asian American and Pacific Island American adolescents. Contextual factors contribute to ethnic differences in mortality rates during adolescence. Specifically, socioeconomic status and community factors place Black and American Indian/Alaskan Native youth, who are disproportionately at risk to live in low SES homes and communities, at risk for higher rates of mortality. Economic disadvantage is one of the most robust predictors of violence, especially in urban settings (Stansfield, Williams, & Parker, 2017). Violence by Black adolescents may be fueled by insufficient home and neighborhood resources and exposure to violence and discrimination in the community (Rojas-Gaona, Hong, & Peguero, 2016). American Indian/Alaskan Native youth also experience high levels of poverty. The perception of discrimination, difficulty acculturating or integrating native customs and beliefs with popular culture, and feeling marginalized contribute to higher rates of suicide in American Indian/Alaskan Native adolescents (Jaramillo, Mello, & Worrell, 2016; Wyatt, Ung, Park, Kwon, & Trinh-Shevrin, 2015).

Physical Activity and Exercise

Regular physical activity is an important component to health throughout life. In adolescence, physical activity promotes cardiovascular health, muscle strength, motor control, cognitive performance,

FIGURE 13.6

Injury- and Violence-Related Deaths Among Youth Age 0–19

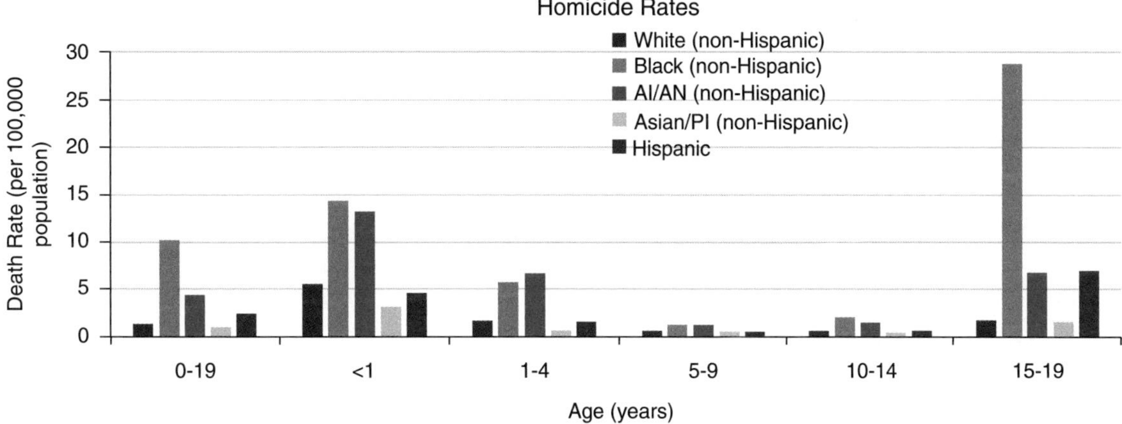

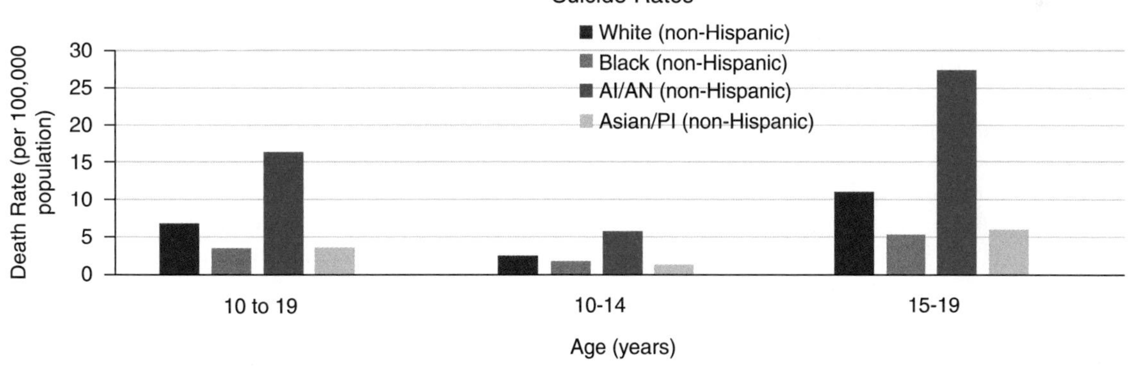

Source: Ballesteros et al. (2018).

mental health, and well-being (Esteban-Cornejo, Tejero-Gonzalez, Sallis, & Veiga, 2015; McMahon et al., 2017). Physical activity tends to decline beginning in middle childhood, about age 7 (Farooq et al., 2018). Although some teens engage in competitive sports, average levels of physical activity decrease throughout adolescence, and many adolescents engage in no regular exercise or activity (Dumith, Gigante, Domingues, & Kohl, 2011; Farooq et al., 2018). Most adolescents in the United States do not meet the federal recommendation guideline of at least 60 minutes of moderate to vigorous physical activity every day. It is estimated that only about 8% of 12- to 15-year-old adolescents are active for 60 minutes per day on at least 5 days per week (Kann et al., 2014). Schools play a role in promoting physical fitness through physical education classes. Participation in physical education is highest among students in ninth grade, decreases among tenth- and eleventh-grade students, and is lowest among twelfth-grade students (Kann et al., 2014).

Longitudinal research with U.S. adolescents has shown that the reductions in physical activity during adolescence are consistent across contextual settings, whether rural or urban, and across SES (Metcalf, Hosking, Jeffery, Henley, & Wilkin, 2015). Adolescents of low SES are more likely to be sedentary and obese than their more affluent peers; this holds true for adolescents from a variety of developed nations, such as Canada, England, Finland, France, and the United States (Frederick, Snellman, & Putnam, 2014; Mielke, Brown, Nunes, Silva, & Hallal, 2017; Y. Wang & Lim, 2012). Socioeconomic disparities may be influenced by opportunities for physical activity, such as the availability of safe parks and outdoor spaces and opportunities for extracurricular activities in the school and community (Watts, Mason, Loth, Larson, & Neumark-Sztainer, 2016). After-school and community sports teams, for example, may be more prominent and available in middle-income and affluent communities.

Eating Disorders

Adolescents' rapidly changing physique, coupled with media portrayals of the ideal woman as thin with few curves, leads many to become dissatisfied with their body image and the dissatisfaction often persists into emerging adulthood (Benowitz-Fredericks, Garcia, Massey, Vasagar, & Borzekowski, 2012). Girls who have a negative body image are at risk of developing **eating disorders**, mental disorders that are characterized by extreme over- or under-control of eating and behaviors intended to control weight such as compulsive exercise, dieting, or purging (American Psychiatric Association, 2013). Eating disorders, such as anorexia nervosa, bulimia nervosa, and binge eating disorder, pose serious challenges to health.

Anorexia Nervosa and Bulimia Nervosa

Anorexia nervosa and bulimia nervosa are eating disorders that are characterized by excessive concern about body weight and attempts to lose weight. However, they differ in how this concern is manifested. Those who suffer from **anorexia nervosa** starve themselves and sometimes engage in extreme exercise in order to achieve thinness and maintain a weight that is substantially lower than expected for height and age (American Psychiatric Association, 2013). A distorted body image leads youth with anorexia to perceive themselves as "fat" despite their emaciated appearance, and they continue to lose weight (Gila, Castro, Cesena, & Toro, 2005; Hagman et al., 2015). Anorexia affects about 2% of girls 19 and younger; however, many more girls show similar poor eating behaviors (Smink, van Hoeken, & Hoek, 2013; Smink, van Hoeken, Oldehinkel, & Hoek, 2014).

Bulimia nervosa is characterized by recurrent episodes of *binge eating*—consuming an abnormally large amount of food (thousands of calories) in a single sitting coupled with a feeling of being out of control—followed by *purging*, inappropriate behavior designed to compensate for the binge, such as vomiting, excessive exercise, or use of laxatives (American Psychiatric Association, 2013). Individuals with bulimia nervosa experience extreme dissatisfaction with body image and attempt to lose weight, but they tend to have a body weight that is normal or high-normal (Golden et al., 2015). Bulimia is more common than anorexia, affecting between 1% and 5% of females across Western Europe and the United States (Kessler et al., 2013; Smink et al., 2014), and many more young people show symptoms of bulimia but remain undiagnosed (Keel, 2014).

Both anorexia and bulimia pose serious health risks. Girls with anorexia may lose 25% to 50% of their body weight (Berkman, Lohr, & Bulik, 2007). They may not experience menarche or may stop menstruating because menstruation is dependent on maintaining at least 15% to 18% body fat (Golden et al., 2015). Starvation and malnutrition not only contribute to extreme sensitivity to cold and to growth of fine hairs all over the body; they can also have serious health consequences such as bone loss, kidney failure, heart and brain damage, and even death (Golden et al., 2015; Reel, 2012). Side effects of bulimia nervosa include nutritional deficiencies. Repeated exposure to stomach acid causes tooth damage, ulcers, and even holes in the mouth and esophagus and increases the risk of throat and esophageal cancer (Katzman, 2005).

Both anorexia and bulimia occur more often in both members of identical twins than fraternal twins, indicating a genetic component (Bulik, Kleiman, & Yilmaz, 2016; Strober, Freeman, Lampert, Diamond, & Kaye, 2014). These disorders are more common in girls (about 6% prevalence) than boys (about 1% prevalence) (Raevuori, Keski-Rahkonen, & Hoek, 2014). Girls who compete in sports and activities that idealize lean figures, such as ballet, figure skating, gymnastics, and long distance running, are at higher risk for disordered eating than are other girls (Nordin, Harris, & Cumming, 2003; Voelker, Gould, & Reel, 2014). Anorexia nervosa is associated with perfectionism and strict regulation of eating; thus, it may be viewed as a way to exert control and reduce negative mood states (Kaye, Wierenga, Bailer, Simmons, & Bischoff-Grethe, 2013; Tyrka, Graber, & Brooks-Gunn, 2000). Anorexia nervosa and bulimia nervosa are associated with altered neural activity in several limbic system structures and parts of the prefrontal cortex, responsible for aspects of emotion, rewards, and decision making (Fuglset, Landrø, Reas, & Rø, 2016; Monteleone et al., 2018; L. Wang et al., 2017).

Anorexia nervosa and bulimia nervosa occur in all ethnic and socioeconomic groups in Western countries and are increasingly common in Asian and Arab cultures (Isomaa, Isomaa, Marttunen, Kaltiala-Heino, & Björkqvist, 2009; Keski-Rahkonen & Mustelin, 2016; Pike, Hoek, & Dunne, 2014; Thomas et al., 2015). In the United States, White and Latina girls, especially those of higher socioeconomic status, are at higher risk for low body image and eating disorders than are Black girls, who may be protected by cultural and media portrayals of African American women that value voluptuous figures (Smink et al., 2013). Some researchers suggest, however, that ethnic differences in eating disorders are not as large as they appear. Instead, eating disorders may exist in Black girls but remain undetected and undiagnosed because of barriers to diagnosis and treatment (Wilson, Grilo, & Vitousek, 2007). This is supported by research with adult women suggesting that the prevalence of anorexia nervosa is similar, but bulimia nervosa is more common in African American women and Latinas than in White women (Marques et al., 2011). In addition, lesbian, gay, and bisexual (LGB) youth report higher rates of dangerous eating behaviors, such as fasting, diet pill use, and purging to control weight than their heterosexual peers (R. J. Watson, Adjei, Saewyc, Homma, & Goodenow, 2017). The experience of stigma and discrimination is associated with higher rates of disordered eating behaviors in LGB youth, whereas social support and connections to family, school, and peers are associated with lower levels of disordered eating (R. J. Watson et al., 2017).

Anorexia nervosa and bulimia nervosa are difficult to treat. In some studies, as many as three-quarters of adolescents diagnosed with an eating disorder continued to show symptoms 5 years later (Ackard, Fulkerson, & Neumark-Sztainer, 2011; Herpertz-Dahlmann et al., 2015). Standard treatment for anorexia includes hospitalization to remedy malnutrition and ensure weight gain, antianxiety or antidepressant medications, and individual and family therapy (Herpertz-Dahlmann, 2017). Therapy is designed to enhance individuals' motivation to change and engage them as collaborators in treatment, providing them with a sense of control. Unfortunately, patients with anorexia tend to deny that there is a problem because they are unable to objectively perceive their bodies and value thinness and restraint, making anorexia very resistant to treatment (Berkman et al., 2007). As a result, only about 50% of girls with anorexia make a full recovery, and anorexia nervosa has the highest mortality rate of all mental disorders (Smink et al., 2013).

Bulimia tends to be more amenable to treatment because girls with bulimia often acknowledge that their behavior is not healthy. Individuals with bulimia tend to feel guilty about binging and purging and are more likely than those with anorexia to seek help. Individual therapy, support groups, nutritional education, and antianxiety or antidepressant medications are the treatments of choice for bulimia nervosa (Hay & Bacaltchuk, 2007; le Grange & Schmidt, 2005). Individual and family-based therapy helps girls become aware of the thoughts and behaviors that cause and maintain their binging and purging behaviors, which decreases binge eating and vomiting and reduces the risk of relapse (Lock, 2011; Smink et al., 2013).

Binge Eating Disorder

It's not uncommon for people to use the word "binge" in reference to their eating (e.g., "I totally binged on pizza!"). **Binge eating disorder**, however, is not simply overeating. Binge eating is uncomfortable. It refers to eating an amount of food much larger than a similar person would eat in a discrete period (such as 2 hours). More important, it is associated with a sense of feeling out of control, as if one cannot stop or control what one is eating. The person eats more quickly, even when not hungry, and feels uncomfortably full. Binge eating typically occurs in private, out of embarrassment, and tends to be accompanied by a sense of guilt, shame, self-disgust, and depression afterward. Notably, the binge eating is not accompanied by compensatory behavior, such as exercising or purging, as with bulimia nervosa (Campbell & Peebles, 2014). Binge eating disorder is diagnosed when binges occur at least once a week for 3 months.

Binge eating disorder is the most prevalent eating disorder and may affect up to 5% of adolescents (Marzilli, Cerniglia, & Cimino, 2018). Although most research has examined adolescent girls, binge eating disorder may occur in 1–2% of boys. Similar rates of binge eating are seen in adolescents of all ethnicities (Rodgers, Watts, Austin, Haines, & Neumark-Sztainer, 2017). Binge eating disorder emerges more frequently in early adolescence and in emerging adulthood (Marzilli et al., 2018). Binge eating disorder often persists from adolescence into emerging adulthood and even into middle adulthood (Goldschmidt, Wall, Zhang, Loth, & Neumark-Sztainer, 2016).

Like other eating disorders, binge eating disorder is associated with internalizing thin body ideals, body dissatisfaction, dieting, and negative affect (Stice, Gau, Rohde, & Shaw, 2017). Experiencing negative emotions may increase the risk for binge eating, as high-calorie "comfort" foods may become more rewarding and enticing and binge eating may be rewarding and improve mood (Lavender et al., 2016). Binge eating is associated with chronic abdominal pain, obesity, diabetes, and other health problems associated with obesity, as well as anxiety, depression, and suicidality (Ágh et al., 2016; Forrest, Zuromski, Dodd, & Smith, 2017; Micali et al., 2015). Treatment for binge eating disorder addresses eating behaviors, patients' weight and shape concerns, and psychological conditions such as anxiety and depression (Berkman et al., 2015). A combination of medication and behavioral training can help adolescents with binge eating disorder manage emotions and learn long-term behavioral strategies for coping with strong emotions and drives.

Alcohol and Substance Use

Nearly half of U.S. teens have tried an illicit drug and two-thirds have tried alcohol by the time they leave high school, as shown in Table 13.2. Experimentation with alcohol, tobacco, and marijuana use, that is, "trying out" these substances, is so common that it may be considered normative for North American adolescents. Rates of experimentation rise during the adolescent years into emerging adulthood (Miech et al., 2017). Perhaps surprising to some adults is that a limited amount of experimentation with drugs and alcohol is common in well-adjusted middle and older adolescents and associated with psychosocial health and well-being (Mason & Spoth, 2011). Why? Alcohol and substance use may serve a developmental function in middle and late adolescence, such as a way of asserting independence and autonomy from parents, sustaining peer relationships, and learning about oneself (Englund et al., 2013; Rulison, Patrick, & Maggs, 2015). Notice, however, that many more adolescents have tried a given substance ("experimented" with it) than use it regularly.

Many adolescents first try alcohol in high school and show steady increases in use throughout the high school years. Marijuana is used nearly as often as alcohol. Alcohol and marijuana use tends to peak in emerging adulthood and then declines (Miech et al., 2017). Although most adolescents experiment with alcohol, tobacco, and marijuana without incident, there are short-term dangers of alcohol and substance use, such as overdose, accidents, and motor impairment, as well as long-term dangers of dependence and abuse. The Lives in Context feature examines the influence of substance use on brain development.

Adolescents are particularly vulnerable to alcohol abuse because they show reduced sensitivity to the effects of alcohol that serve as cues in adults to limit their intake, such as motor impairment, sedation, social impairment, and quietness or distress (Spear, 2011). They develop a tolerance and are at risk for developing dependence for alcohol more quickly than adults (Simons, Wills, & Neal, 2014). Alcohol use in adolescence, even moderate use, is associated with damage to the brain, including reduced volume in the prefrontal cortex and hippocampus (Silveri et al., 2016; Squeglia et al., 2015). Heavy drinking is associated with reduced frontal cortex response during working memory tasks, slower information processing, and reductions in attention, visuospatial functioning, and problem solving (Carbia et al., 2017; Feldstein

TABLE 13.2

Substance Use in U.S. Adolescents, 2017

		LIFETIME PREVALENCE	30-DAY PREVALENCE
Cigarettes			
	Eighth grade	9.4	1.9
	Tenth grade	15.9	5.0
	Twelfth grade	26.6	9.7
Any vaping			
	Eighth grade	18.5	6.6
	Tenth grade	30.9	13.1
	Twelfth grade	35.8	16.6
Alcohol			
	Eighth grade	23.1	8.0
	Tenth grade	42.2	19.7
	Twelfth grade	61.5	33.2
Been drunk			
	Eighth grade	9.2	12.2
	Tenth grade	25.1	8.9
	Twelfth grade	45.3	19.1
Marijuana			
	Eighth grade	13.5	5.5
	Tenth grade	30.7	15.7
	Twelfth grade	45.0	22.9
Other illicit drugs			
	Eighth grade	9.3	2.7
	Tenth grade	13.7	4.5
	Twelfth grade	19.5	6.3

Note: Vaping includes vaping nicotine, marijuana, and flavoring.
Source: Johnston et al. (2018).

LIVES IN CONTEXT: BIOLOGICAL INFLUENCES

Substance Use and the Brain

Experimentation with alcohol and cannabis is a common form of risk taking during adolescence. How do alcohol and substance use affect the developing brain?

Alcohol use is associated with changes in the structure and function of the adolescent brain. Compared with those who do not use alcohol, adolescents who drink alcohol moderately show smaller brain volumes and gray matter density in areas responsible for executive control, including parts of the temporal and parietal lobes and, especially, the frontal cortex (Cservenka & Brumback, 2017; Müller-Oehring et al., 2018). Executive control is responsible for higher-level cognitive functions such as planning, directing attention, and decision making. It also controls response inhibition, the ability to resist temptation, such as the rewards that come with risky but exciting activities, including drinking.

There is a strong dose–response relationship: Greater consumption of alcohol predicts decreased brain volume and less white matter integrity (Cservenka & Brumback, 2017; Silveri, Dager, Cohen-Gilbert, & Sneider, 2016). The effects of adolescent alcohol use on brain function may be long lasting because alcohol use is associated with impaired neurogenesis and long-term reductions in synaptic connections and memory in animals (Spear, 2018; Tapia-Rojas et al., 2017). Yet there is room for optimism because some research has shown that the adolescent brain can increase in volume and show improved executive function when alcohol use is discontinued (Lisdahl, Gilbart, Wright, & Shollenbarger, 2013). The extent and limits of this rebound effect are unclear.

Whereas regular alcohol use is associated predominantly with deficits in attention and executive function, regular cannabis use is associated with a broad set of neurocognitive deficits in attention, learning and memory, processing speed, visuospatial functioning, and executive control (Lisdahl et al., 2013; Meruelo, Castro, Cota, & Tapert, 2017). Like alcohol use, regular cannabis use is associated with brain alterations, including reduced brain and gray matter volumes in the frontal lobe, followed by the parietal and temporal lobes (Lopez-Larson et al., 2012; Takagi et al., 2016). Early onset of cannabis use, before age 18 and especially prior to age 16, is associated with more severe neurocognitive consequences, especially in learning, memory, and executive function (Lubman, Cheetham, & Yücel, 2015; Silveri et al., 2016). One study suggests that cognitive function improved after 3 weeks of abstention, but attention deficits remained (Hanson et al., 2010). It is unknown whether abstinence over a long period is associated with a rebound in function. Other research suggests that attention, verbal and working memory, and processing speed remain impaired up to 2 months later (Hanson, Thayer, & Tapert, 2014; Winward, Hanson, Tapert, & Brown, 2014). Given the plasticity of the brain, some recovery of neurological function after abstention is expected, but the degree of recovery is not clear (Meruelo et al., 2017).

Alcohol and cannabis use tend to co-occur, making it difficult to disentangle the independent effects of each. Regardless, the literature to date suggests that, although normative, alcohol and cannabis use pose serious risks to neurological development in adolescence.

What Do You Think?

How might findings about the effects of alcohol and cannabis on brain development be applied to prevent or change adolescent behavior? Identify challenges that might arise in applying these findings as well as ways of countering challenges. ●

Ewing, Sakhardande, & Blakemore, 2014). Executive function, working memory, and learning suffer—and adolescents become less well able to regulate their behavior. At the same time, some research suggests that preexisting individual differences, such as poor functioning in tests of inhibition and working memory, smaller gray and white matter volume, and altered brain activation, are not only influenced by substance use but also place adolescents at risk for heavy substance use (Brumback et al., 2016; Squeglia & Gray, 2016).

Alcohol and substance use and abuse are associated with negative consequences that can interfere with adolescents' development, such as unwanted sexual encounters and risky sexual activity. Risks and negative consequences of alcohol and substance use include academic problems, social problems, aggression and victimization, unintentional injuries, anxiety, depression, car crashes, and suicide (Marshall, 2014).

Adolescents at risk to abuse alcohol and substances tend to begin drinking earlier than their peers (Palmer et al., 2009). Adolescents are at reduced risk of developing alcohol and substance abuse problems if their parents are involved, warm, supportive, and aware of their children's whereabouts and friends. Low socioeconomic status, family members with poor mental health, drug abuse within the family and community, and disadvantaged neighborhoods increase the risk of alcohol abuse in adolescence (Chaplin et al., 2012; Trucco, Colder, Wieczorek, Lengua, & Hawk, 2014). In turn, adolescents who have mental health problems, have difficulty with self-regulation, or are victims of physical or sexual abuse are at higher risk of alcohol and drug abuse than their peers. However, perhaps the most direct influences on adolescents are their peers' drinking or substance abuse behavior, their perceptions of peer support for such use, and their access to alcohol and substances (Brooks-Russell, Simons-Morton, Haynie, Farhat, & Wang, 2014).

Because adolescent alcohol and substance use is a complex problem with multiple influences, prevention and treatment programs must be multipronged. Effective prevention and intervention programs target parents by encouraging that they be warm and supportive, set rules, and be aware of their children's activities. Effective alcohol and substance abuse prevention and treatment programs educate adolescents about the health risks of substance use and emphasize that, contrary to depictions in the media and society, substance use is not socially acceptable. Such programs teach adolescents how to resist pressure from peers, how to refuse offers, and how to build their coping and self-regulatory skills (Windle & Zucker, 2010).

Health Promotion

The health behaviors established in adolescence tend to last well into adulthood. As a result, there is a growing emphasis on promoting healthy habits by improving access to health care and educating adolescents about health.

Health Care Access

Over the course of adolescence into emerging adulthood, young people become less likely to use health services. One recent study examined health care use by children, adolescents, and adults after the implementation of the Affordable Care Act in 2010, U.S. federal legislation designed to improve access to health insurance coverage (Spencer et al., 2018). From 2010 to 2016, rates of uninsured adolescents dropped from 8% to 5% in early adolescence (age 10–14) and 12% to 8% in late adolescence (age 15–18). The most dramatic changes were observed among emerging adults (age 19–25), dropping from 34% in 2010 to 14% uninsured in 2016. At all ages, but especially in emerging adulthood, young people were more likely to report having a regular source of medical care and having had a doctor or provider visit in the past year, and they were less likely to report having unmet health needs in 2016 than 2010. These findings suggest that improving access to health care can improve young people's use of health resources, with benefits for their health.

There are large economic disparities in health care access. Adolescents of color, especially those from low SES homes and communities, experience more difficulties with health care access than White adolescents (Yoshikawa et al., 2012). Recent research suggests that sexual minority adolescents may be less likely to use health services than their heterosexual peers. For example, in one study, males who reported same-sex, bisexual, and questioning orientations (collectively referred to as sexual minority adolescents) were three times as likely as heterosexual males to report unmet medical needs in the past year (Luk, Gilman, Haynie, & Simons-Morton, 2017). Girls with a same-sex, bisexual, or questioning orientation were nearly twice as likely to have had no routine checkup in the past year relative to heterosexual adolescents. Sexual minority adolescents are more likely than their heterosexual peers to report concerns discussing sexuality with health care providers (Fuzzell, Fedesco, Alexander, Fortenberry, & Shields, 2016). Some sexual minority adolescents report the sense that doctors seem uncomfortable discussing sexuality with them and feel isolated by noninclusive language used in the office and in conversations. Overall, physicians tend to discuss sexual behaviors and attractions rarely relative to other physical health topics, regardless of their patients' sexual orientation (Fuzzell, Shields, Alexander, & Fortenberry, 2017). In fact, communication about sexual topics tends to most frequently mention contraception and rarely discusses sexual attractions and orientations. Health care providers may miss out on important opportunities for helping the young people they treat.

Health Literacy

Adolescents' conceptions of health and health-related attitudes are important influences on their behaviors and have implications for health in adulthood (Michaelson, Pickett, Vandemeer, Taylor, & Davison, 2016). **Health literacy** refers to the knowledge, skills, and attitudes about health and the ability to obtain, process, and understand health information to make appropriate health decisions (Ghaddar, Valerio, Garcia, & Hansen, 2012; Manganello, 2008). Health literacy holds implications for individuals' ability to influence their own and others' health. For example, individuals with low levels of health literacy show more poor health (Peralta, Rowling, Samdal, Hipkins, & Dudley, 2017).

Adolescents and adults may conceptualize health in different ways. Adults often evaluate health based on the presence or absence of self-limiting health problems, but adolescents may emphasize different factors (Peralta et al., 2017). Adolescents tend to focus on specific behaviors and psychological states such physical activity, nutrition, sense of well-being, and specific behaviors such as not smoking. For example, one study of Canadian adolescents born between 1995 and 2002 suggested that they viewed good health as individualized, different for everyone (Michaelson et al., 2016). They tended to explain that good health is subjective. Specifically, how one felt about one's health state and behaviors was considered fundamental in determining one's health. In this study, the majority of adolescents reported that their health was "good" or "excellent," despite often engaging in unhealthy behaviors, in line with the theme expressed by one participant: "You can be healthy without always being healthy." Thus, adolescents may not accurately assess their health.

Educators who seek to improve health literacy are challenged with teaching adolescents the basics of health, how their bodies work, and how to promote health, while balancing adolescents' preferred individualized views of health (Peralta et al., 2017). A customized view of health, recognizing that there are individual differences among adolescents, can help young people value individual differences in health needs and offer protection from unhealthy beliefs (e.g., that everyone's body should look the same) (Michaelson et al., 2016). However, a subjective one-size-does-not-fit-all approach to health can interfere with school and community health promotion efforts that educate students about universal influences on health, such as good nutrition and exercise, as well as the hazards of drug use.

THINKING IN CONTEXT 13.3

1. Were you active in sports or other physical activities in childhood? Did your interests and behaviors change in adolescence? Why do you think many teens become less physically active? Do your own experiences and observations match these findings? How might the home, school, peer, and neighborhood context influence the extent to which adolescents engage in physical activity?
2. Consider eating disorders from a bioecological perspective. Identify factors at the microsystem and mesosystem levels that may influence one's likelihood of developing an eating disorder. How might exosystem factors influence the development of eating disorders? What is the role of the macrosystem? Finally, do you think these factors influence all three eating disorders (anorexia nervosa, bulimia nervosa, and binge eating disorder) in the same way? Why or why not?
3. Imagine that you are a health teacher preparing a curriculum for middle school students. What do they need to know about alcohol and substance use? How might you present this information? Next, consider high school students. How might you present the material to older adolescents? How might their concerns differ from those of middle school students? Discuss similarities and differences in your approach.

ADOLESCENT SEXUALITY

An important dimension of socioemotional development during adolescence is sexual development, a task that entails integrating physical, cognitive, and social domains of functioning. Sexuality encompasses feelings about oneself, appraisals of the self, attitudes, and behaviors (McClelland & Tolman, 2014). With the hormonal changes of puberty, both boys and girls experience an increase in sex drive and sexual interest (Fortenberry, 2013). Social context influences how biological urges are channeled into behavior and adolescents' conceptions of sexuality.

Sexual Activity

Research on adolescent sexuality tends to focus on intercourse, leaving gaps in our knowledge about the range of sexual activity milestones young people experience (Diamond & Savin-Williams, 2009). Sexual behaviors tend to progress from hand-holding to kissing, to touching through clothes and under clothes, to oral sex, and then to genital intercourse. Adolescents are about as likely to engage in oral sex as vaginal intercourse, with male and female high school students showing similar rates of oral sex (Copen, Chandra, & Martinez, 2012; Lefkowitz, Vasilenko, & Leavitt, 2016). Oral sex does not seem to be a substitute for vaginal sex, as the majority of over 12,000 adolescents in one sample initiated oral sex after first experiencing vaginal intercourse, and about one-half initiated oral sex a year or more after the onset of vaginal sex (Haydon, Herring, Prinstein, & Halpern, 2012).

Many adults are surprised to learn that the percentage of high school students who have ever had sexual intercourse has declined from 54% in 1991 to about 40% in 2017 (Kaiser Family Foundation, 2014; Kann et al., 2018). Overall rates of sexual activity are similar internationally, with comparable declines in recent years (Guttmacher Institute, 2014). Most young people have sexual intercourse for the first time at about age 17 (Figure 13.7) (Guttmacher Institute, 2017). About one-third of high school students report being sexually

FIGURE 13.7

Age at Sexual Initiation During Adolescence

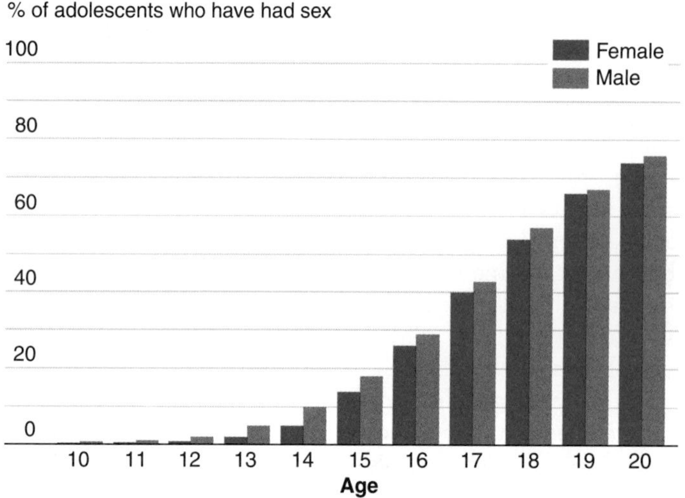

Source: Guttmacher. (2017). Adolescent sexual and reproductive health in the United States. Retrieved from https://www.guttmacher.org/fact-sheet/american-teens-sexual-and-reproductive-health

Many adults are surprised to learn that the percentage of high school students who have ever had sexual intercourse has declined over the past 3 decades.
©iStockphoto.com/stray_cat

active, defined as within the previous 3 months. As shown in Figure 13.8, African American high school students are more likely to report being sexually active compared to White and Hispanic students (Child Trends, 2017).

Ethnic differences in sexual activity are intertwined with the socioeconomic and contextual factors that accompany ethnicity. Early sexual activity and greater sexual experience are more common in adolescents reared in stressful contexts, such as low socioeconomic status homes and poverty-stricken and dangerous neighborhoods where community ties are weak (Carlson, McNulty, Bellair, & Watts, 2014; Warner, 2018). For example, in one study of middle school students, experiencing a direct threat of violence in the school or community predicted early sexual initiation (Coyle, Guinosso, Glassman, Anderson, & Wilson, 2017). In addition, ethnic differences in rates of pubertal maturation, with African American girls experiencing puberty earlier than other girls, influence sexual activity, as early maturation is a risk factor for early sexual activity (Carlson et al., 2014; Moore et al., 2014).

Although sexual activity is normative in late adolescence, early sexual activity, prior to age 15, is associated with problem behaviors, including alcohol and substance use, poor academic achievement, and delinquent activity, as well as having a larger number of sex partners relative to peers (McLeod & Knight, 2010). Risk factors for early sexual activity in U.S. teens are early pubertal maturation, poor parental monitoring, and poor parent–adolescent communication (McClelland & Tolman, 2014; Negriff, Susman, & Trickett, 2011). In one study of nearly 15,000 adolescents, those who perceived that their parents made more warnings emphasizing the negative consequences of sex tended to accumulate more sexual partners (Coley, Lombardi, Lynch, Mahalik, & Sims, 2013). Authoritative parenting, regularly shared family activities (e.g., outings, game nights, or shared dinners), parental monitoring, and parental knowledge are associated with lower rates of sexual activity (Dittus et al., 2015; Huang, Murphy, & Hser, 2011). Having sexually active peers and perceiving positive attitudes about sex among schoolmates predict initiation and greater levels of sexual activity and a greater number of sexual partners (Coley et al., 2013; Moore et al., 2014; White

FIGURE 13.8

Percentage of Sexually Active Students in Grades 9 Through 12

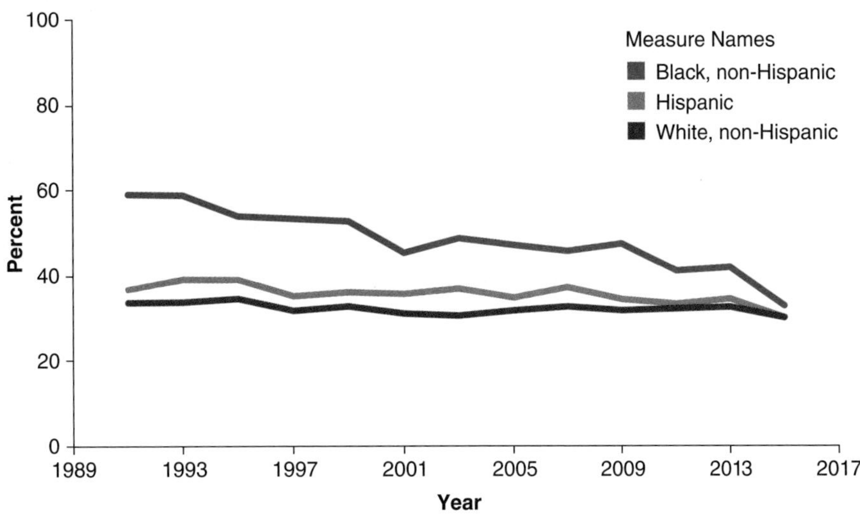

Source: Child Trends (2017).

& Warner, 2015). In addition, adolescents' perceptions of the sexual norms in their neighborhood, as well as siblings' sexual activity, are associated with age of initiation, casual sex, and the number of sexual partners, even after controlling for neighborhood demographic risk factors (Almy et al., 2016; Warner, Giordano, Manning, & Longmore, 2011).

In recent years, parents and health professionals have become increasingly concerned about adolescents' use of technology as tools for sexual exploration and expression. **Sexting**, the exchange of explicit sexual messages or images via mobile phone, is increasingly common among adolescents. Females and older youth are more likely to share sexual photos than males and younger youth. Several studies have found that sexting is associated with sexual activity, especially risky sexual activity, in adolescents as young as 13 (Rice et al., 2012; Romo et al., 2017; Ybarra & Mitchell, 2014; Ševčíková, Blinka, & Daneback, 2018). One study of over 17,000 adolescents aged 11 to 16 from 25 European countries revealed that sexting was associated with emotional problems and alcohol use in girls and boys of all ages (Ševčíková, 2016). Other research supports the link between sexting and adolescent problems such as substance use, depression, and low self-esteem (Van Ouytsel, Van Gool, Ponnet, & Walrave, 2014).

Lesbian, Gay, Bisexual, and Transgender Adolescents

Adolescents are driven to understand the sexual feelings they experience, and their emerging sexual orientation becomes an important contributor to their sense of self (McClelland & Tolman, 2014). Many youth enter a period of questioning in which they are uncertain of their sexuality and attempt to determine their **sexual orientation**, an enduring pattern of emotional, romantic, and sexual attraction to opposite-sex partners (heterosexual or cisgender), same-sex partners (gay or lesbian), or partners of both sexes (bisexual) (Greenberg, 2017). For many adolescents, the process of determining their sexual orientation entails exploring and considering alternatives. For example, many preadolescents and young adolescents engage in sex play with members of the same sex, yet ultimately develop a cisgender orientation. Longitudinal data with over 10,000 seventh- to twelfth-grade students over a 6-year period revealed some migration over time in both directions—from opposite-sex attraction and behavior to same-sex attraction and behavior and vice versa (Saewyc, 2011). Adolescents who identify as transgender do not identify with their sex assigned at birth but instead adopt an alternative gender identity (Diamond et al., 2015). Transgender is distinct from sexual orientation. That is, a transgender identity does not signify sexual orientation, whether one is gay, lesbian, or bisexual (Bosse & Chiodo, 2016). However, research on the intersection of transgender identity and sexual orientation is rare. Consequently, many researchers study transgender adolescents alongside LGB adolescents (Galupo, Davis, Grynkiewicz, & Mitchell, 2014). Wherever possible, the following discussion distinguishes LGB and transgender adolescents.

In North America and many other developed countries, young people are disclosing their sexual orientation—"coming out" as gay or lesbian—at earlier ages than in prior generations, likely due to an increasingly inviting, positive cultural context for LGB young people (Calzo, Antonucci, Mays, & Cochran, 2011; Floyd & Bakeman, 2006; Lucassen et al., 2015). Research suggests that some sexual minority youth may disclose their sexuality starting at around age 14 or 15, yet many wait until late adolescence or emerging adulthood (Calzo, Masyn, Austin, Jun, & Corliss, 2017; Savin-Williams & Ream, 2003). In the annual Youth Risk Behavior Survey conducted by the Centers for Disease Control and Prevention, about half of the adolescents who identified as lesbian, gay, or bisexual reported ever having sex and about a third reported being sexually active (Kann et al., 2018). Adolescents who anticipate negative responses from parents are less likely to disclose their sexual orientation to them and may become emotionally distant (Ueno, 2005). Despite stereotypes, adolescents who come out to a parent are rarely met with ongoing condemnation, severe negative response, or expulsion (Savin-Williams & Dubé, 1998). Most receive responses that range from neutral to positive (Samarova, Shilo, & Diamond, 2014).

Constructing an identity as a young person who is lesbian, gay, bisexual, or transgender can be complicated by the prejudice and discrimination that many LGBT youth experience in their schools and communities. LGBT adolescents experience more harassment and victimization by peers and report a more hostile peer environment than their heterosexual peers (Robinson & Espelage, 2013). Perceived discrimination and victimization by peers contribute to LGBT adolescents' increased risk for psychological and behavioral problems, such as depression, self-harm, suicide, running away, poor academic performance, substance use, and risky sexual practices (Collier, van Beusekom, Bos, & Sandfort, 2013; Haas et al., 2011; Plöderl et al., 2013).

Accepting reactions from parents and peers can buffer the psychological and behavioral risks that accompany perceived discrimination (Birkett, Newcomb, & Mustanski, 2015; Rosario, Schrimshaw, & Hunter, 2009). Developmental scientists have come to conclude that disclosing a sexual minority identity can be a positive event that facilitates the development of identity, self-esteem, and psychological health and can often reduce distress, anxiety, and depression (Juster, Smith, Ouellet, Sindi, & Lupien, 2013; Ueno, 2005; Vincke & van Heeringen, 2002). It can also be a means for obtaining social support and interpersonal closeness (Kosciw, Palmer, & Kull, 2015; Legate, Ryan, & Weinstein, 2012; Savin-Williams & Cohen, 2015). Within the school setting, the presence of gay-straight alliances (GSAs) is an important source of support and education for students and helps sexual minority students connect with peers, reduces hopelessness, and is associated with a lower number of suicide attempts (Davis, Royne Stafford, & Pullig, 2014).

Young people are disclosing their sexual orientation at earlier ages than in prior generations, likely in response to an increasingly inviting, positive political and cultural context for LGB young people.
https://www.shutterstock.com/image-photo/two-women-holding-hands-wooden-background-332181500

Contraceptive Use

Adolescent contraceptive use is at an all-time high, yet only about three-quarters of sexually active 15- to 19-year-olds report using contraception during first intercourse (Kaiser Family Foundation, 2014). Two-thirds of sexually active adolescents report the condom as the method used during the most recent sexual intercourse and the method used at first intercourse (Guttmacher Institute, 2014). Many adolescents use contraceptives only sporadically and not consistently (Pazol et al., 2015). Common reasons given for not using contraceptives include not planning to have sex, the belief that pregnancy is unlikely, and difficulty communicating and negotiating the use of condoms (Johnson, Sieving, Pettingell, & McRee, 2015).

Authoritative parenting combined with open discussions about sex and contraception are associated with increased contraceptive use (Bersamin et al., 2008; Malcolm et al., 2013). Adolescents' knowledge and access to contraceptives are the best predictors of contraceptive use. Boys and girls with more reproductive knowledge report greater use of contraceptives and more consistent use of contraceptives (Jaramillo, Buhi, Elder, & Corliss, 2017; Ryan, Franzetta, & Manlove, 2007).

Sexually Transmitted Infections

With sexual activity comes the risk of transmitting or acquiring sexually transmitted infections (STIs), infections passed from one individual to another through sexual contact. STIs may be caused by viruses, bacteria, or parasites. In 2015, STIs—specifically, cases of chlamydia, gonorrhea, and syphilis—reached an all-time high in the United States (Centers for Disease Control and Prevention, 2016). Although they represent only 25% of the sexually active population, 15- to 24-year-olds account for one-half to two-thirds of all STI diagnoses, depending on illness, each year. Untreated STIs can result in sterility and serious, even life-threatening illnesses such as cancer.

Human papillomavirus (HPV) is the most common STI diagnosed in people of all ages. There are several types of HPV, and some can cause cancer in different areas of the body—most commonly cervical cancer in women (McQuillan, Kruszon-Moran, Markowitz, Unger, & Paulose-Ram, 2017). The U.S. Centers for Disease Control and Prevention recommends HPV vaccinations for males and females starting at age 11. In 2015, 63% of females aged 13 to 17 had received one or more doses of the vaccine against HPV, and 42% had completed the recommended regimen of three doses as compared with 50% and 28% for males, respectively (Reagan-Steiner et al., 2016). Some believe that HPV vaccination rates are low, compared to other vaccinations, because of the erroneous belief that giving the vaccine might condone sexual activity (Holman et al., 2014).

The most serious sexually transmitted infection is **human immunodeficiency virus (HIV)**, which causes acquired immune deficiency syndrome (AIDS). Adolescents and emerging adults aged 13 to 24 represented one in five new HIV/AIDS diagnoses in 2015. Symptoms of AIDS, specifically a deterioration of the immune system, occur about 8 to 10 years after infection with HIV. Although most adolescents (about 85% of high school students) receive education and demonstrate basic knowledge about HIV/AIDS, most underestimate their own risks, know little about other STIs, and are not knowledgeable about how to protect themselves from STIs (Kann et al., 2014). The three ways to avoid STIs are to abstain from sex; to be in a long-term, mutually monogamous relationship with a partner who has been tested and does not have any STIs; or to use condoms consistently and correctly.

Adolescent Pregnancy

In 2017, the birthrate among 15- to 19-year-old girls in the United States was 18.8 per 1,000 girls, down from a high of 117 per 1,000 in 1990 (Martin, Hamilton, & Osterman, 2018). The decline in adolescent birthrates can be attributed to an increase in contraceptive use (Lindberg, Santelli, & Desai, 2016). Despite overall declines over the past 2 decades, the United States continues to have one of the highest teen birthrates in the developed world (Sedgh, Finer, Bankole, Eilers, & Singh, 2015). In addition, ethnic and socioeconomic disparities place vulnerable teens at heightened risk for adolescent pregnancy and birth. Hispanic, African American, and American Indian/Alaska Native adolescents, as well as those from low socioeconomic status homes and communities (both rural and urban), have the highest adolescent birth-rates in the United States (Burrus, 2018). As shown in Figure 13.9, although birthrates have declined dramatically since the 1980s, the birthrate for Hispanic and Black girls is over twice that for non-Hispanic White girls (Child Trends, 2019).

The risks for adolescent parenthood (see Figure 13.10) are much the same as for early sexual activity. Girls who experience menarche early, relative to peers, are at risk as this early maturation predicts early sexual behavior and, in turn, pregnancy (De Genna, Larkby, & Cornelius, 2011). Similarly, poor academic achievement, delinquency, substance use, depression, and affiliation with deviant peers are risk factors for early sexual activity and adolescent pregnancy (Carlson et al., 2014; Fortenberry, 2013). Low socioeconomic status homes, poor neighborhoods, and low levels of parental warmth and monitoring influence early sexual activity and the risk for adolescent childbirth. Involved and firm parenting during early adolescence can buffer the effects of multiple home and community risk factors on the likelihood of early sexual activity and adolescent pregnancy (East, Khoo, Reyes, & Coughlin, 2006).

Adolescent mothers are less likely than their peers to achieve many of the typical markers of adulthood on time, such as completing high school, entering a stable marriage, and becoming financially and residentially independent (Taylor, 2009). Lack of resources such as child care, housing, and financial support is associated with poor educational outcomes; adolescents with child care and financial resources tend to show higher educational attainment (Casares, Lahiff, Eskenazi, & Halpern-Felsher, 2010). Although adolescent pregnancy is associated with negative outcomes, the risk factors for adolescent pregnancy are also those that place youth at risk for negative adult outcomes in general, such as extreme poverty, family instability, and few educational and community supports (Oxford et al., 2005). It is therefore difficult to determine the degree to which outcomes are caused by adolescent pregnancy itself or the contextual conditions that are associated with it. Adolescent fathers are similar to adolescent mothers in that they are more likely than their peers to have poor academic performance, higher school dropout rates, finite financial resources, and lowered income potential (Kiselica & Kiselica, 2014).

FIGURE 13.9

Birthrates for Adolescents Aged 15 to 19, 1960–2017

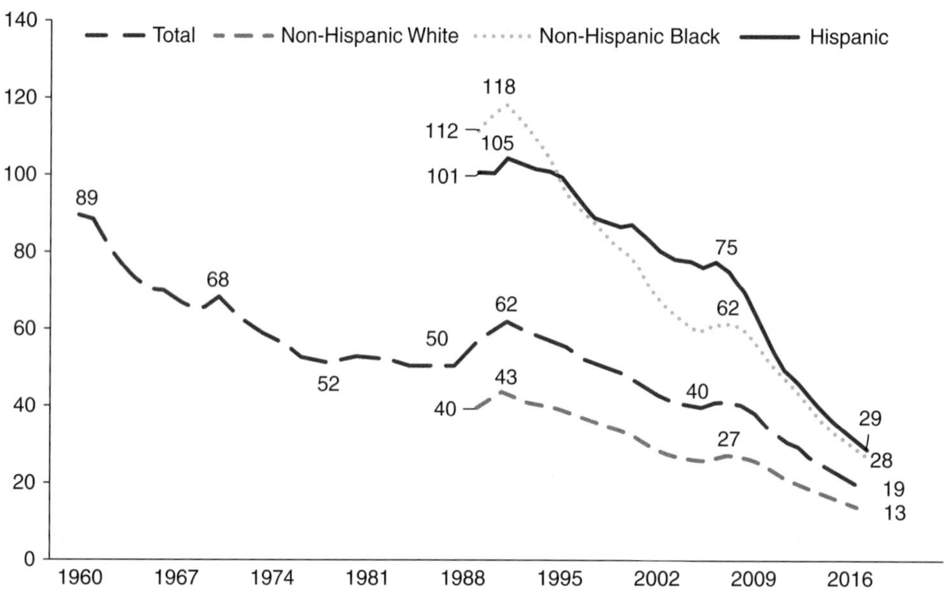

Source: Child Trends (2019).

FIGURE 13.10

Influences on Adolescent Pregnancy

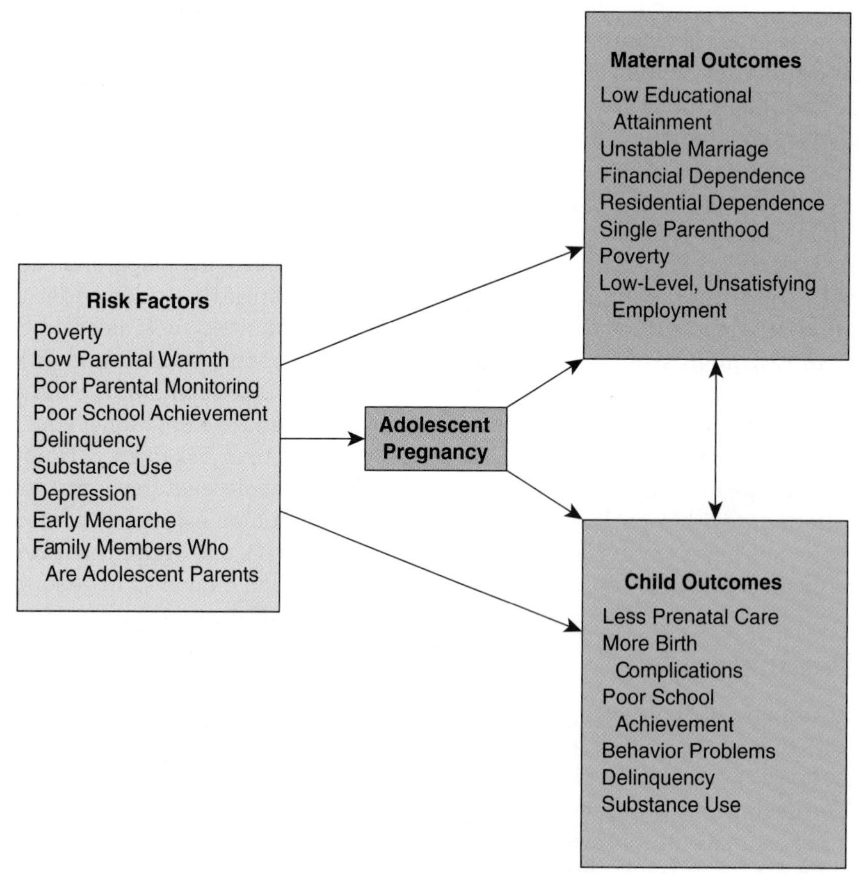

Source: Child Trends (2019).

Infants born to adolescent mothers are at risk for preterm birth and low birthweight (Jeha, Usta, Ghulmiyyah, & Nassar, 2015). Children of adolescent mothers tend to be at risk for a variety of negative developmental outcomes such as conduct and emotional problems, developmental delays, and poor academic achievement (Rafferty, Griffin, & Lodise, 2011; Tang, Davis-Kean, Chen, & Sexton, 2016). These outcomes are influenced by the characteristics of adolescents who are likely to become mothers, as well as the consequences of having a child at a young age (e.g., low level of maternal education, low socioeconomic status, frequent caretaker and residence changes, poor parenting) (De Genna et al., 2011; Rafferty et al., 2011). However, there is variability in outcomes. Many children of adolescent mothers demonstrate resilience and adjustment despite these risks (Levine, Emery, & Pollack, 2007). Positive adjustment is predicted by secure attachment, low maternal depressive symptoms, and positive parenting on the part of the mother, characterized by warmth, discussion, and stimulation.

Adolescent parents can be effective if provided with supports—economic, educational, and social. Effective supports for adolescent parents include access to health care and affordable child care, encouragement to stay in school, and training in vocational skills, parenting skills, and coping skills (Easterbrooks, Chaudhuri, Bartlett, & Copeman, 2011). Social support predicts increased parenting self-efficacy and parental satisfaction (Angley, Divney, Magriples, & Kershaw, 2015; Umaña-Taylor, Guimond, Updegraff, & Jahromi, 2013). Relationships with adults who are close, are supportive, and provide guidance predict completing high school. Adolescent parents who share caregiving with their mothers or other adults learn as apprentices and become increasingly competent at parenting over time (Oberlander, Black, & Starr, 2007). Adolescent parents also benefit from relationships with adults who are sensitive not only to their needs as parents but also to their own developmental needs for autonomy and support.

Sexual Coercion

Healthy sexual activity is consensual sexual activity. It is estimated that about 20% of women experience nonconsensual sexual activity; that is, they experience sexual assault or rape (Breiding et al., 2014b). **Rape** refers to nonconsensual sexual penetration of the body by the body part of another person or object (Federal Bureau of Investigation, 2015), while **sexual assault** is a broader term referring to a wide variety of nonconsensual sexual contact or behavior. *Nonconsensual* is the key to identifying sexual assault: It includes instances in which the victim is coerced by fear tactics, such as threats or use of physical harm; or is incapable of giving consent due to the influence of drugs or alcohol or because of age. Most victims are young, with nearly 80% experiencing sexual assault prior to age 25; 40% of victims are under the age of 18 (Breiding et al., 2014b).

Adolescents are most likely to be assaulted by someone they know (Breiding, Chen, & Black, 2014a; Sinozich & Langton, 2014). The commonly used term "date rape" for nonconsensual sexual activity with an acquaintance downplays the severity of sexual assault. Many cases of date rape are premeditated and involve slipping powerful sedatives such as Rohypnol (roofie) into a young person's drink. The drug makes the victim drowsy, unconscious, or unable to move, and often causes the victim to not recall the event the next day. When alcohol is involved, victims may blame themselves for drinking (Hock, 2015).

Underreporting of rape is high. The actual number of incidents is hard to determine, but one study found that only about 20% of rapes had been reported to the police (Sinozich & Langton, 2014). Sometimes victims believe that their attacker will deny the rape or believe that no assault occurred. They may want to avoid being judged negatively by friends, peers, or future potential dating partners. Many victims do not acknowledge rape or sexual assault, but instead refer to it as miscommunication or sexual activities that "got out of hand." One meta-analysis of 28 studies (with almost 6,000 participants) found that two-thirds of women rape survivors, particularly those who experienced acquaintance rape, did not acknowledge that they had been raped (Wilson & Miller, 2016).

Survivors of sexual assault have a higher than average risk of developing post-traumatic stress disorder (PTSD) and depression and of abusing alcohol and other substances (Ullman, Relyea, Peter-Hagene, & Vasquez, 2013; Zinzow et al., 2010). Women's attributions for the assault influence their adjustment. Those who blame themselves tend to experience more adjustment difficulties, including a higher risk for depression (Vickerman & Margolin, 2009), whereas support from family and friends influences positive adjustment (Orchowski, Untied, & Gidycz, 2013).

THINKING IN CONTEXT 13.4

1. Consider the problem of adolescent pregnancy from the standpoint of Bronfenbrenner's bioecological perspective. Identify individual and microsystem factors that may place girls at risk for adolescent pregnancy and childbearing. At the microsystem level, how might these factors interact to increase or decrease risk for pregnancy and childbirth? How might exosystem factors contribute to (or protect girls from) risk? Identify macrosystem factors that may influence adolescent pregnancy and childbirth.
2. Discuss prevention and intervention for adolescent pregnancy and childbirth referring to the factors identified in item 1. How might this model be applied to prevent pregnancy?
3. Considering that many of the contextual factors that place girls at risk for adolescent parenthood also influence developmental outcomes for mother and child, discuss ways of intervening to help adolescent mothers and their children.

APPLY YOUR KNOWLEDGE

"Here I am, right in the center of the back row," 14-year-old Jimena said, as she reviewed her second-grade class photo. "Now I'm one of the shortest in my grade. And the heaviest. I need to do something about my thighs. They're too thick," she complained to her mother. "Nonsense. I was just like you at your age. You might feel like you stand out now, but the other girls will catch up," her mother said. "Doubt it," Jimena sighed as she went to her room. "The girls in my class just look at me and gossip. They'll never be like me," she said.

Jimena hopped onto her bed and texted Ralph: "U around?" "Can U hang out?" he replied. Jimena loved hanging out with Ralph and his friends. Ralph, a high school senior, knew how to have fun. He and his friends got together almost every day to hang out in the park and vape pot. Sometimes they drank but beer wasn't as easy to get. Ralph made her feel pretty. He appreciated her body. Jimena didn't feel heavy when she was with Ralph and his friends. Plus, she seemed to fit in with the girls in the group.

Jimena's twin brother, Alonzo, was a star on the basketball court. Stronger and faster than his peers, Alonzo was popular with the kids in his class, but his closest friends were not in his class. Like Jimena, Alonzo preferred spending time with the seniors in his school. The girls were cuter than those in his class and the older boys posed more of a challenge on the basketball court. They were also more fun off the court. They often played what they called "sneaking games" and tried to "get away with stuff." Last week they got away with breaking into the corner store and stealing a case of beer. Alonzo was scared but soon was exhilarated that they got away with it.

1. Why are Jimena and Alonzo larger than their peers? How else might they differ physically from their peers?
2. Contrast Jimena and Alonzo's experiences. Identify similarities and differences.
3. What are some of the correlates of early maturation relative to peers?
4. What opportunities does early maturation pose for boys and girls?
5. How might contextual factors influence the effects of early maturation? Imagine that Jimena and Alonzo live in a rural farming community versus a busy urban neighborhood. How might Jimena and Alonzo's experiences differ in these two contexts? What challenges and opportunities might early maturation pose in suburban environments?

WANT A BETTER GRADE?

Get the tools you need to sharpen your study skills. **SAGE edge** offers a robust online environment featuring an impressive array of free tools and resources. Access practice quizzes, eFlashcards, video, and multimedia at **edge.sagepub.com/kutherchild1e.** SAGE edge™

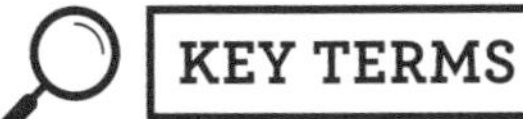

KEY TERMS

Puberty 349
Adolescent growth spurt 350
Secondary sex characteristic 351
Primary sex characteristic 351
Menstruation 351
Menarche 351
Testes 351
Semen 351
Spermarche 351
Nocturnal emissions 351
Delayed phase preference 352
Melatonin 352
Secular trend 355
Limbic system 357
Amygdala 357
Dual-systems model 358
Eating disorder 364
Anorexia nervosa 364
Bulimia nervosa 364
Binge eating disorder 365
Health literacy 368
Sexting 371
Sexual orientation 371
Human papillomavirus (HPV) 373
Human immunodeficiency virus (HIV) 373
Rape 375
Sexual assault 375

SUMMARY

13.1 Summarize the physical changes that accompany puberty and how context influences how it is experienced.

The most noticeable signs of pubertal maturation are the growth spurt and the development of secondary sex characteristics, such as breast development, deepening of the voice, growth of body hair, and changes in the skin. During puberty, the primary sex characteristics, the reproductive organs, grow larger and mature, and adolescents become capable of reproduction. Pubertal timing is influenced by genetic and contextual factors, which also determine adolescents' subjective experiences. Early maturation poses challenges for both boys and girls, with more dramatic effects for girls.

13.2 Describe brain development during adolescence and its effect on behavior.

Changes in the volume of the cortex, interconnections among neurons, and myelination influence the speed and efficiency of thought and the capacity for executive function. According to the dual-systems model, the limbic system undergoes a burst of development well ahead of the prefrontal cortex, and this difference in development can account for many "typical" adolescent behaviors. Changes in the balance of neurotransmitters that are associated with impulsivity and reward salience shift, influencing adolescent engagement in risky behavior.

13.3 Discuss adolescents' health needs and common health problems.

Although adolescence is a generally healthy time in which young people tend to report good or excellent health and low rates of illness, mortality rises mainly due to the risky behavior that is common in adolescence. As in prior periods, nutrition and physical activity are important for health. Many adolescents become dissatisfied with their body shape and are at risk to develop eating disorders, such as anorexia nervosa, bulimia nervosa, and binge eating disorder, all of which pose serious challenges to health. Experimentation with alcohol, tobacco, and cannabis is common and may serve a developmental function in middle and late adolescence. Substances, however, pose risks because adolescents are particularly vulnerable to alcohol and substance abuse and use is associated with damage to the brain. Improving adolescents' health entails increasing access to health care and improving health literacy.

13.4 Distinguish normative sexual development and activity from problematic activities and outcomes.

The average adolescent has sexual intercourse at about age 17. Although normative sexual activity is not associated with problems, early sexual activity, under age 15, is associated with problem behaviors. Risk factors for early sexual activity include early pubertal maturation, poor parental communication and monitoring, sexually active peers, risky behaviors, and stressful homes and neighborhoods. Despite a decline since 1990, and increasing contraceptive use, the United States has one of the highest teen pregnancy rates in the developed world. Adolescent mothers are less likely to achieve many of the typical markers of adulthood. Children born to adolescent mothers are at greater risk for academic and behavioral problems. A substantial number of adolescent girls experience sexual coercion, most commonly being assaulted by someone they know. Sexual assaults are often unreported and pose adjustment risks for victims.

REVIEW QUESTIONS

13.1 What are primary and secondary sex characteristics?

What influences pubertal timing?

What are the effects of early and late pubertal timing in boys and girls?

13.2 What are some changes that take place in the brain during adolescence?

What is the dual-systems model?

What are some of the behavioral effects of brain development?

13.3 What are common health problems in adolescence?

Differentiate among three eating disorders.

What are some reasons why adolescents experiment with alcohol and substances?

What are some risks of alcohol and substance use?

13.4 Describe normative sexual behavior in adolescence.

What are risks for early sexual activity?

What are influences on contraceptive use?

What are risk factors for pregnancy?

©iStockphoto.com/Tomwang

14 Cognitive Development in Adolescence

At 14 years of age, Eric spends much of his time learning about astronomy. He wonders about the existence of dark matter—cosmological matter that cannot be observed but is inferred by its gravitational pull on objects like planets and even galaxies. Eric reads blogs written by astronomers and has started his own blog where he comments on the best websites for teenagers who are interested in learning about the galaxy. Eric's newfound ability and interest in considering complex abstract phenomena illustrates the ways in which adolescents' thinking departs from children's thinking. Moreover, these changes spill over and affect all aspects of adolescents' development, from their understanding of right and wrong, to their relationships, academic success, and plans for the future. In this chapter, we examine the cognitive changes that occur during adolescence and their effects on adolescents' interactions with the people around them and contexts in which they are embedded.

Learning Objectives

14.1 Identify ways in which thinking changes in adolescence and how these changes are reflected in adolescent decision making and behavior.

14.2 Describe moral development and influences on moral reasoning in adolescence.

14.3 Examine the challenges that school transitions pose for adolescents and the role of parents in academic achievement.

Video Activity 14.1: Transition to Middle School

14.4 Discuss the nature of adolescent employment, the influence of college on development, and the challenges faced by noncollege-bound youth.

Video Activity 14.2: Coming of Age: Bat Mitzvah

Chapter Contents

COGNITIVE DEVELOPMENT

As in infancy and childhood, cognitive-developmental theory and information processing theory offer different explanations and accounts of cognitive development in adolescence.

Piaget's Cognitive-Developmental Theory

Piaget's cognitive-developmental theory views individuals as active constructors of their schemes. Through their interactions with the world, adolescents devise new, more mature schemes and undergo a transformation in thought. The result is formal operational reasoning, the final stage of Piaget's cognitive-developmental theory.

Formal Operational Reasoning

In early adolescence, at about 11 years of age, individuals may enter the final stage of Piaget's scheme of cognitive development: formal operations. **Formal operational reasoning** entails the ability to think abstractly, logically, and systematically (Inhelder & Piaget, 1958). Children in the concrete operational stage reason about specific *things*—that is, concepts that exist in reality, such as problems concerning how to equitably divide materials (e.g., dividing candies of different types into equal servings). Adolescents in the formal operational stage, however, reason about *ideas*, possibilities that do not exist in reality and that may have no tangible substance, such as whether it is possible to love equitably (e.g., to distribute love equally among several targets). Adolescents become capable of reasoning about their own thinking and even positing their own existence. Mariana, for instance, wonders, "I know I'm thinking. So, I'm thinking about my thinking . . . and I'm thinking about thinking about how I think. Now, how do I know that I am real? Am I just a thought?" The ability to think about possibilities beyond the here and now permits adolescents to plan for the future, make inferences from available information, and consider ways of solving potential but not yet real problems.

Formal operational thought enables adolescents to engage in **hypothetical–deductive reasoning**, or the ability to consider problems, generate and systematically test hypotheses, and draw conclusions. It is these abilities that underlie the scientific method (Chapter 1). The tasks that Piaget constructed to study formal operational reasoning test adolescents' abilities to use scientific reasoning to approach a problem by developing hypotheses and systematically testing them. For example, consider his famous pendulum task illustrated in Figure 14.1 (Inhelder & Piaget, 1958). Adolescents are presented with a pendulum and are asked what determines the speed with which the pendulum swings. They are given materials and told that there are four variables to consider: (1) length of string (short, medium, long), (2) weight (light, medium, heavy), (3) height at which the weight is dropped, and (4) force with which the weight is dropped. Adolescents who display formal operational reasoning develop hypotheses that they systematically test. For example, they change one variable while holding the others constant (e.g., trying each of the lengths of string while keeping the weight, height, and force the same). Children in the concrete operational stage, on the other hand, do not proceed systematically and fail to test each variable independently. For example, children who reason at the concrete operational stage might test a short string with a heavy weight, then try a long string and short weight. Solving the pendulum problem requires the scientific reasoning capacities that come with formal operational reasoning.

FIGURE 14.1

Measuring Formal Operations: The Pendulum Task

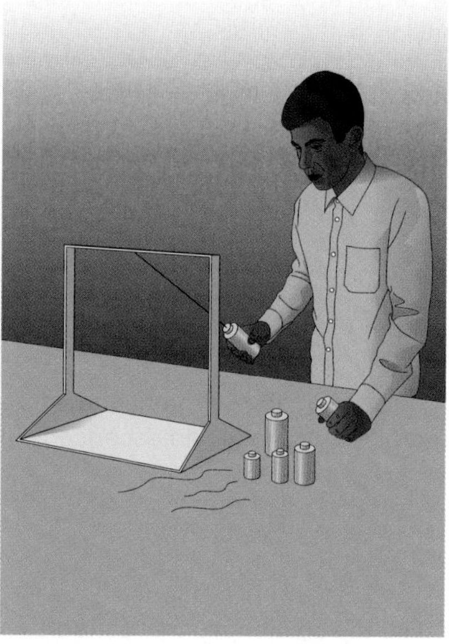

Children and adolescents are presented with a pendulum and are asked what determines the speed with which the pendulum swings. They are given materials and told that there are four variables to consider: (1) length of string (short, medium, long), (2) weight (light, medium, heavy), (3) height at which the weight is dropped, and (4) force with which the weight is dropped.

Evaluating Formal Operational Reasoning

Although Piaget believed that cognitive development is a universal process, individuals show varying abilities. For example, most adolescents and many adults do not display formal operational thinking in Piagetian hypothetical-deductive tasks (Kuhn, 2013). Does this mean that they cannot think abstractly? Likely not. Piaget (1972) explained that opportunities to use formal operational reasoning influence its development. Individuals are more likely to show formal operational reasoning when considering material with which they have a great deal of experience. For example, completing college courses is associated with gains in propositional and statistical thought, skills that are often honed in college as well as measured in Piagetian tasks (Kuhn, 2012; Lehman & Nisbett, 1990). In one study in the early 1990s, adolescents from 10 to 15 years of age performed better on Piagetian tasks such as the pendulum task than adolescents had done over 2 decades before. The researchers attributed the difference to the fact that (in France, where the studies were done) secondary education was less common in the earlier decades; therefore, adolescents had fewer opportunities to practice the reasoning measured by Piagetian tasks (Flieller, 1999).

Ultimately, the appearance of formal operational reasoning varies across individuals as well as within individuals because it is not consistent across intellectual areas. Instead, the appearance of formal operations varies with situation, task, context, and the individual's motivation (Birney & Sternberg, 2011; Labouvie-Vief, 2015; Marti & Rodríguez, 2012). Moreover, formal operational reasoning does not suddenly appear in early adolescence. Instead, cognitive change occurs gradually from childhood on, with gains in knowledge, experience, and information processing capacity (Keating, 2012; Moshman & Moshman, 2011). Finally, most developmental scientists believe that the pinnacle of cognitive development is not in adolescence. Most agree that cognitive development continues throughout adulthood.

Information Processing Theory

From the perspective of information processing theory, improvements in information processing capacities—such as attention, memory, knowledge base, and speed—enable adolescents to think faster, more efficiently, and more complexly than ever before. Specifically, brain development influences adolescents' growing capacities for executive function, permitting greater cognitive control and regulation of attention, thinking, and problem solving (Carlson et al., 2013; Crone, Peters, & Steinbeis, 2018), as described in the following sections.

Attention

Greater control over attention allows adolescents to deploy it selectively. As compared with children, adolescents show improvements in selective attention, focusing on one stimulus while tuning out others and remaining focused even as task demands change, as well as divided attention, attending to two stimuli at once (Hanania & Smith, 2010; Memmert, 2014). With increases in attention, adolescents are better able to hold material in working memory while taking in and processing new material (Barrouillet, Gavens, Vergauwe, Gaillard, & Camos, 2009). Improvements in the ability to monitor information and select the most important parts of it have important implications for classroom performance. Now students can concentrate on more complex tasks. For example, tenth-grader Leon can tune out his giggling friends to pay attention to what the teacher is saying. He can determine what is important and explain the material in his own words as he takes notes. He can shift his attention and focus on each speaker during class discussion and identify new ideas to add to his notes. Advances in information processing support adolescents' abilities to solve geometry problems, employ the scientific method, and solve other complex problems.

Advances in attention, the ability to monitor information and select the most important parts of it, enable adolescents to engage in complicated tasks and better attend in class.
©iStockphoto.com/diego_cervo

Working Memory and Executive Function

Neurological maturation leads to improvements in working memory throughout adolescence. Working memory reaches adult-like levels by about age 19 and continues to improve into the 20s (Isbell, Fukuda, Neville, & Vogel, 2015; Murty, Calabro, & Luna, 2016; Simmonds & Luna, 2015). Advances in working memory are largely driven by changes in the central executive. Advances in executive function permit individuals to effectively deploy their attention and memory to solve problems.

Adolescents become better able to determine what is important to attend to, combine new information with information already in working memory, and select and apply strategies for manipulating the information in order to understand it, make decisions, and solve problems (Andersson, 2008; Baddeley, 2016). Adolescents are more likely than children to use memory strategies such as organizing new material into patterns and connecting new material with what is already known (Camos, Barrouillet, & Barrouillet, 2018). Experience contributes to cognitive advances. Adolescents know more than children, permitting them more opportunities to associate new material with old, enhancing encoding and long-term memory (Keating, 2012). These advances in knowledge and strategy use result in more sophisticated, efficient, and quick thinking and learning. Now adolescents can retain more information at once, better integrate prior experiences and knowledge with new information, and combine information in more complex ways (Cowan et al., 2010; Gaillard, Barrouillet, Jarrold, & Camos, 2011). Specifically, brain development influences adolescents' growing capacities for executive function, permitting greater cognitive control and regulation of attention, thinking, and problem solving (Carlson et al., 2013; Crone et al., 2018),

An important aspect of executive function is **response inhibition**, the ability to control and stop responding to a stimulus (Carlson et al., 2013). The ability to control and inhibit responses advances through childhood, but shows substantial gains in adolescence and increases through emerging adulthood (Crone et al., 2018; Zhai et al., 2015). Advances in response inhibition enable adolescents to adapt their responses to the situation. They can inhibit well-learned responses when they are inappropriate to the situation and thereby speed cognitive processing (Luna, Paulsen, Padmanabhan, & Geier, 2013). Response inhibition improves gradually in adolescence. Immature inhibitory processes can contribute to outbursts where it seems as if adolescents speak before considering their feelings or the potential consequences of their actions. The neurological changes that underlie response inhibition continue to develop into the 20s, and still-immature capacities for response inhibition are thought to underlie the risk-taking behavior common in adolescence (Müller & Kerns, 2015; Peeters et al., 2015).

Working memory and executive function improve with maturation and experience, but are also influenced by contextual factors. For example, some research suggests that the experience of early life stress is associated with impaired inhibition in adolescence (Mueller et al., 2010). Socioeconomic status (SES) is also associated with executive function. In addition, the development of executive function is associated with SES, suggesting that adolescents in low SES homes and neighborhoods may experience greater challenges in developing the cognitive control capacities needed for good decision making (Lawson, Hook, & Farah, 2018). A cross-sectional study of adolescents and emerging adults age 9 to 25 showed an inverse association of SES and executive function for individuals of all ethnicities (Last, Lawson, Breiner, Steinberg, & Farah, 2018). Adolescents from high-income families show greater activation of the prefrontal cortex during working memory tasks than those from low-income families, and prefrontal activity better predicted math achievement in high-income adolescents (Finn et al., 2017). Contextual factors can also buffer the negative effects of low SES. For example, low SES adolescents who perceive greater academic support at school show better performance on executive function tasks, specifically inhibition, than their peers who perceive less support (Piccolo, Merz, & Noble, 2018).

Processing Speed

One important way in which adolescents' thinking improves is that it gets quicker (Kail, 2008). Older adolescents are able to process information to solve problems more quickly than younger adolescents, who are quicker than children. Processing speed reaches adult levels in middle to late adolescence, as early as 15 (Coyle, Pillow, Snyder, & Kochunov, 2011). Part of the gains in speed are biological in origin. Changes in the brain underlie many improvements in information processing capacities. As the structure of the prefrontal cortex changes, with decreases in gray matter and increases in white matter, cognition becomes markedly more efficient (Asato, Terwilliger, Woo, & Luna, 2010). Myelination underlies improvements in processing speed during childhood and adolescence, permitting quicker physical and cognitive responses (Silveri, Tzilos, & Yurgelun-Todd, 2008). Compared to children, not only do adolescents show faster reaction speed in gym class, but they are quicker at connecting ideas, making arguments, and drawing conclusions. Processing speed increases and reaches adult levels at about age 15 and is associated with advances in working memory and cognition, especially reasoning (Coyle et al., 2011).

Advances in processing speed are also due to improvements in working memory and long-term memory. **Automaticity** is the amount of cognitive effort required to process the information; as processes become automatic, they require fewer resources and become quicker (Servant, Cassey, Woodman, & Logan, 2018). Automaticity is a function of experience. Adolescents become more efficient problem solvers as they get better at understanding how their mind works, or metacognition.

Metacognition

Not only are adolescents better at thinking than children, they are more aware of their own thought process. Adolescents become capable of thinking about ideas and the nature of thinking itself, metacognition (Cowan et al., 2010; Gaillard et al., 2011; Murty et al., 2016). Metacognition refers to knowledge of how the mind works and the ability to control the mind. One study of adolescents and adults found that metacognitive ability develops dramatically between ages 11 and 17 (Weil et al., 2013). As metacognition develops, adolescents become better able to think about how their mind works—how they take in, manipulate, and store information (Ardila, 2013; van der Stel & Veenman, 2014). They can monitor their own thinking. They are better able to understand how they learn and remember and to choose and deploy strategies that enhance the representation, storage, and retrieval of information.

Eleventh-grader Jolinda explains: "Studying for a biology exam is really different than studying for a history exam. In biology, I visualize the material, but when I study for history, I make up stories to help me remember it all." Jolinda illustrates the metacognitive skills that emerge in adolescence because she is able to evaluate her understanding, and she adjusts her strategies to the content by applying her understanding of how she learns best. Adolescents' abilities to apply metacognition in real-world settings continue to develop into late adolescence and early adulthood.

The ability to think about one's thinking enables adolescents to reason about problems in new ways. By considering their own cognitive strategies and experimenting and reflecting on their experiences, adolescents begin to appreciate logical reasoning, which they increasingly apply to everyday situations (Ardila, 2013; van der Stel & Veenman, 2014). As adolescents become able to reason about reasoning, they show improvements in manipulating abstract ideas and engaging in the hypothetical-deductive thinking that is characteristic of scientific reasoning (Kuhn, 2013). The development of metacognition proficiency is associated with gains in academic performance (van der Stel & Veenman, 2014).

Social Cognition

Advances in reasoning and metacognition lead adolescents to understand themselves and others in more complex ways. Their growing appreciation for other people's perspectives leads to more mature relationships with parents and peers.

Perspective Taking

Although young children are largely unable to take another person's perspective, perspective taking ability improves alongside cognitive and social development. By adolescence, young people have lots of social experience and their reasoning skills make them much better able to understand different viewpoints, which has implications for social relationships (Carpendale & Lewis, 2015). According to Robert Selman (1980), **social perspective taking** ability follows a developmental path from extreme egocentrism in early childhood to mature perspective taking ability in late adolescence.

Similar to Piaget's ideas about cognition, Selman posed that individuals progress through several stages of social perspective taking. Young children are often unable to separate their own perspective from those of others, believing that others hold their views. With advances in cognitive and social development, 6- to 8-year-old children recognize that others have different thoughts but they have difficulty comparing others' perspectives with their own. As children approach adolescence (age 8–10), they appreciate that others have different perspectives and taking others' points of view offers a valuable window to interpreting their behavior. It is not until early adolescence (age 10–12) that individuals develop the abstract thinking needed to realize that other people can take their perspective. That is, adolescents become capable of **mutual perspective taking,** understanding that they take other people's points of view at the same time as others attempt to take their own point of view. Now adolescents can consider how their behavior appears to others (take a third person's perspective) and modify their behavior accordingly. By middle adolescence (age 12–15), **societal perspective taking** emerges and adolescents recognize that the social environment, including the larger society, influences people's perspectives and beliefs. Research has suggested that perspective taking ability develops from childhood into adolescence, but may not closely follow the age-based timeline advocated by Selman. For example, Selman (1980) found that mutual perspective taking may emerge as early as 11 or as late as 20. Likewise, other research suggests that the ability to use another's perspective in communication and decision making continues to develop in late adolescence (Nilsen & Bacso, 2017).

Perspective taking ability is linked with working memory (Nilsen & Bacso, 2017). Developmental improvements in cognitive control influence social cognitive processing. For example, although attending to social cues is largely automatic, attending to another person's perspective when it differs from one's own requires inhibiting our own perspective, which is an effortful process that requires the cognitive control resources in working memory (Kilford, Garrett, & Blakemore, 2016). This is supported by research demonstrating that adolescents and adults were slower at tasks requiring perspective taking under conditions that required high levels of working memory (such as simultaneously remembering three 2-digit numbers) than when under low cognitive load (such as remembering one 3-digit number), suggesting that taking another's perspective is cognitively demanding (Mills, Dumontheil, Speekenbrink, & Blakemore, 2015). Another study of 9- to 29-year-olds found that inhibitory control ability partly explained errors on a perspective taking task even after age was taken into account, suggesting that working memory contributes to perspective taking abilities (Kilford et al., 2016).

Advances in social perspective taking permit adolescents to better understand others and also to grasp how they are perceived by others. Perspective taking ability predicts peer relations, friendship, and popularity (Nilsen & Bacso, 2017). Yet not all adolescents apply their perspective taking skills (Flannery & Smith, 2017). Similar to abstract thought, perspective taking abilities and the ability to apply their understanding emerges gradually. Teenagers are prone to errors in reasoning and lapses in judgment, as evidenced by the emergence of adolescent egocentrism.

Adolescent Egocentrism

As adolescents get better at reasoning and metacognition, they often direct their abstract thinking abilities toward themselves. Although social perspective taking improves, it often develops slowly and even in a piecemeal fashion. When it comes to considering themselves, adolescents often have difficulty separating their own and others' perspectives. That is, adolescents find it difficult to distinguish their view of what others think of them from reality, what others actually think about them. They show adolescent egocentrism, a perspective taking error that is manifested in two phenomena: the **imaginary audience** and the **personal fable** (Elkind & Bowen, 1979).

The imaginary audience is experienced as self-consciousness, feeling as if all eyes are on them. Adolescents misdirect their own preoccupation about themselves toward others and assume that they are the focus of others' attention (Elkind & Bowen, 1979). In this way, the imaginary audience is an error in perspective taking. The imaginary audience fuels adolescents' concerns with their appearance and can make the slightest criticism sting painfully, as teens are convinced that all eyes are on them. The imaginary audience contributes to the heightened self-consciousness characteristic of adolescence (Alberts, Elkind, & Ginsberg, 2007).

Adolescents' preoccupation with themselves also leads them to believe that they are special, unique, and invulnerable—a belief known as the personal fable (Elkind & Bowen, 1979). They believe that their emotions, the highs of happiness and depths of despair that they feel, are different from and more intense than other people's emotions and that others simply do not understand. The invulnerability aspect of the personal fable may predispose adolescents to seek risks and may lead them to believe that they are immune to the negative consequences of such risky activities as drug use, delinquency, and unsafe sex (Alberts et al., 2007).

Both the imaginary audience and the personal fable are thought to increase in early adolescence, peak in middle adolescence, and decline in late adolescence (Elkind & Bowen, 1979). Recent research suggests that adolescent egocentrism may persist into late adolescence and beyond (Schwartz, Maynard, & Uzelac, 2008). One study examined adolescents in 11 countries in Africa, Asia, Europe, and the Americas and found that sensation seeking increased in preadolescence, peaked at around age 19, and declined thereafter (Steinberg et al., 2018). Indeed, in one recent study, adolescents aged 13–16 showed similar levels of egocentrism as adults; they were just as likely as adults to believe that others could tell when they were lying and when they were nervous (Rai, Mitchell, Kadar, & Mackenzie, 2016). Moreover, for many adolescents (and adults), the audience is not imaginary. When posting to social media, many adolescents painstakingly consider their audience and play to them by sharing content to appear interesting, well liked, and attractive (Yau & Reich, 2018).

Decision Making

Advances in cognition permit adolescents to engage in more sophisticated thinking than ever before and approach decision making in more sophisticated ways than children. Under laboratory conditions, adolescents are capable of demonstrating rational decision making that is in line with their goals and is comparable to that of adults (Reyna & Rivers, 2008). For example, comparisons of adolescents and adults' decisions on hypothetical dilemmas—such as whether to engage in substance use, have surgery, have sex, or drink and drive—show that adolescents and adults generate similar consequences to each decision option, spontaneously mention similar risks and benefits of each option, and rate the harmfulness of risks in similar ways (Furby & Beyth-Marom, 1992; Halpern-Felsher & Cauffman, 2001; Reyna & Farley, 2006). However, laboratory studies of decision making usually present adolescents with hypothetical dilemmas which are very different from the everyday decisions they face.

Everyday decisions have personal relevance, require quick thinking, are emotional, and often are made in the presence and influence of others. Recall the developmental mismatch described by the dual-systems model in Chapter 13. Adolescents often feel strong emotions and impulses that they may be unable to regulate, due to the still-immature condition of their prefrontal cortex (Cohen & Casey, 2017). Therefore, laboratory studies of decision making are less useful in understanding how young people compare with adults when they must make choices that are important or occur in stressful situations in which they must rely on experience, knowledge, and intuition (Steinberg, 2013). Adolescents tend to reason more poorly than adults when faced with unfamiliar, emotionally charged situations, spur-of-the moment decisions, pressures to conform, poor self-control, and risk and benefit estimates that favor good short-term and bad long-term outcomes (Albert, Chein, & Steinberg, 2013; Breiner et al., 2018). Adolescents are susceptible to risk taking in situations of heightened emotional arousal (Figner, Mackinlay, Wilkening, & Weber, 2009; Mills et al., 2014a).

Adolescents are more approach oriented to positive consequences and less responsive to negative consequences than are adults (Cauffman et al., 2010; Javadi, Schmidt, & Smolka, 2014). We have seen that adolescents are neurologically more sensitive to rewards than adults. Adolescents tend to place more importance on the potential benefits of decisions (e.g., social status, pleasure) than on the potential costs or risks (e.g., physical harm, short- and long-term health issues) (Javadi et al., 2014; Shulman & Cauffman, 2013). In the presence of rewards, adolescents show heightened activity in the brain systems that support reward processing and reduced activity in the areas responsible for inhibitory control, compared with adults (Paulsen, Hallquist, Geier, & Luna, 2014; Smith, Steinberg, Strang, & Chein, 2015). Risky activity is thought to decline in late adolescence in part because of increases in adolescents' self-regulatory capacities and their capacities for long-term planning that accompany maturation of the frontal cortex (Albert et al., 2013; Casey, 2015). These research findings have important applied policy value, as discussed in the Applying Developmental Science feature.

APPLYING DEVELOPMENTAL SCIENCE

Legal Implications of Adolescent Decision Making

Neurological and psychological factors play a prominent role in adolescent decision making and behavior, suggesting that courts should treat adolescents differently than adults.
AP Photo/W.A. Bridges Jr.

Developmental scientists' work is often called upon to inform legal issues and influence social policy, as illustrated by a series of Supreme Court cases that examined whether minors should be subject to the same punishments as adults.

The landmark case *Roper v. Simmons*, decided by the Supreme Court in 2005, examined whether adolescents should be sentenced to the death penalty. At the time, 21 states permitted the death penalty for adolescents under the age of 18, and most of them permitted it at the age of 16 (Steinberg & Scott, 2003). As the case moved to the Supreme Court, developmental scientists collaborated with the American Psychological Association to submit an amicus curiae ("friend of the court") brief to inform the justices about developmental research relevant to the case specifically, research on adolescent judgment and decision making.

The brief explained that adolescents' developmental immaturity makes them less culpable for crimes and justifies a more lenient punishment than that of adults—but still holds that they are actors who retain responsibility for the crime (Cauffman & Steinberg, 2012; Steinberg & Scott, 2003).

Research conducted over the past 15 years has supported the brief's conclusion. For example, neurological research suggests that adolescents tend to feel strong emotions and impulses that they may have difficulty controlling (Steinberg, 2017). Adolescents, especially males, react impulsively to threat cues more than do adults or children, even when instructed not to respond (Dreyfuss et al., 2014).

In addition to neurological development, psychosocial development—specifically, susceptibility to peer influence and future orientation—plays a prominent role in adolescent decision making and behavior (Albert et al., 2013). When adolescents make decisions in response to hypothetical dilemmas in which they must choose between engaging in an antisocial behavior suggested by friends and a prosocial one, their choices suggest that susceptibility to peer influence increases between childhood and early adolescence, peaking around age 14 and declining slowly during high school (Allen & Antonishak, 2008). Not only are adolescents' decisions more likely to be influenced by peers, but simply thinking about peer evaluation increases risky behavior. Moreover, the presence of peers can increase risky behavior

(Continued)

(Continued)

even when the probability of a negative outcome is high (Centifanti, Modecki, MacLellan, & Gowling, 2016; Smith, Rosenbaum, Botdorf, Steinberg, & Chein, 2018). Adolescents also have a poor sense of future orientation, envisioning themselves in the future, which is associated with participation in risky activities (Chen & Vazsonyi, 2013). Difficulty envisioning the future coupled with the influence of strong emotions, susceptibility to peers, and poor self-control can compromise adolescents' decision-making ability.

Adolescents and adults weigh the costs and benefits involved in making decisions differently. To the extent that teens are less psychosocially mature than adults, their decisions are likely to be inferior to those of adults, even if they score similarly to adults on cognitive measures (Cauffman & Steinberg, 2012; Modecki, 2014). Therefore, the amicus curiae brief prepared for *Roper v. Simmons* concluded that adolescents' developmental immaturity makes them less culpable for crimes and justifies a more lenient punishment than that for adults—but still holds that they are actors who retain responsibility for the crime (Cauffman & Steinberg, 2012; Steinberg, 2017).

In the case of *Roper v. Simmons*, the Supreme Court ruled against capital punishment for minors on the basis of their lack of maturity and susceptibility to peer influence. In 2010 and 2012, based on a similar rationale, in *Florida v. Graham, Miller v. Alabama*, and *Jackson v. Hobbs*, the Supreme Court ruled that minors cannot be sentenced to life in prison without parole.

What Do You Think?

1. To what degree do you think adolescents should be culpable for criminal offenses they commit? Do you agree with the Supreme Court decisions against the death penalty or life in prison without parole for adolescents? Why or why not?
2. Do you advocate using developmental science research to make policy decisions such as this? Why or why not? ●

THINKING IN CONTEXT 14.1

1. Recall from Chapter 1 that domains of development interact. How might cognitive development in adolescence influence physical and socioemotional functioning? How might aspects of cognition be influenced by physical and socioemotional development?
2. Consider a parent's perspective. Provide examples of how advances in information processing abilities might influence parent–adolescent interactions. What challenges and rewards might these pose for parents?
3. Uncle Bob wisecracks, "If adolescents are so smart, why do they do such dumb things?" How would you respond to Bob, considering the research on adolescent cognition?

ADOLESCENT MORAL DEVELOPMENT

Adolescents' newfound abilities for abstract reasoning lead them to approach problems in different ways, consider multiple perspectives, and delight in the process of thinking itself. It is these cognitive advances that enable adolescents to demonstrate the final and most sophisticated form of reasoning described in Lawrence Kohlberg's theory of moral reasoning: **postconventional moral reasoning.**

Postconventional Moral Reasoning

Much of Kohlberg's theory was based on longitudinal research with a group of boys, ages 10, 13, and 16, who were periodically interviewed over 3 decades (Kohlberg, 1969). Kohlberg discovered that the boys' reasoning progressed through sequential stages and in a predictable order. Kohlberg measured moral reasoning by presenting individuals with hypothetical dilemmas such as the following:

> Near death, a woman with cancer learns of a drug that may save her. The woman's husband, Heinz, approaches the druggist who created the drug, but the druggist refuses to sell the drug for anything less than $2,000. After borrowing from everyone he knows, Heinz has only scraped together $1,000. Heinz asks the druggist to let him have the drug for $1,000 and he will pay him the rest later. The druggist says that it is his right to make money from the drug he developed and refuses to sell it to Heinz. Desperate for the drug,

Heinz breaks into the druggist's store and steals the drug. Should Heinz have done that? Why or why not? (Kohlberg, 1969)

The Heinz dilemma is the most popular example of the hypothetical conflicts that Kohlberg used to study moral development. These problems examine how people make decisions when fairness and people's rights are pitted against obedience to authority and law. Participants' explanations of how they arrived at their decisions reveal developmental shifts through three broad levels of reasoning that correspond to cognitive development.

Recall that young children reason at the preconventional level. Their decisions are influenced by self-interest, the desire to gain rewards and avoid punishments. School-age children's moral decisions tend to be socially driven. Conventional moral reasoning entails internalizing the norms and standards of authority figures, in a desire to be accepted (Stage 3) and to maintain social order (Stage 4).

Not until adolescence, according to Kohlberg, do people become capable of demonstrating the most advanced moral thinking, postconventional moral reasoning, which entails autonomous decision making from moral principles that value respect for individual rights above all else. Postconventional moral thinkers recognize that their self-chosen principles of fairness and justice may sometimes conflict with the law. At Stage 5, Social Contract Orientation, individuals view laws and rules as flexible and part of the social contract or agreement meant to further human interests. Laws and rules are to be followed as they bring good to people, but laws can be changed if they are inconsistent with the needs and rights of the majority. Sometimes, if laws are unjust—if they harm more people than they protect—they can be broken. Stage 6, Universal Ethical Principles, represents the most advanced moral reasoning, defined by abstract ethical principles that are universal, or valid for all people regardless of law, such as equality and respect for human dignity.

A great deal of research has confirmed that individuals proceed through the first four stages of moral reasoning in a slow, gradual, and predictable fashion (Boom, Wouters, & Keller, 2007; Dawson, 2002). Specifically, reasoning at the preconventional level decreases by early adolescence. Conventional reasoning, Stage 3, increases through middle adolescence, and Stage 4 reasoning increases in middle to late adolescence and becomes typical of most individuals by early adulthood. Research suggests that few people advance beyond Stage 4 moral reasoning. Postconventional reasoning is rare and appears as Stage 5 reasoning (Kohlberg, Levine, & Hewer, 1983). The existence of Stage 6, the hypothesized, most advanced type of moral reasoning, is supported only by case-based anecdotal evidence. Kohlberg himself questioned the validity of Stage 6, dropped it from the stage scheme, but later included Stage 6 again because it represented an end goal state to which human development strives (Kohlberg & Ryncarz, 1990).

Kohlberg's theory of moral reasoning has led to 4 decades of research. Most of the research conducted has examined the role of social interaction in promoting development, the role of gender and culture, and the link between reasoning and behavior.

Social Interaction and Moral Reasoning

Moral development occurs within parent, peer, and school contexts and is influenced by social development. Social interactions offer important opportunities for the development of moral reasoning. High-quality parent–child relationships predict advanced moral reasoning (Malti & Latzko, 2010). Reasoning advances when adolescents have opportunities to engage in discussions that are characterized by mutual perspective taking. Engaging adolescents in discussion about personal experiences, local issues, and media events—while presenting alternative points of view and asking questions—advances reasoning. For example, a parent might ask, "Why do you think he did that? Was there something else that he could have done? How do you think other people interpret his actions?" Issue-focused discussions that present adolescents with reasoning that is slightly more advanced than their own prompts them to compare their reasoning with the new reasoning and often internalize the new reasoning, advancing their moral reasoning to a new level.

Parents who engage their children in discussion, listen with sensitivity, ask for children's input, praise them, engage them with questioning, and use humor promote the development of moral reasoning (Carlo et al., 2011). Likewise, interactions with peers in which adolescents confront one another with differing perspectives and engage each other with in-depth discussions promote the development of moral reasoning (Power, Higgins, & Kohlberg, 1989). Adolescents who report having more close friendships in which they engage in deep conversations tend to show more advanced moral reasoning than do teens who have little social contact (Schonert-Reichl, 1999). They also report feeling positive emotions when they make unselfish moral decisions (Malti, Keller, & Buchmann, 2013). Moral reasoning is inherently social. Some have argued, however, that the social basis of morality means that men and women should reason in very different ways.

Gender and Moral Reasoning

A popular criticism of Kohlberg's theory of moral reasoning arises because his initial research was conducted with all-male samples. Early research that studied both males and females suggested gender differences in moral reasoning, with males typically showing Stage 4 reasoning, characterized by concerns about law and order, and females showing Stage 3 reasoning, characterized by concerns about maintaining relationships (Poppen, 1974). Carol Gilligan (1982) argued that Kohlberg's theory neglected a distinctively female mode of moral reasoning, a **care orientation**, which is characterized by empathy, a desire to maintain relationships, and a responsibility not to cause harm. As Gilligan explains, the care orientation contrasts with the distinctively male mode of moral reasoning, a **justice orientation**, which is based on the abstract principles of fairness and individualism captured by Kohlberg. Care and justice represent frameworks modified by experience that influence how people interpret and resolve moral problems.

Although most people are capable of raising both justice and care concerns in describing moral dilemmas, Gilligan argued that care reasoning was thought to be used predominantly by females and justice reasoning by males (Gilligan & Attanucci, 1988). In agreement with Gilligan, most researchers acknowledge that more than one mode of moral reasoning exists (Kohlberg et al., 1983) but instead argue that moral orientations are not linked with gender (Knox, Fagley, & Miller, 2004). Male and female adolescents and adults display similar reasoning that combines concerns of justice (e.g., being fair) with those of care (e.g., being supportive and helpful), and when there are sex differences, they are very small (Jaffee & Hyde, 2000; Weisz & Black, 2002). The most mature forms of moral reasoning incorporate both justice and care concerns.

Culture and Moral Reasoning

Cross-cultural studies of Kohlberg's theory show that the sequence appears in all cultures but that people in non-Western cultures rarely score above Stage 3 (Gibbs, Basinger, Grime, & Snarey, 2007). Like cognitive capacities, morality and appropriate responses to ethical dilemmas are defined by each society and its cultural perspectives. Whereas Western cultures tend to emphasize the rights of the individual (justice-based reasoning), non-Western cultures tend to value collectivism, focusing on human interdependence (care-based reasoning). Individuals in collectivist cultures tend to define moral dilemmas in terms of the responsibility to the entire community rather than simply to the individual (Miller, 2018). Such emphasis on the needs of others is characteristic of Stage 3 in Kohlberg's scheme. However, because moral values are relative to the cultural context, Stage 3 reasoning is an advanced form of reasoning in collectivist cultures, because it embodies what is most valued in these cultures, concepts such as interdependence and relationships.

Despite cross-cultural differences, individuals in many cultures show similarities in reasoning. For example, one study examined Chinese and Canadian 12- to 19-year-old adolescents' views of the fairness of various forms of democratic and nondemocratic government (Helwig, Arnold, Tan, & Boyd, 2007). Adolescents from both China and Canada preferred democratic forms of government and appealed to fundamental democratic justice principles such as representation, voice, and majority rule to support their judgments, suggesting that adolescents in collectivist cultures are able to reason with justice principles in particular contexts. In addition, similar age-related patterns in judgments and reasoning were found across cultures and across diverse regions within China. It appears that the development of moral reasoning progresses in a similar pattern across cultures. People of different cultures are able to reason using both care and justice orientations even though cultures tend to vary in the weight they assign moral orientations, emphasizing one over another.

Moral Reasoning and Behavior

Moral reasoning explains how people think about issues of justice, but reasoning is only moderately related to behavior (Colby & Damon, 1992). People often behave in ways they know they should not. For example, an adolescent who explains that stealing and cheating are wrong may slip a pack of gum into her pocket and leave a store without paying or may peek at a classmate's paper during an exam. Like other decisions, ethical conflicts experienced in real life are complex, accompanied by intense emotions, social obligations, and practical considerations, which lead people to act in ways that contradict their judgments (Walker, 2004).

With advances in moral reasoning, adolescents often begin to coordinate moral, conventional, and personal concepts and are more likely to act in ways that are in line with their beliefs (Smetana et al., 2013). For example, adolescents who demonstrate higher levels of moral reasoning are more likely to share with and help others and are less likely to engage in antisocial behaviors such as cheating, aggression, or delinquency (Brugman, 2010;

Adolescents sometimes behave in ways they know they shouldn't.
©iStockphoto.com/FatCamera

Adolescents who demonstrate higher levels of moral reasoning are more likely to act prosocially by sharing, helping others, and engaging in service.
©iStockphoto.com/mixetto

Comunian & Gielen, 2000). Moral reasoning is associated with volunteerism, as discussed in the Lives in Context feature. Although adolescents who show low levels of moral reasoning are thought to be at greater risk for delinquency, findings are mixed in this area. Some studies find that low levels of reasoning predict delinquency, and others show no relationship (Leenders & Brugman, 2005; Tarry & Emler, 2007). Perhaps the degree to which moral reasoning is associated with behavior varies with whether adolescents perceive the behavior as an issue regarding morality, social convention, or personal choice (Berkowitz & Begun, 1994; Brugman, 2010). Adolescents, particularly early adolescents, tend to overwhelmingly label behaviors as personal issues. Adolescents' moral development influences behaviors they label as moral decisions but not those viewed as social conventions or personal issues. Adolescents who engage in delinquency are more likely than other adolescents to view delinquent behaviors as issues of social convention or personal choice rather than moral issues, suggesting that their level of moral maturity may not influence on their delinquent behavior because they do not label the behavior as entailing a moral decision (Kuther & Higgins-D'Alessandro, 2000; Leenders & Brugman, 2005). A variety of factors influence the development of moral reasoning and how adolescents view and behave in their world.

LIVES IN CONTEXT: COMMUNITY CONTEXT

Volunteer Work and Social Responsibility

In adolescence, moral development often includes a sense of social responsibility, a personal commitment to contribute to community and society (Wray-Lake & Syvertsen, 2011). Social responsibility values predict a variety of prosocial civic behaviors such as volunteering, voting, political activism, and environmental conservation (Caprara, Schwartz, Capanna, Vecchione, & Barbaranelli, 2006; Hart, Donnelly, Youniss, & Atkins, 2007; Pratt, Hunsberger, Pancer, & Alisat, 2003).

How does social responsibility develop? Surprisingly, prosocial behavior, voluntarily helping others, tends to plateau or even dip from late childhood into middle adolescence (Eisenberg et al., 2005; Smetana et al., 2009). The physical and cognitive transitions of adolescence draw adolescents' attention to themselves, and most adolescents tend to prioritize personal issues over social and moral concerns (Wang & Dishion, 2012). For example, a 3-year study following elementary, middle, and high school students ages 9 to 18 found that social responsibility decreased from ages 9 to 16 before leveling off in later adolescence (Wray-Lake, Syvertsen, & Flanagan, 2016). Connections to family, peers, school, and community contributed dynamically to advances in social responsibility. Parents with an authoritative style often model social responsibility values, and their behavior influences children and adolescents. Adolescents who participate in community service tend to have parents who volunteer and talk about volunteering and giving (Ottoni-Wilhelm, Estell, & Perdue, 2014). When parents recruit their children into community service, it transmits prosocial values, including the meaning of service

(Continued)

(Continued)

and its effect on others (White & Mistry, 2016). Parental encouragement and modeling of volunteer work predict sympathy, feeling compassion for another person, and adolescents' volunteer work (McGinley, Lipperman-Kreda, Byrnes, & Carlo, 2010; van Goethem, van Hoof, van Aken, Orobio de Castro, & Raaijmakers, 2014).

Volunteerism itself predicts social responsibility. When youth volunteer and engage in service learning, they demonstrate increases in prosocial attitudes toward others, as well as social responsibility and civic values (Conway, Amel, & Gerwien, 2009; van Goethem et al., 2014). Volunteerism and social responsibility values interact. Community service offers adolescents opportunities to better understand themselves as they interact with a heterogeneous group of people in their community who likely differ from them in age, ethnicity, religion, or social class (Flanagan, Kim, Collura, & Kopish, 2015; Yates & Youniss, 1996). Community service holds the potential to enhance sensitivity toward others. Compared to their nonvolunteer peers, early adolescents who do community volunteer work are more likely to see similarities between themselves and disadvantaged groups, less likely to stereotype outgroups, and more likely to believe that people are capable of change (Flanagan et al., 2015; Karafantis & Levy, 2004). In addition, volunteering during adolescence predicts voting, volunteering, and joining community organizations in adulthood (Hart et al., 2007; McFarland & Thomas, 2006).

What Do You Think?

1. What are some of the potential barriers to engaging in volunteer work during adolescence? How can adolescents overcome those barriers?
2. Do you engage in volunteer work? What does it mean to you? ●

THINKING IN CONTEXT 14.2

1. How might contextual factors influence moral reasoning? For example, consider whether socioeconomic status in the home and community influences the development of moral reasoning. Do race, ethnicity, and culture matter? Why or why not?
2. From Kohlberg's perspective, can morality be taught? Why or why not? Do you think it can be taught? Why or why not?

SCHOOLS AND ACADEMIC FUNCTIONING IN ADOLESCENCE

Apart from the home context, school is the most relevant and immediate context in which adolescents live. Most adolescents transition from an elementary school to a middle school (typically, sixth, seventh, and eighth grades) or junior high school (seventh, eighth, and ninth grades) and then to a high school (ninth through twelfth grades).

Transition to Junior High or Middle School and High School

The structure of schools in the United States has changed dramatically since the mid-20th century. In past generations, students made only one school transition: from elementary school (kindergarten to Grade 8) to high school (Grades 9–12). Today, students make more school changes, or transitions, than ever before. Junior high schools, comprising seventh-, eighth-, and ninth-grade students, were created in the 1960s and were modeled after high schools, serving as mini-high schools. In the late 1970s and 1980s, educators began to recognize that young adolescents have different educational needs than middle and older adolescents, and junior high schools began to be converted and organized into middle schools of Grades 5 or 6 through 8 or 9 (Byrnes & Ruby, 2007). Middle schools are designed to provide more flexibility and autonomy than elementary schools while encouraging strong ties to adults, such as teachers and parents, as well as offering active learning that takes advantage of and stimulates young adolescents' emerging capacities for abstract reasoning (National Middle School Association, 2003).

Change, although often exciting, can cause stress to individuals of all ages. Many students find the transition to a new school, whether middle school or high school, a challenge. Academic motivation and achievement often suffer during school transitions (Booth & Gerard, 2014; Felmlee, McMillan, Inara Rodis, & Osgood, 2018). Many students may feel more lonely and anxious, and they may report depressive symptoms (Benner, Boyle, & Bakhtiari, 2017; Coelho, Marchante, & Jimerson, 2017). For most students, these adjustment difficulties are temporary, and their achievement recovers within 1 to 2 years as they adapt to their new schools (Crosnoe & Benner, 2015). However, students who perceive the school transition as more stressful tend to show greater drops in motivation and academic achievement and less connectedness to school that persists well beyond the school transition (Goldstein, Boxer, & Rudolph, 2015).

School transitions tend to coincide with many developmental and contextual changes. Many young people experience puberty during the transition to middle school. Changing thought capacities, self-perceptions, and relationships as well as new responsibilities and opportunities for independence pose challenges. As friendships become more important, school transitions can disrupt them by dividing friends into different schools. All of these simultaneous changes mean that many adolescents experience school transitions as stressful.

The school environment, teachers, and standards change with each transition. With each transition, adolescents must meet more stringent academic standards, and evaluation becomes more frequent and formal than in elementary school. At the same time, many students feel that they receive less support from teachers (Mueller & Anderman, 2010). Students commonly report feeling less connected to middle school teachers than elementary school teachers and view their middle school teachers as less friendly, supportive, and fair (Way, Reddy, & Rhodes, 2007). High school students often report that they receive less personal attention from teachers, more class lectures, fewer hands-on demonstration activities, and fewer opportunities to participate in class discussions and group decision making than they did in middle school (Gentle-Genitty, 2009; Seidman, Aber, & French, 2004). At the same time, teachers' sense of efficacy, their belief in their abilities as teachers, declines with each grade into secondary school (Eccles & Roeser, 2015). Teachers' sense of competence predicts high expectations for students, which in turn predicts student success. This decline is greater for teachers who educate high proportions of poor children and children of color (Cooper, Kurtz-Costes, & Rowley, 2010), adding to the challenges that at-risk students face. As a result, middle school classrooms tend to be characterized by a greater emphasis on teacher control and offer fewer opportunities for student decision making and autonomy (Eccles & Roeser, 2015).

According to researcher Jacqueline Eccles, negative effects of school transitions occur when there is little **stage–environment fit.** That is, adolescents experience difficulties when there is a poor match between their developmental needs and what the school environment affords in its organization and characteristics (Eccles & Roeser, 2011). Teachers become more stringent, less personal, and more directive at the same time as young people value independence. Adolescents need more guidance and assistance with academic, social, and mental health issues just as teachers report feeling less responsibility for students' problems. The mismatch of adolescents' changing developmental needs and school resources contributes to declines in academic performance, motivation, and overall functioning (Booth & Gerard, 2014). Vulnerable students, such as those from low-income families or those who require special education services, tend to show a larger interruption in academic achievement (Akos, Rose, & Orthner, 2014).

Some adolescents face greater risks with school transitions than others. Changes in school demographics, particularly a mismatch between the ethnic composition of elementary and middle school, or middle and high school, can pose challenges to adolescents' adjustment (Douglass, Yip, & Shelton, 2014). One study of over 900 entering high school students found that students who experienced more ethnic incongruence from middle to high school, a mismatch in demographics, reported declining feelings of connectedness to school over time and increasing worries about their academic success (Benner & Graham, 2009). Students who moved to high schools with fewer students who were ethnically similar to themselves were most likely to experience a disconnect, as were African American male students. This is of particular concern because African American adolescents tend to experience more risk factors to academic achievement, have more difficulties in school transitions, and are more likely to fall behind during school transitions than adolescents of other ethnicities (Burchinal, Roberts, Zeisel, Hennon, & Hooper, 2006). Similarly, Latino students tend to be more sensitive to changes in the school climate and experience school transitions as more challenging than do non-Hispanic White students (Espinoza & Juvonen, 2011). Recent research suggests that students of all ethnicities—African American, Latino, Asian, and White adolescents—fare best in diverse schools with ethnic groups of relatively equal size (Juvonen, Kogachi, & Graham, 2018). Students in diverse schools reported feeling safer, less victimized, and less lonely; perceived teachers as more fair; and reported more favorable attitudes toward students of other ethnicities.

The best student outcomes occur when schools closely match adolescents' developmental needs. Small, tight-knit middle schools may reduce the alienation that some students experience during the middle school transition (Crosnoe & Benner, 2015). Small schools may also foster strong teacher–student relationships through more opportunities for teachers to interact with a smaller student base. Close relationships may help teachers feel comfortable providing opportunities for adolescents to have autonomy in classroom interactions and assignments while providing strong support. Adolescents who report high levels of teacher support and feel connected to their schools tend to show better academic achievement and better emotional health, including lower rates of depressive and anxiety symptoms (Kidger, Araya, Donovan, & Gunnell, 2012).

Adolescents' success in navigating school transitions is also influenced by their experiences outside of school. Adolescents are most vulnerable to the negative effects of school transitions when they lack the social and emotional resources to cope with multiple stressors. Young people who report feeling supported by their families and having many friends are less bothered by day-to-day stressors and experience school transitions with few problems (Kingery, Erdley, & Marshall, 2011; Rueger, Chen, Jenkins, & Choe, 2014).

Parenting and Academic Competence

Close parent–adolescent relationships serve as an important buffer to academic motivation and performance from childhood through adolescence for young people at all socioeconomic levels (Dotterer, Lowe, & McHale, 2014). As in other areas of development, both the overly harsh parenting characterized by the authoritarian parenting style and the lax, permissive parenting style are associated with poor academic performance. Likewise, adolescents reared by uninvolved parents tend to show the poorest school grades (Gonzalez & Wolters, 2006; Heaven & Ciarrochi, 2008). Authoritative parenting, in contrast, is associated with academic achievement in adolescents around the world, including Argentina, Australia, Canada, China, Hong Kong, Iran, Pakistan, Scotland, and the United States (Assadi et al., 2007; Garg, Levin, Urajnik, & Kauppi, 2005; Gonzalez & Wolters, 2006; Spera, 2005).

When parents use the authoritative style, they are open to discussion, involve their adolescents in joint decision making, and firmly but fairly monitor their adolescents' behavior and set limits. This style of parenting helps adolescents feel valued, respected, and encouraged to think for themselves (Dornbusch, Ritter, Mont-Reynaud, & Chen, 1990; Spera, 2005). Adolescents are learning to regulate their emotions and behavior and to set, work toward, and achieve educational goals (Aunola & Stattin, 2000; Moilanen, Rasmussen, & Padilla-Walker, 2015). Authoritative parenting supports these developments.

Parent involvement promotes adolescents' academic achievement.
©iStockphoto.com/monkeybusinessimages

Just as in elementary school, parents can promote high academic achievement in middle and high school students by being active and involved—for example, by knowing their teens' teachers, monitoring progress, ensuring that their teens are taking challenging and appropriate classes, and expressing high expectations (Benner, 2011; Karbach, Gottschling, Spengler, Hegewald, & Spinath, 2013; Wang, Hill, & Hofkens, 2014). Parent–school involvement in eighth grade has been shown to predict tenth-grade students' grade point average regardless of socioeconomic status, previous academic achievement, and ethnicity (Keith et al., 1998). By being involved in the school, parents communicate the importance of education; they also model academic engagement and problem solving, which can help protect against dropout.

School Dropout

School dropout rates in the United States have reached historic lows, with dramatic decreases for African American and Hispanic adolescents (see Figure 14.2). Nevertheless, each year, about 6% of high school students drop out of school (National Center for Education Statistics, 2017b). Students of low socioeconomic status are at high risk of school dropout, and students of color immigrant students are particularly vulnerable.

Students with behavior and substance use problems are most at risk for school dropout, but many who drop out simply have academic problems, skip classes with increasing frequency, and disengage emotionally and behaviorally (Bowers & Sprott, 2012; Henry, Knight, & Thornberry, 2012; Wang & Fredricks, 2014). Lack of parental involvement places students at risk for school dropout—and when parents respond to poor grades with anger and punishment, this can further reduce adolescents' academic motivation and feelings of connectedness to school (Alivernini & Lucidi, 2011).

Students who are engaged and attached to school and who participate in many school-related activities are less likely to drop out than their less engaged peers (Janosz, Archambault, Morizot, & Pagani, 2008; Mahoney, 2014). Conversely, feelings of anonymity at school increase the risk of dropping out. Many of the unfavorable characteristics that students report of their high schools predict dropout: large schools, unsupportive teachers, and few

FIGURE 14.2

Percentage of Grade 10–12 Dropouts Among Persons 15 Through 24 Years Old (Event Dropout Rate), by Race/Ethnicity, October 1976 Through 2016

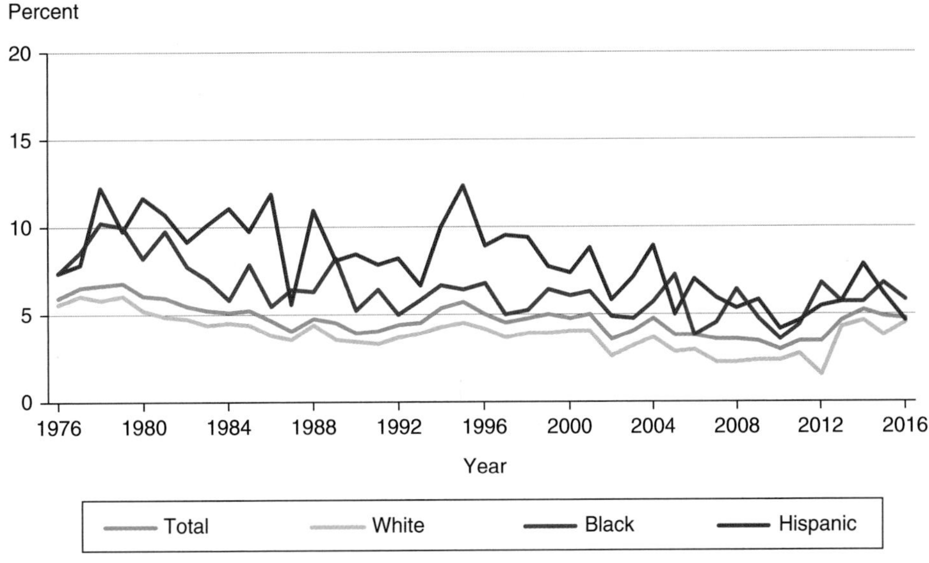

Source: National Center for Education Statistics. Retrieved from https://nces.ed.gov/programs/dropout/ind_01.asp

opportunities to form personal relationships or to speak out in class (Battin-Pearson & Newcomb, 2000; Christenson & Thurlow, 2004; Croninger & Lee, 2001; Freeman & Simonsen, 2015); poor connections with teachers and poor support for meeting academic expectations (Jia, Konold, Cornell & et al., 2016); and bullying and poor relationships with peers (Cornell, Gregory, Huang, & Fan, 2013; Frostad, Pijl, & Mjaavatn, 2014). Students who experience academic difficulties may be more vulnerable than their peers to the structural changes that are common during school transitions.

Although dropout is often the result of extended difficulties, there is heterogeneity in paths. Many students show few problems until a particularly disruptive event or situation, such as severe peer victimization, health problems, family instability, or long work hours, impairs their coping skills (Dupéré et al., 2015). For example, in a study that examined three groups of Canadian high school students—recent dropouts, matched at-risk students who remain in school, and average students—results indicated that in comparison with the two other groups, dropouts were over three times more likely to have experienced recent acute stressors, suggesting that it may be these acute stressors that place students at increased risk for dropout, over and above existing contextual risks (Dupéré et al., 2018).

As adults, high school dropouts experience higher rates of unemployment and, when hired, earn less than high school graduates throughout adulthood. Young people who have dropped out of school have the option of taking a high school equivalency test, the General Educational Development exam (GED). The GED was developed in the late 1940s to certify that returning World War II veterans who had left high school to serve in the military were ready for college or the labor market. Although passing the GED exam can signify that a young person has accumulated the knowledge entailed in earning a high school diploma, GED holders do not fare as well as regular high school graduates in the labor market, and they tend to get much less postsecondary education (Tyler & Lofstrom, 2009).

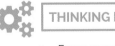

THINKING IN CONTEXT 14.3

1. From your experience and observations, what challenges do adolescents face in middle and high school? How well does the environment match adolescents' developmental needs?
2. What contextual factors might determine goodness of fit? How can we enhance the fit between adolescents' needs and school opportunities and resources?

POSTSECONDARY EDUCATION AND EMPLOYMENT

From an early age most children are asked by well-meaning adults, "What do you want to be when you grow up?" Do you remember your answer to this question? Did it change over time? Many adolescents have their first experiences with paid work during high school.

Adolescent Employment

Working at a part-time job during high school is commonplace in the United States and Canada, with over half of high school students reporting working at some point during the school year (Bachman, Johnston, & O'Malley, 2014). Labor force surveys report fewer employed adolescents (about 30%) than in prior generations, but many of the jobs held by teens are "off the books" and unrecorded (U.S. Bureau of Labor Statistics, 2015). Regardless, adolescent employment today is at its lowest level since World War II (see Figure 14.3) (Greene & Staff, 2012).

Most U.S. adolescents who work come from middle SES families and seek part-time employment as a source of spending money (Bachman, Staff, O'Malley, & Freedman-Doan, 2013). Black adolescents are less likely to work than White adolescents (McLoyd & Hallman, 2018). However, few jobs are available in the economically depressed areas where Black adolescents are likely to live.

Although both adults and adolescents tend to view working as an opportunity to develop a sense of responsibility, research does not support this view (Monahan, Lee, & Steinberg, 2011). For example, one area of responsibility that working is believed to affect is money management (i.e., a job may provide opportunities to learn how to budget, save, and spend wisely), yet most teens spend their earnings on personal expenses, such as clothes, and experience premature affluence—they get used to a luxurious standard of living before they have financial responsibilities (Bachman et al., 2013). Young adults who experienced premature affluence in their teen years may be less satisfied with their financial situation than are their peers who did not work during high school.

The effects of employment on adolescent well-being largely depend on the hours worked. About half of employed adolescents work 15 or fewer hours per week (Bachman et al., 2014). Working few hours (15 or less) appears to have little positive or negative effect on adolescents' academic or psychosocial functioning (Monahan et al., 2011). On the other

FIGURE 14.3

Employment of Adolescents and Adults in the United States, 1948–2014

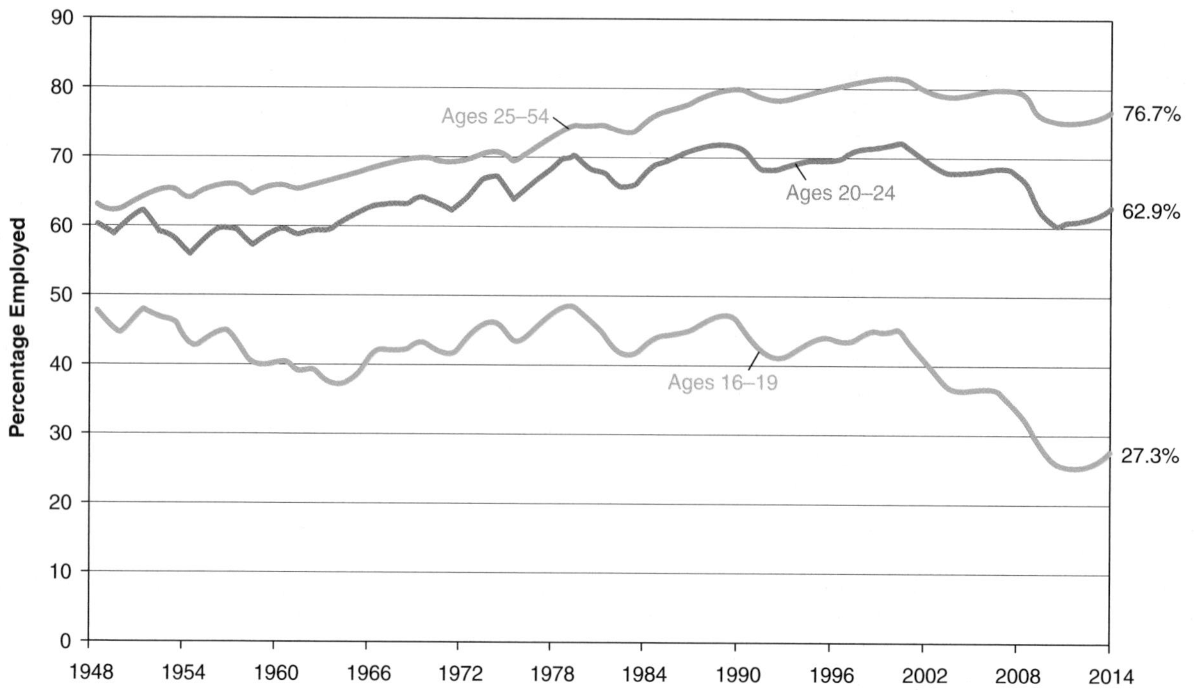

Source: Congressional Research Service (2018), with 2014 data from the U.S. Department of Labor Bureau of Labor Statistics (2014).

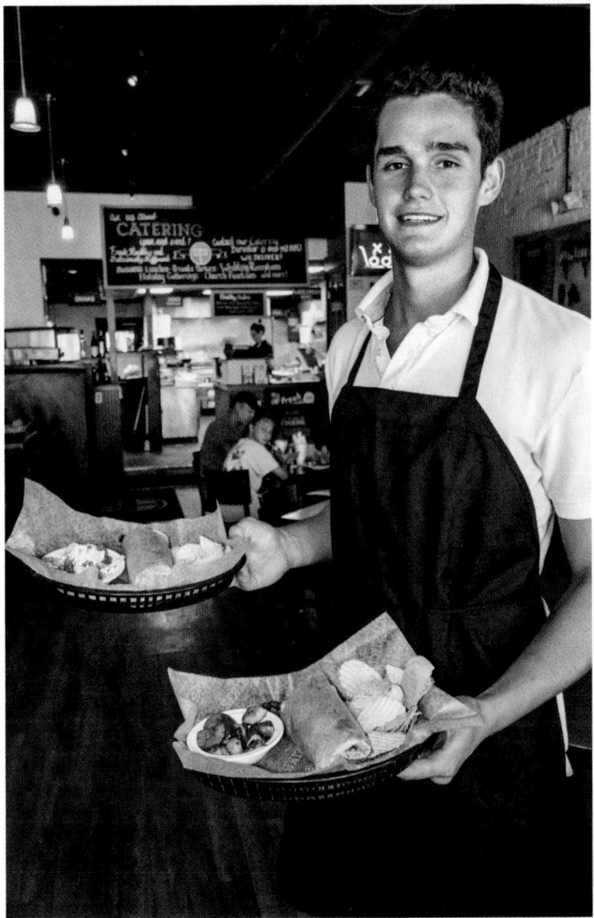

Although working more than 20 hours a week is harmful, adolescent work can be a positive experience if it entails limited hours and if it includes educational and vocational training opportunities and contact with adults.
Jeff Greenberg/Universal Images Group/Getty Images

hand, working more than 20 hours each week, common to about one-third of employed adolescents (Bachman et al., 2014), is associated with many poor outcomes, such as poor school attendance, performance, and motivation; risk of school dropout; and problem behaviors such as smoking, alcohol and substance use, early sexual activity, and delinquency (Bachman et al., 2013; Dumont, Leclerc, & McKinnon, 2009; Godley, Passetti, & White, 2006; Monahan et al., 2011; Staff, Vaneseltine, Woolnough, Silver, & Burrington, 2012). Some research suggests that the negative effects of long hours of employment are most evident for White middle-class adolescents and are associated with fewer disadvantages for Hispanic and African American adolescents from low-income families (Bachman et al., 2013). Yet other research suggests that intense adolescent employment is associated with detrimental developmental outcomes for youth regardless of neighborhood context (Kingston & Rose, 2015).

However, adolescent work can be a positive experience if it entails limited hours and if it includes educational and vocational training opportunities and contact with adults (Greene & Staff, 2012; Mortimer & Johnson, 1998). The most common jobs available to adolescents often entail repetitive simple tasks, such as microwaving meals at a fast-food restaurant (Steinberg, Fegley, & Dornbusch, 1993). Adolescent workers often have little contact with adults—their coworkers tend to be teens; supervisors tend to be not much older than they are; and customers, if the job is in food service or retail, tend to be adolescents (Greenberger & Steinberg, 1986). Work settings that emphasize vocational skills, such as answering phones as a receptionist, and in which adolescents interact with, and work alongside, adults, tend to promote positive attitudes toward work as well as academic motivation and achievement and low levels of delinquency and drug and alcohol use (Staff & Uggen, 2003).

College-Bound Youth

Attending college, at least for a time, has become a normative experience for emerging adults. In 2015, 69% of high school graduates in the United States enrolled in 2- or 4-year colleges (National Center for Education Statistics, 2017b). Students enroll in college to learn about a specific field of study (i.e., a major) and to prepare for careers, but attending college is also associated with many positive developmental outcomes.

Developmental Impact of Attending College

Adults of all ages often view their college years as highly influential in shaping their thoughts, values, and worldview (Patton, Renn, Guido-DiBrito, & Quaye, 2016). In addition to academic learning, college presents young people with various perspectives and encourages experimentation with alternative behavior, beliefs, and values. College students encounter a wealth of new experiences and opportunities for autonomy, ideas, and social demands. College courses often require students to construct arguments and solve complex problems, fostering the development of post-formal reasoning (Perry, 1970; Sinnott, 2003). Attending college is associated with advanced moral reasoning and the ability to synthesize the considerations of autonomy and individual rights with promotion of human welfare (Kohlberg & Ryncarz, 1990). In addition to intellectual growth, college students show advances in social development (Hassan, 2008). The expanded worldview that accompanies college attendance is displayed in young people's tolerance of diversity and their interest in subjects such as art, literature, and philosophy.

The positive impact of attending college is not simply a matter of the type of college one attends; research indicates that all institutions, public and private, selective and open enrollment, advance cognitive and psychological development (Mayhew et al., 2016; Montgomery & Côté, 2003). In addition, students at 2-year community colleges show similar cognitive gains to those of their peers at 4-year institutions (Pascarella, Bohr, & Nora, 1995). Rather than the type of institution attended, developmental outcomes are most influenced by student involvement in campus life and peer interaction in academic and social contexts. Students who live in residence halls have more opportunities to interact with peers and become involved in the academic and social aspects of campus life—and show the greatest cognitive gains in the college years (Reason, Terenzini, & Domingo, 2007; Terenzini, Pascarella, & Blimling, 1999). Education that challenges students and encourages them to consider perspectives other than their own, solve ambiguous, messy problems, and apply course work to real-world problems and activities with the guidance of supportive faculty promotes cognitive-affective complexity, which underlies adaptive functioning in college as well as all of the contexts in which young adults are embedded (Patton et al., 2016; Reason et al., 2007).

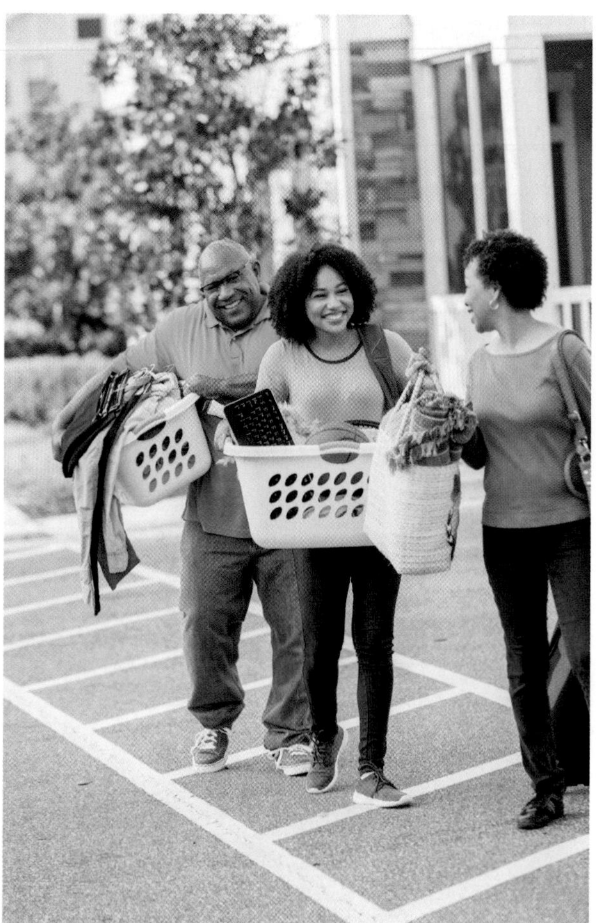

Adolescents' experiences during the transition to college influence their success in college.
©iStockphoto.com/kali9

Transition to College

Despite these benefits, however, many students do not complete college. Only about two-thirds of students who enroll in 4-year institutions graduate within 6 years, and one-third of students enrolled at 2-year institutions graduate within 3 years (National Center for Education Statistics, 2014). Generally, student attrition is highest in colleges with open enrollment and those with relatively low admission requirements. How a student handles the transition to college itself predicts the likelihood of dropping out. While most students find the transition to college challenging, some fail to realize or act upon the fact that they are expected to take the initiative in requesting help as they face new demands. Such demands are not only academic (e.g., more difficult course work) but also social (e.g., changes in living situation, whether a move to a dorm room or off-campus housing) and personal (e.g., new psychological demands for autonomy, motivation, study skills, and self-management) (Cleary, Walter, & Jackson, 2011).

Students who are the first in their families to attend college (known as **first-generation college students**), as well as those who are of color or from low SES homes (who also are often first-generation students), tend to experience the most difficulty transitioning to college and are at highest risk of dropping out or attending discontinuously (Aronson, 2008; Fischer, 2007; Ishitani, 2006). In 2014, about 15% of all college students enrolled in the United States were African American and 17% were Hispanic (as compared with 68% White) (National Center for Education Statistics, 2016). With few family and peer models of how to succeed in college, first-generation students and those of color may feel isolated and find it difficult to understand and adjust to the college student role and expectations (Collier & Morgan, 2008; Orbe, 2008). Compared with White students and those whose parents attended college, they may be assigned to more remedial course work; trail in the number of credits they earn in the first year of college; have difficulty deciding on a major; and be less active in campus, academic, and social activities—all of which are risk factors for college dropout (Aronson, 2008; Walpole, 2008).

Students' transition to college and success in college are also influenced by the college environment (Fischer, 2007). Institutions that are responsive to the academic, social, and cultural needs of students help them adjust to college and, ultimately, succeed (Mayhew et al., 2016). Reaching out to at-risk students during the first weeks of college can help them to feel connected to the institution. Social connection, communication skills, motivation, and study skills are associated with retention (Robbins,

Allen, Casillas, Peterson, & Le, 2006). Students who live on campus, see faculty as concerned with their development, establish relationships with faculty and other students, and become involved in campus life are more likely to succeed and graduate from college (Mayhew et al., 2016; Pike & Kuh, 2005). Colleges and universities can provide opportunities for faculty and students to interact and form connections, help students develop study skills, and assist students in getting involved on campus. Students are more likely to persist and graduate when they feel that they are part of a campus community.

Noncollege-Bound Youth

Although most young people express the desire to go to college, a 2017 report showed that only 34% of adults held college degrees by age 25 (National Center for Education Statistics, 2017a). Each year about one-third of high school graduates in the United States transition from high school to work without attending college. Although some academically well-prepared students report forgoing college because of a desire to work or a lack of interest in academics, many cite economic barriers, such as the high cost of college or the need to support their family, as reasons for nonattendance (Bozick & DeLuca, 2011). The population of noncollege-bound youth has been referred to in the literature as "forgotten" by educators, scholars, and policy makers, because relatively few resources are directed toward learning about them or assisting them, as compared with college-bound young adults.

Young adults who enter the workforce immediately after high school have fewer work opportunities than those of prior generations. In 2018, the rate of unemployment for high school graduates was twice that of bachelor's degree holders (Torpey, 2019). In addition, many young people with high school degrees spend their first working years in jobs that are similar to those they held in high school: unskilled, with low pay and little security (Rosenbaum & Person, 2003). Figure 14.4 shows that across all ages, high school graduates earn less and are more likely to be unemployed than peers with college degrees.

The curricula of most secondary schools tend to be oriented toward college-bound students, and counseling tends to focus on helping students gain admission to college (Krei & Rosenbaum, 2000). Over the past 3 decades, secondary education has shifted toward emphasizing academics and reducing vocational training, leaving young adults who do not attend college ill prepared for the job market (Symonds, Schwartz, & Ferguson, 2011). A solution proposed in the *Pathways to Prosperity* report from Harvard Graduate School of Education is for the U.S. educational system to support multiple pathways in the transition to adulthood (R. F. Ferguson & Lamback, 2014; Symonds et al., 2011). Opportunities for vocational training and to obtain relevant work experience will help young people try out careers and get relevant training for specific jobs.

FIGURE 14.4

Median Weekly Earnings and Unemployment by Educational Attainment, 2018 (Age 25 and Older)

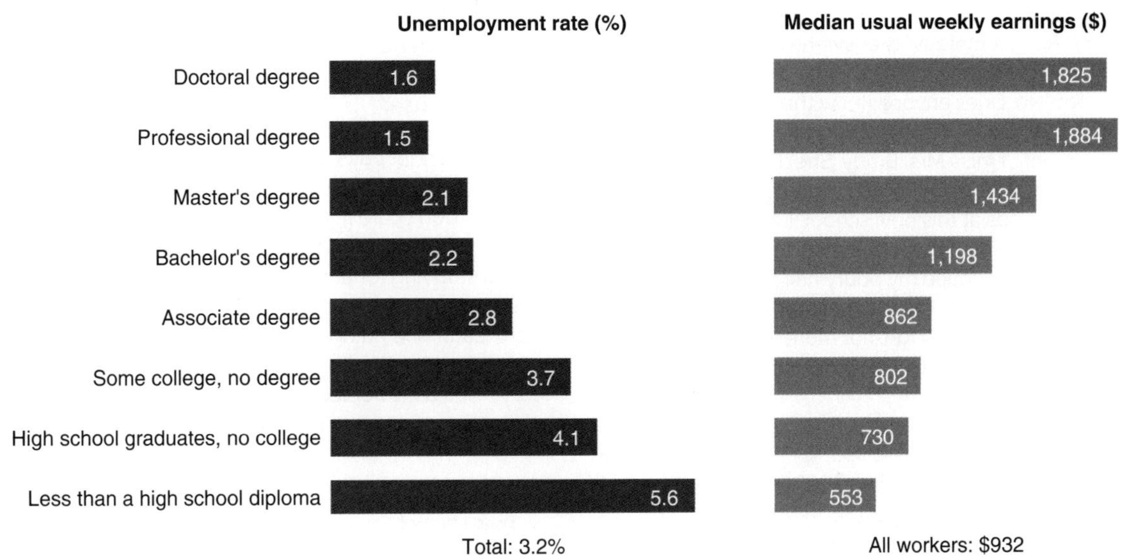

Note: Data are for persons age 25 and over. Earnings are for full-time wage and salary workers.

Source: Torpey (2019). U.S. Bureau of Labor Statistics, Current Population Survey

The U.S. Department of Labor and many states have established a series of registered apprenticeships that combine on-the-job training with theoretical and practical classroom instruction to prepare young people to work in a variety of settings. About 150,000 companies and organizations serve as program sponsors in the Apprenticeship USA registered program, training about 410,000 young people in over 1,000 occupations in industries such as construction, manufacturing, health care, information technology, energy, telecommunications, and more (U.S. Department of Labor, 2015). Apprentices receive on-the-job training and instruction by employers, and earn wages during training. The programs must meet national standards for registration with the U.S. Department of Labor, and training results in an industry-recognized credential. Apprentices who complete the program are often hired by their placement employers—a win-win solution for the program alumni as well as for the employers, which benefit by hiring employees who have acquired the specific skills they need.

Contextual influences such as family and educational opportunities also influence our choice of career. Socioeconomic status and parents' occupational fields influence career choice (Schoon & Polek, 2011). Young people in high SES households are more likely to receive career information from parents. In one study, African American mothers with at least some exposure to college were more likely than other mothers to use a variety of strategies to aid their daughters' progress on academic and career goals, such as gathering information about career options, colleges, and professionals from whom to seek advice (Kerpelman, Shoffner, & Ross-Griffin, 2002). Regardless of socioeconomic status, parents can provide support and motivation. Among low SES first-generation college students, a sense of ethnic identity and maternal support predicted career expectations and, in turn, school engagement—the behavior needed to achieve vocational goals (Kantamneni, McCain, Shada, Hellwege, & Tate, 2018). Other research with college students in the Philippines showed that parent and teacher support predicted career optimism (Garcia, Restubog, Bordia, Bordia, & Roxas, 2015). Parental expectations and encouragement for academic success and pursuit of high-status occupations also predict vocational choice and success (Maier, 2005).

THINKING IN CONTEXT 14.4

1. In your view, what are the pros and cons of adolescent employment? How might contextual factors influence whether adolescents work, their work activities, and the effects of employment?
2. What are some of the reasons why an adolescent might choose not to attend college or drop out? How might contextual circumstances influence their opportunities? What can schools, colleges, parents, or policy makers do to help young adults attend college?

APPLY YOUR KNOWLEDGE

"Uh . . . 44?" Rachel tentatively answered the teacher's question. Her face grew red as she felt the other students' eyes on her. "No. Does anyone know the right answer?" the teacher asked. "I feel so dumb. Everyone is looking at me," Rachel thought. "I miss Mrs. Brady. She'd never put me on the spot and make me feel dumb. None of the teachers care about the kids at this new school. I wish I could get out of here, maybe escape to the restroom, but everyone will look at me and notice my poufy hair and the stain on my pants," she thought. The teacher started distributing packets to the students. "Ugh, not more worksheets. All we do is complete worksheets. I miss my old school," Rachel thought.

"Today we're pairing up to complete this packet," the teacher announced. Rachel's partner had difficulty with the assigned math problems. Rachel patiently showed her partner how to complete the algebra problem. "You just have to remember that the variable X represents the number of apples and Y is the number of oranges," she explained. She talked through the word problem with her partner, saying, "As you work, remind yourself that these aren't just letters. They stand for something else."

At home Rachel pulls out her homework and sighs, "The work is so much harder now. And more boring. And the teachers don't care if you have more than one test in a day. I have to study for English and algebra. Ugh." Rachel begins studying for algebra by reviewing flash cards, noting that she needs to memorize formulas to succeed on the exam. Later she pulls out the assigned novel and her notes to study for her English exam. "What is the theme of this story?" she asks herself. "I need to think about how these ideas relate to the last book we read."

1. Describe Rachel's thinking. Give examples of how Rachel's thinking illustrates the cognitive developmental perspective.
2. What information processing abilities does Rachel show? Explain.

3. To what extent is Rachel's thinking characterized by adolescent egocentrism?
4. Rachel is a first-year high school student. Compare her school experience with what we know about school transitions.
5. How might teachers and schools meet the needs of students like Rachel?

WANT A BETTER GRADE?

Get the tools you need to sharpen your study skills. **SAGE edge** offers a robust online environment featuring an impressive array of free tools and resources. Access practice quizzes, eFlashcards, video, and multimedia at **edge.sagepub.com/kutherchild1e.** SAGE edge™

KEY TERMS

Formal operational reasoning 381

Hypothetical-deductive reasoning 382

Response inhibition 383

Automaticity 384

Social perspective taking 385

Mutual perspective taking 385

Societal perspective taking 385

Imaginary audience 386

Personal fable 386

Postconventional moral reasoning 388

Care orientation 390

Justice orientation 390

Stage-environment fit 393

First-generation college student 398

SUMMARY

14.1 Identify ways in which thinking changes in adolescence and how these changes are reflected in adolescent decision making and behavior.

Adolescents become capable of formal operational reasoning permitting hypothetical-deductive reasoning and the use of propositional logic. Research suggests that formal operational reasoning does not suddenly appear in early adolescence, but instead, cognitive change occurs gradually from childhood onward. Adolescents' advances in cognition are the result of improvements in information processing capacities, such as attention, memory, knowledge base, response inhibition, strategy use, speed, and metacognition. Adolescents' ability to take other people's perspectives advances, yet they also show features of adolescent egocentrism. Adolescents' decision-making competence is more advanced in laboratory settings than everyday settings, which often are charged with emotion.

14.2 Describe moral development and influences on moral reasoning in adolescence.

Adolescents become capable of demonstrating postconventional reasoning. Research has confirmed that individuals proceed through the first four stages of moral reasoning in a slow, gradual, and predictable fashion, but few people advance beyond Stage 4 moral reasoning. Social interactions offer important opportunities for the development of moral reasoning. Moral reasoning is only moderately related with behavior. Cross-cultural studies of Kohlberg's theory show that the sequence appears in all cultures but that cultures differ in the degree to which they value the individual or the collective.

14.3 Examine the challenges that school transitions pose for adolescents and the role of parents in academic achievement.

Many students experience school transitions as stressful, and academic motivation and achievement often decline. Poor stage-environment fit—the mismatch of adolescents' changing developmental needs with school resources—contributes to the challenges of school transitions. Authoritative parenting, parent involvement in the school, and close parent-adolescent relationships are important buffers to academic motivation and performance from childhood through adolescence for young people at all socioeconomic levels. School dropout poses challenges to young people's short- and long-term development.

14.4 Discuss the nature of adolescent employment, the influence of college on development, and the challenges faced by noncollege-bound youth.

Most U.S. adolescents who work come from middle SES families and seek part-time employment as a source of spending money. The effects of employment on adolescent well-being largely depend on the hours worked. However, adolescent work can be a positive experience if it entails limited hours and if it includes educational and vocational training opportunities and contact with adults. Attending college at least for a time has become normative. Attending college is associated with intellectual growth, advanced moral reasoning, and social development. The transition to college predicts the likelihood of dropping out. First-generation college students tend to experience the most difficulty transitioning to college and are at highest risk of dropping out or attending discontinuously. A supportive college environment can aid students' transition and reduce dropout rates. Young people who enter the workforce immediately after high school have fewer work opportunities than those of prior generations. They are more likely to spend their first working years in jobs that are similar to those they held in high school: unskilled, with low pay and little security. Recent initiatives to offer apprenticeships can help young people who do not attend college get skills for competitive jobs.

REVIEW QUESTIONS

14.1 What is formal operational reasoning, and how has it been criticized?

How do attention, working memory, and metacognition contribute to advances in adolescent thinking?

How does adolescent egocentrism develop?

Compare adolescent and adult decision making.

14.2 What is postconventional moral reasoning?

How do social contexts contribute to moral development?

How does culture influence moral reasoning?

How well does moral reasoning predict moral behavior?

14.3 What are some common challenges associated with school transitions?

How can parents and teachers promote adjustment?

What are risk factors for school dropout?

How can parents promote academic motivation and performance?

14.4 What are the effects of adolescent employment?

Why is the transition to college important?

What challenges do noncollege-bound young people face?

15 Socioemotional Development in Adolescence

"Describe yourself in six words." Lilia rolled her eyes as the read the social media meme. "Just six words? I could write a book!" she exclaimed. "I know! How can you sum yourself up in just a couple of words? We're complex ladies," added her best friend, Delia. "And we're always changing. Sometimes I'm shy, but a lot of times I'm outgoing. It all depends. I think I know myself, but I still don't know what I want to do with my life. College? Yes! But then what?" asked Lilia. "Boy, this meme has you all introspective," her friend teased. "Yeah, I guess I'm trying to figure myself out," Lilia responded. "Aren't we all, Lilia?" Lilia and Delia have summed up much of the socioemotional task of adolescence: figuring yourself out. Specifically, adolescents construct a sense of self and identity, an understanding of who they are and who they hope to be. Adolescents' attempts at self-definition and discovery are influenced by their relationships with parents and peers, relationships that become more complex during the adolescent years.

Learning Objectives

15.1 Summarize the processes by which self-concept, self-esteem, and identity change during adolescence.

▶ **Video Activity 15.1:** Teen Shopping Influenced by Social Media

15.2 Discuss the nature of parent–child relationships in adolescence.

15.3 Examine the developmental progression of peer relations in adolescence.

15.4 Describe common psychological and behavioral problems in adolescence.

Chapter Contents

PSYCHOSOCIAL DEVELOPMENT: THE CHANGING SELF

Adolescents spend a great deal of time reflecting on themselves and engaging in introspective activities, such as writing in journals, composing poetry, and posting messages, photos, and videos about their lives on social media. These activities might seem self-indulgent, but they are a means of working on an important developmental task: forming a sense of self. During adolescence, we undergo advances in self-concept and identity.

Self-Concept

A more complex, differentiated, and organized self-concept emerges in adolescence (Harter, 2012a). Adolescents use multiple, abstract, and complex labels to describe themselves (e.g., witty, intelligent). As young people recognize that their feelings, attitudes, and behaviors may change with the situation, they begin to use qualifiers in their self-descriptions (e.g., "I'm sort of shy"). Adolescents' awareness of the situational variability in their psychological and behavioral qualities is evident in statements such as "I'm assertive in class, speaking out and debating my classmates, but I'm quieter with my friends. I don't want to stir up trouble." Many young adolescents find these inconsistencies confusing and wonder who they really are, contributing to their challenge of forming a balanced and consistent sense of self.

Adolescents' views of themselves reflect but also influence their behavior. For example, young adolescents' academic self-concept predicts their academic achievement in middle adolescence (Preckel, Niepel, Schneider, & Brunner, 2013). Adolescents identify a self that they aspire to be, the **ideal self**, which is characterized by traits that they value. Adjustment is influenced by the match between the actual self—the adolescents' personal characteristics—and their aspirational, ideal self. Mismatches between ideal and actual selves are associated with poor school grades, low self-esteem, and symptoms of depression (Ferguson, Hafen, & Laursen, 2010; Stevens, Lovejoy, & Pittman, 2014). In addition, adolescents who show poor stability or consistency in their self-descriptions tend to experience higher rates of depressive and anxiety symptoms throughout adolescence (Van Dijk et al., 2014).

Self-concept is influenced by experiences in the home, school, and community. At home, an authoritative parenting style can provide support, acceptance, and give-and-take to promote the development of adolescent self-concept (Lee, Daniels, & Kissinger, 2006; Van Dijk et al., 2014). At school, particularly among high school students, perceived teacher support predicts positive academic and behavioral self-concept (Dudovitz, Chung, & Wong, 2017). Participation in youth organizations, such as the Boys' and Girls' Clubs of America, has positive effects on the self-concept of young people, especially those reared in impoverished neighborhoods, because such organizations foster competence, positive socialization, and connections with the community (Quane & Rankin, 2006). Adolescents' evaluations of their self-concepts are the basis for self-esteem, as discussed later in this chapter (Harter, 2006; Marsh, Trautwein, Lüdtke, Köller, & Baumert, 2006).

Self-Esteem

The overall evaluation of self-worth, known as **global self-esteem**, tends to decline at about 11 years of age, reaching its lowest point at about 12 or 13 years of age, and then rises (Orth, 2017b). This pattern is true for both boys and girls, with girls tending to show lower self-esteem (von Soest, Wichstrøm, & Kvalem, 2016). Declines in global self-esteem are likely due to the multiple transitions that young adolescents undergo, such as body changes and the emotions that accompany those changes, as well as adolescents' self-comparisons to their peers (Schaffhuser, Allemand, & Schwarz, 2017). Although school transitions are often associated with temporary declines in self-esteem, most adolescents view themselves more positively as they progress from early adolescence through the high school years (von Soest et al., 2016). For example, comparisons of adolescents in Grades 8, 10, and 12 reveal higher ratings of self-esteem with age for European American, African American, Asian American, and Latino youth (Bachman, O'Malley, Freedman-Doan, Trzesniewski, & Donnellan, 2011). Self-esteem tends to rise again from late adolescence and emerging adulthood through middle adulthood (Bleidorn et al., 2016).

As self-conceptions become more differentiated, so do self-evaluations. Adolescents describe and evaluate themselves overall, as well as in specific areas, such as academics, athletic ability, and social competence (Harter, 2012b). Adolescents develop a positive sense of self-esteem when they evaluate themselves favorably in the areas that they view as important. For example, sports accomplishments are more closely associated with physical self-esteem in adolescent athletes, who tend to highly value physical athleticism. Nonathletes tend to place less importance on athleticism (Wagnsson, Lindwall, & Gustafsson, 2014). Similarly, adolescents with high academic self-esteem tend to spend more time and effort on schoolwork, view academics as more important, and continue to demonstrate high academic achievement (Preckel et al., 2013).

Whereas favorable self-evaluations are associated with positive adjustment and sociability in adolescents of all socioeconomic status and ethnic groups, persistently low self-esteem is associated with adjustment difficulties that can persist throughout the lifespan (Orth, 2017b). For example, one longitudinal study assessed self-esteem annually in over 1,500 adolescents ages 12 to 16 years and found that both level and change in self-esteem predicted depression at age 16 and also 2 decades later, at age 35 (Steiger, Allemand, Robins, & Fend, 2014). Individuals who entered adolescence with low self-esteem and whose global or domain-specific self-esteem declined further during the adolescent years were more likely to show depression 2 decades later.

High-quality parent–adolescent relationships, characterized by an authoritative parenting style, are associated with greater self-worth and better adjustment in adolescents from the Netherlands, China, Australia, Germany, Italy, and the United States (Harris et al., 2015; Miconi, Moscardino, Ronconi, & Altoè, 2017; M.-T. Wang & Sheikh-Khalil, 2016; Wouters, Doumen, Germeijs, Colpin, & Verschueren, 2013). In contrast, parent–adolescent conflict and parental feedback that is critical, inconsistent, and not contingent on behavior predict the development of poor self-esteem (Wang et al., 2016).

Peer acceptance can buffer the negative effects of a distant relationship with parents (Birkeland, Breivik, & Wold, 2014). Adolescents who feel supported and well-liked by peers tend to show high self-esteem (Vanhalst, Luyckx, Scholte, Engels, & Goossens, 2013). Positive attachments to peers predict self-esteem in adolescence and emerging adulthood and may have long-lasting effects on self-evaluations (Sánchez-Queija, Oliva, & Parra, 2017). For example, a longitudinal study that spanned 2 decades showed that perceived peer approval predicted self-esteem in early adolescence, and adolescent self-esteem predicted self-esteem in adulthood, at age 35 (Gruenenfelder-Steiger, Harris, & Fend, 2016).

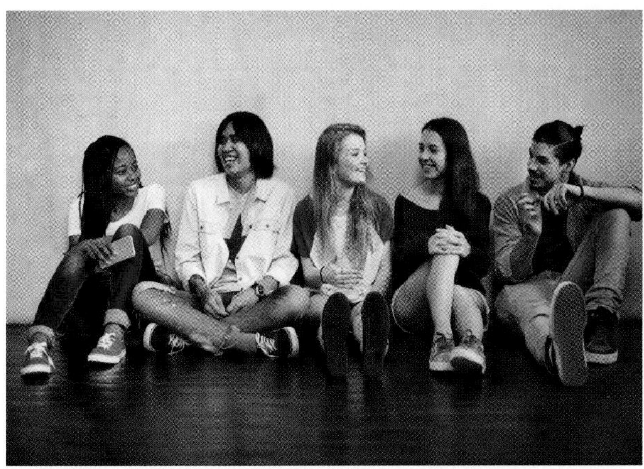

Positive attachments to peers predict self-esteem in adolescence and emerging adulthood and may have long-lasting effects on self-evaluations.
©iStockphoto.com/Rawpixel

Identity

As adolescents come to understand their characteristics, they begin to construct an **identity**, a sense of self that is coherent and consistent over time (Erikson, 1950). According to Erikson, to establish a sense of identity, individuals must consider their past and future and determine a sense of their values, beliefs, and goals with regard to vocation, politics, religion, and sexuality. Identity achievement represents the successful resolution of this process, establishing a coherent sense of self after exploring a range of possibilities.

Adolescents are best positioned to construct an identity when they experience what Erikson referred to as a **psychosocial moratorium**, which is a timeout period that gives adolescents the opportunity to explore possibilities of whom they might become. A psychosocial moratorium provides more freedom and independence than childhood but is without the full responsibilities of adulthood. Adolescents might sample careers, consider becoming an actor one week and a lawyer the next, or explore personalities and desires. Some adolescents examine their religion more closely and consider their own beliefs, perhaps learning about other religions. Young people who successfully engage in this process emerge with a sense of identity—an understanding of who they are and where they are going. The unsuccessful resolution of the identity search is confusion, in which one withdraws from the world, isolating oneself from loved ones, parents, and peers. Erikson's ideas about identity have influenced thinking in this area for the past half century, and researchers have devised ways of measuring identity, permitting his ideas to be tested.

Some adolescents learn about different religions and explore their religious beliefs as part of their identity search.
©iStockphoto.com/FatCamera

Identity Statuses

"Wearing gray on gray? Again?" Rose sighs. Her daughter, Stephanie, retorts, "How can anyone wear too much gray? It's neutral." Rose wonders where last year's preppy girl went and hopes that Stephanie will rediscover colors and wear something other than gray. Stephanie's changing styles of dress reflect her struggle with figuring out who she is—her identity. Researchers classify individuals' progress in identity development into four categories known as **identity status**, the degree to which individuals have explored possible selves and whether they have committed to specific beliefs and goals (Marcia, 1966).

Table 15.1 summarizes four identity statuses, or categories, describing a person's identity development. The least mature status is **identity diffusion** (not having explored or committed to a sense of self), characterized by pervasive uncertainty with little motive for resolution (Berzonsky & Kuk, 2000; Boyes & Chandler, 1992). Individuals who are in the **identity foreclosed status** have prematurely chosen an identity without having engaged in exploration; they tend to be inflexible and view the world in black and white, right and wrong terms. The **moratorium status** involves an active exploration of ideas and a sense of openness to possibilities, coupled with some uncertainty. As the uncertainty is experienced as discomfort, young people are highly motivated to seek resolution and reduce the discomfort. The fourth category, **identity achievement status**, requires that individuals construct a sense of self through reflection, critical examination, and exploring or trying out new ideas and belief systems and that they have formed a commitment to a particular set of ideas, values, and beliefs.

Researchers assess identity status by administering interview and survey measures (Årseth, Kroger, Martinussen, & Marcia, 2009). Young people typically shift among identity statuses over the adolescent years, but the specific pattern

TABLE 15.1

Identity Status

		COMMITMENT	
		PRESENT	ABSENT
EXPLORATION	PRESENT	**Identity Achievement Status** **Description:** Has committed to an identity after exploring multiple possibilities **Characteristics:** Active problem-solving style, high self-esteem, feelings of control, high moral reasoning, and positive views of work and school	**Moratorium Status** **Description:** Has not committed to an identity but is exploring alternatives **Characteristics:** Information-seeking, active problem-solving style, open to experience, anxiety, experimentation with alcohol or substance use
	ABSENT	**Identity Foreclosed Status** **Description:** Has committed to an identity without having explored multiple possibilities **Characteristics:** Avoid reflecting on their identity choice, not open to new information, especially if it contradicts their position, rigid and inflexible	**Identity Diffusion Status** **Description:** Has neither committed to an identity nor explored alternatives **Characteristics:** Avoidance; tend to not solve personal problems in favor of letting issues decide themselves, academic difficulties, apathy, and alcohol and substance use

of identity development varies among adolescents (Meeus, 2011). The most common shifts in identity status are from the least mature statuses, identity diffusion and identity foreclosure, to the most mature statuses, moratorium and achievement, in middle and late adolescence (Al-Owidha, Green, & Kroger, 2009; Yip, 2014). The overall proportion of young people in the moratorium status tends to increase during adolescence, peaking at about age 19 and declining over emerging adulthood as young people gradually commit to identities (Kroger, Martinussen, & Marcia, 2010). People form a sense of identity in many different realms within both the ideological (i.e., occupation, religion, and politics) and interpersonal domains (i.e., friendships and dating) (Grotevant, Thorbecke, & Meyer, 1982). Many adolescents experience daily shifts in identity certainty that accompany shifts in circumstances and moods (Becht et al., 2016).

Although Erikson emphasized identity development as a task for adolescence, researchers today believe that emerging adulthood, particularly the college years, is an important time for identity development (Arnett, 2015). As we will discuss in Chapter 13, the cognitive development that most emerging adults experience in college enables them to consider themselves and their roles in new ways, which contributes to a more complex integrated sense of self. Exposure to new environments and diverse students, coupled with increased independence, makes the college years key for identity development. Identity is revisited and reconstructed again and again (Crocetti, 2017). Identity development continues after college. Most theorists view it as a lifelong task.

Influences on Identity Development

Just as authoritative parenting fosters the development of positive self-concept and self-esteem, it also is associated with identity achievement. When parents provide a sense of security along with autonomy, adolescents tend to explore, much as toddlers do, by using their parents as a secure base (Schwartz, Luyckx, & Crocetti, 2015; Schwartz, Zamboanga, Luyckx, Meca, & Ritchie, 2013). Adolescents who feel connected to their parents, supported, and accepted by them but who also feel that they are free and encouraged to develop and voice their own views are more likely to engage in the exploration necessary to advance to the moratorium and achieved status. In turn, as adolescents commit to identities, their relationships with parents and siblings tend to improve (Crocetti, Branje, Rubini, Koot, & Meeus, 2017). The degree of freedom that adolescents are afforded for exploration varies with family and community contextual factors, such as socioeconomic status. Adolescents from high socioeconomic status homes may have fewer responsibilities to work outside the home, may reside in communities with more extracurricular opportunities, and may be more likely to attend postsecondary education than their peers from low socioeconomic homes—all factors that support the exploration needed for identity achievement (Kroger, 2015; Spencer, Swanson, & Harpalani, 2015).

Peers also influence identity development as they serve as a mirror in which adolescents view their emerging identities, an audience to which they relay their self-narratives (McAdams & Zapata-Gietl, 2015). When adolescents feel supported and respected by peers, they feel more comfortable exploring identity alternatives (Ragelienė, 2016). As with parents, conflict with peers harms identity development as adolescents often feel less free to explore identity alternatives and lack a supportive peer group to offer input on identity alternatives, which holds negative implications for identity development, such as identity foreclosure or diffusion (Hall & Brassard, 2008).

Although the task of forming an identity is first encountered during adolescence, it is often not resolved in adolescence, and the resulting identity is still not final thereafter (Kroger, 2015; Marcia, 2002). For example, one longitudinal study examined change in identity status at ages 18, 22, and 35. Although the overall sample demonstrated a shift toward identity achieved, there was substantial variability among participants in the degree to which they had changed (Cramer, 2017). Other research suggests that identity development continues through early adulthood even after achievement has been reached (Carlsson, Wängqvist, & Frisén, 2015). Changing life circumstances, contexts, and developmental needs spur identity development over adulthood. Adults often move in and out of identity statuses. For example, in one study of young adults, nearly half shifted identity statuses between ages 25 and 29, and all four statuses were represented at both ages (Carlsson, Wängqvist, & Frisén, 2016).

Outcomes Associated With Identity Development

Identity achievement is associated with high self-esteem, a mature sense of self, feelings of control, high moral reasoning, and positive views of work and school (Jespersen, Kroger, & Martinussen, 2013; Spencer et al., 2015). In contrast, young people in the moratorium status often feel puzzled by the many choices before them (Lillevoll, Kroger, & Martinussen, 2013). Sorting through and determining commitments in the educational and relationship domains is stressful and is associated with negative mood and, at its extreme, can be paralyzing and curtail identity exploration (Crocetti, Klimstra, Keijsers, Hale Iii, & Meeus, 2009; Klimstra et al., 2016). Young people who show identity foreclosure tend to take a rigid and inflexible stance. Unopen to new experiences, they avoid reflecting on their identity choice and reject information that may contradict their position.

Finally, while it is developmentally appropriate for early adolescents to have neither explored nor committed to a sense of identity, by late adolescence, identity diffusion is uncommon and has been considered indicative of maladjustment (Kroger et al., 2010). Young people in identity diffusion keep life on hold; they don't seek the meaning-making experiences needed to form a sense of identity (Carlsson et al., 2016). Young people who show identity diffusion tend to use a cognitive style that is characterized by avoidance. Academic difficulties, general apathy, organization and time management problems, and alcohol and substance abuse are associated with identity diffusion and often precede it (Crocetti, Klimstra, Hale, Koot, & Meeus, 2013; Laghi, Baiocco, Lonigro, & Baumgartner, 2013).

Ethnic Identity

An important aspect of identity is **ethnic identity**, or a sense of membership in an ethnic group, including the attitudes, values, and culture associated with that group (whether Latino, Asian American, African American, White, etc.) (Phinney & Ong, 2007; Rivas-Drake et al., 2014; Umaña-Taylor et al., 2014). Some researchers instead refer to ethnic-racial identity, which includes both the aspect of identity that is based on one's ethnic heritage and the aspect based on one's racial group in a specific sociohistorical context (Umaña-Taylor, 2016). Ethnic identity emerges when children begin to identify and categorize themselves and others according to ethnic and racial labels.

Like other aspects of identity, the process of ethnic identity development involves exploring one's sense of self and internalizing values from one's ethnic group (Hughes, Del Toro, & Way, 2017). Adolescents might explore their ethnic identity by learning about the cultural practices associated with their ethnicity by reading, attending cultural events, and talking to members of their culture (Romero, Edwards, Fryberg, & Orduña, 2014). As adolescents develop a sense of belonging to their cultural community, they may become committed to an ethnic identity. However, negative ethnic and

Adolescents can develop a strong sense of ethnic identity by learning about their cultural heritage, including its language, customs, and shared history.
Glow Images/Getty Images

racial stereotypes, discrimination, and inequality often pose challenges to developing a positive sense of ethnic identity development (McLean et al., 2015).

Adolescents from a variety of racial and ethnic groups, both native born and immigrant, often report experiences of discrimination that are associated with low self-esteem, depression, poor social competence, and behavior problems (Mrick & Mrtorell, 2011; Rivas-Drake et al., 2014). Some adolescents of color perceive discrimination in the classroom, such as feeling that their teachers call on them less or grade or discipline them more harshly than other students. Discrimination at school also has negative consequences for grades, academic self-concept, and school engagement, as well as adjustment and ethnic identity (Dotterer, McHale, & Crouter, 2009; Galliher, Jones, & Dahl, 2011). Adolescents of color and from disenfranchised groups often must manage confusing messages to embrace their heritage while confronting discrimination, making the path to exploring and achieving ethnic identity challenging and painful (McLean, Syed, Way, & Rogers, 2015).

A strong positive sense of ethnic identity can reduce the magnitude of the effects of racial discrimination on self-concept, academic achievement, and problem behaviors among African American, Latino, and multiracial adolescents, as well as act as a buffer to stress, including discrimination stress (Douglass & Umaña-Taylor, 2016; Romero et al., 2014; Zapolski, Fisher, Banks, Hensel, & Barnes-Najor, 2017). Adolescents who have achieved a strong sense of ethnic identity tend to have high self-esteem, optimism, and effective coping strategies, and they view their ethnicity positively (Douglass & Umaña-Taylor, 2017; Gonzales-Backen, Bámaca-Colbert, & Allen, 2016; Williams, Aiyer, Durkee, & Tolan, 2014). Ethnic identity is an important contributor to well-being. Adolescents from Mexican, Chinese, Latino, African American, and European heritage and with a strong sense of ethnic identity tend to show better adjustment and coping skills and have fewer academic, emotional, and behavior problems than do those who do not or only weakly identify with ethnicity (Miller-Cotto & Byrnes, 2016; Mrick & Mrtorell, 2011; Umaña-Taylor, 2016).

What fosters ethnic identity development? The exploration and commitment process that is key to identity achievement also underlies establishment of a sense of ethnic identity (Yip, 2014). The family is a particularly important context for ethnic identity formation, as close and warm relationships with parents are associated with more well-developed ethnic identities (Umaña-Taylor et al., 2014). Parents who provide positive ethnic socialization messages promote ethnic identity (Douglass & Umaña-Taylor, 2016). In contrast, adolescents who perceive excessive parental pressure and restrictions might respond with rebellion and rejection of ethnic heritage. Adolescents who learn about their culture, such as values, attitudes, language, and traditions, and regularly interact with parents and peers as members of a cultural community are more likely to construct a favorable ethnic identity (Romero et al., 2014; White, Knight, Jensen, & Gonzales, 2018). For example, ethnic identity is positively associated with an adolescent's proficiency in speaking his or her heritage language (Oh & Fuligni, 2010).

Similar to other aspects of development, perception matters. Adolescents' perception of their ethnic socialization—their view of the degree to which they adopt the customs and values of their culture—predicts ethnic identity rather than simply following their parents' views (Hughes, Hagelskamp, Way, & Foust, 2009). Likewise, among African American adolescents, high levels of peer acceptance and popularity among African American peers are associated with a strong sense of ethnic identity (Rivas-Drake et al., 2014; Rock, Cole, Houshyar, Lythcott, & Prinstein, 2011). Adolescents' perceptions of their ethnicity and ethnic groups are influenced by multiple layers of a dynamic ecological system, including families, schools, and peers, as well as the political social and economic climate (Way, Santos, Niwa, & Kim-Gervey, 2008).

Ethnic identity continues to influence adjustment in adulthood (Syed et al., 2013). Ethnic identity becomes integrated with and interacts with other domains of identity, such as gender, career, and relationship, to create a coherent overall identity (Umaña-Taylor et al., 2014).

Gender Development in Adolescence

In early adolescence, boys and girls experience dramatic physical, cognitive, and social changes. Physical development takes center stage and adolescents think about themselves in new ways, are treated differently by others, and often become acutely aware of their appearance as their bodies become adult-like. The onset of puberty often heightens boys' and girls' awareness of sex differences and gender becomes a more relevant label. Young adolescents become increasingly sensitive to gender stereotypes and their behavior is likely to adhere to gender stereotypes, a phenomenon referred to as the **gender intensification hypothesis** (Galambos, Berenbaum, & McHale, 2009; Priess & Lindberg, 2016). Although adolescents' thinking becomes more flexible and abstract, their views about gender roles become more rigid and their thinking adheres to strict gender stereotypes. Similar to young children, adolescents tend to negatively evaluate peers who violate expectations for gendered behavior by, for example, engaging in behaviors or expressing interests stereotyped for the other sex (Alfieri, Ruble, & Higgins, 1996; Sigelman, Carr, & Begley, 1986; Toomey, Card, & Casper, 2014).

Social pressures may also drive adolescents toward more gender-stereotypic behavior (Galambos et al., 2009). As they begin to date, many adolescents feel it is important to act in gender-consistent ways that are approved of by peers. Boys who are perceived as less masculine and girls as less feminine than peers may feel less accepted, be less popular, and experience higher rates of victimization (Smith & Leaper, 2006; Toomey et al., 2014). Some researchers, however, question whether all adolescents experience gender intensification (Priess & Lindberg, 2016). Research findings examining the gender intensity hypothesis are mixed. For example, Galambos, Almeida, and Petersen (1990) found that

LIVES IN CONTEXT: CULTURAL CONTEXT

Gender Roles and Acculturation in Mexican American Youth

In many cultures, women are expected to take on household duties such as preparing and serving meals.
©iStockphoto.com/fstop123

Gender stereotypes appear in all cultures, but they vary in intensity, prominence, and developmental trajectory (Guimond et al., 2013; Kapadia & Gala, 2015). Similar to findings with White adolescents, longitudinal research with African American youth found that young girls and boys show knowledge of gender stereotypes, but from ages 9 to 15, they show declines in traditional gender attitudes that level off through age 18 (Lam, Stanik, & McHale, 2017). Traditional attitudes in mothers, but not fathers, predict stereotyped attitudes in children. How do cultural factors influence gender attitudes?

In Mexican American families, the traditional role of the female is to care for the children and take care of the home, and males are expected to provide for the family (Cauce & Domenech-Rodríguez, 2002). These differences are related to the concept of machismo, which incorporates many traditional expectations of the male gender role, such as being unemotional, strong, authoritative, and aggressive. Yet gender differences in Mexican American males and females may be declining as women are increasingly providing for the family by working outside the home as well as sharing in decision making in the family. As families become more acculturated to the United States, Mexican American mothers and fathers tend to endorse more gender-egalitarian attitudes, reporting attitudes favoring similar treatment of boys and girls (Leaper & Valin, 1996).

One longitudinal study examined the role of acculturation in Mexican American adolescents' views of gender roles. Mexican American adolescents born in Mexico and the United States were followed from ages 13 to 20 (Updegraff et al., 2014). Among the adolescents born in Mexico, girls showed declines in traditional attitudes from early to late adolescence, but males' attitudes were stable over time. U.S.-born males and females did not differ in their traditional gender attitude trajectories; both declined over time. Mexico-born adolescents' greater exposure to Mexican culture and traditional attitudes about men's and women's roles may influence their views of gender (Cauce & Domenech-Rodríguez, 2002). Yet in this study, only Mexico-born males maintained their traditional gender role attitudes across adolescence (Updegraff et al., 2014). In addition, the differences in trajectories for Mexico-born males versus females suggested that males may be less influenced by acculturation processes, which are expected to lead to less traditional gender role attitudes. One possibility is that traditional gender role values in Mexican American families are advantageous for males, as Latino culture traditionally awards status and privilege (e.g., freedom to spend time outside the home) and fewer responsibilities (e.g., less involvement in housework) for adolescent and young adult males (Raffaelli & Ontai, 2004).

What Do You Think?

What gender-related values are evident within your culture or context, such as race, ethnicity, religion, or even neighborhood or part of the world? What are the accepted roles for men and women? Are gender roles changing over time in your context? ●

sex differences in instrumental (stereotypically masculine) qualities, such as independence and leadership, increased in early adolescence, but sex differences in expressive (stereotypically feminine) qualities, such as sensitivity and kindness, did not. Similarly, a longitudinal study found that adolescents did not become more stereotypical in their gender role identity across adolescence, suggesting that patterns of gender socialization may have shifted in recent decades, perhaps voiding the gender intensification hypothesis (Priess, Lindberg, & Hyde, 2009). In present-day society, boys are free to be more expressive and girls are encouraged to be more independent than they were in the past (Steensma, Kreukels, de Vries, & Cohen-Kettenis, 2013). By late adolescence, even young people who earlier displayed gender intensification tend to become more flexible in their thinking and adoption of gender roles. The Lives in Context feature examines the role of culture in attitudes about gender roles.

THINKING IN CONTEXT 15.1

1. How are adolescents' sense of self and identity influenced by other domains of development? In turn, how might other areas of development influence how adolescents view themselves? For example, consider aspects of physical and cognitive development, such as puberty and decision making. How might adolescents' sense of identity influence other areas of development?
2. Identify contextual influences on the development of a sense of self and identity. In what ways do interactions with contextual influences, such as parents, peers, school, community, and societal forces, shape adolescents' emerging sense of self?
3. Consider your own sense of ethnic identity. Is ethnicity an important part of your sense of self? Why or why not? Have you experienced shifts in your experience of ethnicity from childhood to adulthood? What factors might influence whether an adolescent is aware and feels a sense of ethnic identity?

ADOLESCENTS AND THEIR PARENTS

From middle childhood into adolescence, parents must adapt their parenting strategies to children's increased ability to reason and their desire for independence. Adolescence marks a change in parent–child relationships. As they advance cognitively and develop a more complicated sense of self, adolescents strive for **autonomy**, the ability to make and carry out their own decisions, and they decreasingly rely on parents. Physically, adolescents appear more mature. They also can demonstrate better self-understanding and more rational decision making and problem solving, creating a foundation for parents to treat adolescents less like children and grant them more decision-making responsibility. The parenting challenge of adolescence is to offer increasing opportunities for adolescents to develop and practice autonomy while providing protection from danger and the consequences of poor decisions (Kobak, Abbott, Zisk, & Bounoua, 2017). Parents may doubt their own importance to their adolescent children, but a large body of research shows that parents play a critical role in adolescent development alongside that of peers.

Parent–Adolescent Conflict

Leroy's mother orders, "Clean your room," but Leroy snaps back, "It's my room. I can have it my way!" Conflict between parents and adolescents tends to rise in early adolescence as adolescents begin to seek autonomy and begin to recognize that their parents are fallible and are capable of good and bad decisions. Conflict peaks in middle adolescence and declines from middle to late adolescence and emerging adulthood as young people become more independent and begin to better understand their parents as people (Branje, Laursen, & Collins, 2013). For example, in one longitudinal study, about 14% of participants reported turbulent relationships with parents characterized by low support and high conflict in early adolescence (age 12), rising to 29% at about age 16 and declining to 10% by around age 20 (Hadiwijaya, Klimstra, Vermunt, Branje, & Meeus, 2017). Most teenagers had the same type of relationship with their parents throughout adolescence. Although conflict rises during early adolescence, the majority of adolescents and parents

Parent–adolescent conflict most commonly occurs over mundane everyday issues, such as curfew.
©iStockphoto.com/asiseeit

continue to have warm, close, communicative relationships characterized by love and respect.

Parent–adolescent conflict is generally innocuous bickering over mundane matters: small arguments over the details of life, such as household responsibilities, privileges, relationships, curfews, cleaning of the adolescent's bedroom, choices of media, or music volume (Van Doorn, Branje, & Meeus, 2011). Conflicts over religious, political, or social issues occur less frequently, as do conflicts concerning other potentially sensitive topics (e.g., substance use, dating, sexual relationships) (Renk, Liljequist, Simpson, & Phares, 2005). Adolescents report having three or four conflicts or disagreements with parents over the course of a typical day, but they also report having one or two conflicts with friends (Adams & Laursen, 2007).

Severe parent–adolescent conflict occurs in some families. Like many aspects of development, there tends to be continuity in parenting and parent–child relationships (Huey, Hiatt, Laursen, Burk, & Rubin, 2017). Patterns of harsh verbal discipline (yelling, threatening, punishment, shaming) and insensitive parenting established in early childhood tend to persist and worsen in middle childhood and adolescence (Lansford et al., 2013). Frequent arguments charged with negative emotion are harmful to adolescents (Huey et al., 2017). Parent–adolescent conflict is associated with internalizing problems such as depression, externalizing problems such as aggression and delinquency, and social problems such as social withdrawal and poor conflict resolution with peers, poor school achievement, and early sexual activity (among girls) in adolescents of all ethnicities—African American, Latino, Asian, and White (Hofer et al., 2013; Moreno, Janssen, Cox, Colby, & Jackson, 2017; Skinner & McHale, 2016; Weymouth, Buehler, Zhou, & Henson, 2016).

Some conflict is conducive to adolescent development, helping adolescents learn to regulate emotions and resolve conflicts (Branje, 2018). Developmentally supportive conflict is coupled with acceptance, respect, and autonomy support.

Parenting

Parenting plays a large role in the development of autonomy during adolescence. As Romana explains, "My parents have rules. I hate some of those rules. But I know that my parents will always be there for me. If I needed to, I could tell them anything. They might be mad, but they'll always help me." Romana describes the most positive form of parenting, authoritative parenting. Recall from Chapter 9 that authoritative parenting is characterized by warmth, support, and limits. Across ethnic and socioeconomic groups and in countries around the world, multiple studies have found that authoritative parenting fosters autonomy, self-reliance, self-esteem, a positive view of the value of work, and academic competence in adolescents (Bornstein & Putnick, 2018; McKinney & Renk, 2011; Uji, Sakamoto, Adachi, & Kitamura, 2013). Parental support and acceptance, as characterized by authoritative parenting, is associated with reduced levels of depression, psychological disorders, and behavior problems (Pinquart, 2017). Authoritative parents' use of open discussion, joint decision making, and firm but fair limit setting helps adolescents feel valued, respected, and encouraged to think for themselves. Parents in a given household often share a common parenting style, but when they do not, the presence of authoritative parenting in at least one parent buffers the negative outcomes associated with the other style and predicts positive adjustment (Hoeve, Dubas, Gerris, van der Laan, & Smeenk, 2011). Generally, emotional support by parents tends to increase and psychological control continues to decline during emerging adulthood (Desjardins & Leadbeater, 2017).

In contrast, authoritarian parenting, which emphasizes psychological control and punishment (e.g., "my way or the highway"), is much less successful in promoting healthy adjustment (Milevsky, 2016). Psychological control inhibits the development of autonomy and has been found to be linked with low self-esteem, depression, low academic competence, and antisocial behavior in adolescence through early adulthood in young people from Africa, Asia, Europe, the Middle East, and the Americas (Bornstein & Putnick, 2018; Griffith & Grolnick, 2013; Lansford, Laird, Pettit, Bates, & Dodge, 2014; Uji et al., 2013). Moreover, it is adolescents' perceptions of negative or controlling parenting behavior, not parents' own views, that predict behavior problems (Dimler, Natsuaki, Hastings, Zahn-Waxler, & Klimes-Dougan, 2017). Finally, similar to findings with children, as discussed in Chapter 9, adolescents reared in permissive homes are more likely to show immaturity, have difficulty with self-control, and be more likely to conform to peers (Hoeve et al., 2011).

Parental Monitoring

One way in which parents balance autonomy granting with protection is through parental monitoring, being aware of their teens' whereabouts and companions. **Parental monitoring** is associated with overall well-being in adolescents, including academic achievement, delayed sexual initiation, and low levels of substance use and delinquent activity in youth of all ethnicities (Ethier, Harper, Hoo, & Dittus, 2016; Lopez-Tamayo, LaVome Robinson, Lambert, Jason, & Ialongo, 2016; Malczyk & Lawson, 2017). Effective parental monitoring is accompanied by warmth and is balanced with respect for adolescents' autonomy and privacy. When parents monitor too closely, such that adolescents feel they are intrusive, adolescents are likely to conceal their activities from their parents and continue to do so at least 1 year later (Rote & Smetana, 2016). Adolescents' views of the warmth and control provided by their parents are linked with their psychological adjustment, including conduct, emotional symptoms, and peer relations (Maynard & Harding, 2010). What is considered effective parental monitoring changes as adolescents grow older. From middle to late adolescence, parental knowledge declines as adolescents establish a private sphere and disclose less as parents exert less control (Masche, 2010; Wang, Dishion, Stormshak, & Willett, 2011). Overall, parenting entails a delicate balance of warmth and support, monitoring, and limit setting and enforcement—no easy task indeed.

THINKING IN CONTEXT 15.2

1. Parent–adolescent relationships are commonly viewed as, at best, strained and, at worst, hostile. Compare these popular views of parent–adolescent relationships in the research on parenting.
2. How might exosystem factors, such as neighborhood or a parent's workplace and activities outside of the home, influence parent–adolescent interactions and parenting style?
3. How can parents best support an adolescent's emerging autonomy? What are some of the challenges of encouraging developmentally appropriate autonomy seeking?

ADOLESCENTS AND THEIR PEERS

The most easily recognizable influence on adolescents, and that which gets the most attention from adults and the media, is the peer group. Each week, adolescents spend up to one-third of their waking, nonschool hours with friends (Hartup & Stevens, 1997).

Friendships

The typical adolescent has four to six close friends (French & Cheung, 2018). Adolescent friendships are characterized by intimacy, self-disclosure, trust, and loyalty (Bowker & Ramsay, 2016). Adolescents expect their friends to be there for them, stand up for them, and not share their secrets or harm them. Adolescent friendships tend to include cooperation, sharing, intimacy, and affirmation, which reflect their emerging capacities for perspective taking, social sensitivity, empathy, and social skills (Poulin & Chan, 2010).

Adolescent boys get together for activities, usually sports and competitive games, and tend to be more social and vocal in groups as compared with one-on-one situations. Boys tend to excel at being fun companions, coping with a friend who violates an expectation, and sustaining friendships within the context of having other friends (Rose & Asher, 2017). In contrast, most girls tend to prefer one-on-one interactions and often spend their time together talking, sharing thoughts and feelings, and supporting each other. Overall, girls' friendships tend to be shorter in duration, but characterized by more closeness, than are those of boys (Erdley & Day, 2017). High-quality friendships characterized by sharing, intimacy, and open communication tend to endure over time (Hiatt, Laursen, Mooney, & Rubin, 2015). Among early adolescents, it is estimated that one-third to one-half of friendships are unstable, with young people regularly losing friends and making new friendships (Poulin & Chan, 2010). After early adolescence, friendships become more stable, with young people retaining the majority of their friendships over the course of a school year.

As in childhood, similarity characterizes adolescent friendships. Friends tend to be similar in demographics, such as age, ethnicity, and socioeconomic status (Bowker & Ramsay, 2016). Close friends and best friends tend to be similar in orientation toward risky activity, such as willingness to try drugs and engage in delinquency and dangerous behaviors such as unprotected sex (de Water, Burk, Cillessen, & Scheres, 2017; Hiatt, Laursen, Stattin, & Kerr, 2017; Scalco, Trucco, Coffman, & Colder, 2015).

Most adolescents report having several close friendships that are characterized by trust, intimacy, loyalty, and companionship.

Adolescent friends tend to share interests, such as tastes in music; they are also similar in academic achievement, educational aspirations, and political beliefs; and they show similar trends in psychosocial development, such as identity status (Markiewicz & Doyle, 2016; Shin & Ryan, 2014). Through interaction, friends tend to become even more similar to each other (Scalco et al., 2015). An important predictor of friendship stability in adolescence is similarity. In one study, adolescent friend dyads, or pairs, who differed in peer acceptance, physical aggression, and school competence in seventh grade were more likely to dissolve their friendship during high school than were dyads who were more similar (Hartl, Laursen, & Cillessen, 2015).

Sometimes, however, middle and older adolescents choose friends who are different from them, which encourages them to consider new perspectives. Cross-ethnic friendships, for example, are less common than same-ethnic friendships but are associated with unique benefits. Adolescent members of cross-ethnic friendships show decreases in racial prejudice over time (Titzmann, Brenick, & Silbereisen, 2015). Adolescents of color who have cross-ethnic friends perceive less discrimination, vulnerability, and relational victimization and show higher rates of self-esteem and well-being over time than those without cross-ethnic friends (Bagci, Rutland, Kumashiro, Smith, & Blumberg, 2014; Graham et al., 2014; Kawabata & Crick, 2011).

Close and stable friendships aid adolescents in their social adjustment (French & Cheung, 2018). By communicating with others and forming mutually self-disclosing supportive relationships, adolescents develop perspective taking, empathy, self-concept, and a sense of identity. Friends who are supportive and empathetic encourage prosocial behavior, promote psychological health, reduce the risk of delinquency, and help adolescents manage stress, such as the challenges of school transitions (Hiatt et al., 2015; Wentzel, 2014). Friendship continues to have positive benefits, and the nature of friendship continues to change in emerging adulthood and early adulthood (Miething, Almquist, Edling, Rydgren, & Rostila, 2017), as discussed in Chapter 14.

Cliques and Crowds

Each day after school, Paul, Manny, and Jose go with Pete to Pete's house where they apply what they learn in their automotive class to work on each other's cars and, together, restore a classic car. During adolescence, one-on-one friendships tend to expand into tightly knit peer groups of anywhere from three to about nine but most commonly around five members who are close friends. These close-knit, friendship-based groups are known as **cliques**. Paul, Manny, Jose, and Pete have formed a clique. Like most close friends, members of cliques tend to share similarities such as demographics and attitudes (Lansford et al., 2009). The norms of expected behavior and values that govern cliques derive from interactions among the group members. For example, a norm of spending time exercising together and snacking afterward, as well as valuing health and avoiding smoking, alcohol, and drugs, may emerge in a clique whose members are athletes. Belonging to a peer group provides adolescents with a sense of inclusion, worth, support, and companionship (Ellis & Zarbatany, 2017).

In early adolescence, cliques tend to be sex segregated, with some composed of boys and others composed of girls. Girls' groups tend to be smaller than boys' groups, but both are similarly tight-knit (Gest, Davidson, Rulison, Moody, & Welsh, 2007). By mid-adolescence, cliques become mixed and form the basis for dating. A mixed-sex group of friends provides opportunities for adolescents to learn how to interact with others of the opposite sex in a safe, nonromantic context (Connolly, Craig, Goldberg, & Pepler, 2004). By late adolescence, especially after high school graduation, mixed-sex cliques tend to split up as adolescents enter college, the workforce, and other post–high school activities (Connolly & Craig, 1999).

In contrast with cliques, which are an expansion of intimate friendships, **crowds** are larger and looser groups based on shared characteristics, interests, and reputation. Rather than voluntarily "joining," adolescents are sorted into crowds by their peers. Common categories of peer groups found in Western nations include populars/elites (high in social status), athletes/jocks (athletically oriented), academics/brains (academically oriented), and partiers (highly social; care little about academics). Other types of crowds include nonconformists (unconventional

In early adolescence, same-sex groups are most common. Cliques of boys and girls tend to merge in middle adolescence, creating larger integrated groups.
©iStockphoto.com/Rawpixel

FIGURE 15.1

Age Differences in Resistance to Peer Influence

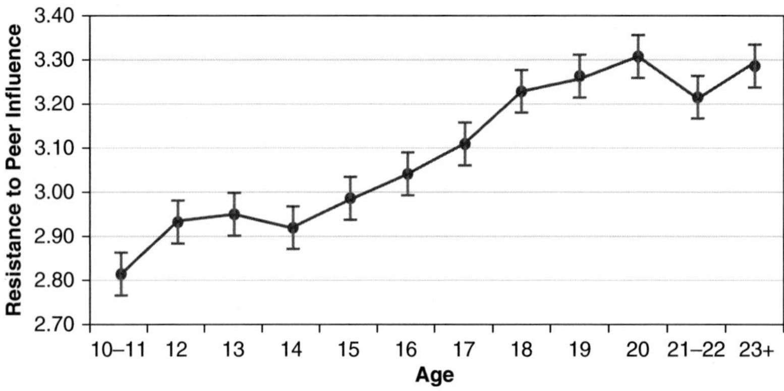

in dress and music), deviants (defiant; engage in delinquent activity), and normals (not clearly distinct on any particular trait) (Delsing, ter Bogt, Engels, & Meeus, 2007; Sussman, Pokhrel, Ashmore, & Brown, 2007; Verkooijen, de Vries, & Nielsen, 2007). Populars and jocks are generally rated by adolescents as higher in social status than brains and partiers (Helms et al., 2014).

Crowd membership is based on an adolescent's image or reputation among peers (Cross & Fletcher, 2009). Members of a crowd may or may not interact with one another; however, because of similarities in appearance, activities, and perceived attitudes, their peers consider them members of the same group (Verkooijen et al., 2007). Crowds differentiate young people on the basis of behaviors such as sexual activity, academic achievement, psychiatric symptoms, and health risks such as alcohol and substance use (Jordan et al., 2018). Some adolescents may use a particular crowd as a reference group and model their behavior and appearance accordingly, but adolescents do not always accurately perceive their own crowd status (Verkooijen et al., 2007). In one study, about one-half of students placed themselves in a crowd different from that assigned by peers—generally most tended to label themselves as normals or as not having a crowd. Only about 20% of adolescents classified in the low-status crowds, such as brains, agreed with their peers on their crowd status (Brown, Bank, & Steinberg, 2008). Adolescents who did not perceive themselves as part of a low-status crowd showed higher self-esteem than did adolescents who agreed with their crowd placement.

In middle adolescence, as their cognitive and classification capacities increase, adolescents begin to classify their peers in more complex ways and hybrid crowds emerge, such as popular-jocks and partier-jocks. As with cliques, crowds decline in late adolescence, especially after young people leave high school. However, recent research suggests that college students self-identify into crowds along four dimensions: social, scholastic, athletic, and counterculture, with social and counterculture affiliation predicting drug use (Hopmeyer & Medovoy, 2017). In contrast, the most social affiliation in adolescent samples, populars, tend to engage in relatively few risk behaviors (Jordan et al., 2018), suggesting that norms regarding substance use may shift from adolescence into emerging adulthood.

Peer Conformity

"Look at these shoes. They're red. Cool, huh?" asks Jamaica's mother. "No. I want the black ones," Jamaica replies. "But honey, these are so different from what everyone else has, you'll really stand out," her mother reasons. Jamaica shakes her head and replies, "I don't want to stand out. The shoes need to be black. That's what everyone wears." Jamaica's insistence on wearing the black shoes that all of her friends own illustrates her desire to conform to peer norms about dressing. The pressure to conform to peers rises in early adolescence, peaks at about age 14, and declines through age 18 and after (see Figure 15.1; Steinberg & Monahan, 2007).

Most adolescents experience pressure to conform to peer norms. Peers tend to exert pressure to conform to day-to-day activities and personal choices such as appearance (clothing, hairstyle, makeup) and music. Adults tend to view peer pressure as a negative influence on adolescents, influencing them to behave in socially undesirable and even harmful ways. Adolescents' reporting of risky behavior such as smoking and unsafe sexual activity correlates with their peers' behaviors (Choukas-Bradley, Giletta, Widman, Cohen, & Prinstein, 2014; van de Bongardt,

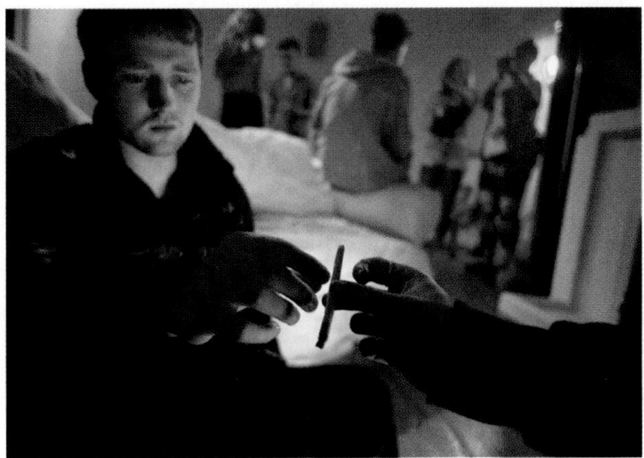

Most adolescents perceive peer pressure to conform to peer norms for both positive and, in this example, negative behavior.
©iStockphoto.com/sturti

Reitz, Sandfort, & Deković, 2014). It is not simply peer behavior that influences adolescent behavior; it is also adolescents' perceptions of peer behavior, as well as beliefs about peers' activity, that predict engaging in risky activities such as smoking, alcohol use, and marijuana use (Duan, Chou, Andreeva, & Pentz, 2009). In addition, adolescents naturally engage in more risk in the presence of peers, even without encouragement (van Hoorn, Crone, & van Leijenhorst, 2017). Young people vary in how they perceive and respond to peer pressure based on factors such as age, personal characteristics, and context, such as the presence of norms. Adolescents are especially vulnerable to the negative effects of peer pressure during transitions such as entering a new school and undergoing puberty (Brechwald & Prinstein, 2011) and when they are uncertain of their status in the peer group (Ellis & Zarbatany, 2017). Adolescents are more likely to conform to best friends' behavior when they share a high-quality and satisfying relationship (Hiatt et al., 2017).

Yet peer pressure is not always negative. Youths also report pressure from their friends to engage in prosocial and positive behaviors such as getting good grades, performing well athletically, getting along with parents, and avoiding smoking (Berndt & Murphy, 2002; Brown et al., 2008; Brown, Lohr, & McClenahan, 1986; Wentzel, 2014). For example, research with youths from Singapore demonstrates that peers exerted pressure on one another to conform to family and academic responsibilities—values that are particularly prized in Singapore culture (Sim & Koh, 2003). In laboratory experiments, U.S. adolescents were likely to show prosocial behavior, such as sharing coins with others, after believing that anonymous peers approved of their prosocial actions (van Hoorn, van Dijk, Meuwese, Rieffe, & Crone, 2016). Peer relationships can be a positive force on adolescent development.

Dating

Establishing romantic relationships, dating, is part of the adolescent experience. Many young people have been involved in at least one romantic relationship by middle adolescence, and by age 18, most young people have some dating experience. By late adolescence, the majority of adolescents have been in an ongoing romantic relationship with one person (O'Sullivan, Cheng, Harris, & Brooks-Gunn, 2007).

Dating typically begins through the intermingling of mixed-sex peer groups and progresses to group dating and then one-on-one dating and romantic relationships (Connolly, Nguyen, Pepler, Craig, & Jiang, 2013). Adolescents with larger social networks and greater access to opposite-sex peers date more than those who are less social. However, some research suggests that adolescents date outside of their friendship networks and that preexisting friendships are not likely to transform into romantic relationships (Kreager, Molloy, Moody, & Feinberg, 2016). Like friendship, romantic partners tend to share similarities, such as in academic achievement (Giordano, Phelps, Manning, & Longmore, 2008).

Adolescents' capacity for romantic intimacy develops slowly and is influenced by the quality of their experiences with intimacy in friendships and their attachments to parents (van de Bongardt, Yu, Deković, & Meeus, 2015). Specifically, one longitudinal study showed that attachment to parents and friendship quality at 10 years of age predicted being in a relationship and relationship quality at ages 12 and 15 (Kochendorfer & Kerns, 2017). Through romantic relationships, adolescents can learn to share, be sensitive to others' needs, and develop the capacity for intimacy. Close romantic relationships provide opportunities to develop and practice sensitivity, cooperation, empathy, and social support, as well as to aid in identity development.

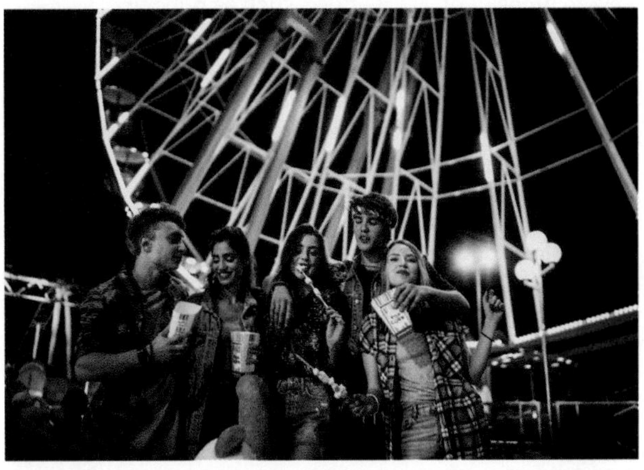

Dating typically begins through the intermingling of mixed-sex peer groups.
©iStockphoto.com/wundervisuals

In middle and late adolescence, romantic relationships are associated with positive self-concept, expectations for success in relationships, fewer feelings of alienation, and good physical and mental health (Connolly & McIsaac, 2011). However, early dating relative to peers is associated with higher rates of alcohol and substance use, smoking, delinquency, and low academic competence over the adolescent years, as well as long-term depression, especially in early-maturing girls (Connolly et al., 2013; Furman & Collibee, 2014).

Adolescent romantic relationships can have consequences for functioning later in life. For example, in one longitudinal study, high-quality romantic relationships at age 17 were associated with fewer externalizing problems, such as substance use and antisocial behavior, in early adulthood at ages 25 to 27 (Kansky & Allen, 2018). Poor relationships, however, predicted increased levels of anxiety and depression in early adulthood. Causality cannot be assumed. It is likely that interpersonal and developmental characteristics that led to poor relationships in adolescence also influenced poor functioning in adulthood. Romantic experiences in adolescence are often continuous with romantic experiences in adulthood, suggesting that building romantic relationships is an important developmental task for adolescents (Collins, Welsh, & Furman, 2009). Adolescents who date fewer partners and experience better quality dating relationships in middle adolescence tend to demonstrate smoother partner interactions and relationship processes in young adulthood (e.g., negotiating conflict, appropriate caregiving) as compared with their peers who are more indiscriminate in their choice of dates (Madsen & Collins, 2011).

Dating violence, the actual or threatened physical or sexual violence or psychological abuse directed toward a current or former boyfriend, girlfriend, or dating partner, is surprisingly prevalent during adolescence. Like adult domestic violence, adolescent dating violence occurs in youth of all socioeconomic, ethnic, and religious groups (Herrman, 2009). This behavior is discussed in the Lives in Context feature.

LIVES IN CONTEXT: FAMILY AND PEER CONTEXT

Adolescent Dating Violence

On average, about 20% of high school students have experienced physical violence, and 9% sexual violence, within a dating relationship (Wincentak, Connolly, & Card, 2017). Both males and females perpetrate dating violence at roughly equal rates and within the context of relationships of mutual partner aggression in which both partners perpetrate and sustain the aggression (Sears, Byers, & Price, 2007; Williams, Connolly, Pepler, Laporte, & Craig, 2008). Girls are more likely to inflict psychological abuse and minor physical abuse (slapping, throwing objects, pinching), and boys are more likely to inflict more severe types of physical abuse, such as punching, as well as sexual abuse, making girls more likely to suffer physical wounds than boys. Physical violence tends to occur alongside other problematic relationship dynamics and behaviors such as verbal conflict, jealousy, and accusations of "cheating" (Giordano, Soto, Manning, & Longmore, 2010).

Risk factors for engaging in dating violence include difficulty with anger management, poor interpersonal skills, early involvement with antisocial peers, a history of problematic relationships with parents and peers, exposure to family violence and community violence, and child maltreatment (Foshee et al., 2014, 2015; Vagi et al., 2013). Many of the risk factors for dating victimization are also outcomes of dating violence, such as depression, anxiety, negative interactions with family and friends, low self-esteem, and substance use (Exner-Cortens, Eckenrode, & Rothman, 2013; Niolon et al., 2015). Victims of dating violence in adolescence are more likely to experience intimate partner violence in adulthood.

Adolescent dating violence is less likely to be reported than adult domestic violence. Only about 1 in 11 cases is reported to adults or authorities (Herrman, 2009). In addition, only one-third of adolescents report that they would intervene if they became aware of a peer's involvement in dating violence, predominately believing that dating violence is the couple's own private business (Weisz & Black, 2008). Encouraging close relationships with parents is an important way of preventing dating violence because adolescents learn about romantic relationships by observing and reflecting on the behaviors of others. Adolescent girls who are close with their parents are more likely to recognize unhealthy relationships, are less likely to be victimized by dating violence, and are more likely to seek help (Leadbeater, Banister, Ellis, & Yeung, 2008).

Developmental interventions to address adolescent dating violence are often housed within high schools. Interventions have been successful in increasing teens' awareness of dating violence, helping them to identify violence, and shifting teens' attitudes to be less supportive of violence in dating relationships (Fellmeth, Heffernan, Nurse, Habibula, & Sethi, 2013). However, school-based programs are generally not successful at reducing the incidence of violence in adolescents' dating relationships (De La Rue, Polanin, Espelage, & Pigott, 2017). It is likely that adolescents must learn skills to change their behavior. Successful interventions help adolescents build skills in regulating their emotions, communicating effectively, and resolving conflicts (Rizzo et al., 2018; Smith-Darden, Kernsmith, Reidy, & Cortina, 2017).

What Do You Think?

1. From your perspective, how prevalent is dating violence in adolescence? Why do you think it occurs?
2. Why is it underreported? What contextual factors might influence whether an adolescent reports dating violence?
3. What can be done to reduce dating violence and help victims of dating violence? ●

THINKING IN CONTEXT 15.3

1. Cliques are commonly viewed as a negative, often harmful, influence on adolescents. Compare the research on cliques with common views about cliques.
2. How might relationships with peers such as friends or dates vary by context? Consider an adolescent from an inner-city neighborhood and another from a rural community. In what ways might their peer interactions and relationships be similar? Different? Compare these adolescents with one from an affluent suburban community. How might contextual factors influence adolescents' peer relationships?
3. When should adolescents date? Provide advice to parents about adolescent dating.

PROBLEMS IN ADOLESCENCE

Most young people traverse the adolescent years without adversity, but about one in five teenagers experiences serious problems that pose risks to their health and development (Lerner & Israeloff, 2007). Common problems during adolescence include depression and delinquency.

Depression and Suicide

The most common psychological problem experienced by adolescents is depression. Although about one-third of adolescents report sometimes feeling hopeless (Kann et al., 2014), only 2% to 8% experience chronic depression that persists over months and years (Substance Abuse and Mental Health Services Administration, 2013). Depression is characterized by feelings of sadness, hopelessness, and frustration; changes in sleep and eating habits; problems with concentration; loss of interest in activities; and loss of energy and motivation. Rates of depression rise in early adolescence, and lifelong sex differences emerge, with girls reporting depression twice as often as boys (Thapar, Collishaw, Pine, & Thapar, 2012).

Genetic factors play a role in depression, as they influence the brain regions responsible for emotional regulation and stress responses as well as the production of neurotransmitters (Maughan, Collishaw, & Stringaris, 2013). Longitudinal research demonstrates a role for epigenetics in depression during adolescence. For example, in one study, boys with a specific neurotransmitter allele showed severe symptoms of depression in the presence of poor family support but showed positive outcomes in the presence of high family support (Li, Berk, & Lee, 2013). The allele may increase reactivity to both negative and positive family influences, serving as a risk factor in an unsupportive family context but a protective factor when coupled with family support.

Contextual factors, such as the extended experience of stress, also influence depression. The longitudinal effects of stressful life events on depression are buffered by parent–child closeness and worsened by parental depression (Ge, Natsuaki, Neiderhiser, & Reiss, 2009; Natsuaki et al., 2014). Cultural factors also play a role in influencing adolescents' susceptibility to depression. Some adolescents find a discrepancy between their level of acculturation and that of their first-generation immigrant parents as stressful. Poor parental acculturation is linked with adolescent depression when adolescent–parent relationships are poor (Kim, Qi, Jing, Xuan, & Ui Jeong, 2009). For example, in one study, Chinese immigrant parents whose level of acculturation differed from their adolescent children tended to show more unsupportive parenting practices and the adolescents reported greater feelings of alienation (Kim, Chen, Wang, Shen, & Orozco-Lapray, 2013). Likewise, Vietnamese fathers who were less acculturated to the United States used more authoritarian parenting methods that fit their

FIGURE 15.2

International Suicide Rates for Adolescents, Age 15–19

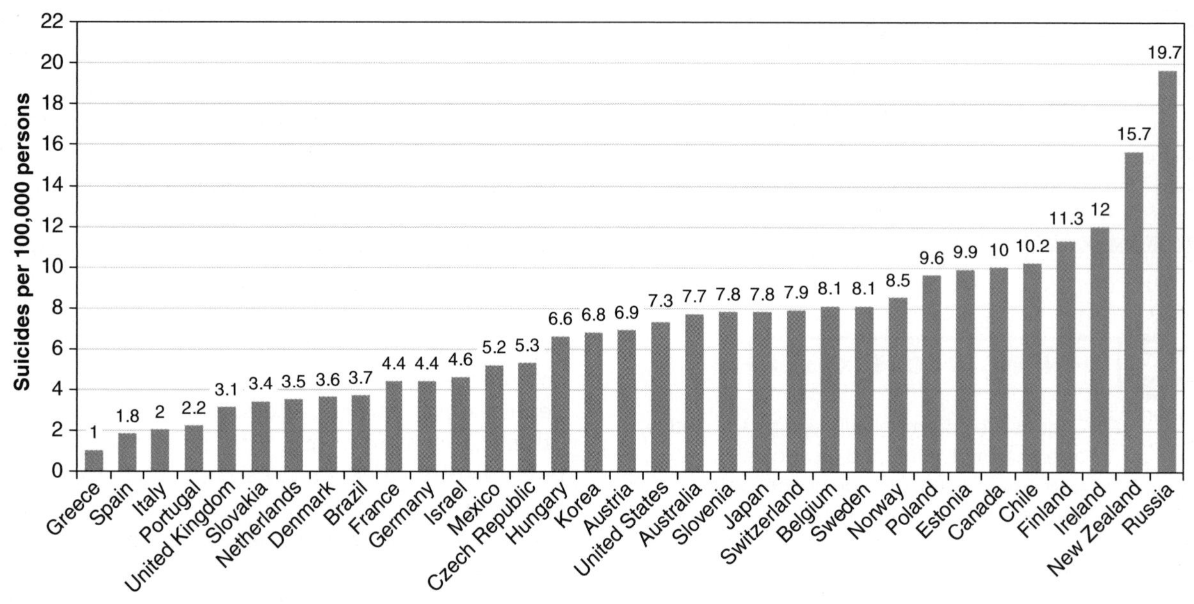

Source: McLoughlin et al. (2015).

society, but their adolescents tended to experience more depression (Nguyen, Kim, Weiss, Ngo, & Lau, 2018). Latino adolescents who experienced a discrepancy in acculturation as compared with their parents also were at risk for depression (Howell et al., 2017; Nair, Roche, & White, 2018). As young people acculturate, they may challenge traditional attitudes and beliefs of their immigrant parents, leading to greater family conflict and emotional distress.

Intense and long-lasting depression can lead to thoughts of suicide. Suicide is among the top three causes of death for adolescents and emerging adults in many Western countries, including the United States, Canada, United Kingdom, and Australia (Australian Institute of Health and Welfare, 2016; Centers for Disease Control and Prevention, 2017f; Office for National Statistics, 2015; Statistics Canada, 2015). Figure 15.2 illustrates international differences in suicide rates. Large gender differences exist in suicide. Although females display higher rates of depression and make more suicide attempts, males are four times more likely to succeed in committing suicide (Xu, Kochanek, Murphy, & Arias, 2014). Girls tend to choose suicide methods that are slow and passive and that they are likely to be revived from, such as overdoses of pills. Boys tend to choose methods that are quick and irreversible, such as firearms. The methods correspond to gender roles that expect males to be active, decisive, aggressive, and less open to discussing emotions than females (Canetto & Sakinofsky, 1998; Hepper, Dornan, & Lynch, 2012).

LGBT youth, especially male and bisexual youth, experience an exceptionally high risk for suicide, with three to four times as many attempts as other youth (Grossman, Park, & Russell, 2016; Miranda-Mendizábal et al., 2017; Pompili et al., 2014). LGBT adolescents who attempt suicide often list family conflict, peer rejection, and inner conflict about their sexuality as influences on their attempts (Liu & Mustanski, 2012; Mustanski & Liu, 2013; Russell & Fish, 2016). Adolescents are more likely to attempt suicide following a friend's attempt (Nanayakkara, Misch, Chang, & Henry, 2013). Some adolescents who commit suicide first express their depression and frustration through antisocial activity such as bullying, fighting, stealing, substance abuse, and risk taking (Fergusson, Woodward, & Horwood, 2000). Peer victimization is a risk factor for suicide attempts (Bauman, Toomey, & Walker, 2013); another risk factor is a high level of anxiety (Hill, Castellanos, & Pettit, 2011).

Preventing suicide relies on recognizing and treating depression and symptoms of suicide. Frequently, however, adolescents who attempt suicide show warning signs beforehand, as listed in Table 15.2. After a suicide, family, friends, and schoolmates of the adolescent require immediate support and assistance in working through their grief and anger. The availability of support and counseling to all

TABLE 15.2

Suicide Warning Signs

Any of the following behaviors can serve as a warning sign of increased suicide risk.
Change in eating and sleeping habits
Withdrawal from friends, family, and regular activities
Violent actions, rebellious behavior, or running away
Drug and alcohol use, especially changes in use
Unusual neglect of personal appearance
Marked personality change
Persistent boredom, difficulty concentrating, or a decline in the quality of schoolwork
Frequent complaints about physical symptoms, such as stomachaches, headaches, and fatigue
Loss of interest in pleasurable activities
Complaints of being a bad person or feeling rotten inside
Verbal hints with statements such as the following: "I won't be a problem for you much longer." "Nothing matters." "It's no use." "I won't see you again."
Affairs are in order—for example, giving away favorite possessions, cleaning his or her room, and throwing away important belongings
Suddenly cheerful after a period of depression
Signs of psychosis (hallucinations or bizarre thoughts)
Most important: Stating "I want to kill myself," or "I'm going to commit suicide."

Source: Adapted from American Academy of Child and Adolescent Psychiatry (2008).

adolescents within the school and community after a suicide is important because adolescent suicides can occur in clusters, increasing the risk of suicide among adolescents in the community (Haw, Hawton, Niedzwiedz, & Platt, 2013).

Nonsuicidal Self-Injury

Brianna closed the door to her room, rolled up her shirtsleeve, and looked down at the scarred and healing gashes in her arm before reaching for a new razor blade. Brianna engages in self-harm, **nonsuicidal self-injury**. This is behavior designed to cause harm, not death. Although self-harm may indicate serious psychological disorders, it is also fairly common among adolescents in Western countries, with lifetime prevalence rates of 13% to 23% of adolescents in the United States, Canada, Australia, and Western Europe (Klemera, Brooks, Chester, Magnusson, & Spencer, 2017; Muehlenkamp, Claes, Havertape, & Plener, 2012). Rates may be even higher because most self-harming adolescents do not seek help or medical attention for their injuries (Hall & Place, 2010). Most adolescents who engage in self-harm behaviors do so a few times, and most do not show recurring self-harm.

Self-harm behaviors, particularly cutting, tend to emerge between ages 12 and 15, on average at about age 13 (Bjärehed, Wångby-Lundh, & Lundh, 2012). Girls are more likely than boys to report harming themselves, most commonly by cutting, but also hitting, biting, or burning, but there are no differences on the basis of ethnicity or socioeconomic status (Klemera et al., 2017; Nock, Prinstein, & Sterba, 2009). Some research has linked self-injurious behavior with impulsivity, perhaps accounting for the onset in early adolescence, when impulsivity tends to rise (Lockwood, Daley, Townsend, & Sayal, 2017; Stanford, Jones, & Hudson, 2017). Psychological and behavioral difficulties such as anxiety, depression, antisocial behavior, and poor problem-solving skills are also associated with self-harm (Bjärehed et al., 2012; Marshall, Tilton-Weaver, & Stattin, 2013). Adolescents who self-harm tend to report being more confused about their emotions, experiencing difficulty recognizing and responding to them and more reluctance to express their feelings and thoughts to others (Bjärehed et al., 2012; Nock et al., 2009). Common reasons that adolescents endorse for self-harm include depression, feeling alone, anger, self-dislike, and inadequacy.

Social problems and a difficulty forming close relationships are common among adolescents who self-harm (Ross, Heath, & Toste, 2009). Social risk factors include high family conflict, poor parent–adolescent communication, low levels of support, and intense conflict with peers and bullying (Claes, Luyckx, Baetens, Van de Ven, & Witteman, 2015; Fisher et al., 2012; Giletta, Burk, Scholte, Engels, & Prinstein, 2013). Yet positive parental involvement and support and close friendships can buffer adolescents against social risks for self-harm (Klemera et al., 2017).

Adolescents who repeatedly engage in cutting and other acts of self-harm often report that the act relieves emotional pain, reducing negative emotions (Scoliers et al., 2009; Selby, Nock, & Kranzler, 2014). Interestingly, self-harming adolescents tend to show little or no pain during the harm episode (Nock et al., 2009). Instead, the act of cutting or other self-harming behavior produces a sense of relief and satisfaction for adolescents who repeatedly self-harm. Soon, they tend to value self-harm as an effective way of relieving anxiety and negative emotions, making it a difficult habit to break (Madge et al., 2008; Selby et al., 2014). The fifth edition of the *Diagnostic and Statistical Manual of Mental Disorders*, or DSM-5 (American Psychiatric Association, 2013), includes a diagnosis for severe self-harm: nonsuicidal self-injury—self-injurious behavior that occurs with the expectation of relief from a negative feeling—to solve an interpersonal problem, or to feel better, and interpersonal difficulty and negative feelings of thoughts, premeditation, or rumination on nonsuicidal self-injury. Many adolescents who self-harm receive treatment similar to other internalizing disorders, including a combination of medication, therapy, and behavioral treatment. However, repeated self-harming behaviors are difficult to treat because the relief they produce is reinforcing to adolescents, making psychologists and other treatment providers' work challenging (Bentley, Nock, & Barlow, 2014; Nock, 2009).

Delinquency

"Have you got it?" asked Corey. "Here it is—right from Ms. Scarcela's mailbox!" Adam announced as he dropped the stolen item on the floor in front of his friends. During adolescence, young people experiment with new ideas, activities, and limits. For many adolescents, like Adam, experimentation takes the form of delinquent activity. Nearly all young people engage in at least one delinquent or illegal act, such as stealing, during the adolescent years, without coming into police contact (Flannery, Hussey, & Jefferis, 2005). In one study, boys admitted to engaging in, on average, three serious delinquent acts and girls reported one serious delinquent act between ages 10 and 20, yet almost none of the adolescents had been arrested (Fergusson & Horwood, 2002). Adolescents account for 8% of police arrests in the United States (Federal Bureau of Investigation, 2015). Males are about four times as likely to be arrested as females. African American youth are disproportionately likely to be arrested as compared with European American and Latino youth, who are similar in their likelihood of arrest; Asian American youth are least likely to be arrested (Andersen, 2015; Federal Bureau of Investigation, 2015). Adolescents' own reports, however, tend to suggest few to no gender or ethnic differences in delinquent activity (Rutter, Giller, & Hagell, 1998). Differences in arrest rates may be influenced by the tendency for police to arrest and charge adolescents of color and those in low SES communities more often than European American and Asian American youth in higher SES communities (Rutter et al., 1998).

Most delinquent acts are limited to the adolescent years and do not continue into adulthood (Piquero & Moffitt, 2013). Antisocial behavior tends to increase during puberty and is sustained by affiliation with similar peers. As described in the Lives in Context feature, adolescents tend to find peer interaction highly rewarding, providing a context for antisocial activity. With advances in cognition, moral reasoning, emotional regulation, social skills, and empathy, antisocial activity declines (Monahan, Steinberg, Cauffman, & Mulvey, 2013). That is, most adolescents tend to show an increase in delinquent activity in early adolescence that continues into middle adolescence and then declines in late adolescence. Although mild delinquency is common and not necessarily cause for concern, about one-quarter of violent offenses in the United States, including murder, rape, robbery, and aggravated assault, are conducted by adolescents (Office of Juvenile Justice and Delinquency Prevention, 2014). Adolescents who engage in serious crime are at risk to become repeat offenders who continue criminal activity into adulthood. Yet most young people whose delinquent activity persists and evolves into a life of crime show multiple problem

LIVES IN CONTEXT: BIOLOGICAL INFLUENCES

Peer Interaction and the Brain

Adolescents spend much of their time with friends, and peer interactions become highly motivating. Adolescents' strong desire to spend time with and earn the approval of peers is accompanied by distinct patterns of neurological activity. For example, in one study, adolescents completed a risky driving task alone or in the presence of peers (Chein, Albert, O'Brien, Uckert, & Steinberg, 2011). The presence of peers was associated with increases in both risk taking and activity in the nucleus accumbens (NAcc), a subcortical structure that is part of the limbic system, a collection of brain structures that is implicated in emotion. The NAcc contains the brain's reward circuitry, playing a critical role in the experience of reward and pleasure, including social rewards and positive feedback, and in motivating goal-directed behavior (Fareri & Delgado, 2014). The NAcc shows greater responsivity to reward during the second decade of life, peaking in mid-to-late adolescence (Braams, van Duijvenvoorde, Peper, & Crone, 2015).

A great deal of adolescents' peer interaction occurs online via social media designed for mobile devices, such as Instagram and Snapchat (Lenhart, Purcell, Smith, & Zickuhr, 2010). Social and emotional processes typical of adolescence, such as peer influence, are also enacted on social media. For example, Smith, Chein, and Steinberg (2014) demonstrated increased NAcc activation and risky activity in a gambling task when adolescents believed

Peer interactions on social media are neurologically reinforcing and hard to resist.
©iStockphoto.com/monkeybusinessimages

that they were interacting with and being observed by an anonymous peer, suggesting that peer influence and its neurological correlates may also occur online. In addition, the level of NAcc response to positive social feedback has been linked to intensity of social media use (Meshi, Morawetz, & Heekeren, 2013), suggesting that social media interactions may also be neurologically rewarding.

A recent study examined whether peer influence processes occur online and whether the effects of peer processes can be observed in the brain (Sherman, Payton, Hernandez, Greenfield, & Dapretto, 2016). Adolescents were recruited to participate in an "internal social network" that simulated Instagram, a popular photo-sharing tool. Participants submitted their own Instagram photos and viewed both their own and other photos that they believed belonged to other members of the social network. The researchers manipulated how many likes accompanied each photo. Adolescents were more likely to like photographs they believed to be popular (those that were assigned many likes), and neural responses differed as a function of photograph popularity. When adolescents' own photographs received many likes (vs. few), they showed significantly greater activation of the NAcc, suggesting that likes may be experienced as rewarding and may motivate online behavior and continued use of social media. These findings are supported by prior research linking NAcc response to social evaluation and the role of the NAcc in reward and reinforcement (Meshi et al., 2013).

A follow-up study compared high school and college students on the Instagram-like social network task to determine whether peer influence and its neurological correlates are particularly high in adolescence as compared with emerging adulthood (Sherman, Greenfield, Hernandez, & Dapretto, 2018). Both high school and college students were more likely to like popular photographs than unpopular photographs and showed greater NAcc activation in response to popular photographs, especially when viewing their own images. Among high school students, the NAcc response when viewing their own photos with many likes over few increased with age, but no age differences emerged among college students. Prior research suggests that both peer influence and NAcc sensitivity to rewarding stimuli increase in adolescence and peak at around ages 16 to 17 (Braams et al., 2015; Steinberg & Monahan, 2007). However, high school and college students did not differ in overall NAcc activation. It appears that peer influence remains important in college, with similar neural correlates, suggesting a gradual path for social and neurological development from adolescence through emerging adulthood.

What Do You Think?

1. Why might adolescents find engaging in social media rewarding? What are the potential rewards? How might the rewards influence adolescents' behavior?
2. How might individuals' experience of social media and its effects change as they progress into and through adulthood? ●

behaviors that begin in childhood (Farrington & Loeber, 2000), and they typically have their first contacts with the criminal justice system by age 12 or earlier (Baglivio, Jackowski, Greenwald, & Howell, 2014).

When biological and individual risk factors are coupled with challenging home and community environments, the risk for childhood onset of serious antisocial behavior that persists into adulthood increases (Dishion & Patterson, 2016). Parenting that is inconsistent, highly controlling and/or negligent, accompanied by harsh punishment, and/or low in monitoring can worsen impulsive, defiant, and aggressive tendencies in children and adolescents (Chen, Voisin, & Jacobson, 2013; Harris-McKoy & Cui, 2012).

Contextual factors in the community also matter. Communities of pervasive poverty are characterized by limited educational, recreational, and employment activities, coupled with access to drugs and firearms, opportunities to witness and be victimized by violence, and offers of protection and companionship by gangs that engage in criminal acts—all of which contribute to the onset of antisocial behavior (Chen et al., 2013). Exposure to high levels of community violence predicts delinquent activity (Jain & Cohen, 2013). Low-income communities tend to have schools that struggle to meet students' educational and developmental needs, with crowding, limited resources, and overtaxed teachers (Flannery et al., 2005). Young people who experience individual, home, community, and school risk factors for

TABLE 15.3

Developmental Assets for Positive Youth Development

INDIVIDUAL	CONTEXT
Self-regulation	Family support
Planning and decision-making competence	Positive family communication
Interpersonal competence	Parental monitoring
Conflict resolution	Positive relationships with other adults
School engagement	High expectations from adults
Hopeful expectations for the future	Caring school climate
Spirituality	Parents' involvement in school
Achievement motivation	Organized out-of-school programs
Self-esteem	Neighborhood members monitor children in the community
Sense of purpose	Availability of youth programs
	Supportive religious community
	Availability of libraries and other community resources
	Neighborhood safety

Source: Lerner et al. (2019) and Search Institute (2017).

antisocial behavior tend to associate with similarly troubled peers, a pattern that tends to increase delinquent activity as well as chronic delinquency (Evans, Simons, & Simons, 2014).

Preventing and intervening in delinquency requires examining individual, family, and community factors. Training parents in discipline, communication, and monitoring fosters healthy parent–child relationships, which buffer young people who are at risk for delinquency (Bowman, Prelow, & Weaver, 2007). High-quality teachers, teacher support, resources, and economic aid foster an educational environment that protects young people from risks for antisocial behavior. A 3-year longitudinal study following adolescents of low-income single mothers transitioning off welfare showed that involvement in school activities protects adolescents from some of the negative effects of low-income contexts and is associated with lower levels of delinquency over time (Mahatmya & Lohman, 2011). Economic, social, and employment resources empower communities to create environments that reduce criminal activity by all age-groups and promote the development of children and adolescents.

Positive Youth Development

Throughout much of history, developmental scientists who study adolescence tended to emphasize treating problems, such as those we have discussed. However, for the majority of adolescents, problem behaviors are mild and temporary when they occur, and most adolescents do not experience serious problems (Boyer & Byrnes, 2016; Lerner et al., 2015a). Rather than emphasizing deficits and problems, today developmental scientists view adolescence as a period of growth and plasticity. Developmental scientists thereby focus on promoting healthy development in children and adolescents rather than simply treating problems. The **positive youth development (PYD)** approach seeks to discover and promote positive qualities that contribute to adolescents' ability to adapt and engage in constructive interactions with their complex and changing contexts (Lerner et al., 2019). Specifically, developmental assets, positive influences on adaptation, can be found within the individual and context. Table 15.3 illustrates some developmental assets within the individual and context. Interventions that promote PYD target both the individual and context.

PYD interventions are commonly implemented at school and involve practices and policies that help students and adults acquire and apply knowledge, skills, and attitudes that enhance personal development, social relationships, ethical behavior, and productive work (Ciocanel, Power, Eriksen, & Gillings, 2017; Taylor, Oberle, Durlak, & Weissberg, 2017). School-based PYD interventions promote asset development by focusing on interrelated cognitive, emotional, and behavioral competencies that are important for success in school and life, such as self-awareness (e.g., recognizing emotions, strengths and limitations, and values), self-management (e.g., regulating emotions and behaviors), social awareness (e.g., taking the perspective of and empathizing with others from diverse backgrounds and cultures), relationship skills (e.g., establishing and maintaining healthy relationships), and responsible decision making (e.g., making constructive choices across varied situations).

PYD interventions applied in family, school, and community settings have shown success in promoting positive development in a broad range of developmental assets, such as self-control, interpersonal skills, problem solving, the quality of their peer and adult relationships, commitment to schooling, and academic achievement (Ciocanel et al., 2017; Eichas, Ferrer-Wreder, & Olsson, 2019). Advances in social and emotional competencies are positively associated with social and academic adjustment and are also associated with fewer behavioral problems and emotional distress (Domitrovich, Durlak, Staley, & Weissberg, 2017; Osher et al., 2016; Weissberg, 2019). Frequently PYD interventions are associated with decreases in substance use, negative risk taking, and problem behaviors, suggesting that in addition to promoting positive outcomes, PYD interventions may protect against negative outcomes (Ciocanel et al., 2017; Waid & Uhrich, 2019). Moreover, the positive effects of interventions tend to persist up to at least 4 years (Taylor et al., 2017).

THINKING IN CONTEXT 15.4

1. What are some contributors to adolescent depression and self-harm? What individual factors might place an adolescent at risk for depression or engaging in self-harm? What role might contextual factors have? How might adolescents' interactions in the home, peer, school, and neighborhood context influence the risk for depression or self-harm? Conversely, how might these interactions protect adolescents?
2. How might adults distinguish normative delinquent activity that declines with age from atypical delinquent activity that continues and escalates? How should each be treated by adults and the legal system?
3. Although often depicted as a time of problems, adolescence is also a time for positive development. Discuss this statement, referring to the positive youth development approach. To what extent do you agree? Why?

APPLY YOUR KNOWLEDGE

"Recording your secrets again?" Janie's mother teased. "It's none of your business. She's so annoying," Janie thought to herself as she picked up her journal and went to her room.

"What did I do?" Janie's mother asked herself. "Janie has no sense of humor anymore. Nothing I say or do is right." She peeked into Janie's room and asked, "Janie, are you going to clean your room today? Or would you rather be grounded?"

"It's my room. If I want it dirty, it's up to me! You can't ground me. I have the party Friday," Janie responded.

"I don't think so, Janie. There will be no adults present at the party. No way."

Janie wrote in her journal, "This is so unfair! If she's not forbidding me to get my nose pierced, she's complaining for me to clean my room or telling me I can't hang out with my friends. I can't wait to move out."

After Janie blew off steam, she started to write about herself. "Who am I?" she asked, writing down adjectives and roles, like happy, thoughtful, friend, girlfriend. She wondered about her future and how she would make sense of it all and make a plan for the future.

At school, Janie met her best friend Hayla who asked, "Are you going Friday?" "No. My mom won't let me," Janie said. "She's such a dud," Hayla said. "Hey! She's still my mom. I love her even though she annoys me. Only I can say that," Janie retorted. "Sorry. Hey, look. There are the girls," Hayla said as they walked toward their group of friends.

1. Evaluate Janie's relationship with her mother. Compare their interactions with what we know about parent–adolescent relationships.
2. Give advice to Janie's mother. How should she handle Janie's emerging desires for independence?
3. Should Janie be allowed to go to the party? Why or why not? As a parent, what would you consider in making that decision?
4. Why does Janie keep a journal? What role might it have in her developing sense of self?

WANT A BETTER GRADE?

KEY TERMS

Ideal self 405
Global self-esteem 406
Identity 407
Psychosocial moratorium 407
Identity status 407
Identity diffusion 407
Identity foreclosed status 407
Moratorium status 407
Identity achievement status 407
Ethnic identity 409
Gender intensification hypothesis 410
Autonomy 412
Parental monitoring 413
Clique 415
Crowd 415
Nonsuicidal self-injury 421
Positive youth development (PYD) 424

SUMMARY

15.1 Summarize the processes by which self-concept, self-esteem, and identity change during adolescence.

Adolescents use more abstract and complex labels to describe and evaluate themselves. Positive self-esteem predicts adjustment and sociability in adolescents of all socioeconomic status and ethnic groups. Adolescents must construct an identity that is coherent and consistent over time. Many adolescents seek to establish a sense of ethnic identity, which is associated with positive outcome and can buffer the negative effects of discrimination and contextual stress. Adolescents may experience shifts in their views of gender stereotypes, or gender intensification, which can influence their behavior.

15.2 Discuss the nature of parent–child relationships in adolescence.

Conflict between parents and adolescents rises in early adolescence and peaks in middle adolescence but takes the form of small arguments over minor details. Authoritative parenting fosters autonomy, self-esteem, and academic competence in adolescents. Authoritarian parenting inhibits the development of autonomy and is linked with poor adjustment. Parental monitoring promotes well-being and is a protective factor against risky behavior.

15.3 Examine the developmental progression of peer relations in adolescence.

In adolescence, friendships are characterized by intimacy, loyalty, self-disclosure, and trust and promote positive adjustment. In early adolescence, cliques emerge and, by mid-adolescence, begin to include both boys and girls, creating opportunities for dating. Dating typically begins through the intermingling of mixed-sex peer groups, progresses to group dating, and then goes to one-on-one dating and romantic relationships. Both cliques and crowds, larger reputation-based groups, tend to decline in late adolescence. Susceptibility to peer conformity for both positive and negative behaviors tends to rise in early adolescence, peaks in middle adolescence, and declines thereafter.

15.4 Describe common psychological and behavioral problems in adolescence.

Several problems may rise during adolescence, such as nonsuicidal self-injury, depression, and suicide. Nearly all adolescents engage in at least one delinquent activity, and overall rates of delinquency rise in early adolescence and decline in late adolescence. The Positive Youth Development (PYD) approach focuses on discovering and promoting adolescents' strengths and the positive qualities that enable them to adapt to challenges.

REVIEW QUESTIONS

15.1 How do self-concept and self-esteem change during adolescence?

What is identity and what are outcomes associated with four identity statuses?

What is ethnic identity?

What are influences on identity development?

15.2 What are examples of typical parent–adolescent conflict?

What parenting style is most effective with adolescents?

How does parental monitoring contribute to positive development in adolescence?

15.3 What are characteristics of adolescent friendships?

What purposes do cliques and crowds serve in adolescence?

To what extent do most adolescents perceive peer pressure?

How does dating typically progress in adolescence?

15.4 Why do some adolescents engage in nonsuicidal self-injury?

What factors contribute to depression and suicide in adolescence?

What are some common patterns of adolescent delinquency?

What is the positive youth development approach?

GLOSSARY

A-not-B error: An object permanence error in which an infant uncovers an object several times in one place (Place A), and continues to search for the object in Place A even after seeing the object moved to a new location, Place B.

academically centered preschool programs: An approach to early childhood education that emphasizes providing children with structured learning environments in which teachers deliver direct instruction on letters, numbers, shapes, and academic skills.

accommodation: In Piaget's theory, the process by which schemas are modified or new schemas are created in light of experience.

achievement motivation: The willingness to persist at challenging tasks and meet high standards of accomplishment.

adolescent growth spurt: The first outward sign of puberty; refers to a rapid gain in height and weight that generally begins in girls at about age 10 and in boys about age 12.

adoption: A legal process in which a person assumes the parenting rights and responsibilities of a child.

adrenarche: Refers to the maturation of adrenal glands.

affordances: Refers to the actional properties of objects—the opportunities and limits they provide for action.

age of viability: The age at which the fetus may survive if born prematurely; begins about 22 weeks after conception.

aggressive behavior: Behavior that harms or violates the rights of others; can be physical or relational.

aggressive-rejected children: Children who are confrontational and hostile toward peers and are shunned by peers.

allele: A variation of a gene that influences an individual's characteristics.

amniocentesis: A prenatal diagnostic procedure in which a small sample of the amniotic fluid is extracted fromthe mother's uterus and subject to genetic analysis.

amnion: A membrane that holds amniotic fluid.

amygdala: A brain structure that is part of the limbic system and plays a role in emotion, especially fear and anger.

anencephaly: A neural tube defect that results in the failure of all or part of the brain to develop, resulting in death prior to or shortly after birth.

animism: The belief that inanimate objects are alive and have feelings and intentions; a characteristic of preoperational reasoning.

anorexia nervosa: An eating disorder characterized by compulsive starvation and extreme weight loss and accompanied by a distorted body image.

Apgar scale: A quick overall assessment of a baby's immediate health at birth, including appearance, pulse, grimace, activity, and respiration.

appearance–reality distinction: The ability to distinguish between what something appears to be and what it really is.

applied developmental science: A field that studies lifespan interactions between individuals and the contexts in which they live and applies research findings to real-world settings, such as to influence social policy and create interventions.

artificial insemination: A means of conception in which sperm are injected into the vagina by a means other than sexual intercourse.

assimilation: In Piaget's theory, the process by which new experiences are interpreted and integrated into preexisting schemas.

asthma: A chronic disease of the respiratory system in which inflammation narrows the airways, causing wheezing, coughing, and difficulty breathing.

attachment: A lasting emotional tie between two individuals.

attention: The ability to direct one's awareness.

attention-deficit/hyperactivity disorder (ADHD): A condition characterized by persistent difficulties with attention and/or impulsivity that interfere with performance and behavior in school and daily life.

authoritarian parenting style: An approach to childrearing that emphasizes high behavioral control and low levels of warmth and autonomy granting.

authoritative parenting style: An approach to childrearing in which parents are warm and sensitive to children's needs, grant appropriate autonomy, and exert firm control.

autism spectrum disorder: Refers to a family of disorders that range in severity and are marked by social and communication deficits, often accompanied by restrictive and repetitive behaviors.

autobiographical memory: The recollection of a personally meaningful event that took place at a specific time and place in one's past.

automaticity: With practice and experience, processes become automatic and require fewer cognitive resources.

autonomous morality: Piaget's second stage of morality in which children have a more flexible view of rules as they begin to value fairness and equality and account for factors like act, intent, and situation.

autonomy: The ability to make and carry out decisions independently.

autonomy versus shame and doubt: In Erikson's theory, the psychosocial crisis of toddlerhood in which individuals must establish the sense that they can make choices and guide their actions and bodies.

babbling: An infant's repetition of syllables such as "ba-ba-ba-ba" and "ma-ma-ma," which begins at about 6 months of age.

basic emotions: Emotions that are universal in humans, appear early in life, and are thought to have a long evolutional history; includes happiness, interest, surprise, fear, anger, sadness, and disgust.

behavioral genetics: The field of study that examines how genes and environment combine to influence the diversity of human traits, abilities, and behaviors.

behaviorism: A theoretical approach that studies how observable behavior is controlled by the physical and social environment through conditioning.

beneficence and nonmaleficence: The ethical principle that requires searchers to adhere to the dual responsibilities to do good and to avoid doing harm.

binge eating disorder: An eating disorder characterized by binges, consuming an abnormally large amount of food (thousands of calories) in a single sitting coupled with a feeling of being out of control.

bioecological systems theory: A theory introduced by Bronfenbrenner that emphasizes the role of context in development, positing that contexts are organized into a series of systems in which individuals are embedded and that interact with one another and the person to influence development.

blastocyst: A thin-walled, fluid-filled sphere containing an inner mass of cells from which the embryo will develop; is implanted into the uterine wall during the germinal period.

body image dissatisfaction: Dissatisfaction with one's physical appearance as shown by a discrepancy between one's ideal body figure and actual body figure.

body mass index (BMI): A measure of body fat based on weight in kilograms divided by height in meters squared (kg/m^2).

Brazelton Neonatal Behavioral Assessment Scale (NBAS): The most common neurobehavioral assessment administered to newborns that is administered a few days after birth to assess neurological functioning, including the strength of 20 inborn reflexes, responsiveness to the physical and social environment, and changes in state.

breech position: A feet-first birth position that poses risks to the neonate's health; often results in a cesarean section.

Broca's area: The region in the brain that controls the ability to use language for expression; damage to the area inhibits fluent speech.

bulimia nervosa: An eating disorder characterized by recurrent episodes of binge eating and subsequent purging usually by induced vomiting and the use of laxatives.

bullying: Refers to an ongoing interaction in which a child repeatedly attempts to inflict physical, verbal, or social harm on another child; also known as *peer victimization*.

canalization: The tendency for a trait that is biologically programmed to be restricted to only a few outcomes.

care orientation: Gilligan's feminine mode of moral reasoning, characterized by a desire to maintain relationships and a responsibility to avoid hurting others.

case study: An in-depth examination of a single individual (or small group of individuals).

categorical self: A classification of the self based on broad ways in which people differ, such as sex, age, and physical characteristics, which children use to guide their behavior.

categorization: An adaptive mental process in which objects are grouped into conceptual categories, allowing for organized storage of information in memory, efficient retrieval of that information, and the capacity to respond with familiarity to new stimuli from a common class.

central executive: In information processing, the part of our mental system that directs the flow of information and regulates cognitive activities such as attention, action, and problem solving.

centration: The tendency to focus on one part of a stimulus, situation, or idea and exclude all others; a characteristic of preoperational reasoning.

cephalocaudal development: The principle that growth proceeds from the head downward; the head and upper regions of the body develop before the lower regions.

cerebellum: Part of the brain at the back of the skull that is responsible for body movements, balance, and coordination.

cesarean section: A surgical procedure that removes the fetus from the uterus through the abdomen; also known as a *C-section*.

child assent: A child's agreement to participate in a study.

child maltreatment: Any intentional harm to a minor, including actions that harm the child physically, emotionally, sexually, or through neglect; also known as *child abuse*.

child-centered preschool programs: A constructivist approach to early childhood education that encourages children to actively build their own understanding of the world through observing, interacting with objects and people, and engaging in a variety of activities that allow them to manipulate materials and interact with teachers and peers.

chorionic villus sampling: Prenatal diagnostic test that is conducted on cells sampled from the chorion to detect chromosomal abnormalities.

chromosome: One of 46 rod-like molecules that contain 23 pairs of DNA found in every body cell and collectively contain all of the genes.

cisgender: An individual who identifies with his or her chromosomal sex.

class inclusion: Involves understanding hierarchical relationships among items.

classical conditioning: A form of learning in which an environmental stimulus becomes associated with stimuli that elicit reflex responses.

classification: The ability to organize things into groups based on similar characteristics.

clique: A tight-knit peer group of about three to eight close friends who share similarities such as demographics and attitudes.

cognitive development: Maturation of mental processes and tools individuals use to obtain knowledge, think, and solve problems.

cognitive disequilibrium: A mismatch between an individual's schemas and the world.

cognitive equilibrium: A balance between the processes of assimilation and accommodation such that an individual's schemas match the world.

cognitive schema: A mental representation, such as concepts, ideas, and ways of interacting with the world.

cognitive-developmental theory: A perspective posited by Piaget that views individuals as active explorers of their world, learning by interacting with the world around them, and describes cognitive development as progressing through stages.

concrete operational stage of reasoning: Piaget's third stage of reasoning, from about 6 to 11, in which thought becomes logical and is applied to direct tangible experiences but not to abstract problems.

conservation: The principle that a physical quantity, such as number, mass, or volume, remains the same even when its appearance changes.

context: Unique conditions in which a person develops, including aspects of the physical and social environment such as family, neighborhood, culture, and historical time period.

continuous change: An aspect of development that unfolds slowly and gradually over time.

conventional moral reasoning: The second level of Kohlberg's theory in which moral decisions are based on conforming to social rules.

cooing: An infant's repetition of sounds, such as "ahhhh," "ohhh," and "eeee," that begins between 2 and 3 months of age.

core knowledge theory: A framework explaining that infants are born with several innate knowledge systems or core domains of thought that enable early rapid learning and adaptation.

correlational research: A research design that measures relationships among participants' measured characteristics, behaviors, and development.

cortex: The outermost part of the brain containing the greatest numbers of neurons and accounting for thought and consciousness.

cross-sectional research study: A developmental research design that compares people of different ages at a single point in time to infer age differences.

cross-sequential research study: A research design that combines the cross-sectional and longitudinal research by assessing multiple cohorts over time.

crowd: A large group of adolescents grouped based on perceived shared characteristics, interests, and reputation.

culture: A set of customs, knowledge, attitudes, and values shared by a group of people and learned through interactions with group members.

deferred imitation: Imitating the behavior of an absent model; illustrates infants' capacity for mental representation.

delayed phase preference: Change in pubertal hormone levels causes adolescents' sleep patterns to shift such that they tend to remain awake late at night and are groggy early in the morning.

deoxyribonucleic acid (DNA): The chemical structure, shaped like a twisted ladder, that contains all of the genes.

dependent variable: The behavior under study in an experiment; it is expected to be affected by changes in the independent variable.

depth perception: The ability to perceive the distance of objects from each other and from ourselves.

development: The processes by which individuals grow and change, as well as the ways in which they stay the same over time.

developmental dyscalculia: A specific learning disorder that affects mathematics ability.

developmental dysgraphia: A specific learning disorder that affects writing abilities.

developmental dyslexia: The most commonly diagnosed learning disability, characterized by unusual difficulty in matching letters to sounds and difficulty with word recognition and spelling despite adequate instruction and intelligence and intact sensory abilities.

developmental science: The study of human development at all points in life, from conception to death.

developmentally appropriate practice: An educational approach that tailors instruction to the age of the child, recognizing individual differences and the need for hands-on active teaching methods.

difficult temperament: A temperament characterized by irregularity in biological rhythms, slow adaptation to change, and a tendency for intense negative reactions.

discipline: The methods a parent uses to teach and socialize children.

discontinuous change: An aspect of development that is characterized by abrupt change.

distributive justice: The moral issue of how to divide goods fairly.

dizygotic (DZ) twin: Occurs when two ova are released and each is fertilized by a different sperm, and the resulting offspring share 50% of the genetic material; also known as a *fraternal twin*.

domains of development: A type or area of development, such as physical, cognitive, or socioemotional.

dominant–recessive inheritance: A form of genetic inheritance in which the phenotype reflects only the dominant allele of a heterozygous pair.

doula: A caregiver who provides support to an expectant mother and her partner throughout the birth process.

Down syndrome: A condition in which a third, extra chromosome appears at the 21st site; also known as *trisomy 21*. Down syndrome is associated with distinctive physical characteristics accompanied by developmental disability.

dual-language learning: An approach in which children are taught and develop skills in two languages; also known as *two-way immersion*.

dual-systems model: A model of the brain consisting of two systems, one emotional and the other rational, that develop on different timeframes, accounting for typical adolescent behavior.

dynamic systems theory: A framework describing motor skills as resulting from ongoing interactions among physical, cognitive, and socioemotional influences and environmental supports in which previously mastered skills are combined to provide more complex and effective ways of exploring and controlling the environment.

easy temperament: A temperament characterized by regularity in biological rhythms, the tendency to adapt easily to new experiences, and a general cheerfulness.

eating disorders: Mental disorders that are characterized by extreme over- or under-control of eating and behaviors intended to control weight such as compulsive exercise, dieting, or purging.

egocentrism: Piaget's term for children's inability to take another person's point of view or perspective and to assume that others share the same feelings, knowledge, and physical view of the world.

elaboration: A memory strategy in which one imagines a scene or story to link the material to be remembered.

embryo: Prenatal organism between about 2 and 8 weeks after conception; a period of major structural development.

embryonic period: Occurs from about 2 to 8 weeks after pregnancy, in which rapid structural development takes place.

emerging adulthood: a developmental period between adolescence and early adulthood, extending from the completion of secondary education to the adoption of adult roles.

emotion regulation: The ability to adjust and control our emotional state to influence how and when emotions are expressed.

emotional display rule: Unstated cultural guidelines for acceptable emotions and emotional expression that are communicated to children via parents' emotional behavior, expressions, and socialization.

empathy: The capacity to understand another person's emotions and concerns.

epigenetics: A perspective that development results from dynamic interactions between genetics and the environment such that the expression of genetic inheritance is influenced by environmental forces.

episodic memory: Memory for everyday experiences.

ethnic identity: A sense of membership in an ethnic group and viewing the attitudes and practices associated with that group as an enduring part of the self.

ethology: Emphasizes the evolutionary basis of behavior and its adaptive value in ensuring survival of a species.

evolutionary developmental theory: A perspective that applies principles of evolution and scientific knowledge about the interactive influence of genetic and environmental mechanisms to understand the adaptive value of developmental changes that are experienced with age.

executive function: The set of cognitive operations that support planning, decision making, and goal-setting abilities, such as the ability to control attention, coordinate information in working memory, and inhibit impulses.

experience-dependent brain development: Brain growth and development in response-specific learning experiences.

experience-expectant brain development: Brain growth and development that are dependent on basic environmental experiences, such as visual and auditory stimulation, in order to develop normally.

experimental research: A research design that permits inferences about cause and effect by exerting control, systematically manipulating a variable, and studying the effects on measured variables.

expressive trait: A trait such as kindness, creativity, gentleness, and cooperation that is a key characteristic of the feminine gender role.

external attributions: Emphasizing external factors that cannot be controlled as causes of an outcome.

externality effect: Refers to a particular pattern of infant visual processing.

extremely low birthweight: Refers to a birthweight of less than 750 grams (1 pound, 10 ounces); poses serious risks for survival, developmental challenges, and handicaps.

fallopian tube: A long, thin tube that connects the ovaries to the uterus.

false-belief task: A task that requires children to understand that someone does not share their knowledge.

fast mapping: A process by which children learn new words after only a brief encounter, connecting them with their own mental categories.

fetal alcohol spectrum disorders: The continuum of physical, mental, and behavioral outcomes caused by prenatal exposure to alcohol.

fetal alcohol syndrome (FAS): The most severe form of fetal alcohol spectrum disorder accompanying heavy prenatal exposure to alcohol, including a distinct pattern of facial characteristics, growth deficiencies, and deficits in intellectual development.

fetal MRI: Applies MRI technology to image the fetus's body and diagnose malformations.

fetal period: Occurs during the ninth week of prenatal development to birth, in which the fetus grows rapidly, and its organs become more complex and begin to function.

fetus: The prenatal organism from about the ninth week of pregnancy to delivery; a period of rapid growth and maturation of body structures.

fine motor development: The ability to control small movements of the fingers such as reaching and grasping.

first-generation college student: A student who is the first in their family to attend college.

fixed mindset: Viewing one's characteristics as enduring and unchangeable.

Flynn effect: The rise in IQ scores over generations in many nations.

formal operational reasoning: Piaget's fourth stage of cognitive development, characterized by abstract, logical, and systematic thinking.

fragile X syndrome: An example of a dominant–recessive disorder carried on the X chromosome characterized by intellectual disability, cardiac defects, and behavioral mannerisms common in individuals with autism spectrum disorder; occurs in both males and females but is more severe in males.

gamete: A reproductive cell; sperm in males and ovum in females.

gender constancy: A child's understanding of the biological permanence of gender and that it does not change regardless of appearance, activities, or attitudes.

gender identity: Awareness of oneself as a male or female.

gender intensification hypothesis: The view that young adolescents become sensitive to gender stereotypes and are increasingly likely to adhere to gender stereotypes.

gender role norms: The activities, attitudes, skills, and characteristics that are considered appropriate for males or females.

gender schema: A concept or a mental structure that organizes gender-related information and embodies a person's understanding of what it means to be a male or female and is used as a guide to attitudes and behaviors.

gender stereotypes: Refer to broad generalized judgments of the activities, attitudes, skills, and characteristics deemed appropriate for males or females in a given culture.

gender typing: The process in which young children acquire the characteristics and attitudes that are considered appropriate for males or females.

gene: The basic unit of heredity; a small section of a chromosome that contains the string of chemicals (DNA) that provide instructions for the cell to manufacture proteins.

gene–environment correlation: The idea that many of an individual's traits are supported by his or her genes and environment; there are three types of correlations: passive, reactive, and active.

gene–environment interactions: Refer to the dynamic interplay between our genes and our environment in determining our characteristics, behavior, and physical, cognitive, and social development as well as health.

genetic counseling: A medical specialty that helps prospective parents determine the probability that their children will inherit genetic defects and chromosomal abnormalities.

genomic imprinting: The instance when the expression of a gene is determined by whether it is inherited from the mother or father.

genotype: An individual's collection of genes that contain instructions for all physical and psychological characteristics, including hair color, eye color, personality, health, and behavior.

germinal period: Also referred to as the period of the zygote; refers to the first 2 weeks after conception.

giftedness: Exceptional intelligence.

glial cell: A type of brain cell that nourishes neurons and provides structure to the brain.

global self-esteem: An overall evaluation of self-worth.

goodness of fit: The compatibility between a child's temperament and his or her environment, especially the parent's temperament and childrearing methods; the greater the degree of match, the more favorable the child's adjustment.

gray matter: Unmyelinated neurons.

gross motor development: The ability to control large movements of the body, such as walking and jumping.

growing pains: Intermittent aches and stiffness in the legs often experienced at night that are caused by the stretching and molding of the muscles to fit the child's growing skeleton.

growth faltering: A condition in which growth and weight are substantially lower than the norm expected for a child's age; also known as *failure to thrive*.

growth hormone deficiency: Too little growth hormone circulating in the blood, which affects an individual's growth rate.

growth mindset: Viewing one's skills and characteristics as malleable or changeable.

growth norm: The expectation for typical gains and variations in height and weight for children based on their chronological age and ethnic background.

growth stunting: A reduced growth rate.

guided participation: The process by which people learn from others who guide them, providing a scaffold to help them accomplish more than the child could do alone; also known as *apprenticeship in thinking*.

habituation: The gradual decline in the intensity, frequency, or duration of a response when repeatedly exposed to a stimulus; indicates learning.

health literacy: Refers to the knowledge, skills, and attitudes about health and the ability to obtain, process, and understand health information to make appropriate health decisions.

hemophilia: An X-linked chromosomal disorder involving abnormal blood clotting.

heritability: The statistic that indicates the extent to which variation of a certain trait can be traced to genes.

heteronomous morality: Piaget's first stage of morality when children become aware of rules and view them as absolute and unalterable.

hippocampus: A structure located in the inner region of the temporal lobe.

holophrase: A one-word expression used to convey a complete thought.

hormone: A chemical that is produced and secreted into the bloodstream to affect and influence physiological functions.

human immunodeficiency virus (HIV): The most serious sexually transmitted infection, which causes acquired immune deficiency syndrome (AIDS).

human papillomavirus (HPV): The most common type of sexually transmitted infection diagnosed in people of all ages; comprises several types, some of which can cause cancer in different areas of the body (e.g., cervical cancer in women).

hypothesis: A proposed explanation for a phenomenon that can be tested.

hypothetical–deductive reasoning: The ability to consider propositions and probabilities, generate and systematically test hypotheses, and draw conclusions.

ideal self: A sense of self that is characterized by traits that one values.

identity: A coherent organized sense of self that includes values, attitudes, and goals to which one is committed.

identity achievement status: The identity state that requires that individuals construct a sense of self through reflection, critical examination, and exploring or trying out new ideas and belief systems.

identity diffusion: The identity state in which an individual has not undergone exploration or committed to self-chosen values and goals.

identity foreclosed status: The identity state in which an individual has not undergone exploration but has committed to values and goals chosen by an authority figure.

identity status: The degree to which individuals have explored possible selves and whether they have committed to specific beliefs and goals, assessed by administering interview and survey measures, and categorized into four identity statuses.

imaginary audience: A manifestation of adolescent egocentrism in which they assume that they are the focus of others' attention.

imaginary companion: A make-believe friend or companion a child comes up with during early childhood.

implantation: The process by which the blastocyst becomes attached to the uterine wall, completed by about 10 days after fertilization.

in vitro fertilization: Fertilization, the creation of zygotes, that takes place outside of a woman's body by mixing sperm with ova that have been surgically removed from the woman's body.

inclusion: The approach in which children with learning disabilities learn alongside other children in the regular classroom for all or part of the day, accompanied by additional educational support of a teacher or paraprofessional who is specially trained to meet their needs.

incomplete dominance: A genetic inheritance pattern in which both genes are expressed in the phenotype.

independent variable: The factor proposed to change the behavior under study in an experiment; it is systematically manipulated during an experiment.

indifferent gonad: A gonad in an embryo that has not yet differentiated into testes or ovaries.

inductive discipline: Strategy to control children's behavior that relies on reasoning and discussion.

infant-directed speech: Uses shorter words and sentences, higher and more varied pitch, repetitions, a slower rate, and longer pauses; also known as *motherese*.

information processing theory: A perspective that uses a computer analogy to describe how the mind receives information and manipulates, stores, recalls, and uses it to solve problems.

informed consent: A participant's informed (knowledge of the scope of the research and potential harm and benefits of participating), rational, and voluntary agreement to participate in a study.

initiative versus guilt: Erikson's third psychosocial stage in which young children develop a sense of purposefulness, try new skills and activities, and take pride in their accomplishments, as well as feel guilty if they are unsuccessful.

insecure–avoidant attachment: An attachment pattern in which an infant avoids connecting with a caregiver, showing no distress when separated from the caregiver, such as during the Strange Situation, and does not seem to care about the caregiver's return.

insecure–disorganized attachment: An attachment in which an infant shows inconsistent, contradictory behavior in the Strange Situation, suggesting a conflict between approaching and fleeing the caregiver and perhaps fear.

insecure–resistant attachment: An attachment pattern in which an infant shows anxiety and uncertainty, showing great distress at separation from the caregiver during the Strange Situation, and simultaneously seeks and avoids contact upon the caregiver's return.

instrumental aggression: Behavior that hurts someone else in order to achieve a goal such as gaining a possession.

instrumental assistance: Tangible help.

Instrumental traits: Traits such as dominance and acting on the world to fulfill the role of provider and protector that are characteristic of the masculine gender role.

integrity: The ethical principle that requires that scientists be accurate, honest, and truthful in their work.

intelligence: An individual's ability to adapt to the environment.

intelligence test (IQ test): A test designed to measure the aptitude to learn at school; intellectual aptitude.

intermodal perception: The process of combining information from more than one sensory system, such as visual and auditory senses.

internal attributions: Emphasizing one's own role influence as the cause of an outcome.

internal working model: A set of expectations about one's worthiness of love and the availability of attachment figures during times of distress.

irreversibility: A characteristic of preoperational thought in which a child does not understand that an action can be reversed and a thing restored to its original state.

justice: The ethical principle that requires that risks and benefits of research participation must be spread equitably across individuals and groups.

justice orientation: A male mode of moral reasoning proposed by Gilligan that emphasizes the abstract principles of fairness and individualism.

kangaroo care: An intervention for low-birthweight babies in which the infant is placed vertically against the parent's chest, under the shirt, providing skin-to-skin contact.

kwashiorkor: A malnutrition disease in children caused by deprivation of protein and calories and characterized by lethargy and the bloating and swelling of the stomach.

labor: Occurs at about 40 weeks of pregnancy, or 38 weeks after conception; also known as *childbirth*.

language acquisition device (LAD): In Chomsky's theory, an innate facilitator of language that allows infants to quickly and efficiently analyze everyday speech and determine its rules, regardless of their native language.

lanugo: A fine, down-like hair that covers the fetus's body.

lateralization: The process by which the two hemispheres of the brain become specialized to carry out different functions.

learned helplessness orientation: An orientation characterized by a fixed mindset and the attribution of poor performance to internal factors.

limbic system: A collection of brain structures responsible for emotion.

logical extension: A strategy children use to increase their vocabulary in which they extend a new word to other objects in the same category.

longitudinal research study: A developmental study in which one group of participants is studied repeatedly to infer age changes.

long-term memory: The component of the information processing system that is an unlimited store that holds information indefinitely, until it is retrieved to manipulate in working memory.

low birthweight: Classifies infants who weigh less than 2,500 grams (5.5 pounds) at birth.

marasmus: A wasting disease in which the body's fat and muscle are depleted; growth stops and the body wastes away, taking on a hollow appearance.

meiosis: The process by which a gamete is formed, containing one-half of the cell's chromosomes, producing ova and sperm with 23 single, unpaired chromosomes.

melatonin: A hormone that influences sleep.

memory strategy: Deliberate cognitive activities that make an individual more likely to remember information.

menarche: A girl's first menstrual period.

menstruation: The monthly shedding of the uterine lining, which has thickened in preparation for the implantation of a fertilized egg.

mental representation: An internal depiction of an object; thinking of an object using mental pictures.

metacognition: The ability to think about thinking; knowledge of how the mind works.

metamemory: An aspect of metacognition that refers to the understanding of memory and how to use strategies to enhance memory.

mitosis: The process of cell duplication in which DNA is replicated and the resulting cell is genetically identical to the original.

monozygotic (MZ) twin: Occurs when the zygote splits apart early in development, and the resulting offspring share 100% of their genetic material; also known as an *identical twin*.

Montessori school: A child-centered educational approach, first created in the early 1900s by the Italian physician and educator Maria Montessori (1870–1952), in which children are viewed as active constructors of their own development and are given freedom in choosing their activities.

moratorium status: The identity state that includes active exploration of ideas and a sense of openness to possibilities, coupled with some uncertainty.

multiple intelligence theory: Gardner's proposition that human intelligence is composed of a varied set of abilities.

mutation: A sudden permanent change in the structure of genes.

mutual exclusivity assumption: When learning new words, young children assume that objects have only one label or name.

mutual perspective taking: Adolescents' understanding that they take other people's point of view at the same time as others attempt to take their own point of view.

myelin: The fatty substance that coats the axons, which speeds the transmission of electrical impulses and neurological function.

myelination: The process in which neurons are coated in a fatty substance, myelin, which contributes to faster neural communication.

natural childbirth: An approach to birth that reduces pain through the use of breathing and relaxation exercises.

naturalistic observation: A research method in which a researcher views and records an individual's behavior in natural, real-world settings.

nature–nurture debate: A debate within the field of human development regarding whether development is caused by nature (genetics or heredity) or nurture (the physical and social environment).

neural tube: Forms during the third week after conception and will develop into the central nervous system (brain and spinal cord).

neurogenesis: The production of new neurons.

neuron: A nerve cell that stores and transmits information; billions of neurons comprise the brain.

niche-picking: An active gene–environment correlation in which individuals seek out experiences and environments that complement their genetic tendencies.

nightmare: An anxiety-provoking dream.

nocturnal emissions: involuntary ejaculations that are sometimes accompanied by erotic dreams; also known as *wet dreams*.

noninvasive prenatal testing (NIPT): A prenatal diagnostic that samples cell-free fetal DNA from the mother's blood for chromosomal abnormalities.

nonsuicidal self-injury: Self-inflicted behavior intended to cause harm, not death.

obesity: In children, defined as having a body mass index at or above the 95th percentile for height and age.

object permanence: The understanding that objects continue to exist outside of sight.

observational learning: Learning that occurs by watching and imitating models, as posited by social learning theory.

open-ended interview: A research method in which a researcher asks a participant questions using a flexible, conversational style and may vary the order of questions, probe, and ask follow-up questions based on the participant's responses.

operant conditioning: A form of learning in which behavior increases or decreases based on environmental consequences.

organization: Memory strategy in which items to remember are categorized or grouped by theme or type.

ossification: The process of cartilage being converted into bone.

overextension: A vocabulary error in which the infant applies a word too broadly to a wider class of objects than appropriate.

overregularization errors: Grammatical mistakes that children make because they apply grammatical rules too stringently to words that are exceptions.

ovulation: An event that takes place about every 28 days, in which an ovum bursts from one of the ovaries into the long, thin fallopian tube that leads to the uterus.

parental monitoring: Parents' awareness of their children's activities, whereabouts, and companions.

parenting style: Enduring sets of childrearing behaviors a parent uses across situations to form a childrearing climate.

peer rejection: An ongoing interaction in which a child is deliberately excluded by peers.

perception: The mental processing of sensory information, which is interpreted as sight, sound, and smell, for example.

perceptual narrowing: A decline in sensitivity to discriminate faces within unfamiliar groups.

permissive parenting style: A childrearing approach characterized by high levels of warmth and low levels of control or discipline.

personal fable: A manifestation of adolescent egocentrism in which adolescents believe their thoughts, feelings, and experiences are more special and unique than anyone else's, as well as the sense that they are invulnerable.

phenotype: The observable physical or behavioral characteristics of a person's eye color, hair color, or height.

phenylketonuria (PKU): A recessive disorder that prevents the body from producing an enzyme that breaks down phenylalanine (an amino acid) from proteins that, without treatment, leads to buildup that damages the central nervous system.

physical development: Body maturation, including body size, proportion, appearance, health, and perceptual abilities.

placenta: The principal organ of exchange between the mother and the developing organism, enabling the exchange of nutrients, oxygen, and wastes via the umbilical cord.

plasticity: A characteristic of development that refers to malleability or openness to change in response to experience.

polygenic inheritance: Occurs when a trait is a function of the interaction of many genes, such as with height, intelligence, and temperament.

popular children: Children who receive many positive ratings from peers indicating that they are accepted and valued by peers.

positive youth development (PYD): An approach that seeks to discover and promote positive qualities that contribute to adolescents' ability to adapt and engage in constructive interactions with their complex and changing contexts.

postconventional moral reasoning: Kohlberg's third level of moral reasoning emphasizing autonomous decision making based on principles such as valuing human dignity.

pragmatics: The practical application of language for everyday communication.

preconventional reasoning: Kohlberg's first level of reasoning in which young children's behavior is governed by punishment and gaining rewards.

prefrontal cortex: Located in the front of the brain, responsible for higher thought, such as planning, goal setting, controlling impulses, and using cognitive skills and memory to solve problems.

prenatal care: A set of services provided to improve pregnancy outcomes and engage the expectant mother, family members, and friends in pregnancy-related health care decisions.

prenatal development: The development process from conception until birth.

preoperational reasoning: Piaget's second stage of cognitive development, between about ages 2 and 6, characterized by advances in symbolic thought, but thought is not yet logical.

preterm: A birth that occurs 35 or fewer weeks after conception.

primary circular reaction: In Piaget's theory, repeating an action that produced a chance event involving the infant's body.

primary sex characteristic: The reproductive organs; in females, this includes the ovaries, fallopian tubes, uterus, and vagina, and in males, this includes the penis, testes, scrotum, seminal vesicles, and prostate gland.

private speech: Self-directed speech that children use to guide their behavior.

productive language: Language individuals can produce for themselves.

Project Head Start: Early childhood intervention program funded by the U.S. federal government that provides low-income children with nutritional, health, and educational services, as well as helps parents become involved in their children's development.

prosocial behavior: Actions that are oriented toward others for the pure sake of helping, without a reward.

proximodistal development: The principle that growth and development proceed from the center of the body outward.

psychoanalytic theory: A perspective introduced by Freud that development and behavior are stage-like and influenced by inner drives, memories, and conflicts of which an individual is unaware and which the individual cannot control.

psychosocial moratorium: In Erikson's theory, a period in which the individual is free to explore identity possibilities before committing to an identity.

puberty: The biological transition to adulthood, in which hormones cause the body to physically mature and permit sexual reproduction.

punishment: In operant conditioning, the process in which a behavior is followed by an aversive or unpleasant outcome that decreases the likelihood of a response.

questionnaire: A research method in which researchers use a survey or set of questions to collect data from large samples of people.

random assignment: A method of assigning participants that ensures each participant has an equal chance of being assigned to the experimental group or control group.

range of reaction: The concept that a genetic trait may be expressed in a wide range of phenotypes dependent on environmental opportunities and constraints.

rape: Refers to nonconsensual sexual penetration of the body by a body part of another person or by an object.

recall memory: The ability to generate a memory of a stimulus encountered before without seeing it again.

receptive language: Language that one can understand.

recess: Unstructured play that allocates time for free play and social growth.

reciprocal determinism: A perspective positing that individuals and the environment interact and influence each other.

recognition memory: The ability to identify a previously encountered stimulus.

reflex: Involuntary and automatic responses to stimuli such as touch, light, and sound.

rehearsal: A mnemonic strategy that involves systematically repeating information to retain it in working memory.

reinforcement: In operant conditioning, the process by which a behavior is followed by a desirable outcome that increases the likelihood of a response.

REM sleep: Rapid eye movement sleep, in which an individual's brain wave activity is remarkably similar to that of the waking state but the individual is asleep.

representational play: Make-believe play in which children often pretend that one object is something else.

resilience: The ability to adapt to serious adversity.

respect for autonomy: The ethical principle that states researchers have a special obligation to respect participants' autonomy, their ability to make and implement decisions.

response inhibition: Part of executive function, the ability to control and stop responding to a stimulus.

responsibility: The ethical principle that requires researchers to act responsibly by adhering to professional standards of conduct and clarifying their obligations and roles to others.

rough-and-tumble play: Social interaction involving chasing and play fighting with no intent to harm.

scaffolding: Temporary support that permits a child to bridge the gap between his or her current competence level and the task at hand.

scientific method: The process of forming and answering questions using systematic observations and gathering information.

script: Description of what occurs in a certain situation and used as a guide to understand and organize daily experiences.

secondary circular reaction: In Piaget's theory, repeating an action that produced a chance event that triggers a response in the external environment.

secondary sex characteristic: Physical traits that indicate sexual maturity but are not directly related to fertility, such as breast development and the growth of body hair.

secular trend: The change from one generation to the next in an aspect of development, such as body size or the timing of puberty.

secure attachment: The attachment pattern in which an infant uses the caregiver as a secure base from which to explore, seeks contact during reunions, and is easily comforted by the caregiver.

selective attention: The ability to focus on relevant stimuli and ignore others.

self-concept: The set of attributes, abilities, and characteristics that a person uses to describe and define himself or herself.

self-conscious emotion: Emotion that requires cognitive development and an awareness of self, such as empathy, embarrassment, shame, and guilt.

self-esteem: The emotional evaluation of one's own worth.

self-recognition: The ability to identify the self, typically measured as mirror recognition.

semen: The fluid that contains sperm.

sensation: The physical response of sensory receptors when a stimulus is detected (e.g., activity of the sensory receptors in the eye in response to light); awareness of stimuli in the senses.

sensitive period: A period during which experience has a particularly powerful role in shaping developmental outcomes.

sensory memory: The first step in the information processing system in which a stimulus is stored for a brief moment in its original form to enable it to be processed.

sensory processing disorder (SPD): An extreme difficulty processing and responding to sensory stimuli that interferes with daily functioning.

separation anxiety: Occurs when infants respond to the departure of an attachment figure with distress and crying; also known as *separation protest*.

seriation: A type of classification that involves ordering objects in a series according to a physical dimension such as height, weight, or color.

sexting: The exchange of explicit sexual messages or images via mobile phone.

sexual assault: A broader term than rape, refers to a wide variety of nonconsensual sexual contact or behavior.

sexual orientation: A term that refers to whether someone is sexually attracted to others of the same sex, opposite sex, or both.

sickle cell trait: A recessive trait, most often affecting African Americans, that causes red blood cells to become crescent or sickle shaped, resulting in difficulty distributing oxygen throughout the circulatory system.

sleep terror: An episode of screaming, flailing, and fear while asleep.

sleeper effects: Teratogenic outcomes or effects that are not visible until many years later.

slow-to-warm-up temperament: A temperament characterized by mild irregularity in biological rhythms, slow adaptation to change, and mildly negative mood.

small for date: Describes an infant who is full term but who has significantly lower weight than expected for the gestational age.

social comparison: The tendency to compare and judge one's abilities, achievements, and behaviors in relation to others.

social learning theory: An approach that emphasizes the role of modeling and observational learning over people's behavior in addition to reinforcement and punishment.

social perspective taking: The ability to understand different viewpoints.

social referencing: Seeking information from caregivers about how to interpret unfamiliar or ambiguous events by observing their emotional expressions and reactions.

social smile: A smile that emerges between 6 and 10 weeks in response to seeing familiar people.

societal perspective taking: The understanding that societal factors influence people's perspectives and beliefs.

sociocultural theory: Vygotsky's theory that individuals acquire culturally relevant ways of thinking through social interactions with members of their culture.

sociodramatic play: Make-believe play in which children act out roles and themes.

socioemotional development: Maturation of social and emotional functioning, which includes changes in personality, emotions, personal perceptions, social skills, and interpersonal relationships.

special education: Education tailored to meet the needs of a child with special needs, such as a specific learning disability.

specific learning disorder (SLD): Diagnosed in children who demonstrate a measurable discrepancy between aptitude and achievement in a particular academic area given their age, intelligence, and amount of schooling.

spermarche: A boy's first ejaculation of sperm.

spina bifida: A neural tube that results in spinal nerves growing outside of the vertebrae, often resulting in paralysis and developmental disability.

stage-environment fit: Refers to the match between the characteristics and supports of the school environment and the developing person's needs and capacities. Influences well-being.

states of arousal: Degrees of wakefulness; newborns shift among five states of arousal ranging from regular sleep to waking activity.

Strange Situation: A structured laboratory procedure that measures the security of attachment by observing infants' reactions to being separated from the caregiver in an unfamiliar environment.

stranger wariness: An infant's expression of fear of unfamiliar people; also known as *stranger anxiety*.

structured interview: A research method in which each participant is asked the same set of questions in the same way.

structured observation: An observational measure in which an individual's behavior is viewed and recorded in a controlled environment; a situation created by the experimenter.

sudden infant death syndrome (SIDS): The sudden unexpected death of an infant less than 1 year of age that occurs seemingly during sleep and remains unexplained after a thorough investigation.

surrogacy: An alternative form of reproduction in which a woman (the surrogate) is impregnated and carries a fetus to term and agrees to turn the baby over to a woman, man, or couple who will raise the child.

sustained attention: The ability to remain focused on a stimulus for an extended period of time.

synapse: The intersection or gap between the axon of one neuron and the dendrites of other neurons; the gap that neurotransmitters must cross.

synaptic pruning: The process by which synapses, neural connections that are seldom used, disappear.

synaptogenesis: The process in which neurons form synapses and increase connections between neurons.

telegraphic speech: Two-word utterances produced by toddlers that communicate only the essential words.

temperament: Characteristic differences among individuals in emotional reactivity, self-regulation, and activity that influence reactions to the environment and are stable and appear early in life.

teratogen: An environmental factor that causes damage to prenatal development.

tertiary circular reaction: In Piaget's theory, repeating an action to explore and experiment in order to see the results and learn about the world.

testes: The glands that produce sperm.

theory: An organized set of observations to describe, explain, and predict a phenomenon.

theory of mind: Children's awareness of their own and other people's mental processes and realization that other people do not share their thoughts.

three-mountains task: A classic Piagetian task used to illustrate preoperational children's egocentrism.

transgender: Denotes when a person's sense of identity and gender do not correspond to that person's biological sex.

transitive inference: A classification skill in which a child can infer the relationship between two objects by understanding each object's relationship to a third object.

triarchic theory of intelligence: Sternberg's theory positing three independent forms of intelligence: analytical, creative, and applied.

trust versus mistrust: The first psychosocial crisis in Erikson's theory in which infants must develop a basic sense of trust of the world as a safe place where their basic needs will be met.

ultrasound: Prenatal diagnostic procedure in which high-frequency sound waves are directed at the mother's abdomen to provide clear images of the womb projected onto a video monitor.

underextension: A vocabulary error in which the infant applies a word too narrowly to a single object rather than the more appropriate, wider class of objects.

uninvolved parenting style: A childrearing style characterized by low levels of warmth and acceptance coupled with little control or discipline.

vaccine: A small dose of inactive virus that is injected into the body to stimulate the production of antibodies to guard against a disease.

verbal aggression: A form of relational aggression, intended to harm others' social relationships.

vernix caseosa: Greasy material that protects the fetal skin from abrasions, chapping, and hardening that can occur from exposure to amniotic fluid.

very low birthweight: Refers to a birthweight less than 1,500 grams (3.5 pounds); poses risks for developmental disabilities and handicaps.

violation-of-expectation task: A task in which a stimulus appears to violate physical laws.

visual acuity: Sharpness of vision.

Wernicke's area: The region of the brain that is responsible for language comprehension; damage to this area impairs the ability to understand others' speech and sometimes the ability to speak coherently.

white matter: Myelinated brain tissue.

withdrawn-rejected children: Children who are withdrawn and passive and are shunned by peers.

working memory: The component of the information processing system that holds and processes information that is being manipulated, encoded, or retrieved and is responsible for maintaining and processing information used in cognitive tasks.

zone of proximal development: Vygotsky's term for the tasks that children cannot do alone but can exercise with the aid of more skilled partners.

zygote: A fertilized ovum.

REFERENCES

AAP Committee on Psychosocial Aspects of Child and Family Health. (1998). Guidance for effective discipline. *Pediatrics, 101*, 723–728.

AAP Task Force on Circumcision. (2012). Circumcision policy statement. *Pediatrics, 130*(3), 585–586. https://doi.org/10.1542/peds.2012-1989

Abbasi, J. (2017). The paternal epigenome makes its mark. *JAMA, 317*(20), 2049. https://doi.org/10.1001/jama.2017.1566

Abdallah, B., Badr, L. K., & Hawwari, M. (2013). The efficacy of massage on short and long term outcomes in preterm infants. *Infant Behavior and Development, 36*(4), 662–669. https://doi.org/10.1016/j.infbeh.2013.06.009

Ablewhite, J., Peel, I., McDaid, L., Hawkins, A., Goodenough, T., Deave, T., . . . Kessel, A. (2015). Parental perceptions of barriers and facilitators to preventing child unintentional injuries within the home: A qualitative study. *BMC Public Health, 15*(1), 280. https://doi.org/10.1186/s12889-015-1547-2

Abraham, L. M., Crais, E., & Vernon-Feagans, L. (2013). Early maternal language use during book sharing in families from low-income environments. *American Journal of Speech-Language Pathology, 22*(1), 71–83. https://doi.org/10.1044/1058-0360(2012/11-0153)

Acar, E., Dursun, O. B., Esin, İ. S., Öğütlü, H., Özcan, H., & Mutlu, M. (2015). Unintentional injuries in preschool age children: Is there a correlation with parenting style and parental attention deficit and hyperactivity symptoms? *Medicine, 94*(32), e1378. https://doi.org/10.1097/MD.0000000000001378

Ackard, D. M., Fulkerson, J. A., & Neumark-Sztainer, D. (2011). Stability of eating disorder diagnostic classifications in adolescents: Five-year longitudinal findings from a population-based study. *Eating Disorders, 19*(4), 308–322. https://doi.org/10.1080/10640266.2011.584804

Acredolo, L. P., & Goodwyn, S. (1988). Symbolic gesturing in normal infants. *Child Development, 59*(2), 450–466.

Acredolo, L. P., Goodwyn, S., & Abrams, D. (2009). *Baby signs: How to talk with your baby before your baby can talk* (3rd ed.). New York, NY: McGraw-Hill.

Adams, R. E., & Laursen, B. (2007). The correlates of conflict: Disagreement is not necessarily detrimental. *Journal of Family Psychology, 21*(3), 445–458.

Adams-Chapman, I., Hansen, N. I., Shankaran, S., Bell, E. F., Boghossian, N. S., Murray, J. C., . . . Stoll, B. J. (2013). Ten-year review of major birth defects in VLBW infants. *Pediatrics, 132*(1), 49–61. https://doi.org/10.1542/peds.2012-3111

Addabbo, M., Longhi, E., Marchis, I. C., Tagliabue, P., & Turati, C. (2018). Dynamic facial expressions of emotions are discriminated at birth. *PLoS ONE, 13*(3), e0193868. https://doi.org/10.1371/journal.pone.0193868

Adolph, K. E., Cole, W. G., Komati, M., Garciaguirre, J. S., Badaly, D., Lingeman, J. M., . . . Sotsky, R. B. (2012). How do you learn to walk? Thousands of steps and dozens of falls per day. *Psychological Science, 23*(11), 1387–1394. https://doi.org/10.1177/0956797612446346

Adolph, K. E., & Franchak, J. M. (2017). The development of motor behavior. *Wiley Interdisciplinary Reviews: Cognitive Science, 8*(1–2), e1430. https://doi.org/10.1002/wcs.1430

Adolph, K. E., & Kretch, K. S. (2015). Gibson's theory of perceptual learning. In J. D. Wright (Ed.), *International encyclopedia of social and behavioral sciences* (2nd ed., pp. 127–134). New York, NY: Elsevier. https://doi.org/10.1016/B978-0-08-097086-8.23096-1

Adolph, K. E., Kretch, K. S., & LoBue, V. (2014). Fear of heights in infants? *Current Directions in Psychological Science, 23*(1), 60–66. https://doi.org/10.1177/0963721413498895

Adolph, K. E., & Robinson, S. R. (2015). Motor development. In L. S. Liben & U. Müller (Eds.), *Handbook of child psychology and developmental science* (pp. 1–45). Hoboken, NJ: John Wiley & Sons. https://doi.org/10.1002/9781118963418.childpsy204

Adolph, K. E., & Tamis-LeMonda, C. S. (2014). The costs and benefits of development: The transition from crawling to walking. *Child Development Perspectives, 8*(4), 187–192. https://doi.org/10.1111/cdep.12085

Afifi, T. O., & MacMillan, H. L. (2011). Resilience following child maltreatment: A review of protective factors. *La Résilience Aprés La Maltraitance Clans l'enfance: Une Revue Des Facteurs Protecteurs, 56*(5), 266–272.

Afshin, A., Reitsma, M. B., & Murray, C. J. L. (2017). Health effects of overweight and obesity in 195 countries. *New England Journal of Medicine, 377*(15), 1496–1497. https://doi.org/10.1056/NEJMc1710026

Ágh, T., Kovács, G., Supina, D., Pawaskar, M., Herman, B. K., Vokó, Z., & Sheehan, D. V. (2016). A systematic review of the health-related quality of life and economic burdens of anorexia nervosa, bulimia nervosa, and binge eating disorder. *Eating and Weight Disorders: Studies on Anorexia, Bulimia and Obesity, 21*(3), 353–364. https://doi.org/10.1007/s40519-016-0264-x

Aguiar, A., Eubig, P. A., & Schantz, S. L. (2010). Attention deficit/hyperactivity disorder: A focused overview for children's environmental health researchers. *Environmental Health Perspectives, 118*(12), 1646–1653. https://doi.org/10.1289/ehp.1002326

Aguiar, N. R., Mottweilier, C. M., Taylor, M., & Fisher, P. A. (2017). The imaginary companions created by children who have lived in foster care. *Imagination, Cognition and Personality, 36*(4), 340–355. https://doi.org/10.1177/0276236617700590

Agyei, S. B., van der Weel, F. R. R., & van der Meer, A. L. H. (2016). Development of visual motion perception for prospective control: Brain and behavioral studies in infants. *Frontiers in Psychology, 7*, 100. https://doi.org/10.3389/fpsyg.2016.00100

Ahmed, A., & Ruffman, T. (1998). Why do infants make A not B errors in a search task, yet show memory for location of hidden objects in a non-search task? *Developmental Psychology, 34*, 441–453.

Ahn, R. R., Miller, L. J., Milberger, S., & McIntosh, D. N. (2004). Prevalence of parents' perceptions of sensory processing disorders among kindergarten children. *American Journal of Occupational Therapy, 58*(3), 287–293. https://doi.org/10.5014/ajot.58.3.287

Aiello, L. C., & Dunbar, R. I. M. (1993). Neocortex size, group size, and the evolution of language. *Current Anthropology, 34*(2), 184–193. https://doi.org/10.1086/204160

Ainsworth, M. D. S., Blehar, M. C., Waters, E., & Wall, S. (1978). *Patterns of attachment*. Hillsdale, NJ: Erlbaum.

Aïte, A., Cassotti, M., Linzarini, A., Osmont, A., Houdé, O., & Borst, G. (2018). Adolescents' inhibitory control: Keep it cool or lose control. *Developmental Science, 21*(1), e12491. https://doi.org/10.1111/desc.12491

Aizer, A. (2017). The role of children's health in the intergenerational transmission of economic status. *Child Development Perspectives, 11*(3), 167–172. https://doi.org/10.1111/cdep.12231

Akhtar, N., Jipson, J., & Callanan, M. A. (2001). Learning words through overhearing. *Child Development, 72*, 416–430.

Akinbami, L. J., Moorman, J. E., Garbe, P. L., & Sondik, E. J. (2009). Status of childhood asthma in the United States, 1980-2007. *Pediatrics, 123*(Suppl. 3), S131–S145. https://doi.org/10.1542/peds.2008-2233C

Akolekar, R., Beta, J., Picciarelli, G., Ogilvie, C., & D'Antonio, F. (2015). Procedure-related risk of miscarriage following amniocentesis and chorionic villus sampling: A systematic review and meta-analysis. *Ultrasound in Obstetrics & Gynecology, 45*(1), 16–26. https://doi.org/10.1002/uog.14636

Akos, P., Rose, R. A., & Orthner, D. (2014). Sociodemographic moderators of middle school transition effects on academic achievement. *Journal of Early Adolescence, 35*(2), 170–198. https://doi.org/10.1177/0272431614529367

Alaggia, R., Collin-Vézina, D., & Lateef, R. (2018). Facilitators and barriers to child sexual abuse (CSA) disclosures. *Trauma, Violence, & Abuse, 20*(2), 260–283. https://doi.org/10.1177/1524838017697312

Alanis, M. C., & Lucidi, R. S. (2004). Neonatal circumcision: A review of the world's oldest and most controversial operation. *Obstetrical and Gynecological Survey, 59*(5), 379–395.

Alarcón-Rubio, D., Sánchez-Medina, J. A., & Prieto-García, J. R. (2014). Executive function and verbal self-regulation in childhood: Developmental linkages between partially internalized private speech and cognitive flexibility. *Early Childhood Research Quarterly, 29*(2), 95–105. https://doi.org/10.1016/j.ecresq.2013.11.002

Alati, R., Davey Smith, G., Lewis, S. J., Sayal, K., Draper, E. S., Golding, J., . . . Gray, R. (2013). Effect of prenatal alcohol exposure on childhood academic outcomes: Contrasting maternal and paternal associations in the ALSPAC study. *PLoS One, 8*(10), e74844.

https://doi.org/10.1371/journal.pone.0074844

Albert, D., Chein, J., & Steinberg, L. (2013). The teenage brain: Peer influences on adolescent decision making. *Current Directions in Psychological Science, 22*(2), 114–120. https://doi.org/10.1177/0963721412471347

Alberts, A., Elkind, D., & Ginsberg, S. (2007). The personal fable and risk-taking in early adolescence. *Journal of Youth & Adolescence, 36*(1), 71–76.

Albuquerque, D., Nóbrega, C., Manco, L., & Padez, C. (2017). The contribution of genetics and environment to obesity. *British Medical Bulletin, 123*(1), 159–173. https://doi.org/10.1093/bmb/ldx022

Alcohol Policy Information System. (2018). Reporting requirements: Data on a specific date - 2017. Retrieved from https://alcoholpolicy.niaaa.nih.gov/apis-policy-topics/reporting-requirements/23?sd=2017-01-01

Aldercotte, A., White, N., & Hughes, C. (2016). Sibling and peer relationships in early childhood. In *Child psychology: A handbook of contemporary issues* (pp. 141–165). New York, NY: Routledge.

Alexander, G. M., & Wilcox, T. (2012). Sex differences in early infancy. *Child Development Perspectives, 6*(4), 400–406.

Alferink, L. A., & Farmer-Dougan, V. (2010). Brain-(not) based education: Dangers of misunderstanding and misapplication of neuroscience research. *Exceptionality, 18*(1), 42–52. https://doi.org/10.1080/09362830903462573

Alfieri, T., Ruble, D. N., & Higgins, E. T. (1996). Gender stereotypes during adolescence: Developmental changes and the transition to junior high school. *Developmental Psychology, 32*(6), 1129–1137. https://doi.org/10.1037/0012-1649.32.6.1129

Alisic, E., Krishna, R. N., Robbins, M. L., & Mehl, M. R. (2016). A comparison of parent and child narratives of children's recovery from trauma. *Journal of Language and Social Psychology, 35*(2), 224–235. https://doi.org/10.1177/0261927X15599557

Alivernini, F., & Lucidi, F. (2011). Relationship between social context, self-efficacy, motivation, academic achievement, and intention to drop out of high school: A longitudinal study. *Journal of Educational Research, 104*(4), 241–252. https://doi.org/10.1080/00220671003728062

Allen, J. P., & Antonishak, J. (2008). Adolescent peer influences: Beyond the dark side. In M. J. Prinstein & K. A. Dodge (Eds.), *Understanding peer influence in children and adolescents* (pp. 141–160). New York, NY: Guilford.

Allen, S. E. M., & Crago, M. B. (1996). Early passive acquisition in Inukitut. *Journal of Child Language, 23*, 129–156.

Allen, T. (2007). Witchcraft, sexuality and HIV/AIDS among the Azande of Sudan. *Journal of Eastern African Studies, 1*(3), 359–396. https://doi.org/10.1080/17531050701625789

Almeida, J., Bécares, L., Erbetta, K., Bettegowda, V. R., & Ahluwalia, I. B. (2018). Racial/ethnic inequities in low birth weight and preterm birth: The role of multiple forms of stress. *Maternal and Child Health Journal, 22*(8), 1154–1163. https://doi.org/10.1007/s10995-018-2500-7

Almy, B., Long, K., Lobato, D., Plante, W., Kao, B., & Houck, C. (2016). Perceptions of siblings' sexual activity predict sexual attitudes among at-risk adolescents. *Journal of Developmental and Behavioral Pediatrics, 36*(4), 258–266.

Al-Namlah, A. S., Meins, E., & Fernyhough, C. (2012). Self-regulatory private speech relates to children's recall and organization of autobiographical memories. *Early Childhood Research Quarterly, 27*(3), 441–446. https://doi.org/10.1016/j.ecresq.2012.02.005

Al-Owidha, A., Green, K. E., & Kroger, J. (2009). On the question of an identity status category order: Rasch model step and scale statistics used to identify category order. *International Journal of Behavioral Development, 33*(1), 88–96. https://doi.org/10.1177/0165025408100110

Alshaarawy, O., Breslau, N., & Anthony, J. C. (2016). Monthly estimates of alcohol drinking during pregnancy: United States, 2002-2011. *Journal of Studies on Alcohol and Drugs, 77*(2), 272–276. https://doi.org/10.15288/JSAD.2016.77.272

Alvarez, A. V. G., Rubin, D., Pina, P., & Velasquez, M. S. (2018). Neurodevelopmental outcomes and prenatal exposure to marijuana [Abstract]. *Pediatrics, 142*(1), 787. https://doi.org/10.1542/PEDS.142.1_MEETINGABSTRACT.787

Álvarez, M. J., Fernández, D., Gómez-Salgado, J., Rodríguez-González, D., Rosón, M., & Lapeña, S. (2017). The effects of massage therapy in hospitalized preterm neonates: A systematic review. *International Journal of Nursing Studies, 69*, 119–136. https://doi.org/10.1016/J.IJNURSTU.2017.02.009

Alviola, P. A., Nayga, R. M., Thomsen, M. R., Danforth, D., & Smartt, J. (2014). The effect of fast-food restaurants on childhood obesity: A school level analysis. *Economics & Human Biology, 12*, 110–119. https://doi.org/10.1016/j.ehb.2013.05.001

Amato, P. R. (2010). Research on divorce: Continuing trends and new developments. *Journal of Marriage & Family, 72*(3), 650–666. https://doi.org/10.1111/j.1741-3737.2010.00723.x

Amato, P. R., & Anthony, C. J. (2014). Estimating the effects of parental divorce and death with fixed effects models. *Journal of Marriage and Family, 76*(2), 370–386. https://doi.org/10.1111/jomf.12100

Amberger, J. S., & Hamosh, A. (2017). Searching Online Mendelian Inheritance in Man (OMIM): A knowledgebase of human genes and genetic phenotypes. In *Current protocols in bioinformatics* (Vol. 58, pp. 1.2.1–1.2.12). Hoboken, NJ: John Wiley & Sons Inc. https://doi.org/10.1002/cpbi.27

American Academy of Child and Adolescent Psychiatry. (2008). Teen suicide: Facts for families. Retrieved from https://www.aacap.org/App_Themes/AACAP/docs/facts_for_families/10_teen_suicide.pdf

American Academy of Pediatrics. (1992). American Academy of Pediatrics AAP Task Force on Infant Positioning and SIDS: Positioning and SIDS. *Pediatrics, 89*(6, Pt. 1), 1120–1126. Retrieved from https://pediatrics.aappublications.org/content/89/6/1120.long

American Academy of Pediatrics. (2017). AAP Agenda for Children. Retrieved from https://www.aap.org/en-us/about-the-aap/aap-facts/AAP-Agenda-for-Children-Strategic-Plan/Pages/AAP-Agenda-for-Children-Strategic-Plan.aspx

American Academy of Pediatrics (AAP) Task Force on Circumcision Policy. (1999). Circumcision policy statement. *Pediatrics, 103*, 686–693.

American Academy of Pediatrics Council on Communications and Media. (2016). Media and young minds. *Pediatrics, 138*(5), e20162591. https://doi.org/10.1542/peds.2016-2591

American College of Obstetricians and Gynecologists. (2011). *Substance abuse reporting and pregnancy: The role of the obstetrician-gynecologist.* Washington, DC: Author. Retrieved from http://www.acog.org/~/media/Committee Opinions/Committee on Health Care for Underserved Women/co473.pdf?dmc=1&ts=20140604T1051541013

American College of Obstetricians and Gynecologists. (2017). Obstetric analgesia and anesthesia: Practice Bulletin No. 177. *Obstetrics & Gynecology, 129*(4), e73–e89. https://doi.org/10.1097/AOG.0000000000002018

American Medical Association. (1999). *Neonatal circumcision.* Chicago: Author.

American Medical Association. (2014). *Pregnant women's rights.* Retrieved from https://policysearch.ama-assn.org/policyfinder/detail/Substance%20Use%20Disorder?uri=%2FAMADoc%2FHOD.xml-H-420.950.xml

American Psychiatric Association. (2013). *Diagnostic and statistical manual of mental disorders* (5th ed.). Washington, DC: Author.

American Psychological Association. (2010). *Ethical principles of psychologists and code of conduct.* Retrieved from http://www.apa.org/ethics/code/principles.pdf

Amir, D., Jordan, M. R., & Bribiescas, R. G. (2016). A longitudinal assessment of associations between adolescent environment, adversity perception, and economic status on fertility and age of menarche. *PLoS ONE, 11*(6), e0155883. https://doi.org/10.1371/journal.pone.0155883

Amitay, E. L., Dubnov Raz, G., & Keinan-Boker, L. (2016). Breastfeeding, other early life exposures and childhood leukemia and lymphoma. *Nutrition and Cancer, 68*(6), 968–977. https://doi.org/10.1080/01635581.2016.1190020

Ammerman, S., Ryan, S., Adelman, W. P., Committee on Substance Abuse, & Committee on Adolescence. (2015). The impact of marijuana policies on youth: Clinical, research, and legal update. *Pediatrics, 135*(3), e769–e785. https://doi.org/10.1542/peds.2014-4147

Ampaabeng, S. K., & Tan, C. M. (2013). The long-term cognitive consequences of early childhood malnutrition: The case of famine in Ghana. *Journal of Health Economics, 32*(6), 1013–1027. https://doi.org/10.1016/j.jhealeco.2013.08.001

Andersen, T. S. (2015). Race, ethnicity, and structural variations in youth risk of arrest: Evidence from a national longitudinal sample. *Criminal Justice and Behavior, 42*, 900–916. https://doi.org/10.1177/0093854815570963

Anderson, C. A., & Bushman, B. J. (2002). Human aggression. *Annual Review of Psychology, 53*, 27–51.

Anderson, D. R., Huston, A. C., Schmitt, K. L., Lineberger, D. L., & Wright, J. C. (2001). Early childhood television viewing and adolescent behavior: The recontact study. *Monographs of the Society for Research in Child Development, 66*(Serial No. 264).

Anderson, D. R., & Pempek, T. A. (2005). Television and very young children. *American Behavioral Scientist, 48*(5), 505–522. https://doi.org/10.1177/0002764204271506

Anderson, M. (2018). About a quarter of rural Americans say access to high-speed internet is a major problem. *Pew Research Center Fact Tank*. Retrieved from https://www.pewresearch.org/fact-tank/2018/09/10/about-a-quarter-of-rural-americans-say-access-to-high-speed-internet-is-a-major-problem/

Anderson, S., & Phillips, D. (2017). Is pre-K classroom quality associated with kindergarten and middle-school academic skills? *Developmental Psychology, 53*(6), 1063–1078. https://doi.org/10.1037/dev0000312

Anderson, V. A., Spencer-Smith, M. M., Coleman, L., Anderson, P. J., Greenham, M., Jacobs, R., . . . Leventer, R. J. (2014). Predicting neurocognitive and behavioural outcome after early brain insult. *Developmental Medicine and Child Neurology, 56*(4), 329–336. https://doi.org/10.1111/dmcn.12387

Andersson, B.-E. (1989). Effects of public day-care: A longitudinal study. *Child Development, 60*(4), 857. https://doi.org/10.1111/1467-8624.ep9676141

Andersson, U. (2008). Working memory as a predictor of written arithmetical skills in children: The importance of central executive functions. *British Journal of Educational Psychology, 78*(2), 181–203.

Andescavage, N. N., du Plessis, A., McCarter, R., Serag, A., Evangelou, I., Vezina, G., . . . Limperopoulos, C. (2016). Complex trajectories of brain development in the healthy human fetus. *Cerebral Cortex, 27*(11), 5274–5283. https://doi.org/10.1093/cercor/bhw306

Andruski, J. E., Casielles, E., & Nathan, G. (2013). Is bilingual babbling language-specific? Some evidence from a case study of Spanish-English dual acquisition. *Bilingualism: Language and Cognition, 17*(03), 660–672. https://doi.org/10.1017/S1366728913000655

Angley, M., Divney, A., Magriples, U., & Kershaw, T. (2015). Social support, family functioning and parenting competence in adolescent parents. *Maternal and Child Health Journal, 19*(1), 67–73. https://doi.org/10.1007/s10995-014-1496-x

Apgar, V. (1953). A proposal for a new method of evaluation in the newborn infant. *Current Research in Anesthesia and Analgesia, 32*, 260–267.

Archer, L., DeWitt, J., Osborne, J., Dillon, J., Willis, B., & Wong, B. (2012). Science aspirations, capital, and family habitus: How families shape children's engagement and identification with science. *American Educational Research Journal, 49*(5), 881–908. https://doi.org/10.3102/0002831211433290

Ardila, A. (2013). Development of metacognitive and emotional executive functions in children. *Applied Neuropsychology. Child, 2*(2), 82–87. https://doi.org/10.1080/21622965.2013.748388

Ardila, A., Rosselli, M., Matute, E., & Inozemtseva, O. (2011). Gender differences in cognitive development. *Developmental Psychology, 47*(4), 984–990. https://doi.org/10.1037/a002381910.1037/a0023819.supp

Arditi-Babchuk, H., Feldman, R., & Eidelman, A. I. (2009). Rapid eye movement (REM) in premature neonates and developmental outcome at 6 months. *Infant Behavior & Development, 32*(1), 27–32. https://doi.org/10.1016/j.infbeh.2008.09.001

Ari-Even Roth, D., Hildesheimer, M., Roziner, I., & Henkin, Y. (2016). Evidence for a right-ear advantage in newborn hearing screening results. *Trends in Hearing, 20*, 233121651668116. https://doi.org/10.1177/2331216516681168

Armon-Lotem, S., Haman, E., Jensen de López, K., Smoczynska, M., Yatsushiro, K., Szczerbinski, M., . . . van der Lely, H. (2016). A large-scale cross-linguistic investigation of the acquisition of passive. *Language Acquisition, 23*(1), 27–56. https://doi.org/10.1080/10489223.2015.1047095

Arnett, J. J. (2000). Emerging adulthood: A theory of development from the late teens through the twenties. *American Psychologist, 55*(5), 469–480. https://doi.org/10.1037/0003-066X.55.5.469

Arnett, J. J. (2015). Identity development from adolescence to emerging adulthood. In K. C. McLean & M. Syed (Eds.), *The Oxford handbook of identity development* (pp. 53–64). Oxford, England: Oxford University Press. https://doi.org/10.1093/oxfordhb/9780199936564.013.009

Aronson, P. (2008). Breaking barriers or locked out? Class-based perceptions and experiences of postsecondary education. *New Directions for Child & Adolescent Development, 2008*(119), 41–54. https://doi.org/10.1002/cd.208

Arseneault, L. (2018). Annual research review: The persistent and pervasive impact of being bullied in childhood and adolescence: Implications for policy and practice. *Journal of Child Psychology and Psychiatry, 59*(4), 405–421. https://doi.org/10.1111/jcpp.12841

Årseth, A. K., Kroger, J., Martinussen, M., & Marcia, J. E. (2009). Meta-analytic studies of identity status and the relational issues of attachment and intimacy. *Identity, 9*(1), 1–32. https://doi.org/10.1080/15283480802579532

Arthur, A. E., Bigler, R. S., & Ruble, D. N. (2009). An experimental test of the effects of gender constancy on sex typing. *Journal of Experimental Child Psychology, 104*(4), 427–446. https://doi.org/10.1016/j.jecp.2009.08.002

Artman, L., & Cahan, S. (1993). Schooling and the development of transitive inference. *Developmental Psychology, 29*(4), 753–759.

Asato, M. R., Terwilliger, R., Woo, J., & Luna, B. (2010). White matter development in adolescence: A DTI study. *Cerebral Cortex, 20*(9), 2122–2131. https://doi.org/10.1093/cercor/bhp282

Aslan, A., & Bäuml, K.-H. T. (2010). Retrieval-induced forgetting in young children. *Psychonomic Bulletin & Review, 17*(5), 704–709. https://doi.org/10.3758/pbr.17.5.704

Aslin, R. N. (2014). Infant learning: Historical, conceptual, and methodological challenges. *Infancy, 19*(1), 2–27. https://doi.org/10.1111/infa.12036

Assadi, S. M., Zokaei, N., Kaviani, H., Mohammadi, M. R., Ghaeli, P., Gohari, M. R., & van de Vijver, F. J. R. (2007). Effect of sociocultural context and parenting style on scholastic achievement among Iranian adolescents. *Social Development, 16*, 169–180.

Astington, J. W. (1993). *The child's discovery of the mind*. Cambridge, MA: Harvard University Press.

Atkinson, R. C., & Shiffrin, R. M. (1968). Human memory: A proposed system and its control processes. *Psychology of Learning and Motivation, 2*, 89–195. https://doi.org/10.1016/S0079-7421(08)60422-3

Auchus, R. J., & Rainey, W. E. (2004). Adrenarche: Physiology, biochemistry and human disease. *Clinical Endocrinology, 60*(3), 288–296. https://doi.org/10.1046/j.1365-2265.2003.01858.x

Aunola, K., & Stattin, H. (2000). Parenting styles and adolescents' achievement strategies. *Journal of Adolescence, 23*(2), 205–223.

Australian Institute of Health and Welfare. (2016). *Leading causes of death*. Retrieved from https://www.aihw.gov.au/reports/life-expectancy-death/deaths-in-australia/contents/leading-causes-of-death

Axe, J. B. (2007). Child care and child development: Results from the NICHD Study of Early Child Care and Youth Development. *Education & Treatment of Children, 30*(3), 129–136.

Axelsson, J., Sabra, S., Rylander, L., Rignell-Hydbom, A., Lindh, C. H., & Giwercman, A. (2018). Association between paternal smoking at the time of pregnancy and the semen quality in sons. *PLoS ONE, 13*(11), e0207221. https://doi.org/10.1371/journal.pone.0207221

Axia, V. D., & Weisner, T. S. (2002). Infant stress reactivity and home cultural ecology of Italian infants and families. *Infant Behavior & Development, 25*(3), 255.

Baams, L., Dubas, J. S., Overbeek, G., & van Aken, M. A. G. (2015). Transitions in body and behavior: A meta-analytic study on the relationship between pubertal development and adolescent sexual behavior. *Journal of Adolescent Health, 56*(6), 586–598. https://doi.org/10.1016/j.jadohealth.2014.11.019

Bachman, J. G., Johnston, L. D., & O'Malley, P. M. (2014). *Monitoring the future: Questionnaire responses from the nation's high school seniors, 2012*. Ann Arbor, MI: Monitoring the Future. Retrieved from http://monitoringthefuture.org/datavolumes/2012/2012dv.pdf

Bachman, J. G., O'Malley, P. M., Freedman-Doan, P., Trzesniewski, K. H., & Donnellan, M. B. (2011). Adolescent self-esteem: Differences by race/ethnicity, gender, and age. *Self and Identity, 10*(4), 445–473. https://doi.org/10.1080/15298861003794538

Bachman, J. G., Staff, J., O'Malley, P. M., & Freedman-Doan, P. (2013). Adolescent work intensity, school performance, and substance use: Links vary by race/ethnicity and socioeconomic status. *Developmental Psychology, 49*(11), 2125–2134. https://doi.org/10.1037/a0031464

Backschneider, A. G., Shatz, M., & Gelman, S. A. (1993). Preschoolers' ability to distinguish living kinds as a function of regrowth. *Child Development, 64*, 1242–1257.

Bada, H. S., Bann, C. M., Whitaker, T. M., Bauer, C. R., Shankaran, S., Lagasse, L., . . . Higgins, R. (2012). Protective factors can mitigate behavior problems after prenatal cocaine and other drug exposures. *Pediatrics, 130*(6), e1479-88. https://doi.org/10.1542/peds.2011-3306

Baddeley, A. (2012). Working memory: Theories, models, and controversies. *Annual Review of Psychology, 63*, 1–29. https://doi.org/10.1146/annurev-psych-120710-100422

Baddeley, A. (2016). Working memory. In R. J. Sternberg, S. T. Fiske, & D. J. Foss (Eds.), *Scientists making a difference: One hundred eminent behavioral and brain scientists talk about their most important contributions* (pp. 119–122). New York, NY: Cambridge University Press.

Baer, R. J., Altman, M. R., Oltman, S. P., Ryckman, K. K., Chambers, C. D., Rand, L., & Jelliffe-Pawlowski, L. L. (2019). Maternal factors influencing late entry into prenatal care: A stratified analysis by race or ethnicity and insurance status. *Journal of Maternal-Fetal & Neonatal Medicine, 32*(20), 3336–3342. https://doi.org/10.1080/14767058.2018.1463366

Bagci, S. C., Rutland, A., Kumashiro, M., Smith, P. K., & Blumberg, H. (2014). Are minority status children's cross-ethnic friendships beneficial in a multiethnic context? *British Journal of Developmental Psychology, 32*(1), 107–115. https://doi.org/10.1111/bjdp.12028

Baglivio, M. T., Jackowski, K., Greenwald, M. A., & Howell, J. C. (2014). Serious, violent, and chronic juvenile offenders. *Criminology & Public Policy, 13*(1), 83–116. https://doi.org/10.1111/1745-9133.12064

Baillargeon, R. (1987). Object permanence in 3 1/2- and 4 1/2-month-old-infants. *Developmental Psychology, 23*(5), 655–664.

Baillargeon, R., Scott, R. M., & Bian, L. (2016). Psychological reasoning in infancy. *Annual Review of Psychology, 67*(1), 159–186. https://doi.org/10.1146/annurev-psych-010213-115033

Bajanowski, T., & Vennemann, M. (2017). Sudden infant death syndrome (SIDS). In M. M. Houck (Ed.), *Forensic pathology* (pp. 259–266). London, England: Elsevier.

Baker, E. R., Tisak, M. S., & Tisak, J. (2016). What can boys and girls do? Preschoolers' perspectives regarding gender roles across domains of behavior. *Social Psychology of Education, 19*(1), 23–39. https://doi.org/10.1007/s11218-015-9320-z

Bakermans-Kranenburg, M. J., & van IJzendoorn, M. H. (2015). The hidden efficacy of interventions: Gene × environment experiments from a differential susceptibility perspective. *Annual Review of Psychology, 66*(1), 381–409. https://doi.org/10.1146/annurev-psych-010814-015407

Baker-Ward, L., Gordon, B. N., Ornstein, P. A., Larus, D. M., & Clubb, P. A. (1993). Young children's long-term retention of a pediatric examination. *Child Development, 64*, 1519–1533.

Balan, R., Dobrean, A., Roman, G. D., & Balazsi, R. (2017). Indirect effects of parenting practices on internalizing problems among adolescents: The role of expressive suppression. *Journal of Child and Family Studies, 26*(1), 40–47. https://doi.org/10.1007/s10826-016-0532-4

Baldwin, D. A., Markman, E. M., Bill, B., Desjardins, R. N., Irwin, J. M., & Tidball, G. (1996). Infants' reliance on social criteria for establishing word-object relations. *Child Development, 67*, 3135–3153.

Bale, T. L. (2015). Epigenetic and transgenerational reprogramming of brain development. *Nature Reviews Neuroscience, 16*(6), 332–344. https://doi.org/10.1038/nrn3818

Balenzano, C., Coppola, G., Cassibba, R., & Moro, G. (2018). Pre-adoption adversities and adoptees' outcomes: The protective role of post-adoption variables in an Italian experience of domestic open adoption. *Children and Youth Services Review, 85*, 307–318. https://doi.org/10.1016/J.CHILDYOUTH.2018.01.012

Ball, C. L., Smetana, J. G., & Sturge-Apple, M. L. (2017). Following my head and my heart: Integrating preschoolers' empathy, theory of mind, and moral judgments. *Child Development, 88*(2), 597–611. https://doi.org/10.1111/cdev.12605

Ball, H. L., Hooker, E., & Kelly, P. J. (1999). Where will the baby sleep? Attitudes and practices of new and experienced parents regarding co-sleeping with their new-born infants. *American Anthropologist, 101*(1), 143–151.

Ball, H. L., Hooker, E., & Kelly, P. J. (2000). Parent-infant co-sleeping: Fathers' roles and perspectives. *Infant and Child Development, 9*, 67–74.

Ball, J. W., Bindler, R. C., Cowen, K., & Shaw, M. R. (2017). *Principles of pediatric nursing: Caring for children* (7th ed.). New York, NY: Pearson.

Ballesteros, M. F., Williams, D. D., Mack, K. A., Simon, T. R., & Sleet, D. A. (2018). The epidemiology of unintentional and violence-related injury morbidity and mortality among children and adolescents in the United States. *International Journal of Environmental Research and Public Health, 15*(4), 616. https://doi.org/10.3390/ijerph15040616

Bandettini, P. A. (2012). Twenty years of functional MRI: The science and the stories. *NeuroImage, 62*(2), 575–588. https://doi.org/10.1016/j.neuroimage.2012.04.026

Bandura, A. (1977). *Social learning theory*. Englewood Cliffs, NJ: Prentice Hall.

Bandura, A. (1986). *Social foundations of thought and action: A social cognitive theory*. Englewood Cliffs, NJ: Prentice Hall.

Bandura, A. (2010). Vicarious learning. In D. Matsumoto (Ed.), *Cambridge dictionary of psychology* (p. 344). New York, NY: Cambridge University Press.

Bandura, A. (2011). But what about that gigantic elephant in the room? In R. M. Arkin (Ed.), *Most underappreciated: 50 prominent social psychologists describe their most unloved work* (pp. 51–59). New York, NY: Oxford University Press.

Bandura, A. (2012). Social cognitive theory. In P. A. M. Van Lange, A. W. Kruglanski, & E. T. Higgins (Eds.), *Handbook of theories of social psychology* (Vol. 1, pp. 349–373). Thousand Oaks, CA: Sage.

Bandura, A., & Bussey, K. (2004). On broadening the cognitive, motivational, and sociostructural scope of theorizing about gender development and functioning: Comment on Martin, Ruble, and Szkrybalo (2002). *Psychological Bulletin, 130*(5), 691–701.

Bandura, A., & McDonald, F. J. (1963). The influence of social reinforcement and the behavior of models in shaping children's moral judgments. *Journal of Abnormal and Social Psychology, 67*, 274–281.

Bandura, A., Ross, D., & Ross, S. A. (1963). Imitation of film-mediated aggressive models. *Journal of Abnormal and Social Psychology, 66*, 3–11.

Banfield, E. C., Liu, Y., Davis, J. S., Chang, S., & Frazier-Wood, A. C. (2016). Poor adherence to US dietary guidelines for children and adolescents in the National Health and Nutrition Examination Survey Population. *Journal of the Academy of Nutrition and Dietetics, 116*(1), 21–27. https://doi.org/10.1016/j.jand.2015.08.010

Bangsbo, J., Krustrup, P., Duda, J., Hillman, C., Andersen, L. B., Weiss, M., . . . Elbe, A. (2016). The Copenhagen Consensus Conference 2016: Children, youth, and physical activity in schools and during leisure time. *British Journal of Sports Medicine, 50*(19), 1177–1178. https://doi.org/10.1136/bjsports-2016-096325

Banse, R., Gawronski, B., Rebetez, C., Gutt, H., & Morton, J. B. (2010). The development of spontaneous gender stereotyping in childhood: Relations to stereotype knowledge and stereotype flexibility. *Developmental Science, 13*(2), 298–306. https://doi.org/10.1111/j.1467-7687.2009.00880.x

Barac, R., & Bialystok, E. (2012). Bilingual effects on cognitive and linguistic development: Role of language, cultural background, and education. *Child Development, 83*(2), 413–422. https://doi.org/10.1111/j.1467-8624.2011.01707.x

Barac, R., Bialystok, E., Castro, D. C., & Sanchez, M. (2014). The cognitive development of young dual language learners: A critical review. *Early Childhood Research Quarterly, 29*(4), 699–714. https://doi.org/10.1016/j.ecresq.2014.02.003

Barba-Müller, E., Craddock, S., Carmona, S., & Hoekzema, E. (2019). Brain plasticity in pregnancy and the postpartum period: Links to maternal caregiving and mental health. *Archives of Women's Mental Health, 22*(2), 289–299. https://doi.org/10.1007/s00737-018-0889-z

Bard, K. A., Todd, B. K., Bernier, C., Love, J., & Leavens, D. A. (2006). Self-awareness in human and chimpanzee infants: What is measured and what is meant by the mark and mirror test? *Infancy, 9*(2), 191–219. https://doi.org/10.1207/s15327078in0902_6

Barendse, M. E. A., Simmons, J. G., Byrne, M. L., Seal, M. L., Patton, G., Mundy, L., . . . Whittle, S. (2018). Brain structural connectivity during adrenarche: Associations between hormone levels and white matter microstructure. *Psychoneuroendocrinology, 88*, 70–77. https://doi.org/10.1016/J.PSYNEUEN.2017.11.009

Bargh, J. A. (2013). Our unconscious mind. *Scientific American, 310*(1), 30–37. https://doi.org/10.1038/scientificamerican0114-30

Barlow-Stewart, K., & Saleh, M. (2012). *Prenatal testing: Overview*. Centre for Genetics Education. Retrieved from https://www.genetics.edu.au/publications-and-resources/facts-sheets/fact-sheet-24-prenatal-testing-overview

Barnett, L. M., Lai, S. K., Veldman, S. L., Hardy, L. L., Cliff, D. P., Morgan, P. J., . . . Rush, E. (2016). Correlates of gross motor competence in children and adolescents: A systematic review and meta-analysis. *Sports Medicine, 46*(11), 1663–1688.

Barnett, S. M., Ceci, S. J., & Williams, W. M. (2006). Is the ability to make a bacon sandwich a mark of intelligence? and other issues: Some reflections on Gardner's theory of multiple intelligences. In J. A. Schaler (Ed.), *Howard Gardner under fire: The rebel psychologist faces his critics* (pp. 95–114). Chicago, IL: Open Court.

Barnett, W. S., Carolan, M. E., Squires, J. H., Clarke Brown, K., & Horowitz, M. (2015). *The state of preschool 2014: State preschool yearbook.* New Brunswick, NJ: National Institute for Early Education Research.

Barone, L., Lionetti, F., & Green, J. (2017). A matter of attachment? How adoptive parents foster post-institutionalized children's social and emotional adjustment. *Attachment & Human Development, 19*(4), 323–339. https://doi.org/10.1080/14616734.2017.1306714

Barr, R. (2010). Transfer of learning between 2D and 3D sources during infancy: Informing theory and practice. *Developmental Review, 30*(2), 128–154. https://doi.org/10.1016/j.dr.2010.03.001

Barr, R. (2013). Memory constraints on infant learning from picture books, television, and touchscreens. *Child Development Perspectives, 7*(4), 205–210. https://doi.org/10.1111/cdep.12041

Barr, R., Lauricella, A., Zack, E., & Calvert, S. L. (2010). Infant and early childhood exposure to adult-directed and child-directed television programming. *Merrill-Palmer Quarterly, 56*(1), 21–48.

Barr, R., Marrott, H., & Rovee-Collier, C. (2003). The role of sensory preconditioning in memory retrieval by preverbal infants. *Learning & Behavior, 31*(2), 111–123.

Barr, R. G., Konner, M., Bakeman, R., & Adamson, L. (1991). Crying in pKung San infants: A test of the cultural specificity hypothesis. *Developmental Medicine & Child Neurology, 33*(7), 601–610.

Barros, M. C. M., Mitsuhiro, S., Chalem, E., Laranjeira, R. R., & Guinsburg, R. (2011). Neurobehavior of late preterm infants of adolescent mothers. *Neonatology, 99*(2), 133–139. https://doi.org/10.1159/000313590

Barrouillet, P., Gavens, N., Vergauwe, E., Gaillard, V., & Camos, V. (2009). Working memory span development: A time-based resource-sharing model account. *Developmental Psychology, 45*(2), 477–490. https://doi.org/10.1037/a0014615

Bartel, K. A., Gradisar, M., & Williamson, P. (2015). Protective and risk factors for adolescent sleep: A meta-analytic review. *Sleep Medicine Reviews, 21*, 72–85. https://doi.org/10.1016/j.smrv.2014.08.002

Barth, R. P., Scarborough, A., Lloyd, E. C., Losby, J., Casanueva, C., & Mann, T. (2007). *Developmental status and early intervention service needs of maltreated children.* Washington, DC: U.S. Department of Health and Human Services, Office of the Assistant Secretary for Planning and Evaluation.

Bartram, S. C., Barlow, J., & Wolke, D. (2015). The Neonatal Behavioral Assessment Scale (NBAS) and Newborn Behavioral Observations system (NBO) for supporting caregivers and improving outcomes in caregivers and their infants. In S. C. Bartram (Ed.), *Cochrane database of systematic reviews.* Chichester, England: John Wiley & Sons Ltd. https://doi.org/10.1002/14651858.CD011754

Basow, S. (2008). Gender socialization, or how long a way has baby come? In J. C. Chrisler, C. Golden, & P. D. Rozee (Eds.), *Lectures on the psychology of women* (4th ed., pp. 81–95). New York, NY: McGraw-Hill.

Bass, R. W., Brown, D. D., Laurson, K. R., & Coleman, M. M. (2013). Physical fitness and academic performance in middle school students. *Acta Paediatrica, 102*(8), 832–837. https://doi.org/10.1111/apa.12278

Bassano, D. (2000). Early development of nouns and verbs in French: Exploring the interface between lexicon and grammar. *Journal of Child Language, 27*, 521–559.

Bastaits, K., & Mortelmans, D. (2016). Parenting as mediator between post-divorce family structure and children's well-being. *Journal of Child and Family Studies, 25*(7), 2178–2188. https://doi.org/10.1007/s10826-016-0395-8

Bates, E. (1990). Language about me and you: Pronominal reference and the emerging concept of self. In D. Cicchetti & M. Beeghly (Eds.), *The self in transition: Infancy to childhood* (pp. 165–182). Chicago, IL: University of Chicago Press.

Bates, E., Bretherton, I., & Snyder, L. (1988). *From first words to grammar.* Cambridge, England: Cambridge University Press.

Bates, J., Pettit, G., Dodge, K., & Ridge, B. (1998). Interaction of temperamental resistance to control and restrictive parenting in the development of externalizing behavior. *Developmental Psychology, 34*, 982–995.

Bateson, P. (2015). Human evolution and development: An ethological perspective. In W. F. Overton & P. C. M. Molenaar (Eds.), *Handbook of child psychology and developmental science: Vol. 1. Theory and method* (7th ed., pp. 208–243). Hoboken, NJ: John Wiley & Sons.

Battin-Pearson, S., & Newcomb, M. D. (2000). Predictors of early high school dropout: A test of five theories. *Journal of Educational Psychology, 92*(3), 568–582.

Battistella, G., Fornari, E., Annoni, J.-M., Chtioui, H., Dao, K., Fabritius, M., . . . Giroud, C. (2014). Long-term effects of cannabis on brain structure. *Neuropsychopharmacology, 39*(9), 2041–2048. https://doi.org/10.1038/npp.2014.67

Bauer, P. J. (1996). Development of memory in early childhood. In N. Cowan (Ed.), *The development of memory in childhood* (pp. 83–112). Hove, England: Psychology Press.

Bauer, P. J. (2007). Recall in infancy. *Current Directions in Psychological Science, 16*(3), 142–146. https://doi.org/10.1111/j.1467-8721.2007.00492.x

Bauer, P. J. (2015). Development of episodic and autobiographical memory: The importance of remembering forgetting. *Developmental Review, 38*, 146–166. https://doi.org/10.1016/J.DR.2015.07.011

Bauer, P. J., Burch, M. M., & Kleinknecht, E. E. (2002). Developments in early recall memory: Normative trends and individual differences. *Advances in Child Development and Behavior, 30*, 103–152. Retrieved from http://www.ncbi.nlm.nih.gov/pubmed/12402673

Bauer, P. J., Wenner, J. A., Dropik, P. L., & Wewerka, S. S. (2000). Parameters of remembering and forgetting in the transition from infancy to early childhood. *Monographs of the Society for Research in Child Development, 65*(4), i–vi, 1–204. Retrieved from http://www.ncbi.nlm.nih.gov/pubmed/12467092

Bauman, S., Toomey, R. B., & Walker, J. L. (2013). Associations among bullying, cyberbullying, and suicide in high school students. *Journal of Adolescence, 36*(2), 341–350. https://doi.org/10.1016/j.adolescence.2012.12.001

Baumrind, D. (1971). Current patterns of parental authority. *Developmental Psychology, 4*(Monograph 1), 1–103.

Baumrind, D. (2012). Differentiating between confrontive and coercive kinds of parental power-assertive disciplinary practices. *Human Development, 55*(2), 35–51. https://doi.org/10.1159/000337962

Baumrind, D. (2013). Authoritative parenting revisited: History and current status. In R. E. Larzelere, A. S. Morris, & A. W. Harrist (Eds.), *Authoritative parenting: Synthesizing nurturance and discipline for optimal child development* (pp. 11–34). Washington, DC: American Psychological Association. Retrieved from http://psycnet.apa.org/buy/2012-15622-002

Baumrind, D., Larzelere, R. E., & Owens, E. B. (2010). Effects of preschool parents' power assertive patterns and practices on adolescent development. *Parenting: Science & Practice, 10*(3), 157–201. https://doi.org/10.1080/15295190903290790

Baus, C., Costa, A., & Carreiras, M. (2013). On the effects of second language immersion on first language production. *Acta Psychologica, 142*(3), 402–409. https://doi.org/10.1016/j.actpsy.2013.01.010

Bava, S., & Tapert, S. F. (2010). Adolescent brain development and the risk for alcohol and other drug problems. *Neuropsychology Review, 20*(4), 398–413. https://doi.org/10.1007/s11065-010-9146-6

Bayefsky, M. J. (2016). Comparative preimplantation genetic diagnosis policy in Europe and the USA and its implications for reproductive tourism. *Reproductive Biomedicine & Society Online, 3*, 41–47. https://doi.org/10.1016/j.rbms.2017.01.001

Bayet, L., Quinn, P. C., Tanaka, J. W., Lee, K., Gentaz, É., & Pascalis, O. (2015). Face gender influences the looking preference for smiling expressions in 3.5-month-old human infants. *PLoS ONE, 10*(6), e0129812. https://doi.org/10.1371/journal.pone.0129812

Bayley, N. (1949). Consistency and variability in the growth of intelligence from birth to eighteen years. *Pedagogical Seminary and Journal of Genetic Psychology, 75*(2), 165–196. https://doi.org/10.1080/08856559.1949.10533516

Bayley, N. (1969). *Manual for the Bayley Scales of Infant Development.* San Antonio, TX: Psychological Corporation.

Bayley, N. (2005). *Bayley Scales of Infant and Toddler Development* (3rd ed.). San Antonio, TX: Psychological Corporation.

Bazinet, A. D., Squeglia, L., Riley, E., & Tapert, S. F. (2016). *Effects of drug exposure on development* (K. J. Sher, Ed., Vol. 1). Oxford, England: Oxford University Press. https://doi.org/10.1093/oxfordhb/9780199381708.013.21

Bazzano, A. N., Kirkwood, B., Tawiah-Agyemang, C., Owusu-Agyei, S., & Adongo, P. (2008). Social costs of skilled attendance at birth in rural Ghana. *International Journal of Gynecology & Obstetrics, 102*(1), 91–94. https://doi.org/10.1016/j.ijgo.2008.02.004

Beach, S. R. H., Brody, G. H., Gunter, T. D., Packer, H., Wernett, P., & Philibert, R. A. (2010). Child maltreatment moderates the association of MAOA with symptoms of depression and antisocial personality disorder. *Journal of Family Psychology, 24*(1), 12–20. https://doi.org/10.1037/a0018074

Beal, C. R. (1994). *Boys and girls: The development of gender roles.* New York, NY: McGraw-Hill.

Beal, J. A. (2017). Neonatal male circumcision. *American Journal of Maternal/Child Nursing, 42*(4), 233. https://doi.org/10.1097/NMC.0000000000000352

Beal, M. A., Yauk, C. L., & Marchetti, F. (2017). From sperm to offspring: Assessing the heritable genetic consequences of paternal smoking and potential public health impacts. *Mutation Research/Reviews in Mutation Research, 773*, 26–50. https://doi.org/10.1016/J.MRREV.2017.04.001

Beauchamp, G. K., & Mennella, J. A. (2011). Flavor perception in human infants: Development and functional significance. *Digestion, 83*(Suppl. 1), 1–6. https://doi.org/10.1159/000323397

Becht, A. I., Nelemans, S. A., Branje, S. J. T., Vollebergh, W. A. M., Koot, H. M., Denissen, J. J. A., & Meeus, W. H. J. (2016). The quest for identity in adolescence: Heterogeneity in daily identity formation and psychosocial adjustment across 5 years. *Developmental Psychology, 52*(12), 2010–2021. https://doi.org/10.1037/dev0000245

Becker, A. E., Keel, P., Anderson-Fye, E. P., & Thomas, J. J. (2004). Genes and/or jeans? Genetic and socio-cultural contributions to risk for eating disorders. *Journal of Addictive Diseases, 23*(3), 81–103. https://doi.org/10.1300/J069v23n03_07

Bednarczyk, R. A., King, A. R., Lahijani, A., & Omer, S. B. (2019). Current landscape of nonmedical vaccination exemptions in the United States: Impact of policy changes. *Expert Review of Vaccines, 18*(2), 175–190. https://doi.org/10.1080/14760584.2019.1562344

Beebe, B., Jaffe, J., Markese, S., Buck, K., Chen, H., Cohen, P., . . . Feldstein, S. (2010). The origins of 12-month attachment: A microanalysis of 4-month mother-infant interaction. *Attachment & Human Development, 12*(1/2), 3–141. https://doi.org/10.1080/14616730903338985

Beebe, B., Messinger, D., Bahrick, L. E., Margolis, A., Buck, K. A., & Chen, H. (2016). A systems view of mother–infant face-to-face communication. *Developmental Psychology, 52*(4), 556–571. https://doi.org/10.1037/a0040085

Behera, D., Sivakami, M., & Behera, M. R. (2015). Menarche and menstruation in rural adolescent girls in Maharashtra, India. *Journal of Health Management, 17*(4), 510–519. https://doi.org/10.1177/0972063415612581

Behnke, M., & Smith, V. C. (2013). Prenatal substance abuse: Short- and long-term effects on the exposed fetus. *Pediatrics, 131*(3), e1009–e1024. https://doi.org/10.1542/peds.2012-3931

Behrend, D. A., Scofield, J., & Kleinknecht, E. E. (2001). Beyond fast mapping: Young children's extensions of novel words and novel facts. *Developmental Psychology, 37*, 698–705.

Behrens, K. Y., Parker, A. C., & Haltigan, J. D. (2011). Maternal sensitivity assessed during the Strange Situation procedure predicts child's attachment quality and reunion behaviors. *Infant Behavior & Development, 34*(2), 378–381. https://doi.org/10.1016/j.infbeh.2011.02.007

Beitsch, R. (2017). As surrogacy surges, new parents seek legal protections. *Pew Stateline.* https://www.pewtrusts.org/en/research-and-analysis/blogs/stateline/2017/06/29/as-surrogacy-surges-new-parents-seek-legal-protections

Bellows, L. L., Davies, P. L., Courtney, J. B., Gavin, W. J., Johnson, S. L., & Boles, R. E. (2017). Motor skill development in low-income, at-risk preschoolers: A community-based longitudinal intervention study. *Journal of Science and Medicine in Sport, 20*(11), 997–1002. https://doi.org/10.1016/J.JSAMS.2017.04.003

Belsky, J. (2005). Attachment theory and research in ecological perspective: Insights from the Pennsylvania Infant and Family Development Project and the NICHD Study of Early Child Care. In K. E. Grossmann, K. Grossmann, & E. Waters (Eds.), *Attachment from infancy to adulthood: The major longitudinal studies* (pp. 71–97). New York, NY: Guilford.

Belsky, J., & Hartman, S. (2014). Gene-environment interaction in evolutionary perspective: Differential susceptibility to environmental influences. *World Psychiatry, 13*(1), 87–89. https://doi.org/10.1002/wps.20092

Beltramini, A. U., & Hertzig, M. E. (1983). Sleep and bedtime behavior in preschool-aged children. *Pediatrics, 71*(2), 153–158. Retrieved from https://pediatrics.aappublications.org/content/71/2/153.short

Bem, S. L. (1974). The measurement of psychological androgyny. *Journal of Consulting and Clinical Psychology, 42*(2), 155–162. Retrieved from http://www.ncbi.nlm.nih.gov/pubmed/4823550

Benasich, A. A., & Brooks-Gunn, J. (1996). Maternal attitudes and knowledge of child-rearing: Associations with family and child outcomes. *Child Development, 67*, 1186–1205.

Benatar, M., & Benatar, D. (2003). Between prophylaxis and child abuse: The ethics of neonatal male circumcision. *American Journal of Bioethics, 3*(2), 35–48.

Benigno, J. P., Byrd, D. L., McNamara, J. P., Berg, W. K., & Farrar, M. J. (2011). Talking through transitions: Microgenetic changes in preschoolers' private speech and executive functioning. *Child Language Teaching and Therapy, 27*(3), 269–285. https://doi.org/10.1177/0265659010394385

Benjamin Neelon, S. E., Vaughn, A., Ball, S. C., McWilliams, C., & Ward, D. S. (2012). Nutrition practices and mealtime environments of North Carolina child care centers. *Childhood Obesity, 8*(3), 216–223. https://doi.org/10.1089/chi.2011.0065

Benner, A. D. (2011). The transition to high school: Current knowledge, future directions. *Educational Psychology Review, 23*(3), 299–328. https://doi.org/10.1007/s10648-011-9152-0

Benner, A. D., Boyle, A. E., & Bakhtiari, F. (2017). Understanding students' transition to high school: Demographic variation and the role of supportive relationships. *Journal of Youth and Adolescence, 46*(10), 2129–2142. https://doi.org/10.1007/s10964-017-0716-2

Benner, A. D., & Graham, S. (2009). The transition to high school as a developmental process among multiethnic urban youth. *Child Development, 80*(2), 356–376. https://doi.org/10.1111/j.1467-8624.2009.01265.x

Benner, G. J., Nelson, J. R., & Epstein, M. H. (2002). The language skills of students with emotional and behavioral disorders: A literature review. *Journal of Emotional and Behavioral Disorders, 10*, 43–59.

Bennett, D. S., Bendersky, M., & Lewis, M. (2005). Does the organization of emotional expression change over time? Facial expressivity from 4 to 12 months. *Infancy, 8*(2), 167–187. https://doi.org/10.1207/s15327078in0802_4

Bennett, K. M. (2006). Does marital status and marital status change predict physical health in older adults? *Psychological Medicine, 36*(9), 1313–1320.

Benoit, A., Lacourse, E., & Claes, M. (2013). Pubertal timing and depressive symptoms in late adolescence: The moderating role of individual, peer, and parental factors. *Development and Psychopathology, 25*(2), 455–471. https://doi.org/10.1017/S0954579412001174

Benowitz-Fredericks, C. A., Garcia, K., Massey, M., Vasagar, B., & Borzekowski, D. L. G. (2012). Body image, eating disorders, and the relationship to adolescent media use. *Pediatric Clinics of North America, 59*(3), 693–704, ix. https://doi.org/10.1016/j.pcl.2012.03.017

Ben-Sasson, A., Carter, A. S., & Briggs-Gowan, M. J. (2009). Sensory over-responsivity in elementary school: Prevalence and social-emotional correlates. *Journal of Abnormal Child Psychology, 37*(5), 705–716. https://doi.org/10.1007/s10802-008-9295-8

Benson, J. E., Sabbagh, M. A., Carlson, S. M., & Zelazo, P. D. (2013). Individual differences in executive functioning predict preschoolers' improvement from theory-of-mind training. *Developmental Psychology, 49*(9), 1615–1627. https://doi.org/10.1037/a0031056

Bentley, K. H., Nock, M. K., & Barlow, D. H. (2014). The four-function model of nonsuicidal self-injury: Key directions for future research. *Clinical Psychological Science, 2*(5), 638–656. https://doi.org/10.1177/2167702613514563

Benzies, K. M., Magill-Evans, J. E., Hayden, K., Ballantyne, M., Raju, T., Higgins, R., . . . Dahl, L. (2013). Key components of early intervention programs for preterm infants and their parents: A systematic review and meta-analysis. *BMC Pregnancy and Childbirth, 13*(Suppl. 1), S10. https://doi.org/10.1186/1471-2393-13-S1-S10

Beran, T. N., Ramirez-Serrano, A., Kuzyk, R., Fior, M., & Nugent, S. (2011). Understanding how children understand robots: Perceived animism in child–robot interaction. *International Journal of Human-Computer Studies, 69*(7–8), 539–550.

Berardi, N., Sale, A., & Maffei, L. (2015). Brain structural and functional development:

Genetics and experience. *Developmental Medicine & Child Neurology, 57*(Suppl. 2), 4–9. https://doi.org/10.1111/dmcn.12691

Beratis, I. N., Rabavilas, A. D., Kyprianou, M., Papadimitriou, G. N., & Papageorgiou, C. (2013). Investigation of the link between higher order cognitive functions and handedness. *Journal of Clinical and Experimental Neuropsychology, 35*(4), 393–403. https://doi.org/10.1080/13803395.2013.778231

Berenbaum, S. A. (2018). Beyond pink and blue: The complexity of early androgen effects on gender development. *Child Development Perspectives, 12*(1), 58–64. https://doi.org/10.1111/cdep.12261

Berenbaum, S. A., Beltz, A. M., & Corley, R. (2015). The importance of puberty for adolescent development: Conceptualization and measurement. *Advances in Child Development and Behavior, 48*, 53–92. https://doi.org/10.1016/BS.ACDB.2014.11.002

Berge, J. M., MacLehose, R. F., Larson, N., Laska, M., & Neumark-Sztainer, D. (2016). Family food preparation and its effects on adolescent dietary quality and eating patterns. *Journal of Adolescent Health*. https://doi.org/10.1016/j.jadohealth.2016.06.007

Berge, J. M., Wall, M., Hsueh, T.-F., Fulkerson, J. A., Larson, N., & Neumark-Sztainer, D. (2015). The protective role of family meals for youth obesity: 10-year longitudinal associations. *Journal of Pediatrics, 166*(2), 296–301. https://doi.org/10.1016/j.jpeds.2014.08.030

Bergelson, E., & Swingley, D. (2012). At 6–9 months, human infants know the meanings of many common nouns. *Proceedings of the National Academy of Sciences of the United States of America, 109*(9), 3253–3258. https://doi.org/10.1073/pnas.1113380109

Berger, L. M., Font, S. A., Slack, K. S., & Waldfogel, J. (2017). Income and child maltreatment in unmarried families: Evidence from the earned income tax credit. *Review of Economics of the Household, 15*(4), 1345–1372. https://doi.org/10.1007/s11150-016-9346-9

Berger, P. K., Hohman, E. E., Marini, M. E., Savage, J. S., & Birch, L. L. (2016). Girls' picky eating in childhood is associated with normal weight status from ages 5 to 15 y. *American Journal of Clinical Nutrition, 104*(6), 1577–1582. https://doi.org/10.3945/ajcn.116.142430

Berger, R. H., Miller, A. L., Seifer, R., Cares, S. R., & Lebourgeois, M. K. (2012). Acute sleep restriction effects on emotion responses in 30- to 36-month-old children. *Journal of Sleep Research, 21*(3), 235–246. https://doi.org/10.1111/j.1365-2869.2011.00962.x

Berger, S. E., Theuring, C., & Adolph, K. E. (2007). How and when infants learn to climb stairs. *Infant Behavior & Development, 30*(1), 36–49. https://doi.org/10.1016/j.infbeh.2006.11.002

Bergman, N. J. (2015). Proposal for mechanisms of protection of supine sleep against sudden infant death syndrome: An integrated mechanism review. *Pediatric Research, 77*(1-1), 10–19. https://doi.org/10.1038/pr.2014.140

Berk, L. E. (1986). Development of private speech among preschool children. *Early Child Development and Care, 24*, 113–136.

Berk, L. E. (1992). The extracurriculum. In P. W. Jackson (Ed.), *Handbook of research on curriculum* (pp. 1003–1043). New York, NY: Macmillan.

Berk, L. E., & Garvin, R. A. (1984). Development of private speech among low-income Appalachian children. *Developmental Psychology, 20*, 271–286.

Berk, L. E., & Winsler, A. (1995). *Scaffolding children's learning: Vygotsky and early childhood education.* Washington, DC: National Association for the Education of Young Children.

Berkman, N. D., Brownley, K. A., Peat, C. M., Lohr, K. N., Cullen, K. E., Morgan, L. C., . . . Bulik, C. M. (2015). *Management and outcomes of binge-eating disorder.* Rockville, MD: Agency for Healthcare Research and Quality. Retrieved from http://www.ncbi.nlm.nih.gov/pubmed/26764442

Berkman, N. D., Lohr, K. N., & Bulik, C. M. (2007). Outcomes of eating disorders: A systematic review of the literature. *International Journal of Eating Disorders, 40*(4), 293–309.

Berkowitz, M. W., & Begun, A. L. (1994). Assessing how adolescents think about the morality of substance use. *Drugs & Society, 8*(3/4), 111.

Berlin, I., Golmard, J.-L., Jacob, N., Tanguy, M.-L., & Heishman, S. J. (2017). Cigarette smoking during pregnancy: Do complete abstinence and low level cigarette smoking have similar impact on birth weight? *Nicotine & Tobacco Research, 19*(5), 518–524. https://doi.org/10.1093/ntr/ntx033

Bernard, S., & Deleau, M. (2007). Conversational perspective-taking and false belief attribution: A longitudinal study. *British Journal of Developmental Psychology, 25*(3), 443–460. https://doi.org/10.1348/026151006X171451

Berndt, T. J., & Murphy, L. M. (2002). Influences of friends and friendships: Myths, truths, and research recommendations. In R. V. Kail (Ed.), *Advances in child development and behavior* (Vol. 30, pp. 275–310). San Diego, CA: Academic Press.

Bernier, A., Calkins, S. D., & Bell, M. A. (2016). Longitudinal associations between the quality of mother-infant interactions and brain development across infancy. *Child Development, 87*(4), 1159–1174. https://doi.org/10.1111/cdev.12518

Berninger, V., Abbott, R., Cook, C. R., & Nagy, W. (2017). Relationships of attention and executive functions to oral language, reading, and writing skills and systems in middle childhood and early adolescence. *Journal of Learning Disabilities, 50*(4), 434–449. https://doi.org/10.1177/0022219415617167

Berninger, V. W., & Wolf, B. J. (2009). *Teaching students with dyslexia and dysgraphia: Lessons from teaching and science.* Baltimore, MD: Paul H. Brookes Publishing. Retrieved from https://psycnet.apa.org/record/2009-08969-000

Bernstein, D. M., Atance, C., Meltzoff, A. N., & Loftus, G. R. (2007). Hindsight bias and developing theories of mind. *Child Development, 78*(4), 1374–1394. https://doi.org/10.1111/j.1467-8624.2007.01071.x

Berry, D., Blair, C., Willoughby, M., Garrett-Peters, P., Vernon-Feagans, L., & Mills-Koonce, W. R. (2016). Household chaos and children's cognitive and socio-emotional development in early childhood: Does childcare play a buffering role? *Early Childhood Research Quarterly, 34*, 115–127. https://doi.org/10.1016/J.ECRESQ.2015.09.003

Bersamin, M., Todd, M., Fisher, D. A., Hill, D. L., Grube, J. W., & Walker, S. (2008). Parenting practices and adolescent sexual behavior: A longitudinal study. *Journal of Marriage & Family, 70*(1), 97–112. https://doi.org/10.1111/j.1741-3737.2007.00464.x

Bertenthal, B. I., Campos, J. J., & Barrett, K. (1984). Self-produced locomotion: An organizer of emotional, cognitive, and social development in infancy. In R. Emde & R. Harmon (Eds.), *Continuities and discontinuities in development* (pp. 174–210). New York, NY: Plenum.

Berwick, R. C., & Chomsky, N. (2016). *Why only us: Language and evolution.* Cambridge, MA: MIT Press.

Berwick, R. C., Chomsky, N., & Piattelli-Palmarini, M. (2013). Poverty of the stimulus stands: Why recent challenges fail. In M. Piattelli-Palmarini & R. C. Berwick (Eds.), *Rich languages from poor inputs* (pp. 18–42). Oxford, England: Oxford University Press. https://doi.org/10.1093/acprof:oso/9780199590339.003.0002

Berzonsky, M. D., & Kuk, L. S. (2000). Identity status, identity processing style, and the transition to university. *Journal of Adolescent Research, 15*, 81–99.

Best, D. L., & Bush, C. D. (2016). Gender roles in childhood and adolescence. In U. P. Gielen & J. L. Roopnarine (Eds.), *Childhood and adolescence: Cross-cultural perspectives and applications* (pp. 209–240). Santa Barbara, CA: Praeger.

Best, D. L., House, A. S., Barnard, A. E., & Spicker, B. S. (1994). Parent-child interactions in France, Germany, and Italy: The effects of gender and culture. *Journal of Cross-Cultural Psychology, 25*(2), 181–193. https://doi.org/10.1177/0022022194252002

Best, J. R. (2012). Exergaming immediately enhances children's executive function. *Developmental Psychology, 48*(5), 1501–1510. https://doi.org/10.1037/a0026648

Best, R. M., Dockrell, J. E., & Braisby, N. R. (2006). Real-world word learning: Exploring children's developing semantic representations of a science term. *British Journal of Developmental Psychology, 24*(2), 265–282.

Beta, J., Lesmes-Heredia, C., Bedetti, C., & Akolekar, R. (2018). Risk of miscarriage following amniocentesis and chorionic villus sampling: A systematic review of the literature. *Minerva Ginecologica, 70*(2), 215–219. https://doi.org/10.23736/S0026-4784.17.04178-8

Betancourt, L. M., Avants, B., Farah, M. J., Brodsky, N. L., Wu, J., Ashtari, M., & Hurt, H. (2016). Effect of socioeconomic status (SES) disparity on neural development in female African-American infants at age 1 month. *Developmental Science, 19*(6), 947–956. https://doi.org/10.1111/desc.12344

Bhatia, R. (2010). Constructing gender from the inside out: Sex-selection practices in the United States. *Feminist Studies, 36*(2), 260–291.

Bhatia, R. (2018). The development of sex-selective reproductive technologies within Fertility, Inc. and the anticipation of lifestyle sex selection. In *Selective reproduction in the 21st century* (pp. 45–66). Cham, Switzerland:

Springer International Publishing. https://doi.org/10.1007/978-3-319-58220-7_3

Białecka-Pikul, M., Byczewska-Konieczny, K., Kosno, M., Białek, A., & Stępień-Nycz, M. (2018). Waiting for a treat: Studying behaviors related to self-regulation in 18- and 24-month-olds. *Infant Behavior and Development*, *50*, 12–21. https://doi.org/10.1016/J.INFBEH.2017.10.004

Bialik, K. (2018). Middle children have become rarer, but a growing share of Americans now say three or more kids are "ideal." *Pew Research Center Fact Tank*. Retrieved from https://www.pewresearch.org/fact-tank/2018/08/09/middle-children-have-become-rarer-but-a-growing-share-of-americans-now-say-three-or-more-kids-are-ideal/

Bialystok, E. (2015). Bilingualism and the development of executive function: The role of attention. *Child Development Perspectives*, *9*(2), 117–121. https://doi.org/10.1111/cdep.12116

Bialystok, E., Peets, K. F., & Moreno, S. (2014). Producing bilinguals through immersion education: Development of metalinguistic awareness. *Applied Psycholinguistics*, *35*(1), 177–191. https://doi.org/10.1017/S0142716412000288

Bian, L., Leslie, S.-J., & Cimpian, A. (2017). Gender stereotypes about intellectual ability emerge early and influence children's interests. *Science*, *355*(6323), 389–391. https://doi.org/10.1126/science.aah6524

Bianchi, E., & Wright, G. J. (2016). Sperm meets egg: The genetics of mammalian fertilization. *Annual Review of Genetics*, *50*(1), 93–111. https://doi.org/10.1146/annurev-genet-121415-121834

Bick, J., & Nelson, C. A. (2017). Early experience and brain development. *Wiley Interdisciplinary Reviews: Cognitive Science*, *8*(1–2), e1387. https://doi.org/10.1002/wcs.1387

Biehl, M., Natsuaki, M., & Ge., X. (2007). The influence of pubertal timing on alcohol use and heavy drinking trajectories. *Journal of Youth & Adolescence*, *36*(2), 153–167.

Bienstock, J. L., Fox, H. E., & Wallach, E. E. (2015). *The Johns Hopkins manual of gynecology and obstetrics*. Retrieved from https://shop.lww.com/Johns-Hopkins-Manual-of-Gynecology-and-Obstetrics/p/9781451188806

Bierman, K. L., Kalvin, C. B., & Heinrichs, B. S. (2014). Early childhood precursors and adolescent sequelae of grade school peer rejection and victimization. *Journal of Clinical Child and Adolescent Psychology*, *44*(3), 367–379. https://doi.org/10.1080/15374416.2013.873983

Bigelow, A. E. (2017). Self knowledge. In *Reference module in neuroscience and biobehavioral psychology*. Amsterdam, Netherlands: Elsevier. https://doi.org/10.1016/B978-0-12-809324-5.05882-X

Binder, E., Dovern, A., Hesse, M. D., Ebke, M., Karbe, H., Saliger, J., . . . Weiss, P. H. (2017). Lesion evidence for a human mirror neuron system. *Cortex*, *90*, 125–137. https://doi.org/10.1016/J.CORTEX.2017.02.008

Bing, N. M., Nelson, W. M., & Wesolowski, K. L. (2009). Comparing the effects of amount of conflict on children's adjustment following parental divorce. *Journal of Divorce & Remarriage*, *50*(3), 159–171. https://doi.org/10.1080/10502550902717699

Birch, S. A. J. (2005). When knowledge is a curse: Biases in mental state attribution. *Current Directions in Psychological Science*, *14*, 25–29.

Birditt, K. S., & Fingerman, K. L. (2003). Age and gender differences in adults' descriptions of emotional reactions to interpersonal problems. *Journals of Gerontology Series B: Psychological Sciences and Social Sciences*, *58*(4), P237–P245. https://doi.org/10.1093/geronb/58.4.P237

Birkeland, M. S., Breivik, K., & Wold, B. (2014). Peer acceptance protects global self-esteem from negative effects of low closeness to parents during adolescence and early adulthood. *Journal of Youth and Adolescence*, *43*(1), 70–80. https://doi.org/10.1007/s10964-013-9929-1

Birkett, M., Newcomb, M. E., & Mustanski, B. (2015). Does it get better? A longitudinal analysis of psychological distress and victimization in lesbian, gay, bisexual, transgender, and questioning youth. *Journal of Adolescent Health*, *56*(3), 280–285. https://doi.org/10.1016/j.jadohealth.2014.10.275

Birney, D. P., & Sternberg, R. J. (2011). The development of cognitive abilities. In M. H. Bornstein & M. E. Lamb (Eds.), *Developmental science: An advanced textbook* (6th ed., pp. 353–388). New York, NY: Psychology Press.

Biro, F. M., Greenspan, L. C., & Galvez, M. P. (2012). Puberty in girls of the 21st century. *Journal of Pediatric and Adolescent Gynecology*, *25*(5), 289–294. https://doi.org/10.1016/j.jpag.2012.05.009

Biro, F. M., Pajak, A., Wolff, M. S., Pinney, S. M., Windham, G. C., Galvez, M. P., . . . Teitelbaum, S. L. (2018). Age of menarche in a longitudinal US cohort. *Journal of Pediatric and Adolescent Gynecology*, *31*(4), 339–345. https://doi.org/10.1016/j.jpag.2018.05.002

Biro, S., Alink, L. R. A., van IJzendoorn, M. H., & Bakermans-Kranenburg, M. J. (2014). Infants' monitoring of social interactions: The effect of emotional cues. *Emotion*, *14*(2), 263–271.

Bjärehed, J., Wångby-Lundh, M., & Lundh, L.-G. (2012). Nonsuicidal self-injury in a community sample of adolescents: Subgroups, stability, and associations with psychological difficulties. *Journal of Research on Adolescence*, *22*(4), 678–693. https://doi.org/10.1111/j.1532-7795.2012.00817.x

Bjorklund, D. F. (2018a). A metatheory for cognitive development (or "Piaget is dead" revisited). *Child Development*. https://doi.org/10.1111/cdev.13019

Bjorklund, D. F. (2018b). Behavioral epigenetics: The last nail in the coffin of genetic determinism. *Human Development*, *61*(1), 54–59. https://doi.org/10.1159/000481747

Bjorklund, D. F., & Myers, A. (2015). The development of cognitive abilities. In M. H. Bornstein & M. E. Lamb (Eds.), *Developmental science: An advanced textbook* (pp. 391–441). New York, NY: Psychology Press.

Björkqvist, K. (2018). Gender differences in aggression. *Current Opinion in Psychology*, *19*, 39–42. https://doi.org/10.1016/J.COPSYC.2017.03.030

Black, I. E., Menzel, N. N., & Bungum, T. J. (2015). The relationship among playground areas and physical activity levels in children. *Journal of Pediatric Health Care*, *29*(2), 156–168. https://doi.org/10.1016/j.pedhc.2014.10.001

Black, K., Marola, J., Littman, A., Chrisler, J., & Neace, W. (2009). Gender and form of cereal box characters: Different medium, same disparity. *Sex Roles*, *60*(11/12), 882–889. https://doi.org/10.1007/s11199-008-9579-z

Blair, C. (2010). Stress and the development of self-regulation in context. *Child Development Perspectives*, *4*(3), 181–188. https://doi.org/10.1111/j.1750-8606.2010.00145.x

Blair, P. S., Sidebotham, P., Berry, P. J., Evans, M., & Fleming, P. J. (2006). Major epidemiological changes in sudden infant death syndrome: A 20-year population-based study in the UK. *Lancet*, *367*(9507), 314–319. https://doi.org/10.1016/S0140-6736(06)67968-3

Blakemore, J. E. O. (2003). Children's beliefs about violating gender norms: Boys shouldn't look like girls, and girls shouldn't act like boys. *Sex Roles*, *48*(9/10), 411–419. https://doi.org/10.1023/A:1023574427720

Blakemore, J. E. O., Berenbaum, S. A., & Liben, L. S. (2009). *Gender development*. New York, NY: Psychology Press.

Blakemore, S.-J. (2012). Imaging brain development: The adolescent brain. *NeuroImage*, *61*(2), 397–406. https://doi.org/10.1016/j.neuroimage.2011.11.080

Blakemore, S.-J., & Mills, K. L. (2014). Is adolescence a sensitive period for sociocultural processing? *Annual Review of Psychology*, *65*, 187–207. https://doi.org/10.1146/annurev-psych-010213-115202

Blanchette, N., Smith, M., Fernandes-Penney, A., King, S., & Read, S. (2001). Cognitive and motor development in children with vertically transmitted HIV infection. *Brain and Cognition*, *46*(1–2), 50–53.

Blandon, A. Y., Calkins, S. D., Grimm, K. J., Keane, S. P., & O'Brien, M. (2010). Testing a developmental cascade model of emotional and social competence and early peer acceptance. *Development and Psychopathology*, *22*(4), 737–748. https://doi.org/10.1017/S0954579410000428

Blankenship, S. L., Redcay, E., Dougherty, L. R., & Riggins, T. (2017). Development of hippocampal functional connectivity during childhood. *Human Brain Mapping*, *38*(1), 182–201. https://doi.org/10.1002/hbm.23353

Blass, E. M., Ganchrow, J. R., & Steiner, J. E. (1984). Classical conditioning in newborn humans 2–48 hours of age. *Infant Behavior and Development*, *7*, 223–235.

Blau, N. (2016). Genetics of phenylketonuria: Then and now. *Human Mutation*, *37*(6), 508–515. https://doi.org/10.1002/humu.22980

Blau, N., Shen, N., & Carducci, C. (2014). Molecular genetics and diagnosis of phenylketonuria: State of the art. *Expert Review of Molecular Diagnostics*, *14*(6), 655–671. https://doi.org/10.1586/14737159.2014.923760

Bleah, D. A., & Ellett, M. L. (2010). Infant crying among recent African immigrants. *Health Care for Women International*, *31*(7), 652–663. https://doi.org/10.1080/07399331003628446

Bleidorn, W., Arslan, R. C., Denissen, J. J. A., Rentfrow, P. J., Gebauer, J. E., Potter, J., & Gosling, S. D. (2016). Age and gender differences in self-esteem—A cross-cultural window. *Journal of Personality and*

Social Psychology, 111(3), 396–410. https://doi.org/10.1037/pspp0000078

Bloom, L. (2000). Commentary: Breaking the language barrier: An emergentist coalition model for the origins of word learning. *Monographs of the Society for Research in Child Development, 65*(3, Serial No. 262), 124–135.

Bloomfield, F. H., Alexander, T., Muelbert, M., & Beker, F. (2017). Smell and taste in the preterm infant. *Early Human Development, 114*, 31–34. https://doi.org/10.1016/J.EARLHUMDEV.2017.09.012

Bloss, C. S., Delis, D. C., Salmon, D. P., & Bondi, M. W. (2010). APOE genotype is associated with left-handedness and visuospatial skills in children. *Neurobiology of Aging, 31*(5), 787–795. https://doi.org/10.1016/j.neurobiolaging.2008.05.021

Blumberg, M. S., Gall, A. J., & Todd, W. D. (2014). The development of sleep-wake rhythms and the search for elemental circuits in the infant brain. *Behavioral Neuroscience, 128*(3), 250–263. https://doi.org/10.1037/a0035891

Bo, X., & Goldman, H. (2008). Newborn circumcision in Victoria, Australia: Reasons and parental attitudes. *ANZ Journal of Surgery, 78*(11), 1019–1022. https://doi.org/10.1111/j.1445-2197.2008.04723.x

Boazman, J., & Sayler, M. (2011). Personal well-being of gifted students following participation in an early college-entrance program. *Roeper Review, 33*(2), 76–85. https://doi.org/10.1080/02783193.2011.554153

Bodrova, E., & Leong, D. J. (2018). Tools of the mind: A Vygotskian early childhood curriculum. In M. Fleer & B. van Oers (Eds.), *International handbook of early childhood education* (pp. 1095–1111). Dordrecht, The Netherlands: Springer. https://doi.org/10.1007/978-94-024-0927-7_56

Bogartz, R. S., Shinskey, J. L., & Schilling, T. H. (2000). Object permanence in five-and-a-half-month-old infants? *Infancy, 1*(4), 403–428. https://doi.org/10.1207/S15327078IN0104_3

Bohannon, J. N., Padgett, R. J., Nelson, K. E., & Mark, M. (1996). Useful evidence on negative evidence. *Developmental Psychology, 32*, 551–555.

Bohannon, J. N., & Stanowicz, L. (1988). The issue of negative evidence: Adult responses to children's language errors. *Developmental Psychology, 24*, 684–689.

Boivin, M., Brendgen, M., Vitaro, F., Forget-Dubois, N., Feng, B., Tremblay, R. E., & Dionne, G. (2013). Evidence of gene–environment correlation for peer difficulties: Disruptive behaviors predict early peer relation difficulties in school through genetic effects. *Development and Psychopathology, 25*(01), 79–92. https://doi.org/10.1017/S0954579412000910

Boivin, M., & Hassan, G. (2015). Ethnic identity and psychological adjustment in transracial adoptees: A review of the literature. *Ethnic and Racial Studies, 38*(7), 1084–1103. https://doi.org/10.1080/01419870.2014.992922

Boldt, L. J., Kochanska, G., Yoon, J. E., & Koenig Nordling, J. (2014). Children's attachment to both parents from toddler age to middle childhood: Links to adaptive and maladaptive outcomes. *Attachment & Human Development, 16*(3), 211–229. https://doi.org/10.1080/14616734.2014.889181

Boom, J. J., Wouters, H., & Keller, M. (2007). A cross-cultural validation of stage development: A Rasch re-analysis of longitudinal socio-moral reasoning data. *Cognitive Development, 22*(2), 213–229.

Boor-Klip, H. J., Cillessen, A. H. N., & van Hell, J. G. (2014). Social understanding of high-ability children in middle and late childhood. *Gifted Child Quarterly, 58*(4), 259–271. https://doi.org/10.1177/0016986214547634

Booth, M. Z., & Gerard, J. M. (2014). Adolescents' stage-environment fit in middle and high school: The relationship between students' perceptions of their schools and themselves. *Youth & Society, 46*(6), 735–755. https://doi.org/10.1177/0044118X12451276

Booth-LaForce, C., Groh, A. M., Burchinal, M. R., Roisman, G. I., Owen, M. T., & Cox, M. J. (2014). V. Caregiving and contextual sources of continuity and change in attachment security from infancy to late adolescence. *Monographs of the Society for Research in Child Development, 79*(3), 67–84. https://doi.org/10.1111/mono.12114

Borges, E., Braga, D. P. de A. F., Provenza, R. R., Figueira, R. de C. S., Iaconelli, A., & Setti, A. S. (2018). Paternal lifestyle factors in relation to semen quality and in vitro reproductive outcomes. *Andrologia, 50*(9), e13090. https://doi.org/10.1111/and.13090

Borich, G. D. (2017). *Effective teaching methods: Research-based practice* (9th ed.). New York, NY: Pearson.

Bornstein, M. H, & Arterberry, M. E. (2010). The development of object categorization in young children: Hierarchical inclusiveness, age, perceptual attribute, and group versus individual analyses. *Developmental Psychology, 46*(2), 350–365. https://doi.org/10.1037/a0018411

Bornstein, M. H., Arterberry, M. E., & Lamb, M. E. (2013). *Development in infancy: A contemporary introduction.* Philadelphia, PA: Psychology Press.

Bornstein, M. H., Arterberry, M. E., & Mash, C. (2004). Long-term memory for an emotional interpersonal interaction occurring at 5 months of age. *Infancy, 6*(4), 407–416.

Bornstein, M. H., Cote, L. R., Maital, S., Painter, K., Park, S.-Y., Pascual, L., . . . Vyt, A. (2004). Cross-linguistic analysis of vocabulary in young children: Spanish, Dutch, French, Hebrew, Italian, Korean, and American English. *Child Development, 75*(4), 1115–1139.

Bornstein, M. H., Hahn, C.-S., Suwalsky, J. T. D., & Haynes, O. M. (2011). Maternal and infant behavior and context associations with mutual emotion availability. *Infant Mental Health Journal, 32*(1), 70–94. https://doi.org/10.1002/imhj.20284

Bornstein, M. H., & Lamb, M. E. (1992). *Development in infancy* (3rd ed.). New York, NY: McGraw-Hill.

Bornstein, M. H., & Lamb, M. E. (2011). *Developmental science: An advanced textbook* (6th ed.). Philadelphia, PA: Psychology Press.

Bornstein, M. H., & Putnick, D. L. (2018). Parent–adolescent relationships in global perspective. In J. E. Lansford & P. Banati (Eds.), *Handbook of adolescent development research and its impact on global policy.* Oxford, England: Oxford University Press.

Bornstein, M. H., Putnick, D. L., Gartstein, M. A., Hahn, C.-S., Auestad, N., & O'Connor, D. L. (2015). Infant temperament: Stability by age, gender, birth order, term status, and socioeconomic status. *Child Development, 86*(3), 844–863. https://doi.org/10.1111/cdev.12367

Bornstein, M. H., Putnick, D. L., Rigo, P., Esposito, G., Swain, J. E., Suwalsky, J. T. D., . . . Venuti, P. (2017). Neurobiology of culturally common maternal responses to infant cry. *Proceedings of the National Academy of Sciences of the United States of America, 114*(45), E9465–E9473. https://doi.org/10.1073/pnas.1712022114

Bornstein, M. H., Slater, A., Brown, E., Roberts, E., & Barrett, J. (1997). Stability of mental development from infancy to later childhood: Three "waves" of research. In G. Bremner, A. Slater, & G. Butterworth (Eds.), *Infant development: Recent advances* (pp. 191–215). Philadelphia, PA: Psychology Press.

Bornstein, M. H., Suwalsky, J. T. D., & Breakstone, D. A. (2012). Emotional relationships between mothers and infants: Knowns, unknowns, and unknown unknowns. *Development and Psychopathology, 24*(1), 113–123. https://doi.org/10.1017/S0954579411000708

Borst, G., Poirel, N., Pineau, A., Cassotti, M., & Houdé, O. (2013). Inhibitory control efficiency in a Piaget-like class-inclusion task in school-age children and adults: A developmental negative priming study. *Developmental Psychology, 49*(7), 1366–1374. https://doi.org/10.1037/a0029622

Bos, H. M. W., Knox, J. R., van Rijn-van Gelderen, L., & Gartrell, N. K. (2016). Same-sex and different-sex parent households and child health outcomes. *Journal of Developmental & Behavioral Pediatrics, 37*(3), 179–187. https://doi.org/10.1097/DBP.0000000000000288

Bosch, A. M., Hutter, I., & van Ginneken, J. K. (2008). Perceptions of adolescents and their mothers on reproductive and sexual development in Matlab, Bangladesh. *International Journal of Adolescent Medicine and Health, 20*(3), 329–342.

Bosch, L., & Ramon-Casas, M. (2014). First translation equivalents in bilingual toddlers' expressive vocabulary: Does form similarity matter? *International Journal of Behavioral Development, 38*(4), 317–322. https://doi.org/10.1177/0165025414532559

Boseovski, J. J. (2010). Evidence for "rosecolored glasses": An examination of the positivity bias in young children's personality judgments. *Child Development Perspectives, 4*(3), 212–218. https://doi.org/10.1111/j.1750-8606.2010.00149.x

Bošković, A., & Rando, O. J. (2018). Transgenerational epigenetic inheritance. *Annual Review of Genetics, 52*(1), 21–41. https://doi.org/10.1146/annurev-genet-120417-031404

Bosse, J. D., & Chiodo, L. (2016). It is complicated: Gender and sexual orientation identity in LGBTQ youth. *Journal of Clinical Nursing, 25*(23–24), 3665–3675. https://doi.org/10.1111/jocn.13419

Boterberg, S., & Warreyn, P. (2016). Making sense of it all: The impact of sensory processing sensitivity on daily functioning of children. *Personality and Individual Differences, 92*, 80–86. https://doi.org/10.1016/J.PAID.2015.12.022

Bouchard, T. J. (2014). Genes, evolution and intelligence. *Behavior Genetics, 44*(6),

549–577. https://doi.org/10.1007/s10519-014-9646-x

Bouchard, T. J., & McGue, M. (1981). Familial studies of intelligence: A review. *Science, 212*(4498), 1055–1059.

Bouldin, P. (2006). An investigation of the fantasy predisposition and fantasy style of children with imaginary companions. *Journal of Genetic Psychology, 167*, 17–29.

Boundy, E. O., Dastjerdi, R., Spiegelman, D., Fawzi, W. W., Missmer, S. A., Lieberman, E., . . . Guedes, Z. (2015). Kangaroo mother care and neonatal outcomes: A meta-analysis. *Pediatrics, 365*(9462), 891–900. https://doi.org/10.1542/peds.2015-2238

Bourgeron, T. (2015). From the genetic architecture to synaptic plasticity in autism spectrum disorder. *Nature Reviews Neuroscience, 16*(9), 551–563. https://doi.org/10.1038/nrn3992

Bouthry, E., Picone, O., Hamdi, G., Grangeot-Keros, L., Ayoubi, J.-M., & Vauloup-Fellous, C. (2014). Rubella and pregnancy: Diagnosis, management and outcomes. *Prenatal Diagnosis, 34*(13), 1246–1253. https://doi.org/10.1002/pd.4467

Boutwell, B. B., Meldrum, R. C., & Petkovsek, M. A. (2017). General intelligence in friendship selection: A study of preadolescent best friend dyads. *Intelligence, 64*, 30–35. https://doi.org/10.1016/J.INTELL.2017.07.002

Bower, B. (1993). A child's theory of mind. *Science News, 144*, 40–42.

Bower, T. G. R., Broughton, J. M., & Moore, M. K. (1970). The coordination of vision and tactile input in infancy. *Perception and Psychophysics, 8*, 51–53.

Bowers, A. J., & Sprott, R. (2012). Examining the multiple trajectories associated with dropping out of high school: A growth mixture model analysis. *Journal of Educational Research, 105*(3), 176–195. https://doi.org/10.1080/00220671.2011.552075

Bowers, J. S. (2016). The practical and principled problems with educational neuroscience. *Psychological Review, 123*(5), 600–612. https://doi.org/10.1037/rev0000025

Bowker, A., & Ramsay, K. (2016). Friendship characteristics. In R. J. R. Levesque (Ed.), *Encyclopedia of adolescence* (pp. 1–8). Cham, Switzerland: Springer. https://doi.org/10.1007/978-3-319-32132-5_49-2

Bowker, J. C., Fredstrom, B. K., Rubin, K. H., Rose-Krasnor, L., Booth-LaForce, C., & Laursen, B. (2010). Distinguishing children who form new best-friendships from those who do not. *Journal of Social and Personal Relationships, 27*(6), 707–725. https://doi.org/10.1177/0265407510373259

Bowlby, J. (1969). *Attachment and loss: Vol. 1.*

Bowlby, J. (1973). *Attachment and loss: Vol. 2. Separation: Anxiety and anger.* New York, NY: Basic Books.

Bowlby, J. (1988). *A secure base: Clinical applications of attachment theory.* New York, NY: Routledge.

Bowman, L. J. (2005). Grade retention: Is it a help or hindrance to student academic success? *Preventing School Failure, 49*(3), 42–46.

Bowman, M. A., Prelow, H. M., & Weaver, S. R. (2007). Parenting behaviors, association with deviant peers, and delinquency in African American adolescents: A mediated-moderation model. *Journal of Youth & Adolescence, 36*, 517–527.

Bowman, S. A., Gortmaker, S. L., Ebbeling, C. B., Pereira, M. A., & Ludwig, D. S. (2004). Effects of fast-food consumption on energy intake and diet quality among children in a national household survey. *Pediatrics, 113*(1), 112–118.

Boyer, T. W., & Byrnes, J. P. (2016). Risk-taking. In J. R. Levesque (Ed.), *Encyclopedia of adolescence* (pp. 1–5). Cham, Switzerland: Springer International Publishing. https://doi.org/10.1007/978-3-319-32132-5_15-2

Boyes, M. C., & Chandler, M. (1992). Cognitive development, epistemic doubt, and identity formation in adolescence. *Journal of Youth and Adolescence, 21*(3), 277–304.

Boysson-Bardies, B. De, Sagart, L., Durand, C., Eimas, P. D., Siqueland, E. R., Jusczyk, P., . . . Oller, D. K. (1984). Discernible differences in the babbling of infants according to target language. *Journal of Child Language, 11*(1), 1–15. https://doi.org/10.1017/S0305000900005559

Bozick, R., & DeLuca, S. (2011). Not making the transition to college: School, work, and opportunities in the lives of American youth. *Social Science Research, 40*(4), 1249–1262. https://doi.org/10.1016/j.ssresearch.2011.02.003

Braams, B. R., van Duijvenvoorde, A. C. K., Peper, J. S., & Crone, E. A. (2015). Longitudinal changes in adolescent risk-taking: A comprehensive study of neural responses to rewards, pubertal development, and risk-taking behavior. *Journal of Neuroscience, 35*(18), 7226–7238.

Bradley, R. H., & Corwyn, R. F. (2008). Infant temperament, parenting, and externalizing behavior in first grade: A test of the differential susceptibility hypothesis. *Journal of Child Psychology & Psychiatry, 49*(2), 124–131. https://doi.org/10.1111/j.1469-7610.2007.01829.x

Bradley, R. H., Iida, M., Pennar, A., Owen, M. T., & Vandell, D. L. (2017). The dialectics of parenting: Changes in the interplay of maternal behaviors during early and middle childhood. *Journal of Child and Family Studies, 26*(11), 3214–3225. https://doi.org/10.1007/s10826-017-0805-6

Bradman, A., Quirós-Alcalá, L., Castorina, R., Aguilar Schall, R., Camacho, J., Holland, N. T., . . . Eskenazi, B. (2015). Effect of organic diet intervention on pesticide exposures in young children living in low-income urban and agricultural communities. *Environmental Health Perspectives, 123*(10), 1086–1093. https://doi.org/10.1289/ehp.1408660

Brady, S. A. (2011). Efficacy of phonics teaching for reading outcomes: Indications from post-NRP research. In S. A. Brady, D. Braze, & C. A. Fowler (Eds.), *Explaining individual differences in reading: Theory and evidence.* New York, NY: Psychology Press.

Brain Development Cooperative Group. (2011). Total and regional brain volumes in a population-based normative sample from 4 to 18 years: The NIH MRI Study of Normal Brain Development. *Cerebral Cortex, 22*(1), 1–12. https://doi.org/10.1093/cercor/bhr018

Brandl, J. L. (2018). The puzzle of mirror self-recognition. *Phenomenology and the Cognitive Sciences, 17*(2), 1–26. https://doi.org/10.1007/s11097-016-9486-7

Brandler, W. M., Morris, A. P., Evans, D. M., Scerri, T. S., Kemp, J. P., Timpson, N. J., . . . Paracchini, S. (2013). Common variants in left/right asymmetry genes and pathways are associated with relative hand skill. *PLoS Genetics, 9*(9), e1003751. https://doi.org/10.1371/journal.pgen.1003751

Branje, S. (2018). Development of parent-adolescent relationships: Conflict interactions as a mechanism of change. *Child Development Perspectives, 12*(3), 171–176. https://doi.org/10.1111/cdep.12278

Branje, S., Laursen, B., & Collins, W. A. (2013). Parent-child communication during adolescence. In A. L. Vangelisti (Ed.), *Routledge handbook of family communication* (p. 601). New York, NY: Routledge. Retrieved from https://www.routledge.com/The-Routledge-Handbook-of-Family-Communication-2nd-Edition/Vangelisti/p/book/9780415881975

Brassard, M. R., & Fiorvanti, C. M. (2015). School-based child abuse prevention programs. *Psychology in the Schools, 52*(1), 40–60. https://doi.org/10.1002/pits.21811

Bratberg, E., & Tjøtta, S. (2008). Income effects of divorce in families with dependent children. *Journal of Population Economics, 21*(2), 439–461. https://doi.org/10.1007/s00148-005-0029-8

Braungart-Rieker, J. M., Hill-Soderlund, A. L., & Karrass, J. (2010). Fear and anger reactivity trajectories from 4 to 16 months: The roles of temperament, regulation, and maternal sensitivity. *Developmental Psychology, 46*(4), 791–804. https://doi.org/10.1037/a0019673

Braveman, P. A., Heck, K., Egerter, S., Marchi, K. S., Dominguez, T. P., Cubbin, C., . . . Curtis, M. (2015). The role of socioeconomic factors in Black-White disparities in preterm birth. *American Journal of Public Health, 105*(4), 694–702. https://doi.org/10.2105/AJPH.2014.302008

Brazelton, T. B. (1977). Implications of infant development among the Mayan Indians of Mexico. In P. H. Liederman, S. R. Tulikn, & A. Rosenfeld (Eds.), *Culture and infancy* (pp. 336–352). New York, NY: Academic Press.

Brechwald, W. A., & Prinstein, M. J. (2011). Beyond homophily: A decade of advances in understanding peer influence processes. *Journal of Research on Adolescence, 21*(1), 166–179. https://doi.org/10.1111/j.1532-7795.2010.00721.x

Breiding, M. J., Chen, J., & Black, M. C. (2014). *Intimate partner violence in the United States—2010.* Retrieved from https://www.ncjrs.gov/App/Publications/abstract.aspx?ID=267363

Breiding, M. J., Smith, S. G., Basile, K. C., Walters, M. L., Chen, J., & Merrick, M. T. (2014). Prevalence and characteristics of sexual violence, stalking, and intimate partner violence victimization—National Intimate Partner and Sexual Violence Survey, United States, 2011. *Morbidity and Mortality Weekly Report, 63*(SS08), 1–18. Retrieved from https://www.cdc.gov/mmwr/preview/mmwrhtml/ss6308a1.htm

Breiner, K., Li, A., Cohen, A. O., Steinberg, L., Bonnie, R. J., Scott, E. S., . . . Galván, A. (2018). Combined effects of peer presence, social cues, and rewards on cognitive control in adolescents. *Developmental Psychobiology, 60*(3), 292–302. https://doi.org/10.1002/dev.21599

Bremner, J. G., Slater, A. M., & Johnson, S. P. (2015). Perception of object persistence: The origins of object permanence in infancy. *Child Development Perspectives, 9*(1), 7–13. https://doi.org/10.1111/cdep.12098

Bretherton, I., Fritz, J., Zahn-Waxler, C., & Ridgeway, D. (1986). Learning to talk about emotions: A functionalist perspective. *Child Development, 57*, 529–548.

Bretherton, I., & Munholland, K. (2016). The internal working model construct in light of contemporary neuroimaging research. In *Handbook of attachment: Theory, research, and clinical applications* (pp. 63–88). New York, NY: Guilford.

Bridgett, D. J., Gartstein, M. A., Putnam, S. P., McKay, T., Iddins, E., Robertson, C., . . . Rittmueller, A. (2009). Maternal and contextual influences and the effect of temperament development during infancy on parenting in toddlerhood. *Infant Behavior & Development, 32*(1), 103–116. https://doi.org/10.1016/j.infbeh.2008.10.007

Brinums, M., Imuta, K., & Suddendorf, T. (2018). Practicing for the future: Deliberate practice in early childhood. *Child Development*. https://doi.org/10.1111/cdev.12938

Broberg, A. G., Wessels, H., Lamb, M. E., & Hwang, C. P. (1997). Effects of day care on the development of cognitive abilities in 8-year-olds: A longitudinal study. *Developmental Psychology, 33*(1), 62–69. https://doi.org/10.1037/0012-1649.33.1.62

Brocklehurst, P., Hardy, P., Hollowell, J., Linsell, L., Macfarlane, A., McCourt, C., . . . Stewart, M. (2011). Perinatal and maternal outcomes by planned place of birth for healthy women with low risk pregnancies: The Birthplace in England national prospective cohort study. *BMJ (Clinical Research Ed.), 343*, d7400. https://doi.org/10.1136/BMJ.D7400

Brodie, B. (1974). Views of healthy children towards illness. *American Journal of Public Health, 64*(12), 1156–1159.

Broekhuizen, M. L., van Aken, M. A. G., Dubas, J. S., & Leseman, P. P. M. (2018). Child care quality and Dutch 2- and 3-year-olds' socio-emotional outcomes: Does the amount of care matter? *Infant and Child Development, 27*(1), e2043. https://doi.org/10.1002/icd.2043

Broesch, T., Rochat, P., Olah, K., Broesch, J., & Henrich, J. (2016). Similarities and differences in maternal responsiveness in three societies: Evidence from Fiji, Kenya, and the United States. *Child Development, 87*(3), 700–711. https://doi.org/10.1111/cdev.12501

Broesch, T. L., & Bryant, G. A. (2015). Prosody in infant-directed speech is similar across Western and traditional cultures. *Journal of Cognition and Development, 16*(1), 31–43. https://doi.org/10.1080/15248372.2013.833923

Bronfenbrenner, U. (1979). *The ecology of human development: Experiments by nature and design*. Cambridge, MA: Harvard University Press.

Bronfenbrenner, U., & Morris, P. A. (2006). The bioecological model of human development. In R. M. Lerner & W. Damon (Eds.), *Handbook of child psychology* (Vol. 1, pp. 793–828). Hoboken, NJ: John Wiley & Sons.

Brooker, R. J., Buss, K. A., Lemery-Chalfant, K., Aksan, N., Davidson, R. J., & Goldsmith, H. H. (2013). The development of stranger fear in infancy and toddlerhood: Normative development, individual differences, antecedents, and outcomes. *Developmental Science, 16*(6), 864–878. https://doi.org/10.1111/desc.12058

Brooks, P. J., & Kempe, V. (2014). *Encyclopedia of language development*. Thousand Oaks, CA: Sage.

Brooks, R., & Meltzoff, A. N. (2008). Infant gaze following and pointing predict accelerated vocabulary growth through two years of age: A longitudinal, growth curve modeling study. *Journal of Child Language, 35*(1), 207–220. https://doi.org/10.1017/s030500090700829x

Brooks-Gunn, J., & Ruble, D. N. (2013). Developmental processes in the experience of menarche. In A. Baum, J. E. Singer, & J. L. Singer (Eds.), *Issues in child health and adolescent health: Handbook of psychology and health* (pp. 117–148). New York, NY: Psychology Press.

Brooks-Russell, A., Simons-Morton, B., Haynie, D., Farhat, T., & Wang, J. (2014). Longitudinal relationship between drinking with peers, descriptive norms, and adolescent alcohol use. *Prevention Science, 15*(4), 497–505. https://doi.org/10.1007/s11121-013-0391-9

Brown, A., Waters, C. S., & Shelton, K. H. (2017). A systematic review of the school performance and behavioural and emotional adjustments of children adopted from care. *Adoption & Fostering, 41*(4), 346–368. https://doi.org/10.1177/0308575917731064

Brown, B., Bank, H., & Steinberg, L. (2008). Smoke in the looking glass: Effects of discordance between self- and peer rated crowd affiliation on adolescent anxiety, depression and self-feelings. *Journal of Youth & Adolescence, 37*(10), 1163–1177. https://doi.org/10.1007/s10964-007-9198-y

Brown, B. B., Lohr, M. J., & McClenahan, E. L. (1986). Early adolescents' perceptions of peer pressure. *Journal of Early Adolescence, 6*(2), 139–154.

Brown, D. A., & Lamb, M. E. (2015). Can children be useful witnesses? It depends how they are questioned. *Child Development Perspectives, 9*(4), 250–255. https://doi.org/10.1111/cdep.12142

Brown, G. L., Mangelsdorf, S. C., & Neff, C. (2012). Father involvement, paternal sensitivity, and father-child attachment security in the first 3 years. *Journal of Family Psychology, 26*(3), 421–430. https://doi.org/10.1037/a0027836

Brown, H. R., Harvey, E. A., Griffith, S. F., Arnold, D. H., & Halgin, R. P. (2017). Assent and dissent: Ethical considerations in research with toddlers. *Ethics & Behavior, 27*(8), 651–664. https://doi.org/10.1080/10508422.2016.1277356

Brown, S. L., Manning, W. D., & Stykes, J. B. (2015). Family structure and child well-being: Integrating family complexity. *Journal of Marriage and the Family, 77*(1), 177–190. https://doi.org/10.1111/jomf.12145

Brownell, C. A. (2016). Prosocial behavior in infancy: The role of socialization. *Child Development Perspectives, 10*(4), 222–227. https://doi.org/10.1111/cdep.12189

Brubacher, S. P., Glisic, U. N. A., Roberts, K. P., & Powell, M. (2011). Children's ability to recall unique aspects of one occurrence of a repeated event. *Applied Cognitive Psychology, 25*(3), 351–358. https://doi.org/10.1002/acp.1696

Bruer, J. T. (2008). In search of. . . brain-based education. In M. H. Immordino-Yang (Ed.), *The Jossey-Bass reader on the brain and learning* (pp. 51–69). San Francisco, CA: Jossey-Bass.

Brugman, D. (2010). Moral reasoning competence and the moral judgment-action discrepancy in young adolescents. In A. F. S. W. Koops, D. Brugman, & T. J. Ferguson (Eds.), *The development and structure of conscience* (pp. 119–133). New York, NY: Psychology Press.

Brumariu, L. E. (2015). Parent-child attachment and emotion regulation. *New Directions for Child and Adolescent Development, 2015*(148), 31–45. https://doi.org/10.1002/cad.20098

Brumback, T., Worley, M., Nguyen-Louie, T. T., Squeglia, L. M., Jacobus, J., & Tapert, S. F. (2016). Neural predictors of alcohol use and psychopathology symptoms in adolescents. *Development and Psychopathology, 28*(4, Pt. 1), 1209–1216. https://doi.org/10.1017/S0954579416000766

Brummelman, E. (2018). The emergence of narcissism and self-esteem: A social-cognitive approach. *European Journal of Developmental Psychology, 15*(6), 756–767. https://doi.org/10.1080/17405629.2017.1419953

Bryant, B. R., Bryant, D. P., Porterfield, J., Dennis, M. S., Falcomata, T., Valentine, C., . . . Bell, K. (2016). The effects of a tier 3 intervention on the mathematics performance of second grade students with severe mathematics difficulties. *Journal of Learning Disabilities, 49*(2), 176–188. https://doi.org/10.1177/0022219414538516

Bryant, G. A., Liénard, P., & Barrett, H. C. (2012). Recognizing infant-directed speech across distant cultures: Evidence from Africa. *Journal of Evolutionary Psychology, 10*(2), 47–59. https://doi.org/10.1556/jep.10.2012.2.1

Bryck, R. L., & Fisher, P. A. (2012). Training the brain: Practical applications of neural plasticity from the intersection of cognitive neuroscience, developmental psychology, and prevention science. *American Psychologist, 67*(2), 87–100.

Buckingham-Howes, S., Berger, S. S., Scaletti, L. A., & Black, M. M. (2013). Systematic review of prenatal cocaine exposure and adolescent development. *Pediatrics, 131*(6), e1917–e1936. https://doi.org/10.1542/peds.2012-0945

Buckley, C. (2015). China ends one-child policy, allowing families two children. *New York Times*. Retrieved from https://www.nytimes.com/2015/10/30/world/asia/china-end-one-child-policy.html

Buist, K. L., & Vermande, M. (2014). Sibling relationship patterns and their associations with child competence and problem behavior. *Journal of Family Psychology, 28*(4), 529–537. https://doi.org/10.1037/a0036990

Buiting, K., Williams, C., & Horsthemke, B. (2016). Angelman syndrome—insights into a rare neurogenetic disorder. *Nature Reviews Neurology, 12*(10), 584–593. https://doi.org/10.1038/nrneurol.2016.133

Bulik, C. M., Kleiman, S. C., & Yilmaz, Z. (2016). Genetic epidemiology of eating disorders. *Current Opinion in Psychiatry, 29*(6), 383–388. https://doi.org/10.1097/YCO.0000000000000275

Bullock, M., & Lutkenhaus, P. (1990). Who am I? Self-understanding in toddlers. *Merrill-Palmer Quarterly, 36*, 217–238.

Bundak, R., Darendeliler, F., Gunoz, H., Bas, F., Saka, N., & Neyzi, O. (2007). Analysis of puberty and pubertal growth in healthy boys. *European Journal of Pediatrics, 166*(6), 595–600.

Burchinal, M., Roberts, J. E., Zeisel, S. A., Hennon, E. A., & Hooper, S. (2006). Social risk and protective child, parenting, and child care factors in early elementary school years. *Parenting: Science & Practice, 6*(1), 79–113.

Burden, P. R., & Byrd, D. M. (2019). *Methods for effective teaching: Meeting the needs of all students* (8th ed.). New York, NY: Pearson.

Burgdorf, J., Kroes, R. A., & Moskal, J. R. (2017). Rough-and-tumble play induces resilience to stress in rats. *NeuroReport, 28*(17), 1122–1126. https://doi.org/10.1097/WNR.0000000000000864

Burnham, D., Kitamura, C., & Vollmer-Conna, U. (2002). What's new pussycat? On talking to babies and animals. *Science, 296*, 1435.

Burrus, B. B. (2018). Decline in adolescent pregnancy in the United States: A success not shared by all. *American Journal of Public Health, 108*(S1), S5–S6. https://doi.org/10.2105/AJPH.2017.304273

Burt, A. (2009). A mechanistic explanation of popularity: Genes, rule breaking, and evocative gene–environment correlations. *Journal of Personality and Social Psychology, 96*(4), 783–794. https://doi.org/10.1037/a0013702

Bush, N. R., Allison, A. L., Miller, A. L., Deardorff, J., Adler, N. E., & Boyce, W. T. (2017). Socioeconomic disparities in childhood obesity risk: Association with an oxytocin receptor polymorphism. *JAMA Pediatrics, 171*(1), 61. https://doi.org/10.1001/jamapediatrics.2016.2332

Buss, A. H., & Plomin, R. (1984). *Temperament: Early developing personality traits.* Hillsdale, NJ: Erlbaum.

Bussey, K. (1992). Lying and truthfulness: Children's definitions, standards, and evaluative reactions. *Child Development, 63*, 129–137.

Bussey, K. (2013). Gender development. In M. K. Ryan & N. R. Branscombe (Eds.), *The SAGE handbook of gender and psychology* (pp. 81–100). Thousand Oaks: Sage.

Busso, D. S., & Pollack, C. (2014). No brain left behind: Consequences of neuroscience discourse for education. *Learning, Media and Technology, 40*(2), 168–186. https://doi.org/10.1080/17439884.2014.908908

Butler, M. G., Manzardo, A. M., Heinemann, J., Loker, C., & Loker, J. (2016). Causes of death in Prader-Willi syndrome: Prader-Willi Syndrome Association (USA) 40-year mortality survey. *Genetics in Medicine, 19*(6), 635. https://doi.org/10.1038/gim.2016.178

Butterworth, G. (1992). Origins of self-perception in infancy. *Psychological Inquiry, 3*(2), 103–111. https://doi.org/10.1207/s15327965pli0302_1

Bygdell, M., Vandenput, L., Ohlsson, C., & Kindblom, J. M. (2014). A secular trend for pubertal timing in Swedish men born 1946–1991—the Best Cohort. Puberty: From bench to bedside [Abstract OR11-3]. In *ENDO Meetings*. Retrieved from https://www.endocrine.org/meetings/endo-annual-meetings/abstract-details?ID=14868

Byrd, A. L., & Manuck, S. B. (2014). MAOA, childhood maltreatment, and antisocial behavior: Meta-analysis of a gene-environment interaction. *Biological Psychiatry, 75*(1), 9–17. https://doi.org/10.1016/j.biopsych.2013.05.004

Byrd, A. L., Manuck, S. B., Hawes, S. W., Vebares, T. J., Nimgaonkar, V., Chowdari, K. V., . . . Stepp, S. D. (2018). The interaction between monoamine oxidase A (MAOA) and childhood maltreatment as a predictor of personality pathology in females: Emotional reactivity as a potential mediating mechanism. *Development and Psychopathology.* https://doi.org/10.1017/S0954579417001900

Byrne, M. L., Whittle, S., Vijayakumar, N., Dennison, M., Simmons, J. G., & Allen, N. B. (2017). A systematic review of adrenarche as a sensitive period in neurobiological development and mental health. *Developmental Cognitive Neuroscience, 25*, 12–28. https://doi.org/10.1016/J.DCN.2016.12.004

Byrnes, J. P., & Takahira, S. (1993). Explaining gender differences on SAT-math items. *Developmental Psychology, 29*(5), 805–810. https://doi.org/10.1037/0012-1649.29.5.805

Byrnes, J. P., & Vu, L. T. (2015). Educational neuroscience: Definitional, methodological, and interpretive issues. *Wiley Interdisciplinary Reviews: Cognitive Science, 6*(3), 221–234. https://doi.org/10.1002/wcs.1345

Byrnes, V., & Ruby, A. (2007). Comparing achievement between K–8 and middle schools: A large-scale empirical study. *American Journal of Education, 114*(1), 101–135.

Cabeza, R., & Nyberg, L. (2000). Neural bases of learning and memory: Functional neuroimaging evidence. *Current Opinion in Neurology, 13*(4), 415–421. Retrieved from http://www.ncbi.nlm.nih.gov/pubmed/10970058

Cabinian, A., Sinsimer, D., Tang, M., Zumba, O., Mehta, H., Toma, A., . . . Richardson, B. (2016). Transfer of maternal immune cells by breastfeeding: Maternal cytotoxic T lymphocytes present in breast milk localize in the Peyer's patches of the nursed infant. *PLoS ONE, 11*(6), e0156762. https://doi.org/10.1371/journal.pone.0156762

Cabrera, N. J., Fitzgerald, H. E., Bradley, R. H., & Roggman, L. (2014). The ecology of father child relationships: An expanded model. *Journal of Family Theory & Review, 6*(4), 336–354. https://doi.org/10.1111/jftr.12054

Cabrera, N. J., Volling, B. L., & Barr, R. (2018). Fathers are parents, too! Widening the lens on parenting for children's development. *Child Development Perspectives, 12*(3), 152–157. https://doi.org/10.1111/cdep.12275

Cadima, J., Doumen, S., Verschueren, K., & Buyse, E. (2015). Child engagement in the transition to school: Contributions of self-regulation, teacher–child relationships and classroom climate. *Early Childhood Research Quarterly, 32*, 1–12. https://doi.org/10.1016/J.ECRESQ.2015.01.008

Caldas, S. J., & Reilly, M. S. (2018). The influence of race–ethnicity and physical activity levels on elementary school achievement. *Journal of Educational Research, 111*(4), 473–486. https://doi.org/10.1080/00220671.2017.1297925

Calhoun, S., Conner, E., Miller, M., & Messina, N. (2015). Improving the outcomes of children affected by parental substance abuse: A review of randomized controlled trials. *Substance Abuse and Rehabilitation, 6*, 15–24. https://doi.org/10.2147/SAR.S46439

Callaghan, T., & Corbit, J. (2015). The development of symbolic representation. In *Handbook of child psychology and developmental science* (pp. 1–46). Hoboken, NJ: John Wiley & Sons Inc. https://doi.org/10.1002/9781118963418.childpsy207

Callaghan, T., Rochat, P., Lillard, A., Claux, M. L., Odden, H., Itakura, S., . . . Singh, S. (2005). Synchrony in the onset of mental-state reasoning. *Psychological Science, 16*(5), 378–384. https://doi.org/10.1111/j.0956-7976.2005.01544.x

Callaghan, T. C. (1999). Early understanding and production of graphic symbols. *Child Development, 70*, 1314–1324.

Calvert, H. G., Mahar, M. T., Flay, B., & Turner, L. (2018). Classroom-based physical activity: Minimizing disparities in school-day physical activity among elementary school students. *Journal of Physical Activity and Health, 15*(3), 161–168. https://doi.org/10.1123/jpah.2017-0323

Calzo, J. P., Antonucci, T. C., Mays, V. M., & Cochran, S. D. (2011). Retrospective recall of sexual orientation identity development among gay, lesbian, and bisexual adults. *Developmental Psychology, 47*(6), 1658–1673. https://doi.org/10.1037/a0025508

Calzo, J. P., Masyn, K. E., Austin, S. B., Jun, H.-J., & Corliss, H. L. (2017). Developmental latent patterns of identification as mostly heterosexual versus lesbian, gay, or bisexual. *Journal of Research on Adolescence, 27*(1), 246–253. https://doi.org/10.1111/jora.12266

Cameron, C. E., Brock, L. L., Murrah, W. M., Bell, L. H., Worzalla, S. L., Grissmer, D., & Morrison, F. J. (2012). Fine motor skills and executive function both contribute to kindergarten achievement. *Child Development, 83*(4), 1229–1244. https://doi.org/10.1111/j.1467-8624.2012.01768.x

Camerota, M., Willoughby, M. T., Cox, M., Greenberg, M., & the Family Life Project Investigators. (2015). Executive function in low birth weight preschoolers: The moderating effect of parenting. *Journal of Abnormal Child Psychology, 43*(8), 1551–1562. https://doi.org/10.1007/s10802-015-0032-9

Camos, V., Barrouillet, P., & Barrouillet, P. (2018). *Working memory in development.* New York, NY: Routledge. https://doi.org/10.4324/9781315660851

Campbell, B. C. (2011). Adrenarche and middle childhood. *Human Nature, 22*(3), 327–349. https://doi.org/10.1007/s12110-011-9120-x

Campbell, F. A., Pungello, E. P., Burchinal, M., Kainz, K., Pan, Y., Wasik, B. H., . . . Ramey, C. T. (2012). Adult outcomes as a function of an early childhood educational program: An Abecedarian Project follow-up. *Developmental Psychology, 48*(4), 1033–1043. https://doi.org/10.1037/a0026644

Campbell, F. A., & Ramey, C. T. (1994). Effects of early intervention on intellectual and academic achievement: A follow-up study of children from low-income families. *Child Development, 65*(2), 684–698. https://doi.org/10.1111/j.1467-8624.1994.tb00777.x

Campbell, F. A., Ramey, C. T., Pungello, E., Sparling, J., & Miller-Johnson, S. (2002). Early childhood education: Young adult outcomes from the Abecedarian Project. *Applied Developmental Science, 6*(1), 42–57. https://doi.org/10.1207/S1532480XADS0601_05

Campbell, K., & Peebles, R. (2014). Eating disorders in children and adolescents: State of the art review. *Pediatrics, 134*(3), 582–592. https://doi.org/10.1542/peds.2014-0194

Camras, L. A., & Halberstadt, A. G. (2017). Emotional development through the lens of affective social competence. *Current Opinion in Psychology, 17*, 113–117. https://doi.org/10.1016/J.COPSYC.2017.07.003

Canetto, S. S., & Sakinofsky, I. (1998). The gender paradox in suicide. *Suicide and Life-Threatening Behavior, 28*, 1–23.

Canevello, A. (2016). Gender schema theory. In V. Zeigler-Hill & T. K. Shackelford (Eds.), *Encyclopedia of personality and individual differences* (pp. 1–3). Cham, Switzerland: Springer International Publishing. https://doi.org/10.1007/978-3-319-28099-8_978-1

Caprara, G. V., Schwartz, S., Capanna, C., Vecchione, M., & Barbaranelli, C. (2006). Personality and politics: Values, traits, and political choice. *Political Psychology, 27*(1), 1–28. https://doi.org/10.1111/j.1467-9221.2006.00447.x

Carbia, C., Cadaveira, F., López-Caneda, E., Caamaño-Isorna, F., Rodriguez Holguin, S., & Corral, M. (2017). Working memory over a six-year period in young binge drinkers. *Alcohol, 61*, 17–23. https://doi.org/10.1016/j.alcohol.2017.01.013

Carbonneau, K. J., Marley, S. C., & Selig, J. P. (2013). A meta-analysis of the efficacy of teaching mathematics with concrete manipulatives. *Journal of Educational Psychology, 105*(2), 380–400. https://doi.org/10.1037/a0031084

Cardona Cano, S., Hoek, H. W., van Hoeken, D., de Barse, L. M., Jaddoe, V. W. V., Verhulst, F. C., & Tiemeier, H. (2016). Behavioral outcomes of picky eating in childhood: A prospective study in the general population. *Journal of Child Psychology and Psychiatry, 57*(11), 1239–1246. https://doi.org/10.1111/jcpp.12530

Carey, S., Zaitchik, D., & Bascandziev, I. (2015). Theories of development: In dialog with Jean Piaget. *Developmental Review, 38*, 36–54. https://doi.org/10.1016/J.DR.2015.07.003

Carlin, R. F., & Moon, R. Y. (2017). Risk factors, protective factors, and current recommendations to reduce sudden infant death syndrome. *JAMA Pediatrics, 171*(2), 175. https://doi.org/10.1001/jamapediatrics.2016.3345

Carlo, G., Mestre, M. V., Samper, P., Tur, A., & Armenta, B. E. (2011). The longitudinal relations among dimensions of parenting styles, sympathy, prosocial moral reasoning, and prosocial behaviors. *International Journal of Behavioral Development, 35*(2), 116–124. https://doi.org/10.1177/0165025410375921

Carlson, D. L., McNulty, T. L., Bellair, P. E., & Watts, S. (2014). Neighborhoods and racial/ethnic disparities in adolescent sexual risk behavior. *Journal of Youth and Adolescence, 43*(9), 1536–1549. https://doi.org/10.1007/s10964-013-0052-0

Carlson, M., Oshri, A., & Kwon, J. (2015). Child maltreatment and risk behaviors: The roles of callous/unemotional traits and conscientiousness. *Child Abuse & Neglect, 50*, 234–243. https://doi.org/10.1016/j.chiabu.2015.07.003

Carlson, S. M., Zelazo, P. D., & Faja, S. (2013). *Executive function* (P. D. Zelazo, Ed.). Oxford, England: Oxford University Press. https://doi.org/10.1093/oxfordhb/9780199958450.013.0025

Carlson, V. J., & Harwood, R. L. (2003). Attachment, culture, and the caregiving system: The cultural patterning of everyday experiences among Anglo and Puerto Rican mother-infant pairs. *Infant Mental Health Journal, 24*, 53–73.

Carlsson, J., Wängqvist, M., & Frisén, A. (2015). Identity development in the late twenties: A never ending story. *Developmental Psychology, 51*(3), 334–345. https://doi.org/10.1037/a0038745

Carlsson, J., Wängqvist, M., & Frisén, A. (2016). Life on hold: Staying in identity diffusion in the late twenties. *Journal of Adolescence, 47*, 220–229. https://doi.org/10.1016/j.adolescence.2015.10.023

Carone, N., Lingiardi, V., Chirumbolo, A., & Baiocco, R. (2018). Italian gay father families formed by surrogacy: Parenting, stigmatization, and children's psychological adjustment. *Developmental Psychology, 54*(10), 1904–1916. https://doi.org/10.1037/dev0000571

Carpendale, J. I. M., & Lewis, C. (2015). The development of social understanding. In *Handbook of child psychology and developmental science* (pp. 1–44). Hoboken, NJ: John Wiley & Sons. https://doi.org/10.1002/9781118963418.childpsy210

Carrion-Castillo, A., Franke, B., & Fisher, S. E. (2013). Molecular genetics of dyslexia: An overview. *Dyslexia, 19*(4), 214–240. https://doi.org/10.1002/dys.1464

Carskadon, M. A. (2009). Adolescents and sleep: Why teens can't get enough of a good thing. *Brown University Child & Adolescent Behavior Letter, 25*(4), 1–6.

Carskadon, M. A., Acebo, C., & Jenni, O. G. (2004). Regulation of adolescent sleep: Implications for behavior. *Annals of the New York Academy of Sciences, 1021*, 276–291. https://doi.org/10.1196/annals.1308.032

Carskadon, M. A., & Tarokh, L. (2014). Developmental changes in sleep biology and potential effects on adolescent behavior and caffeine use. *Nutrition Reviews, 72*(Suppl. 1), 60–64. https://doi.org/10.1111/nure.12147

Carson, A. S., & Banuazizi, A. (2008). "That's not fair": Similarities and differences in distributive justice reasoning between American and Filipino children. *Journal of Cross-Cultural Psychology, 39*(4), 493–514.

Carson, N. (2014). *Foundations of behavioral neuroscience*. New York, NY: Pearson.

Carson, V., Lee, E.-Y., Hewitt, L., Jennings, C., Hunter, S., Kuzik, N., . . . Tremblay, M. S. (2017). Systematic review of the relationships between physical activity and health indicators in the early years (0-4 years). *BMC Public Health, 17*(S5), 854. https://doi.org/10.1186/s12889-017-4860-0

Carson, V., Ridgers, N. D., Howard, B. J., Winkler, E. A. H., Healy, G. N., Owen, N., . . . Zheng, Y. (2013). Light-intensity physical activity and cardiometabolic biomarkers in US adolescents. *PLoS ONE, 8*(8), e71417. https://doi.org/10.1371/journal.pone.0071417

Carter, C. S. (2014). Oxytocin pathways and the evolution of human behavior. *Annual Review of Psychology, 65*(1), 17–39. https://doi.org/10.1146/annurev-psych-010213-115110

Carter, R. (2015). Anxiety symptoms in African American youth. *Journal of Early Adolescence, 35*(3), 281–307. https://doi.org/10.1177/0272431614530809

Carter, R., Halawah, A., & Trinh, S. L. (2018). Peer exclusion during the pubertal transition: The role of social competence. *Journal of Youth and Adolescence, 47*(1), 121–134. https://doi.org/10.1007/s10964-017-0682-8

Carter, R., Mustafaa, F. N., & Leath, S. (2018). Teachers' expectations of girls' classroom performance and behavior. *Journal of Early Adolescence, 38*(7), 885–907. https://doi.org/10.1177/0272431617699947

Casanueva, C., Goldman-Fraser, J., Ringeisen, H., Lederman, C., Katz, L., & Osofsky, J. (2010). Maternal perceptions of temperament among infants and toddlers investigated for maltreatment: Implications for services need and referral. *Journal of Family Violence, 25*(6), 557–574. https://doi.org/10.1007/s10896-010-9316-6

Casares, W. N., Lahiff, M., Eskenazi, B., & Halpern-Felsher, B. L. (2010). Unpredicted trajectories: The relationship between race/ethnicity, pregnancy during adolescence, and young women's outcomes. *Journal of Adolescent Health, 47*(2), 143–150. https://doi.org/10.1016/j.jadohealth.2010.01.013

Case, R. (1999). Cognitive development. In M. Bennett (Ed.), *Developmental psychology: Achievements and prospects* (pp. 36–54). Philadelphia, PA: Taylor & Francis.

Casey, B. J. (2015). Beyond simple models of self-control to circuit-based accounts of adolescent behavior. *Annual Review of Psychology, 66*, 295–319. https://doi.org/10.1146/annurev-psych-010814-015156

Caspi, A., McClay, J., Moffitt, T. E., Mill, J., Martin, J., Craig, I. W., . . . Poulton, R. (2002). Role of genotype in the cycle of violence in maltreated children. *Science, 297*(5582), 851–854. https://doi.org/10.1126/science.1072290

Cassibba, R., Sette, G., Bakermans-Kranenburg, M. J., & van IJzendoorn, M. H. (2013). Attachment the Italian way: In search of specific patterns of infant and adult attachments in Italian typical and atypical samples. *European Psychologist, 18*(1), 47–58.

Castillo, J. C., Clark, B. R., Butler, C. E., & Racette, S. B. (2015). Support for physical education as a core subject in urban elementary schools. *American Journal of Preventive Medicine, 49*(5), 753–756. https://doi.org/10.1016/j.amepre.2015.04.015

Castro, D. C., Páez, M. M., Dickinson, D. K., & Frede, E. (2011). Promoting language and literacy in young dual language learners: Research, practice, and policy. *Child Development Perspectives, 5*(1), 15–21. https://doi.org/10.1111/j.1750-8606.2010.00142.x

Cauce, A., & Domenech-Rodríguez, M. (2002). Latino families: Myths and realities. In J. Contreras, A. Neal-Barnett, & K. Kerns (Eds.), *Latino children and families in the United States* (pp. 2–25). Westport, CT: Praeger.

Cauce, A. M. (2008). Parenting, culture, and context: Reflections on excavating culture. *Applied Developmental Science, 12*(4), 227–229. https://doi.org/10.1080/10888690802388177

Cauffman, E., Shulman, E., Bechtold, J., & Steinberg, L. (2015). Children and the law. In M. H. Bornstein & T. Leventhal (Eds.), *Handbook of child psychology and developmental science* (pp. 1–49). Hoboken, NJ: John Wiley & Sons. https://doi.org/10.1002/9781118963418.childpsy312

Cauffman, E., Shulman, E. P., Steinberg, L., Claus, E., Banich, M. T., Graham, S., & Woolard, J. (2010). Age differences in affective decision making as indexed by performance on the Iowa Gambling Task. *Developmental Psychology, 46*(1), 193–207. https://doi.org/10.1037/a0016128

Cauffman, E., & Steinberg, L. (2012). Emerging findings from research on adolescent justice. *Victims & Offenders, 7*(4), 428–449. https://doi.org/10.1080/15564886.2012.713901

Ceci, S. J., & Bruck, M. (1998). The ontogeny and durability of true and false memories: A fuzzy trace account. *Journal of Experimental Child Psychology, 71*, 165–169.

Ceci, S. J., Ginther, D. K., Kahn, S., & Williams, W. M. (2014). Women in academic science. *Psychological Science in the Public Interest, 15*(3), 75–141. https://doi.org/10.1177/1529100614541236

Ceci, S. J., Huffman, M. L., Smith, E., & Loftus, E. F. (1994). Repeatedly thinking about a non-event: Source misattributions among preschoolers. *Consciousness and Cognition, 3*, 388–407.

Cecil, C. A. M., Viding, E., Fearon, P., Glaser, D., & McCrory, E. J. (2017). Disentangling the mental health impact of childhood abuse and neglect. *Child Abuse & Neglect, 63*, 106–119. https://doi.org/10.1016/j.chiabu.2016.11.024

Celeghin, A., Diano, M., Bagnis, A., Viola, M., & Tamietto, M. (2017). Basic emotions in human neuroscience: Neuroimaging and beyond. *Frontiers in Psychology, 8*, 1432. https://doi.org/10.3389/fpsyg.2017.01432

Centers for Disease Control and Prevention. (2013). Progress in increasing breastfeeding and reducing racial/ethnic differences - United States, 2000-2008 births. *MMWR. Morbidity and Mortality Weekly Report, 62*(5), 77–80. Retrieved from http://www.ncbi.nlm.nih.gov/pubmed/23388550

Centers for Disease Control and Prevention. (2014). *Results from the School Health Policies and Practices Study 2014*. Retrieved from https://www.cdc.gov/healthyyouth/data/shpps/pdf/shpps-508-final_101315.pdf

Centers for Disease Control and Prevention. (2016). *Sexually transmitted disease surveillance 2015*. Atlanta. Retrieved from https://www.cdc.gov/std/stats15/default.htm

Centers for Disease Control and Prevention. (2017a). *Birth defects: Data and statistics*. Retrieved from https://www.cdc.gov/ncbddd/birthdefects/data.html

Centers for Disease Control and Prevention. (2017b). *Breastfeeding among U.S. children born 2002–2014, CDC National Immunization Survey*. Retrieved December 22, 2017, from https://www.cdc.gov/breastfeeding/data/nis_data/results.html

Centers for Disease Control and Prevention. (2017c). *Infertility*. Retrieved from https://www.cdc.gov/reproductivehealth/infertility/index.htm

Centers for Disease Control and Prevention. (2017d). *Microcephaly & other birth defects*. Retrieved from https://www.cdc.gov/zika/healtheffects/

Centers for Disease Control and Prevention. (2017e). *Preterm birth*. Retrieved from https://www.cdc.gov/

Centers for Disease Control and Prevention. (2017f). *Ten leading causes of injury deaths by age group highlighting unintentional injury deaths, United States - 2015*. Retrieved from https://www.cdc.gov/injury/images/lc-charts/leading_causes_of_death_age_group_2015_1050w740h.gif

Centers for Disease Control and Prevention. (2018a). *National estimates of the 10 leading causes of nonfatal injuries treated in hospital emergency departments - 2017*. Retrieved from https://www.cdc.gov/injury/wisqars/pdf//leading_causes_of_nonfatal_injury_2017-508.pdf

Centers for Disease Control and Prevention. (2018b). *Results from the School Health Policies and Practices Study 2016*. Retrieved from https://www.cdc.gov/healthyyouth/data/shpps/pdf/shpps-results_2016.pdf#page=26

Centers for Disease Control and Prevention. (2018c). *Table 5: Low birthweight live births, by detailed race and Hispanic origin of mother: United States, selected years 1970–2015*. Retrieved from https://www.cdc.gov/nchs/data/hus/2016/005.pdf

Centers for Disease Control and Prevention. (2019a). *Data and statistics about hearing loss in children*. Retrieved from https://www.cdc.gov/ncbddd/hearingloss/data.html

Centers for Disease Control and Prevention. (2019b). *Measles: Cases and outbreaks*. Retrieved from https://www.cdc.gov/measles/cases-outbreaks.html

Centers for Disease Control and Prevention. (2019c). *Most recent national asthma data*. Retrieved from https://www.cdc.gov/asthma/most_recent_national_asthma_data.htm

Centers for Disease Control and Prevention. (2019d). *WISQARS leading causes of nonfatal injury reports*. Retrieved from https://webappa.cdc.gov/sasweb/ncipc/nfilead.html

Centers for Disease Control and Prevention. (2019e). *WISQARS nonfatal injury reports*. Retrieved from https://www.cdc.gov/injury/wisqars/nonfatal.html

Centifanti, L. C. M., Modecki, K. L., MacLellan, S., & Gowling, H. (2016). Driving under the influence of risky peers: An experimental study of adolescent risk taking. *Journal of Research on Adolescence, 26*(1), 207–222. https://doi.org/10.1111/jora.12187

Chabris, C. F., Lee, J. J., Cesarini, D., Benjamin, D. J., & Laibson, D. I. (2015). The fourth law of behavior genetics. *Current Directions in Psychological Science, 24*(4), 304–312. https://doi.org/10.1177/0963721415580430

Chaibal, S., Bennett, S., Rattanathanthong, K., & Siritaratiwat, W. (2016). Early developmental milestones and age of independent walking in orphans compared with typical home-raised infants. *Early Human Development, 101*, 23–26. https://doi.org/10.1016/j.earlhumdev.2016.06.008

Chakravorty, S., & Williams, T. N. (2015). Sickle cell disease: A neglected chronic disease of increasing global health importance. *Archives of Disease in Childhood, 100*(1), 48–53. https://doi.org/10.1136/archdischild-2013-303773

Chambers, A. M. (2017). The role of sleep in cognitive processing: Focusing on memory consolidation. *Wiley Interdisciplinary Reviews: Cognitive Science, 8*(3), e1433. https://doi.org/10.1002/wcs.1433

Champagne, F. A. (2018). Beyond the maternal epigenetic legacy. *Nature Neuroscience, 21*(6), 773–774. https://doi.org/10.1038/s41593-018-0157-6

Chan, W., Kwok, Y., Choy, K., Leung, T., & Wang, C. (2013). Single fetal cells for non-invasive prenatal genetic diagnosis: Old myths new prospective. *Medical Journal of Obstetrics and Gynecology, 1*(1), 1004.

Chandler, M. J., & Carpendale, J. I. (1998). Inching toward a mature theory of mind. In M. Ferrari & R. J. Sternberg (Eds.), *Self-awareness: Its nature and development* (pp. 148–190). New York, NY: Guilford.

Chandra-Mouli, V., & Patel, S. V. (2017). Mapping the knowledge and understanding of menarche, menstrual hygiene and menstrual health among adolescent girls in low- and middle-income countries. *Reproductive Health, 14*(1), 30. https://doi.org/10.1186/s12978-017-0293-6

Chang, D. S., Lasley, F. D., Das, I. J., Mendonca, M. S., & Dynlacht, J. R. (2014). Radiation effects in the embryo and fetus. In *Basic radiotherapy physics and biology* (pp. 313–316). Cham, Switzerland: Springer International Publishing. https://doi.org/10.1007/978-3-319-06841-1_32

Chang, S. M., Grantham-McGregor, S. M., Powell, C. A., Vera-Hernández, M., Lopez-Boo, F., Baker-Henningham, H., . . . Aboud, F. (2015). Integrating a parenting intervention with routine primary health care: A cluster randomized trial. *Pediatrics, 136*(2), 272–280. https://doi.org/10.1542/peds.2015-0119

Chang, Y.-S., Gratiot, M., Owen, J. P., Brandes-Aitken, A., Desai, S. S., Hill, S. S., . . . Mukherjee, P. (2016). White matter microstructure is associated with auditory and tactile processing in children with and without sensory processing disorder. *Frontiers in Neuroanatomy, 9*, 169. https://doi.org/10.3389/fnana.2015.00169

Chao, R. K. (1995). Chinese and European American cultural models of the self related in mothers' child rearing beliefs. *Ethos, 23*(3), 328–354.

Chao, R. K. (2001). Extending research on the consequences of parenting style for Chinese Americans and European Americans. *Child Development, 72*, 1832–1843.

Chaplin, T. M. (2015). Gender and emotion expression: A developmental contextual perspective. *Emotion Review, 7*(1), 14–21. https://doi.org/10.1177/1754073914544408

Chaplin, T. M., & Aldao, A. (2013). Gender differences in emotion expression in children: A meta-analytic review. *Psychological Bulletin, 139*(4), 735–765. https://doi.org/10.1037/a0030737

Chaplin, T. M., Sinha, R., Simmons, J. A., Healy, S. M., Mayes, L. C., Hommer, R. E., & Crowley,

M. J. (2012). Parent-adolescent conflict interactions and adolescent alcohol use. *Addictive Behaviors, 37*(5), 605–612. https://doi.org/10.1016/j.addbeh.2012.01.004

Charness, M. E., Riley, E. P., & Sowell, E. R. (2016). Drinking during pregnancy and the developing brain: Is any amount safe? *Trends in Cognitive Sciences, 20*(2), 80–82. https://doi.org/10.1016/j.tics.2015.09.011

Charpak, N., Gabriel Ruiz, J., Zupan, J., Cattaneo, A., Figueroa, Z., Tessier, R., . . . Worku, B. (2005). Kangaroo mother care: 25 years after. *Acta Paediatrica, 94*(5), 514–522. https://doi.org/10.1111/j.1651-2227.2005.tb01930.x

Chasnoff, I. J. (2017). Medical marijuana laws and pregnancy: Implications for public health policy. *American Journal of Obstetrics and Gynecology, 216*(1), 27–30. https://doi.org/10.1016/J.AJOG.2016.07.010

Chauhan, S. (2017). A meta-analysis of the impact of technology on learning effectiveness of elementary students. *Computers & Education, 105*, 14–30. https://doi.org/10.1016/J.COMPEDU.2016.11.005

Chavajay, P., & Rogoff, B. (1999). Cultural variation in management of attention by children and their caregivers. *Developmental Psychology, 35*(4), 1079–1090. Retrieved from http://www.ncbi.nlm.nih.gov/pubmed/10442876

Cheah, C. S. L., Leung, C. Y. Y., Tahseen, M., & Schultz, D. (2009). Authoritative parenting among immigrant Chinese mothers of preschoolers. *Journal of Family Psychology, 23*(3), 311–320. https://doi.org/10.1037/a0015076

Chein, J., Albert, D., O'Brien, L., Uckert, K., & Steinberg, L. (2011). Peers increase adolescent risk taking by enhancing activity in the brain's reward circuitry. *Developmental Science, 14*(2), F1–F10. https://doi.org/10.1111/J.1467-7687.2010.01035.X

Chemin, A. (2014). Handwriting vs typing: Is the pen still mightier than the keyboard? *The Guardian*. Retrieved from https://www.theguardian.com/science/2014/dec/16/cognitive-benefits-handwriting-decline-typing

Chen, F. R., Rothman, E. F., & Jaffee, S. R. (2017). Early puberty, friendship group characteristics, and dating abuse in US girls. *Pediatrics, 139*(6), e20162847. https://doi.org/10.1542/peds.2016-2847

Chen, J.-H. (2014). Asthma and child behavioral skills: Does family socioeconomic status matter? *Social Science & Medicine (1982), 115*, 38–48. https://doi.org/10.1016/j.socscimed.2014.05.048

Chen, L.-M., & Kent, R. D. (2010). Segmental production in Mandarin-learning infants. *Journal of Child Language, 37*(2), 341–371. https://doi.org/10.1017/s0305000909009581

Chen, L.-W., Wu, Y., Neelakantan, N., Chong, M. F.-F., Pan, A., & van Dam, R. M. (2014). Maternal caffeine intake during pregnancy is associated with risk of low birth weight: A systematic review and dose-response meta-analysis. *BMC Medicine, 12*(1), 174. https://doi.org/10.1186/s12916-014-0174-6

Chen, L.-W., Wu, Y., Neelakantan, N., Chong, M. F.-F., Pan, A., & van Dam, R. M. (2016). Maternal caffeine intake during pregnancy and risk of pregnancy loss: A categorical and dose–response meta-analysis of prospective studies. *Public Health Nutrition, 19*(07), 1233–1244. https://doi.org/10.1017/S1368980015002463

Chen, P., & Vazsonyi, A. T. (2013). Future orientation, school contexts, and problem behaviors: A multilevel study. *Journal of Youth and Adolescence, 42*(1), 67–81. https://doi.org/10.1007/s10964-012-9785-4

Chen, P., Voisin, D. R., & Jacobson, K. C. (2013). Community violence exposure and adolescent delinquency: Examining a spectrum of promotive factors. *Youth & Society, 48*, 33–57. https://doi.org/10.1177/0044118X13475827

Chen, X., Rubin, K. H., & Li, B. (1994). Only children and sibling children in urban China: A re-examination. *International Journal of Behavioral Development, 17*(3), 413–421.

Chen, X., & Schmidt, L. A. (2015). Temperament and personality. In R. Lerner (Ed.), *Handbook of child psychology and developmental science* (pp. 1–49). Hoboken, NJ: John Wiley & Sons. https://doi.org/10.1002/9781118963418.childpsy305

Chen, X., Striano, T., & Rakoczy, H. (2004). Auditory–oral matching behavior in newborns. *Developmental Science, 7*(1), 42–47.

Chen, Y.-C., Sudre, G., Sharp, W., Donovan, F., Chandrasekharappa, S. C., Hansen, N., . . . Shaw, P. (2018). Neuroanatomic, epigenetic and genetic differences in monozygotic twins discordant for attention deficit hyperactivity disorder. *Molecular Psychiatry, 23*(3), 683–690. https://doi.org/10.1038/mp.2017.45

Cheng, D. T., Meintjes, E. M., Stanton, M. E., Dodge, N. C., Pienaar, M., Warton, C. M. R., . . . Jacobson, S. W. (2016). Functional MRI of human eyeblink classical conditioning in children with fetal alcohol spectrum disorders. *Cerebral Cortex, 27*(7), 3752–3767. https://doi.org/10.1093/cercor/bhw273

Cheng, N., Lu, S., Archer, M., & Wang, Z. (2018). Quality of maternal parenting of 9-month-old infants predicts executive function performance at 2 and 3 years of age. *Frontiers in Psychology, 8*, 2293. https://doi.org/10.3389/fpsyg.2017.02293

Cheng, W., Rolls, E. T., Gu, H., Zhang, J., & Feng, J. (2015). Autism: Reduced connectivity between cortical areas involved in face expression, theory of mind, and the sense of self. *Brain, 138*(Pt. 5), 1382–1393. https://doi.org/10.1093/brain/awv051

Cheour, M., Ceponiene, R., Leppanen, P., Alho, K., Kujala, T., Renlund, M., . . . Naatanen, R. (2002). The auditory sensory memory trace decays rapidly in newborns. *Scandinavian Journal of Psychology, 43*(1), 33–39. https://doi.org/10.1111/1467-9450.00266

Chess, S., & Thomas, A. (1984). *Origins and evolution of behavior disorders*. New York, NY: Brunner/Mazel.

Chess, S., & Thomas, A. (1991). Temperament and the concept of goodness of fit. In J. Strelau & A. Angleitner (Eds.), *Explorations in temperament: International perspectives on theory and measurement* (pp. 15–28). New York, NY: Plenum.

Chevalier, N., Kurth, S., Doucette, M. R., Wiseheart, M., Deoni, S. C. L. S., Dean, D. C. D., . . . Greenstein, D. (2015). Myelination is associated with processing speed in early childhood: Preliminary insights. *PLoS ONE, 10*(10), e0139897. https://doi.org/10.1371/journal.pone.0139897

Chhangur, R. R., Weeland, J., Overbeek, G., Matthys, W., Orobio de Castro, B., van der Giessen, D., & Belsky, J. (2017). Genetic moderation of intervention efficacy: Dopaminergic genes, the incredible years, and externalizing behavior in children. *Child Development, 88*(3), 796–811. https://doi.org/10.1111/cdev.12612

Child Care Aware of America. (2014). *Parents and the high cost of child care: 2013 report*. Retrieved from https://usa.childcareaware.org/2013/11/parents-and-the-high-cost-of-child-care-a-report/

Child Trends. (2013). *Measures of flourishing*. Retrieved from http://www.childtrends.org

Child Trends. (2015). *Immunization*. Retrieved from https://www.childtrends.org

Child Trends. (2017). *Sexually active teens*. Retrieved from https://www.childtrends.org/indicators/sexually-active-teens/

Child Trends. (2018a). *Infant, child, and teen mortality*. Retrieved from https://www.childtrends.org/indicators/infant-child-and-teen-mortality

Child Trends. (2018b). *Overweight children and youth*. Retrieved from https://www.childtrends.org/indicators/overweight-children-and-youth

Child Trends. (2019). *Key facts about teen births*. Retrieved from https://www.childtrends.org/indicators/teen-births

Child Welfare Information Gateway. (2013). *What is child abuse and neglect? Recognizing the signs and symptoms*. Retrieved from https://www.childwelfare.gov/pubpdfs/whatiscan.pdf

Chmurzynska, A. (2010). Fetal programming: Link between early nutrition, DNA methylation, and complex diseases. *Nutrition Reviews, 68*(2), 87–98. https://doi.org/10.1111/j.1753-4887.2009.00265.x

Choe, D. E., Olson, S. L., & Sameroff, A. J. (2013). The interplay of externalizing problems and physical and inductive discipline during childhood. *Developmental Psychology, 49*(11), 2029–2039. https://doi.org/10.1037/a0032054

Choi, J., & Silverman, I. (2003). Processes underlying sex differences in route-learning strategies in children and adolescents. *Personality and Individual Differences, 34*(7), 1153–1166. https://doi.org/10.1016/S0191-8869(02)00105-8

Chomsky, N. (1959). Review of B. F. Skinner's *Verbal Behavior. Language, 35*, 26–58.

Chomsky, N. (2017). Language architecture and its import for evolution. *Neuroscience & Biobehavioral Reviews, 81*, 295–300. https://doi.org/10.1016/J.NEUBIOREV.2017.01.053

Choukas-Bradley, S., Giletta, M., Widman, L., Cohen, G. L., & Prinstein, M. J. (2014). Experimentally measured susceptibility to peer influence and adolescent sexual behavior trajectories: A preliminary study. *Developmental Psychology, 50*(9), 2221–2227. https://doi.org/10.1037/a0037300

Christenson, S. L., & Thurlow, M. L. (2004). School dropouts: Prevention considerations, interventions, and challenges. *Current Directions in Psychological Science, 13*(1), 36–39. https://doi.org/10.1111/j.0963-7214.2004.01301010.x

Christodoulou, J., Lac, A., & Moore, D. S. (2017). Babies and math: A meta-analysis of infants' simple arithmetic competence. *Developmental Psychology, 53*(8), 1405–1417. https://doi.org/10.1037/dev0000330

Chung, A., Backholer, K., Wong, E., Palermo, C., Keating, C., & Peeters, A. (2016). Trends in child and adolescent obesity prevalence in economically advanced countries according to socioeconomic position: A systematic review. *Obesity Reviews, 17*(3), 276–295. https://doi.org/10.1111/obr.12360

Cicchetti, D. (2016). Socioemotional, personality, and biological development: Illustrations from a multilevel developmental psychopathology perspective on child maltreatment. *Annual Review of Psychology, 67*(1), 187–211. https://doi.org/10.1146/annurev-psych-122414-033259

Cicchetti, D., & Banny, A. (2014). A developmental psychopathology perspective on child maltreatment. In M. Lewis & K. D. Rudolph (Eds.), *Handbook of developmental psychopathology* (pp. 723–741). Boston, MA: Springer. https://doi.org/10.1007/978-1-4614-9608-3

Cicchetti, D., Rogosch, F. A., & Sturge-Apple, M. L. (2007). Interactions of child maltreatment and serotonin transporter and monoamine oxidase A polymorphisms: Depressive symptomatology among adolescents from low socioeconomic status backgrounds. *Development and Psychopathology, 19*(4), 1161–1180. https://doi.org/10.1017/S0954579407000600

Cicchetti, D., Rogosch, F. A., Toth, S. L., & Spagnola, M. (1997). Affect, cognition, and the emergence of self-knowledge in the toddler offspring of depressed mothers. *Journal of Experimental Child Psychology, 67*(3), 338.

Cicchetti, D., & Toth, S. L. (2015). Child maltreatment. In M. E. Lamb (Ed.), *Handbook of child psychology and developmental science* (Vol. 3, pp. 1–51). Hoboken, NJ: John Wiley & Sons. https://doi.org/10.1002/9781118963418.childpsy313

Cierniak, R. (2011). Some words about the history of computed tomography. In *X-ray computed tomography in biomedical engineering* (pp. 7–19). London, England: Springer London. https://doi.org/10.1007/978-0-85729-027-4_2

Cimpian, A., Hammond, M. D., Mazza, G., & Corry, G. (2017). Young children's self-concepts include representations of abstract traits and the global self. *Child Development, 88*(6), 1786–1798. https://doi.org/10.1111/cdev.12925

Cimpian, J. R., Lubienski, S. T., Timmer, J. D., Makowski, M. B., & Miller, E. K. (2016). Have gender gaps in math closed? Achievement, teacher perceptions, and learning behaviors across two ECLS-K cohorts. *AERA Open, 2*(4), 233285841667361. https://doi.org/10.1177/2332858416673617

Ciocanel, O., Power, K., Eriksen, A., & Gillings, K. (2017). Effectiveness of positive youth development interventions: A meta-analysis of randomized controlled trials. *Journal of Youth and Adolescence, 46*(3), 483–504. https://doi.org/10.1007/s10964-016-0555-6

Claes, L., Luyckx, K., Baetens, I., Van de Ven, M., & Witteman, C. (2015). Bullying and victimization, depressive mood, and non-suicidal self-injury in adolescents: The moderating role of parental support. *Journal of Child and Family Studies, 24*(11), 3363–3371. https://doi.org/10.1007/s10826-015-0138-2

Clark, E. V. (2017). *Language in children: A brief introduction*. New York, NY: Routledge. Retrieved from https://www.routledge.com/Language-in-Children/Clark/p/book/9781138906075

Clark, K. A., Helland, T., Specht, K., Narr, K. L., Manis, F. R., Toga, A. W., & Hugdahl, K. (2014). Neuroanatomical precursors of dyslexia identified from pre-reading through to age 11. *Brain, 137*, 3136–3141. https://doi.org/10.1093/brain/awu229

Clark, L., & Tiggemann, M. (2008). Sociocultural and individual psychological predictors of body image in young girls: A prospective study. *Developmental Psychology, 44*(4), 1124–1134. https://doi.org/10.1037/0012-1649.44.4.1124

Clearfield, M. W. (2011). Learning to walk changes infants' social interactions. *Infant Behavior & Development, 34*(1), 15–25. https://doi.org/10.1016/j.infbeh.2010.04.008

Cleary, M., Walter, G., & Jackson, D. (2011). "Not always smooth sailing": Mental health issues associated with the transition from high school to college. *Issues in Mental Health Nursing, 32*(4), 250–254. https://doi.org/10.3109/01612840.2010.548906

Clifford, A., Franklin, A., Davies, I. R. L., & Holmes, A. (2009). Electrophysiological markers of categorical perception of color in 7-month old infants. *Brain & Cognition, 71*(2), 165–172. https://doi.org/10.1016/j.bandc.2009.05.002

Cliffordson, C., & Gustafsson, J.-E. (2008). Effects of age and schooling on intellectual performance: Estimates obtained from analysis of continuous variation in age and length of schooling. *Intelligence, 36*(2), 143–152. https://doi.org/10.1016/j.intell.2007.03.006

Clifton, R. K., Rochat, P., Robin, D. J., & Berthier, N. E. (1994). Multimodal perception in the control of infant reaching. *Journal of Experimental Psychology: Human Perception and Performance, 20*, 876–886.

Coelho, V. A., Marchante, M., & Jimerson, S. R. (2017). Promoting a positive middle school transition: A randomized-controlled treatment study examining self-concept and self-esteem. *Journal of Youth and Adolescence, 46*(3), 558–569. https://doi.org/10.1007/s10964-016-0510-6

Cohen, A. O., & Casey, B. J. (2017). The neurobiology of adolescent self-control. In T. Egner (Ed.), *The Wiley handbook of cognitive control* (pp. 455–475). Chichester, England: John Wiley & Sons, Ltd. https://doi.org/10.1002/9781118920497.ch26

Cohen, K. K., Johnson, M. H., Dick, F., Cohen Kadosh, R., & Blakemore, S.-J. (2013). Effects of age, task performance, and structural brain development on face processing. *Cerebral Cortex, 23*(7), 1630–1642. https://doi.org/10.1093/cercor/bhs150

Cohen, L. B., & Cashon, C. H. (2006). Infant cognition. In D. Kuhn, R. S. Siegler, W. Damon, & R. M. Lerner (Eds.), *Handbook of child psychology: Vol. 2. Cognition, perception, and language* (6th ed., pp. 214–251). Hoboken, NJ: John Wiley & Sons.

Colby, A., & Damon, W. (1992). *Some do care: Contemporary lives of moral commitment*. New York, NY: Free Press.

Cole, E. B., & Flexer, C. A. (2016). *Children with hearing loss: Developing listening and talking, birth to six*. San Diego, CA: Plural Publishing.

Cole, M., & Packer, M. (2015). A bio-cultural-historical approach to the study of development. In M. J. Gelfand, C. Chiu, & Y. Hong (Eds.), *Handbook of advances in culture and psychology*. New York, NY: Oxford University Press.

Cole, W. G., Lingeman, J. M., & Adolph, K. E. (2012). Go naked: Diapers affect infant walking. *Developmental Science, 15*(6), 783–790. https://doi.org/10.1111/j.1467-7687.2012.01169.x

Cole, W. G., Robinson, S. R., & Adolph, K. E. (2016). Bouts of steps: The organization of infant exploration. *Developmental Psychobiology, 58*(3), 341–354. https://doi.org/10.1002/dev.21374

Coleman-Jensen, A., Rabbitt, M. P., Gregory, C. A., & Singh, A. (2018). Household food security in the United States in 2017. *U.S. Department of Agriculture Economic Research Report No. (ERR-256)*. Retrieved from https://www.ers.usda.gov/publications/pub-details/?pubid=90022

Coley, R. L., Kull, M. A., & Carrano, J. (2014). Parental endorsement of spanking and children's internalizing and externalizing problems in African American and Hispanic families. *Journal of Family Psychology, 28*(1), 22–31. https://doi.org/10.1037/a0035272

Coley, R. L., Lombardi, C. M., Lynch, A. D., Mahalik, J. R., & Sims, J. (2013). Sexual partner accumulation from adolescence through early adulthood: The role of family, peer, and school social norms. *Journal of Adolescent Health, 53*(1), 91–97. https://doi.org/10.1016/j.jadohealth.2013.01.005

Collette, F., & Van der Linden, M. (2002). Brain imaging of the central executive component of working memory. *Neuroscience & Biobehavioral Reviews, 26*(2), 105–125.

Collier, K. L., van Beusekom, G., Bos, H. M. W., & Sandfort, T. G. M. (2013). Sexual orientation and gender identity/expression related peer victimization in adolescence: A systematic review of associated psychosocial and health outcomes. *Journal of Sex Research, 50*(3–4), 299–317. https://doi.org/10.1080/00224499.2012.750639

Collier, P., & Morgan, D. (2008). "Is that paper really due today?": Differences in first-generation and traditional college students' understandings of faculty expectations. *Higher Education, 55*(4), 425–446. https://doi.org/10.1007/s10734-007-9065-5

Collins, J. E., Gill, T. K., Chittleborough, C. R., Martin, A. J., Taylor, A. W., & Winefield, H. (2008). Mental, emotional, and social problems among school children with asthma. *Journal of Asthma, 45*(6), 489–493. https://doi.org/10.1080/02770900802074802

Collins, J. W., Papacek, E., Schulte, N. F., & Drolet, A. (2001). Differing postneonatal mortality rates of Mexican-American infants with United-States-born and Mexico-born mothers in Chicago. *Ethnicity & Disease, 11*(4), 606–613. Retrieved from http://www.ncbi.nlm.nih.gov/pubmed/11763285

Collins, W. A., Welsh, D. P., & Furman, W. (2009). Adolescent romantic relationships. *Annual Review of Psychology, 60*, 631–652. https://doi.org/10.1146/annurev.psych.60.110707.163459

Colls, P., Silver, L., Olivera, G., Weier, J., Escudero, T., Goodall, N., . . . Munné, S. (2009). Preimplantation genetic diagnosis for gender selection in the USA. *Reproductive BioMedicine Online, 19*(S2), 16–22.

Collura, T. F. (1993). History and evolution of electroencephalographic instruments and techniques. *Journal of Clinical Neurophysiology, 10*(4), 476–504. Retrieved from http://www.ncbi.nlm.nih.gov/pubmed/8308144

Colombo, J., Brez, C. C., & Curtindale, L. M. (2015). Infant perception and cognition. In I. B. Weiner, R. M. Lerner, M. A. Easterbrooks, & J. Mistry (Eds.), *Handbook of psychology: Developmental psychology* (pp. 61–90). Hoboken, NJ: John Wiley & Sons.

Colrain, I. M., & Baker, F. C. (2011). Changes in sleep as a function of adolescent development. *Neuropsychology Review, 21*(1), 5–21. https://doi.org/10.1007/s11065-010-9155-5

Colson, E. R., Willinger, M., Rybin, D., Heeren, T., Smith, L. A., Lister, G., & Corwin, M. J. (2013). Trends and factors associated with infant bed sharing, 1993-2010. *JAMA Pediatrics, 167*(11), 1032. https://doi.org/10.1001/jamapediatrics.2013.2560

Combs-Orme, T., & Renkert, L. E. (2009). Fathers and their infants: Caregiving and affection in the modern family. *Journal of Human Behavior in the Social Environment, 19*(4), 394–418. https://doi.org/10.1080/10911350902790753

Comstock, G., & Scharrer, E. (1999). *Television: What's on, who's watching, and what it means.* San Diego, CA: Academic Press.

Comunian, A. L., & Gielen, U. P. (2000). Sociomoral reflection and prosocial and antisocial behavior: Two Italian studies. *Psychological Reports, 87*(1), 161–176.

Conboy, B. T., & Thal, D. J. (2006). Ties between the lexicon and grammar: Cross-sectional and longitudinal studies of bilingual toddlers. *Child Development, 77*(3), 712–735. https://doi.org/10.1111/j.1467-8624.2006.00899.x

Congressional Research Service. (2018). *Youth and the labor force: Background and trends.* Retrieved from https://fas.org/sgp/crs/misc/R42519.pdf

Conlon, J. L. (2017). Diethylstilbestrol. *Journal of the American Academy of Physician Assistants, 30*(2), 49–52. https://doi.org/10.1097/01.JAA.0000511800.91372.34

Connolly, J., & Craig, W. (1999). Conceptions of cross-sex friendships and romantic relationships in early adolescence. *Journal of Youth & Adolescence, 28*(4), 481–494.

Connolly, J., Craig, W., Goldberg, A., & Pepler, D. (2004). Mixed-gender groups, dating, and romantic relationships in early adolescence. *Journal of Research on Adolescence, 14*, 185–207.

Connolly, J., & McIsaac, C. (2011). Romantic relationships in adolescence. In M. K. Underwood & L. H. Rosen (Eds.), *Social development: Relationships in infancy, childhood, and adolescence* (pp. 180–203). New York, NY: Guilford.

Connolly, J., Nguyen, H. N. T., Pepler, D., Craig, W., & Jiang, D. (2013). Developmental trajectories of romantic stages and associations with problem behaviours during adolescence. *Journal of Adolescence, 36*(6), 1013–1024. https://doi.org/10.1016/j.adolescence.2013.08.006

Conradt, E. (2017). Using principles of behavioral epigenetics to advance research on early-life stress. *Child Development Perspectives, 11*(2), 107–112. https://doi.org/10.1111/cdep.12219

Conron, K. J., Scott, G., Stowell, G. S., & Landers, S. J. (2012). Transgender health in Massachusetts: Results from a household probability sample of adults. *American Journal of Public Health, 102*(1), 118–122. https://doi.org/10.2105/AJPH.2011.300315

Conway, J. M., Amel, E. L., & Gerwien, D. P. (2009). Teaching and learning in the social context: A meta-analysis of service learning's effects on academic, personal, social, and citizenship outcomes. *Teaching of Psychology, 36*(4), 233–245. https://doi.org/10.1080/00986280903172969

Cook, R., Bird, G., Catmur, C., Press, C., & Heyes, C. (2014). Mirror neurons: From origin to function. *Behavioral and Brain Sciences, 37*(2), 177–192. https://doi.org/10.1017/S0140525X13000903

Cooley, J. L., & Fite, P. J. (2016). Peer victimization and forms of aggression during middle childhood: The role of emotion regulation. *Journal of Abnormal Child Psychology, 44*(3), 535–546. https://doi.org/10.1007/s10802-015-0051-6

Cooper, S. M., Kurtz-Costes, B., & Rowley, S. J. (2010). The schooling of African American children. In J. L. Meece & J. S. Eccles (Eds.), *Handbook of research on schools, schooling and human development* (pp. 275–292). New York, NY: Routledge.

Copeland, K. A., Khoury, J. C., & Kalkwarf, H. J. (2016). Child care center characteristics associated with preschoolers' physical activity. *American Journal of Preventive Medicine, 50*(4), 470–479. https://doi.org/10.1016/j.amepre.2015.08.028

Copen, C. E., Chandra, A., & Martinez, G. (2012). Prevalence and timing of oral sex with opposite-sex partners among females and males aged 15–24 years: United States, 2007–2010. *National Health Statistics Reports, 56*, 1–14. Retrieved from https://www.ncbi.nlm.nih.gov/pubmed/24979976

Copen, C. E., Daniels, K., & Mosher, W. D. (2013). First premarital cohabitation in the United States: 2006–2010 National Survey of Family Growth. *National Health Statistics Reports, 64*, 1–15. Retrieved from http://bibliobase.sermais.pt:8008/BiblioNET/Upload/PDF3/002491.pdf

Copen, C. E., Daniels, K., Vespa, J., & Mosher, W. D. (2012). First marriages in the United States: Data from the 2006–2010 National Survey of Family Growth. *National Health Statistics Reports, 49*(49), 1–21. Retrieved from http://www.ncbi.nlm.nih.gov/pubmed/22803221

Coplan, R. J., & Arbeau, K. A. (2009). Peer interactions and play in early childhood. In K. H. Rubin, W. M. Bukowski, & B. Laursen (Eds.), *Handbook of peer interactions, relationships, and groups* (pp. 143–161). New York, NY: Guilford.

Coplan, R. J., Ooi, L. L., & Nocita, G. (2015). When one is company and two is a crowd: Why some children prefer solitude. *Child Development Perspectives, 9*(3), 133–137. https://doi.org/10.1111/cdep.12131

Coplan, R. J., Rose-Krasnor, L., Weeks, M., Kingsbury, A., Kingsbury, M., & Bullock, A. (2013). Alone is a crowd: Social motivations, social withdrawal, and socioemotional functioning in later childhood. *Developmental Psychology, 49*(5), 861-875.

Corballis, M. C., Lalueza-Fox, C., Orlando, L., Enard, W., & Green, R. (2014). Left brain, right brain: Facts and fantasies. *PLoS Biology, 12*(1), e1001767. https://doi.org/10.1371/journal.pbio.1001767

Corbetta, D., & Snapp-Childs, W. (2009). Seeing and touching: The role of sensory-motor experience on the development of infant reaching. *Infant Behavior & Development, 32*(1), 44–58. https://doi.org/10.1016/j.infbeh.2008.10.004

Cordaro, D. T., Sun, R., Keltner, D., Kamble, S., Huddar, N., & McNeil, G. (2018). Universals and cultural variations in 22 emotional expressions across five cultures. *Emotion, 18*(1), 75–93. https://doi.org/10.1037/emo0000302

Cormier, D. C., McGrew, K. S., Bulut, O., & Funamoto, A. (2017). Revisiting the relations between the WJ-IV measures of Cattell-Horn-Carroll (CHC) cognitive abilities and reading achievement during the school-age years. *Journal of Psychoeducational Assessment, 38*(8), 731–754. https://doi.org/10.1177/0734282916659208

Cornell, D., Gregory, A., Huang, F., & Fan, X. (2013). Perceived prevalence of teasing and bullying predicts high school dropout rates. *Journal of Educational Psychology, 105*(1), 138–149.

Cornell, D., & Limber, S. P. (2015). Law and policy on the concept of bullying at school. *American Psychologist, 70*(4), 333–343. https://doi.org/10.1037/a0038558

Corrigall, K. A., & Schellenberg, E. G. (2015). Predicting who takes music lessons: Parent and child characteristics. *Frontiers in Psychology, 6*, 282. https://doi.org/10.3389/fpsyg.2015.00282

Cosbey, J., Johnston, S. S., Dunn, M. L., & Bauman, M. (2012). Playground behaviors of children with and without sensory processing disorders. *OTJR: Occupation, Participation and Health, 32*(2), 39–47. https://doi.org/10.3928/15394492-20110930-01

Costa, L. da C. F., Silva, D. A. S., Alvarenga, M. dos S., & de Vasconcelos, F. de A. G. (2016). Association between body image dissatisfaction and obesity among schoolchildren aged 7–10 years. *Physiology & Behavior, 160*, 6–11. https://doi.org/10.1016/J.PHYSBEH.2016.03.022

Côté, S. M. (2009). A developmental perspective on sex differences in aggressive behaviours. In R. E. Tremblay, M. A. G. van Aken, & W. Koops (Eds.), *Development and prevention of behaviour problems: From genes to social policy* (pp. 143–163). New York, NY: Psychology Press.

Cottini, M., Basso, D., & Palladino, P. (2018). The role of declarative and procedural metamemory in event-based prospective memory in school-aged children. *Journal of Experimental Child Psychology, 166*, 17–33. https://doi.org/10.1016/J.JECP.2017.08.002

Coubart, A., Izard, V., Spelke, E. S., Marie, J., & Streri, A. (2014). Dissociation between small and large numerosities in newborn infants. *Developmental Science, 17*(1), 11–22. https://doi.org/10.1111/desc.12108

Coughlin, C., Leckey, S., & Ghetti, S. (2018). Development of episodic memory: Processes and implications. In S. Ghetti

(Ed.), *Stevens' handbook of experimental psychology and cognitive neuroscience* (pp. 1–25). Hoboken, NJ: John Wiley & Sons. https://doi.org/10.1002/9781119170174.epcn404

Courage, M. L. (2017). Screen media and the youngest viewers: Implications for attention and learning. In F. C. Blumberg & P. J. Brooks (Eds.), *Cognitive development in digital contexts* (pp. 3–28). Cambridge, MA: Elsevier. https://doi.org/10.1016/B978-0-12-809481-5.00001-8

Courage, M. L., & Cowan, N. (2009). *The development of memory in infancy and childhood* (2nd ed.). New York, NY: Psychology Press.

Courage, M. L., Edison, S. C., & Howe, M. L. (2004). Variability in the early development of visual self-recognition. *Infant Behavior & Development, 27*(4), 509–532. https://doi.org/10.1016/j.infbeh.2004.06.001

Courage, M. L., & Howe, M. L. (2010). To watch or not to watch: Infants and toddlers in a brave new electronic world. *Developmental Review, 30*(2), 101–115. https://doi.org/10.1016/j.dr.2010.03.002

Courage, M. L., Reynolds, G. D., & Richards, J. E. (2006). Infants' attention to patterned stimuli: Developmental change from 3 to 12 months of age. *Child Development, 77*(3), 680–695. https://doi.org/10.1111/j.1467-8624.2006.00897.x

Cousminer, D. L., Stergiakouli, E., Berry, D. J., Ang, W., Groen-Blokhuis, M. M., Körner, A., . . . for the Early Growth Genetics Consortium (EGG). (2014). Genome-wide association study of sexual maturation in males and females highlights a role for body mass and menarche loci in male puberty. *Human Molecular Genetics, 23*(16), 4452–4464. https://doi.org/10.1093/hmg/ddu150

Coutelle, C., & Waddington, S. N. (2012). The concept of prenatal gene therapy. In C. Coutelle & S. N. Waddington (Eds.), *Methods in molecular biology* (Vol. 891, pp. 1–7). Clifton, NJ: Springer. https://doi.org/10.1007/978-1-61779-873-3_1

Covelli, V., Raggi, A., Meucci, P., Paganelli, C., & Leonardi, M. (2016). Ageing of people with Down's syndrome. *International Journal of Rehabilitation Research, 39*(1), 20–28. https://doi.org/10.1097/MRR.0000000000000147

Cowan, N., Hismjatullina, A., AuBuchon, A. M., Saults, J. S., Horton, N., Leadbitter, K., & Towse, J. (2010). With development, list recall includes more chunks, not just larger ones. *Developmental Psychology, 46*(5), 1119–1131. https://doi.org/10.1037/a0020618

Cowell, P., & Gurd, J. (2018). Handedness and the corpus callosum: A review and further analyses of discordant twins. *Neuroscience, 388*, 57–68. https://doi.org/10.1016/J.NEUROSCIENCE.2018.06.017

Cox, M., & Littlejohn, K. (1995). Children's use of converging obliques in their perspective drawings. *Educational Psychology, 15*, 127–139.

Cox, M. V. (1993). *Children's drawings of the human figure*. Hillsdale, NJ: Erlbaum.

Cox, M. V. (1997). *Drawings of people by the under-5s*. London, England: Falmer Press.

Coyle, K. K., Guinosso, S. A., Glassman, J. R., Anderson, P. M., & Wilson, H. W. (2017). Exposure to violence and sexual risk among early adolescents in urban middle schools. *Journal of Early Adolescence, 37*(7), 889–909. https://doi.org/10.1177/0272431616642324

Coyle, S., Demaray, M. K., Malecki, C. K., Tennant, J. E., & Klossing, J. (2017). The associations among sibling and peer-bullying, social support and internalizing behaviors. *Child & Youth Care Forum, 46*(6), 895–922. https://doi.org/10.1007/s10566-017-9412-3

Coyle, T. R., Pillow, D. R., Snyder, A. C., & Kochunov, P. (2011). Processing speed mediates the development of general intelligence (*g*) in adolescence. *Psychological Science, 22*(10), 1265–1269. https://doi.org/10.1177/0956797611418243

Coyne, S. M., Linder, J. R., Rasmussen, E. E., Nelson, D. A., & Birkbeck, V. (2016). Pretty as a princess: Longitudinal effects of engagement with Disney princesses on gender stereotypes, body esteem, and prosocial behavior in children. *Child Development, 87*(6), 1909–1925. https://doi.org/10.1111/cdev.12569

Crain, W. C. (2016). *Theories of development: Concepts and applications* (4th ed.). New York, NY: Routledge.

Cramer, P. (2017). Identity change between late adolescence and adulthood. *Personality and Individual Differences, 104*, 538–543. https://doi.org/10.1016/j.paid.2016.08.044

Crespo, L. M., Trentacosta, C. J., Aikins, D., & Wargo-Aikins, J. (2017). Maternal emotion regulation and children's behavior problems: The mediating role of child emotion regulation. *Journal of Child and Family Studies, 26*(10), 2797–2809. https://doi.org/10.1007/s10826-017-0791-8

Critz, C., Blake, K., & Nogueira, E. (2015). Sensory processing challenges in children. *Journal for Nurse Practitioners, 11*(7), 710–716. https://doi.org/10.1016/j.nurpra.2015.04.016

Crnic, K., & Ross, E. (2017). Parenting stress and parental efficacy. In K. Deater-Deckard & R. Panneton (Eds.), *Parental stress and early child development* (pp. 263–284). Cham, Switzerland: Springer International Publishing. https://doi.org/10.1007/978-3-319-55376-4_11

Crocetti, E. (2017). Identity formation in adolescence: The dynamic of forming and consolidating identity commitments. *Child Development Perspectives, 11*(2), 145–150. https://doi.org/10.1111/cdep.12226

Crocetti, E., Branje, S., Rubini, M., Koot, H. M., & Meeus, W. (2017). Identity processes and parent-child and sibling relationships in adolescence: A five-wave multi-informant longitudinal study. *Child Development, 88*(1), 210–228. https://doi.org/10.1111/cdev.12547

Crocetti, E., Klimstra, T. A., Hale, W. W., Koot, H. M., & Meeus, W. H. J. (2013). Impact of early adolescent externalizing problem behaviors on identity development in middle to late adolescence: A prospective 7-year longitudinal study. *Journal of Youth and Adolescence, 42*(11), 1745–1758. https://doi.org/10.1007/s10964-013-9924-6

Crocetti, E., Klimstra, T., Keijsers, L., Hale III, W. W. & Meeus, W. H. J. (2009). Anxiety trajectories and identity development in adolescence: A five-wave longitudinal study. *Journal of Youth & Adolescence, 38*(6), 839–849. https://doi.org/10.1007/s10964-008-9302-y

Crockenberg, S. C., & Leerkes, E. M. (2004). Infant and maternal behaviors regulate infant reactivity to novelty at 6 months. *Developmental Psychology, 40*(6), 1123–1132.

Crockett, L. J., Carlo, G., Wolff, J. M., & Hope, M. O. (2013). The role of pubertal timing and temperamental vulnerability in adolescents' internalizing symptoms. *Development and Psychopathology, 25*(2), 377–389. https://doi.org/10.1017/S0954579412001125

Croke, K., Ishengoma, D. S., Francis, F., Makani, J., Kamugisha, M. L., Lusingu, J., . . . Mmbando, B. P. (2017). Relationships between sickle cell trait, malaria, and educational outcomes in Tanzania. *BMC Infectious Diseases, 17*(1), 568. https://doi.org/10.1186/s12879-017-2644-x

Crone, E. A., Peters, S., & Steinbeis, N. (2018). Executive function: Development in adolescence. In S. A. Wiebe & J. Karbach (Eds.), *Executive function: Development across the life span* (pp. 58–72). New York, NY: Routledge.

Crone, E. A., & Steinbeis, N. (2017). Neural perspectives on cognitive control development during childhood and adolescence. *Trends in Cognitive Sciences, 21*(3), 205–215. https://doi.org/10.1016/J.TICS.2017.01.003

Croninger, R. G., & Lee, V. E. (2001). Social capital and dropping out of high school: Benefits to at-risk students of teachers' support and guidance. *Teachers College Record, 103*(4), 548–582.

Crosnoe, R., & Benner, A. D. (2015). Children at school. In M. H. Bornstein & T. Leventhal (Eds.), *Handbook of child psychology and developmental science* (pp. 1–37). Hoboken, NJ: John Wiley & Sons. https://doi.org/10.1002/9781118963418.childpsy407

Cross, C. P., Copping, L. T., & Campbell, A. (2011). Sex differences in impulsivity: A meta-analysis. *Psychological Bulletin, 137*(1), 97–130. https://doi.org/10.1037/a0021591

Cross, J. R., & Fletcher, K. L. (2009). The challenge of adolescent crowd research: Defining the crowd. *Journal of Youth & Adolescence, 38*(6), 747–764. https://doi.org/10.1007/s10964-008-9307-6

Crowley, S. J., Acebo, C., & Carskadon, M. A. (2007). Sleep, circadian rhythms, and delayed phase in adolescence. *Sleep Medicine, 8*(6), 602–612. https://doi.org/10.1016/j.sleep.2006.12.002

Crowley, S. J., Cain, S. W., Burns, A. C., Acebo, C., & Carskadon, M. A. (2015). Increased sensitivity of the circadian system to light in early/mid-puberty. *Journal of Clinical Endocrinology & Metabolism, 100*(11), 4067–4073. https://doi.org/10.1210/jc.2015-2775

Cservenka, A., & Brumback, T. (2017). The burden of binge and heavy drinking on the brain: Effects on adolescent and young adult neural structure and function. *Frontiers in Psychology, 8*, 1111. https://doi.org/10.3389/fpsyg.2017.01111

Cuartas, J. (2018). Neighborhood crime undermines parenting: Violence in the vicinity of households as a predictor of aggressive discipline. *Child Abuse & Neglect, 76*, 388–399. https://doi.org/10.1016/J.CHIABU.2017.12.006

Cuellar, J., Jones, D. J., & Sterrett, E. (2013). Examining parenting in the neighborhood context: A review. *Journal of Child and Family Studies, 24*(1), 195–219. https://doi.org/10.1007/s10826-013-9826-y

Cuevas, K., & Bell, M. A. (2010). Developmental progression of looking and reaching performance on the A-not-B task. *Developmental Psychology, 46*(5), 1363–1371. https://doi.org/10.1037/a0020185

Cummings, E. M., Goeke-Morey, M. C., Merrilees, C. E., Taylor, L. K., & Shirlow, P. (2014). A social-ecological, process-oriented perspective on political violence and child development. *Child Development Perspectives, 8*(2), 82–89. https://doi.org/10.1111/cdep.12067

Cunningham, P. M. (2013). *Phonics they use: Words for reading and writing.* New York, NY: Pearson.

Currie, C., Ahluwalia, N., Godeau, E., Nic Gabhainn, S., Due, P., & Currie, D. B. (2012). Is obesity at individual and national level associated with lower age at menarche? Evidence from 34 countries in the Health Behaviour in School-aged Children Study. *Journal of Adolescent Health, 50*(6), 621–626. https://doi.org/10.1016/j.jadohealth.2011.10.254

Curtin, S. C., Heron, M., Miniño, A. M., & Warner, M. (2018). Recent increases in injury mortality among children and adolescents aged 10-19 years in the United States: 1999-2016. *National Vital Statistics Reports, 67*(4), 1–16. Retrieved from http://www.ncbi.nlm.nih.gov/pubmed/29874162

Cutuli, J. J., Ahumada, S. M., Herbers, J. E., Lafavor, T. L., Masten, A. S., & Oberg, C. N. (2017). Adversity and children experiencing family homelessness: Implications for health. *Journal of Children and Poverty, 23*(1), 41–55. https://doi.org/10.1080/10796126.2016.1198753

Cvencek, D., Meltzoff, A. N., & Greenwald, A. G. (2011). Math-gender stereotypes in elementary school children. *Child Development, 82*(3), 766–779. https://doi.org/10.1111/j.1467-8624.2010.01529.x

D'Souza, A. J., Russell, M., Wood, B., Signal, L., & Elder, D. (2016). Attitudes to physical punishment of children are changing. *Archives of Disease in Childhood, 101*(8), 690–693. https://doi.org/10.1136/archdischild-2015-310119

D'Souza, H., Cowie, D., Karmiloff-Smith, A., & Bremner, A. J. (2017). Specialization of the motor system in infancy: From broad tuning to selectively specialized purposeful actions. *Developmental Science, 20*(4), e12409. https://doi.org/10.1111/desc.12409

Dąbrowska, E. (2015). What exactly is universal grammar, and has anyone seen it? *Frontiers in Psychology, 6*, 852. https://doi.org/10.3389/fpsyg.2015.00852

Dagan, O., & Sagi-Schwartz, A. (2018). Early attachment network with mother and father: An unsettled issue. *Child Development Perspectives, 12*(2), 115–121. https://doi.org/10.1111/cdep.12272

Dahl, A. (2015). The developing social context of infant helping in two U.S. samples. *Child Development, 86*(4), 1080–1093. https://doi.org/10.1111/cdev.12361

Dahl, A., Campos, J. J., Anderson, D. I., Uchiyama, I., Witherington, D. C., Ueno, M., & Barbu-Roth, M. (2013). The epigenesis of wariness of heights. *Psychological Science, 24*, 1361–1367. https://doi.org/10.1177/0956797613476047

Dajani, D. R., & Uddin, L. Q. (2016). Local brain connectivity across development in autism spectrum disorder: A cross-sectional investigation. *Autism Research, 9*(1), 43–54. https://doi.org/10.1002/aur.1494

Daley, C. E., & Onwuegbuzie, A. J. (2011). Race and intelligence. In R. J. Sternberg & S. B. Kaufman (Eds.), *The Cambridge handbook of intelligence* (pp. 293–308). New York, NY: Cambridge University Press.

Damaske, S., Bratter, J. L., & Frech, A. (2017). Single mother families and employment, race, and poverty in changing economic times. *Social Science Research, 62*, 120–133. https://doi.org/10.1016/j.ssresearch.2016.08.008

Damon, W. (1977). *The social world of the child.* San Francisco, CA: Jossey-Bass.

Damon, W. (1980). Patterns of change in children's social reasoning: A two-year longitudinal study. *Child Development, 51*(4), 1010–1017.

Damon, W. (1988). *The moral child.* New York, NY: Free Press.

Daniels, P., Noe, G. F., & Mayberry, R. (2006). Barriers to prenatal care among black women of low socioeconomic status. *American Journal of Health Behavior, 30*(2), 188–198.

Danovitch, J., & Bloom, P. (2009). Children's extension of disgust to physical and moral events. *Emotion, 9*(1), 107–112. https://doi.org/10.1037/a0014113

Darchia, N., & Cervena, K. (2014). The journey through the world of adolescent sleep. *Reviews in the Neurosciences, 25*(4), 585–604. https://doi.org/10.1515/revneuro-2013-0065

Das, J. K., Salam, R. A., Thornburg, K. L., Prentice, A. M., Campisi, S., Lassi, Z. S., . . . Bhutta, Z. A. (2017). Nutrition in adolescents: Physiology, metabolism, and nutritional needs. *Annals of the New York Academy of Sciences, 1393*(1), 21–33. https://doi.org/10.1111/nyas.13330

Dasen, P. R. (1994). Culture and cognitive development from a Piagetian perspective. In W. J. Lonner & R. Malpass (Eds.), *Psychology and culture* (pp. 145–149). Boston, MA: Allyn & Bacon.

Dasgupta, N., & Stout, J. G. (2014). Girls and women in science, technology, engineering, and mathematics. *Policy Insights from the Behavioral and Brain Sciences, 1*(1), 21–29. https://doi.org/10.1177/2372732214549471

Davidson, R. D., O'Hara, K. L., & Beck, C. J. A. (2014). Psychological and biological processes in children associated with high conflict parental divorce. *Juvenile and Family Court Journal, 65*(1), 29–44. https://doi.org/10.1111/jfcj.12015

Davies, P., & Martin, M. (2014). Children's coping and adjustment in high-conflict homes: The reformulation of emotional security theory. *Child Development Perspectives, 8*(4), 242–249. https://doi.org/10.1111/cdep.12094

Davis, A. S., & Escobar, L. F. (2013). Early childhood cognitive disorders: Down syndrome. In A. S. Davis (Ed.), *Psychopathology of childhood and adolescence: A neuropsychological approach* (pp. 569–580). New York, NY: Springer.

Davis, B., Royne Stafford, M. B., & Pullig, C. (2014). How gay-straight alliance groups mitigate the relationship between gay-bias victimization and adolescent suicide attempts. *Journal of the American Academy of Child and Adolescent Psychiatry, 53*(12), 1271–1278. https://doi.org/10.1016/j.jaac.2014.09.010

Davis, E. P., Glynn, L. M., Waffarn, F., & Sandman, C. A. (2011). Prenatal maternal stress programs infant stress regulation. *Journal of Child Psychology and Psychiatry, and Allied Disciplines, 52*(2), 119–129. https://doi.org/10.1111/j.1469-7610.2010.02314.x

Davis, P. E., Meins, E., & Fernyhough, C. (2014). Children with imaginary companions focus on mental characteristics when describing their real-life friends. *Infant and Child Development, 23*(6), 622–633. https://doi.org/10.1002/icd.1869

Davis-Kean, P. E., Jager, J., & Andrew Collins, W. (2009). The self in action: An emerging link between self-beliefs and behaviors in middle childhood. *Child Development Perspectives, 3*(3), 184–188. https://doi.org/10.1111/j.1750-8606.2009.00104.x

Dawson, T. L. (2002). New tools, new insights: Kohlberg's moral judgement stages revisited. *International Journal of Behavioral Development, 26*(2), 154–166.

Day, F. R., Thompson, D. J., Helgason, H., Chasman, D. I., Finucane, H., Sulem, P., . . . Perry, J. R. B. (2017). Genomic analyses identify hundreds of variants associated with age at menarche and support a role for puberty timing in cancer risk. *Nature Genetics, 49*(6), 834–841. https://doi.org/10.1038/ng.3841

Day, J., Savani, S., Krempley, B. D., Nguyen, M., & Kitlinska, J. B. (2016). Influence of paternal preconception exposures on their offspring: Through epigenetics to phenotype. *American Journal of Stem Cells, 5*(1), 11–18.

De Genna, N., Larkby, C., & Cornelius, M. (2011). Pubertal timing and early sexual intercourse in the offspring of teenage mothers. *Journal of Youth & Adolescence, 40*(10), 1315–1328. https://doi.org/10.1007/s10964-010-9609-3

de Graaf, G., Buckley, F., Dever, J., & Skotko, B. G. (2017). Estimation of live birth and population prevalence of Down syndrome in nine U.S. states. *American Journal of Medical Genetics Part A, 173*(10), 2710–2719. https://doi.org/10.1002/ajmg.a.38402

de Houwer, A., & Gillis, S. (1998). *The acquisition of Dutch.* Amsterdam, Netherlands: Benjamins.

de Jonge, A., Geerts, C., van der Goes, B., Mol, B., Buitendijk, S., & Nijhuis, J. (2015). Perinatal mortality and morbidity up to 28 days after birth among 743 070 low-risk planned home and hospital births: A cohort study based on three merged national perinatal databases. *BJOG, 122*(5), 720–728. https://doi.org/10.1111/1471-0528.13084

de Kovel, C. G. F., Carrión-Castillo, A., & Francks, C. (2019). A large-scale population study of early life factors influencing left-handedness. *Scientific Reports, 9*(1), 584. https://doi.org/10.1038/s41598-018-37423-8

De La Rue, L., Polanin, J. R., Espelage, D. L., & Pigott, T. D. (2017). A meta-analysis of school-based interventions aimed to prevent or reduce violence in teen dating relationships. *Review of Educational Research, 87*(1), 7–34. https://doi.org/10.3102/0034654316632061

De Maio, F., Ansell, D., & Shah, R. C. (2018). Racial/ethnic minority segregation and low birth weight in five North American cities. *Ethnicity & Health*, 1–10. https://doi.org/10.1080/13557858.2018.1492706

De Meester, A., Stodden, D., Brian, A., True, L., Cardon, G., Tallir, I., & Haerens, L. (2016). Associations among elementary school children's actual motor competence, perceived motor competence, physical activity and BMI: A cross-sectional study. *PLoS ONE, 11*(10), e0164600. https://doi.org/10.1371/journal.pone.0164600

de Onis, M., Blössner, M., & Borghi, E. (2010). Global prevalence and trends of overweight and obesity among preschool children. *American Journal of Clinical Nutrition, 92*(5), 1257–1264. https://doi.org/10.3945/ajcn.2010.29786

de Onis, M., & Branca, F. (2016). Childhood stunting: A global perspective. *Maternal & Child Nutrition, 12*(S1), 12–26. https://doi.org/10.1111/mcn.12231

de Villiers, J. G., & de Villiers, P. A. (2014). The role of language in theory of mind development. *Topics in Language Disorders, 34*(4), 313–328. https://doi.org/10.1097/TLD.0000000000000037

de Waal, F. B. M. (1993). Sex differences in chimpanzee (and human) behavior: A matter of social values? In M. Hechter, L. Nadel, & R. E. Michod (Eds.), *The origin of values* (pp. 285–303). New York, NY: Aldine de Gruyter.

de Water, E., Burk, W. J., Cillessen, A. H. N., & Scheres, A. (2017). Substance use and decision-making in adolescent best friendship dyads: The role of popularity. *Social Development, 26*(4), 860–875. https://doi.org/10.1111/sode.12227

de Wilde, A., Koot, H. M., & van Lier, P. A. C. (2016). Developmental links between children's working memory and their social relations with teachers and peers in the early school years. *Journal of Abnormal Child Psychology, 44*(1), 19–30. https://doi.org/10.1007/s10802-015-0053-4

de Wit, J. B. F., Stok, F. M., Smolenski, D. J., de Ridder, D. D. T., de Vet, E., Gaspar, T., . . . Luszczynska, A. (2015). Food culture in the home environment: Family meal practices and values can support healthy eating and self-regulation in young people in four European countries. *Applied Psychology. Health and Well-Being, 7*(1), 22–40. https://doi.org/10.1111/aphw.12034

Deák, G. O. (2006). Do children really confuse appearance and reality? *Trends in Cognitive Sciences, 10*(12), 546–550.

Deák, G. O., Krasno, A. M., Triesch, J., Lewis, J., & Sepeta, L. (2014). Watch the hands: Infants can learn to follow gaze by seeing adults manipulate objects. *Developmental Science, 17*(2), 270–281. https://doi.org/10.1111/desc.12122

Dean, D. C., O'Muircheartaigh, J., Dirks, H., Waskiewicz, N., Walker, L., Doernberg, E., . . . Deoni, S. C. L. (2014). Characterizing longitudinal white matter development during early childhood. *Brain Structure & Function, 220*(4), 1921–1933. https://doi.org/10.1007/s00429-014-0763-3

Deardorff, J., Abrams, B., Ekwaru, J. P., & Rehkopf, D. H. (2014). Socioeconomic status and age at menarche: An examination of multiple indicators in an ethnically diverse cohort. *Annals of Epidemiology, 24*(10), 727–733. https://doi.org/10.1016/j.annepidem.2014.07.002

Deardorff, J., Ekwaru, J. P., Kushi, L. H., Ellis, B. J., Greenspan, L. C., Mirabedi, A., . . . Hiatt, R. A. (2011). Father absence, body mass index, and pubertal timing in girls: Differential effects by family income and ethnicity. *Journal of Adolescent Health, 48*(5), 441–447. https://doi.org/10.1016/j.jadohealth.2010.07.032

Deater-Deckard, K. (2001). Nonshared environmental processes in social emotional development: An observational study of identical twin differences in the preschool period. *Developmental Science, 4*(2), 1–7.

Deater-Deckard, K., & O'Connor, T. (2000). Parent-child mutuality in early childhood: Two behavioral genetic studies. *Developmental Psychology, 36*(5), 561–571.

Deaton, A. E., Sheiner, E., Wainstock, T., Landau, D., & Walfisch, A. (2017). Does lack of prenatal care predict later lack of child care? *American Journal of Obstetrics and Gynecology, 216*(1), S359–S360. https://doi.org/10.1016/j.ajog.2016.11.347

Declercq, E. R., Sakala, C., Corry, M. P., Applebaum, S., & Herrlich, A. (2014). Major survey findings of Listening to Mothers(SM) III: Pregnancy and Birth: Report of the Third National U.S. Survey of Women's Childbearing Experiences. *Journal of Perinatal Education, 23*(1), 9–16. https://doi.org/10.1891/1058-1243.23.1.9

Dediu, D., & Christiansen, M. H. (2016). Language evolution: Constraints and opportunities from modern genetics. *Topics in Cognitive Science, 8*(2), 361–370. https://doi.org/10.1111/tops.12195

Deeney, M. (2013). Bioethical considerations of preimplantation genetic diagnosis for sex selection. *Washington University Jurisprudence Review*. Retrieved from http://digitalcommons.law.wustl.edu/jurisprudence/vol5/iss2/5

Dehaan, L. (2006). Child care and development: Results from the NICHD Study of Early Child Care and Youth Development. The NICHD Early Child Care Research Network. *Journal of Marriage & Family, 68*(1), 252–253. https://doi.org/10.1111/j.1741-3737.2006.00245.x

Dehaene-Lambertz, G. (2017). The human infant brain: A neural architecture able to learn language. *Psychonomic Bulletin & Review, 24*(1), 48–55. https://doi.org/10.3758/s13423-016-1156-9

Dehaene-Lambertz, G., & Spelke, E. S. (2015). The infancy of the human brain. *Neuron, 88*(1), 93–109. https://doi.org/10.1016/j.neuron.2015.09.026

DelGiudice, M. (2018). Middle childhood: An evolutionary-developmental synthesis. In N. Halfon, C. B. Forrest, R. M. Lerner, & E. M. Faustman (Eds.), *Handbook of life course health development* (pp. 95–107). Cham, Switzerland: Springer International Publishing. https://doi.org/10.1007/978-3-319-47143-3_5

Della Longa, L. (2019). Tune to touch: Affective touch enhances learning of face identity in 4-month-old infants. *Developmental Cognitive Neuroscience, 35*, 42–46. https://doi.org/10.1016/J.DCN.2017.11.002

Dellinger, A., & Gilchrist, J. (2018). Leading causes of fatal and nonfatal unintentional injury for children and teens and the role of lifestyle clinicians. *American Journal of Lifestyle Medicine, 13*(1), 7–21. https://doi.org/10.1177/1559827617696297

DeLoache, J. S., Chiong, C., Sherman, K., Islam, N., Vanderborght, M., Troseth, G. L., . . . O'Doherty, K. (2010). Do babies learn from baby media? *Psychological Science, 21*(11), 1570–1574. https://doi.org/10.1177/0956797610384145

Delsing, M. J. M. H., ter Bogt, T. F. M., Engels, R. C. M. E., & Meeus, W. H. J. (2007). Adolescents' peer crowd identification in the Netherlands: Structure and associations with problem behaviors. *Journal of Research on Adolescence, 17*(2), 467–480. https://doi.org/10.1111/j.1532-7795.2007.00530.x

Demissie, Z., Eaton, D. K., Lowry, R., Nihiser, A. J., & Foltz, J. L. (2018). Prevalence and correlates of missing meals among high school students—United States, 2010. *American Journal of Health Promotion, 32*(1), 89–95. https://doi.org/10.1177/0890117116667348

Dempsey, J., McQuillin, S., Butler, A. M., & Axelrad, M. E. (2016). Maternal depression and parent management training outcomes. *Journal of Clinical Psychology in Medical Settings, 23*(3), 240–246. https://doi.org/10.1007/s10880-016-9461-z

DeNavas-Walt, C., & Proctor, B. D. (2014). *Income and poverty in the United States: 2013*. Washington, DC: U.S. Census Bureau. Retrieved from https://www2.census.gov/library/publications/2014/demographics/p60-249.pdf

Denbow, J. R., & Thebe, P. C. (2006). *Culture and customs of Botswana*. Westport, CT: Greenwood Press.

Deneault, J., & Ricard, M. (2006). The assessment of children's understanding of inclusion relations: Transitivity, asymmetry, and quantification. *Journal of Cognition & Development, 7*(4), 551–570.

Deneault, J., & Ricard, M. (2013). Are emotion and mind understanding differently linked to young children's social adjustment? Relationships between behavioral consequences of emotions, false belief, and SCBE. *Journal of Genetic Psychology, 174*(1), 88–116. https://doi.org/10.1080/00221325.2011.642028

Denissen, J. J. A., Zarrett, N. R., & Eccles, J. S. (2007). I like to do it, I'm able, and I know I am: Longitudinal couplings between domain-specific achievement, self-concept, and interest. *Child Development, 78*(2), 430–447.

Dennis, T. A., Cole, P. M., Zahn-Waxler, C., & Mizuta, I. (2002). Self in context: Autonomy and relatedness in Japanese and U. S. mother-preschooler dyads. *Child Development, 73*, 1803–1817.

Dennis, W. (1960). Causes of retardation among institutional children: Iran. *Journal of Genetic Psychology, 96*, 47–59.

Dennis, W., & Dennis, M. G. (1991). The effect of cradling practices upon the onset of walking in Hopi children. *Journal of Genetic Psychology, 152*(4), 563–572.

Deprest, J. A., Devlieger, R., Srisupundit, K., Beck, V., Sandaite, I., Rusconi, S., . . . Lewi, L. (2010). Fetal surgery is a clinical reality. *Seminars in Fetal & Neonatal Medicine, 15*(1), 58–67. https://doi.org/10.1016/j.siny.2009.10.002

Der, G., Batty, G. D., & Deary, I. J. (2006). Effect of breast feeding on intelligence in children: Prospective study, sibling pairs analysis, and meta-analysis. *BMJ, 333*(7575), 945–948.

DeRose, L. M., & Brooks-Gunn, J. (2006). Transition into adolescence: The role of pubertal processes. In L. Balter & C. S. Tamis-LeMonda (Eds.), *Child psychology: A handbook of contemporary issues* (2nd ed., pp. 385–414). New York, NY: Psychology Press.

Desjardins, T., & Leadbeater, B. J. (2017). Changes in parental emotional support and psychological control in early adulthood. *Emerging Adulthood, 5*(3), 177–190. https://doi.org/10.1177/2167696816666974

Devine, R. T., & Hughes, C. H. (2018). Let's talk: Parents' mental talk (not mind-mindedness or mindreading capacity) predicts children's false belief understanding. *Child Development, 90*(4), 1236–1253. https://doi.org/10.1111/cdev.12990

DeVries, R. (1969). Constancy of generic identity in the years three to six. *Monographs of the Society for Research in Child Development, 34*(Serial No. 127), iii–67.

DeVries, R., & Zan, B. (2003). When children make rules. *Educational Leadership, 61*(1), 64–67.

Diamandopoulos, K., & Green, J. (2018). Down syndrome: An integrative review. *Journal of Neonatal Nursing, 24*(5), 235–241. https://doi.org/10.1016/J.JNN.2018.01.001

Diamond, A. (1991). Neuropsychological insights into the meaning of object concept development. In S. Carey & R. Gelman (Eds.), *The epigenesis of mind: Essays on biology and cognition* (pp. 67–110). Hillsdale, NJ: Lawrence Erlbaum.

Diamond, A. (2013). Executive functions. *Annual Review of Psychology, 64*, 135–168. https://doi.org/10.1146/annurev-psych-113011-143750

Diamond, K., & Hong, S.-Y. (2010). Young children's decisions to include peers with physical disabilities in play. *Journal of Early Intervention, 32*(3), 163–177. https://doi.org/10.1177/1053815110371332

Diamond, K., & Kensinger, K. R. (2002). Vignettes from *Sesame Street*: Preschooler's ideas about children with Down syndrome and physical disability. *Early Education & Development, 13*(4), 409–422. https://doi.org/10.1207/s15566935eed1304_5

Diamond, K., & Tu, H. (2009). Relations between classroom context, physical disability and preschool children's inclusion decisions. *Journal of Applied Developmental Psychology, 30*(2), 75–81. https://doi.org/10.1016/J.APPDEV.2008.10.008

Diamond, L. M., Bonner, S. B., & Dickenson, J. (2015). The development of sexuality. In *Handbook of child psychology and developmental science* (pp. 1–44). Hoboken, NJ: John Wiley & Sons. https://doi.org/10.1002/9781118963418.childpsy321

Diamond, L. M., & Savin-Williams, R. C. (2009). Adolescent Sexuality. In R. M. Lerner & L. Steinberg (Eds.), *Handbook of adolescent psychology* (p. 479). Hoboken, NJ: John Wiley & Sons.

Dickerson, A., & Popli, G. K. (2016). Persistent poverty and children's cognitive development: Evidence from the UK Millennium Cohort Study. *Journal of the Royal Statistical Society: Series A (Statistics in Society), 179*(2), 535–558. https://doi.org/10.1111/rssa.12128

Dieke, A. C., Zhang, Y., Kissin, D. M., Barfield, W. D., & Boulet, S. L. (2017). Disparities in assisted reproductive technology utilization by race and ethnicity, United States, 2014: A commentary. *Journal of Women's Health, 26*(6), 605–608. https://doi.org/10.1089/jwh.2017.6467

Diener, M. (2000). Gift from the Gods: A Balinese guide to early child rearing. In J. DeLoache & A. Gotleib (Eds.), *A world of babies: Imagined childcare guiles for seven societies*. Cambridge, England: Cambridge University Press.

Dimler, L. M., Natsuaki, M. N., Hastings, P. D., Zahn-Waxler, C., & Klimes-Dougan, B. (2017). Parenting effects are in the eye of the beholder: Parent-adolescent differences in perceptions affects adolescent problem behaviors. *Journal of Youth and Adolescence, 46*(5), 1076–1088. https://doi.org/10.1007/s10964-016-0612-1

Dinehart, L., & Manfra, L. (2013). Associations between low-income children's fine motor skills in preschool and academic performance in second grade. *Early Education & Development, 24*(2), 138–161. https://doi.org/10.1080/10409289.2011.636729

Dinehart, L. H. (2015). Handwriting in early childhood education: Current research and future implications. *Journal of Early Childhood Literacy, 15*(1), 97–118. https://doi.org/10.1177/1468798414522825

Ding, G., Ji, R., & Bao, Y. (2014). Risk and protective factors for the development of childhood asthma. *Paediatric Respiratory Reviews, 16*(2), 133–139. https://doi.org/10.1016/j.prrv.2014.07.004

Ding, Y., Xu, X., Wang, Z., Li, H., & Wang, W. (2014). The relation of infant attachment to attachment and cognitive and behavioural outcomes in early childhood. *Early Human Development, 90*(9), 459–464. https://doi.org/10.1016/J.EARLHUMDEV.2014.06.004

Dion, J., Hains, J., Vachon, P., Plouffe, J., Laberge, L., Perron, M., . . . Leone, M. (2016). Correlates of body dissatisfaction in children. *Journal of Pediatrics, 171*, 202–207. https://doi.org/10.1016/J.JPEDS.2015.12.045

DiPietro, J. A. (2000). Baby and the brain: Advances in child development. *Annual Review of Public Health, 21*, 455–471.

Dirix, C. E. H., Nijhuis, J. G., Jongsma, H. W., & Hornstra, G. (2009). Aspects of fetal learning and memory. *Child Development, 80*(4), 1251–1258. https://doi.org/10.1111/j.1467-8624.2009.01329.x

Dishion, T. J., & Patterson, G. R. (2016). The development and ecology of antisocial behavior: Linking etiology, prevention, and treatment. In D. Cicchetti (Ed.), *Developmental psychopathology* (pp. 1–32). Hoboken, NJ: John Wiley & Sons. https://doi.org/10.1002/9781119125556.devpsy315

Dittus, P. J., Michael, S. L., Becasen, J. S., Gloppen, K. M., McCarthy, K., & Guilamo-Ramos, V. (2015). Parental monitoring and its associations with adolescent sexual risk behavior: A meta-analysis. *Pediatrics, 136*(6), e1587–e1599.

Dixson, H. G. W., Komugabe-Dixson, A. F., Dixson, B. J., & Low, J. (2018). Scaling theory of mind in a small-scale society: A case study from Vanuatu. *Child Development, 89*(6), 2157–2175. https://doi.org/10.1111/cdev.12919

Dodge, K. A., & Rutter, M. (2011). *Gene-environment interactions in developmental psychopathology*. New York, NY: Guilford.

Doenyas, C., Yavuz, H. M., & Selcuk, B. (2018). Not just a sum of its parts: How tasks of the theory of mind scale relate to executive function across time. *Journal of Experimental Child Psychology, 166*, 485–501. https://doi.org/10.1016/J.JECP.2017.09.014

Doherty, B. R., & Scerif, G. (2017). Genetic syndromes and developmental risk for autism spectrum and attention deficit hyperactivity disorders: Insights from fragile X syndrome. *Child Development Perspectives, 11*(3), 161–166. https://doi.org/10.1111/cdep.12227

Doherty-Sneddon, G. (2008). The great baby signing debate: Academia meets public interest. *British Psychological Society*. Retrieved from https://dspace.stir.ac.uk/handle/1893/385

Döhla, D., & Heim, S. (2016). Developmental dyslexia and dysgraphia: What can we learn from the one about the other? *Frontiers in Psychology, 6*, 2045. https://doi.org/10.3389/fpsyg.2015.02045

Dohnt, H. K., & Tiggemann, M. (2005). Peer influences on body dissatisfaction and dieting awareness in young girls. *British Journal of Developmental Psychology, 23*, 103–116.

Domhardt, M., Münzer, A., Fegert, J. M., & Goldbeck, L. (2015). Resilience in survivors of child sexual abuse: A systematic review of the literature. *Trauma, Violence & Abuse, 16*(4), 476–493. https://doi.org/10.1177/1524838014557288

Domitrovich, C. E., Durlak, J. A., Staley, K. C., & Weissberg, R. P. (2017). Social-emotional competence: An essential factor for promoting positive adjustment and reducing risk in school children. *Child Development, 88*(2), 408–416. https://doi.org/10.1111/cdev.12739

Domsch, H., Thomas, H., & Louhas, A. (2010). Infant attention, heart rate, and looking time during habituation/dishabituation. *Infant Behavior & Development, 33*(3), 321–329. https://doi.org/10.1016/j.infbeh.2010.03.008

Dondi, M., Simion, F., & Caltran, G. (1999). Can newborns discriminate between their own cry and the cry of another newborn infant? *Developmental Psychology, 35*, 418–426.

Dondorp, W., De Wert, G., Pennings, G., Shenfield, F., Devroey, P., Tarlatzis, B., . . . Diedrich, K. (2013). ESHRE Task Force on Ethics and Law 20: Sex selection for non-medical reasons. *Human Reproduction, 28*(6), 1448–1454. https://doi.org/10.1093/humrep/det109

Donnan, J., Walsh, S., Sikora, L., Morrissey, A., Collins, K., & MacDonald, D. (2017). A systematic review of the risk factors associated with the onset and natural progression of spina bifida. *NeuroToxicology, 61*, 20–31. https://doi.org/10.1016/J.NEURO.2016.03.008

Doodson, L., & Morley, D. (2006). Understanding the roles of non-residential stepmothers. *Journal of Divorce & Remarriage, 45*(3/4), 109–130. https://doi.org/10.1300/J087v45n03-06

Dorn, L. D., Dahl, R. E., Woodward, H. R., & Biro, F. (2006). Defining the boundaries of early adolescence: A user's guide to assessing pubertal status and pubertal timing in research with adolescents. *Applied Developmental Science, 10*(1), 30–56.

Dornbusch, S. M., Ritter, P. L., Mont-Reynaud, R., & Chen, Z. (1990). Family decision making and academic performance in a diverse high school population. *Journal of Adolescent Research, 5*(2), 143–160.

Dorsey, E. A., Mouzourou, C., Park, H., Ostrosky, M. M., & Favazza, P. C. (2016). Teacher perceptions of two multi-component interventions. *Topics in Early Childhood Special Education, 36*(2), 103–114. https://doi.org/10.1177/0271121415626711

Dotterer, A. M., Lowe, K., & McHale, S. M. (2014). Academic growth trajectories and family relationships among African American youth. *Journal of Research on Adolescence, 24*(4), 734–747. https://doi.org/10.1111/jora.12080

Dotterer, A. M., McHale, S. M., & Crouter, A. C. (2009). Sociocultural factors and school engagement among African American youth: The roles of racial discrimination, racial socialization, and ethnic identity. *Applied Developmental Science, 13*(2), 61–73. https://doi.org/10.1080/10888690902801442

Douglass, S., & Umaña-Taylor, A. J. (2016). Time-varying effects of family ethnic socialization on ethnic-racial identity development among Latino adolescents. *Developmental Psychology, 52*(11), 1904–1912. https://doi.org/10.1037/dev0000141

Douglass, S., & Umaña-Taylor, A. J. (2017). Examining discrimination, ethnic-racial identity status, and youth public regard among Black, Latino, and White adolescents. *Journal of Research on Adolescence, 27*(1), 155–172. https://doi.org/10.1111/jora.12262

Douglass, S., Yip, T., & Shelton, J. N. (2014). Intragroup contact and anxiety among ethnic minority adolescents: Considering ethnic identity and school diversity transitions. *Journal of Youth and Adolescence, 43*(10), 1628–1641. https://doi.org/10.1007/s10964-014-0144-5

Downey, D. B., Condron, D. J., & Yucel, D. (2015). Number of siblings and social skills revisited among American fifth graders. *Journal of Family Issues, 36*(2), 273–296. https://doi.org/10.1177/0192513X13507569

Downs, A. C., & Fuller, M. J. (1991). Recollections of spermarche: An exploratory investigation. *Current Psychology, 10*(1/2), 93–102. https://doi.org/10.1007/BF02686783

Doyle-Thomas, K. A. R., Lee, W., Foster, N. E. V., Tryfon, A., Ouimet, T., Hyde, K. L., . . . Anagnostou, E. (2015). Atypical functional brain connectivity during rest in autism spectrum disorders. *Annals of Neurology, 77*(5), 866–876. https://doi.org/10.1002/ana.24391

Doyon, J., Gabitov, E., Vahdat, S., Lungu, O., & Boutin, A. (2018). Current issues related to motor sequence learning in humans. *Current Opinion in Behavioral Sciences, 20*, 89–97. https://doi.org/10.1016/j.cobeha.2017.11.012

Drapeau, S., Gagne, M.-H., Saint-Jacques, M.-C., Lepine, R., & Ivers, H. (2009). Post-separation conflict trajectories: A longitudinal study. *Marriage & Family Review, 45*(4), 353–373. https://doi.org/10.1080/01494920902821529

Dreyfuss, M., Caudle, K., Drysdale, A. T., Johnston, N. E., Cohen, A. O., Somerville, L. H., . . . Casey, B. J. (2014). Teens impulsively react rather than retreat from threat. *Developmental Neuroscience, 36*(3–4), 220–227. https://doi.org/10.1159/000357755

Du Toit, G., Roberts, G., Sayre, P. H., Bahnson, H. T., Radulovic, S., Santos, A. F., . . . LEAP Study Team. (2015). Randomized trial of peanut consumption in infants at risk for peanut allergy. *New England Journal of Medicine, 372*(9), 803–813. https://doi.org/10.1056/NEJMoa1414850

Du Toit, G., Sayre, P. H., Roberts, G., Sever, M. L., Lawson, K., Bahnson, H. T., . . . Lack, G. (2016). Effect of avoidance on peanut allergy after early peanut consumption. *New England Journal of Medicine, 374*(15), 1435–1443. https://doi.org/10.1056/NEJMoa1514209

Duan, L., Chou, C.-P., Andreeva, V., & Pentz, M. (2009). Trajectories of peer social influences as long-term predictors of drug use from early through late adolescence. *Journal of Youth & Adolescence, 38*(3), 454–465. https://doi.org/10.1007/s10964-008-9310-y

Duboc, V., Dufourcq, P., Blader, P., & Roussigné, M. (2015). Asymmetry of the brain: Development and implications. *Annual Review of Genetics, 49*(1), 647–672. https://doi.org/10.1146/annurev-genet-112414-055322

Dubois, J., Dehaene-Lambertz, G., Kulikova, S., Poupon, C., Hüppi, P. S., & Hertz-Pannier, L. (2013). The early development of brain white matter: A review of imaging studies in fetuses, newborns and infants. *Neuroscience, 276*, 48–71. https://doi.org/10.1016/j.neuroscience.2013.12.044

Dubois, L., Ohm Kyvik, K., Girard, M., Tatone-Tokuda, F., Pérusse, D., Hjelmborg, J., . . . Martin, N. G. (2012). Genetic and environmental contributions to weight, height, and BMI from birth to 19 years of age: An international study of over 12,000 twin pairs. *PLoS One, 7*(2), e30153. https://doi.org/10.1371/journal.pone.0030153

Duchin, O., Marin, C., Mora-Plazas, M., Mendes de Leon, C., Lee, J. M., Baylin, A., & Villamor, E. (2015). A prospective study of body image dissatisfaction and BMI change in school-age children. *Public Health Nutrition, 18*(02), 322–328. https://doi.org/10.1017/S1368980014000366

Dudovitz, R. N., Chung, P. J., & Wong, M. D. (2017). Teachers and coaches in adolescent social networks are associated with healthier self-concept and decreased substance use. *Journal of School Health, 87*(1), 12–20. https://doi.org/10.1111/josh.12462

Duell, N., Steinberg, L., Icenogle, G., Chein, J., Chaudhary, N., Di Giunta, L., . . . Chang, L. (2018). Age patterns in risk taking across the world. *Journal of Youth and Adolescence, 47*(5), 1052–1072. https://doi.org/10.1007/s10964-017-0752-y

Dumith, S. C., Gigante, D. P., Domingues, M. R., & Kohl, H. W. (2011). Physical activity change during adolescence: A systematic review and a pooled analysis. *International Journal of Epidemiology, 40*(3), 685–698. https://doi.org/10.1093/ije/dyq272

Dumont, M., Leclerc, D., & McKinnon, S. (2009). Consequences of part-time work on the academic and psychosocial adaptation of adolescents. *Canadian Journal of School Psychology, 24*(1), 58–75. https://doi.org/10.1177/0829573509333197

Dumontheil, I. (2016). Adolescent brain development. *Current Opinion in Behavioral Sciences, 10*, 39–44. https://doi.org/10.1016/j.cobeha.2016.04.012

Duncan, G. J., Ludwig, J., & Magnuson, K. A. (2007). Reducing poverty through preschool interventions. *The Future of Children, 17*(2), 143–160.

Duncan, G. J., & Magnuson, K. (2013). Investing in preschool programs. *Journal of Economic Perspectives, 27*(2), 109–132. https://doi.org/10.1257/jep.27.2.109

Dunn, J. (2002). Sibling relationships. In P. K. Smith & C. H. Hart (Eds.), *Blackwell handbook of childhood social development* (pp. 223–237). Oxford, England: Blackwell.

Dunn, J., Gray, C., Moffett, P., & Mitchell, D. (2018). "It's more funner than doing work": Children's perspectives on using tablet computers in the early years of school. *Early Child Development and Care, 188*(6), 819–831. https://doi.org/10.1080/03004430.2016.1238824

Dunst, C. J., & Gorman, E. (2009). Development of infant and toddler mark making and scribbling. *Cell Reviews, 2*(2), 1–16.

Dupéré, V., Dion, E., Leventhal, T., Archambault, I., Crosnoe, R., & Janosz, M. (2018). High school dropout in proximal context: The triggering role of stressful life events. *Child Development, 89*(2), e107–e122. https://doi.org/10.1111/cdev.12792

Dupéré, V., Leventhal, T., Dion, E., Crosnoe, R., Archambault, I., & Janosz, M. (2015). Stressors and turning points in high school and dropout: A stress process, life course framework. *Review of Educational Research, 85*(4), 591–629. https://doi.org/10.3102/0034654314559845

Durik, A., Hyde, J., & Clark, R. (2000). Sequelae of cesarean and vaginal deliveries: Psychosocial outcomes for mothers and infants. *Developmental Psychology, 36*, 251–260.

Durkin, M. S., Benedict, R. E., Christensen, D., Dubois, L. A., Fitzgerald, R. T., Kirby, R. S., . . . Yeargin-Allsopp, M. (2016). Prevalence of cerebral palsy among 8-year-old children in 2010 and preliminary evidence of trends in its relationship to low birthweight. *Paediatric and Perinatal Epidemiology, 30*(5), 496–510. https://doi.org/10.1111/ppe.12299

Durwood, L., McLaughlin, K. A., & Olson, K. R. (2017). Mental health and self-worth in socially transitioned transgender youth. *Journal of the American Academy of Child and Adolescent Psychiatry, 56*(2), 116–123. https://doi.org/10.1016/j.jaac.2016.10.016

Duschinsky, R. (2015). The emergence of the disorganized/disoriented (D) attachment classification, 1979–1982. *History of Psychology, 18*(1), 32–46. https://doi.org/10.1037/a0038524

Duyme, M., Dumaret, A. C., & Tomkiewicz, S. (1999). How can we boost IQs of "dull children"? A late adoption study. *Proceedings of the National Academy of Sciences of the United States of America, 96*(15), 8790–8794. https://doi.org/10.1073/PNAS.96.15.8790

Dweck, C. S. (2017). The journey to children's mindsets—and beyond. *Child Development Perspectives, 11*(2), 139–144. https://doi.org/10.1111/cdep.12225

Dyer, S., & Moneta, G. B. (2006). Frequency of parallel, associative, and cooperative play in British children of different socioeconomic status. *Social Behavior & Personality, 34*(5), 587–592.

Dyson, L. L. (2005). Kindergarten children's understanding of and attitudes toward people with disabilities. *Topics in Early Childhood Special Education, 25*(2), 95–105. https://doi.org/10.1177/02711214050250020601

Dyson, M. W., Olino, T. M., Durbin, C. E., Goldsmith, H. H., Bufferd, S. J., Miller, A. R., & Klein, D. N. (2015). The structural and rank-order stability of temperament in young children based on a laboratory-observational measure. *Psychological Assessment, 27*(4), 1388–1401. https://doi.org/10.1037/pas0000104

Dziewolska, H., & Cautilli, J. (2006). The effects of a motor training package on minimally assisted standing behavior in a three-month-old infant. *The Behavior Analyst Today, 7*(1), 111–120.

East, P. L., Khoo, S. T., Reyes, B. T., & Coughlin, L. (2006). AAP report on pregnancy in adolescents. *Perspectives on Sexual & Reproductive Health, 10*, 12p.

Easterbrooks, M. A., Bartlett, J. D., Beeghly, M., & Thompson, R. A. (2012). Social and emotional development in infancy. In I. B. Weiner, R. M. Lerner, M. A. Easterbrooks, & J. Mistry (Eds.), *Handbook of psychology, developmental psychology* (p. 752). Hoboken, NJ: John Wiley & Sons.

Easterbrooks, M. A., Chaudhuri, J. H., Bartlett, J. D., & Copeman, A. (2011). Resilience in parenting among young mothers: Family and ecological risks and opportunities. *Children and Youth Services Review, 33*(1), 42–50. https://doi.org/10.1016/j.childyouth.2010.08.010

Eccles, J. S., & Roeser, R. W. (2011). Schools as developmental contexts during adolescence. *Journal of Research on Adolescence, 21*(1), 225–241. https://doi.org/10.1111/j.1532-7795.2010.00725.x

Eccles, J. S., & Roeser, R. W. (2015). School and community influences on human development. In M. H. Bornstein & M. E. Lamb (Eds.), *Developmental science: An advanced textbook* (7th ed., pp. 645–727). New York, NY: Psychology Press.

Eccles, J. S., & Wang, M.-T. (2016). What motivates females and males to pursue careers in mathematics and science? *International Journal of Behavioral Development, 40*(2), 100–106. https://doi.org/10.1177/0165025415616201

Eckerman, C. O., Hsu, H. C., Molitor, A., Leung, E. H. L., & Goldstein, R. F. (1999). Infant arousal as an en-face exchange with a new partner: Effects of prematurity and perinatal biological risk. *Developmental Psychology, 35*, 282–293.

Education Commission of the States. (2014). *Child must attend kindergarten*. Retrieved from https://www.ecs.org

Edwards, C. P. (2000). Children's play in cross-cultural perspective: A new look at the six cultures study. *Cross-Cultural Research, 34*(4), 318.

Ehmke, T., Drechsel, B., & Carstensen, C. H. (2010). Effects of grade retention on achievement and self-concept in science and mathematics. *Studies in Educational Evaluation, 36*(1/2), 27–35. https://doi.org/10.1016/j.stueduc.2010.10.003

Eichas, K., Ferrer-Wreder, L., & Olsson, T. M. (2019). Contributions of positive youth development to intervention science. *Child & Youth Care Forum, 48*(2), 279–287. https://doi.org/10.1007/s10566-018-09486-1

Eigsti, I.-M., Weitzman, C., Schuh, J., de Marchena, A., & Casey, B. J. (2011). Language and cognitive outcomes in internationally adopted children. *Development and Psychopathology, 23*(02), 629–646. https://doi.org/10.1017/S0954579411000204

Eisbach, A. O. (2004). Children's developing awareness of diversity in people's trains of thoughts. *Child Development, 75*(6), 1694–1707.

Eisenberg, N., Cumberland, A., Guthrie, I. K., Murphy, B. C., & Shepard, S. A. (2005). Age changes in prosocial responding and moral reasoning in adolescence and early adulthood. *Journal of Research on Adolescence, 15*(3), 235–260. https://doi.org/10.1111/j.1532-7795.2005.00095.x

Eisenberg, N., Haugen, R., Spinrad, T. L., Hofer, C., Chassin, L., Qing, Z., . . . Liew, J. (2010). Relations of temperament to maladjustment and ego resiliency in at-risk children. *Social Development, 19*(3), 577–600. https://doi.org/10.1111/j.1467-9507.2009.00550.x

Eisenberg, N., Spinrad, T. L., & Knafo-Noam, A. (2015). Prosocial development. In *Handbook of child psychology and developmental science* (pp. 1–47). Hoboken, NJ: John Wiley & Sons. https://doi.org/10.1002/9781118963418.childpsy315

Eisenberg, N., Spinrad, T. L., & Morris, A. S. (2013). Prosocial development. In P. D. Zelazo (Ed.), *The Oxford handbook of developmental psychology: Vol. 2. Self and other* (pp. 300–324). New York, NY: Oxford University Press. https://doi.org/10.1093/oxfordhb/9780199958474.013.0013

Eisenberg, S. L., Guo, L.-Y., & Germezia, M. (2012). How grammatical are 3-year-olds? *Language, Speech, and Hearing Services in Schools, 43*(1), 36–52. https://doi.org/10.1044/0161-1461(2011/10-0093)

Eisner, M. P., & Malti, T. (2015). Aggressive and violent behavior. In *Handbook of child psychology and developmental science* (pp. 1–48). Hoboken, NJ: John Wiley & Sons. https://doi.org/10.1002/9781118963418.childpsy319

El Hassan, K. (2008). Identifying indicators of student development in college. *College Student Journal, 42*(2), 517–530.

El Marroun, H., Brown, Q. L., Lund, I. O., Coleman-Cowger, V. H., Loree, A. M., Chawla, D., & Washio, Y. (2018). An epidemiological, developmental and clinical overview of cannabis use during pregnancy. *Preventive Medicine, 116*, 1–5. https://doi.org/10.1016/J.YPMED.2018.08.036

El Marroun, H., Tiemeier, H., Franken, I. H. A., Jaddoe, V. W. V., van der Lugt, A., Verhulst, F. C., . . . White, T. (2016). Prenatal cannabis and tobacco exposure in relation to brain morphology: A prospective neuroimaging study in young children. *Biological Psychiatry, 79*(12), 971–979. https://doi.org/10.1016/J.BIOPSYCH.2015.08.024

Elder, G. H., Jr., Shanahan, M. J., & Jennings, J. A. (2016). Human development in time and place. In M. H. Bornstein & T. Leventhal (Eds.), *Handbook of child psychology: Vol. 4. Ecological settings and processes* (7th ed., pp. 6–54). Hoboken, NJ: John Wiley & Sons, Inc.

Elkind, D., & Bowen, R. (1979). Imaginary audience behavior in children and adolescents. *Developmental Psychology, 15*(1), 38–44.

Ellemers, N. (2018). Gender stereotypes. *Annual Review of Psychology, 69*(1), 275–298. https://doi.org/10.1146/annurev-psych-122216-011719

Ellis, A. E., Xiao, N. G., Lee, K., & Oakes, L. M. (2017). Scanning of own- versus other-race faces in infants from racially diverse or homogenous communities. *Developmental Psychobiology, 59*(5), 613–627. https://doi.org/10.1002/dev.21527

Ellis, B. J., Bianchi, J., Griskevicius, V., & Frankenhuis, W. E. (2017). Beyond risk and protective factors: An adaptation-based approach to resilience. *Perspectives on Psychological Science, 12*(4), 561–587. https://doi.org/10.1177/1745691617693054

Ellis, K. J., Abrams, S. A., & Wong, W. W. (1997). Body composition of a young, multiethnic female population. *American Journal of Clinical Nutrition, 65*, 724–731.

Ellis, W. E., & Zarbatany, L. (2017). Understanding processes of peer clique influence in late childhood and early adolescence. *Child Development Perspectives, 11*(4), 227–232. https://doi.org/10.1111/cdep.12248

Elsabbagh, M., Hohenberger, A., Campos, R., Van Herwegen, J., Serres, J., de Schonen, S., . . . Karmiloff-Smith, A. (2013). Narrowing perceptual sensitivity to the native language in infancy: Exogenous influences on developmental timing. *Behavioral Sciences, 3*(1), 120–132. https://doi.org/10.3390/bs3010120

Else-Quest, N. M., Higgins, A., Allison, C., & Morton, L. C. (2012). Gender differences in self-conscious emotional experience: A meta-analysis. *Psychological Bulletin, 138*(5), 947–981. https://doi.org/10.1037/a0027930

Else-Quest, N. M., Hyde, J. S., Goldsmith, H. H., & Van Hulle, C. A. (2006). Gender differences in temperament: A meta-analysis. *Psychological Bulletin, 132*(1), 33–72. https://doi.org/10.1037/0033-2909.132.1.33

El-Sheikh, M., & Kelly, R. J. (2017). Family functioning and children's sleep. *Child Development Perspectives, 11*(4), 264–269. https://doi.org/10.1111/cdep.12243

Emmanuel, M., & Bokor, B. R. (2017). Tanner stages. *StatPearls*. Retrieved from http://www.ncbi.nlm.nih.gov/pubmed/29262142

Emond, J. A., Tantum, L. K., Gilbert-Diamond, D., Kim, S. J., Lansigan, R. K., & Neelon, S. B. (2018). Household chaos and screen media use among preschool-aged children: A cross-sectional study. *BMC Public Health, 18*(1), 1210. https://doi.org/10.1186/s12889-018-6113-2

Endendijk, J. J., Groeneveld, M. G., van der Pol, L. D., van Berkel, S. R., Hallers-Haalboom, E. T., Bakermans-Kranenburg, M. J., & Mesman, J. (2017). Gender differences in child aggression: Relations with gender-differentiated parenting and parents' gender-role stereotypes. *Child Development, 88*(1), 299–316. https://doi.org/10.1111/cdev.12589

England, D. E., Descartes, L., & Collier-Meek, M. A. (2011). Gender role portrayal and the Disney princesses. *Sex Roles, 64*(7–8), 555–567. https://doi.org/10.1007/s11199-011-9930-7

Englund, K., & Behne, D. (2006). Changes in infant directed speech in the first six months. *Infant & Child Development, 15*, 139–160.

Englund, M. M., Siebenbruner, J., Oliva, E. M., Egeland, B., Chung, C.-T., & Long, J. D. (2013). The developmental significance of late adolescent substance use for early adult functioning. *Developmental Psychology, 49*(8), 1554–1564. https://doi.org/10.1037/a0030229

Enlow, M. B., King, L., Schreier, H. M., Howard, J. M., Rosenfield, D., Ritz, T., & Wright, R. J. (2014). Maternal sensitivity and infant autonomic and endocrine stress responses. *Early Human Development, 90*(7), 377–385. https://doi.org/10.1016/J.EARLHUMDEV.2014.04.007

Ennouri, K., & Bloch, H. (1996). Visual control of hand approach movements in newborns. *British Journal of Developmental Psychology, 14*(3), 327–338. https://doi.org/10.1111/j.2044-835X.1996.tb00709.x

Enright, R. D., Bjerstedt, Å., Enright, W. F., Levy, Jr., V. M., Lapsley, D. K., Buss, R. R., . . . Zindler, M. (1984). Distributive justice development: Cross-cultural, contextual, and longitudinal evaluations. *Child Development, 55*(5), 1737. https://doi.org/10.1111/1467-8624.ep7304494

Entwisle, D. R., Alexander, K. L., & Steffel Olson, L. (2005). First grade and educational attainment by age 22: A new story. *American Journal of Sociology, 110*(5), 1458–1502.

Erdley, C. A., & Day, H. J. (2017). Friendship in childhood and adolescence. In M. Hojjat & A. Moyer (Eds.), *The psychology of friendship* (pp. 3–19). Oxford University Press.

Ericsson, K. A., & Moxley, J. H. (2013). Experts' superior memory: From accumulation of chunks to building memory skills that mediate improved performance and learning. In T. J. Perfect & D. S. Lindsay (Eds.), *The SAGE handbook of applied memory* (pp. 404–420). Thousand Oaks, CA: Sage.

Erikson, E. H. (1950). *Childhood and society* (2nd ed.). New York, NY: Norton.

Errisuriz, V. L., Golaszewski, N. M., Born, K., & Bartholomew, J. B. (2018). Systematic review of physical education-based physical activity interventions among elementary school children. *Journal of Primary Prevention, 39*(3), 303–327. https://doi.org/10.1007/s10935-018-0507-x

Eryigit Madzwamuse, S., Baumann, N., Jaekel, J., Bartmann, P., & Wolke, D. (2015). Neuro-cognitive performance of very preterm or very low birth weight adults at 26 years. *Journal of Child Psychology and Psychiatry, 56*(8), 857–864. https://doi.org/10.1111/jcpp.12358

Esakky, P., & Moley, K. H. (2016). Paternal smoking and germ cell death: A mechanistic link to the effects of cigarette smoke on spermatogenesis and possible long-term sequelae in offspring. *Molecular and Cellular Endocrinology, 435*, 85–93. https://doi.org/10.1016/J.MCE.2016.07.015

Eshraghi, A. A., Liu, G., Kay, S.-I. S., Eshraghi, R. S., Mittal, J., Moshiree, B., & Mittal, R. (2018). Epigenetics and autism spectrum disorder: Is there a correlation? *Frontiers in Cellular Neuroscience, 12*, 78. https://doi.org/10.3389/fncel.2018.00078

Espelage, D. L., Low, S. K., & Jimerson, S. R. (2014). Understanding school climate, aggression, peer victimization, and bully perpetration: Contemporary science, practice, and policy. *School Psychology Quarterly, 29*(3), 233–237.

Espinoza, G., & Juvonen, J. (2011). Perceptions of the school social context across the transition to middle school: Heightened sensitivity among Latino students? *Journal of Educational Psychology, 103*(3), 749–758. https://doi.org/10.1037/a0023811

Esposito, G., Truzzi, A., Setoh, P., Putnick, D. L., Shinohara, K., & Bornstein, M. H. (2017). Genetic predispositions and parental bonding interact to shape adults' physiological responses to social distress. *Behavioural Brain Research, 325*, 156–162. https://doi.org/10.1016/J.BBR.2016.06.042

Esteban-Cornejo, I., Tejero-Gonzalez, C. M., Sallis, J. F., & Veiga, O. L. (2015). Physical activity and cognition in adolescents: A systematic review. *Journal of Science and Medicine in Sport, 18*(5), 534–539. https://doi.org/10.1016/J.JSAMS.2014.07.007

Estes, K. G., & Hurley, K. (2013). Infant-directed prosody helps infants map sounds to meanings. *Infancy, 18*(5), 797–824. https://doi.org/10.1111/infa.12006

Esteve-Gilbert, N., Prieto, P., Balog, H. L., Brentari, D., Davis, B. L., MacNeilage, P. F., . . . Liszkowski, U. (2013). Prosody signals the emergence of intentional communication in the first year of life: Evidence from Catalan-babbling infants. *Journal of Child Language, 40*(5), 919–944. https://doi.org/10.1017/S0305000912000359

Estill, M. S., & Krawetz, S. A. (2016). The epigenetic consequences of paternal exposure to environmental contaminants and reproductive toxicants. *Current Environmental Health Reports, 3*(3), 202–213. https://doi.org/10.1007/s40572-016-0101-4

Ethier, K. A., Harper, C. R., Hoo, E., & Dittus, P. J. (2016). The longitudinal impact of perceptions of parental monitoring on adolescent initiation of sexual activity. *Journal of Adolescent Health, 59*(5), 570–576. https://doi.org/10.1016/j.jadohealth.2016.06.011

Ettekal, I., & Ladd, G. W. (2015). Developmental pathways from childhood aggression-disruptiveness, chronic peer rejection, and deviant friendships to early-adolescent rule breaking. *Child Development, 86*(2), 614–631. https://doi.org/10.1111/cdev.12321

Evans, A., Bagnall, R. D., Duflou, J., & Semsarian, C. (2013). Postmortem review and genetic analysis in sudden infant death syndrome: An 11-year review. *Human Pathology, 44*(9), 1730–1736. https://doi.org/10.1016/j.humpath.2013.01.024

Evans, D. W., Milanak, M. E., Medeiros, B., & Ross, J. L. (2002). Magical beliefs and rituals in young children. *Child Psychiatry and Human Development, 33*, 43–58.

Evans, E. H., Tovée, M. J., Boothroyd, L. G., & Drewett, R. F. (2013). Body dissatisfaction and disordered eating attitudes in 7- to 11-year-old girls: Testing a sociocultural model. *Body Image, 10*(1), 8–15. https://doi.org/10.1016/j.bodyim.2012.10.001

Evans, G. W., & Kim, P. (2013). Childhood poverty, chronic stress, self-regulation, and coping. *Child Development Perspectives, 7*(1), 43–48. https://doi.org/10.1111/cdep.12013

Evans, G. W., Li, D., & Whipple, S. S. (2013). Cumulative risk and child development. *Psychological Bulletin, 139*(6), 1342–1396. https://doi.org/10.1037/a0031808

Evans, J. (1998). "Princesses are not into war 'n things, they always scream and run off": Exploring gender stereotypes in picture books. *Reading, 32*(3), 5–11.

Evans, S. W., Owens, J. S., Wymbs, B. T., & Ray, A. R. (2018). Evidence-based psychosocial treatments for children and adolescents with attention deficit/hyperactivity disorder. *Journal of Clinical Child & Adolescent Psychology, 47*(2), 157–198. https://doi.org/10.1080/15374416.2017.1390757

Evans, S. Z., Simons, L. G., & Simons, R. L. (2014). Factors that influence trajectories of delinquency throughout adolescence. *Journal of Youth and Adolescence, 45*, 156–171. https://doi.org/10.1007/s10964-014-0197-5

Evans-Lacko, S., Takizawa, R., Brimblecombe, N., King, D., Knapp, M., Maughan, B., & Arseneault, L. (2017). Childhood bullying victimization is associated with use of mental health services over five decades: A longitudinal nationally representative cohort study. *Psychological Medicine, 47*(01), 127–135. https://doi.org/10.1017/S0033291716001719

Exner-Cortens, D., Eckenrode, J., & Rothman, E. (2013). Longitudinal associations between teen dating violence victimization and adverse health outcomes. *Pediatrics, 131*(1), 71–78. https://doi.org/10.1542/peds.2012-1029

Fagan, J. F. (2011). Intelligence in infancy. In R. J. Sternberg & S. B. Kaufman (Eds.), *The Cambridge handbook of intelligence* (pp. 130–142). Cambridge University Press.

Fagard, J., Spelke, E., & von Hofsten, C. (2009). Reaching and grasping a moving object in 6-, 8-, and 10-month-old infants: Laterality and performance. *Infant Behavior & Development, 32*(2), 137–146. https://doi.org/10.1016/j.infbeh.2008.12.002

Fakhouri, T. H. I., Hughes, J. P., Brody, D. J., Kit, B. K., & Ogden, C. L. (2013). Physical activity and screen-time viewing among elementary school-aged children in the United States from 2009 to 2010. *JAMA Pediatrics, 167*(3), 223–229. https://doi.org/10.1001/2013.jamapediatrics.122

Falbe, J., Davison, K. K., Franckle, R. L., Ganter, C., Gortmaker, S. L., Smith, L., . . . Taveras, E. M. (2015). Sleep duration, restfulness, and screens in the sleep environment. *Pediatrics, 135*(2), e367–e375. https://doi.org/10.1542/peds.2014-2306

Falbo, T., & Polit, D. F. (1986). Quantitative review of the only child literature: Research evidence and theory development. *Psychological Bulletin, 100*(2), 176–189. https://doi.org/10.1037/0033-2909.100.2.176

Falbo, T., Poston, D. L., Jr.,Triscari, R. S., & Zhang, X. (1997). Self-enhancing illusions among Chinese schoolchildren. *Journal of Cross-Cultural Psychology, 28*, 172–191.

Fallone, M. D., LaGasse, L. L., Lester, B. M., Shankaran, S., Bada, H. S., & Bauer, C. R. (2014). Reactivity and regulation of motor responses in cocaine-exposed infants. *Neurotoxicology and Teratology, 43*, 25–32. https://doi.org/10.1016/j.ntt.2014.02.005

Fan, M., & Jin, Y. (2014). Do neighborhood parks and playgrounds reduce childhood obesity? *American Journal of Agricultural Economics, 96*(1), 26–42. https://doi.org/10.1093/ajae/aat047

Fantz, R. L. (1961). The origin of form perception. *Scientific American, 204*, 66–72.

Farber, D. A., & Beteleva, T. G. (2011). Development of the brain's organization of working memory in young schoolchildren.

Human Physiology, 37(1), 1–13. https://doi.org/10.1134/s0362119710061015

Fareri, D. S., & Delgado, M. R. (2014). Social rewards and social networks in the human brain. *The Neuroscientist, 20*(4), 387–402. https://doi.org/10.1177/1073858414521869

Farooq, M. A., Parkinson, K. N., Adamson, A. J., Pearce, M. S., Reilly, J. K., Hughes, A. R., . . . Reilly, J. J. (2018). Timing of the decline in physical activity in childhood and adolescence: Gateshead Millennium Cohort Study. *British Journal of Sports Medicine, 52*, 1002–1006. https://doi.org/10.1136/bjsports-2016-096933

Farr, R. H. (2017). Does parental sexual orientation matter? A longitudinal follow-up of adoptive families with school-age children. *Developmental Psychology, 53*(2), 252–264. https://doi.org/10.1037/dev0000228

Farrington, D. P., & Loeber, R. (2000). Epidemiology of juvenile violence. *Juvenile Violence, 9*, 733–748.

Farroni, T., & Menon, E. (2008). Visual perception and early brain development. In R. E. Tremblay, R. G. Barr, R. DeV. Peters, & M. Boivin (Eds.), *Encyclopedia on early childhood development* (pp. 1–6). Montreal, Quebec, Canada: Centre of Excellence for Early Childhood Development. Retrieved from http://www.child-encyclopedia.com/documents/Farroni-MenonANGxp.pdf

Farroni, T., Menon, E., Rigato, S., & Johnson, M. H. (2007). The perception of facial expressions in newborns. *European Journal of Developmental Psychology, 4*(1), 2–13. https://doi.org/10.1080/17405620601046832

Farver, J. A. M., Xu, Y., Eppe, S., Fernandez, A., & Schwartz, D. (2005). Community violence, family conflict, and preschoolers' socioemotional functioning. *Developmental Psychology, 41*, 160–170.

Fast, A. A., & Olson, K. R. (2018). Gender development in transgender preschool children. *Child Development, 89*(2), 620–637. https://doi.org/10.1111/cdev.12758

Fauser, B. C. J. M., Devroey, P., Diedrich, K., Balaban, B., Bonduelle, M., Delemarre-van de Waal, H. A., . . . Wells, D. (2014). Health outcomes of children born after IVF/ICSI: A review of current expert opinion and literature. *Reproductive BioMedicine Online, 28*(2), 162–182. https://doi.org/10.1016/J.RBMO.2013.10.013

Fay-Stammbach, T., Hawes, D. J., & Meredith, P. (2014). Parenting influences on executive function in early childhood: A review. *Child Development Perspectives, 8*(4), 258–264. https://doi.org/10.1111/cdep.12095

Federal Bureau of Investigation. (2015). *Crime in the United States, 2015*. Washington, DC: Author.

Federal Interagency Forum on Child and Family Statistics. (2014). *America's children: Key national indicators of well-being, 2013*. Retrieved from https://www.childstats.gov/pdf/ac2013/ac_13.pdf

Federal Interagency Forum on Child and Family Statistics. (2017). *America's children: Key national indicators of well-being, 2017*. Retrieved from https://www.childstats.gov/pdf/ac2017/ac_17.pdf

Fedewa, A. L., Black, W. W., & Ahn, S. (2014). Children and adolescents with same-gender parents: A meta-analytic approach in assessing outcomes. *Journal of GLBT Family Studies, 11*(1), 1–34. https://doi.org/10.1080/1550428X.2013.869486

Feeney, B. C., & Monin, J. K. (2016). Divorce through the lens of attachment theory. In J. Shaver & P. R. Cassidy (Eds.), *Handbook of attachment: Theory, research, and clinical applications* (pp. 941–965). New York, NY: Guilford.

Feigelman, S., & Keane, V. (2017). Failure to thrive. In R. Kliegman, P. S. Lye, B. J. Bordini, H. Toth, & D. Basel (Eds.), *Nelson pediatric symptom-based diagnosis* (p. 896). Philadelphia, PA: Elsevier.

Feigenson, L., & Carey, S. (2003). Tracking individuals via object-files: Evidence from infants' manual search. *Developmental Science, 6*(5), 568–584. https://doi.org/10.1111/1467-7687.00313

Feinberg, M. E., Solmeyer, A. R., & McHale, S. M. (2012). The third rail of family systems: Sibling relationships, mental and behavioral health, and preventive intervention in childhood and adolescence. *Clinical Child and Family Psychology Review, 15*(1), 43–57. https://doi.org/10.1007/s10567-011-0104-5

Feldman, P. J., Dunkel-Schetter, C., Sandman, C. A., & Wadhwa, P. D. (2000). Maternal social support predicts birth weight and fetal growth in human pregnancy. *Psychosomatic Medicine, 62*, 715–725.

Feldman, R. (2003). Infant–mother and infant–father synchrony: The coregulation of positive arousal. *Infant Mental Health Journal, 24*(1), 1–23. https://doi.org/10.1002/imhj.10041

Feldman, R., Dollberg, D., & Nadam, R. (2011). The expression and regulation of anger in toddlers: Relations to maternal behavior and mental representations. *Infant Behavior & Development, 34*(2), 310–320. https://doi.org/10.1016/j.infbeh.2011.02.001

Feldstein Ewing, S. W., Sakhardande, A., & Blakemore, S.-J. (2014). The effect of alcohol consumption on the adolescent brain: A systematic review of MRI and fMRI studies of alcohol-using youth. *NeuroImage: Clinical, 5*, 420–437. https://doi.org/10.1016/j.nicl.2014.06.011

Fellmeth, G. L., Heffernan, C., Nurse, J., Habibula, S., & Sethi, D. (2013). Educational and skills-based interventions for preventing relationship and dating violence in adolescents and young adults. *Cochrane Database of Systematic Reviews, 6*, 1465–1858. https://doi.org/10.1002/14651858.CD004534.pub3

Felmlee, D., McMillan, C., Inara Rodis, P., & Osgood, D. W. (2018). Falling behind: Lingering costs of the high school transition for youth friendships and grades. *Sociology of Education, 91*(2), 159–182. https://doi.org/10.1177/0038040718762136

Fenstermacher, S. K., Barr, R., Salerno, K., Garcia, A., Shwery, C. E., Calvert, S. L., & Linebarger, D. L. (2010). Infant-directed media: An analysis of product information and claims. *Infant & Child Development, 19*(6), 556–557. https://doi.org/10.1002/icd.718

Ferguson, C. J., & Donnellan, M. B. (2014). Is the association between children's baby video viewing and poor language development robust? A reanalysis of Zimmerman, Christakis, and Meltzoff (2007). *Developmental Psychology, 50*(1), 129–137. https://doi.org/10.1037/a0033628

Ferguson, G. M., Hafen, C. A., & Laursen, B. (2010). Adolescent psychological and academic adjustment as a function of discrepancies between actual and ideal self-perceptions. *Journal of Youth and Adolescence, 39*(12), 1485–1497. https://doi.org/10.1007/s10964-009-9461-5

Ferguson, R. F., & Lamback, S. (2014). *Creating pathways to prosperity: A blueprint for action. Report issued by the Pathways to Prosperity Project at the Harvard Graduate School of Education and the Achievement Gap Initiative at Harvard University.* Retrieved from http://www.agi.harvard.edu/pathways/CreatingPathwaystoProsperityReport2014.pdf

Fergusson, D. M., Boden, J. M., Horwood, L. J., Miller, A. L., & Kennedy, M. A. (2011). MAOA, abuse exposure and antisocial behaviour: 30-year longitudinal study. *British Journal of Psychiatry, 198*(6), 457–463. https://doi.org/10.1192/bjp.bp.110.086991

Fergusson, D. M., & Horwood, L. J. (2002). Male and female offending trajectories. *Development and Psychopathology, 14*(1), 159–177.

Fergusson, D. M., McLeod, G. F. H., & Horwood, L. J. (2013). Childhood sexual abuse and adult developmental outcomes: Findings from a 30-year longitudinal study in New Zealand. *Child Abuse & Neglect, 37*(9), 664–674. https://doi.org/10.1016/j.chiabu.2013.03.013

Fergusson, D. M., Woodward, L. J., & Horwood, L. J. (2000). Risk factors and life processes associated with the onset of suicidal behaviour during adolescence and early adulthood. *Psychological Medicine, 30*, 23–39.

Ferjan Ramirez, N., Ramirez, R. R., Clarke, M., Taulu, S., & Kuhl, P. K. (2017). Speech discrimination in 11-month-old bilingual and monolingual infants: A magnetoencephalography study. *Developmental Science, 20*(1), e12427. https://doi.org/10.1111/desc.12427

Fernald, A., Marchman, V. A., & Weisleder, A. (2013). SES differences in language processing skill and vocabulary are evident at 18 months. *Developmental Science, 16*(2), 234–248. https://doi.org/10.1111/desc.12019

Fernald, A. & Morikawa, H. (1993). Common themes and cultural variations in Japanese and American mothers' speech to infants. *Child Development, 64*, 657–674.

Fetters, L., & Huang, H. (2007). Motor development and sleep, play, and feeding positions in very-low-birthweight infants with and without white matter disease. *Developmental Medicine & Child Neurology, 49*(11), 807–813. https://doi.org/10.1111/j.1469-8749.2007.00807.x

Field, T. (2011). Prenatal depression effects on early development: A review. *Infant Behavior & Development, 34*(1), 1–14. https://doi.org/10.1016/j.infbeh.2010.09.008

Figner, B., Mackinlay, R. J., Wilkening, F., & Weber, E. U. (2009). Affective and deliberative processes in risky choice: Age differences in risk taking in the Columbia Card Task. *Journal of Experimental Psychology: Learning, Memory, and Cognition, 35*(3), 709–730. https://doi.org/10.1037/a0014983

Figueiredo, B., Dias, C. C., Pinto, T. M., & Field, T. (2016). Infant sleep-wake behaviors at two weeks, three and six months. *Infant Behavior and Development, 44*, 169–178. https://doi.org/10.1016/J.INFBEH.2016.06.011

Fildes, A., Llewellyn, C., Van Jaarsveld, C. H. M., Fisher, A., Cooke, L., & Wardle, J. (2014). Common genetic architecture underlying food fussiness in children, and preference for fruits and vegetables. *Appetite, 76*, 200. https://doi.org/10.1016/j.appet.2014.01.023

Filiano, J. J., & Kinney, H. C. (1994). A perspective on neuropathologic findings in victims of the sudden infant death syndrome: The triple-risk model. *Neonatology, 65*(3–4), 194–197. https://doi.org/10.1159/000244052

Filippova, E., & Astington, J. W. (2008). Further development in social reasoning revealed in discourse irony understanding. *Child Development, 79*(1), 126–138.

Finegold, D. N. (2017). Overview of genetics. *Merck Manual*. Retrieved from http://www.merckmanuals.com/professional/special-subjects/general-principles-of-medical-genetics/overview-of-genetics

Fink, E., Begeer, S., Peterson, C. C., Slaughter, V., & de Rosnay, M. (2015). Friendlessness and theory of mind: A prospective longitudinal study. *British Journal of Developmental Psychology, 33*(1), 1–17. https://doi.org/10.1111/bjdp.12060

Fink, E., Patalay, P., Sharpe, H., & Wolpert, M. (2018). Child- and school-level predictors of children's bullying behavior: A multilevel analysis in 648 primary schools. *Journal of Educational Psychology, 110*(1), 17–26. https://doi.org/10.1037/edu0000204

Fink, S. K., Racine, E. F., Mueffelmann, R. E., Dean, M. N., & Herman-Smith, R. (2014). Family meals and diet quality among children and adolescents in North Carolina. *Journal of Nutrition Education and Behavior, 46*(5), 418–422. https://doi.org/10.1016/J.JNEB.2014.05.004

Finkelhor, D., Ormrod, R. K., & Turner, H. A. (2009). The developmental epidemiology of childhood victimization. *Journal of Interpersonal Violence, 24*(5), 711–731.

Finkelhor, D., Shattuck, A., Turner, H. A., & Hamby, S. L. (2014). The lifetime prevalence of child sexual abuse and sexual assault assessed in late adolescence. *Journal of Adolescent Health, 55*(3), 329–333. https://doi.org/10.1016/j.jadohealth.2013.12.026

Finn, A. S., Minas, J. E., Leonard, J. A., Mackey, A. P., Salvatore, J., Goetz, C., . . . Gabrieli, J. D. E. (2017). Functional brain organization of working memory in adolescents varies in relation to family income and academic achievement. *Developmental Science, 20*(5), e12450. https://doi.org/10.1111/desc.12450

Fischer, M. J. (2007). Settling into campus life: Differences by race/ethnicity in college involvement and outcomes. *Journal of Higher Education, 78*, 125–161.

Fischer, U., Suggate, S. P., Schmirl, J., & Stoeger, H. (2018). Counting on fine motor skills: Links between preschool finger dexterity and numerical skills. *Developmental Science, 21*(4), e12623. https://doi.org/10.1111/desc.12623

Fisher, H. L., Moffitt, T. E., Houts, R. M., Belsky, D. W., Arseneault, L., & Caspi, A. (2012). Bullying victimisation and risk of self harm in early adolescence: Longitudinal cohort study. *BMJ (Clinical Research Ed.), 344*(apr26_2), e2683. https://doi.org/10.1136/bmj.e2683

Fisher, S. E. (2017). Evolution of language: Lessons from the genome. *Psychonomic Bulletin & Review, 24*(1), 34–40. https://doi.org/10.3758/s13423-016-1112-8

Fite, P. J., Hendrickson, M., Rubens, S. L., Gabrielli, J., & Evans, S. (2013). The role of peer rejection in the link between reactive aggression and academic performance. *Child & Youth Care Forum, 42*(3), 193–205. https://doi.org/10.1007/s10566-013-9199-9

Fitneva, S. A., & Matsui, T. (2015). The emergence and development of language across cultures. In L. A. Jensen (Ed.), *The Oxford handbook of human development and culture*. Oxford, England: Oxford University Press. https://doi.org/10.1093/oxfordhb/9780199948550.013.8

Fitzpatrick, M., & McPherson, B. (2010). Coloring within the lines: Gender stereotypes in contemporary coloring books. *Sex Roles, 62*(1/2), 127–137. https://doi.org/10.1007/s11199-009-9703-8

Fitzsimmons, P., Leddy, D., Johnson, L., Biggam, S., & Locke, S. (2013). The moon challenge. *Science and Children, 051*(01), 36–41. https://doi.org/10.2505/4/sc13_051_01_36

Fivush, R. (2011). The development of autobiographical memory. *Annual Review of Psychology, 62*, 559–582. https://doi.org/10.1146/annurev.psych.121208.131702

Fivush, R., Hudson, J., & Nelson, K. (1983). Children's long-term memory for a novel event: An exploratory study. *Merrill-Palmer Quarterly, 30*, 303–316.

Flak, A. L., Su, S., Bertrand, J., Denny, C. H., Kesmodel, U. S., & Cogswell, M. E. (2014). The association of mild, moderate, and binge prenatal alcohol exposure and child neuropsychological outcomes: A meta-analysis. *Alcoholism: Clinical and Experimental Research, 38*(1), 214–226. https://doi.org/10.1111/acer.12214

Flanagan, C. A., Kim, T., Collura, J., & Kopish, M. A. (2015). Community service and adolescents' social capital. *Journal of Research on Adolescence, 25*(2), 295–309. https://doi.org/10.1111/jora.12137

Flanagan, D. P., & Alfonso, V. C. (2017). *Essentials of WISC-V assessment*. Hoboken, NJ: John Wiley & Sons, Inc.

Flanders, J. L., Leo, V., Paquette, D., Pihl, R. O., & Séguin, J. R. (2009). Rough-and-tumble play and the regulation of aggression: An observational study of father–child play dyads. *Aggressive Behavior, 35*(4), 285–295. https://doi.org/10.1002/ab.20309

Flannery, D. J., Hussey, D., & Jefferis, E. (2005). Adolescent delinquency and violent behavior. In T. P. Gullotta & G. R. Adams (Eds.), *Handbook of adolescent behavioral problems: Evidence-based approaches to prevention and treatment* (pp. 415–438). New York, NY: Springer Science + Business Media.

Flannery, K. M., & Smith, R. L. (2017). The effects of age, gender, and gender role ideology on adolescents' social perspective-taking ability and tendency in friendships. *Journal of Social and Personal Relationships, 34*(5), 617–635. https://doi.org/10.1177/0265407516650942

Flatt, T. (2005). The evolutionary genetics of canalization. *Quarterly Review of Biology, 80*(3), 287–316.

Flavell, J. H. (1992). Cognitive development: Past, present, and future. *Developmental Psychology, 28*, 998–1005.

Flavell, J. H. (1993). The development of children's understanding of false belief and the appearance-reality distinction. *International Journal of Psychology, 28*, 595–604.

Flavell, J. H. (1999). Cognitive development: Children's knowledge about the mind. *Annual Review of Psychology, 50*, 21–45.

Flavell, J. H., Everett, B. H., Croft, K., & Flavell, E. R. (1981). Young children's knowledge about visual perception: Further evidence for the level 1-level 2 distinction. *Developmental Psychology, 17*, 99–103.

Flavell, J. H., Green, F. L., & Flavell, E. R. (1986). Development of knowledge about the appearance-reality distinction. *Monographs of the Society for Research in Child Development, 51*(1, Serial No. 212).

Flavell, J. H., Green, F. L., & Flavell, E. R. (1995). Young children's knowledge about thinking. *Monographs of the Society for Research in Child Development, 60*(1, Serial No. 243), i–113.

Flieller, A. (1999). Comparison of the development of formal thought in adolescent cohorts aged 10 to 15 (1967–1996). *Developmental Psychology, 35*(4), 1048–1058. https://doi.org/10.1037/0012-1649.35.4.1048

Floccia, C., Christophe, A., & Bertoncini, J. (1997). High-amplitude sucking and newborns: The quest for underlying mechanisms. *Journal of Experimental Child Psychology, 64*, 175–198.

Floyd, F. J., & Bakeman, R. (2006). Coming-out across the life course: Implications of age and historical context. *Archives of Sexual Behavior, 35*(3), 287–296. https://doi.org/10.1007/s10508-006-9022-x

Flynn, J. R. (1987). Massive IQ gains in 14 nations: What IQ tests really measure. *Psychological Bulletin of the World Health Organization, 101*, 171–191.

Flynn, J. R. (1998). IQ gains over time: Toward finding the causes. In I. U. Neisser (Ed.), *The rising curve: Long-term gains in IQ and related measures* (pp. 25–66). Washington, DC: American Psychological Association.

Flynn, J. R., & Weiss, L. G. (2007). American IQ gains from 1932 to 2002: The WISC subtests and educational progress. *International Journal of Testing, 7*(2), 209–224. https://doi.org/10.1080/15305050701193587

Fogel, A. (2007). *Infancy: Infant, family, and society* (7th ed.). Cornwall-on-Hudson, NY: Sloan Educational Publishing.

Font, S. A., & Berger, L. M. (2014). Child maltreatment and children's developmental trajectories in early to middle childhood. *Child Development, 86*(2), 536–556. https://doi.org/10.1111/cdev.12322

Forestell, C. A. (2016). The development of flavor perception and acceptance: The roles of nature and nurture. *Nestle Nutrition Institute Workshop Series, 85*, 135–143. https://doi.org/10.1159/000439504

Forrest, L. N., Zuromski, K. L., Dodd, D. R., & Smith, A. R. (2017). Suicidality in adolescents and adults with binge-eating disorder: Results from the national comorbidity survey replication and adolescent supplement. *International Journal of Eating Disorders, 50*(1), 40–49. https://doi.org/10.1002/eat.22582

Fortenberry, J. D. (2013). Puberty and adolescent sexuality. *Hormones and Behavior, 64*(2), 280–287. https://doi.org/10.1016/j.yhbeh.2013.03.007

Foshee, V. A., McNaughton Reyes, H. L., Vivolo-Kantor, A. M., Basile, K. C., Chang, L.-Y., Faris, R., & Ennett, S. T. (2014). Bullying as a longitudinal predictor of adolescent dating violence. *Journal of Adolescent Health, 55*(3), 439–444. https://doi.org/10.1016/j.jadohealth.2014.03.004

Foshee, V. A., McNaughton Reyes, L., Tharp, A. T., Chang, L.-Y., Ennett, S. T., Simon, T. R., . . . Suchindran, C. (2015). Shared longitudinal predictors of physical peer and dating violence. *Journal of Adolescent Health, 56*(1), 106–112. https://doi.org/10.1016/j.jadohealth.2014.08.003

Fowler, P. J., Tompsett, C. J., Braciszewski, J. M., Jacques-Tiura, A. J., & Baltes, B. B. (2009). Community violence: A meta-analysis on the effect of exposure and mental health outcomes of children and adolescents. *Development and Psychopathology, 21*(1), 227–259. https://doi.org/10.1017/s0954579409000145

Fox, K. A., & Saade, G. (2012). Fetal blood sampling and intrauterine transfusion. *NeoReviews, 13*(11), e661–e669. https://doi.org/10.1542/neo.13-11-e661

Fracasso, M. P., & Busch-Rossnagel, N. A. (1992). Children and parents of Hispanic origin. In M. E. Procidano & C. B. Fisher (Eds.), *Families: A handbook for school professionals* (pp. 83–98). New York, NY: Teachers College Press.

Fraga, L. R., Diamond, A. J., Vargesson, N., Fraga, L. R., Diamond, A. J., & Vargesson, N. (2016). Thalidomide and birth defects. In *eLS* (pp. 1–11). Chichester, England: John Wiley & Sons, Ltd. https://doi.org/10.1002/9780470015902.a0026052

Frahsek, S., Mack, W., Mack, C., Pfalz-Blezinger, C., & Knopf, M. (2010). Assessing different aspects of pretend play within a play setting: Towards a standardized assessment of pretend play in young children. *British Journal of Developmental Psychology, 28*(2), 331–345. https://doi.org/10.1348/026151009x413666

Franić, S., Dolan, C. V., Broxholme, J., Hu, H., Zemojtel, T., Davies, G. E., . . . Boomsma, D. I. (2015). Mendelian and polygenic inheritance of intelligence: A common set of causal genes? Using next-generation sequencing to examine the effects of 168 intellectual disability genes on normal-range intelligence. *Intelligence, 49*, 10–22. https://doi.org/10.1016/j.intell.2014.12.001

Frank, M. C., Vul, E., & Johnson, S. P. (2009). Development of infants' attention to faces during the first year. *Cognition, 110*(2), 160–170. https://doi.org/10.1016/j.cognition.2008.11.010

Frankel, L. L. (2002). "I've never thought about it": Contradictions and taboos surrounding American males' experiences of first ejaculation (semenarche). *Journal of Men's Studies, 11*(1), 37–54.

Frankenhuis, W. E., & Tiokhin, L. (2018). Bridging evolutionary biology and developmental psychology: Toward an enduring theoretical infrastructure. *Child Development*. https://doi.org/10.1111/cdev.13021

Frawley, T. J. (2008). Gender schema and prejudicial recall: How children misremember, fabricate, and distort gendered picture book information. *Journal of Research in Childhood Education, 22*(3), 291–303.

Frazier-Wood, A. C., Banfield, E. C., Liu, Y., Davis, J. S., & Chang, S. (2015). Poor adherence to US dietary guidelines for children and adolescents in the National Health and Nutrition Examination Survey (NHANES) 2005–2010 population [Abstract]. *Circulation, 131*(Suppl. 1), 27. Retrieved from http://circ.ahajournals.org/content/131/Suppl_1/A27.short

Frederick, C. B., Snellman, K., & Putnam, R. D. (2014). Increasing socioeconomic disparities in adolescent obesity. *Proceedings of the National Academy of Sciences of the United States of America, 111*(4), 1338–1342. https://doi.org/10.1073/pnas.1321355110

Frederickson, N. L., & Simmonds, E. A. (2008). Special needs, relationship type and distributive justice norms in early and later years of middle childhood. *Social Development, 17*(4), 1056–1073. https://doi.org/10.1111/j.1467-9507.2008.00477.x

Frederiksen, L. E., Ernst, A., Brix, N., Braskhøj Lauridsen, L. L., Roos, L., Ramlau-Hansen, C. H., & Ekelund, C. K. (2018). Risk of adverse pregnancy outcomes at advanced maternal age. *Obstetrics & Gynecology, 131*(3), 457–463. https://doi.org/10.1097/AOG.0000000000002504

Freedman, A. L. (2016). The circumcision debate: Beyond benefits and risks. *Pediatrics, 137*(5), e20160594. https://doi.org/10.1542/peds.2016-0594

Freeman, J., & Simonsen, B. (2015). Examining the impact of policy and practice interventions on high school dropout and school completion rates: A systematic review of the literature. *Review of Educational Research, 85*(2), 205–248. https://doi.org/10.3102/0034654314554431

Freeman, N. (2007). Preschoolers' perceptions of gender appropriate toys and their parents' beliefs about genderized behaviors: Miscommunication, mixed messages, or hidden truths? *Early Childhood Education Journal, 34*(5), 357–366. https://doi.org/10.1007/s10643-006-0123-x

French, D. C., & Cheung, H. S. (2018). Peer relationships. In J. E. Lansford & P. Banati (Eds.), *Handbook of adolescent development research and its impact on global policy*. New York, NY: Oxford University Press.

Frey, N. (2005). Retention, social promotion, and academic redshirting: What do we know and need to know? *Remedial and Special Education, 26*(6), 332–346.

Friederici, A. D. (2017). Evolution of the neural language network. *Psychonomic Bulletin & Review, 24*(1), 41–47. https://doi.org/10.3758/s13423-016-1090-x

Friedlmeier, W., Çorapçi, F., & Benga, O. (2015). Early emotional development in cultural perspective. In L. A. Jensen (Ed.), *The Oxford handbook of human development and culture* (pp. 127–148). Oxford, England: Oxford University Press. https://doi.org/10.1093/oxfordhb/9780199948550.013.9

Friedrich, M., Wilhelm, I., Mölle, M., Born, J., & Friederici, A. D. (2017). The sleeping infant brain anticipates development. *Current Biology, 27*(15), 2374–2380. https://doi.org/10.1016/J.CUB.2017.06.070

Frisch, M., Aigrain, Y., Barauskas, V., Bjarnason, R., Boddy, S.-A., Czauderna, P., . . . Wijnen, R. (2013). Cultural bias in the AAP's 2012 technical report and policy statement on male circumcision. *Pediatrics, 131*(4), 796–800. https://doi.org/10.1542/peds.2012-2896

Frodi, A. M., Lamb, M. E., Hwang, C.-P., & Frodi, M. (1983). Father-mother infant interaction in traditional and nontraditional Swedish families: A longitudinal study. *Alternative Lifestyles, 5*(3), 142–163. https://doi.org/10.1007/bf01091325

Frost, J. L., Wortham, S. C., & Reifel, S. C. (2012). *Play and child development*. New York, NY: Pearson.

Frostad, P., Pijl, S. J., & Mjaavatn, P. E. (2014). Losing all interest in school: Social participation as a predictor of the intention to leave upper secondary school early. *Scandinavian Journal of Educational Research, 59*(1), 110–122. https://doi.org/10.1080/00313831.2014.904420

Fry, A. F., & Hale, S. (1996). Processing speed, working memory, and fluid intelligence: Evidence for a developmental cascade. *Psychological Science, 7*, 237–241.

Fryda, C. M., & Hulme, P. A. (2015). School-based childhood sexual abuse prevention programs: An integrative review. *Journal of School Nursing, 31*(3), 167–182. https://doi.org/10.1177/1059840514544125

Fuchs, L. S., Malone, A. S., Schumacher, R. F., Namkung, J., & Wang, A. (2017). Fraction intervention for students with mathematics difficulties: Lessons learned from five randomized controlled trials. *Journal of Learning Disabilities, 50*(6), 631–639. https://doi.org/10.1177/0022219416677249

Fuglset, T. S., Landrø, N. I., Reas, D. L., & Rø, Ø. (2016). Functional brain alterations in anorexia nervosa: A scoping review. *Journal of Eating Disorders, 4*, 32. https://doi.org/10.1186/s40337-016-0118-y

Fuhrmann, D., Knoll, L. J., & Blakemore, S.-J. (2015). Adolescence as a sensitive period of brain development. *Trends in Cognitive Sciences, 19*(10), 558–566. https://doi.org/10.1016/j.tics.2015.07.008

Fuligni, A. J., Arruda, E. H., Krull, J. L., & Gonzales, N. A. (2018). Adolescent sleep duration, variability, and peak levels of achievement and mental health. *Child Development, 89*(2), e18–e28. https://doi.org/10.1111/cdev.12729

Furby, L., & Beyth-Marom, R. (1992). Risk taking in adolescence: A decision-making perspective. *Developmental Review, 12*(1), 1–44.

Furman, W., & Collibee, C. (2014). A matter of timing: Developmental theories of romantic involvement and psychosocial adjustment. *Development and Psychopathology, 26*(4, Pt. 1), 1149–1160. https://doi.org/10.1017/S0954579414000182

Fuss, J., Auer, M. K., & Briken, P. (2015). Gender dysphoria in children and adolescents. *Current Opinion in Psychiatry, 28*(6), 430–434. https://doi.org/10.1097/YCO.0000000000000203

Fuzzell, L., Fedesco, H. N., Alexander, S. C., Fortenberry, J. D., & Shields, C. G. (2016). "I just think that doctors need to ask more questions": Sexual minority and majority adolescents' experiences talking about sexuality with healthcare providers. *Patient Education and Counseling, 99*(9), 1467–1472. https://doi.org/10.1016/J.PEC.2016.06.004

Fuzzell, L., Shields, C. G., Alexander, S. C., & Fortenberry, J. D. (2017). Physicians talking about sex, sexuality, and protection with adolescents. *Journal of Adolescent Health, 61*(1), 6–23. https://doi.org/10.1016/J.JADOHEALTH.2017.01.017

Gabbard, C. P. (2018). *Lifelong motor development* (6th ed.). Philadelphia, PA: Pearson.

Gabbe, S. G., Niebyl, J. R., Simpson, J. L., Landon, M. B., Galan, H. L., Jauniaux, E. R., . . . Grobman, W. A. (2016). *Obstetrics: Normal and problem pregnancies*. Philadelphia, PA: Elsevier.

Gabriel, M. A. M., Alonso, C. R. P., Bértolo, J. D. L. C., Carbonero, S. C., Maestro, M. L., Pumarega, M. M., . . . Pablos, D. L. (2009). Age of sitting unsupported and independent walking in very low birth weight preterm infants with normal motor development at 2 years. *Acta Paediatrica, 98*(11), 1815–1821. https://doi.org/10.1111/j.1651-2227.2009.01475.x

Gaddis, A., & Brooks-Gunn, J. (1985). The male experience of pubertal change. *Journal of Youth and Adolescence, 14*(1), 61–69.

Gagnier, C., & Collin-Vézina, D. (2016). The disclosure experiences of male child sexual abuse survivors. *Journal of Child Sexual Abuse, 25*(2), 221–241. https://doi.org/10.1080/10538712.2016.1124308

Gagnon, S. G., Huelsman, T. J., Reichard, A. E., Kidder-Ashley, P., Griggs, M. S., Struby, J., & Bollinger, J. (2013). Help me play! Parental behaviors, child temperament, and preschool peer play. *Journal of Child and Family Studies, 23*(5), 872–884. https://doi.org/10.1007/s10826-013-9743-0

Gaillard, V., Barrouillet, P., Jarrold, C., & Camos, V. (2011). Developmental differences in working memory: Where do they come from? *Journal of Experimental Child Psychology, 110*(3), 469–479. https://doi.org/10.1016/j.jecp.2011.05.004

Galambos, N. L., Almeida, D. M., & Petersen, A. C. (1990). Masculinity, femininity, and sex role attitudes in early adolescence: Exploring gender intensification. *Child Development, 61*(6), 1905–1914. https://doi.org/10.1111/j.1467-8624.1990.tb03574.x

Galambos, N. L., Berenbaum, S. A., & McHale, S. M. (2009). Gender development in adolescence. In R. M. Lerner & L. Steinberg (Eds.), *Handbook of adolescent psychology* (Vol. 1, pp. 305–357). Hoboken, NJ: John Wiley & Sons. https://doi.org/10.1002/9780470479193.adlpsy001011

Gallagher, A. (2008). *Developing thinking with four and five year old pupils: The impact of a cognitive acceleration programme through early science skill development*. Dublin, Ireland: Dublin City University, Education Department and School of Chemical Sciences.

Galland, B. C., Taylor, B. J., Elder, D. E., & Herbison, P. (2012). Normal sleep patterns in infants and children: A systematic review of observational studies. *Sleep Medicine Reviews, 16*(3), 213–222. https://doi.org/10.1016/J.SMRV.2011.06.001

Galler, J. R., Bryce, C. P., Waber, D., Hock, R. S., Exner, N., Eaglesfield, D., . . . Harrison, R. (2010). Early childhood malnutrition predicts depressive symptoms at ages 11–17. *Journal of Child Psychology & Psychiatry, 51*(7), 789–798. https://doi.org/10.1111/j.1469-7610.2010.02208.x

Galler, J. R., Bryce, C. P., Zichlin, M. L., Fitzmaurice, G., Eaglesfield, G. D., & Waber, D. P. (2012). Infant malnutrition is associated with persisting attention deficits in middle adulthood. *Journal of Nutrition, 142*(4), 788–794. https://doi.org/10.3945/jn.111.145441

Galliher, R. V., Jones, M. D., & Dahl, A. (2011). Concurrent and longitudinal effects of ethnic identity and experiences of discrimination on psychosocial adjustment of Navajo adolescents. *Developmental Psychology, 47*(2), 509–526. https://doi.org/10.1037/a0021061

Galloway, J. C., & Thelen, E. (2004). Feet first: Object exploration in young infants. *Infant Behavior & Development, 27*(1), 107–112.

Galupo, M. P., Davis, K. S., Grynkiewicz, A. L., & Mitchell, R. C. (2014). Conceptualization of sexual orientation identity among sexual minorities: Patterns across sexual and gender identity. *Journal of Bisexuality, 14*(3–4), 433–456. https://doi.org/10.1080/15299716.2014.933466

Ganong, L., & Coleman, M. (2017). Siblings, half-siblings, and stepsiblings. In *Stepfamily relationships* (pp. 191–204). Boston, MA: Springer. https://doi.org/10.1007/978-1-4899-7702-1_10

Ganong, L., Coleman, M., & Russell, L. T. (2015). Children in diverse families. In M. H. Bornstein & T. Leventhal (Eds.), *Handbook of child psychology and developmental science* (pp. 1–42). Hoboken, NJ: John Wiley & Sons. https://doi.org/10.1002/9781118963418.childpsy404

Gao, G. (2015). Americans' ideal family size is smaller than it used to be. *Pew Research Fact Tank*. Retrieved from http://www.pewresearch.org/fact-tank/2015/05/08/ideal-size-of-the-american-family/

Garber, K. J., & Grotevant, H. D. (2015). "*YOU* were adopted?!" *The Counseling Psychologist, 43*(3), 435–462. https://doi.org/10.1177/0011000014566471

Garcia, P. R. J. M., Restubog, S. L. D., Bordia, P., Bordia, S., & Roxas, R. E. O. (2015). Career optimism: The roles of contextual support and career decision-making self-efficacy. *Journal of Vocational Behavior, 88*, 10–18. https://doi.org/10.1016/j.jvb.2015.02.004

Garcia-Sierra, A., Rivera-Gaxiola, M., Percaccio, C. R., Conboy, B. T., Romo, H., Klarman, L., . . . Kuhl, P. K. (2011). Bilingual language learning: An ERP study relating early brain responses to speech, language input, and later word production. *Journal of Phonetics, 39*(4), 546–557. https://doi.org/10.1016/J.WOCN.2011.07.002

Gardiner, H. W., & Kosmitzki, C. (2018). *Lives across cultures: Cross-cultural human development* (6th ed.). Boston, MA: Pearson.

Gardner, H. (2013). *The unschooled mind: How children think and how schools should teach* (Vol. 25). New York, NY: Basic Books.

Gardner, H. (2016). Multiple intelligences: Prelude, theory, and aftermath. In R. J. Sternberg, S. T. Fiske, & D. J. Foss (Eds.), *Scientists making a difference: One hundred eminent behavioral and brain scientists talk about their most important contributions* (pp. 167–170). New York, NY: Cambridge University Press.

Gardner, H. (2017). Taking a multiple intelligences (MI) perspective. *Behavioral and Brain Sciences, 40*, e203. https://doi.org/10.1017/S0140525X16001631

Garg, R., Levin, E., Urajnik, D., & Kauppi, C. (2005). Parenting style and academic achievement for East Indian and Canadian adolescents. *Journal of Comparative Family Studies, 36*(4), 653–661.

Gartstein, M. A., & Iverson, S. (2014). Attachment security: The role of infant, maternal, and contextual factors. *International Journal of Psychology & Psychological Therapy, 14*(2), 261–276.

Gartstein, M. A., Putnam, S. P., Aron, E. N., & Rothbart, M. K. (2016). *Temperament and personality* (S. Maltzman, Ed.) (Vol. 1). Oxford, England: Oxford University Press. https://doi.org/10.1093/oxfordhb/9780199739134.013.2

Gaskins, S. (2014). Children's play as cultural activity. In E. Brooker, M. Blaise, & S. Edwards (Eds.), *SAGE handbook of play and learning in early childhood* (pp. 31–42). Thousand Oaks, CA: Sage.

Gaskins, S., & Paradise, R. (2010). Learning through observation in daily life. In D. F. Lancy, J. Bock, & S. Gaskins (Eds.), *The anthropology of learning in childhood* (pp. 85–117). Walnut Creek, CA: AltaMira Press. Retrieved from https://psycnet.apa.org/record/2010-03678-005

Gass, K., Jenkins, J., & Dunn, J. (2007). Are sibling relationships protective? A longitudinal study. *Journal of Child Psychology & Psychiatry, 48*(2), 167–175.

Gasser, U. E., & Hatten, M. E. (1990). Central nervous system neurons migrate on astroglial fibers from heterotypic brain regions in vitro. *Proceedings of the National Academy of Sciences of the United States of America, 87*(12), 4543-4547. https://doi.org/10.1073/pnas.87.12.4543

Gates, G. J. (2011). *How many people are lesbian, gay, bisexual and transgender?* Retrieved from https://escholarship.org/uc/item/09h684x2

Gates, G. J. (2015). Marriage and family: LGBT individuals and same-sex couples. *The Future of Children, 25*(2), 67–87. https://doi.org/10.1353/foc.2015.0013

Gathercole, S. E., Pickering, S. J., Ambridge, B., & Wearing, H. (2004). A structural analysis of working memory from 4 to 15 years of age. *Developmental Psychology, 40*, 177–190.

Gathercole, V. C. M., & Thomas, E. M. (2009). Bilingual first-language development: Dominant language takeover, threatened minority language take-up. *Bilingualism: Language and Cognition, 12*(2), 213–237. https://doi.org/10.1017/S1366728909004015

Gattario, K. H., Frisén, A., & Anderson-Fye, E. (2014). Body image and child well-being. In A. Ben-Arieh, F. Casas, I. Frønes, & J. E. Korbin (Eds.), *Handbook of child well-being* (pp. 2409–2436). Dordrecht, Netherlands: Springer.

Gaultney, J. F., & Gingras, J. L. (2005). Fetal rate of behavioral inhibition and preference for novelty during infancy. *Early Human Development, 81*(4), 379–386.

Gauvain, M. (2018). From developmental psychologist to water scientist and back again: The role of interdisciplinary research in developmental science. *Child Development Perspectives, 12*(1), 45–50. https://doi.org/10.1111/cdep.12255

Gauvain, M., & Perez, S. (2015). Cognitive development and culture. In L. S. Liben & U. Müller (Eds.), *Handbook of child psychology and developmental science* (pp. 1–43). Hoboken, NJ: John Wiley & Sons. https://doi.org/10.1002/9781118963418.childpsy220

Ge, X., Natsuaki, M. N., Neiderhiser, J. M., & Reiss, D. (2009). The longitudinal effects of stressful life events on adolescent depression are buffered by parent-child closeness. *Development & Psychopathology, 21*(2), 621–635. https://doi.org/10.1017/s0954579409000339

Geier, C. F. (2013). Adolescent cognitive control and reward processing: Implications for risk taking and substance use. *Hormones and Behavior, 64*(2), 333–342. https://doi.org/10.1016/j.yhbeh.2013.02.008

Genesee, F., & Nicoladis, E. (2007). Bilingual first language acquisition. In E. Hoff & M. Shatz (Eds.), *Blackwell handbook of language development* (pp. 324–344). Oxford, England: Blackwell.

Gentile, D. A., Bender, P. K., & Anderson, C. A. (2017). Violent video game effects on salivary cortisol, arousal, and aggressive thoughts in children. *Computers in Human Behavior, 70*, 39–43. https://doi.org/10.1016/j.chb.2016.12.045

Gentle-Genitty, C. (2009). Best practice program for low-income African American students transitioning from middle to high school. *Children & Schools, 31*(2), 109–117.

Georgas, J., Weiss, L. G., van de Vijver, F. J. R., & Saklofske, D. H. (2003). Cross-cultural psychology, intelligence, and cognitive processes. In J. Georgas, L. G. Weiss, F. J. Van de Vijver, & D. H. Saklofske (Eds.), *Culture and children's intelligence: Cross-cultural analysis of the WISC-III* (pp. 23–37). San Diego, CA: Academic Press.

Georgsdottir, I., Haraldsson, A., & Dagbjartsson, A. (2013). Behavior and well-being of extremely low birth weight teenagers in Iceland. *Early Human Development, 89*(12), 999–1003. https://doi.org/10.1016/j.earlhumdev.2013.08.018

Gerhardt, C. (2016). Only children. In *Encyclopedia of family studies* (pp. 1–3). Hoboken, NJ: John Wiley & Sons. https://doi.org/10.1002/9781119085621.wbefs042

Gershkoff-Stowe, L. (2002). Object naming, vocabulary growth, and the development of word retrieval abilities. *Journal of Memory & Language, 46*(4), 665.

Gershoff, E. T. (2013). Spanking and child development: We know enough now to stop hitting our children. *Child Development Perspectives, 7*(3), 133–137. https://doi.org/10.1111/cdep.12038

Gershoff, E. T., & Grogan-Kaylor, A. (2016). Spanking and child outcomes: Old controversies and new meta-analyses. *Journal of Family Psychology, 30*(4), 453–469. https://doi.org/10.1037/fam0000191

Gervain, J., Macagno, F., Cogoi, S., Peña, M., & Mehler, J. (2008). The neonate brain detects speech structure. *Proceedings of the National Academy of Sciences of the United States of America, 105*(37), 14222–14227. https://doi.org/10.1073/pnas.0806530105

Gervain, J., & Mehler, J. (2010). Speech perception and language acquisition in the first year of life. *Annual Review of Psychology, 61*, 191–218. https://doi.org/10.1146/annurev.psych.093008.100408

Gest, S. D., Davidson, A. J., Rulison, K. L., Moody, J., & Welsh, J. A. (2007). Features of groups and status hierarchies in girls' and boys' early adolescent peer networks. *New Directions for Child & Adolescent Development, 2007*(118), 43–60.

Gettler, L. T., & McKenna, J. J. (2011). Evolutionary perspectives on mother-infant sleep proximity and breastfeeding in a laboratory setting. *American Journal of Physical Anthropology, 144*(3), 454–462. https://doi.org/10.1002/ajpa.21426

Geva, R., Yaron, H., & Kuint, J. (2016). Neonatal sleep predicts attention orienting and distractibility. *Journal of Attention Disorders, 20*(2), 138–150. https://doi.org/10.1177/1087054713491493

Ghaddar, S. F., Valerio, M. A., Garcia, C. M., & Hansen, L. (2012). Adolescent health literacy: The importance of credible sources for online health information. *Journal of School Health, 82*, 28–36. Retrieved from https://deepblue.lib.umich.edu/bitstream/handle/2027.42/89464/j.1746-1561.2011.00664.x.pdf?sequence=1&isAllowed=y

Ghassabian, A., Sundaram, R., Bell, E., Bello, S. C., Kus, C., & Yeung, E. (2016). Gross motor milestones and subsequent development. *Pediatrics, 138*(1), e20154372. https://doi.org/10.1542/peds.2015-4372

Ghezzo, A., Salvioli, S., Solimando, M. C., Palmieri, A., Chiostergi, C., Scurti, M., . . . Franceschi, C. (2014). Age-related changes of adaptive and neuropsychological features in persons with Down syndrome. *PLoS ONE, 9*(11), e113111. https://doi.org/10.1371/journal.pone.0113111

Ghosh, J. K. C., Wilhelm, M. H., Dunkel-Schetter, C., Lombardi, C. A., & Ritz, B. R. (2010). Paternal support and preterm birth, and the moderation of effects of chronic stress: A study in Los Angeles County mothers. *Archives of Women's Mental Health, 13*(4), 327–338. https://doi.org/10.1007/s00737-009-0135-9

Giagazoglou, P., Fotiadou, E., Angelopoulou, N., Tsikoulas, J., & Tsimaras, V. (2001). Gross and fine motor skills of left-handed preschool children. *Perceptual and Motor Skills, 92*(3, Suppl.), 1122–1128. https://doi.org/10.2466/pms.2001.92.3c.1122

Gialamas, A., Mittinty, M. N., Sawyer, M. G., Zubrick, S. R., & Lynch, J. (2014). Child care quality and children's cognitive and socio-emotional development: An Australian longitudinal study. *Early Child Development and Care, 184*(7), 977–997. https://doi.org/10.1080/03004430.2013.847835

Gibb, R., & Kovalchuk, A. (2018). Brain development. In R. Gibb & B. Kolb (Eds.), *The neurobiology of brain and behavioral development* (pp. 3–27). Cambridge, MA: Academic Press. https://doi.org/10.1016/B978-0-12-804036-2.00001-7

Gibbs, J. C. (1991). Sociomoral developmental delay and cognitive distortion: Implications for the treatment of antisocial youth. In W. M. Kurtines & J. L. Gewirtz (Eds.), *Handbook of moral behavior and development: Vol. 3. Application* (pp. 95–110). Hillsdale, NJ: Erlbaum.

Gibbs, J. C. (2003). *Moral development and reality: Beyond the theories of Kohlberg and Hoffman.* Thousand Oaks, CA: Sage.

Gibbs, J. C., Basinger, K. S., Grime, R. L., & Snarey, J. R. (2007). Moral judgment development across cultures: Revisiting Kohlberg's universality claims. *Developmental Review, 27*(4), 443–500. https://doi.org/10.1016/j.dr.2007.04.001

Gibson, E. J., & Pick, A. D. (2000). *An ecological approach to perceptual learning and development.* New York, NY: Oxford University Press. Retrieved from http://psycnet.apa.org/psycinfo/2001-18056-000

Gibson, E. J., & Walk, R. D. (1960). The "visual cliff." *Scientific American, 202*, 64–71.

Gibson, J. (1979). *The ecological approach to visual perception.* Boston, MA: Houghton Mifflin. Retrieved from http://psycnet.apa.org/psycinfo/2003-00063-000

Giedd, J. N. (2018). A ripe time for adolescent research. *Journal of Research on Adolescence, 28*(1), 157–159. https://doi.org/10.1111/jora.12378

Giedd, J. N., Lalonde, F. M., Celano, M. J., White, S. L., Wallace, G. L., Lee, N. R., & Lenroot, R. K. (2009). Anatomical brain magnetic resonance imaging of typically developing children and adolescents. *Journal of the American Academy of Child & Adolescent Psychiatry, 48*(5), 465–470. https://doi.org/10.1097/CHI.0b013e31819f215

Gila, A., Castro, J., Cesena, J., & Toro, J. (2005). Anorexia nervosa in male adolescents: Body image, eating attitudes and psychological traits. *Journal of Adolescent Health, 36*, 221–226.

Gilbert, A. N., & Wysocki, C. J. (1992). Hand preference and age in the United States. *Neuropsychologia, 30*(7), 601–608. https://doi.org/10.1016/0028-3932(92)90065-T

Giletta, M., Burk, W. J., Scholte, R. H. J., Engels, R. C. M. E., & Prinstein, M. J. (2013). Direct and indirect peer socialization of adolescent nonsuicidal self-injury. *Journal of Research on Adolescence, 23*(3), 450–463. https://doi.org/10.1111/jora.12036

Gilliard, J. L., & Moore, R. A. (2007). An investigation of how culture shapes curriculum in early care and education programs on a Native American Indian reservation. *Early Childhood Education Journal, 34*(4), 251–258. https://doi.org/10.1007/s10643-006-0136-5

Gilligan, C. (1982). *In a different voice: Psychological theory and women's development.* Cambridge, MA: Harvard University Press.

Gilligan, C., & Attanucci, J. (1988). Two moral orientations: Gender differences and similarities. *Merrill-Palmer Quarterly, 34*(3), 223–237.

Gilmore, C. K., McCarthy, S. E., & Spelke, E. S. (2010). Non-symbolic arithmetic abilities and mathematics achievement in the first year of formal schooling. *Cognition, 115*(3), 394–406. https://doi.org/10.1016/j.cognition.2010.02.002

Gilmore, J. H., Knickmeyer Santelli, R. C., & Gao, W. (2018). Imaging structural and functional brain development in early childhood. *Nature Reviews Neuroscience, 19*(3), 123–137. https://doi.org/10.1038/nrn.2018.1

Gilmore, J. H., Shi, F., Woolson, S. L., Knickmeyer, R. C., Short, S. J., Lin, W., . . . Shen, D. (2012). Longitudinal development of cortical and subcortical gray matter from birth to 2 years. *Cerebral Cortex, 22*(11), 2478–2485. https://doi.org/10.1093/cercor/bhr327

Giménez-Dasí, M., Pons, F., & Bender, P. K. (2016). Imaginary companions, theory of mind and emotion understanding in young children.

European Early Childhood Education Research Journal, 24(2), 186–197. https://doi.org/10.1080/1350293X.2014.919778

Ginsburg, H. P. (1997). *Entering the child's mind: The clinical interview in psychological research & practice.* New York, NY: Cambridge University Press.

Ginsburg, K. R. (2007). The importance of play in promoting healthy child development and maintaining strong parent-child bonds. *Pediatrics, 119*(1), 182–191.

Giofrè, D., Mammarella, I. C., & Cornoldi, C. (2013). The structure of working memory and how it relates to intelligence in children. *Intelligence, 41*(5), 396–406. https://doi.org/10.1016/j.intell.2013.06.006

Gioia, K. A., & Tobin, R. M. (2010). Role of sociodramatic play in promoting self-regulation. In C. E. Schaefer (Ed.), *Play therapy for preschool children* (pp. 181–198). Washington, DC: American Psychological Association. https://doi.org/10.1037/12060-009

Giordano, P. C., Phelps, K. D., Manning, W. D., & Longmore, M. A. (2008). Adolescent academic achievement and romantic relationships. *Social Science Research, 37*(1), 37–54. https://doi.org/10.1016/j.ssresearch.2007.06.004

Giordano, P. C., Soto, D. A., Manning, W. D., & Longmore, M. A. (2010). The characteristics of romantic relationships associated with teen dating violence. *Social Science Research, 39*(6), 863–874. https://doi.org/10.1016/j.ssresearch.2010.03.009

Gjersoe, N. L., Hall, E. L., & Hood, B. (2015). Children attribute mental lives to toys when they are emotionally attached to them. *Cognitive Development, 34*, 28–38. https://doi.org/10.1016/j.cogdev.2014.12.002

Glasson, E. J., Dye, D. E., & Bittles, A. H. (2014). The triple challenges associated with age-related comorbidities in Down syndrome. *Journal of Intellectual Disability Research, 58*(4), 393–398. https://doi.org/10.1111/jir.12026

Gleason, T. R. (2017). The psychological significance of play with imaginary companions in early childhood. *Learning & Behavior, 45*(4), 432–440. https://doi.org/10.3758/s13420-017-0284-z

Gleason, T. R., & Kalpidou, M. (2014). Imaginary companions and young children's coping and competence. *Social Development, 23*(4), 820–839. https://doi.org/10.1111/sode.12078

Gleason, T. R., Sebanc, A. M., & Hartup, W. W. (2000). Imaginary companions of preschool children. *Developmental Psychology, 36*, 419–428.

Glennen, S. (2014). A longitudinal study of language and speech in children who were internationally adopted at different ages. *Language, Speech, and Hearing Services in Schools, 45*(3), 185–203. https://doi.org/10.1044/2014_LSHSS-13-0035

Glennen, S., & Masters, M. (2002). Typical and atypical language development in infants and toddlers adopted from Eastern Europe. *American Journal of Speech-Language Pathology, 11*, 417–433.

Glenwright, M., & Pexman, P. M. (2010). Development of children's ability to distinguish sarcasm and verbal irony. *Journal of Child Language, 37*(2), 429–451. https://doi.org/10.1017/S0305000909009520

Glover, V. (2011). Annual research review: Prenatal stress and the origins of psychopathology: An evolutionary perspective. *Journal of Child Psychology and Psychiatry, 52*(4), 356–367. https://doi.org/10.1111/j.1469-7610.2011.02371.x

Goddings, A.-L., Mills, K. L., Clasen, L. S., Giedd, J. N., Viner, R. M., & Blakemore, S.-J. (2014). The influence of puberty on subcortical brain development. *NeuroImage, 88*, 242–251. https://doi.org/10.1016/j.neuroimage.2013.09.073

Godfrey, J. R., & Lawrence, R. A. (2010). Toward optimal health: The maternal benefits of breastfeeding. *Journal of Women's Health (15409996), 19*(9), 1597–1602. https://doi.org/10.1089/jwh.2010.2290

Godley, S. H., Passetti, L. L., & White, M. K. (2006). Employment and adolescent alcohol and drug treatment and recovery: An exploratory study. *American Journal on Addictions, 15*, 137–143.

Goldberg, A. E., Downing, J. B., & Moyer, A. M. (2012). Why parenthood, and why now? Gay men's motivations for pursuing parenthood. *Family Relations, 61*(1), 157–174.

Golden, N. H., Katzman, D. K., Sawyer, S. M., Ornstein, R. M., Rome, E. S., Garber, A. K., . . . Kreipe, R. E. (2015). Update on the medical management of eating disorders in adolescents. *Journal of Adolescent Health*, 56(4), 370–375. https://doi.org/10.1016/j.jadohealth.2014.11.020

Goldizen, F. C., Sly, P. D., & Knibbs, L. D. (2016). Respiratory effects of air pollution on children. *Pediatric Pulmonology, 51*(1), 94–108. https://doi.org/10.1002/ppul.23262

Goldschmidt, A. B., Wall, M. M., Zhang, J., Loth, K. A., & Neumark-Sztainer, D. (2016). Overeating and binge eating in emerging adulthood: 10-year stability and risk factors. *Developmental Psychology, 52*(3), 475–483. https://doi.org/10.1037/dev0000086

Goldsmith, H. H., Buss, A. H., Plomin, R., Rothbart, M. K., Thomas, A., Chess, S., . . . McCall, R. B. (1987). Roundtable: What is temperament? Four approaches. *Child Development, 58*, 505–529.

Goldstein, M. H., & Schwade, J. A. (2008). Social feedback to infants' babbling facilitates rapid phonological learning. *Psychological Science, 19*(5), 515–523. https://doi.org/10.1111/j.1467-9280.2008.02117.x

Goldstein, S. E., Boxer, P., & Rudolph, E. (2015). Middle school transition stress: Links with academic performance, motivation, and school experiences. *Contemporary School Psychology, 19*(1), 21–29. https://doi.org/10.1007/s40688-014-0044-4

Goldstein, T. R., & Lerner, M. D. (2018). Dramatic pretend play games uniquely improve emotional control in young children. *Developmental Science, 21*(4), e12603. https://doi.org/10.1111/desc.12603

Golinkoff, R. M., Hirsh-Pasek, K., Grob, R., & Schlesinger, M. (2017). "Oh, the places you'll go" by bringing developmental science into the world! *Child Development, 88*(5), 1403–1408. https://doi.org/10.1111/cdev.12929

Golombok, S. (2013). Families created by reproductive donation: Issues and research. *Child Development Perspectives, 7*(1), 61–65. https://doi.org/10.1111/cdep.12015

Golombok, S., Blake, L., Slutsky, J., Raffanello, E., Roman, G. D., & Ehrhardt, A. (2018). Parenting and the adjustment of children born to gay fathers through surrogacy. *Child Development, 89*, 1223–1233. https://doi.org/10.1111/cdev.12728

Golombok, S., Ilioi, E., Blake, L., Roman, G., & Jadva, V. (2017). A longitudinal study of families formed through reproductive donation: Parent-adolescent relationships and adolescent adjustment at age 14. *Developmental Psychology, 53*(10), 1966–1977. https://doi.org/10.1037/dev0000372

Golombok, S., Mellish, L., Jennings, S., Casey, P., Tasker, F., & Lamb, M. E. (2014). Adoptive gay father families: Parent-child relationships and children's psychological adjustment. *Child Development, 85*(2), 456–468. https://doi.org/10.1111/cdev.12155

Golombok, S., & Tasker, F. (2015). Socioemotional development in changing families. In M. E. Lamb (Ed.), *Handbook of child psychology and developmental science* (pp. 1–45). Hoboken, NJ: John Wiley & Sons. https://doi.org/10.1002/9781118963418.childpsy311

Gómez, R. L., & Edgin, J. O. (2015). Sleep as a window into early neural development: Shifts in sleep-dependent learning effects across early childhood. *Child Development Perspectives, 9*(3), 183–189. https://doi.org/10.1111/cdep.12130

Gómez-Ortiz, O., Romera, E. M., & Ortega-Ruiz, R. (2016). Parenting styles and bullying: The mediating role of parental psychological aggression and physical punishment. *Child Abuse & Neglect, 51*, 132–143. https://doi.org/10.1016/j.chiabu.2015.10.025

Göncü, A., & Gauvain, M. (2012). Sociocultural approaches to educational psychology: Theory, research, and application. In J. Harris, K. R. Graham, S. Urdan, T. McCormick, C. B. Sinatra, & G. M. Sweller (Eds.), *APA educational psychology handbook: Vol 1. Theories, constructs, and critical issues* (pp. 125–154). Washington, DC: American Psychological Association. https://doi.org/10.1037/13273-006

Gong, L., Parikh, S., Rosenthal, P. J., & Greenhouse, B. (2013). Biochemical and immunological mechanisms by which sickle cell trait protects against malaria. *Malaria Journal, 12*, 317. https://doi.org/10.1186/1475-2875-12-317

Gonzales-Backen, M. A., Bámaca-Colbert, M. Y., & Allen, K. (2016). Ethnic identity trajectories among Mexican-origin girls during early and middle adolescence: Predicting future psychosocial adjustment. *Developmental Psychology, 52*(5), 790–797. https://doi.org/10.1037/a0040193

Gonzalez, A.-L., & Wolters, C. A. (2006). The relation between perceived parenting practices and achievement motivation in mathematics. *Journal of Research in Childhood Education, 21*(2), 203–217.

Goodarzi, M. O. (2018). Genetics of obesity: What genetic association studies have taught us about the biology of obesity and its complications. *Lancet Diabetes & Endocrinology, 6*(3), 223–236. https://doi.org/10.1016/S2213-8587(17)30200-0

Goodman, G. S., & Aman, C. J. (1990). Children's use of anatomically detailed dolls to recount an event. *Child Development, 61*, 1859–1871.

Goodman, G. S., Rudy, L., Bottoms, B. L., & Aman, C. (1990). Children's concerns and memory: Issues of ecological validity in the study of children's eyewitness testimony. In R.

Fivush & J. A. Hudson (Eds.), *Knowing and remembering in young children* (pp. 249–284). New York, NY: Cambridge University Press.

Goodman, S. H., & Garber, J. (2017). Evidence-based interventions for depressed mothers and their young children. *Child Development, 88*(2), 368–377. https://doi.org/10.1111/cdev.12732

Goodman-Scott, E., & Lambert, S. F. (2015). Professional counseling for children with sensory processing disorder. *The Professional Counselor, 5*(2), 273–292. https://doi.org/10.15241/egs.5.2.273

Goodnow, J. J., & Lawrence, J. A. (2015). Children and cultural context. In M. H. Bornstein & T. Leventhal (Eds.), *Handbook of child psychology and developmental science* (Vol. 4, pp. 1–41). Hoboken, NJ: John Wiley & Sons. https://doi.org/10.1002/9781118963418.childpsy419

Goodvin, R., Meyer, S., Thompson, R. A., & Hayes, R. (2008). Self-understanding in early childhood: Associations with child attachment security and maternal negative affect. *Attachment & Human Development, 10*(4), 433–450. https://doi.org/10.1080/14616730802461466

Goodvin, R., Thompson, R. A., & Winer, A. C. (2015). The individual child: Temperament, emotion, self, and personality. In M. Bornstein & M. Lamb (Eds.), *Developmental psychology: An advanced textbook* (pp. 491–533). New York, NY: Psychology Press.

Goodwin, G. P., & Johnson-Laird, P. N. (2008). Transitive and pseudo-transitive inferences. *Cognition, 108*(2), 320–352. https://doi.org/10.1016/j.cognition.2008.02.010

Goodwin, P., Mosher, W., & Chandra, A. (2010). Marriage and cohabitation in the United States: A statistical portrait based on cycle 6 (2002) of the National Survey of Family Growth. *Vital and Health Statistics, 23*(28), 1–45.

Goodwyn, S. W., & Acredolo, L. P. (1998). Encouraging symbolic gestures: A new perspective on the relationship between gesture and speech. *New Directions for Child and Adolescent Development, 1998*(79), 61–73. https://doi.org/10.1002/cd.23219987905

Gopinath, B., Flood, V. M., Burlutsky, G., Louie, J. C. Y., Baur, L. A., & Mitchell, P. (2016). Frequency of takeaway food consumption and its association with major food group consumption, anthropometric measures and blood pressure during adolescence. *British Journal of Nutrition, 115*(11), 2025–2030. https://doi.org/10.1017/S000711451600101X

Gopnik, A., & Choi, S. (1995). *Beyond names for things: Children's acquisition of verbs.* Hillsdale, NJ: Erlbaum.

Gordon, A. M., & Browne, K. W. (2016). *Beginning essentials in early childhood education.* Belmont, CA: Cengage Learning.

Gormley, W. T., Jr., Phillips, D., Adelstein, S., & Shaw, C. (2010). Head Start's comparative advantage: Myth or reality? *Policy Studies Journal, 38*(3), 397–418. https://doi.org/10.1111/j.1541-0072.2010.00367.x

Gothe-Snape, J. (2017). *How other countries address affordable childcare.* Retrieved from https://www.sbs.com.au/news/how-other-countries-address-affordable-childcare

Gottlieb, G. (2000). Environmental and behavioral influences on gene activity. *Current Directions in Psychological Science, 9*, 93–97. https://doi.org/10.1111/1467-8721.00068

Gottlieb, G. (2007). Probabilistic epigenesis. *Developmental Science, 10*(1), 1–11. https://doi.org/10.1111/j.1467-7687.2007.00556.x

Goubet, N., Strasbaugh, K., & Chesney, J. (2007). Familiarity breeds content? Soothing effect of a familiar odor on full-term newborns. *Journal of Developmental & Behavioral Pediatrics, 28*(3), 189–194. https://doi.org/10.1097/dbp.0b013e31802d0b8d

Gourley, L., Wind, C., Henninger, E. M., & Chinitz, S. (2013). Sensory processing difficulties, behavioral problems, and parental stress in a clinical population of young children. *Journal of Child and Family Studies, 22*(7), 912–921. https://doi.org/10.1007/s10826-012-9650-9

Gower, A. L., Lingras, K. A., Mathieson, L. C., Kawabata, Y., & Crick, N. R. (2014). The role of preschool relational and physical aggression in the transition to kindergarten: Links with social-psychological adjustment. *Early Education and Development, 25*(5), 619–640. https://doi.org/10.1080/10409289.2014.844058

Graber, J. A., Nichols, T. R., & Brooks-Gunn, J. (2010). Putting pubertal timing in developmental context: Implications for prevention. *Developmental Psychobiology, 52*(3), 254–262. https://doi.org/10.1002/dev.20438

Gradin, M., Eriksson, M., Schollin, J., Holmqvist, G., & Holstein, A. (2002). Pain reduction at venipuncture in newborns: Oral glucose compared with local anesthetic cream. *Pediatrics, 110*(6), 1053–1057.

Grady, J. S., & Karraker, K. (2017). Mother and child temperament as interacting correlates of parenting sense of competence in toddlerhood. *Infant and Child Development, 26*(4), e1997. https://doi.org/10.1002/icd.1997

Graham, S., Munniksma, A., & Juvonen, J. (2014). Psychosocial benefits of cross-ethnic friendships in urban middle schools. *Child Development, 85*(2), 469–483. https://doi.org/10.1111/cdev.12159

Granat, A., Gadassi, R., Gilboa-Schechtman, E., & Feldman, R. (2017). Maternal depression and anxiety, social synchrony, and infant regulation of negative and positive emotions. *Emotion, 17*(1), 11–27. https://doi.org/10.1037/emo0000204

Granier-Deferre, C., Ribeiro, A., Jacquet, A.-Y., & Bassereau, S. (2011). Near-term fetuses process temporal features of speech. *Developmental Science, 14*, 336–352. https://doi.org/10.1111/j.1467-7687.2010.00978.x

Granqvist, P., Sroufe, L. A., Dozier, M., Hesse, E., Steele, M., van IJzendoorn, M., . . . Duschinsky, R. (2017). Disorganized attachment in infancy: A review of the phenomenon and its implications for clinicians and policy-makers. *Attachment & Human Development, 19*(6), 534–558. https://doi.org/10.1080/14616734.2017.1354040

Grant, K. S., Petroff, R., Isoherranen, N., Stella, N., & Burbacher, T. M. (2018). Cannabis use during pregnancy: Pharmacokinetics and effects on child development. *Pharmacology & Therapeutics, 182*, 133–151. https://doi.org/10.1016/J.PHARMTHERA.2017.08.014

Grassetti, S. N., Hubbard, J. A., Smith, M. A., Bookhout, M. K., Swift, L. E., & Gawrysiak, M. J. (2018). Caregivers' advice and children's bystander behaviors during bullying incidents. *Journal of Clinical Child & Adolescent Psychology*, 1–12. https://doi.org/10.1080/15374416.2017.1295381

Gray, C., & MacBlain, S. (2015). *Learning theories in childhood.* Thousand Oaks, CA: Sage.

Greenberg, J. S. (2017). *Exploring the dimensions of human sexuality.* Burlington, MA: Jones & Bartlett.

Greenberger, E., & Steinberg, L. (1986). *When teenagers work: The psychological and social costs of adolescent employment.* New York, NY: Basic Books.

Greene, K. M., & Staff, J. (2012). Teenage employment and career readiness. *New Directions for Youth Development, 2012*(134), 23–31, 7–8. https://doi.org/10.1002/yd.20012

Gregg, A. R., Gross, S. J., Best, R. G., Monaghan, K. G., Bajaj, K., Skotko, B. G., . . . Watson, M. S. (2013). ACMG statement on noninvasive prenatal screening for fetal aneuploidy. *Genetics in Medicine, 15*(5), 395–398. https://doi.org/10.1038/gim.2013.29

Grewen, K., Burchinal, M., Vachet, C., Gouttard, S., Gilmore, J. H., Lin, W., . . . Gerig, G. (2014). Prenatal cocaine effects on brain structure in early infancy. *NeuroImage, 101*, 114–123. https://doi.org/10.1016/J.NEUROIMAGE.2014.06.070

Grieco, J., Pulsifer, M., Seligsohn, K., Skotko, B., & Schwartz, A. (2015). Down syndrome: Cognitive and behavioral functioning across the lifespan. *American Journal of Medical Genetics Part C: Seminars in Medical Genetics, 169*(2), 135–149. https://doi.org/10.1002/ajmg.c.31439

Griffith, S. F., & Grolnick, W. S. (2013). Parenting in Caribbean families: A look at parental control, structure, and autonomy support. *Journal of Black Psychology, 40*(2), 166–190. https://doi.org/10.1177/0095798412475085

Griffiths, L. J., Tate, A. R., & Lucy, J. G. (2007). Do early infant feeding practices vary by maternal ethnic group? *Public Health Nutrition, 10*(9), 957–964.

Griffiths, P. D., Bradburn, M., Campbell, M. J., Cooper, C. L., Graham, R., Jarvis, D., . . . Wailoo, A. (2017). Use of MRI in the diagnosis of fetal brain abnormalities in utero (MERIDIAN): A multicentre, prospective cohort study. *Lancet, 389*(10068), 538–546. https://doi.org/10.1016/S0140-6736(16)31723-8

Grigg-Damberger, M. M., & Wolfe, K. M. (2017). Infants sleep for brain. *Journal of Clinical Sleep Medicine, 13*(11), 1233–1234. https://doi.org/10.5664/jcsm.6786

Grimberg, A., & Allen, D. B. (2017). Growth hormone treatment for growth hormone deficiency and idiopathic short stature: New guidelines shaped by the presence and absence of evidence. *Current Opinion in Pediatrics, 29*(4), 466–471. https://doi.org/10.1097/MOP.0000000000000505

Grogan-Kaylor, A., Ma, J., & Graham-Bermann, S. A. (2018). The case against physical punishment. *Current Opinion in Psychology, 19*, 22–27. https://doi.org/10.1016/j.copsyc.2017.03.022

Groh, A. M., Fearon, R. M. P., van IJzendoorn, M. H., Bakermans-Kranenburg, M. J., & Roisman, G. I. (2017). Attachment in the early life course: Meta-analytic evidence for its role in socioemotional development. *Child Development Perspectives, 11*(1), 70–76. https://doi.org/10.1111/cdep.12213

Grosse Wiesmann, C., Friederici, A. D., Singer, T., & Steinbeis, N. (2017). Implicit and explicit false belief development in preschool children. *Developmental Science, 20*(5), e12445. https://doi.org/10.1111/desc.12445

Grossman, A. H., Park, J. Y., & Russell, S. T. (2016). Transgender youth and suicidal behaviors: Applying the interpersonal psychological theory of suicide. *Journal of Gay & Lesbian Mental Health, 20*(4), 329–349. https://doi.org/10.1080/19359705.2016.1207581

Grossmann, K., Grossman, K. E., Fremmer-Bombik, E., Kindler, H., Scheuerer-Englisch, H., & Zimmermann, P. (2002). The uniqueness of the child–father attachment relationship: Fathers' sensitive and challenging play as a pivotal variable in a 16-year longitudinal study. *Social Development, 11*(3), 301–337.

Grossmann, K. E., Spangler, G., Suess, G., & Unzner, L. (1985). Maternal sensitivity and newborns' orientation responses as related to quality of attachment in Northern Germany. In I. Bretherton & E. Waters (Eds.), *Growing points of attachment theory and research: Monographs of the Society for Research in Child Development, 50*(1–2, Serial No. 209), 233–256.

Grotegut, C. A., Chisholm, C. A., Johnson, L. N. C., Brown, H. L., Heine, R. P., & James, A. H. (2014). Medical and obstetric complications among pregnant women aged 45 and older. *PLoS One, 9*(4), e96237. https://doi.org/10.1371/journal.pone.0096237

Grotevant, H. D., Lo, A. Y. H., Fiorenzo, L., & Dunbar, N. D. (2017). Adoptive identity and adjustment from adolescence to emerging adulthood: A person-centered approach. *Developmental Psychology, 53*(11), 2195–2204. https://doi.org/10.1037/dev0000352

Grotevant, H. D., & McDermott, J. M. (2014). Adoption: Biological and social processes linked to adaptation. *Annual Review of Psychology, 65*(1), 235–265. https://doi.org/10.1146/annurev-psych-010213-115020

Grotevant, H. D., Thorbecke, W., & Meyer, M. L. (1982). An extension of Marcia's Identity Status Interview into the interpersonal domain. *Journal of Youth and Adolescence, 11*(1), 33–47. https://doi.org/10.1007/BF01537815

Gruenenfelder-Steiger, A. E., Harris, M. A., & Fend, H. A. (2016). Subjective and objective peer approval evaluations and self-esteem development: A test of reciprocal, prospective, and long-term effects. *Developmental Psychology, 52*(10), 1563–1577. https://doi.org/10.1037/dev0000147

Grusec, J. E. (1992). Social learning theory and developmental psychology: The legacies of Robert Sears and Albert Bandura. *Developmental Psychology, 28*(5), 776–786.

Grusec, J. E., & Goodnow, J. J. (1994). Impact of parental discipline methods on the child's internalization of values: A reconceptualization of current points of view. *Developmental Psychology, 30*, 4–19.

Guignard, J.-H., & Lubart, T. (2006). Is it reasonable to be creative? In J. C. Kaufman & J. Baer (Eds.), *Creativity and reason in cognitive development* (pp. 269–281). Cambridge, England: Cambridge University Press. https://doi.org/10.1017/CBO9780511606915.016

Guimond, S., Chatard, A., & Lorenzi-Cioldi, F. (2013). The social psychology of gender across cultures. In M. K. Ryan (Ed.), *The SAGE handbook of gender and psychology* (pp. 216–233). Thousand Oaks, CA: Sage. https://doi.org/10.4135/9781446269930.n14

Gunn, J. K. L., Rosales, C. B., Center, K. E., Nuñez, A., Gibson, S. J., Christ, C., & Ehiri, J. E. (2016). Prenatal exposure to cannabis and maternal and child health outcomes: A systematic review and meta-analysis. *BMJ Open, 6*(4), e009986. https://doi.org/10.1136/bmjopen-2015-009986

Guo, L., Yang, L., Liu, Z., & Song, T. (2005). An experimental research on the formation of primary school pupils' self-confidence. *Psychological Science (China), 28*(5), 1068–1071.

Guo, M., O'Connor Duffany, K., Shebl, F. M., Santilli, A., & Keene, D. E. (2018). The effects of length of residence and exposure to violence on perceptions of neighborhood safety in an urban sample. *Journal of Urban Health, 95*(2), 245–254. https://doi.org/10.1007/s11524-018-0229-7

Guo, Y., Garfin, D. R., Ly, A., & Goldberg, W. A. (2017). Emotion coregulation in mother-child dyads: A dynamic systems analysis of children with and without autism spectrum disorder. *Journal of Abnormal Child Psychology, 45*(7), 1369–1383. https://doi.org/10.1007/s10802-016-0234-9

Guo, Y., Leu, S.-Y., Barnard, K. E., Thompson, E. A., & Spieker, S. J. (2015). An examination of changes in emotion co-regulation among mother and child dyads during the strange situation. *Infant and Child Development, 24*(3), 256–273. https://doi.org/10.1002/icd.1917

Guo, Y., Sun, S., Breit-Smith, A., Morrison, F. J., & Connor, C. M. (2015). Behavioral engagement and reading achievement in elementary-school-age children: A longitudinal cross-lagged analysis. *Journal of Educational Psychology, 107*(2), 332–347. https://doi.org/10.1037/a0037638

Gupta, K. K., Gupta, V. K., & Shirasaka, T. (2016). An update on fetal alcohol syndrome-pathogenesis, risks, and treatment. *Alcoholism: Clinical and Experimental Research, 40*(8), 1594–1602. https://doi.org/10.1111/acer.13135

Gupta, R. C. (2017). *Reproductive and developmental toxicology.* Cambridge, MA: Elsevier Science.

Guralnick, M. J., Hammond, M. A., Connor, R. T., & Neville, B. (2006). Stability, change, and correlates of the peer relationships of young children with mild developmental delays. *Child Development, 77*(2), 312–324. https://doi.org/10.1111/j.1467-8624.2006.00872.x

Gurd, J. M., Schulz, J., Cherkas, L., & Ebers, G. C. (2006). Hand preference and performance in 20 pairs of monozygotic twins with discordant handedness. *Cortex, 42*(6), 934–945. https://doi.org/10.1016/S0010-9452(08)70438-6

Guttmacher Institute. (2014). *American teens' sexual and reproductive health.* Retrieved from http://www.guttmacher.org/pubs/fb_ATSRH.html

Guttmacher Institute. (2017). *Adolescent sexual and reproductive health in the United States.* Retrieved from https://www.guttmacher.org/fact-sheet/american-teens-sexual-and-reproductive-health

Guttmacher Institute. (2018). *Substance use during pregnancy—May 1, 2018.* Retrieved from https://www.guttmacher.org/state-policy/explore/substance-use-during-pregnancy

Guzman, M. R. de, Do, K.-A., & Kok, C. (2014). The cultural contexts of children's prosocial behaviors. *Faculty Publications, Department of Child, Youth, and Family Studies.* Retrieved from http://digitalcommons.unl.edu/famconfacpub/103

Haas, A. P., Eliason, M., Mays, V. M., Mathy, R. M., Cochran, S. D., D'Augelli, A. R., . . . Clayton, P. J. (2011). Suicide and suicide risk in lesbian, gay, bisexual, and transgender populations: Review and recommendations. *Journal of Homosexuality, 58*(1), 10–51. https://doi.org/10.1080/00918369.2011.534038

Hacker, N. F., Gambone, J. C., & Hobel, C. J. (2016). *Hacker & Moore's essentials of obstetrics and gynecology.* Philadelphia, PA: Elsevier.

Hackman, D. A., Gallop, R., Evans, G. W., & Farah, M. J. (2015). Socioeconomic status and executive function: Developmental trajectories and mediation. *Developmental Science, 18*(5), 686–702. https://doi.org/10.1111/desc.12246

Haden, C. A., & Fivush, F. (1996). Contextual variation in maternal conversational styles. *Merrill-Palmer Quarterly, 42*, 200–227.

Hadiwijaya, H., Klimstra, T. A., Vermunt, J. K., Branje, S. J. T., & Meeus, W. H. J. (2017). On the development of harmony, turbulence, and independence in parent–adolescent relationships: A five-wave longitudinal study. *Journal of Youth and Adolescence, 46*, 1772–1788. https://doi.org/10.1007/s10964-016-0627-7

Hadley, P. A., Rispoli, M., Fitzgerald, C., & Bahnsen, A. (2011). Predictors of morphosyntactic growth in typically developing toddlers: Contributions of parent input and child sex. *Journal of Speech Language and Hearing Research, 54*(2), 549. https://doi.org/10.1044/1092-4388(2010/09-0216)

Hafstad, G. S., Abebe, D. S., Torgersen, L., & von Soest, T. (2013). Picky eating in preschool children: The predictive role of the child's temperament and mother's negative affectivity. *Eating Behaviors, 14*(3), 274–277. https://doi.org/10.1016/j.eatbeh.2013.04.001

Hagerman, R. J., Berry-Kravis, E., Hazlett, H. C., Bailey, D. B., Moine, H., Kooy, R. F., . . . Hagerman, P. J. (2017). Fragile X syndrome. *Nature Reviews Disease Primers, 3*, 17065. https://doi.org/10.1038/nrdp.2017.65

Hagman, J., Gardner, R. M., Brown, D. L., Gralla, J., Fier, J. M., & Frank, G. K. W. (2015). Body size overestimation and its association with body mass index, body dissatisfaction, and drive for thinness in anorexia nervosa. *Eating and Weight Disorders–Studies on Anorexia, Bulimia and Obesity, 20*(4), 449–455. https://doi.org/10.1007/s40519-015-0193-0

Hahamy, A., Behrmann, M., & Malach, R. (2015). The idiosyncratic brain: Distortion of spontaneous connectivity patterns in autism spectrum disorder. *Nature Neuroscience, 18*(2), 302–309. https://doi.org/10.1038/nn.3919

Haimovitz, K., & Dweck, C. S. (2017). The origins of children's growth and fixed mindsets: New research and a new proposal. *Child Development, 88*(6), 1849–1859. https://doi.org/10.1111/cdev.12955

Hair, N. L., Hanson, J. L., Wolfe, B. L., Pollak, S. D., & Knight, R. T. (2015). Association of child poverty, brain development, and academic achievement. *JAMA Pediatrics, 169*(9), 822. https://doi.org/10.1001/jamapediatrics.2015.1475

Haith, M. M. (1993). Preparing for the 21st century: Some goals and challenges for studies of infant sensory and perceptual development. *Developmental Review, 13*, 354–371.

Hakvoort, E. M., Bos, H. M. W., van Balen, F., & Hermanns, J. M. A. (2010). Family relationships and the psychosocial adjustment of school-aged children in intact families. *Journal of Genetic Psychology, 171*(2), 182–201.

Halberstadt, A. G., & Lozada, F. T. (2011). Emotion development in infancy through the lens of culture. *Emotion Review, 3*(2), 158–168. https://doi.org/10.1177/1754073910387946

Hale, L., & Guan, S. (2015). Screen time and sleep among school-aged children and adolescents: A systematic literature review. *Sleep Medicine Reviews, 21*, 50–58. https://doi.org/10.1016/j.smrv.2014.07.007

Hales, C. M., Fryar, C. D., Carroll, M. D., Freedman, D. S., & Ogden, C. L. (2018). Trends in obesity and severe obesity prevalence in US youth and adults by sex and age, 2007-2008 to 2015-2016. *JAMA, 319*(16), 1723–1725. https://doi.org/10.1001/jama.2018.3060

Halevi, G., Djalovski, A., Vengrober, A., & Feldman, R. (2016). Risk and resilience trajectories in war-exposed children across the first decade of life. *Journal of Child Psychology and Psychiatry, 57*(10), 1183–1193. https://doi.org/10.1111/jcpp.12622

Halford, G. S., & Andrews, G. (2011). Information-processing models of cognitive development. In U. Goswami (Ed.), *The Wiley-Blackwell handbook of childhood cognitive development* (2nd ed., pp. 697–721). Hoboken, NJ: John Wiley & Sons, Inc.

Halim, M. L., Ruble, D., Tamis-LeMonda, C., & Shrout, P. E. (2013). Rigidity in gender-typed behaviors in early childhood: A longitudinal study of ethnic minority children. *Child Development, 84*(4), 1269–1284. https://doi.org/10.1111/cdev.12057

Halim, M. L., Ruble, D. N., Tamis-LeMonda, C. S., Zosuls, K. M., Lurye, L. E., & Greulich, F. K. (2014). Pink frilly dresses and the avoidance of all things "girly": Children's appearance rigidity and cognitive theories of gender development. *Developmental Psychology, 50*(4), 1091–1101. https://doi.org/10.1037/a0034906

Halim, M. L. D. (2016). Princesses and superheroes: Social-cognitive influences on early gender rigidity. *Child Development Perspectives, 10*(3), 155–160. https://doi.org/10.1111/cdep.12176

Halim, M. L. D., Ruble, D. N., Tamis-LeMonda, C. S., Shrout, P. E., & Amodio, D. M. (2017). Gender attitudes in early childhood: Behavioral consequences and cognitive antecedents. *Child Development, 88*(3), 882–899. https://doi.org/10.1111/cdev.12642

Hall, B., & Place, M. (2010). Cutting to cope—a modern adolescent phenomenon. *Child: Care, Health & Development, 36*(5), 623–629. https://doi.org/10.1111/j.1365-2214.2010.01095.x

Hall, L. J. (2018). *Autism spectrum disorders: From theory to practice*. New York, NY: Pearson.

Hall, S. P., & Brassard, M. R. (2008). Relational support as a predictor of identity status in an ethnically diverse early adolescent sample. *Journal of Early Adolescence, 28*(1), 92–114. https://doi.org/10.1177/0272431607308668

Halpern, D. F., & LaMay, M. L. (2000). The smarter sex: A critical review of sex differences in intelligence. *Educational Psychology Review, 12*(2), 229–246. https://doi.org/10.1023/A:1009027516424

Halpern, H. P., & Perry-Jenkins, M. (2016). Parents' gender ideology and gendered behavior as predictors of children's gender-role attitudes: A longitudinal exploration. *Sex Roles, 74*(11–12), 527–542. https://doi.org/10.1007/s11199-015-0539-0

Halpern-Felsher, B. L., & Cauffman, E. (2001). Costs and benefits of a decision: Decision-making competence in adolescents and adults. *Journal of Applied Developmental Psychology, 22*(3), 257–273.

Hamilton, B. E., Martin, J. A., Osterman, M. J. K. S., Driscoll, A. K., & Rossen, L. M. (2017). *Vital statistics rapid release births: Provisional data for 2016*. Retrieved from https://www.cdc.gov/nchs/data/vsrr/report002.pdf

Hamm, M. P., Newton, A. S., Chisholm, A., Shulhan, J., Milne, A., Sundar, P., . . . Hartling, L. (2015). Prevalence and effect of cyberbullying on children and young people. *JAMA Pediatrics, 169*(8), 770–777. https://doi.org/10.1001/jamapediatrics.2015.0944

Hammond, S. I., & Carpendale, J. I. M. (2015). Helping children help: The relation between maternal scaffolding and children's early help. *Social Development, 24*(2), 367–383. https://doi.org/10.1111/sode.12104

Hanania, R., & Smith, L. B. (2010). Selective attention and attention switching: Towards a unified developmental approach. *Developmental Science, 13*(4), 622–635. https://doi.org/10.1111/j.1467-7687.2009.00921.x

Hanish, L. D., Fabes, R. A., Leaper, C., Bigler, R., Hayes, A. R., Hamilton, V., & Beltz, A. M. (2013). Gender: Early socialization. In E. T. Gershoff, R. S. Mistry, & D. A. Crossby (Eds.), *Societal contexts of child development: Pathways of influence and implications for practice and policy*. New York, NY: Oxford University Press.

Hanley, J. R., Cortis, C., Budd, M.-J., & Nozari, N. (2016). Did I say dog or cat? A study of semantic error detection and correction in children. *Journal of Experimental Child Psychology, 142*, 36–47. https://doi.org/10.1016/j.jecp.2015.09.008

Hannon, P. A., Bowen, D. J., Moinpour, C. M., & McLerran, D. F. (2003). Correlations in perceived food use between the family food preparer and their spouses and children. *Appetite, 40*(1), 77–83. https://doi.org/10.1016/S0195-6663(02)00140-X

Hansen, M. B., & Markman, E. M. (2009). Children's use of mutual exclusivity to learn labels for parts of objects. *Developmental Psychology, 45*(2), 592–596. https://doi.org/10.1037/a0014838

Hanson, J. J. L., Hair, N., Shen, D. G., Shi, F., Gilmore, J. H. J., Wolfe, B. B. L., . . . Hickie, I. (2013). Family poverty affects the rate of human infant brain growth. *PLoS ONE, 8*(12), e80954. https://doi.org/10.1371/journal.pone.0080954

Hanson, K. L., Thayer, R. E., & Tapert, S. F. (2014). Adolescent marijuana users have elevated risk-taking on the balloon analog risk task. *Journal of Psychopharmacology, 28*(11), 1080–1087. https://doi.org/10.1177/0269881114550352

Hanson, K. L., Winward, J. L., Schweinsburg, A. D., Medina, K. L., Brown, S. A., & Tapert, S. F. (2010). Longitudinal study of cognition among adolescent marijuana users over three weeks of abstinence. *Addictive Behaviors, 35*(11), 970–976. https://doi.org/10.1016/j.addbeh.2010.06.012

Harker, A. (2018). Social dysfunction. In R. Gibb & B. Kolb (Eds.), *The neurobiology of brain and behavioral development* (pp. 439–467). Philadelphia, PA: Elsevier. https://doi.org/10.1016/B978-0-12-804036-2.00016-9

Harlow, H. F., & Zimmerman, R. (1959). Affectional responses in the infant monkey. *Science, 130*, 421–432.

Harper, S., & Ruicheva, I. (2010). Grandmothers as replacement parents and partners: The role of grandmotherhood in single parent families. *Journal of Intergenerational Relationships, 8*(3), 219–233. https://doi.org/10.1080/15350770.2010.498779

Harriman, A. E., & Lukosius, P. A. (1982). On why Wayne Dennis found Hopi infants retarded in age at onset of walking. *Perceptual & Motor Skills, 55*(1), 79–86.

Harris, J., Golinkoff, R. M., & Hirsh-Pasek, K. (2011). Lessons from the crib for the classroom: How children really learn vocabulary. In S. B. Neuman & D. K. Dickinson (Eds.), *Handbook of early literacy research* (Vol. 3, pp. 49–65). New York, NY: Guilford.

Harris, M. A., Gruenenfelder-Steiger, A. E., Ferrer, E., Donnellan, M. B., Allemand, M., Fend, H., . . . Trzesniewski, K. H. (2015). Do parents foster self-esteem? Testing the prospective impact of parent closeness on adolescent self-esteem. *Child Development, 86*(4), 995–1013. https://doi.org/10.1111/cdev.12356

Harris-McKoy, D., & Cui, M. (2012). Parental control, adolescent delinquency, and young adult criminal behavior. *Journal of Child and Family Studies, 22*(6), 836–843. https://doi.org/10.1007/s10826-012-9641-x

Harrison, L. J., & Ungerer, J. A. (2002). Maternal employment and infant-mother attachment security at 12 months postpartum. *Developmental Psychology, 38*(5), 758–773.

Harrist, A. W., Swindle, T. M., Hubbs-Tait, L., Topham, G. L., Shriver, L. H., & Page, M. C. (2016). The social and emotional lives of overweight, obese, and severely obese children. *Child Development, 87*(5), 1564–1580. https://doi.org/10.1111/cdev.12548

Hart, D., Atkins, R., & Tursi, N. (2006). Origins and developmental influences on self-esteem. In M. H. Kernis (Ed.), *Self-esteem issues and answers: A sourcebook of current perspectives* (pp. 157–162). New York, NY: Psychology Press.

Hart, D., Donnelly, T. M., Youniss, J., & Atkins, R. (2007). High school community service as a predictor of adult voting and volunteering. *American Educational Research Journal, 44*(1), 197–219. https://doi.org/10.3102/0002831206298173

Harter, S. (2006). The self. In N. Eisenberg, W. Damon, & R. M. Lerner (Eds.), *Handbook of child psychology: Vol. 3. Social, emotional, and personality development* (6th ed., pp. 505–570). Hoboken, NJ: John Wiley & Sons.

Harter, S. (2012a). Emerging self-processes during childhood and adolescence. In M. R. Leary & J. P. Tangney (Eds.), *Handbook of self and identity* (pp. 680–715). New York, NY: Guilford.

Harter, S. (2012b). *The construction of the self: Developmental and sociocultural foundations* (2nd ed.). New York, NY: Guilford.

Hartl, A. C., Laursen, B., & Cillessen, A. H. N. (2015). A survival analysis of adolescent friendships. *Psychological Science, 26*(8), 1304–1315. https://doi.org/10.1177/0956797615588751

Hartup, W. W. (2006). Relationships in early and middle childhood. In A. L. Vangelisti & D. Perlman (Eds.), *The Cambridge handbook of personal relationships* (pp. 177–190). New York, NY: Cambridge University Press.

Hartup, W. W., & Stevens, N. (1997). Friendships and adaptation in the life course. *Psychological Bulletin, 121*, 355–370.

Harwood, R., Feng, X., & Yu, S. (2013). Preadoption adversities and postadoption mediators of mental health and school outcomes among international, foster, and private adoptees in the United States. *Journal of Family Psychology, 27*(3), 409–420. https://doi.org/10.1037/a0032908

Harwood, R. L., Scholmerich, A., Schulze, P. A., & Gonzalez, Z. (1999). Cultural differences in maternal beliefs and behaviors: A study of middle class Anglo and Puerto Rican mother-infant pairs in four everyday situations. *Child Development, 70*, 1005–1016.

Hatzis, D., Dawe, S., Harnett, P., & Barlow, J. (2017). Quality of caregiving in mothers with illicit substance use: A systematic review and meta-analysis. *Substance Abuse: Research and Treatment, 11*, 1178221817694038. https://doi.org/10.1177/1178221817694038

Hauck, Y. L., Fenwick, J., Dhaliwal, S. S., & Butt, J. (2011). A Western Australian survey of breastfeeding initiation, prevalence and early cessation patterns. *Maternal & Child Health Journal, 15*(2), 260–268. https://doi.org/10.1007/s10995-009-0554-2

Hauser, M. D., Yang, C., Berwick, R. C., Tattersall, I., Ryan, M. J., Watumull, J., . . . Lewontin, R. C. (2014). The mystery of language evolution. *Frontiers in Psychology, 5*, 401. https://doi.org/10.3389/fpsyg.2014.00401

Haw, C., Hawton, K., Niedzwiedz, C., & Platt, S. (2013). Suicide clusters: A review of risk factors and mechanisms. *Suicide & Life-Threatening Behavior, 43*(1), 97–108. https://doi.org/10.1111/j.1943-278X.2012.00130.x

Hawk, L. W., Fosco, W. D., Colder, C. R., Waxmonsky, J. G., Pelham, W. E., & Rosch, K. S. (2018). How do stimulant treatments for ADHD work? Evidence for mediation by improved cognition. *Journal of Child Psychology and Psychiatry*. https://doi.org/10.1111/jcpp.12917

Hawks, Z. W., Strube, M. J., Johnson, N. X., Grange, D. K., & White, D. A. (2018). Developmental trajectories of executive and verbal processes in children with phenylketonuria. *Developmental Neuropsychology, 43*(3), 207–218. https://doi.org/10.1080/87565641.2018.1438439

Hawkyard, R., Dempsey, I., & Arthur-Kelly, M. (2014). The handwriting experiences of left-handed primary school students in a digital age: Australian data and critique. *Australian Journal of Education, 58*(2), 123–138. https://doi.org/10.1177/0004944114530062

Hay, D. F., Hurst, S.-L., Waters, C. S., & Chadwick, A. (2011). Infants' use of force to defend toys: The origins of instrumental aggression. *Infancy, 16*(5), 471–489. https://doi.org/10.1111/j.1532-7078.2011.00069.x

Hay, P. J., & Bacaltchuk, J. (2007). Bulimia nervosa. *American Family Physician, 75*, 1699–1702.

Haydon, A. A., Herring, A. H., Prinstein, M. J., & Halpern, C. T. (2012). Beyond age at first sex: Patterns of emerging sexual behavior in adolescence and young adulthood. *Journal of Adolescent Health, 50*(5), 456–463. https://doi.org/10.1016/j.jadohealth.2011.09.006

Hayne, H., Boniface, J., & Barr, R. (2000). The development of declarative memory in human infants: Age-related changes in deferred imitation. *Behavioral Neuroscience, 114*(1), 77–83. https://doi.org/10.1037/0735-7044.114.1.77

Hazlett, H. C., Hammer, J., Hooper, S. R., & Kamphaus, R. W. (2011). Down syndrome. In S. Goldstein & C. R. Reynolds (Eds.), *Handbook of neurodevelopmental and genetic disorders in children* (2nd ed., pp. 362–381). New York, NY: Guilford.

He, M., Walle, E. A., & Campos, J. J. (2015). A cross-national investigation of the relationship between infant walking and language development. *Infancy, 20*(3), 283–305. https://doi.org/10.1111/infa.12071

He, Y., Chen, J., Zhu, L.-H., Hua, L.-L., & Ke, F.-F. (2017). Maternal smoking during pregnancy and ADHD. *Journal of Attention Disorders*, 108705471769676. https://doi.org/10.1177/1087054717696766

Heaman, M. I., Sword, W., Elliott, L., Moffatt, M., Helewa, M. E., Morris, H., . . . Brown, J. (2015). Barriers and facilitators related to use of prenatal care by inner-city women: Perceptions of health care providers. *BMC Pregnancy and Childbirth, 15*(1), 2. https://doi.org/10.1186/s12884-015-0431-5

Heath, S. B. (1989). Oral and literate tradition among black Americans living in poverty. *American Psychologist, 44*, 367–373.

Heaven, P. C. L., & Ciarrochi, J. (2008). Parental styles, conscientiousness, and academic performance in high school: A three-wave longitudinal study. *Personality and Social Psychology Bulletin, 34*(4), 451–461. https://doi.org/10.1177/0146167207311909

Heimann, M., & Meltzoff, A. N. (1996). Deferred imitation in 9- and 14-month-old infants: A longitudinal study of a Swedish sample. *British Journal of Developmental Psychology, 14*(1), 55–64. https://doi.org/10.1111/j.2044-835X.1996.tb00693.x

Hein, T. C., & Monk, C. S. (2017). Research review: Neural response to threat in children, adolescents, and adults after child maltreatment—a quantitative meta-analysis. *Journal of Child Psychology and Psychiatry, 58*(3), 222–230. https://doi.org/10.1111/jcpp.12651

Heinrich, J. (2011). Influence of indoor factors in dwellings on the development of childhood asthma. *International Journal of Hygiene & Environmental Health, 214*(1), 1–25. https://doi.org/10.1016/j.ijheh.2010.08.009

Helming, K. A., Strickland, B., & Jacob, P. (2014). Making sense of early false-belief understanding. *Trends in Cognitive Sciences, 18*(4), 167–170. https://doi.org/10.1016/j.tics.2014.01.005

Helms, J. E. (1992). Why is there no study of cultural equivalence in standardized cognitive ability testing? *American Psychologist, 47*, 1083–1101.

Helms, S. W., Choukas-Bradley, S., Widman, L., Giletta, M., Cohen, G. L., & Prinstein, M. J. (2014). Adolescents misperceive and are influenced by high-status peers' health risk, deviant, and adaptive behavior. *Developmental Psychology, 50*(12), 2697–2714. https://doi.org/10.1037/a0038178

Helwig, C. C., Arnold, M. L., Tan, D., & Boyd, D. (2007). Mainland Chinese and Canadian adolescents' judgments and reasoning about the fairness of democratic and other forms of government. *Cognitive Development, 22*(1), 96–109.

Helwig, C. C., & Prencipe, A. (1999). Children's judgments of flags and flag-burning. *Child Development, 70*, 132–143.

Henry, D., Dormuth, C., Winquist, B., Carney, G., Bugden, S., Teare, G., . . . CNODES (Canadian Network for Observational Drug Effect Studies) Investigators. (2016). Occurrence of pregnancy and pregnancy outcomes during isotretinoin therapy. *CMAJ, 188*(10), 723–730. https://doi.org/10.1503/cmaj.151243

Henry, K. L., Knight, K. E., & Thornberry, T. P. (2012). School disengagement as a predictor of dropout, delinquency, and problem substance use during adolescence and early adulthood. *Journal of Youth and Adolescence, 41*(2), 156–166. https://doi.org/10.1007/s10964-011-9665-3

Henry, O., Brzostek, J., Czajka, H., Leviniene, G., Reshetko, O., Gasparini, R., . . . Innis, B. (2018). One or two doses of live varicella virus-containing vaccines: Efficacy, persistence of immune responses, and safety six years after administration in healthy children during their second year of life. *Vaccine, 36*(3), 381–387. https://doi.org/10.1016/J.VACCINE.2017.11.081

Hensch, T. K. (2018). Critical periods in cortical development. In R. Gibb & B. Kolb (Eds.), *The neurobiology of brain and behavioral development* (pp. 133–151). Philadelphia, PA: Elsevier. https://doi.org/10.1016/B978-0-12-804036-2.00006-6

Hepach, R., Vaish, A., & Tomasello, M. (2012). Young children are intrinsically motivated to see others helped. *Psychological Science, 23*(9), 967–972. https://doi.org/10.1177/0956797612440571

Hepper, P. (2015). Behavior during the prenatal period: Adaptive for development and survival. *Child Development Perspectives, 9*(1), 38–43. https://doi.org/10.1111/cdep.12104

Hepper, P. G. (2013). The developmental origins of laterality: Fetal handedness. *Developmental Psychobiology, 55*(6), 588–595. https://doi.org/10.1002/dev.21119

Hepper, P. G., Dornan, J. C., & Lynch, C. (2012). Sex differences in fetal habituation. *Developmental Science, 15*(3), 373–383. https://doi.org/10.1111/j.1467-7687.2011.01132.x

Herati, A. S., Zhelyazkova, B. H., Butler, P. R., & Lamb, D. J. (2017). Age-related alterations in the genetics and genomics of the male germ line. *Fertility and Sterility, 107*(2), 319–323. https://doi.org/10.1016/J.FERTNSTERT.2016.12.021

Herbert, J., Eckerman, C. O., Goldstein, R. F., & Stanton, M. E. (2004). Contrasts in classical eyeblink conditioning as a function of premature birth. *Infancy, 5*(3), 367–383.

Herman-Giddens, M. E. (2006). Recent data on pubertal milestones in United States children: The secular trend toward earlier development. *International Journal of Andrology, 29*(1), 241–246.

Herman-Giddens, M. E., Steffes, J., Harris, D., Slora, E., Hussey, M., Dowshen, S. A., . . . Reiter, E. O. (2012). Secondary sexual characteristics in boys: Data from the Pediatric Research in Office Settings Network. *Pediatrics, 130*(5), e1058–e1068. https://doi.org/10.1542/peds.2011-3291

Hernandez-Pavon, J. C., Sosa, M., Lutter, W. J., Maier, M., & Wakai, R. T. (2008). Auditory evoked responses in neonates by MEG. *AIP Conference Proceedings, 1032*(1), 114–117. https://doi.org/10.1063/1.2979244

Herpertz-Dahlmann, B. (2017). Treatment of eating disorders in child and adolescent psychiatry. *Current Opinion in Psychiatry, 30*(6), 438–445. https://doi.org/10.1097/YCO.0000000000000357

Herpertz-Dahlmann, B., Dempfle, A., Konrad, K., Klasen, F., Ravens-Sieberer, U., & the BELLA Study Group. (2015). Eating disorder symptoms do not just disappear: The implications of adolescent eating-disordered behaviour for body weight and mental health in young adulthood. *European Child & Adolescent Psychiatry, 24*(6), 675–684. https://doi.org/10.1007/s00787-014-0610-3

Herrenkohl, T. I., Hong, S., Klika, J. B., Herrenkohl, R. C., & Russo, M. J. (2013). Developmental impacts of child abuse and neglect related to adult mental health, substance use, and physical health. *Journal of Family Violence, 28*(2), 191–199. https://doi.org/10.1007/s10896-012-9474-9

Herrera-Gómez, A., Luna-Bertos, E. De, Ramos-Torrecillas, J., Ocaña-Peinado, F. M., García-Martínez, O., & Ruiz, C. (2017). The effect of epidural analgesia alone and in association with other variables on the risk of cesarean section. *Biological Research for Nursing, 19*(4), 393–398. https://doi.org/10.1177/1099800417706023

Herrman, J. W. (2009). There's a fine line . . . adolescent dating violence and prevention. *Pediatric Nursing, 35*(3), 164–170.

Hesketh, K. R., Lakshman, R., & van Sluijs, E. M. F. (2017). Barriers and facilitators to young children's physical activity and sedentary behaviour: A systematic review and synthesis of qualitative literature. *Obesity Reviews, 18*(9), 987–1017. https://doi.org/10.1111/obr.12562

Hespos, S. J., & Baillargeon, R. (2008). Young infants' actions reveal their developing knowledge of support variables: Converging evidence for violation-of-expectation findings. *Cognition, 107*(1), 304–316. https://doi.org/10.1016/J.COGNITION.2007.07.009

Hespos, S. J., Ferry, A. L., Anderson, E. M., Hollenbeck, E. N., & Rips, L. J. (2016). Five-month-old infants have general knowledge of how nonsolid substances behave and interact. *Psychological Science, 27*(2), 244–256. https://doi.org/10.1177/0956797615617897

Hess, J., & Slavin, J. (2014). Snacking for a cause: Nutritional insufficiencies and excesses of U.S. children, a critical review of food consumption patterns and macronutrient and micronutrient intake of U.S. children. *Nutrients, 6*(11), 4750–4759. https://doi.org/10.3390/nu6114750

Heward, W. L. (2018). *Exceptional children: An introduction to special education* (11th ed.). New York, NY: Pearson.

Hewlett, B. S. (2008). Fathers and infants among Aka pygmies. In R. A. LeVine & R. S. New (Eds.), *Anthropology and child development: A cross-cultural reader* (pp. 84–99). Malden, MA: Blackwell Publishing.

Hewlett, B S., Lamb, M. E., Shannon, D., Leyendecker, B., & Scholmerich, A. (1998). Culture and early infancy among central African foragers and farmers. *Developmental Psychology, 34*, 653–661.

Hewlett, B. S., & MacFarlan, S. J. (2010). Fathers, roles in hunter-gatherer and other small-scale cultures. In M. E. Lamb (Ed.), *The roles of the father in child development* (5th ed., pp. 413–434). Hoboken, NJ: John Wiley & Sons.

Heyes, C. (2014). False belief in infancy: A fresh look. *Developmental Science, 17*(5), 647–659. https://doi.org/10.1111/desc.12148

Hiatt, C., Laursen, B., Mooney, K. S., & Rubin, K. H. (2015). Forms of friendship: A person-centered assessment of the quality, stability, and outcomes of different types of adolescent friends. *Personality and Individual Differences, 77*, 149–155. https://doi.org/10.1016/j.paid.2014.12.051

Hiatt, C., Laursen, B., Stattin, H., & Kerr, M. (2017). Best friend influence over adolescent problem behaviors: Socialized by the satisfied. *Journal of Clinical Child & Adolescent Psychology, 46*(5), 695–708. https://doi.org/10.1080/15374416.2015.1050723

Hicks-Pass, S. (2009). Corporal punishment in America today: Spare the rod, spoil the child? A systematic review of the literature. *Best Practice in Mental Health, 5*(2), 71–88.

Hill, H. A., Elam-Evans, L. D., Yankey, D., Singleton, J. A., & Kang, Y. (2018). Vaccination coverage among children aged 19–35 months—United States, 2017. *MMWR. Morbidity and Mortality Weekly Report, 67*(40), 1123–1128. https://doi.org/10.15585/mmwr.mm6740a4

Hill, N. E., Bush, K. R., & Roosa, M. W. (2003). Parenting and socialization strategies and children's mental health: Low-income Mexican-American and Euro-American mothers and children. *Child Development, 74*, 189–204.

Hill, R. M., Castellanos, D., & Pettit, J. W. (2011). Suicide-related behaviors and anxiety in children and adolescents: A review. *Clinical Psychology Review, 31*(7), 1133–1144. https://doi.org/10.1016/j.cpr.2011.07.008

Hillerer, K. M., Jacobs, V. R., Fischer, T., & Aigner, L. (2014). The maternal brain: An organ with peripartal plasticity. *Neural Plasticity, 2014*, 574159. https://doi.org/10.1155/2014/574159

Hillis, S., Mercy, J., Amobi, A., & Kress, H. (2016). Global prevalence of past-year violence against children: A systematic review and minimum estimates. *Pediatrics, 137*(3), e20154079. https://doi.org/10.1542/peds.2015-4079

Hindman, A. H., & Wasik, B. A. (2015). Building vocabulary in two languages: An examination of Spanish-speaking dual language learners in Head Start. *Early Childhood Research Quarterly, 31*, 19–33. https://doi.org/10.1016/j.ecresq.2014.12.006

Hinduja, S., & Patchin, J. (2015). *State cyberbullying laws: A brief review of state cyberbullying laws and policies.* Retrieved from http://www.cyberbullying.us/Bullying-and-Cyberbullying-Laws.pdf

Hines, M. (2013). Sex and sex differences. In P. D. Zelazo (Ed.), *The Oxford handbook of developmental psychology: Vol. 1. Body and mind.* New York, NY: Oxford University Press. https://doi.org/10.1093/oxfordhb/9780199958450.013.0007

Hines, M. (2015). Gendered development. In *Handbook of child psychology and developmental science* (pp. 1–46). Hoboken, NJ: John Wiley & Sons. https://doi.org/10.1002/9781118963418.childpsy320

Hines, M., Pasterski, V., Spencer, D., Neufeld, S., Patalay, P., Hindmarsh, P. C., . . . Acerini, C. L. (2016). Prenatal androgen exposure alters girls' responses to information indicating gender-appropriate behaviour. *Philosophical Transactions of the Royal Society of London B: Biological Sciences, 371*(1688), 20150125. Retrieved from http://rstb.royalsocietypublishing.org/content/371/1688/20150125

Hinkelman, L., & Bruno, M. (2008). Identification and reporting of child sexual abuse: The role of elementary school professionals. *Elementary School Journal, 108*(5), 376–391.

Hinshaw, S. P. (2018). Attention deficit hyperactivity disorder (ADHD): Controversy, developmental mechanisms, and multiple levels of analysis. *Annual Review of Clinical Psychology, 14*(1), 291–316. https://doi.org/10.1146/annurev-clinpsy-050817-084917

Hitch, G. J., Towse, J. N., & Hutton, U. (2001). What limits children's working memory span? Theoretical accounts and applications for scholastic development. *Journal of Experimental Psychology: General, 130*(2), 184–198.

Hithersay, R., Hamburg, S., Knight, B., & Strydom, A. (2017). Cognitive decline and dementia in Down syndrome. *Current Opinion in Psychiatry, 30*(2), 102–107. https://doi.org/10.1097/YCO.0000000000000307

Hock, A., Oberst, L., Jubran, R., White, H., Heck, A., & Bhatt, R. S. (2017). Integrated emotion processing in infancy: Matching of faces and bodies. *Infancy, 22*(5), 608–625. https://doi.org/10.1111/infa.12177

Hock, R. (2015). *Human sexuality.* Boston, MA: Pearson.

Hoddinott, J., Alderman, H., Behrman, J. R., Haddad, L., & Horton, S. (2013). The economic rationale for investing in stunting reduction. *Maternal & Child Nutrition, 9*(Suppl. 2), 69–82. https://doi.org/10.1111/mcn.12080

Hodel, A. S. (2018). Rapid infant prefrontal cortex development and sensitivity to early environmental experience. *Developmental Review, 48*, 113–144. https://doi.org/10.1016/J.DR.2018.02.003

Hodel, A. S., Hunt, R. H., Cowell, R. A., Van Den Heuvel, S. E., Gunnar, M. R., & Thomas, K. M. (2015). Duration of early adversity and structural brain development in post-institutionalized adolescents. *NeuroImage,*

105, 112–119. https://doi.org/10.1016/J.NEUROIMAGE.2014.10.020

Hodges-Simeon, C. R., Gurven, M., Cárdenas, R. A., & Gaulin, S. J. C. (2013). Voice change as a new measure of male pubertal timing: A study among Bolivian adolescents. *Annals of Human Biology, 40*(3), 209–219. https://doi.org/10.3109/03014460.2012.759622

Hoekzema, E., Barba-Müller, E., Pozzobon, C., Picado, M., Lucco, F., García-García, D., . . . Vilarroya, O. (2017). Pregnancy leads to long-lasting changes in human brain structure. *Nature Neuroscience, 20*(2), 287–296. https://doi.org/10.1038/nn.4458

Hoeve, M., Dubas, J. S., Gerris, J. R. M., van der Laan, P. H., & Smeenk, W. (2011). Maternal and paternal parenting styles: Unique and combined links to adolescent and early adult delinquency. *Journal of Adolescence, 34*(5), 813–827. https://doi.org/10.1016/j.adolescence.2011.02.004

Hofer, C., Eisenberg, N., Spinrad, T. L., Morris, A. S., Gershoff, E., Valiente, C., . . . Eggum, N. D. (2013). Mother-adolescent conflict: Stability, change, and relations with externalizing and internalizing behavior problems. *Social Development (Oxford, England), 22*(2), 259–279. https://doi.org/10.1111/sode.12012

Hoff, E. (2014). *Language development*. New York, NY: Cengage Learning.

Hoff, E. (2015). Language development. In M. H. Bornstein & M. E. Lamb (Eds.), *Developmental science: An advanced textbook* (5th ed., pp. 443–488). New York, NY: Psychology Press.

Hoff, E., & Core, C. (2015). What clinicians need to know about bilingual development. *Seminars in Speech and Language, 36*(02), 089–099. https://doi.org/10.1055/s-0035-1549104

Hoff, E., Core, C., Place, S., & Rumiche, R. (2012). Dual language exposure and early bilingual development. *Journal of Child Language, 39*(01), 1–27. https://doi.org/10.1017/S0305000910000759

Hoff, E., Naigles, L., & Nigales, L. (2002). How children use input to acquire a lexicon. *Child Development, 73*(2), 418–433.

Hoff, E., Rumiche, R., Burridge, A., Ribot, K. M., & Welsh, S. N. (2014). Expressive vocabulary development in children from bilingual and monolingual homes: A longitudinal study from two to four years. *Early Childhood Research Quarterly, 29*(4), 433–444. https://doi.org/10.1016/j.ecresq.2014.04.012

Hoffman, M. L. (1970). Conscience, personality, and socialization technique. *Human Development, 13*, 90–126.

Hoffmann, J., & Russ, S. (2012). Pretend play, creativity, and emotion regulation in children. *Psychology of Aesthetics, Creativity, and the Arts, 6*(2), 175–184.

Hoggatt, K. J., Flores, M., Solorio, R., Wilhelm, M., & Ritz, B. (2012). The "Latina epidemiologic paradox" revisited: The role of birthplace and acculturation in predicting infant low birth weight for Latinas in Los Angeles, CA. *Journal of Immigrant and Minority Health, 14*(5), 875–884. https://doi.org/10.1007/s10903-011-9556-4

Holliday, K. (2014, October 21). China to ease 1-child rule further, but do people care? *CNBC News*. Retrieved from http://www.cnbc.com/id/102104640#

Hollis, J. L., Williams, A. J., Sutherland, R., Campbell, E., Nathan, N., Wolfenden, L., . . . Wiggers, J. (2016). A systematic review and meta-analysis of moderate-to-vigorous physical activity levels in elementary school physical education lessons. *Preventive Medicine, 86*, 34–54. https://doi.org/10.1016/J.YPMED.2015.11.018

Hollon, S. D., DeRubeis, R. J., Fawcett, J., Amsterdam, J. D., Shelton, R. C., Zajecka, J., . . . Gallop, R. (2016). Notice of Retraction and Replacement. Hollon et al. Effect of cognitive therapy with antidepressant medications vs antidepressants alone on the rate of recovery in major depressive disorder: A randomized clinical trial. *JAMA Psychiatry*. 2014;71(10):1157–1164. *JAMA Psychiatry, 73*(6), 639. https://doi.org/10.1001/jamapsychiatry.2016.0756

Holloway, S. D. (1999). Divergent cultural models of child rearing and pedagogy in Japanese preschools. *New Directions for Child and Adolescent Development, 83*, 61–75.

Holman, D. M., Benard, V., Roland, K. B., Watson, M., Liddon, N., & Stokley, S. (2014). Barriers to human papillomavirus vaccination among US adolescents. *JAMA Pediatrics, 168*(1), 76–82. https://doi.org/10.1001/jamapediatrics.2013.2752

Homan, G. J. (2016). Failure to thrive: A practical guide. *American Family Physician, 94*(4), 295–299.

Homma, Y., Wang, N., Saewyc, E., & Kishor, N. (2012). The relationship between sexual abuse and risky sexual behavior among adolescent boys: A meta-analysis. *Journal of Adolescent Health, 51*(1), 18–24. https://doi.org/10.1016/j.jadohealth.2011.12.032

Honaker, S. M., & Meltzer, L. J. (2014). Bedtime problems and night wakings in young children: An update of the evidence. *Paediatric Respiratory Reviews, 15*(4), 333–339. https://doi.org/10.1016/j.prrv.2014.04.011

Hong, G., & Yu, B. (2007). Early-grade retention and children's reading and math learning in elementary years. *Educational Evaluation and Policy Analysis, 29*(4), 239–261.

Honomichl, R. D., & Zhe, C. (2011). Relations as rules: The role of attention in the dimensional change card sort task. *Developmental Psychology, 47*(1), 50–60. https://doi.org/10.1037/a0021025

Hopkins, B. (1991). Facilitating early motor development: An intercultural study of West Indian mothers and their infants living in Britain. In J. K. Nugent, B. M. Lester, & T. B. Brazelton (Eds.), *The cultural context of infancy: Vol. 2. Multicultural and interdisciplinary approaches to parent-infant relations*. Norwood, NJ: Ablex.

Hopkins, B., & Westra, T. (1989). Maternal expectations of their infants' development: Some cultural differences. *Developmental Medicine & Child Neurology, 31*(3), 384–390.

Hopkins, B., & Westra, T. (1990). Motor development, maternal expectations, and the role of handling. *Infant Behavior & Development, 13*(1), 117–122.

Hopkins, K. D., Taylor, C. L., D'Antoine, H., & Zubrick, S. R. (2012). Predictors of resilient psychosocial functioning in Western Australian Aboriginal young people exposed to high family-level risk. In M. Ungar (Ed.), *The social ecology of resilience* (pp. 425–440). New York, NY: Springer. https://doi.org/10.1007/978-1-4614-0586-3_33

Hopmeyer, A., & Medovoy, T. (2017). Emerging adults' self-identified peer crowd affiliations, risk behavior, and social–emotional adjustment in college. *Emerging Adulthood, 5*(2), 143–148. https://doi.org/10.1177/2167696816665055

Horning, M. L., Schow, R., Friend, S. E., Loth, K., Neumark-Sztainer, D., & Fulkerson, J. A. (2017). Family dinner frequency interacts with dinnertime context in associations with child and parent BMI outcomes. *Journal of Family Psychology, 31*(7), 945–951. https://doi.org/10.1037/fam0000330

Horowitz, F. D., & O'Brien, M. (1986). Gifted and talented children: State of knowledge and directions for research. *American Psychologist, 41*(10), 1147–1152. https://doi.org/10.1037/0003-066X.41.10.1147

Horowitz, S. H., Rawe, J., & Whittaker, M. C. (2017). *The state of learning disabilities: Understanding the 1 in 5*. New York, NY: National Center for Learning Disabilities.

Hossain, Z., Field, T., Pickens, J., Malphurs, J., & Del Valle, C. (1997). Fathers' caregiving in low-income African-American and Hispanic-American families. *Early Development & Parenting, 6*(2), 73–82. https://doi.org/10.1002/(sici)1099-0917(199706)6:2<73:: aid-edp145>3.0.co;2-o

Hossain, Z., Roopnarine, J. L., Ismail, R., Hashmi, S. I., & Sombuling, A. (2007). Fathers' and mothers' reports of involvement in caring for infants in Kadazan families in Sabah, Malaysia. *Fathering, 5*(1), 58–72. https://doi.org/10.3149/fth.0501.58

Houdé, O., Pineau, A., Leroux, G., Poirel, N., Perchey, G., Lanoë, C., . . . Mazoyer, B. (2011). Functional magnetic resonance imaging study of Piaget's conservation-of-number task in preschool and school-age children: A neo-Piagetian approach. *Journal of Experimental Child Psychology, 110*(3), 332–346. https://doi.org/10.1016/j.jecp.2011.04.008

Howard-Jones, P. A. (2014). Neuroscience and education: Myths and messages. *Nature Reviews Neuroscience, 15*(12), 817–824. https://doi.org/10.1038/nrn3817

Howe, M. L. (2015). Memory development. In *Handbook of child psychology and developmental science* (pp. 1–47). Hoboken, NJ: John Wiley & Sons. https://doi.org/10.1002/9781118963418.childpsy206

Howe, N., Della Porta, S., Recchia, H., & Ross, H. (2016). "Because if you don't put the top on, it will spill": A longitudinal study of sibling teaching in early childhood. *Developmental Psychology, 52*(11), 1832–1842. https://doi.org/10.1037/dev0000193

Howe, T.-H., Sheu, C.-F., Wang, T.-N., & Hsu, Y.-W. (2014). Parenting stress in families with very low birth weight preterm infants in early infancy. *Research in Developmental Disabilities, 35*(7), 1748–1756. https://doi.org/10.1016/j.ridd.2014.02.015

Howell, B. R., McMurray, M. S., Guzman, D. B., Nair, G., Shi, Y., McCormack, K. M., . . . Sanchez, M. M. (2017). Maternal buffering beyond glucocorticoids: Impact of early life stress on corticolimbic circuits that control infant responses to novelty. *Social Neuroscience, 12*(1), 50–64. https://doi.org/10.1080/17470919.2016.1200481

Hoyme, H. E., Kalberg, W. O., Elliott, A. J., Blankenship, J., Buckley, D., Marais, A.-S., . . . May, P. A. (2016). Updated clinical guidelines for diagnosing fetal alcohol spectrum disorders. *Pediatrics, 138*(2), e20154256. https://doi.org/10.1542/peds.2015-4256

Hrapczynski, K. M., & Leslie, L. A. (2018). Engagement in racial socialization among transracial adoptive families with white parents. *Family Relations, 67*(3), 354–367. https://doi.org/10.1111/fare.12316

Huang, D. Y. C., Murphy, D. A., & Hser, Y.-I. (2011). Parental monitoring during early adolescence deters adolescent sexual initiation: Discrete-time survival mixture analysis. *Journal of Child and Family Studies, 20*(4), 511–520. https://doi.org/10.1007/s10826-010-9418-z

Huang, X. N., Wang, H. S., Zhang, L. J., & Liu, X. C. (2010). Co-sleeping and children's sleep in China. *Biological Rhythm Research, 41*(3), 169–181. https://doi.org/10.1080/09291011003687940

Huang, Z. J., Lewin, A., Mitchell, S. J., & Zhang, J. (2012). Variations in the relationship between maternal depression, maternal sensitivity, and child attachment by race/ethnicity and nativity: Findings from a nationally representative cohort study. *Maternal and Child Health Journal, 16*(1), 40–50. https://doi.org/10.1007/s10995-010-0716-2

Hudson, J. A., Fivush, R., & Kuebli, J. (1992). Scripts and episodes: The development of event memory. *Applied Cognitive Psychology, 6*, 483–505.

Huelke, D. F. (1998). An overview of anatomical considerations of infants and children in the adult world of automobile safety design. In *Annual proceedings of the Association for the Advancement of Automotive Medicine*. Chicago, IL: Association for the Advancement of Automotive Medicine.

Huesmann, L. R., Dubow, E. F., Boxer, P., Landau, S. F., Gvirsman, S. D., Shikaki, K., . . . Sapolsky, R. M. (2016). Children's exposure to violent political conflict stimulates aggression at peers by increasing emotional distress, aggressive script rehearsal, and normative beliefs favoring aggression. *Development and Psychopathology, 36*(7), 1–12. https://doi.org/10.1017/S0954579416001115

Hueston, C. M., Cryan, J. F., & Nolan, Y. M. (2017). Stress and adolescent hippocampal neurogenesis: Diet and exercise as cognitive modulators. *Translational Psychiatry, 7*(4), e1081. https://doi.org/10.1038/tp.2017.48

Huey, M., Hiatt, C., Laursen, B., Burk, W. J., & Rubin, K. (2017). Mother–adolescent conflict types and adolescent adjustment: A person-oriented analysis. *Journal of Family Psychology, 31*(4), 504–512. https://doi.org/10.1037/fam0000294

Hughes, C., McHarg, G., & White, N. (2018). Sibling influences on prosocial behavior. *Current Opinion in Psychology, 20*, 96–101. https://doi.org/10.1016/J.COPSYC.2017.08.015

Hughes, C. H., & Devine, R. T. (2015). A social perspective on theory of mind. In M. E. Lamb (Ed.), *Handbook of child psychology and developmental science* (pp. 1–46). Hoboken, NJ: John Wiley & Sons. https://doi.org/10.1002/9781118963418.childpsy314

Hughes, C. H., & Ensor, R. (2007). Executive function and theory of mind: Predictive relations from ages 2 to 4. *Developmental Psychology, 43*(6), 1447–1459. https://doi.org/10.1037/0012-1649.43.6.1447

Hughes, D., Hagelskamp, C., Way, N., & Foust, M. D. (2009). The role of mothers' and adolescents' perceptions of ethnic-racial socialization in shaping ethnic-racial identity among early adolescent boys and girls. *Journal of Youth & Adolescence, 38*(5), 605–626. https://doi.org/10.1007/s10964-009-9399-7

Hughes, D. L., Del Toro, J., & Way, N. (2017). Interrelations among dimensions of ethnic-racial identity during adolescence. *Developmental Psychology, 53*(11), 2139–2153. https://doi.org/10.1037/dev0000401

Hughes, J. N., Cao, Q., West, S. G., Allee Smith, P., & Cerda, C. (2017). Effect of retention in elementary grades on dropping out of school early. *Journal of School Psychology, 65*, 11–27. https://doi.org/10.1016/J.JSP.2017.06.003

Hughes, J. N., Chen, Q., Thoemmes, F., & Kwok, O. (2010). An investigation of the relationship between retention in first grade and performance on high stakes tests in third grade. *Educational Evaluation and Policy Analysis, 32*(2), 166–182. https://doi.org/10.3102/0162373710367682

Hui, K., Angelotta, C., & Fisher, C. E. (2017). Criminalizing substance use in pregnancy: Misplaced priorities. *Addiction, 112*(7), 1123–1125. https://doi.org/10.1111/add.13776

Hull, J. V., Dokovna, L. B., Jacokes, Z. J., Torgerson, C. M., Irimia, A., & Van Horn, J. D. (2017). Resting-state functional connectivity in autism spectrum disorders: A review. *Frontiers in Psychiatry, 7*, 205. https://doi.org/10.3389/fpsyt.2016.00205

Hunnius, S., & Geuze, R. H. (2004). Developmental changes in visual scanning of dynamic faces and abstract stimuli in infants: A longitudinal study. *Infancy, 6*(2), 231–255.

Huntsinger, C. S., Jose, P. E., & Larson, S. L. (1998). Do parent practices to encourage academic competence influence the social adjustment of young European American and Chinese American children? *Developmental Psychology, 34*, 747–756.

Hurtado, N., Marchman, V. A., & Fernald, A. (2008). Does input influence uptake? Links between maternal talk, processing speed and vocabulary size in Spanish-learning children. *Developmental Science, 11*(6), F31–F39. https://doi.org/10.1111/j.1467-7687.2008.00768.x

Hussain, F. N., & Ashmead, G. G. (2017). The safety of over-the-counter medications in pregnancy. *Topics in Obstetrics & Gynecology 3, 37*(14), 1–7. https://doi.org/10.1097/01.PGO.0000524651.99411.37

Huston, A. C. (2008). From research to policy and back. *Child Development, 79*(1), 1–12. https://doi.org/10.1111/j.1467-8624.2007.01107.x

Huston, A. C. (2018). A life at the intersection of science and social issues. *Child Development Perspectives, 12*(2), 75–79. https://doi.org/10.1111/cdep.12265

Huston, A. C., Bobbitt, K. C., & Bentley, A. (2015). Time spent in child care: How and why does it affect social development? *Developmental Psychology, 51*(5), 621–634. https://doi.org/10.1037/a0038951

Hutchinson, E. A., De Luca, C. R., Doyle, L. W., Roberts, G., Anderson, P. J., & Victorian Infant Collaborative Study Group. (2013). School-age outcomes of extremely preterm or extremely low birth weight children. *Pediatrics, 131*(4), e1053–e1061. https://doi.org/10.1542/peds.2012-2311

Hutchison, J. E., Lyons, I. M., & Ansari, D. (2019). More similar than different: Gender differences in children's basic numerical skills are the exception not the rule. *Child Development, 90*(1), e66–e79. https://doi.org/10.1111/cdev.13044

Hutson, E., Kelly, S., & Militello, L. K. (2018). Systematic review of cyberbullying interventions for youth and parents with implications for evidence-based practice. *Worldviews on Evidence-Based Nursing, 15*(1), 72–79. https://doi.org/10.1111/wvn.12257

Huttenlocher, J., Levine, S., & Vevea, J. (1998). Environmental input and cognitive growth: A study using time-period comparisons. *Child Development, 69*, 1012–1029.

Huttenlocher, J., Vasilyeva, M., Cymerman, E., & Levine, S. (2002). Language input and child syntax. *Cognitive Psychology, 45*(3), 337–374.

Huttenlocher, J., Waterfall, H., Vasilyeva, M., Vevea, J., & Hedges, L. V. (2010). Sources of variability in children's language growth. *Cognitive Psychology, 61*(4), 343–365. https://doi.org/10.1016/j.cogpsych.2010.08.002

Huynh, H. T., Demeter, N. E., Burke, R. V., & Upperman, J. S. (2017). The role of adult perceptions and supervision behavior in preventing child injury. *Journal of Community Health, 42*(4), 649–655. https://doi.org/10.1007/s10900-016-0300-9

Hwang, G.-J., Chiu, L.-Y., & Chen, C.-H. (2015). A contextual game-based learning approach to improving students' inquiry-based learning performance in social studies courses. *Computers & Education, 81*, 13–25. https://doi.org/10.1016/J.COMPEDU.2014.09.006

Hyde, J. S. (2014). Gender similarities and differences. *Annual Review of Psychology, 65*, 373–398. https://doi.org/10.1146/annurev-psych-010213-115057

Hyde, J. S. (2016). Sex and cognition: Gender and cognitive functions. *Current Opinion in Neurobiology, 38*, 53–56. https://doi.org/10.1016/j.conb.2016.02.007

Hyde, K. L., Lerch, J., Norton, A., Forgeard, M., Winner, E., Evans, A. C., & Schlaug, G. (2009). Musical training shapes structural brain development. *Journal of Neuroscience, 29*(10), 3019–3025. https://doi.org/10.1523/JNEUROSCI.5118-08.2009

Hymel, S., & Swearer, S. M. (2015). Four decades of research on school bullying: An introduction. *American Psychologist, 70*(4), 293–299. https://doi.org/10.1037/a0038928

Ibbotson, P., & Tomasello, M. (2016). Evidence rebuts Chomsky's theory of language learning. *Scientific American, 315*(5), 70–75. https://doi.org/10.1038/scientificamerican1116-70

Ilmarinen, V.-J., Vainikainen, M.-P., Verkasalo, M. J., & Lönnqvist, J.-E. (2017). Homophilous friendship assortment based on personality traits and cognitive ability in middle childhood: The moderating effect of peer network size. *European Journal of Personality, 31*(3), 208–219. https://doi.org/10.1002/per.2095

Imdad, A., Yakoob, M. Y., & Bhutta, Z. A. (2011). Effect of breastfeeding promotion interventions on breastfeeding rates, with special focus on developing countries. *BMC Public Health, 11*(Suppl. 3), S24. https://doi.org/10.1186/1471-2458-11-s3-s24

Immler, S. (2018). The sperm factor: Paternal impact beyond genes. *Heredity, 121*(3), 239–247. https://doi.org/10.1038/s41437-018-0111-0

Inhelder, B., & Piaget, J. (1958). *The growth of logical thinking: From childhood to adolescence.* New York, NY: Basic Books.

Inhelder, B., & Piaget, J. (1964). *The early growth of logic in the child: Classification and seriation.* New York, NY: Harper and Row.

Ioannides, A. S. (2017). Preconception and prenatal genetic counselling. *Best Practice & Research Clinical Obstetrics & Gynaecology, 42*, 2–10. https://doi.org/https://doi.org/10.1016/j.bpobgyn.2017.04.003

Iqbal, H., Neal, S., & Vincent, C. (2017). Children's friendships in super-diverse localities: Encounters with social and ethnic difference. *Childhood, 24*(1), 128–142. https://doi.org/10.1177/0907568216633741

Isaacs, E. B., Fischl, B. R., Quinn, B. T., Chong, W. K., Gadian, D. G., & Lucas, A. (2010). Impact of breast milk on intelligence quotient, brain size, and white matter development. *Pediatric Research, 67*(4), 357–362.

Isbell, E., Fukuda, K., Neville, H. J., & Vogel, E. K. (2015). Visual working memory continues to develop through adolescence. *Frontiers in Psychology, 6*, 696. https://doi.org/10.3389/fpsyg.2015.00696

Ishitani, T. T. (2006). Studying attrition and degree completion behavior among first-generation college students in the United States. *Journal of Higher Education, 77*, 861–885.

Islami, F., Liu, Y., Jemal, A., Zhou, J., Weiderpass, E., Colditz, G., . . . Weiss, M. (2015). Breastfeeding and breast cancer risk by receptor status—a systematic review and meta-analysis. *Annals of Oncology, 26*(12), mdv379. https://doi.org/10.1093/annonc/mdv379

Isomaa, R., Isomaa, A.-L., Marttunen, M., Kaltiala-Heino, R., & Björkqvist, K. (2009). The prevalence, incidence and development of eating disorders in Finnish adolescents—a two-step 3-year follow-up study. *European Eating Disorders Review, 17*(3), 199–207. https://doi.org/10.1002/erv.919

Iverson, J. M., & Goldin-Meadow, S. (2005). Gesture paves the way for language development. *Psychological Science, 16*(5), 367–371. https://doi.org/10.1111/j.0956-7976.2005.01542.x

Izard, C. E., Woodburn, E. M., & Finlon, K. J. (2010). Extending emotion science to the study of discrete emotions in infants. *Emotion Review, 2*(2), 134–136. https://doi.org/10.1177/1754073909355003

Jacob, J. I. (2009). The socio-emotional effects of non-maternal childcare on children in the USA: A critical review of recent studies. *Early Child Development & Care, 179*(5), 559–570. https://doi.org/10.1080/03004430701292988

Jacobs, E., Miller, L. C., & Tirella, L. G. (2010). Developmental and behavioral performance of internationally adopted preschoolers: A pilot study. *Child Psychiatry & Human Development, 41*(1), 15–29. https://doi.org/10.1007/s10578-009-0149-6

Jacobson, L. A., Crocetti, D., Dirlikov, B., Slifer, K., Denckla, M. B., Mostofsky, S. H., & Mahone, E. M. (2018). Anomalous brain development is evident in preschoolers with attention-deficit/hyperactivity disorder. *Journal of the International Neuropsychological Society, 24*(6), 531–539. https://doi.org/10.1017/S1355617718000103

Jacobus, J., Squeglia, L. M., Infante, M. A., Castro, N., Brumback, T., Meruelo, A. D., & Tapert, S. F. (2015). Neuropsychological performance in adolescent marijuana users with co-occurring alcohol use: A three-year longitudinal study. *Neuropsychology, 29*(6), 829–843. https://doi.org/10.1037/neu0000203

Jacoby, S. F., Tach, L., Guerra, T., Wiebe, D. J., & Richmond, T. S. (2017). The health status and well-being of low-resource, housing-unstable, single-parent families living in violent neighbourhoods in Philadelphia, Pennsylvania. *Health & Social Care in the Community, 25*(2), 578–589. https://doi.org/10.1111/hsc.12345

Jadva, V., Imrie, S., & Golombok, S. (2015). Surrogate mothers 10 years on: A longitudinal study of psychological well-being and relationships with the parents and child. *Human Reproduction, 30*(2), 373–379. https://doi.org/10.1093/humrep/deu339

Jaeger, E. L. (2016). Negotiating complexity: A bioecological systems perspective on literacy development. *Human Development, 59*(4), 163–187. https://doi.org/10.1159/000448743

Jaeger, M. M. (2012). The extended family and children's educational success. *American Sociological Review, 77*(6), 903–922. https://doi.org/10.1177/0003122412464040

Jaekel, J., Pluess, M., Belsky, J., & Wolke, D. (2015). Effects of maternal sensitivity on low birth weight children's academic achievement: A test of differential susceptibility versus diathesis stress. *Journal of Child Psychology and Psychiatry, 56*(6), 693–701. https://doi.org/10.1111/jcpp.12331

Jaffee, S., & Hyde, J. S. (2000). Gender differences in moral orientation: A meta-analysis. *Psychological Bulletin, 126*(5), 703.

Jagers, R. J., Bingham, K., & Hans, S. L. (1996). Socialization and social judgments among inner-city African-American kindergartners. *Child Development, 67*, 140–150.

Jahja, R., Huijbregts, S. C. J., de Sonneville, L. M. J., van der Meere, J. J., Legemaat, A. M., Bosch, A. M., . . . van Spronsen, F. J. (2017). Cognitive profile and mental health in adult phenylketonuria: A PKU-COBESO study. *Neuropsychology, 31*(4), 437–447. https://doi.org/10.1037/neu0000358

Jahns, L., Siega-Riz, A. M., & Popkin, B. M. (2001). The increasing prevalence of snacking among US children from 1977 to 1996. *Journal of Pediatrics, 138*, 493–498.

Jahromi, L. B., & Stifter, C. A. (2007). Individual differences in the contribution of maternal soothing to infant distress reduction. *Infancy, 11*(3), 255–269. https://doi.org/10.1080/15250000701310371

Jain, S., & Cohen, A. K. (2013). Behavioral adaptation among youth exposed to community violence: A longitudinal multidisciplinary study of family, peer and neighborhood-level protective factors. *Prevention Science, 14*(6), 606–617. https://doi.org/10.1007/s11121-012-0344-8

Jambon, M., & Smetana, J. G. (2014). Moral complexity in middle childhood: Children's evaluations of necessary harm. *Developmental Psychology, 50*(1), 22–33. https://doi.org/10.1037/a0032992

James, D. K. (2010). Fetal learning: A critical review. *Infant & Child Development, 19*(1), 45–54. https://doi.org/10.1002/icd.653

Janitz, A., Peck, J. D., & Craig, L. B. (2016). Ethnic and racial differences in the utilization of infertility services: National Survey of Family Growth (NSFG). *Fertility and Sterility, 106*(3), e112–e113. https://doi.org/10.1016/j.fertnstert.2016.07.337

Janosz, M., Archambault, I., Morizot, J., & Pagani, L. S. (2008). School engagement trajectories and their differential predictive relations to dropout. *Journal of Social Issues, 64*(1), 21–40. https://doi.org/10.1111/j.1540-4560.2008.00546.x

Jansen, I. (2006). Decision making in childbirth: The influence of traditional structures in a Ghanaian village. *International Nursing Review, 53*(1), 41–46.

Jansen, P. W., de Barse, L. M., Jaddoe, V. W. V., Verhulst, F. C., Franco, O. H., & Tiemeier, H. (2017). Bi-directional associations between child fussy eating and parents' pressure to eat: Who influences whom? *Physiology & Behavior, 176*, 101–106. https://doi.org/10.1016/j.physbeh.2017.02.015

Janssen, H. G., Davies, I. G., Richardson, L. D., & Stevenson, L. (2018). Determinants of takeaway and fast food consumption: A narrative review. *Nutrition Research Reviews, 31*(1), 16–34. https://doi.org/10.1017/S0954422417000178

Janssen, I., Katzmarzyk, P. T., Boyce, W. F., Vereecken, C., Mulvihill, C., Roberts, C., . . . Health Behaviour in School-Aged Children Obesity Working Group. (2005). Comparison of overweight and obesity prevalence in school-aged youth from 34 countries and their relationships with physical activity and dietary patterns. *Obesity Reviews, 6*, 123–132.

Janssen, I., & LeBlanc, A. G. (2010). Systematic review of the health benefits of physical activity and fitness in school-aged children and youth. *International Journal of Behavioral Nutrition and Physical Activity, 7*(1), 40. https://doi.org/10.1186/1479-5868-7-40

Janssens, J. M. A. M., & Dekovic, M. (1997). Child rearing, prosocial moral reasoning, and prosocial behaviour. *International Journal of Behavioral Development, 20*, 509–527.

Jaramillo, J., Mello, Z. R., & Worrell, F. C. (2016). Ethnic identity, stereotype threat, and perceived discrimination among Native American adolescents. *Journal of Research on Adolescence, 26*(4), 769–775. https://doi.org/10.1111/jora.12228

Jaramillo, N., Buhi, E. R., Elder, J. P., & Corliss, H. L. (2017). Associations between sex education and contraceptive use among heterosexually active, adolescent males in the United States. *Journal of Adolescent Health, 60*(5), 534–540. https://doi.org/10.1016/j.jadohealth.2016.11.025

Jaswal, V. K. (2010). Believing what you're told: Young children's trust in unexpected testimony about the physical world. *Cognitive Psychology, 61*(3), 248–272. https://doi.org/10.1016/j.cogpsych.2010.06.002

Javadi, A. H., Schmidt, D. H. K., & Smolka, M. N. (2014). Differential representation of feedback and decision in adolescents and adults. *Neuropsychologia, 56*, 280–288. https://doi.org/10.1016/j.neuropsychologia.2014.01.021

Jayakody, R., & Kalil, A. (2002). Social fathering in low-income, African American families with preschool children. *Journal of Marriage and Family, 64*, 504–516.

Jean, A. D. L., & Stack, D. M. (2012). Full-term and very-low-birth-weight preterm infants' self-regulating behaviors during a still-face interaction: Influences of maternal touch. *Infant Behavior and Development, 35*(4), 779–791. https://doi.org/10.1016/j.infbeh.2012.07.023

Jefferies, A. L. (2012). Kangaroo care for the preterm infant and family. *Paediatrics & Child Health, 17*(3), 141–146. Retrieved from https://www.ncbi.nlm.nih.gov/pmc/articles/PMC3287094/

Jeha, D., Usta, I., Ghulmiyyah, L., & Nassar, A. (2015). A review of the risks and consequences of adolescent pregnancy. *Journal of Neonatal-Perinatal Medicine, 8*(1), 1–8. https://doi.org/10.3233/NPM-15814038

Jelenkovic, A., Sund, R., Hur, Y.-M., Yokoyama, Y., Hjelmborg, J. v. B., Möller, S., . . . Silventoinen, K. (2016). Genetic and environmental influences on height from infancy to early adulthood: An individual-based pooled analysis of 45 twin cohorts. *Scientific Reports, 6*(1), 28496. https://doi.org/10.1038/srep28496

Jenkins, J. M., & Foster, E. M. (2014). The effects of breastfeeding exclusivity on early childhood outcomes. *American Journal of Public Health, 104*(Suppl.), S128–S135. https://doi.org/10.2105/AJPH.2013.301713

Jenni, O. G., & O'Connor, B. B. (2005). Children's sleep: An interplay between culture and biology. *Pediatrics, 115*(1), 204–216. https://doi.org/10.1542/peds.2004-0815B

Jennings, K. D., Sandberg, I., Kelley, S. A., Valdes, L., Yaggi, K., Abrew, A., & Macey-Kalcevic, M. (2008). Understanding of self and maternal warmth predict later self-regulation in toddlers. *International Journal of Behavioral Development, 32*(2), 108–118. https://doi.org/10.1177/0165025407087209

Jennings, S., Mellish, L., Tasker, F., Lamb, M., & Golombok, S. (2014). Why adoption? Gay, lesbian, and heterosexual adoptive parents' reproductive experiences and reasons for adoption. *Adoption Quarterly, 17*(3), 205–226. https://doi.org/10.1080/10926755.2014.891549

Jensen, E. (2008). *Brain-based learning: The new paradigm of teaching*. Thousand Oaks, CA: Sage.

Jernigan, T. L., & Stiles, J. (2017). Construction of the human forebrain. *Wiley Interdisciplinary Reviews: Cognitive Science, 8*(1–2), e1409. https://doi.org/10.1002/wcs.1409

Jespersen, K., Kroger, J., & Martinussen, M. (2013). Identity status and moral reasoning: A meta-analysis. *Identity, 13*(3), 266–280. https://doi.org/10.1080/15283488.2013.799472

Jewell, J. D., Krohn, E. J., Scott, V. G., Carlton, M., & Meinz, E. (2008). The differential impact of mothers' and fathers' discipline on preschool children's home and classroom behavior. *North American Journal of Psychology, 10*(1), 173–188.

Jha, A. K., Baliga, S., Kumar, H. H., Rangnekar, A., & Baliga, B. S. (2015). Is there a preventive role for vernix caseosa? An in vitro study. *Journal of Clinical and Diagnostic Research, 9*(11), SC13–SC16. https://doi.org/10.7860/JCDR/2015/14740.6784

Jia, G., & Aaronson, D. (2003). A longitudinal study of Chinese children and adolescents learning English in the United States. *Applied Psycholinguistics, 24*(1), 131–161. https://doi.org/10.1017/S0142716403000079

Jia, Y., Konold, T. R., & Cornell, D. (2016). Authoritative school climate and high school dropout rates. *School Psychology Quarterly, 31*(2), 289–303. https://doi.org/10.1037/spq0000139

Jin, M. K., Jacobvitz, D., Hazen, N., & Jung, S. H. (2012). Maternal sensitivity and infant attachment security in Korea: Cross-cultural validation of the Strange Situation. *Attachment & Human Development, 14*(1), 33–44. https://doi.org/10.1080/14616734.2012.636656

Jipson, J. L., Gülgöz, S., & Gelman, S. A. (2016). Parent–child conversations regarding the ontological status of a robotic dog. *Cognitive Development, 39*, 21–35. https://doi.org/10.1016/j.cogdev.2016.03.001

Ji-Yeon, K., McHale, S. M., Crouter, A. C., & Osgood, D. W. (2007). Longitudinal linkages between sibling relationships and adjustment from middle childhood through adolescence. *Developmental Psychology, 43*(4), 960–973.

Johnson, A. Z., Sieving, R. E., Pettingell, S. L., & McRee, A.-L. (2015). The roles of partner communication and relationship status in adolescent contraceptive use. *Journal of Pediatric Health Care, 29*(1), 61–69. https://doi.org/10.1016/j.pedhc.2014.06.008

Johnson, S. B., Riis, J. L., & Noble, K. G. (2016). State of the art review: Poverty and the developing brain. *Pediatrics, 137*(4), e20153075. https://doi.org/10.1542/peds.2015-3075

Johnson, S. P., & Hannon, E. E. (2015). Perceptual development. In L. S. Liben & U. Müller (Eds.), *Handbook of child psychology and developmental science* (pp. 1–50). Hoboken, NJ: John Wiley & Sons. https://doi.org/10.1002/9781118963418.childpsy203

Johnston, D. W., Nicholls, M. E. R., Shah, M., & Shields, M. A. (2009). Nature's experiment? Handedness and early childhood development. *Demography, 46*(2), 281–301. https://doi.org/10.1353/dem.0.0053

Johnston, D. W., Nicholls, M. E. R., Shah, M., & Shields, M. A. (2013). Handedness, health and cognitive development: Evidence from children in the National Longitudinal Survey of Youth. *Journal of the Royal Statistical Society: Series A (Statistics in Society), 176*(4), 841–860. https://doi.org/10.1111/j.1467-985X.2012.01074.x

Johnston, J. C. (2005). Teaching gestural signs to infants to advance child development: A review of the evidence. *First Language, 25*(2), 235–251. https://doi.org/10.1177/0142723705050340

Johnston, L. D., Miech, R. A., O 'Malley, P. M., Bachman, J. G., Schulenberg, J. E., & Patrick, M. E. (2018). *2017 overview: Key findings on adolescent drug use*. Retrieved from http://www.monitoringthefuture.org/pubs/monographs/mtf-overview2017.pdf

Jonas, W., Atkinson, L., Steiner, M., Meaney, M. J., Wazana, A., & Fleming, A. S. (2015). Breastfeeding and maternal sensitivity predict early infant temperament. *Acta Paediatrica, 104*(7), 678–686. https://doi.org/10.1111/apa.12987

Jones, D. J., Lewis, T., Litrownik, A., Thompson, R., Proctor, L. J., Isbell, P., . . . Runyan, D. (2013). Linking childhood sexual abuse and early adolescent risk behavior: The intervening role of internalizing and externalizing problems. *Journal of Abnormal Child Psychology, 41*(1), 139–150. https://doi.org/10.1007/s10802-012-9656-1

Jones, E. J. H., & Herbert, J. S. (2006). Exploring memory in infancy: Deferred imitation and the development of declarative memory. *Infant & Child Development, 15*, 195–205.

Jones, L., Rowe, J., & Becker, T. (2009). Appraisal, coping, and social support as predictors of psychological distress and parenting efficacy in parents of premature infants. *Children's Health Care, 38*(4), 245–262. https://doi.org/10.1080/02739610903235976

Jones, W., & Klin, A. (2013). Attention to eyes is present but in decline in 2–6-month-old infants later diagnosed with autism. *Nature, 504*(7480), 427–431. https://doi.org/10.1038/nature12715

Jonsson, B., Wiklund-Hörnqvist, C., Nyroos, M., & Börjesson, A. (2014). Self-reported memory strategies and their relationship to immediate and delayed text recall and working memory capacity. *Education Inquiry, 5*, 22850. https://doi.org/10.3402/edui.v5.22850

Joo, M. (2010). Long-term effects of Head Start on academic and school outcomes of children in persistent poverty: Girls vs. boys. *Children & Youth Services Review, 32*(6), 807–814. https://doi.org/10.1016/j.childyouth.2010.01.018

Joos, C. M., Wodzinski, A. M., Wadsworth, M. E., & Dorn, L. D. (2018). Neither antecedent nor consequence: Developmental integration of chronic stress, pubertal timing, and conditionally adapted stress response. *Developmental Review, 48*, 1–23. https://doi.org/10.1016/J.DR.2018.05.001

Jordan, J. W., Stalgaitis, C. A., Charles, J., Madden, P. A., Radhakrishnan, A. G., & Saggese, D. (2018). Peer crowd identification and adolescent health behaviors: Results from a statewide representative study. *Health Education & Behavior*, 109019811875914. https://doi.org/10.1177/1090198118759148

Joubert, B. R., Felix, J. F., Yousefi, P., Bakulski, K. M., Just, A. C., Breton, C., . . . London, S. J. (2016). DNA methylation in newborns and maternal smoking in pregnancy: Genome-wide consortium meta-analysis. *American Journal of Human Genetics, 98*(4), 680–696. https://doi.org/10.1016/J.AJHG.2016.02.019

Jouhki, M.-R., Suominen, T., & Åstedt-Kurki, P. (2017). Giving birth on our own terms—Women's experience of childbirth at home. *Midwifery, 53*, 35–41. https://doi.org/10.1016/j.midw.2017.07.008

Juárez, S. P., & Merlo, J. (2013). Revisiting the effect of maternal smoking during pregnancy on offspring birthweight: A quasi-experimental sibling analysis in

Sweden. *PLoS One, 8*(4), e61734. https://doi.org/10.1371/journal.pone.0061734

Juffer, F., & van IJzendoorn, M. H. (2007). Adoptees do not lack self-esteem: A meta-analysis of studies on self-esteem of transracial, international, and domestic adoptees. *Psychological Bulletin, 133*(6), 1067–1083. https://doi.org/10.1037/0033-2909.133.6.1067

Julian, M. M., Muzik, M., Kees, M., Valenstein, M., Dexter, C., & Rosenblum, K. L. (2018a). Intervention effects on reflectivity explain change in positive parenting in military families with young children. *Journal of Family Psychology, 32*(6), 804–815. https://doi.org/10.1037/fam0000431

Julian, M. M., Muzik, M., Kees, M., Valenstein, M., & Rosenblum, K. L. (2018b). Strong military families intervention enhances parenting reflectivity and representations in families with young children. *Infant Mental Health Journal, 39*(1), 106–118. https://doi.org/10.1002/imhj.21690

Junaid, K. A., & Fellowes, S. (2006). Gender differences in the attainment of motor skills on the Movement Assessment Battery for Children. *Physical & Occupational Therapy in Pediatrics, 26*(1/2), 5–11.

Just, M. A., & Carpenter, P. A. (1992). A capacity theory of comprehension: Individual differences in working memory. *Psychological Review, 99*, 122–149.

Juster, R.-P., Smith, N. G., Ouellet, É., Sindi, S., & Lupien, S. J. (2013). Sexual orientation and disclosure in relation to psychiatric symptoms, diurnal cortisol, and allostatic load. *Psychosomatic Medicine, 75*(2), 103–116. https://doi.org/10.1097/PSY.0b013e3182826881

Juvonen, J., & Graham, S. (2014). Bullying in schools: The power of bullies and the plight of victims. *Annual Review of Psychology, 65*, 159–185. https://doi.org/10.1146/annurev-psych-010213-115030

Juvonen, J., Kogachi, K., & Graham, S. (2018). When and how do students benefit from ethnic diversity in middle school? *Child Development, 89*(4), 1268–1282. https://doi.org/10.1111/cdev.12834

Kagan, J. (2013). Temperamental contributions to inhibited and uninhibited profiles. In P. D. Zelazo (Ed.), *The Oxford handbook of developmental psychology: Vol. 2. Self and other* (pp. 142–165). New York, NY: Oxford University Press. https://doi.org/10.1093/oxfordhb/9780199958474.013.0007

Kagan, J., Arcus, D., Snidman, N., Feng, W., Handler, J., & Greene, S. (1994). Reactivity in infants: A cross national comparison. *Developmental Psychology, 30*, 342–345.

Kahlenberg, S. G., & Hein, M. M. (2010). Progression on Nickelodeon? Gender-role stereotypes in toy commercials. *Sex Roles, 62*(11–12), 830–847. https://doi.org/10.1007/s11199-009-9653-1

Kahn, J., Koh, A., Luckcuck, R., McNeice, J., Walter, E., Yao, W., . . . Link, T. (2016). A phenylalanine fiasco: The structure of phenylalanine hydroxylase and its impact on phenylketonuria. *FASEB Journal, 30*(1 Suppl.), 665.8.

Kail, R. V. (2003). Information processing and memory. In M. H. Bornstein & L. Davidson (Eds.), *Well-being: Positive development across the life course* (pp. 269–279). Mahwah, NJ: Erlbaum.

Kail, R. V. (2008). Speed of processing in childhood and adolescence: Nature, consequences, and implications for understanding atypical development. In J. DeLuca & J. H. Kalmar (Eds.), *Information processing speed in clinical populations* (pp. 101–123). Philadelphia, PA: Taylor & Francis.

Kaiser Family Foundation. (2014). *Sexual health of adolescents and young adults in the United States*. Retrieved from http://kff.org/womens-health-policy/fact-sheet/sexual-health-of-adolescents-and-young-adults-in-the-united-states/

Kaiser, L., Allen, L., & American Dietetic Association. (2008). Position of the American Dietetic Association: Nutrition and lifestyle for a healthy pregnancy outcome. *Journal of the American Dietetic Association, 108*(3), 553–561. https://doi.org/10.1016/j.jada.2008.01.030

Kalashnikova, M., Mattock, K., & Monaghan, P. (2016). Flexible use of mutual exclusivity in word learning. *Language Learning and Development, 12*(1), 79–91. https://doi.org/10.1080/15475441.2015.1023443

Kaler, S. B., & Kopp, C. B. (1990). Compliance and comprehension in very young toddlers. *Child Development, 61*, 1997–2003.

Kalsner, L., & Chamberlain, S. J. (2015). Prader-Willi, Angelman, and 15q11-q13 duplication syndromes. *Pediatric Clinics of North America, 62*(3), 587–606. https://doi.org/10.1016/j.pcl.2015.03.004

Kamper-DeMarco, K. E., & Ostrov, J. M. (2017). Prospective associations between peer victimization and social-psychological adjustment problems in early childhood. *Aggressive Behavior, 43*(5), 471–482. https://doi.org/10.1002/ab.21705

Kan, P. F., & Kohnert, K. (2008). Fast mapping by bilingual preschool children. *Journal of Child Language, 35*(3), 495–514. https://doi.org/10.1017/S0305000907008604

Kana, R. K., Maximo, J. O., Williams, D. L., Keller, T. A., Schipul, S. E., Cherkassky, V. L., . . . Müller, R. (2015). Aberrant functioning of the theory-of-mind network in children and adolescents with autism. *Molecular Autism, 6*(1), 59. https://doi.org/10.1186/s13229-015-0052-x

Kang, H.-K. (2014). Influence of culture and community perceptions on birth and perinatal care of immigrant women: Doulas' perspective. *Journal of Perinatal Education, 23*(1), 25–32. https://doi.org/10.1891/1058-1243.23.1.25

Kann, L., Kinchen, S., Shanklin, S. L., Flint, K. H., Kawkins, J., Harris, W. A., . . . Centers for Disease Control and Prevention (CDC). (2014). Youth risk behavior surveillance–United States, 2013. *Morbidity and Mortality Weekly Report, Surveillance Summaries, 63*(Suppl. 4), 1–168.

Kann, L., McManus, T., Harris, W. A., Shanklin, S. L., Flint, K. H., Queen, B., . . . Ethier, K. A. (2018). Youth Risk Behavior Surveillance — United States, 2017. *MMWR Surveillance Summaries, 67*(8), 1. https://doi.org/10.15585/MMWR.SS6708A1

Kansky, J., & Allen, J. P. (2018). Long-term risks and possible benefits associated with late adolescent romantic relationship quality. *Journal of Youth and Adolescence, 47*(7), 1531–1544. https://doi.org/10.1007/s10964-018-0813-x

Kantamneni, N., McCain, M. R. C., Shada, N., Hellwege, M. A., & Tate, J. (2018). Contextual factors in the career development of prospective first-generation college students. *Journal of Career Assessment, 26*(1), 183–196. https://doi.org/10.1177/1069072716680048

Kantomaa, M. T., Stamatakis, E., Kankaanpää, A., Kaakinen, M., Rodriguez, A., Taanila, A., . . . Tammelin, T. (2013). Physical activity and obesity mediate the association between childhood motor function and adolescents' academic achievement. *Proceedings of the National Academy of Sciences of the United States of America, 110*(5), 1917–1922. https://doi.org/10.1073/pnas.1214574110

Kapadia, S., & Gala, J. (2015). Gender Across Cultures. In L. A. Jensen (Ed.), *The Oxford handbook of human development and culture* (pp. 307–326). Oxford, England: Oxford University Press. https://doi.org/10.1093/oxfordhb/9780199948550.013.19

Kaplan, H., & Dove, H. (1987). Infant development among the Ache of eastern Paraguay. *Developmental Psychology, 23*(2), 190–198.

Kapoor, A., Lubach, G. R., Ziegler, T. E., & Coe, C. L. (2016). Hormone levels in neonatal hair reflect prior maternal stress exposure during pregnancy. *Psychoneuroendocrinology, 66*, 111–117. https://doi.org/10.1016/j.psyneuen.2016.01.010

Karafantis, D. M., & Levy, S. R. (2004). The role of children's lay theories about the malleability of human attributes in beliefs about and volunteering for disadvantaged groups. *Child Development, 75*(1), 236–250. https://doi.org/10.1111/j.1467-8624.2004.00666.x

Karasik, L. B., Tamis-LeMonda, C. S., Adolph, K. E., & Bornstein, M. H. (2015). Places and postures: A cross-cultural comparison of sitting in 5-month-olds. *Journal of Cross-Cultural Psychology, 46*(8), 1023–1038. https://doi.org/10.1177/0022022115593803

Karbach, J., Gottschling, J., Spengler, M., Hegewald, K., & Spinath, F. M. (2013). Parental involvement and general cognitive ability as predictors of domain-specific academic achievement in early adolescence. *Learning and Instruction, 23*, 43–51. https://doi.org/10.1016/j.learninstruc.2012.09.004

Kärnä, A., Voeten, M., Poskiparta, E., & Salmivalli, C. (2010). Vulnerable children in varying classroom contexts: Bystanders' behaviors moderate the effects of risk factors on victimization. *Merrill-Palmer Quarterly, 56*(3), 261–282.

Kärtner, J., Keller, H., Lamm, B., Abels, M., Yovsi, R. D., Chaudhary, N., & Su, Y. (2008). Similarities and differences in contingency experiences of 3-month-olds across sociocultural contexts. *Infant Behavior and Development*, 31(3), 488–500.

Kassa, G. M. (2018). Mother-to-child transmission of HIV infection and its associated factors in Ethiopia: A systematic review and meta-analysis. *BMC Infectious Diseases, 18*(1), 216. https://doi.org/10.1186/s12879-018-3126-5

Katz, A. M. (2017). Psycholinguistic approaches to metaphor acquisition and use. In E. Semino & Z. Demjén (Eds.), *The Routledge handbook of metaphor and language*. New York, NY: Routledge.

Katz, J. C., & Buchholz, E. S. (1999). "I did it myself": The necessity of solo play for preschoolers. *Early Child Development and Care, 155*(1), 39–50. https://doi.org/10.1080/0030443991550104

Katz, V. S., Moran, M. B., & Gonzalez, C. (2018). Connecting with technology in lower-income US families. *New Media & Society, 20*(7), 2509–2533. https://doi.org/10.1177/1461444817726319

Katzman, D. K. (2005). Medical complications in adolescents with anorexia nervosa: A review of the literature. *International Journal of Eating Disorders, 37*, 52–59.

Kaufman, J. C., Kaufman, S. B., & Plucker., J. A. (2013). Contemporary theories of intelligence. In D. Reisberg (Ed.), *Oxford handbook of cognitive psychology* (pp. 811–822). Oxford, England: Oxford University Press.

Kaufman, J. C., Plucker, J. A., & Russell, C. M. (2012). Identifying and assessing creativity as a component of giftedness. *Journal of Psychoeducational Assessment, 30*(1), 60–73. https://doi.org/10.1177/0734282911428196

Kaufmann, L., Mazzocco, M. M., Dowker, A., von Aster, M., Göbel, S. M., Grabner, R. H., . . . Nuerk, H.-C. (2013). Dyscalculia from a developmental and differential perspective. *Frontiers in Psychology, 4*, 516. https://doi.org/10.3389/fpsyg.2013.00516

Kaufmann, W. E., Kidd, S. A., Andrews, H. F., Budimirovic, D. B., Esler, A., Haas-Givler, B., . . . Berry-Kravis, E. (2017). Autism spectrum disorder in fragile X syndrome: Cooccurring conditions and current treatment. *Pediatrics, 139*(Suppl. 3), S194–S206. https://doi.org/10.1542/peds.2016-1159F

Kavšek, M. (2004). Predicting later IQ from infant visual habituation and dishabituation: A meta-analysis. *Journal of Applied Developmental Psychology, 25*(3), 369–393. https://doi.org/10.1016/j.appdev.2004.04.006

Kavšek, M. (2013). The comparator model of infant visual habituation and dishabituation: Recent insights. *Developmental Psychobiology, 55*(8), 793–808. https://doi.org/10.1002/dev.21081

Kavšek, M., & Bornstein, M. H. (2010). Visual habituation and dishabituation in preterm infants: A review and meta-analysis. *Research in Developmental Disabilities, 31*(5), 951–975. https://doi.org/10.1016/j.ridd.2010.04.016

Kawabata, Y., & Crick, N. R. (2011). The significance of cross-racial/ethnic friendships: Associations with peer victimization, peer support, sociometric status, and classroom diversity. *Developmental Psychology, 47*(6), 1763–1775. https://doi.org/10.1037/a0025399

Kawabata, Y., Crick, N. R., & Hamaguchi, Y. (2010). The role of culture in relational aggression: Associations with social-psychological adjustment problems in Japanese and US school-aged children. *International Journal of Behavioral Development, 34*(4), 354–362. https://doi.org/10.1177/0165025409339151

Kawai, N. (2010). Towards a new study on associative learning in human fetuses: Fetal associative learning in primates. *Infant & Child Development, 19*(1), 55–59. https://doi.org/10.1002/icd.654

Kawakami, K., Takai-Kawakami, K., Kawakami, F., Tomonaga, M., Suzuki, M., & Shimizu, Y. (2008). Roots of smile: A preterm neonates' study. *Infant Behavior & Development, 31*(3), 518–522. https://doi.org/10.1016/j.infbeh.2008.03.002

Kaye, W. H., Wierenga, C. E., Bailer, U. F., Simmons, A. N., & Bischoff-Grethe, A. (2013). Nothing tastes as good as skinny feels: The neurobiology of anorexia nervosa. *Trends in Neurosciences, 36*(2), 110–120. https://doi.org/10.1016/j.tins.2013.01.003

Kayed, N. S., Farstad, H., & van der Meer, A. L. H. (2008). Preterm infants' timing strategies to optical collisions. *Early Human Development, 84*(6), 381–388. https://doi.org/10.1016/j.earlhumdev.2007.10.006

Keating, D. P. (2012). Cognitive and brain development in adolescence. *Enfance, 2012*(3), 267–279. https://doi.org/10.4074/S0013754512003035

Keefe-Cooperman, K., & Brady-Amoon, P. (2014). Preschooler sleep patterns related to cognitive and adaptive functioning. *Early Education and Development, 25*(6), 859–874. https://doi.org/10.1080/10409289.2014.876701

Keel, P. K. (2014). Bulimia nervosa. In R. L. Cautin & S. O. Lilienfeld (Eds.), *The encyclopedia of clinical psychology*. Hoboken, NJ: John Wiley & Sons.

Keijsers, L., Loeber, R., Branje, S., & Meeus, W. H. J. (2011). Bidirectional links and concurrent development of parent-child relationships and boys' offending behavior. *Journal of Abnormal Psychology, 120*(4), 878–889. https://doi.org/10.1037/a0024588

Keith, T. Z., Keith, P. B., Quirk, K. J., Sperduto, J., Santillo, S., & Killings, S. (1998). Longitudinal effects of parent involvement on high school grades: Similarities and differences. *Journal of School Psychology, 35*(3), 335–364.

Kell, H. J., Lubinski, D., Benbow, C. P., & Steiger, J. H. (2013). Creativity and technical innovation: Spatial ability's unique role. *Psychological Science, 24*(9), 1831–1836. https://doi.org/10.1177/0956797613478615

Keller, H. (2003). Socialization for competence: Cultural models of infancy. *Human Development, 46*(5), 288–311.

Keller, H. (2017). Culture and development: A systematic relationship. *Perspectives on Psychological Science, 12*(5), 833–840. https://doi.org/10.1177/1745691617704097

Keller, H., Borke, J., Staufenbiel, T., Yovsi, R. D., Abels, M., Papaligoura, Z., . . . Su, Y. (2009). Distal and proximal parenting as alternative parenting strategies during infants' early months of life: A cross-cultural study. *International Journal of Behavioral Development, 33*(5), 412–420. https://doi.org/10.1177/0165025409338441

Kellogg, R. (1970). Understanding children's art. In P. Cramer (Ed.), *Readings in developmental psychology today*. Delmar, CA: CRM.

Kelly, K. (1999). Retention vs. promotion: Schools search for alternatives. *Harvard Education Letter Research Online*. Retrieved from http://www.edletter.org/past/issues/1999-jf/retention.shtml

Kelly, S. T., & Spencer, H. G. (2017). Population-genetic models of sex-limited genomic imprinting. *Theoretical Population Biology, 115*, 35–44. https://doi.org/10.1016/j.tpb.2017.03.004

Kelly, Y., Zilanawala, A., Sacker, A., Hiatt, R., & Viner, R. (2017). Early puberty in 11-year-old girls: Millennium Cohort Study findings. *Archives of Disease in Childhood, 102*(3), 232–237. https://doi.org/10.1136/archdischild-2016-310475

Kendrick, D., Barlow, J., Hampshire, A., Stewart-Brown, S., & Polnay, L. (2008). Parenting interventions and the prevention of unintentional injuries in childhood: Systematic review and meta-analysis. *Child: Care, Health and Development, 34*(5), 682–695. https://doi.org/10.1111/j.1365-2214.2008.00849.x

Kennedy, S., & Bumpass, L. (2008). Cohabitation and children's living arrangements: New estimates from the United States. *Demographic Research, 19*, 1663–1692.

Kennedy, S., & Fitch, C. A. (2012). Measuring cohabitation and family structure in the United States: Assessing the impact of new data from the Current Population Survey. *Demography, 49*(4), 1479–1498. https://doi.org/10.1007/s13524-012-0126-8

Kennedy, T. M., & Ceballo, R. (2014). Who, what, when, and where? Toward a dimensional conceptualization of community violence exposure. *Review of General Psychology, 18*(2), 69–81. https://doi.org/10.1037/gpr0000005

Kenny, D. (2018). *Children, sexuality and child sexual abuse*. New York, NY: Routledge.

Kenny, L. C., Lavender, T., McNamee, R., O'Neill, S. M., Mills, T., & Khashan, A. S. (2013). Advanced maternal age and adverse pregnancy outcome: Evidence from a large contemporary cohort. *PLoS One, 8*(2), e56583. https://doi.org/10.1371/journal.pone.0056583

Kenny, M. C., & McEachern, A. (2009). Children's self-concept: A multicultural comparison. *Professional School Counseling, 12*(3), 207–212.

Kenward, B., & Dahl, M. (2011). Preschoolers distribute scarce resources according to the moral valence of recipients' previous actions. *Developmental Psychology, 47*(4), 1054–1064. https://doi.org/10.1037/a002386910.1037/a0023869.supp

Keresztes, A., Ngo, C. T., Lindenberger, U., Werkle-Bergner, M., & Newcombe, N. S. (2018). Hippocampal maturation drives memory from generalization to specificity. *Trends in Cognitive Sciences, 22*(8), 676–686. https://doi.org/10.1016/J.TICS.2018.05.004

Kerpelman, J. L., Shoffner, M. F., & Ross-Griffin, S. (2002). African American mothers' and daughters' beliefs about possible selves and their strategies for reaching the adolescents' future academic and career goals. *Journal of Youth & Adolescence, 31*(4), 289–302.

Keski-Rahkonen, A., & Mustelin, L. (2016). Epidemiology of eating disorders in Europe. *Current Opinion in Psychiatry, 29*(6), 340–345. https://doi.org/10.1097/YCO.0000000000000278

Kessler, R. C., Berglund, P. A., Chiu, W. T., Deitz, A. C., Hudson, J. I., Shahly, V., . . . Xavier, M. (2013). The prevalence and correlates of binge eating disorder in the World Health Organization World Mental Health Surveys. *Biological Psychiatry, 73*(9), 904–914. https://doi.org/10.1016/j.biopsych.2012.11.020

Keven, N., & Akins, K. A. (2017). Neonatal imitation in context: Sensorimotor development in the perinatal period. *Behavioral and Brain Sciences, 40*, e381. https://doi.org/10.1017/S0140525X16000911

Khalil, A., Syngelaki, A., Maiz, N., Zinevich, Y., & Nicolaides, K. H. (2013). Maternal age and adverse pregnancy outcome: A cohort study. *Ultrasound in Obstetrics & Gynecology, 42*(6), 634–643. https://doi.org/10.1002/uog.12494

Khan, A. J., Nair, A., Keown, C. L., Datko, M. C., Lincoln, A. J., & Müller, R.-A. (2015). Cerebro-cerebellar resting state functional connectivity in children and adolescents with autism spectrum disorder. *Biological Psychiatry, 78*(9), 625. https://doi.org/10.1016/J.BIOPSYCH.2015.03.024

Kharitonova, M., Winter, W., & Sheridan, M. A. (2015). As working memory grows: A developmental account of neural bases of working memory capacity in 5- to 8-year old children and adults. *Journal of Cognitive Neuroscience, 27*(9), 1775–1788. https://doi.org/10.1162/jocn_a_00824

Kidger, J., Araya, R., Donovan, J., & Gunnell, D. (2012). The effect of the school environment on the emotional health of adolescents: A systematic review. *Pediatrics, 129*(5), 925–949. https://doi.org/10.1542/peds.2011-2248

Kiechl-Kohlendorfer, U., Horak, E., Mueller, W., Strobl, R., Haberland, C., Fink, F.-M., . . . Kiechl, S. (2007). Neonatal characteristics and risk of atopic asthma in schoolchildren: Results from a large prospective birth-cohort study. *Acta Paediatrica, 96*(11), 1606–1610.

Kilford, E. J., Garrett, E., & Blakemore, S.-J. (2016). The development of social cognition in adolescence: An integrated perspective. *Neuroscience & Biobehavioral Reviews, 70*, 106–120. https://doi.org/10.1016/J.NEUBIOREV.2016.08.016

Killen, M., Kelly, M., Richardson, C., Crystal, D., & Ruck, M. (2010). European-American children's and adolescents' evaluations of interracial exclusion. *Group Processes & Intergroup Relations, 13*(3), 283–300. https://doi.org/10.1177/1368430209346700

Killen, M., McGlothlin, H., & Lee-Kim, J. (2002). Between individuals and culture: Individuals' evaluations of exclusion from social groups. In H. Keller, Y. Poortinga, & A. Schoelmerich (Eds.), *Between biology and culture: Perspectives on ontogenetic development* (pp. 159–190). Cambridge, England: Cambridge University Press.

Killen, M., & Nucci, L. P. (1995). Morality, autonomy, and social conflict. In M. Killen & D. Hart (Eds.), *Morality in everyday life: Developmental perspectives* (pp. 52–86). Cambridge, England: Cambridge University Press.

Killen, M., & Smetana, J. G. (2015). Origins and development of morality. In *Handbook of child psychology and developmental science* (pp. 1–49). Hoboken, NJ: John Wiley & Sons. https://doi.org/10.1002/9781118963418.childpsy317

Kim, B.-R., & Teti, D. M. (2014). Maternal emotional availability during infant bedtime: An ecological framework. *Journal of Family Psychology, 28*(1), 1–11. https://doi.org/10.1037/a0035157

Kim, H., Drake, B., & Jonson-Reid, M. (2018). An examination of class-based visibility bias in national child maltreatment reporting. *Children and Youth Services Review, 85*, 165–173. https://doi.org/10.1016/J.CHILDYOUTH.2017.12.019

Kim, H., Wildeman, C., Jonson-Reid, M., & Drake, B. (2017). Lifetime prevalence of investigating child maltreatment among US children. *American Journal of Public Health, 107*(2), 274–280. https://doi.org/10.2105/AJPH.2016.303545

Kim, M. (2016). A meta-analysis of the effects of enrichment programs on gifted students. *Gifted Child Quarterly, 60*(2), 102–116. https://doi.org/10.1177/0016986216630607

Kim, S., Fleisher, B., & Sun, J. Y. (2017). The long-term health effects of fetal malnutrition: Evidence from the 1959-1961 China great leap forward famine. *Health Economics, 26*(10), 1264–1277. https://doi.org/10.1002/hec.3397

Kim, S. Y., Chen, Q., Wang, Y., Shen, Y., & Orozco-Lapray, D. (2013). Longitudinal linkages among parent-child acculturation discrepancy, parenting, parent-child sense of alienation, and adolescent adjustment in Chinese immigrant families. *Developmental Psychology, 49*(5), 900–912. https://doi.org/10.1037/a0029169

Kim, S. Y., Qi, C., Jing, L., Xuan, H., & Ui Jeong, M. (2009). Parent-child acculturation, parenting, and adolescent depressive symptoms in Chinese immigrant families. *Journal of Family Psychology, 23*(3), 426–437. https://doi.org/10.1037/a0016019

Kimball, M. M. (1986). Television and sex-role attitudes. In T. M. Williams (Ed.), *The impact of television: A natural experiment in three communities* (pp. 265–301). Orlando, FL: Academic Press.

Kingery, J. N., Erdley, C. A., & Marshall, K. C. (2011). Peer acceptance and friendship as predictors of early adolescents' adjustment across the middle school transition. *Merrill-Palmer Quarterly, 57*(3), 215–243. https://doi.org/10.1353/mpq.2011.0012

Kingston, D., Tough, S., & Whitfield, H. (2012). Prenatal and postpartum maternal psychological distress and infant development: A systematic review. *Child Psychiatry and Human Development, 43*(5), 683–714. https://doi.org/10.1007/s10578-012-0291-4

Kingston, S., & Rose, A. (2015). Do the effects of adolescent employment differ by employment intensity and neighborhood context? *American Journal of Community Psychology, 55*(1–2), 37–47. https://doi.org/10.1007/s10464-014-9690-y

Kinsley, C. H., & Amory-Meyer, E. (2011). Why the maternal brain? *Journal of Neuroendocrinology, 23*(11), 974–983. https://doi.org/10.1111/j.1365-2826.2011.02194.x

Király, I., Takács, S., Kaldy, Z., & Blaser, E. (2017). Preschoolers have better long-term memory for rhyming text than adults. *Developmental Science, 20*(3), e12398. https://doi.org/10.1111/desc.12398

Kirk, E., Howlett, N., Pine, K. J., & Fletcher, B. C. (2013). To sign or not to sign? The impact of encouraging infants to gesture on infant language and maternal mind-mindedness. *Child Development, 84*(2), 574–590. https://doi.org/10.1111/j.1467-8624.2012.01874.x

Kirkorian, H. L., Wartella, E. A., & Anderson, D. R. (2008). Media and young children's learning. *The Future of Children, 18*(1), 39–61. https://doi.org/10.1353/foc.0.0002

Kiselica, M. S., & Kiselica, A. M. (2014). The complicated worlds of adolescent fathers: Implications for clinical practice, public policy, and research. *Psychology of Men & Masculinity, 15*(3), 260.

Kisilevsky, B. S. (2016). Fetal auditory processing: Implications for language development? In N. Reissland & B. S. Kisilevsky (Eds.), *Fetal development* (pp. 133–152). Cham, Switzerland: Springer International Publishing. https://doi.org/10.1007/978-3-319-22023-9_8

Kisilevsky, B. S., & Hains, S. M. (2011). Onset and maturation of fetal heart rate response to the mother's voice over late gestation. *Developmental Science, 14*, 214–223. https://doi.org/10.1111/j.1467-7687.2010.00970.x

Kit, B. K., Akinbami, L. J., Isfahani, N. S., & Ulrich, D. A. (2017). Gross motor development in children aged 3–5 years, United States 2012. *Maternal and Child Health Journal, 21*(7), 1–8. https://doi.org/10.1007/s10995-017-2289-9

Kitamura, C., & Burnham, D. (2003). Pitch and communicative intent in mother's speech: Adjustments for age and sex in the first year. *Infancy, 4*(1), 85–110.

Kitsao-Wekulo, P. K., Holding, P., Taylor, H. G., Abubakar, A., Kvalsvig, J., & Connolly, K. (2013). Nutrition as an important mediator of the impact of background variables on outcome in middle childhood. *Frontiers in Human Neuroscience, 7*, 713. https://doi.org/10.3389/fnhum.2013.00713

Klahr, A. M., Thomas, K. M., Hopwood, C. J., Klump, K. L., & Burt, S. A. (2013). Evocative gene–environment correlation in the mother–child relationship: A twin study of interpersonal processes. *Development and Psychopathology, 25*(01), 105–118. https://doi.org/10.1017/S0954579412000934

Kleanthous, K., Dermitzaki, E., Papadimitriou, D. T., Papaevangelou, V., & Papadimitriou, A. (2017). Secular changes in the final height of Greek girls are levelling off. *Acta Paediatrica, 106*(2), 341–343. https://doi.org/10.1111/apa.13677

Klemera, E., Brooks, F. M., Chester, K. L., Magnusson, J., & Spencer, N. (2017). Self-harm in adolescence: Protective health assets in the family, school and community. *International Journal of Public Health, 62*(6), 631–638. https://doi.org/10.1007/s00038-016-0900-2

Kliegman, R., Stanton, B., St. Geme, J. W., Schor, N. F., Behrman, R. E., & Nelson, W. E. (2016). *Nelson textbook of pediatrics*. Philadelphia, PA: Elsevier.

Klima, T., & Repetti, R. L. (2008). Children's peer relations and their psychological adjustment: Differences between close friendships and the larger peer group. *Merrill-Palmer Quarterly, 54*(2), 151–178.

Klimstra, T. A., Kuppens, P., Luyckx, K., Branje, S., Hale, W. W., Oosterwegel, A., . . . Meeus, W. H. J. (2016). Daily dynamics of adolescent mood and identity. *Journal of Research on Adolescence, 26*(3), 459–473. https://doi.org/10.1111/jora.12205

Knafo, A., & Jaffee, S. R. (2013). Gene–environment correlation in developmental psychopathology. *Development and Psychopathology, 25*(1), 1–6. https://doi.org/10.1017/S0954579412000855

Knafo-Noam, A., Uzefovsky, F., Israel, S., Davidov, M., & Zahn-Waxler, C. (2015). The prosocial personality and its facets: Genetic and environmental architecture of mother-reported behavior of 7-year-old twins. *Frontiers in Psychology, 6*, 112. https://doi.org/10.3389/fpsyg.2015.00112

Knopik, V. S., Neiderhiser, J. M., DeFries, J. C., & Plomin, R. (2017). *Behavioral genetics*. New York, NY: Macmillan Higher Education.

Knopman, J. M., Krey, L. C., Oh, C., Lee, J., McCaffrey, C., & Noyes, N. (2014). What makes them split? Identifying risk factors that lead to monozygotic twins after in vitro fertilization. *Fertility and Sterility, 102*(1), 82–89. https://doi.org/10.1016/j.fertnstert.2014.03.039

Knox, P. L., Fagley, N. S., & Miller, P. M. (2004). Care and justice moral orientation among African American college students. *Journal of Adult Development, 11*(1), 41–45.

Kobak, R., Abbott, C., Zisk, A., & Bounoua, N. (2017). Adapting to the changing needs of adolescents: Parenting practices and challenges to sensitive attunement. *Current Opinion in Psychology, 15*, 137–142. https://doi.org/10.1016/j.copsyc.2017.02.018

Koball, H., & Jiang, Y. (2018). *Basic facts about low income children*. Retrieved from http://www.nccp.org/publications/pub_1194.html

Kobayashi, T., Good, C., Mamiya, K., Skinner, R., & Garcia-Rill, E. (2004). Development of REM sleep drive and clinical implications. *Journal of Applied Physiology, 96*(2), 735–746.

Kochanek, K. D., Murphy, S. L., Xu, J., & Arias, E. (2017). Mortality in the United States, 2016: Key findings data from the National Vital Statistics System. *NCHS Data Brief, 293*. Retrieved from https://www.cdc.gov/nchs/data/databriefs/db293.pdf

Kochanska, G. (2000). Mother-child mutually responsive orientation and conscience development: From toddler to early school age. *Child Development, 71*(2), 417.

Kochanska, G., Casey, R. J., & Fukumoto, A. (1995). Toddlers' sensitivity to standard violations. *Child Development, 66*, 643–656.

Kochanska, G., & Kim, S. (2013). Early attachment organization with both parents and future behavior problems: From infancy to middle childhood. *Child Development, 84*(1), 283–296. https://doi.org/10.1111/j.1467-8624.2012.01852.x

Kochendorfer, L. B., & Kerns, K. A. (2017). Perceptions of parent-child attachment relationships and friendship qualities: Predictors of romantic relationship involvement and quality in adolescence. *Journal of Youth and Adolescence, 46*(5), 1009–1021. https://doi.org/10.1007/s10964-017-0645-0

Koehn, A. J., & Kerns, K. A. (2018). Parent–child attachment: Meta-analysis of associations with parenting behaviors in middle childhood and adolescence. *Attachment & Human Development, 20*(4), 378–405. https://doi.org/10.1080/14616734.2017.1408131

Koenen, K. C., Amstadter, A. B., & Nugent, N. (2012). Genetic methods in psychology. In H. Cooper, P. M. Camic, D. L. Long, A. T. Panter, D. Rindskopf, & K. J. Sher (Eds.), *APA handbook of research methods in psychology: Vol 2. Research designs: Quantitative, qualitative, neuropsychological, and biological* (pp. 663–680). Washington, DC: American Psychological Association. https://doi.org/10.1037/13620-000

Kohlberg, L. (1966). A cognitive-developmental analysis of children's sex-role concepts and attitudes. In E. E. Maccoby (Ed.), *The development of sex differences* (pp. 82–173). Stanford, CA: Stanford University Press.

Kohlberg, L. (1969). Stage and sequence: The cognitive-developmental approach to socialization. In D. A. Goslin (Ed.), *Handbook of socialization* (pp. 347–480). Chicago, IL: Rand McNally.

Kohlberg, L. (1976). Moral stages and moralization: The cognitive developmental approach. In T. Lickona (Ed.), *Moral development and moral behavior: Theory, research, and social issues* (pp. 31–53). New York, NY: Holt, Rinehart & Winston.

Kohlberg, L. (1981). *Essays on moral development*. San Francisco, CA: Harper & Row.

Kohlberg, L., Levine, C., & Hewer, A. (1983). Moral stages: A current formulation and a response to critics. *Contributions to Human Development, 10*, 174.

Kohlberg, L., & Ryncarz, R. A. (1990). Beyond justice reasoning: Moral development and consideration of a seventh stage. In C. N. Alexander & E. J. Langer (Eds.), *Higher stages of human development: Perspectives on adult growth* (pp. 191–207). New York, NY: Oxford University Press.

Kohn, T. P., Kohn, J. R., Darilek, S., Ramasamy, R., & Lipshultz, L. (2016). Genetic counseling for men with recurrent pregnancy loss or recurrent implantation failure due to abnormal sperm chromosomal aneuploidy. *Journal of Assisted Reproduction and Genetics, 33*(5), 571–576. https://doi.org/10.1007/s10815-016-0702-8

Kohnert, K. J., & Bates, E. (2002). Balancing bilinguals II. *Journal of Speech Language and Hearing Research, 45*(2), 347. https://doi.org/10.1044/1092-4388(2002/027)

Kojima, H. (1986). Becoming nurturant in Japan: Past and present. In A. Fogel & G. F. Melson (Eds.), *Origins of nurturance: Developmental, biological, and cultural perspectives on caregiving* (pp. 359–376). Hillsdale, NJ: Erlbaum.

Kolata, G. (2019). These patients had sickle-cell disease. Experimental therapies might have cured them. *New York Times*. Retrieved from https://www.nytimes.com/2019/01/27/health/sickle-cell-gene-therapy.html

Kolb, B. (2018). Overview of factors influencing brain development. In R. Gibb & B. Kolb (Eds.), *The neurobiology of brain and behavioral development* (pp. 51–79). Philadelphia, PA: Elsevier. https://doi.org/10.1016/B978-0-12-804036-2.00003-0

Kolb, B., Mychasiuk, R., & Gibb, R. (2014). Brain development, experience, and behavior. *Pediatric Blood & Cancer, 61*(10), 1720–1723. https://doi.org/10.1002/pbc.24908

Kolb, B., Whishaw, I., & Teskey, G. C. (2016). *An introduction to brain and behavior*. New York, NY: Worth.

Kolling, T., Goertz, C., Stefanie, F., & Knopf, M. (2010). Memory development throughout the second year: Overall developmental pattern, individual differences, and developmental trajectories. *Infant Behavior & Development, 33*(2), 159–167. https://doi.org/10.1016/j.infbeh.2009.12.007

Konijnenberg, C., & Melinder, A. (2015). Executive function in preschool children prenatally exposed to methadone or buprenorphine. *Child Neuropsychology, 21*(5), 570–585. https://doi.org/10.1080/09297049.2014.967201

Konner, M. (2017). Hunter-gatherer infancy and childhood. In B. S. Hewlett (Ed.), *Hunter-gatherer childhoods* (pp. 19–64). New York, NY: Routledge. https://doi.org/10.4324/9780203789445-3

Kornbluh, M., & Neal, J. W. (2016). Examining the many dimensions of children's popularity. *Journal of Social and Personal Relationships, 33*(1), 62–80. https://doi.org/10.1177/0265407514562562

Korotchikova, I., Stevenson, N. J., Livingstone, V., Ryan, C. A., & Boylan, G. B. (2016). Sleep–wake cycle of the healthy term newborn infant in the immediate postnatal period. *Clinical Neurophysiology, 127*(4), 2095–2101. https://doi.org/10.1016/j.clinph.2015.12.015

Kosciw, J. G., Palmer, N. A., & Kull, R. M. (2015). Reflecting resiliency: Openness about sexual orientation and/or gender identity and its relationship to well-being and educational outcomes for LGBT students. *American Journal of Community Psychology, 55*(1–2), 167–178. https://doi.org/10.1007/s10464-014-9642-6

Kostelnik, M. J., Soderman, A. K., Whiren, A. P., & Rupiper, M. Q. (2015). *Developmentally appropriate curriculum: Best practices in early childhood education*. Boston, MA: Pearson.

Kowalski, R. M., Giumetti, G. W., Schroeder, A. N., & Lattanner, M. R. (2014). Bullying in the digital age: A critical review and meta-analysis of cyberbullying research among youth. *Psychological Bulletin, 140*(4), 1073–1137. https://doi.org/10.1037/a0035618

Kozhimannil, K. B., Hardeman, R. R., Alarid-Escudero, F., Vogelsang, C. A., Blauer-Peterson, C., & Howell, E. A. (2016). Modeling the cost-effectiveness of doula care associated with reductions in preterm birth and cesarean delivery. *Birth, 43*(1), 20–27. https://doi.org/10.1111/birt.12218

Krafchuk, E. E., Tronick, E. Z., & Clifton, R. K. (1983). Behavioral and cardiac responses to sound in preterm infants varying in risk status: A hypothesis of their paradoxical reactivity. In T. Field & A. Sostek (Eds.), *Infants born at risk: Physiological, perceptual, and cognitive processes* (pp. 99–128). New York, NY: Grune & Stratton.

Kragel, P. A., & LaBar, K. S. (2016). Decoding the nature of emotion in the brain. *Trends in Cognitive Sciences, 20*(6), 444–455. https://doi.org/10.1016/J.TICS.2016.03.011

Kramer, L. (2010). The essential ingredients of successful sibling relationships: An emerging framework for advancing theory and practice. *Child Development Perspectives, 4*(2), 80–86. https://doi.org/10.1111/j.1750-8606.2010.00122.x

Kramer, L. (2014). Learning emotional understanding and emotion regulation through sibling interaction. *Early Education and Development, 25*(2), 160–184. https://doi.org/10.1080/10409289.2014.838824

Kramer, M. S., Fombonne, E., Igumnov, S., Vanilovich, I., Matush, L., Mironova, E., . . . Platt, R. W. (2008). Effects of prolonged and exclusive breastfeeding on child behavior and maternal adjustment: Evidence from a large, randomized trial. *Pediatrics, 121*(3), e435–e440.

Krassner, A. M., Gartstein, M. A., Park, C., Dragan, W. Ł., Lecannelier, F., & Putnam, S. P. (2016). East–west, collectivist-individualist: A cross-cultural examination of temperament in toddlers from Chile, Poland, South Korea, and the U.S. *European Journal of Developmental Psychology, 14*(4), 449–464. https://doi.org/10.1080/17405629.2016.1236722

Kreager, D. A., Molloy, L. E., Moody, J., & Feinberg, M. E. (2016). Friends first? The peer network origins of adolescent dating. *Journal of Research on Adolescence, 26*(2), 257–269. https://doi.org/10.1111/jora.12189

Krei, M. S., & Rosenbaum, J. E. (2000). Career and college advice to the forgotten half: What do counselors and vocational teachers advise? *Teachers College Record, 103*(5), 823–842. Retrieved from http://eric.ed.gov/?id=EJ638357

Kremen, W. S., Panizzon, M. S., & Cannon, T. D. (2016). Genetics and neuropsychology: A merger whose time has come. *Neuropsychology, 30*(1), 1–5. https://doi.org/10.1037/neu0000254

Kressley-Mba, R. A., Lurg, S., & Knopf, M. (2005). Testing for deferred imitation of 2- and 3-step action sequences with 6-month-olds. *Infant Behavior & Development, 28*(1), 82–86.

Kretch, K. S., & Adolph, K. E. (2017). The organization of exploratory behaviors in infant locomotor planning. *Developmental Science, 20*(4), e12421. https://doi.org/10.1111/desc.12421

Kretch, K. S., Franchak, J. M., & Adolph, K. E. (2014). Crawling and walking infants see the world differently. *Child Development, 85*(4), 1503–1518. https://doi.org/10.1111/cdev.12206

Kretsch, N., Mendle, J., Cance, J. D., & Harden, K. P. (2016). Peer group similarity in perceptions of pubertal timing. *Journal of Youth and Adolescence, 45*(8), 1696–1710. https://doi.org/10.1007/s10964-015-0275-3

Kretsch, N., Mendle, J., & Harden, K. P. (2016). A twin study of objective and subjective pubertal timing and peer influence on risk-taking. *Journal of Research on Adolescence, 26*(1), 45–59. https://doi.org/10.1111/jora.12160

Kringelbach, M. L., Stark, E. A., Alexander, C., Bornstein, M. H., & Stein, A. (2016). On cuteness: Unlocking the parental brain and beyond. *Trends in Cognitive Sciences, 20*(7), 545–558. https://doi.org/10.1016/J.TICS.2016.05.003

Kroger, J. (2015). Identity development through adulthood: The move toward "wholeness." In K. C. McLean & M. Syed (Eds.), *The Oxford handbook of identity development* (pp. 65–80). Oxford, England: Oxford University Press.

Kroger, J., Martinussen, M., & Marcia, J. E. (2010). Identity status change during adolescence and young adulthood: A meta-analysis. *Journal of Adolescence, 33*(5), 683–698. https://doi.org/10.1016/j.adolescence.2009.11.002

Kronenberger, W., & Pisoni, D. (2018). Neurocognitive functioning in deaf children with cochlear implants. In H. Knoors & M. Marschark (Eds.), *Evidence-based practices in deaf education* (pp. 363–398). New York, NY: Oxford University Press.

Krueger, J. M., Frank, M. G., Wisor, J. P., & Roy, S. (2016). Sleep function: Toward elucidating an enigma. *Sleep Medicine Reviews, 28*, 46–54. https://doi.org/10.1016/J.SMRV.2015.08.005

Krüger, O., Korsten, P., & Hoffman, J. I. (2017). The rise of behavioral genetics and the transition to behavioral genomics and beyond. In *APA handbook of comparative psychology: Basic concepts, methods, neural substrate, and behavior* (pp. 365–379). Washington, DC: American Psychological Association. https://doi.org/10.1037/0000011-018

Kruszka, P., Porras, A. R., Sobering, A. K., Ikolo, F. A., La Qua, S., Shotelersuk, V., . . . Muenke, M. (2017). Down syndrome in diverse populations. *American Journal of Medical Genetics Part A, 173*(1), 42–53. https://doi.org/10.1002/ajmg.a.38043

Kucian, K., & von Aster, M. (2015). Developmental dyscalculia. *European Journal of Pediatrics, 174*(1), 1–13. https://doi.org/10.1007/s00431-014-2455-7

Kucker, S. C., McMurray, B., & Samuelson, L. K. (2015). Slowing down fast mapping: Redefining the dynamics of word learning. *Child Development Perspectives, 9*(2), 74–78. https://doi.org/10.1111/cdep.12110

Kuhl, P. K. (2015). Baby talk. *Scientific American, 313*(5), 64–69. https://doi.org/10.1038/scientificamerican1115-64

Kuhl, P. K. (2016). Language and the social brain: The power of surprise in science. In R. J. Sternberg, S. T. Fiske, & D. J. Foss (Eds.), *Scientists making a difference: One hundred eminent behavioral and brain scientists talk about their most important contributions* (pp. 206–209). New York, NY: Cambridge University Press.

Kuhl, P. K., Andruski, J. E., Chistovich, I. A., Chistovich, L. A., Kozhevnikova, E. V., Ryskina, V. L., . . . Lacerda, F. (1997). Cross-language analysis of phonetic units in language addressed to infants. *Science, 277*, 684–686.

Kuhl, P., & Ramirez, N. F. (2016). *Bilingual language learning in children*. Retrieved from http://ilabs.washington.edu/sites/default/files/Ramirez_WhiteHouse_Paper.pdf

Kuhl, P. K., Stevens, E., Hayashi, A., Deguchi, T., Kiritani, S., & Iverson, P. (2006). Infants show a facilitation effect for native language phonetic perception between 6 and 12 months. *Developmental Science, 9*(2), F13–F21. https://doi.org/10.1111/j.1467-7687.2006.00468.x

Kuhl, P. K, Tsao, F.-M., & Liu, H.-M. (2003). Foreign-language experience in infancy: Effects of short-term exposure and social interaction on phonetic learning. *Proceedings of the National Academy of Sciences of the United States of America, 100*(15), 9096–9101. https://doi.org/10.1073/pnas.1532872100

Kuhlmeier, V., Dunfield, K., & O'Neill, A. (2014). Selectivity in early prosocial behavior. *Frontiers in Psychology, 5*(00836). https://doi.org/10.3389/fpsyg.2014.00836

Kuhn, D. (2012). The development of causal reasoning. *Wiley Interdisciplinary Reviews: Cognitive Science, 3*(3), 327–335. https://doi.org/10.1002/wcs.1160

Kuhn, D. (2013). Reasoning. In P. D. Zelazo (Ed.), *The Oxford handbook of developmental psychology: Vol. 1. Body and mind* (pp. 744–764). New York, NY: Oxford University Press. https://doi.org/10.1093/oxfordhb/9780199958450.013.0026

Kumar, S., & Kelly, A. S. (2017). Review of childhood obesity: From epidemiology, etiology, and comorbidities to clinical assessment and treatment. *Mayo Clinic Proceedings, 92*(2), 251–265. https://doi.org/10.1016/j.mayocp.2016.09.017

Kuo, Y.-L., Liao, H.-F., Chen, P.-C., Hsieh, W.-S., & Hwang, A.-W. (2008). The influence of wakeful prone positioning on motor development during the early life. *Journal of Developmental and Behavioral Pediatrics, 29*(5), 367–376. https://doi.org/10.1097/DBP.0b013e3181856d54

Kurosky, S. K., Davis, K. L., & Krishnarajah, G. (2017). Effect of combination vaccines on completion and compliance of childhood vaccinations in the United States. *Human Vaccines & Immunotherapeutics, 13*(11), 2494–2502. https://doi.org/10.1080/21645515.2017.1362515

Kurtz-Costes, B., Copping, K. E., Rowley, S. J., & Kinlaw, C. R. (2014). Gender and age differences in awareness and endorsement of gender stereotypes about academic abilities. *European Journal of Psychology of Education, 29*(4), 603–618. https://doi.org/10.1007/s10212-014-0216-7

Kuther, T. L., & Higgins-D'Alessandro, A. (2000). Bridging the gap between moral reasoning and adolescent engagement in risky behavior. *Journal of Adolescence, 23*(4), 409–423.

La Rooy, D., Lamb, M. E., & Pipe, M. (2011). Repeated interviewing: A critical evaluation of the risks and potential benefits. In K. Kuehnle & M. Connell (Eds.), *The evaluation of child sexual abuse allegations: A comprehensive guide to assessment and testimony* (pp. 327–361). Chichester, England: Wiley-Blackwell.

Labella, M. H., Narayan, A. J., McCormick, C. M., Desjardins, C. D., & Masten, A. S. (2018). Risk and adversity, parenting quality, and children's social-emotional adjustment in families experiencing homelessness. *Child Development, 90*(1), 227–244. https://doi.org/10.1111/cdev.12894

Labouvie-Vief, G. (2015). *Integrating emotions and cognition throughout the lifespan*. New York, NY: Springer. https://doi.org/10.1007/978-3-319-09822-7

Lacroix, A. E., & Whitten, R. A. (2017). Menarche. *StatPearls*. Retrieved from http://www.ncbi.nlm.nih.gov/pubmed/29261991

Ladd, G. W., & Kochenderfer-Ladd, B. (2016). Research in educational psychology: Social exclusion in school. In P. Riva & J. Eck (Eds.), *Social Exclusion* (pp. 109–132). Cham, Switzerland: Springer International Publishing. https://doi.org/10.1007/978-3-319-33033-4_6

LaFontana, K. M., & Cillessen, A. H. N. (2010). Developmental changes in the priority of perceived status in childhood and adolescence. *Social Development, 19*(1), 130–147. https://doi.org/10.1111/j.1467-9507.2008.00522.x

Laghi, F., Baiocco, R., Lonigro, A., & Baumgartner, E. (2013). Exploring the relationship between identity status development and alcohol consumption among Italian adolescents. *Journal of Psychology, 147*(3), 277–292. https://doi.org/10.1080/00223980.2012.688075

Laible, D., McGinley, M., Carlo, G., Augustine, M., & Murphy, T. (2014). Does engaging in prosocial behavior make children see the world through rose-colored glasses? *Developmental Psychology, 50*(3), 872–880.

Lam, C. B., Stanik, C., & McHale, S. M. (2017). The development and correlates of gender role attitudes in African American youth. *British Journal of Developmental Psychology, 35*, 406–419. https://doi.org/10.1111/bjdp.12182

Lamaze, F. (1956). *Painless childbirth: Psychoprophylactic method*. New York, NY: Contemporary Books.

Lamb, M. E. (2012). Mothers, fathers, families, and circumstances: Factors affecting children's adjustment. *Applied Developmental Science, 16*(2), 98–111. https://doi.org/10.1080/10888691.2012.667344

Lamb, M. E., & Lewis, C. (2015). The role of parent-child relationships in child development. In M. H. Bornstein & M. E. Lamb (Eds.), *Developmental science: An advanced textbook* (7th ed., pp. 469–517). New York, NY: Psychology Press.

Lamb, M. E., & Lewis, C. (2016). The role of parent-child relationships in development. In M. H. Bornstein & M. E. Lamb (Eds.), *Developmental science: An advanced textbook* (7th ed., pp. 535–585). New York, NY: Psychology Press.

Lambert, B. L., & Bauer, C. R. (2012). Developmental and behavioral consequences of prenatal cocaine exposure: A review. *Journal of Perinatology, 32*(11), 819–828. https://doi.org/10.1038/jp.2012.90

Lambert, M. C., & Kelley, H. M. (2011). Initiative versus guilt. In S. Goldstein & J. A. Naglieri (Eds.), *Encyclopedia of child behavior and development* (pp. 816–817). Boston, MA: Springer. https://doi.org/10.1007/978-0-387-79061-9_1499

Lampl, M., & Johnson, M. L. (2011). Infant growth in length follows prolonged sleep and increased naps. *Sleep, 34*(5), 641–650. https://doi.org/10.1093/sleep/34.5.641

Lampl, M., Johnson, M. L., & Frongillo, E. A. Jr. (2001). Mixed distribution analysis identifies saltation and stasis growth. *Annals of Human Biology, 28*(4), 403–411.

Lancy, D. (2008). The anthropology of childhood: Cherubs, chattel, changelings. *Utah State University Faculty Monographs*. Retrieved from http://digitalcommons.usu.edu/usufaculty_monographs/15

Landrigan, P. J., Fuller, R., Fisher, S., Suk, W. A., Sly, P., Chiles, T. C., & Bose-O'Reilly, S. (2019). Pollution and children's health. *Science of The Total Environment, 650*, 2389–2394. https://doi.org/10.1016/J.SCITOTENV.2018.09.375

Lange, H., Buse, J., Bender, S., Siegert, J., Knopf, H., & Roessner, V. (2016). Accident proneness in children and adolescents affected by ADHD and the impact of medication. *Journal of Attention Disorders, 20*(6), 501–509. https://doi.org/10.1177/1087054713518237

Langfur, S. (2013). The You-I event: On the genesis of self-awareness. *Phenomenology and the Cognitive Sciences, 12*(4), 769–790. https://doi.org/10.1007/s11097-012-9282-y

Lansford, J. E. (2014). Parenting across cultures. In H. Selin (Ed.), *Parenting across cultures* (Vol. 7, pp. 445–458). Dordrecht, Netherlands: Springer. https://doi.org/10.1007/978-94-007-7503-9

Lansford, J. E., Costanzo, P. R., Grimes, C., Putallaz, M., Miller, S., & Malone, P. S. (2009). Social network centrality and leadership status: Links with problem behaviors and tests of gender differences. *Merrill-Palmer Quarterly, 55*(1), 1–25.

Lansford, J. E., Deater-Deckard, K., Dodge, K. A., Bates, J. E., & Pettit, G. S. (2004). Ethnic differences in the link between physical discipline and later adolescent externalizing behaviors. *Journal of Child Psychology & Psychiatry, 45*(4), 801–812. https://doi.org/10.1111/j.1469-7610.2004.00273.x

Lansford, J. E., Laird, R. D., Pettit, G. S., Bates, J. E., & Dodge, K. A. (2014). Mothers' and fathers' autonomy-relevant parenting: Longitudinal links with adolescents' externalizing and internalizing behavior. *Journal of Youth and Adolescence, 43*(11), 1877–1889. https://doi.org/10.1007/s10964-013-0079-2

Lansford, J. E., Staples, A. D., Bates, J. E., Pettit, G. S., & Dodge, K. A. (2013). Trajectories of mothers' discipline strategies and interparental conflict: Interrelated change during middle childhood. *Journal of Family Communication, 13*(3), 178–195. https://doi.org/10.1080/15267431.2013.796947

Lany, J., Shoaib, A., Thompson, A., & Estes, K. G. (2018). Infant statistical-learning ability is related to real-time language processing. *Journal of Child Language, 45*(02), 368–391. https://doi.org/10.1017/S0305000917000253

Larion, S., Warsof, S., Maher, K., Peleg, D., & Abuhamad, A. (2016). Success of universal carrier screening for fetal diagnosis of genetic disease. *Obstetrics & Gynecology, 127*, 128S. https://doi.org/10.1097/01.AOG.0000483518.67531.79

Larson-Nath, C., & Biank, V. F. (2016). Clinical review of failure to thrive in pediatric patients. *Pediatric Annals, 45*(2), e46–e49. https://doi.org/10.3928/00904481-20160114-01

Last, B. S., Lawson, G. M., Breiner, K., Steinberg, L., & Farah, M. J. (2018). Childhood socioeconomic status and executive function in childhood and beyond. *PLoS ONE, 13*(8), e0202964. https://doi.org/10.1371/journal.pone.0202964

Lau, R., & Morse, C. A. (2003). Stress experiences of parents with premature infants in a special care nursery. *Stress and Health, 19*, 69–78.

Laughton, B., Cornell, M., Boivin, M., & Van Rie, A. (2013). Neurodevelopment in perinatally HIV-infected children: A concern for adolescence. *Journal of the International AIDS Society, 16*(1), 18603. https://doi.org/10.7448/IAS.16.1.18603

Laukkanen, A., Pesola, A., Havu, M., Sääkslahti, A., & Finni, T. (2014). Relationship between habitual physical activity and gross motor skills is multifaceted in 5- to 8-year-old children. *Scandinavian Journal of Medicine & Science in Sports, 24*(2), e102-10. https://doi.org/10.1111/sms.12116

Laurent, H. K., & Ablow, J. C. (2013). A face a mother could love: Depression-related maternal neural responses to infant emotion faces. *Social Neuroscience, 8*(3), 228–239. https://doi.org/10.1080/17470919.2012.762039

Laurent, H. K., Harold, G. T., Leve, L., Shelton, K. H., & Van Goozen, S. H. M. (2016). Understanding the unfolding of stress regulation in infants. *Development and Psychopathology, 28*(4pt2), 1431–1440. https://doi.org/10.1017/S0954579416000171

Laurin, J. C., & Joussemet, M. (2017). Parental autonomy-supportive practices and toddlers' rule internalization: A prospective observational study. *Motivation and Emotion, 41*(5), 562–575. https://doi.org/10.1007/s11031-017-9627-5

Laursen, B. (2017). Making and keeping friends: The importance of being similar. *Child Development Perspectives, 11*(4), 282–289. https://doi.org/10.1111/cdep.12246

Lavender, J. M., Utzinger, L. M., Cao, L., Wonderlich, S. A., Engel, S. G., Mitchell, J. E., & Crosby, R. D. (2016). Reciprocal associations between negative affect, binge eating, and purging in the natural environment in women with bulimia nervosa. *Journal of Abnormal Psychology, 125*(3), 381–386. https://doi.org/10.1037/abn0000135

Lawrence, K., Campbell, R., & Skuse, D. (2015). Age, gender, and puberty influence the development of facial emotion recognition. *Frontiers in Psychology, 6*, 761. https://doi.org/10.3389/fpsyg.2015.00761

Lawson, G. M., Hook, C. J., & Farah, M. J. (2018). A meta-analysis of the relationship between socioeconomic status and executive function performance among children. *Developmental Science, 21*(2), e12529. https://doi.org/10.1111/desc.12529

Layne, C. M., Saltzman, W. R., Poppleton, L., Burlingame, G. M., Pašalić, A., Duraković, E., . . . Pynoos, R. S. (2008). Effectiveness of a school-based group psychotherapy program for war-exposed adolescents: A randomized controlled trial. *Journal of the American Academy of Child & Adolescent Psychiatry, 47*(9), 1048–1062. https://doi.org/10.1097/CHI.0b013e31817eecae

le Grange, D., & Schmidt, U. (2005). The treatment of adolescents with bulimia nervosa. *Journal of Mental Health, 14*(6), 587–597.

Leadbeater, B., Banister, E., Ellis, W., & Yeung, R. (2008). Victimization and relational aggression in adolescent romantic relationships: The influence of parental and peer behaviors, and individual adjustment. *Journal of Youth & Adolescence, 37*(3), 359–372. https://doi.org/10.1007/s10964-007-9269-0

Leahey, E., & Guo, G. (2001). Gender differences in mathematical trajectories. *Social Forces, 80*(2), 713–732. https://doi.org/10.1353/sof.2001.0102

Leaper, C. (2013). Gender development during childhood. In P. D. Zelaz (Ed.), *The Oxford handbook of developmental psychology: Vol. 2. Self and other* (pp. 326–376). New York, NY: Oxford University Press.

Leaper, C., & Valin, D. (1996). Predictors of Mexican American mothers' and fathers' attitudes toward gender equality. *Hispanic Journal of Behavioral Sciences, 18*(3), 343–355. https://doi.org/10.1177/07399863960183005

Learmonth, A. E., Lamberth, R., & Rovee-Collier, C. (2004). Generalizations of deferred imitation during the first year of life. *Journal of Experimental Child Psychology, 88*(4), 297–318.

Leat, S. J., Yadav, N. K., & Irving, E. L. (2009). Development of visual acuity and contrast sensitivity in children. *Journal of Optometry,*

2(1), 19–26. https://doi.org/10.3921/joptom.2009.19

Leather, C. V., & Henry, L. A. (1994). Working memory span and phonological awareness tasks as predictors of early reading ability. *Journal of Experimental Child Psychology, 58*, 88–111.

Lebel, C., & Beaulieu, C. (2011). Longitudinal development of human brain wiring continues from childhood into adulthood. *Journal of Neuroscience, 31*(30), 10937–10947. https://doi.org/10.1523/JNEUROSCI.5302-10.2011

Lebel, C., & Deoni, S. (2018). The development of brain white matter microstructure. *NeuroImage*. https://doi.org/10.1016/J.NEUROIMAGE.2017.12.097

Lebel, C., Walker, L., Leemans, A., Phillips, L., & Beaulieu, C. (2008). Microstructural maturation of the human brain from childhood to adulthood. *NeuroImage, 40*(3), 1044–1055. https://doi.org/10.1016/J.NEUROIMAGE.2007.12.053

Lecce, S., Demicheli, P., Zocchi, S., & Palladino, P. (2015). The origins of children's metamemory: The role of theory of mind. *Journal of Experimental Child Psychology, 131*, 56–72. https://doi.org/10.1016/j.jecp.2014.11.005

Leclerc, B., & Wortley, R. (2015). Predictors of victim disclosure in child sexual abuse: Additional evidence from a sample of incarcerated adult sex offenders. *Child Abuse & Neglect, 43*, 104–111. https://doi.org/10.1016/J.CHIABU.2015.03.003

Lederberg, A. R., Schick, B., & Spencer, P. E. (2013). Language and literacy development of deaf and hard-of-hearing children: Successes and challenges. *Developmental Psychology, 49*(1), 15–30. https://doi.org/10.1037/a0029558

Lee, B. K., & McGrath, J. J. (2015). Advancing parental age and autism: Multifactorial pathways. *Trends in Molecular Medicine, 21*(2), 118–125. https://doi.org/10.1016/J.MOLMED.2014.11.005

Lee, H., & Galloway, J. C. (2012). Control in very young infants. *Physical Therapy, 92*(7), 935–947.

Lee, J. M., Wasserman, R., Kaciroti, N., Gebremariam, A., Steffes, J., Dowshen, S., . . . Herman-Giddens, M. E. (2016). Timing of puberty in overweight versus obese boys. *Pediatrics, 137*(2), e20150164. https://doi.org/10.1542/peds.2015-0164

Lee, K., Quinn, P. C., & Pascalis, O. (2017). Face race processing and racial bias in early development: A perceptual-social linkage. *Current Directions in Psychological Science, 26*(3), 256–262. https://doi.org/10.1177/0963721417690276

Lee, L., Howes, C., & Chamberlain, B. (2007). Ethnic heterogeneity of social networks and cross-ethnic friendships of elementary school boys and girls. *Merrill-Palmer Quarterly, 53*(3), 325–346.

Lee, L. J., & Lupo, P. J. (2013). Maternal smoking during pregnancy and the risk of congenital heart defects in offspring: A systematic review and metaanalysis. *Pediatric Cardiology, 34*(2), 398–407. https://doi.org/10.1007/s00246-012-0470-x

Lee, N.-C., Chien, Y.-H., & Hwu, W.-L. (2017). A review of biomarkers for Alzheimer's disease in Down syndrome. *Neurology and Therapy, 6*(S1), 69–81. https://doi.org/10.1007/s40120-017-0071-y

Lee, S. J., Altschul, I., & Gershoff, E. T. (2013). Does warmth moderate longitudinal associations between maternal spanking and child aggression in early childhood? *Developmental Psychology, 49*(11), 2017–2028. https://doi.org/10.1037/a0031630

Lee, S. M., Daniels, M. H., & Kissinger, D. B. (2006). Parental influences on adolescent adjustment: Parenting styles versus parenting practices. *Family Journal, 14*, 253–259.

Lee, Y.-E., Brophy-Herb, H. E., Vallotton, C. D., Griffore, R. J., Carlson, J. S., & Robinson, J. L. (2016). Do young children's representations of discipline and empathy moderate the effects of punishment on emotion regulation? *Social Development, 25*(1), 120–138. https://doi.org/10.1111/sode.12141

Leenders, I., & Brugman, D. D. (2005). Moral/non-moral domain shift in young adolescents in relation to delinquent behaviour. *British Journal of Developmental Psychology, 23*(1), 65–79.

Lefkowitz, E. S., Vasilenko, S. A., & Leavitt, C. E. (2016). Oral vs. vaginal sex experiences and consequences among first-year college students. *Archives of Sexual Behavior, 45*(2), 329–337. https://doi.org/10.1007/s10508-015-0654-6

Legare, C. H., Clegg, J. M., & Wen, N. J. (2018). Evolutionary developmental psychology: 2017 redux. *Child Development*. https://doi.org/10.1111/cdev.13018

Legare, C. H., Evans, E. M., Rosengren, K. S., & Harris, P. L. (2012). The coexistence of natural and supernatural explanations across cultures and development. *Child Development, 83*(3), 779–793. https://doi.org/10.1111/j.1467-8624.2012.01743.x

Legare, C. H., & Gelman, S. A. (2008). Bewitchment, biology, or both: The co-existence of natural and supernatural explanatory frameworks across development. *Cognitive Science, 32*(4), 607–642. https://doi.org/10.1080/03640210802066766

Legare, C. H., Wen, N. J., Herrmann, P. A., & Whitehouse, H. (2015). Imitative flexibility and the development of cultural learning. *Cognition, 142*, 351–361. https://doi.org/10.1016/J.COGNITION.2015.05.020

Legate, N., Ryan, R. M., & Weinstein, N. (2012). Is coming out always a "good thing"? Exploring the relations of autonomy support, outness, and wellness for lesbian, gay, and bisexual individuals. *Social Psychological and Personality Science, 3*(2), 145–152. https://doi.org/10.1177/1948550611411929

Lehman, D. R., & Nisbett, R. E. (1990). A longitudinal study of the effects of undergraduate training on reasoning. *Developmental Psychology, 26*, 952–960.

Leiden Conference on the Development and Care of Children Without Permanent Parents. (2012). The development and care of institutionally reared children. *Child Development Perspectives, 6*(2), 174–180. https://doi.org/10.1111/j.1750-8606.2011.00231.x

Lemerise, E. A., & Dodge, K. A. (2008). The development of anger and hostile interactions. In M. Lewis, J. M. Haviland-Jones, & L. F. Barrett (Eds.), *Handbook of emotions* (3rd ed., pp. 730–741). New York, NY: Guilford.

Lemery-Chalfant, K., Kao, K., Swann, G., & Goldsmith, H. H. (2013). Childhood temperament: Passive gene–environment correlation, gene–environment interaction, and the hidden importance of the family environment. *Development and Psychopathology, 25*(1), 51–63. https://doi.org/10.1017/S0954579412000892

Lench, H. C., Baldwin, C. L., An, D., & Garrison, K. E. (2018). The emotional toolkit: Lessons from the science of emotion. In H. C. Lench (Ed.), *The function of emotions* (pp. 253–261). Cham, Switzerland: Springer International Publishing. https://doi.org/10.1007/978-3-319-77619-4_13

Lenhart, A., Purcell, K., Smith, A., & Zickuhr, K. (2010). Social media and young adults. *Pew Research Center Internet & Technology*. Retrieved from http://www.pewinternet.org/2010/02/03/social-media-and-young-adults/

Leow, C., & Wen, X. (2017). Is full day better than half day? A propensity score analysis of the association between Head Start program intensity and children's school performance in kindergarten. *Early Education and Development, 28*(2), 224–239. https://doi.org/10.1080/10409289.2016.1208600

Leppanen, J. M. (2011). Neural and developmental bases of the ability to recognize social signals of emotions. *Emotion Review, 3*(2), 179–188. https://doi.org/10.1177/1754073910387942

Lerkkanen, M.-K., Kiuru, N., Pakarinen, E., Poikkeus, A.-M., Rasku-Puttonen, H., Siekkinen, M., & Nurmi, J.-E. (2016). Child-centered versus teacher-directed teaching practices: Associations with the development of academic skills in the first grade at school. *Early Childhood Research Quarterly, 36*, 145–156. https://doi.org/10.1016/j.ecresq.2015.12.023

Lerner, R. M., Agans, J. P., DeSouza, L. M., & Hershberg, R. M. (2014). Developmental science in 2025: A predictive review. *Research in Human Development, 11*(4), 255–272. https://doi.org/10.1080/15427609.2014.967046

Lerner, R. M., Buckingham, M. H., Champine, R. B., Greenman, K. N., Warren, D. J. A., Weiner, M. B., . . . Weiner, M. B. (2015a). Positive development among diverse youth. In R. A. Scott, S. M. Kosslyn, & M. Buchmann (Eds.), *Emerging trends in the social and behavioral sciences* (pp. 1–14). Hoboken, NJ: John Wiley & Sons. https://doi.org/10.1002/9781118900772.etrds0260

Lerner, R. M., & Israeloff, R. (2007). *The good teen: Rescuing adolescence from the myths of the storm and stress years*. New York, NY: Crown.

Lerner, R. M., Johnson, S. K., & Buckingham, M. H. (2015b). Relational developmental systems-based theories and the study of children and families: Lerner and Spanier (1978) revisited. *Journal of Family Theory & Review, 7*(2), 83–104. https://doi.org/10.1111/jftr.12067

Lerner, R. M., & Overton, W. F. (2017). Reduction to absurdity: Why epigenetics invalidates all models involving genetic reduction. *Human Development, 60*(2–3), 107–123. https://doi.org/10.1159/000477995

Lerner, R. M., Tirrell, J. M., Dowling, E. M., Geldhof, G. J., Gestsdóttir, S., Lerner, J. V., . . . Sim, A. T.

R. (2019). The end of the beginning: Evidence and absences studying positive youth development in a global context. *Adolescent Research Review, 4*(1), 1–14. https://doi.org/10.1007/s40894-018-0093-4

Lester, B. M., Conradt, E., & Marsit, C. (2016). Introduction to the special section on epigenetics. *Child Development, 87*(1), 29–37. https://doi.org/10.1111/cdev.12489

Levenson, E. (2017). China's two-child policy sparks immediate increase in babies. *CNN*. Retrieved from https://www.cnn.com/2017/01/23/world/china-two-child/index.html

Leventon, J. S., & Bauer, P. J. (2013). The sustained effect of emotional signals on neural processing in 12-month-olds. *Developmental Science, 16*(4), 485–498. https://doi.org/10.1111/desc.12041

Levine, D., Strother-Garcia, K., Golinkoff, R. M., & Hirsh-Pasek, K. (2016). Language development in the first year of life. *Otology & Neurotology, 37*(2), e56–e62. https://doi.org/10.1097/MAO.0000000000000908

Levine, J. A., Emery, C. R., & Pollack, H. (2007). The well-being of children born to teen mothers. *Journal of Marriage and Family, 69*(1), 105–122. https://doi.org/10.1111/j.1741-3737.2006.00348.x

Levine, L. E. (1983). Mine: Self-definition in 2-year-old boys. *Developmental Psychology, 19*, 544–549.

Levine, L. E., & Munsch, J. (2010). *Child development: An active learning approach*. Thousand Oaks, CA: Sage.

Levine, R. A., Levine, S., Dixon, S., Richman, A., Keefer, C. H., Leiderman, P. H., & Brazelton, T. B. (1994). *Child care and culture: Lessons from Africa*. New York, NY: Cambridge University Press.

Levine, T. A., & Woodward, L. J. (2018). Early inhibitory control and working memory abilities of children prenatally exposed to methadone. *Early Human Development, 116*, 68–75. https://doi.org/10.1016/j.earlhumdev.2017.11.010

Levitt, A. G., Aydelott Utman, J. G., Jakobson, R., Menn, L., Oller, D. K., & Stark, R. E. (1992). From babbling towards the sound systems of English and French: A longitudinal two-case study. *Journal of Child Language, 19*(1), 19. https://doi.org/10.1017/S0305000900013611

Levy, G. D., & Haaf, R. A. (1994). Detection of gender-related categories by 10-month-old infants. *Infant Behavior & Development, 17*(4), 457–459. https://doi.org/10.1016/0163-6383(94)90037-x

Levy, G. D., Taylor, M. G., & Gelman, S. A. (1995). Traditional and evaluative aspects of flexibility in gender roles, social conventions, moral rules, and physical laws. *Child Development, 66*(2), 515–531.

Levy, J. (1976). A review of evidence for a genetic component in the determination of handedness. *Behavior Genetics, 6*(4), 429–453. https://doi.org/10.1007/BF01065700

Lewis, B. A., Minnes, S., Short, E. J., Min, M. O., Wu, M., Lang, A., . . . Singer, L. T. (2013). Language outcomes at 12 years for children exposed prenatally to cocaine. *Journal of Speech, Language, and Hearing Research, 56*(5), 1662–1676. https://doi.org/10.1044/1092-4388(2013/12-0119)

Lewis, M (2011). Inside and outside: The relation between emotional states and expressions. *Emotion Review, 3*(2), 189–196. https://doi.org/10.1177/1754073910387947

Lewis, M. (2016). Self-conscious emotions: Embarrassment, pride, shame, guilt, and hubris. In L. F. Barrett, M. Lewis, & J. M. Haviland-Jones (Eds.), *Handbook of emotions* (p. 928). New York, NY: Guilford.

Lewis, M., & Brooks-Gunn, J. (1979). *Social cognition and the acquisition of self*. New York, NY: Plenum Press.

Lewis, M, & Carmody, D. P. (2008). Self-representation and brain development. *Developmental Psychology, 44*(5), 1329–1334. https://doi.org/10.1037/a0012681

Lewis, M, Hitchcock, D. F. A., & Sullivan, M. W. (2004). Physiological and emotional reactivity to learning and frustration. *Infancy, 6*(1), 121–143.

Lewis, M, Ramsay, D. S., & Kawakami, K. (1993). Differences between Japanese infants and Caucasian American infants in behavioral and cortisol response to inoculation. *Child Development, 64*(6), 1722–1731. https://doi.org/10.1111/j.1467-8624.1993.tb04209.x

Lewis, M., Takai-Kawakami, K., Kawakami, K., & Sullivan, M. W. (2010). Cultural differences in emotional responses to success and failure. *International Journal of Behavioral Development, 34*(1), 53–61. https://doi.org/10.1177/0165025409348559

Lewis, R. (2017). *Human genetics*. New York, NY: McGraw-Hill Education.

Lewis, R. B., Wheeler, J. J., & Carter, S. L. (2017). *Teaching students with special needs in general education classrooms*. Boston, MA: Pearson.

Lewis, S. (2017). Sleep: Dream a little dream. *Nature Reviews Neuroscience, 18*(6), 324–324. https://doi.org/10.1038/nrn.2017.66

Lewkowicz, D. J., Leo, I., & Simion, F. (2010). Intersensory perception at birth: Newborns match nonhuman primate faces and voices. *Infancy, 15*(1), 46–60. https://doi.org/10.1111/j.1532-7078.2009.00005.x

Lew-Williams, C., Ferguson, B., Abu-Zhaya, R., & Seidl, A. (2019). Social touch interacts with infants' learning of auditory patterns. *Developmental Cognitive Neuroscience, 35*, 66–74. https://doi.org/10.1016/J.DCN.2017.09.006

Li, D., Liu, L., & Odouli, R. (2003). Exposure to non-steroidal anti-inflammatory drugs during pregnancy and risk of miscarriage: Population based cohort study. *British Medical Journal, 327*, 368–371.

Li, J. J., Berk, M. S., & Lee, S. S. (2013). Differential susceptibility in longitudinal models of gene-environment interaction for adolescent depression. *Development and Psychopathology, 25*(4, Pt. 1), 991–1003. https://doi.org/10.1017/S0954579413000321

Liben, L. S., Bigler, R. S., & Hilliard, L. J. (2013). Gender development. In E. T. Gershoff, R. S. Mistry, & D. A. Crossby (Eds.), *Societal contexts of child development: Pathways of influence and implications for practice and policy* (pp. 3–18). New York, NY: Oxford University Press.

Libertus, K., Gibson, J., Hidayatallah, N. Z., Hirtle, J., Adcock, R. A., & Needham, A. (2013). Size matters: How age and reaching experiences shape infants' preferences for different sized objects. *Infant Behavior & Development, 36*(2), 189–198. https://doi.org/10.1016/j.infbeh.2013.01.006

Libertus, K., Joh, A. S., & Needham, A. W. (2016). Motor training at 3 months affects object exploration 12 months later. *Developmental Science, 19*(6), 1058–1066. https://doi.org/10.1111/desc.12370

Libertus, K., & Needham, A. (2010). Teach to reach: The effects of active vs. passive reaching experiences on action and perception. *Vision Research, 50*(24), 2750–2757. https://doi.org/10.1016/j.visres.2010.09.001

Libertus, M. E., Starr, A., & Brannon, E. M. (2014). Number trumps area for 7-month-old infants. *Developmental Psychology, 50*(1), 108. https://doi.org/10.1037/a0032986

Lickenbrock, D. M., & Braungart-Rieker, J. M. (2015). Examining antecedents of infant attachment security with mothers and fathers: An ecological systems perspective. *Infant Behavior and Development, 39*, 173–187. https://doi.org/10.1016/J.INFBEH.2015.03.003

Lickliter, R., & Witherington, D. C. (2017). Towards a truly developmental epigenetics. *Human Development, 60*(2–3), 124–138. https://doi.org/10.1159/000477996

Lieven, E., & Stoll, S. (2010). Language. In M. H. Bornstein (Ed.), *Handbook of cultural developmental science* (pp. 143–160). New York, NY: Psychology Press.

Lilienfeld, S. O. (2002). When worlds collide. Social science, politics, and the Rind et al. (1998). Child sexual abuse meta-analysis. *The American Psychologist, 57*(3), 176–188.

Lillard, A. S. (2015). The development of play. In *Handbook of child psychology and developmental science* (pp. 1–44). Hoboken, NJ: John Wiley & Sons. https://doi.org/10.1002/9781118963418.childpsy211

Lillevoll, K. R., Kroger, J., & Martinussen, M. (2013). Identity status and anxiety: A meta-analysis. *Identity, 13*(3), 214–227. https://doi.org/10.1080/15283488.2013.799432

Limber, S. P., & Small, M. A. (2003). State laws and policies to address bullying in schools. *School Psychology Review, 32*(3), 445–455.

Lindberg, L., Santelli, J., & Desai, S. (2016). Understanding the decline in adolescent fertility in the United States, 2007–2012. *Journal of Adolescent Health, 59*(5), 577–583. https://doi.org/10.1016/j.jadohealth.2016.06.024

Lindberg, S. M., Hyde, J. S., Petersen, J. L., & Linn, M. C. (2010). New trends in gender and mathematics performance: A meta-analysis. *Psychological Bulletin, 136*(6), 1123–1135. https://doi.org/10.1037/a0021276

Lindenburg, I. T. M., van Kamp, I. L., & Oepkes, D. (2014). Intrauterine blood transfusion: Current indications and associated risks. *Fetal Diagnosis and Therapy, 36*(4), 263–271. https://doi.org/10.1159/000362812

Lindsay, A. C., Greaney, M. L., Wallington, S. F., Mesa, T., & Salas, C. F. (2017). A review of early influences on physical activity and sedentary behaviors of preschool-age children in high-income countries. *Journal for Specialists in Pediatric Nursing, 22*(3), e12182. https://doi.org/10.1111/jspn.12182

Lindsey, E. W., & Colwell, M. J. (2013). Pretend and physical play: Links to preschoolers' affective social competence. *Merrill-Palmer Quarterly, 59*(3), 330–360. https://doi.org/10.1353/mpq.2013.0015

Linebarger, D. L., & Vaala, S. E. (2010). Screen media and language development in infants and toddlers: An ecological perspective. *Developmental Review, 30*(2), 176–202. https://doi.org/10.1016/j.dr.2010.03.006

Lipsitt, L. P., & Kaye, H. (1964). Conditioned sucking in the human newborn. *Psychonomic Science, 1*, 29–30.

Lisdahl, K. M., Gilbart, E. R., Wright, N. E., & Shollenbarger, S. (2013). Dare to delay? The impacts of adolescent alcohol and marijuana use onset on cognition, brain structure, and function. *Frontiers in Psychiatry, 4*, 53. https://doi.org/10.3389/fpsyt.2013.00053

Litovsky, R. Y., & Ashmead, D. H. (1997). Developmental of binaural and spatial hearing in infants and children. In R. H. Gilkey & T. R. Anderson (Eds.), *Binaural and special hearing in real and virtual environments* (pp. 571–592). Mahwah, NJ: Erlbaum.

Little, A. H., Lipsitt, L. P., & Rovee-Collier, C. K. (1984). Classical conditioning and retention of the infants eyelid response: Effects of age and interstimulus interval. *Journal of Experimental Child Psychology, 37*, 512–524.

Little, E. E., Carver, L. J., & Legare, C. H. (2016). Cultural variation in triadic infant-caregiver object exploration. *Child Development, 87*(4), 1130–1145. https://doi.org/10.1111/cdev.12513

Littschwager, J. C., & Markman, E. M. (1994). Sixteen- and 24-month-olds' use of mutual exclusivity as a default assumption in second-label learning. *Developmental Psychology, 30*, 955–968.

Liu, D., Wellman, H. M., Tardif, T., & Sabbagh, M. A. (2008). Theory of mind development in chinese children: A meta-analysis of false-belief understanding across cultures and languages. *Developmental Psychology, 44*(2), 523–531. https://doi.org/10.1037/0012-1649.44.2.523

Liu, M., Wu, L., & Ming, Q. (2015). How does physical activity intervention improve self-esteem and self-concept in children and adolescents? Evidence from a meta-analysis. *PLoS One, 10*(8), e0134804. https://doi.org/10.1371/journal.pone.0134804

Liu, R. T., & Mustanski, B. (2012). Suicidal ideation and self-harm in lesbian, gay, bisexual, and transgender youth. *American Journal of Preventive Medicine, 42*(3), 221–228. https://doi.org/10.1016/j.amepre.2011.10.023

Liu, Y., Kaaya, S., Chai, J., McCoy, D. C., Surkan, P. J., Black, M. M., . . . Smith-Fawzi, M. C. (2017). Maternal depressive symptoms and early childhood cognitive development: A meta-analysis. *Psychological Medicine, 47*(04), 680–689. https://doi.org/10.1017/S003329171600283X

Livingston, G. (2013). The rise of single fathers. *Pew Research Center Social & Demographic Trends*. Retrieved from http://www.pewsocialtrends.org/2013/07/02/the-rise-of-single-fathers/

Lloyd, B. J., Coller, R., & Miller, L. T. (2019). *BRS pediatrics*. Philadelphia PA: Wolters Kluwer.

Lobo, M. A., & Galloway, J. C. (2012). Enhanced handling and positioning in early infancy advances development throughout the first year. *Child Development, 83*(4), 1290–1302. https://doi.org/10.1111/j.1467-8624.2012.01772.x

Lobstein, T., Jackson-Leach, R., Moodie, M. L., Hall, K. D., Gortmaker, S. L., Swinburn, B. A., . . . McPherson, K. (2015). Child and adolescent obesity: Part of a bigger picture. *Lancet (London, England), 385*(9986), 2510–2520. https://doi.org/10.1016/S0140-6736(14)61746-3

LoBue, V., Nishida, T., Chiong, C., DeLoache, J. S., & Haidt, J. (2011). When getting something good is bad: Even three-year-olds react to inequality. *Social Development, 20*(1), 154–170. https://doi.org/10.1111/j.1467-9507.2009.00560.x

Lock, J. (2011). Evaluation of family treatment models for eating disorders. *Current Opinion in Psychiatry, 24*(4), 274–279. https://doi.org/10.1097/YCO.0b013e328346f71e

Lockenhoff, C. E., Chan, W., McCrae, R. R., De Fruyt, F., Jussim, L., De Bolle, M., . . . Terracciano, A. (2014). Gender stereotypes of personality: Universal and accurate? *Journal of Cross-Cultural Psychology, 45*(5), 675–694. https://doi.org/10.1177/0022022113520075

Lockl, K., & Schneider, W. (2007). Knowledge about the mind: Links between theory of mind and later metamemory. *Child Development, 78*(1), 148–167. https://doi.org/10.1111/j.1467-8624.2007.00990.x

Lockwood, J., Daley, D., Townsend, E., & Sayal, K. (2017). Impulsivity and self-harm in adolescence: A systematic review. *European Child & Adolescent Psychiatry, 26*(4), 387–402. https://doi.org/10.1007/s00787-016-0915-5

Loessl, B., Valerius, G., Kopasz, M., Hornyak, M., Riemann, D., & Voderholzer, U. (2008). Are adolescents chronically sleep-deprived? An investigation of sleep habits of adolescents in the Southwest of Germany. *Child: Care, Health & Development, 34*(5), 549–556. https://doi.org/10.1111/j.1365-2214.2008.00845.x

Lohaus, A., Keller, H., Lamm, B., Teubert, M., Fassbender, I., Freitag, C., . . . Schwarzer, G. (2011). Infant development in two cultural contexts: Cameroonian Nso farmer and German middleclass infants. *Journal of Reproductive and Infant Psychology, 29*(2), 148–161. https://doi.org/10.1080/02646838.2011.558074

Lohmann, H., & Tomasello, M. (2003). The role of language in the development of false belief understanding: A training study. *Child Development, 74*(4), 1130–1144. https://doi.org/10.1111/1467-8624.00597

Lonigan, C. J. (2015). Literacy Development. In L. S. Liben & U. Muller (Eds.), *Handbook of child psychology and developmental science* (pp. 763–804). Hoboken, NJ: John Wiley & Sons. https://doi.org/10.1002/9781118963418.childpsy218

Lopez-Larson, M. P., Rogowska, J., Bogorodzki, P., Bueler, C. E., McGlade, E. C., & Yurgelun-Todd, D. A. (2012). Cortico-cerebellar abnormalities in adolescents with heavy marijuana use. *Psychiatry Research: Neuroimaging, 202*(3), 224–232. https://doi.org/10.1016/j.pscychresns.2011.11.005

Lopez-Tamayo, R., LaVome Robinson, W., Lambert, S. F., Jason, L. A., & Ialongo, N. S. (2016). Parental monitoring, association with externalized behavior, and academic outcomes in urban African-American youth: A moderated mediation analysis. *American Journal of Community Psychology, 57*(3–4), 366–379. https://doi.org/10.1002/ajcp.12056

Lorenz, K. (1952). *King Solomon's ring*. New York, NY: Crowell.

Lottero-Leconte, R., Isidro Alonso, C. A., Castellano, L., & Perez Martinez, S. (2017). Mechanisms of the sperm guidance, an essential aid for meeting the oocyte. *Translational Cancer Research, 6*(2), S427–S430. https://doi.org/10.21037/12829

Lozoff, B., Wolf, A. W., & Davis, N. S. (1984). Cosleeping in urban families with young children in the United States. *Pediatrics, 74*, 171–182.

Lubinski, D., Benbow, C. P., Webb, R. M., & Bleske-Rechek, A. (2006). Tracking exceptional human capital over two decades. *Psychological Science, 17*(3), 194–199. https://doi.org/10.1111/j.1467-9280.2006.01685.x

Lubman, D. I., Cheetham, A., & Yücel, M. (2015). Cannabis and adolescent brain development. *Pharmacology & Therapeutics, 148*, 1–16. https://doi.org/10.1016/j.pharmthera.2014.11.009

Lucassen, M. F., Clark, T. C., Denny, S. J., Fleming, T. M., Rossen, F. V, Sheridan, J., . . . Robinson, E. M. (2015). What has changed from 2001 to 2012 for sexual minority youth in New Zealand? *Journal of Paediatrics and Child Health, 51*(4), 410–418. https://doi.org/10.1111/jpc.12727

Lucassen, N., Tharner, A., Van IJzendoorn, M. H., Bakermans-Kranenburg, M. J., Volling, B. L., Verhulst, F. C., . . . Tiemeier, H. (2011). The association between paternal sensitivity and infant-father attachment security: A meta-analysis of three decades of research. *Journal of Family Psychology, 25*(6), 986–992. https://doi.org/10.1037/a0025855

Luckey, A. J., & Fabes, R. A. (2005). Understanding Nonsocial Play in Early Childhood. *Early Childhood Education Journal, 33*(2), 67–72.

Luders, E., Gingnell, M., Poromaa, I. S., Engman, J., Kurth, F., & Gaser, C. (2018). Potential brain age reversal after pregnancy: Younger brains at 4–6 weeks postpartum. *Neuroscience, 386*, 309–314. https://doi.org/10.1016/J.NEUROSCIENCE.2018.07.006

Luders, E., Thompson, P. M., & Toga, A. W. (2010). The development of the corpus callosum in the healthy human brain. *Journal of Neuroscience, 30*(33), 10985–10990. https://doi.org/10.1523/JNEUROSCI.5122-09.2010

Luk, J. W., Gilman, S. E., Haynie, D. L., & Simons-Morton, B. G. (2017). Sexual orientation differences in adolescent health care access and health-promoting physician advice. *Journal of Adolescent Health, 61*, 555–561. https://doi.org/10.1016/j.jadohealth.2017.05.032

Luna, B., Marek, S., Larsen, B., Tervo-Clemmens, B., & Chahal, R. (2015). An integrative model of the maturation of cognitive control. *Annual Review of Neuroscience, 38*(1), 151–170. https://doi.org/10.1146/annurev-neuro-071714-034054

Luna, B., Paulsen, D. J., Padmanabhan, A., & Geier, C. (2013). The teenage brain: Cognitive control and motivation. *Current Directions in*

Psychological Science, 22(2), 94–100. https://doi.org/10.1177/0963721413478416

Lundsberg, L. S., Illuzzi, J. L., Belanger, K., Triche, E. W., & Bracken, M. B. (2015). Low-to-moderate prenatal alcohol consumption and the risk of selected birth outcomes: A prospective cohort study. *Annals of Epidemiology, 25*(1), 46–54.e3. https://doi.org/10.1016/j.annepidem.2014.10.011

Luthar, S. S., Crossman, E. J., & Small, P. J. (2015). Resilience and adversity. In M. E. Lamb (Ed.), *Handbook of child psychology and developmental science* (pp. 1–40). Hoboken, NJ: John Wiley & Sons. https://doi.org/10.1002/9781118963418.childpsy307

Luttikhuizen dos Santos, E. S., de Kieviet, J. F., Königs, M., van Elburg, R. M., & Oosterlaan, J. (2013). Predictive value of the Bayley scales of infant development on development of very preterm/very low birth weight children: A meta-analysis. *Early Human Development, 89*(7), 487–496. https://doi.org/10.1016/j.earlhumdev.2013.03.008

Lyall, A. E., Shi, F., Geng, X., Woolson, S., Li, G., Wang, L., . . . Gilmore, J. H. (2015). Dynamic development of regional cortical thickness and surface area in early childhood. *Cerebral Cortex, 25*(8), 2204–2212. https://doi.org/10.1093/cercor/bhu027

Lynch, A., Lee, H. M., Bhat, A., & Galloway, J. C. (2008). No stable arm preference during the pre-reaching period: A comparison of right and left hand kinematics with and without a toy present. *Developmental Psychobiology, 50*(4), 390–398. https://doi.org/10.1002/dev.20297

Lynch, K. (2016). Gene-environment correlation. In *Encyclopedia of personality and individual differences* (pp. 1–4). Cham, Switzerland: Springer International Publishing. https://doi.org/10.1007/978-3-319-28099-8_1470-1

Lynn, R. (2013). Who discovered the Flynn effect? A review of early studies of the secular increase of intelligence. *Intelligence, 41*(6), 765–769. https://doi.org/10.1016/j.intell.2013.03.008

Lyons, R. A., Delahunty, A. M., Heaven, M., McCabe, M., Allen, H., & Nash, P. (2000). Incidence of childhood fractures in affluent and deprived areas: Population based study. *BMJ (Clinical Research Ed.), 320*(7228), 149.

Lyons-Ruth, K., & Jacobvitz, D. (2016). Attachment disorganization from infancy to adulthood: Neurobiological correlates, parenting contexts, and pathways to disorder. In J. Cassidy & P. R. Shaver (Eds.), *Handbook of attachment: Theory, research, and clinical applications*, (pp. 667–695). New York, NY: Guilford.

Ma, L., & Ganea, P. A. (2010). Dealing with conflicting information: Young children's reliance on what they see versus what they are told. *Developmental Science, 13*(1), 151–160. https://doi.org/10.1111/j.1467-7687.2009.00878.x

Maakaron, J. E., & Taher, A. (2012). Sickle cell anemia. *Medscape*. Retrieved from http://emedicine.medscape.com/article/205926-overview#a0156

Maccoby, E. E., & Jacklin, C. N. (1987). Gender segregation in childhood. *Advances in Child Development and Behavior*, 20, 239–287. https://doi.org/10.1016/S0065-2407(08)60404-8

MacConnell, A., & Daehler, M. W. (2004). The development of representational insight: Beyond the model/room paradigm. *Cognitive Development, 19*(3), 345–362.

MacDorman, M. F., & Declercq, E. (2016). Trends and characteristics of United States out-of-hospital births 2004-2014: New information on risk status and access to care. *Birth, 43*(2), 116–124. https://doi.org/10.1111/birt.12228

Macfarlane, A. J. (1975). Olfaction in the development of social preferences in the human neonate. *Ciba Foundation Symposia, 33*, 103–117.

MacKay, D. F., Smith, G. C. S., Dobbie, R., & Pell, J. P. (2010). Gestational age at delivery and special educational need: Retrospective cohort study of 407,503 schoolchildren. *PLoS Medicine, 7*(6), e1000289. https://doi.org/10.1371/journal.pmed.1000289

Mackintosh, J. N. (2011). *IQ and human intelligence*. (2nd ed.). Oxford, England: Oxford University Press.

MacWhinney, B. (2015). Language development. In L. S. Liben & U. Müller (Eds.), *Handbook of child psychology and developmental science* (pp. 296–338). Hoboken, NJ: John Wiley & Sons. https://doi.org/10.1002/9781118963418.childpsy208

Madge, N., Hewitt, A., Hawton, K., De Wilde, E. J., Corcoran, P., Fekete, S., . . . Ystgaard, M. (2008). Deliberate self-harm within an international community sample of young people: Comparative findings from the Child & Adolescent Self-Harm in Europe (CASE) Study. *Journal of Child Psychology & Psychiatry, 49*(6), 667–677. https://doi.org/10.1111/j.1469-7610.2008.01879.x

Madsen, S. D., & Collins, W. A. (2011). The Salience of adolescent romantic experiences for romantic relationship qualities in young adulthood. *Journal of Research on Adolescence, 21*(4), 789–801. https://doi.org/10.1111/j.1532-7795.2011.00737.x

Magee, C. A., Gordon, R., & Caputi, P. (2014). Distinct developmental trends in sleep duration during early childhood. *Pediatrics, 133*(6), e1561–e1567. https://doi.org/10.1542/peds.2013-3806

Mahatmya, D., & Lohman, B. (2011). Predictors of late adolescent delinquency: The protective role of after-school activities in low-income families. *Children and Youth Services Review, 33*(7), 1309–1317. https://doi.org/10.1016/j.childyouth.2011.03.005

Mahoney, J. L. (2014). School extracurricular activity participation and early school dropout: A mixed-method study of the role of peer social networks. *Journal of Educational and Developmental Psychology, 4*(1), p143. https://doi.org/10.5539/jedp.v4n1p143

Maier, K. S. (2005). Transmitting educational values: Parent occupation and adolescent development. In B. Schneider & L. J. Waite (Eds.), *Being together, working apart: Dual-career families and the work-life balance* (pp. 396–418). New York, NY: Cambridge University Press.

Maikovich-Fong, A. K., & Jaffee, S. R. (2010). Sex differences in childhood sexual abuse characteristics and victims' emotional and behavioral problems: Findings from a national sample of youth. *Child Abuse & Neglect, 34*(6), 429–437. https://doi.org/10.1016/j.chiabu.2009.10.006

Main, M., & Solomon, J. (1986). Discovery of an insecure, disorganized/disoriented attachment pattern: Procedures, findings, and implications for the classification of behavior. In M. Yogman & T. B. Brazelton (Eds.), *Affective development in infancy* (pp. 95–124). Norwood, NJ: Ablex.

Maital, S. L., Dromi, E., Sagi, A., & Bornstein, M. H. (2000). The Hebrew Communicative Development Inventory: Language specific properties and cross-linguistic generalizations. *Journal of Child Language, 27*, 43–67.

Makel, M. C., Kell, H. J., Lubinski, D., Putallaz, M., & Benbow, C. P. (2016). When lightning strikes twice: Profoundly gifted, profoundly accomplished. *Psychological Science, 27*(7), 1004–1018. https://doi.org/10.1177/0956797616644735

Mäkelä, T. E., Peltola, M. J., Nieminen, P., Paavonen, E. J., Saarenpää-Heikkilä, O., Paunio, T., & Kylliäinen, A. (2018). Night awakening in infancy: Developmental stability and longitudinal associations with psychomotor development. *Developmental Psychology, 54*(7), 1208–1218. https://doi.org/10.1037/dev0000503

Malatesta, C. Z., & Haviland, J. M. (1982). Learning display rules: The socialization of emotion expression in infancy. *Child Development, 53*(4), 991–1003.

Malcolm, S., Huang, S., Cordova, D., Freitas, D., Arzon, M., Jimenez, G. L., . . . Prado, G. (2013). Predicting condom use attitudes, norms, and control beliefs in Hispanic problem behavior youth: The effects of family functioning and parent-adolescent communication about sex on condom use. *Health Education & Behavior, 40*(4), 384–391. https://doi.org/10.1177/1090198112440010

Malczyk, B. R., & Lawson, H. A. (2017). Parental monitoring, the parent-child relationship and children's academic engagement in mother-headed single-parent families. *Children and Youth Services Review, 73*, 274–282. https://doi.org/10.1016/j.childyouth.2016.12.019

Maldonado-Carreño, C., & Votruba-Drzal, E. (2011). Teacher-child relationships and the development of academic and behavioral skills during elementary school: A within- and between-child analysis. *Child Development, 82*(2), 601–616. https://doi.org/10.1111/j.1467-8624.2010.01533.x

Malm, K., & Welti, K. (2010). Exploring motivations to adopt. *Adoption Quarterly, 13*(3–4), 185–208. https://doi.org/10.1080/10926755.2010.524872

Malti, T., & Dys, S. P. (2018). From being nice to being kind: Development of prosocial behaviors. *Current Opinion in Psychology, 20*, 45–49. https://doi.org/10.1016/J.COPSYC.2017.07.036

Malti, T., & Latzko, B. (2010). Children's moral emotions and moral cognition: Towards an integrative perspective. *New Directions for Child & Adolescent Development, 2010*(129), 1–10. https://doi.org/10.1002/cd.272

Malti, T., Keller, M., & Buchmann, M. (2013). Do moral choices make us feel good? The development of adolescents' emotions following moral decision making. *Journal of Research on Adolescence, 23*(2), 389–397. https://doi.org/10.1111/jora.12005

Mamluk, L., Edwards, H. B., Savović, J., Leach, V., Jones, T., Moore, T. H. M., . . . Zuccolo,

L. (2016). Prenatal alcohol exposure and pregnancy and childhood outcomes: A systematic review of alternative analytical approaches. *Lancet, 388*, S73. https://doi.org/10.1016/S0140-6736(16)32309-1

Mamluk, L., Edwards, H. B., Savović, J., Leach, V., Jones, T., Moore, T. H. M., . . . Zuccolo, L. (2017). Low alcohol consumption and pregnancy and childhood outcomes: Time to change guidelines indicating apparently "safe" levels of alcohol during pregnancy? A systematic review and meta-analyses. *BMJ Open, 7*(7), e015410. https://doi.org/10.1136/bmjopen-2016-015410

Mandel, D. R., Jusczyk, P. W., & Pisoni, D. B. (1995). Infants' recognition of the sound patterns of their own names. *Psychological Science, 6*(5), 314–317.

Mandler, J. M. (2004). *The foundations of mind: Origins of conceptual thought*. New York, NY: Oxford University Press.

Mandler, J. M., & McDonough, L. (1998). On developing a knowledge base in infancy. *Developmental Psychology, 34*, 1274–1288.

Manfra, L., & Winsler, A. (2006). Preschool children's awareness of private speech. *International Journal of Behavioral Development, 30*(6), 537–549.

Manganello, J. A. (2008). Health literacy and adolescents: A framework and agenda for future research. *Health Education Research, 23*(5), 840–847. https://doi.org/10.1093/her/cym069

Mangelsdorf, S. C. (1992). Developmental changes in infant-stranger interaction. *Infant Behavior & Development, 15*(2), 191–208. https://doi.org/10.1016/0163-6383(92)80023-n

Mangelsdorf, S. C., Shapiro, J. R., & Marzolf, D. (1995). Developmental and temperamental differences in emotion regulation in infancy. *Child Development, 66*, 1817–1828.

Mani, N., & Ackermann, L. (2018). Why do children learn the words they do? *Child Development Perspectives, 12*(4), 253–257. https://doi.org/10.1111/cdep.12295

Maniglio, R. (2011). The role of child sexual abuse in the etiology of substance-related disorders. *Journal of Addictive Diseases, 30*(3), 216–228. https://doi.org/10.1080/10550887.2011.581987

Maniglio, R. (2013). Child sexual abuse in the etiology of anxiety disorders: A systematic review of reviews. *Trauma, Violence & Abuse, 14*(2), 96–112. https://doi.org/10.1177/1524838012470032

Manning, W. D. (2015). Cohabitation and child wellbeing. *The Future of Children, 25*(2), 51–66.

Manning, W. D., & Brown, S. (2006). Children's economic well-being in married and cohabiting parent families. *Journal of Marriage & Family, 68*(2), 345–362.

Manoach, D. S., Schlaug, G., Siewert, B., Darby, D. G., Bly, B. M., Benfield, A., . . . Warach, S. (1997). Prefrontal cortex fMRI signal changes are correlated with working memory load. *NeuroReport, 8*, 545–549.

Manuck, S. B., & McCaffery, J. M. (2014). Gene-environment interaction. *Annual Review of Psychology, 65*, 41–70. https://doi.org/10.1146/annurev-psych-010213-115100

Marceau, K., Ram, N., Houts, R. M., Grimm, K. J., & Susman, E. J. (2011). Individual differences in boys' and girls' timing and tempo of puberty: Modeling development with nonlinear growth models. *Developmental Psychology, 47*(5), 1389–1409. https://doi.org/10.1037/a0023838

March of Dimes. (2015). *Caffeine in pregnancy*. Retrieved from https://www.marchofdimes.org/pregnancy/caffeine-in-pregnancy.aspx

Marcia, J. E. (1966). Development and validation of ego-identity status. *Journal of Personality and Social Psychology, 3*(5), 551–558.

Marcia, J. E. (2002). Identity and psychosocial development in adulthood. *Identity, 2*(1), 7–28. https://doi.org/10.1207/S1532706XID0201_02

Marcon, R. A. (1999). Positive relationships between parent-school involvement and public school inner-city preschoolers' development and academic performance. *School Psychology Review, 28*, 395–412.

Marcovitch, S., Clearfield, M. W., Swingler, M., Calkins, S. D., & Bell, M. A. (2016). Attentional predictors of 5-month-olds' performance on a looking A-not-B task. *Infant and Child Development, 25*(4), 233–246. https://doi.org/10.1002/icd.1931

Marcus, G. (2000). Children's overregularization and its implications for cognition. In P. Broeder & J. Murre (Eds.), *Models of language acquisition* (pp. 154–176). Oxford, England: Oxford University Press.

Marin, M. M., Rapisardi, G., & Tani, F. (2015). Two-day-old newborn infants recognise their mother by her axillary odour. *Acta Paediatrica, 104*(3), 237–240. https://doi.org/10.1111/apa.12905

Marinellie, S. A., & Kneile, L. A. (2012). Acquiring knowledge of derived nominals and derived adjectives in context. *Language Speech and Hearing Services in Schools, 43*(1), 53. https://doi.org/10.1044/0161-1461(2011/10-0053)

Markant, J., & Scott, L. S. (2018). Attention and perceptual learning interact in the development of the other-race effect. *Current Directions in Psychological Science, 27*(3), 163–169. https://doi.org/10.1177/0963721418769884

Markiewicz, D., & Doyle, A. B. (2016). Best friends. In *Encyclopedia of adolescence* (pp. 1–8). Cham, Switzerland: Springer. https://doi.org/10.1007/978-3-319-32132-5_314-2

Markman, E. M., & Wachtel, G. F. (1988). Children's use of mutual exclusivity to constrain the meaning of words. *Cognitive Psychology, 20*(2), 121–157. https://doi.org/10.1016/0010-0285(88)90017-5

Markman, E. M., Wasow, J. L., & Hansen, M. B. (2003). Use of the mutual exclusivity assumption by young word learners. *Cognitive Psychology, 47*(3), 241–275. https://doi.org/10.1016/S0010-0285(03)00034-3

Markowitz, A. J., Bassok, D., & Hamre, B. (2018). Leveraging developmental insights to improve early childhood education. *Child Development Perspectives, 12*(2), 87–92. https://doi.org/10.1111/cdep.12266

Marks, A. K., Szalacha, L. A., Lamarre, M., Boyd, M. J., & Coll, C. G. (2007). Emerging ethnic identity and interethnic group social preferences in middle childhood: Findings from the Children of Immigrants Development in Context (CIDC) study. *International Journal of Behavioral Development, 31*(5), 501–513.

Marks, P. E. L. (2017). Introduction to the special issue: 20th-century origins and 21st-century developments of peer nomination methodology. *New Directions for Child and Adolescent Development, 2017*(157), 7–19. https://doi.org/10.1002/cad.20205

Markus, H. R., & Kitayama, S. (1991). Culture and the self: Implications for cognition, emotion, and motivation. *Psychological Review, 98*(2), 224–253. https://doi.org/10.1037/0033-295X.98.2.224

Markus, H. R., & Kitayama, S. (2010). Cultures and selves: A cycle of mutual constitution. *Perspectives on Psychological Science, 5*(4), 420–430. https://doi.org/10.1177/1745691610375557

Marlier, L., & Schaal, B. (2005). Human newborns prefer human milk: Conspecific milk odor is attractive without postnatal exposure. *Child Development, 76*(1), 155–168.

Marotz, L. R. (2015). *Health, safety, and nutrition for the young child*. Stamford, CT: Cengage.

Marques, L., Alegria, M., Becker, A. E., Chen, C., Fang, A., Chosak, A., & Diniz, J. B. (2011). Comparative prevalence, correlates of impairment, and service utilization for eating disorders across US ethnic groups: Implications for reducing ethnic disparities in health care access for eating disorders. *International Journal of Eating Disorders, 44*(5), 412–420. https://doi.org/10.1002/eat.20787

Marr, E. (2017). U.S. transracial adoption trends in the 21st century. *Adoption Quarterly, 20*(3), 222–251. https://doi.org/10.1080/10926755.2017.1291458

Marriott, C., Hamilton-Giachritsis, C., & Harrop, C. (2014). Factors promoting resilience following childhood sexual abuse: A structured, narrative review of the literature. *Child Abuse Review, 23*(1), 17–34. https://doi.org/10.1002/car.2258

Marsh, H. W., Trautwein, U., Lüdtke, O., Köller, O., & Baumert, J. (2006). Integration of multidimensional self-concept and core personality constructs: Construct validation and relations to well-being and achievement. *Journal of Personality, 74*, 403–456.

Marshall, E. J. (2014). Adolescent alcohol use: Risks and consequences. *Alcohol and Alcoholism, 49*(2), 160–164. https://doi.org/10.1093/alcalc/agt180

Marshall, L. (1999). *Nyae! Kung beliefs and rites*. Boston, MA: Peabody Museum of Archaeology and Ethnology, Harvard University.

Marshall, S. K., Tilton-Weaver, L. C., & Stattin, H. (2013). Non-suicidal self-injury and depressive symptoms during middle adolescence: A longitudinal analysis. *Journal of Youth and Adolescence, 42*(8), 1234–1242. https://doi.org/10.1007/s10964-013-9919-3

Marti, E., & Rodriguez, C. (2012). *After Piaget*. New Brunswick, NJ: Transaction Publishers.

Martin, C., Fabes, R., Hanish, L., Leonard, S., & Dinella, L. (2011). Experienced and expected similarity to same-gender peers: Moving toward a comprehensive model of gender segregation. *Sex Roles, 65*(5/6), 421–434. https://doi.org/10.1007/s11199-011-0029-y

Martin, C. L., Kornienko, O., Schaefer, D. R., Hanish, L. D., Fabes, R. A., & Goble, P. (2013). The role of sex of peers and gender-typed activities in young children's peer affiliative networks: A longitudinal analysis of selection and influence. *Child Development, 84*(3), 921–937. https://doi.org/10.1111/cdev.12032

Martin, C. L., & Ruble, D. N. (2010). Patterns of gender development. *Annual Review of Psychology, 61*, 353–381.

https://doi.org/10.1146/annurev.psych.093008.100511

Martin, C. L., Ruble, D. N., & Szkrybalo, J. (2002). Cognitive theories of early gender development. *Psychological Bulletin, 128*, 903–933.

Martin, J., Hamilton, B., & Osterman, M. (2018). Births in the United States, 2017. *NCHS Data Brief, 318*. Retrieved from https://www.cdc.gov/nchs/data/databriefs/db318.pdf

Martin, J. A., Hamilton, B. E., Osterman, M. J., Driscoll, A. K., & Drake, P. (2018). Births: Final data for 2016. *National Vital Statistics Reports, 67*(1). Retrieved from https://stacks.cdc.gov/view/cdc/51199

Martin, Joyce A., Hamilton, B. E., Osterman, M. J. K., Curtin, S. C., & Mathews, T. J. (2013). Births: Final data for 201 2. *National Vital Statistics Reports, 62*(9). Retrieved from http://www.cdc.gov/nchs/data/nvsr/nvsr62/nvsr62_09.pdf#table21

Martin, L. R., & Petrie, K. J. (2017). Understanding the dimensions of anti-vaccination attitudes: The Vaccination Attitudes Examination (VAX) Scale. *Annals of Behavioral Medicine, 51*(5), 652–660. https://doi.org/10.1007/s12160-017-9888-y

Martinson, M. L., & Reichman, N. E. (2016). Socioeconomic inequalities in low birth weight in the United States, the United Kingdom, Canada, and Australia. *American Journal of Public Health, 106*(4), 748–754. https://doi.org/10.2105/AJPH.2015.303007

Marvin, R. S., Britner, P. A., & Russell, B. S. (2016). Normative development: The ontogeny of attachment in childhood. In J. Cassidy & P. R. Shaver (Eds.), *Handbook of attachment: Theory, research, and clinical applications* (3rd ed., pp. 273–289). New York, NY: Guilford.

Marzilli, E., Cerniglia, L., & Cimino, S. (2018). A narrative review of binge eating disorder in adolescence: Prevalence, impact, and psychological treatment strategies. *Adolescent Health, Medicine and Therapeutics, 9*, 17–30. https://doi.org/10.2147/AHMT.S148050

Masche, J. G. (2010). Explanation of normative declines in parents' knowledge about their adolescent children. *Journal of Adolescence, 33*(2), 271–284. https://doi.org/10.1016/j.adolescence.2009.08.002

Mascolo, M. F., van Geert, P., Steenbeek, H., & Fischer, K. W. (2016). What can dynamic systems models of development offer to the study of developmental psychopathology? In D. Cicchetti (Ed.), *Developmental psychopathology* (pp. 1–52). Hoboken, NJ: John Wiley & Sons. https://doi.org/10.1002/9781119125556.devpsy115

Masi, A., DeMayo, M. M., Glozier, N., & Guastella, A. J. (2017). An overview of autism spectrum disorder, heterogeneity and treatment options. *Neuroscience Bulletin, 33*(2), 183–193. https://doi.org/10.1007/s12264-017-0100-y

Mason, P., & Narad, C. (2005). International adoption: A health and developmental perspective. *Seminars in Speech and Language, 26*(1), 1–9.

Mason, W. A., & Spoth, R. L. (2011). Longitudinal associations of alcohol involvement with subjective well-being in adolescence and prediction to alcohol problems in early adulthood. *Journal of Youth and Adolescence, 40*(9), 1215–1224. https://doi.org/10.1007/s10964-011-9632-z

Masten, A. S. (2016). Resilience in developing systems: The promise of integrated approaches. *European Journal of Developmental Psychology, 13*(3), 297–312. https://doi.org/10.1080/17405629.2016.1147344

Masten, A. S., & Cicchetti, D. (2016). Resilience in development: Progress and transformation. In D. Cicchetti (Ed.), *Developmental psychopathology* (pp. 1–63). Hoboken, NJ: John Wiley & Sons. https://doi.org/10.1002/9781119125556.devpsy406

Masten, A. S., & Monn, A. R. (2015). Child and family resilience: A call for integrated science, practice, and professional training. *Family Relations, 64*(1), 5–21. https://doi.org/10.1111/fare.12103

Masten, A. S., Narayan, A. J., Silverman, W. K., & Osofsky, J. D. (2015). Children in war and disaster. In M. H. Bornstein & T. Leventhal (Eds.), *Handbook of child psychology and developmental science* (pp. 1–42). Hoboken, NJ: John Wiley & Sons. https://doi.org/10.1002/9781118963418.childpsy418

Mastropieri, M. A., & Scruggs, T. E. (2017). *The inclusive classroom: Strategies for effective differentiated instruction*. Boston, MA: Pearson.

Mathews, T. J., & MacDorman, M. F. (2013). Infant mortality statistics from the 2010 Period Linked Birth/Infant Death Data Set. *National Vital Statistics Reports, 62*(8). Retrieved from http://www.cdc.gov/nchs/data/nvsr/nvsr62/nvsr62_08.pdf

Matlin, M. W., & Foley, H. J. (1997). *Sensation and perception* (4th ed.). Boston, MA: Allyn & Bacon.

Matsuda, E. (2017). Sucrose for analgesia in newborn infants undergoing painful procedures. *Nursing Standard, 31*(30), 61–63. https://doi.org/10.7748/ns.2017.e10827

Maughan, B., Collishaw, S., & Stringaris, A. (2013). Depression in childhood and adolescence. *Journal of the Canadian Academy of Child and Adolescent Psychiatry, 22*(1), 35–40.

Maurer, D. (2017). Critical periods re-examined: Evidence from children treated for dense cataracts. *Cognitive Development, 42*, 27–36. https://doi.org/10.1016/j.cogdev.2017.02.006

May, L., Gervain, J., Carreiras, M., & Werker, J. F. (2018). The specificity of the neural response to speech at birth. *Developmental Science, 21*(3), e12564. https://doi.org/10.1111/desc.12564

May, P. A., Chambers, C. D., Kalberg, W. O., Zellner, J., Feldman, H., Buckley, D., . . . Hoyme, H. E. (2018). Prevalence of fetal alcohol spectrum disorders in 4 US communities. *JAMA, 319*(5), 474. https://doi.org/10.1001/jama.2017.21896

May, P. P. A., Baete, A., Russo, J., Elliott, A. J., Blankenship, J., Kalberg, W. O. W., . . . Vagnarelli, F. (2014). Prevalence and characteristics of fetal alcohol spectrum disorders. *Pediatrics, 134*(5), 855–866. https://doi.org/10.1542/peds.2013-3319

Mayer, A., & Träuble, B. (2015). The weird world of cross-cultural false-belief research: A true- and false-belief study among Samoan children based on commands. *Journal of Cognition and Development, 16*(4), 650–665. https://doi.org/10.1080/15248372.2014.926273

Mayhew, M. J., Rockenbach, A. N., Bowman, N. A., Seifert, T. A., Wolniak, G. C., Pascarella, E. T., & Terenzini, P. Y. (2016). *How college affects students: Vol. 3. 21st century evidence that higher education works*. Hoboken, NJ: John Wiley & Sons.

Maynard, M. J., & Harding, S. (2010). Perceived parenting and psychological well-being in UK ethnic minority adolescents. *Child: Care, Health and Development, 36*(5), 630–638. https://doi.org/10.1111/j.1365-2214.2010.01115.x

Mayo Clinic. (2016). *Food allergies: Understanding food labels*. Retrieved from https://www.mayoclinic.org/diseases-conditions/food-allergy/in-depth/food-allergies/art-20045949

Mazul, M. C., Salm Ward, T. C., & Ngui, E. M. (2016). Anatomy of good prenatal care: Perspectives of low income African-American women on barriers and facilitators to prenatal care. *Journal of Racial and Ethnic Health Disparities, 4*(1), 79–86. https://doi.org/10.1007/s40615-015-0204-x

McAdams, D. P., & Zapata-Gietl, C. (2015). Three strands of identity development across the human life course. In K. C. McLean & M. Syed (Eds.), *The Oxford handbook of identity development* (pp. 81–96). Oxford, England: Oxford University Press. https://doi.org/10.1093/oxfordhb/9780199936564.013.006

McAlister, A. R., & Peterson, C. C. (2013). Siblings, theory of mind, and executive functioning in children aged 3-6 years: New longitudinal evidence. *Child Development, 84*(4), 1442–1458. https://doi.org/10.1111/cdev.12043

McCabe, M. P., Connaughton, C., Tatangelo, G., Mellor, D., & Busija, L. (2017). Healthy me: A gender-specific program to address body image concerns and risk factors among preadolescents. *Body Image, 20*, 20–30. https://doi.org/10.1016/J.BODYIM.2016.10.007

McCall, R. B. (1994). What process mediates predictions of childhood IQ from infant habituation and recognition memory? Speculations on the roles of inhibition and rate of information processing. *Intelligence, 18*(2), 107–125.

Mcclain, M.-C., & Pfeiffer, S. (2012). Identification of gifted students in the United States today: A look at state definitions, policies, and practices. *Journal of Applied School Psychology, 28*(1), 59–88. https://doi.org/10.1080/15377903.2012.643757

McCleery, J. P., Akshoomoff, N., Dobkins, K. R., & Carver, L. J. (2009). Atypical face versus object processing and hemispheric asymmetries in 10-month-old infants at risk for autism. *Biological Psychiatry, 66*(10), 950–957. https://doi.org/10.1016/j.biopsych.2009.07.031

McClelland, M. M., & Cameron, C. E. (2011). Self-regulation and academic achievement in elementary school children. *New Directions for Child and Adolescent Development, 2011*(133), 29–44. https://doi.org/10.1002/cd.302

McClelland, S. I., & Tolman, D. L. (2014). Adolescent sexuality. In T. Tio (Ed.), *Encyclopedia of critical psychology* (pp. 40–47). New York, NY: Springer.

McClure, E. R., Chentsova-Dutton, Y. E., Holochwost, S. J., Parrott, W. G., & Barr, R. (2018). Look at that! Video chat and joint visual attention development among babies and toddlers. *Child Development, 89*(1), 27–36. https://doi.org/10.1111/cdev.12833

McClure, J., Meyer, L. H., Garisch, J., Fischer, R., Weir, K. F., & Walkey, F. H. (2011). Students' attributions for their best and worst marks: Do they relate to achievement?

Contemporary Educational Psychology, 36(2), 71–81. https://doi.org/10.1016/j.cedpsych.2010.11.001

McClure, R., Kegler, S., Davey, T., & Clay, F. (2015). Contextual determinants of childhood injury: A systematic review of studies with multilevel analytic methods. *American Journal of Public Health, 105*(12), e37–e43. https://doi.org/10.2105/AJPH.2015.302883

McCord, J. (1996). Unintended consequences of punishment. *Pediatrics, 88*, 832–834.

McCorry, N. K., & Hepper, P. G. (2007). Fetal habituation performance: Gestational age and sex effects. *British Journal of Developmental Psychology, 25*(2), 277–292.

McDevitt, T. M., & Ormrod, J. E. (2016). *Child development and education* (6th ed.). Boston, MA: Pearson.

McDonald, K. L., Dashiell-Aje, E., Menzer, M. M., Rubin, K. H., Oh, W., & Bowker, J. C. (2013). Contributions of racial and sociobehavioral homophily to friendship stability and quality among same-race and cross-race friends. *Journal of Early Adolescence, 33*(7), 897–919. https://doi.org/10.1177/0272431612472259

McDonald, N. M., & Perdue, K. L. (2018). The infant brain in the social world: Moving toward interactive social neuroscience with functional near-infrared spectroscopy. *Neuroscience & Biobehavioral Reviews, 87*, 38–49. https://doi.org/10.1016/J.NEUBIOREV.2018.01.007

McDougall, P., & Vaillancourt, T. (2015). Long-term adult outcomes of peer victimization in childhood and adolescence: Pathways to adjustment and maladjustment. *The American Psychologist, 70*(4), 300–310. https://doi.org/10.1037/a0039174

McFarland, D. A., & Thomas, R. J. (2006). Bowling young: How youth voluntary associations influence adult political participation. *American Sociological Review, 71*(3), 401–425. https://doi.org/10.1177/000312240607100303

McGinley, M., Lipperman-Kreda, S., Byrnes, H. F., & Carlo, G. (2010). Parental, social and dispositional pathways to Israeli adolescents' volunteering. *Journal of Applied Developmental Psychology, 31*(5), 386–394. https://doi.org/10.1016/j.appdev.2010.06.001

McGlade, M. S., Saha, S., & Dahlstrom, M. E. (2004). The Latina paradox: An opportunity for restructuring prenatal care delivery. *American Journal of Public Health, 94*(12), 2062–2065.

McGlothlin, H., & Killen, M. (2006). Intergroup attitudes of European American children attending ethnically homogeneous schools. *Child Development, 77*(5), 1375–1386.

McGonigle-Chalmers, M., Slater, H., & Smith, A. (2014). Rethinking private speech in preschoolers: The effects of social presence. *Developmental Psychology, 50*(3), 829–836. https://doi.org/10.1037/a0033909

McGue, M., & Christensen, K. (2013). Growing old but not growing apart: Twin similarity in the latter half of the lifespan. *Behavior Genetics, 43*(1), 1–12. https://doi.org/10.1007/s10519-012-9559-5

McHale, S. M., Updegraff, K. A., & Whiteman, S. D. (2012). Sibling relationships and influences in childhood and adolescence. *Journal of Marriage and the Family, 74*(5), 913–930. Retrieved from https://www.ncbi.nlm.nih.gov/pmc/articles/PMC3956653/

McKenna, J. J. (2001). Why we never ask "Is it safe for infants to sleep alone?" *Academy of Breast Feeding Medicine News and Views, 7*(4), 32, 38.

McKenna, J. J., & Volpe, L. E. (2007). Sleeping with baby: An internet-based sampling of parental experiences, choices, perceptions, and interpretations in a Western industrialized context. *Infant and Child Development, 16*(4), 359–385. https://doi.org/10.1002/icd.525

McKinney, C., & Renk, K. (2011). A multivariate model of parent-adolescent relationship variables in early adolescence. *Child Psychiatry and Human Development, 42*(4), 442–462. https://doi.org/10.1007/s10578-011-0228-3

McKinney, S. (2017). Cochlear implantation in children under 12 months of age. *Current Opinion in Otolaryngology & Head and Neck Surgery, 25*(5), 400–404. https://doi.org/10.1097/MOO.0000000000000400

McKusick, V. A. (1998). *Mendelian inheritance in man: A catalog of human genes and genetic disorders* (12th ed.). Baltimore, MD: Johns Hopkins University Press.

McKusick, V. A. (2007). Mendelian inheritance in man and its online version, OMIM. *American Journal of Human Genetics, 80*, 588–604. https://doi.org/10.1086/514346

McKusick-Nathans Institute of Genetic Medicine. (2019). *OMIM—Online Mendelian Inheritance in Man*. Retrieved from http://www.omim.org/about

McLaughlin, K. A., Sheridan, M. A., & Nelson, C. A. (2017). Neglect as a violation of species-expectant experience: Neurodevelopmental consequences. *Biological Psychiatry, 82*(7), 462–471. https://doi.org/10.1016/J.BIOPSYCH.2017.02.1096

McLean, K. C., Syed, M., Way, N., & Rogers, O. (2015). "[T]hey say black men won't make it, but I know I'm gonna make it." In K. C. McLean & M. Syed (Eds.), *The Oxford handbook of identity development* (pp. 269–287). Oxford, England: Oxford University Press. https://doi.org/10.1093/oxfordhb/9780199936564.013.032

McLeod, J. D., & Knight, S. (2010). The association of socioemotional problems with early sexual initiation. *Perspectives on Sexual and Reproductive Health, 42*(2), 93–101. https://doi.org/10.1363/4209310

McLoughlin, C. S. (2005). The coming-of-age of China's single-child policy. *Psychology in the Schools, 42*(3), 305–313. https://doi.org/10.1002/pits.20081

McLoyd, V. C., & Hallman, S. K. (2018). Antecedents and correlates of adolescent employment: Race as a moderator of psychological predictors. *Youth & Society, 2018*, 0044118X1878163. https://doi.org/10.1177/0044118X18781637

McLoyd, V. C., & Smith, J. (2002). Physical discipline and behavior problems in African American, European American, and Hispanic children: Emotional support as a moderator. *Journal of Marriage and Family, 64*, 40–53.

McMahan True, M., Pisani, L., & Oumar, F. (2001). Infant–mother attachment among the Dogon of Mali. *Child Development, 72*(5), 1451.

McMahon, E. M., Corcoran, P., O'Regan, G., Keeley, H., Cannon, M., Carli, V., . . . Wasserman, D. (2017). Physical activity in European adolescents and associations with anxiety, depression and well-being. *European Child & Adolescent Psychiatry, 26*(1), 111–122. https://doi.org/10.1007/s00787-016-0875-9

McMahon, S. D., Todd, N. R., Martinez, A., Coker, C., Sheu, C.-F., Washburn, J., & Shah, S. (2013). Aggressive and prosocial behavior: Community violence, cognitive, and behavioral predictors among urban African American youth. *American Journal of Community Psychology, 51*(3–4), 407–421. https://doi.org/10.1007/s10464-012-9560-4

McManus, I. C., Moore, J., Freegard, M., & Rawles, R. (2010). Science in the making: Right hand, left hand. III: Estimating historical rates of left-handedness. *Laterality: Asymmetries of Body, Brain and Cognition, 15*(1–2), 186–208. https://doi.org/10.1080/13576500802565313

McMurray, B. (2007). Defusing the childhood vocabulary explosion. *Science, 317*(5838), 631. https://doi.org/10.1126/science.1144073

McQuillan, G., Kruszon-Moran, D., Markowitz, L. E., Unger, E. R., & Paulose-Ram, R. (2017). Prevalence of HPV in adults aged 18–69: United States, 2011–2014. *NCHS Data Brief, 280*. Retrieved from https://www.cdc.gov/nchs/data/databriefs/db280.pdf

McRae, K., Rhee, S. H., Gatt, J. M., Godinez, D., Williams, L. M., & Gross, J. J. (2017). Genetic and environmental influences on emotion regulation: A twin study of cognitive reappraisal and expressive suppression. *Emotion, 17*(5), 772–777. https://doi.org/10.1037/emo0000300

McVey, G. L., Levine, M., Piran, N., & Ferguson, H. B. (2013). *Preventing eating-related and weight-related disorders: Collaborative research, advocacy, and policy change*. Waterloo, Ontario, Canada: Wilfrid Laurier University Press.

Mead, M. (1970). Children and ritual in Bali. In B. J (Ed.), *Traditional Balinese culture* (pp. 198–211). New York, NY: Columbia University Press.

Meaney, M. J. (2017). Epigenetics and the biology of gene × environment interactions. In P. H. Tolan & B. L. Leventhal (Eds.), *Gene-environment transactions in developmental psychopathology* (pp. 59–94). Cham, Switzerland: Springer International Publishing. https://doi.org/10.1007/978-3-319-49227-8_4

Medford, E., Hare, D. J., & Wittkowski, A. (2017). Demographic and psychosocial influences on treatment adherence for children and adolescents with PKU: A systematic review. *JIMD Reports, 39*, 107–116. https://doi.org/10.1007/8904_2017_52

Meece, J. L., Anderman, E. M., & Anderman, L. H. (2006). Classroom goal structure, student motivation, and academic achievement. *Annual Review of Psychology, 57*(1), 487–503. https://doi.org/10.1146/annurev.psych.56.091103.070258

Meehan, C. L., & Hawks, S. (2013). Cooperative breeding and attachment among the Aka foragers. In N. Quinn & J. M. Mageo (Eds.), *Attachment reconsidered* (pp. 85–113). New York, NY: Palgrave Macmillan. https://doi.org/10.1057/9781137386724_4

Meeus, W. H. J. (2011). The study of adolescent identity formation 2000-2010: A review of longitudinal research. *Journal of Research on Adolescence, 21*(1), 75–94. https://doi.org/10.1111/j.1532-7795.2010.00716.x

Mehl, M. R. (2017). The electronically activated recorder (EAR). *Current Directions in Psychological Science, 26*(2), 184–190. https://doi.org/10.1177/0963721416680611

Mehta, P. K. (2016). Pregnancy with chicken pox. In A. Gandhi, N. Malhotra, J. Malhotra, N. Gupta, & N. M. Bora (Eds.), *Principles of critical care in obstetrics* (pp. 21–30). New Delhi, India: Springer India. https://doi.org/10.1007/978-81-322-2686-4_4

Meier, M. H., Caspi, A., Ambler, A., Harrington, H., Houts, R., Keefe, R. S. E., . . . Moffitt, T. E. (2012). Persistent cannabis users show neuropsychological decline from childhood to midlife. *Proceedings of the National Academy of Sciences of the United States of America, 109*(40), E2657–E2664. https://doi.org/10.1073/pnas.1206820109

Meisel, J. M. (1989). Early differentiation of languages in bilingual children. In K. Hyltenstam & L. K. Obler (Eds.), *Bilingualism across the lifespan: Aspects of acquisition, maturity and loss* (pp. 13–40). Cambridge, England: Cambridge University Press.

Meléndez, L. (2005). Parental beliefs and practices around early self-regulation: The impact of culture and immigration. *Infants & Young Children, 18*(2), 136–146.

Meltzoff, A. N. (1990). Towards a developmental cognitive science. *Annals of the New York Academy of Sciences, 608*, 1–37.

Meltzoff, A. N. (2007). 'Like me': A foundation for social cognition. *Developmental Science, 10*(1), 126–134. https://doi.org/10.1111/j.1467-7687.2007.00574.x

Meltzoff, A. N., & Borton, R. W. (1979). Intermodal matching by human neonates. *Nature, 282*, 403–404.

Meltzoff, A. N., & Kuhl, P. K. (1994). Faces and speech: Intermodal processing of biologically relevant signals in infants and adults. In D. J. Lewkowicz & R. Lickliter (Eds.), *The development of intersensory perception* (pp. 335–369). Hillsdale, NJ: Erlbaum.

Meltzoff, A. N., & Moore, M. K. (1977). Imitation of facial and manual gestures by human neonates. *Science, 198*, 75–78.

Meltzoff, A. N., & Moore, M. K. (1994). Imitation, memory, and the representation of persons. *Infant Behavior & Development, 17*(1), 83–99. https://doi.org/10.1016/0163-6383(94)90024-8

Memmert, D. (2014). Inattentional blindness to unexpected events in 8–15-year-olds. *Cognitive Development, 32*, 103–109. https://doi.org/10.1016/J.COGDEV.2014.09.002

Mendez, M., Durtschi, J., Neppl, T. K., & Stith, S. M. (2016). Corporal punishment and externalizing behaviors in toddlers: The moderating role of positive and harsh parenting. *Journal of Family Psychology, 30*(8), 887–895. http://doi.org/10.1037/fam0000187

Mendle, J. (2014). Beyond pubertal timing: New directions for studying individual differences in development. *Current Directions in Psychological Science, 23*(3), 215–219. https://doi.org/10.1177/0963721414530144

Mendle, J., & Ferrero, J. (2012). Detrimental psychological outcomes associated with pubertal timing in adolescent boys. *Developmental Review, 32*(1), 49–66. https://doi.org/10.1016/j.dr.2011.11.001

Mendle, J., Turkheimer, E., D'Onofrio, B. M., Lynch, S. K., Emery, R. E., Slutske, W. S., & Martin, N. G. (2006). Family structure and age at menarche: A children-of-twins approach. *Developmental Psychology, 42*, 533–542.

Menesini, E., & Salmivalli, C. (2017). Bullying in schools: The state of knowledge and effective interventions. *Psychology, Health & Medicine, 22*(Suppl. 1), 240–253. https://doi.org/10.1080/13548506.2017.1279740

Meng, J., Martinez, L., Holmstrom, A., Chung, M., & Cox, J. (2017). Research on social networking sites and social support from 2004 to 2015: A narrative review and directions for future research. *Cyberpsychology, Behavior, and Social Networking, 20*(1), 44–51. https://doi.org/10.1089/cyber.2016.0325

Mennella, J. A., & Beauchamp, G. K. (2002). Flavor experiences during formula feeding are related to preferences during childhood. *Early Human Development, 68*(2), 71–82.

Menon, V. (2016). Working memory in children's math learning and its disruption in dyscalculia. *Current Opinion in Behavioral Sciences, 10*, 125–132. https://doi.org/10.1016/j.cobeha.2016.05.014

Menting, B., Koot, H., & van Lier, P. (2014). Peer acceptance and the development of emotional and behavioural problems: Results from a preventive intervention study. *International Journal of Behavioral Development, 39*(6), 530–540. https://doi.org/10.1177/0165025414558853

Menting, B., van Lier, P. A. C., & Koot, H. M. (2011). Language skills, peer rejection, and the development of externalizing behavior from kindergarten to fourth grade. *Journal of Child Psychology & Psychiatry, 52*(1), 72–79. https://doi.org/10.1111/j.1469-7610.2010.02279.x

Mercuri, E., Baranello, G., Romeo, D. M. M., Cesarini, L., & Ricci, D. (2007). The development of vision. *Early Human Development, 83*(12), 795–800. https://doi.org/10.1016/j.earlhumdev.2007.09.014

Mermelshtine, R. (2017). Parent-child learning interactions: A review of the literature on scaffolding. *British Journal of Educational Psychology, 87*(2), 241–254. https://doi.org/10.1111/bjep.12147

Meruelo, A. D., Castro, N., Cota, C. I., & Tapert, S. F. (2017). Cannabis and alcohol use, and the developing brain. *Behavioural Brain Research, 325*(Pt. A), 44–50. https://doi.org/10.1016/j.bbr.2017.02.025

Merz, E. C., Harlé, K. M., Noble, K. G., & McCall, R. B. (2016). Executive function in previously institutionalized children. *Child Development Perspectives, 10*(2), 105–110. https://doi.org/10.1111/cdep.12170

Meshi, D., Morawetz, C., & Heekeren, H. R. (2013). Nucleus accumbens response to gains in reputation for the self relative to gains for others predicts social media use. *Frontiers in Human Neuroscience, 7*, 439. https://doi.org/10.3389/fnhum.2013.00439

Mesman, J., van IJzendoorn, M. H., & Sagi-Schwartz, A. (2016). Cross-cultural patterns of attachment: Universal and contextual dimensions. In J. Cassidy & P. R. Shaver (Eds.), *Handbook of attachment: Theory, research, and clinical applications* (3rd ed., pp. 852–876). New York, NY: Guilford.

Messer, E. P., Ammerman, R. T., Teeters, A. R., Bodley, A. L., Howard, J., Van Ginkel, J. B., & Putnam, F. W. (2018). Treatment of maternal depression with in-home cognitive behavioral therapy augmented by a parenting enhancement: A case report. *Cognitive and Behavioral Practice, 25*(3), 402–415. https://doi.org/10.1016/J.CBPRA.2017.10.002

Messinger, D., & Fogel, A. (2007). The interactive development of social smiling. In R. V Kail (Ed.), *Advances in child development and behavior* (Vol. 35, pp. 327–366). San Diego, CA: Elsevier Academic Press.

Metcalf, B. S., Hosking, J., Jeffery, A. N., Henley, W. E., & Wilkin, T. J. (2015). Exploring the adolescent fall in physical activity: A 10-yr cohort study (EarlyBird 41). *Medicine and Science in Sports and Exercise, 47*(10), 2084–2092. https://doi.org/10.1249/MSS.0000000000000644

Micali, N., Solmi, F., Horton, N. J., Crosby, R. D., Eddy, K. T., Calzo, J. P., . . . Field, A. E. (2015). Adolescent eating disorders predict psychiatric, high-risk behaviors and weight outcomes in young adulthood. *Journal of the American Academy of Child & Adolescent Psychiatry, 54*(8), 652–659. https://doi.org/10.1016/J.JAAC.2015.05.009

Michael, S. L., Wentzel, K., Elliott, M. N., Dittus, P. J., Kanouse, D. E., Wallander, J. L., . . . Schuster, M. A. (2014). Parental and peer factors associated with body image discrepancy among fifth-grade boys and girls. *Journal of Youth and Adolescence, 43*(1), 15–29. https://doi.org/10.1007/s10964-012-9899-8

Michaelson, V., Pickett, W., Vandemeer, E., Taylor, B., & Davison, C. (2016). A mixed methods study of Canadian adolescents' perceptions of health. *International Journal of Qualitative Studies on Health and Well-Being, 11*(1), 32891. https://doi.org/10.3402/

Miconi, D., Moscardino, U., Ronconi, L., & Altoè, G. (2017). Perceived parenting, self-esteem, and depressive symptoms in immigrant and non-immigrant adolescents in Italy: A multigroup path analysis. *Journal of Child and Family Studies, 26*(2), 345–356. https://doi.org/10.1007/s10826-016-0562-y

Miech, R. A., Johnston, L. D., O'Malley, P. M., Bachman, J. G., Schulenberg, J. E., & Patrick, M. E. (2017). *Monitoring the Future national survey results on drug use, 1975–2016: Vol. 1. Secondary school students.* Retrieved from http://www.monitoringthefuture.org/pubs/monographs/mtf-vol1_2016.pdf

Mielke, G. I., Brown, W. J., Nunes, B. P., Silva, I. C. M., & Hallal, P. C. (2017). Socioeconomic correlates of sedentary behavior in adolescents: Systematic review and meta-analysis. *Sports Medicine, 47*(1), 61–75. https://doi.org/10.1007/s40279-016-0555-4

Miething, A., Almquist, Y. B., Edling, C., Rydgren, J., & Rostila, M. (2017). Friendship trust and psychological well-being from late adolescence to early adulthood: A structural equation modelling approach. *Scandinavian Journal of Public Health, 45*(3), 244–252. https://doi.org/10.1177/1403494816680784

Milani, H. J., Araujo Júnior, E., Cavalheiro, S., Oliveira, P. S., Hisaba, W. J., Barreto, E. Q. S., . . . Moron, A. F. (2015). Fetal brain tumors: Prenatal diagnosis by ultrasound and magnetic resonance imaging. *World Journal of Radiology, 7*(1), 17–21. https://doi.org/10.4329/wjr.v7.i1.17

Milevsky, A. (2016). Parenting styles. In *Encyclopedia of adolescence* (pp. 1–6). Cham, Switzerland: Springer International Publishing. https://doi.org/10.1007/978-3-319-32132-5_38-2

Miller, A. L., Seifer, R., Crossin, R., & Lebourgeois, M. K. (2015). Toddler's self-regulation strategies in a challenge context are nap-dependent. *Journal of Sleep Research, 24*(3), 279–287. https://doi.org/10.1111/jsr.12260

Miller, B. D., Wood, B. L., & Smith, B. A. (2010). Respiratory illness. In R. J. Shaw & D. R. DeMaso (Eds.), *Textbook of pediatric psychosomatic medicine* (pp. 303–317). Arlington, VA: American Psychiatric Publishing, Inc.

Miller, B. G., Kors, S., & Macfie, J. (2017). No differences? Meta-analytic comparisons of psychological adjustment in children of gay fathers and heterosexual parents. *Psychology of Sexual Orientation and Gender Diversity, 4*(1), 14–22. https://doi.org/10.1037/sgd0000203

Miller, C. F., Trautner, H. M., & Ruble, D. N. (2006). The role of gender stereotypes in children's preferences and behavior. In L. Balter & C. S. Tamis-LeMonda (Eds.), *Child psychology: A handbook of contemporary issues* (2nd ed., pp. 293–323). New York, NY: Psychology Press.

Miller, D. I., & Halpern, D. F. (2014). The new science of cognitive sex differences. *Trends in Cognitive Sciences, 18*(1), 37–45. https://doi.org/10.1016/j.tics.2013.10.011

Miller, J. E., Hammond, G. C., Strunk, T., Moore, H. C., Leonard, H., Carter, K. W., . . . Burgner, D. P. (2016). Association of gestational age and growth measures at birth with infection-related admissions to hospital throughout childhood: A population-based, data-linkage study from Western Australia. *Lancet Infectious Diseases, 16*(8), 952–961. https://doi.org/10.1016/S1473-3099(16)00150-X

Miller, J. G. (2018). Physiological mechanisms of prosociality. *Current Opinion in Psychology, 20*, 50–54. https://doi.org/10.1016/J.COPSYC.2017.08.018

Miller, L., Nielsen, D. M., Schoen, S. A., & Brett-Green, B. A. (2009). Perspectives on sensory processing disorder: A call for translational research. *Frontiers in Integrative Neuroscience, 3*, 22. https://doi.org/10.3389/neuro.07.022.2009

Miller, L., Tseng, B., Tirella, L., Chan, W., & Feig, E. (2008). Health of children adopted from Ethiopia. *Maternal & Child Health Journal, 12*(5), 599–605. https://doi.org/10.1007/s10995-007-0274-4

Miller, M. B., Janssen, T., & Jackson, K. M. (2017). The prospective association between sleep and initiation of substance use in young adolescents. *Journal of Adolescent Health, 60*(2), 154–160. https://doi.org/10.1016/j.jadohealth.2016.08.019

Miller, P. H. (2016). *Theories of developmental psychology* (6th ed.). New York, NY: Worth.

Miller, S., McCulloch, S., & Jarrold, C. (2015). The development of memory maintenance strategies: Training cumulative rehearsal and interactive imagery in children aged between 5 and 9. *Frontiers in Psychology, 6*, 524. https://doi.org/10.3389/fpsyg.2015.00524

Miller-Cotto, D., & Byrnes, J. P. (2016). Ethnic/racial identity and academic achievement: A meta-analytic review. *Developmental Review, 41*, 51–70. https://doi.org/10.1016/j.dr.2016.06.003

Milligan, K., Astington, J. W., & Dack, L. A. (2007). Language and theory of mind: Meta-analysis of the relation between language ability and false-belief understanding. *Child Development, 78*(2), 622–646.

Mills, K. L., Dumontheil, I., Speekenbrink, M., & Blakemore, S.-J. (2015). Multitasking during social interactions in adolescence and early adulthood. *Royal Society Open Science, 2*(11), 150117. https://doi.org/10.1098/rsos.150117

Mills, K. L., Goddings, A.-L., Clasen, L. S., Giedd, J. N., & Blakemore, S.-J. (2014a). The developmental mismatch in structural brain maturation during adolescence. *Developmental Neuroscience, 36*(3–4), 147–160. https://doi.org/10.1159/000362328

Mills, K. L., Goddings, A.-L., Herting, M. M., Meuwese, R., Blakemore, S.-J., Crone, E. A., . . . Tamnes, C. K. (2016). Structural brain development between childhood and adulthood: Convergence across four longitudinal samples. *NeuroImage, 141*, 273–281. https://doi.org/10.1016/J.NEUROIMAGE.2016.07.044

Mills, K. L., Lalonde, F., Clasen, L. S., Giedd, J. N., & Blakemore, S.-J. (2014b). Developmental changes in the structure of the social brain in late childhood and adolescence. *Social Cognitive and Affective Neuroscience, 9*(1), 123–131. https://doi.org/10.1093/scan/nss113

Mills, K., & Tamnes, C. K. (2018). Longitudinal structural and functional brain development in childhood and adolescence. *PsyArXiv*. https://doi.org/10.31234/OSF.IO/87KFT

Min, M. O., Minnes, S., Yoon, S., Short, E. J., & Singer, L. T. (2014). Self-reported adolescent behavioral adjustment: Effects of prenatal cocaine exposure. *Journal of Adolescent Health, 55*(2), 167–174. https://doi.org/10.1016/j.jadohealth.2013.12.032

Mindell, J. A., Meltzer, L. J., Carskadon, M. A., & Chervin, R. D. (2009). Developmental aspects of sleep hygiene: Findings from the 2004 National Sleep Foundation Sleep in America Poll. *Sleep Medicine, 10*(7), 771–779. https://doi.org/10.1016/j.sleep.2008.07.016

Mindell, J. A., Sadeh, A., Kwon, R., & Goh, D. Y. T. (2013). Cross-cultural differences in the sleep of preschool children. *Sleep Medicine, 14*(12), 1283–1289. https://doi.org/10.1016/j.sleep.2013.09.002

Mindell, J. A., Sadeh, A., Wiegand, B., How, T. H., & Goh, D. Y. T. (2010). Cross-cultural differences in infant and toddler sleep. *Sleep Medicine, 11*(3), 274–280. https://doi.org/10.1016/J.SLEEP.2009.04.012

Minges, K. E., & Redeker, N. S. (2016). Delayed school start times and adolescent sleep: A systematic review of the experimental evidence. *Sleep Medicine Reviews, 28*, 86–95. https://doi.org/10.1016/j.smrv.2015.06.002

Minkoff, H., & Berkowitz, R. (2014). The case for universal prenatal genetic counseling. *Obstetrics & Gynecology, 123*(6), 1335–1338. https://doi.org/10.1097/AOG.0000000000000267

Miranda-Mendizábal, A., Castellví, P., Parés-Badell, O., Almenara, J., Alonso, I., Blasco, M. J., . . . Alonso, J. (2017). Sexual orientation and suicidal behaviour in adolescents and young adults: Systematic review and meta-analysis. *British Journal of Psychiatry, 211*(2), 77–87. https://doi.org/10.1192/bjp.bp.116.196345

Misca, G. (2014). The "quiet migration": Is intercountry adoption a successful intervention in the lives of vulnerable children? *Family Court Review, 52*(1), 60–68. https://doi.org/10.1111/fcre.12070

Mishna, F., Cook, C., Gadalla, T., Daciuk, J., & Solomon, S. (2010). Cyber bullying behaviors among middle and high school students. *American Journal of Orthopsychiatry, 80*(3), 362–374. https://doi.org/10.1111/j.1939-0025.2010.01040.x

Mistry, J. (2013). Integration of culture and biology in human development. *Advances in Child Development and Behavior, 45*, 287–314.

Mistry, J., & Dutta, R. (2015). Human development and culture. *Handbook of Child Psychology and Developmental Science, 1*(10), 1–38. https://doi.org/10.1002/9781118963418.childpsy110

Mistry, J., Li, J., Yoshikawa, H., Tseng, V., Tirrell, J., Kiang, L., . . . Wang, Y. (2016). An integrated conceptual framework for the development of Asian American children and youth. *Child Development, 87*(4), 1014–1032. https://doi.org/10.1111/cdev.12577

Mitchell, E. A. (2009). Risk factors for SIDS. *BMJ, 339*, b3466. https://doi.org/10.1136/bmj.b3466

Mitchell, J. A., Rodriguez, D., Schmitz, K. H., & Audrain-McGovern, J. (2013a). Greater screen time is associated with adolescent obesity: A longitudinal study of the BMI distribution from ages 14 to 18. *Obesity, 21*(3), 572–575. https://doi.org/10.1002/oby.20157

Mitchell, J. A., Rodriguez, D., Schmitz, K. H., & Audrain-McGovern, J. (2013b). Sleep duration and adolescent obesity. *Pediatrics, 131*(5), e1428–e1434. https://doi.org/10.1542/peds.2012-2368

Mix, K. S., Huttenlocher, J., & Levine, S. C. (2002). Multiple cues for quantification in infancy: Is number one of them? *Psychological Bulletin, 128*(2), 278–294.

Miyake, A., & Friedman, N. P. (2012). The nature and organization of individual differences in executive functions. *Current Directions in Psychological Science, 21*(1), 8–14. https://doi.org/10.1177/0963721411429458

Modabbernia, A., Velthorst, E., & Reichenberg, A. (2017). Environmental risk factors for autism: An evidence-based review of systematic reviews and meta-analyses. *Molecular Autism, 8*(1), 13. https://doi.org/10.1186/s13229-017-0121-4

Modecki, K. L. (2014). Maturity of judgment. In *Encyclopedia of adolescence* (pp. 1660–1665). New York, NY: Springer. https://doi.org/10.1007/978-1-4419-1695-2_213

Mohanty, J. (2015). Ethnic identity and psychological well-being of international transracial adoptees: A curvilinear relationship. *New Directions for Child and Adolescent Development, 2015*(150), 33–45. https://doi.org/10.1002/cad.20117

Moilanen, K. L., Rasmussen, K. E., & Padilla-Walker, L. M. (2015). Bidirectional associations between self-regulation and parenting styles in early adolescence. *Journal of Research on Adolescence, 25*(2), 246–262. https://doi.org/10.1111/jora.12125

Molnar, B. E., Goerge, R. M., Gilsanz, P., Hill, A., Subramanian, S. V, Holton, J. K., . . . Beardslee, W. R. (2016). Neighborhood-level social processes and substantiated cases of child maltreatment. *Child Abuse & Neglect, 51*, 41–53. https://doi.org/10.1016/j.chiabu.2015.11.007

Monahan, K. C., Lee, J. M., & Steinberg, L. (2011). Revisiting the impact of part-time work on adolescent adjustment: Distinguishing between selection and socialization using propensity score matching. *Child Development, 82*(1), 96–112. https://doi.org/10.1111/j.1467-8624.2010.01543.x

Monahan, K. C., Steinberg, L., Cauffman, E., & Mulvey, E. P. (2013). Psychosocial (im) maturity from adolescence to early adulthood: Distinguishing between adolescence-limited and persisting antisocial behavior. *Development and Psychopathology, 25*(4, Pt. 1), 1093–1105. https://doi.org/10.1017/S0954579413000394

Monnelly, V. J., Anblagan, D., Quigley, A., Cabez, M. B., Cooper, E. S., Mactier, H., . . . Boardman, J. P. (2018). Prenatal methadone exposure is associated with altered neonatal brain development. *NeuroImage: Clinical, 18*, 9–14. https://doi.org/10.1016/J.NICL.2017.12.033

Monteleone, A. M., Castellini, G., Volpe, U., Ricca, V., Lelli, L., Monteleone, P., & Maj, M. (2018). Neuroendocrinology and brain imaging of reward in eating disorders: A possible key to the treatment of anorexia nervosa and bulimia nervosa. *Progress in Neuro-Psychopharmacology and Biological Psychiatry, 80*, 132–142. https://doi.org/10.1016/J.PNPBP.2017.02.020

Montgomery, J. E., & Jordan, N. A. (2018). Racial–ethnic socialization and transracial adoptee outcomes: A systematic research synthesis. *Child and Adolescent Social Work Journal, 35*(5), 439–458. https://doi.org/10.1007/s10560-018-0541-9

Montgomery, M. J., & Côté, J. E. (2003). College as a transition to adulthood. In G. R. Adams & M. D. Berzonsky (Eds.), *Blackwell handbook of adolescence* (pp. 149–172). Malden, MA: Blackwell Publishing.

Moon, C., Cooper, R. P., & Fifer, W. P. (1993). Two-day-old infants prefer their native language. *Infant Behavior and Development, 16*, 495–500.

Moon, R. Y., & Task Force on Sudden Infant Death Syndrome. (2016). SIDS and other sleep-related infant deaths: Evidence base for 2016 updated recommendations for a safe infant sleeping environment. *Pediatrics, 138*(5), e20162940. https://doi.org/10.1542/peds.2016-2940

Moore, C., Angelopoulos, M., & Bennett, P. (1999). Word learning in the context of referential and salience cues. *Developmental Psychology, 35*, 60–68.

Moore, D. S. (2017). Behavioral epigenetics. *Wiley Interdisciplinary Reviews: Systems Biology and Medicine, 9*(1), e1333. https://doi.org/10.1002/wsbm.1333

Moore, J. S. B., & Smith, M. (2018). Children's levels of contingent self-esteem and social and emotional outcomes. *Educational Psychology in Practice, 34*(2), 113–130. https://doi.org/10.1080/02667363.2017.1411786

Moore, K. L., & Persaud, T. V. N. (2016). *Before we are born: Essentials of embryology and birth defects* (9th ed.). Philadelphia, PA: Saunders.

Moore, R., Vitale, D., & Stawinoga, N. (2018). *The digital divide and educational equity: A look at students with very limited access to electronic devices at home.* Retrieved from https://equityinlearning.act.org/wp-content/themes/voltron/img/tech-briefs/the-digital-divide.pdf

Moore, S. E., Norman, R. E., Suetani, S., Thomas, H. J., Sly, P. D., & Scott, J. G. (2017). Consequences of bullying victimization in childhood and adolescence: A systematic review and meta-analysis. *World Journal of Psychiatry, 7*(1), 60–76. https://doi.org/10.5498/wjp.v7.i1.60

Moore, S. R., Harden, K. P., & Mendle, J. (2014). Pubertal timing and adolescent sexual behavior in girls. *Developmental Psychology, 50*(6), 1734–1745. https://doi.org/10.1037/a0036027

Morawska, A., & Sanders, M. (2011). Parental use of time out revisited: A useful or harmful parenting strategy? *Journal of Child & Family Studies, 20*(1), 1–8. https://doi.org/10.1007/s10826-010-9371-x

Morcillo, C., Ramos-Olazagasti, M. A., Blanco, C., Sala, R., Canino, G., Bird, H., & Duarte, C. S. (2015). Socio-cultural context and bullying others in childhood. *Journal of Child and Family Studies, 24*(8), 2241–2249. https://doi.org/10.1007/s10826-014-0026-1

Morelli, G. (2015). The evolution of attachment theory and cultures of human attachment in infancy and early childhood. In L. A. Jensen (Ed.), *The Oxford handbook of human development and culture* (pp. 149–164). Oxford, England: Oxford University Press. https://doi.org/10.1093/oxfordhb/9780199948550.013.10

Morelli, G., Rogoff, B., Oppenheim, D., & Goldsmith, D. (1992). Cultural variation in infants' sleeping arrangements: Questions of independence. *Developmental Psychology, 28*, 604–613.

Moreno, O., Janssen, T., Cox, M. J., Colby, S., & Jackson, K. M. (2017). Parent-adolescent relationships in Hispanic versus Caucasian families: Associations with alcohol and marijuana use onset. *Addictive Behaviors, 74*, 74–81. https://doi.org/10.1016/J.ADDBEH.2017.05.029

Morey, C. C., Mareva, S., Lelonkiewicz, J. R., & Chevalier, N. (2018). Gaze-based rehearsal in children under 7: A developmental investigation of eye movements during a serial spatial memory task. *Developmental Science, 21*(3), e12559. https://doi.org/10.1111/desc.12559

Mori, A., & Cigala, A. (2016). Perspective taking: Training procedures in developmentally typical preschoolers. Different intervention methods and their effectiveness. *Educational Psychology Review, 28*(2), 267–294. https://doi.org/10.1007/s10648-015-9306-6

Moriguchi, Y. (2014). The early development of executive function and its relation to social interaction: A brief review. *Frontiers in Psychology, 5*, 388. https://doi.org/10.3389/fpsyg.2014.00388

Moriguchi, Y., Kanda, T., Ishiguro, H., Shimada, Y., & Itakura, S. (2011). Can young children learn words from a robot? *Interaction Studies: Social Behaviour and Communication in Biological and Artificial Systems, 12*(1), 107–118.

Morley, D., Till, K., Ogilvie, P., & Turner, G. (2015). Influences of gender and socioeconomic status on the motor proficiency of children in the UK. *Human Movement Science, 44*, 150–156. https://doi.org/10.1016/J.HUMOV.2015.08.022

Morley, J. E. (2016). Protein-energy undernutrition (PEU). *Merck Manual*. Retrieved from http://www.merckmanuals.com/professional/nutritional-disorders/undernutrition/protein-energy-undernutrition-peu

Morokuma, S., Fukushima, K., Kawai, N., Tomonaga, M., Satoh, S., & Nakano, H. (2004). Fetal habituation correlates with functional brain development. *Behavioural Brain Research, 153*(2), 459–463.

Morris, A. S., Criss, M. M., Silk, J. S., & Houltberg, B. J. (2017). The impact of parenting on emotion regulation during childhood and adolescence. *Child Development Perspectives, 11*(4), 233–238. https://doi.org/10.1111/cdep.12238

Morris, A. S., Squeglia, L. M., Jacobus, J., & Silk, J. S. (2018). Adolescent brain development: Implications for understanding risk and resilience processes through neuroimaging research. *Journal of Research on Adolescence, 28*(1), 4–9. https://doi.org/10.1111/jora.12379

Morris, B. J., Kennedy, S. E., Wodak, A. D., Mindel, A., Golovsky, D., Schrieber, L., . . . Ziegler, J. B. (2017). Early infant male circumcision: Systematic review, risk-benefit analysis, and progress in policy. *World Journal of Clinical Pediatrics, 6*(1), 89–102. https://doi.org/10.5409/wjcp.v6.i1.89

Morris, B. J., Wamai, R. G., Henebeng, E. B., Tobian, A. A., Klausner, J. D., Banerjee, J., & Hankins, C. A. (2016). Estimation of country-specific and global prevalence of male circumcision. *Population Health Metrics, 14*(1), 4. https://doi.org/10.1186/s12963-016-0073-5

Morrison, M. L., & McMahon, C. J. (2018). Congenital heart disease in Down syndrome. In S. Dey (Ed.), *Advances in research on Down syndrome* (pp. 128–144). London, England: InTech. https://doi.org/10.5772/intechopen.71060

Morrongiello, B. A., Corbett, M., McCourt, M., & Johnston, N. (2006). Understanding unintentional injury risk in young children II. The contribution of caregiver supervision, child attributes, and parent attributes. *Journal of Pediatric Psychology, 31*(6), 540–551. https://doi.org/10.1093/jpepsy/jsj073

Mortensen, J. A., & Barnett, M. A. (2015). Teacher–child interactions in infant/toddler child care and socioemotional development. *Early Education and Development, 26*(2), 209–229. https://doi.org/10.1080/10409289.2015.985878

Mortimer, J. T., & Johnson, M. K. (1998). New perspectives on adolescent work and the transition to adulthood. In R. Jessor (Ed.), *New perspectives on adolescent risk behavior* (pp. 425–496). New York, NY: Cambridge University Press.

Moses, A. M. (2008). Impacts of television viewing on young children's literacy development in the USA: A review of the literature. *Journal of Early Childhood Literacy, 8*(1), 67–102. https://doi.org/10.1177/1468798407087162

Moses, L. J., Coon, J. A., & Wusinich, N. (2000). Young children's understanding of desire information. *Developmental Psychology, 36*, 77–90.

Mosher, S. W. (2006). China's one-child policy: Twenty-five years later. *Human Life Review, 32*(1), 76–101.

Moshman, D., & Moshman, D. (2011). *Adolescent rationality and development: Cognition, morality, and identity.* New York, NY: Psychology Press.

Motta-Mena, N. V., & Scherf, K. S. (2017). Pubertal development shapes perception of complex facial expressions. *Developmental Science, 20*(4), e12451. https://doi.org/10.1111/desc.12451

Mõttus, R., Indus, K., & Allik, J. (2008). Accuracy of only children stereotype. *Journal of Research in Personality, 42*(4), 1047–1052. https://doi.org/10.1016/J.JRP.2007.10.006

Mouratidi, P.-S., Bonoti, F., & Leondari, A. (2016). Children's perceptions of illness and health: An analysis of drawings. *Health Education Journal, 75*(4), 434–447. https://doi.org/10.1177/0017896915599416

Mowery, T. M., Kotak, V. C., & Sanes, D. H. (2016). The onset of visual experience gates auditory cortex critical periods. *Nature Communications, 7*, 10416. https://doi.org/10.1038/ncomms10416

Mpofu, E., & Vijver, F. J. R. van de. (2000). Taxonomic structure in early to middle childhood: A longitudinal study with Zimbabwean schoolchildren. *International Journal of Behavioral Development, 24*(2), 204–212.

Mrick, S. E., & Mrtorell, G. A. (2011). Sticks and stones may break my bones: Protective factors for the effects of perceived discrimination on social competence in adolescence. *Personal Relationships, 18*(3), 487–501. https://doi.org/10.1111/j.1475-6811.2010.01320.x

Mrug, S., Elliott, M. N., Davies, S., Tortolero, S. R., Cuccaro, P., & Schuster, M. A. (2014). Early puberty, negative peer influence, and problem behaviors in adolescent girls. *Pediatrics, 133*(1), 7–14. https://doi.org/10.1542/peds.2013-0628

Muehlenkamp, J. J., Claes, L., Havertape, L., & Plener, P. L. (2012). International prevalence of adolescent non-suicidal self-injury and deliberate self-harm. *Child and Adolescent Psychiatry and Mental Health, 6*, 10. https://doi.org/10.1186/1753-2000-6-10

Mueller, C. E., & Anderman, E. M. (2010). Middle school transitions and adolescent development. In J. L. Meece & J. S. Eccles (Eds.), *Handbook of research on schools, schooling and human development* (pp. 216–233). New York, NY: Routledge. https://doi.org/10.4324/9780203874844-24

Mueller, S. C., Maheu, F. S., Dozier, M., Peloso, E., Mandell, D., Leibenluft, E., . . . Ernst, M. (2010). Early-life stress is associated with impairment in cognitive control in adolescence: An fMRI study. *Neuropsychologia, 48*(10), 3037–3044. https://doi.org/10.1016/j.neuropsychologia.2010.06.013

Mueller, V., & Sepulveda, A. (2014). Parental perception of a baby sign workshop on stress and parent–child interaction. *Early Child Development and Care, 184*(3), 450–468. https://doi.org/10.1080/03004430.2013.797899

Muenks, K., Wigfield, A., & Eccles, J. S. (2018). I can do this! The development and calibration of children's expectations for success and competence beliefs. *Developmental Review, 48*, 24–39. https://doi.org/10.1016/J.DR.2018.04.001

Muennig, P., Robertson, D., Johnson, G., Campbell, F., Pungello, E. P., & Neidell, M. (2011). The effect of an early education program on adult health: The Carolina Abecedarian Project randomized controlled trial. *American Journal of Public Health, 101*(3), 512–516. https://doi.org/10.2105/AJPH.2010.200063

Muenssinger, J., Matuz, T., Schleger, F., Kiefer-Schmidt, I., Goelz, R., Wacker-Gussmann, A., . . . Preissl, H. (2013). Auditory habituation in the fetus and neonate: An fMEG study. *Developmental Science, 16*(2), 287–295. https://doi.org/10.1111/desc.12025

Muggli, E., Matthews, H., Penington, A., Claes, P., O'Leary, C., Forster, D., . . . Halliday, J. (2017). Association between prenatal alcohol exposure and craniofacial shape of children at 12 months of age. *JAMA Pediatrics, 171*(8), 771. https://doi.org/10.1001/jamapediatrics.2017.0778

Müller, U., & Kerns, K. (2015). The development of executive function. In L. Liben & U. Müller (Eds.), *Handbook of child psychology and developmental science* (pp. 1–53). Hoboken, NJ: John Wiley & Sons. https://doi.org/10.1002/9781118963418.childpsy214

Müller-Oehring, E. M., Kwon, D., Nagel, B. J., Sullivan, E. V, Chu, W., Rohlfing, T., . . . Pohl, K. M. (2018). Influences of age, sex, and moderate alcohol drinking on the intrinsic functional architecture of adolescent brains. *Cerebral Cortex, 28*(3), 1049–1063. https://doi.org/10.1093/cercor/bhx014

Mummert, A., Schoen, M., & Lampl, M. (2018). Growth and life course health development. In N. Halfon, C. B. Forrest, R. M. Lerner, & E. M. Faustman (Eds.), *Handbook of life course health development* (pp. 405–429). Cham, Switzerland: Springer International Publishing. https://doi.org/10.1007/978-3-319-47143-3_17

Munniksma, A., & Juvonen, J. (2012). Cross-ethnic friendships and sense of social-emotional safety in a multiethnic middle school: An exploratory study. *Merrill-Palmer Quarterly, 58*(4), 489–506. https://doi.org/10.1353/mpq.2012.0023

Munthali, A. C., & Zulu, E. M. (2007). The timing and role of initiation rites in preparing young people for adolescence and responsible sexual and reproductive behaviour in Malawi. *African Journal of Reproductive Health, 11*(3), 150–167. Retrieved from https://journals.co.za/content/ajrh/11/3/EJC134431

Murachver, T., Pipe, M., Gordon, R., Owens, J. L., & Fivush, R. (1996). Do, show, and tell: Children's event memories acquired through direct experience, observation, and stories. *Child Development, 67*, 3029–3044.

Murdock, G. P. (1980). *Theories of illness: A world survey.* University of Pittsburgh. eweb:30999. Retrieved from https://repository.library.georgetown.edu/handle/10822/785785

Muris, P., & Meesters, C. (2014). Small or big in the eyes of the other: On the developmental psychopathology of self-conscious emotions as shame, guilt, and pride. *Clinical Child and Family Psychology Review, 17*(1), 19–40. https://doi.org/10.1007/s10567-013-0137-z

Murray, P. G., Dattani, M. T., & Clayton, P. E. (2016). Controversies in the diagnosis and management of growth hormone deficiency in childhood and adolescence. *Archives of Disease in Childhood, 101*(1), 96–100. https://doi.org/10.1136/archdischild-2014-307228

Murray, R., Ramstetter, C., Council on School Health, & American Academy of Pediatrics. (2013). The crucial role of recess in school. *Pediatrics, 131*(1), 183–188. https://doi.org/10.1542/peds.2012-2993

Murray-Close, D., Nelson, D. A., Ostrov, J. M., Casas, J. F., & Crick, N. R. (2016). Relational aggression: A developmental psychopathology perspective. In D. Cicchetti (Ed.), *Developmental psychopathology* (pp. 1–63). Hoboken, NJ: John Wiley. https://doi.org/10.1002/9781119125556.devpsy413

Murry, V. M., Brody, G. H., Simons, R. L., Cutrona, C. E., & Gibbons, F. X. (2008). Disentangling ethnicity and context as predictors of parenting within rural African American families. *Applied Developmental Science, 12*(4), 202–210. https://doi.org/10.1080/10888690802388144

Murty, V. P., Calabro, F., & Luna, B. (2016). The role of experience in adolescent cognitive development: Integration of executive, memory, and mesolimbic systems. *Neuroscience & Biobehavioral Reviews, 70*, 46–58. https://doi.org/10.1016/j.neubiorev.2016.07.034

Mussen, P., & Eisenberg-Berg, N. (1977). *Roots of caring, sharing, and helping.* San Francisco, CA: Freeman.

Mustanski, B., & Liu, R. T. (2013). A longitudinal study of predictors of suicide attempts among lesbian, gay, bisexual, and transgender youth. *Archives of Sexual Behavior, 42*(3), 437–448. https://doi.org/10.1007/s10508-012-0013-9

Myant, K. A., & Williams, J. M. (2005). Children's concepts of health and illness: Understanding of contagious illnesses, non-contagious illnesses and injuries. *Journal of Health Psychology, 10*(6), 805–819.

Myers, L. J., LeWitt, R. B., Gallo, R. E., & Maselli, N. M. (2017). Baby FaceTime: Can toddlers learn from online video chat? *Developmental Science, 20*(4), e12430. https://doi.org/10.1111/desc.12430

Myers, N. A., & Perlmutter, M. (2014). Memory in the years from two to five. In P. A. Ornstein (Ed.), *Memory development in children* (pp. 191–218). New York, NY: Psychology Press.

Nabors, L., & Keyes, L. (1995). Preschoolers' reasons for accepting peers with and without disabilities. *Journal of Developmental and Physical Disabilities, 7*(4), 335–355. https://doi.org/10.1007/BF02578435

Nadel, J., & Butterworth, G. (1999). *Imitation in infancy.* Cambridge, England: Cambridge University Press.

Næss, K.-A. B., Nygaard, E., Ostad, J., Dolva, A.-S., & Lyster, S.-A. H. (2017). The profile of social functioning in children with Down syndrome. *Disability and Rehabilitation, 39*(13), 1320–1331. https://doi.org/10.1080/09638288.2016.1194901

Nagayama, M., & Gilliard, J. L. (2005). An investigation of Japanese and American early care and education. *Early Childhood Education Journal, 33*(3), 137–143.

Nagy, E., Pilling, K., Orvos, H., & Molnar, P. (2013). Imitation of tongue protrusion in human neonates: Specificity of the response in a large sample. *Developmental Psychology, 49*(9), 1628–1638. https://doi.org/10.1037/a0031127

Nagy, G. R., Győrffy, B., Nagy, B., & Rigó, J. (2013). Lower risk for Down syndrome associated with longer oral contraceptive use: A case-control study of women of advanced maternal age presenting for prenatal diagnosis. *Contraception, 87*(4), 455–458.

https://doi.org/10.1016/j.contraception.2012.08.040

Nair, R. L., Roche, K. M., & White, R. M. B. (2018). Acculturation gap distress among Latino youth: Prospective links to family processes and youth depressive symptoms, alcohol use, and academic performance. *Journal of Youth and Adolescence, 47*(1), 105–120. https://doi.org/10.1007/s10964-017-0753-x

Naito, M., & Koyama, K. (2006). The development of false-belief understanding in Japanese children: Delay and difference? *International Journal of Behavioral Development, 30*(4), 290-304. https://doi.org/10.1177/0165025406063622

Nakano, T., Watanabe, H., Homae, F., & Taga, G. (2009). Prefrontal cortical involvement in young infants' analysis of novelty. *Cerebral Cortex, 19*(2), 455–463. https://doi.org/10.1093/cercor/bhn096

Nanayakkara, S., Misch, D., Chang, L., & Henry, D. (2013). Depression and exposure to suicide predict suicide attempt. *Depression and Anxiety, 30*(10), 991–996. https://doi.org/10.1002/da.22143

Nance, M. A. (2017). Genetic counseling and testing for Huntington's disease: A historical review. *American Journal of Medical Genetics Part B: Neuropsychiatric Genetics, 174*(1), 75–92. https://doi.org/10.1002/ajmg.b.32453

Náñez Sr., J. E., & Yonas, A. (1994). Effects of luminance and texture motion on infant defensive reactions to optical collision. *Infant Behavior & Development, 17*, 165–174.

Natale, V., & Rajagopalan, A. (2014). Worldwide variation in human growth and the World Health Organization growth standards: A systematic review. *BMJ Open, 4*(1), e003735. https://doi.org/10.1136/bmjopen-2013-003735

National Association for Down Syndrome. (2017). *Facts about down syndrome*. Retrieved from http://www.nads.org/resources/facts-about-down-syndrome/

National Association of School Psychologists. (2003). *Position statement on student grade retention and social promotion*. Retrieved from https://www.nasponline.org

National Center for Education Statistics. (2014). *The condition of education - 2014*. Retrieved from http://nces.ed.gov/pubsearch/pubsinfo.asp?pubid=2014083

National Center for Education Statistics. (2016). *Fall enrollment of U.S. residents in degree-granting postsecondary institutions, by race/ethnicity: Selected years, 1976 through 2025*. Retrieved from https://nces.ed.gov/programs/digest/d15/tables/dt15_306.30.asp? current=ye

National Center for Education Statistics. (2017a). *Digest of education statistics, 2017*. Retrieved from https://nces.ed.gov/pubsearch/pubsinfo.asp?pubid=2018070

National Center for Education Statistics. (2017b). *Dropout rates*. Retrieved from https://nces.ed.gov/programs/coe/indicator_coj.asp

National Center for Education Statistics. (2019). *Digest of education statistics, 2018*. Washington DC: National Center for Education Statistics.

National Center for Health Statistics. (2015). *National marriage and divorce rate trends*. Washington, DC: National Center for Health Statistics.

National Center for Health Statistics. (2017). *Table C-6: Number of school days missed in the past 12 months because of illness or injury for children aged 5-17 years, by selected characteristics: United States, 2017--National Health Interview Survey*. Retrieved from https://www.cdc.gov/nchs/data/series/sr_02/sr02_175.pdf

National Center for Health Statistics. (2018). *Table 66: Vaccination coverage for selected diseases among children aged 19-35 months, by race, Hispanic origin, poverty level, and location of residence in metropolitan statistical area: United States, selected years 1998-2016*. Retrieved from https://www.ncbi.nlm.nih.gov/books/NBK532684/table/ch4.tab66/

National Center for Hearing Assessment and Management. (2019). *Early hearing detection and intervention components*. Retrieved from https://www.infanthearing.org/components/

National Coalition for Health Professional Education in Genetics. (2012). *Non-invasive prenatal testing (NIPT) factsheet*. Retrieved from http://www.acog.org/Resources_And_Publications/Committee_Opinions/Committee_on_Genetics/Noninvasive_Prenatal_Testing_for_Fetal_Aneuploidy

National Institute of Allergy and infectious Diseases. (2014). *NIH trial tests very early anti-HIV therapy in HIV-infected newborns*. Retrieved from https://aidsinfo.nih.gov/news/1511/nih-trial-tests-very-early-anti-hiv-therapy-in-hiv-infected-newborns

National Library of Medicine. (2019). *Help me understand genetics. Genetics Home Reference*. Bethesda, MD: U.S. National Library of Medicine. Retrieved from http://ghr.nlm.nih.gov/handbook

National Middle School Association. (2003). *This we believe: Successful schools for young adolescents*. Westerville, OH: Author.

National Physical Activity Plan Alliance. (2018). *The 2018 United States report card on physical activity for children and youth*. Washington DC. Retrieved from http://physicalactivityplan.org/projects/PA/2018/2018 US Report Card Full Version_WEB.PDF? pdf=page-link

National Science Foundation. (2018). *Instructional technology and digital learning. Science and engineering indicators*. Retrieved from https://www.nsf.gov/statistics/2018/nsb20181/report/sections/elementary-and-secondary-mathematics-and-science-education/instructional-technology-and-digital-learning

National Survey of Children's Health. (2014). Asthma: Chronic health conditions. Data query from the Child and Adolescent Health Measurement Initiative NSCH 2011/12. *Data Resource Center for Child and Adolescent Health website*. Retrieved from http://www.childhealthdata.org/browse/survey/results? q=2401&r=1

Natsuaki, M. N., Samuels, D., & Leve, L. D. (2015). Puberty, Identity, and context. In K. C. McLean & M. Syed (Eds.), *The Oxford handbook of identity development* (pp. 389–405). Oxford, England: Oxford University Press. https://doi.org/10.1093/oxfordhb/9780199936564.013.005

Natsuaki, M. N., Shaw, D. S., Neiderhiser, J. M., Ganiban, J. M., Harold, G. T., Reiss, D., & Leve, L. D. (2014). Raised by depressed parents: Is it an environmental risk? *Clinical Child and Family Psychology Review, 17*(4), 357–367. https://doi.org/10.1007/s10567-014-0169-z

NCD Risk Factor Collaboration (NCD-RisC). (2016). A century of trends in adult human height. *ELife, 5*, e13410. https://doi.org/10.7554/eLife.13410

Ncube, C. N., Enquobahrie, D. A., Albert, S. M., Herrick, A. L., & Burke, J. G. (2016). Association of neighborhood context with offspring risk of preterm birth and low birthweight: A systematic review and meta-analysis of population-based studies. *Social Science & Medicine, 153*, 156–164. https://doi.org/10.1016/J.SOCSCIMED.2016.02.014

Nederkoorn, C., Jansen, A., & Havermans, R. C. (2015). Feel your food. The influence of tactile sensitivity on picky eating in children. *Appetite, 84*, 7–10. https://doi.org/10.1016/J.APPET.2014.09.014

Negriff, S., & Susman, E. J. (2011). Pubertal timing, depression, and externalizing problems: A framework, review, and examination of gender differences. *Journal of Research on Adolescence, 21*(3), 717–746. https://doi.org/10.1111/j.1532-7795.2010.00708.x

Negriff, S., Blankson, A. N., & Trickett, P. K. (2015). Pubertal timing and tempo: Associations with childhood maltreatment. *Journal of Research on Adolescence, 25*(2), 201–213. https://doi.org/10.1111/jora.12128

Negriff, S., Susman, E. J., & Trickett, P. K. (2011). The developmental pathway from pubertal timing to delinquency and sexual activity from early to late adolescence. *Journal of Youth and Adolescence, 40*(10), 1343–1356. https://doi.org/10.1007/s10964-010-9621-7

Neisser, U. (1993). *The perceived self: Ecological and interpersonal sources of self-knowledge*. New York, NY: Cambridge University Press.

Neisser, U., Boodoo, G., Bouchard Jr., T. J., Boykin, A. W., Brody, N., Ceci, S. J., . . . Urbina, S. (1996). Intelligence: Knowns and unknowns. *American Psychologist, 51*(2), 77–101.

Nelson, C. A. (2011). Neural development and lifelong plasticity. In D. P. Keating (Ed.), *Nature and nurture in early child development* (pp. 45–69). New York, NY: Cambridge University Press.

Nelson, C. A., Fox, N. A., Zeanah, C. H., Nelson, C. A., Fox, N. A., & Zeanah, C. H. (2016). the effects of early psychosocial deprivation on brain and behavioral development: Findings from the Bucharest Early Intervention Project. In D. Cicchetti (Ed.), *Developmental psychopathology* (pp. 1–37). Hoboken, NJ: John Wiley & Sons. https://doi.org/10.1002/9781119125556.devpsy418

Nelson, L. H., White, K. R., & Grewe, J. (2012). Evidence for Website claims about the benefits of teaching sign language to infants and toddlers with normal hearing. *Infant and Child Development, 21*(5), 474–502. https://doi.org/10.1002/icd.1748

Nemeroff, C. B. (2016). Paradise lost: The neurobiological and clinical consequences of child abuse and neglect. *Neuron, 89*(5), 892–909. https://doi.org/10.1016/J.NEURON.2016.01.019

Neradugomma, N. K., Drafton, K., O'Day, D. R., Liao, M. Z., Han, L. W., Glass, I. A., & Mao, Q. (2018). Marijuana use differentially affects cannabinoid receptor expression in early gestational human endometrium and placenta. *Placenta, 66*, 36–39. https://doi.org/10.1016/J.PLACENTA.2018.05.002

Nese, R. N. T., Horner, R. H., Dickey, C. R., Stiller, B., & Tomlanovich, A. (2014). Decreasing bullying behaviors in middle school: Expect respect. *School Psychology Quarterly, 29(3)*(3), 272–286.

Neshat, H., Jebreili, M., Seyyedrasouli, A., Ghojazade, M., Hosseini, M. B., & Hamishehkar, H. (2016). Effects of breast milk and vanilla odors on premature neonate's heart rate and blood oxygen saturation during and after venipuncture. *Pediatrics & Neonatology, 57*(3), 225–231. https://doi.org/10.1016/J.PEDNEO.2015.09.004

Neuburger, S., Ruthsatz, V., Jansen, P., & Quaiser-Pohl, C. (2015). Can girls think spatially? Influence of implicit gender stereotype activation and rotational axis on fourth graders' mental-rotation performance. *Learning and Individual Differences, 37*, 169–175. https://doi.org/10.1016/J.LINDIF.2014.09.003

Neuman, S. B., Kaefer, T., Pinkham, A., & Strouse, G. (2014). Can babies learn to read? A randomized trial of baby media. *Journal of Educational Psychology, 106*(3), 815.

New York City Department of Health. (2019). Measles. Retrieved from https://www1.nyc.gov/site/doh/health/health-topics/measles.page

Newcombe, N., & Huttenlocher, J. (1992). Children's early ability to solve perspective-taking problems. *Developmental Psychology, 28*, 635–643.

Newell, F. N. (2004). Cross-modal object recognition. In G. A. Calvert, C. Spence, & B. E. Stein (Eds.), *The handbook of multisensory processes* (pp. 123–139). Cambridge, MA: MIT Press.

Newland, R. P., Parade, S. H., Dickstein, S., & Seifer, R. (2016). The association between maternal depression and sensitivity: Child-directed effects on parenting during infancy. *Infant Behavior and Development, 45*, 47–50. https://doi.org/10.1016/J.INFBEH.2016.09.001

Newton, E. K., Laible, D., Carlo, G., Steele, J. S., & McGinley, M. (2014). Do sensitive parents foster kind children, or vice versa? Bidirectional influences between children's prosocial behavior and parental sensitivity. *Developmental Psychology, 50*(6), 1808–1816. https://doi.org/10.1037/a0036495

Newton, E., & Jenvey, V. (2011). Play and theory of mind: Associations with social competence in young children. *Early Child Development & Care, 181*(6), 761–773. https://doi.org/10.1080/03004430.2010.486898

Ng, F. F.-Y., Pomerantz, E. M., & Lam, S. (2007). European American and Chinese parents' responses to children's success and failure: Implications for children's responses. *Developmental Psychology, 43*(5), 1239–1255. https://doi.org/10.1037/0012-1649.43.5.1239

Nguyen, D. J., Kim, J. J., Weiss, B., Ngo, V., & Lau, A. S. (2018). Prospective relations between parent–adolescent acculturation conflict and mental health symptoms among Vietnamese American adolescents. *Cultural Diversity and Ethnic Minority Psychology, 24*, 151–161. https://doi.org/10.1037/cdp0000157

Nguyen, T., Li, G. E., Chen, H., Cranfield, C. G., McGrath, K. C., & Gorrie, C. A. (2018). Maternal E-cigarette exposure results in cognitive and epigenetic alterations in offspring in a mouse model. *Chemical Research in Toxicology, 31*(7), 601–611. https://doi.org/10.1021/acs.chemrestox.8b00084

Nguyen-Louie, T. T., Brumback, T., Worley, M. J., Colrain, I. M., Matt, G. E., Squeglia, L. M., & Tapert, S. F. (2018). Effects of sleep on substance use in adolescents: A longitudinal perspective. *Addiction Biology, 23*(2), 750–760. https://doi.org/10.1111/adb.12519

Nhlekisana, R. O. (2017). From childhood to womanhood: Puberty rites of !Xoo girls of Zutshwa. *Marang: Journal of Language and Literature, 29*(0), 31–41. Retrieved from http://168.167.8.131/ojs/index.php/marang/article/view/1135

NICHD Early Child Care Research Network. (2005). Early child care and children's development in the primary grades: Follow-up results from the NICHD Study of Early Child Care. *American Educational Research Journal, 42*(3), 537–570. https://doi.org/10.3102/00028312042003537

Nieto, M., Ros, L., Ricarte, J. J., & Latorre, J. M. (2018). The role of executive functions in accessing specific autobiographical memories in 3- to 6- year-olds. *Early Childhood Research Quarterly, 43*, 23–32. https://doi.org/10.1016/j.ecresq.2017.11.004

Nikolaou, D. (2017). Do anti-bullying policies deter in-school bullying victimization? *International Review of Law and Economics, 50*, 1–6. https://doi.org/10.1016/J.IRLE.2017.03.001

Nikulina, V., Widom, C. S., & Brzustowicz, L. M. (2012). Child abuse and neglect, MAOA, and mental health outcomes: A prospective examination. *Biological Psychiatry, 71*(4), 350–357. https://doi.org/10.1016/j.biopsych.2011.09.008

Nilsen, E. S., & Bacso, S. A. (2017). Cognitive and behavioural predictors of adolescents' communicative perspective-taking and social relationships. *Journal of Adolescence, 56*, 52–63. https://doi.org/10.1016/J.ADOLESCENCE.2017.01.004

Ninio, A. (2014). Pragmatic development. In P. J. Brooks & V. Kempe (Eds.), *Encyclopedia of language development*. Thousand Oaks, CA: Sage. https://doi.org/10.4135/9781483346441.n153

Niolon, P. H., Vivolo-Kantor, A. M., Latzman, N. E., Valle, L. A., Kuoh, H., Burton, T., . . . Tharp, A. T. (2015). Prevalence of Teen dating violence and co-occurring risk factors among middle school youth in high-risk urban communities. *Journal of Adolescent Health, 56*(2), S5–S13. https://doi.org/10.1016/j.jadohealth.2014.07.019

Nisbett, R. E., Aronson, J., Blair, C., Dickens, W., Flynn, J., Halpern, D. F., & Turkheimer, E. (2013). Intelligence: New findings and theoretical developments. *American Psychologist, 67*(2), 130–159. https://doi.org/10.1037/a0026699

Nishitani, S., Miyamura, T., Tagawa, M., Sumi, M., Takase, R., Doi, H., . . . Shinohara, K. (2009). The calming effect of a maternal breast milk odor on the human newborn infant. *Neuroscience Research, 63*(1), 66–71. https://doi.org/10.1016/j.neures.2008.10.007

Nishiyori, R., Bisconti, S., Meehan, S. K., & Ulrich, B. D. (2016). Developmental changes in motor cortex activity as infants develop functional motor skills. *Developmental Psychobiology, 58*(6), 773–783. https://doi.org/10.1002/dev.21418

Nixon, E., & Hadfield, K. (2016). Blended families. In C. L. Shehan (Ed.), *Encyclopedia of family studies* (pp. 1–5). Hoboken, NJ: John Wiley & Sons. https://doi.org/10.1002/9781119085621.wbefs207

Nobes, G., & Pawson, C. (2003). Children's understanding of social rules and social status. *Merrill-Palmer Quarterly, 49*, 77–99.

Noble, K. G., Houston, S. M., Brito, N. H., Bartsch, H., Kan, E., Kuperman, J. M., . . . Sowell, E. R. (2015). Family income, parental education and brain structure in children and adolescents. *Nature Neuroscience, 18*(5), 773–778. https://doi.org/10.1038/nn.3983

Nock, M. K. (2009). Why do people hurt themselves? New insights into the nature and functions of self-injury. *Current Directions in Psychological Science, 18*(2), 78–83. https://doi.org/10.1111/j.1467-8721.2009.01613.x

Nock, M. K., Prinstein, M. J., & Sterba, S. K. (2009). Revealing the form and function of self-injurious thoughts and behaviors: A real-time ecological assessment study among adolescents and young adults. *Journal of Abnormal Psychology, 118*(4), 816–827. https://doi.org/10.1037/a0016948

Noll, J. G., Trickett, P. K., Long, J. D., Negriff, S., Susman, E. J., Shalev, I., . . . Putnam, F. W. (2017). Childhood sexual abuse and early timing of puberty. *Journal of Adolescent Health, 60*(1), 65–71. https://doi.org/10.1016/j.jadohealth.2016.09.008

Nordin, S. M., Harris, G., & Cumming, J. (2003). Disturbed eating in young, competitive gymnasts: Differences between three gymnastics disciplines. *European Journal of Sport Science, 3*(5), 1–14.

Nørgaard, M., Nielsson, M. S., & Heide-Jørgensen, U. (2015). Birth and neonatal outcomes following opioid use in pregnancy: A Danish population-based study. *Substance Abuse: Research and Treatment, 9s2*, SART.S23547. https://doi.org/10.4137/SART.S23547

Northern, J. L., & Downs, M. P. (2014). Hearing in children (6th ed.). San Diego, CA: Plural Publishing.

Northoff, G., & Hayes, D. J. (2011). Is our self nothing but reward? *Biological Psychiatry, 69*(11), 1019–1025. https://doi.org/10.1016/j.biopsych.2010.12.014

Nugent, B. M., & McCarthy, M. M. (2011). Epigenetic underpinnings of developmental sex differences in the brain. *Neuroendocrinology, 93*(3), 150–158. https://doi.org/10.1159/000325264

Nugent, J. K. (2013). The Competent Newborn and the Neonatal Behavioral Assessment Scale: T. Berry Brazelton's legacy. *Journal of Child and Adolescent Psychiatric Nursing, 26*(3), 173–179. https://doi.org/10.1111/jcap.12043

Nuttall, A. K., Valentino, K., Comas, M., McNeill, A. T., & Stey, P. C. (2014). Autobiographical memory specificity among preschool-aged children. *Developmental Psychology, 50*, 1963–1972.

Nygaard, E., Moe, V., Slinning, K., & Walhovd, K. B. (2015). Longitudinal cognitive development of children born to mothers with opioid and polysubstance use. *Pediatric Research, 78*(3), 330–335. https://doi.org/10.1038/pr.2015.95

Nygaard, E., Slinning, K., Moe, V., Due-Tønnessen, P., Fjell, A., & Walhovd, K. B. (2018). Neuroanatomical characteristics of youths with prenatal opioid and poly-drug exposure. *Neurotoxicology and Teratology, 68*, 13–26. https://doi.org/10.1016/J.NTT.2018.04.004

O'Dea, J. A., & Yager, Z. (2011). School-based psychoeducational approaches to prevention. In I. T. F. Cash & L. Smolak (Eds.), *Body image: A handbook of science, practice, and prevention* (pp. 434–441). New York, NY: Guilford.

O'Sullivan, L. F., Cheng, M. M., Harris, K. M., & Brooks-Gunn, J. (2007). I wanna hold your hand: The progression of social, romantic and sexual events in adolescent relationships. *Perspectives on Sexual & Reproductive Health, 39*(2), 100–107. https://doi.org/10.1363/3910007

Oakes, L. M. (2010). Using habituation of looking time to assess mental processes in infancy. *Journal of Cognition & Development, 11*(3), 255–268. https://doi.org/10.1080/15248371003699977

Obeidallah, D. A., Brennan, R. T., Brooks-Gunn, J., & Earls, F. (2004). Links between pubertal timing and neighborhood contexts: Implications for girls' violent behavior. *Journal of the American Academy of Child & Adolescent Psychiatry, 43*(12), 1460–1468.

Obeidallah, D. A., Brennan, R. T., Brooks-Gunn, J., Kindlon, D., & Earls, F. (2000). Socioeconomic status, race, and girls' pubertal maturation: Results from the Project on Human Development in Chicago Neighborhoods. *Journal of Research on Adolescence (Lawrence Erlbaum), 10*(4), 443–464.

Oberauer, K., Farrell, S., Jarrold, C., & Lewandowsky, S. (2016). What limits working memory capacity? *Psychological Bulletin, 142*(7), 758–799.

Oberlander, S. E., Black, M. M., & Starr, J. R. H. (2007). African American adolescent mothers and grandmothers: A multigenerational approach to parenting. *American Journal of Community Psychology, 39*(1/2), 37–46. https://doi.org/10.1007/s10464-007-9087-2

Ochs, E., & Izquierdo, C. (2009). Responsibility in childhood: Three developmental trajectories. *Ethos, 37*(4), 391–413. https://doi.org/10.1111/j.1548-1352.2009.01066.x

Ochs, E., & Schieffein, B. (1984). Language acquisition and socialization: Three developmental stories and their implications. In R. A. Shweder & R. A. LeVine (Eds.), *Culture theory: Essays on mind, self, and emotion* (pp. 276–320). Cambridge, England: Cambridge University Press.

Oddi, K. B., Murdock, K. W., Vadnais, S., Bridgett, D. J., & Gartstein, M. A. (2013). Maternal and infant temperament characteristics as contributors to parenting stress in the first year postpartum. *Infant and Child Development, 22*(6), 553–579. https://doi.org/10.1002/icd.1813

Odibo, A. O. (2015). Amniocentesis, chorionic villus sampling, and fetal blood sampling. In A. Milunsky & J. M. Milunsky (Eds.), *Genetic disorders and the fetus* (pp. 68–97). Hoboken, NJ: John Wiley & Sons. https://doi.org/10.1002/9781118981559.ch2

Odom, S. L., Zercher, C., Li, S., Marquart, J. M., Sandall, S., & Brown, W. H. (2006). Social acceptance and rejection of preschool children with disabilities: A mixed-method analysis. *Journal of Educational Psychology, 98*(4), 807–823. https://doi.org/10.1037/0022-0663.98.4.807

Office for National Statistics. (2015). What are the top causes of death by age and gender? Retrieved from http://visual.ons.gov.uk/what-are-the-top-causes-of-death-by-age-and-gender/

Office of Juvenile Justice and Delinquency Prevention. (2014). *Statistical briefing book.* Retrieved from http://www.ojjdp.gov/ojstatbb/

Oh, J. S., & Fuligni, A. J. (2010). The role of heritage language development in the ethnic identity and family relationships of adolescents from immigrant backgrounds. *Social Development, 19*(1), 202–220. https://doi.org/10.1111/j.1467-9507.2008.00530.x

Ojodu, J., Hulihan, M. M., Pope, S. N., & Grant, A. M. (2014). Incidence of sickle cell trait — United States, 2010. *Morbidity and Mortality Weekly Report, 63*(49), 1155–1158. Retrieved from https://www.cdc.gov/mmwr/preview/mmwrhtml/mm6349a3.htm

Okagaki, L., & Sternberg, R. J. (1993). Parental beliefs and children's school performance. *Child Development, 64*, 36–56.

Oller, D. K., Eilers, R. E., & Basinger, D. (2001). Intuitive identification of infant vocal sounds by parents. *Developmental Science, 4*(1), 49–60.

Olsen, E. M. (2006). Failure to thrive: Still a problem of definition. *Clinical Pediatrics, 45*(1), 1–6.

Olson, K. R., Durwood, L., DeMeules, M., & McLaughlin, K. A. (2016). Mental health of transgender children who are supported in their identities. *Pediatrics, 137*(3), e20153223. https://doi.org/10.1542/peds.2015-3223

Olson, K. R., & Enright, E. A. (2018). Do transgender children (gender) stereotype less than their peers and siblings? *Developmental Science, 21*(4), e12606. https://doi.org/10.1111/desc.12606

Olson, K. R., Key, A. C., & Eaton, N. R. (2015). Gender cognition in transgender children. *Psychological Science, 26*(4), 467–474. https://doi.org/10.1177/0956797614568156

Olweus, D. (2013). School bullying: Development and some important challenges. *Annual Review of Clinical Psychology, 9*(1), 751–780. https://doi.org/10.1146/annurev-clinpsy-050212-185516

Olweus, D., & Limber, S. P. (2010). Bullying in school: Evaluation and dissemination of the Olweus Bullying Prevention Program. *American Journal of Orthopsychiatry, 80*(1), 124–134. https://doi.org/10.1111/j.1939-0025.2010.01015.x

Omar, H., McElderry, D., & Zakharia, R. (2003). Educating adolescents about puberty: What are we missing? *International Journal of Adolescent Medicine and Health, 15*, 79–83.

Oostenbroek, J., Suddendorf, T., Nielsen, M., Redshaw, J., Kennedy-Costantini, S., Davis, J., . . . Slaughter, V. Comprehensive longitudinal study challenges the existence of neonatal imitation in humans. *Current Biology, 26*(10), 1334–1338. https://doi.org/10.1016/j.cub.2016.03.047

Orbe, M. P. (2008). Theorizing multidimensional identity negotiation: Reflections on the lived experiences of first-generation college students. *New Directions for Child & Adolescent Development, 2008*(120), 81–95.

Orchowski, L. M., Untied, A. S., & Gidycz, C. A. (2013). Social Reactions to disclosure of sexual victimization and adjustment among survivors of sexual assault. *Journal of Interpersonal Violence, 28*(10), 2005–2023. https://doi.org/10.1177/0886260512471085

Orkin, M., May, S., & Wolf, M. (2017). How parental support during homework contributes to helpless behaviors among struggling readers. *Reading Psychology, 38*(5), 506–541. https://doi.org/10.1080/02702711.2017.1299822

Orth, U. (2017a). The family environment in early childhood has a long-term effect on self-esteem: A longitudinal study from birth to age 27 years. *Journal of Personality and Social Psychology, 114*(4), 637–655. https://doi.org/10.1037/pspp0000143

Orth, U. (2017b). The lifespan development of self-esteem. In J. Specht (Ed.), *Personality Development Across the Lifespan* (pp. 181–195). New York, NY: Elsevier. https://doi.org/10.1016/B978-0-12-804674-6.00012-0

Osborne, C., Manning, W. D., & Smock, P. J. (2007). Married and cohabiting parents' relationship stability: A focus on race and ethnicity. *Journal of Marriage & Family, 69*(5), 1345–1366.

Osher, D., Kidron, Y., Brackett, M., Dymnicki, A., Jones, S., & Weissberg, R. P. (2016). Advancing the science and practice of social and emotional learning. *Review of Research in Education, 40*(1), 644–681. https://doi.org/10.3102/0091732X16673595

Osofsky, J. D., & Chartrand, L. C. M. M. (2013). Military children from birth to five years. *The Future of Children, 23*(2), 61–77. https://doi.org/10.1353/foc.2013.0011

Ostrosky, M. M., Mouzourou, C., Dorsey, E. A., Favazza, P. C., & Leboeuf, L. M. (2015). Pick a book, any book. *Young Exceptional Children, 18*(1), 30–43. https://doi.org/10.1177/1096250613512666

Ostrov, J. M., & Godleski, S. A. (2010). Toward an integrated gender-linked model of aggression subtypes in early and middle childhood. *Psychological Review, 117*(1), 233–242. https://doi.org/10.1037/a0018070

Otgaar, H., Howe, M. L., Merckelbach, H., & Muris, P. (2018). Who is the better eyewitness? Adults and children—city research online. *Current Directions in Psychological Science.* Retrieved from http://openaccess.city.ac.uk/19272/

Ottoni-Wilhelm, M., Estell, D. B., & Perdue, N. H. (2014). Role-modeling and conversations about giving in the socialization of adolescent charitable giving and volunteering. *Journal of Adolescence, 37*(1), 53–66. https://doi.org/10.1016/j.adolescence.2013.10.010

Oulton, K., Gibson, F., Sell, D., Williams, A., Pratt, L., & Wray, J. (2016). Assent for children's participation in research: Why it matters and making it meaningful. *Child: Care, Health and Development, 42*(4), 588–597. https://doi.org/10.1111/cch.12344

Outhwaite, L. A., Gulliford, A., & Pitchford, N. J. (2017). Closing the gap: Efficacy of a tablet intervention to support the development of early mathematical skills in UK primary school children. *Computers & Education, 108*, 43–58. https://doi.org/10.1016/J.COMPEDU.2017.01.011

Oveisi, S., Eftekhare Ardabili, H., Majdzadeh, R., Mohammadkhani, P., Alaqband Rad, J., & Loo, J. (2010). Mothers' attitudes toward corporal punishment of children in Qazvin-Iran. *Journal of Family Violence, 25*(2), 159–164. https://doi.org/10.1007/s10896-009-9279-7

Owen, J. P., Marco, E. J., Desai, S., Fourie, E., Harris, J., Hill, S. S., . . . Mukherjee, P. (2013). Abnormal white matter microstructure in children with sensory processing disorders. *NeuroImage: Clinical, 2*, 844–853. https://doi.org/10.1016/J.NICL.2013.06.009

Owens, J. A. (2004). Sleep in children: Cross-cultural perspectives. *Sleep and Biological Rhythms, 2*(3), 165–173. https://doi.org/10.1111/j.1479-8425.2004.00147.x

Owens, J. A., Belon, K., & Moss, P. (2010). Impact of delaying school start time on adolescent sleep, mood, and behavior. *Archives of Pediatrics & Adolescent Medicine, 164*(7), 608–614. https://doi.org/10.1001/archpediatrics.2010.96

Owens, J. A., Dearth-Wesley, T., Herman, A. N., Oakes, J. M., & Whitaker, R. C. (2017). A quasi-experimental study of the impact of school start time changes on adolescent sleep. *Sleep Health, 3*(6), 437–443. https://doi.org/10.1016/j.sleh.2017.09.001

Owens, R. E. (2016). *Language development: An introduction*. Boston, MA: Pearson.

Owings, M., Uddin, S., & Williams, S. (2013). Trends in circumcision among male newborns born in U.S. hospitals: 1979–2010. *NCHS Health E-Stat*. Retrieved from http://www.cdc.gov/nchs/data/hestat/circumcision_2013/circumcision_2013.htm

Oxford, M. L., Gilchrist, L. D., Lohr, M. J., Gillmore, M. R., Morrison, D. M., & Spieker, S. J. (2005). Life course heterogeneity in the transition from adolescence to adulthood among adolescent mothers. *Journal of Research on Adolescence, 15*(4), 479–504.

Oyserman, D. (2016). What does a priming perspective reveal about culture? Culture-as-situated cognition. *Current Opinion in Psychology, 12*, 94–99. https://doi.org/10.1016/j.copsyc.2016.10.002

Oyserman, D. (2017). Culture three ways: Cultures and subcultures within countries. *Annual Review of Psychology, 68*(15), 1–29.

Paix, B. R., & Peterson, S. E. (2012). Circumcision of neonates and children without appropriate anaesthesia is unacceptable practice. *Anaesthesia & Intensive Care, 40*(3), 511.

Paksarian, D., Rudolph, K. E., He, J.-P., & Merikangas, K. R. (2015). School start time and adolescent sleep patterns: Results from the U.S. National Comorbidity Survey--Adolescent Supplement. *American Journal of Public Health, 105*(7), 1351–1357. https://doi.org/10.2105/AJPH.2015.302619

Palacios, J., & Brodzinsky, D. (2010). Review: Adoption research: Trends, topics, outcomes. *International Journal of Behavioral Development, 34*(3), 270–284. https://doi.org/10.1177/0165025410362837

Palacios, J., Román, M., Moreno, C., León, E., & Peñarrubia, M.-G. (2014). Differential plasticity in the recovery of adopted children after early adversity. *Child Development Perspectives, 8*(3), 169–174. https://doi.org/10.1111/cdep.12083

Paley, B., Lester, P., & Mogil, C. (2013). Family systems and ecological perspectives on the impact of deployment on military families. *Clinical Child and Family Psychology Review, 16*(3), 245–265. https://doi.org/10.1007/s10567-013-0138-y

Pallini, S., Chirumbolo, A., Morelli, M., Baiocco, R., Laghi, F., & Eisenberg, N. (2018). The relation of attachment security status to effortful self-regulation: A meta-analysis. *Psychological Bulletin, 144*(5), 501–531. https://doi.org/10.1037/bul0000134

Palmer, R. H. C., Young, S. E., Hopfer, C. J., Corley, R. P., Stallings, M. C., Crowley, T. J., & Hewitt, J. K. (2009). Developmental epidemiology of drug use and abuse in adolescence and young adulthood: Evidence of generalized risk. *Drug & Alcohol Dependence, 102*(1–3), 78–87. https://doi.org/10.1016/j.drugalcdep.2009.01.012

Paltrow, L. M., & Flavin, J. (2013). Arrests of and forced interventions on pregnant women in the United States, 1973–2005: Implications for women's legal status and public health. *Journal of Health Politics, Policy and Law, 38*(2), 299–343. https://doi.org/10.1215/03616878-1966324

Panczakiewicz, A. L., Glass, L., Coles, C. D., Kable, J. A., Sowell, E. R., Wozniak, J. R., . . . CIFASD. (2016). Neurobehavioral deficits consistent across age and sex in youth with prenatal alcohol exposure. *Alcoholism, Clinical and Experimental Research, 40*(9), 1971–1981. https://doi.org/10.1111/acer.13153

Pandita, A., Panghal, A., Gupta, G., Verma, A., Pillai, A., Singh, A., & Naranje, K. (2018). Is kangaroo mother care effective in alleviating vaccination associated pain in early infantile period? A RCT. *Early Human Development, 127*, 69–73. https://doi.org/10.1016/J.EARLHUMDEV.2018.10.001

Pantell, R. H., & Committee on Psychosocial Aspects of Child and Family Health. (2017). The child witness in the courtroom. *Pediatrics, 139*(3), e20164008. https://doi.org/10.1542/peds.2016-4008

Papadimitriou, A. (2016a). The evolution of the age at menarche from prehistorical to modern times. *Journal of Pediatric and Adolescent Gynecology, 29*(6), 527–530. https://doi.org/10.1016/j.jpag.2015.12.002

Papadimitriou, A. (2016b). Timing of puberty and secular trend in human maturation. In P. Kumanov & A. Agarwal (Eds.), *Puberty* (pp. 121–136). Cham, Switzerland: Springer International Publishing. https://doi.org/10.1007/978-3-319-32122-6_9

Papageorgiou, K. a, Smith, T. J., Wu, R., Johnson, M. H., Kirkham, N. Z., & Ronald, A. (2014). Individual differences in infant fixation duration relate to attention and behavioral control in childhood. *Psychological Science, 25*(7), 1371–1379. https://doi.org/10.1177/0956797614531295

Papousek, H. (1967). Conditioning during early postnatal development. In Y. Brackbill & G. G. Thompson (Eds.), *Behavior in infancy and early childhood* (pp. 268–284). New York, NY: Free Press.

Papoušek, M., & Papoušek, H. (1990). Excessive infant crying and intuitive parental care: Buffering support and its failures in parent-infant interaction. *Early Child Development and Care, 65*, 117–126. https://doi.org/10.1080/0300443900650114

Papp, Z., & Fekete, T. (2003). The evolving role of ultrasound in obstetrics/gynecology practice. *International Journal of Gynecology & Obstetrics, 82*(3), 339–347.

Pappas, K. B., & Migeon, C. J. (2017). Sex Chromosome Abnormalities. In D. N. Cooper (Ed.), *eLS* (pp. 1–9). Chichester, England: John Wiley & Sons Ltd. https://doi.org/10.1002/9780470015902.a0005943.pub2

Paquette, N., Lassonde, M., Vannasing, P., Tremblay, J., González-Frankenberger, B., Florea, O., . . . Gallagher, A. (2015). Developmental patterns of expressive language hemispheric lateralization in children, adolescents and adults using functional near-infrared spectroscopy. *Neuropsychologia, 68*, 117–125. https://doi.org/10.1016/J.NEUROPSYCHOLOGIA.2015.01.007

Paracchini, S., & Scerri, T. (2017). Genetics of human handedness and laterality. In L. J. Rogers & G. Vallortigara (Eds.), *Lateralized brain functions* (pp. 523–552). New York, NY: Humana Press. https://doi.org/10.1007/978-1-4939-6725-4_16

Paradise, R., & Rogoff, B. (2009). Side by side: Learning by observing and pitching in. *Ethos, 37*(1), 102–138. https://doi.org/10.1111/j.1548-1352.2009.01033.x

Parazzini, F., Cipriani, S., Bianchi, S., Bulfoni, C., Bortolus, R., & Somigliana, E. (2016). Risk of monozygotic twins after assisted reproduction: A population-based approach. *Twin Research and Human Genetics, 19*(01), 72–76. https://doi.org/10.1017/thg.2015.96

Parent, J., Sanders, W., & Forehand, R. (2016). Youth Screen time and behavioral health problems: The role of sleep duration and disturbances. *Journal of Developmental and Behavioral Pediatrics, 37*(4), 277–284. https://doi.org/10.1097/DBP.0000000000000272

Paris, R., DeVoe, E. R., Ross, A. M., & Acker, M. L. (2010). When a parent goes to war: Effects of parental deployment on very young children and implications for intervention. *American Journal of Orthopsychiatry, 80*(4), 610–618. https://doi.org/10.1111/j.1939-0025.2010.01066.x

Park, C. J., Yelland, G. W., Taffe, J. R., & Gray, K. M. (2012). Brief report: The relationship between language skills, adaptive behavior, and emotional and behavior problems in pre-schoolers with autism. *Journal of Autism and Developmental Disorders, 42*(12), 2761–2766. https://doi.org/10.1007/s10803-012-1534-8

Parks, S. E., Erck Lambert, A. B., & Shapiro-Mendoza, C. K. (2017). Racial and ethnic trends in sudden unexpected infant deaths: United States, 1995–2013. *Pediatrics, 139*(6), e20163844. https://doi.org/10.1542/peds.2016-3844

Parra, M., Hoff, E., & Core, C. (2011). Relations among language exposure, phonological memory, and language development in Spanish–English bilingually developing 2-year-olds. *Journal of Experimental Child Psychology, 108*(1), 113–125. https://doi.org/10.1016/j.jecp.2010.07.011

Parra-Cardona, J. R., Cordova, D., Holtrop, K., Villarruel, F. A., & Wieling, E. (2008). Shared ancestry, evolving stories: Similar and contrasting life experiences described by foreign born and U.S. born Latino parents. *Family Process, 47*(2), 157–172. https://doi.org/10.1111/j.1545-5300.2008.00246.x

Parten, M. (1932). Social participation among preschool children. *Journal of Abnormal and Social Psychology, 27*, 243–269.

Partridge, S., Balayla, J., Holcroft, C., & Abenhaim, H. (2012). Inadequate prenatal care utilization and risks of infant mortality and poor birth outcome: A retrospective analysis of 28,729,765 U.S. deliveries over 8 years. *American Journal of Perinatology, 29*(10), 787–794. https://doi.org/10.1055/s-0032-1316439

Paruthi, S., Brooks, L. J., D'Ambrosio, C., Hall, W. A., Kotagal, S., Lloyd, R. M., . . . Wise, M. S. (2016). Recommended Amount of sleep for pediatric populations: A consensus statement of the American Academy of Sleep Medicine. *Journal of Clinical Sleep Medicine, 12*(06), 785–786. https://doi.org/10.5664/jcsm.5866

Pascalis, O., Dechonen, S., Morton, J., Duruelle, C., & Grenet, F. (1995). Mother's face recognition in neonates: A replication and an extension. *Infant Behavior and Development, 18*, 79–85.

Pascarella, E., Bohr, L., & Nora, A. (1995). Cognitive effects of 2-year and 4-year colleges: New evidence. *Educational Evaluation and Policy Analysis, 17*(1), 83–96.

Pascoe, J. M., Wood, D. L., Duffee, J. H., & Kuo, A. (2016). Mediators and adverse effects of child poverty in the United States. *Pediatrics, 137*(4), e20160340. https://doi.org/10.1542/peds.2016-0340

Passolunghi, M. C., Rueda Ferreira, T. I., & Tomasetto, C. (2014). Math–gender stereotypes and math-related beliefs in childhood and early adolescence. *Learning and Individual Differences, 34*, 70–76. https://doi.org/10.1016/j.lindif.2014.05.005

Pate, R. R., O'Neill, J. R., Brown, W. H., Pfeiffer, K. A., Dowda, M., & Addy, C. L. (2015). Prevalence of compliance with a new physical activity guideline for preschool-age children. *Childhood Obesity (Print), 11*(4), 415–420. https://doi.org/10.1089/chi.2014.0143

Patel, S., Gaylord, S., & Fagen, J. (2013). Generalization of deferred imitation in 6-, 9-, and 12-month-old infants using visual and auditory contexts. *Infant Behavior and Development, 36*(1), 25–31. https://doi.org/10.1016/J.INFBEH.2012.09.006

Patenaude, Y., Pugash, D., Lim, K., Morin, L., Lim, K., Bly, S., . . . Salem, S. (2014). The use of magnetic resonance imaging in the obstetric patient. *Journal of Obstetrics and Gynaecology Canada, 36*(4), 349–355. https://doi.org/10.1016/S1701-2163(15)30612-5

Patterson, C. J. (2017). Parents' sexual orientation and children's development. *Child Development Perspectives, 11*(1), 45–49. https://doi.org/10.1111/cdep.12207

Patton, L. D., Renn, K. A., Guido-DiBrito, F., & Quaye, S. J. (2016). *Student development in college: Theory, research, and practice*. New York, NY: Wiley.

Paulsen, D. J., Hallquist, M. N., Geier, C. F., & Luna, B. (2014). Effects of incentives, age, and behavior on brain activation during inhibitory control: A longitudinal fMRI study. *Developmental Cognitive Neuroscience, 11*, 105–115. https://doi.org/10.1016/j.dcn.2014.09.003

Paulus, M., & Moore, C. (2014). The development of recipient-dependent sharing behavior and sharing expectations in preschool children. *Developmental Psychology, 50*(3), 914–921. https://doi.org/10.1037/a0034169

Paulussen-Hoogeboom, M. C., Stams, G. J. J. M., Hermanns, J. M. A., & Peetsma, T. T. D. (2007). Child negative emotionality and parenting from infancy to preschool: A meta-analytic review. *Developmental Psychology, 43*(2), 438–453. https://doi.org/10.1037/0012-1649.43.2.438

Pavarini, G., Hollanda Souza, D., & Hawk, C. K. (2012). Parental practices and theory of mind development. *Journal of Child and Family Studies, 22*(6), 844–853. https://doi.org/10.1007/s10826-012-9643-8

Pavone, V., Lionetti, E., Gargano, V., Evola, F. R., Costarella, L., & Sessa, G. (2011). Growing pains: A study of 30 cases and a review of the literature. *Journal of Pediatric Orthopedics, 31*(5), 606–609. https://doi.org/10.1097/BPO.0b013e318220ba5e

Payne, V. G., & Isaacs, L. D. (2016). *Human motor development: A lifespan approach*. New York, NY: McGraw-Hill. Retrieved from http://dl.acm.org/citation.cfm?id=1214267

Pazol, K., Whiteman, M. K., Folger, S. G., Kourtis, A. P., Marchbanks, P. A., & Jamieson, D. J. (2015). Sporadic contraceptive use and nonuse: Age-specific prevalence and associated factors. *American Journal of Obstetrics and Gynecology, 212*(3), 324.e1-8. https://doi.org/10.1016/j.ajog.2014.10.004

Pearson, R. M., Lightman, S. L., & Evans, J. (2009). Emotional sensitivity for motherhood: Late pregnancy is associated with enhanced accuracy to encode emotional faces. *Hormones and Behavior, 56*(5), 557–563. https://doi.org/10.1016/j.yhbeh.2009.09.013

Pecker, L. H., & Little, J. (2018). Clinical manifestations of sickle cell disease across the lifespan. In E. R. Meier, A. Abraham, & R. M. Fasano (Eds.), *Sickle cell disease and hematopoietic stem cell transplantation* (pp. 3–39). Cham, Switzerland: Springer International Publishing. https://doi.org/10.1007/978-3-319-62328-3_1

Peeters, M., Janssen, T., Monshouwer, K., Boendermaker, W., Pronk, T., Wiers, R., & Vollebergh, W. (2015). Weaknesses in executive functioning predict the initiating of adolescents' alcohol use. *Developmental Cognitive Neuroscience, 16*, 139–146. https://doi.org/10.1016/j.dcn.2015.04.003

Pelaez, M., Virues-Ortega, J., & Gewirtz, J. L. (2011). Reinforcement of vocalizations through contingent vocal imitation. *Journal of Applied Behavior Analysis, 44*(1), 33–40. https://doi.org/10.1901/jaba.2011.44-33

Pellegrini, A. D. (2013). Play. In P. D. Zelazo (Ed.), *The Oxford handbook of developmental psychology: Vol. 2. Self and Other* (pp. 276–299). New York, NY: Oxford University Press. https://doi.org/10.1093/oxfordhb/9780199958474.013.0012

Pellegrini, A. D., & Roseth, C. J. (2006). Relational aggression and relationships in preschoolers: A discussion of methods, gender differences, and function. *Journal of Applied Developmental Psychology, 27*(3), 269–276.

Pemberton Roben, C. K., Bass, A. J., Moore, G. A., Murray-Kolb, L., Tan, P. Z., Gilmore, R. O., . . . Teti, L. O. (2012). Let me go: The influences of crawling experience and temperament on the development of anger expression. *Infancy, 17*(5), 558–577. https://doi.org/10.1111/j.1532-7078.2011.00092.x

Peng, P., Barnes, M., Wang, C., Wang, W., Li, S., Swanson, H. L., . . . Tao, S. (2018). A meta-analysis on the relation between reading and working memory. *Psychological Bulletin, 144*(1), 48–76. https://doi.org/10.1037/bul0000124

Penke, L., & Jokela, M. (2016). The evolutionary genetics of personality revisited. *Current Opinion in Psychology, 7*, 104–109. https://doi.org/10.1016/J.COPSYC.2015.08.021

Peralta, L., Rowling, L., Samdal, O., Hipkins, R., & Dudley, D. (2017). Conceptualising a new approach to adolescent health literacy. *Health Education Journal, 76*(7), 787-801. https://doi.org/10.1177/0017896917714812

Pérez-Fuentes, G., Olfson, M., Villegas, L., Morcillo, C., Wang, S., & Blanco, C. (2013). Prevalence and correlates of child sexual abuse: A national study. *Comprehensive Psychiatry, 54*(1), 16–27. https://doi.org/10.1016/j.comppsych.2012.05.010

Pérez-González, A., Guilera, G., Pereda, N., & Jarne, A. (2017). Protective factors promoting resilience in the relation between child sexual victimization and internalizing and externalizing symptoms. *Child Abuse & Neglect, 72*, 393–403. https://doi.org/10.1016/J.CHIABU.2017.09.006

Perlman, S. B., Huppert, T. J., & Luna, B. (2016). Functional near-infrared spectroscopy evidence for development of prefrontal engagement in working memory in early through middle childhood. *Cerebral Cortex, 26*(6), 2790–2799. https://doi.org/10.1093/cercor/bhv139

Perone, S., Almy, B., & Zelazo, P. D. (2018). Toward an understanding of the neural basis of executive function development. In R. Gibb & B. Kolb (Eds.), *The neurobiology of brain and behavioral development* (pp. 291–314). New York, NY: Elsevier. https://doi.org/10.1016/B978-0-12-804036-2.00011-X

Perren, S., Ettekal, I., & Ladd, G. (2013). The impact of peer victimization on later maladjustment: Mediating and moderating effects of hostile and self-blaming attributions. *Journal of Child Psychology and Psychiatry, and Allied Disciplines, 54*(1), 46–55. https://doi.org/10.1111/j.1469-7610.2012.02618.x

Perrin, E. C., & Siegel, B. S. (2013). Promoting the well-being of children whose parents are gay or lesbian. *Pediatrics, 131*(4), e1374-83. https://doi.org/10.1542/peds.2013-0377

Perry, L. K. (2015). To have and to hold: Looking vs. touching in the study of categorization. *Frontiers in Psychology, 6*, 178. https://doi.org/10.3389/fpsyg.2015.00178

Perry, W. G. (1970). *Forms of intellectual and ethical development in the college years: A scheme*. San Francisco, CA: Jossey-Bass.

Perszyk, D. R., & Waxman, S. R. (2018). Linking language and cognition in infancy. *Annual Review of Psychology, 69*(1), 231–250. https://doi.org/10.1146/annurev-psych-122216-011701

Pesu, L., Viljaranta, J., & Aunola, K. (2016). The role of parents' and teachers' beliefs in children's self-concept development. *Journal of Applied Developmental Psychology, 44*, 63–71. https://doi.org/10.1016/j.appdev.2016.03.001

Peter, C. J., Fischer, L. K., Kundakovic, M., Garg, P., Jakovcevski, M., Dincer, A., . . . Akbarian, S. (2016). DNA methylation signatures of early childhood malnutrition associated with impairments in attention and cognition. *Biological Psychiatry, 80*(10), 765–774.

https://doi.org/10.1016/J.BIOPSYCH.2016.03.2100

Peter, V., Kalashnikova, M., Santos, A., & Burnham, D. (2016). Mature neural responses to infant-directed speech but not adult-directed speech in pre-verbal infants. *Scientific Reports, 6*, 34273. https://doi.org/10.1038/srep34273

Peterson, R. L., & Pennington, B. F. (2012). Developmental dyslexia. *Lancet, 379*(9830), 1997–2007. https://doi.org/10.1016/S0140-6736(12)60198-6

Petitto, L. A., Berens, M. S., Kovelman, I., Dubins, M. H., Jasinska, K., & Shalinsky, M. (2012). The "Perceptual Wedge Hypothesis" as the basis for bilingual babies' phonetic processing advantage: New insights from fNIRS brain imaging. *Brain and Language, 121*(2), 130–143. https://doi.org/10.1016/j.bandl.2011.05.003

Petteway, R. J., Valerio, M. A., & Patel, M. R. (2011). What about your friends? Exploring asthma-related peer interactions. *Journal of Asthma, 48*(4), 393–399. https://doi.org/10.3109/02770903.2011.563807

Petursdottir, A. I., & Mellor, J. R. (2017). Reinforcement contingencies in language acquisition. *Policy Insights from the Behavioral and Brain Sciences, 4*(1), 25–32. https://doi.org/10.1177/2372732216686083

Pew Research Center. (2015). Parenting in America: The American family today. *Pew Research Center Social & Demographic Trends*. Retrieved from http://www.pewsocialtrends.org/2015/12/17/1-the-american-family-today/

Pexman, P. M. (2014). Nonliteral language use. In P. J. Brooks & V. Kempe (Eds.), *Encyclopedia of language development*. Thousand Oaks, CA: Sage. https://doi.org/10.4135/9781483346441.n132

Pezaro, N., Doody, J. S., & Thompson, M. B. (2017). The ecology and evolution of temperature-dependent reaction norms for sex determination in reptiles: A mechanistic conceptual model. *Biological Reviews, 92*(3), 1348–1364. https://doi.org/10.1111/brv.12285

Pfeifer, J. H., & Peake, S. J. (2012). Self-development: Integrating cognitive, socioemotional, and neuroimaging perspectives. *Developmental Cognitive Neuroscience, 2*(1), 55–69. https://doi.org/10.1016/j.dcn.2011.07.012

Pfeifer, J. H., Kahn, L. E., Merchant, J. S., Peake, S. J., Veroude, K., Masten, C. L., . . . Dapretto, M. (2013). Longitudinal change in the neural bases of adolescent social self-evaluations: Effects of age and pubertal development. *Journal of Neuroscience, 33*(17), 7415–7419. https://doi.org/10.1523/JNEUROSCI.4074-12.2013

Pfeifer, J. H., Lieberman, M. D., & Dapretto, M. (2007). "I know you are but what am I?!": Neural bases of self- and social knowledge retrieval in children and adults. *Journal of Cognitive Neuroscience, 19*(8), 1323–1337. https://doi.org/10.1162/jocn.2007.19.8.1323

Pfeiffer, S. I. (2012). Current perspectives on the identification and assessment of gifted students. *Journal of Psychoeducational Assessment, 30*(1), 3–9. https://doi.org/10.1177/0734282911428192

Phillips, D., Gormley, W., & Anderson, S. (2016). The effects of Tulsa's CAP Head Start program on middle-school academic outcomes and progress. *Developmental Psychology, 52*(8), 1247–1261. https://doi.org/10.1037/dev0000151

Phinney, J. S., & Ong, A. D. (2007). Conceptualization and measurement of ethnic identity: Current status and future directions. *Journal of Counseling Psychology, 54*(3), 271–281. https://doi.org/10.1037/0022-067.54.3.271

Piaget, J. (1929). *The child's conception of the world*. London, England: Routledge & Kegan Paul.

Piaget, J. (1932). *The moral judgment of the child*. New York, NY: Harcourt Brace.

Piaget, J. (1952). *The origins of intelligence in children*. New York, NY: International Universities Press. (Original work published in 1936)

Piaget, J. (1962). *Play, dreams, and imitation in childhood*. New York, NY: Norton.

Piaget, J. (1972). Intellectual evolution from adolescence to adulthood. *Human Development, 51*(1), 40–47. https://doi.org/10.1159/000112531

Piaget, J., & Inhelder, B. (1967). *The child's conception of space*. New York, NY: Norton.

Piantadosi, S. T., & Cantlon, J. F. (2017). True numerical cognition in the wild. *Psychological Science, 28*(4), 462–469. https://doi.org/10.1177/0956797616686862

Picci, G., & Scherf, K. S. (2016). From caregivers to peers. *Psychological Science, 27*(11), 1461–1473. https://doi.org/10.1177/0956797616663142

Piccolo, L. R., Merz, E. C., & Noble, K. G. (2018). School climate is associated with cortical thickness and executive function in children and adolescents. *Developmental Science*, e12719. https://doi.org/10.1111/desc.12719

Piek, J. P., Dawson, L., Smith, L. M., & Gasson, N. (2008). The role of early fine and gross motor development on later motor and cognitive ability. *Human Movement Science, 27*(5), 668–681. https://doi.org/10.1016/j.humov.2007.11.002

Piercy, K. L., Troiano, R. P., Ballard, R. M., Carlson, S. A., Fulton, J. E., Galuska, D. A., . . . Olson, R. D. (2018). The physical activity guidelines for Americans. *JAMA, 320*(19), 2020–2028.

Pierrehumbert, B., Nicole, A., Muller-Nix, C., Forcada-Guex, M., & Ansermet, F. (2003). Parental post-traumatic reactions after premature birth: Implications for sleeping and eating problems in the infant. *Archives of Disease in Childhood: Fetal and Neonatal Edition, 88*(5), 400F–404F. https://doi.org/10.1136/fn.88.5.F400

Pieters, S., Burk, W. J., Van der Vorst, H., Dahl, R. E., Wiers, R. W., & Engels, R. C. M. E. (2015). Prospective relationships between sleep problems and substance use, internalizing and externalizing problems. *Journal of Youth and Adolescence, 44*(2), 379–388. https://doi.org/10.1007/s10964-014-0213-9

Pike, A., & Oliver, B. R. (2017). Child behavior and sibling relationship quality: A cross-lagged analysis. *Journal of Family Psychology, 31*(2), 250–255. https://doi.org/10.1037/fam0000248

Pike, G. R., & Kuh, G. D. (2005). First- and second-generation college students: A comparison of their engagement and intellectual development. *Journal of Higher Education, 76*(3), 276–300.

Pike, K. M., Hoek, H. W., & Dunne, P. E. (2014). Cultural trends and eating disorders. *Current Opinion in Psychiatry, 27*(6), 436–442. https://doi.org/10.1097/YCO.0000000000000100

Pillow, B. H. (2008). Development of children's understanding of cognitive activities. *Journal of Genetic Psychology, 169*(4), 297–321.

Pinderhughes, E. E., Zhang, X., & Agerbak, S. (2015). "American" or "multiethnic"? Family ethnic identity among transracial adoptive families, ethnic-racial socialization, and children's self-perception. *New Directions for Child and Adolescent Development, 2015*(150), 5–18. https://doi.org/10.1002/cad.20118

Pinquart, M. (2017). Associations of parenting dimensions and styles with externalizing problems of children and adolescents: An updated meta-analysis. *Developmental Psychology, 53*(5), 873–932. https://doi.org/10.1037/dev0000295

Pinquart, M., Feußner, C., & Ahnert, L. (2013). Meta-analytic evidence for stability in attachments from infancy to early adulthood. *Attachment & Human Development, 15*(2), 189–218. https://doi.org/10.1080/14616734.2013.746257

Piotrowski, J. T., Lapierre, M. A., & Linebarger, D. L. (2013). Investigating correlates of self-regulation in early childhood with a representative sample of English-speaking American families. *Journal of Child and Family Studies, 22*(3), 423–436. https://doi.org/10.1007/s10826-012-9595-z

Piquero, A. R., & Moffitt, T. E. (2013). Moffitt's developmental taxonomy of antisocial behavior. In G. Bruinsma & D. Weisburd (Eds.), *Encyclopedia of criminology and criminal justice* (pp. 3121–3127). New York, NY: Springer.

Pison, G., Monden, C., & Smits, J. (2015). Twinning rates in developed countries: Trends and explanations. *Population and Development Review, 41*(4), 629–649. https://doi.org/10.1111/j.1728-4457.2015.00088.x

Planalp, E. M., Van Hulle, C., Lemery-Chalfant, K., & Goldsmith, H. H. (2017). Genetic and environmental contributions to the development of positive affect in infancy. *Emotion, 17*(3), 412–420. https://doi.org/10.1037/emo0000238

Plöderl, M., Wagenmakers, E.-J., Tremblay, P., Ramsay, R., Kralovec, K., Fartacek, C., & Fartacek, R. (2013). Suicide risk and sexual orientation: A critical review. *Archives of Sexual Behavior, 42*(5), 715–727. https://doi.org/10.1007/s10508-012-0056-y

Plomin, R, & Deary, I. J. (2015). Genetics and intelligence differences: Five special findings. *Molecular Psychiatry, 20*(1), 98–108. https://doi.org/10.1038/mp.2014.105

Plomin, R., & Spinath, F. M. (2004). Intelligence: Genetics, genes, and genomics. *Journal of Personality & Social Psychology, 86*(1), 112–129. https://doi.org/10.1037/0022-3514.86.1.112

Plomin, R., DeFries, J. C., Knopik, V. S., & Neiderhiser, J. M. (2013). *Behavioral genetics* (6th ed.). New York, NY: Worth.

Plomin, R., DeFries, J. C., Knopik, V. S., & Neiderhiser, J. M. (2016). Top 10 replicated findings from behavioral genetics. *Perspectives on Psychological Science, 11*(1), 3–23. https://doi.org/10.1177/1745691615617439

Pluess, M. (2015). Individual differences in environmental sensitivity. *Child Development*

Perspectives, *9*(3), 138–143. https://doi.org/10.1111/cdep.12120

Pluess, M., Birkbeck, J. B., & Belsky, J. (2010). Differential susceptibility to parenting and quality child care. *Developmental Psychology*, *46*(2), 379–390. https://doi.org/10.1037/a0015203

Poehlmann, J., Schwichtenberg, A. J. M., Shlafer, R. J., Hahn, E., Bianchi, J.-P., & Warner, R. (2011). Emerging self-regulation in toddlers born preterm or low birth weight: Differential susceptibility to parenting? *Development & Psychopathology*, *23*(1), 177–193. https://doi.org/10.1017/s0954579410000726

Poirel, N., Borst, G. G., Simon, G., Rossi, S., Cassotti, M., Pineau, A., . . . Jouvent, R. (2012). Number conservation is related to children's prefrontal inhibitory control: An fMRI study of a Piagetian task. *PLoS ONE*, *7*(7), e40802. https://doi.org/10.1371/journal.pone.0040802

Poitras, V. J., Gray, C. E., Borghese, M. M., Carson, V., Chaput, J.-P., Janssen, I., . . . Tremblay, M. S. (2016). Systematic review of the relationships between objectively measured physical activity and health indicators in school-aged children and youth. *Applied Physiology, Nutrition, and Metabolism*, *41*(6 Suppl. 3), S197–S239. https://doi.org/10.1139/apnm-2015-0663

Pollack, A., & McNeil, D. G., Jr. (2013). In medical first, a baby with H.I.V. is deemed cured. *New York Times*. Retrieved from http://www.nytimes.com/2013/03/04/health/for-firsttime-baby-cured-of-hivdoctors-say.html?pagewanted=all&_r=0

Pomerantz, E. M., & Dong, W. (2006). Effects of mothers' perceptions of children's competence: The moderating role of mothers' theories of competence. *Developmental Psychology*, *42*(5), 950–961. https://doi.org/10.1037/0012-1649.42.5.950

Pomerantz, E. M., Ng, F. F.-Y., Cheung, C. S.-S., & Qu, Y. (2014). Raising happy children who succeed in school: Lessons from China and the United States. *Child Development Perspectives*, *8*(2), 71–76. https://doi.org/10.1111/cdep.12063

Pomerantz, E. M., & Saxon, J. L. (2001). Conceptions of ability as stable and self-evaluative processes: A longitudinal examination. *Child Development*, *72*(1), 152–173. https://doi.org/10.1111/1467-8624.00271

Pompili, M., Lester, D., Forte, A., Seretti, M. E., Erbuto, D., Lamis, D. A., . . . Girardi, P. (2014). Bisexuality and suicide: A systematic review of the current literature. *Journal of Sexual Medicine*, *11*(8), 1903–1913. https://doi.org/10.1111/jsm.12581

Poole, D. A., & White, L. T. (1991). Effects of question repetition on the eyewitness testimony of children and adults. *Developmental Psychology*, *27*, 975–986.

Poole, D. A., & White, L. T. (1993). Two years later: Effects of question repetition and retention interval on the eyewitness testimony of children and adults. *Developmental Psychology*, *29*, 844–853.

Popova, S., Lange, S., Probst, C., Parunashvili, N., & Rehm, J. (2017). Prevalence of alcohol consumption during pregnancy and fetal alcohol spectrum disorders among the general and Aboriginal populations in Canada and the United States. *European Journal of Medical Genetics*, *60*(1), 32–48. Retrieved from https://www.sciencedirect.com/science/article/pii/S1769721216303159

Poppen, P. (1974). Sex differences in moral judgment. *Personality and Social Psychology Bulletin*, *1*(1), 313–315. https://doi.org/10.1177/014616727400100106

Portnow, L. H., Vaillancourt, D. E., & Okun, M. S. (2013). The history of cerebral PET scanning: From physiology to cutting-edge technology. *Neurology*, *80*(10), 952–956. https://doi.org/10.1212/WNL.0b013e318285c135

Posadas, D. M., & Carthew, R. W. (2014). MicroRNAs and their roles in developmental canalization. *Current Opinion in Genetics & Development*, *27*, 1–6. https://doi.org/10.1016/j.gde.2014.03.005

Posner, M. I. (2001). The developing human brain. *Developmental Science*, *4*(3), 253–387.

Posner, M. I., & Rothbart, M. K. (2018). Temperament and brain networks of attention. *Philosophical Transactions of the Royal Society of London. Series B, Biological Sciences*, *373*(1744), 20170254. https://doi.org/10.1098/rstb.2017.0254

Potegal, M., Robison, S., Anderson, F., Jordan, C., & Shapiro, E. (2007). Sequence and priming in 15 month-olds' reactions to brief arm restraint: Evidence for a hierarchy of anger responses. *Aggressive Behavior*, *33*(6), 508–518. https://doi.org/10.1002/ab.20207

Potter, D. (2010). Psychosocial well-being and the relationship between divorce and children's academic achievement. *Journal of Marriage & Family*, *72*(4), 933–946. https://doi.org/10.1111/j.1741-3737.2010.00740.x

Poulin, F., & Chan, A. (2010). Friendship stability and change in childhood and adolescence. *Developmental Review*, *30*(3), 257–272. https://doi.org/10.1016/j.dr.2009.01.001

Powell, S. D. (2019). *Your introduction to education: Explorations in teaching*. New York, NY: Pearson.

Power, F. C., Higgins, A., & Kohlberg, L. (1989). *Lawrence Kohlberg's approach to moral education*. New York, NY: Columbia University Press.

Pozzoli, T., Gini, G., & Vieno, A. (2012). The role of individual correlates and class norms in defending and passive bystanding behavior in bullying: A multilevel analysis. *Child Development*, *83*(6), 1917–1931. https://doi.org/10.1111/j.1467-8624.2012.01831.x

Prady, S. L., Kiernan, K., Fairley, L., Wilson, S., & Wright, J. (2014). Self-reported maternal parenting style and confidence and infant temperament in a multi-ethnic community: Results from the Born in Bradford cohort. *Journal of Child Health Care*, *18*(1), 31–46. https://doi.org/10.1177/1367493512473855

Prakalapakorn, S. G., Meaney-Delman, D., Honein, M. A., & Rasmussen, S. A. (2017). The eyes as a window to improved understanding of the prenatal effects of Zika virus infection. *Journal of AAPOS*, *21*(4), 259–261. https://doi.org/10.1016/j.jaapos.2017.07.001

Pratt, M. W., Hunsberger, B., Pancer, S. M., & Alisat, S. (2003). A longitudinal analysis of personal values socialization: Correlates of a moral self-ideal in late adolescence. *Social Development*, *12*(4), 563–585. https://doi.org/10.1111/1467-9507.00249

Prechtl, H. F. R. (1974). The behavioural states of the newborn infant (a review). *Brain Research*, *76*(2), 185–212. https://doi.org/10.1016/0006-8993(74)90454-5

Preckel, F., Niepel, C., Schneider, M., & Brunner, M. (2013). Self-concept in adolescence: A longitudinal study on reciprocal effects of self-perceptions in academic and social domains. *Journal of Adolescence*, *36*(6), 1165–1175. https://doi.org/10.1016/j.adolescence.2013.09.001

Prenoveau, J. M., Craske, M. G., West, V., Giannakakis, A., Zioga, M., Lehtonen, A., . . . Stein, A. (2017). Maternal postnatal depression and anxiety and their association with child emotional negativity and behavior problems at two years. *Developmental Psychology*, *53*(1), 50–62. https://doi.org/10.1037/dev0000221

Previc, F. H. (1991). A general theory concerning the prenatal origins of cerebral lateralization in humans. *Psychological Review*, *98*(3), 299–334. https://doi.org/10.1037/0033-295x.98.3.299

Priel, B., & deSchonen, S. (1986). Self-recognition: A study of a population without mirrors. *Journal of Experimental Child Psychology*, *41*, 237–250.

Priess, H. A., & Lindberg, S. M. (2016). Gender intensification. In R. J. R. Levesque (Ed.), *Encyclopedia of adolescence* (pp. 1135–1142). New York, NY: Springer. https://doi.org/10.1007/978-1-4419-1695-2_391

Priess, H. A., Lindberg, S. M., & Hyde, J. S. (2009). Adolescent gender-role identity and mental health: Gender intensification revisited. *Child Development*, *80*(5), 1531–1544. https://doi.org/10.1111/j.1467-8624.2009.01349.x

Procianoy, R. S., Mendes, E. W., & Silveira, R. C. (2010). Massage therapy improves neurodevelopment outcome at two years corrected age for very low birth weight infants. *Early Human Development*, *86*(1), 7–11. https://doi.org/10.1016/j.earlhumdev.2009.12.001

Przybylski, A. K. (2019). Digital screen time and pediatric sleep: Evidence from a preregistered cohort study. *Journal of Pediatrics*, *205*, 218–223.e1. https://doi.org/10.1016/J.JPEDS.2018.09.054

Przybylski, A. K., & Weinstein, N. (2019). Digital screen time limits and young children's psychological well-being: Evidence from a population-based study. *Child Development*, *90*(1), e56. https://doi.org/10.1111/cdev.13007

Pulgarón, E. R. (2013). Childhood obesity: A review of increased risk for physical and psychological comorbidities. *Clinical Therapeutics*, *35*(1), A18–A32. https://doi.org/10.1016/j.clinthera.2012.12.014

Punamäki, R.-L., Palosaari, E., Diab, M., Peltonen, K., & Qouta, S. R. (2014). Trajectories of posttraumatic stress symptoms (PTSS) after major war among Palestinian children: Trauma, family- and child-related predictors. *Journal of Affective Disorders*, *172C*, 133–140. https://doi.org/10.1016/j.jad.2014.09.021

Qiu, A., Mori, S., & Miller, M. I. (2015). Diffusion tensor imaging for understanding brain development in early life. *Annual Review of Psychology*, *66*(1), 853–876. https://doi.org/10.1146/annurev-psych-010814-015340

Quane, J. M., & Rankin, B. H. (2006). Does it pay to participate? Neighborhood-based organizations and the social development of urban adolescents. *Children & Youth Services Review, 28*, 1229–1250.

Quek, Y.-H., Tam, W. W. S., Zhang, M. W. B., & Ho, R. C. M. (2017). Exploring the association between childhood and adolescent obesity and depression: A meta-analysis. *Obesity Reviews, 18*(7), 742–754. https://doi.org/10.1111/obr.12535

Quinn, M., & Hennessy, E. (2010). Peer relationships across the preschool to school transition. *Early Education & Development, 21*(6), 825–842. https://doi.org/10.1080/10409280903329013

Quinn, P. C. (2016). Establishing cognitive organization in infancy. In L. Balter & C. S. Tamis-LeMonda (Eds.), *Child psychology: A handbook of contemporary issues*. Philadelphia, PA: Psychology Press.

Quinn, P. C., Doran, M. M., Reiss, J. E., & Hoffman, J. E. (2010). Neural markers of subordinate-level categorization in 6- to 7-month-old infants. *Developmental Science, 13*(3), 499–507. https://doi.org/10.1111/j.1467-7687.2009.00903.x

Quinn, P. C., Eimas, P. D., & Rosenkrantz, S. L. (1993). Evidence for representations of perceptual similar natural categories by 3 and 4 month old infants. *Perception, 22*, 463–475.

Quinn, P. C., Lee, K., & Pascalis, O. (2018). Perception of face race by infants: Five developmental changes. *Child Development Perspectives, 12*(3), 204–209. https://doi.org/10.1111/cdep.12286

Quinn, P. C., Lee, K., & Pascalis, O. (2019). Face processing in infancy and beyond: The case of social categories. *Annual Review of Psychology, 70*(1), 165–189. https://doi.org/10.1146/annurev-psych-010418-102753

Quinn, P. C., & Liben, L. S. (2014). A sex difference in mental rotation in infants: Convergent evidence. *Infancy, 19*(1), 103–116. https://doi.org/10.1111/infa.12033

Quinn, P. C., Yahr, J., Kuhn, A., Slater, A. M., & Pascalis, O. (2002). Representation of the gender of human faces by infants: A preference for female. *Perception, 31*(9), 1109–1121. https://doi.org/10.1068/p3331

Raab, C. (2017). Failure to thrive (FTT). *Merck Manual*. Retrieved from https://www.merckmanuals.com/professional/pediatrics/miscellaneous-disorders-in-infants-and-children/failure-to-thrive-ftt

Raby, K. L., Steele, R. D., Carlson, E. A., & Sroufe, L. A. (2015). Continuities and changes in infant attachment patterns across two generations. *Attachment & Human Development, 17*(4), 414–428. https://doi.org/10.1080/14616734.2015.1067824

Racine, E. F., Frick, K., Guthrie, J. F., & Strobino, D. (2009). Individual net-benefit maximization: A model for understanding breastfeeding cessation among low-income women. *Maternal & Child Health Journal, 13*(2), 241–249. https://doi.org/10.1007/s10995-008-0337-1

Radvansky, G. A. (2017). *Human memory*. New York, NY: Routledge. https://doi.org/10.4324/9781315542768

Raevuori, A., Keski-Rahkonen, A., & Hoek, H. W. (2014). A review of eating disorders in males. *Current Opinion in Psychiatry, 27*(6), 426–430. https://doi.org/10.1097/YCO.0000000000000113

Raffaeli, G., Cavallaro, G., Allegaert, K., Wildschut, E. D., Fumagalli, M., Agosti, M., . . . Mosca, F. (2017). Neonatal abstinence syndrome: Update on diagnostic and therapeutic strategies. *Pharmacotherapy, 37*(7), 814–823. https://doi.org/10.1002/phar.1954

Raffaelli, M., & Ontai, L. L. (2004). Gender socialization in Latino/a families: Results from two retrospective studies. *Sex Roles, 50*(5/6), 287–299. https://doi.org/10.1023/B:SERS.0000018886.58945.06

Rafferty, Y., Griffin, K. W., & Lodise, M. (2011). Adolescent motherhood and developmental outcomes of children in early Head Start: The influence of maternal parenting behaviors, well-being, and risk factors within the family setting. *American Journal of Orthopsychiatry, 81*(2), 228–245. https://doi.org/10.1111/j.1939-0025.2011.01092.x

Raftery, J. N., Grolnick, W. S., & Flamm, E. S. (2012). Families as facilitators of student engagement: Toward a home-school partnership model. In S. L. Christenson, A. L. Reschly, & C. Wylie (Eds.), *Handbook of research on student engagement* (pp. 343–364). Boston, MA: Springer. https://doi.org/10.1007/978-1-4614-2018-7_16

Ragelienė, T. (2016). Links of adolescents identity development and relationship with peers: A systematic literature review. *Journal of the Canadian Academy of Child and Adolescent Psychiatry, 25*(2), 97–105. Retrieved from http://www.ncbi.nlm.nih.gov/pubmed/27274745

Rai, R., Mitchell, P., Kadar, T., & Mackenzie, L. (2016). Adolescent egocentrism and the illusion of transparency: Are adolescents as egocentric as we might think? *Current Psychology, 35*(3), 285–294. https://doi.org/10.1007/s12144-014-9293-7

Rainwater-Lovett, K., Luzuriaga, K., & Persaud, D. (2015). Very early combination antiretroviral therapy in infants: Prospects for cure. *Current Opinion in HIV and AIDS, 10*, 4–11. https://doi.org/10.1097/COH.0000000000000127

Rajendran, K., Kruszewski, E., & Halperin, J. M. (2016). Parenting style influences bullying: A longitudinal study comparing children with and without behavioral problems. *Journal of Child Psychology and Psychiatry, 57*(2), 188–195. https://doi.org/10.1111/jcpp.12433

Rakhlin, N., Hein, S., Doyle, N., Hart, L., Macomber, L., Ruchkin, V., . . . Grigorenko, E. L. (2015). Language development of internationally adopted children: Adverse early experiences outweigh the age of acquisition effect. *Journal of Communication Disorders, 57*, 66–80.

Rakison, D. H., & Butterworth, G. E. (1998). Infants' use of object parts in early categorization. *Developmental Psychology, 34*, 49–62.

Rakoczy, H., Warneken, F., & Tomasello, M. (2007). "This way!" "No! That way!" 3-year olds know that two people can have mutually incompatible desires. *Cognitive Development, 22*(1), 47–68.

Ram, G., & Chinen, J. (2011). Infections and immunodeficiency in Down syndrome. *Clinical and Experimental Immunology, 164*(1), 9–16. https://doi.org/10.1111/j.1365-2249.2011.04335.x

Ramey, C. T., & Ramey, S. L. (1998). Prevention of intellectual disabilities: Early interventions to improve cognitive development. Preventive Medicine, 27, 224–232.

Ramírez-Esparza, N., García-Sierra, A., & Kuhl, P. K. (2017). The Impact of early social interactions on later language development in Spanish-English bilingual infants. *Child Development, 88*(4), 1216–1234. https://doi.org/10.1111/cdev.12648

Ramos, D. K., & Melo, H. M. (2019). Can digital games in school improve attention? A study of Brazilian elementary school students. *Journal of Computers in Education, 6*(1), 5–19. https://doi.org/10.1007/s40692-018-0111-3

Ramsdell, H. L., Oller, D. K., Buder, E. H., Ethington, C. A., & Chorna, L. (2012). Identification of prelinguistic phonological categories. *Journal of Speech, Language, and Hearing Research, 55*(6), 1626–1639. https://doi.org/10.1044/1092-4388(2012/11-0250)

Ramus, F. (2014). Neuroimaging sheds new light on the phonological deficit in dyslexia. *Trends in Cognitive Sciences, 18*(6), 274–275. https://doi.org/10.1016/j.tics.2014.01.009

Rangmar, J., Hjern, A., Vinnerljung, B., Strömland, K., Aronson, M., & Fahlke, C. (2015). Psychosocial outcomes of fetal alcohol syndrome in adulthood. *Pediatrics, 135*(1), e52-8. https://doi.org/10.1542/peds.2014-1915

Rapin, I. (2016). Dyscalculia and the calculating brain. *Pediatric Neurology, 61*, 11–20. https://doi.org/10.1016/j.pediatrneurol.2016.02.007

Raspa, M., Wheeler, A. C., & Riley, C. (2017). Public health literature review of fragile X syndrome. *Pediatrics, 139*(Suppl. 3), S153–S171. https://doi.org/10.1542/peds.2016-1159C

Ratnarajah, N., Rifkin-Graboi, A., Fortier, M. V, Chong, Y. S., Kwek, K., Saw, S.-M., . . . Qiu, A. (2013). Structural connectivity asymmetry in the neonatal brain. *NeuroImage, 75*, 187–194. https://doi.org/10.1016/j.neuroimage.2013.02.052

Rattaz, C., Goubet, N., & Bullinger, A. (2005). The calming effect of a familiar odor on full-term newborns. *Journal of Developmental and Behavioral Pediatrics, 26*(2), 86–92.

Reagan-Steiner, S., Yankey, D., Jeyarajah, J., Elam-Evans, L. D., Curtis, C. R., MacNeil, J., . . . Singleton, J. A. (2016). National, regional, state, and selected local area vaccination coverage among adolescents aged 13–17 years — United States, 2015. *MMWR. Morbidity and Mortality Weekly Report, 65*(33), 850–858. https://doi.org/10.15585/mmwr.mm6533a4

Reason, R. D., Terenzini, P. T., & Domingo, R. J. (2007). Developing social and personal competence in the first year of college. *Review of Higher Education, 30*(3), 271–299.

Reavis, R. D., Keane, S. P., & Calkins, S. D. (2010). Trajectories of peer victimization: The role of multiple relationships. *Merrill-Palmer Quarterly, 56*(3), 303–332.

Redick, T. S., Unsworth, N., Kelly, A. J., & Engle, R. W. (2012). Faster, smarter? Working memory capacity and perceptual speed in relation to fluid intelligence. *Journal of Cognitive Psychology, 24*(7), 844–854. https://doi.org/10.1080/20445911.2012.704359

Reel, J. J. (2012). *Eating disorders: An encyclopedia of causes, treatment, and prevention*. Santa Barbara, CA: ABC-CLIO.

Reese, E., & Fivush, R. (1993). Parental styles for talking about the past. *Developmental Psychology, 29*, 596–606.

Reid Chassiakos, Y. (Linda), Radesky, J., Christakis, D., Moreno, M. A., Cross, C., & Council on Communications and Media. (2016). Children and adolescents and digital media. *Pediatrics, 138*(5), e20162593. https://doi.org/10.1542/peds.2016-2593

Reilly, J. J. (2007). Childhood obesity: An overview. *Children & Society, 21*(5), 390–396.

Reising, M. M., Watson, K. H., Hardcastle, E. J., Merchant, M. J., Roberts, L., Forehand, R., & Compas, B. E. (2013). Parental depression and economic disadvantage: The role of parenting in associations with internalizing and externalizing symptoms in children and adolescents. *Journal of Child and Family Studies, 22*(3), 335–343. https://doi.org/10.1007/s10826-012-9582-4

Reissland, N., Francis, B., & Mason, J. (2013). Can healthy fetuses show facial expressions of "pain" or "distress"? *PLoS ONE, 8*(6), e65530. https://doi.org/10.1371/journal.pone.0065530

Relji, G., Ferring, D., & Martin, R. (2015). A Meta-analysis on the effectiveness of bilingual programs in Europe. *Review of Educational Research, 85*(1), 92–128. https://doi.org/10.3102/0034654314548514

Rembeck, G., Möller, M., & Gunnarsson, R. (2006). Attitudes and feelings towards menstruation and womanhood in girls at menarche. *Acta Paediatrica, 95*(6), 707–714.

Remer, J., Croteau-Chonka, E., Dean, D. C., D'Arpino, S., Dirks, H., Whiley, D., & Deoni, S. C. L. (2017). Quantifying cortical development in typically developing toddlers and young children, 1–6 years of age. *NeuroImage, 153*, 246–261. https://doi.org/10.1016/J.NEUROIMAGE.2017.04.010

Remington, A., Añez, E., Croker, H., Wardle, J., & Cooke, L. (2012). Increasing food acceptance in the home setting: A randomized controlled trial of parent-administered taste exposure with incentives. *American Journal of Clinical Nutrition, 95*(1), 72–77. https://doi.org/10.3945/ajcn.111.024596

Renfrew, M. J., McFadden, A., Bastos, M. H., Campbell, J., Channon, A. A., Cheung, N. F., . . . Declercq, E. (2014). Midwifery and quality care: Findings from a new evidence-informed framework for maternal and newborn care. *Lancet, 384*(9948), 1129–1145. https://doi.org/10.1016/S0140-6736(14)60789-3

Renk, K., Liljequist, L., Simpson, J. E., & Phares, V. (2005). Gender and age differences in the topics of parent-adolescent conflict. *Family Journal, 13*(2), 139–149. https://doi.org/10.1177/1066480704271190

Rennels, J. L., & Kayl, A. J. (2017). How experience affects infants' facial categorization. In H. Cohen & C. Lefebvre (Eds.), *Handbook of categorization in cognitive science* (pp. 637–652). Amsterdam, Netherlands: Elsevier. https://doi.org/10.1016/B978-0-08-101107-2.00026-9

Resch, F., Haffner, J., Parzer, P., Pfueller, U., Strehlow, U., & Zerahn-Hartung, C. (1997). Testing the hypothesis of the relationships between laterality and ability according to Annett's right-shift theory: Findings in an epidemiological sample of young adults. *British Journal of Psychology, 88*(4), 621–635. https://doi.org/10.1111/j.2044-8295.1997.tb02661.x

Reuben, A., Caspi, A., Belsky, D. W., Broadbent, J., Harrington, H., Sugden, K., . . . Moffitt, T. E. (2017). Association of Childhood blood lead levels with cognitive function and socioeconomic status at age 38 years and with IQ change and socioeconomic mobility between childhood and adulthood. *JAMA, 317*(12), 1244. https://doi.org/10.1001/jama.2017.1712

Reyna, C. (2008). Ian is intelligent but Leshaun is lazy: Antecedents and consequences of attributional stereotypes in the classroom. *European Journal of Psychology of Education, 23*(4), 439–458. https://doi.org/10.1007/BF03172752

Reyna, V. F., & Farley, F. (2006). Risk and rationality in adolescent decision making: Implications for theory, practice, and public policy. *Psychological Science in the Public Interest, 7*(1), 1–44.

Reyna, V. F., & Rivers, S. E. (2008). Current theories of risk and rational decision making. *Developmental Review, 28*(1), 1–11. https://doi.org/10.1016/j.dr.2008.01.002

Reynolds, B. M., & Juvonen, J. (2011). The role of early maturation, perceived popularity, and rumors in the emergence of internalizing symptoms among adolescent girls. *Journal of Youth and Adolescence, 40*(11), 1407–1422. https://doi.org/10.1007/s10964-010-9619-1

Reynolds, G. D., & Romano, A. C. (2016). The development of attention systems and working memory in infancy. *Frontiers in Systems Neuroscience, 10*, 15. https://doi.org/10.3389/fnsys.2016.00015

Reynolds, G. D., Zhang, D., & Guy, M. W. (2013). Infant attention to dynamic audiovisual stimuli: Look duration from 3 to 9 months of age. *Infancy, 18*(4), 554–577. https://doi.org/10.1111/j.1532-7078.2012.00134.x

Reznick, J. S. (2009). Working memory in infants and toddlers. In M. Courage & N. Cowan (Eds.), *The development of memory in infancy and childhood* (pp. 355–378). New York, NY: Psychology Press. https://doi.org/10.4324/9780203934654-17

Rice, E., Rhoades, H., Winetrobe, H., Sanchez, M., Montoya, J., Plant, A., & Kordic, T. (2012). Sexually explicit cell phone messaging associated with sexual risk among adolescents. *Pediatrics, 130*(4), 667–673. https://doi.org/10.1542/peds.2012-0021

Richards, J. E. (1997). Effects of attention on infant's preference for briefly exposed visual stimuli in the paired-comparison recognition-memory paradigm. *Developmental Psychology, 32*, 22–31.

Richards, J. E. (2010). The development of attention to simple and complex visual stimuli in infants: Behavioral and psychophysiological measures. *Developmental Review, 30*(2), 203–219. https://doi.org/10.1016/j.dr.2010.03.005

Richards, J. E., & Holley, F. B. (1999). Infant attention and the development of smooth pursuit tracking. *Developmental Psychology, 35*, 856–867.

Richards, T. L., Grabowski, T. J., Boord, P., Yagle, K., Askren, M., Mestre, Z., . . . Berninger, V. (2015). Contrasting brain patterns of writing-related DTI parameters, fMRI connectivity, and DTI–fMRI connectivity correlations in children with and without dysgraphia or dyslexia. *NeuroImage: Clinical, 8*, 408–421. https://doi.org/10.1016/J.NICL.2015.03.018

Richardson, G. A., Goldschmidt, L., Larkby, C., & Day, N. L. (2015). Effects of prenatal cocaine exposure on adolescent development. *Neurotoxicology and Teratology, 49*, 41–48. https://doi.org/10.1016/J.NTT.2015.03.002

Richardson, S. M., Paxton, S. J., & Thomson, J. S. (2009). Is BodyThink an efficacious body image and self-esteem program? A controlled evaluation with adolescents. *Body Image, 6*(2), 75–82. https://doi.org/10.1016/j.bodyim.2008.11.001

Richert, R. A., Robb, M. B., & Smith, E. I. (2011). Media as social partners: The social nature of young children's learning from screen media. *Child Development, 82*(1), 82–95. https://doi.org/10.1111/j.1467-8624.2010.01542.x

Richmond, S., Johnson, K. A., Seal, M. L., Allen, N. B., & Whittle, S. (2016). Development of brain networks and relevance of environmental and genetic factors: A systematic review. *Neuroscience & Biobehavioral Reviews, 71*, 215–239. https://doi.org/10.1016/j.neubiorev.2016.08.024

Rickard, I. J., Frankenhuis, W. E., & Nettle, D. (2014). Why are childhood family factors associated with timing of maturation? A role for internal prediction. *Perspectives on Psychological Science, 9*(1), 3–15. https://doi.org/10.1177/1745691613513467

Rideout, V. (2015). *The Common Sense census: Media use by tweens and teens.* San Francisco, CA: Common Sense Media. Retrieved from https://static1.squarespace.com/static/5ba15befec4eb7899898240d/t/5ba261f24fa51a7fb2c19904/1537368577261/CSM_TeenTween_MediaCensus_FinalWebVersion_1%281%29.pdf

Rideout, V. (2018). *The Common Sense census: Media use by kids age zero to eight.* San Francisco, CA: Common Sense Media.

Rideout, V. V. S. (2016). Opportunity for all? Technology and learning in lower-income families. *Joan Ganz Cooney Center at Sesame Workshop.* Retrieved from https://eric.ed.gov/?id=ED574416

Riggins, T., Geng, F., Botdorf, M., Canada, K., Cox, L., & Hancock, G. R. (2018). Protracted hippocampal development is associated with age-related improvements in memory during early childhood. *NeuroImage, 174*, 127–137. https://doi.org/10.1016/J.NEUROIMAGE.2018.03.009

Rigney, J., & Wang, S. (2015). Delineating the boundaries of infants' spatial categories: The case of containment. *Journal of Cognition and Development, 16*(3), 420–441. https://doi.org/10.1080/15248372.2013.848868

Rindermann, H., & Thompson, J. (2013). Ability rise in NAEP and narrowing ethnic gaps? *Intelligence, 41*(6), 821–831. https://doi.org/10.1016/j.intell.2013.06.016

Ristic, J., & Enns, J. T. (2015a). Attentional development. In *Handbook of child psychology and developmental science* (pp. 1–45). Hoboken, NJ: John Wiley & Sons. https://doi.org/10.1002/9781118963418.childpsy205

Ristic, J., & Enns, J. T. (2015b). The changing face of attentional development. *Current Directions in Psychological Science, 24*(1), 24–31. https://doi.org/10.1177/0963721414551165

Ritchie, K., Bora, S., & Woodward, L. J. (2015). Social development of children born very preterm: A systematic review. *Developmental Medicine & Child Neurology, 57*(10), 899–918. https://doi.org/10.1111/dmcn.12783

Ritz, B. R., Chatterjee, N., Garcia-Closas, M., Gauderman, W. J., Pierce, B. L., Kraft, P., . . . McAllister, K. (2017). Lessons Learned from past gene-environment interaction successes. *American Journal of Epidemiology, 186*(7), 778–786. https://doi.org/10.1093/aje/kwx230

Rivas-Drake, D., Seaton, E. K., Markstrom, C., Quintana, S., Syed, M., Lee, R. M., . . . Yip, T. (2014). Ethnic and racial identity in adolescence: Implications for psychosocial, academic, and health outcomes. *Child Development, 85*(1), 40–57. https://doi.org/10.1111/cdev.12200

Rivera, S. M., Wakely, A., & Langer, J. (1999). The drawbridge phenomenon: Representational reasoning or perceptual preference? *Developmental Psychology, 35*(2), 427–435.

Rizzo, C. J., Joppa, M., Barker, D., Collibee, C., Zlotnick, C., & Brown, L. K. (2018). Project Date SMART: A dating violence (DV) and sexual risk prevention program for adolescent girls with prior DV exposure. *Prevention Science, 19*, 416–442. https://doi.org/10.1007/s11121-018-0871-z

Rizzolatti, G., Sinigaglia, C., & Anderson, F. (2008). *Mirrors in the brain: How our minds share actions and emotions*. New York, NY: Oxford University Press.

Roa, J., & Tena-Sempere, M. (2014). Connecting metabolism and reproduction: Roles of central energy sensors and key molecular mediators. *Molecular and Cellular Endocrinology, 397*(1–2), 4–14. https://doi.org/10.1016/J.MCE.2014.09.027

Robb, M. B., Richert, R. A., & Wartella, E. A. (2009). Just a talking book? Word learning from watching baby videos. *British Journal of Developmental Psychology, 27*(1), 27–45. https://doi.org/10.1348/026151008X320156

Robbins, E., Starr, S., & Rochat, P. (2016). Fairness and distributive justice by 3- to 5-year-old Tibetan children. *Journal of Cross-Cultural Psychology, 47*(3), 333–340. https://doi.org/10.1177/0022022115620487

Robbins, J. (2005). Contexts, collaboration, and cultural tools: A sociocultural perspective on researching children's thinking. *Contemporary Issues in Early Childhood, 6*(2), 140. https://doi.org/10.2304/ciec.2005.6.2.4

Robbins, S. B., Allen, J., Casillas, A., Peterson, C. H., & Le, H. (2006). Unraveling the differential effects of motivational and skills, social, and self-management measures from traditional predictors of college outcomes. *Journal of Educational Psychology, 98*(3), 598–616.

Roben, C. K. P., Cole, P. M., & Armstrong, L. M. (2013). Longitudinal relations among language skills, anger expression, and regulatory strategies in early childhood. *Child Development, 84*(3), 891–905. https://doi.org/10.1111/cdev.12027

Roben, C. K. P., Moore, G. A., Cole, P. M., Molenaar, P., Leve, L. D., Shaw, D. S., . . . Neiderhiser, J. M. (2015). Transactional patterns of maternal depressive symptoms and mother-child mutual negativity in an adoption sample. *Infant and Child Development, 24*(3), 322–342. https://doi.org/10.1002/icd.1906

Roberge, S., Bujold, E., & Nicolaides, K. H. (2017). Aspirin for the prevention of preterm and term preeclampsia: Systematic review and meta-analysis. *American Journal of Obstetrics and Gynecology, 218*(3), 287–293. https://doi.org/10.1016/J.AJOG.2017.11.561

Roberts, G., Quach, J., Mensah, F., Gathercole, S., Gold, L., Anderson, P., . . . Wake, M. (2015). Schooling duration rather than chronological age predicts working memory between 6 and 7 years. *Journal of Developmental & Behavioral Pediatrics, 36*(2), 68–74. https://doi.org/10.1097/DBP.0000000000000121

Roberts, G., Quach, J., Spencer-Smith, M., Anderson, P. J., Gathercole, S., Gold, L., . . . Wake, M. (2016). Academic outcomes 2 years after working memory training for children with low working memory. *JAMA Pediatrics, 170*(5), e154568. https://doi.org/10.1001/jamapediatrics.2015.4568

Roberts, J. E., & Bell, M. A. (2002). The effects of age and sex on mental rotation performance, verbal performance, and brain electrical activity. *Developmental Psychobiology, 40*(4), 391–407. https://doi.org/10.1002/dev.10039

Roberts, J. R., Dawley, E. H., & Reigart, J. R. (2019). Children's low-level pesticide exposure and associations with autism and ADHD: A review. *Pediatric Research, 85*(2), 234–241. https://doi.org/10.1038/s41390-018-0200-z

Roberts, S. C. M., & Nuru-Jeter, A. (2012). Universal screening for alcohol and drug use and racial disparities in child protective services reporting. *Journal of Behavioral Health Services & Research, 39*(1), 3–16. https://doi.org/10.1007/s11414-011-9247-x

Robertson, J. A., & Hickman, T. (2013). Should PGD be used for elective gender selection? *American Society for Reproductive Medicine*. Retrieved from https://www.contemporaryobgyn.net/infertility/should-pgd-be-used-elective-gender-selection

Robinson, J. B., Burns, B. M., & Davis, D. W. (2009). Maternal scaffolding and attention regulation in children living in poverty. *Journal of Applied Developmental Psychology, 30*(2), 82–91. https://doi.org/10.1016/j.appdev.2008.10.013

Robinson, J. P., & Espelage, D. L. (2013). Peer victimization and sexual risk differences between lesbian, gay, bisexual, transgender, or questioning and nontransgender heterosexual youths in grades 7-12. *American Journal of Public Health, 103*(10), 1810–1819. https://doi.org/10.2105/AJPH.2013.301387

Robinson, T. N., Banda, J. A., Hale, L., Lu, A. S., Fleming-Milici, F., Calvert, S. L., & Wartella, E. (2017). Screen media exposure and obesity in children and adolescents. *Pediatrics, 140*(Suppl. 2), S97–S101. https://doi.org/10.1542/peds.2016-1758K

Roby, A. C., & Kidd, E. (2008). The referential communication skills of children with imaginary companions. *Developmental Science, 11*(4), 531–540. https://doi.org/10.1111/j.1467-7687.2008.00699.x

Rochat, P. (1998). Self-perception and action in infancy. *Experimental Brain Research, 123*(1–2), 102–109. https://doi.org/10.1007/s002210050550

Rochat, P. (2010). Emerging Self-concept. In J. G. Bremner & T. D. Wachs (Eds.), *The Wiley-Blackwell handbook of infant development* (pp. 320–344). Oxford, England: Wiley-Blackwell. https://doi.org/10.1002/9781444327564.ch10

Rochat, P. (2013). Self-conceptualizing in development. In P. D. Zelazo (Ed.), *The Oxford handbook of developmental psychology: Vol. 2. Self and other* (pp. 378–396). New York, NY: Oxford University Press. https://doi.org/10.1093/oxfordhb/9780199958474.013.0015

Rochat, P., Dias, M. D. G., Guo Liping, G., Broesch, T., Passos-Ferreira, C., Winning, A., & Berg, B. (2009). Fairness in distributive justice by 3- and 5-year-olds across seven cultures. *Journal of Cross-Cultural Psychology, 40*(3), 416–442. https://doi.org/10.1177/0022022109332844

Rock, P. F., Cole, D. J., Houshyar, S., Lythcott, M., & Prinstein, M. J. (2011). Peer status in an ethnic context: Associations with African American adolescents' ethnic identity. *Journal of Applied Developmental Psychology, 32*(4), 163–169. https://doi.org/10.1016/j.appdev.2011.03.002

Rodgers, R. F., Watts, A. W., Austin, S. B., Haines, J., & Neumark-Sztainer, D. (2017). Disordered eating in ethnic minority adolescents with overweight. *International Journal of Eating Disorders, 50*(6), 665–671. https://doi.org/10.1002/eat.22652

Rodriguez, E. T., & Tamis-LeMonda, C. S. (2011). Trajectories of the home learning environment across the first 5 years: Associations with children's vocabulary and literacy skills at prekindergarten. *Child Development, 82*(4), 1058–1075. https://doi.org/10.1111/j.1467-8624.2011.01614.x

Roediger, H. L., & Marsh, E. J. (2003). Episodic and autobiographical memory. In I. B. Weiner (Ed.), *Handbook of psychology, Part 6: Complex learning and memory processes*. Hoboken, NJ: John Wiley & Sons.

Roelants, M., Hauspie, R., & Hoppenbrouwers, K. (2010). Breastfeeding, growth and growth standards: Performance of the WHO growth standards for monitoring growth of Belgian children. *Annals of Human Biology, 37*(1), 2–9. https://doi.org/10.3109/03014460903089500

Rogoff, B. (2014). Learning by observing and pitching in to family and community endeavors: An orientation. *Human Development, 57*(2–3), 69–81. https://doi.org/10.1159/000356757

Rogoff, B. (2016). Culture and participation: A paradigm shift. *Current Opinion in Psychology, 8*, 182–189. https://doi.org/10.1016/j.copsyc.2015.12.002

Rogoff, B., Callanan, M., Gutiérrez, K. D., & Erickson, F. (2016). The organization of informal learning. *Review of Research in Education, 40*(1), 356–401. https://doi.org/10.3102/0091732X16680994

Rogoff, B., & Chavajay, P. (1995). What's become of research on the cultural basis of cognitive development? *American Psychologist, 50*, 859–877.

Rogoff, B., Mistry, J., Goncu, A., & Mosier, C. (1993a). Guided participation in cultural activity by toddlers and caregivers. *Monographs of the Society for Research in Child Development, 58*(8), v–179. http://dx.doi.org/10.2307/1166109

Rogoff, B., Moore, L. C., Correa-Chavez, M., & Dexter, A. L. (2014). Children develop cultural repertoires through engaging in everyday routines and practices. In J. Grusec & P.

Hastings (Eds.), *Handbook of socialization: Theory and research* (pp. 472–498). New York, NY: Guilford.

Rogoff, B., Mosier, C., Mistry, J., & Goncu, A. (1993b). Toddlers' guided participation with their caregivers in cultural activity. In E. Foreman, N. Minnick, & C. Stone (Eds.), *Contexts for learning: Sociocultural dynamics in children's development* (pp. 230–253). New York, NY: Oxford University Press.

Rogoff, B., & Waddell, K. J. (1982). Memory for information organized in a scene by children from two cultures. *Child Development, 53*(5), 1224–1228. Retrieved from http://www.ncbi.nlm.nih.gov/pubmed/7140428

Rojas-Gaona, C. E., Hong, J. S., & Peguero, A. A. (2016). The significance of race/ethnicity in adolescent violence: A decade of review, 2005–2015. *Journal of Criminal Justice, 46*, 137–147. https://doi.org/10.1016/J.JCRIMJUS.2016.05.001

Rolls, E. T. (2017). Evolution of the Emotional Brain. In S. Watanabe, M. A. Hofman, & T. Shimizu (Eds.), *Evolution of the brain, cognition, and emotion in vertebrates* (pp. 251–272). Tokyo, Japan: Springer. https://doi.org/10.1007/978-4-431-56559-8_12

Romani, C., Palermo, L., MacDonald, A., Limback, E., Hall, S. K., & Geberhiwot, T. (2017). The impact of phenylalanine levels on cognitive outcomes in adults with phenylketonuria: Effects across tasks and developmental stages. *Neuropsychology, 31*(3), 242–254. https://doi.org/10.1037/neu0000336

Romeo, R. D. (2017). The impact of stress on the structure of the adolescent brain: Implications for adolescent mental health. *Brain Research, 1654*, 185–191. https://doi.org/10.1016/J.BRAINRES.2016.03.021

Romero, A. J., Edwards, L. M., Fryberg, S. A., & Orduña, M. (2014). Resilience to discrimination stress across ethnic identity stages of development. *Journal of Applied Social Psychology, 44*(1), 1–11. https://doi.org/10.1111/jasp.12192

Romo, D. L., Garnett, C., Younger, A. P., Stockwell, M. S., Soren, K., Catallozzi, M., & Neu, N. (2017). Social media use and its association with sexual risk and parental monitoring among a primarily Hispanic adolescent population. *Journal of Pediatric and Adolescent Gynecology, 30*(4), 466–473. https://doi.org/10.1016/j.jpag.2017.02.004

Roopnarine, J. L., Hossain, Z., Gill, P., & Brophy, H. (1994). Play in the East Indian context. In J. L. Roopnarine, J. E. Johnson, & F. H. Hooper (Eds.), *Children's play in diverse cultures* (pp. 9–30). Albany, NY: State University of New York Press.

Roopnarine, J. L., Lasker, J., Sacks, M., & Stores, M. (1998). The cultural contexts of children's play. In O. N. Saracho & B. Spodek (Eds.), *Multiple perspectives on play in early childhood education* (pp. 194–219). Albany, NY: State University of New York Press.

Roopnarine, J. L., Talukder, E., Jain, D., Joshi, P., & Srivastav, P. (1992). Personal well-being, kinship tie, and mother-infant and father-infant interactions in single-wage and dual-wage families in New Delhi, India. *Journal of Marriage & Family, 54*(2), 293–301.

Rosario, M., Schrimshaw, E. W., & Hunter, J. (2009). Disclosure of sexual orientation and subsequent substance use and abuse among lesbian, gay, and bisexual youths: Critical role of disclosure reactions. *Psychology of Addictive Behaviors, 23*(1), 175–184. https://doi.org/10.1037/a0014284

Rose, A. J., & Asher, S. R. (2017). The social tasks of friendship: Do boys and girls excel in different tasks? *Child Development Perspectives, 11*(1), 3–8. https://doi.org/10.1111/cdep.12214

Rose, J., Roman, N., Mwaba, K., & Ismail, K. (2018). The relationship between parenting and internalizing behaviours of children: A systematic review. *Early Child Development and Care, 188*(10), 1468–1486. https://doi.org/10.1080/03004430.2016.1269762

Rose, S. A., & Feldman, J. F. (1995). Prediction of IQ and specific cognitive abilities from infancy measures. *Developmental Psychology, 31*, 685–696.

Rose, S. A., Feldman, J. F., & Jankowski, J. J. (2009). Information processing in toddlers: Continuity from infancy and persistence of preterm deficits. *Intelligence, 37*(3), 311–320. https://doi.org/10.1016/j.intell.2009.02.002

Rose, S. A., Feldman, J. F., & Jankowski, J. J. (2012). Implications of infant cognition for executive functions at age 11. *Psychological Science, 23*(11), 1345–1355. https://doi.org/10.1177/0956797612444902

Rose, S. A., Feldman, J. F., Jankowski, J. J., & Van Rossem, R. (2011). The structure of memory in infants and toddlers: An SEM study with full-terms and preterms. *Developmental Science, 14*(1), 83–91. https://doi.org/10.1111/j.1467-7687.2010.00959.x

Rose, S. A., Feldman, J. F., Jankowski, J. J., & Van Rossem, R. (2012). Information processing from infancy to 11 years: Continuities and prediction of IQ. *Intelligence, 40*(5), 445–457. https://doi.org/10.1016/j.intell.2012.05.007

Roseberry, S., Hirsh-Pasek, K., & Golinkoff, R. M. (2014). Skype me! Socially contingent interactions help toddlers learn language. *Child Development, 85*(3), 956–970. https://doi.org/10.1111/cdev.12166

Rose-Greenland, F., & Smock, P. J. (2013). Living together unmarried: What do we know about cohabiting families? In G. W. Peterson & K. R. Bush (Eds.), *Handbook of marriage and the family* (pp. 255–273). New York, NY: Springer.

Rosenbaum, J. E., & Person, A. E. (2003). Beyond college for all: Policies and practices to improve transitions into college and jobs. *Professional School Counseling, 6*(4), 252.

Rosenberg, R. D., & Feigenson, L. (2013). Infants hierarchically organize memory representations. *Developmental Science, 16*(4), 610–621. https://doi.org/10.1111/desc.12055

Rosenkoetter, L. I. (1973). Resistance to temptation: Inhibitory and disinhibitory effects of models. *Developmental Psychology, 8*, 80–84.

Rosnati, R., Pinderhughes, E. E., Baden, A. L., Grotevant, H. D., Lee, R. M., & Mohanty, J. (2015). New trends and directions in ethnic identity among internationally transracially adopted persons: Summary of special issue. *New Directions for Child and Adolescent Development, 2015*(150), 91–95. https://doi.org/10.1002/cad.20121

Ross, E. S. (2017). Flavor and taste development in the first years of life. *Nestle Nutrition Institute Workshop Series, 87*, 49–58. https://doi.org/10.1159/000448937

Ross, J. (2017). You and me: Investigating the role of self-evaluative emotion in preschool prosociality. *Journal of Experimental Child Psychology, 155*, 67–83. https://doi.org/10.1016/J.JECP.2016.11.001

Ross, S., Heath, N. L., & Toste, J. R. (2009). Non-suicidal self-injury and eating pathology in high school students. *American Journal of Orthopsychiatry, 79*(1), 83–92. https://doi.org/10.1037/a0014826

Rote, W. M., & Smetana, J. G. (2016). Beliefs about parents' right to know: Domain differences and associations with change in concealment. *Journal of Research on Adolescence, 26*, 334–344. https://doi.org/10.1111/jora.12194

Rothbart, M. K. (2011). *Becoming who we are: Temperament and personality in development*. New York, NY: Guilford.

Rothbart, M. K., & Bates, J. E. (1998). Temperament. In N. Eisenberg (Ed.), *Handbook of child psychology: Vol. 3. Social, emotional, and personality development* (5th ed., pp. 105–176). New York, NY: Wiley.

Rothbart, M. K., & Bates, J. E. (2007). Temperament. In *Handbook of child psychology* (pp. 207–212). Hoboken, NJ: John Wiley & Sons. https://doi.org/10.1002/9780470147658.chpsy0303

Rothbaum, F., Pott, M., Azuma, H., Miyake, K., & Weisz, J. (2000a). The development of close relationships in Japan and the United States: Paths of symbiotic harmony and generative tension. *Child Development, 71*, 1121–1142.

Rothbaum, F., Weisz, J., Pott, M., Miyake, K., & Morelli, G. (2000b). Attachment and culture: Security in the United States and Japan. *American Psychologist, 55*, 1093–1104.

Roth-Cline, M., & Nelson, R. M. (2013). Parental permission and child assent in research on children. *Yale Journal of Biology and Medicine, 86*(3), 291–301. Retrieved from http://www.ncbi.nlm.nih.gov/pubmed/24058304

Rotstein, M., Stolar, O., Uliel, S., Mandel, D., Mani, A., Dollberg, S., . . . Leitner, Y. (2015). Facial expression in response to smell and taste stimuli in small and appropriate for gestational age newborns. *Journal of Child Neurology, 30*(11), 1466–1471. https://doi.org/10.1177/0883073815570153

Rovee-Collier, C. K. (1987). Learning and memory. In J. D. Osofsky (Ed.), *Handbook of infant development* (2nd ed., pp. 98–148). New York, NY: Wiley.

Rovee-Collier, C. K., & Bhatt, R. S. (1993). Evidence of long-term memory in infancy. *Annals of Child Development, 9*, 1–45.

Rowe, M. L. (2012). A longitudinal investigation of the role of quantity and quality of child-directed speech in vocabulary development. *Child Development, 83*(5), 1762–1774. https://doi.org/10.1111/j.1467-8624.2012.01805.x

Rubin, K. H., Bukowski, W. M., & Bowker, J. C. (2015a). Children in peer groups. In M. H. Bornstein & T. Leventhal (Eds.), *Handbook of child psychology and developmental science* (pp. 1–48). Hoboken, NJ: John Wiley & Sons. https://doi.org/10.1002/9781118963418.childpsy405

Rubin, K. H., Coplan, R. J., & Bowker, J. C. (2009). Social withdrawal in childhood.

Annual Review of Psychology, 60(1), 141–171. https://doi.org/10.1146/annurev.psych.60110707.163642

Rubin, K. H., Coplan, R. J., Chen, X., Bowker, J. C., McDonald, K. L., & Heverly-Fitt, S. (2015b). Peer relationships. In *Developmental science: An advanced textbook* (pp. 587–644). New York, NY: Psychology Press.

Rubin, K. H., Hastings, P., Chen, X., Stewart, S., & McNichol, K. (1998). Interpersonal and maternal correlates of aggression, conflict, and externalizing problems in toddlers. *Child Development, 69*, 1614–1629.

Rubin, K. H., Wojslawowicz, J. C., Rose-Krasnor, L., Booth-LaForce, C., & Burgess, K. B. (2006). The best friendships of shy/withdrawn children: Prevalence, stability, and relationship quality. *Journal of Abnormal Child Psychology, 34*(2), 143–157. https://doi.org/10.1007/s10802-005-9017-4

Ruble, D. N., Taylor, L. J., Cyphers, L., Greulich, F. K., Lurye, L. E., & Shrout, P. E. (2007). The role of gender constancy in early gender development. *Child Development, 78*(4), 1121–1136. https://doi.org/10.1111/j.1467-8624.2007.01056.x

Rudolph, K. D., Troop-Gordon, W., Lambert, S. F., & Natsuaki, M. N. (2014). Long-term consequences of pubertal timing for youth depression: Identifying personal and contextual pathways of risk. *Development and Psychopathology, 26*(4pt2), 1423–1444. https://doi.org/10.1017/S0954579414001126

Rueda, M. R. (2013). Development of attention. In K. Ochsner & S. M. Kosslyn (Eds.), *The Oxford handbook of cognitive neuroscience: Vol: 1. Core topics* (p. 656). Oxford, England: Oxford University Press.

Rueger, S. Y., Chen, P., Jenkins, L. N., & Choe, H. J. (2014). Effects of perceived support from mothers, fathers, and teachers on depressive symptoms during the transition to middle school. *Journal of Youth and Adolescence, 43*(4), 655–670. https://doi.org/10.1007/s10964-013-0039-x

Ruiz, J. M., Hamann, H. A., Mehl, M. R., & O'Connor, M.-F. (2016). The Hispanic health paradox: From epidemiological phenomenon to contribution opportunities for psychological science. *Group Processes & Intergroup Relations, 19*(4), 462–476. https://doi.org/10.1177/1368430216638540

Rulison, K., Patrick, M. E., & Maggs, J. (2015). Linking peer relationships to substance use across adolescence. In R. A. Zucker & S. A. Brown (Eds.), *The Oxford handbook of adolescent substance abuse* (Vol. 1). Oxford, England: Oxford University Press. https://doi.org/10.1093/oxfordhb/9780199735662.013.019

Runions, K. C., Vitaro, F., Cross, D., Shaw, T., Hall, M., & Boivin, M. (2014). Teacher–child relationship, parenting, and growth in likelihood and severity of physical aggression in the early school years. *Merrill-Palmer Quarterly, 60*(3), 274–301. Retrieved from http://muse.jhu.edu/journals/merrill-palmer_quarterly/v060/60.3.runions.html

Rushton, J. P., & Bons, T. A. (2005). Mate choice and friendship in twins: Evidence for genetic similarity. *Psychological Science, 16*(7), 555–559. https://doi.org/10.1111/j.0956-7976.2005.01574.x

Russell, S. T., & Fish, J. N. (2016). Mental health in lesbian, gay, bisexual, and transgender (LGBT) youth. *Annual Review of Clinical Psychology, 12*(1), 465–487. https://doi.org/10.1146/annurev-clinpsy-021815-093153

Rutter, M. (2012). Gene–environment interdependence. *European Journal of Developmental Psychology, 9*(4), 391–412.

Rutter, M. (2014). Nature–nurture integration. In M. Lewis & K. D. Rudolph (Eds.), *Handbook of developmental psychopathology* (pp. 45–65). Boston, MA: Springer. https://doi.org/10.1007/978-1-4614-9608-3_3

Rutter, M., Giller, H., & Hagell, A. (1998). *Antisocial behavior by young people*. New York, NY: Cambridge University Press.

Ruzgis, P., & Grigorenko, E. L. (1994). Cultural meaning systems, intelligence, and personality. In R. J. Sternberg & P. Ruzgis (Eds.), *Personality and intelligence* (pp. 248–270). New York, NY: Cambridge University Press.

Ryalls, B. O. (2000). Dimensional adjectives: Factors affecting children's ability to compare objects using novel words. *Journal of Experimental Child Psychology, 76*(1), 26–49.

Ryan, C., Russell, S. T., Huebner, D., Diaz, R., & Sanchez, J. (2010). Family acceptance in adolescence and the health of LGBT young adults. *Journal of Child and Adolescent Psychiatric Nursing, 23*(4), 205–213. https://doi.org/10.1111/j.1744-6171.2010.00246.x

Ryan, R. M., Claessens, A., & Markowitz, A. J. (2015). Associations between family structure change and child behavior problems: The moderating effect of family income. *Child Development, 86*, 112–127. https://doi.org/10.1111/cdev.12283

Ryan, S., Franzetta, K., & Manlove, J. (2007). Knowledge, perceptions, and motivations for contraception. *Youth & Society, 39*(2), 182–208.

Saarni, C., Mumme, D. L., & Campos, J. J. (1998). Emotional development: Action, communication, and understanding. In N. Eisenberg & W. Damon (Eds.), *Handbook of child psychology: Vol: 3. Social, emotional, and personality development* (5th ed., pp. 237–309). Hoboken, NJ: John Wiley & Sons.

Sabbagh, M. A., Xu, F., Carlson, S. M., Moses, L. J., & Lee., K. (2006). The development of executive functioning and theory of mind. *Psychological Science, 17*(1), 74–81.

Sabia, J. J., & Bass, B. (2017). Do anti-bullying laws work? New evidence on school safety and youth violence. *Journal of Population Economics, 30*(2), 473–502. https://doi.org/10.1007/s00148-016-0622-z

Sadeh, A., De Marcas, G., Guri, Y., Berger, A., Tikotzky, L., & Bar-Haim, Y. (2015). Infant sleep predicts attention regulation and behavior problems at 3–4 years of age. *Developmental Neuropsychology, 40*(3), 122–137. https://doi.org/10.1080/87565641.2014.973498

Sadler, K. (2017). Pubertal Development. In M. A. Goldstein (Ed.), *The MassGeneral Hospital for Children adolescent medicine handbook* (pp. 19–26). Cham, Switzerland: Springer International Publishing. https://doi.org/10.1007/978-3-319-45778-9_3

Sadler, T. L. (2015). *Langman's medical embryology* (13th ed.). New York, NY: Lippincott Williams & Wilkins.

Sadler, T. L. (2018). *Langman's medical embryology* (14th ed.). Philadelphia, PA: Lippincott Williams & Wilkins.

Saewyc, E. M. (2011). Research on adolescent sexual orientation: Development, health disparities, stigma, and resilience. *Journal of Research on Adolescence, 21*(1), 256–272. https://doi.org/10.1111/j.1532-7795.2010.00727.x

Safdar, S., Friedlmeier, W., Matsumoto, D., Yoo, S. H., Kwantes, C. T., Kakai, H., & Shigemasu, E. (2009). Variations of emotional display rules within and across cultures: A comparison between Canada, USA, and Japan. *Canadian Journal of Behavioural Science, 41*(1), 1–10. https://doi.org/10.1037/a0014387

Saffran, J. R., & Kirkham, N. Z. (2018). Infant statistical learning. *Annual Review of Psychology, 69*(1), 181–203. https://doi.org/10.1146/annurev-psych-122216-011805

Sagi, A., Lamb, M. E., Lewkowicz, K. S., Shoham, R., Dvir, R., & Estes, D. (1985). Security of infant-mother, -father, and -metapelet attachments among kibbutz-reared Israeli children. *Monographs of the Society for Research in Child Development, 50*(1/2), 257–275. https://doi.org/10.1111/1540-5834.ep11890146

Sagi, A., Van IJzendoorn, M. H., & Koren-Karie, N. (1991). Primary appraisal of the Strange Situation: A cross-cultural analysis of preseparation episodes. *Developmental Psychology, 27*(4), 587–596.

Sai, F. Z. (2005). The role of the mother's voice in developing mother's face preference: Evidence for intermodal perception at birth. *Infant & Child Development, 14*, 29–50.

Sala, M. N., Pons, F., & Molina, P. (2014). Emotion regulation strategies in preschool children. *British Journal of Developmental Psychology, 32*(4), 440–453. https://doi.org/10.1111/bjdp.12055

Sala, P., Prefumo, F., Pastorino, D., Buffi, D., Gaggero, C. R., Foppiano, M., & De Biasio, P. (2014). Fetal surgery. *Obstetrical & Gynecological Survey, 69*(4), 218–228. https://doi.org/10.1097/OGX.0000000000000061

Saleem, S. N. (2014). Fetal MRI: An approach to practice: A review. *Journal of Advanced Research, 5*(5), 507–523. https://doi.org/10.1016/J.JARE.2013.06.001

Salend, S. J. (2015). *Creating inclusive classrooms: Effective, differentiated and reflective practices*. Boston, MA: Pearson.

Salmivalli, C. (2014). Participant roles in bullying: How can peer bystanders be utilized in interventions? *Theory Into Practice, 53*(4), 286–292. https://doi.org/10.1080/00405841.2014.947222

Salmon, D. A., Dudley, M. Z., Glanz, J. M., & Omer, S. B. (2015). Vaccine hesitancy: Causes, consequences, and a call to action. *Vaccine, 33*, D66–D71. https://doi.org/10.1016/J.VACCINE.2015.09.035

Salo, V. C., Rowe, M. L., & Reeb-Sutherland, B. C. (2018). Exploring infant gesture and joint attention as related constructs and as predictors of later language. *Infancy, 23*(3), 432–452. https://doi.org/10.1111/infa.12229

Salter, M. D. (1940). *An evaluation of adjustment based upon the concept of security*. Toronto, ON, Canada: University of Toronto Press.

Samarova, V., Shilo, G., & Diamond, G. M. (2014). Changes in youths' perceived parental acceptance of their sexual minority status over time. *Journal of Research on*

Adolescence, 24(4), 681–688. https://doi.org/10.1111/jora.12071

Samour, P. Q., & King, K. (2013). *Essentials of pediatric nutrition*. Burlington, MA: Jones & Bartlett Learning.

Samuelson, L. K., & McMurray, B. (2017). What does it take to learn a word? *Wiley Interdisciplinary Reviews: Cognitive Science, 8*(1–2), e1421. https://doi.org/10.1002/wcs.1421

Sánchez-Queija, I., Oliva, A., & Parra, Á. (2017). Stability, change, and determinants of self-esteem during adolescence and emerging adulthood. *Journal of Social and Personal Relationships, 34*(8), 1277–1294. https://doi.org/10.1177/0265407516674831

Sanchez-Vaznaugh, E. V., Braveman, P. A., Egerter, S., Marchi, K. S., Heck, K., & Curtis, M. (2016). Latina birth outcomes in California: Not so paradoxical. *Maternal and Child Health Journal, 20*(9), 1849–1860. https://doi.org/10.1007/s10995-016-1988-y

Sanders, J. O., Qiu, X., Lu, X., Duren, D. L., Liu, R. W., Dang, D., . . . Cooperman, D. R. (2017). The uniform pattern of growth and skeletal maturation during the human adolescent growth spurt. *Scientific Reports, 7*(1), 16705. https://doi.org/10.1038/s41598-017-16996-w

Sandin, S., Lichtenstein, P., Kuja-Halkola, R., Hultman, C., Larsson, H., & Reichenberg, A. (2017). The heritability of autism spectrum disorder. *JAMA, 318*(12), 1182–1184. https://doi.org/10.1001/jama.2017.12141

Sann, C., & Streri, A. (2007). Perception of object shape and texture in human newborns: Evidence from cross-modal transfer tasks. *Developmental Science, 10*(3), 399–410. https://doi.org/10.1111/j.1467-7687.2007.00593.x

Sansavini, A., Bertoncini, J., & Giovanelli, G. (1997). Newborns discriminate the rhythm of multisyllabic stressed words. *Developmental Psychology, 33*(1), 3–11.

Sapp, F., Lee, K., & Muir, D. (2000). Three-year-olds' difficulty with the appearance-reality distinction: Is it real or is it apparent? *Developmental Psychology, 36*, 547–560.

Saraiya, A., Garakani, A., & Billick, S. B. (2013). Mental health approaches to child victims of acts of terrorism. *Psychiatric Quarterly, 84*(1), 115–124. https://doi.org/10.1007/s11126-012-9232-4

Sarkadi, A., Kristiansson, R., Oberklaid, F., & Bremberg, S. (2008). Fathers' involvement and children's developmental outcomes: A systematic review of longitudinal studies. *Acta Paediatrica, 97*(2), 153–158. https://doi.org/10.1111/j.1651-2227.2007.00572.x

Sasaki, J. Y., & Kim, H. S. (2017). Nature, nurture, and their interplay. *Journal of Cross-Cultural Psychology, 48*(1), 4–22. https://doi.org/10.1177/0022022116680481

Saswati, S., Kissin, D. M., Crawford, S. B., Folger, S. G., Jamieson, D. J., Warner, L., & Barfield, W. D. (2017). Assisted reproductive technology surveillance — United States, 2014. *Morbidity and Mortality Weekly Report, 66*(6), 1–24.

Sattler, J. M. (2014). *Foundations of behavioral, social and clinical assessment of children*. La Mesa, CA: Jerome M. Sattler, Publisher.

Saudino, K. J., & Micalizzi, L. (2015). Emerging trends in behavioral genetic studies of child temperament. *Child Development Perspectives, 9*(3), 144–148. https://doi.org/10.1111/cdep.12123

Savelsbergh, G., van der Kamp, J., & van Wermeskerken, M. (2013). The development of reaching actions. In P. D. Zelazo (Ed.), *The Oxford handbook of developmental psychology, Vol. 1*. New York, NY: Oxford University Press. https://doi.org/10.1093/oxfordhb/9780199958450.013.0014

Savin-Williams, R. C., & Cohen, K. M. (2015). Developmental trajectories and milestones of lesbian, gay, and bisexual young people. *International Review of Psychiatry, 27*(5), 357–366. https://doi.org/10.3109/09540261.2015.1093465

Savin-Williams, R. C., & Dubé, E. M. (1998). Parental reactions to their child's disclosure of a gay/lesbian identity. *Family Relations, 47*(1), 7. https://doi.org/10.2307/584845

Saxton, M. (1997). The contrast theory of negative input. *Journal of Child Language, 24*, 139–161.

Savin-Williams, R. C., & Ream, G. L. (2003). Sex variations in the disclosure to parents of same-sex attractions. *Journal of Family Psychology, 17*(3), 429–438. https://doi.org/10.1037/0893-3200.17.3.429

Scalco, M. D., Trucco, E. M., Coffman, D. L., & Colder, C. R. (2015). Selection and socialization effects in early adolescent alcohol use: A propensity score analysis. *Journal of Abnormal Child Psychology, 43*(6), 1131–1143. https://doi.org/10.1007/s10802-014-9969-3

Scarr, S. (1992). Developmental theories for the 1990s: Development and individual differences. *Child Development, 63*(1), 1–19. https://doi.org/10.1111/1467-8624.ep9203091721

Scarr, S., & McCartney, K. (1983). How people make their own environments: A theory of genotype environment effects. *Child Development, 54*(2), 424. https://doi.org/10.1111/1467-8624.ep8877295

Schaal, B. (2017). Infants and children making sense of scents. In *Springer handbook of odor* (pp. 107–108). Cham, Switzerland: Springer International Publishing. https://doi.org/10.1007/978-3-319-26932-0_43

Schachar, R. (2014). Genetics of attention deficit hyperactivity disorder (ADHD): Recent updates and future prospects. *Current Developmental Disorders Reports, 1*(1), 41–49. https://doi.org/10.1007/s40474-013-0004-0

Schachner, A., & Hannon, E. E. (2011). Infant-directed speech drives social preferences in 5-month-old infants. *Developmental Psychology, 47*(1), 19–25. https://doi.org/10.1037/a0020740

Schaffhuser, K., Allemand, M., & Schwarz, B. (2017). The development of self-representations during the transition to early adolescence: The role of gender, puberty, and school transition. *Journal of Early Adolescence, 37*(6), 774–804. https://doi.org/10.1177/0272431615624841

Schelleman-Offermans, K., Knibbe, R. A., & Kuntsche, E. (2013). Are the effects of early pubertal timing on the initiation of weekly alcohol use mediated by peers and/or parents? A longitudinal study. *Developmental Psychology, 49*(7), 1277–1285.

Schetter, C. D., & Tanner, L. (2012). Anxiety, depression and stress in pregnancy: Implications for mothers, children, research, and practice. *Current Opinion in Psychiatry, 25*(2), 141–148. https://doi.org/10.1097/YCO.0b013e3283503680

Schneider, B. H. (2016). *Childhood friendships and peer relations: Friends and enemies*. New York, NY: Routledge.

Schneider, W., & Bjorklund, D. F. (1992). Expertise, aptitude, and strategic remembering. *Child Development, 63*(2), 461–473. https://doi.org/10.1111/j.1467-8624.1992.tb01640.x

Schneider, W., & Ornstein, P. A. (2015). The development of children's memory. *Child Development Perspectives, 9*(3), 190–195. https://doi.org/10.1111/cdep.12129

Schneider, W., & Pressley, M. (2013). *Memory development between two and twenty* (3rd ed.). Mahwah, NJ: Erlbaum.

Schnur, E., & Belanger, S. (2000). What works in Head Start. In M. P. Kluger, G. Alexander, & P. A. Curtis (Eds.), *What works in child welfare* (pp. 277–284). Washington, DC: Child Welfare League of America.

Schoenmaker, C., Juffer, F., van IJzendoorn, M. H., van den Dries, L., Linting, M., van der Voort, A., & Bakermans-Kranenburg, M. J. (2015). Cognitive and health-related outcomes after exposure to early malnutrition: The Leiden longitudinal study of international adoptees. *Children and Youth Services Review, 48*, 80–86. https://doi.org/10.1016/j.childyouth.2014.12.010

Schonert-Reichl, K. A. (1999). Relations of peer acceptance, friendship adjustment, and social behavior to moral reasoning during early adolescence. *Journal of Early Adolescence, 19*(2), 249–279.

Schoon, I., & Polek, E. (2011). Teenage career aspirations and adult career attainment: The role of gender, social background and general cognitive ability. *International Journal of Behavioral Development, 35*(3), 210–217. https://doi.org/10.1177/0165025411398183

Schreiber, J. (1977). Birth, the family and the community: A southern Italian example. *Birth and the Family Journal, 4*, 153–157.

Schuldiner, O., & Yaron, A. (2015). Mechanisms of developmental neurite pruning. *Cellular and Molecular Life Sciences, 72*(1), 101–119. https://doi.org/10.1007/s00018-014-1729-6

Schulte, B., & Durana, A. (2016). *The New America care report*. Retrieved from https://www.newamerica.org/better-life-lab/policy-papers/new-america-care-report/

Schulze, P. A., & Carlisle, S. A. (2010). What research does and doesn't say about breastfeeding: A critical review. *Early Child Development & Care, 180*(6), 703–718. https://doi.org/10.1080/03004430802263870

Schumacher, A. M., Miller, A. L., Watamura, S. E., Kurth, S., Lassonde, J. M., & LeBourgeois, M. K. (2017). Sleep moderates the association between response inhibition and self-regulation in early childhood. *Journal of Clinical Child and Adolescent Psychology 46*(2), 222–235. https://doi.org/10.1080/15374416.2016.1204921

Schurz, M., Wimmer, H., Richlan, F., Ludersdorfer, P., Klackl, J., & Kronbichler, M. (2015). Resting-state and task-based functional brain connectivity in developmental dyslexia. *Cerebral Cortex, 25*, 3502–3514. https://doi.org/10.1093/cercor/bhu184

Schwartz, D., Lansford, J. E., Dodge, K. A., Pettit, G. S., & Bates, J. E. (2015). Peer victimization during middle childhood as a lead indicator of internalizing problems and diagnostic outcomes in late adolescence. *Journal of Clinical Child and Adolescent Psychology, 44*(3), 393–404. https://doi.org/10.1080/15374416.2014.881293

Schwartz, P. D., Maynard, A. M., & Uzelac, S. M. (2008). Adolescent egocentrism: A contemporary view. *Adolescence, 43*(171), 441–448.

Schwartz, S. J., Luyckx, K., & Crocetti, E. (2015). What have we learned since Schwartz (2001)? In K. C. McLean & M. Syed (Eds.), *The Oxford handbook of identity development* (pp. 539–561). Oxford, England: Oxford University Press. https://doi.org/10.1093/oxfordhb/9780199936564.013.028

Schwartz, S. J., Zamboanga, B. L., Luyckx, K., Meca, A., & Ritchie, R. A. (2013). Identity in emerging adulthood: Reviewing the field and looking forward. *Emerging Adulthood, 1*(2), 96–113. https://doi.org/10.1177/2167696813479781

Schwebel, D. C., Rosen, C. S., & Singer, J. L. (1999). Preschoolers' pretend play and theory of mind: The role of jointly constructed pretence. *British Journal of Developmental Psychology, 17*(3), 333–348. https://doi.org/10.1348/026151099165320

Schweinhart, L. J., Montie, J., Iang, Z., Barnett, W. S., Belfield, C. R., & Nores, M. (2005). *Lifetime effects: The High/Scope Perry Preschool study through age 40.* Ypsilanti, MI: High/Scope Press.

Schwerdt, G., West, M. R., & Winters, M. A. (2017). The effects of test-based retention on student outcomes over time: Regression discontinuity evidence from Florida. *Journal of Public Economics, 152*, 154–169. https://doi.org/10.1016/J.JPUBECO.2017.06.004

Scoliers, G., Portzky, G., Madge, N., Hewitt, A., Hawton, K., de Wilde, E. J., . . . Van Heeringen, K. (2009). Reasons for adolescent deliberate self-harm: A cry of pain and/or a cry for help? *Social Psychiatry & Psychiatric Epidemiology, 44*(8), 601–607. https://doi.org/10.1007/s00127-008-0469-z

Scott Adzick, N. (2013). Fetal surgery for spina bifida: Past, present, future. *Seminars in Pediatric Surgery, 22*(1), 10–17. https://doi.org/10.1053/j.sempedsurg.2012.10.003

Scott, E. S., Duell, N., & Steinberg, L. (2018, January 8). Brain development, social context and justice policy. Retrieved from https://papers.ssrn.com/sol3/papers.cfm?abstract_id=3118366

Scott, E., & Panksepp, J. (2003). Rough-and-tumble play in human children. *Aggressive Behavior, 29*(6), 539–551. https://doi.org/10.1002/ab.10062

Scott, L. S., Pascalis, O., & Nelson, C. A. (2007). A domain-general theory of the development of perceptual discrimination. *Current Directions in Psychological Science, 16*(4), 197–201. https://doi.org/10.1111/j.1467-8721.2007.00503.x

Scott, R. M., & Baillargeon, R. (2017). Early false-belief understanding. *Trends in Cognitive Sciences, 21*(4), 237–249. https://doi.org/10.1016/J.TICS.2017.01.012

Scutti, S. (2015). Puberty comes earlier and earlier for girls. *Newsweek.* Retrieved from http://www.newsweek.com/2015/02/06/puberty-comes-earlier-and-earlier-girls-301920.html

Search Institute. (2017). *The asset approach: 40 Elements of healthy development, 2017 update.* Minneapolis, MN: Author. Retrieved from https://www.search-institute.org/product/the-asset-approach-40-elements-of-healthy-development-2017-update/

Sears, H. A., Byers, S. E., & Price, L. E. (2007). The co-occurrence of adolescent boys' and girls' use of psychologically, physically, and sexually abusive behaviours in their dating relationships. *Journal of Adolescence, 30*(3), 487–504. https://doi.org/10.1016/j.adolescence.2006.05.002

Seaton, E. K., & Carter, R. (2018). Pubertal timing, racial identity, neighborhood, and school context among Black adolescent females. *Cultural Diversity and Ethnic Minority Psychology, 24*(1), 40–50. https://doi.org/10.1037/cdp0000162

Sebanc, A. M., Kearns, K. T., Hernandez, M. D., & Galvin, K. B. (2007). Predicting having a best friend in young children: Individual characteristics and friendship features. *Journal of Genetic Psychology, 168*(1), 81–96. https://doi.org/10.3200/GNTP.168.1.81-96

Sedgh, G., Finer, L. B., Bankole, A., Eilers, M. A., & Singh, S. (2015). Adolescent pregnancy, birth, and abortion rates across countries: Levels and recent trends. *Journal of Adolescent Health, 56*(2), 223–230. https://doi.org/10.1016/j.jadohealth.2014.09.007

Segal, J., & Newman, R. S. (2015). Infant preferences for structural and prosodic properties of infant-directed speech in the second year of life. *Infancy, 20*(3), 339–351. https://doi.org/10.1111/infa.12077

Seger, J. Y., & Thorstensson, A. (2000). Muscle strength and electromyogram in boys and girls followed through puberty. *European Journal of Applied Physiology, 81*(1–2), 54–61. https://doi.org/10.1007/PL00013797

Seggers, J., Pontesilli, M., Ravelli, A. C. J., Painter, R. C., Hadders-Algra, M., Heineman, M. J., . . . Ensing, S. (2016). Effects of in vitro fertilization and maternal characteristics on perinatal outcomes: A population-based study using siblings. *Fertility and Sterility, 105*(3), 590-598.e2. https://doi.org/10.1016/J.FERTNSTERT.2015.11.015

Seidman, E., Aber, J. L., & French, S. E. (2004). The organization of schooling and adolescent development. In K. I. Maton, C. J. Schellenbach, B. J. Leadbeater, & A. L. Solarz (Eds.), *Investing in children, youth, families, and communities: Strengths-based research and policy* (pp. 233–250). Washington, DC: American Psychological Association.

Seifer, R., Dickstein, S., Parade, S., Hayden, L. C., Magee, K. D., & Schiller, M. (2014). Mothers' appraisal of goodness of fit and children's social development. *International Journal of Behavioral Development, 38*(1), 86–97. https://doi.org/10.1177/0165025413507172

Seiler, N. K. (2016). Alcohol and pregnancy: CDC's health advice and the legal rights of pregnant women. *Public Health Reports 131*(4), 623–627. https://doi.org/10.1177/003335491666222

Selby, E. A., Nock, M. K., & Kranzler, A. (2014). How does self-injury feel? Examining automatic positive reinforcement in adolescent self-injurers with experience sampling. *Psychiatry Research, 215*(2), 417–423. https://doi.org/10.1016/j.psychres.2013.12.005

Selman, R. L. (1980). *The growth of interpersonal understanding.* New York, NY: Academic Press.

Senbanjo, I. O., Oshikoya, K. A., Odusanya, O. O., & Njokanma, O. F. (2011). Prevalence of and risk factors for stunting among school children and adolescents in Abeokuta, southwest Nigeria. *Journal of Health, Population, and Nutrition, 29*(4), 364–370. Retrieved from https://www.ncbi.nlm.nih.gov/pmc/articles/PMC3190367/

Senju, A. (2012). Spontaneous theory of mind and its absence in autism spectrum disorders. *Neuroscientist, 18*(2), 108–113. https://doi.org/10.1177/1073858410397208

Serbin, L. A., Powlishta, K. K., & Gulko, J. (1993). The development of sex typing in middle childhood. *Monographs of the Society for Research in Child Development, 58*(2), 1–99. Retrieved from http://www.ncbi.nlm.nih.gov/pubmed/8474512

Serpell, R. (1974). Aspects of intelligence in a developing country. *African Social Research, 17*, 578–596.

Serpell, R., & Jere-Folotiya, J. (2008). Developmental assessment, cultural context, gender, and schooling in Zambia. *International Journal of Psychology, 43*(2), 88–96.

Serra, A. E., Lemon, L. S., Mokhtari, N. B., Parks, W. T., Catov, J. M., Venkataramanan, R., & Caritis, S. N. (2017). Delayed villous maturation in term placentas exposed to opioid maintenance therapy: A retrospective cohort study. *American Journal of Obstetrics and Gynecology, 216*(4), 418.e1–418.e5. https://doi.org/10.1016/J.AJOG.2016.12.016

Servant, M., Cassey, P., Woodman, G. F., & Logan, G. D. (2018). Neural bases of automaticity. *Journal of Experimental Psychology: Learning, Memory, and Cognition, 44*(3), 440–464. https://doi.org/10.1037/xlm0000454

Servey, J., & Chang, J. (2014). Over-the-counter medications in pregnancy. *American Family Physician, 90*(8), 548–555. Retrieved from http://www.ncbi.nlm.nih.gov/pubmed/25369643

Sethna, V. F., Perry, E., Domoney, J., Iles, J., Psychogiou, L., Rowbotham, N. E. L., . . . Ramchandani, P. G. (2016). Father-child interactions at 3-months and 2 years: contributions to children's cognitive development at 2 years. *Infant Mental Health Journal, 38*(3), 378–390. https://doi.org/10.1002/imhj.21642

Ševčiková, A. (2016). Girls' and boys' experience with teen sexting in early and late adolescence. *Journal of Adolescence, 51*, 156–162. https://doi.org/10.1016/j.adolescence.2016.06.007

Ševčiková, A., Blinka, L., & Daneback, K. (2018). Sexting as a predictor of sexual behavior in a sample of Czech adolescents. *European Journal of Developmental Psychology, 15*, 426–437. https://doi.org/10.1080/17405629.2017.1295842

Shaffer, D. R. (2002). *Developmental psychology: Childhood and adolescence* (6th ed.). Belmont, CA: Wadsworth/Thomson.

Shah, K., DeRemigis, A., Hageman, J. R., Sriram, S., & Waggoner, D. (2017). Unique characteristics of the X chromosome and related disorders. *NeoReviews, 18*(4), e209–e216. https://doi.org/10.1542/neo.18-4-e209

Shahaeian, A., Peterson, C. C., Slaughter, V., & Wellman, H. M. (2011). Culture and the sequence of steps in theory of mind development. *Developmental Psychology, 47*(5), 1239–1247. https://doi.org/10.1037/a0023899

Shahbazian, N., Barati, M., Arian, P., & Saadati, N. (2012). Comparison of complications of chorionic villus sampling and amniocentesis. *International Journal of Fertility & Sterility, 5*(4), 241–244.

Shankar, P., Chung, R., & Frank, D. A. (2017). Association of food insecurity with children's behavioral, emotional, and academic outcomes: A systematic review. *Journal of Developmental and Behavioral Pediatrics, 38*(2), 135–150. https://doi.org/10.1097/DBP.0000000000000383

Shapiro, B., Fagen, J., Prigot, J., Carroll, M., & Shalan, J. (1998). Infants' emotional and regulatory behaviors in response to violations of expectancies. *Infant Behavior and Development, 27*, 299–313.

Shapiro-Mendoza, C. K., Colson, E. R., Willinger, M., Rybin, D. V., Camperlengo, L., & Corwin, M. J. (2014). Trends in infant bedding use: National Infant Sleep Position Study, 1993–2010. *Pediatrics, 135*(1), 10–17. https://doi.org/10.1542/peds.2014-1793

Sharapova, S. R., Phillips, E., Sirocco, K., Kaminski, J. W., Leeb, R. T., & Rolle, I. (2018). Effects of prenatal marijuana exposure on neuropsychological outcomes in children aged 1-11 years: A systematic review. *Paediatric and Perinatal Epidemiology, 32*(6), 512–532. https://doi.org/10.1111/ppe.12505

Sharma, P., McAlinden, K., Chan, Y., Kota, A., Komalla, V., Chen, H., & Oliver, B. (2017). Maternal eCigarette vaping enhances Th2 driven asthma in the offspring. *Airway Pharmacology and Treatment*, 50, PA4694). https://doi.org/10.1183/1393003.congress-2017.PA4694

Shaw, D. J., & Czekóová, K. (2013). Exploring the development of the mirror neuron system: Finding the right paradigm. *Developmental Neuropsychology, 38*(4), 256–271. https://doi.org/10.1080/87565641.2013.783832

Shearer, C. B., & Karanian, J. M. (2017). The neuroscience of intelligence: Empirical support for the theory of multiple intelligences? *Trends in Neuroscience and Education, 6*, 211–223. https://doi.org/10.1016/J.TINE.2017.02.002

Sheehy, A. T. Gasser, L. Molinari, R. H. L. (2009). An analysis of variance of the pubertal and midgrowth spurts for length and width. *Annals of Human Biology, 26*(4), 309–331. https://doi.org/10.1080/030144699282642

Shepard, L. S., & Smith, M. L. (1990). Synthesis of research on grade retention. *Educational Leadership, 47*(8), 84–88.

Sheppard, L. D. (2008). Intelligence and speed of information-processing: A review of 50 years of research. *Personality & Individual Differences, 44*(3), 533–549.

Sheridan, M. A., & McLaughlin, K. A. (2014). Dimensions of early experience and neural development: Deprivation and threat. *Trends in Cognitive Sciences, 18*(11), 580–585. https://doi.org/10.1016/J.TICS.2014.09.001

Sheridan, M. A., Sarsour, K., Jutte, D., D'Esposito, M., & Boyce, W. T. (2012). The impact of social disparity on prefrontal function in childhood. *PLoS ONE, 7*(4), e35744. https://doi.org/10.1371/journal.pone.0035744

Sherman, L. E., Greenfield, P. M., Hernandez, L. M., & Dapretto, M. (2018). Peer influence via Instagram: Effects on brain and behavior in adolescence and young adulthood. *Child Development, 89*(1), 37–47. https://doi.org/10.1111/cdev.12838

Sherman, L. E., Payton, A. A., Hernandez, L. M., Greenfield, P. M., & Dapretto, M. (2016). The power of the *like* in adolescence. *Psychological Science, 27*(7), 1027–1035. https://doi.org/10.1177/0956797616645673

Sherr, L., Mueller, J., & Varrall, R. (2009). A systematic review of cognitive development and child human immunodeficiency virus infection. *Psychology, Health & Medicine, 14*(4), 387–404. https://doi.org/10.1080/13548500903012897

Shetgiri, R., Lin, H., & Flores, G. (2013). Trends in risk and protective factors for child bullying perpetration in the United States. *Child Psychiatry and Human Development, 44*(1), 89–104. https://doi.org/10.1007/s10578-012-0312-3

Shi, B., & Xie, H. (2012). Popular and nonpopular subtypes of physically aggressive preadolescents: Continuity of aggression and peer mechanisms during the transition to middle school. *Merrill-Palmer Quarterly, 58*(4), 530–553. https://doi.org/10.1353/mpq.2012.0025

Shim, S.-S., Malone, F., Canick, J., Ball, R., Nyberg, D., Comstock, C., . . . Abuhamad, A. (2014). Chorionic villus sampling. *Journal of Genetic Medicine, 11*(2), 43–48. https://doi.org/10.5734/JGM.2014.11.2.43

Shin, H., & Ryan, A. M. (2014). Early adolescent friendships and academic adjustment: Examining selection and influence processes with longitudinal social network analysis. *Developmental Psychology, 50*(11), 2462–2472. https://doi.org/10.1037/a0037922

Shinskey, J. L. (2012). Disappearing décalage: Object search in light and dark at 6 months. *Infancy, 17*(3), 272–294. https://doi.org/10.1111/j.1532-7078.2011.00078.x

Shmaya, Y., Eilat-Adar, S., Leitner, Y., Reif, S., & Gabis, L. V. (2017). Meal time behavior difficulties but not nutritional deficiencies correlate with sensory processing in children with autism spectrum disorder. *Research in Developmental Disabilities, 66*, 27–33. https://doi.org/10.1016/J.RIDD.2017.05.004

Shulman, E. P., & Cauffman, E. (2013). Reward-biased risk appraisal and its relation to juvenile versus adult crime. *Law and Human Behavior, 37*(6), 412–423. https://doi.org/10.1037/lhb0000033

Shulman, E. P., Smith, A. R., Silva, K., Icenogle, G., Duell, N., Chein, J., & Steinberg, L. (2016). The dual systems model: Review, reappraisal, and reaffirmation. *Developmental Cognitive Neuroscience, 17*, 103–117. https://doi.org/10.1016/j.dcn.2015.12.010

Shutts, K., Kenward, B., Falk, H., Ivegran, A., & Fawcett, C. (2017). Early preschool environments and gender: Effects of gender pedagogy in Sweden. *Journal of Experimental Child Psychology, 162*, 1–17. https://doi.org/10.1016/J.JECP.2017.04.014

Shwe, H. I., & Markman, E. M. (1997). Young children's appreciation of the mental impact of their communicative signals. *Developmental Psychology, 33*, 630–636.

Siegel, L. S. (1994). Working memory and reading: A life-span perspective. *International Journal of Behavioural Development, 17*, 109–124.

Siegler, R. S. (2016). How does change occur? In R. Sternberg, S. Fiske, & D. Foss (Eds.), *Scientists making a difference: One hundred eminent behavioral and brain scientists talk about their most important contributions* (pp. 223–227). New York, NY: Cambridge University Press.

Siekerman, K., Barbu-Roth, M., Anderson, D. I., Donnelly, A., Goffinet, F., & Teulier, C. (2015). Treadmill stimulation improves newborn stepping. *Developmental Psychobiology, 57*(2), 247–254. https://doi.org/10.1002/dev.21270

Sigelman, C. K., Carr, M. B., & Begley, N. L. (1986). Developmental changes in the influence of sex-role stereotypes on person perception. *Child Study Journal, 16*(3), 191–205. Retrieved from http://psycnet.apa.org/psycinfo/1987-10006-001

Signorella, M., & Liben, L. S. (1984). Recall and reconstruction of gender-related pictures: Effects of attitude, task difficulty, and age. *Child Development, 55*, 393–405.

Silkenbeumer, J. R., Schiller, E.-M., & Kärtner, J. (2018). Co- and self-regulation of emotions in the preschool setting. *Early Childhood Research Quarterly, 44*, 72–81. https://doi.org/10.1016/J.ECRESQ.2018.02.014

Sills, J., Rowse, G., & Emerson, L.-M. (2016). The role of collaboration in the cognitive development of young children: A systematic review. *Child: Care, Health and Development, 42*(3), 313–324. https://doi.org/10.1111/cch.12330

Silva, M., Strasser, K., & Cain, K. (2014). Early narrative skills in Chilean preschool: Questions scaffold the production of coherent narratives. *Early Childhood Research Quarterly, 29*(2), 205–213. https://doi.org/10.1016/j.ecresq.2014.02.002

Silveri, M. M., Dager, A. D., Cohen-Gilbert, J. E., & Sneider, J. T. (2016). Neurobiological signatures associated with alcohol and drug use in the human adolescent brain. *Neuroscience & Biobehavioral Reviews, 70*, 244–259. https://doi.org/10.1016/J.NEUBIOREV.2016.06.042

Silveri, M. M., Tzilos, G. K., & Yurgelun-Todd, D. A. (2008). Relationship between white matter volume and cognitive performance during adolescence: Effects of age, sex and risk for drug use. *Addiction, 103*(9), 1509–1520. https://doi.org/10.1111/j.1360-0443.2008.02272.x

Sim, A., Fazel, M., Bowes, L., & Gardner, F. (2018). Pathways linking war and displacement to parenting and child adjustment: A qualitative study with Syrian refugees in Lebanon. *Social Science & Medicine, 200*, 19–26. https://doi.org/10.1016/J.SOCSCIMED.2018.01.009

Sim, T. N., & Koh, S. F. (2003). A domain conceptualization of adolescent susceptibility to peer pressure. *Journal of Research on Adolescence, 13*, 58–80.

Simard, D., & Gutiérrez, X. (2018). The study of metalinguistic constructs in second language acquisition research. In P. Garrett & J. M. Cots (Eds.), *The Routledge handbook of language awareness*. New York, NY: Routledge. Retrieved from https://www.routledge.com/The-Routledge-Handbook-of-Language-Awareness/Garrett-Cots/p/book/9781138937048

Simmering, V. R. (2016). I. Working memory capacity in context: Modeling dynamic processes of behavior, memory, and development. *Monographs of the Society for Research in Child Development, 81*(3), 7–24. https://doi.org/10.1111/mono.12249

Simmonds, D., & Luna, B. (2015). *Protracted development of brain systems underlying working memory in adolescence: A longitudinal study* (Doctoral dissertation). University of Pittsburgh, Pittsburg, PA.

Simmons, K. (2015). Sub-Saharan Africa makes progress against poverty but has long way to go. Retrieved from http://www.pewresearch.org/fact-tank/2015/09/24/sub-saharan-africa-makes-progress-against-poverty-but-has-long-way-to-go/

Simons, J. S., Wills, T. A., & Neal, D. J. (2014). The many faces of affect: A multilevel model of drinking frequency/quantity and alcohol dependence symptoms among young adults. *Journal of Abnormal Psychology, 123*(3), 676–694. https://doi.org/10.1037/a0036926

Simons, L., Schrager, S. M., Clark, L. F., Belzer, M., & Olson, J. (2013). Parental support and mental health among transgender adolescents. *Journal of Adolescent Health, 53*(6), 791–793. https://doi.org/10.1016/j.jadohealth.2013.07.019

Simons, S. S. H., Cillessen, A. H. N., & de Weerth, C. (2017). Cortisol stress responses and children's behavioral functioning at school. *Developmental Psychobiology, 59*(2), 217–224. https://doi.org/10.1002/dev.21484

Simonton, D. K., & Song, A. V. (2009). Eminence, IQ, physical and mental health, and achievement domain: Cox's 282 geniuses revisited. *Psychological Science, 20*(4), 429–434. https://doi.org/10.1111/J.1467-9280.2009.02313.X

Simpkins, S. D., Delgado, M. Y., Price, C. D., Quach, A., & Starbuck, E. (2013). Socioeconomic status, ethnicity, culture, and immigration: Examining the potential mechanisms underlying Mexican-origin adolescents' organized activity participation. *Developmental Psychology, 49*(4), 706–721. https://doi.org/10.1037/a0028399

Sinclair, K. D., & Watkins, A. J. (2013). Parental diet, pregnancy outcomes and offspring health: Metabolic determinants in developing oocytes and embryos. *Reproduction, Fertility, and Development, 26*(1), 99–114. https://doi.org/10.1071/RD13290

Singer, L. T., Minnes, S., Min, M. O., Lewis, B. A., & Short, E. J. (2015). Prenatal cocaine exposure and child outcomes: A conference report based on a prospective study from Cleveland. *Human Psychopharmacology: Clinical and Experimental, 30*(4), 285–289. https://doi.org/10.1002/hup.2454

Singh, G. K., & Kogan, M. D. (2007). Widening socioeconomic disparities in US childhood mortality, 1969--2000. *American Journal of Public Health, 97*(9), 1658–1665.

Singh, L., Fu, C. S. L., Tay, Z. W., & Golinkoff, R. M. (2018). Novel word learning in bilingual and monolingual infants: Evidence for a bilingual advantage. *Child Development, 89*(3), e183–e198. https://doi.org/10.1111/cdev.12747

Singh, L., Nestor, S., Parikh, C., & Yull, A. (2009). Influences of infant-directed speech on early word recognition. *Infancy, 14*(6), 654–666. https://doi.org/10.1080/15250000903263973

Sinnott, J. D. (2003). Postformal thought and adult development: Living in balance. In J. Demick & C. Andreoletti (Eds.), *Handbookof adult development* (pp. 221–238). New York, NY: Kluwer.

Sinozich, S., & Langton, L. (2014). *Rape and sexual assault victimization among college-age females, 1995–2013*. Washington, DC: U.S. Department of Justice. Retrieved from https://assets.documentcloud.org/documents/1378364/rsavcaf9513.pdf

Sirnes, E., Oltedal, L., Bartsch, H., Eide, G. E., Elgen, I. B., & Aukland, S. M. (2017). Brain morphology in school-aged children with prenatal opioid exposure: A structural MRI study. *Early Human Development, 106–107*, 33–39. https://doi.org/10.1016/J.EARLHUMDEV.2017.01.009

Sisk, C. L. (2017). Development: Pubertal hormones meet the adolescent brain. *Current Biology, 27*(14), R706–R708. https://doi.org/10.1016/J.CUB.2017.05.092

Skinner, B. F. (1957). *Verbal behavior*. New York, NY: Appleton-Century-Crofts.

Skinner, O. D., & McHale, S. M. (2016). Parent–adolescent conflict in African American families. *Journal of Youth and Adolescence, 45*(10), 2080–2093. https://doi.org/10.1007/s10964-016-0514-2

Skitka, L. J., Bauman, C. W., & Mullen, E. (2016). Morality and justice. In C. Sabbagh & M. Schmitt (Eds.), *Handbook of social justice theory and research* (pp. 407–423). New York, NY: Springer. https://doi.org/10.1007/978-1-4939-3216-0_22

Skoog, T., & Özdemir, S. B. (2016). Explaining why early-maturing girls are more exposed to sexual harassment in early adolescence. *Journal of Early Adolescence, 36*(4), 490–509. https://doi.org/10.1177/0272431614568198

Skoog, T., Özdemir, S. B., & Stattin, H. (2016). Understanding the link between pubertal timing in girls and the development of depressive symptoms: The role of sexual harassment. *Journal of Youth and Adolescence, 45*(2), 316–327. https://doi.org/10.1007/s10964-015-0292-2

Skoog, T., & Stattin, H. (2014). Why and under what contextual conditions do early-maturing girls develop problem behaviors? *Child Development Perspectives, 8*(3), 158–162. https://doi.org/10.1111/cdep.12076

Slaby, R. G., Roedell, W. C., Arezzo, D., & Hendrix, K. (1995). *Early violence prevention*. Washington, DC: National Association for the Education of Young Children.

Slater, A., Rose, D., & Morison, V. (1984). Newborn infants' perception of similarities and differences between two- and three-dimensional stimuli. *British Journal of Developmental Psychology, 3*, 211–220.

Slater, A., & Tiggemann, M. (2016). Little girls in a grown up world: Exposure to sexualized media, internalization of sexualization messages, and body image in 6–9 year-old girls. *Body Image, 18*, 19–22. https://doi.org/10.1016/j.bodyim.2016.04.004

Slaughter, V., Imuta, K., Peterson, C. C., & Henry, J. D. (2015). Meta-analysis of theory of mind and peer popularity in the preschool and early school years. *Child Development, 86*(4), 1159–1174. https://doi.org/10.1111/cdev.12372

Slaughter, V., & Perez-Zapata, D. (2014). Cultural variations in the development of mind reading. *Child Development Perspectives, 8*(4), 237–241. https://doi.org/10.1111/cdep.12091

Slaughter, V., Peterson, C. C., & Mackintosh, E. (2007). Mind what mother says: Narrative input and theory of mind in typical children and those on the autism spectrum. *Child Development, 78*(3), 839–858. https://doi.org/10.1111/j.1467-8624.2007.01036.x

Sloan, S., Stewart, M., & Dunne, L. (2010). The effect of breastfeeding and stimulation in the home on cognitive development in one-year-old infants. *Child Care in Practice, 16*(2), 101–110. https://doi.org/10.1080/13575270903529136

Slone, M., & Mann, S. (2016). Effects of war, terrorism and armed conflict on young children: A systematic review. *Child Psychiatry & Human Development, 47*(6), 950–965. https://doi.org/10.1007/s10578-016-0626-7

Slutzky, C. B., & Simpkins, S. D. (2009). The link between children's sport participation and self-esteem: Exploring the mediating role of sport self-concept. *Psychology of Sport & Exercise, 10*(3), 381–389. https://doi.org/10.1016/j.psychsport.2008.09.006

Smetana, J. G. (1995). Morality in context: Abstractions, ambiguities, and applications. In R. Vasta (Ed.), *Annals of child development* (Vol. 10, pp. 83–130). London, England: Jessica Kingsley.

Smetana, J. G., & Braeges, J. L. (1990). The development of toddler's moral and conventional judgments. *Merrill-Palmer Quarterly, 36*, 329–346.

Smetana, J. G., Jambon, M., & Ball, C. (2013). The social domain approach to children's moral and social judgments. In M. Killen & J. G. Smetana (Eds.), *Handbook of moral development* (pp. 23–44). New York, NY: Psychology Press. https://doi.org/10.4324/9780203581957

Smetana, J. G., Tasopoulos-Chan, M., Gettman, D. C., Villalobos, M., Campione-Barr, N., & Metzger, A. (2009). Adolescents' and parents' evaluations of helping versus fulfilling personal desires in family situations. *Child Development, 80*(1), 280–294. https://doi.org/10.1111/j.1467-8624.2008.01259.x

Smink, F. R. E., van Hoeken, D., & Hoek, H. W. (2013). Epidemiology, course, and outcome of eating disorders. *Current Opinion in Psychiatry, 26*(6), 543–548. https://doi.org/10.1097/YCO.0b013e328365a24f

Smink, F. R. E., van Hoeken, D., Oldehinkel, A. J., & Hoek, H. W. (2014). Prevalence and severity of DSM-5 eating disorders in a community cohort of adolescents. *International Journal of Eating Disorders, 47*(6), 610–619. https://doi.org/10.1002/eat.22316

Smith, A. M., Mioduszewski, O., Hatchard, T., Byron-Alhassan, A., Fall, C., & Fried, P. A. (2016). Prenatal marijuana exposure impacts executive functioning into young adulthood: An fMRI study. *Neurotoxicology and Teratology, 58*, 53–59. https://doi.org/10.1016/J.NTT.2016.05.010

Smith, A. R., Chein, J., & Steinberg, L. (2013). Impact of socio-emotional context, brain development, and pubertal maturation on adolescent risk-taking. *Hormones and Behavior, 64*(2), 323–332. https://doi.org/10.1016/j.yhbeh.2013.03.006

Smith, A. R., Chein, J., & Steinberg, L. (2014). Peers increase adolescent risk taking even when the probabilities of negative outcomes are known. *Developmental Psychology, 50*(5), 1564–1568. https://doi.org/10.1037/a0035696

Smith, A. R., Rosenbaum, G. M., Botdorf, M. A., Steinberg, L., & Chein, J. M. (2018). Peers influence adolescent reward processing, but not response inhibition. *Cognitive, Affective, & Behavioral Neuroscience, 18*(2), 284–295. https://doi.org/10.3758/s13415-018-0569-5

Smith, A. R., Steinberg, L., Strang, N., & Chein, J. (2015). Age differences in the impact of peers on adolescents' and adults' neural response to reward. *Developmental Cognitive Neuroscience, 11*, 75–82. https://doi.org/10.1016/j.dcn.2014.08.010

Smith, C. E., Blake, P. R., & Harris, P. L. (2013). I should but I won't: Why young children endorse norms of fair sharing but do not follow them. *PLoS ONE, 8*(3), e59510. https://doi.org/10.1371/journal.pone.0059510

Smith, C. E., & Warneken, F. (2016). Children's reasoning about distributive and retributive justice across development. *Developmental Psychology, 52*(4), 613–628. https://doi.org/10.1037/a0040069

Smith, T. E., & Leaper, C. (2006). Self-perceived gender typicality and the peer context during adolescence. *Journal of Research on Adolescence, 16*(1), 91–104. https://doi.org/10.1111/j.1532-7795.2006.00123.x

Smith-Darden, J. P., Kernsmith, P. D., Reidy, D. E., & Cortina, K. S. (2017). In search of modifiable risk and protective factors for teen dating violence. *Journal of Research on Adolescence, 27*(2), 423–435. https://doi.org/10.1111/jora.12280

Smith-Gagen, J., Hollen, R., Walker, M., Cook, D. M., & Yang, W. (2014). Breastfeeding laws and breastfeeding practices by race and ethnicity. *Women's Health Issues, 24*(1), e11–e19. https://doi.org/10.1016/J.WHI.2013.11.001

Smolak, L. (2011). Body image development in childhood. In T. F. Cash & L. Smolak (Eds.), *Body image: A handbook of science, practice, and prevention* (pp. 67–75). New York, NY: Guilford.

Snowling, M. J. (2013). Early identification and interventions for dyslexia: A contemporary view. *Journal of Research in Special Educational Needs, 13*(1), 7–14. https://doi.org/10.1111/j.1471-3802.2012.01262.x

Society for Research in Child Development. (2007). *Ethical standards in research.* Retrieved from http://www.srcd.org/about-us/ethical-standards-research

Söderström-Anttila, V., Wennerholm, U.-B., Loft, A., Pinborg, A., Aittomäki, K., Romundstad, L. B., & Bergh, C. (2015). Surrogacy: Outcomes for surrogate mothers, children and the resulting families—a systematic review. *Human Reproduction Update, 22*(2), dmv046. https://doi.org/10.1093/humupd/dmv046

Somers, M., Shields, L. S., Boks, M. P., Kahn, R. S., & Sommer, I. E. (2015). Cognitive benefits of right-handedness: A meta-analysis. *Neuroscience & Biobehavioral Reviews, 51*, 48–63. https://doi.org/10.1016/J.NEUBIOREV.2015.01.003

Song, Y., Ma, J., Li, L.-B., Dong, B., Wang, Z., & Agardh, A. (2016). Secular trends for age at spermarche among Chinese boys from 11 ethnic minorities, 1995-2010: A multiple cross-sectional study. *BMJ Open, 6*(2), e010518. https://doi.org/10.1136/bmjopen-2015-010518

Sørensen, K., Mouritsen, A., Aksglaede, L., Hagen, C. P., Mogensen, S. S., & Juul, A. (2012). Recent secular trends in pubertal timing: Implications for evaluation and diagnosis of precocious puberty. *Hormone Research in Paediatrics, 77*(3), 137–145. https://doi.org/10.1159/000336325

Sorkhabi, N. (2005). Applicability of Baumrind's parent typology to collective cultures: Analysis of cultural explanations of parent socialization effects. *International Journal of Behavioral Development, 29*(6), 552–563.

Sosic-Vasic, Z., Kröner, J., Schneider, S., Vasic, N., Spitzer, M., & Streb, J. (2017). The association between parenting behavior and executive functioning in children and young adolescents. *Frontiers in Psychology, 8*, 472. https://doi.org/10.3389/fpsyg.2017.00472

Soubry, A., Hoyo, C., Jirtle, R. L., & Murphy, S. K. (2014). A paternal environmental legacy: Evidence for epigenetic inheritance through the male germ line. *BioEssays, 36*(4), 359–371. https://doi.org/10.1002/bies.201300113

Sours, C., Raghavan, P., Foxworthy, W. A., Meredith, M. A., El Metwally, D., Zhuo, J., . . . Gullapalli, R. P. (2017). Cortical multisensory connectivity is present near birth in humans. *Brain Imaging and Behavior, 11*(4), 1207–1213. https://doi.org/10.1007/s11682-016-9586-6

Sousa, D. A. (2001). *How the brain learns: A classroom teacher's guide.* Thousand Oaks, CA: Corwin.

Spear, L. P. (2011). Adolescent neurobehavioral characteristics, alcohol sensitivities, and intake: Setting the stage for alcohol use disorders? *Child Development Perspectives, 5*(4), 231–238. https://doi.org/10.1111/j.1750-8606.2011.00182.x

Spear, L. P. (2018). Effects of adolescent alcohol consumption on the brain and behaviour. *Nature Reviews Neuroscience, 19*(4), 197–214. https://doi.org/10.1038/nrn.2018.10

Spelke, E. (2016a). Cognitive abilities of infants. In R. J. Sternberg, S. T. Fiske, & D. J. Foss (Eds.), *Scientists making a difference: One hundred eminent behavioral and brain scientists talk about their most important contributions* (pp. 228–232). New York, NY: Cambridge University Press.

Spelke, E. S. (2016b). Core knowledge and conceptual change. In D. Barner & A. S. Baron (Eds.), *Core knowledge and conceptual change* (pp. 279–300). New York, NY: Oxford University Press.

Spelke, E. S. (2017). Core knowledge, language, and number. *Language Learning and Development, 13*(2), 147–170. https://doi.org/10.1080/15475441.2016.1263572

Spencer, D. L., McManus, M., Call, K. T., Turner, J., Harwood, C., White, P., & Alarcon, G. (2018). Health care coverage and access among children, adolescents, and young adults, 2010-2016: Implications for future health reforms. *Journal of Adolescent Health, 62*(6), 667–673. https://doi.org/10.1016/j.jadohealth.2017.12.012

Spencer, J. P., Vereijken, B., Diedrich, F. J., & Thelen, E. (2000). Posture and the emergence of manual skills. *Developmental Science, 3*(2), 216–217.

Spencer, M. B., Swanson, D. P., & Harpalani, V. (2015). Development of the self. In M. E. Lamb (Ed.), *Handbook of child psychology and developmental science* (pp. 1–44). Hoboken, NJ: John Wiley & Sons. https://doi.org/10.1002/9781118963418.childpsy318

Spencer, R. M. C., Walker, M. P., & Stickgold, R. (2017). Sleep and memory consolidation. In S. Chokroverty (Ed.), *Sleep disorders medicine* (pp. 205–223). New York, NY: Springer. https://doi.org/10.1007/978-1-4939-6578-6_13

Spera, C. (2005). A review of the relationship among parenting practices, parenting styles, and adolescent school achievement. *Educational Psychology Review, 17*(2), 125–146.

Spiegel, C., & Halberda, J. (2011). Rapid fast-mapping abilities in 2-year-olds. *Journal of Experimental Child Psychology, 109*(1), 132–140. https://doi.org/10.1016/j.jecp.2010.10.013

Spielberg, J. M., Olino, T. M., Forbes, E. E., & Dahl, R. E. (2014). Exciting fear in adolescence: Does pubertal development alter threat processing? *Developmental Cognitive Neuroscience, 8*, 86–95. https://doi.org/10.1016/j.dcn.2014.01.004

Spielvogel, I., Matthes, J., Naderer, B., & Karsay, K. (2018). A treat for the eyes. An eye-tracking study on children's attention to unhealthy and healthy food cues in media content. *Appetite, 125*, 63–71. https://doi.org/10.1016/J.APPET.2018.01.033

Spilt, J. L., Hughes, J. N., Wu, J.-Y., & Kwok, O.-M. (2012). Dynamics of teacher-student relationships: Stability and change across elementary school and the influence on children's academic success. *Child Development, 83*(4), 1180–1195. https://doi.org/10.1111/j.1467-8624.2012.01761.x

Spinelli, J., Collins-Praino, L., Van Den Heuvel, C., & Byard, R. W. (2017). Evolution and significance of the triple risk model in sudden infant death syndrome. *Journal of Paediatrics and Child Health, 53*(2), 112–115. https://doi.org/10.1111/jpc.13429

Spinelli, M., & Mesman, J. (2018). The regulation of infant negative emotions: The role of maternal sensitivity and infant-directed speech prosody. *Infancy, 23*(4), 502–518. https://doi.org/10.1111/infa.12237

Spinrad, T. L., & Gal, D. E. (2018). Fostering prosocial behavior and empathy in young children. *Current Opinion in Psychology, 20*, 40–44. https://doi.org/10.1016/J.COPSYC.2017.08.004

Spruyt, K., Braam, W., & Curfs, L. M. (2018). Sleep in Angelman syndrome: A review of evidence. *Sleep Medicine Reviews, 37*, 69–84. https://doi.org/10.1016/J.SMRV.2017.01.002

Squeglia, L. M., & Gray, K. M. (2016). Alcohol and drug use and the developing brain. *Current Psychiatry Reports, 18*(5), 46. https://doi.org/10.1007/s11920-016-0689-y

Squeglia, L. M., Tapert, S. F., Sullivan, E. V., Jacobus, J., Meloy, M. J., Rohlfing, T., & Pfefferbaum, A. (2015). Brain development in heavy-drinking adolescents. *American Journal of Psychiatry, 172*(6), 531–542. https://doi.org/10.1176/appi.ajp.2015.14101249

Srabstein, J., Joshi, P. T., Due, P., Wright, J., Leventhal, B., Merrick, J., . . . Riibner, K. (2008). Antibullying legislation: A public health perspective. *Journal of Adolescent Health, 42*(1), 11–20. https://doi.org/10.1016/j.jadohealth.2007.10.007

Sroufe, L. A. (1977). Wariness of strangers and the study of infant development. *Child Development, 48*(3), 731–746.

Sroufe, L. A. (1997). Psychopathology as an outcome of development. *Development and Psychopathology, 7*, 323–336.

Sroufe, L. A. (2016). The place of attachment in development. In J. Cassidy & P. R. Shaver (Eds.), *Handbook of attachment: Theory, research, and clinical applications* (pp. 997–1010). New York, NY: Guilford. Retrieved from https://www.guilford.com/books/Handbook-of-Attachment/Cassidy-Shaver/9781462525294/contents

Sroufe, L. A., & Waters, E. (1976). The ontogenesis of smiling and laughter: A perspective on the organization of development in infancy. *Psychological Review, 83*(3), 173–189. https://doi.org/10.1037/0033-295x.83.3.173

Stacks, A. M., Oshio, T., Gerard, J., & Roe, J. (2009). The moderating effect of parental warmth on the association between spanking and child aggression: A longitudinal approach. *Infant & Child Development, 18*(2), 178–194. https://doi.org/10.1002/icd.596

Staff, J., & Uggen, C. (2003). The fruits of good work: Early work experiences and adolescent deviance. *Journal of Research in Crime & Delinquency, 40*(3), 263–290.

Staff, J., Vaneseltine, M., Woolnough, A., Silver, E., & Burrington, L. (2012). Adolescent work experiences and family formation behavior. *Journal of Research on Adolescence, 22*(1), 150–164. https://doi.org/10.1111/j.1532-7795.2011.00755.x

Stagi, S., Scalini, P., Farello, G., & Verrotti, A. (2017). Possible effects of an early diagnosis and treatment in patients with growth hormone deficiency: The state of art. *Italian Journal of Pediatrics, 43*(1), 81. https://doi.org/10.1186/s13052-017-0402-8

Stams, G.-J. J. M., Juffer, F., & van IJzendoorn, M. H. (2002). Maternal sensitivity, infant attachment, and temperament in early childhood predict adjustment in middle childhood: The case of adopted children and their biologically unrelated parents. *Developmental Psychology, 38*(5), 806–821. https://doi.org/10.1037/0012-1649.38.5.806

Stanford, S., Jones, M. P., & Hudson, J. L. (2017). Rethinking pathology in adolescent self-harm: Towards a more complex understanding of risk factors. *Journal of Adolescence, 54*, 32–41. https://doi.org/10.1016/j.adolescence.2016.11.004

Stang, J. S., & Stotmeister, B. (2017). Nutrition in adolescence. In N. J. Temple, T. Wilson, & G. A. Bray (Eds.), *Nutrition guide for physicians and related healthcare professionals* (pp. 29–39). Cham, Switzerland: Springer International Publishing. https://doi.org/10.1007/978-3-319-49929-1_4

Stansfield, R., Williams, K. R., & Parker, K. F. (2017). Economic disadvantage and homicide. *Homicide Studies, 21*(1), 59–81. https://doi.org/10.1177/1088767916647990

Stapel, J. C., van Wijk, I., Bekkering, H., & Hunnius, S. (2017). Eighteen-month-old infants show distinct electrophysiological responses to their own faces. *Developmental Science, 20*(5), e12437. https://doi.org/10.1111/desc.12437

Stark, A. D., Bennet, G. C., Stone, D. H., & Chishti, P. (2002). Association between childhood fractures and poverty: Population based study. *BMJ (Clinical Research Ed.), 324*(7335), 457. https://doi.org/10.1136/bmj.324.7335.457

Statistics Canada. (2015). *The 10 leading causes of death, 2011*. Retrieved from http://www.statcan.gc.ca/pub/82-625-x/2014001/article/11896-eng.htm

Steensma, T. D., & Cohen-Kettenis, P. T. (2011). Gender transitioning before puberty? *Archives of Sexual Behavior, 40*(4), 649–650. https://doi.org/10.1007/s10508-011-9752-2

Steensma, T. D., Kreukels, B. P. C., de Vries, A. L. C., & Cohen-Kettenis, P. T. (2013). Gender identity development in adolescence. *Hormones and Behavior, 64*(2), 288–297. https://doi.org/10.1016/j.yhbeh.2013.02.020

Ştefan, C. A., & Avram, J. (2018). The multifaceted role of attachment during preschool: Moderator of its indirect effect on empathy through emotion regulation. *Early Child Development and Care, 188*(1), 62–76. https://doi.org/10.1080/03004430.2016.1246447

Steiger, A. E., Allemand, M., Robins, R. W., & Fend, H. A. (2014). Low and decreasing self-esteem during adolescence predict adult depression two decades later. *Journal of Personality and Social Psychology, 106*(2), 325–338. https://doi.org/10.1037/a0035133

Stein, A. D., Wang, M., Martorell, R., Norris, S. A., Adair, L. S., Bas, I., . . . Victora, C. G. (2010). Growth patterns in early childhood and final attained stature: data from five birth cohorts from low- and middle-income countries. *American Journal of Human Biology, 22*(3), 353–359. https://doi.org/10.1002/ajhb.20998

Stein, J. H., & Reiser, L. W. (1994). A study of white middle-class adolescent boys' responses to semenarche? (the first ejaculation). *Journal of Youth and Adolescence, 23*(3), 373–384. https://doi.org/10.1007/BF01536725

Stein, R. (2019). First U.S. patients treated with CRISPR as human gene-editing trials get underway. *NPR*. Retrieved from https://www.npr.org/sections/health-shots/2019/04/16/712402435/first-u-s-patients-treated-with-crispr-as-gene-editing-human-trials-get-underway

Steinberg, L. (2008). A social neuroscience perspective on adolescent risk-taking. *Developmental Review, 28*(1), 78–106. https://doi.org/10.1016/j.dr.2007.08.002

Steinberg, L. (2013). Does recent research on adolescent brain development inform the mature minor doctrine? *Journal of Medicine and Philosophy, 38*, 256–267. https://doi.org/10.1093/jmp/jht017

Steinberg, L. (2017). Adolescent brain science and juvenile justice policymaking. *Psychology, Public Policy, and Law, 23*(4), 410–420. https://doi.org/10.1037/law0000128

Steinberg, L., Fegley, S., & Dornbusch, S. M. (1993). Negative impact of part-time work on adolescent adjustment: Evidence from a longitudinal study. *Developmental Psychology, 29*(2), 171–180.

Steinberg, L., Icenogle, G., Shulman, E. P., Breiner, K., Chein, J., Bacchini, D., . . . Takash, H. M. S. (2018). Around the world, adolescence is a time of heightened sensation seeking and immature self-regulation. *Developmental Science, 21*(2), e12532. https://doi.org/10.1111/desc.12532

Steinberg, L., & Monahan, K. C. (2007). Age differences in resistance to peer influence. *Developmental Psychology, 43*(6), 1531–1543. https://doi.org/10.1037/0012-1649.43.6.1531

Steinberg, L., & Scott, E. S. (2003). Less guilty by reason of adolescence: Developmental immaturity, diminished responsibility, and the juvenile death penalty. *American Psychologist, 58*(12), 1009–1018.

Steiner, J. E. (1979). Human facial expressions in response to taste and smell stimulations. In L. P. Lipsitt & H. W. Reese (Eds.), *Advances in child development: Vol. 13* (pp. 257–295). New York, NY: Academic Press.

Steinsbekk, S., Bonneville-Roussy, A., Fildes, A., Llewellyn, C. H., & Wichstrøm, L. (2017). Child and parent predictors of picky eating from preschool to school age. *International Journal of Behavioral Nutrition and Physical Activity, 14*(1), 87. https://doi.org/10.1186/s12966-017-0542-7

Stenberg, G. (2017). Does contingency in adults' responding influence 12-month-old infants' social referencing? *Infant Behavior and Development, 46*, 67–79. https://doi.org/10.1016/j.infbeh.2016.11.013

Stephenson, J. (2005). Fetal ultrasound safety. *JAMA, 293*(3), 286.

Stern, J. A., & Cassidy, J. (2018). Empathy from infancy to adolescence: An attachment perspective on the development of individual differences. *Developmental Review, 47*, 1–22. https://doi.org/10.1016/J.DR.2017.09.002

Sternberg, R. J. (1985). *Beyond IQ: A triarchic theory of human intelligence*. Cambridge, England: Cambridge University Press.

Sternberg, R. J. (2011). The theory of successful intelligence. In R. J. Sternberg & S. B. Kaufman (Eds.), *The Cambridge handbook of intelligence* (pp. 504–527). Cambridge University Press.

Sternberg, R. J. (2014a). Teaching about the nature of intelligence. *Intelligence, 42*, 176–179. https://doi.org/10.1016/j.intell.2013.08.010

Sternberg, R. J. (2014b). The development of adaptive competence: Why cultural psychology is necessary and not just nice. *Developmental Review, 34*(3), 208–224. https://doi.org/10.1016/j.dr.2014.05.004

Sternberg, R. J., & Grigorenko, E. L. (2008). Ability testing across cultures. In L. A. Suzuki & J. G. Ponterotto (Eds.), *Handbook of multicultural assessment: Clinical, psychological, and educational applications* (pp. 449–470). San Francisco, CA: Jossey-Bass.

Sternberg, R. J., Grigorenko, E. L., & Bundy, D. A. (2001). The predictive value of IQ. *Merrill-Palmer Quarterly, 47*, 1–41.

Stevens, E. N., Lovejoy, M. C., & Pittman, L. D. (2014). Understanding the relationship between actual: ideal discrepancies and depressive symptoms: a developmental examination. *Journal of Adolescence, 37*(5), 612–621. https://doi.org/10.1016/j.adolescence.2014.04.013

Stevenson, H. W., Lee, S., & Mu, X. (2000). Successful achievement in mathematics: China and the United States. In C. F. M. van Lieshout & P. G. Heymans (Eds.), *Developing talent across the life span* (pp. 167–183). New York, NY: Psychology Press.

Stice, E., Gau, J. M., Rohde, P., & Shaw, H. (2017). Risk factors that predict future onset of each DSM-5 eating disorder: Predictive specificity in high-risk adolescent females. *Journal of Abnormal Psychology, 126*(1), 38–51. https://doi.org/10.1037/abn0000219

Stidham-Hall, K., Moreau, C., & Trussell, J. (2012). Patterns and correlates of parental and formal sexual and reproductive health communication for adolescent women in the United States, 2002-2008. *Journal of Adolescent Health, 50*(4), 410–413. https://doi.org/10.1016/j.jadohealth.2011.06.007

Stiles, J. (2017). Principles of brain development. *Wiley Interdisciplinary Reviews: Cognitive Science, 8*(1–2), e1402. https://doi.org/10.1002/wcs.1402

Stiles, J., Brown, T. T., Haist, F., Jernigan, T. L., Stiles, J., Brown, T. T., . . . Jernigan, T. L. (2015). Brain and cognitive development. In *Handbook of Child Psychology and Developmental Science* (pp. 1–54). Hoboken, NJ: John Wiley & Sons. https://doi.org/10.1002/9781118963418.childpsy202

Stipek, D. (1995). *The development of pride and shame in toddlers.* (J. P. Tangney & K. W. Fischer, Eds.). New York, NY: Guilford.

Stipek, D., Feiler, R., Daniels, D., & Milburn, S. (1995). Effects of different instructional approaches on young children's achievement and motivation. *Child Development, 66*, 209–223.

Stipek, D., Gralinski, J. H., & Kopp, C. B. (1990). Self-concept development in the toddler years. *Developmental Psychology, 26*(6), 972–977. https://doi.org/10.1037/0012-1649.26.6.972

Stojković, I. (2013). Pubertal timing and self-esteem in adolescents: The mediating role of body-image and social relations. *European Journal of Developmental Psychology, 10*(3), 359–377. https://doi.org/10.1080/17405629.2012.682145

Stoll, B. J., Hansen, N. I., Bell, E. F., Walsh, M. C., Carlo, W. A., Shankaran, S., . . . Higgins, R. D. (2015). Trends in care practices, morbidity, and mortality of extremely preterm neonates, 1993-2012. *JAMA, 314*(10), 1039. https://doi.org/10.1001/jama.2015.10244

Stone, M. M., Blumberg, F. C., Blair, C., & Cancelli, A. A. (2016). *The "EF" in deficiency:* Examining the linkages between executive function and the utilization deficiency observed in preschoolers. *Journal of Experimental Child Psychology, 152*, 367–375. https://doi.org/10.1016/j.jecp.2016.07.003

Strathearn, L., Jian, L., Fonagy, P., & Montague, P. R. (2008). What's in a smile? Maternal brain responses to infant facial cues. *Pediatrics, 122*(1), 40–51. https://doi.org/10.1542/peds.2007-1566

Streri, A., Hevia, M., Izard, V., & Coubart, A. (2013). What do we know about neonatal cognition? *Behavioral Sciences, 3*(1), 154–169. https://doi.org/10.3390/bs3010154

Strober, M., Freeman, R., Lampert, C., Diamond, J., & Kaye, W. (2014). Controlled family study of anorexia nervosa and bulimia nervosa: Evidence of shared liability and transmission of partial syndromes. *American Journal of Psychiatry, 157*(3), 393–401.

Strohschein, L. (2005). Parental divorce and child mental health trajectories. *Journal of Marriage and Family, 67*(5), 1286–1300.

Stroud, C. B., & Davila, J. (2016). Pubertal timing. In *Encyclopedia of adolescence* (pp. 1–9). Cham, Switzerland: Springer International Publishing. https://doi.org/10.1007/978-3-319-32132-5_14-2

Stulp, G., & Barrett, L. (2016). Evolutionary perspectives on human height variation. *Biological Reviews, 91*(1), 206–234. https://doi.org/10.1111/brv.12165

Su, J. R., Leroy, Z., Lewis, P. W., Haber, P., Marin, M., Leung, J., . . . Shimabukuro, T. T. (2017). Safety of second-dose single-antigen varicella vaccine. *Pediatrics, 139*(3), e20162536. https://doi.org/10.1542/peds.2016-2536

Suarez, S. S. (2016). Mammalian sperm interactions with the female reproductive tract. *Cell and Tissue Research, 363*(1), 185–194. https://doi.org/10.1007/s00441-015-2244-2

Subotnik, R. F., Olszewski-Kubilius, P., & Worrell, F. C. (2011). Rethinking giftedness and gifted education: A proposed direction forward based on psychological science. *Psychological Science in the Public Interest, 12*(1), 3–54. https://doi.org/10.1177/1529100611418056

Subrahmanyam, K., & Greenfield, P. M. (1996). Effect of video game practice on spatial skills in girls and boys. In P. M. Greenfield & R. R. Cocking (Eds.), *Interacting with video* (pp. 95–114). Norwood, NJ: Ablex.

Substance Abuse and Mental Health Services Administration. (2013). *Results from the 2012 National Survey on Drug Use and Health: Mental Health Findings.* Rockville, MD: Author.

Suddendorf, T., Oostenbroek, J., Nielsen, M., & Slaughter, V. (2013). Is newborn imitation developmentally homologous to later social-cognitive skills? *Developmental Psychobiology, 55*(1), 52–58. https://doi.org/10.1002/dev.21005

Sugden, N. A., Mohamed-Ali, M. I., & Moulson, M. C. (2014). I spy with my little eye: Typical, daily exposure to faces documented from a first-person infant perspective. *Developmental Psychobiology, 56*(2), 249–261. https://doi.org/10.1002/dev.21183

Sugita, Y. (2004). Experience in early infancy is indispensable for color perception. *American Journal of Ophthalmology, 138*(5), 902.

Suk, W. A., Ahanchian, H., Asante, K. A., Carpenter, D. O., Diaz-Barriga, F., Ha, E.-H., . . . Landrigan, P. J. (2016). Environmental pollution: An under-recognized threat to children's health, especially in low- and middle-income countries. *Environmental Health Perspectives, 124*(3). https://doi.org/10.1289/ehp.1510517

Sullivan, J. L. (2003). Prevention of mother-to-child transmission of HIV: What next? *Journal of Acquired Immune Deficiency Syndromes, 34*(Suppl. 1), S67–S72.

Sullivan, M. W., Carmody, D. P., & Lewis, M. (2010). How neglect and punitiveness influence emotion knowledge. *Child Psychiatry and Human Development, 41*(3), 285–298. https://doi.org/10.1007/s10578-009-0168-3

Sullivan, M. W., & Lewis, M. (2003). Contextual determinants of anger and other negative expressions in young infants. *Developmental Psychology, 39*(4), 693–705. https://doi.org/10.1037/0012-1649.39.4.693

Sullivan-Pyke, C. S., Senapati, S., Mainigi, M. A., & Barnhart, K. T. (2017). In Vitro fertilization and adverse obstetric and perinatal outcomes. *Seminars in Perinatology, 41*(6), 345–353. https://doi.org/10.1053/J.SEMPERI.2017.07.001

Sun, Y., Mensah, F. K., Azzopardi, P., Patton, G. C., & Wake, M. (2017). Childhood social disadvantage and pubertal timing: A national birth cohort from Australia. *Pediatrics, 139*(6), e20164099. https://doi.org/10.1542/peds.2016-4099

Sundberg, U. (1998). *Mother tongue-phonetic aspects of infant-directed speech* (Doctoral dissertation). PERILUS, Stockholm, Sweden.

Sunderam, S., Kissin, D. M., Crawford, S. B., Folger, S. G., Jamieson, D. J., Warner, L., & Barfield, W. D. (2017). Assisted reproductive technology surveillance—United States, 2014. *MMWR Surveillance Summaries, 66*(6), 1–24.

Super, C. M. (1981). Cross-cultural research on infancy. In H. C. Triandis & A. Heron (Eds.), *Handbook of cross-cultural psychology: Vol. 4. Developmental psychology.* Boston, MA: Allyn & Bacon.

Super, C. M., & Harkness, S. (1982). The infant's niche in rural Kenya and metropolitan America. In L. L. Adler (Ed.), *Cross-cultural research at issue* (pp. 247–255). New York, NY: Academic Press.

Super, C. M., & Harkness, S. (2010). Culture and infancy. In J. G. Bremner & T. D. Wachs (Eds.), *The Wiley-Blackwell handbook of infant development* (pp. 623–649). Oxford, England: Wiley-Blackwell. https://doi.org/10.1002/9781444327564.ch21

Super, C. M., & Harkness, S. (2015). Charting infant development. In L. A. Jensen (Ed.), *The Oxford handbook of human development and culture.* Oxford, England: Oxford University Press. https://doi.org/10.1093/oxfordhb/9780199948550.013.6

Sussman, S., Pokhrel, P., Ashmore, R. D., & Brown, B. B. (2007). Adolescent peer group identification and characteristics: A review of the literature. *Addictive Behaviors, 32*, 1602–1627.

Sutin, A. R., Flynn, H. A., & Terracciano, A. (2017). Maternal cigarette smoking during pregnancy and the trajectory of externalizing and internalizing symptoms across childhood: Similarities and differences across parent, teacher, and self reports. *Journal of Psychiatric Research, 91*, 145–148. https://doi.org/10.1016/J.JPSYCHIRES.2017.03.003

Suurland, J., van der Heijden, K. B., Smaling, H. J. A., Huijbregts, S. C. J., van Goozen, S. H. M., & Swaab, H. (2017). Infant autonomic nervous system response and recovery: Associations with maternal risk status and infant emotion regulation. *Development and Psychopathology, 29*(03), 759–773. https://doi.org/10.1017/S0954579416000456

Suzuki, K., Ando, J., & Satou, N. (2009). Genetic effects on infant handedness under spatial constraint conditions. *Developmental Psychobiology, 51*(8), 605–615. https://doi.org/10.1002/dev.20395

Svetlova, M., Nichols, S. R., & Brownell, C. A. (2010). Toddlers prosocial behavior: From instrumental to empathic to altruistic helping. *Child Development, 81*(6), 1814–1827. https://doi.org/10.1111/j.1467-8624.2010.01512.x

Swartz, H. A., Cyranowski, J. M., Cheng, Y., Zuckoff, A., Brent, D. A., Markowitz, J. C., . . . Frank, E. (2016). Brief psychotherapy for maternal depression: Impact on mothers and children. *Journal of the American Academy of Child & Adolescent Psychiatry, 55*(6), 495-503.e2. https://doi.org/10.1016/J.JAAC.2016.04.003

Swearer, S. M., & Hymel, S. (2015). Understanding the psychology of bullying: Moving toward a social-ecological diathesis-stress model. *American Psychologist, 70*(4), 344–353. https://doi.org/10.1037/a0038929

Syed, M., Walker, L. H. M., Lee, R. M., Umana-Taylor, A. J., Zamboanga, B. L., Schwartz, S. J., . . . Huynh, Q.-L. (2013). A two-factor model of ethnic identity exploration: Implications for identity coherence and well-being. *Cultural Diversity and Ethnic Minority Psychology, 19*(2), 143–154. https://doi.org/10.1037/a0030564

Symonds, W. C., Schwartz, R., & Ferguson., R. F. (2011). *Pathways to prosperity: Meeting the challenge of preparing young Americans.* Retrieved from https://www.gse.harvard.edu/sites/default/files/documents/Pathways_to_Prosperity_Feb2011-1.pdf

Szyf, M. (2015). Nongenetic inheritance and transgenerational epigenetics. *Trends in Molecular Medicine, 21*(2), 134–144. https://doi.org/10.1016/j.molmed.2014.12.004

Tabor, H. K., Murray, J. C., Gammill, H. S., Kitzman, J. O., Snyder, M. W., Ventura, M., . . . Shendure, J. (2012). Non-invasive fetal genome sequencing: Opportunities and challenges. *American Journal of Medical Genetics, Part A, 158A*(10), 2382–2384. https://doi.org/10.1002/ajmg.a.35545

Taggart, J., Eisen, S., & Lillard, A. S. (2019). The current landscape of US children's television: Violent, prosocial, educational, and fantastical content. *Journal of Children and Media*, 1–19. https://doi.org/10.1080/17482798.2019.1605916

Tait, A. R., & Geisser, M. E. (2017). Development of a consensus operational definition of child assent for research. *BMC Medical Ethics, 18*(1), 41. https://doi.org/10.1186/s12910-017-0199-4

Takagi, M., Youssef, G., & Lorenzetti, V. (2016). Neuroimaging of the human brain in adolescent substance users. In D. De Micheli, A. L. M. Andrade, E. A. da Silva, & M. L. O. de Souza Formigoni (Eds.), *Drug abuse in adolescence* (pp. 69–99). Cham, Switzerland: Springer International Publishing. https://doi.org/10.1007/978-3-319-17795-3_6

Takahashi, K. (1990). Are the key assumptions of the "Strange Situation" procedure universal? A view from Japanese research. *Human Development, 33*, 23–30.

Tamariz, M., & Kirby, S. (2016). The cultural evolution of language. *Current Opinion in Psychology, 8*, 37–43. https://doi.org/10.1016/J.COPSYC.2015.09.003

Tamis-LeMonda, C. S., & Bornstein, M. H. (1989). Habituation and maternal encouragement of attention in infancy as predictors of toddler language, play, and representational competence. *Child Development, 60*, 738–751.

Tamis-Lemonda, C., & Bornstein, M. (2015). Infant word learning in biopsychosocial perspective. In S. Calkins (Ed.), *Handbook of infant development: A biopsychosocial perspective.* Retrieved from https://nyuscholars.nyu.edu/en/publications/infant-word-learning-in-biopsychosocial-perspective

Tamis-LeMonda, C. S., Bornstein, M. H., & Baumwell, L. (2001). Maternal responsiveness and children's achievement of language milestones. *Child Development, 72*(3), 748–767.

Tamis-Lemonda, C., Bornstein, M. H., Cyphers, L., Toda, S., & Ogino, M. (1992). Language and play at one year: A comparison of toddlers and mothers in the United States and Japan. *International Journal of Behavioral Development, 15*, 19–42.

Tamis-LeMonda, C. S., Briggs, R. D., McClowry, S. G., & Snow, D. L. (2009a). Maternal control and sensitivity, child gender, and maternal education in relation to children's behavioral outcomes in African American families. *Journal of Applied Developmental Psychology, 30*(3), 321–331. https://doi.org/10.1016/j.appdev.2008.12.018

Tamis-LeMonda, C. S., Kahana-Kalman, R., & Yoshikawa, H. (2009b). Father involvement in immigrant and ethnically diverse families from the prenatal period to the second year: Prediction and mediating mechanisms. *Sex Roles, 60*(7), 496–509. https://doi.org/10.1007/s11199-009-9593-9

Tamis-LeMonda, C. S., Kuchirko, Y., & Song, L. (2014). Why is infant language learning facilitated by parental responsiveness? *Current Directions in Psychological Science, 23*(2), 121–126. https://doi.org/10.1177/0963721414522813

Tamis-LeMonda, C. S., Shannon, J. D., Cabrera, N. J., & Lamb, M. E. (2004). Fathers and mothers at play with their 2- and 3-year-olds: Contributions to language and cognitive development. *Child Development, 75*(6), 1806–1820. https://doi.org/10.1111/j.1467-8624.2004.00818.x

Tamnes, C. K., Herting, M. M., Goddings, A.-L., Meuwese, R., Blakemore, S.-J., Dahl, R. E., . . . Mills, K. L. (2017). Development of the cerebral cortex across adolescence: A multisample study of inter-related longitudinal changes in cortical volume, surface area, and thickness. *Journal of Neuroscience, 37*(12), 3402–3412. https://doi.org/10.1523/JNEUROSCI.3302-16.2017

Tan, E. S., McIntosh, J. E., Kothe, E. J., Opie, J. E., & Olsson, C. A. (2018). Couple relationship quality and offspring attachment security: A systematic review with meta-analysis. *Attachment & Human Development, 20*(4), 349–377. https://doi.org/10.1080/14616734.2017.1401651

Tanaka, K., Kon, N., Ohkawa, N., Yoshikawa, N., & Shimizu, T. (2009). Does breastfeeding in the neonatal period influence the cognitive function of very-low-birth-weight infants at 5 years of age? *Brain & Development, 31*(4), 288–293. https://doi.org/10.1016/j.braindev.2008.05.011

Tanaka, Y., Kanakogi, Y., Kawasaki, M., & Myowa, M. (2018). The integration of audio-tactile information is modulated by multimodal social interaction with physical contact in infancy. *Developmental Cognitive Neuroscience, 30*, 31–40. https://doi.org/10.1016/J.DCN.2017.12.001

Tang, S., Davis-Kean, P. E., Chen, M., & Sexton, H. R. (2016). Adolescent pregnancy's intergenerational effects: Does an adolescent mother's education have consequences for her children's achievement? *Journal of Research on Adolescence, 26*, 180–193. https://doi.org/10.1111/jora.12182

Tanner, J. M. (1990). *Foetus into man: Physical growth from conception to maturity.* Boston, MA: Harvard University Press.

Tannock, M. (2011). Observing young children's rough-and-tumble play. *Australasian Journal of Early Childhood, 36*(2), 13–20.

Tapia-Rojas, C., Carvajal, F. J., Mira, R. G., Arce, C., Lerma-Cabrera, J. M., Orellana, J. A., . . . Quintanilla, R. A. (2017). Adolescent binge alcohol exposure affects the brain function through mitochondrial impairment. *Molecular Neurobiology, 55*(5), 4473–4491. https://doi.org/10.1007/s12035-017-0613-4

Tardif, T., Fletcher, P., Liang, W., Zhang, Z., Kaciroti, N., & Marchman, V. A. (2008). Baby's first 10 words. *Developmental Psychology, 44*(4), 929–938. https://doi.org/10.1037/0012-1649.44.4.929

Tardif, T., Shatz, M., & Naigles, L. (1997). Caregiver speech and children's use of nouns versus verbs: A comparison of English, Italian, and Mandarin. *Journal of Child Language, 24*, 535–565.

Tarry, H., & Emler, N. (2007). Attitude, values and moral reasoning as predictors of delinquency. *British Journal of Developmental Psychology, 25*(2), 169–183. https://doi.org/10.1348/026151006x113671

Tarullo, A. R., Isler, J. R., Condon, C., Violaris, K., Balsam, P. D., & Fifer, W. P. (2016). Neonatal eyelid conditioning during sleep. *Developmental Psychobiology, 58*(7), 875–882. https://doi.org/10.1002/dev.21424

Tarver, J., Daley, D., & Sayal, K. (2014). Attention-deficit hyperactivity disorder (ADHD): An updated review of the essential facts. *Child: Care, Health and Development, 40*(6), 762–774. https://doi.org/10.1111/cch.12139

Task Force on Sudden Infant Death Syndrome. (2016). SIDS and other sleep-related infant deaths: Updated 2016 recommendations for a safe infant sleeping environment. *Pediatrics, 138*(5), e20162938. https://doi.org/10.1542/peds.2016-2938

Tasker, F., & Patterson, C. J. (2007). Research on gay and lesbian parenting: Retrospect and prospect. *Journal of GLBT Family Studies, 3*(2/3), 9–34.

Taumoepeau, M. (2015). From talk to thought. *Journal of Cross-Cultural Psychology, 46*(9), 1169–1190. https://doi.org/10.1177/0022022115604393

Taylor, A. W., Nesheim, S. R., Zhang, X., Song, R., FitzHarris, L. F., Lampe, M. A., . . . Sweeney, P. (2017). Estimated perinatal HIV infection among infants born in the United States, 2002-2013. *JAMA Pediatrics, 171*(5), 435. https://doi.org/10.1001/jamapediatrics.2016.5053

Taylor, C. M., Wernimont, S. M., Northstone, K., & Emmett, P. M. (2015). Picky/fussy eating in children: Review of definitions, assessment, prevalence and dietary intakes. *Appetite, 95*, 349–359. https://doi.org/10.1016/J.APPET.2015.07.026

Taylor, H. G., Klein, N., Minich, N. M., & Hack, M. (2001). Long-term family outcomes for children with very low birth weights. *Archives of Pediatrics & Adolescent Medicine, 155*(2), 155–161.

Taylor, J. L. (2009). Midlife impacts of adolescent parenthood. *Journal of Family Issues, 30*(4), 484–510.

Taylor, K. (2017, April 24). New York City will offer free preschool for all 3-year-olds. *New York Times*. Retrieved from https://www.nytimes.com/2017/04/24/nyregion/de-blasio-pre-k-expansion.html?_r=0

Taylor, L. E., Swerdfeger, A. L., & Eslick, G. D. (2014). Vaccines are not associated with autism: An evidence-based meta-analysis of case-control and cohort studies. *Vaccine, 32*(29), 3623–3629. https://doi.org/10.1016/j.vaccine.2014.04.085

Taylor, M. (1999). *Imaginary companions and the children who create them*. New York, NY: Oxford University Press.

Taylor, M., Shawber, A. B., & Mannering, A. M. (2009). Children's imaginary companions: What is it like to have an invisible friend? In K. D. Markman, W. M. P. Klein, & J. A. Suhr (Eds.), *Handbook of imagination and mental simulation* (pp. 211–224). New York, NY: Psychology Press.

Taylor, N., Donovan, W., & Leavitt, L. (2008). Consistency in infant sleeping arrangements and mother-infant interaction. *Infant Mental Health Journal, 29*(2), 77–94. https://doi.org/10.1002/imhj.20170

Taylor, R. D., Oberle, E., Durlak, J. A., & Weissberg, R. P. (2017). Promoting positive youth development through school-based social and emotional learning interventions: A meta-analysis of follow-up effects. *Child Development, 88*(4), 1156–1171. https://doi.org/10.1111/cdev.12864

Taylor, Z. E., & Conger, R. D. (2017). Promoting strengths and resilience in single-mother families. *Child Development, 88*(2), 350–358. https://doi.org/10.1111/cdev.12741

Taylor, Z. E., Eisenberg, N., Spinrad, T. L., Eggum, N. D., & Sulik, M. J. (2013). The relations of ego-resiliency and emotion socialization to the development of empathy and prosocial behavior across early childhood. *Emotion, 13*(5), 822–831

Tchaconas, A., & Adesman, A. (2013). Autism spectrum disorders. *Current Opinion in Pediatrics, 25*(1), 130–144. https://doi.org/10.1097/MOP.0b013e32835c2b70

te Nijenhuis, J. (2013). The Flynn effect, group differences, and g loadings. *Personality and Individual Differences, 55*(3), 224–228. https://doi.org/10.1016/j.paid.2011.12.023

Tehranifar, P., Wu, H.-C., McDonald, J. A., Jasmine, F., Santella, R. M., Gurvich, I., . . . Terry, M. B. (2017). Maternal cigarette smoking during pregnancy and offspring DNA methylation in midlife. *Epigenetics*, 00–00. https://doi.org/10.1080/15592294.2017.1325065

Teller, D. Y. (1997). First glances: The vision of infants. *Investigative Ophthalmology & Visual Science, 38*, 2183–2203.

Teller, D. Y. (1998). Spatial and temporal aspects of infant color vision. *Vision Research, 38*, 3275–3282.

Telzer, E. H., Fuligni, A. J., Lieberman, M. D., & Galván, A. (2013). The effects of poor quality sleep on brain function and risk taking in adolescence. *NeuroImage, 71*, 275–283. https://doi.org/10.1016/j.neuroimage.2013.01.025

Temoka, E. (2013). Becoming a vaccine champion: Evidence-based interventions to address the challenges of vaccination. *South Dakota Medicine*, Special Issue, 68–72. Retrieved from http://www.sdsma.org/docs/pdfs-new_site/Journal/2013/SDMSpecial%20Issue2013l.pdf#page=70

Teoh, P. J., & Maheshwari, A. (2014). Low-cost in vitro fertilization: Current insights. *International Journal of Women's Health, 6*, 817–827. https://doi.org/10.2147/IJWH.S51288

Terenzini, P. T., Pascarella, E. T., & Blimling, G. S. (1999). Students' out-of-class experiences and their influence on learning and cognitive development: A literature review. *Journal of College Student Development, 40*(5), 610–623.

Tham, E. K., Schneider, N., & Broekman, B. F. (2017). Infant sleep and its relation with cognition and growth: A narrative review. *Nature and Science of Sleep, 9*, 135–149. https://doi.org/10.2147/NSS.S125992

Thapar, A., Collishaw, S., Pine, D. S., & Thapar, A. K. (2012). Depression in adolescence. *Lancet, 379*(9820), 1056–1067. https://doi.org/10.1016/S0140-6736(11)60871-4

Thapar, A., Cooper, M., Eyre, O., & Langley, K. (2013). What have we learnt about the causes of ADHD? *Journal of Child Psychology and Psychiatry, and Allied Disciplines, 54*(1), 3–16. https://doi.org/10.1111/j.1469-7610.2012.02611.x

The Annie E. Casey Foundation. (2017). *Children who speak a language other than English at home: Kids Count national indicators*. Baltimore, MD: Author. Retrieved from https://datacenter.kidscount.org/data#USA/1/0/char/0

Thelen, E. (1995). Motor development: A new synthesis. *American Psychologist, 50*(2), 79–95. https://doi.org/10.1037/0003-066X.50.2.79

Thelen, E. (2000). Motor development as foundation and future of developmental psychology. *International Journal of Behavioral Development, 24*(4), 385–397.

Theodora, M., Antsaklis, A., Antsaklis, P., Blanas, K., Daskalakis, G., Sindos, M., . . . Papantoniou, N. (2016). Fetal loss following second trimester amniocentesis. Who is at greater risk? How to counsel pregnant women? *Journal of Maternal-Fetal & Neonatal Medicine, 29*(4), 590–595. https://doi.org/10.3109/14767058.2015.1012061

Thiessen, E. D., Hill, E. A., & Saffran, J. R. (2005). Infant-directed speech facilitates word segmentation. *Infancy, 7*(1), 53–71.

Thoma, M. E., McLain, A. C., Louis, J. F., King, R. B., Trumble, A. C., Sundaram, R., & Buck Louis, G. M. (2013). Prevalence of infertility in the United States as estimated by the current duration approach and a traditional constructed approach. *Fertility and Sterility, 99*(5), 1324-1331.e1. https://doi.org/10.1016/j.fertnstert.2012.11.037

Thomaes, S., Reijntjes, A., Orobio de Castro, B., Bushman, B. J., Poorthuis, A., & Telch, M. J. (2010). I like me if you like me: On the interpersonal modulation and regulation of preadolescents' state self-esteem. *Child Development, 81*(3), 811–825. https://doi.org/10.1111/j.1467-8624.2010.01435.x

Thoman, E. B., & Ingersoll, E. W. (1993). Learning in premature infants. *Developmental Psychology, 28*, 692–700.

Thomas, A., & Chess, S. (1977). *Temperament and development*. New York, NY: Brunner/Mazel.

Thomas, A., Chess, S., & Birch, H. G. (1970). The origin of personality. *Scientific American, 223*, 102–109.

Thomas, H. J., Connor, J. P., & Scott, J. G. (2017). Why do children and adolescents bully their peers? A critical review of key theoretical frameworks. *Social Psychiatry and Psychiatric Epidemiology, 53*(5), 437–451. https://doi.org/10.1007/s00127-017-1462-1

Thomas, J. C., Letourneau, N., Campbell, T. S., Tomfohr-Madsen, L., & Giesbrecht, G. F. (2017). Developmental origins of infant emotion regulation: Mediation by temperamental negativity and moderation by maternal sensitivity. *Developmental Psychology, 53*(4), 611–628. https://doi.org/10.1037/dev0000279

Thomas, J. J., Eddy, K. T., Ruscio, J., Ng, K. L., Casale, K. E., Becker, A. E., & Lee, S. (2015). Do Recognizable lifetime eating disorder phenotypes naturally occur in a culturally Asian population? A combined latent profile and taxometric approach. *European Eating Disorders Review, 23*(3), 199–209. https://doi.org/10.1002/erv.2357

Thomas, J. R., & French, K. E. (1985). Gender differences across age in motor performance: A meta-analysis. *Psychological Bulletin, 98*(2), 260.

Thomas, M. S. C., Ansari, D., & Knowland, V. C. P. (2019). Annual research review: Educational neuroscience: Progress and prospects. *Journal of Child Psychology and Psychiatry, 60*(4), 477–492. https://doi.org/10.1111/jcpp.12973

Thompson, A. E., & Voyer, D. (2014). Sex differences in the ability to recognise non-verbal displays of emotion: A meta-analysis. *Cognition and Emotion, 28*(7), 1164–1195. https://doi.org/10.1080/02699931.2013.875889

Thompson, J. (2014). The common cold: "Why is my child always sick?" *HealthCentral*. Retrieved from https://www.healthcentral.com/article/the-common-cold-why-is-my-child-always-sick

Thompson, R., Kaczor, K., Lorenz, D. J., Bennett, B. L., Meyers, G., & Pierce, M. C. (2017). Is the use of physical discipline associated with aggressive behaviors in young children? *Academic Pediatrics, 17*(1), 34–44. https://doi.org/10.1016/J.ACAP.2016.02.014

Thompson, R. A. (2013). Attachment theory and research: Précis and prospect. In P. D. Zelazo (Ed.), *The Oxford handbook of developmental psychology: Vol. 2. Self and other* (2nd ed., pp. 191–216). New York, NY: Oxford University Press. https://doi.org/10.1093/oxfordhb/9780199958474.013.0009

Thompson, R. A. (2016). Early attachment and later development: Reframing the questions. In J. Cassidy & P. R. Shaver (Eds.), *Handbook of attachment: Theory, research, and clinical applications* (3rd ed., pp. 330–347). New York, NY: Guilford.

Thompson, R. A., & Goodvin, R. (2007). Taming the tempest in the teapot: Emotion regulation in toddlers. In C. A. Brownell & C. B. Kopp (Eds.), *Transitions in early socioemotional development: The toddler years* (pp. 320–341). New York, NY: Guilford.

Thompson, R. A., & Limber, S. (1991). "Social anxiety" in infancy: Stranger wariness and separation distress. In H. Leitenberg (Ed.), *Handbook of social and evaluation anxiety* (pp. 85–137). New York, NY: Plenum.

Thompson, R. A., & Newton, E. K. (2013). Baby altruists? Examining the complexity of prosocial motivation in young children. *Infancy, 18*(1), 120–133. https://doi.org/10.1111/j.1532-7078.2012.00139.x

Thompson, R. A., & Virmani, E. A. (2010). Self and personality. In M. H. Bornstein (Ed.), *Handbook of cultural developmental science* (pp. 195–207). New York, NY: Psychology Press.

Thomsen, S. F., van der Sluis, S., Kyvik, K. O., Skytthe, A., & Backer, V. (2010). Estimates of asthma heritability in a large twin sample. *Clinical & Experimental Allergy*, *40*(7), 1054–1061. https://doi.org/10.1111/j.1365-2222.2010.03525.x

Thornberg, R., Thornberg, U. B., Alamaa, R., & Daud, N. (2016). Children's conceptions of bullying and repeated conventional transgressions: Moral, conventional, structuring and personal-choice reasoning. *Educational Psychology*, *36*(1), 95–111. https://doi.org/10.1080/01443410.2014.915929

Thurman, S. L., & Corbetta, D. (2017). Spatial exploration and changes in infant–mother dyads around transitions in infant locomotion. *Developmental Psychology*, *53*(7), 1207–1221. https://doi.org/10.1037/dev0000328

Tiemeier, H., Lenroot, R. K., Greenstein, D. K., Tran, L., Pierson, R., & Giedd, J. N. (2010). Cerebellum development during childhood and adolescence: A longitudinal morphometric MRI study. *NeuroImage*, *49*(1), 63–70. https://doi.org/10.1016/j.neuroimage.2009.08.016

Tinggaard, J., Mieritz, M. G., Sørensen, K., Mouritsen, A., Hagen, C. P., Aksglaede, L., . . . Juul, A. (2012). The physiology and timing of male puberty. *Current Opinion in Endocrinology, Diabetes, and Obesity*, *19*(3), 197–203. https://doi.org/10.1097/MED.0b013e3283535614

Tinker, S. C., Cogswell, M. E., Devine, O., & Berry, R. J. (2010). Folic acid intake among U.S. women aged 15–44 years, National Health and Nutrition Examination Survey, 2003–2006. *American Journal of Preventive Medicine*, *38*(5), 534–542. https://doi.org/10.1016/j.amepre.2010.01.025

Titz, C., & Karbach, J. (2014). Working memory and executive functions: Effects of training on academic achievement. *Psychological Research*, *78*(6), 852–868. https://doi.org/10.1007/s00426-013-0537-1

Titzmann, P. F., Brenick, A., & Silbereisen, R. K. (2015). Friendships fighting prejudice: A longitudinal perspective on adolescents' cross-group friendships with immigrants. *Journal of Youth and Adolescence*, *44*(6), 1318–1431. https://doi.org/10.1007/s10964-015-0256-6

Tobiansky, D. J., Wallin-Miller, K. G., Floresco, S. B., Wood, R. I., & Soma, K. K. (2018). Androgen regulation of the mesocorticolimbic system and executive function. *Frontiers in Endocrinology*, *9*, 279. https://doi.org/10.3389/fendo.2018.00279

Toft, D. J. (2018). *Growth hormone therapy: The most common growth hormone deficiency treatment*. Retrieved from https://www.endocrineweb.com/conditions/growth-disorders/growth-hormone-therapy

Togias, A., Cooper, S. F., Acebal, M. L., Assa'ad, A., Baker, J. R., Beck, L. A., . . . Boyce, J. A. (2017). Addendum guidelines for the prevention of peanut allergy in the United States: Report of the National Institute of Allergy and Infectious Diseases-sponsored expert panel. *Allergy, Asthma & Clinical Immunology*, *13*(1), 1. https://doi.org/10.1186/s13223-016-0175-4

Tomalski, P., Marczuk, K., Pisula, E., Malinowska, A., Kawa, R., & Niedźwiecka, A. (2017). Chaotic home environment is associated with reduced infant processing speed under high task demands. *Infant Behavior and Development*, *48*, 124–133. https://doi.org/10.1016/J.INFBEH.2017.04.007

Tomasello, M. (2012). A usage-based approach to child language acquisition. *Proceedings of the Annual Meeting of the Berkeley Linguistics Society*, *26*(1), 305–319.

Tomova, A, Lalabonova, C., Robeva, R. N., & Kumanov, P. T. (2011). Timing of pubertal maturation according to the age at first conscious ejaculation. *Andrologia*, *43*(3), 163–166. https://doi.org/10.1111/j.1439-0272.2009.01037.x

Tomova, Analia. (2016). Body weight and puberty. In P. Kumanov & A. Agarwal (Eds.), *Puberty* (pp. 95–108). Cham, Switzerland: Springer International Publishing. https://doi.org/10.1007/978-3-319-32122-6_7

Tong, V. T., England, L. J., Rockhill, K. M., & D'Angelo, D. V. (2017). Risks of preterm delivery and small for gestational age infants: Effects of nondaily and low-intensity daily smoking during pregnancy. *Paediatric and Perinatal Epidemiology*, *31*(2), 144–148. https://doi.org/10.1111/ppe.12343

Tønnessen, E., Svendsen, I. S., Olsen, I. C., Guttormsen, A., & Haugen, T. (2015). Performance development in adolescent track and field athletes according to age, sex and sport discipline. *PLoS ONE*, *10*(6), e0129014. https://doi.org/10.1371/journal.pone.0129014

Tononi, G., & Cirelli, C. (2014). Sleep and the price of plasticity: From synaptic and cellular homeostasis to memory consolidation and integration. *Neuron*, *81*(1), 12–34. https://doi.org/10.1016/j.neuron.2013.12.025

Toomela, A. (2003). Developmental stages in children's drawings of a cube and a doll. *TRAMES*, *7*(3), 164–182.

Toomey, R. B., Card, N. A., & Casper, D. M. (2014). Peers' perceptions of gender nonconformity: Associations with overt and relational peer victimization and aggression in early adolescence. *Journal of Early Adolescence*, *34*(4), 463–485. https://doi.org/10.1177/0272431613495446

Torpey, E. (2019). Education pays: Career outlook. *U.S. Bureau of Labor Statistics*. Retrieved from https://www.bls.gov/careeroutlook/2019/data-on-display/education_pays.htm

Torpey, K., Kabaso, M., Kasonde, P., Dirks, R., Bweupe, M., Thompson, C., & Mukadi, Y. D. (2010). Increasing the uptake of prevention of mother-to- child transmission of HIV services in a resource-limited setting. *BMC Health Services Research*, *10*, 29–36. https://doi.org/10.1186/1472-6963-10-29

Tottenham, N., & Galván, A. (2016). Stress and the adolescent brain: Amygdala-prefrontal cortex circuitry and ventral striatum as developmental targets. *Neuroscience & Biobehavioral Reviews*, *70*, 217–227. https://doi.org/10.1016/J.NEUBIOREV.2016.07.030

Towers, C. V, Hyatt, B. W., Visconti, K. C., Chernicky, L., Chattin, K., & Fortner, K. B. (2019). Neonatal head circumference in newborns with neonatal abstinence syndrome. *Pediatrics*, *143*(1), e20180541. https://doi.org/10.1542/peds.2018-0541

Toyama, M. (2001). Developmental changes in social comparison in pre-school and elementary school children: Perceptions, feelings, and behavior. *Japanese Journal of Educational Psychology*, *49*, 500–507.

Tramacere, A., Pievani, T., & Ferrari, P. F. (2017). Mirror neurons in the tree of life: Mosaic evolution, plasticity and exaptation of sensorimotor matching responses. *Biological Reviews*, *92*(3), 1819–1841. https://doi.org/10.1111/brv.12310

Traub, F., & Boynton-Jarrett, R. (2017). Modifiable resilience factors to childhood adversity for clinical pediatric practice. *Pediatrics*, *139*(5), e20162569. https://doi.org/10.1542/peds.2016-2569

Trautmann, J., Alhusen, J., & Gross, D. (2015). Impact of deployment on military families with young children: A systematic review. *Nursing Outlook*, *63*(6), 656–679. https://doi.org/10.1016/J.OUTLOOK.2015.06.002

Trautner, H. M., Ruble, D. N., Cyphers, L., Kirsten, B., Behrendt, R., & Hartmann, P. (2005). Rigidity and flexibility of gender stereotypes in childhood: Developmental or differential? *Infant and Child Development*, *14*(4), 365–381. https://doi.org/10.1002/icd.399

Trawick-Smith, J., & Dziurgot, T. (2011). 'Good-fit' teacher–child play interactions and the subsequent autonomous play of preschool children. *Early Childhood Research Quarterly*, *26*(1), 110–123. https://doi.org/10.1016/j.ecresq.2010.04.005

Tremblay, L., & Limbos, M. (2009). Body image disturbance and psychopathology in children: Research evidence and implications for prevention and treatment. *Current Psychiatry Reviews*, *5*(1), 62–72. https://doi.org/10.2174/157340009787315307

Tremblay, R. E. (2014). Early development of physical aggression and early risk factors for chronic physical aggression in humans. *Current Topics in Behavioral Neurosciences*, *17*, 315–327. https://doi.org/10.1007/7854_2013_262

Tremblay, R. E., Nagin, D. S., Séguin, J. R., Zoccolillo, M., Zelazo, P. D., Boivin, M., . . . Japel, C. (2004). Physical aggression during early childhood: Trajectories and predictors. *Pediatrics*, *114*(1), e43–e50.

Trettien, A. W. (1990). Creeping and walking. *American Journal of Psychology*, *12*, 1–57.

Trionfi, G., & Reese, E. (2009). A good story: Children with imaginary companions create richer narratives. *Child Development*, *80*(4), 1301–1313. https://doi.org/10.1111/j.1467-8624.2009.01333.x

Tronick, E. Z., Als, H., Adamson, L., Wise, S., & Brazelton, B. (1978). The infants' response to entrapment between contradictory messages in face-to-face interaction. *American Academy of Child Psychiatry*, *1*, 1–13.

Tronick, E. Z., Morelli, G. A., & Ivey, P. K. (1992). The Efe forager infant and toddler's pattern of social relationships: Multiple and simultaneous. *Developmental Psychology*, *28*, 568–577.

Troutman, B. (2015). Viewing parent-child interactions through the lens of behaviorism. In B. Troutman (Ed.), *Integrating behaviorism and attachment theory in parent coaching* (pp. 3–20). New York, NY: Springer, Cham. https://doi.org/10.1007/978-3-319-15239-4_1

Troutman, D. R., & Fletcher, A. C. (2010). Context and companionship in children's short-term versus long-term friendships. *Journal of Social & Personal Relationships, 27*(8), 1060–1074. https://doi.org/10.1177/0265407510381253

Troxel, W. M., Shih, R. A., Ewing, B., Tucker, J. S., Nugroho, A., & D'Amico, E. J. (2017). Examination of neighborhood disadvantage and sleep in a multi-ethnic cohort of adolescents. *Health & Place, 45*, 39–45. https://doi.org/10.1016/j.healthplace.2017.03.002

Trucco, E. M., Colder, C. R., Wieczorek, W. F., Lengua, L. J., & Hawk, L. W. (2014). Early adolescent alcohol use in context: How neighborhoods, parents, and peers impact youth. *Development and Psychopathology, 26*(2), 425–436. https://doi.org/10.1017/S0954579414000042

Tsai, K. M., Dahl, R. E., Irwin, M. R., Bower, J. E., McCreath, H., Seeman, T. E., . . . Fuligni, A. J. (2017). The roles of parental support and family stress in adolescent sleep. *Child Development*. https://doi.org/10.1111/cdev.12917

Tsimis, M. E., & Sheffield, J. S. (2017). Update on syphilis and pregnancy. *Birth Defects Research, 109*(5), 347–352. https://doi.org/10.1002/bdra.23562

Tsujimoto, S., Kuwajima, M., & Sawaguchi, T. (2007). Developmental fractionation of working memory and response inhibition during childhood. *Experimental Psychology, 54*(1), 30–37.

Tucker, B., & Young, A. (2005). Growing up Mikea: Children's time allocation and tuber foraging in southwestern Madagascar. In B. S. Hewlett & M. E. Lamb. (Eds.), *Huntergatherer childhoods: Evolutionary, developmental and cultural perspectives* (pp. 147–174). New Brunswick, NJ: Transaction.

Tucker, C. J., Finkelhor, D., & Turner, H. (2019). Patterns of sibling victimization as predictors of peer victimization in childhood and adolescence. *Journal of Family Violence*, 1–11. https://doi.org/10.1007/s10896-018-0021-1

Tudge, J. R. H., Payir, A., Merçon-Vargas, E., Cao, H., Liang, Y., Li, J., & O'Brien, L. (2016). Still misused after all these years? A reevaluation of the uses of Bronfenbrenner's bioecological theory of human development. *Journal of Family Theory & Review, 8*(4), 427–445. https://doi.org/10.1111/jftr.12165

Tulving, E. (2002). Episodic memory: From mind to brain. *Annual Review of Psychology, 53*, 1–25.

Tunau, K., Adamu, A., Hassan, M., Ahmed, Y., & Ekele, B. (2012). Age at menarche among school girls in Sokoto, Northern Nigeria. *Annals of African Medicine*. Usmanu Danfodiyo University Teaching Hospital. Retrieved from http://www.ajol.info/index.php/aam/article/view/75230

Turcotte Benedict, F., Vivier, P. M., & Gjelsvik, A. (2015). Mental health and bullying in the United States among children aged 6 to 17 years. *Journal of Interpersonal Violence, 30*(5), 782–795. https://doi.org/10.1177/0886260514536279

Turecki, G., & Meaney, M. J. (2016). Effects of the social environment and stress on glucocorticoid receptor gene methylation: A systematic review. *Biological Psychiatry, 79*(2), 87–96. https://doi.org/10.1016/j.biopsych.2014.11.022

Turfkruyer, M., & Verhasselt, V. (2015). Breast milk and its impact on maturation of the neonatal immune system. *Current Opinion in Infectious Diseases, 28*(3), 199–206. https://doi.org/10.1097/QCO.0000000000000165

Turiel, E. (1998). The development of morality. In N. Eisenberg (Ed.), *Handbook of child psychology: Vol. 3. Social, emotional, and personality development* (5th ed., pp. 863–932). New York, NY: Wiley.

Turiel, E., & Nucci, L. (2017). Moral development in context. In A. Dick & U. Muller (Eds.), *Advancing developmental science: Philosophy, theory, and method* (pp. 107–121). New York, NY: Routledge.

Turnbull, K., & Justice, L. M. (2016). *Language development from theory to practice*. New York, NY: Pearson.

Turner, J. H. (2014). In the evolution of human emotions. In J. E. Stets & J. H. Turner (Eds.), *Handbook of the sociology of emotions* (Vol. 2, pp. 11–31). Dordrecht, Netherlands: Springer. https://doi.org/10.1007/978-94-017-9130-4_2

Turner, P. J., & Gervai, J. (1995). A multidimensional study of gender typing in preschool children and their parents: Personality, attitudes, preferences, behavior, and cultural differences. *British Journal of Developmental Psychology, 11*, 323–342.

Turner, P. L., & Mainster, M. A. (2008). Circadian photoreception: Ageing and the eye's important role in systemic health. *British Journal of Ophthalmology, 92*(11), 1439–1444. https://doi.org/10.1136/bjo.2008.141747

Tuulari, J. J., Scheinin, N. M., Lehtola, S., Merisaari, H., Saunavaara, J., Parkkola, R., . . . Björnsdotter, M. (2019). Neural correlates of gentle skin stroking in early infancy. *Developmental Cognitive Neuroscience, 35*, 36–41. https://doi.org/10.1016/J.DCN.2017.10.004

Tyler, J. H., & Lofstrom, M. (2009). Finishing high school: Alternative pathways and dropout recovery. *The Future of Children, 19*(1), 77–103. Retrieved from http://europepmc.org/abstract/med/21141706

Tyrka, A. R., Graber, J. A., & Brooks-Gunn, J. (2000). The development of disordered eating: Correlates and predictors of eating problems in the context of adolescence. In A. J. Sameroff, M. Lewis, & S. M. Miller (Eds.), *Handbook of developmental psychopathology* (2nd ed., pp. 607–624). Dordrecht, Netherlands: Kluwer Academic Publishers.

Tzeng, O., Jackson, J., & Karlson, H. (1991). *Theories of child abuse and neglect: Differential perspectives, summaries, and evaluations*. New York, NY: Praeger Publishers.

U.S. Bureau of Labor Statistics. (2015). *Labor force statistics from the current population survey: Employment status of the civilian noninstitutional population by age, sex, and race*. Retrieved from http://www.bls.gov/cps/cpsaat03.htm

U.S. Bureau of Labor Statistics. (2016). *Employment characteristics of families—2015*. Retrieved from https://www.bls.gov/news.release/pdf/famee.pdf

U.S. Bureau of the Census. (2018). *America's families and living arrangements: 2017*. Retrieved from https://www.census.gov/data/tables/2017/demo/families/cps-2017.html

U.S. Department of Agriculture. (2017). *Food security status of U.S. households in 2016*. Retrieved from https://www.ers.usda.gov/topics/food-nutrition-assistance/food-security-in-the-us/key-statistics-graphics.aspx

U.S. Department of Health and Human Services, & Administration for Children and Families. (2010). *Head Start impact study: Final report*. Washington, DC: Author.

U.S. Department of Health and Human Services. (2011). *The Surgeon General's call to action to support breastfeeding* (Office of the Surgeon General., Ed.). Washington, DC: U.S. Department of Health and Human Services.

U.S. Department of Health and Human Services. (2013). *Child maltreatment 2012*. Retrieved from http://www.acf.hhs.gov/programs/cb/resource/child-maltreatment-2012

U.S. Department of Health and Human Services. (2014). *Child health USA 2014*. Retrieved from http://www.mchb.hrsa.gov/chusa14/index.html

U.S. Department of Health and Human Services. (2016). *Child maltreatment, 2014*. Retrieved from http://www.acf.hhs.gov/sites/default/files/cb/cm2014.pdf

U.S. Department of Health and Human Services. (2017a). *Laws & policies*. Retrieved from https://www.stopbullying.gov/laws/index.html

U.S. Department of Health and Human Services. (2017b). *United States adolescent physical health facts*. Retrieved from https://www.hhs.gov/ash/oah/facts-and-stats/national-and-state-data-sheets/adolescent-physical-health-and-nutrition/united-states/index.html

U.S. Department of Health and Human Services. (2018a). *Child maltreatment, 2016*. Retrieved from https://www.acf.hhs.gov/cb/resource/child-maltreatment-2016

U.S. Department of Health and Human Services. (2018b). *The physical activity guidelines for Americans* (2nd ed.). Retrieved from https://www.hhs.gov/fitness/be-active/physical-activity-guidelines-for-americans/index.html

U.S. Department of Labor Bureau of Labor Statistics. (2014). *Labor force statistics from the current population survey*. Retrieved from https://www.bls.gov/cps/cpsaat03.htm

U.S. Department of State. (2014). *FY 2013 annual report on intercountry adoption*. Retrieved from http://adoption.state.gov/content/pdf/fy2013_annual_report.pdf

U.S. Food and Drug Administration. (2010). *iPLEDGE information*. Retrieved from https://www.fda.gov/Drugs/DrugSafety/PostmarketDrugSafetyInformationforPatientsandProviders/ucm094307.htm

Ueno, K. (2005). Sexual orientation and psychological distress in adolescence: Examining interpersonal stressors and social support processes. *Social Psychology Quarterly, 68*(3), 258–277.

Uhl, E. R., Camilletti, C. R., Scullin, M. H., & Wood, J. M. (2016). Under pressure: Individual differences in children's suggestibility in response to intense social influence. *Social Development, 25*(2), 422–434. https://doi.org/10.1111/sode.12156

Uhlmann, W. R., Schuette, J. L., & Yashar, B. (2009). *A guide to genetic counseling* (2nd ed.). Hoboken, NJ: Wiley-Blackwell.

Uji, M., Sakamoto, A., Adachi, K., & Kitamura, T. (2013). The Impact of authoritative, authoritarian, and permissive parenting styles on children's later mental health in Japan: Focusing on parent and child gender. *Journal of Child and Family Studies, 23*(2), 293–302. https://doi.org/10.1007/s10826-013-9740-3

U.K. Department of Health. (2005). *Reduce the risk of cot death: An easy guide.* London, England: U.K. Department of Health.

Ullman, H., Almeida, R., & Klingberg, T. (2014). Structural maturation and brain activity predict future working memory capacity during childhood development. *Journal of Neuroscience, 34*(5), 1592–1598. https://doi.org/10.1523/jneurosci.0842-13.2014

Ullman, S. E., Relyea, M., Peter-Hagene, L., & Vasquez, A. L. (2013). Trauma histories, substance use coping, PTSD, and problem substance use among sexual assault victims. *Addictive Behaviors, 38*(6), 2219–2223. https://doi.org/10.1016/j.addbeh.2013.01.027

Ullsperger, J. M., & Nikolas, M. A. (2017). A meta-analytic review of the association between pubertal timing and psychopathology in adolescence: Are there sex differences in risk? *Psychological Bulletin, 143*(9), 903–938. https://doi.org/10.1037/bul0000106

Ulrich, D. A., Lloyd, M. C., Tiernan, C. W., Looper, J. E., & Angulo-Barroso, R. M. (2008). Effects of intensity of treadmill training on developmental outcomes and stepping in infants with Down syndrome: A randomized trial. *Physical Therapy, 88*(1), 114–122.

Umaña-Taylor, A. J. (2016). Ethnic-racial identity conceptualization, development, and youth adjustment. In L. Balter & C. S. Tamis-LeMonda (Eds.), *Child psychology: A handbook of contemporary issues* (p. 505). New York, NY: Routledge.

Umaña-Taylor, A. J., Guimond, A. B., Updegraff, K. A., & Jahromi, L. (2013). A longitudinal examination of support, self-esteem, and Mexican-origin adolescent mothers' parenting efficacy. *Journal of Marriage and the Family, 75*(3), 746–759. https://doi.org/10.1111/jomf.12019

Umaña-Taylor, A. J., Quintana, S. M., Lee, R. M., Cross, W. E., Rivas-Drake, D., Schwartz, S. J., . . . Seaton, E. (2014). Ethnic and racial identity during adolescence and into young adulthood: An integrated conceptualization. *Child Development, 85*(1), 21–39. https://doi.org/10.1111/cdev.12196

Umstad, M., Calais-Ferreira, L., Scurrah, K.J., Hall, J., & Craig, J. (2019). Twins and twinning. In Reed E. Pyeritz, Bruce R. Korf, & Wayne W. Grody (Eds.), *Emery and Rimoin's principles and practice of medical genetics and genomics* (pp. 387-414). London, England: Academic Press. https://doi.org/10.1016/B978-0-12-812537-3.00014-7

Ungar, M. (2015). Practitioner review: Diagnosing childhood resilience - a systemic approach to the diagnosis of adaptation in adverse social and physical ecologies. *Journal of Child Psychology and Psychiatry, 56*(1), 4–17. https://doi.org/10.1111/jcpp.12306

United Nations Children's Fund. (2013). *Towards an AIDS-free generation: Children and AIDS, sixth stocktaking report.* New York. Retrieved from http://www.childinfo.org/files/str6_full_report_29-11-2013.pdf

United Nations General Assembly. (2015). *Transforming our world: The 2030 agenda for sustainable development.* Retrieved from undocs.org/A/RES/70/1.

Updegraff, K. A., McHale, S. M., Zeiders, K. H., Umaña-Taylor, A. J., Perez-Brena, N. J., Wheeler, L. A., & Rodríguez De Jesús, S. A. (2014). Mexican-American adolescents' gender role attitude development: The role of adolescents' gender and nativity and parents' gender role attitudes. *Journal of Youth and Adolescence, 43*(12), 2041–2053. https://doi.org/10.1007/s10964-014-0128-5

Ursache, A., & Noble, K. G. (2016). Neurocognitive development in socioeconomic context: Multiple mechanisms and implications for measuring socioeconomic status. *Psychophysiology, 53*(1), 71–82. https://doi.org/10.1111/psyp.12547

Ursache, A., Blair, C., Stifter, C., Voegtline, K., & The Family Life Project Investigators. (2013). Emotional reactivity and regulation in infancy interact to predict executive functioning in early childhood. *Developmental Psychology, 40*(1), 760.

U.S. Department of Health and Human Services. (2013). Prenatal care utilization. Retrieved from https://mchb.hrsa.gov/chusa13/dl/pdf/hsu.pdf

U.S. Department of Health and Human Services, & Administration for Children and Families. (2010). *Head Start impact study: Final report.* Washington, DC: Author.

U.S. Department of Labor. (2015). *Registered apprenticeship national results fiscal year 2014.* Retrieved from http://doleta.gov/oa/data_statistics.cfm

Utriainen, P., Laakso, S., Liimatta, J., Jaaskelainen, J., & Voutilainen, R. (2015). Premature adrenarche - a common condition with variable presentation. *Hormone Research in Paediatrics, 83*(4), 221–231. https://doi.org/10.1159/000369458

Vaala, S. E., & LaPierre, M. A. (2014). Marketing genius: The impact of educational claims and cues on parents' reactions to infant/toddler DVDs. *Journal of Consumer Affairs, 48*(2), 323–350. https://doi.org/10.1111/joca.12023

Vagi, K. J., Rothman, E. F., Latzman, N. E., Tharp, A. T., Hall, D. M., & Breiding, M. J. (2013). Beyond correlates: A review of risk and protective factors for adolescent dating violence perpetration. *Journal of Youth and Adolescence, 42*(4), 633–649. https://doi.org/10.1007/s10964-013-9907-7

Vaillancourt, T., Faris, R., & Mishna, F. (2017). Cyberbullying in children and youth: Implications for health and clinical practice. *Canadian Journal of Psychiatry, 62*(6), 368–373. https://doi.org/10.1177/0706743716684791

Vaish, A. (2018). The prosocial functions of early social emotions: the case of guilt. *Current Opinion in Psychology, 20*, 25–29. https://doi.org/10.1016/J.COPSYC.2017.08.008

Vaish, A., Grossmann, T., & Woodward, A. (2008). Not all emotions are created equal: The negativity bias in social-emotional development. *Psychological Bulletin, 134*(3), 383–403. https://doi.org/10.1037/0033-2909.134.3.383

Vallotton, C. D., Decker, K. B., Kwon, A., Wang, W., & Chang, T. (2017). Quantity and quality of gestural input: Caregivers' sensitivity predicts caregiver-infant bidirectional communication through gestures. *Infancy, 22*(1), 56–77. https://doi.org/10.1111/infa.12155

Vallotton, C., & Ayoub, C. (2011). Use your words: The role of language in the development of toddlers' self-regulation. *Early Childhood Research Quarterly, 26*(2), 169–181.

Van Craeyevelt, S., Verschueren, K., Vancraeyveldt, C., Wouters, S., & Colpin, H. (2017). The role of preschool teacher-child interactions in academic adjustment: An intervention study with Playing-2-gether. *British Journal of Educational Psychology, 87*(3), 345–364. https://doi.org/10.1111/bjep.12153

van de Bongardt, D., Reitz, E., Sandfort, T., & Deković, M. (2014). A meta-analysis of the relations between three types of peer norms and adolescent sexual behavior. *Personality and Social Psychology Review, 19*, 203–234. https://doi.org/10.1177/1088868314544223

van de Bongardt, D., Yu, R., Deković, M., & Meeus, W. H. J. (2015). Romantic relationships and sexuality in adolescence and young adulthood: The role of parents, peers, and partners. *European Journal of Developmental Psychology, 12*(5), 497–515. https://doi.org/10.1080/17405629.2015.1068689

Van de Vondervoort, J. W., & Hamlin, J. K. (2016). Evidence for intuitive morality: Preverbal infants make sociomoral evaluations. *Child Development Perspectives, 10*(3), 143–148. https://doi.org/10.1111/cdep.12175

van den Bemt, L., Kooijman, S., Linssen, V., Lucassen, P., Muris, J., Slabbers, G., & Schermer, T. (2010). How does asthma influence the daily life of children? Results of focus group interviews. *Health & Quality of Life Outcomes, 8*, 1–10. https://doi.org/10.1186/1477-7525-8-5

van den Berg, Y. H. M., Deutz, M. H. F., Smeekens, S., & Cillessen, A. H. N. (2017). Developmental pathways to preference and popularity in middle childhood. *Child Development, 88*(5), 1629–1641. https://doi.org/10.1111/cdev.12706

Van den Bergh, B. R. H., van den Heuvel, M. I., Lahti, M., Braeken, M., de Rooij, S. R., Entringer, S., . . . Schwab, M. (2017). Prenatal developmental origins of behavior and mental health: The influence of maternal stress in pregnancy. *Neuroscience & Biobehavioral Reviews*. https://doi.org/10.1016/J.NEUBIOREV.2017.07.003

van der Niet, A. G., Smith, J., Scherder, E. J. A., Oosterlaan, J., Hartman, E., & Visscher, C. (2015). Associations between daily physical activity and executive functioning in primary school-aged children. *Journal of Science and Medicine in Sport, 18*(6), 673–677. https://doi.org/10.1016/j.jsams.2014.09.006

van der Stel, M., & Veenman, M. V. J. (2014). Metacognitive skills and intellectual ability of young adolescents: A longitudinal study from a developmental perspective. *European Journal of Psychology of Education, 29*(1), 117–137. https://doi.org/10.1007/s10212-013-0190-5

van Dijk, A., Poorthuis, A. M. G., & Malti, T. (2017). Psychological processes in young bullies versus bully-victims. *Aggressive Behavior, 43*(5), 430–439. https://doi.org/10.1002/ab.21701

Van Dijk, M. P. A., Branje, S., Keijsers, L., Hawk, S. T., Hale, W. W., & Meeus, W. H. J. (2014). Self-concept clarity across adolescence: Longitudinal associations with open communication with parents and internalizing symptoms. *Journal of Youth and Adolescence, 43*(11), 1861–1876. https://doi.org/10.1007/s10964-013-0055-x

van Dijken, M. W., Stams, G. J. J. M., & de Winter, M. (2016). Can community-based interventions prevent child maltreatment? *Children and Youth Services Review, 61*, 149–158. https://doi.org/10.1016/j.childyouth.2015.12.007

van Dommelen, P., Koledova, E., & Wit, J. M. (2018). Effect of adherence to growth hormone treatment on 0–2 year catch-up growth in children with growth hormone deficiency. *PLoS ONE, 13*(10), e0206009. https://doi.org/10.1371/journal.pone.0206009

Van Doorn, M. D., Branje, S. J. T., & Meeus, W. H. J. (2011). Developmental changes in conflict resolution styles in parent-adolescent relationships: A four-wave longitudinal study. *Journal of Youth and Adolescence, 40*(1), 97–107. https://doi.org/10.1007/s10964-010-9516-7

van Duijvenvoorde, A. C. K., Peters, S., Braams, B. R., & Crone, E. A. (2016). What motivates adolescents? Neural responses to rewards and their influence on adolescents' risk taking, learning, and cognitive control. *Neuroscience & Biobehavioral Reviews, 70*, 135–147. https://doi.org/10.1016/J.NEUBIOREV.2016.06.037

van Goethem, A. A. J., van Hoof, A., van Aken, M. A. G., Orobio de Castro, B., & Raaijmakers, Q. A. W. (2014). Socialising adolescent volunteering: How important are parents and friends? Age dependent effects of parents and friends on adolescents' volunteering behaviours. *Journal of Applied Developmental Psychology, 35*(2), 94–101. https://doi.org/10.1016/j.appdev.2013.12.003

van Heteren, C. F., Boekkooi, P. F., Jongsma, H. W., & Nijhuis, J. G. (2000). Fetal learning and memory. *Lancet, 356*(9236), 1169–1170. https://doi.org/10.1016/S0140-6736(00)02766-5

van Hoogdalem, A.-G., Singer, E., Eek, A., & Heesbeen, D. (2013). Friendship in young children: Construction of a behavioural sociometric method. *Journal of Early Childhood Research, 11*(3), 236–247. https://doi.org/10.1177/1476718X13488337

van Hoorn, J., Crone, E. A., & Van Leijenhorst, L. (2017). Hanging out with the right crowd: Peer influence on risk-taking behavior in adolescence. *Journal of Research on Adolescence, 27*(1), 189–200. https://doi.org/10.1111/jora.12265

van Hoorn, J., van Dijk, E., Meuwese, R., Rieffe, C., & Crone, E. A. (2016). Peer influence on prosocial behavior in adolescence. *Journal of Research on Adolescence, 26*(1), 90–100. https://doi.org/10.1111/jora.12173

Van IJzendoorn, M. H., & Kroonenberg, P. M. (1988). Cross-cultural patterns of attachment: A meta-analysis of the strange situation. *Child Development, 59*, 147–156.

Van Ouytsel, J., Van Gool, E., Ponnet, K., & Walrave, M. (2014). Brief report: The association between adolescents' characteristics and engagement in sexting. *Journal of Adolescence, 37*(8), 1387–1391. https://doi.org/10.1016/j.adolescence.2014.10.004

Van Ryzin, M. J., Carlson, E. A., & Sroufe, L. A. (2011). Attachment discontinuity in a high-risk sample. *Attachment & Human Development, 13*(4), 381–401. https://doi.org/10.1080/14616734.2011.584403

Vandell, D. L., Belsky, J., Burchinal, M., Steinberg, L., & Vandergrift, N. (2010). Do effects of early child care extend to age 15 years? Results from the NICHD study of early child care and youth development. *Child Development, 81*(3), 737–756. https://doi.org/10.1111/j.1467-8624.2010.01431.x

Vandell, D. L., Burchinal, M., & Pierce, K. M. (2016). Early child care and adolescent functioning at the end of high school: Results from the NICHD Study of Early Child Care and Youth Development. *Developmental Psychology, 52*(10), 1634–1645. https://doi.org/10.1037/dev0000169

Vandenbroucke, A. R. E., Sligte, I. G., Barrett, A. B., Seth, A. K., Fahrenfort, J. J., & Lamme, V. A. F. (2014). Accurate metacognition for visual sensory memory representations. *Psychological Science, 25*(4), 861–873. https://doi.org/10.1177/0956797613516146

Vandermaas-Peeler, M., Massey, K., & Kendall, A. (2016). Parent guidance of young children's scientific and mathematical reasoning in a science museum. *Early Childhood Education Journal, 44*(3), 217–224. https://doi.org/10.1007/s10643-015-0714-5

Vanhalst, J., Luyckx, K., Scholte, R. H. J., Engels, R. C. M. E., & Goossens, L. (2013). Low self-esteem as a risk factor for loneliness in adolescence: Perceived - but not actual - social acceptance as an underlying mechanism. *Journal of Abnormal Child Psychology, 41*(7), 1067–1081. https://doi.org/10.1007/s10802-013-9751-y

Vanhees, K., Vonhögen, I. G. C., van Schooten, F. J., & Godschalk, R. W. L. (2014). You are what you eat, and so are your children: The impact of micronutrients on the epigenetic programming of offspring. *Cellular and Molecular Life Sciences, 71*(2), 271–285. https://doi.org/10.1007/s00018-013-1427-9

Vannasing, P., Florea, O., González-Frankenberger, B., Tremblay, J., Paquette, N., Safi, D., . . . Gallagher, A. (2016). Distinct hemispheric specializations for native and non-native languages in one-day-old newborns identified by fNIRS. *Neuropsychologia, 84*, 63–69. https://doi.org/10.1016/j.neuropsychologia.2016.01.038

Varnum, M. E. W., & Grossmann, I. (2017). Cultural change: The how and the why. *Perspectives on Psychological Science, 12*(6), 956–972. https://doi.org/10.1177/1745691617699971

Vaughn, B. E., Elmore-Staton, L., Shin, N., & El-Sheikh, M. (2015). Sleep as a support for social competence, peer relations, and cognitive functioning in preschool children. *Behavioral Sleep Medicine, 13*(2), 92–106. https://doi.org/10.1080/15402002.2013.845778

Vaughn, S., & Klingner, J. K. (1998). Students' perceptions of inclusion and resource room settings. *Journal of Special Education, 32*, 79–88.

Veer, I. M., Luyten, H., Mulder, H., van Tuijl, C., & Sleegers, P. J. C. (2017). Selective attention relates to the development of executive functions in 2,5- to 3-year-olds: A longitudinal study. *Early Childhood Research Quarterly, 41*, 84–94. https://doi.org/10.1016/J.ECRESQ.2017.06.005

Vélez-Agosto, N. M., Soto-Crespo, J. G., Vizcarrondo-Oppenheimer, M., Vega-Molina, S., & Garcia Coll, C. (2017). Bronfenbrenner's bioecological theory revision: Moving culture from the macro into the micro. *Perspectives on Psychological Science, 12*(5), 900–910. https://doi.org/10.1177/1745691617704397

Ventola, C. L. (2016). Immunization in the United States: Recommendations, barriers, and measures to improve compliance: Part 1: Childhood vaccinations. *P & T, 41*(7), 426–436. Retrieved from http://www.ncbi.nlm.nih.gov/pubmed/27408519

Ventura, A. K., & Worobey, J. (2013). Early influences on the development of food preferences. *Current Biology, 23*(9), R401–R408. https://doi.org/10.1016/J.CUB.2013.02.037

Vereijken, B., & Thelen, E. (1997). Training infant treadmill stepping: The role of individual pattern stability. *Developmental Psychobiology, 30*, 89–102.

Verhage, M. L., Oosterman, M., & Schuengel, C. (2013). Parenting self-efficacy predicts perceptions of infant negative temperament characteristics, not vice versa. *Journal of Family Psychology, 27*(5), 844–849. https://doi.org/10.1037/a0034263

Verissimo, M., J. Santos, A. J., Fernandes, C., Shin, N., & Vaughn, B. E. (2014). Associations between attachment security and social competence in preschool children. *Merrill-Palmer Quarterly, 60*(1), 80. https://doi.org/10.13110/merrpalmquar1982.60.1.0080

Verkooijen, K. T., de Vries, N. K., & Nielsen, G. A. (2007). Youth crowds and substance use: The impact of perceived group norm and multiple group identification. *Psychology of Addictive Behaviors, 21*(1), 55–61. https://doi.org/10.1037/0893-164x.21.1.55

Vernon, L., Modecki, K. L., & Barber, B. L. (2018). Mobile phones in the bedroom: Trajectories of sleep habits and subsequent adolescent psychosocial development. *Child Development, 89*(1), 66–77. https://doi.org/10.1111/cdev.12836

Vickerman, K. A., & Margolin, G. (2009). Rape treatment outcome research: Empirical findings and state of the literature. *Clinical Psychology Review, 29*(5), 431–448. https://doi.org/10.1016/j.cpr.2009.04.004

Victora, C. G., Bahl, R., Barros, A. J. D., França, G. V. A., Horton, S., Krasevec, J., . . . Rollins, N. C. (2016). Breastfeeding in the 21st century: Epidemiology, mechanisms, and lifelong effect. *Lancet, 387*(10017), 475–490. https://doi.org/10.1016/S0140-6736(15)01024-7

Victora, M. D., Victora, C. G., & Barros, F. C. (1990). Cross-cultural differences in developmental rates: A comparison between British and Brazilian children. *Child: Care, Health and Development, 16*(3), 151–164. https://doi.org/10.1111/j.1365-2214.1990.tb00647.x

Vigeh, M., Yokoyama, K., Matsukawa, T., Shinohara, A., & Ohtani, K. (2014). Low level prenatal blood lead adversely affects early childhood mental development. *Journal of Child Neurology, 29*(10), 1305–1311. https://doi.org/10.1177/0883073813516999

Vijayakumar, N., Allen, N. B., Youssef, G., Dennison, M., Yücel, M., Simmons, J. G., & Whittle, S. (2016). Brain development during adolescence: A mixed-longitudinal investigation of cortical thickness, surface area, and volume. *Human Brain Mapping, 37*(6), 2027–2038. https://doi.org/10.1002/hbm.23154

Vikraman, S., Fryar, C. D., & Ogden, C. L. (2015). Caloric intake from fast food among children and adolescents in the United States, 2011-2012. *NCHS Data Brief*, (213), 1–8. Retrieved from http://www.ncbi.nlm.nih.gov/pubmed/26375457

Villamor, E., & Jansen, E. C. (2016). Nutritional determinants of the timing of puberty, *37*(1), 33–46. https://doi.org/10.1146/annurev-publhealth-031914-122606

Vincent, N. J. (2009). Exposure to community violence and the family: Disruptions in functioning and relationships. *Families in Society, 90*(2), 137–143.

Vincini, S., Jhang, Y., Buder, E. H., & Gallagher, S. (2017). Neonatal imitation: Theory, experimental design, and significance for the field of social cognition. *Frontiers in Psychology, 8*, 1323. https://doi.org/10.3389/fpsyg.2017.01323

Vincke, J., & van Heeringen, K. (2002). Confidant support and the mental wellbeing of lesbian and gay young adults: Aa longitudinal analysis. *Journal of Community & Applied Social Psychology, 12*(3), 181–193. https://doi.org/10.1002/casp.671

Vinden, P. (1996). Junin Quechua children's understanding of mind. *Child Development, 67*, 1707–1716.

Vink, J., & Quinn, M. (2018a). Amniocentesis. In J. Copel, M. E. D'Alton, H. Feltovich, E. Gratacos, A. O. Odibo, L. Platt, & B. Tutschek (Eds.), *Obstetric imaging: Fetal diagnosis and care* (pp. 473–475.e1). Philadelphia, PA: Elsevier. https://doi.org/10.1016/B978-0-323-44548-1.00111-X

Vink, J., & Quinn, M. (2018b). Chorionic villus sampling. In J. Copel, M. E. D'Alton, H. Feltovich, E. Gratacos, A. O. Odibo, L. Platt, & B. Tutschek (Eds.), *Obstetric imaging: Fetal diagnosis and care* (pp. 479–481). Philadelphia, PA: Elsevier. https://doi.org/10.1016/B978-0-323-44548-1.00113-3

Virtanen, M., Kivimäki, H., Ervasti, J., Oksanen, T., Pentti, J., Kouvonen, A., . . . Vahtera, J. (2015). Fast-food outlets and grocery stores near school and adolescents' eating habits and overweight in Finland. *European Journal of Public Health, 25*(4), 650–655. https://doi.org/10.1093/eurpub/ckv045

Visscher, M., & Narendran, V. (2014). Vernix caseosa: Formation and functions. *Newborn and Infant Nursing Reviews, 14*(4), 142–146. https://doi.org/10.1053/j.nainr.2014.10.005

Visser, S. N., Danielson, M. L., Bitsko, R. H., Holbrook, J. R., Kogan, M. D., Ghandour, R. M., . . . Blumberg, S. J. (2014). Trends in the parent-report of health care provider-diagnosed and medicated attention-deficit/hyperactivity disorder: United States, 2003-2011. *Journal of the American Academy of Child and Adolescent Psychiatry, 53*(1), 34–46. https://doi.org/10.1016/j.jaac.2013.09.001

Vissers, L. E. L. M., Gilissen, C., & Veltman, J. A. (2016). Genetic studies in intellectual disability and related disorders. *Nature Reviews Genetics, 17*(1), 9–18. https://doi.org/10.1038/nrg3999

Viswanathan, M., Treiman, K. A., Kish-Doto, J., Middleton, J. C., Coker-Schwimmer, E. J. L., & Nicholson, W. K. (2017). Folic acid supplementation for the prevention of neural tube defects. *JAMA, 317*(2), 190. https://doi.org/10.1001/jama.2016.19193

Viteri, O., Soto, E., Bahado-Singh, R., Christensen, C., Chauhan, S., & Sibai, B. (2015). Fetal anomalies and long-term effects associated with substance abuse in pregnancy: A literature review. *American Journal of Perinatology, 32*(5), 405–416. https://doi.org/10.1055/s-0034-1393932

Voelker, D. K., Gould, D., & Reel, J. J. (2014). Prevalence and correlates of disordered eating in female figure skaters. *Psychology of Sport and Exercise, 15*(6), 696–704. https://doi.org/10.1016/j.psychsport.2013.12.002

von Hofsten, C., & Rönnqvist, L. (1993). The structuring of neonatal arm movements. *Child Development, 64*(4), 1046–1057. Retrieved from http://www.ncbi.nlm.nih.gov/pubmed/8404256

von Hofsten, C., Kochukhova, O., & Rosander, K. (2007). Predictive tracking over occlusions by 4-month-old infants. *Developmental Science, 10*(5), 625–640. https://doi.org/10.1111/j.1467-7687.2006.00604.x

von Soest, T., Wichstrøm, L., & Kvalem, I. L. (2016). The development of global and domain-specific self-esteem from age 13 to 31. *Journal of Personality and Social Psychology, 110*(4), 592–608. https://doi.org/10.1037/pspp0000060

Voorhies, W., Dajani, D. R., Vij, S. G., Shankar, S., Turan, T. O., & Uddin, L. Q. (2018). Aberrant functional connectivity of inhibitory control networks in children with autism spectrum disorder. *Autism Research, 11*(11), 1468–1478. https://doi.org/10.1002/aur.2014

Vouloumanos, A., Hauser, M. D., Werker, J. F., & Martin, A. (2010). The tuning of human neonates' preference for speech. *Child Development, 81*(2), 517–527. https://doi.org/10.1111/j.1467-8624.2009.01412.x

Vrijheid, M., Casas, M., Gascon, M., Valvi, D., & Nieuwenhuijsen, M. (2016). Environmental pollutants and child health—A review of recent concerns. *International Journal of Hygiene and Environmental Health, 219*(4–5), 331–342. https://doi.org/10.1016/J.IJHEH.2016.05.001

Vygotsky, L. S. (1962). *Thought and language*. Cambridge, MA: MIT Press. (Original work published in 1934)

Vygotsky, L. S. (1976) Play and its role in the mental development of the child. In: J. S. Bruner, A. Jolly, & K. Sylva (Eds.) *Play: Its role in development and evolution* (pp. 537–554). New York, NY: Basic Books.

Vygotsky, L. S. (1978). *Mind in society: The development of higher psychological processes*. Cambridge, MA: Harvard University Press.

Vygotsky, L. S., & Minick, N. (1987). *Thinking and speech* (T. N. Minick, Ed.). New York, NY: Plenum Press.

Waasdorp, T. E., & Bradshaw, C. P. (2015). The overlap between cyberbullying and traditional bullying. *Journal of Adolescent Health, 56*(5), 483–488. https://doi.org/10.1016/j.jadohealth.2014.12.002

Waasdorp, T. E., & Bradshaw, C. P. (2011). Examining student responses to frequent bullying: A latent class approach. *Journal of Educational Psychology, 103*(2), 336–352. https://doi.org/10.1037/a0022747

Waber, D. P., Bryce, C. P., Fitzmaurice, G. M., Zichlin, M. L., McGaughy, J., Girard, J. M., & Galler, J. R. (2014). Neuropsychological outcomes at midlife following moderate to severe malnutrition in infancy. *Neuropsychology, 28*(4), 530–540. https://doi.org/10.1037/neu0000058

Waddington, C. H. (1971). Concepts of development. In E. Tobach, L. R. Aronson, & E. Shaw (Eds.), *The biopsychology of development* (pp. 17–23). San Diego, CA: Academic Press.

Wagner, M. F., Milner, J. S., McCarthy, R. J., Crouch, J. L., McCanne, T. R., & Skowronski, J. J. (2015). Facial emotion recognition accuracy and child physical abuse: An experiment and a meta-analysis. *Psychology of Violence, 5*(2), 154–162. https://doi.org/10.1037/a0036014

Wagnsson, S., Lindwall, M., & Gustafsson, H. (2014). Participation in organized sport and self-esteem across adolescence: The mediating role of perceived sport competence. *Journal of Sport & Exercise Psychology, 36*(6), 584–594. https://doi.org/10.1123/jsep.2013-0137

Waid, J., & Uhrich, M. (2019). A scoping review of the theory and practice of positive youth development. *British Journal of Social Work*. https://doi.org/10.1093/bjsw/bcy130

Waldfogel, J., Craigie, T.-A., & Brooks-Gunn, J. (2010). Fragile families and child wellbeing. *The Future of Children, 20*(2), 87–112. Retrieved from https://www.ncbi.nlm.nih.gov/pubmed/20964133

Waldman, I. D., Tackett, J. L., Van Hulle, C. A., Applegate, B., Pardini, D., Frick, P. J., & Lahey, B. B. (2011). Child and adolescent conduct disorder substantially shares genetic influences with three socioemotional dispositions. *Journal of Abnormal Psychology, 120*(1), 57–70. https://doi.org/10.1037/a0021351

Walk, R. D. (1968). Monocular compared to binocular depth perception in human infants. *Science, 162*, 473–475.

Walker, L. J. (2004). Progress and prospects in the psychology of moral development. *Merrill-Palmer Quarterly, 50*(4), 546–557.

Walker, L. J., & Taylor, J. H. (1991). Family interactions and the development of moral reasoning. *Child Development, 62*, 264–283.

Walle, E. A., & Campos, J. J. (2013). Infant language development is related to the acquisition of walking. *Developmental Psychology, 50*(2), 336–348.

Walle, E. A., Reschke, P. J., & Knothe, J. M. (2017). Social referencing: Defining and delineating a basic process of emotion. *Emotion Review, 9*(3), 245–252. https://doi.org/10.1177/1754073916669594

Walpole, M. (2008). Emerging from the pipeline: African American students, socioeconomic status, and college experiences and outcomes. *Research in Higher Education, 49*(3), 237–255. https://doi.org/10.1007/s11162-007-9079-y

Waltes, R., Duketis, E., Knapp, M., Anney, R. J. L., Huguet, G., Schlitt, S., . . . Chiocchetti, A. G. (2014). Common variants in genes of the postsynaptic FMRP signalling pathway are risk factors for autism spectrum disorders. *Human Genetics, 133*(6), 781–792. https://doi.org/10.1007/s00439-013-1416-y

Walton, G. M., & Spencer, S. J. (2009). Latent ability: Grades and test scores systematically underestimate the intellectual ability of negatively stereotyped students. *Psychological Science, 20*(9), 1132–1139. https://doi.org/10.1111/j.1467-9280.2009.02417.x

Walton, K., Kuczynski, L., Haycraft, E., Breen, A., & Haines, J. (2017). Time to re-think picky eating? A relational approach to understanding picky eating. *International Journal of Behavioral Nutrition and Physical Activity, 14*(1), 62. https://doi.org/10.1186/s12966-017-0520-0

Walton, M., Dewey, D., & Lebel, C. (2018). Brain white matter structure and language ability in preschool-aged children. *Brain and Language, 176*, 19–25. https://doi.org/10.1016/J.BANDL.2017.10.008

Wang, C., Xia, Y., Li, W., Wilson, S. M., Bush, K., & Peterson, G. (2016). Parenting behaviors, adolescent depressive symptoms, and problem behavior: The role of self-esteem and school adjustment difficulties among Chinese adolescents. *Journal of Family Issues, 37*, 520–542. https://doi.org/10.1177/0192513X14542433

Wang, D., Kato, N., Inaba, Y., Tango, T., Yoshida, Y., Kusaka, Y., . . . Zhang, Q. (2000). Physical and personality traits of preschool children in Fuzhou, China: Only child vs sibling. *Child: Care, Health & Development, 26*(1), 49–60.

Wang, E., Clymer, J., Davis-Hayes, C., & Buttenheim, A. (2014). Nonmedical exemptions from school immunization requirements: A systematic review. *American Journal of Public Health, 104*(11), e62–e84. https://doi.org/10.2105/AJPH.2014.302190

Wang, F., Christ, S. L., Mills-Koonce, W. R., Garrett-Peters, P., & Cox, M. J. (2013). Association between maternal sensitivity and externalizing behavior from preschool to preadolescence. *Journal of Applied Developmental Psychology, 34*(2), 89–100. https://doi.org/10.1016/j.appdev.2012.11.003

Wang, L., Kong, Q.-M., Li, K., Li, X.-N., Zeng, Y.-W., Chen, C., . . . Si, T.-M. (2017). Altered intrinsic functional brain architecture in female patients with bulimia nervosa. *Journal of Psychiatry & Neuroscience, 42*(6), 414–423. https://doi.org/10.1503/JPN.160183

Wang, L., Yang, Y., Liu, F., Yang, A., Xu, Q., Wang, Q., . . . He, Y. (2018). Paternal smoking and spontaneous abortion: A population-based retrospective cohort study among non-smoking women aged 20–49 years in rural China. *J Epidemiol Community Health, 72*(9), 783-789.

Wang, M.-T., & Dishion, T. J. (2012). The trajectories of adolescents' perceptions of school climate, deviant peer affiliation, and behavioral problems during the middle school years. *Journal of Research on Adolescence, 22*(1), 40–53. https://doi.org/10.1111/j.1532-7795.2011.00763.x

Wang, M.-T., Dishion, T. J., Stormshak, E. A., & Willett, J. B. (2011). Trajectories of family management practices and early adolescent behavioral outcomes. *Developmental Psychology, 47*(5), 1324–1341. https://doi.org/10.1037/a0024026

Wang, M.-T., & Fredricks, J. A. (2014). The reciprocal links between school engagement, youth problem behaviors, and school dropout during adolescence. *Child Development, 85*(2), 722–737. https://doi.org/10.1111/cdev.12138

Wang, M.-T., Hill, N. E., & Hofkens, T. (2014) Parental involvement and African American and European American adolescents' academic, behavioral, and emotional development in secondary school. *Child Development, 85*(6), 2151–2168. https://doi.org/10.1111/cdev.12284

Wang, M.-T., & Sheikh-Khalil, S. (2014). Does parental involvement matter for student achievement and mental health in high school? *Child Development, 85*(2), 610–625. https://doi.org/10.1111/cdev.12153

Wang, Q. (2004). The emergence of cultural self-constructs: Autobiographical memory and self-description in European American and Chinese children. *Developmental Psychology, 40*, 3–15.

Wang, Q., Zheng, S.-X., Ni, Y.-F., Lu, Y.-Y., Zhang, B., Lian, Q.-Q., & Hu, M.-P. (2018). The effect of labor epidural analgesia on maternal–fetal outcomes: A retrospective cohort study. *Archives of Gynecology and Obstetrics, 298*(1), 89–96. https://doi.org/10.1007/s00404-018-4777-6

Wang, X., Bernas, R., & Eberhard, P. (2008). Responding to children's everyday transgressions in Chinese working-class families. *Journal of Moral Education, 37*(1), 55–79. https://doi.org/10.1080/03057240701803684

Wang, Y., & Lim, H. (2012). The global childhood obesity epidemic and the association between socio-economic status and childhood obesity. *International Review of Psychiatry, 24*(3), 176–188. https://doi.org/10.3109/09540261.2012.688195

Wang, Y., Shafto, C. L., & Houston, D. M. (2018b). Attention to speech and spoken language development in deaf children with cochlear implants: A 10-year longitudinal study. *Developmental Science, 21*(6), e12677. https://doi.org/10.1111/desc.12677

Wang, Y., Zhang, Y., Liu, L., Cui, J., Wang, J., Shum, D. H. K., . . . Chan, R. C. K. (2017). A meta-analysis of working memory impairments in autism spectrum disorders. *Neuropsychology Review, 27*(1), 46–61. https://doi.org/10.1007/s11065-016-9336-y

Ware, R. E., de Montalembert, M., Tshilolo, L., & Abboud, M. R. (2017). Sickle cell disease. *Lancet, 390*(10091), 15–21. https://doi.org/https://doi.org/10.1016/S0140-6736(17)30193-9

Warneken, F., Lohse, K., Melis, A. P., & Tomasello, M. (2011). Young children share the spoils after collaboration. *Psychological Science, 22*(2), 267–273. https://doi.org/10.1177/0956797610395392

Warner, T. D. (2018). Adolescent sexual risk taking: The distribution of youth behaviors and perceived peer attitudes across neighborhood contexts. *Journal of Adolescent Health, 62*(2), 226–233. https://doi.org/10.1016/J.JADOHEALTH.2017.09.007

Warner, T. D., Giordano, P. C., Manning, W. D., & Longmore, M. A. (2011). Everybody's doin' it (right?): Neighborhood norms and sexual activity in adolescence. *Social Science Research, 40*(6), 1676–1690. https://doi.org/10.1016/j.ssresearch.2011.06.009

Warren, J. R., & Saliba, J. (2012). First through eighth grade retention rates for all 50 states: A new method and initial results. *Educational Researcher, 41*(8), 320–329. https://doi.org/10.3102/0013189X12457813

Warsof, S. L., Larion, S., & Abuhamad, A. Z. (2015). Overview of the impact of noninvasive prenatal testing on diagnostic procedures. *Prenatal Diagnosis, 35*(10), 972–979. https://doi.org/10.1002/pd.4601

Wass, R., & Golding, C. (2014). Sharpening a tool for teaching: The zone of proximal development. *Teaching in Higher Education, 19*(6), 671–684. https://doi.org/10.1080/13562517.2014.901958

Watamura, S. E., Phillips, D. A., Morrissey, T. W., McCartney, K., & Bub, K. (2011). Double jeopardy: Poorer social-emotional outcomes for children in the NICHD SECCYD experiencing home and child-care environments that confer risk. *Child Development, 82*(1), 48–65. https://doi.org/10.1111/j.1467-8624.2010.01540.x

Waterhouse, L. (2006). Multiple intelligences, the Mozart effect, and emotional intelligence: A critical review. *Educational Psychologist, 41*(4), 207–225. https://doi.org/10.1207/s15326985ep4104_1

Waterland, R. A., & Jirtle, R. L. (2003). Transposable elements: Targets for early nutritional effects on epigenetic gene regulation. *Molecular and Cellular Biology, 23*(15), 5293–5300. https://doi.org/10.1128/MCB.23.15.5293-5300.2003

Waters, S. F., West, T. V., Karnilowicz, H. R., & Mendes, W. B. (2017). Affect contagion between mothers and infants: Examining valence and touch. *Journal of Experimental Psychology: General, 146*(7), 1043–1051. https://doi.org/10.1037/xge0000322

Waters, S. F., West, T. V, & Mendes, W. B. (2014). Stress contagion: Physiological covariation between mothers and infants. *Psychological Science, 25*(4), 934–942. https://doi.org/10.1177/0956797613518352

Watson, J. (1925). *Behaviorism*. New York, NY: Norton.

Watson, J. B., & Raynor, R. (1920). Conditioned emotional reactions. *Journal of Experimental Psychology, 3*, 1–14.

Watson, N. F., Martin, J. L., Wise, M. S., Carden, K. A., Kirsch, D. B., Kristo, D. A., . . . American Academy of Sleep Medicine Board of Directors. (2017). Delaying middle school and high school start times promotes student health and performance: An American Academy of Sleep Medicine position statement. *Journal of Clinical Sleep Medicine, 13*(04), 623–625. https://doi.org/10.5664/jcsm.6558

Watson, R. J., Adjei, J., Saewyc, E., Homma, Y., & Goodenow, C. (2017). Trends and disparities in disordered eating among heterosexual and sexual minority adolescents. *International Journal of Eating Disorders, 50*(1), 22–31. https://doi.org/10.1002/eat.22576

Watson, S. M. R., & Gable, R. A. (2013). Unraveling the complex nature of mathematics learning disability: Implications for research and practice. *Learning Disability Quarterly, 36*(3), 178–187. https://doi.org/10.1177/0731948712461489

Watson-Jones, R. E., Busch, J. T. A., & Legare, C. H. (2015). Interdisciplinary and cross-cultural perspectives on explanatory coexistence. *Topics in Cognitive Science, 7*(4), 611–623. https://doi.org/10.1111/tops.12162

Watts, A. W., Loth, K., Berge, J. M., Larson, N., & Neumark-Sztainer, D. (2017). No time for family meals? Parenting practices associated with adolescent fruit and vegetable intake when family meals are not an option. *Journal of the Academy of Nutrition and Dietetics, 117*(5), 707–714. https://doi.org/10.1016/j.jand.2016.10.026

Watts, A. W., Mason, S. M., Loth, K., Larson, N., & Neumark-Sztainer, D. (2016). Socioeconomic differences in overweight and weight-related behaviors across adolescence and young adulthood: 10-year longitudinal findings from Project EAT. *Preventive Medicine, 87*, 194–199. https://doi.org/10.1016/j.ypmed.2016.03.007

Waxman, S., Fu, X., Arunachalam, S., Leddon, E., Geraghty, K., & Song, H. (2013). Are nouns learned before verbs? Infants provide insight into a long-standing debate. *Child Development Perspectives, 7*(3), 155–159. https://doi.org/10.1111/cdep.12032

Way, N., Reddy, R., & Rhodes, J. (2007). Students' perceptions of school climate during the middle school years: Associations with trajectories of psychological and behavioral adjustment. *American Journal of Community Psychology, 40*(3–4), 194–213. https://doi.org/10.1007/s10464-007-9143-y

Way, N., Santos, C., Niwa, E. Y., & Kim-Gervey, C. (2008). To be or not to be: An exploration of ethnic identity development in context. *New Directions for Child & Adolescent Development, 2008*(120), 61–79.

Weaver, J. M., & Schofield, T. J. (2015). Mediation and moderation of divorce effects on children's behavior problems. *Journal of Family Psychology, 29*(1), 39–48. https://doi.org/10.1037/fam0000043

Weaver, J., Crespi, S., Tosetti, M., & Morrone, M. (2015). Map of visual activity in the infant brain sheds light on neural development. *PLoS Biology, 13*(9), e1002261. https://doi.org/10.1371/journal.pbio.1002261

Webb, R., & Ayers, S. (2015). Cognitive biases in processing infant emotion by women with depression, anxiety and post-traumatic stress disorder in pregnancy or after birth: A systematic review. *Cognition and Emotion, 29*(7), 1278–1294. https://doi.org/10.1080/02699931.2014.977849

Webster, G. D., Graber, J. A., Gesselman, A. N., Crosier, B. S., & Schember, T. O. (2014). A life history theory of father absence and menarche: A meta-analysis. *Evolutionary Psychology, 12*(2), 147470491401200. https://doi.org/10.1177/147470491401200202

Webster, S., Morris, G., & Kevelighan, E. (2018). *Essential human development*. Hoboken, NJ: John Wiley & Sons, Inc.

Wechsler, D. (1944). *The measurement of adult intelligence* (3rd ed.). Baltimore, MD: Williams & Wilkins.

Wechsler, D. (2014a). *Wechsler Intelligence Scale for Children* (5th ed.). San Antonio, TX: NCS Pearson.

Wechsler, D. (2014b). *WISC®-V CDN (Wechsler Intelligence Scale for Children®-Fifth Edition: Canadian)*. Toronto, ON, Canada: Pearson. Retrieved from https://www.pearsonclinical.ca/en/products/product-master/item-84.html

Wei, W., Lu, H., Zhao, H., Chen, C., Dong, Q., & Zhou, X. (2012). Gender differences in children's arithmetic performance are accounted for by gender differences in language abilities. *Psychological Science, 23*(3), 320–330. https://doi.org/10.1177/0956797611427168

Weil, L. G., Fleming, S. M., Dumontheil, I., Kilford, E. J., Weil, R. S., Rees, G., . . . Blakemore, S.-J. (2013). The development of metacognitive ability in adolescence. *Consciousness and Cognition, 22*(1), 264–271. https://doi.org/10.1016/J.CONCOG.2013.01.004

Weinberg, M. K., & Tronick, E. Z. (1994). Beyond the face: An empirical study of infant affective configurations of facial, vocal, gestural, and regulatory behaviors. *Child Development, 65*, 1503–1515.

Weinberg, M. K., Tronick, E. Z., Cohn, J. F., & Olson, K. L. (1999). Gender differences in emotional expressivity and self-regulation during early infancy. *Developmental Psychology, 35*(1), 175–188. https://doi.org/10.1037/0012-1649.35.1.175

Weinfield, N. S., Sroufe, L. A., Egeland, B., & Carlson, E. (2008). Individual differences in infant-caregiver attachment: Conceptual and empirical aspects of security. In J. Cassidy & P. R. Shaver (Eds.), *Handbook of attachment: Theory, research, and clinical applications* (pp. 78–101). New York, NY: Guilford.

Weinhold, B. (2009). Environmental factors in birth defects. *Environmental Health Perspectives, 117*(10), A440–A447.

Weis, R., & Toolis, E. E. (2010). Parenting across cultural contexts in the USA: Assessing parenting behaviour in an ethnically and socioeconomically diverse sample. *Early Child Development & Care, 180*(7), 849–867. https://doi.org/10.1080/03004430802472083

Weisgram, E. S. (2016). The cognitive construction of gender stereotypes: Evidence for the dual pathways model of gender differentiation. *Sex Roles, 75*(7–8), 301–313. https://doi.org/10.1007/s11199-016-0624-z

Weisleder, A., & Fernald, A. (2013). Talking to children matters: Early language experience strengthens processing and builds vocabulary. *Psychological Science, 24*(11), 2143–2152. https://doi.org/10.1177/0956797613488145

Weissberg, R. P. (2019). Promoting the social and emotional learning of millions of school children. *Perspectives on Psychological Science, 14*(1), 65–69. https://doi.org/10.1177/1745691618817756

Weisz, A. N., & Black, B. M. (2002). Gender and moral reasoning: African American youth respond to dating dilemmas. *Journal of Human Behavior in the Social Environment, 5*(1), 35–52.

Weisz, A. N., & Black, B. M. (2008). Peer intervention in dating violence: Beliefs of African-American middle school adolescents. *Journal of Ethnic & Cultural Diversity in Social Work, 17*(2), 177–196. https://doi.org/10.1080/15313200801947223

Wellman, H. M. (2017). The development of theory of mind: Historical reflections. *Child Development Perspectives, 11*(3), 207–214. https://doi.org/10.1111/cdep.12236

Wellman, H. M., & Banerjee, M. (1991). Mind and emotion: Children's understanding of the emotional consequences of beliefs and desires. *British Journal of Developmental Psychology, 9*, 191–214.

Wellman, H. M., Cross, D., & Watson, J. (2001). Meta-analysis of theory-of-mind development: The truth about false belief. *Child Development, 72*(3), 655. https://doi.org/10.1111/1467-8624.00304

Wellman, H. M., Fang, F., & Peterson, C. C. (2011). Sequential progressions in a theory-of-mind scale: Longitudinal perspectives. *Child Development, 82*(3), 780–792. https://doi.org/10.1111/j.1467-8624.2011.01583.x

Wellman, H. M., Somerville, S. C., & Haake, R. J. (1979). Development of search procedures in real-life spatial environments. *Developmental Psychology, 15*, 530–542.

Welshman, J. (2010). From Head Start to sure start: Reflections on policy transfer. *Children & Society, 24*(2), 89–99. https://doi.org/10.1111/j.1099-0860.2008.00201.x

Wenger, Y. (2018). Baltimore tries to close digital divide with free tablets, internet. Retrieved from https://www.govtech.com/network/Baltimore-Tries-to-Close-Digital-Divide-with-Free-Tablets-Internet.html

Wentz, E. E. (2017). Importance of initiating a "tummy time" intervention early in infants with Down syndrome. *Pediatric Physical Therapy, 29*(1), 68–75. https://doi.org/10.1097/PEP.0000000000000335

Wentzel, K. R. (2002). Are effective teachers like good parents? Teaching styles and student adjustment in early adolescence. *Child Development, 73*(1), 287–301. Retrieved from http://www.ncbi.nlm.nih.gov/pubmed/14717258

Wentzel, K. R. (2014). Prosocial behavior and peer relations in adolescence. In G. C. Laura M. Padilla-Walker (Ed.), *Prosocial development: A multidimensional approach* (pp. 178-200). Oxford, England: Oxford University Press.

Werker, J. (2012). Perceptual foundations of bilingual acquisition in infancy. *Annals of the New York Academy of Sciences, 1251*(1), 50–61. https://doi.org/10.1111/j.1749-6632.2012.06484.x

Werker, J. F., Yeung, H. H., & Yoshida, K. A. (2012). How do infants become experts at native-speech perception? *Current Directions in Psychological Science, 21*(4), 221–226. https://doi.org/10.1177/0963721412449459

Werner, E. E. (2012). Children and war: Risk, resilience, and recovery. *Development and Psychopathology, 24*(2), 553–558. https://doi.org/10.1017/S0954579412000156

Wertsch, J. V. (1998). *Mind as action*. New York, NY: Oxford University Press.

Wessel, L. (2017). Vaccine myths. *Science, 356*(6336), 368–372. https://doi.org/10.1126/science.356.6336.368

Westen, D. (1998). The scientific legacy of Sigmund Freud: Toward a psychodynamically informed psychological science. *Psychological Bulletin, 124*, 333–371.

Westermann, G. (2016). Experience-dependent brain development as a key to understanding the language system. *Topics in Cognitive Science, 8*(2), 446–458. https://doi.org/10.1111/tops.12194

Wetzel, N., Buttelmann, D., Schieler, A., & Widmann, A. (2016). Infant and adult pupil dilation in response to unexpected sounds. *Developmental Psychobiology, 58*(3), 382–392. https://doi.org/10.1002/dev.21377

Weymouth, B. B., Buehler, C., Zhou, N., & Henson, R. A. (2016). A meta-analysis of parent-adolescent conflict: Disagreement, hostility, and youth maladjustment. *Journal of Family Theory & Review, 8*(1), 95–112. https://doi.org/10.1111/jftr.12126

White, C. N., & Warner, L. A. (2015). Influence of family and school-level factors on age of sexual initiation. *Journal of Adolescent Health, 56*(2), 231–237. https://doi.org/10.1016/j.jadohealth.2014.09.017

White, E. S., & Mistry, R. S. (2016). Parent civic beliefs, civic participation, socialization practices, and child civic engagement. *Applied Developmental Science, 20*(1), 44–60. https://doi.org/10.1080/10888691.2015.1049346

White, K. M. (2013). Associations between teacher–child relationships and children's writing in kindergarten and first grade. *Early Childhood Research Quarterly, 28*(1), 166–176. https://doi.org/10.1016/j.ecresq.2012.05.004

White, R. M. B., Knight, G. P., Jensen, M., & Gonzales, N. A. (2018). Ethnic socialization in neighborhood contexts: Implications for ethnic attitude and identity development among Mexican-origin adolescents. *Child Development, 89*(3), 1004–1021. https://doi.org/10.1111/cdev.12772

Whitehouse, A. J. O., Robinson, M., Li, J., & Oddy, W. H. (2011). Duration of breast feeding and language ability in middle childhood. *Paediatric & Perinatal Epidemiology, 25*(1), 44–52. https://doi.org/10.1111/j.1365-3016.2010.01161.x

Whiteside, M. F., & Becker, B. J. (2000). Parental factors and the young child's postdivorce adjustment: A meta-analysis with implications for parenting arrangements. *Journal of Family Psychology, 14*, 5–26.

Whiting, B. B., & Whiting, J. W. (1975). *Children of six cultures: A psycho-cultural analysis.* Cambridge, MA: Harvard University Press.

Whittle, S., Vijayakumar, N., Simmons, J. G., Dennison, M., Schwartz, O., Pantelis, C., . . . Allen, N. B. (2017). Role of positive parenting in the association between neighborhood social disadvantage and brain development across adolescence. *JAMA Psychiatry, 74*(8), 824. https://doi.org/10.1001/jamapsychiatry.2017.1558

Wichmann, J., Wolvaardt, J. E., Maritz, C., & Voyi, K. V. V. (2009). Household conditions, eczema symptoms and rhinitis symptoms: Relationship with wheeze and severe wheeze in children living in the Polokwane Area, South Africa. *Maternal & Child Health Journal, 13*(1), 107–118. https://doi.org/10.1007/s10995-007-0309-x

Widom, C. S. (2014). Handbook of Child Maltreatment. In J. E. Korbin & R. D. Krugman (Eds.), *Handbook of child maltreatment* (Vol. 2, pp. 225–247). Dordrecht, Netherlands: Springer. https://doi.org/10.1007/978-94-007-7208-3

Wigby, K., D'Epagnier, C., Howell, S., Reicks, A., Wilson, R., Cordeiro, L., & Tartaglia, N. (2016). Expanding the phenotype of triple X syndrome: A comparison of prenatal versus postnatal diagnosis. *American Journal of Medical Genetics Part A, 170*(11), 2870–2881. https://doi.org/10.1002/ajmg.a.37688

Wigfield, A., Eccles, J. S., Fredricks, J. A., Simpkins, S., Roeser, R. W., & Schiefele, U. (2015). Development of achievement motivation and engagement. In M. Lamb (Ed.), *Handbook of child psychology and developmental science* (pp. 1–44). Hoboken, NJ: John Wiley & Sons. https://doi.org/10.1002/9781118963418.childpsy316

Wigfield, A., Gladstone, J. R., & Turci, L. (2016). Beyond cognition: Reading motivation and reading comprehension. *Child Development Perspectives, 10*(3), 190–195. https://doi.org/10.1111/cdep.12184

Wigfield, A., Muenks, K., & Rosenzweig, E. Q. (2015). Children's achievement motivation in school. In C. M. Rubie-Davies, J. M. Stephens, & P. Watson (Eds.), *Routledge international handbook of social psychology of the classroom* (pp. 1–12). New York, NY: Routledge. https://doi.org/10.4324/9781315716923

Wiik, K. L., Loman, M. M., Van Ryzin, M. J., Armstrong, J. M., Essex, M. J., Pollak, S. D., & Gunnar, M. R. (2011). Behavioral and emotional symptoms of post-institutionalized children in middle childhood. *Journal of Child Psychology & Psychiatry, 52*(1), 56–63. https://doi.org/10.1111/j.1469-7610.2010.02294.x

Wijeakumar, S., Kumar, A., M. Delgado Reyes, L., Tiwari, M., & Spencer, J. P. (2019). Early adversity in rural India impacts the brain networks underlying visual working memory. *Developmental Science*, e12822. https://doi.org/10.1111/desc.12822

Wilbur, M. B., Little, S., & Szymanski, L. M. (2015). Is home birth safe? *New England Journal of Medicine, 373*(27), 2683–2685. https://doi.org/10.1056/NEJMclde1513623

Wiley, M. O. (2017). Adoption research, practice, and societal trends: Ten years of progress. *American Psychologist, 72*(9), 985–995. https://doi.org/10.1037/amp0000218

Wilhoit, L. F., Scott, D. A., & Simecka, B. A. (2017). Fetal alcohol spectrum disorders: Characteristics, complications, and treatment. *Community Mental Health Journal, 53*(6), 711–718. https://doi.org/10.1007/s10597-017-0104-0

Wilkinson, P. O., Trzaskowski, M., Haworth, C. M. A., & Eley, T. C. (2013). The role of gene–environment correlations and interactions in middle childhood depressive symptoms. *Development and Psychopathology, 25*(01), 93–104. https://doi.org/10.1017/S0954579412000922

Will, G.-J., van Lier, P. A. C., Crone, E. A., & Güroğlu, B. (2016). Chronic childhood peer rejection is associated with heightened neural responses to social exclusion during adolescence. *Journal of Abnormal Child Psychology, 44*(1), 43–55. https://doi.org/10.1007/s10802-015-9983-0

Williams, E. (2015). Pre-kindergarten across states. *Education Policy.* Retrieved from http://www.edcentral.org/prekstatefunding/

Williams, J., Mai, C. T., Mulinare, J., Isenburg, J., Flood, T. J., Ethen, M., . . . Centers for Disease Control and Prevention. (2015). Updated estimates of neural tube defects prevented by mandatory folic acid fortification - United States, 1995-2011. *MMWR. Morbidity and Mortality Weekly Report, 64*(1), 1–5.

Williams, J. E., & Best, D. L. (1982). *Measuring sex stereotypes: A thirty-nation study.* Beverly Hills, CA: Sage.

Williams, J. L., Aiyer, S. M., Durkee, M. I., & Tolan, P. H. (2014). The protective role of ethnic identity for urban adolescent males facing multiple stressors. *Journal of Youth and Adolescence, 43*(10), 1728–1741. https://doi.org/10.1007/s10964-013-0071-x

Williams, N. A., Fournier, J., Coday, M., Richey, P. A., Tylavsky, F. A., & Hare, M. E. (2013). Body esteem, peer difficulties and perceptions of physical health in overweight and obese urban children aged 5 to 7 years. *Child: Care, Health and Development, 39*(6), 825–834. https://doi.org/10.1111/j.1365-2214.2012.01401.x

Williams, T. S., Connolly, J., Pepler, D., Laporte, L., & Craig, W. (2008). Risk models of dating aggression across different adolescent relationships: A developmental psychopathology approach. *Journal of Consulting and Clinical Psychology, 76*(4), 622–632. https://doi.org/10.1037/0022-006x.76.4.622

Willis-Owen, S. A. G., Cookson, W. O. C., & Moffatt, M. F. (2018). The genetics and genomics of asthma. *Annual Review of Genomics and Human Genetics, 19*(1), 223–246. https://doi.org/10.1146/annurev-genom-083117-021651

Wilson, G. T., Grilo, C. M., & Vitousek, K. M. (2007). Psychological treatment of eating disorders. *American Psychologist, 62*(3), 199–216.

Wilson, L. C., & Miller, K. E. (2016). Meta-analysis of the prevalence of unacknowledged rape. *Trauma, Violence, & Abuse, 17*(2), 149–159. https://doi.org/10.1177/1524838015576391

Wilson, R. D. (2016). A preventable teratology: Isotretinoin. *CMAJ, 188*(12), 901. https://doi.org/10.1503/cmaj.1150114

Wilson, R. S., & Harpring, E. B. (1972). Mental and motor development in infant twins. *Developmental Psychology, 7*(3), 277–287.

Wilson, S. L., & Weaver, T. L. (2009). Follow-up of developmental attainment and behavioral adjustment for toddlers adopted internationally into the USA. *International Social Work, 52*(5), 679–684. https://doi.org/10.1177/0020872809337684

Wincentak, K., Connolly, J., & Card, N. (2017). Teen dating violence: A meta-analytic review of prevalence rates. *Psychology of Violence, 7*(2), 224–241. https://doi.org/10.1037/a0040194

Windle, M., & Zucker, R. A. (2010). Reducing underage and young adult drinking: How to address critical drinking problems during this developmental period. *Alcohol Research & Health, 33*(1/2), 29–44.

Winner, E. (1986). Where pelicans kiss seals. *Psychology Today, 20*(8), 25–35.

Winsler, A., Fernyhough, C., & Montero, I. (2009). *Private speech, executive functioning, and the development of verbal self-regulation.* Cambridge, England: Cambridge University Press.

Winward, J. L., Hanson, K. L., Tapert, S. F., & Brown, S. A. (2014). Heavy alcohol use, marijuana use, and concomitant use by adolescents are associated with unique and shared cognitive decrements. *Journal of the International Neuropsychological Society, 20*(8), 784–795. https://doi.org/10.1017/S1355617714000666

Wiseman, F. K., Al-Janabi, T., Hardy, J., Karmiloff-Smith, A., Nizetic, D., Tybulewicz, V. L. J., . . . Strydom, A. (2015). A genetic cause of Alzheimer disease: Mechanistic insights from Down syndrome. *Nature Reviews Neuroscience, 16*(9), 564–574. https://doi.org/10.1038/nrn3983

Wistuba, J., Brand, C., Zitzmann, M., & Damm, O. S. (2017). Genetics of Klinefelter syndrome: Experimental exploration. In P. H. Vogt (Ed.), *Genetics of human infertility* (Vol. 21, pp. 40–56). Basel, Switzerland: Karger. https://doi.org/10.1159/000477277

Witchel, S. F., & Topaloglu, A. K. (2019). Puberty: Gonadarche and adrenarche. In J. F. Strauss, R. L. Barbieri, & A. R. Gargiulo (Eds.), *Yen and Jaffe's reproductive endocrinology* (pp. 394–446). NewYork, NY: Elsevier. https://doi.org/10.1016/B978-0-323-47912-7.00017-2

Witherington, D. C., Campos, J. J., Anderson, D. I., Lejeune, L., & Seah, E. (2005). Avoidance of heights on the Visual Cliff in newly walking infants. *Infancy, 7*(3), 285–298. https://doi.org/10.1207/s15327078in0703_4

Witherington, D. C., & Lickliter, R. (2016). Integrating development and evolution in psychological science: Evolutionary developmental psychology, developmental systems, and explanatory pluralism. *Human Development, 59*(4), 200–234. https://doi.org/10.1159/000450715

Wohlfahrt-Veje, C., Mouritsen, A., Hagen, C. P., Tinggaard, J., Mieritz, M. G., Boas, M., . . . Main, K. M. (2016). Pubertal onset in boys and girls is influenced by pubertal timing of both parents, *101*(7), 2667–2674. https://doi.org/10.1210/jc.2016-1073

Wojciak, A. S., McWey, L. M., & Waid, J. (2018). Sibling relationships of youth in foster care: A predictor of resilience. *Children and Youth Services Review, 84*, 247–254. https://doi.org/10.1016/J.CHILDYOUTH.2017.11.030

Wojcicki, J. M., Heyman, M. B., Elwan, D., Lin, J., Blackburn, E., & Epel, E. (2016). Early exclusive breastfeeding is associated with longer telomeres in Latino preschool children. *American Journal of Clinical Nutrition, 104*(2), 397–405. https://doi.org/10.3945/ajcn.115.115428

Wojslawowicz Bowker, J. C., Rubin, K. H., Burgess, K. B., Booth-Laforce, C., & Rose-Krasnor, L. (2006). Behavioral characteristics associated with stable and fluid best friendship patterns in middle childhood. *Merrill-Palmer Quarterly, 52*(4), 671–693.

Wolf, R. M., & Long, D. (2016). Pubertal development. *Pediatrics in Review, 37*(7), 292–300. https://doi.org/10.1542/pir.2015-0065

Wolff, P. H. (1966). The causes, controls and organization of behavior in the neonate. *Psychological Issues Monograph Series, 5*(1), 1–105.

Wolke, D., Eryigit-Madzwamuse, S., & Gutbrod, T. (2014). Very preterm/very low birthweight infants' attachment: Infant and maternal characteristics. *Archives of Disease in Childhood. Fetal and Neonatal Edition, 99*(1), F70-5. https://doi.org/10.1136/archdischild-2013-303788

Womack, L. S., Rossen, L. M., & Martin, J. A. (2018). Singleton low birthweight rates, by race and Hispanic origin: United States, 2006-2016. *NCHS Data Brief*, (306), 1–8. Retrieved from http://www.ncbi.nlm.nih.gov/pubmed/29616897

Wong, M. M., & Brower, K. J. (2012). The prospective relationship between sleep problems and suicidal behavior in the National Longitudinal Study of Adolescent Health. *Journal of Psychiatric Research, 46*(7), 953–959. https://doi.org/10.1016/j.jpsychires.2012.04.008

Wong, M. M., Robertson, G. C., & Dyson, R. B. (2015). Prospective relationship between poor sleep and substance-related problems in a national sample of adolescents. *Alcoholism, Clinical and Experimental Research, 39*, 355–362. https://doi.org/10.1111/acer.12618

Woodward, A. L., Markman, E. M., & Fitzsimmons, C. M. (1994). Rapid word learning in 13- and 18-month-olds. *Developmental Psychology, 30*, 553–556.

Woolley, J. D., & E Ghossainy, M. (2013). Revisiting the fantasy-reality distinction: Children as naïve skeptics. *Child Development, 84*(5), 1496–1510. https://doi.org/10.1111/cdev.12081

World Health Organization. (2009). *BMI classification*. Retrieved from http://apps.who.int/bmi/index.jsp? introPage=intro_3.html

World Health Organization. (2010). *Guidelines on HIV and infant feeding 2010: Principles and recommendations for feeding in the context of HIV and a summary of evidence*. Geneva: Switzerland: Author.

World Health Organization. (2011). *Progress report 2011: Global HIV/AIDS response*. Retrieved from http://www.who.int/hiv/pub/progress_report2011/en/

World Hunger Education Service. (2017). *2016 world hunger and poverty facts and statistics*. Retrieved from https://www.worldhunger.org/2015-world-hunger-and-poverty-facts-and-statistics/

Worobey, J. (2014). Physical activity in infancy: Developmental aspects, measurement, and importance. *American Journal of Clinical Nutrition, 99*(3), 729S–733S. https://doi.org/10.3945/ajcn.113.072397

Wouters, S., Doumen, S., Germeijs, V., Colpin, H., & Verschueren, K. (2013). Contingencies of self-worth in early adolescence: The antecedent role of perceived parenting. *Social Development, 22*(2), 242–258. https://doi.org/10.1111/sode.12010

Wray-Lake, L., & Syvertsen, A. K. (2011). The developmental roots of social responsibility in childhood and adolescence. *New Directions for Child and Adolescent Development, 2011*(134), 11–25. https://doi.org/10.1002/cd.308

Wray-Lake, L., Syvertsen, A. K., & Flanagan, C. A. (2016). Developmental change in social responsibility during adolescence: An ecological perspective. *Developmental Psychology, 52*(1), 130–142. https://doi.org/10.1037/dev0000067

Wright, B. C., & Smailes, J. (2015). Factors and processes in children's transitive deductions. *Journal of Cognitive Psychology, 27*(8), 967–978. https://doi.org/10.1080/20445911.2015.1063641

Wright, J. C., Huston, A. C., Murphy, K. C., St. Peters, M., Pinon, M., Scantlin, R., & Kotler, J. (2001). The relations of early television viewing to school readiness and vocabulary of children from low-income families: The Early Window Project. *Child Development, 72*, 1347–1366.

Wu, R., Gopnik, A., Richardson, D. C., & Kirkham, N. Z. (2011). Infants learn about objects from statistics and people. *Developmental Psychology, 47*(5), 1220–1229. https://doi.org/10.1037/a0024023

Wu, W., West, S. G., & Hughes, J. N. (2010). Effect of grade retention in first grade on psychosocial outcomes. *Journal of Educational Psychology, 102*(1), 135–152. https://doi.org/10.1037/a0016664

Wu, Y., Gong, Q., Zou, Z., Li, H., & Zhang, X. (2017). Short sleep duration and obesity among children: A systematic review and meta-analysis of prospective studies. *Obesity Research & Clinical Practice, 11*(2), 140–150. https://doi.org/10.1016/J.ORCP.2016.05.005

Wyatt, L. C., Ung, T., Park, R., Kwon, S. C., & Trinh-Shevrin, C. (2015). Risk factors of suicide and depression among Asian American, Native Hawaiian, and Pacific Islander Youth: A systematic literature review. *Journal of Health Care for the Poor and Underserved, 26*(2 Suppl.), 191–237. https://doi.org/10.1353/hpu.2015.0059

Wysman, L., Scoboria, A., Gawrylowicz, J., & Memon, A. (2014). The cognitive interview buffers the effects of subsequent repeated questioning in the absence of negative feedback. *Behavioral Sciences & the Law, 32*(2), 207–219. https://doi.org/10.1002/bsl.2115

Xie, X., Ding, G., Cui, C., Chen, L., Gao, Y., Zhou, Y., . . . Tian, Y. (2013). The effects of low-level prenatal lead exposure on birth outcomes. *Environmental Pollution, 175*, 30–34. https://doi.org/10.1016/j.envpol.2012.12.013

Xu, F., & Kushnir, T. (2013). Infants are rational constructivist learners. *Current Directions in Psychological Science, 22*(1), 28–32.

Xu, J., Kochanek, K. D., Murphy, S. L., & Arias, E. (2014). Mortality in the United States, 2012. *NCHS Data Brief*, (168), 1–8. Retrieved from http://europepmc.org/abstract/med/25296181

Xu, J., Murphy, S. L., Kochanek, K. D., & Bastian, B. A. (2016). Deaths: Final data for 2013. *National Vital and Statistics Reports,1, 64*(2). Retrieved from http://www.cdc.gov/nchs/data/nvsr/nvsr64/nvsr64_02.pdf

Xu, Y., Farver, J. A. M., Zhang, Z., Zeng, Q., Yu, L., & Cai., B. (2005). Mainland Chinese parenting styles and parent-child interaction. *International Journal of Behavioral Development, 29*(6), 524–531.

Yamagata, K. (2007). Differential emergence of representational systems: Drawings, letters, and numerals. *Cognitive Development, 22*(2), 244–257.

Yang, C., Crain, S., Berwick, R. C., Chomsky, N., & Bolhuis, J. J. (2017). The growth of language: Universal grammar, experience, and principles of computation. *Neuroscience & Biobehavioral Reviews, 81*, 103–119. https://doi.org/10.1016/J.NEUBIOREV.2016.12.023

Yang, J. (2007). The one-child policy and school attendance in China. *Comparative Education Review, 51*(4), 471–495.

Yang, S., & Sternberg, R. J. (1997). Conceptions of intelligence in ancient Chinese philosophy. *Journal of Theoretical and Philosophical Psychology, 17*(2), 101–119.

Yaniv, S. S., Levy, A., Wiznitzer, A., Holcberg, G., Mazor, M., & Sheiner, E. (2011). A significant linear association exists between advanced maternal age and adverse perinatal outcome. *Archives of Gynecology and Obstetrics, 283*(4), 755–759. https://doi.org/10.1007/s00404-010-1459-4

Yaoying, X., & Xu, Y. (2010). Children's social play sequence: Parten's classic theory revisited. *Early Child Development* and Care, 180(4), 489–498. https://doi.org/10.1080/03004430802090430

Yarrow, M. R., Scott, P. M., & Waxler, C. Z. (1973). Learning concern for others. *Developmental Psychology, 8*, 240–260.

Yates, M., & Youniss, J. (1996). Community service and political-moral identity in adolescents. *Journal of Research on Adolescence, 6*, 271–284.

Yau, G., Schluchter, M., Taylor, H. G., Margevicius, S., Forrest, C. B., Andreias, L., . . . Hack, M. (2013). Bullying of extremely low birth weight children: Associated risk factors during adolescence. *Early Human Development, 89*(5), 333–338. https://doi.org/10.1016/j.earlhumdev.2012.11.004

Yau, J., & Smetana, J. G. (2003). Conceptions of moral, social-conventional, and personal events among Chinese preschoolers in Hong Kong. *Child Development, 74*(3), 647–658.

Yau, J. C., & Reich, S. M. (2018). "It's just a lot of work": Adolescents' self-presentation norms and practices on Facebook and Instagram. *Journal of Research on Adolescence*. https://doi.org/10.1111/jora.12376

Ybarra, M. L., & Mitchell, K. J. (2014). "Sexting" and its relation to sexual activity and sexual risk behavior in a national survey of adolescents. *Journal of Adolescent Health, 55*(6), 757–764. https://doi.org/10.1016/j.jadohealth.2014.07.012

Yeager, D. S., & Dweck, C. S. (2012). Mindsets that promote resilience: When students believe that personal characteristics can be developed. *Educational Psychologist, 47*(4), 302–314. https://doi.org/10.1080/00461520.2012.722805

Yip, T. (2014). Ethnic identity in everyday life: The influence of identity development status. *Child Development, 85*(1), 205–219. https://doi.org/10.1111/cdev.12107

Yoshikawa, H., Aber, J. L., & Beardslee, W. R. (2012). The effects of poverty on the mental, emotional, and behavioral health of children and youth: Implications for prevention. *American Psychologist, 67*(4), 272–284. https://doi.org/10.1037/a0028015

Yoshikawa, H., Mistry, R., & Wang, Y. (2016). Advancing methods in research on Asian American children and youth. *Child Development, 87*(4), 1033–1050. https://doi.org/10.1111/cdev.12576

Young, G. (2016). Lateralization and specialization of the brain. In G. Young (Ed.), *Unifying causality and psychology* (pp. 177–200). Cham, Switzerland: Springer International Publishing. https://doi.org/10.1007/978-3-319-24094-7_8

Yousefi, M., Karmaus, W., Zhang, H., Roberts, G., Matthews, S., Clayton, B., & Arshad, S. H. (2013). Relationships between age of puberty onset and height at age 18 years in girls and boys. *World Journal of Pediatrics, 9*(3), 230–238. https://doi.org/10.1007/s12519-013-0399-z

Yu, S., Ostrosky, M. M., & Fowler, S. A. (2012). Measuring young children's attitudes toward peers with disabilities. *Topics in Early Childhood Special Education, 32*(3), 132–142. https://doi.org/10.1177/0271121412453175

Yu, S., Ostrosky, M. M., & Fowler, S. A. (2015). The relationship between preschoolers' attitudes and play behaviors toward classmates with disabilities. *Topics in Early Childhood Special Education, 35*(1), 40–51. https://doi.org/10.1177/0271121414554432

Yücel, M. A., Selb, J. J., Huppert, T. J., Franceschini, M. A., & Boas, D. A. (2017). Functional near infrared spectroscopy: Enabling routine functional brain imaging. *Current Opinion in Biomedical Engineering, 4*, 78–86. https://doi.org/10.1016/J.COBME.2017.09.011

Yuill, N., & Perner, J. (1988). Intentionality and knowledge in children's judgments of actor's responsibility and recipient's emotional reaction. *Developmental Psychology, 24*, 358–365.

Yuma-Guerrero, P., Orsi, R., Lee, P.-T., & Cubbin, C. (2018). A systematic review of socioeconomic status measurement in 13 years of U.S. injury research. *Journal of Safety Research, 64*, 55–72. https://doi.org/10.1016/J.JSR.2017.12.017

Yurgelun-Todd, D. (2007). Emotional and cognitive changes during adolescence. *Current Opinion in Neurobiology, 17*(2), 251–257.

Zafiropoulou, M., Sotiriou, A., & Mitsiouli, V. (2007). Relation of self-concept in kindergarten and first grade to school adjustment. *Perceptual & Motor Skills, 104*(3), 1313–1327. https://doi.org/10.2466/PMS.104.4.1313-1327

Zahn-Waxler, C., Friedman, R. J., Cole, P. M., Mizuta, I., & Hiruma, N. (1996). Japanese and United States preschool children's responses to conflict and distress. *Child Development, 67*, 2462–2477.

Zaitchik, D., Iqbal, Y., & Carey, S. (2014). The effect of executive function on biological reasoning in young children: An individual differences study. *Child Development, 85*(1), 160–175. https://doi.org/10.1111/cdev.12145

Zammit, M., & Atkinson, S. (2017). The relations between 'babysigning', child vocabulary and maternal mind-mindedness. *Early Child Development and Care, 187*(12), 1887–1895. https://doi.org/10.1080/03004430.2016.1193502

Zampieri, B. L., Biselli-Périco, J. M., de Souza, J. E. S., Bürger, M. C., Silva Júnior, W. A., Goloni-Bertollo, E. M., . . . Flavell, R. (2014). Altered expression of immune-related genes in children with Down syndrome. *PLoS ONE, 9*(9), e107218. https://doi.org/10.1371/journal.pone.0107218

Zapolski, T. C. B., Fisher, S., Banks, D. E., Hensel, D. J., & Barnes-Najor, J. (2017). Examining the protective effect of ethnic identity on drug attitudes and use among a diverse youth population. *Journal of Youth and Adolescence, 46*(8), 1702–1715. https://doi.org/10.1007/s10964-016-0605-0

Zelazo, N. A., Zelazo, P. R. D. R., Cohen, K. M., & Zelazo, P. R. D. R. (1993). Specificity of practice effects on elementary neuromotor patterns. *Developmental Psychology, 29*(4), 686–691. https://doi.org/10.1037/0012-1649.29.4.686

Zelazo, P. D., Reznick, J. S., & Spinazzola, J. (1998). Representational flexibility and response control in a multistep, multilocation search task. *Developmental Psychology, 34*, 203–214.

Zelazo, P. R. (1983). The development of walking: New findings on old assumptions. *Journal of Motor Behavior, 2*, 99–137.

Zeman, J., Cassano, M., & Adrian, M. C. (2013). Socialization influences on children's and adolescents' emotional self-regulation processes. In K. C. Barrett, N. A. Fox, G. A. Morgan, D. J. Fidler, & L. A. Daunhauer (Eds.), *Handbook of self-regulatory processes in development* (pp. 79–107). New York, NY: Psychology Press. https://doi.org/10.4324/9780203080719.ch5

Zhai, F., Brooks-Gunn, J., & Waldfogel, J. (2011). Head Start and urban children's school readiness: A birth cohort study in 18 cities. *Developmental Psychology, 47*(1), 134–152. https://doi.org/10.1037/a0020784

Zhai, Z. W., Pajtek, S., Luna, B., Geier, C. F., Ridenour, T. a., & Clark, D. B. (2015). Reward-modulated response inhibition, cognitive shifting, and the orbital frontal cortex in early adolescence. *Journal of Research on Adolescence, 25*(4), 753–764. https://doi.org/10.1111/jora.12168

Zhang, N., Baker, H. W., Tufts, M., Raymond, R. E., Salihu, H., & Elliott, M. R. (2013). Early childhood lead exposure and academic achievement: Evidence from Detroit public schools, 2008–2010. *American Journal of Public Health, 103*(3), e72–e77.

Zhou, D., Lebel, C., Treit, S., Evans, A., & Beaulieu, C. (2015). Accelerated longitudinal cortical thinning in adolescence. *NeuroImage, 104*, 138–145. https://doi.org/10.1016/j.neuroimage.2014.10.005

Zhu, J., Kusa, T. O., & Chan, Y.-M. (2018). Genetics of pubertal timing. *Current Opinion in Pediatrics, 30*(4), 532–540. https://doi.org/10.1097/MOP.0000000000000642

Zhu, L., Liu, G., & Tardif, T. (2009). Chinese children's explanations for illness. *International Journal of Behavioral Development, 33*(6), 516–519. https://doi.org/10.1177/0165025409343748

Zhu, W. X., Lu, L., & Hesketh, T. (2009). China's excess males, sex selective abortion, and one child policy: Analysis of data from 2005 national intercensus survey. *BMJ, 338*(7700), 920–923.

Zhu, Y., Mangini, L. D., Dong, Y., & Forman, F. (2017). Episodes of food insecurity and linear growth in childhood: A prospective cohort study. *FASEB Journal, 31*(1 Suppl.), 297. Retrieved from https://www.fasebj.org/doi/abs/10.1096/fasebj.31.1_supplement.297.1

Zielinski, R., Ackerson, K., & Kane Low, L. (2015). Planned home birth: Benefits, risks, and opportunities. *International Journal of Women's Health, 7*, 361–377. https://doi.org/10.2147/IJWH.S55561

Zigler, E., & Styfco, S. J. (2004). Moving Head Start to the states: One experiment too many. *Applied Developmental Science, 8*(1), 51–55.

Zill, N. (2015). The paradox of adoption. *Institute for Family Studies*. Retrieved from https://ifstudies.org/blog/the-paradox-of-adoption/

Zimmer-Gembeck, M. J., Webb, H. J., Farrell, L. J., & Waters, A. M. (2018). Girls' and boys' trajectories of appearance anxiety from age 10 to 15 years are associated with earlier maturation and appearance-related teasing. *Development and Psychopathology, 30*(1), 337–350. https://doi.org/10.1017/S0954579417000657

Zimmer-Gembeck, M. J., Webb, H. J., Pepping, C. A., Swan, K., Merlo, O., Skinner, E. A., . . . Dunbar, M. (2017). Is parent–child attachment a correlate of children's emotion regulation and coping? *International Journal of Behavioral Development, 41*(1), 74–93. https://doi.org/10.1177/0165025415618276

Zimmermann, P., & Iwanski, A. (2014). Emotion regulation from early adolescence to emerging adulthood and middle adulthood: Age differences, gender differences, and emotion-specific developmental variations. *International Journal of Behavioral Development, 38*(2), 182–194. https://doi.org/10.1177/0165025413515405

Zinzow, H. M., Resnick, H. S., McCauley, J. L., Amstadter, A. B., Ruggiero, K. J., & Kilpatrick, D. G. (2010). The role of rape tactics in risk for posttraumatic stress disorder and major depression: Results from a national sample of college women. *Depression and Anxiety, 27*(8), 708–715. https://doi.org/10.1002/da.20719

Zosh, J. M., Brinster, M., & Halberda, J. (2013). Optimal contrast: Competition between two referents improves word learning. *Applied Developmental Science, 17*(1), 20–28. https://doi.org/10.1080/10888691.2013.748420

Zosuls, K. M., Andrews, N. C. Z., Martin, C. L., England, D. E., & Field, R. D. (2016). Developmental changes in the link between gender typicality and peer victimization and exclusion. *Sex Roles, 75*(5–6), 243–256. https://doi.org/10.1007/s11199-016-0608-z

Zosuls, K. M., Ruble, D. N., Tamis-LeMonda, C. S., Shrout, P. E., Bornstein, M. H., & Greulich, F. K. (2009). The acquisition of gender labels in infancy: Implications for gender-typed play. *Developmental Psychology, 45*(3), 688–701. https://doi.org/10.1037/a0014053

Zucker, K. J., Wood, H., Singh, D., & Bradley, S. J. (2012). A developmental, biopsychosocial model for the treatment of children with gender identity disorder. *Journal of Homosexuality, 59*(3), 369–397. https://doi.org/10.1080/00918369.2012.653309

Zuckerman, G. (2007). Child-adult interaction that creates a zone of proximal development. *Journal of Russian & East European Psychology, 45*(3), 43–69. https://doi.org/10.2753/RPO1061-0405450302

Zych, I., Farrington, D. P., Llorent, V. J., & Ttofi, M. M. (2017). *Protecting children against bullying and its consequences*. Cham, Switzerland: Springer International Publishing. https://doi.org/10.1007/978-3-319-53028-4

NAME INDEX

SUBJECT INDEX